Professional JSP, 2nd Edition

Simon Brown

Robert Burdick

Jayson Falkner

Ben Galbraith

Rod Johnson

Larry Kim

Casey Kochmer

Thor Kristmundsson

Sing Li

Dan Malks

Mark Nelson

Grant Palmer

Bob Sullivan

Geoff Taylor

John Timney

Sameer Tyagi

Geert Van Damme

Steve Wilkinson

Wrox Press Ltd. ®

Professional JSP, 2nd Edition

Published by Wrox Press Ltd,
Arden House, 1102 Warwick Road, Acocks Green,
Birmingham, B27 6BH, UK
Printed in Canada
ISBN 1-861004-95-8

Trademark Acknowledgements

Wrox has endeavored to provide trademark information about all the companies and products mentioned in this book by the appropriate use of capitals. However, Wrox cannot guarantee the accuracy of this information.

Credits

Authors
Simon Brown
Robert Burdick
Jayson Falkner
Ben Galbraith
Rod Johnson
Larry Kim
Casey Kochmer
Thor Kristmundsson
Sing Li
Dan Malks
Mark Nelson
Grant Palmer
Bob Sullivan
Geoff Taylor
John Timney
Sameer Tyagi
Geert Van Damme
Steve Wilkinson

Additional Material
Darko Cokor

Category Manager
Viv Emery

Technical Architect
Richard Huss

Technical Editors
Matthew Moodie
Christian Peak
Mark Waterhouse

Author Agent
Emma Batch

Project Administrators
Laura Hall
Nicola Phillips

Technical Reviewers
A. Rick Anderson
Michael Boerner
Vik David
Phil Hanna
Ethan Henry
Brian Hickey
Brian Higdon
Jim Johnson
Andrew Jones
Sachin S. Khanna
Lance Lavandowska
Gamaliel Masters
Stéphane Osmont
Pradyumnajit Pathy
Phil Powers-DeGeorge
Vikram Rajan
David Schultz
Sébastien Stormacq
John Timney
Andrew Watt
Paul Wilt

Production Coordinator
Pip Wonson

Index
Alessandro Ansa

Figures
Shabnam Hussain

Cover
Shelley Frazier

Proof Reader
Fiona Berryman

About the Authors

Simon Brown

Based in London, Simon is a Technical Architect with the Concise Group Ltd and has over 4 years experience of Java and related technologies. He has acted as technical lead and mentor to others in addition to writing and delivering training material. Outside of work he has spoken at several Java events including JavaOne, and has been published in JavaWorld.

Simon graduated from the University of Reading in 1996 with a First class BSc (hons) degree in Computer Science, and is now also a Sun Certified Enterprise Architect for J2EE, and a Certified Developer for the Java 2 Platform. He can be e-mailed at simon_g_brown@yahoo.com.

Simon contributed Chapter 24 to this book.

I would like to dedicate this to my family and friends who have helped me get to where I am today, and especially to my fiancée Kirstie for her understanding and encouragement in the various projects that I've been involved in.

Robert Burdick

Robert Burdick is an industry veteran with 14 years software design and development experience. He is president and founder of wAppearances, a consulting and training firm specializing in mobile and wireless computing.

Mr. Burdick is the author of '*Essential Windows CE Application Programming*', published by John Wiley and Sons in 1999. He lives in Los Altos, California with his wife and daughter.

Robert contributed Chapter 22 to this book.

First and foremost, thanks to my wife Kate for her support during my second publishing project. Thanks also go to my daughter, Mallory Rose, for providing important comic relief. I would also like to thank James Klicman of Megatomic Internet for introducing me to this project and the Wrox team. I would also like to thank The Residents, wherever and whoever you are, for keeping me company while working on this project.

Jayson Falkner

Jayson Falkner is a full time student at the University of Miami pursuing a degree in Information Technology. He has been programming in Java for the past year and a half and is now focusing on JSP. Jayson is the CTO of Amberjack Software LLC and Webmaster of JSP Insider. In his spare time Jayson likes to program in binary and write not-so-funny jokes using XML.

Jayson contributed Chapters 8 and 12 to this book, with Casey Kochmer.

Dedicated to James and Joleen Falkner for countless hours of long distance support and love.

Ben Galbraith

Ben Galbraith first started programming when he was eight years old. He spent a considerable amount of his youth as a hobby programmer. In his late teens, he was hired by a Silicon Valley computer manufacturer to develop Windows-based client-server applications. In 1995, Mr. Galbraith began developing for the web and fell in love with Unix, vi, and Perl. After some years as an Internet consultant, Mr. Galbraith now leads the Java development team at an insurance company in Salt Lake City. He regularly lectures, evangelizes and gives classes on Java technology.

Ben contributed Chapters 1, 2, and 20 to this book.

To Jessica

Rod Johnson

Rod Johnson is an enterprise Java architect specializing in scalable web applications. He is currently designing a J2EE solution for FT.com, Europe's largest business portal.

After an arts degree majoring in music and computer science, Rod completed a Ph.D. in musicology before returning to software development.

Rod has worked with Java on both client and server since its release, and has concentrated on Internet development since 1996. His main interests are J2EE architecture, EJB, and OO web development.

Rod divides his time between London and Sydney, and enjoys tennis, skiing and playing the piano. He can be reached at rod.johnson@bigfoot.com.

Rod contributed Chapters 17 and 18 to this book.

Thanks to Kerry for her love and encouragement.

Larry Kim

Larry Kim is a Technologist with netNumina, a systems integrator of customized distributed financial applications. He completed an undergraduate degree in Electrical Engineering from the University of Waterloo, and is finishing graduate studies in distributed computing. He was the former Product Manager for the JRun Server at Allaire, and has co-authored several other books on Java Server Programming. Please come see his technical session on JSP web application frameworks and tag patterns at JavaOne 2001, the official Sun Microsystems Java Developer Conference.

Larry contributed Chapter 13 to this book.

I acknowledge my professors at Waterloo: Dr. Paul Dasiewicz, Dr. Kostas Kontogiannis and Dr. Frank Tompa for supervising my research; Dr. Jon Christensen and the cs162 gang for all the Java fun; my boss Max Grasso, co-workers Jay Walters, Ed Lyons & roommate Dilip Ogale for sharing their greatness with me.

Casey Kochmer

Casey Kochmer's professional programming experience spans the past 11 years. Since 1996 his emphasis has been on web development using the server side web languages. Now actively promoting JSP, Casey is a co-founder of JSPInsider.com, a web site devoted to technical support for programmers making the jump to this development environment. Casey is also President of Amberjack Software LLC. When not programming, Casey loves to spend time with his family at a lake or hiking in the Olympic Mountains near his home.

Casey contributed Chapters 8 and 12 to this book, with Jayson Falkner.

Dedicated to Kenneth Joseph Kochmer, who would have smiled if he had known all his children became authors.

Thor Kristmundsson

Thor Kristmundsson is freelance developer specializing in distributed computing. He lives in Aalborg, Denmark with his wife Unnur and son Arnar (4).

Thor contributed Chapter 11 to this book.

Sing Li

First bitten by the computer bug in 1978, Sing has grown up with the microprocessor revolution. His first PC was a $99 do-it-yourself COSMIC ELF computer with 256 bytes of memory and a 1 bit LED display. For two decades, Sing has been an active author, consultant, speaker, instructor, and entrepreneur. His wide-ranging experience spans distributed architectures, multi-tiered Internet/Intranet systems, computer telephony, call center technology, and embedded systems. Sing has participated in several Wrox projects in the past, has been working with (and writing about) Java and Jini since their very first alpha releases, and is an active participant in the Jini community.

Sing contributed Chapters 14 and 15 to this book.

Dan Malks

Dan Malks is an Enterprise Java Architect with Sun Microsystems, working in the Sun Java Center in McLean, VA. He received a Master of Science degree in Computer Science from Johns Hopkins University in 1996 after having earned a Bachelor of Science in Computer Science from The College of William and Mary in 1987.

While focusing on Object Oriented technologies, he has developed in a variety of environments, including Smalltalk and most recently Java. He has published articles about Java in leading industry periodicals, in addition to being a contributing author to *Professional JSP*, Wrox 2000 and *Professional Java Server Programming, J2EE Edition*, Wrox 2000. Additionally, he presented at JavaOne 2000 and will present at JavaOne 2001. Currently he has been focusing on Distributed, Service-based designs, patterns and implementations, and is author of the book *Core J2EE Patterns*, Prentice Hall 2001.

Dan contributed Chapter 7 to this book.

Thanks to my wife and children for their support. Also, thanks again to the Wrox staff.

Mark Nelson

Mark Nelson is currently a Software Engineer for Distributed Object Technologies (DOTech), Inc., a Sun Microsystems Authorized Java Center. A graduate of the University of Connecticut, Mark holds a degree in Computer Engineering. He has been developing in Java since 1996 with a focus on applications and server side programming. Mark can be contacted at mark@dotech.com.

Mark contributed Chapters 3, 4, 5, 6, and 23 to this book, with Bob Sullivan.

To my wife Laura, for without her nothing would be possible.

Grant Palmer

Grant Palmer is the IT tool development lead for the Eloret Corporation. He uses Java to develop standalone and web-based programs for scientific applications. Grant lives in Chandler, Arizona with his beautiful wife, Lisa, and his two sons, Jackson and Zachary.

Grant contributed Appendix C to this book.

Bob Sullivan

Bob Sullivan has been building large-scale software systems for almost 20 years. He is a co-founder of Distributed Object Technologies (DOTech), Inc., a Sun Microsystems Authorized Java Center that enables its clients to leverage Java, XML and related technologies to construct IT systems and solutions that provide a competitive edge. He has been developing and teaching Object Oriented systems since 1985. Prior to starting DOTech, he was a Systems Engineer with Sun Microsystems where he architected enterprise solutions for large corporate customers. He has a Bachelor of Science in Electrical Engineering from the University of Hartford (1982), and a Masters of Science in Computer Engineering from Rensselaer Polytechnic Institute (1987).

He can be reached at sully@dotech.com.

Bob contributed Chapters 3, 4, 5, 6, and 23 to this book, along with Mark Nelson.

To my wife Viv for her love and support. Your love is a gift from God!

Geoff Taylor

Geoff Taylor (g.taylor@kainos.com) is a Senior Software Engineer and has worked at Kainos Software Ltd for the last 8 years. He wrote his first web application in PL-SQL in 1995 (back when web programming was hard) and is impressed with how much simpler it all is now. He lives in Carrickfergus, Northern Ireland, with Shereen, two cats, two guitars and unfortunately only one computer.

Geoff contributed Chapters 9 and 10 to this book.

John Timney

John lives in the UK with his lovely wife Philippa in a small town called Chester-le-Street in the North of England. He is a postgraduate of Nottingham University having gained an MA in Information Technology following a BA Honours Degree from Humberside University. John specialises in Internet Solutions and his computing expertise has gained him a Microsoft MVP (Most Valuable Professional) award. His hobbies include martial arts, and he has black belts in two different styles of Karate.

John wishes to acknowledge Dan Adler, author of the JACOB Java-COM Bridge.

John contributed Appendix G to this book.

Thanks Pippa, for letting me spend hours glued to the web, feeding me biscuits, bringing me tea and not complaining much.

Sameer Tyagi

Sameer works with the Java Center at Sun Microsystems and writes regularly.

Sameer contributed Chapter 16 to this book.

Geert Van Damme

Geert lives in Leuven (Belgium) with his wife Sofie and his two little sons. He studied Mathematical Psychology and Philosophy but ended up working in the IT business after a short while. In 1997 he started his own development and consulting company Darling, currently focusing on server side Java. Since then he has worked as an independant consultant on a number of projects, mainly from his home office, and as a Java trainer for Sun Belgium.

Geert can be reached at geert.vandamme@darling.be.

Geert contributed Chapter 19 to this book.

Steve Wilkinson

Steve is a hands-on software developer with over 13 years experience and is based in Denver, Colorado. Steve is founder of his own company Elkhorn Creek Software, Incorporated. He is also employed full-time by New Particles, Incorporated. Steve currently is working in J2EE technologies in the Denver area. He has developed software using Java technologies since 1996. He has worked on projects for the following Fortune 500 companies: Sun Microsystems, MCI, BellSouth, IBM, and British Airways. He has also assisted several start-ups in the Denver area. He received a B.S. in Electrical Engineering from the University of Kentucky, and is working on his M.S. in Computer Information Systems at Regis University. Steve has contributed to *Developing Java Servlets*, Sams 1999, by Jim Goodwill, and *Professional JSP*, Wrox 2000.

Steve would like to dedicate his work to his daughters, Cayleigh and Ashleigh. He would also like to thank the employees of New Particles, Incorporated for hosting a series of pages dedicated to the Struts framework (http://www.newparticles.com/struts/). Lastly, Steve would like to thank Craig McClanahan for donating Struts to the Apache Software Foundation.

Steve contributed Chapter 21 to this book.

itionProfessionalJSP2ndEditionProfessionalJSP2ndEditionProfessiona
onProfessionalJSP2ndEditionProfessionalJSP2ndEditionProfessionalJS
rofessionalJSP2ndEditionProfessionalJSP2ndEditionProfessionalJSP2n
essionalJSP2ndEditionProfessionalJSP2ndEditionProfessionalJSP2ndEd
ionalJSP2ndEditionProfessionalJSP2ndEditionProfessionalJSP2ndEditi
alJSP2ndEditionProfessionalJSP2ndEditionProfessionalJSP2ndEditionP
SP2ndEditionProfessionalJSP2ndEditionProfessionalJSP2ndEditionProf
ndEditionProfessionalJSP2ndEditionProfessionalJSP2ndEditionProfess

Table of Contents

Table of Contents

Table of Contents

Table of Contents

Table of Contents

Table of Contents

Table of Contents

Table of Contents

Table of Contents

xvi

Table of Contents

Table of Contents

xxi

xxii

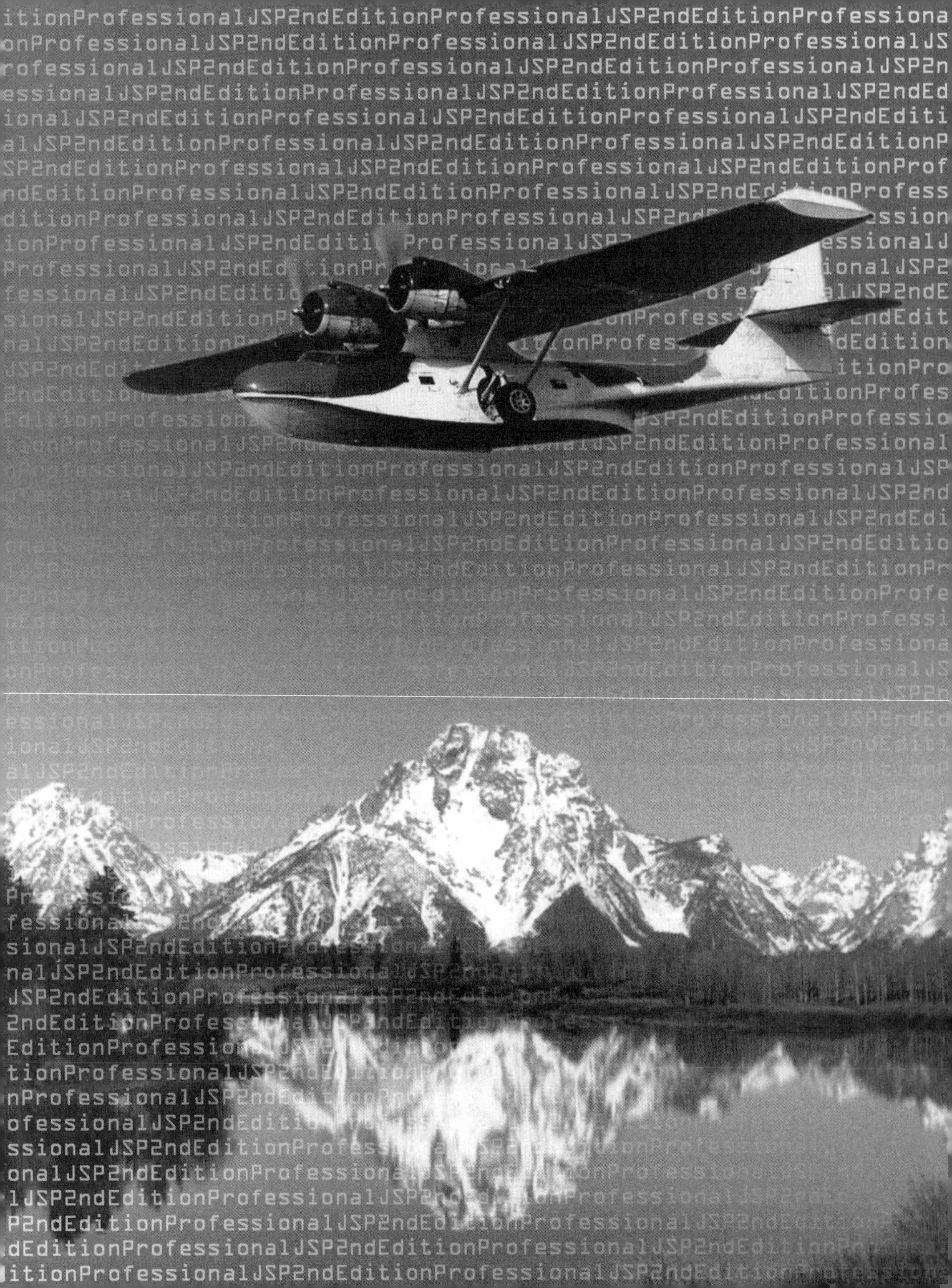
ProfessionalJSP2ndEdition

Introduction

Welcome

Welcome to *Professional JSP, 2nd Edition*, which is designed to help new and experienced Java developers alike discover the power (and even the joy) of creating Java-based server-side solutions for the web.

JavaServer Pages (**JSP**) and **Java Servlets** are complementary technologies that form a fundamental part of the **Java 2 Enterprise Edition** (**J2EE**). J2EE turns Java into a wide-ranging platform for enterprise development, by defining a set of useful APIs, a runtime platform, and a coherent model for how best to combine their features into a scalable, portable, and well-designed application.

The J2EE platform is built upon the premise that its job is to remove from the developer as much hard work as possible, by abstracting away much of the messy, low-level code that can so easily clog enterprise applications and divert developers' attention from the real task of writing their business and presentation logic. Its container-based architecture provides the context in which this happens, containers providing many services to the application via XML-based deployment descriptor files. In the J2EE model, JavaServer Pages and servlets are the components that are deployed in a web container to provide an interactive web interface to enterprise-level processing and data.

Who is this Book For?

This book is aimed at anyone who knows the Java language and core APIs – through reading *Beginning Java 2, JDK 1.3 Edition* (ISBN 1-861003-668) or some other tutorial book that covers similar ground –and wants to learn about web programming with the latest versions of the JSP and servlet APIs.

Familiarity with HTML is required; however, no prior knowledge of server-side Java programming is necessary. Having said that, this book does not claim to be exhaustive in all areas, particularly in relation to other Java APIs such as Enterprise JavaBeans, JavaMail, and JMS. *Professional Java Server Programming, J2EE Edition* (ISBN 1-861004-65-6) is an excellent introduction to the whole Java 2 Enterprise Edition platform.

This book covers the latest versions of the JSP and Servlet specifications – versions 1.2 and 2.3 respectively. These new specifications are being developed through the **Java Community Process** (http://java.sun.com/aboutJava/communityprocess/), and as of this writing are at the Proposed Final Draft stage.

> *It is possible that some small changes might be made before they are finally released; however any*
> *modifications are likely to be minor and the new specifications are already being implemented by a*
> *number of products including the reference implementation, Tomcat 4.0.*

Those who have read the first edition of this book will notice that this edition is not a revision of *Professional JSP, 1ˢᵗ Edition*; rather, it has been 're-coded from the ground up' to address the newest features of Java web development. A lot has changed since the first edition, which was only a year ago!

If you already have some exposure to server Java web development, you should pay attention to the *"What's New"* sections of Chapter 1, and then perhaps skip ahead to the sections that most interest you. On the other hand, if all this JSP and servlet stuff is new and somewhat confusing, you've come to the right place; the first section of this book (especially Chapters 1-6) was written with you in mind.

What's Covered in this Book

This book has the following structure:

- ❑ We start with an introduction to the Web, and the HTTP protocol that makes it work.

- ❑ JSP and Servlets are then introduced. We show the fundamental programming models, the JSP tags, using JavaBeans to remove business logic from the JSP, and how to combine JSPs and Servlets to create a well-structured, easily-maintainable application.

- ❑ The next section covers the JSP custom tag mechanism, which enables developers to extend the vocabulary of JSP. As well as describing how to develop custom tags, we look at why and how you would want to do this, and at some of the third-party tag libraries that are available.

- ❑ Further chapters cover database access, using the eXtensible Markup Language (XML) in connection with JSP, the powerful new filtering mechanism in Servlet 2.3, application events, and configuring web applications for security.

- ❑ Once we've finished looking at the key Java web technologies, we step back and spend some time considering best practices, debugging and performance, and the increasingly popular Struts framework that provides a solid foundation for extensible, flexible applications.

- ❑ Finally, we look at how JSPs and Servlets can be used to generate web content that is not purely HTML, before closing with an examination of how they fit into the larger Java 2 Enterprise Edition, and particularly how they relate to Enterprise JavaBeans.

Appendices cover installation and configuration of a JSP/Servlet environment, provide detailed references for JSP, Servlets, and the HTTP protocol, and finally JSP for ASP programmers.

What You Need to Use this Book

Most of the code in this book was tested with the Java 2 Platform, Standard Edition SDK (JDK 1.3) and Tomcat 4.0, the reference implementation of the JSP 1.2 and Servlet 2.3 specifications. JDK 1.3 is obtainable from http://java.sun.com/j2se/, and Tomcat from http://jakarta.apache.org/tomcat/.

See Appendix A for Tomcat installation and configuration instructions.

However, for some of the chapters you will need some additional software:

Databases

Several of the chapters also require access to a database. For these chapters we used a mixture of:

❑ MySQL, from http://www.mysql.com/

❑ Microsoft Access 2000

EJB Container

For Chapter 24 you will also need an EJB container supporting 1.1 version of the EJB specification. We used jBoss 2.0, from http://www.jboss.org.

Image Creation and Rendering Tools

For Chapter 23, several image viewing and creation tools are required:

❑ The Adobe SVG Viewer 2.0 from http://www.adobe.com/svg/viewer/install/beta.html

❑ The Batik 1.0 Beta distribution from http://xml.apache.org/batik/

❑ The FOP Project, from http://xml.apache.org/fop

Additional Software

Finally, there are a few additional pieces of software that a number of chapters also require:

❑ The Java API for XML Parsing (JAXP), version 1.1, from http://java.sun.com/xml/

❑ Xerces XML Parser and Xalan XSLT Processor, from http://xml.apache.org

❑ For the SSL example in Chapter 16, the Java Secure Sockets Extension (JSSE) version 1.0.1, from http://java.sun.com/products/jsse/

❑ For Chapter 21, the Struts application framework, from http://jakarta.apache.org/struts/

❑ For Chapter 22, the Openwave UP.SDK WAP simulator, from http://developer.phone.com/download/

❑ An SMTP mail service for the JavaMail example in Chapter 24

Conventions

To help you get the most from the text and keep track of what's happening, we've used a number of conventions throughout the book. For instance:

> **These boxes hold important, not-to-be forgotten information, which is directly relevant to the surrounding text.**

While this background style is used for asides to the current discussion.

As for styles in the text:

❑ When we introduce them, we **highlight** important words.

❑ We show keyboard strokes like this: *Ctrl-A*.

❑ We show filenames and code within the text like so: doGet().

❑ Text on user interfaces and URLs are shown as: Menu.

We present code in three different ways. Definitions of methods and properties are shown as follows:

```
protected void doGet(HttpServletRequest req, HttpServletResponse resp)
                     throws ServletException, IOException
```

Example code is shown:

```
In our code examples, the code foreground style shows new, important,
   pertinent code
while code background shows code that is less important in the present context,
   or has been seen before.
```

Customer Support

We've tried to make this book as accurate and enjoyable as possible, but what really matters is what the book actually does for you. Please let us know your views, either by returning the reply card in the back of the book, or by contacting us via email at feedback@wrox.com.

Source Code and Updates

As you work through the examples in this book, you may decide that you prefer to type in all the code by hand. Many readers prefer this because it's a good way to get familiar with the coding techniques that are being used.

Whether you want to type the code in or not, we have made all the source code for this book available at our web site at the following address:

http://www.wrox.com/

If you're one of those readers who likes to type in the code, you can use our files to check the results you should be getting - they should be your first stop if you think you might have typed in an error. If you're one of those readers who doesn't like typing, then downloading the source code from our web site is a must!

Either way, it'll help you with updates and debugging.

Errata

We've made every effort to make sure that there are no errors in the text or the code. However, to err is human, and as such we recognize the need to keep you informed of any mistakes as they're spotted and corrected. Errata sheets are available for all our books at http://www.wrox.com. If you find an error that hasn't already been reported, please let us know.

Our web site acts as a focus for other information and support, including the code from all our books, sample chapters, previews of forthcoming titles, and articles and opinion on related topics.

P2P Online Forums

Join the mailings lists at http://www.p2p.wrox.com for author and peer support. Be confident that your query is not just being examined by a support professional, but by the many Wrox authors and other industry experts present on our mailing lists.

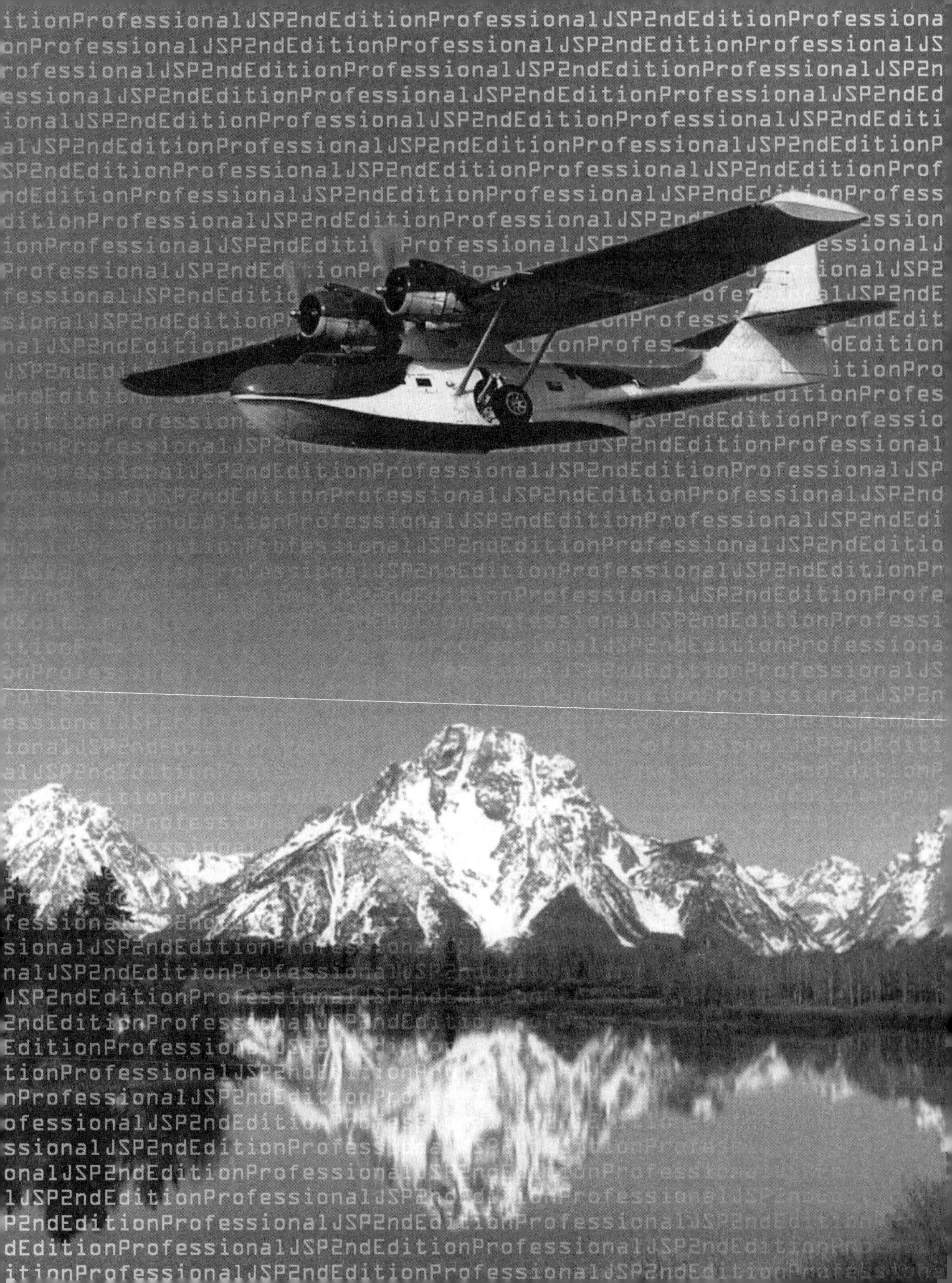
ProfessionalJSP2ndEdition

1

Introducing JSP 1.2
and Servlet 2.3

In this first chapter we will set the scene for the rest of the book by answering a number of important questions:

- ❑ Why is Java an effective web platform?
- ❑ What is the Java 2 Enterprise Edition?
- ❑ What role do JSP and Servlets play in J2EE?
- ❑ Why is this book worth reading?
- ❑ What are the latest JSP and Servlet features?

Java and the Web

When the Java programming language was first introduced, many thought it would play an important role in the emerging World Wide Web. Yet the initial excitement that Java applets provoked didn't last long, especially as products such as Macromedia Director and Flash stole the client-side thunder. As the language has matured over the past few years, it turns out that Java has indeed found an important role to fill, although not in the way that was initially intended. It is on the server, not the client, that Java has taken the web world by storm. In just a few years, Java has arguably become the premier server-side programming language for the web. In fact, a search on a popular job placement website for career opportunities in Silicon Valley showed more software development positions available to Java programmers than for any other language. (A search of http://www.monster.com/ for "Computers, Software" jobs in the "California-Silicon Valley/San Jose" location on January 13, 2001 revealed 287 Java, 154 C/C++, 87 Perl, and 34 Visual Basic jobs.)

Why has Java become so popular despite the existence of many other established programming languages? The following are a few probable reasons:

- **Java is platform independent**

  Java's "Write Once, Run Anywhere" technology let's you deploy the same Servlets and JSPs on many different platforms, be it Solaris, Linux, or Win32 (to name a few). In fact, switching platforms with Servlet/JSP applications can be as simple as copying a single file into the proper directory. No other web development solution provides such flexibility.

- **Java is web-centric**

  While other languages have had modules or add-ons incorporated into them to support the web, Java was built from the ground up with Internet support in mind. Java's net-centric architecture makes creating efficient server-side applications remarkably easy.

- **Java is a simple, elegant language**

  In order to maintain platform independence, Java does not allow developers to get deep into the nuts and bolts of the host operating system. This is a hurdle for graphically intensive applications (such as games) that want to get as close to the hardware as possible to gain performance, but for the rest of us it provides the pleasant, streamlined environment that allows developers to concern themselves more with the fundamental architecture of their applications and less with the housekeeping details.

  Furthermore, Java's highly object-oriented nature encourages developers to write maintainable and reusable code, which is ideal for the ever-changing nature of web applications in a work climate that tends towards frequent developer turnover.

- **Sun Microsystems controls Java**

  Sun has taken flak over the years by not relinquishing control of Java to a neutral standards body. Without making a case for either side of this issue, as a result Sun has prevented Java from splintering off into different so-called flavors (avoiding the fate of C, SQL, etc.) and also ensures that new updates to the language consistently arrive to market.

  It should also be noted that Sun's "Java Community Process" helps ensure that those of us in the trenches can both influence the direction that Java is headed and learn about upcoming changes long before they are implemented. In contrast, as of this writing the Visual Basic community is up in arms over a significant amount of core changes made to the upcoming Visual Basic.NET, revealed only after beta copies of the new VB were made available.

The Big Picture

Servlets and JavaServer Pages are a subset of the overall collection of Java server-side APIs called the **Java 2 Enterprise Edition** (**J2EE**). The J2EE technologies are designed to provide a highly scalable and easily maintainable software infrastructure well suited for medium to large organizations (in other words, 'enterprises'). Servlets and JavaServer Pages together form the presentation layer of J2EE web applications, while another technology, **Enterprise JavaBeans** (EJBs), is used to form the logic and data layers.

Enterprise JavaBeans are designed to encapsulate the interfaces of all types of disparate database management systems. They are also intended to encapsulate business logic that is reused across an organization in many different applications. For example, an insurance company might create an EJB to perform the complex calculations used to determine an insurance policy's future values. This same EJB could then be reused by a financial tracking system, insurance sales software, and even web applications. EJBs can thus help servlet/JSP developers create flexible and reusable solutions that can interface with multiple data sources and leverage existing business logic. The diagram below summarizes the whole enterprise application architecture, as seen by J2EE:

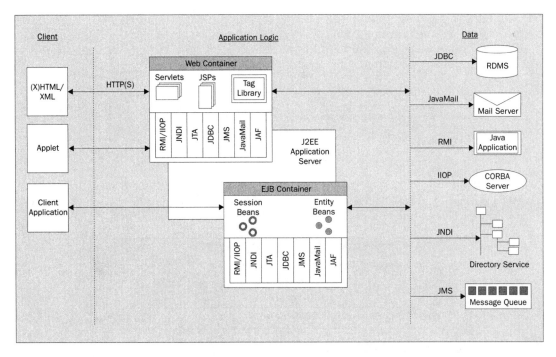

If you are creating a simple to moderately complex website, it is unlikely that you will incorporate EJB technology into your applications; servlets/JSP may very well meet all your needs by themselves, or with the help of normal JavaBeans. However, if you are creating web-enabled applications in an enterprise environment, you will likely find EJB and other J2EE components highly useful to your organization. While this book is focused on the Servlet and JSP technologies, a related Wrox work, *Professional Java Server Programming, J2EE Edition* (ISBN 1-861004-65-6), addresses these J2EE issues.

Servlets

Servlets are the Java way to create web-enabled applications. It may help to think of a servlet as a 'mini-web server'; each servlet extends the capability of a web server by providing additional custom functionality. This functionality can be used to create an e-commerce website, a database front-end, an image converter, etc. A servlet receives an HTTP request, and returns an HTTP response, and fortunately most of the underlying details of the process have been abstracted from the developer. Servlets can therefore be compared to other technologies such as CGI scripts, NSAPI applications, or any other solution that interfaces with a web server to produce web content. Servlets have gained market share from these alternative technologies because of their simplicity, extensibility, efficiency, and performance.

Even a novice developer should have no problems creating a Servlet – if you've written a simple Java class before, you've got all the skills you need. The following is an extremely simple Servlet that outputs "Hello world!" to a browser:

```
package com.wrox.projsp.ch01;

import javax.servlet.*;
import javax.servlet.http.*;
```

```
import java.io.*;

public class SimpleServlet extends HttpServlet {

  public void doGet(HttpServletRequest req, HttpServletResponse resp)
          throws ServletException, IOException {

    PrintWriter pw = resp.getWriter();
    pw.print("<html><body>Hello world!</body></html>");
    pw.close();
  }
}
```

We'll be looking at Servlets – both how they are written and how to configure the web server to process them – in Chapter 3. However, the screenshot below shows the result of executing this Servlet:

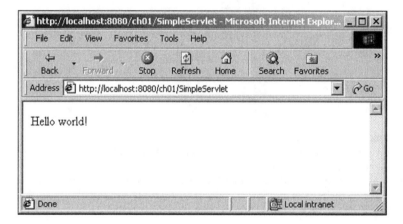

JavaServer Pages

JavaServer Pages perform the same task as Servlets (programmatically generating web content), but use a different development paradigm. While Servlets are created by writing Java classes, JavaServer Pages (JSP) are created using a syntax very similar to HTML, not unlike Microsoft's Active Server Pages (ASP) technology. The JSPs are then converted into servlets at run-time automatically. Here's an example of a JSP:

```
<html>
  <body>
    Hello <%= new String("world!") %>
  </body>
</html>
```

Note how the HTML is seamlessly combined with a form of in-line Java code. JSP syntax will be introduced in Chapters 4 and 5; for now, the screenshot below shows the output from this JSP (which is just the same as that produced by the Servlet above):

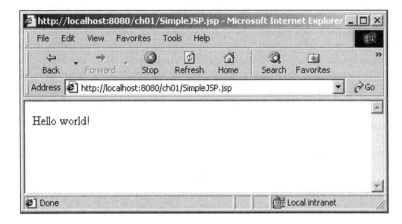

While the functionality of Servlets and JSP are redundant, the two different development styles lend themselves quite nicely to effective web development:

❑ JavaServer Pages are ideal for creating dynamic web pages. HTML developers can use the tools with which they are already familiar to develop normal HTML, adding dynamic functionality by inserting custom JSP tags here and there as Java developers instruct. Using this type of development methodology, development shops can cleanly separate the HTML presentation layer from the logic layer.

❑ Servlets on the other hand, are ideal for creation of highly programmatic content, such as images created on demand. Servlets are also often used as Controllers in so-called Model 2 Model-View-Controller applications (if that sounded Greek to you, don't panic, just check out Chapter 20 when you get a chance).

Thus, Servlets and JSPs can be and are often used together effectively in the same project. In fact, a **web application** in Java is a collection of various JSPs and Servlets that form components of the same project or application.

Why Read This Book?

With the incredible popularity of Servlets and JSP over the past two years, many books on the topic have come to market. Here are some reasons to spend your time studying this text (besides the handsome photographs on the cover):

❑ **This book covers the latest standards**
As of this writing (March 2001), the Java Servlet Specification 2.3 and the JavaServer Pages Specification 1.2, both of which introduce powerful new functionality, have reached 'Proposed Final Draft' status, and servers that implement these standards are becoming available. Any server-side Java developer will want to familiarize himself with these new standards immediately.

❑ **This book provides equal coverage of Servlets and JSP**
Experience has shown that for the majority of developers, *both* technologies fill important roles in web applications. We will consider both JSP and Servlets, and their respective roles, in this book rather than focusing entirely on one.

❑ **This book discusses architectural issues in depth**
JavaServer Pages are an excellent way to separate the presentation layer from the logic layer in a web application. However, to do so you need a good understanding of the architectural decisions to be made and the options open to you. There issues are discussed in depth, and the Apache Struts project (a ready-made and increasingly popular application framework) is covered extensively in Chapter 21.

❑ **This book covers a rich selection of topics**
By utilizing the wealth of experience of our team of experts, we are able to explore many advanced topics in depth. In addition to the basics of writing JSPs and Servlets, and JSP custom tags, this book discusses data access strategies with databases and XML; good practice in web application design; maintainability, debugging, and performance; how to generate non-textual content such as images and PDF files on-the-fly; and integrating JSPs and Servlets into a full-blown J2EE application. Extensive examples and case studies are provided.

What's New in the Servlet 2.3 Specification?

The Servlet 2.3 Specification doesn't introduce any significant fixes, but it does introduce two very significant new features:

Application Lifecycle Events

An individual Servlet does a good job of managing its own lifecycle; an `init()` method is called when the Servlet is first instantiated, and a `destroy()` method is called when the Servlet is terminated. Within these methods, a developer can deal with resource management efficiently. However, a group of Servlets may share the same resources (such as a pool of database connections) amongst themselves. They do this by all sharing a `ServletContext` object, which functions as a container for the Servlets' shared resources. Because no individual Servlet owns the `ServletContext` object, managing the lifecycle of shared resources can get hairy.

This inefficiency is resolved with the use of two new `ServletContext` event listener interfaces that let the application know when information is added to, modified, or deleted from a `ServletContext` object, and also when such objects are being created and destroyed. Event listeners are part of Java's way of event handling; 'listener' objects are registered to 'listen' for specific types of events. Thus, special `ServletContext` listeners can be used to listen for changes to the `ServletContext` object itself, and manage any resources in the `ServletContext` independent of the servlets/JSPs that use them.

Similarly, two new `HttpSession` event listeners have been added that enable a developer to know when information is added, modified or removed from an `HttpSession`, and when an `HttpSession` object is created or destroyed. The `HttpSession` object stores information about an individual web client. Because web connections are stateless (in other words, the web server can never know for certain when a client has finished requesting information), `HttpSession` objects periodically expire. It is therefore desirable to know when the objects expire, and it can be useful to know when new information is made available in the `HttpSession`, tasks which the new listeners make feasible.

Application lifecycle events are covered in more detail in Chapter 16.

Filtering

The concept of filtering is simple: instead of one Servlet performing many unrelated functions, such as authentication, encryption, and data processing, a series of specialized Java objects can be 'chained', each performing its own task before passing responsibility on to the next in the chain. The term 'filter' is used because each of these specialized objects filters the HTTP request and/or response data, making changes as necessary, much like an oil or air filter in an automobile.

Filtering is really a new name for an older concept that is familiar to experienced Servlet developers, and was previously implemented through a mechanism known as 'Servlet chaining'. However, servlet chaining was not an official part of the Servlet specification but was implemented in different, vendor-specific ways.

The Servlet 2.3 Specification introduces the chaining/filtering concept through the use of the new `Filter` interface. Filters are able to view and modify both the HTTP request and the HTTP response before they arrive at their intended destinations, as one would expect. However, Filters are not limited to filtering requests for Servlets; they can also acts as filters for requests to and responses from static HTML, and of course, JSP pages. Filters themselves may also be chained together in a specific order.

Filtering is covered thoroughly in Chapters 14 and 15.

What's New in the JSP 1.2 Specification?

The new JSP Specification 1.2 includes a number of new features and fixes:

Custom Tag Enhancements

A powerful feature of JSP is the ability to create custom tags in addition to the simple standard actions that the JSP standard defines. As a consequence, many third-party JSP tag libraries are becoming available. JSP 1.2 introduces several enhancements to this mechanism:

- ❑ **New type of custom tag**
  JSP 1.2 introduces the `IterationTag`, making custom tags that can loop over their contents much simpler to create and more efficient.

- ❑ **Improvements to translation-time JSP tag validation**
  There are now two tag validator classes, which JSP tag libraries may utilize at page-translation time to perform a custom developer-defined validation. Tags that use the new `TagLibraryValidator` class can validate themselves within the context of the entire document, while the other validator class, `TagExtraInfo`, only looks at the JSP tag itself to validate the isolated action that the tag is performing.

Custom tag libraries are covered in detail in Chapters 8 to 11.

New XML Syntax for JSP Pages

A new option is available for JSP authors: defining JSP pages using XML instead of the normal JSP syntax. The tighter XML syntax allows for programmatic interaction with the source of the JSP page, such as automatically transforming other XML documents into an XML JSP document via a transformation language such as XSLT (Extensible Stylesheet Language Transformations). XSLT works with an XML document and a special XSL stylesheet to transform all or part of an XML document into a different form, such as HTML, JSP, or PDF.

13

The XML syntax is covered in Chapter 10.

"Flush on Include" Limitation Removed

While not a major new feature, I couldn't pass up mentioning this fix here. In previous versions of JSP, the ubiquitous `<jsp:include>` tag came with a serious limitation: once used, the HTTP response output buffers were flushed. Since includes are very common, this limited a JSP author's options for error handling and page redirecting.

Thankfully, the limitation has been removed from JSP 1.2, and the revised `<jsp:include>` tag doesn't flush the output buffers by default. This also makes it possible for a JSP custom tag to post-process the output of a `<jsp:include>` tag.

Forthcoming Attractions

In addition to these new features, there are also several new specifications in development that are of particular interest to JSP and Servlet developers:

❑ **Standard JSP Tag Library**
A standardized tag library (or, more likely, collection of tag libraries) is under development under the Java Community Process. These will very significantly enhance the functionality of JSP, though the precise scope of the library that will result is still unclear. Tags for conditional and iterative processing are certain, and tags for accessing JNDI and JDBC data sources likely, but as of this writing little is known beyond that.

Many JSP and Servlet container vendors already provide a tag library that supply facilities of this sort, but the benefit of a standard library over multiple vendor-specific options is clear.

❑ **JSP Debugging Enhancements**
Another forthcoming standard relates to the debugging of code that, whilst not written in Java, is executed within a Java Virtual Machine; JSP is a prime example of such code. While certain Java development environments have already provided JSP debugging features, to date they have all been proprietary.

Summary

By providing platform independence, extensive Internet functionality, and a simple yet powerful syntax, Java is an excellent platform on which to build an application. Sun's continued support ensures that Java will continue to be competitive in the marketplace.

The Java 2 Enterprise Edition (J2EE) libraries provide a rich set of functionality for server-side application developers. Servlets and JavaServer Pages are part of the J2EE libraries, and can be used either by themselves or with some or all of the other J2EE APIs to create powerful web-enabled applications.

This book covers the latest Servlet and JSP standards and provides you with the necessary information and examples to learn and exploit Servlet and JSP technology. As you study this book, it should become clear why Servlet and JSP technology has become popular amongst web developers. They are simple enough to pick up in a few hours, but extensible enough to suit the large and complex projects that come across the desks of today's enterprise developers.

Chapter 2 starts our exploration of these technologies by exploring HTTP, the protocol that defines how the web itself 'works', and how JSPs and Servlets fit into its model. Happy web developing!

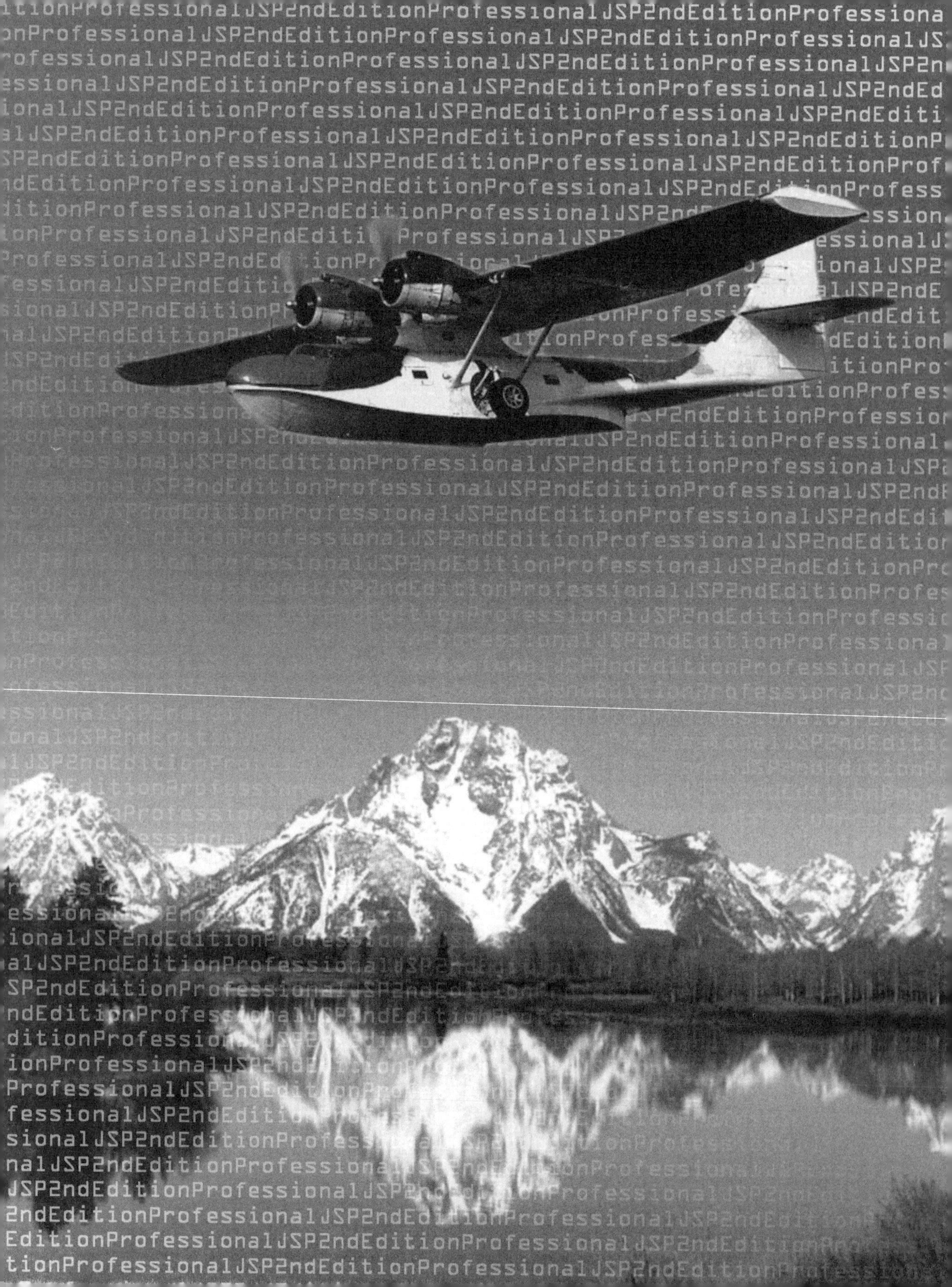
ProfessionalJSP2ndEdition

2

Web Application Concepts

Hard to imagine a world without the Web, isn't it? Think of some of the almost magical scenarios that the Web makes possible:

❑   A single store in Washington state can service the entire world

❑   A news magazine can revise its content ten times a day and be distributed to every country in the world, all without even one printing press

❑   And perhaps the most amazing one of all: it's now cool to be a computer nerd!

But just how does the Web work? This question will be answered in this chapter. We'll start off by looking at:

❑   How content is transferred across the Web using the **HTTP protocol**

❑   The **request/response** model, and how we can **preserve state** information between requests

❑   The concept of a server **port**

Then, in the remaining half of the chapter, we will explain the differences between **static** and **dynamic** web resources, and this will lead us onto the role that **Servlets** and **JSP** play in creating applications for the Web. Finally, we will finish the chapter by discussing how we can collect up static and dynamic Java-based resources into a **web application**.

Web Basics

The World Wide Web was created in 1990 by a scientist named Tim Berners-Lee. He created it while working for the European Organization for Nuclear Research (CERN) with the goal of facilitating more timely collaboration among the world community of physicists. Berners-Lee built the Web as an additional service on top of the existing Internet, which provided the hardware connections between thousands of computer systems across the world (to learn more about the history of Internet, see http://www.isoc.org/internet/history/). It is interesting to note that Berners-Lee and a collaborator, Robert Cailliau, used the object-oriented tools of the NeXTStep operating system to create the world's first web browser and web server. Shame on those of us who thought that NeXT machines were only good for reading the complete works of Shakespeare.

The Web gradually gained momentum, and comprised around 50 known web servers by 1993. A significant event occurred in the same year that would light the fuse of the Internet explosion: the National Center for Supercomputing Applications (NCSA) at the University of Illinois released the first version of the Mosaic web browser for Unix, PC, and Macintosh systems. Prior to Mosaic, the only fully featured browser available was on the NeXT platform.

With the Mosaic foundation laid, 1994 saw the emergence of the Web into pop culture. The general public began to regard the Internet as somewhat useful, and Netscape was founded by some of the same folks who made Mosaic. The so-called 'New Economy' consisting of e-land grabs and irrationally valuated companies was just around the corner. And the rest is, well, history.

The HTTP Connection

The Web defines how two parties, a web browser (or web **client**) and a web **server** communicate. When you visit a website, you are creating a relationship between these two parties. In this relationship, the two parties communicate by sending a series of brief messages. First, the web browser sends a message to the web server requesting a particular web page it wishes to receive, and if the web page exists, the web server responds with a message containing the appropriate web page. For each additional page that is viewed, the web browser sends additional requests to the web server, which likewise responds with the appropriate web pages.

In technical lingo, this type of relationship is called a **request/response model**. The client, in this case the web browser, requests a specific resource (for instance a web page) and the server then responds with the requested resource, if it's available. The Web is based on this request/response model, which is implemented via the **HyperText Transfer Protocol (HTTP)**. Just as 'protocol' in diplomatic settings governs how two parties should conduct their relationship with each other, a 'protocol' in the networking sense is a definition of how one device or program communicates with another. HTTP therefore defines how a web browser and a web server communicate.

A web address, such as http://www.yahoo.com/, is known as a **URL** (Universal Resource Locator). When you enter a URL into a web browser, the browser converts the URL into an HTTP request, and sends that request to the appropriate web server. Since HTTP is a plain-text protocol, we can easily take a closer look at how this process works:

1. A user types a URL into his web browser: http://www.yahoo.com/.

2. The browser determines from the first part of the URL, http://, that this is to be an HTTP request. The next part of the URL, www.yahoo.com, tells the browser the name of the server (also called a **host**) with which it needs to communicate. Finally, the last part of the URL, /, indicates the resource (in other words the web page) that the browser is requesting of the server.

Some web browsers, such as later versions of Internet Explorer and Netscape Navigator, permit the user to be lazy and type in an improperly formatted URL such as www.yahoo.com instead of the properly formatted http://www.yahoo.com/. In these cases, the browser automatically assumes default values for the information omitted from the malformed URL.

3. The web browser establishes a connection (called a **socket**) to the host in the URL, and sends it the following HTTP request:

```
GET / HTTP/1.1
```

(Note that this is a partial excerpt.)

4. The web server analyses the HTTP request. While the full request contains a lot of information, the first line, called the **request line**, is the most important. It's composed of three values delimited by a space: GET, /, and HTTP/1.1. Let's examine each one:

"**GET**" – This first field is the *method* that the web server should perform. The GET method instructs the web server to 'get' a web page from its storage device and send it back to the web browser.

"**/**" – The *resource* (for example the file) that the web server should act on (in this case, should get). If the name of the resource is omitted and only the directory name is indicated, as is the case here, the web server will search for a default file name in the indicated directory, which is usually index.html. In some situations, the web server may actually serve up a listing of all files in a given directory. This option is usually disabled for security reasons.

"**HTTP/1.1**" – The version of HTTP that the client supports, which in this case is of course 1.1. At present, the only other valid value would be "HTTP/1.0".

The remainder of the request is composed of various **HTTP headers**, which contain miscellaneous information about the client that the server may find of use. We'll discuss more about HTTP headers in this and other chapters.

5. The web server sends the client an HTTP response, which looks something like this:

```
HTTP/1.1 200 OK
Date: Sat, 13 Jan 2001 02:45:21 GMT
Connection: close
Content-Type: text/html

<html>
...
```

6. The browser parses the response and displays the resulting HTML page. The first line of the response, called the **status line**, is the most interesting, and just like the request line, it's three values delimited by a space. Let's look at each value:

"**HTTP/1.1**" – The version of HTTP that the server is using. Often it is desirable even for modern servers to use HTTP/1.0 instead of HTTP/1.1 for backwards compatibility, although only the earliest of browsers didn't support HTTP 1.1. All HTTP 1.1 browsers are backwards compatible with HTTP 1.0.

"**200**" – This is the status code that the server returns. The status code tells the browser if the request was successful, and if it wasn't, it provides a reason as to why the request failed.

"**OK**" – The *reason phrase*; this provides a brief textual explanation of the status code. Some examples of common status code/reason phrase combinations are: "`200 OK`" (resource found and served successfully); "`404 Not Found`" (resource not found – a standard error page is usually served in place of the requested resource); "`500 Internal Server Error`" (the familiar bane of the web developerwhich occurs when either a programmatic extension to the web server fails, or in some cases the web server itself).

Just as the request includes a number of informational headers, so does the response. Following the headers is the **message body**, which contains the requested resource.

Usually, a web browser sends several requests to a web server in order to render a single HTML document. For example, if an HTML document contains any images, the browser must send a separate request to the web server for each of the images. It is not unusual for a web page to require 25 or more requests. When a web page uses frames, the web browser treats each frame as an HTML page and so must send at least one additional request to the web server for each frame.

We've just covered some of the basics of HTTP. If your applications demand a more comprehensive understanding, or you're just a curious person, the document RFC2616 provides a detailed specification of HTTP/1.1, including a complete list of all status codes.

> *Contained among the many RFC (Request for Comments) documents are the specifications for many Internet protocols. You can find all RFC documents at http://www.rfc-editor.org.*

MIME Types

Our discussion of HTTP illustrates how a web browser and a web server communicate. The browser requests a resource, and the web server responds with it. A resource can be a web page, an image, a sound clip, a compressed file archive, and so on. When the browser receives the requested resource, it must know what to do with it. For example, an HTML page should be parsed and displayed according to specific rules, an image should be decoded using a specific algorithm, and a compressed archive needs to be decompressed with the appropriate program. For this to occur, the web browser must know what type of resource it is receiving. Because the URL contains no indication of the resource type, the web browser would logically either need to analyze the resource content and determine what type of resource it is, or be told what type of resource it is receiving by the web server. HTTP uses the latter approach.

Recall for a moment the HTTP response we analyzed earlier, without the message body:

```
HTTP/1.1 200 OK
Date: Sat, 13 Jan 2001 02:45:21 GMT
Connection: close
Content-Type: text/html
```

This response is composed of the status line and three headers. The third header, `Content-Type`, indicates the type of resource that the web server is sending to the browser. In this case, the resource type is defined as `text/html`. Because defining resource types for use all around the world could leave plenty of room for conflicts, it's important that the types be unambiguously and authoritatively defined. Fortunately, such a resource classification system existed prior to the web: **MIME types**.

MIME stands for Multipurpose Internet Mail Extensions. The MIME standard allows disparate e-mail systems to interoperate by defining how the text and attachments of an e-mail are to be formatted and stored. As part of this standard, the MIME standard uniquely defines pretty much every distributed file format in existence using 'MIME types'. Here are a few examples:

- ❏   `text/plain` – normal text file

- ❏   `text/html` – HTML files

- ❏   `image/jpeg` – JPG image files

- ❏   `image/gif` – GIF image

The complete list of MIME types can be accessed at:
http://www.isi.edu/in-notes/iana/assignments/media-types/media-types.
The MIME standard is defined in RFC2045, RFC2046, RFC2047, RFC2048, and RFC2049.

If a web browser provides internal support for the MIME type of the resource it receives, it deals with it as programmed. Otherwise, the web browser can either be told what to do with the specific MIME type, or it simply prompts the user to tell it what to do. If a `Content-Type` header is not present in the HTTP response, web browsers differ in their behavior. For example, Internet Explorer 5.x simply assumes that the resource is HTML, while Netscape Navigator 4.x assumes that the resource is simple text. In all cases, it's always a good idea for a web server to specify the MIME type of the HTTP response.

HTTP Headers

We first mentioned HTTP headers in our initial discussion of HTTP, and we've now seen how headers are used to convey the MIME type of an HTTP response and also to set and retrieve cookies. Headers are informational additions to both the HTTP request and response that convey both essential and non-essential details about them. The full list of possible headers and footers is fairly long, so we'll just take a look at some common headers used in a browsing session. For our analysis, we'll take a look at the first request sent by Internet Explorer 5.5 to **www.slashdot.org** and the subsequent response. First the request:

1. `GET / HTTP/1.1`

2. `Accept: image/gif, image/x-xbitmap, image/jpeg, image/pjpeg, application/vnd.ms-powerpoint, application/vnd.ms-excel, application/msword, */*`

3. `Accept-Language: en-us`

4. `Accept-Encoding: gzip, deflate`

5. `User-Agent: Mozilla/4.0 (compatible; MSIE 5.5; Windows NT 5.0)`

6. `Host: www.slashdot.org`

7. `Connection: Keep-Alive`

Line 1 is of course not a header; it's the request line. The remaining six lines all provide non-vital information via headers that aid the web server in determining how to respond to the request. Line 2, the `Accept` header, enumerates the various MIME types that the browser supports. While "`*/*`" indicates that the browser will accept any MIME type, the types that are specifically enumerated indicate those types that the browser prefers. Line 3 tells the web server what language the browser's user prefers. `en-us` refers to the English spoken in the United States. If the browser were to send the following header:

```
Accept-Language: es-cl
```

the web server might choose to redirect the user to a Spanish translation of the web site (`es-cl` is the Chilean dialect of Spanish). Line 4, the `Accept-Encoding` header, indicates the *content codings* schemes that the browser supports. Content codings are any transformation that the content has undergone in the process of being transported from the server to the browser, such as compression. Line 5, `User-Agent`, tells the web server which type of browser is being used to request the resource. In addition to providing useful statistics, this header also allows web developers to provide custom content for differing browsers.

Line 6, the `Host` header, is especially important. At first, it may seem that the value of the `Host` header is redundant since a connection to `www.slashdot.org` must already be open for the client to send the request; isn't it a bit silly to tell the server what its own name is? As it happens, this information is quite necessary. Because the cost of purchasing and configuring a physical web server and connecting it to the Internet is rather high, a single physical server often contains multiple websites (a practice known as **subhosting** or **virtual hosting**). While it is technically possible to assign each of these subhosted websites their own unique Internet address (called an **IP address**; each web server must have one), it is far easier to have each of them share the IP address of the physical server. Thus, it is often necessary for a browser to specify with which website it wishes to communicate *after* the connection to the server has been established.

> *The `Host` header was introduced in the HTTP/1.1 spec, so if you were to browse the web with an older HTTP/1.0 compliant browser, such as Netscape 1.x, any website that is subhosted (and vast numbers are) would be inaccessible. This is probably a minor issue since the HTML would be in most cases rendered rather poorly by such a browser.*

Line 7, the `Connection` header, indicates the browser's preference as to the persistence of the connection. While HTTP is not guaranteed to be persistent, the connection may be maintained for a brief period of time should the browser immediately request additional resources. The value in this example, "`Keep-Alive`", indicates just such a preference. The server may or may not honor this preference.

Now, let's take a look at the HTTP response that was sent back:

1. `HTTP/1.1 200 OK`

2. `Date: Mon, 29 Jan 2001 07:58:05 GMT`

3. `Server: Apache/1.3.12 (Unix) mod_perl/1.24`

4. `Connection: close`

5. `Transfer-Encoding: chunked`

6. `Content-Type: text/html`

7.

8. `(html page)`

As you can see, lines 2-6 provide some interesting data. Line 2 indicates the date and time that the response originated. Line 3, the `Server` header, tells the browser some information about the server that generated the response. Any proxy server sitting between the browser and the server will not modify this header, although it may add a new `Via` header containing information about itself. Line 4 indicates what the browser may do with the connection once the response has been received. Line 5, `Transfer-Encoding:` `chunked` indicates that the message body is being sent as a series of chunks, rather than one long string of data. Line 6 indicates the MIME type of the response. Line 7 is simply a blank line, which is used to separate the header information from the actual resource that has been requested. Line 8 and all subsequent lines contain the actual resource.

I have only briefly summarized the headers contained in the example request and response that we've looked at. You can find complete definitions of all the HTTP headers in the HTTP 1.1 Specification document (RFC2616).

Persistence and Cookies

One of the 'features' of HTTP is its simplicity. We discussed earlier that when a user views a web page, a relationship is formed between the browser and the web server. This relationship is short: the browser requests a resource, and the web server responds with it. While the user could continue to visit other pages on the same website, each time the browser requests an additional web page from the web server, it is a new relationship. The web server is unaware that it has ever communicated with a particular user in the past. Thus, the relationship between the browser and the server is not **persistent**; the link between the browser and the server is not maintained from one request to another. This same concept is described by the term **stateless**. Because information on the state of the relationship between the client and the server is not preserved between connections, HTTP is said to be a stateless protocol.

> *Because opening a socket adds expense to the transaction of requesting and responding for both parties, some web servers do maintain a persistent connection with the browser for a limited amount of time on the assumption that the browser will shortly request more information. However, this persistence is not guaranteed and only available for a very short amount of time. Such connections are called 'keep-alives'.*

A lack of persistence is fine if a website's sole functionality is serving up simple web pages. However, e-commerce sites require much more complex functionality. Isn't it nice that Amazon.com can track all the items you want to purchase in a 'shopping cart' while you browse their website? Yet because HTTP isn't persistent, whenever a website tracks information about you, (such as your name or the items you want to purchase) across multiple page views on a daily or even a weekly or annual basis, the website must rely on additional mechanisms to create persistence.

Enter cookies. A **cookie** is a seemingly non-intuitive name for a piece of information that a web server stores on your local system via the browser. Cookies are simply name/value pairs, and are available only to the web server that created them.

> *Before you rely on cookies for highly secure information, be aware that some browsers have known security holes that when exploited allow cookies to be viewed by unauthorized hosts. You should use cookies for non-sensitive information and store any sensitive information you wish to retain on the server.*

The process that a web server uses to create and retrieve cookies is quite simple. Since www.altavista.com stores a cookie on every visitor's browser, let's take a look at this process:

1. The browser sends a request to the web server:

```
GET / HTTP/1.1
...
```

2. The server replies with the following response:

```
HTTP/1.1 200 OK
Date: Mon, 29 Jan 2001 07:23:37 GMT
Content-Type: text/html; CHARSET=ISO-8859-1
Set-Cookie: AV_USERKEY=AVSe4596f6c1b0000da0810ac000a05c; expires=Tuesday, 31-Dec-
2013 12:00:00 GMT; path=/; domain=.altavista.com;
...
```

The fourth line of the response contains the HTTP header Set-Cookie, which instructs the browser to store a cookie with the name AV_USERKEY and the cryptic value shown above. The expires value indicates when the browser should delete the cookie; domain is used to determine which web servers can see the cookie; path indicates the resources on the web server that can see the cookie. For more information on cookies, refer to http://www.cookiecentral.com.

3. The browser requests another page from the website by sending:

```
GET / HTTP/1.1
Cookie: AV_USERKEY=AVSe4596f6c1b0000da0810ac000a05c
...
```

Now that a cookie has been set, the browser includes an HTTP header named Cookie with each subsequent request.

Cookies are a crucial way to establish persistence. While there are other methods that can provide persistence while a user continues to browse a website, cookies are the only method that reliably provide persistence once a user leaves a website and comes back again later.

Ports

In most cases, the average web server is not a dedicated web server. In fact, the web server is one of many **services** that a **physical server** (an actual computer) provides. Other common services provided on the physical server include FTP (transferring files), POP (receiving e-mail), SMTP (sending e-mail), TELNET (logging into a server), and so on. Each of these services is constantly 'listening' for new clients attempting to establish a connection. This means one of two things: either a single server program is listening for all these different types of connections, or each service has its own server program. Of course, the former wouldn't be practical; it would require that the server program be modified each time an additional service was added to the physical server. Generally, each service has its own unique server program. Yet, if a physical server has five or more services constantly listening for connection requests, how does each service know which of the incoming requests correspond to it? This problem is addressed through the concept of a *port*.

The term **port** comes from the hardware side of computers. Just as I/O with external devices flows through hardware ports (for example serial ports, parallel ports, USB ports, and so on), network I/O flows through software ports. While hardware ports involve a physical route through which signals flow to the computer's bus, software ports are really nothing more than a table that defines the correlation between a port number and a service. The following are some common port numbers and their corresponding services:

❏   80 – web server

❏   110 – POP server

❏   25 – SMTP server

❏   23 – TELNET server

You can find the authoritative list of port assignments at http://www.isi.edu/in-notes/iana/assignments/port-numbers.

In terms of web development, ports are interesting because while a web server listens by default on port 80, it can be set up on any port. Before we elaborate on this concept, let's take a look at how a port is controlled in a URL. Recall our earlier example URL, http://www.yahoo.com/.

We discussed above three basic components of a URL: the protocol (http://), the host (www.yahoo.com), and the resource (/). There's actually another component: the port. Because web servers use port 80 by default, a URL is not required to enumerate a specific port. However, if you knew that a web server was listening on a different port, say, port 8080, you could specify that port in the following way: http://www.someserver.com:8080/.

When do web developers ever start dealing with ports? Configuring a web server to listen on a custom port can be the ideal solution for websites that wish to reside on the Internet but restrict access to a subset of users. Often, a new version of a website will be made available for limited access on a custom port before it becomes the default public website. Additionally, when multiple web servers reside on the same machine, they must listen on different ports; otherwise, both servers would attempt to respond to the same requests. Such a scenario is discussed a little later in this chapter in the 'Servlets' section.

Before we end our discussion of ports, let me mention that you can't just go around picking port numbers out of the air for your web server to listen on. Ports 0 through 1023, called the 'Well Known Ports', are reserved for important (and often critical) system processes. Don't pick a port number in this range, ever. Ports 1024 through 49151 are the 'Registered Ports'. You can generally pick a port number in this range for experimenting and temporary solutions with little trouble, but be aware that many network-aware programs, from Quake to AOL, often use these ports. If you want to live a truly stress-free existence, choose a port from the 'Dynamic and/or Private Ports' collection, ranging from 49152 to 65535.

Using Servlets/JSP with the Web

When a browser requests a resource from a web server, that resource can either be an existing file, or content that is generated on the fly when requested. For example, the home page of www.yahoo.com is the same for all users and is likely an existing file. However, when a user performs a search, the resulting page is created specifically for the user who performed the search; it would be impractical and inflexible to generate thousands of files at design time anticipating the possible searches that a user could perform. Content that is the same for all users and is composed of a simple, unchanging file is referred to as **static** content. While a website's design team can update static content quite often, the key point is that static web pages are stored as files at the time they are requested. On the other hand, web pages that are custom-generated for the requesting user are said to be **dynamic**.

Web servers are designed to process requests for static content. However, because the needs of dynamic content are usually very specific, web servers cannot themselves generate dynamic content. Instead, web servers communicate with custom programs written to generate dynamic data. The most popular mechanism that web servers use to communicate with external programs is the **Common Gateway Interface (CGI)**.

CGI

Under the CGI model, the web server receives the HTTP request from the browser, determines that the request is for dynamic data, launches an external program, and passes it the HTTP request. The external program then executes, and upon terminating passes back to the web server the message body of an appropriate HTTP response and optionally some HTTP headers. The web server then sends an HTTP response to the web browser. Virtually every popular programming language has been used to provide CGI solutions, from C to Perl to Visual Basic. Because CGI programs are typically relatively simple in size and scope, they are often called **CGI scripts**.

> *It is not always possible to tell whether a URL corresponds to a static or a dynamic resource. In the early days of the web the form of the URLs would indicate this, for example* http://www.domain.com/index.html *or* http://www.domain.com/cgi-bin/funanddynamic.cgi. *However, because the web server acts as a gateway between the web browser and the web server, the web server can be configured to route requests in custom, non-intuitive ways. For example, a web server could be configured to route requests to a CGI program if the URL ends in .html or contains the string /hello/. A web server could even be configured to treat all files with the .html extension as GIF files, since HTTP uses MIME types, not file extensions, to determine the content type.*

Problems with CGI

As ubiquitous as CGI has become, it is plagued with a major flaw: it is does not scale well (in other words it falls flat on its face for large websites). Under the CGI model, each time a request is received for dynamic content, the CGI program must be launched. This creates a glaring inefficiency in terms of resource management. For example, if two or three users request a CGI program simultaneously, a web server is usually able to handle the request gracefully. But what happens if 100-200 users request the resource? Imagine the web server attempting to launch a separate copy of the CGI program for each of those requests. Even if the CGI program were written efficiently in a compact language such as C, the performance penalty in terms of memory and speed would still be somewhat significant. The situation would be worse if the CGI program were written in the much more popular PERL language, which launches a large interpreter with each request.

Alternatives to CGI

Over the years, several attempts to address the inefficiency of CGI have been made. One strategy is to create a web server API that enables developers to create solutions that are tightly integrated with the web server. Two examples are **NSAPI** (for Netscape web servers) and **ISAPI** (for Microsoft's IIS web server). These solutions allow developers to write add-in functions to the web server that reside in the same memory space as the web server itself. Thus, an external program is not spawned each time a request for dynamic content is made, which results in faster performance and greater efficiency than CGI solutions. Yet, NSAPI and ISAPI haven't become very popular for the following reasons:

❑   They reside in the same memory space as the web server itself. A buggy program written using NSAPI or ISAPI could bring down the whole web server.

❑   They are proprietary. A solution written using NSAPI will only work on Netscape (now called iPlanet) web servers. ISAPI solutions only work on IIS.

❑ The learning curve is much higher than CGI.

The popular open-source Apache web server (http://www.apache.org) also has an API that allows developers to extend its functionality, called the **module API**. While few developers actually create modules themselves, many third-party modules exist that provide a framework for developers to create applications that are much more efficient than normal CGI. Here are a few examples:

❑ mod_perl – maintains the Perl binary in memory, thus freeing Perl scripts from the overhead of loading a separate instance of the Perl interpreter for each request. mod_perl is very popular.

❑ mod_php4 – does for the popular PHP language what mod_perl does for Perl.

❑ mod_fastcgi – similar to CGI but enables programs to stay resident in memory rather than terminate upon completion.

These three modules form the tip of an ever-growing iceberg full of Apache modules that function as efficient replacements for the aging CGI standard. The key thread in all of the module solutions is that they provide a persistent vehicle for servicing requests.

Java's CGI solution: Servlets

Java provides support for CGI functionality through its **Servlet** API. **Servlets** are simple Java classes that inherit the javax.servlet.http.HttpServlet abstract class.

*Actually, the **Servlet** architecture is designed to support any protocol following the request/response model. The javax.servlet.Servlet interface defines the basic Servlet methods, and the javax.servlet.GenericServlet abstract class provides a limited implementation of that interface. At present, the only protocol specifically supported is HTTP, via the javax.servlet.http.HttpServlet abstract class. So feel free to write your own SMTP server.*

Servlets are not stand-alone applications; they must be managed by a **Servlet container**. The Servlet container manages the lifecycle of the Servlet and handles the socket-level communication. This lets the Servlet developer focus on what matters most: what to do with the HTTP request. A Servlet container may function as a complete web server, or it may be integrated with a third-party web server. The popular Tomcat Servlet container is often paired with the Apache web server. This type of pairing is ideal as it combines the strengths of both applications: Tomcat is excellent at managing Servlets but not optimized for static content, whereas Apache has been rigorously optimized for serving up static content but doesn't natively support Servlets. In such a scenario, Apache is often configured to listen for web requests on the default port 80, while Tomcat listens for Servlet requests on a custom port, which by default is port 8080.

Servlets are a very efficient way of generating dynamic content for the following reasons:

❑ **Servlets are persistent**. Unlike CGI scripts, a Servlet's lifecycle extends beyond HTTP each request.

❑ **Servlets exist in a separate memory space**. Other CGI alternatives often share memory space with the web server, which creates the possibility of crashing the web server.

❑ **Servlets are simple**. In two senses: first, Servlets are easy to write – the Servlet container handles the messy stuff; second, because Java is a relatively high-level language, Servlet developers can't directly manipulate system memory, which decreases the likelihood and severity of bugs.

❑ **Servlets are flexible**. A Servlet has full access to the entire range of Java APIs. While many CGI solutions have extension API libraries, few if any have the amount of *standardized* APIs that Java has. Standardized APIs, as opposed to third-party add-on APIs, are important because a developer knows that when he uses them he can expect a certain level of support and experience from the Java community.

The following code is an example of a complete Servlet:

```
import javax.servlet.*;
import javax.servlet.http.*;
import java.io.*;

public class ExampleServlet extends HttpServlet {

  public void doGet(HttpServletRequest req, HttpServletResponse resp)
            throws ServletException, java.io.IOException {

    PrintWriter pw = resp.getWriter();
    pw.print("<html><body>Hello world! The time is ");
    pw.print(new java.util.Date());
    pw.println("</body></html>");
    pw.close();
  }

}
```

The above Servlet is a very simple and its resulting output should be very predictable; it generates a "Hello World" HTML page with the current date/time displayed:

Hello world. The time is Sat Jan 20 17:23:21 MST 2001

The next chapter will explain Servlets in more detail.

JavaServer Pages

While our example "Hello World" Servlet is technically viable, it actually contains something that should usually be avoided: it has so-called 'hard-coded' HTML. That is, the code controlling the presentation of the Servlet's logic is embedded within the Servlet's Java code. If a Servlet is created by a hobby programmer for a simple purpose, hard-coding the HTML into the Servlet isn't such an evil thing. However, consider the implications of hard-coding the HTML into a Servlet if it is to be integrated into an enterprise website maintained by a team of HTML wranglers and backend programmers. Imagine if the programmers had to change their code whenever the HTML folks wanted to redesign or update the HTML portions of the website for which the Servlet was responsible. Such a scenario is inefficient. The solution is to separate the **presentation layer** of a website (or any application) from the **business logic** (and indeed both of those layers from the **database layer**), freeing all parties to do their job largely independent of one another.

JavaServer Pages (JSPs) help us to achieve this separation of presentation from logic. JSPs provide an alternative to developing Servlets by defining a syntax for integrating dynamic content into an HTML document. The JSP syntax is somewhat similar to Microsoft's **ActiveServer Pages** technology, which enables ASP developers to step into the Java world holding on to some familiar paradigms.

Appendix G gives an introduction to JSP and Servlets for ASP developers.

Here's an example JSP:

```
<html>
  <body>
    Hello world! The time is <%= new java.util.Date() %>
  </body>
</html>
```

And the resulting output of the JSP is very similar to the output of our earlier Servlet:

Hello world! The time is Sat Jan 20 17:25:15 MST 2001

JavaServer Pages give a developer access to the same range of functionality that Servlets do. In general, Servlets are best used when the developer needs to do more than provide an HTML response, such as dynamically generating an image, while JSPs are ideal if the developer is creating an HTML response.

Chapter 4 onwards will explain JSP technology in more detail.

Web Applications

Often a website or web-enabled application will consist of many static and dynamic resources, including multiple Servlets and JSPs. In the official Servlet jargon, such a collection of resources is called a **web application**. Hereafter, the term web application will be used in this Java-centric sense.

As discussed previously, a Servlet container (or combination Servlet container/web server configuration) can be used to manage and execute the web application. Another type of program, an **application server**, can also be used for the same purpose. An application server is a Servlet container and more. It supports additional features, such as full J2EE compliance, and often it is more robust and capable of higher performance than a stand-alone Servlet container. A small to medium organization with limited capital typically uses only a Servlet container, while a large capital-rich enterprise favors application servers.

Traditionally, web developers and system administrators have suffered through the hassles of learning about the proprietary configuration mechanisms necessary for deploying their applications. Fortunately, the Servlet specification dictates a configuration standard that all Servlet containers must support. This standard includes the following structure:

Path	Explanation
/	The root directory of the web application. All static resources and JSPs are placed here. These **public resources** are typically directly available to web clients.
/WEB-INF/web.xml	This is known as the **deployment descriptor**, which contains various configuration options for the web application. All files contained in /WEB-INF/ and its subdirectories are not directly accessible by web clients.
/WEB-INF/classes/	All class files, such as Servlets or JavaBeans, are placed in this directory.
/WEB-INF/lib/	JAR files can be placed here, and they will be automatically included in the web application's CLASSPATH.

A sample web application might consist of the following files:

```
/index.html
/contactus.html
/status.jsp
/images/us.jpg
/WEB-INF/web.xml
/WEB-INF/lib/framework.jar
/WEB-INF/classes/com/ourcompany/website/MainServlet.class
/WEB-INF/classes/com/ourcompany/util/MainUtilities.class
```

Thus, deploying web applications into new and unknown third-party Servlet containers is straightforward, and yes, even easy. Here's the best part: web applications can be compressed into an archive, called a **WAR** (**Web ARchive**) file, and deployed in archived format into the Servlet container. The Servlet container will either decompress the WAR file or execute it in its compressed format. Relations between developers and system administrators have never been so stress-free.

Summary

We've covered the following concepts in this chapter:

- ❑ Web browsers and web servers communicate via **HTTP**, a request/response protocol. **HTTP headers** are used to send various data between the client and server, while **MIME types** define the type of content that a server sends to a browser in the HTTP response.

- ❑ HTTP is **stateless,** but other mechanisms such as **cookies** can be used to preserve state.

- ❑ **Ports** can be used to provide distinct servers on a single physical server, or distinct web sites on a single web server.

- ❑ Web servers can send either **static** or **dynamic** resources to a browser. A static resource is an unchanging resource, such as an HTML page or a GIF image; a dynamic resource is generated for each request.

- ❑ **CGI scripts** were the original mechanism used to generate dynamic content but they are very inefficient. **Servlets** and **JavaServer Pages** are efficient alternatives to CGI scripts.

- ❑ A Java **web application** is a collection of related static and dynamic resources and is exceptionally easy to deploy.

Because these concepts form the foundation of Servlet/JSP development, if you do not understand any of them, you should definitely take a moment to go back and review the appropriate sections of this chapter. Otherwise, you're well on your way to using the Web for fun and profit!

In the next chapter we start our detailed exploration of Java web development by introducing the Servlet API.

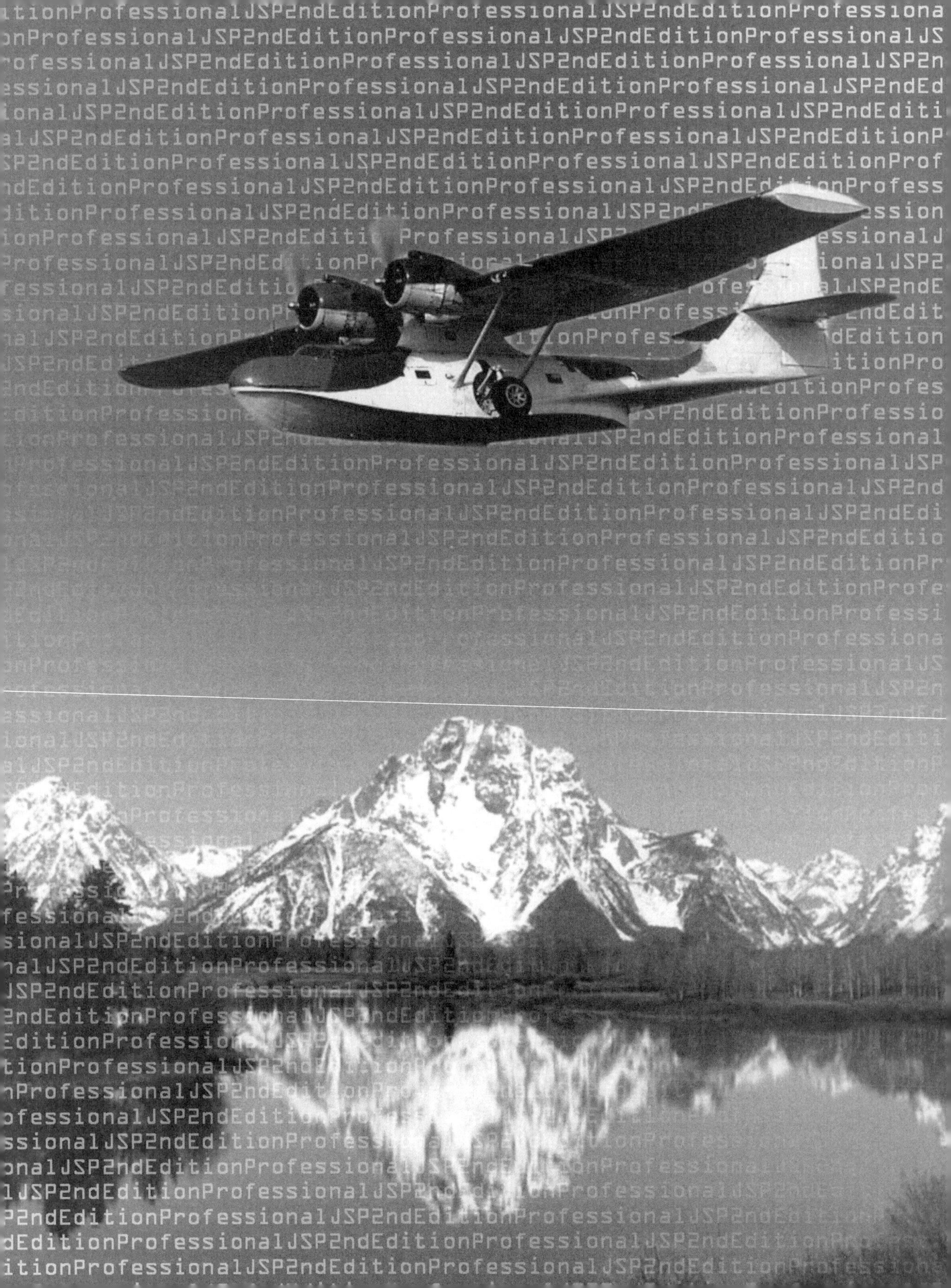
ProfessionalJSP2ndEdition

3

Basic Servlets

Before we explore JavaServer Pages, we should first understand that each JSP gets transparently translated into a Servlet before being executed. Therefore, virtually anything that is available programmatically to a Servlet is also available to a JSP, and a thorough discussion of Servlets should get us on the right path before tackling JSP.

In addition, as you will see in subsequent chapters, JSPs are often most effective when used in conjunction with Servlets; thus, a solid foundation in Servlets is essential. We will cover the following topics in this chapter to give you this foundation:

- ❑ The various moving parts of Servlets and their environment
- ❑ How to develop and compile your own Servlets
- ❑ The dynamics of a Servlet's lifecycle
- ❑ The various Servlet API's available including general, environmental, request and response
- ❑ Session Management
- ❑ Advanced topics

The Moving Parts

There are several moving parts to the operation of Servlets. Servlets themselves are really protocol independent, meaning that they could be built to run over CORBA or RMI, not just HTTP. However, since this book is dedicated to JSP, which is protocol dependent, we will focus on the HTTP implementation and use of Servlets. The major parts are:

❏   Client – typically a web browser

❏   Web Server – handles the HTTP protocol to/from the client

❏   Servlet Engine – supports the execution of Servlets

❏   JSP Engine – supports the compilation of JSP files into Servlets (discussed in Chapter 4)

To start things going, the client sends a request to the web server. The web server then needs to interpret the request and decide either to handle it, or to pass it off to a helper. In our case, the Servlet and JSP engines are helpers to the web server.

These helpers are typically implemented using a web server specific protocol, often called a connector. The web server must be configured to know what helpers are installed, and what URLs are to be mapped to the helpers for processing:

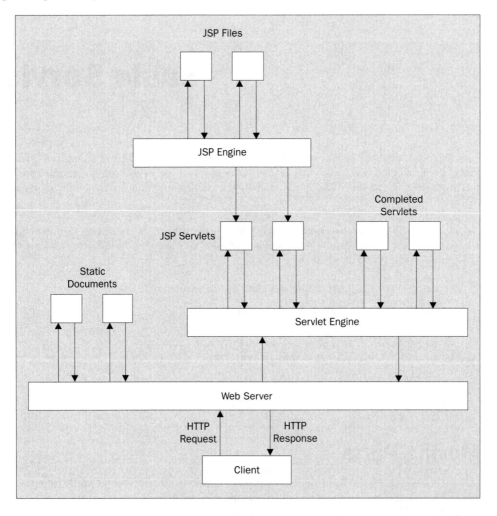

Just from this picture, we can draw a few conclusions:

- The web server needs to know what URL patterns to pass to the Servlet engine (often via the `/servlet/` pattern)

- The web server needs to know what URL patterns to pass to the JSP engine (usually `*.jsp`)

- The HTTP request contains everything sent by the client

- The HTTP response contains everything sent by the server (in response to the request)

We'll cover shortly how to obtain and install Tomcat. Once installed, we will explore how Tomcat supports these details.

A Word about the Specifications

It is worth discussing the scope and intent of the Servlet and JSP specifications before we go rushing into using Tomcat. The talented individuals that worked on these standards strived to achieve a document that specified required Servlet/JSP engine behavior to the point that software developers could write code based on a set of assumptions that would guarantee behavior on any vendor's engine, thus achieving the 'Write once, Run anywhere' goal of Java.

Deployment and configuration were typically left to implementation details (that is, they were vendor specific). While not perfect, this morphs the goal to a very realistic and achievable 'Write once, Run anywhere (once you deploy it)', which is still a huge potential gain in most cases.

While Tomcat is the reference platform for the specifications, there is some **implementation specific behavior** in its configuration and deployment. In this and the next couple of chapters, we will strive to point out where a presented feature or behavior is unique to Tomcat. Otherwise, you can assume that the item is part of the standards and therefore reliably available on each compliant implementation (that is, to the extent that implementation is faithful to the standards).

> *You can obtain copies of the specifications from* http://java.sun.com/products/Servlet/index.html *and* http://java.sun.com/products/jsp/index.html.

Obtaining, Installing, and Running Tomcat

Let's get right into the thick of it. This section discusses the basics on how to obtain a binary version of Tomcat 4.0, install it in its default configuration, and how to run it. Because Tomcat includes several Servlet and JSP examples, it is very useful as a first step on our journey to writing our own.

> *As this book goes to press, Tomcat 4 Beta 3 has just been released. Tomcat 4.0 cannot be finalized until the Servlet 2.3 and JSP 1.2 specifications have been finalized by the Java Community Process. Until this happens you should use the most recent Milestone or Beta version.*

Refer to Appendix A for all the details of installing advanced configurations, installing other versions of Tomcat, or for installing the JRun server. Here, we want to give you a quick start guide to the basic configuration and startup. If your situation calls for something outside of these basic steps, refer to the appendix.

Since Tomcat contains an integrated web server, and it is enabled by default, we will use it in that mode for our examples. Thus Tomcat supports all necessary server components.

Obtaining Tomcat

To obtain Tomcat, download the appropriate binary set from http://jakarta.apache.org/tomcat/.

Most of the examples in this book focus on the latest version available of Tomcat 4.0, the version that supports Sun's specifications for Servlets, version 2.3, and JSP, version 1.2. Tomcat 3.2.1 is the official reference implementation for Servlets, version 2.2, and JSP, version 1.1. Follow the links to the binary downloads section, and select a suitable 4.0 build.

If you select a milestone build, the directory will contain the Servlet API (`jakarta-Servletapi-4.0-xx.*`, where xx reflects the build number such as b3 for Beta 3), Tomcat itself (`jakarta-tomcat-4.0-xx.*`), an Apache module for Linux to connect Tomcat to the Apache web server (the `linux` directory), RPM files to install Tomcat on Linux (the `rpms` directory), and of course the source code (the `src` directory).

The Servlet API contains the official reference implementation of the Servlet and JSP API, including the appropriate JavaDocs. Tomcat includes them so if you are using Tomcat, you don't need to download them separately. However, if you are not using Tomcat, you may wish to use them for compiling or for accessing the JavaDoc for the Servlet and JSP API.

Download the appropriate "`jakarta-tomcat-4.0.xx`" file for your platform and save it wherever you keep your binary downloads (for installing via the RPMs, refer to the Tomcat appendix).

Installing Tomcat

The install for Tomcat is easy, and only slightly platform specific. In general, the steps you must take include the following:

❑ Extract the contents of the downloaded file to an installation directory (say `c:\work\pkgs` on a Windows platform, or `/usr/local` on a Unix/Linux platform)

❑ Set the `JAVA_HOME` environment variable so Tomcat knows where your Java installation is located

❑ Make sure the `javac` command is on your `PATH` environment variable

❑ Start Tomcat by running the `startup` script file provided (`.bat` for Windows, `.sh` for Linux) and off you go

It is useful to install all the tools from the Jakarta project (such as Ant – a Java based build tool) that you plan on using into the same base directory (in our examples above, that would be `c:\work\pkgs` and `/usr/local`). If you aren't using anything else from the Jakarta project, you can install the content anywhere you want.

The extracted contents will create a subdirectory (`jakarta-tomcat-4.0-xx`), under the installation directory where all the files will be placed. This is referred to as the `CATALINA_HOME` directory (although you don't always need to set this environment variable).

From this point forward, we will refer to the `CATALINA_HOME` variable and use the Windows file naming conventions (using the "\" as the pathname separator), unless we are dealing with a Unix/Linux specific issue.

Under the CATALINA_HOME directory, a number of subdirectories will be created:

- ❏ bin – binary files for Tomcat and friends
- ❏ common – library files needed by Tomcat and web applications
- ❏ conf – configuration files
- ❏ jasper – JAR files that make up the JSP engine part of Tomcat
- ❏ lib – library JAR files needed by web applications
- ❏ logs – server log files for use by Tomcat while it is executing
- ❏ server – JAR files that make up the Servlet engine part of Tomcat
- ❏ src – the source code for Tomcat itself
- ❏ webapps – the area Tomcat looks to for web applications, which contain Servlets, JSP files, and other content
- ❏ work – working space for holding translated JSP files

When referencing a file from the installation, we will typically use the shorthand bin\startup.bat to indicate the startup.bat file in the bin directory in the CATALINA_HOME directory.

> **Note that in order to run Tomcat you need to have installed the JDK version 1.2 or above. Also note that if you are using JDK 1.2, you will need to obtain the jndi.jar file from http://java.sun.com/products/jndi and make sure it is on the classpath (see *Compiling Your Own Servlets* for instructions on setting the classpath). jndi.jar is included with JDK 1.3.**

Below are the platform specific instructions.

Windows

Using WinZip, or equivalent tool, extract the contents to the selected install directory. Note that the contents will unpack into the jakarta-tomcat-4.0-xx subdirectory under your selected install directory. Note also that some problems have been reported on Windows 95/98 with these long filenames. If you run into trouble, rename the directory to something like tomcat.

Set the environment variable JAVA_HOME to be equal to the base directory where the JDK is installed. For example, on Windows, if you installed JDK 1.3 into c:\jdk1.3, you would set JAVA_HOME as follows:

```
set JAVA_HOME=c:\jdk1.3
```

On Windows 95/98, this is typically done in the autoexec.bat file. Once set, you must reboot.

On Windows NT or 2000 Professional, open up the Control Panel, double click on the System icon, select the Advanced tab, select the Environment Variables button (on Windows NT there is no Advanced tab, just an Environment Variables tab), and select the New... button in the System Variables section, and enter the appropriate values. Once saved, the new value is active – no rebooting is required (although existing command windows will need to be closed and reopened to see the changes).

This is illustrated below (for Windows 2000 Professional):

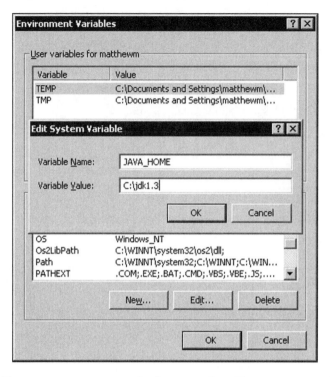

Similarly, you should set CATALINA_HOME to the directory where Tomcat was unpacked.

Finally, make sure the javac program is on the system PATH variable. This is typically set when installing the JDK. To validate this, either look at where the PATH variable is set (in autoexec.bat or via the Command Tool), or enter javac from a command prompt. If javac is not on your path, you will get an error. Correct it and continue.

> **Due to a Windows 95/98 anomaly, you must change the initial memory allocated by Windows to the Tomcat startup and shutdown programs. To do this, open Windows Explorer, right click on bin\startup.bat and bin\shutdown.bat, and select the Properties option. Select the Memory tab and change the Initial Environment to 4096. Select OK to accept the changes.**

Once you debug the Tomcat setup, you may want to go into the properties of the startup.bat and shutdown.bat files; select the Program tab, and change the run mode to Minimized and select Close on Exit. This will keep the Tomcat windows out of your way.

Unix or Linux

Using gunzip and tar, or equivalent tools, extract the contents to the selected install directory. Note that the contents will unpack into the jakarta-tomcat-4.0-xx subdirectory under your selected install directory. Here is an example, which assumes the downloaded jakarta-tomcat-4.0-xx.tar.gz file is in /usr/local:

```
cd /usr/local
gunzip jakarta-tomcat-4.0-xx.tar.gz
tar xf jakarta-tomcat-4.0-xx.tar
```

The `gunzip` command will uncompress the file and leave the `jakarta-tomcat-4.0-xx.tar` file, which is an archive file (just a bundle of files). Use the `tar` command to extract the files as shown.

Set the environment variable `JAVA_HOME` to be equal to the base directory where the JDK is installed. If we installed the JDK in `/usr/local/pkgs/jdk1.2.2`, for example, you would set `JAVA_HOME` as follows:

```
set JAVA_HOME=/usr/local/pkgs/jdk1.2.2
```

If you are using JDK 1.2, add the `jndi.jar` file to your classpath:

```
set CLASSPATH=$CLASSPATH:/usr/local/pkgs/jndi.jar
```

You probably want to set these variables in your `.profile` or `.cshrc` (or `.bashrc`, etc) file, depending on what shell you use. That way it is set each time you login.

Finally, make sure the `javac` program is on the system `PATH` variable. This is typically set when installing the JDK. To validate this, view the current value of the `PATH` variable (via echo `$PATH`) to verify that it is set properly.

Running Tomcat

Once installed, you are ready to run Tomcat. To do this, you simply execute the appropriate startup file. On Windows, execute `%CATALINA_HOME%\bin\startup.bat`. On Unix/Linux, execute `$CATALINA_HOME/bin/startup.sh`.

You should see the following screen displayed in a command window:

Catalina (displayed at the top of the window) is simply the name of Tomcat's Servlet Engine. This command window will stay active as long as Tomcat is running. It is also where standard error outputs are sent (via calls to `out.printer()`).

Test your installation by opening up your web browser and viewing the location http://localhost:8080. This should display the Tomcat welcome page. You should see something similar to the following screenshot:

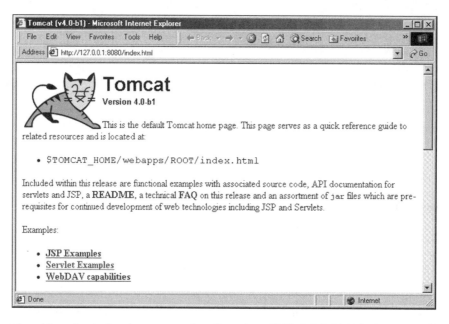

Note that the address bar in the above screenshot shows http://127.0.0.1:8080/index.html. This is because 127.0.0.1 is the IP address for localhost; the two names are functionally identical in that they both point to the same entity – the local computer.

To shutdown Tomcat, you guessed it, execute %CATALINE_HOME%\bin\shutdown.bat or CATALINA_HOME/bin/shutdown.sh.

If you cannot display the Tomcat welcome page, refer to the appendix for help with debugging your Tomcat configuration.

Changing the Default Port

The only configuration change we will discuss here involves modifying the default port that Tomcat listens on. By default, it listens to port 8080. If you want to change it to, say, port 80 (the normal default for http), on Unix/Linux, you must then start Tomcat as root (only the root user can access ports 0 through 1023).

To modify the default port, open the CATALINA_HOME\conf\server.xml file with your favorite text editor (say WordPad, vi, emacs, or whatever you like). Find the line that defines the Connector for port 8080, as shown below, and change it to 80:

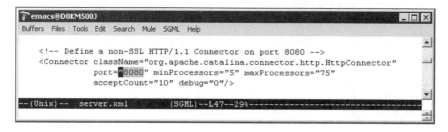

Save the file and the next time you start Tomcat, it will listen on port 80.

Under the Hood

This section will examine the mechanics of Tomcat as a web server and as a Servlet engine. We will map the URLs submitted by the browser to the actual files that are served up by Tomcat in order to illustrate how you would go about deploying your own content.

In order to get a good idea of what Tomcat is doing, follow the following URLs and watch what happens:

- ❏ http://localhost:8080
- ❏ http://localhost:8080/examples/servlets
- ❏ http://localhost:8080/examples/servlets/HelloWorldExample

The following picture illustrates the dynamic behavior of what takes place. We will explore the details in this section.

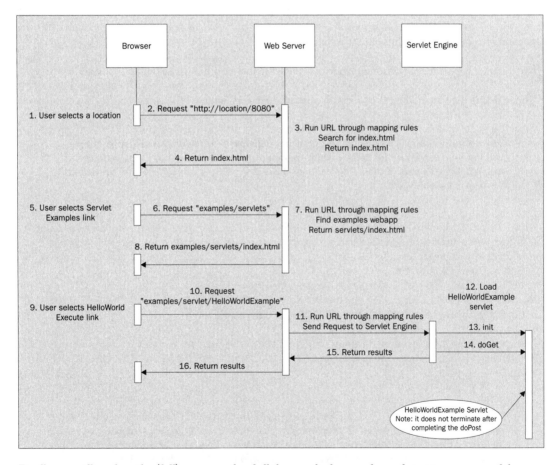

Finally, we will explore the (full) source code of all the supplied examples and start to see some of the capability of Servlets.

Tomcat as a Web Server

First, let's explore the web server functionality of Tomcat and how that fits into what we already know about the moving parts. This foundation is critical before we advance to the Servlet engine's functionality.

In your browser, go back to the http://localhost:8080 location. Notice the hint the page designers gave us to finding out where to look for the corresponding html file:
CATALINA_HOME\webapps\ROOT\index.html.

Let's dissect the pathname CATALINA_HOME\webapps\ROOT\index.html.

First, the CATALINA_HOME\webapps portion is effectively the server root of Tomcat, for both the web server and Servlet engine (and JSP engine portions of Tomcat).

Second, the ROOT portion refers to what's the ROOT **web application**, or webapp for short. As discussed in the previous chapter, a webapp is a Java-centric concept that is a collection of all the components that make up a web based application (hence, the name), including any Servlets, JSP files, HTML files, images, and so on. Adding ROOT to the previous portion of the pathname gives us effectively the document root directory (or **document root**, for short) of the ROOT webapp (that is, CATALINA_HOME\webapps\ROOT).

Finally, the index.html portion refers to a specific file that is to be served within the ROOT webapp.

Notice that in the case of the ROOT webapp, it is not specified in the URL. This is called the **default** webapp.

> **The default webapp is a special case and is implementation specific. Most Servlet engines will have the capability for some default webapp, where you do not have to specify the webapp name as part of the URL. Versions 3.2 and greater of Tomcat assume the default webapp is named ROOT.**

Now let's look at the URL http://localhost:8080. Standard behavior for a web server when the requested URL maps to a directory is to either display the contents of that directory, or to search for a (server configurable) default file, usually index.html. In this case, the URL refers to the document root of the default webapp (a.k.a., ROOT).

Now hold your cursor over the link for the Servlet Examples and notice the URL that it displays at the bottom of your browser: http://localhost:8080/examples/servlets/.

In this case, Tomcat looks in the document root of the ROOT webapp for the examples subdirectory. Since it doesn't exist, Tomcat looks in its own server root (CATALINA_HOME\webapps). If it still doesn't find it there, it will generate an error.

> **The behavior of Tomcat's web server is implementation specific. Other implementations may reverse the search order. If your web server and Servlet engine are separate, you will have to configure your web server so it knows what URLs to pass to the Servlet engine. Make sure you check your web server's documentation for details. Finally, take care in naming subdirectories under the ROOT webapp, so you don't inadvertently hide another webapp.**

Since the `examples` directory exists in the server root, Tomcat recognizes it as a webapp (more on that later). The `servlets/` portion of the URL is treated as the normal pathname portion of the URL. In this case it is a totally arbitrary value. There is nothing special about the use of the name `servlets/` here. It could just as easily have been named `html/` or `myStuff/`. Since the URL ends with a trailing "`/`", it implies a directory which will trigger Tomcat to search for `index.html`.

Go ahead and select the link, and notice that the location display on your browser indicates that we were right, that http://localhost:8080/examples/servlets/index.html was in fact displayed. This may seem like a somewhat trivial point, but one of the common sticking points when getting started is finding out where things are, and where to put your new code and files. We will expand these details as we go along.

Now let's look in the `CATALINA_HOME` directory to see which file is being returned for the request. We can start at the `webapps` directory (where Tomcat keeps the contents of each webapp) and drill down to the `examples` directory. In there, we see the `Servlets` directory, and in there we find `index.html`. This is in fact the file that was just displayed. The full path would be `CATALINA_HOME\webapps\examples\Servlets\index.html`.

To illustrate this, we can say that Tomcat (as a web server) maps URLs to HTML files, by default, as follows (remember the `<webapp name>` in the URL is not required for the default webapp, but still maps to the `<webapp name>` subdirectory on the server):

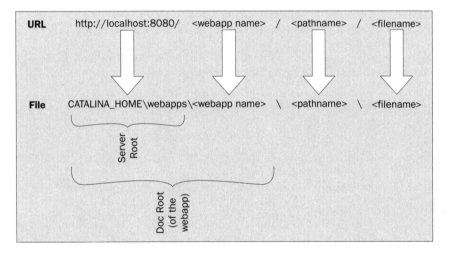

Tomcat as a Servlet Engine

Now if you put your cursor over the Hello World **Execute** link, notice the link displayed at the bottom of the browser: http://localhost:8080/examples/servlet/HelloWorldExample.

Note the use of `servlet` in this case vs. `servlets` from the previous case. In this situation, the use of `servlet` is not arbitrary. It is built into Tomcat as being a default mapping of the URL to a special directory in a webapp named `WEB-INF\classes`. This directory is specified by the standard as the directory that holds the (you guessed it) Servlet class files.

By making the directory structure a standard, webapps may be bundled up and moved onto different Servlet engines without concern for these details. Only the deployment configuration issues of the engine must be dealt with, the webapp itself does not need to change.

As you would expect from any software from the Apache Software Foundation, Tomcat allows you to configure the URL to Servlet class file mapping in almost any way you can imagine (and probably in some ways you couldn't imagine). However, the WEB-INF\classes portion of the filename is set by the Servlet Specification and should not be changed, so the mapping simply ties the pathname and filename of a URL with specific files under this directory.

> **The Servlet specification defines a set of mapping capabilities that is required by each compliant Servlet engine. That mapping has become more formal in version 2.3 of the Servlet specification. Expect individual implementations to catch up with the new specification over time.**

Also note the lack of an extension on HelloWorldExample or a trailing "/". This is a default mapping that allows the Servlet engine to map references to the Servlet directory to the corresponding class file. Thus Tomcat would look for the HelloWorldExample.class file to execute in response to the URL.

Note that the filename mapping is also configurable per the Servlet specification. For example, you could map all URL filenames that end in .do to a specific Servlet. This is in fact how Struts (a full featured Servlet and JSP application framework) is configured, as you will see in Chapter 21.

Putting it all together, we end up with the final pathname of:
CATALINA_HOME\webapps\examples\WEB-INF\classes\HelloWorldExample.class.

Summarizing Servlet mapping, we end up with the following default behavior for Tomcat (which, as we said before, can be enhanced dramatically by setting up specific mapping rules):

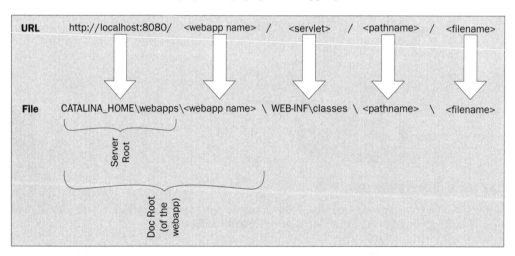

Running Tomcat's Servlet Examples

Tomcat comes with several excellent examples that demonstrate the capabilities of Servlets. So rather than introduce yet another HelloWorld Servlet or have you type in a useless example (or load it off a CD or website), we thought it would be a good idea if we explored what comes built-in with Tomcat.

This section will look at the implementation of each example Servlet in detail. If you have never developed Servlets, don't try to absorb every detail presented here. We will cover the full spectrum of Servlet capabilities as we go on. This section is intended as a quick overview of the structure and capabilities of Servlets.

Since we will be looking at source code, get your favorite text editor ready. The source code for the examples is in `CATALINA_HOME\webapps\examples\WEB-INF\classes`. Note that this directory is the required home for Servlet class files. Servlet source files can be located anywhere, and don't even need to be in the webapp's document root, since they are not required to execute.

> **Since Windows and Unix/Linux don't agree on the end-of-line semantics (carriage return vs. carriage return + line feed), and many of the Tomcat developers prefer the latter environment, some text editors such as Notepad may not display the source files properly. Use WordPad or some other platform-savvy editor instead.**

As illustrated in the above picture of the Tomcat home page, the examples are broken out into the categories of JSP, Servlet, and WebDAV (WebDAV is the remote Web authoring capability that Tomcat supports, and is beyond the scope of this book).

The Snoop Servlet

The Snoop Servlet is not listed on the Servlet Examples page but you can run it by going to http://localhost:8080/examples/servlet/SnoopServlet. Like the Unix snoop utility, this Servlet dumps all the data received in the request. The concept is worth consideration as a logging mode to assist with debugging. You could enable the logging during development and disable it during production (to minimize the performance impact) by changing the setting in a properties file that your Servlet reads (or via an initialization parameter – we'll see how to do that later in the chapter).

We'll use this Servlet to verify some of the browser to server traffic, as we explore the various properties of HTTP through the example Servlets.

Because the Snoop Servlet covers many components of the `request` object, we won't cover it in detail here and won't look at its source until later, when we get into the details of the `HttpServletRequest` class.

The Hello World Servlet

For now, let's explore the Servlet examples. Go ahead and select the **Servlet Examples** link. Select the **Execute** link next to **Hello World**. Your browser should display the famous computer science saying, as shown below:

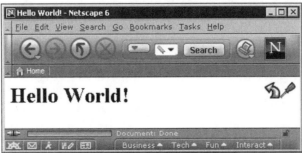

If your browser does not display this, chances are your JAVA_HOME environment variable is not set properly. Refer to the Tomcat appendix for other debugging options.

Now let's look at the source code for this example. To display the source code, click on the icon of the screwdriver or go back to the **Servlet Examples** page and select the **Source** link for the Hello World Servlet. Your browser should display a subset of the following source code (which of course can be found in CATALINA_HOME\webapps\examples\WEB-INF\classes):

```
import java.io.*;
import java.text.*;
import java.util.*;
import javax.servlet.*;
import javax.servlet.http.*;
```

You can see that the class HelloWorld extends HttpServlet (which is in the javax.servlet.http package). The Servlet defines a single method named doGet(), which takes two parameters named request and response (and throws two exceptions):

```
public class HelloWorldExample extends HttpServlet {

    public void doGet(HttpServletRequest request,
                HttpServletResponse response) throws IOException,
                ServletException {
```

The first line below gets a ResourceBundle object named rb, for the locale of the request. The bundle name is LocalStrings. We'll explore internationalization in detail later but for now you should understand these concepts:

❑ The user can set his or her locale (language & dialect preference) in their browser to be a specific language. This value is transmitted via HTTP in the request from the browser to the server (and on to the Servlet). It is available via the request.getLocale() method.

❑ The rb object is created based on the browser's locale and the filename LocalStrings.properties (the normal message bundle/properties file technique in Java).

❑ The rb object is used to obtain language specific strings for ultimate display by the browser. This is illustrated in the line String title = rb.getString ("helloworld.title"). The object title is set to the appropriate string, based on the value returned by request.getLocale(), and then output to the browser as described below.

```
    ResourceBundle rb = ResourceBundle.getBundle("LocalStrings",
                                            request.getLocale());
```

The next line (response.setContentType("text/html")) sets the content type in the response object. This tells the browser the MIME type of the incoming response. In this case the value is set to "text/html", indicating to the browser that it should try to parse it as a normal textual HTML file:

```
    response.setContentType("text/html");
```

The next section of code obtains a PrintWriter object called out from the supplied response input parameter. The out object is used to write the HTML (via its println() method) for what becomes the HelloWorld page we see in the browser:

```
       PrintWriter out = response.getWriter();

       out.println("<html>");
       out.println("<head>");

       String title = rb.getString("helloworld.title");
```

In this case, there is no interaction with the incoming `request` object, which would encapsulate everything the browser sent to the server, but you can clearly see the generation of the `response` back to the browser, and thus the way the HTTP request/response protocol maps to Servlets. Everything else that we do with Servlets and JSP builds off this basic structure:

```
       out.println("<title>" + title + "</title>");
       out.println("</head>");
       out.println("<body bgcolor=\"white\">");
       out.println("<body>");

       out.println("<a href=\"/examples/servlets/helloworld.html\">");
       out.println("<img src=\"/examples/images/code.gif\" height=24 "
               + "width=24 align=right border=0 alt=\"view code\"></a>");
       out.println("<a href=\"/examples/servlets/index.html\">");
       out.println("<img src=\"/examples/images/return.gif\" height=24 "
               + "width=24 align=right border=0 alt=\"return\"></a>");
       out.println("<h1>" + title + "</h1>");
       out.println("</body>");
       out.println("</html>");
     }

   }
```

From this simple example, you can easily see that generating web pages within Servlets can quickly become unwieldy for even the most basic webapps. This illustrates the need for JSP and hence, for this book.

The RequestInfo Servlet

The `RequestInfo` Servlet (refer to the `RequestInfoExample.java` file in the classes directory) illustrates some of the resources available in the `request` object. The file is included here for convenience:

```
/* $Id: RequestInfoExample.java,v 1.1 2000/08/17 00:57:53 horwat Exp $
 *
 */

import java.io.*;
import java.text.*;
import java.util.*;
import javax.servlet.*;
import javax.servlet.http.*;


/**
 * Example servlet showing request information.
 *
```

```
 * @author James Duncan Davidson <duncan@eng.sun.com>
 */

public class RequestInfoExample extends HttpServlet {

    ResourceBundle rb = ResourceBundle.getBundle("LocalStrings");

    public void doGet(HttpServletRequest request,
                      HttpServletResponse response)
        throws IOException, ServletException
    {

        response.setContentType("text/html");

        PrintWriter out = response.getWriter();
        out.println("<html>");
        out.println("<body>");
        out.println("<head>");

        String title = rb.getString("requestinfo.title");
        out.println("<title>" + title + "</title>");
        out.println("</head>");
        out.println("<body bgcolor=\"white\">");

        out.println("<a href=\"/examples/servlets/reqinfo.html\">");
        out.println("<img src=\"/examples/images/code.gif\" height=24 " +
                    "width=24 align=right border=0 alt=\"view code\"></a>");
        out.println("<a href=\"/examples/servlets/index.html\">");
        out.println("<img src=\"/examples/images/return.gif\" height=24 " +
                    "width=24 align=right border=0 alt=\"return\"></a>");

        out.println("<h3>" + title + "</h3>");
        out.println("<table border=0><tr><td>");
        out.println(rb.getString("requestinfo.label.method"));
        out.println("</td><td>");
        out.println(request.getMethod());
        out.println("</td></tr><tr><td>");
        out.println(rb.getString("requestinfo.label.requesturi"));
        out.println("</td><td>");
        out.println(request.getRequestURI());
        out.println("</td></tr><tr><td>");
        out.println(rb.getString("requestinfo.label.protocol"));
        out.println("</td><td>");
        out.println(request.getProtocol());
        out.println("</td></tr><tr><td>");
        out.println(rb.getString("requestinfo.label.pathinfo"));
        out.println("</td><td>");
        out.println(request.getPathInfo());
        out.println("</td></tr><tr><td>");
        out.println(rb.getString("requestinfo.label.remoteaddr"));
        out.println("</td><td>");
        out.println(request.getRemoteAddr());
        out.println("</table>");
    }
```

```
    public void doPost(HttpServletRequest request,
                       HttpServletResponse response)
        throws IOException, ServletException
    {
        doGet(request, response);
    }

}
```

Specifically, key lines include:

Method	Description
getMethod()	Returns the HTTP request method (typically GET or POST for most requests)
getRequestURI()	Returns the requested URI up to but not including the query string (the query string is the optional set of name-value pairs after the ? in the URI)
getProtocol()	Returns the protocol used by the client (the browser)
getPathInfo()	Returns the extra path information in the URI (following the Servlet path, up to the query string)
getRemoteAddr()	Returns the remote IP address of the client (the browser's machine)

Note also the introduction of a new method named doPost(). This maps to the HTTP POST method. In this case, doPost() simply calls the doGet() method, relaying the request and response variables. This is commonly done to provide identical behavior for the two different HTTP methods.

The output of this Servlet should look like this:

The RequestHeaders Servlet

As discussed in the previous chapter, headers play an important role in HTTP. As such, the request object provides convenient mechanisms to access them. The RequestHeaderExample.java file illustrates the use of the request.getHeaderNames() method to obtain an Enumeration object with the name of all the headers in the request. The value of a specific header can be retrieved with the getHeader() method.

The relevant code is included below:

```
Enumeration e = request.getHeaderNames();
while (e.hasMoreElements()) {
    String headerName = (String)e.nextElement();
    String headerValue = request.getHeader(headerName);
    out.println("<tr><td bgcolor=\"#CCCCCC\">" + headerName);
    out.println("</td><td>" + headerValue + "</td></tr>");
}
```

Note that if a headerValue contains certain HTML characters such as <, >, &, ", or ', a badly formed HTML document will result. This is because the balance of the document will be thrown off by the extraneous character, resulting in an incomplete expression. We will discuss techniques for handling this in the *Advanced Servlet Topics* section.

The output of this Servlet is displayed below. Note the list of header names in the left column and the associated values in the right column:

Note that under the user-agent header, Windows NT 5.0 actually corresponds to Windows 2000.

The RequestParameters Servlet

HTML forms have become ubiquitous (and, some would say, annoying) as a way of sending information from the browser to the server. So obviously the Servlet must have a mechanism to obtain the information.

The browser encodes information into name-value pairs within the HTTP protocol. Using the same technique as the headers in the previous example, the set of names are easily obtainable (into an Enumeration object) via the request.getParameterNames() method.

Individual parameter values are available (either once you obtain the name or by prior convention) with the request.getParameter(paramName) call.

The RequestParamExample.java file illustrates obtaining specific parameters with the following code:

```
String firstName = request.getParameter("firstname");
String lastName = request.getParameter("lastname");
out.println(rb.getString("requestparams.params-in-req") + "<br>");
if (firstName != null || lastName != null) {
    out.println(rb.getString("requestparams.firstname"));
    out.println(" = " + firstName + "<br>");
    out.println(rb.getString("requestparams.lastname"));
    out.println(" = " + lastName);
} else {
    out.println(rb.getString("requestparams.no-params"));
}
```

The first time this Servlet is executed, it outputs the following screen:

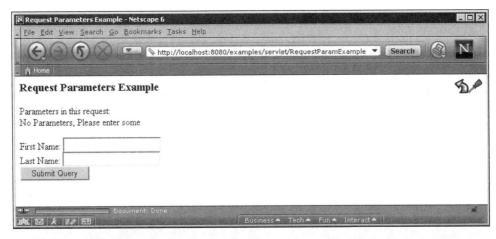

Now if we enter a value into the **First Name** and **Last Name** text boxes, as shown and then if we hit the **Submit Query** button, the following display indicates the expected behavior:

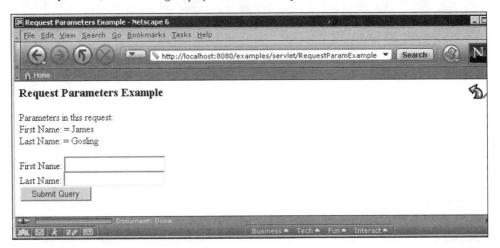

One point is worth mentioning for this example. As we saw, when the Servlet is run, it generates an HTML page that includes a form. Submitting the form sends another request back to that same Servlet, which generates another HTML page in response. The connection between the submitted form and the responding Servlet is linked together through the HTML `<form>` tag as follows (from the `RequestParamsExample.java` file:

```
out.print("<form action=\"");
out.print("RequestParamExample\" ");
out.println("method=POST>");
```

The HTML generated by these statements is:

```
<form action="RequestParamExample" method=POST>
```

Building a Servlet that both generates a page with a form and responds to the submission of that form requires a clear program flow (and is yet another example of the need for Servlets and JSP to co-exist).

Also note the use of the method `out.print()` to concatenate two lines together.

Now look at the code again and notice that like the previous examples, the `doGet()` is defined and the `doPost()` method simply calls the `doGet()` method. Typically application designers want both methods to provide the same result. This provides flexibility to the page designers by allowing either HTTP method to be invoked to get the parameters to the Servlet.

By selecting the Submit Query button, we are submitting the HTML form via the POST method. The `doPost()` method will handle this request (and subsequently pass control to the `doGet()` method). We can also pass the parameters in the query string of the URL. In this case, the HTTP method is of type GET, and the `doGet()` method will handle the request, with the same results.

We can illustrate this by entering
http://localhost:8080/examples/Servlet/RequestParamExample?firstname=Scott&lastname=McNealy
into the location field of the browser. The result demonstrates the same behavior (albeit with a different set of values) as the previous example:

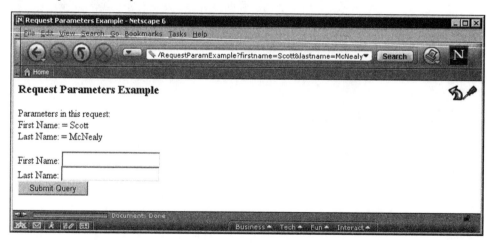

The Cookie Servlet

Cookies have become widely used (and hotly debated) as a technique for storing information on the client (browser). We will discuss cookies in more detail later but for now, understand that a server (in our case a Servlet) can send a name-value pair to the browser (via HTTP of course). The server can also set attributes of the cookie such as the expiration date, and domain that created the cookie (the domain of the server). For any subsequent requests to a server in the domain of the cookie, the browser sends the name-value pair back to the server in the request.

To see this in operation, if your browser allows it, set your preferences to warn you before accepting a cookie. On Netscape, it is configured as follows via the Edit | Preferences menu. In Internet Explorer select Tools | Internet Options, then the Security tab. Select Local intranet and press the Custom Level... button. Scroll down to the Cookies options and select Prompt for per-session cookies.

Now select the Execute link for the Cookie example Servlet. This Servlet displays a form allowing you to enter a name-value pair for defining a cookie. It also indicates that the browser hasn't sent any cookies to the server. Enter a value as shown below:

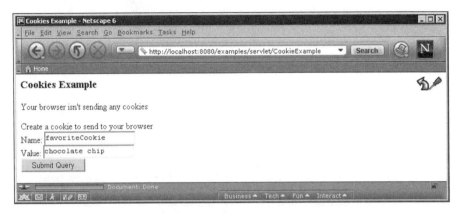

Submit the form. If your browser is set to warn you before accepting a cookie, it will prompt you with a dialog, asking you to accept or reject the cookie:

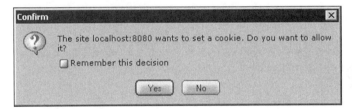

Go ahead and accept the cookie. The cookie will then be set in your browser. The screen says that you sent a cookie to the browser as shown below:

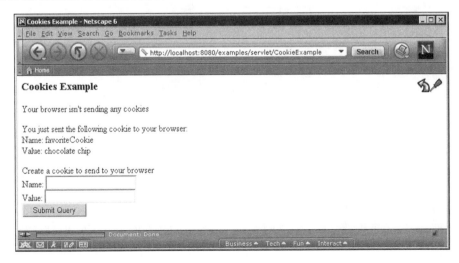

Since we just sent the cookie to the browser, this page indicates the browser hasn't yet sent any cookies to the server. On the very next request (actually on all subsequent requests until changed) to the server (localhost), the browser will send the cookie. We can see this by reloading this page, by creating another cookie, or by running the Snoop Servlet. The relevant output of the Snoop Servlet is shown below. Notice that a cookie is also an HTTP header:

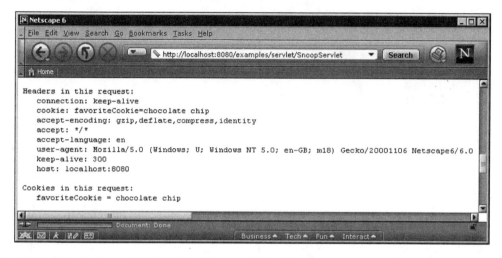

Now let's look at the key code behind this behavior. Like the `RequestParamExample.java` file, the `CookiesExample.java` file makes use of a form that submits back to the same Servlet. The relevant code behind this Servlet is reproduced below. This code relies on the `Cookie` class, which encapsulates the behavior of HTTP cookies.

The first important section gets the cookies from the `request`, extracts their names and values, and echoes it back as text to the `response` (via the `out` object):

```
Cookie[] cookies = request.getCookies();
if (cookies.length > 0) {
    out.println(rb.getString("cookies.cookies") + "<br>");
    for (int i = 0; i < cookies.length; i++) {
        Cookie cookie = cookies[i];
        out.print("Cookie Name: " + cookie.getName() + "<br>");
        out.println("  Cookie Value: " + cookie.getValue() +
          "<br><br>");
    }
} else {
    out.println(rb.getString("cookies.no-cookies"));
}
```

Notice how the `request.getCookies()` method returns an array of `Cookie` objects instead of the familiar `Enumeration` object that encapsulated a list of names. This is because `Cookies`, unlike parameters, which are just name-value pairs of `Strings`, are their own class. Thus we must use the `cookie.getName()` and `cookie.getValue()` method for each individual `Cookie` object in the array.

Note that you don't normally see web sites echoing the cookies they produce. This example only does this so that you can see what is going on here. For a real use of cookies, the contents of the cookie will be used to remember the user for future visits to the site.

The next section of code involves the setting of a new cookie to the browser. If the `cookiename` and `cookievalue` parameters are not `null`, then a new `Cookie` (named `cookie`) is instantiated with those values. Then this `cookie` is added to the `response` via the `response.addCookie(cookie)` method:

```
String cookieName = request.getParameter("cookiename");
String cookieValue = request.getParameter("cookievalue");
if (cookieName != null && cookieValue != null) {
    Cookie cookie = new Cookie(cookieName, cookieValue);
    response.addCookie(cookie);
    out.println("<P>");
    out.println(rb.getString("cookies.set") + "<br>");
    out.print(rb.getString("cookies.name") + "   " + cookieName +
        "<br>");
    out.print(rb.getString("cookies.value") + "   " + cookieValue);
}
```

The Naming Servlet

The Java Naming and Directory Interface (JNDI) allows a Java program (such as a Servlet) to get access to an external object such as an EJB. When used with Servlets, the connection between the Servlet and the external object is linked through the name entered in the `web.xml` file for the associated webapp.

The `web.xml` file is an optional **deployment descriptor** file for a webapp – in this case the `examples` webapp. The Servlet specification describes the format and behavior of the `web.xml` file (there should be no vendor specific formatting or behavior in `web.xml`). The `web.xml` file for each webapp must reside in its corresponding `WEB-INF` directory (also mandated by the Servlet spec). If no deployment information is required for the webapp, the `web.xml` file may be omitted.

Lets look at the syntax in the `web.xml` file for the examples webapp (in `CATALINA_HOME\webapps\examples\WEB-INF\web.xml`):

```
<env-entry>
    <env-entry-name>minExemptions</env-entry-name>
    <env-entry-value>1</env-entry-value>
    <env-entry-type>java.lang.Integer</env-entry-type>
</env-entry>
<env-entry>
    <env-entry-name>foo/name1</env-entry-name>
    <env-entry-value>value1</env-entry-value>
    <env-entry-type>java.lang.String</env-entry-type>
</env-entry>
<env-entry>
    <env-entry-name>foo/bar/name2</env-entry-name>
    <env-entry-value>true</env-entry-value>
    <env-entry-type>java.lang.Boolean</env-entry-type>
</env-entry>
<env-entry>
    <env-entry-name>name3</env-entry-name>
    <env-entry-value>1</env-entry-value>
    <env-entry-type>java.lang.Integer</env-entry-type>
</env-entry>
<env-entry>
    <env-entry-name>foo/name4</env-entry-name>
    <env-entry-value>10</env-entry-value>
    <env-entry-type>java.lang.Integer</env-entry-type>
</env-entry>
```

These <env-entry> tags define environment entries – essentially environment variables – that each Servlet in the examples webapp can access. Each entry has a name, value, and type (class). In this example, five separate names are defined (minExemptions, foo/name1, foo/bar/name2, name3, and foo/name4).

The example references the "java:/comp/env" namespace, which is the default value (hence it isn't shown explicitly).

Also note that another variable is defined in the CATALINA_HOME\conf\web.xml file as a demonstration of the ability in Tomcat to define global variables:

```
<Environment name="maxExemptions" type="java.lang.Integer" value="15"/>
```

The full set of variables defined is listed in the following table:

Variable	Type	Value	Visibility
minExemptions	Integer	1	Webapp
foo/name1	String	value1	Webapp
foo/bar/name2	Boolean	True	Webapp
name3	Integer	1	Webapp
foo/name4	Integer	10	Webapp
maxExemptions	Integer	15	Server

If we execute the Servlet, we see the following display:

This display indicates the bindings of the names with their types, as well as the dynamic looking up of the names and retrieval of their values. This technique is much more flexible than properties files or static parameters in the web.xml file.

Note that not all of our variables were displayed. This is because of the JNDI naming rules. Notice how three of the variables begin with the name "foo":

- ❑   foo/name1

- ❑   foo/bar/name2

- ❑   foo/name4

However, only foo is displayed. In addition, the value displayed for foo by the Servlet indicates org.apache.naming.NamingContext.

Within JNDI, names are treated similar to a directory or pathname. At the highest level (/comp/env), the only names visible are the simple names minExemptions, maxExemptions, name3, and foo (which is what was displayed). If we were to ask for names at the /comp/env/foo level, it would be as if we opened the foo directory. Here we would see name1, bar, and name4. If we were to ask for names at the /comp/env/foo/bar level, it would be as if we opened the bar directory and we would see name2.

Below is the code for this behavior in the Servlet. J2EE interfaces will be covered in depth in later chapters, but you can see the lookup(), list(), and listBindings() methods doing most of the work in this example. Notice how we can perform a simple lookup of an individual variable as well as retrieve the entire context (or set of variable names):

```
Context ctx = null;

try {
    ctx = new InitialContext();
} catch (NamingException e) {
    out.println("Couldn't build an initial context : " + e);
    return;
    }

    try {
        Object value = ctx.lookup("java:/comp/env/maxExemptions");
        out.println("Simple lookup test : ");
        out.println("Max exemptions value : " + value);
    } catch (NamingException e) {
        out.println("JNDI lookup failed : " + e);
    }

    try {
        Context envCtx = (Context) ctx.lookup("java:/comp/env/");
        out.println("list() on /comp/env Context : ");
        NamingEnumeration enum = ctx.list("java:/comp/env/");
        while (enum.hasMoreElements()) {
            out.print("Binding : ");
            out.println(enum.nextElement().toString());
        }
        out.println("listBindings() on /comp/env Context : ");
        enum = ctx.listBindings("java:/comp/env/");
        while (enum.hasMoreElements()) {
            out.print("Binding : ");
            out.println(enum.nextElement().toString());
        }
    } catch (NamingException e) {
        out.println("JNDI lookup failed : " + e);
    }
```

The Session Servlet

Session management is arguably one of the most beneficial attributes of Servlets. They easily transform the stateless HTTP protocol into an integrated seamless thread of activity, thus making a web application truly feel like an application.

To simplify session management, think of it as a technique the Servlet engine employs to keep track of each client-server connection. Essentially, the engine assigns each connection a unique ID and gives that to the client (via one of the techniques described below) when the session gets established. You can think of the session being established at a particular `request` (more on that later), and the ID is passed to the client in the subsequent `response`. The client then sends that ID to the server for all subsequent `requests` until the session ends. Thus the engine can map each request to a particular session.

There are three techniques for giving the client the session ID:

❑ **URL Rewriting**
A name-value pair encapsulating the session ID is added to the URL (hence, the phrase rewriting). The name must be `jsessionid` (per the Servlet specification) and the value is any unique identifier assigned by the server. This technique is referred to as the lowest common denominator of session management because all other techniques require additional assumptions. This technique will always work, with the following caveat: All pages must be handled by the Servlet engine. We will explore this in more detail shortly.

❑ **Via a Cookie**
The cookie name must be `JSESSIONID` (note the upper case-parameter – cookie names are case sensitive) and the value is any unique identifier assigned by the server. Obviously this technique relies on the browser allowing cookies.

❑ **Secure Sockets Layer (SSL)**
The SSL of the HTTPS protocol has built in session management that may be used.

Session management goes beyond just identifying the connection. Each `session` is a Java object, of the `HttpSession` class. The class has been given the capability of associating arbitrary data to it. This data can represent anything your webapp needs to relate to each user's session, such as profile information, user preferences, the current selections (like in a shopping cart), and so on.

The mechanism allows a name-value pair to be 'saved' into the session. The name is a string value, which must be unique for the session itself. The value is any Java object. Since the Servlet is persistent on the server, the Java objects stay in memory and are made available to future requests. In other words, the value that was saved into the session may be retrieved. A useful way to think of this capability is that you have the ability to store data into the session, and retrieve data out of the session at a later point in time (in a subsequent request).

Note that the objects saved should implement the `java.io.Serializable` interface. Otherwise the Servlet engine may have trouble saving the object to disk. The engine may need to serialize an object when performing load balancing, sending a snapshot to another engine for failover capabilities, or for recovery from a restart. All of these scenarios are implemented in vendor specific ways, but if your objects all implement the `java.io.Serializable` interface, your design should be portable.

Let's look at sessions in action. Select the Execute link for the Sessions example Servlet. If you have your browser set to warn you before accepting a cookie, you will see the same warning as before.

If you accept the cookie, the browser will display the following page, indicating the session ID, and a section for data in the session. Since we just created the session, there is no data saved in the session:

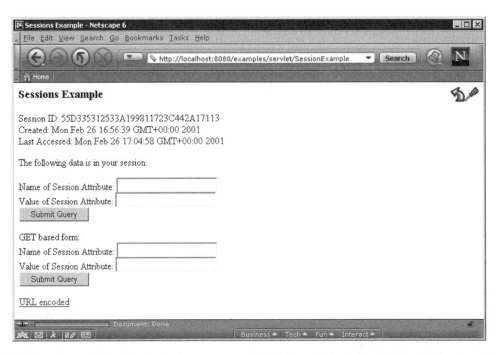

Let's look at the new behavior for the browser, now that we've set this cookie. We can do this by running the Snoop Servlet. The relevant output is shown in the next screenshot:

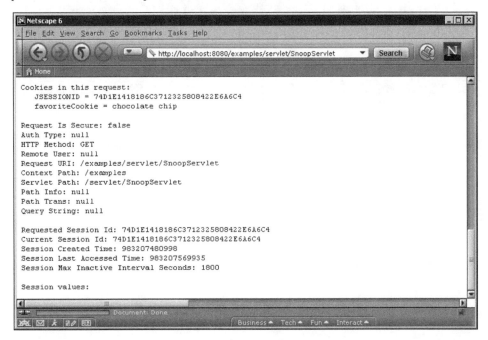

Note that our `favoriteCookie` hasn't changed from our previous cookie example, but the `JSESSIONID` has been set as a cookie in the browser. In addition, the session has some attributes such as a create time, last accessed time, and max inactive interval. In addition, there is a section for Session Values – for which we don't have any yet. We will cover these details later but you can probably imagine their usefulness.

Now let's go back to the Session Servlet display. The display allows for the setting of parameters three different ways. The first Submit Query button corresponds to a POST based form request. The second Submit Query is a GET based form request. The URL encoded link encodes the parameters in the query string of the URL.

Enter a name-value pair through one of the Submit Query forms and select the submit button (or through the URL encoded link, which sets the name equal to foo and the value equal to bar). The Session Servlet will save that pair in the session and make it available to subsequent requests.

The following display illustrates a name-value pair entered in via the POST method:

After submitting this form, the Session Servlet now displays the name-value pair that is stored in the session, as shown below:

Go ahead and experiment with this form. You can add as many name-value pairs as you want. Just remember that since the name is a string, if you enter the same name twice, the second value will overwrite the first.

Now that we've stored some data into the session, lets look again at the Snoop Servlet:

Notice that the **Session values:** section contains our empty `shoppingCart` object.

After having seen sessions in action, you can probably envision the APIs available to Servlets. Let's quickly look at the code for the Session Servlet from `SessionServlet.java`.

The first new piece of code we notice is the following two lines:

```
HttpSession session = request.getSession();
out.println(rb.getString("sessions.id") + " " + session.getId());
```

Remember that the Servlet engine is managing sessions for the Servlets, and it is building the `request` object from the incoming HTTP request. Because of this, the designers of the API conveniently bundled the `session` object (of class `HttpSession`) into the `request` object and made it available via the `getSession()` method.

The `session.getId()` method returns a string value representing the ID.

The next significant code we want to highlight involves saving the supplied parameters in the session:

```
String dataName = request.getParameter("dataname");
String dataValue = request.getParameter("datavalue");
if (dataName != null && dataValue != null) {
    session.setAttribute(dataName, dataValue);
}
```

As you can see, the `session.setAttribute()` method associates the value of `dataValue` with the name of `dataName`. This effectively saves the pair in the session for subsequent requests to access. The second parameter to `setAttribute()` should be of class `Object`. Since `dataValue` is a `String`, the Java compiler allows the translation up the object hierarchy. If `dataValue` was an `int`, it would first have to be converted to an `Integer`, and that `Integer` could then be passed into `setAttribute()`.

Next, let's examine how to get data out of the session. The following code performs this trick using our familiar `Enumeration` to get the list of names that are saved in the session:

```
Enumeration names = session.getAttributeNames();
while (names.hasMoreElements()) {
    String name = (String) names.nextElement();
    String value = session.getAttribute(name).toString();
    out.println(name + " = " + value + "<br>");
}
```

As you might expect from previous features we have already seen, the `getAttributeNames()` method returns an `Enumeration` with all the available object names that are stored in the `session`. The `getAttribute()` method returns the `Object` that corresponds to name. This `Object` must be converted to a `String` via the `toString()` method (as shown), or cast to the appropriate object.

Finally, we can see the use of the `encodeURL()` method in action. This method ensures proper encoding of the supplied `String` parameter. The `String` represents a URL that is being sent to the browser for use as a subsequent `request` URL – thus accurate encoding is essential for proper operation. The benefit is twofold. First, the query string is properly represented. Second, if URL rewriting is used to maintain the session, it will be accurately preserved:

```
out.print(response.encodeURL("SessionExample"));
...
out.print(response.encodeURL("SessionExample?dataname=foo&datavalue=bar"));
```

Problems with URL Rewriting

As mentioned earlier, the Servlet engine must handle all pages if URL rewriting is to efficiently handle session management. This is because all pages must utilize URL rewriting in order for the Servlet engine to keep track of the thread of requests (to keep track of the session). Lets use an example to illustrate the issue. In the following table, we describe the sequence of requests and Servlet engine actions.

Request	Servlet Engine Action
Servlet Examples	No Action
Execute Sessions example Servlet	Create a new session
Back Button (back to the Servlet Examples page)	No action
Execute Sessions example Servlet	Create a new session

To test this, close all browser windows, restart the browser (to eliminate any session information already stored in the browser), make sure cookies are disabled, and go to the **Servlet Examples** page (http://localhost:8080/examples/servlets). Then execute the Sessions example Servlet. You should see a display similar to the following:

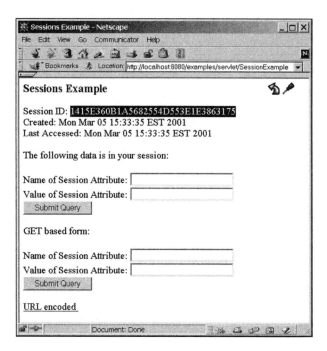

Now hit the back button on your browser. Then execute the Sessions example Servlet again. You should see a display similar to this:

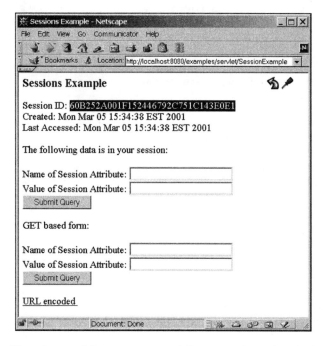

Note that the session ID in the two different screens is different, implying that the Servlet engine lost the thread of the Servlet when we went back to the Servlet Examples page and then created a new session when we executed the Sessions example Servlet a second time.

Thus, if you are going to rely on URL Rewriting for session management (that is, you are not going to force users to enable cookies), make sure every URL goes through your Servlet engine.

Compiling Your Own Servlets

OK, enough examples. Lets code our own Servlet.

This section will introduce you to the basics of how to set up your own web application and make your first Servlet. We prefer starting you off right with your own web application, rather than putting your code into the examples webapp.

Using webapps is analogous to using Java packages. There are a few common mistakes that everyone will make the first few times you try it, but eventually you are going to need the skill. Besides, it's not hard.

Your First Web Application

Creating a basic web application is very anti-climactic. All you need to do is pick a name (try and avoid spaces in the name – in this example we will use mywebapp but you can use whatever you like) and create the following directories:

❑   CATALINA_HOME\webapps\ch03

❑   CATALINA_HOME\webapps\ch03\WEB-INF

❑   CATALINA_HOME\webapps\ch03\WEB-INF\classes

> **Note that even though Windows does not treat filenames as case sensitive, the WEB-INF must be all upper case. If it is not, Tomcat will not behave properly. The Servlet Specification mandates this file naming convention.**

This is the standard file structure for a Tomcat webapp. As we will be using packages in this example create subdirectories of classes following the structure com\wrox\projsp\ch03\myfirstwebapp.

Of course, if you have a more complex webapp, you will eventually run into the need to define some configuration information. This is done in a file called web.xml – also called the webapp deployment descriptor. This file must be located in the WEB-INF directory and is read by the Servlet engine when your webapp is started (usually when the Servlet engine starts).

We will expand on our use of web.xml as it is needed below.

Your First Servlet

In the classes\com\wrox\projsp\ch03\myfirstwebapp directory you just created, create MyFirstServlet.java using a text editor, and enter the following code and save the file:

```
package com.wrox.projsp.ch03.myfirstwebapp;

import java.io.IOException;
```

```
import java.io.PrintWriter;

import javax.servlet.http.HttpServlet;
import javax.servlet.http.HttpServletRequest;
import javax.servlet.http.HttpServletResponse;

import javax.servlet.ServletException;

public class MyFirstServlet extends HttpServlet {

  public void doGet(HttpServletRequest request,
                    HttpServletResponse response) throws ServletException,
                    IOException {
    response.setContentType("text/plain");

    PrintWriter out = response.getWriter();
    out.println("This is my first Servlet");

  }
}
```

Add the Servlet API jar file to your CLASSPATH (note that environment variable names are not case sensitive on Windows, but they are on Unix/Linux). The servlet.jar file implements the Servlet API and is shipped in the CATALINA_HOME\common\lib directory with Tomcat. Now compile your file using javac.

Here is an example on Windows (note the CATALINA_HOME variable is being used here as shorthand – if you do not have this environment variable set you can set it as the first line in the example, making sure that you specify the directory Tomcat is installed in on your computer (the example here uses c:\jakarta-tomcat-4.0-b1)):

```
set CATALINA_HOME=c:\jakarta-tomcat-4.0-xx
set CLASSPATH=%CLASSPATH%;%CATALINA_HOME%\common\lib\servlet.jar
cd %CATALINA_HOME%\webapps\ch03
cd WEB-INF\classes\com\wrox\projsp\ch03\myfirstwebapp
javac MyFirstServlet.java
```

Shutdown Tomcat (via the CATALINA_HOME\bin\shutdown(.bat or .sh))file. Tomcat has some experimental functionality that supports the reloading of modified Servlets – but only if they are already known by Tomcat. Since we are adding an entire webapp (including a previously unknown Servlet, from Tomcat's perspective), we definitely need to restart Tomcat. Once the shutdown is complete, start Tomcat again by executing the appropriate startup script.

Now let's see if it works. Remember that <webapp name>/servlet in a URL maps to <webapp name>\WEB-INF\Servlet in the file system. So you should be able to visit the http://localhost:8080/ch03/servlet/com.wrox.projsp.ch03.MyFirstServlet to run your new Servlet. The results should look like this:

If this seems too clunky to you, you could always use one of those fancy mappings we keep telling you about to make the URL cleaner. We will cover that later in the chapter.

Deploying a Webapp

Now let's say we are happy with our webapp, and want to put it into production. Usually this means we have to copy a bunch of stuff from our development environment and paste it into the production environment. More often than not, this is tedious and error prone.

Webapps provide a simple technique to bundle up the entire webapp and deploy it on any compliant server. Using the `jar` command (for creating a Java ARchive), simply 'jar' up your webapp into what's called a 'war' file (for Web ARchive) and you are free to drop it into the `webapp` directory on any other server. It gets expanded automatically (or executed in place) the next time the server is started. All you need to deploy is the single file.

Of course, there are all those cool configuration options for Servlets that we've only alluded to. If you take advantage of any of those (such as automatically loading the Servlet on startup, or passing initialization parameters to the Servlet), there might be a small additional set of configuration actions you will need to do to deploy them on another machine, but that is it. If you don't use any of those options, you simply deploy the `war` file.

`jar` comes with the Java Development Kit. Typing `jar` at the command prompt will give a fill list of options for use. Typical `jar` command invocations include:

❑ `jar -cvf myJar.jar classes` – creates `myJar.jar` and includes all files under the `classes` directory

❑ `jar -xvf myJar.jar` – extracts `myJar.jar` into the current directory

❑ `jar -tvf myJar.jar` – prints the table of contents (the list of all files contained in the jar file) of `myJar.jar`

The following example creates a `war` file for `myfirstwebapp`:

```
C:\jakarta-tomcat-4.0-b1\webapps\ch03>jar -cvf myfirstwebapp.war *
added manifest
adding: WEB-INF/(in = 0) (out= 0)(stored 0%)
adding: WEB-INF/classes/(in = 0) (out= 0)(stored 0%)
adding: WEB-INF/classes/com/(in = 0) (out= 0)(stored 0%)
adding: WEB-INF/classes/com/wrox/(in = 0) (out= 0)(stored 0%)
adding: WEB-INF/classes/com/wrox/projsp/(in = 0) (out= 0)(stored 0%)
adding: WEB-INF/classes/com/wrox/projsp/ch03/(in = 0) (out= 0)(stored 0%)
adding: WEB-INF/classes/com/wrox/projsp/ch03/myfirstwebapp/(in = 0) (out= 0)(stored 0%)
adding: WEB-INF/classes/com/wrox/projsp/ch03/myfirstwebapp/MyFirstServlet.class(in = 727)
(out= 443)(deflated 39%)
adding: WEB-INF/classes/com/wrox/projsp/ch03/myfirstwebapp/MyFirstServlet.java(in = 649) (
out= 282)(deflated 56%)

C:\jakarta-tomcat-4.0-b1\webapps\ch03>
```

Notice that we ran the jar command from inside the `ch03` directory and told it to grab all the files in that directory and in any subdirectories (via the `*`). Now if we move `myfirstwebapp.war` to the `\webapps` directory of another server and restart it, we should be able to access `myfirstwebapp` on that server just as we did on our development machine, apart from replacing `ch03` in the URL with `myfirstwebapp`. Deployment of a webapp is really that simple.

A Word About Style

Without getting off on a controversial tangent, some points about style and good habits should be made. We have found the following techniques useful:

❑   Use good judgment in your design when partitioning your application into separate webapps. If separate webapps is the best way to go, don't avoid it (of course, when we talk about security, that complicates this decision quite a bit).

❑   Just like when you are developing other Java programs, use packages often and wisely.

❑   Consider separating your Java source code from the webapps classes directory. Build tools such as Ant make this easy, convenient, less error-prone, and manageable.

❑   If you are going to use something like JavaDoc for documenting your source code, start using it from the beginning. Some will argue that when you first start coding on a project, you don't usually have time to document it. But if you don't do it from the start, you'll rarely (if ever) have time to go back and document it later. So either use it from the start, or accept the fact that it will never get done (don't kid yourself).

❑   Use library class and jar files for common utilities such as JDBC drivers. These should go in the WEB-INF\lib directory.

A Day in the Life of a Servlet

So far, we've seen several Servlets in action as well as understood the interaction between the moving parts (browser, web server, and Servlet engine). Now we would like to provide a more thorough discussion of the life of a Servlet and the APIs available to Servlet programmers.

This section will focus on the life cycle of a Servlet, and the environment in which a Servlet performs its job. Subsequent sections will cover the input (request) and output (response), sessions, and advanced topics.

The Life of a Servlet

The following diagram illustrates the steps a Servlet goes through to come into existence and service requests.

The Servlet engine loads the Servlet and then initializes it. The loading involves instantiating the Servlet as an object in memory. The initializing involves calling the Servlet's init() method.

This sequence can be triggered for one of two reasons:

❑   The Servlet was configured to be loaded on startup (of the Servlet engine, that is), in which case when the Servlet engine starts, it will load the Servlet

❑   The Servlet engine received a request for the Servlet

We say that these two steps are effectively synchronous from the Servlet engine's perspective because it must keep track of the completion of both events. The init() method is guaranteed to be called once and only once for the life of a given Servlet. In addition, init() is allowed to complete, guaranteed, before any service methods are invoked.

Finally, when a request is received for a Servlet, the Servlet engine spawns a new thread and calls the appropriate `service()` method of the Servlet. This is illustrated in the following diagram. The 'main thread' for the Servlet visually conveys the difference between the thread that handled the `init()` and the threads that will handle the requests.

The ramification of this multithreading behavior is that Servlet programmers must be conscious of shared objects amongst the various `service()` methods (`doGet()`, `doPost()`, etc.).

On the positive side, Servlets scale extremely well because of this behavior:

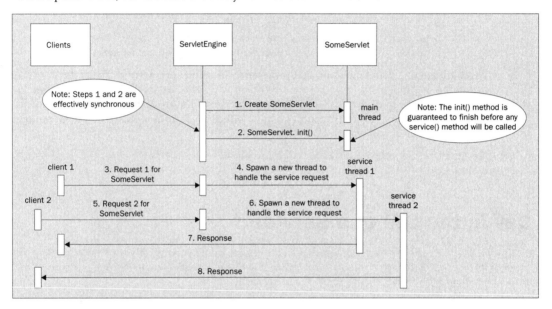

Servlet Entry Points

From the outside looking in, that is, from the Servlet engine's perspective, a Servlet provides the following entry points (consider these the mutator methods of a Servlet):

❏ `init()`
Initialize the Servlet before handling any service requests. This is typically used to open shared resources such as JDBC connections, properties files, etc. It is called only once for the Servlet's lifecycle.

❏ `destroy()`
Used to close down those shared resources and other cleanup required before the Servlet is taken out of service. It is called at most once for the Servlet's lifecycle.

❏ `service()`
Used to handle an incoming request and generate a response. This is further broken down for HTTP Servlets (the only kind we are dealing with in this book) into `doGet()`, `doPost()`, `doDelete()`, `doOptions()`, `doPut()`, and `doTrace()`. This corresponds precisely with the HTTP request methods. It is called once for each incoming HTTP request.

We say these are entry points because the Servlet engine is the primary invoker (although the service methods can call each other, as we have seen from the example Servlets where `doGet()` called `doPost()`, or vice versa).

Servlet APIs

The Servlet APIs are broken up into two packages: `javax.servlet` and `javax.servlet.http`. The `javax` implies it is part of an official Java extension. As mentioned earlier, Tomcat is the official reference implementation platform for these packages. You can reference the API documentation for your Tomcat installation at http://localhost:8080/servletapi-javadoc/index.html.

`javax.servlet` contains classes and interfaces that implement generic, protocol independent Servlets. In addition to code savings, introducing this generic layer allows it to be extended into various flavors for various protocols. Since HTTP is so prevalent and was the initial focus of Servlets, it is included as a standard extension to the generic layer.

`javax.servlet.http` extends the capabilities of the generic Servlets layer for the HTTP protocol.

These two packages can be organized into the groups identified below. This structure helps to serve as a convenient grouping to help understand the full scope of the APIs that are available. It also helps isolate and tackle this information, one digestible topic at a time.

This roadmap will also serve as the outline for the rest of the chapter, as we cover these APIs in depth:

Category	From `javax.servlet`	From `javax.servlet.http`
General	Servlet, GenericServlet, ServletException, UnavailableException	HttpServlet
Environmental	Config, ServletConfig, ServletContext, ServletContextAttributesListener, ServletContextListener, ServletContextAttributeEvent, ServletContextEvent	
Request	ServletRequest, ServletRequestWrapper, ServletInputStream	HttpServletRequest, HttpServletRequestWrapper
Response	ServletResponse, ServletResponseWrapper, ServletOutputStream	HttpServletResponse, HttpServletResponseWrapper
Session	N/A	HttpSession, HttpSessionAttributesListener, HttpSessionBindingListener, HttpSessionListener, HttpSessionBindingEvent, HttpSessionEvent
Miscellaneous	Filter, FilterConfig, RequestDispatcher, SingleThreadModel	Cookie, HttpUtils

Object Scope

Before delving into the APIs, we will take a look at a more global topic. A major feature (and often a major conceptual hurdle) available with Servlets and JSP is **scope**. We've already seen this in action with our session examples, where we were able to save an object into the session.

These objects, when saved into one of the scope objects (or holders), are called **attributes**. They are distinct from **parameters**, which are extracted from the HTTP request.

In scope lingo, we would say that object that we saved was **session scoped**. That is, the object was effectively visible to all invocations of a service method for the same client session. Let's look at the following diagram to illustrate session scope:

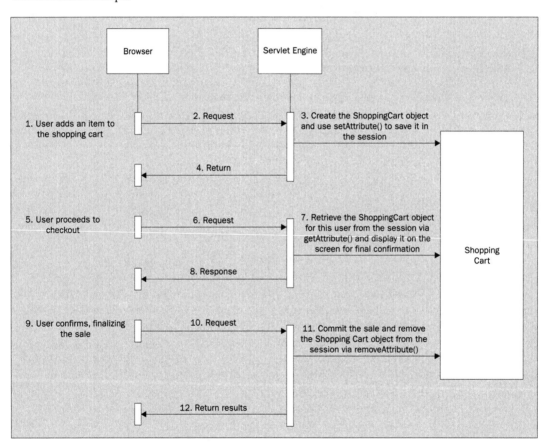

Between Servlets and JSP, there are four different values of scope. They are:

Level of Scope	APIs of interest	Comments
Page	N/A (local variables in the service methods)	Available to the handling Servlet only (within its service method). These are usually method instance variables.
Request	`request.setAttribute(key, obj)` `request.getAttribute(key)`	Available to the handling Servlet and to any Servlet or JSP that control is forwarded to.
Session	`session.setAttribute(key, obj)` `session.getAttribute(key)`	Available to any Servlet or JSP within the same scope. The most common example of a session-scoped object would be a shopping cart.

Application	`getServletContext()`
	`setAttribute(key, obj)`
	
	`getServletContext()`
	`getAttribute(key)`
		Available to any Servlet or JSP within the same webapp. Usually obtained in the `init()` method. Note that the `ServletContext` object holds objects of application scope. A typical application scoped object for an e-commerce application might be a daily special.

The APIs follow a similar structure with `getAttribute()`, `setAttribute()`, and `removeAttribute()` methods to retrieve, save, and delete an attribute from the scope. In addition, there is a `getAttributeNames()` method to obtain the full set of names of attributes in the scope.

The following diagram illustrates all forms of scope. Note that the responses are omitted for clarity.

The diagram shows two sets of client requests, corresponding to two sessions. The webapp's context holds a `dailySpecials` object, which is an application scoped attribute. When client 1 issues a checkout request, the Servlet that handles the request forwards it to another Servlet, including extra information (request attributes) in the request for the other Servlet to use.

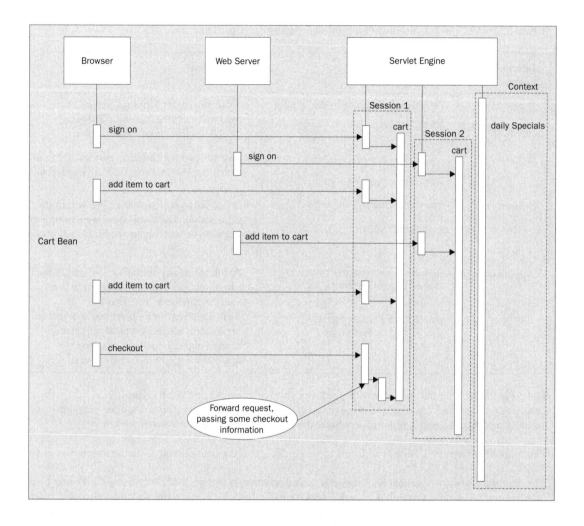

General Servlet APIs

What we call the general Servlet APIs consist of the basic lifecycle oriented APIs. They include the following:

❑ `javax.servlet.Servlet`
An interface that defines the `init()`, `destroy()`, `service()`, `getServletConfig()` and `getServletInfo()` methods

❑ `javax.servlet.GenericServlet`
A class that implements `Servlet` in a protocol independent way and adds a variety of methods useful to all Servlets

❑ `javax.servlet.http.HttpServlet`
A class that extends `GenericServlet` for the HTTP protocol

❑ `javax.servlet.servletException`
A general exception that a Servlet can throw

❑   `javax.servlet.UnavailableException`
A specific exception that indicates the Servlet is unavailable to handle service requests

In this section, we will focus most of our attention on the `HttpServlet` class.

HttpServlet

We have already seen `HttpServlet` in action. One detail we skipped over was the fact that it is declared `abstract`, forcing us to `extend` it before using it. The designers implemented the common and generic functionality, allowing you to focus on the unique behavior you require, allowing the other details to be inherited, unchanged.

Here is a summary of what is available via `HttpServlet`:

Category	Methods	Comments
Lifecycle Methods	`init()`, `destroy()`	For startup and shutdown of global resources
Get and Post Methods	`doGet()`, `doPost()`	Main service methods used, usually one calls the other to provide identical behavior
WebDAV Methods	`doDelete()`, `doPut()`	The service methods are used only if implementing WebDAV functionality
Miscellaneous	`doOptions()`, `doTrace()`, `service()`	The service methods are usually not overridden
Other Miscellaneous	`log()`, `getLastModified()`, `getServletInfo()`, `getServletName()`	Various methods
Environment	`getInitParameter()`, `getInitParameterNames()`, `getServletConfig()`, `getServletContext()`	These are discussed in the next section

Lifecycle Methods

Let's explore the `init()` method a little more closely. There are actually two flavors – one with no parameters, and one that accepts a `ServletConfig` parameter. Remember that `init()` is being called by the Servlet engine, so the `ServletConfig` parameter is set by the engine based on configuration information the engine has access to (we'll expand this later in the chapter when we show examples of initialization parameters).

`HttpServlet` inherits these methods from `GenericServlet`, so there are some class issues to be aware of. Both methods tell the Servlet it is being brought into use (a service request could come at any time after the completion of the `init()` method). When designing your Servlet, choose between the two flavors based on whether or not you need to utilize the `ServletConfig` object in the initialization of your Servlet. The `ServletConfig` is always available via the `getServletConfig()` method anyway. The next section illustrates the use of `ServletConfig`.

Note that you don't have to override either method if you have no initialization required before handling service methods. The amount of initialization required depends on what you're using the Servlet for – database connections, say, would generally be instantiated during initialization.

The destroy() method is also inherited from GenericServlet and only needs to be implemented if you have any required cleanup that must take place before the Servlet is taken out of service. The Servlet spec doesn't say when a Servlet engine might want to do this, but scenarios could include:

❑ An orderly shutdown of the Servlet engine.

❑ An orderly shutdown of selected Servlets. This capability might enable the hot swapping of individual webapps or individual Servlets while preserving the rest of the system.

Service

We have already seen the doGet() and doPost() in action. These two methods will usually handle the bulk of the servicing and are often the only ones implemented (overridden). Indeed, one usually calls the other since most situations will require the GET and POST HTTP methods to have the same response.

The doDelete() and doPut() methods are used to implement WebDAV for remote publishing.

The doOptions() and doTrace(), methods are usually not overridden. The inherited behavior fully supports HTTP version 1.1 and is usually adequate. The doOptions() method returns a header with the supported options that this Servlet provides (for example HEAD, TRACE, OPTIONS, and GET and/or POST if they are overridden). The doTrace() method echoes the headers of the request back to the client for debugging (per the HTTP spec).

Both service() methods are usually not overridden. The default behavior of these methods receives HTTP requests and dispatches the request to the specific HTTP method (such as doGet(), doPost(), and so on).

Miscellaneous

We have a few methods that don't fit into one of the other categories. They are:

❑ log()
Has two flavors – one accepts a message String, the other accepts a message String and a Throwable parameter which would correspond to an exception that occurred. Both methods write the parameters to the Servlet's log file (preceded by the Servlet's name). An example of both types is shown below:

```
// within a method such as doGet()
log ("doGet was just called");
. . .

// as part of an error handling routine
try {
    . . .
} catch (Exception e) {
    log ("exception caught in doGet", e);
}
```

❑ getLastModified()
This method accepts an HttpServletRequest parameter and returns the last modified date of that resource. This method should be overridden to return something appropriate for the Servlet. The HTTP protocol makes use of this information to enable caching and proxy servers, reducing network traffic.

❑ `getServletInfo()`
This method is called by the Servlet engine and could be overridden to provide something appropriate such as a version number (it returns an empty `String` by default). The Servlet engine's use of the return value is vendor specific but one use might be in a management console. The information returned by this method could be displayed in a list of all running Servlets.

❑ `getServletName()`
This method returns the Servlet name from the `web.xml` file (if defined) or the class name (if not defined).

Example

Let's see some of the new features in action. From this point through the next few chapters, we are going to use a common application for many of our illustrations. Since these chapters build upon themselves, we feel it will make for a better learning experience to build upon the same application.

Our example is a Time Entry System, for entering timesheet information. Our first example only illustrates several of the APIs we just learned about.

We will introduce the `ch03` webapp, which you can download from http://www.wrox.com. The Java code for this webapp will be in the `com.wrox.projsp.ch03.time` package (and subpackages including `controller` and `beans`). This will enforce our belief to start early with packages.

If you install this webapp, go to the `CATALINA_HOME\webapps\ch03\WEB-INF\classes\com\wrox\projsp\ch03\time\controller` directory. The first example we are interested in is in the `TimeServlet1.java` file. Its contents are listed below. We will add to this Servlet in subsequent examples, renaming it along the way so we can see each version:

```
package com.wrox.projsp.ch03.time.controller;

import java.util.Enumeration;

import java.io.IOException;
import java.io.PrintWriter;

import javax.servlet.http.HttpServlet;
import javax.servlet.http.HttpServletRequest;
import javax.servlet.http.HttpServletResponse;

import javax.servlet.ServletException;

public class TimeServlet1 extends HttpServlet {
  public void init() {
    log("init was called");
  }

  public void doGet(HttpServletRequest request,
                    HttpServletResponse response) throws ServletException,
                    IOException {
    log("doGet called");

    response.setContentType("text/html");

    PrintWriter out = response.getWriter();

    out.println("<html>");
```

```
        out.println("<head><title>");
        out.println("Time Entry System");
        out.println("</title></head>");

        out.println("<body>");

        out.println("<h2>Welcome to the Time Entry System</h2>");

        out.println("<form action=Time1 method=POST>");
```

We will use the parameter "EVENT" as the key to telling the Servlet what to do. We can pass this in on the URL (in the query string) or as a variable in the form, based on user action. As we add functionality (events) to our Servlet, we simply add "else if (event.equals())" cases to handle the new situations.

```
        String event = request.getParameter("EVENT");
        if (event == null) {

          // default case
        } else if (event.equals("ADMIN")) {
          out.println("<h3>Administration Information</h3>");
          out.println("<ul>");
          out.println("<li>Last Modified: " + getLastModified(request));
          out.println("<li>Servlet Info: " + getServletInfo());
          out.println("<li>Servlet Name: " + getServletName());
          out.println("<li>Init Parameters:");

          Enumeration initParams = getInitParameterNames();
          out.println("<ul>");
          while (initParams.hasMoreElements()) {
            String paramName = (String) initParams.nextElement();
            String paramValue = getInitParameter(paramName);
            out.println("<li>" + paramName + "=" + paramValue);
          }
          out.println("</ul>");
          out.println("</ul>");

        }

        out.println("</form>");

        out.println("</body>");
        out.println("</html>");

      }
  public void doPost(HttpServletRequest request,
                     HttpServletResponse response) throws ServletException,
                     IOException {
    log("doPost called");
    doGet(request, response);
  }
}
```

If you compile this file (as with MyFirstServlet, allowing for location and file name differences) and restart Tomcat, you can execute it via the following URL:

http://localhost:8080/ch03/servlet/com.wrox.projsp.ch03.time.controller.TimeServlet1?EVENT=ADMIN

We apologize for the ridiculously long name, but we haven't learned about mapping URLs to Servlets yet. But think of it this way, when we do cover mapping, you will really learn it.

If you execute this link, you will see the following display:

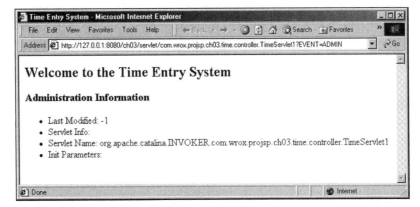

Environmental Servlet APIs

It is useful to use the following picture to visualize a Servlet's execution environment. Note that `ServletContext` and `ServletConfig` objects are discussed in their own section below:

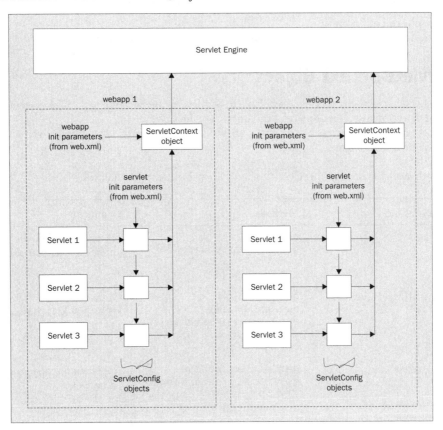

Note that there is one `ServletContext` per webapp.

The `ServletConfig` object (actually an interface implemented by `GenericServlet`) receives Servlet specific initialization parameters, while `ServletContext` receives webapp specific initialization parameters. It is useful to think of the `ServletConfig` as the Servlet specific configuration, and the `ServletContext` as an interface to resources available from the Servlet engine (no client communication is involved).

Also note that all environmental APIs are independent of protocol. That is, none of them have anything to do with HTTP. Therefore, all are found in the `javax.servlet` package.

The ServletConfig Object

The `ServletConfig` object is available from the Servlet engine via the `init(ServletConfig)` method and via the `GenericServlet.getServletConfig()` method. This object provides the following methods:

❑ `getServletName()`
Retrieves the name of the Servlet from (in order of precedence) a server administration mechanism (vendor specific), the `web.xml` file, or the Servlet's class name.

❑ `getInitParameter()`
Retrieves a named parameter (more on this later) for this Servlet.

❑ `getInitParameterNames()`
Retrieves the full set of initialization parameters for this Servlet.

❑ `getServletContext()`
Retrieves the `ServletContext` object for the webapp that this Servlet belongs to.

The ServletContext Object

The `ServletContext` object is made available to Servlets by the Servlet engine. The object is accessible via the `ServletConfig.getServletContext()` method or the `GenericServlet.getServletContext()` method. This object provides a Servlet with a view into the resources of the Servlet engine.

The methods available through `ServletContext` are presented in the following table:

Category	Methods	Comments
Attributes	`getAttribute()` `getAttributeNames()` `removeAttribute()` `setAttribute()`	For saving and obtaining application scoped objects
URL and MIME Resources	`getContext()` `getResource()` `getResourceAsStream()` `getMimeType()` `getRealPath()`	Obtain information for and from URLs and MIME types
Init Parameters	`getInitParameter()` `getInitParameterNames()`	Application scoped init parameters

Category	Methods	Comments
Server Info	getServerInfo() log() getMajorVersion() getMinorVersion()	Log mechanism and specifics on the Servlet engine and API supported
Request Dispatcher	getNamedDispatcher() getRequestDispatcher()	Allows forwarding of requests to other Servlets or JSP

Initialization Parameters

Initialization parameters come in 3 flavors:

- ❑ Servlet specific initialization parameters
- ❑ Webapp specific initialization parameters
- ❑ Webapp specific named objects

Servlet Specific Initialization Parameters

Servlet engines provide a convenient, platform independent mechanism to pass initialization parameters to individual Servlets. They may be passed to any specific Servlet and are made available via the ServletConfig object.

To make use of initialization parameters, all you need to do is the following:

- ❑ Decide on the names of your parameters.

- ❑ Code your Servlet to obtain the initialization parameters via the getInitParameter() method. You can also get all the parameter names via getInitParameterNames().

- ❑ Define the initialization parameters in the web.xml configuration file for your webapp. This file is formatted as per the Servlet specifications and is therefore vendor neutral. The file should be placed in your webapp's WEB-INF directory. This way, it gets bundled up when you make your war file. Valid value types are Boolean, Double, Float, Integer, and String.

That's it – no vendor specific effort is required.

The relevant syntax for the web.xml file is shown below (note that a full example will be included shortly):

```
<web-app>
    <Servlet>
        <Servlet-name>
            Time2
        </Servlet-name>
        <Servlet-class>
            com.wrox.projsp.time.controller.TimeServlet2
        </Servlet-class>

        <init-param>
            <param-name>thisIsMyFirstparam</param-name>
            <param-value>1</param-value>
```

```
            </init-param>

        </Servlet>
    </web-app>
```

Note that in the process of defining the parameters, we also defined an alias for the Servlet. The `<servlet-name>` tag assigned the name `Time2` to the Servlet defined in by the `<servlet-class>` tag, in this case the shortly to be discussed `com.wrox.projsp.ch03.time.controller.TimeServlet2`. The Servlet can now be referenced by the URL http://localhost:8080/ch03/servlet/Time2 – the short cut we've been talking about for so long.

Webapp Specific Initialization Parameters

The Servlet specification also provides a mechanism to pass parameters that are global to a specific webapp. The mechanism is similar to that above but it is implemented via the `ServletContext` object instead of the `ServletConfig` object.

The `ServletContext` object may be obtained via the `ServletConfig.getServletContext()` method. Then the `getInitParameter()` method of the context object can retrieve parameters that are webapp scoped.

The relevant syntax for the `web.xml` file is shown below:

```
<web-app>

    <context-param>
        <param-name>thisIsMyThirdParam</param-name>
        <param-value>3</param-value>
    </context-param>
    <context-param>
        <param-name>thisIsMyFourthParam</param-name>
        <param-value>4</param-value>
    </context-param>

    <Servlet>
        ...
    </Servlet>
</web-app>
```

Similar to Servlet specific parameters, webapp specific parameters may only be of type `Boolean`, `Double`, `Float`, `Integer`, and `String`.

Webapp Specific Named Objects

Webapp specific named objects may be set via the `env-entry` tags in a `web.xml` file. Refer to *The Naming Servlet* section earlier.

These variables allow connectivity to something like an EJB to provide the values. They are much more flexible than the normal initialization parameters.

Preloading a Servlet

As we saw earlier, the normal behavior for a Servlet engine is to load a given Servlet when the first request for it shows up. This cuts down on the startup time of the engine but depending on the tasks required in the `init()` method, may cause the first user to run into unacceptable delays.

The relevant syntax for the `web.xml` file is shown below:

```
<web-app>
  <Servlet>
    <Servlet-name>
      Time2
    </Servlet-name>
    <Servlet-class>
      com.wrox.projsp.time.controller.TimeServlet2
    </Servlet-class>

    <init-param>
      <param-name>thisIsMyFirstparam</param-name>
      <param-value>1</param-value>
    </init-param>
    <init-param>
      <param-name>thisIsMySecondparam</param-name>
      <param-value>2</param-value>
    </init-param>
```

The Servlet spec defines a technique to preload your Servlet when the engine starts. It is called `load-on-startup`. To enable it, simply add the highlighted line in the example below, to your `web.xml` file. The value (in this case 1) determines the order in which the Servlet is loaded. If you have other Servlets being preloaded, you can control the sequence of the load process.

```
      <load-on-startup>1</load-on-startup>
  </Servlet>
  </web-app>
```

Lower values are loaded first. If you do not specify a value for a particular Servlet (or if you specify 0 or a negative number), the engine will load that Servlet at any point it chooses in the engine's startup sequence (most likely after it loads all the other Servlets that are tagged as `load-on-startup`). If you have multiple Servlets with the same value (let's call those Servlets part of the same load group), the engine is free to choose the load order within the group (the order will be unique to the specific engine and may not be portable). In other words, if you require Servlet A to load before Servlet B, make sure Servlet A has a lower value than Servlet B.

Environment Example

Now let's include an example to tie all these environment features together. Let's expand on our previous `TimeServlet1.java` file by making `TimeServlet2.java`. The file is shown below:

```
package com.wrox.projsp.ch03.time.controller;

import java.util.Enumeration;
```

```
import java.io.IOException;
import java.io.PrintWriter;

import javax.servlet.http.HttpServlet;
import javax.servlet.http.HttpServletRequest;
import javax.servlet.http.HttpServletResponse;

import javax.servlet.ServletConfig;
import javax.servlet.ServletContext;
import javax.servlet.ServletException;

public class TimeServlet2 extends HttpServlet {
  public void init() {
    log("init was called");
  }

  public void doGet(HttpServletRequest request,
                    HttpServletResponse response) throws ServletException,
                    IOException {
    log("doGet called");

    response.setContentType("text/html");

    PrintWriter out = response.getWriter();

    out.println("<html>");
    out.println("<head><title>");
    out.println("Time Entry System");
    out.println("</title></head>");

    out.println("<body>");

    out.println("<h2>Welcome to the Time Entry System</h2>");

    out.println("<form action=Time2 method=POST>");

    String event = request.getParameter("EVENT");
    if (event == null) {

      // default case
    } else if (event.equals("ADMIN")) {
      out.println("<h2>Administration Information</h2>");

      out.println("<h3>Webapp and Servlet Engine Info</h3>");
```

You can see how the ServletContext and ServletConfig lead parallel lives, one dealing with webapp resources, the other with Servlet resources:

```
ServletContext context = getServletContext();

out.println("<ul>");
out.println("<li>Server Info: " + context.getServerInfo());
out.println("<li>Major Version: " + context.getMajorVersion());
out.println("<li>Minor Version: " + context.getMinorVersion());
out.println("<li>Webapp Init Parameters:");
```

```
            Enumeration webappParams = context.getInitParameterNames();
            out.println("<ul>");
            while (webappParams.hasMoreElements()) {
               String paramName = (String) webappParams.nextElement();
               String paramValue = context.getInitParameter(paramName);

               // assume paramName and paramValue don't contain any
               // HTML formatting characters such as <, >, &, " or '
               out.println("<li>" + paramName + "=" + paramValue);
            }
            out.println("</ul>");

            out.println("<h3>Servlet Info</h3>");

            ServletConfig config = getServletConfig();

            out.println("<li>Last Modified: " + getLastModified(request));
            out.println("<li>Servlet Info: " + getServletInfo());
            out.println("<li>Servlet Name: " + config.getServletName());

            out.println("<li>Servlet Init Parameters:");

            Enumeration ServletParams = config.getInitParameterNames();
            out.println("<ul>");
            while (ServletParams.hasMoreElements()) {
               String paramName = (String) ServletParams.nextElement();
               String paramValue = config.getInitParameter(paramName);
               out.println("<li>" + paramName + "=" + paramValue);
            }
            out.println("</ul>");
            out.println("</ul>");

         }

      out.println("</form>");

      out.println("</body>");
      out.println("</html>");

   }
   public void doPost(HttpServletRequest request,
                      HttpServletResponse response) throws ServletException,
                      IOException {
      log("doPost called");
      doGet(request, response);
   }

}
```

Now let's look at the web.xml file. In this file, we set some webapp and Servlet initialization parameters, as well as set the load-on-startup for this Servlet:

```
<?xml version="1.0" encoding="ISO-8859-1"?>

<!DOCTYPE web-app
    PUBLIC "-//Sun Microsystems, Inc.//DTD Web Application 2.3//EN"
    "http://java.sun.com/j2ee/dtds/web-app_2_3.dtd">

<web-app>
  <context-param>
```

83

```
        <param-name>thisIsMyThirdParam</param-name>
        <param-value>3</param-value>
    </context-param>
    <context-param>
        <param-name>thisIsMyFourthParam</param-name>
        <param-value>4</param-value>
    </context-param>

    <Servlet>
        <Servlet-name>
            Time2
        </Servlet-name>
        <Servlet-class>
            com.wrox.projsp.ch03.time.controller.TimeServlet2
        </Servlet-class>

        <init-param>
            <param-name>thisIsMyFirstparam</param-name>
            <param-value>1</param-value>
        </init-param>
        <init-param>
            <param-name>thisIsMySecondparam</param-name>
            <param-value>2</param-value>
        </init-param>
        <load-on-startup>1</load-on-startup>
    </Servlet>
</web-app>
```

Notice how we identified the Servlet. This creates a map from the URL to the Servlet, so that once Tomcat has read web.xml (you'll need to restart Tomcat for this to happen) we can reference our Servlet using http://localhost:8080/ch03/servlet/Time2?EVENT=ADMIN.

The display is as follows:

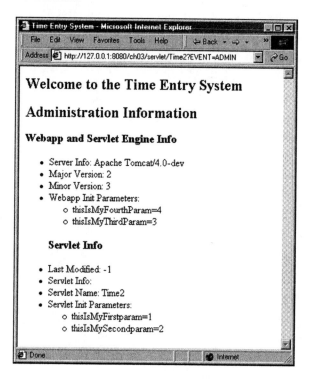

Notice that the Major and Minor Versions map to the specification of the Servlet API. Also notice that our parameters were set properly.

However, if we reference the Servlet by its full name instead of the alias (that is, by http://127.0.0.1:8080/ch03/servlet/com.wrox.projsp.ch03.time.controller.TimeServlet2?EVENT=ADMIN), the initialization parameters are not recognized by the Servlet. This is because the parameters are associated with the alias in web.xml, not with the full name.

Finally, since we aren't doing anything significant in the init() method, we can't tell if the load-on-startup worked or not. Typically the init() method opens connections to databases, reads properties files, and generally carries out all those global startup preparations your Servlet will need. However, we can look at Tomcat's log files to notice the new behavior.

Restart Tomcat and open CATALINA_HOME\logs\localhost_log.<date>, where <date> is the latest date available (sort the directory to find this file). Go to the bottom of the file, where you should see something like the following display (which has admittedly got the information at the top):

```
localhost_log.2001-03-08.txt - Notepad
File  Edit  Format  Help
2001-03-08 17:22:54 StandardHost[localhost]: Deploying web application at
context path /ch03 from URL file:C:\jakarta-tomcat-4.0\webapps\ch03
2001-03-08 17:22:54 Manager[/ch03]: Seeding random number generator class
java.security.SecureRandom
2001-03-08 17:22:54 Manager[/ch03]: Seeding of random number generator has been
completed
2001-03-08 17:22:54 Time2: init
2001-03-08 17:22:54 Time2: init was called
2001-03-08 17:22:54 StandardWrapper[/ch03:default]: Loading container servlet
default
2001-03-08 17:22:54 default: init
2001-03-08 17:22:54 StandardWrapper[/ch03:invoker]: Loading container servlet
invoker
2001-03-08 17:22:54 invoker: init
2001-03-08 17:22:54 jsp: init
```

This section includes the initialization for the ch03 webapp. Notice the line that says "Time2: init". This is the Servlet engine indicating that it started a Servlet and called its init() method. The next line that says "Time2: init was called" is actually our call to log() from within the init() method. At this point, we haven't sent a request to the Servlet yet. Thus we can conclude that Tomcat did as we told it to do and loaded the Servlet when it initialized.

Request APIs

As we have already seen from our tour of the Tomcat examples, the HttpServletRequest object provides methods to obtain (sometimes through other objects) all the information known about the incoming request. This object inherits from ServletRequest and adds protocol specific methods for HTTP. The resources available through this object can be summarized in the following table:

Category	Methods	Comments
Protocol	getMethod getProtocol getScheme	Protocol information for the request

Table continued on following page

Category	Methods	Comments
Client Information	getRemoteAddr getRemoteHost	Client information
Request URL	getContextPath getPathInfo getPathTranslated getQueryString getRequestURI getRequestURL getServletPath getRealPath	Attributes of the request URL
Headers	getDateHeader getHeader getHeaderNames getHeaders getIntHeader	Header information
Cookies	getCookies	Cookie information
Session	getRequestedSessionId getSession isRequestedSessionIdFromCookie isRequestedSessionIdFromURL isRequestedSessionIdValid	Session information
Security	getAuthType getRemoteUser getUserPrincipal isUserInRole isSecure	Security information
Internationalization	getCharacterEncoding getLocale getLocales setCharacterEncoding	Internationalization information
Input Data	getContentLength getContentType getInputStream getParameter getParameterMap getParameterNames getParameterValues getReader	Data in the form of parameters, content information, Stream and Reader objects
Server Information	getRequestDispatcher getServerName getServerPort	Server side information
Attributes	getAttribute getAttributeNames removeAttribute setAttribute	Request scoped attributes

We have already seen many of the major methods through the examples including the use of parameters, sessions, headers, and cookies. Session, cookies, and the request dispatcher will be discussed in more depth in their own sections later in this chapter.

Response APIs

In a similar fashion to the request, the HttpServletResponse object contains everything that there is to know about the outgoing response, along with methods to extract the information. This object inherits from ServletResponse and adds protocol specific methods for HTTP. The resources available through this object can be summarized in the following table:

Category	Methods	Comments
Buffer	flushBuffer getBufferSize isCommitted reset setBufferSize	Response buffers

Category	Methods	Comments

Response URL	`encodeRedirectUrl`
	`encodeRedirectURL encodeURL`
	`sendRedirect`
		Operations for the Response URL

Headers	`addHeader addDateHeader`
	`addIntHeader containsHeader`
	`setDateHeader setHeader`
	`setIntHeader`
		Header information

Cookies	`addCookie`	Cookie information
Internationalization	`getCharacterEncoding getLocale` `setLocale`	Internationalization information
Output Data	`setContentLength setContentType` `getOutputStream getWriter`	Content, Stream and Writer objects
Status and Errors	`sendError setStatus`	Status and Errors

Session Management APIs

As discussed in the examples section, session management within Servlets is a very powerful concept. The APIs provided make management relatively easy. Here are the key APIs:

Category	Methods	Comments
Attributes	`getAttribute() getAttributeNames()` `removeAttribute() setAttribute()`	For storing and retrieving objects into the session.

Session Values	`getCreationTime() getId()`
	`getLastAccessedTime()`
	`getMaxInactiveInterval() isNew()`
	`setMaxInactiveInterval()`
		Note the ability to set the maximum inactive interval. See notes below.

Lifecycle	`invalidate()`	Note: creating a session is done through the `HttpServletRequest.getSession()` method.

Note that the default timeout is Servlet engine specific. Tomcat defaults to 30 minutes. All Servlet engines should support the definition of the timeout in a server-wide configuration file (Tomcat uses `CATALINA_HOME/conf/web.xml` file), as well as an optional timeout for each webapp in the webapp's `WEB-INF/web.xml` file. A value of 0 indicates the sessions never time out due to inactivity (a dangerous design choice – it will be easy to overload your available resources if you don't eliminate unused sessions).

The syntax for setting a webapp's session timeout to 45 minutes looks like this (from the webapp's `WEB-INF/web.xml` file):

```
<session-config>
  <session-timeout>45</session-timeout>
</session-config>
```

A Day in the Life of a Session

Sessions are created due to requests (and somewhat under arbitrary program control) and can either be invalidated by the Servlet engine due to inactivity, or invalidated explicitly by program control.

There are two flavors of the `HttpServletRequest.getSession()` method – one with no parameters, and one with a `boolean` variable named `create`.

With both methods, if a session exists, it will be returned. With the first method, if a session does not exist (or is invalid), a new session will be created. With the second method, if a session does not exist (or is invalid) and the `create` variable is `true`, a new session will be created. If `create` is `false`, a new session is not created.

The `isNew()` method is useful to call after obtaining the session. Since the `getSession()` method will either return an existing session or create a new session, `isNew()` is required to figure out which path `getSession()` took.

This allows the Servlet to react appropriately for a new session. A common use for this feature would be to display the daily specials only when the `request` corresponds to a new session (when `isNew()` returns `true`).

A Session Example

Actually this example builds on the previous `TimeServlet` examples, plus it adds in some of our new request and response knowledge. We'll call this one `TimeServlet3`, and add the following entry to `web.xml` to map it to `Time3`:

```
<servlet>
  <servlet-name>
    Time3
  </servlet-name>
  <servlet-class>
    com.wrox.projsp.ch03.time.controller.TimeServlet3
  </servlet-class>
</servlet>
```

To make use of sessions, we first have to start supplying some data. We will introduce the concept of a `charge` – a set of data that keeps track of the user, project, date, and number of hours (that is, the number of hours to charge). We will use the bean (in the `ch03\WEB-INF\classes\com\wrox\projsp\ch03\time\beans` directory of the webapp) shown below to represent these objects:

```
package com.wrox.projsp.ch03.time.beans;

public class Charge implements java.io.Serializable {

  private String name;
  private String project;
  private String hours;
  private String date;

  public Charge() {}
```

```
public String getName() {
  return name;
}
public void setName(String n) {
  name = n;
}

public String getProject() {
  return project;
}
public void setProject(String proj) {
  project = proj;
}

public String getHours() {
  return hours;
}
public void setHours(String h) {
  hours = h;
}

public String getDate() {
  return date;
}
public void setDate(String d) {
  date = d;
}

}
```

This is just a basic bean – there is nothing interesting about it yet. Note that to give the
TimeServlet3.java file visibility to this bean for compilation, add the classes directory to the
CLASSPATH. A Windows example follows:

```
set CLASSPATH=%CLASSPATH%;%CATALINA_HOME%\webapps\ch03\WEB-INF\classes
```

During execution by a Servlet engine, the CLASSPATH includes the
CATALINA_HOME/webapps/<yourwebapp>/WEB-INF/classes and each jar file in
CATALINA_HOME/webapps/<yourwebapp>/WEB-INF/lib. Global jar files such as JDBC drivers are
typically placed in the lib directory.

The entire Servlet is shown here for clarity:

```
package com.wrox.projsp.ch03.time.controller;

import com.wrox.projsp.ch03.time.beans.Charge;

import java.util.Enumeration;
import java.util.Hashtable;

import java.io.IOException;
import java.io.PrintWriter;
```

```
import javax.servlet.http.HttpSession;
import javax.servlet.http.HttpServlet;
import javax.servlet.http.HttpServletRequest;
import javax.servlet.http.HttpServletResponse;

import javax.servlet.ServletConfig;
import javax.servlet.ServletContext;
import javax.servlet.ServletException;


public class TimeServlet3 extends HttpServlet {
  public void init() {
    log("init was called");
  }

  public void doGet(HttpServletRequest request,
                    HttpServletResponse response) throws ServletException,
                    IOException {
    log("doGet called");

    response.setContentType("text/html");

    PrintWriter out = response.getWriter();

    out.println("<html>");
    out.println("<head><title>");
    out.println("Time Entry System");
    out.println("</title></head>");

    out.println("<body>");

    out.println("<h2>Welcome to the Time Entry System</h2>");

    out.println("<form action=Time3 method=POST>");
```

Notice how we get the session using `request.getSession()`:

```
HttpSession session = request.getSession();

// find out what we were told to do (if anything)
String event = request.getParameter("EVENT");
if (event == null) {
  event = "ENTER_RECORD";   // catch this special case
} else if (event.equals("")) {
  event = "ENTER_RECORD";   // catch this special case
}
```

Now let's create a form to handle the data entry of these charges. Notice the use of named parameters of name, `project`, `hours`, `date`, and `EVENT`. Also notice the use of a `hidden` input type to set the `EVENT` value to `NEW_RECORD`. This is a common practice with web applications because it keeps the user's perspective cleaner by keeping parameters off the query string and out of the visible portion of the form:

```
// main dispatch center
if (event.equals("ENTER_RECORD")) {

  // default case
  out.println("<h3>Enter Charge Record</h3>");
  out.println("<p>User Name<input type=text name=name>");
```

```
out.println("<p>Project<input type=text name=project>");
out.println("<p>Hours<input type=text name=hours>");
out.println("<p>Date<input type=text name=date>");
out.println("<input type=hidden name=EVENT value=NEW_RECORD>");
out.println("<p><input type=submit>");
out.println("<input type=reset>");
```

Next we need to be able to read the parameters. Each time we read them, we will add them to a `Hashtable` that we will store on the session. The `NEW_RECORD` event handler will perform this processing:

```
} else if (event.equals("NEW_RECORD")) {

out.println("<h3>Your Charge Record has been saved</h3>");
String name = request.getParameter("name");
String project = request.getParameter("project");
String hours = request.getParameter("hours");
String date = request.getParameter("date");
```

Notice how we retrieve the parameters and use them to create a `Charge` object and populate it:

```
Charge c = new Charge();
c.setName(name);
c.setProject(project);
c.setHours(hours);
c.setDate(date);
```

Also notice the handling of the `Hashtable` named h (not a very creative name, I know, but it conveys the meaning). We first try and get it off the `session` using `getAttribute()`. If `getAttribute()` returns `null`, this means it hasn't been saved into this `session` yet, so we must instantiate it first. If `getAttribute()` doesn't return `null`, we just use the `Hashtable` it returns. Also notice how we only need to set the attribute to the session once – if it hasn't been set previously. This is because the object reference is kept in the session. Thus all changes to that object (new additions to the `Hashtable`) are effectively preserved in the session automatically.

```
Hashtable h = (Hashtable) session.getAttribute("charges");
if (h == null) {
   h = new Hashtable();    // first charge
   session.setAttribute("charges", h);
}
h.put(project, c);          // use project as the key
out.println("Record Details: <p>");
out.println("Name = " + name + ", Project = " + project
            + ", Hours = " + hours + ", Date = " + date);
```

The event handler for SUMMARY looks like this:

```
} else if (event.equals("SUMMARY")) {

out.println("<h3>Summary of your Charge Records</h3>");
Hashtable h = (Hashtable) session.getAttribute("charges");
if (h != null) {
   out.println("<ul>");
   Enumeration charges = h.keys();
   while (charges.hasMoreElements()) {
      String proj = (String) charges.nextElement();
      Charge ch = (Charge) h.get(proj);
```

```
            out.println("<li>");
            out.println("name = " + ch.getName());
            out.println(", project = " + proj);
            out.println(", hours = " + ch.getHours());
            out.println(", date = " + ch.getDate());
        }
        out.println("</ul>");
    }
```

The ADMIN event is essentially the code from the previous example in `TimeServlet2.java`. It displays the webapp and Servlet engine data:

```
} else if (event.equals("ADMIN")) {
    out.println("<h2>Administration Information</h2>");

    out.println("<h3>Webapp and Servlet Engine Info</h3>");

    ServletContext context = getServletContext();

    out.println("<ul>");
    out.println("<li>Server Info: " + context.getServerInfo());
    out.println("<li>Major Version: " + context.getMajorVersion());
    out.println("<li>Minor Version: " + context.getMinorVersion());
    out.println("<li>Webapp Init Parameters:");

    Enumeration webappParams = context.getInitParameterNames();
    out.println("<ul>");
    while (webappParams.hasMoreElements()) {
        String paramName = (String) webappParams.nextElement();
        String paramValue = context.getInitParameter(paramName);
        out.println("<li>" + paramName + "=" + paramValue);
    }
    out.println("</ul>");

    out.println("<h3>Servlet Info</h3>");

    ServletConfig config = getServletConfig();

    out.println("<li>Last Modified: " + getLastModified(request));
    out.println("<li>Servlet Info: " + getServletInfo());
    out.println("<li>Servlet Name: " + config.getServletName());

    out.println("<li>Servlet Init Parameters:");

    Enumeration ServletParams = config.getInitParameterNames();
    out.println("<ul>");
    while (ServletParams.hasMoreElements()) {
        String paramName = (String) ServletParams.nextElement();
        String paramValue = config.getInitParameter(paramName);
        out.println("<li>" + paramName + "=" + paramValue);
    }
    out.println("</ul>");
    out.println("</ul>");

}

out.println("</form>");

out.println("<hr>");
```

Finally, we need a way to access the saved charges. We will use a separate form with a different value of EVENT as shown here:

```
        out.println("<form action=Time3 method=POST>");
        out.println("<input type=hidden name=EVENT value=SUMMARY>");
        out.println("<input type=submit value=Summary>");
        out.println("</form>");

        out.println("</body>");
        out.println("</html>");

    }
    public void doPost(HttpServletRequest request,
                       HttpServletResponse response) throws ServletException,
                       IOException {
      log("doPost called");
      doGet(request, response);
    }

}
```

Note that the use of String literal constants as illustrated in the values for EVENT in the previous example is a dangerous practice. Bugs can often creep in due to typos in when programmers have to type them into different sections of code. Two possible design considerations to lessen the problem include the use of a Constants class to define the constants used by the package, and the forcing of parameter values to upper (or lower) case prior to any compare logic is performed.

Executing this Servlet by going to http://localhost:8080/ch03/servlet/Time3 results in the following display:

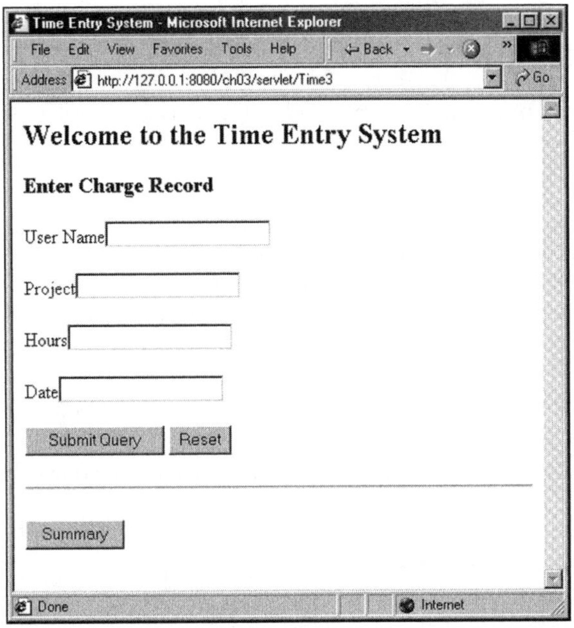

Enter a few charge records, press the **Submit Query** of the form and then the Back button of the browser in between each record. Then press the **Summary** button. You should see a display similar to the following:

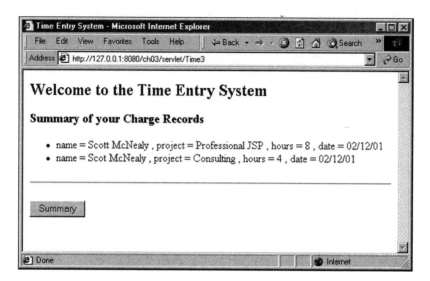

This illustrates how the session kept track of all of our charge records.

Advanced Servlet Topics

Before leaving Servlets, there are a few advanced topics that we should cover before focusing on JSP. These topics will be revisited as we apply these concepts to JSP and ultimately when we integrate JSP and Servlets.

Request Dispatcher

Your Servlet can obtain a `RequestDispatcher` object from its context. The `RequestDispatcher` interface defines the following methods:

❑ `forward()`
Passes control to another entity such as a Servlet or JSP. This mechanism allows for much cleaner designs by enabling control to be passed to the best handler for the circumstances. For example, a Servlet could validate the data from the `request` and then pass control to another Servlet (or JSP) to generate the `response` (we'll see much more of this as we go on). The `request` and `response` object are passed to the target of the forward operation (the Servlet or JSP that will be resuming control). Note that the request attributes (set via the `request.setAttribute()` method) are available to the target Servlet or JSP (via the `request.getAttribute()` method).

Typically you will use something like the following code example inside one of your service methods:

```
// ... inside doGet() or doPost()
ServletContext    sc = getServletContext();
String            url = "CommonErrorPage";
RequestDispatcher rd = sc.getRequestDispatcher(url);
rd.forward(request, response);
// end of processing for this request within this Servlet
```

This example obtains a RequestDispatcher for the url which points to the CommonErrorPage. Then control is forwarded to that url, passing the request and response objects. That would conclude the processing for the request within the Servlet shown. The url that control was forwarded to would complete the processing.

If this Servlet set any attributes in the request such as validation results, the CommonErrorPage would be able to get them and use them.

❑ include()
Includes the contents of a resource such as a JSP, HTML file, or another Servlet into the calling Servlet's response. This allows functionality such as common header/footer generation to be inserted into the response of the processing Servlet.

In the following example, a common header is included into the Servlet:

```
// ... inside doGet() or doPost()
ServletContext     sc = getServletContext();
String             url = "commonHeader.html";
RequestDispatcher rd = sc.getRequestDispatcher(url);
rd.include (request, response);
// continue processing this request
```

Note how the processing of the request continues in this Servlet once the url is included.

Servlet Cookies

As we saw in the example section, cookies provide a useful mechanism for storing data on the client machine for eventual transmission back to the server. This may not seem as useful with the advent of session management, but cookies remain a powerful tool when trying to identify users across sessions.

The following table summarizes the APIs available for cookies:

Category	Methods	Comments
HttpServletRequest	getCookies()	Returns an array of Cookie objects.
The Cookie class itself	clone() Cookie() getComment() setComment() getDomain() setDomain() getMaxAge() setMaxAge() getName() getPath() setPath() getSecure() setSecure() getValue() setValue() getVersion() setVersion()	Because the name is the unique identifier from an HTTP stand point, it must be set in the constructor.
HttpServletResponse	addCookie()	Allows the Servlet to add a Cookie object to the response.

For more details on cookies, reference the section in Chapter 2.

Servlet Logging

Debugging Servlets can be a challenge. A good strategy is to start off with a sound design for logging information that can be used to help track down problems.

The Servlet API includes a `log()` method that enables you to write strings to the Servlets log file. The location of the file is vendor specific. For Tomcat, it is located in `CATALINA_HOME\logs\localhost_log.<todays date>`.

An example of the `log()` output is shown below:

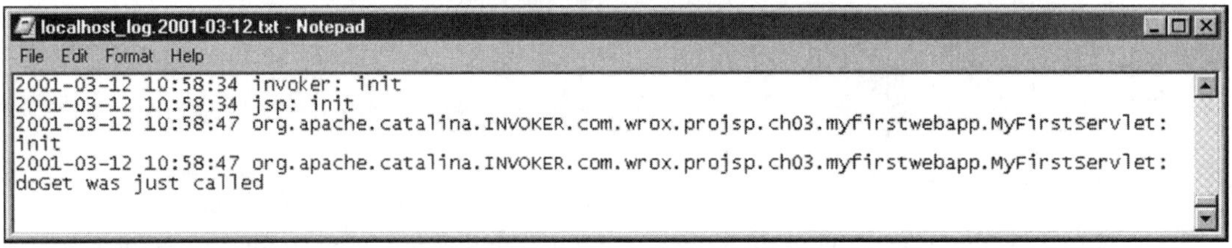

In the above example, we added the following line to `MyFirstServlet` (notice how the `log()` method added the timestamp and our Servlet's name):

```
log("doGet was just called");
```

In addition, Tomcat has an advanced logging feature that allows you to tailor it to suit your application. An example is included with the Tomcat distribution. Reference the `CATALINA_HOME/conf/server.xml` file. Note the following lines:

```
<Context path="/examples" docBase="examples" debug="0" reloadable="true">
  <Logger className="org.apache.catalina.logger.FileLogger"
          prefix="localhost_examples_log." suffix=".txt" timestamp="true"/>
  . . .
```

The first line defines the start of context information for the `examples` webapp. The debug variable can be set to a number other than 0 (typically 0 is the lowest level of debugging and 9 is the highest – meaning the most information is logged).

The next two lines define a separate log file – `localhost_examples_log.txt` – for this webapp (which can be found in `CATALINA_HOME/logs`). This definition also enables the automatic time stamping of entries logged.

Internationalization

We have seen internationalization in action (sort of). Now let's explore the details.

From a sequence point of view, the request contains the requested locale. Locale is the two-character representation for the language plus an optional two-character representation for the localization or dialect within the language.

For example, en_US is the representation for the English language spoken in the United States. es_ES is the version of Spanish spoken in Spain. If no dialect is specified, the default for the language is used. Refer to the java.util.locale class for more details. The default country is set by the JDK (or JRE – the Java runtime environment) and is available via the java.util.Locale.getDefault().getCountry() method.

To change the setting on your browser, first add Spanish as a language supported by your browser. Here is an example with the Internet Explorer browser (note the use of all lower case within the browser – technically the two character locale code is capitalized in Java):

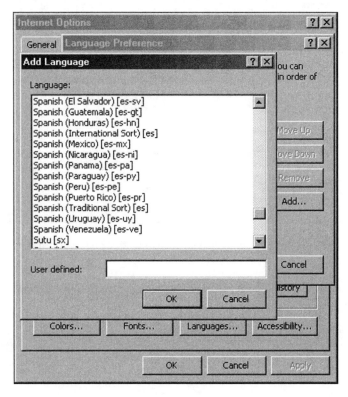

Netscape follows the same process. Go to **Preferences** and select the **Navigator** section. Click on the **Languages** section, and follow the above procedure. The following screenshot shows the Netscape **Add Languages** dialog:

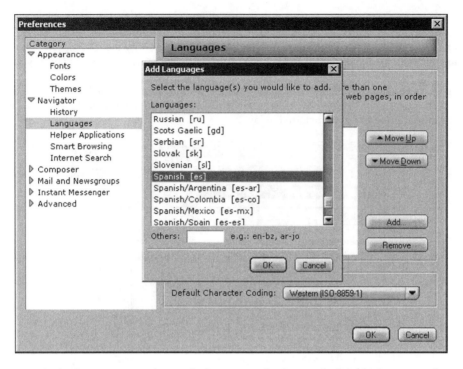

The next step for both systems is to change the language to be first on the list (the browser only sends one to the server).

Now go to the `HelloWorld` example Servlet. It should display the message in Spanish now (don't forget to change the order of the languages back).

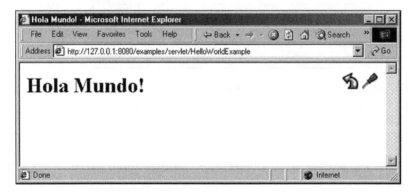

Let's look under the hood at what just happened.

First, by changing the language list in the browser, we changed the locale reported in the `request`. Second, the `HelloWorld` Servlet is coded to use the locale and select locale specific strings for display.

We already saw the use of the `ResourceBundle` in obtaining the string. Here is the code from `HelloWorldExample.java`:

```
ResourceBundle rb = ResourceBundle.getBundle("LocalStrings",request.getLocale());
```

Notice how the `getBundle()` method takes the name of the bundle ("LocalStrings") and the locale from the `request`. We don't even need to worry about the details (well, almost).

Now let's look at the `example` webapp and find the `LocalStrings` files. If we look in CATALINA_HOME\webapps\example\WEB-INF\classes, we find `LocalStrings_en.properties` and `LocalStrings_es.properties`. The locale is appended to the name of the bundle (and as always for Java properties files, appended with the ".properties" extension).

If we open up the two files, we can see the same set of names, but a language specific set of values, as we would expect.

First the English version (note that this is only the code for `HelloWorldExample`. Code for the other examples is included in the property file):

```
helloworld.title=Hello World!

requestinfo.title=Request Information Example
requestinfo.label.method=Method:
requestinfo.label.requesturi=Request URI:
requestinfo.label.protocol=Protocol:
requestinfo.label.pathinfo=Path Info:
requestinfo.label.remoteaddr=Remote Address:
```

Now the Spanish version:

```
helloworld.title=Hola Mundo!

requestinfo.title=Ejemplo de Informacion de Request
requestinfo.label.method=Metodo:
requestinfo.label.requesturi=Request URI:
requestinfo.label.protocol=Protocolo:
requestinfo.label.pathinfo=Path Info:
requestinfo.label.remoteaddr=Direccion Remota:
```

The tedious part of internationalizing your webapp is to remember to always use a `ResourceBundle` to get a string that will be displayed. Then all you need to do is translate each string to each new language that you will support (not that the translation is easy, but at least you don't have to recode anything). Note however that sometimes things will get lost (or at least misplaced) in the translation. Formatting can easily be thrown off when switching between languages. Budget extra time to review all displays when introducing a new language into your application.

Generating Well Formed HTML Documents

We have seen examples where we had to assume that certain parameters or variables contained none of the special HTML control characters such as >, <, &, " or ', such as:

```
out.println("<li>" + paramName + "=" + paramValue);
```

If `paramName` contained a < character, the resulting line would have been off balance and corrupted the intended look of the HTML document. Fortunately HTML (via the ISO-8859-1 standard) has shortcuts that may be substituted. When the browser receives one of these substitutions, it simply displays it instead of parsing it (as part of the HTML syntax).

Character	HTML Substitution
>	>
<	<
&	&
"	"
'	'

A simple filtering algorithm can be employed to eliminate these characters prior to sending them to the output. Similar to the technique used with resource bundles, we must remember to obtain any potential offender through our filter instead of directly obtaining the value.

Here is an example filter algorithm:

```
static String validHtml (String original) {

   StringBuffer new = new StringBuffer(original.length);
   char next;
   for (int i = 0; i < original.length(); i++) {
     next = original.charAt(i);
     if (n == '>') {
       new.append ("&gt;");
     else if (n == '<') {
       new.append ("&lt;");
     else if (n == '&') {
       new.append ("&amp;");
     else if (n == '"') {
       new.append ("&quot;");
     else if (n == ''') {
       new.append ("&$#39;");
     else {
       new.append (next);
     }
   }
   return new.toString();
}
```

To use it in the original line shown above, we would simply obtain the text for `paramName` and `paramValue` via the `htmlFilter` method as shown:

```
out.println("<li>" + validHtml(paramName) + "=" + validHtml(paramValue));
```

Servlet Mapping

We have alluded often to the capability of mapping URLs to Servlets via the Servlet engine. The Servlet spec defines a minimal set of required functionality that must be implemented by each compliant engine for mapping defined in the webapp's web.xml file.

By associating the mapping with each webapp, deployment issues with co-resident webapps are eliminated. Each webapp need only define the mappings it requires with no regard to its deployment environment.

The only minor exceptions are the global mappings such as '*.jsp' files, which are mapped to the JSP engine.

We have already seen an example where we defined an alias for a Servlet. Here was the relevant section from web.xml:

```
<servlet>
  <servlet-name>
    Time3
  </servlet-name>
  <servlet-class>
    com.wrox.projsp.ch03.time.controller.TimeServlet3
  </servlet-class>
</servlet>
```

In this case, the <servlet-name> tag provided an alias to the class specified by the <servlet-class> tag.

This simple example still requires us to specify http://localhost:8080/ch03/servlet/Time3, signifying the use of a Servlet. There is nothing wrong with this, but a more elegant solution exists with the use of a <servlet-mapping> tag.

With a <servlet-mapping> tag, we can map URL patterns to previously defined Servlets (via the above construct).

Below is a simple mapping that binds the Time3 Servlet to the URL pattern ending with /Time:

```
<servlet-mapping>
  <servlet-name>Time3</servlet-name>
  <url-pattern>/Time</url-pattern>
</servlet-mapping>
```

After you've included this mapping in the web.xml file for the webapp, outside any <servlet> tags, visiting the URL http://localhost:8080/ch03/Time will now be mapped to the Time3 Servlet:

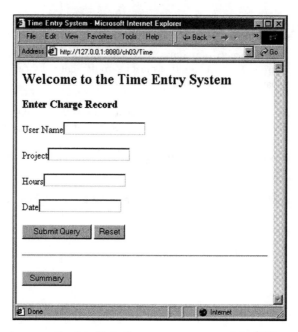

We can also map extensions to a Servlet. This allows us to use part of the URL as information to the Servlet. For example, consider the following mapping:

```
<servlet-mapping>
  <servlet-name>Time3</servlet-name>
  <url-pattern>*.do</url-pattern>
</servlet-mapping>
```

We can now execute our Time3 Servlet with any URL that ends with .do. The following example illustrates this:

We can redesign Time3 to make use of the information just prior to the .do. For example, we could use this information (in the above example – something) as a substitute for the EVENT parameter.

Summary

This chapter presented us with a solid foundation of Servlets, including:

- How to obtain, install, and configure Tomcat, the reference implementation for Servlets and JSP (as well as a web server). Because Tomcat is a Java program, the JAVA_HOME environment variable must be set. Tomcat's examples are good for demonstrating Servlet concepts and capabilities, and are not necessarily implemented using the most appropriate style.

- How the components of the HTTP protocol map to Servlet components and APIs including javax.servlet.* and javax.servlet.http.*. We also covered how a request URL, once passed to the Servlet Engine from the web server, gets mapped to an individual Servlet. We also discussed how the Servlet Engine initializes the Servlet only once, and spawns a separate thread for each incoming HTTP request that is passed to the Servlet.

- How a Servlet obtains access to the parameters from the request, and generates the response by using a java.io.PrintWriter object and executing println() calls. We also saw a technique for preventing the introduction of badly formed HTML when dealing with dynamic data (such as parameters from the request or other Servlet variables).

- How a web application, or webapp, is generated and the mandatory WEB-INF and WEB-INF/classes directories. We introduced the Web ARchive file (a war file) – built using the standard jar command. We also discussed the use and format of the optional web.xml deployment descriptor file for defining configuration information in a vendor neutral way. This file also allows us to set initialization parameters for individual Servlets, or the entire webapp. It also enables us to force a Servlet to be loaded when the Servlet engine initializes, instead of waiting until the first request for the Servlet.

- How to compile and deploy your own Servlets. For Tomcat, the servlet.jar file is required for compiling your own Servlets (as it contains the javax.servlet.* and javax.servlet.http.* packages). Each vendor will supply their own implementation of these packages.

- The various techniques a Servlet engine may employ to keep track of client sessions. We saw some problems with URL rewriting – the lowest common denominator. If you do not mandate that your clients enable cookies, URL rewriting may be your only option for tracking sessions. If you must use it, ensure that all URLs get mapped to your Servlet engine (do not have any URLs within your application that get mapped to normal files that are serviced by the web server). If you do not, you may end up with more sessions than you need because the Servlet engine will lose track of existing sessions and create new ones for the same client.

- How to save information on the client via Cookies.

- How to set and get attributes of the request, session, and context objects. Any valid Java object can be set as an attribute. ServletConfig objects provide Servlet specific information. ServletContext objects provide webapp specific information and information on the Servlet engine.

- How to include or forward control to another URL with the RequestDispatcher object.

Generating HTML from within a Servlet is cumbersome and produces a rigid design where business logic is intertwined with presentation logic, and the proper generation of an HTML page is difficult. The next three chapters will show different approaches and start to evolve a strategy of using the best that each implementation technology (Servlets and JSP) has to offer.

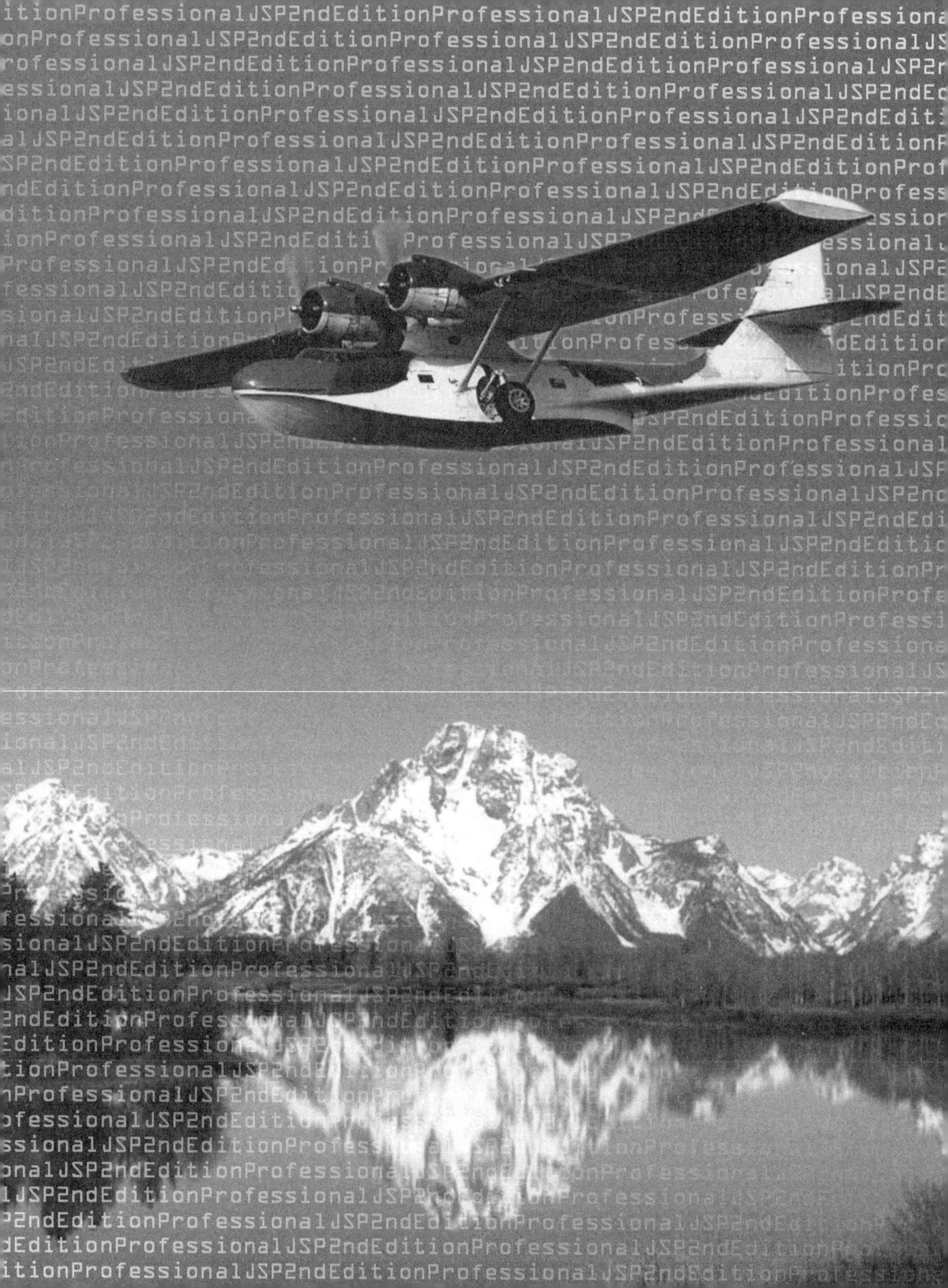
ProfessionalJSP2ndEdition

4

Basic JSP

Well, our harmless little `TimeServlet` is already starting to grow and show some danger signs. The Servlet is being asked to do the following:

- ❑ Determine what type of request has been received
- ❑ Read and validate data in the request
- ❑ Take action on the data, based on the type of request
- ❑ Generate a response based on the data by hard-coding HTML statements into `println()` calls

Adding these together you can see that without a solid infrastructure around it, performing these tasks within Servlets can get unmanageable very quickly. This chapter takes us in the opposite direction – to the use of JSP.

With JSP, we can overcome some of the problems with Servlets, although we end up generating some other problems in the process. As we said at the beginning of the last chapter, for complex applications, often the most effective architecture is a combination of JSPs and Servlets. In a combined architecture, page designers are free to focus on presentation and Java developers can concentrate on control and business logic.

So let's add stand-alone JSP to our toolbox next. This chapter will:

- ❑ Look at what JSPs are and detail the behind the scenes operations of how JSPs work
- ❑ Define the JSP syntax
- ❑ Explore the JSP examples that are provided with Tomcat
- ❑ Redesign the TimeServlet from the previous chapter using JSPs

The Moving Parts

Let's revisit the Moving Parts picture introduced in the previous chapter, but this time focus on the JSP component. Remember, the major parts are:

- ❑ Client – typically a web browser
- ❑ Web Server – handles the HTTP protocol to / from the client
- ❑ Servlet Engine – supports the execution of Servlets
- ❑ JSP Engine – supports the translation and compilation of JSP files into Servlets

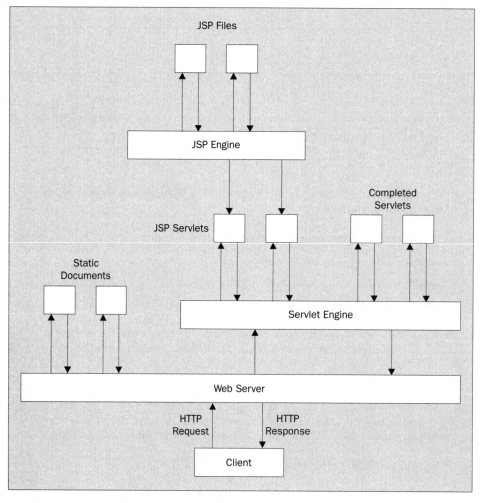

Let's take the case of a request that maps to a JSP file. As with Servlets, the web server must have a mapping definition that tells it what files to pass to the JSP Engine. Typically a default map will translate all URLs ending with *.jsp to the JSP Engine.

The web server passes the request to the JSP Engine. The JSP Engine performs the following processing for each request it receives:

- ❏ Locates the JSP file

- ❏ If the file is newer than the corresponding Servlet (or if the corresponding Servlet doesn't exist – in other words, it hasn't been translated yet), the Engine translates the JSP file into a Servlet

- ❏ Compiles the Servlet and registers it with the Servlet Engine

- ❏ Transfers control to the newly registered Servlet and passes it the request (in other words, forwards the request via the `RequestDispatcher()` method we saw in the previous chapter)

The following figure illustrates the sequencing between the components for a scenario where the user requests a `HelloWorld.jsp` URL for the first time:

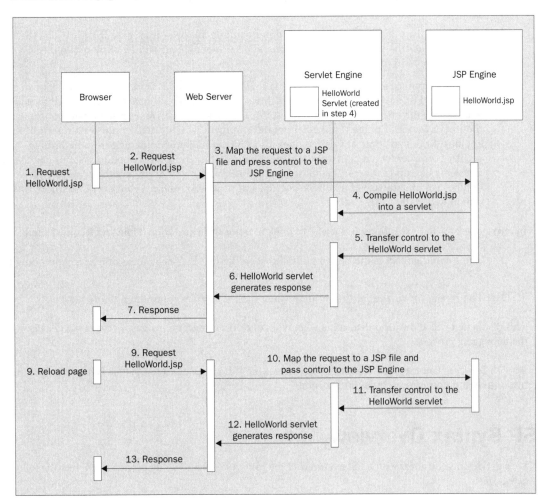

When the user requests a JSP file (step 1), the browser sends a request to the web server (step 2) which is then mapped to the JSP engine (step 3). The JSP Engine looks to see if this JSP file has been translated and compiled into a Servlet. If it hasn't, or if the JSP file is newer than the Servlet (specifically the class file that represents the Servlet), then the Engine translates and compiles the JSP file, creating a Servlet (step 4), and passes the request to it (step 5). The Servlet then generates the response (step 6), which is returned to the browser via the web server (step 7).

109

The JSP spec calls this newly created Servlet the **JSP Page Implementation Class**. We will call it the **JSP Servlet** as a shorthand notation.

The second time the user requests the same `HelloWorld.jsp` URL (steps 8 through 10 – including the browser request and the web server mapping the request to the JSP Engine), the JSP Engine determines that the JSP Servlet is up to date with respect to the `HelloWorld.jsp` file (the class file of the JSP Servlet is newer than the JSP file) and immediately passes control to the JSP Servlet (step 11).

There are some implications of this process:

❑ The first execution of a JSP file may result in a slight delay while the JSP is being translated and compiled into a Servlet.

❑ A JSP compile utility would be useful to pre-compile all (or at least key) JSP files. The JSP spec mandates the support of a pre-compilation protocol. This will be explored in the advanced section of this chapter.

❑ The development and debugging cycle is slightly simplified (at least for this point – it can be complicated on several other points which we will see later) because changes to JSP files are available to the client at the next request (for instance, via a browser reload) without restarting the JSP or Servlet Engine (unlike Servlet development which usually requires a restart of the engine). Note that some Servlet engines also support dynamic reloading in some fashion, usually controlled via a configuration file. Enabling this flag on production systems can lead to problems like un-recovered database connections, which can drain an otherwise relatively lightly-loaded database of available cursors and processes, and prevent access. Explore this option with care.

In terms of errors and exceptions, it is useful to think in terms of **Translation Time** and **Request Time**:

❑ The *translation time* is the portion of time when the JSP Engine is translating and compiling the JSP file.

❑ The *request time* is the portion of time when the JSP Servlet is handling the request.

This distinction will allow us to determine what types of errors or exceptions may occur and will assist with the debugging process.

As with Servlets, Tomcat is the reference platform for the JSP 1.2 specification, which can be obtained from http://java.sun.com/products/jsp/index.html.

JSP Syntax Overview

Let's get down to business with a full overview of the JSP syntax. This can be broken down into the following categories:

❑ **Scripting elements** – dynamic elements that allow access to the native Servlet resources

❑ **Directives** – directives for guiding the translation process

❑ **Action Elements** – dynamic elements that allow a more abstract interface to objects and functionality

A note on URLs: unless explicitly mentioned otherwise, URL references within JSP tags are either relative to the invoking page (if the URL doesn't start with a "/"), or relative to the document root of the webapp (if the URL starts with a "/"). Also note that the WEB-INF directory introduced in the previous chapter (the home of servlet class files) is inaccessible except via the servlet mechanism (that is, by referencing a servlet class file that resides in WEB-INF).

Before we go on, let's get some terminology defined:

❏ Scripting elements and directives follow the format `<% stuff %>`.

❏ Action elements may be of the format `<jsp:tag stuff/>` or as follows:

```
<jsp:tag stuff>
the body of the tag
</jsp:tag>
```

We refer to the `<jsp:tag>` portion as the **start** of the tag (or start tag), the `</jsp:tag>` portion as the end of the tag (or end tag), and the middle as the **body** of the tag. Inside the start of the tag, zero or more attributes may be defined as name-value pairs.

Here is an example with three attributes (named `start`, `end`, and `variable`), and a body.

```
<ul>
<myLib:loop start=0 end=5 variable=i>
    <li> count = <%= i %>
</myLib:loop>
</ul>
```

In this example, `<myLib:loop ...>` is the start tag, `</myLib:loop>` is the end tag, and the `<li> count = <% i %>` portion is the body.

❏ Scripting elements and directives can have attributes but no body:

```
<%@ page import="java.util.Date" %>
```

Anatomy of a JSP File

A JSP file can contain any number of the following items:

❏ **Template Data** – static portions of HTML and text

❏ **JSP Directives** – translation and compilation commands

❏ **Dynamic Data** – dynamic JSP tags (scripting elements and action elements)

Below, we have highlighted the directives (`<%@ page ...>`) and dynamic data (`<%= new Date() %>`) in myFirstJsp.jsp (available from the ch04 webapp in ch04/jsp/myFirstJsp.jsp). The rest of the file is static HTML, or template data:

```
<%@ page import="java.util.Date" %>

<html>
```

```
<body>
<h2>This is my first JSP file.

<p>Today is
<%= new Date() %>
</h2>

</body>
</html>
```

JSP tags may be intermixed within HTML tags, or vice versa. In the simple taglib example JSP file that comes with Tomcat (CATALINA_HOME/webapps/examples/jsp/simpletag/foo.jsp), the <eg:foo> tag is embedded in the body of the <ul> tag. Likewise, the <%= member %> expression tag is contained in the body of the <li> tag. The relevant section of the file is shown below with its indentation exaggerated to illustrate the nesting:

```
<ul>
    <eg:foo att1="98.5" att2="92.3" att3="107.7">
        <li>
            <%= member %>
        </li>
    </eg:foo>
</ul>
```

Running JSP Examples on Tomcat

In order to run the examples we are about to show, download the ch04.war file from http://www.wrox.com. Place it in the CATALINA_HOME/webapps directory and restart Tomcat.

Directives

Directives can be thought of as controlling the translation and compilation phase. They do not directly produce any output. Directives have the following general syntax:

```
<%@ directive {attribute="value"}* %>
```

In other words, a directive can have zero or more attributes.

Directives (except the include directive) should be placed at the top of the JSP page.

The page Directive

The page directive has the following syntax:

```
<%@ page page_directive_attribute_list %>
```

The page_directive_attribute_list is typically in the format of attributeName="attributeValue", and may be one or more of the following:

Attribute Name	Possible Values	Comments
language	"scriptingLanguage"	Obviously the default for scriptingLanguage is Java and currently it is the only defined and required value. However, vendors may implement others (like JavaScript).
extends	"className"	Directs the translation process to *extend* the generated servlet from className. This technique is not to be used lightly as it prevents the JSP engine from doing some things on your behalf. Better techniques involve the use of tag libraries, and these will be explored in later chapters.
import	"importList"	Imports the comma-separated list of packages and/or classes/interfaces into the generated servlet. Note that java.lang.*, javax.servlet.*, javax.servlet.jsp.*, and javax.servlet.http.* are implicitly imported. Note that this is the only directive that may appear more than once in a given JSP file.
session	"true|false"	If set to true, the generated servlet will create an implicit object named session (for each unique user) and set it to the new or current session (identical to HttpServletRequest.getSession(true) method). If set to false, the session object will not be used. The default is true.
buffer	"none|size*kb*"	Specifies the size of the out buffer. If set to none, no buffering is performed (in other words, all output is directly written through to the response). Note that the *kb* should be specified (although Tomcat doesn't currently require it). The default is not less than 8kb.
autoFlush	"true|false"	If set to true, the out buffer will be automatically flushed when full. If set to false, an exception will be raised when the buffer is full. A translation time error should be generated if autoFlush is false and buffer is none. The default for autoFlush is true.
isThreadSafe	"true|false"	If set to true, the JSP engine will spawn a thread for each new request to the page (as with a normal servlet request). If set to false, the JSP engine will send requests synchronously (that is, one at a time). The default is true.

Table continued on following page

Attribute Name	Possible Values	Comments
info	"info_text"	If this attribute is provided, the servlet will override the getServletInfo() method and return info_text.
errorPage	"error_url"	If defined, any un-handled exceptions generated in this page will be passed (in other words, forwarded) to error_url. The error_url script **must** be another JSP. Each JSP engine may define a default.
isErrorPage	"true|false"	If set to true, the object exception is defined and set to the exception (of class Throwable) that was thrown but not caught by the previous page (in other words, that is what invoked this page). If set to false, exception is not defined. The default is false.
contentType	"contentInfo"	Defines the type and charset for use with the setContentType() method. The default value for type is text/html. The default value for charset is ISO-8859-1.
pageEncoding	"pageEncodingInfo"	Defines the character encoding for the page. The default is the value used in the charset attribute of contentType, if set. If not set, ISO-8859-1 is used.

The taglib Directive

The taglib directive will be explored in detail in Chapters 8-11. Here we will introduce a formal definition of this directive; later in the chapter we will see this directive in use.

A **Tag Library** (or taglib) contains custom tags that are developed to give JSP page designers new features to use within a JSP. Each tag library requires a **Tag Library Descriptor** file (or TLD file) to describe its resources to potential users, and may be distributed in a JAR file.

The taglib directive effectively performs three functions:

❑ Imports the taglib into the page

❑ Associates a URI with the taglib to uniquely identify it

❑ Maps that URI to a prefix for use within the page

The syntax is as follows:

```
<%@ taglib uri="taglibURI" prefix="prefix" %>
```

The uri is used to locate a description of the taglib (the TLD file) through one of the following mechanisms:

❑ **Via the** `web.xml` **file**

If the `web.xml` file contains a map of the URI to a TLD file. This takes the form of the following:

```
<taglib>
  <taglib-uri>
    taglibURI
  </taglib-uri>
  <taglib-location>
    /WEB-INF/jsp/my_taglib.tld
  </taglib-location>
</taglib>
```

❑ **Via an implicit map from a packaged taglib**

A taglib may package its TLD file into the JAR file it is distributed in. In this case, the JSP engine automatically builds a map like in the previous step.

The `prefix` is only used within the defining page and allows reference to tags from the library in the following format:

```
<prefix:tag>
```

The include Directive

The `include` directive allows the insertion of another file into the defining page. This insertion happens at translation time. The syntax is:

```
<%@ include file="URL" %>
```

Let's look at an example. Here's the file `jsp/first.jsp`:

```
<html>
<body>

<h2>This is the beginning of first.jsp</h2>

<%@ include file="second.jsp" %>

<%@ include file="third.html" %>

<h2>This is the end of first.jsp</h2>
</body>
</html>
```

This script includes two files. Below is `second.jsp`:

```
<center>
<h3>This is from second.jsp.
The date is
<%= new java.util.Date() %>
</h3>
</center>
```

Here's `third.html`:

```
<h3>This is from third.html</h3>
```

Executing http://localhost:8080/ch04/jsp/first.jsp gives us the following display:

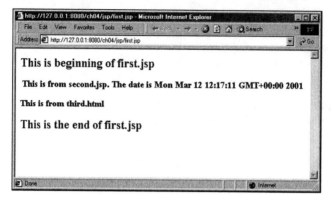

Now edit `second.jsp` and change it to the following (add the `<p>` tag):

```
<center>
<h3>This is from second.jsp.
<p>
The date is
<%= new java.util.Date() %>
</h3>
</center>
```

Reload the browser. Notice now the display did not reflect the changes to `second.jsp`. This is because `second.jsp` was included into `first.jsp` at translation time. Since `first.jsp` has not changed, the JSP engine considers its Servlet up to date.

If you want the changes to be reflected, you will have to change the modification date of `first.jsp` (with Unix/Linux, you can execute the `touch` command, on Windows you can re-save it without making changes to the file).

If we change the modification date of `first.jsp` and reload the browser, now the display reflects our changes (namely the paragraph tag forcing **The date is**... onto a new line):

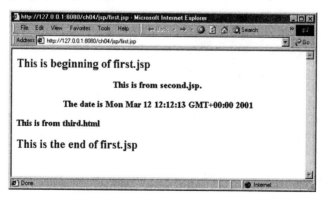

> When developing and debugging, if a simple reload does not give you the effect you were expecting, double-check your use of the `include` tag.

If you need request-time inclusion of a file, consider using the `<jsp:include>` tag (covered later in this chapter) instead.

Scripting Elements

Scripting elements can be broken down into the following categories:

- **Comments** – JSP comments
- **Declarations** – declarations of Java variables and methods
- **Expressions** – short hand notation for evaluating an object and returning its string equivalent value
- **Scriptlets** – sections of Java code within a JSP

We will begin by examining each element type in more detail, and then we will look at an example that makes use of them.

Comments

JSP comments are only intended to assist with understanding the JSP file itself, so they get stripped out before the response page is sent. Contrast this with HTML comments, which are available in the response (in other words, if you view the page source in the browser, you will see the HTML comments but not the JSP comments).

The syntax for a JSP comment is as follows:

```
<%-- jsp comment --%>
```

The syntax for an HTML comment is this:

```
<!-- html comment -->
```

Note that you can also include JSP expressions in HTML comments. The following example:

```
<!-- html comment <%= new java.util.Date() %> -->
```

would produce this comment in the final output to the browser:

```
<!-- html comment Sun Feb 18 00:28:09 EST 2001 -->
```

Declarations

Declarations provide a mechanism to define Java variables and methods. The declarations are available for reference by subsequent scriptlets, expressions, or other declarations.

The general syntax is:

```
<%! JavaDeclaration %>
```

The `JavaDeclaration` must be one or more valid Java declarative statements.

Note that declarations end up in the generated Servlet's class body, not within the body of the request handler method. Since multiple users may simultaneously issue requests, any variables in the class body must be thread-safe.

> **If you define variables via declarations, ensure that their use is thread-safe. (Ensure their access from the request handler is either limited to read-only, or synchronized.)**

Expressions

As mentioned earlier, expressions are an evaluation of some Java statement (without the ";"). The result must be able to be cast to a `String`, and is included in the Servlet's output.

Expressions may be used to set attributes of the following action tags: `<jsp:setProperty>`, `<jsp:include>`, `<jsp:forward>`, and `<jsp:param>` tags.

The general syntax is:

```
<%= validJavaExpression %>
```

Scriptlets

Scriptlets allow the introduction of any valid Java code. The syntax is:

```
<% java statements %>
```

The code is inserted into Servlet's `_jspService()` method, which handles the request.

Scripting Element Examples

Let's tie the definitions of this section together with an example and then look at the underlying Servlet code to reinforce our understanding.

The following example is available in the `ch04` webapp and is in the `/jsp/scriptingTest.jsp` file:

```
<%@ page import="java.util.Calendar" %>

<html>
<body>
<h2>This is a scripting test</h2>

<%! Calendar c = Calendar.getInstance(); %>

<%-- JSP comment --%>
<!-- HTML comment -->
```

```
<%

if ((c.DAY_OF_WEEK == Calendar.SATURDAY) ||
    (c.DAY_OF_WEEK == Calendar.SUNDAY))
{
  out.println("Its the weekend, I don't know what time it is");
} else {
  out.println("today is");
%>
  <%= c.getTime() %>

<%
  }
%>

</body>
</html>
```

In this example, we have used a declaration to define the object c (of type `Calendar`). Then in a scriptlet we test to see if c corresponds to SATURDAY or SUNDAY. If it is, we display some output. If it is not, we display the value of `c.getTime()` using an expression:

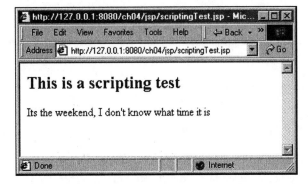

> Note that the declaration of the object will result in an instance variable. Ensure that their use in subsequent scriptlets is thread-safe. In this case it is only read, so it is safe. If we invoked any mutator methods on the variable (we changed its state), we should have synchronized the variable.

Action Elements

Action elements are, as the name implies, request-time oriented. Actions are broken down into the following categories:

- **Control Tags** – tags for flow and plugin control including `<jsp:include>`, `<jsp:forward>`, `<jsp:param>`, and `<jsp:plugin>`
- **Bean Tags** – tags specifically for use with JavaBeans
- **Custom Tags** – tags that allow the definition and use of custom JSP tags

As in the previous section, we will begin by defining these tags in more depth, and then we will look at an example.

Control Tags

What we are calling the Control Tags are a set of tags that allow a JSP to pass control (and parameters) to another JSP file, or control the operation of the browser Java Plug-in.

Each tag is defined below.

The `<jsp:param>` Action Tag

This tag performs just what the name implies – defines a parameter to be passed to an included or forwarded page, or a page that uses the `<jsp:plug-in>` tag.

The syntax is:

```
<jsp:param name="name" value="value"/>
```

Note that `value` may be populated with an expression, as in:

```
<jsp:param name="today" value="<%= new java.util.Date() %>" />
```

The mechanism used to pass the parameters to the included and forwarded page is to add it to the `request` object as an attribute. However, the parameters are only valid to the included or forwarded page, not to the defining page.

The receiving page (the page that is included or forwarded) obtains the parameters via the `request.getParameter("name")` method.

We will illustrate this in an example in a moment.

The `<jsp:include>` Action Tag

We have already seen this tag in use earlier in the chapter. In this section we will look at it in more detail, and contrast it with the `<%@ include %>` directive we discussed earlier.

> **Note that the included page cannot set any headers in the response. Any operations that involve headers such as `setCookie()` must be invoked by the "including" page.**

The syntax for using the tag is:

```
<jsp:include page="URL" {flush="true|false"} />
```

The default for `flush` is `false`. The `<jsp:param>` tag can also be used here to pass parameters to an included file:

```
<jsp:include page="URL" {flush="true|false"}>
    { <jsp:param ... > }*
</jsp:include>
```

You should note that for JSP 1.1, true was the only valid value. This prevented the use of the `<jsp:include>` tag within the body of a custom tag (custom tags can not flush the buffer). JSP 1.2 eliminates this restriction.

Another point to consider is that, unlike the `<%@ include %>` directive, which takes action at translation time, the `<jsp:include>` tag takes action at request time. Therefore, if you change the included file, this update will be noted at the next request.

We will look at an example of using this tag in a moment.

> **It is a good idea to always supply the flush attribute for compatibility with JSP engines that support version 1.1 of the JSP spec.**

The `<jsp:forward>` Action Tag

The forward tag is similar to the include tag, except control is given over to the target page and then never returned to the original page for this request.

The syntax for using `<jsp:forward>` is:

```
<jsp:forward page="URL" />
```

As with `<jsp:include>`, we can use `<jsp:param>` to pass parameters:

```
<jsp:forward page="URL" >
   { <jsp:param ... > }*
</jsp:forward>
```

> **If the "forwarding" page was buffered, the buffer is cleared prior to forwarding. If the page was unbuffered and anything was written to it, the forward operation will generate an IllegalStateException. In other words, the page that control is being forwarded to is expected to provide all of the output to the response.**

The `<jsp:plugin>` Action Tag

The Java Plug-in is a software program, available from http://java.sun.com/products/plug-in, that contains a JVM and bolts onto a web browser. The plug-in registers with the browser to receive the downloaded applets or beans. The browser hands the classes over to the plug-in, which then executes them.

A good analogy is the Real Audio Player. Once installed, it is registered with the browser to handle certain types of files (ithat is, audio files). When the browser is sent a file type that the player is registered for, it pipes the file to the player and the player executes the file (that is, plays the audio file).

In the case of the Java Plug-in, it plays Java files (applets or beans). Applets are Java programs that can execute and display user interfaces in environments such as the plug-in. Beans are reusable Java components (we'll cover Beans in the next chapter).

The `<jsp:plug-in>` tag allows the JSP page to direct the plug-in in the client browser. The plug-in allows itself to be told to load and execute applets or beans. The syntax for using the `<jsp:plug-in>` tag is as follows:

```
<jsp: plugin type="bean|applet"
   code="class filename, relative to codebase"
   codebase="the URI for the root directory of the class filename"
   align="top|middle|bottom|left|right"
   archive="jar file list to download"
   height="height of frame in pixels"
   hspace="# of pixels for a horizontal border"
   jreversion="minimum JRE version required"
   name="name of the object"
   vspace="# of pixels for a vertical border"
   width="width of frame in pixels"
   nspluginurl="URL to load plugin for Netscape"
   iepluginurl="URL to load plugin for IE"
   <jsp:params>
      {<jsp:param name="name" value="value" />}*
   </jsp:params>
   <jsp:fallback>Text message </jsp:fallback>
</jsp:plugin>
```

Note that the `type`, `code`, and `codebase` are required attributes. We will see this tag in action when we explore the examples that are included with Tomcat.

Running Tomcat's JSP Examples

Tomcat provides 13 JSP examples that cover most of the major features of JSP. We will look at the basics of running the examples, followed by an in depth look at a few examples and what each is trying to show.

Getting Started

From the main Tomcat menu (at http://localhost:8080/), select the JSP Examples link. Your display should look like this:

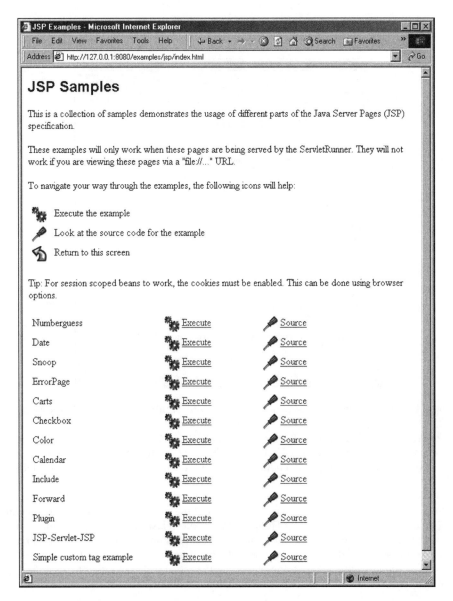

Notice the comment on the page about not viewing the pages via a "file://..." URL. This is a common mistake people make when first developing JSP files. When using a "file://..." URL (or using the File I Open menu option on the browser), the browser treats the file as a text file because there is no web server (or Servlet engine) to tell it what content type to use (via the setContentType() method).

To see the output of a JSP file, we must execute its corresponding Servlet. Viewing a JSP file through the "file://..." technique will end up reading the file directly (instead of requesting it from the web server – which would trigger the above processes). The end result is the browser will treat the entire file as a pure HTML file, skipping over the JSP specific parts.

Let's start out with the **Snoop** example. Select the Execute link next to Snoop. You should see the following display:

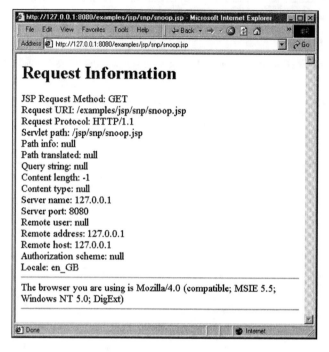

The Snoop JSP returned a slew of information on the request, similar to the Snoop Servlet example.

If your browser does not display this, chances are your JAVA_HOME environment variable is not set properly (on the machine running Tomcat). Once Tomcat translates the JSP file into a Servlet, it needs JAVA_HOME to execute the Java compiler to compile the new Servlet. Refer to Appendix A for additional debugging help.

Now let's look at the source code for this example. To display the source code, click the back icon of your browser to return to the JSP examples page, and then select the Source link for the Snoop example. Your browser should display Source Code for Request Parameters Example, an icon for an arrow going back to the examples page, and a pair of cogs indicating the example should be run. If you click on the text, you should now see the source code as shown below (note that Internet Explorer has display issues with this part of the Tomcat examples, inasmuch as it doesn't display the actual code but rather treats it like a file it should display and presents the HTML parts only with no dynamic content):

```
<html>
<!--
   Copyright (c) 1999 The Apache Software Foundation.  All rights
   reserved.
-->

<body bgcolor="white">
<h1> Request Information </h1>
<font size="4">
JSP Request Method: <%= request.getMethod() %>
<br>
```

```
Request URI: <%= request.getRequestURI() %>
<br>
Request Protocol: <%= request.getProtocol() %>
<br>
Servlet path: <%= request.getServletPath() %>
<br>
Path info: <%= request.getPathInfo() %>
<br>
Path translated: <%= request.getPathTranslated() %>
<br>
Query string: <%= request.getQueryString() %>
<br>
Content length: <%= request.getContentLength() %>
<br>
Content type: <%= request.getContentType() %>
<br>
Server name: <%= request.getServerName() %>
<br>
Server port: <%= request.getServerPort() %>
<br>
Remote user: <%= request.getRemoteUser() %>
<br>
Remote address: <%= request.getRemoteAddr() %>
<br>
Remote host: <%= request.getRemoteHost() %>
<br>
Authorization scheme: <%= request.getAuthType() %>
<hr>
The browser you are using is <%= request.getHeader("User-Agent") %>
<hr>
</font>
</body>
</html>
```

Notice how the source code looks just like any other HTML file, with the exception of the <%= and %> tags. These are expression tags, which we defined earlier. The expressions get executed dynamically, and the results are inserted into the response, in between the static HTML parts.

For some reason, the <%= request.getLocale() %> line is omitted from the provided source listing at CATALINA_HOME/webapps/examples/jsp/snp/snoop.txt.

Specifically, the JSP Engine will parse the JSP file and expand the JSP tags into fully functional Java code in the resultant Servlet. The static HTML portions will get translated in such a way as to fully preserve their representation in the resultant Servlet. Typically this is accomplished by translating each static HTML portion into a sequence of out.write() calls.

Let's now look at the JSP tags more closely. They are all of the form:

```
<%= request.getSomething() %>
```

The method calls were all introduced in the previous chapter on Servlets. Notice the absence of the trailing semicolon with the expression tags. It is a shorthand notation to evaluate an expression, convert the results to a String, and insert it directly into the response.

The contents of the expression are coerced into a `String`. That is, the JSP and Servlet Engines will try to manipulate the output of the expression into a legitimate `String` value, including attempting to use the `toString()` method. Failure to obtain a valid `String` value will result in an error or exception, which will be returned in the response.

The static HTML portions of the file are called **Template Data**, while the JSP tags are called **Dynamic Data**.

At a first glance, JSP gives us the power to design an HTML page and insert dynamic behavior via the JSP tags. With the powerful HTML development tools on the market, this becomes a compelling strategy, albeit applied with some degree of caution (we will find out more about this later).

Under the Hood

We have already seen how Tomcat works as a Web Server and as a Servlet Engine. This section will add the mechanics of Tomcat's JSP Engine to complete the picture.

In addition, we will explore the source code of all the supplied examples and start to see some of the capability of JSP.

Tomcat as a JSP Engine

In this section we turn our attention to the mechanics of Tomcat as a JSP Engine. We will also look at the files that the JSP Engine creates and see how they can assist in the debugging process.

URL to JSP File Mapping

Go back to the JSP Examples page. Notice the URL is http://localhost:8080/examples/jsp/index.html. If we look behind the scenes at the file system, we find the `index.html` file in `CATALINA_HOME/webapps/examples/jsp/index.html`. Unlike the Servlet directory we saw previously, there is no significance to the `jsp` subdirectory in this path – it is completely arbitrary.

Execute the Snoop JSP example again, and notice the location in the browser. It should indicate the request was to http://localhost:8080/examples/jsp/snp/snoop.jsp. If we look for this file in the file system, we find it in `CATALINA_HOME/webapps/examples/jsp/snp/snoop.jsp`.

Formalizing it into an algorithm for Tomcat, we can illustrate the default mapping of URLs to JSP files in the following diagram:

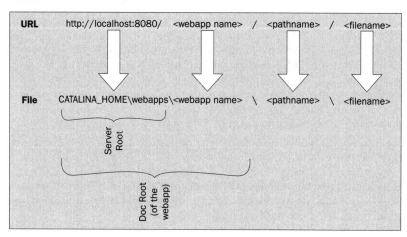

Note that the web server maps the `.jsp` extension to the JSP Engine, while the JSP Engine maps the pathname, filename and extension, to the actual JSP file.

Tomcat's JSP Work Directory

The Servlet spec mandates that all Servlet engines create a temporary working directory on the local file system with a private directory per Servlet context. It must be made available via the `javax.servlet.context.tempdir` context attribute.

This directory becomes useful for JSP developers as a place to view the translated JSP Servlet. Often times when trying to debug a JSP file, it is useful to view the translated JSP Servlet to see where the error may be coming from.

For Tomcat, the directory is kept in `CATALINA_HOME/work`. Tomcat 4.0 breaks this work directory down into a separate subdirectory for each virtual host. Each virtual host directory is broken down into subdirectories for each webapp too. Finally, a `jsp` directory is created below the webapp directory.

Note that a virtual host is an alias for this machine – a technique of supporting the illusion of multiple hosts on the same machine. In our case, we have only been using the hostname localhost, which is only valid for local requests (localhost is the TCP/IP alias for the local machine (127.0.0.1) and is always valid on a TCP/IP machine).

If we look at the `examples/jsp/snp` webapp under the `work` directory, we see a display similar to the following screenshot (note that versions of Tomcat up to and including version 4.0 Beta 1 use a different and more complex naming scheme in the work directory – you may have to browse around to get the hang of how your version of Tomcat is structured):

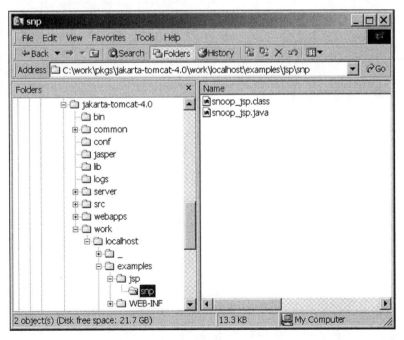

Notice how we have a pair of files (a `.java` file and a `.class` file) corresponding to each translated JSP Servlet (at this point we have only executed the snoop JSP file Servlet). The file naming convention used by Tomcat allows, among other things, the ability to keep multiple versions of each translated Servlet. This can assist tracking down problems during development and debugging.

Now, if we open the Java file with a text editor, we can start to get a feel for the translation process. The JSP Servlet code for the translated Snoop JSP file is included below (slightly edited for clarity).

```java
package org.apache.jsp;

import javax.servlet.*;
import javax.servlet.http.*;
import javax.servlet.jsp.*;
import javax.servlet.jsp.tagext.*;
import org.apache.jasper.runtime.*;


public class snoop_jsp extends HttpJspBase {


  static {
  }
  public snoop_jsp( ) {
  }

  private static boolean _jspx_inited = false;

  public final void _jspx_init() throws org.apache.jasper.JasperException {
  }

  public void _jspService(
      HttpServletRequest request, HttpServletResponse  response)
      throws java.io.IOException, ServletException {

    JspFactory _jspxFactory = null;
    PageContext pageContext = null;
    HttpSession session = null;
    ServletContext application = null;
    ServletConfig config = null;
    JspWriter out = null;
    Object page = this;
    String  _value = null;
    try {

      if (_jspx_inited == false) {
        synchronized (this) {
          if (_jspx_inited == false) {
            _jspx_init();
            _jspx_inited = true;
          }
        }
      }
      _jspxFactory = JspFactory.getDefaultFactory();
      response.setContentType("text/html;charset=8859_1");
      pageContext = _jspxFactory.getPageContext(
          this, request, response, "", true, 8192, true);
      application = pageContext.getServletContext();
      config = pageContext.getServletConfig();
      session = pageContext.getSession();
      out = pageContext.getOut();
```

```
        // HTML // begin

        out.write("<html>\r\n<!--\r\n  Copyright (c) 1999 The Apache Software
Foundation.  All rights \r\n  reserved.\r\n-->\r\n\r\n<body
bgcolor=\"white\">\r\n<h1> Request Information </h1>\r\n<font size=\"4\">\r\nJSP
Request Method: ");

        // end
        // begin

        out.print( request.getMethod() );

        // ...

        out.write("\r\n<hr>\r\n</font>\r\n</body>\r\n</html>\r\n");

    } catch (Throwable t) {
      if (out != null && out.getBufferSize() != 0)
        out.clearBuffer();
          if (pageContext != null) pageContext.handlePageException(t);
    } finally {
      if (_jspxFactory != null)
        _jspxFactory.releasePageContext(pageContext);
    }
  }
}
```

Several points are worth highlighting about this code. First, the class definition extends `HttpJspBase`:

```
public class snoop_jsp extends HttpJspBase {
```

This is a Tomcat-specific class that all JSP Servlets derive from. `HttpJspBase` extends `HttpServlet` (the standard Servlet API's base package from which all HTTP Servlets derive) and implements `HttpJspPage` (the standard JSP API's base interface which all HTTP JSP Pages must implement).

Next notice two of the methods defined:

❑ `snoop_jsp()` – this is the constructor for the class. No action is required in this method:

```
public snoop_jsp( ) {}
```

❑ `_jspService()` – this method is analogous to a Servlet's `service()` method (notice it has the same method signature). This is where all the processing to handle the request takes place:

```
public void _jspService(
   HttpServletRequest request, HttpServletResponse  response)
   throws java.io.IOException, ServletException { ... }
```

Finally, within the `_jspService()` method, note the following:

❑ The use of familiar Servlet methods such as `setContentType()`, `getPageContext()`, `getServletContext()`, `getServletConfig()`, and `getSession()`:

```
        response.setContentType("text/html;charset=8859_1");
        pageContext = _jspxFactory.getPageContext(
            this, request, response, "", true, 8192, true);
        application = pageContext.getServletContext();
        config = pageContext.getServletConfig();
        session = pageContext.getSession();
```

❑   The use of `pageContext.getOut()` to obtain a `JspWriter` object named `out()`:

```
    JspWriter out = null;
// ...
        out = pageContext.getOut();
```

❑   The use of `out.write()` to output data to the response. Notice specifically the `// HTML //` begin and `// end` 'delimiters' in the comments. These give a roadmap from the source JSP file to the translated Servlet, and illustrate how the static HTML portion is just translated into a `String` in the `write()` method. The static HTML from the beginning of the file until the first `<% %>` tag is all represented in the first `write()` call.

In the next line, the effective Java code representing the `<%= request.getMethod()%>` tag is substituted. Tomcat helps even further by indicating the row and column from the source JSP file that it is working on (notice the `from=(0,0);to=(9,20)`, which indicates row 0, column 0 through row 9, column 20; these weren't included in the first listing for reasons of clarity). In the listing below, the comments are not highlighted to help with clarity – note that the lines are wrapped (difficult to show in print – view the files yourself with a text editor for the best representation).

```
// HTML // begin [file="C:\\work\\pkgs\\jakarta-tomcat-
4.0\\bin\\..\\webapps\\examples\\jsp\\snp\\snoop.jsp";from=(0,0);to=(9,20)]
out.write("<html>\r\n<!--\r\n Copyright (c) 1999 The Apache Software Foundation.
All rights \r\n reserved.\r\n-->\r\n\r\n<body bgcolor=\"white\">\r\n<h1> Request
Information </h1>\r\n<font size=\"4\">\r\nJSP Request Method: ");
// end
// begin [file="C:\\work\\pkgs\\jakarta-tomcat-
4.0\\bin\\..\\webapps\\examples\\jsp\\snp\\snoop.jsp";from=(9,23);to=(9,44)]
out.print( request.getMethod() );
// end
```

Objects in a JSP File

Since JSP files get translated into Servlets, and we already know a fair amount about Servlets, let's look at the relationship between items in a JSP file and objects in the Servlet world.

The ease of use of JSP can sometimes produce a conceptual hurdle when using objects. Let's look at an example and try to bridge some of the gaps by looking at the generated Servlet.

We'll start with this example (available in the `ch04/jsp/sessionTest.jsp` file):

```
<%@ page session="true" %>

<html>
```

```
<body>
<h2>This is static template data</h2>

<% if (session.isNew()) {
  out.println("<h3>New Session</h3>");
    }
%>

</body>
</html>
```

Notice the use of the implicit `session` and `out` objects in the scriptlet. The `isNew()` method returns `true` when the `session` object is newly created (in other words, it was created on this request).

If we execute this JSP by going to the location http://localhost:8080/ch04/jsp/sessionTest.jsp, we should see the following display:

Subsequent reloads of this page would not display the "New Session" text since the session was already created in a previous request:

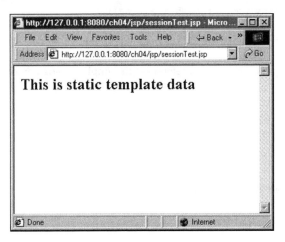

Now let's look at the code Tomcat generated for this Servlet (edited for clarity and found in CATALINA_HOME/work/localhost/ch04/jsp/sessionTest_jsp.java).

First, there is a page directive setting the session attribute to true:

```
<%@ page session="true" %>
```

This directive tells the translator to make the session object available to the page. The resulting Servlet code is as shown below:

```
HttpSession session = null;
//...
session = pageContext.getSession();
```

Note that you can convince yourself of this by changing the session attribute to false (and removing any references to session). Then re-execute the JSP file and view the generated Servlet. There will be no session object created. Next we'll focus on the static template text. There are two sections of it in the JSP file; here's the first:

```
<html>
<body>
<h2>This is static template data</h2>
```

And the last:

```
</body>
</html>
```

We can find these in the generated Servlet. They get translated into the following lines (edited slightly for clarity – added whitespace and line wrapping):

```
out.write("\r\n\r\n<html>\r\n<body>\r\n<h2>This is static template" +
          "data</h2>\r\n\r\n");
//...
out.write("\r\n\r\n</body>\r\n</html>\r\n");
```

So, we can see from this how the static data was mapped directly to the output stream.

Next let's look at the scriptlet. The scriptlet references this implicit session object and then utilizes the implicit out object.

```
<% if (session.isNew()) {
   out.println("<h3>New Session</h3>");
   }
%>
```

Here is the equivalent code in the Servlet:

```
JspWriter out = null;
//...
out = pageContext.getOut();
```

```
//...
if(session.isNew()) {
   out.println("<h3>New Session</h3>");
}
```

The following picture illustrates the translation for this JSP file:

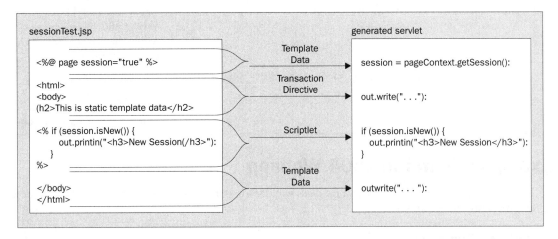

Default Objects

The JSP engine will provide the objects listed below for each JSP. The named objects and all of their associated resources are available to page designers.

Object	Class	Scope	Comments
request	javax.Servlet.http. HttpServletRequest	Request	The request.
response	javax.Servlet.http. HttpServletResponse	Page	The response.
pageContext	javax.sevlet.jsp. PageContext	Page	The environment for this page. This object is used by the Servlet engine to manage such features as error pages and parameters for included / forwarded pages.
session	javax.Servlet.http. HttpSession	Session	Created as long as the `<%@ page session="false" %>` is not used.
application	javax.Servlet. ServletContext	Application	Identical to the Servlet GenericServlet. getServletContext() (see Chapter 3).
out	javax.Servlet.jsp. JspWriter	Page	An object for writing to the output stream.

Table continued on following page

Object	Class	Scope	Comments
config	`javax.Servlet.ServletConfig`	Page	Identical to the Servlet `GenericServlet.getServletConfig()` (see Chapter 3).
page	`java.lang.object`	Page	The instance of this page's Servlet (the 'this' object within the class of the generated Servlet).
exception	`java.lang.Throwable`	Page	Created only if `<%@ page isErrorPage="true" %>` is used (in other words, only available within the error page).

Examples from the ch04 Webapp

Having seen in general terms how Tomcat deals with JSPs and their various elements, let's take a closer look at some individual examples.

Directives Example

Earlier in the chapter we gave formal definitions for the page directives. Now let's take a look at some of them in action. We will introduce a JSP file that highlights some of the directives. Then we will take a look at the generated JSP Servlet to illustrate the behavior. Note that the generated code is Tomcat specific, but it illustrates how Tomcat adheres to the JSP spec, and thus should give us a good conceptual foundation for developing on any JSP engine.

The following JSP file contains some of the directives we just talked about. The file is part of the ch04 webapp and is located in the `/jsp/directives.jsp` file:

```
<%@ page import="java.util.Date" %>
<%@ page session="true" %>
<%@ page buffer="16kb" autoFlush="true" %>
<%@ page errorPage="errorPage.jsp" %>
<%@ page info="this JSP illustrates several JSP directives" %>
<%@ page contentType="text/plain" %>
This JSP illustrates several JSP directives.

Look at the generated servlet to find the impact of these directives.
```

If we execute this JSP (via http://localhost:8080/ch04/jsp/directives.jsp), it should create a Servlet in the work directory. Find that Servlet and examine it with a text editor.

The Servlet created (`CATALINA_HOME/work/localhost/ch04/directives_jsp.java`, although your system might generate a slightly different filename) with Tomcat is included here (edited slightly for clarity):

```java
package org.apache.jsp;
import java.util.Date;
import javax.servlet.*;
import javax.servlet.http.*;
import javax.servlet.jsp.*;
import javax.servlet.jsp.tagext.*;
import org.apache.jasper.runtime.*;

public class directives_jsp extends HttpJspBase {

  public String getServletInfo() {
    return "this JSP illustrates several JSP directives";
  }

  static {     }

  public directives_jsp( ) {
  }

  private static boolean _jspx_inited = false;

  public final void _jspx_init() throws org.apache.jasper.JasperException {
  }

  public void _jspService(
    HttpServletRequest request, HttpServletResponse  response)
    throws java.io.IOException, ServletException {

    JspFactory _jspxFactory = null;
    PageContext pageContext = null;
    HttpSession session = null;
    ServletContext application = null;
    ServletConfig config = null;
    JspWriter out = null;
    Object page = this;
    String  _value = null;

    try {

      if (_jspx_inited == false) {
        synchronized (this) {
          if (_jspx_inited == false) {
            _jspx_init();
            _jspx_inited = true;
          }
        }
      }

      _jspxFactory = JspFactory.getDefaultFactory();
      response.setContentType("text/plain");

      pageContext = _jspxFactory.getPageContext(this, request,
                          response, "errorPage.jsp", true, 16384, true);

      application = pageContext.getServletContext();
      config = pageContext.getServletConfig();
```

```
        session = pageContext.getSession();
        out = pageContext.getOut();

          out.write("\r\n");
          out.write("\r\n");
          out.write("\r\n");
          out.write("\r\n");
          out.write("\r\n");
          out.write("\r\nThis JSP illustrates several JSP directives.\r\n\r\nLook at
the generated servlet to find the impact of these directives.\r\n\r\n");

      } catch (Throwable t) {
        if (out != null && out.getBufferSize() != 0)
          out.clearBuffer();
        if (pageContext != null) pageContext.handlePageException(t);
      } finally {
        if (_jspxFactory != null)
          _jspxFactory.releasePageContext(pageContext);
      }
    }
  }
```

Now we will go through some of the lines in the JSP file and find their corresponding line in the Servlet to illustrate the feature. First, the `import` attribute:

```
<%@ page import="java.util.Date" %>
```

The generated code simply provides the proper Java import statement (and adds the semicolon):

```
import java.util.Date;
```

Next let's look at the `session` attribute:

```
<%@ page session="true" %>
```

The generated Servlet created a session object from the page context. Remember that the default behavior for the `getSession()` method is to generate a new session if one does not exist:

```
HttpSession session = null;
//...
session = pageContext.getSession();
```

Now let's take a look at both the `buffer` and `errorPage` attribute. From the JSP file we have:

```
<%@ page buffer="16kb" autoFlush="true" %>
<%@ page errorPage="errorPage.jsp" %>
```

These attributes get used during the construction of the `pageContext` object. Note the passing of the `errorPage.jsp` for the error page URL, and `16384` for the buffer size, as parameters to the `getPageContext()` method.

```
            pageContext = _jspxFactory.getPageContext(this, request,
                            response, "errorPage.jsp", true, 16384, true);
```

Also notice in the `catch` clause how the `pageContext.handlePageException()` is called (if `pageContext` is not `null`). This is the mechanism that Tomcat is using to forward control to an error page. If we didn't set an error page, Tomcat's default error page would be invoked:

```
//...
    } catch (Throwable t) {
      if (out != null && out.getBufferSize() != 0)
        out.clearBuffer();
      if (pageContext != null) pageContext.handlePageException(t);
```

Next we have the `info` attribute. From the JSP file:

```
<%@ page info="this JSP illustrates several JSP directives" %>
```

The generated Servlet overrides the `getServletInfo()` method and returns the text specified in the `info` attribute.

```
public String getServletInfo() {
   return "this JSP illustrates several JSP directives";
}
```

Finally we have the `contentType` attribute. From the JSP file:

```
<%@ page contentType="text/plain" %>
```

The generated Servlet uses this value in the `setContentType()` method:

```
response.setContentType("text/plain");
```

Experiment with this test file. Change values or remove some of the attributes, and see what that does to the generated Servlet. This will help solidify your understanding of these important directives.

Scriptlet Example

Let's revisit the `scriptingTest.jsp` file introduced earlier:

```
<%@ page import="java.util.Calendar" %>

<html>
<body>
<h2>This is a scripting test</h2>

<%! Calendar c = Calendar.getInstance(); %>

<%-- JSP comment --%>
<!-- HTML comment -->

<%
```

```
if ((c.DAY_OF_WEEK == Calendar.SATURDAY) ||
    (c.DAY_OF_WEEK == Calendar.SUNDAY))
{
  out.println("Its the weekend, I don't know what time it is");
} else {
  out.println("today is");
%>
  <%= c.getTime() %>

<%
  }
%>

</body>
</html>
```

Now lets take a look at the relevant code in the generated Servlet (available at CATALINA_HOME/work/localhost/ch04/jsp/scriptingTest_jsp.java).

First, the declaration ends up as follows in the class body:

```
Calendar c = Calendar.getInstance();
```

Note that the declaration ends up outside the service method. This introduces a potential side effect. If multiple simultaneous threads of the service method need to access this declaration, you may need to synchronize any variables you declare to avoid inconsistent behavior.

Once defined, c can be referenced by the scriptlet. Here is the scriptlet code from the Servlet within the _jspService() method:

```
if ((c.DAY_OF_WEEK == Calendar.SATURDAY) ||
    (c.DAY_OF_WEEK == Calendar.SUNDAY)) {

  out.println("Its the weekend, I don't know what time it is");
} else {
  out.println("today is");
//...
```

Finally, the expression also references c (as part of the else clause):

```
out.print( c.getTime() );
}
```

Also notice the passing of the HTML comment through to the output stream. The JSP comment is not reflected in the generated Servlet.

```
out.write("\r\n<!-- HTML comment -->\r\n\r\n");
```

Tomcat Example JSPs

This section will look at the implementation of some of the Tomcat example JSP files in detail. Some of the examples we skip over will be examined in the next chapter when we discuss JSP and JavaBean interaction. The fact that this eliminates about half of the examples should give you a clear indication of the power and importance of using JavaBeans in conjunction with JSP.

Since we will be looking at source code, get your favorite text editor ready. As we have already seen, the source code for the examples are in CATALINA_HOME/webapps/examples/jsp/.

Plugin JSP Example

The next example illustrates the use of the `<jsp:plugin>` tag for downloading and executing an applet via the **Java Plug-in**. The Java plug-in is a client piece of software that bolts onto the browser. From the browser's perspective, the plug-in works like any other plug-in. Specific types of data are passed from the browser to the registered plug-in. In the case of the Java plug-in, the data type is an applet. The Java plug-in is available as part of the Java JDK.

The `plugin.jsp` file is listed below:

```
<html>
<!--
   Copyright (c) 1999 The Apache Software Foundation. All rights
   reserved.
-->
<title> Plugin example </title>
<body bgcolor="white">
<h3> Current time is : </h3>
```

The next part of the code involves the use of the `<jsp:plugin>` tag. Notice the `codebase` attribute refers to `"/examples/jsp/plugin/applet"`, and the `code` attribute refers to `"Clock2.class"`. We should then expect to find the `Clock2.class` file at `/webapps/examples/jsp/plugin/applet/Clock2.class`. Also notice the use of the `<jsp:fallback>` tag, which allows the browser to display something in case it can't load the plug-in. This is similar to the `ALT` attribute of the HTML `IMG` tag, which displays a text message if the image can't be loaded.

```
<jsp:plugin type="applet" code="Clock2.class"
codebase="/examples/jsp/plugin/applet" jreversion="1.2" width="160" height="150" >
    <jsp:fallback>
        Plugin tag OBJECT or EMBED not supported by browser.
    </jsp:fallback>
</jsp:plugin>
<p>
<h4>
<font color=red>
The above applet is loaded using the Java Plugin from a jsp page using the
plugin tag.
</font>
</h4>
</body>
</html>
```

Executing the Plug-in example results in the browser attempting to load the plug-in. If you have the plug-in installed properly, the following will be displayed:

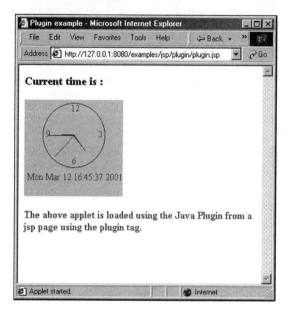

Refer to http://java.sun.com/products/plugin for more details on, and to obtain the plug-in.

The plug-in may be a practical option in an intranet situation where fast networking binds all of your client machines. The plug-in effectively gives all of your browsers a known JDK so your applets can be developed and deployed without concern of browser incompatibilities (assuming you have a technique to maintain the same version of the plug-in on each client machine).

Having applet capabilities provides some compelling capability for interacting with Servlets and JSP. If you can solve the distribution and installation of the plug-in for your organization, you should consider its use.

JSP-Servlet-JSP JSP Example

We introduced the `RequestDispatcher` in the previous chapter on Servlets. This object provides the underlying mechanisms for the `include` and `forward` capabilities we have seen so far demonstrated with JSP. The JSP-Servlet-JSP example demonstrates the use of this capability between Servlets and JSP.

This example demonstrates a JSP file forwarding control to a Servlet, which sets an attribute and forwards control to a JSP file. The last JSP file reads the attribute and displays it.

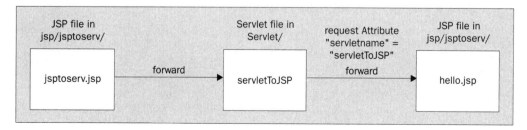

Refer to the /webapps/examples/jsp/jsptoserv directory. Now look at the jsptoserv.jsp file. Its contents are included below:

```
<html>
<!--
  Copyright (c) 1999 The Apache Software Foundation. All rights
  reserved.
-->
<body bgcolor="white">

<!-- Forward to a servlet -->
<jsp:forward page="/servlet/servletToJsp" />

</html>
```

The only line of real interest to us is the <jsp:forward> tag. Notice that the page it refers to is "/servlet/servletToJsp". Remember that Tomcat automatically maps references to the Servlet directory to the /WEB-INF/classes directory and appends .class to the end of the filename, so this forward will be directed to the servletToJsp Servlet.

Let's follow the trail to the servletToJsp.java file (in the classes directory for the examples webapp). This file is reprinted below:

```
import javax.servlet.*;
import javax.servlet.http.*;

public class servletToJsp extends HttpServlet {

    public void doGet (HttpServletRequest request,
        HttpServletResponse response) {

      try {
        // Set the attribute and Forward to hello.jsp
        request.setAttribute ("servletName", "servletToJsp");
```

Note the setting of the request attribute named servletName to the value servletToJsp. Remember from the Servlet chapter that we said the request object follows along with a forward operation? Thus, setting attributes in the request object should make them available to the target of the forward operation:

```
        getServletConfig().getServletContext().getRequestDispatcher(
                  "/jsp/jsptoserv/hello.jsp").forward(request, response);
      } catch (Exception ex) {
        ex.printStackTrace ();
      }
    }
}
```

Finally, notice the complex line to forward the request to the "/jsp/jsptoserv/hello.jsp" file. If you break this line down into its individual steps, you will see the same effect as introduced in the Servlets chapter. The line obtains the Servlet config, which gets the Servlet context. The Servlet context lets us get the request dispatcher for the specified URL. Ultimately, the dispatcher performs the forward operation, passing the request and response parameters.

141

Note that the URL used starts with a "/". This becomes a relative URL from the root of the webapp – in our case from CATALINA_HOME/webapps/examples.

Now let's look at the hello.jsp file:

```
<html>
<!--
   Copyright (c) 1999 The Apache Software Foundation. All rights
   reserved.
-->
<body bgcolor="white">
```

The significant line is a scriptlet that obtains and prints the request attribute named ServletName, which was set by the Servlet to ServletToJsp:

```
<h1>
I have been invoked by
<% out.print (request.getAttribute("servletName").toString()); %>
Servlet.
</h1>

</html>
```

Executing the jsptoserv.jsp file (from the JSP examples page), we see the following display:

This JSP therefore demonstrates the successful passing of a request scoped parameter between a Servlet and a JSP file.

Simple Custom Tag Example JSP

The definition of custom tags is beyond the scope of this chapter (they are introduced in depth in Chapter 8), but we will briefly introduce the use of existing custom tags.

This example demonstrates how to include a tag library into your JSP file, and how to make use of the resources that are in that library. For this example, a tag library is used that defined two custom tags – the foo tag and the log tag. Their syntax is described here:

```
<eg:foo att1="attribute 1" att2="attribute 2" att3="attribute 3" >
  body
</eg:foo>
```

```
<eg:log [toBrowser="true|false"] >
  body
</eg:log>
```

The foo tag takes three attributes and makes each one available to its body in the variable named member (in a loop). The log tag has an optional toBrowser attribute. This tag writes the body to the standard error file. If the toBrowser attribute is true, it also writes the body to the browser (in the response).

We will be exploring the /webapps/examples/jsp/simpletag/foo.jsp file, shown below:

```
<html>
<!--
   Copyright (c) 1999 The Apache Software Foundation. All rights
   reserved.
-->
<body>
<%@ taglib uri="http://java.apache.org/tomcat/examples-taglib"
           prefix="eg" %>

Radio stations that rock:

<ul>
```

The <%@ taglib> tag above brings in a specified library identified by the uri attribute and assigns it the prefix "eg" for use in references within this file. We will explore the linking implied by the uri attribute shortly.

Now let's consider the next highlighted line; it is using the foo tag from the eg library. This tag takes three attributes as shown. Note that the line after this references a previously undefined object named member. What is implied here (and you will learn how to implement this in the upcoming custom tag chapters) is that the body of the foo tag defined an object named member. Since we have not terminated the foo tag yet (with a </eg:foo> tag), you can think of this situation as if we are within the scope of the foo tag and the member object is public.

```
<eg:foo att1="98.5" att2="92.3" att3="107.7">
<li><%= member %></li>
</eg:foo>
</ul>

<eg:log>
Did you see me on the stderr window?
</eg:log>

<eg:log toBrowser="true">
Did you see me on the browser window as well?
</eg:log>

</body>
</html>
```

Now let's follow the trail of the uri in the taglib tag. Our first stop is our old friend the webapp deployment descriptor file web.xml, for the example webapp. In here we find the following relevant lines:

```
...
    <taglib>
        <taglib-uri>
     http://java.apache.org/tomcat/examples-taglib
        </taglib-uri>
        <taglib-location>
            /WEB-INF/jsp/example-taglib.tld
        </taglib-location>
    </taglib>
...
```

Notice how the `<taglib-uri>` tag identifies the uri from the `<%@ taglib%>` usage in the `foo.jsp` SP file:

```
<%@ taglib uri="http://java.apache.org/tomcat/examples-taglib"
           prefix="eg" %>
```

This section in `web.xml` binds the uri from the `<%@ taglib%>` referenced in the JSP file to a specific location in the webapp. In this example, it binds it to `/WEB-INF/jsp/example-taglib.tld`, as seen in the `<taglib-location>` tag.

This reference is to a **Tag Library Descriptor** file, or TLD file for short. For tag libraries, this file is analogous to the `web.xml` file for webapps. In a vendor-neutral way, the TLD file describes the resources available in the tag library.

> Note that the **uri** attribute does not map to a displayable or downloadable entity. Its value is often something that looks like a URL that points to the supplier of the tag library. However, it is not intended to function as a URL (**http://javav.apache.org/tomcat/examples-taglib** does not exist) – it is only intended as a unique identifier of the tag library.

Below is the `example-taglib.tld` file:

```
<?xml version="1.0" encoding="ISO-8859-1" ?>
<!DOCTYPE taglib
        PUBLIC "-//Sun Microsystems, Inc.//DTD JSP Tag Library 1.1//EN"
        "http://java.sun.com/j2ee/dtds/web-jsptaglibrary_1_1.dtd">

<!-- a tag library descriptor -->

<taglib>
  <!-- after this the default space is
       "http://java.sun.com/j2ee/dtds/jsptaglibrary_1_2.dtd"
  -->

  <tlibversion>1.0</tlibversion>
  <jspversion>1.1</jspversion>
  <shortname>simple</shortname>
  <uri></uri>
  <info>
    A simple tag library for the examples
  </info>
```

```
<!-- A simple Tag -->
<!-- foo tag -->
<tag>
  <name>foo</name>
  <tagclass>examples.FooTag</tagclass>
  <teiclass>examples.FooTagExtraInfo</teiclass>
  <bodycontent>JSP</bodycontent>
  <info>
    Perform a server side action; uses 3 mandatory attributes
  </info>

  <attribute>
    <name>att1</name>
    <required>true</required>
  </attribute>
  <attribute>
    <name>att2</name>
    <required>true</required>
  </attribute>
  <attribute>
    <name>att3</name>
    <required>true</required>
  </attribute>
</tag>

<!-- Another simple tag -->
<!-- log tag -->
<tag>
  <name>log</name>
  <tagclass>examples.LogTag</tagclass>
  <bodycontent>TAGDEPENDENT</bodycontent>
  <info>
Perform a server side action; Log the message.
  </info>
  <attribute>
<name>toBrowser</name>
<required>false</required>
  </attribute>
</tag>
```

Notice the two tags defined in the TLD file – foo and log. These tags are referenced in our JSP file above.

Now if we execute the example, we should see a display like this:

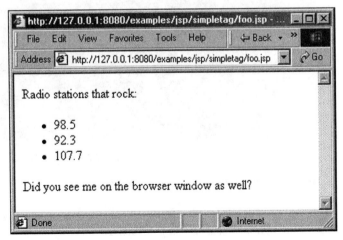

Let's look back at the following lines from the source JSP file (`foo.jsp`):

```
<ul>
<eg:foo att1="98.5" att2="92.3" att3="107.7">
<li><%= member %></li>
</eg:foo>
</ul>
```

We can conclude that the three parameters passed into the `<eg:foo>` tag were each assigned to the `member` object and then evaluated to produce the `<li>` we see on the browser.

This may seem like an overly simple example for three parameters but what if we had a `Hashtable` of values that we wanted to display in a list like this? With custom tags we could literally pass the `Hashtable` to a tag and have the tag print the contents in a list. Now that would dramatically simplify the page.

Moving on to the use of the `<eg:log>` tag, we see two invocations of it – one with no attributes and one with the `toBrowser` attribute set to `true`:

```
<eg:log>
Did you see me on the stderr window?
</eg:log>

<eg:log toBrowser="true">
Did you see me on the browser window as well?
</eg:log>
```

Matching this up with the browser leads us to believe that when the `toBrowser` attribute is to `true`, the `log` tag writes the contents of its body to the browser.

Taking a look at the window where we started Tomcat (which, by the way, is the `stderr` for Tomcat), we can see that the `log` tag always writes the contents of its body to `stderr`.

Hopefully this simple example fires your imagination regarding the power and usefulness of custom tags.

A custom tag has a `.java` file which conducts the processing required from the tags. We won't look at this class here – that's a topic for Chapters 8 to 11.

A Day in the Life of a JSP

Although JSP files ultimately end up as a Servlet before servicing any requests, there are some conceptual hurdles often that must be bridged before we can fully utilize their power, while reaping the benefits of their ease of use.

This section will give us that understanding.

The JSP Life Cycle

From our discussions earlier, we can derive the following states that each JSP file lives through:

❑ **Pre-translation** – before a JSP file has been parsed and translated into a Servlet.

❑ **Translated** – once the JSP file has been successfully translated and compiled as a Servlet. This process can be performed off-line.

❑ **Initialized** – prior to handling a service call, the JSP (or more specifically, the JSP Servlet) must be initialized. Like Servlets, JSPs can be loaded on startup (of the JSP/Servlet engine).

❑ **Servicing** – the point in time when the JSP file is servicing a request.

❑ **Out of service** – when the JSP or Servlet engine takes the JSP out of service, it must be shut down (destroyed) and can no longer service requests.

The first two states – pre-translation and translated – cover the time before the JSP is aware, so to speak. Once in the translated state, a JSP can be called by the JSP/Servlet engine.

In the final three states – initialized, servicing, and out of service –the JSP is a participant in the process and specific methods are defined for them. They are:

❑ `jspInit()` – this method may be overridden in a declaration in the JSP file. This allows you to specify initialization behavior identical to the Servlets `init()` method. If you must open database connections or other initialization-oriented activities, it could be placed here. However, it may be better to utilize a Servlet in conjunction with your JSP files to perform this operation.

❑ `_jspService()` – all items in the JSP page except directives and declarations end up in this method. It may not be overridden or defined in any other way.

❑ `jspDestroy()` – this method may be overridden in a declaration in the JSP file. This allows you to specify shutdown behavior identical to the Servlet's `destroy()` method.

Object Scope

Similar to Servlets, JSPs can have objects in any of the four scopes. The mechanisms to access these objects are similar to those used with Servlets.

Level of Scope	APIs of interest	Comments
Page	Not applicable (local variables in the page)	Available to the handling page only.
Request	`request.setAttribute(key, obj)` `request.getAttribute(key)`	Available to the handling JSP and to any Servlet or JSP that control is forwarded to, or any JSP that is included.
Session	`session.setAttribute(key, obj)` `session.getAttribute(key)`	Available to any Servlet or JSP within the same session.
Application	`application.setAttribute(key, obj)` `application.getAttribute(key)`	Available to any Servlet or JSP within the same webapp.

Writing Your Own JSPs

To write and execute your own JSP files, you simply have to create the file (with a text editor) and put it into a directory under the webapp of your choice (excluding the WEB-INF directory which cannot serve normal content). In this chapter we have used the convention of a /jsp subdirectory to hold the JSP, HTML, and image files.

Control Tags Example

Let's revisit our Time Entry System that we started building in Chapter 3. This simplified system allows the user to enter information (a charge record) for a project in order to charge their hours against it. The information contains the user's name, the project name, the date, and the number of hours to charge.

In Chapter 3 we started with a Servlet design that utilized a Charge class to hold charge records. Problems with that design included too much HTML embedded in the Servlet – difficult to maintain in the same code as business logic. In this chapter we will go in the opposite direction with a complete JSP design.

The files are available in the ch04 webapp, under the /jsp directory. The main JSP – time.jsp – is shown below. This JSP file implements our main control logic and passes control off to 'sub-pages' as necessary:

```
<%
  String event = request.getParameter("EVENT");
  if (event == null) {
    event = "ENTER_RECORD";
  } else if (event.equals ("")) {
    event = "ENTER_RECORD";
  } else if (event.equals ("ADMIN")) {
%>
    <jsp:forward page="admin.jsp"/>
<%
```

```
  }
%>

<jsp:include page="header.jsp" flush="true" >
  <jsp:param name="title" value="Time Entry System" />
  <jsp:param name="heading" value="<%= event %>" />
</jsp:include>

<form action=time.jsp method=POST>

<%
  // main dispatch center
  if (event.equals ("ENTER_RECORD")) {
%>
    <jsp:include page="enterRecord.jsp" flush="true"/>
<%
  } else if (event.equals ("NEW_RECORD")) {
%>
    <jsp:include page="newRecord.jsp" flush="true"/>
<%
  } else if (event.equals ("SUMMARY")) {
%>
    <jsp:include page="summary.jsp" flush="true"/>
<%
  } else {
      // put in error handler
  }
%>

</form>

<hr>
<form action=time.jsp method=POST>
    <input type=hidden name=EVENT value=SUMMARY>
    <input type=submit value=Summary>
</form>

</body>
</html>
```

There are several points to note about this script. First, notice how we replicated some of the Servlet code for managing the control flow using the EVENT parameter:

```
String event = request.getParameter("EVENT");
```

Also notice how we didn't generate any output before forwarding control to the admin.jsp page. Recall the following warning from earlier in the chapter about the <jsp:forward> tag:

If the 'forwarding' page was buffered, the buffer is cleared prior to forwarding. If the page was un-buffered and anything was written to it, the forward operation will generate an IllegalStateException. *In other words, the page that control is being forwarded to is expected to provide all of the output to the response.*

However, when we included the other pages such as enterRecord.jsp, they were included after the header.jsp page was included (in other words, after some data was already output to the response object). This is the typical use of included pages – as a cooperative in the generation of the response.

Finally notice the passing of parameters to the header.jsp file:

```
<jsp:include page="header.jsp" flush="true" >
  <jsp:param name="title" value="Time Entry System" />
  <jsp:param name="heading" value="<%= event %>" />
</jsp:include>
```

Let's take a look at each of the files that are included or forwarded to. First, the header.jsp file; notice how it retrieves the title and heading parameters from the request object:

```
<html>
<head><title>
<%= request.getParameter("title") %>
</title></head>

<body>
<h2>Operation = <%= request.getParameter("heading") %></h2>
```

Here's the enterRecord.jsp file, which displays the input form:

```
<h3>Enter Charge Record</h3>

<p>User Name<input type=text name=name>
<p>Project<input type=text name=project>
<p>Hours<input type=text name=hours>
<p>Date<input type=text name=date>
<input type=hidden name=EVENT value=NEW_RECORD>

<p><input type=submit>
<input type=reset>
```

The newRecord.jsp file, included below, processes form submissions:

```
<%@ page import="com.wrox.projsp.ch03.time.controller.beans.Charge " %>
<%@ page import="java.util.Hashtable" %>

<h3>Your Charge Record has been saved</h3>

<%

  String name = request.getParameter("name");
  String project = request.getParameter("project");
  String hours = request.getParameter("hours");
  String date = request.getParameter("date");
  Charge c = new Charge();
  c.setName(name);
```

```
    c.setProject(project);
    c.setHours(hours);
    c.setDate(date);

    Hashtable h = (Hashtable) session.getAttribute("charges");
    if (h == null) {
      h = new Hashtable();  // first charge
      session.setAttribute ("charges", h);
    }
    h.put (project, c);  // use project as the key
%>


Record Details: <p>
Name = <%= name %>, Project = <%= project %>, Hours = <%= hours %>, Date = <%=date
%>
```

As you will notice, the first line imports the JavaBean we used in the last chapter, `Charge`. In order for the code to work, you will need to have this class accessible to the current webapp. Next we have the `summary.jsp` file, which generates the summary report:

```
<%@ page import="com.wrox.projsp.ch03.time.controller.beans.Charge " %>
<%@ page import="java.util.Enumeration" %>
<%@ page import="java.util.Hashtable" %>

<h3>Summary of your Charge Records</h3>

<%
  Hashtable h = (Hashtable) session.getAttribute("charges");
  if (h != null) {
%>
    <ul>

<%
    Enumeration charges = h.keys();
    while (charges.hasMoreElements()) {
      String proj = (String) charges.nextElement();
      Charge ch = (Charge) h.get(proj);
%>
      <li>
      name = <%= ch.getName() %>
      , project = <%= proj %>
      , hours = <%= ch.getHours() %>
      , date = <%= ch.getDate() %><%
    }
%>
    </ul>
<%
  }
%>
```

time.jsp may also forward control to admin.jsp (below). Notice the difference between the Servlet and the JSP file in the use of the application object for retrieving context information:

```jsp
<%@ page import="java.util.Enumeration" %>

<html>
<head><title>Time Entry System - Admin Page </title></head>

<body>

<h2>Adminstration Page</h2>

<h3>Webapp and Servlet Engine Info</h3>

<ul>
   <li>Server Info: <%= application.getServerInfo() %>
   <li>Major Version: <%= application.getMajorVersion() %>
   <li>Minor Version: <%= application.getMinorVersion() %>
   <li>Webapp Init Parameters:

   <ul>
<%
   Enumeration webappParams = application.getInitParameterNames();
   while (webappParams.hasMoreElements()) {
     String paramName = (String) webappParams.nextElement();
     String paramValue = application.getInitParameter(paramName);
%>
     <li><%= paramName%>=<%=paramValue%>
<%
   }
%>
   </ul>
</ul>

<h3>Servlet Info</h3>

<ul>
   <li>Servlet Name: <%= config.getServletName() %>
   <li>Servlet Init Parameters:

   <ul>
<%
Enumeration servletParams = config.getInitParameterNames();
while (servletParams.hasMoreElements()) {
   String paramName = (String) servletParams.nextElement();
   String paramValue = config.getInitParameter(paramName);
%>
   <li><%= paramName%>=<%=paramValue%>
<%
   }
%>

   </ul>
</ul>
```

Executing http://localhost:8080/ch04/jsp/time.jsp, we get the following display:

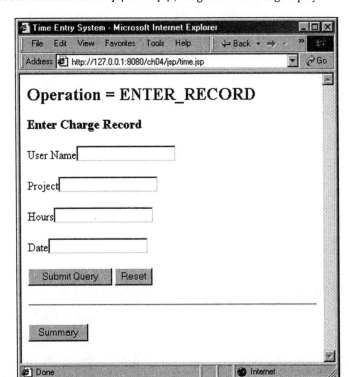

Recall that the time.jsp file sets the event variable to ENTER_RECORD if the EVENT parameter is not set:

```
if (event == null) {
    event = "ENTER_RECORD";
```

The file enterRecord.jsp is then included:

```
<%
  // main dispatch center
  if (event.equals ("ENTER_RECORD")) {
%>
    <jsp:include page="enterRecord.jsp" flush="true"/>
```

enterRecord.jsp sets the EVENT parameter to NEW_RECORD:

```
<input type=hidden name=EVENT value=NEW_RECORD>
```

If we enter some data and press the **Submit Query** button, we will re-invoke `time.jsp` with the EVENT parameter set to NEW_RECORD. The display looks like this:

If we enter another charge record and then press the **Summary** button, we will see something like this display:

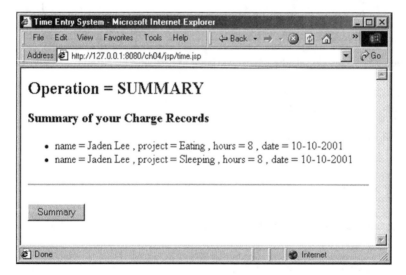

Looking back at our design, you can see some of the JSP files look somewhat maintainable while others look like they are already unmanageable. Breaking up the separate pages like we did could result in a better focus on the look and feel for the pages. However, interweaving scriptlets within HTML often results in a file that is difficult to understand and debug. Indentation can help, but often a better approach is with a Servlet, or the use of bean tags or custom tags.

Bean tags allow the instantiation of JavaBean objects, and the setting and getting of attributes from those objects. These tags will be discussed in detail in the next chapter.

Custom tags are a mechanism that allows the functionality of JSP to be extended. When used in conjunction with the bean tags, custom tags allow the full separation of presentation logic (in a JSP file) from business logic (in the custom tags, beans, and any Servlets). We will explore these architectures as well as the use of custom tags in later chapters.

Advanced JSP Topics

This section explores some of the more advanced JSP topics that are not discussed further in the book. Specifically, we will get a broad overview of the JSP APIs, discuss pre-compilation, and show an example of defining and using an error page.

JSP APIs

The JSP APIs expand on the API's introduced in the previous chapter. The following packages hold all of the standard JSP APIs:

- ❑ `javax.servlet.jsp`
- ❑ `javax.servlet.jsp.tagext`

They build on other items in `javax.servlet` and `javax.servlet.http` packages. Note that the `tagext` package will be covered in later chapters (Chapters 8 to 11) devoted to tag libraries.

While these API's are important, if you find yourself spending too much time studying the JSP API's to implement some feature (with the exception of when building or using tag libraries) consider switching to a Servlet for that feature. As mentioned earlier, embedding Java code in JSP files via scriptlets can quickly result in a maintenance nightmare. With the exception of building custom tags, you should be very sensitive to utilizing these API's.

The package `javax.Servlet.jsp` contains the following resources (note that Tomcat bundles the API documentation and makes it available at http://localhost:8080/servletapi-javadoc/index.html):

Resource	Type	Comments
JspPage	Interface	Extends `javax.servlet.Servlet`.
HttpJspPage	Interface	Extends `HttpJspPage`. Each JSP page implements this interface (or a subclass that also implements this interface).
JspWriter	Class	Extends `java.io.Writer`. This is the normal mechanism for JSP pages to produce output to the response.
PageContext	Class	A `PageContext` instance provides access to all the namespaces associated with a JSP page, provides access to several page attributes, as well as a layer above the implementation details.
JspException	Exception	Extends `Exception`. Generated by code within the page (scriptlets, etc.). If it is not caught, it triggers the error page mechanisms.

This is not an exhaustive list of resources available in this package, but these are the key ones that advanced pages may need to consider utilizing. These API's will be covered in detail in the chapters that discuss creating your own tag libraries.

Precompilation of JSP Files

The JSP specifications define a precompilation protocol that allows pages to be precompiled prior to the receipt of a request. The JSP spec defines a special parameter named `jsp_precompile`. According to the spec, the attribute may be set to the following values:

- ❏ no value – `somePage.jsp?jsp_precompile`

- ❏ `"true"` – `somePage.jsp?jsp_precompile="true"`

- ❏ `"false"` – `somePage.jsp?jsp_precompile="false"`

All other values should be illegal and result in a server error. In all cases, the request is not delivered to the page. If an illegal value is given, an error page will be displayed. If a valid value is given, the page will be precompiled.

> **Note that all request attributes that begin with `jsp` are reserved by the JSP spec and should not be used except as mandated in the spec.**

At the time of this writing, the latest nightly builds for Tomcat generate an error for all values, but properly precompile the page when there is no value given. We can see this in action if we shut down Tomcat and clear out any files in the work directory for our webapp (remove all files in `CATALINA_HOME/work/ch04/jsp`).

Then restart Tomcat. If we go to the following location:
http://localhost:8080/ch04/jsp/time.jsp?jsp_precompile, what we will get depends on which browser we are using. Internet Explorer will present us with a blank screen, while Netscape will show us a useful message telling us "The document contained no data. Try again later, or contact the server's administrator."

This is not an error – it simply means that Tomcat precompiled the page and returned no output. Granted they could have made a nicer response but this mechanism isn't usually meant to work this way (we'll explain in a minute). If we look in the `work/ch04/jsp` directory, we should see the Java file for the JSP Servlet and the compiled class file:

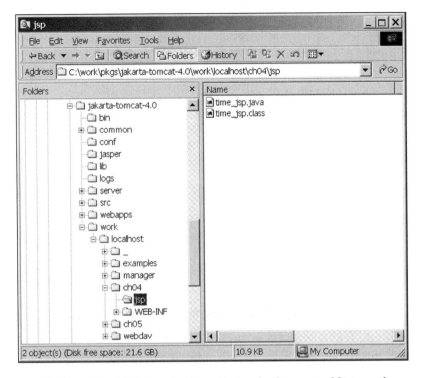

Now since we are dealing with a URL based protocol to invoke this, we could trigger the precompilation through invoking the `java.net.URL.getContent()` method of a `java.net.URL` object. The following code illustrates the point:

```
package com.wrox.projsp.util;

import java.io.File;
import java.io.IOException;
import java.net.URL;

public class Precompile {

  public static void main(String[] args) {

    String pathname = args[0];
    String queryString = "?jsp_precompile";
    String urlBase = "/ch04/jsp/";

    try {
      File dir = new File(pathname);
      if (!dir.exists()) {
        throw new IOException("pathname " + pathname + " not found");
      }
      File[] files = dir.listFiles();
      for (int i = 0; i < files.length; i++) {
        String jspFile = files[i].getName();
        if (jspFile.endsWith(".jsp")) {
          System.out.println("working on " + files[i].getName());
          try {
```

```
                 URL url = new URL("http", "localhost", 8080,
                             urlBase + jspFile + queryString);
                 System.out.println("compiling " + jspFile + " using " + urlBase
                             + jspFile + queryString);
                 url.getContent();
             } catch (Exception e) {

                 // add error handling
             }
         }
     }
     } catch (Exception e) {
         System.out.println("exception raised:" + e);
     }
   }
 }
```

This `Precompile` class has a `main()` method that takes the first command line parameter as the base directory to find all JSP files (note – for simplicity, it does not go recursively into subdirectories in that base directory). For each `.jsp` file in that directory, it will obtain a URL of the format http://localhost:8080/ch04/jsp/<jspFile>?jsp_precompile. It will use this URL to obtain the content – in other words, to issue a request to the URL. This will trigger the precompilation sequence.

Executing the method we see the following (make sure your `CLASSPATH` variable includes the current directory):

```
Command Prompt                                                          _ □ ×
C:\jakarta-tomcat-4.0\webapps\ch04\WEB-INF\classes>java com.wrox.projsp.ch03.util.Precompile c:\jaka
rta-tomcat-4.0\webapps\ch04\jsp
working on admin.jsp
compiling admin.jsp using /ch04/jsp/admin.jsp?jsp_precompile
working on directives.jsp
compiling directives.jsp using /ch04/jsp/directives.jsp?jsp_precompile
working on enterRecord.jsp
compiling enterRecord.jsp using /ch04/jsp/enterRecord.jsp?jsp_precompile
working on first.jsp
compiling first.jsp using /ch04/jsp/first.jsp?jsp_precompile
working on header.jsp
compiling header.jsp using /ch04/jsp/header.jsp?jsp_precompile
working on newRecord.jsp
compiling newRecord.jsp using /ch04/jsp/newRecord.jsp?jsp_precompile
working on scriptingTest.jsp
compiling scriptingTest.jsp using /ch04/jsp/scriptingTest.jsp?jsp_precompile
working on second.jsp
compiling second.jsp using /ch04/jsp/second.jsp?jsp_precompile
working on sessionTest.jsp
compiling sessionTest.jsp using /ch04/jsp/sessionTest.jsp?jsp_precompile
working on summary.jsp
compiling summary.jsp using /ch04/jsp/summary.jsp?jsp_precompile
working on time.jsp
compiling time.jsp using /ch04/jsp/time.jsp?jsp_precompile

C:\jakarta-tomcat-4.0\webapps\ch04\WEB-INF\classes>_
```

If we look at the work directory again, we now see each of the JSP files has been compiled:

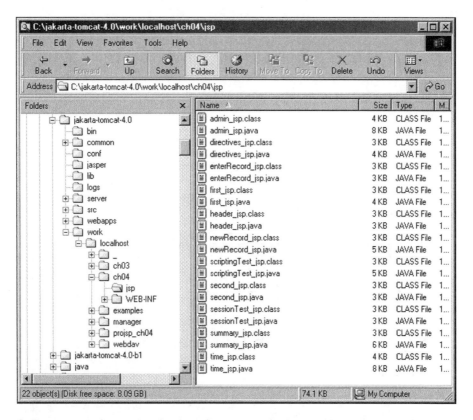

Obviously Tomcat must be running for this scheme to work. You could experiment with this approach and have the mechanism triggered by a Servlet that is set to load-on-startup.

The side affect of not doing a precompilation is that the first time a user hits each page, the JSP engine must translate and compile the Servlet. This delay may or may not be tolerable. If it is not tolerable, experiment with a program similar to the one introduced here.

Note that Tomcat also has an off-line compilation utility. At the time of this writing it was not operational. Other vendors may also experiment with off-line compilation (also called manual compilation). The benefit of this experimentation is a more robust deployment strategy. The downside is the solutions will typically be proprietary.

Error Handling

Let's now add an error page to our Time Entry application. If the EVENT is not set properly, it could be due to user manipulation or a bug. In either case, we could pass control off to a common error page.

We should first throw a JspException if we discover an event that we are not programmed to handle. Simply add the highlighted line to time.jsp (as reflected in time2.jsp in the code dowload). Notice that we pass the name of the event in question to the JspException.

```
<%
    } else if (event.equals ("SUMMARY")) {
%>
```

```
        <jsp:include page="summary.jsp" flush="true"/>
<%
    } else {
        throw new JspException ("illegal event of " + event);
    }
%>
```

If we enter the URL http://localhost:8080/ch04/jsp/time2.jsp?EVENT=bogusEvent, we would again get a different screen depending upon which browser we use. Internet Explorer 5.0 does not display server based error messages the same way as Netscape – they often substitute a 'friendly' HTTP message. So, if you enter the above URL in IE 5.0 (or 5.5), you'll get a "The page cannot be displayed" message; using Netscape, however, we get a Tomcat Exception Report:

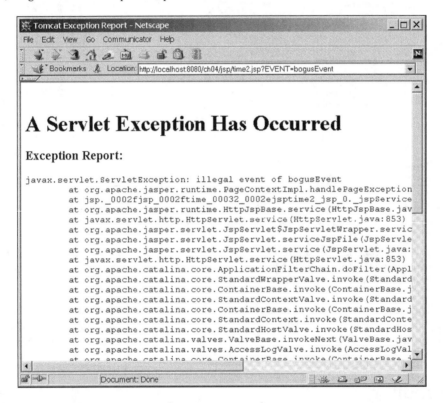

Now let's define the following error page (errorPage.jsp):

```
<%@ page isErrorPage="true" %>

<h2>Error Page</h2>

The exception <%= exception.toString() %> was raised.

<p>The exception reported this message:
<p><%= exception.getMessage() %>
```

To use this error page, enter the following directive to the source page (reflected in `time3.jsp` in the code download):

```
<%@ page errorPage="errorPage.jsp" %>
```

> Note that the value of the **errorPage** attribute must be a URL that points to a JSP file.

Now go to http://localhost:8080/ch04/jsp/time3.jsp?EVENT=bogusEvent; you should get the following screen:

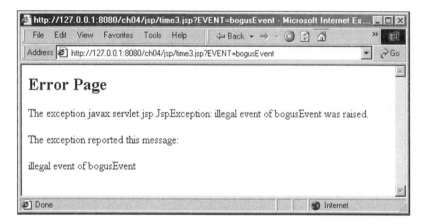

Notice how the URL does not reflect the passing of control to the error page. As with forwarding, this prevents users from book-marking internal URL's to your application, and allows flexibility in design.

Summary

This chapter gave us a broad exposure to the capability of JSP. Some key points to remember:

- ❑ JSP files are translated into Servlets. The translated Servlet processes the request and produces the response.

- ❑ JSP syntax is broken up into scripting elements, directives, and action elements.

- ❑ Scripting elements allow the declaration of variables, methods, or classes. When using declarations for defining variables, take care to ensure they are accessed in a thread-safe manner.

- ❑ Directives are translation time statements to guide the translation process.

- ❑ Action elements are powerful tags that allow the inclusion of another JSP file, the forwarding of control to a Servlet or JSP file, passing parameters to one of the above, and control over the browser's Java plug-in.

- ❑ Be aware of buffer issues when including or forwarding.

❑ JSP Engines are required to have a work directory where translated Servlets reside. Tomcat uses `CATALINA_HOME/work/<virtualHost>/<webapp>/jsp` to hold translated JSP files.

❑ The use of too much scriptlet code makes for a difficult file to maintain and debug.

The last point – too much scriptlet code in a JSP file – is arguably one of the most dangerous side effects of JSP. This problem is partially addressed in the next chapter, where we will introduce JavaBeans and show how we can easily remove some scriptlet code and replace it with some easy to use tags.

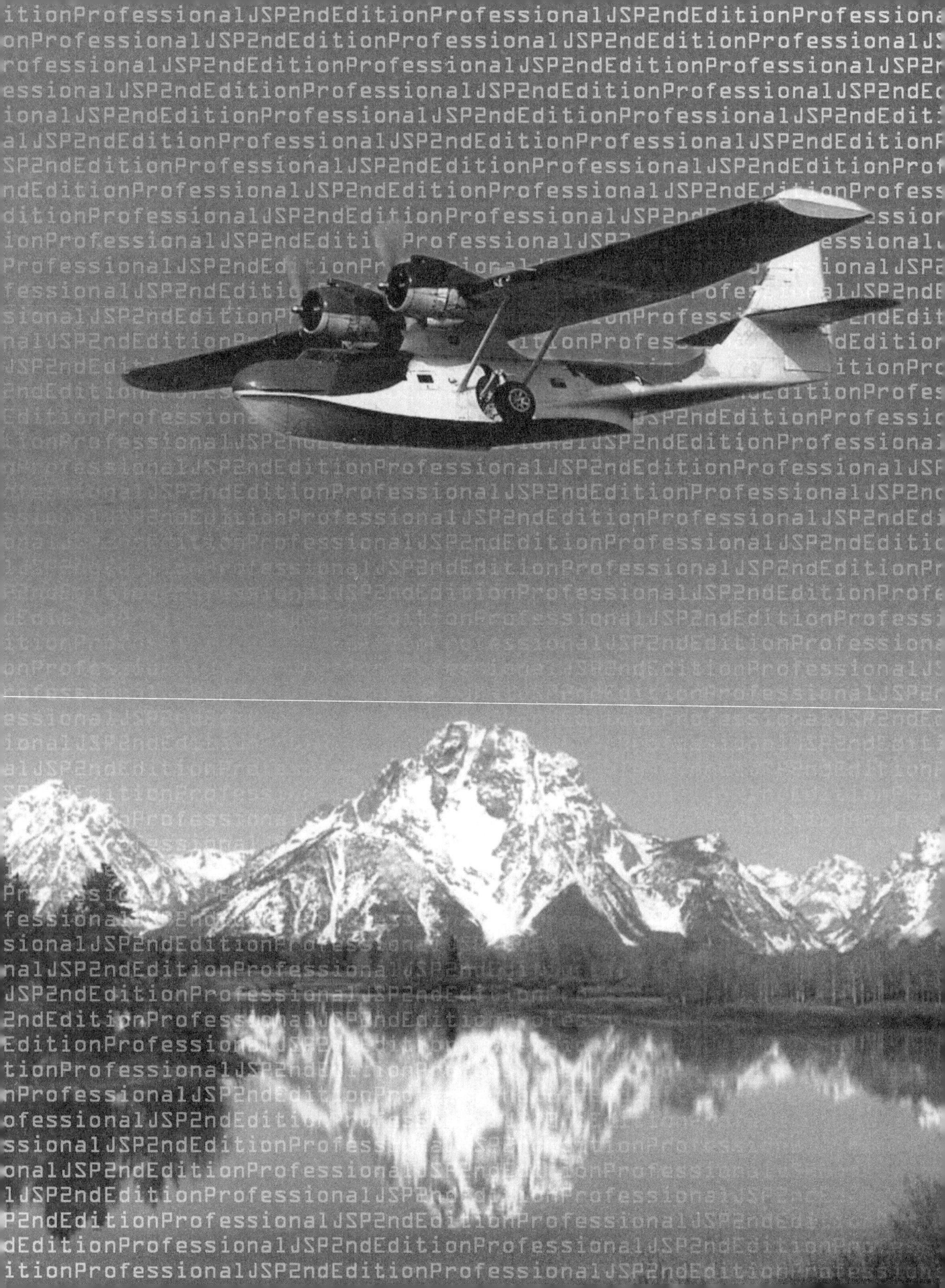
ProfessionalJSP2ndEdition

5

JSP and JavaBeans

JavaBeans ('beans') have achieved widespread popularity amongst developers as a convenient mechanism to encapsulate functionality that also enables powerful tool support and automation. This chapter focuses on integrating beans with JSP.

There are some easy yet powerful tags that unleash the power and flexibility of Beans in a JSP environment. In the process they also simplify the design of pages and help partition the presentation from the business logic. In addition, the use of Beans with JSP eliminates messy scriptlet code. This chapter will:

❑   Provide a definition of JavaBeans and how we should write them to work in conjunction with JSP

❑   Define the set of JSP tags that are used with Beans

❑   Analyze the examples that come with Tomcat

❑   Provide a redesign of the previously introduced Time Entry System using Beans and JSP

Definition of JavaBeans

JavaBeans have become a popular technique for building reusable Java components. Initially focused as building blocks that can be manipulated in a visual development environment, beans have found widespread use for encapsulating business logic. It is this secondary usage of beans that we will focus on in this chapter.

However, as the industry quickly adopts JSP, we are seeing widespread support for integrated development environments that provide seamless development from beans to JSPs and everything in between. This industry trend is exciting because it provides advanced tool support for open standards.

Previously, this advanced integration was only available in proprietary systems.

Let's formally define beans, as they apply to JSP and Servlets.

A JavaBean is really nothing more than a class that maintains some data (called properties) and follows certain coding conventions. These conventions, in conjunction with features of the Java environment and runtime (such as reflection and introspection), provide a powerful mechanism for reuse and automated support.

The JavaBeans API defines the following items that classes must adhere to in order to take full advantage of everything beans has to offer:

❑   Implement the `java.io.Serializable` or the `java.io.Externalizable` interface.

❑   Provide a no-arguments constructor.

❑   Private properties must have corresponding get/set methods using the appropriate naming patterns.

Each of these requirements is explained in detail below.

Note that events, constrained and bound properties, and customization (via a user interface) features of beans do not apply to their use with JSP and Servlets. They are more geared towards visual components, where the beans must inherit from `java.awt.Component`.

Serializable

By implementing either of the `Serializable` or `Externalizable` interfaces (you only need implement one or the other, not both), it signals to the Java runtime that the class supports persistence. There are no methods to implement with this interface; you simply have to add the keyword `implements` and one of the above interfaces to your class definition (reference example below):

```
import java.io.Serializable;

public class MyFirstBean implements Serializable {
    //...
}
```

This enables the runtime to save and restore the bean to/from disk or the network, through Java's serialization mechanism. If your class implements one of these interfaces, the runtime assumes your class supports persistence. **Persistence** simply means the important state (as determined by the bean designer) can be saved and retrieved in a consistent manner.

Before describing what one must do in order to 'support persistence', it is useful to recognize why the requirement is levied in the first place. The original intent for beans in a visual development environment was to allow development and deployment tools to create, manipulate, save (their current state), and restore (to their previous state) instances of beans in a controlled and consistent manner. The saving and restoring is accomplished through a process called **serialization**. Serialization requires certain behavior, which we will discuss shortly.

In order to enable Servlets and JSPs to operate in environments that must support features such as load balancing and failover, similar restrictions for serialized behavior apply. Over the course of the execution of our web application in one of those environments, we might expect an instance of a bean we are using to be saved from one server to another as part of a snapshot of the current state. This snapshot would give the second server a picture of the inner state of the first server, and would allow it to take over from the point where the first server failed (or at least close to the point – depending on the frequency of the snapshots).

Serialization is the process by which a Java object can be saved in its present state to a file or network stream. Conversely, the object can be reconstructed through the same mechanism (sometimes called **deserialization**). All non-static and non-transient variables of the object being serialized are preserved or restored.

Transient variables are marked with the `transient` keyword, which implies that the variable must be recreated on the fly during the serialization reconstruction process (during deserialization). Examples of `transient` variables are file or socket references. Restoring a variable that represented a file reference would likely be inconsistent because the reference may no longer be valid (or may not even apply to the machine that is executing the deserialization) and should be reconstructed from scratch – usually by invoking the same method that originally populated it.

When designing our beans, it is useful to study each variable with the thought of saving and restoring it at any point in time. If the variable cannot be reliably deserialized, it should be marked as `transient`.

For more complex situations, we may override the default serialization technique. If you need to utilize this technique, refer to *Professional Java Programming* from Wrox Press, ISBN 1-861003-82-x.

It is important to remember that once we have convinced ourselves that all variables are set properly (with or without the `transient` keyword – and assuming we don't have to override the default serialization mechanism), we do not have to do any additional work to enable the runtime to serialize our bean.

No-Arguments Constructor

Remember where beans were originally intended to be used – visual development tools. In the course of using beans we will need to instantiate objects. Generating tool support for the myriad set of constructors each bean designer might create would be overly complex and/or slow. Thus by mandating support of a no-arguments constructor, this allows the runtime system to instantiate all beans the same way – via `java.beans.Beans.instantiate()`.

With Servlets and JSP, we want the Servlet/JSP engine to be able to easily instantiate any requested beans using this same technique. Thus any beans we use should have a no-arguments constructor:

```
MyFirstBean () {
    //...
}
```

Properties

Each discrete piece of internal state information that a bean publicly exposes is called a **property**. Properties should be implemented as private instance variables. They are made public via accessor (also called getter) methods for reading, and via mutator (also called setter) methods for modifying.

The naming conventions for the methods are as follows:

Property Name	getter Method Name	setter Method Name
propertyName	getPropertyName()	SetPropertyName()
booleanProperty Name	getBooleanPropertyName() or isBooleanPropertyName()	setBooleanProperty Name()

Note that the method names mimic the property name with the get or set prefixed, and the initial character of the property name changed to upper case. For boolean properties, the isBooleanPropertyName() style of syntax for the getter method is acceptable but not often used and not recommended.

Also note there are not really any enforced naming conventions for the actual property names within the bean itself. Most programmers however follow the conventions shown above for property names.

For a given property of type <type>, the signature of the getter and setter methods are as follows:

```
public <type> getPropertyName();
public void setPropertyName(<type> name);
```

The following example demonstrates two properties – a boolean named autoFlush, and an int named period – and their corresponding getter/setter methods:

```
//...
private boolean autoFlush;
private int period;

public void setAutoFlush (boolean b) {
   autoFlush = a;
}
public boolean getAutoFlush() {  // could have also called it isAutoFlush()
   return autoFlush;
}

public void setPeriod (int p) {
   period = p;
}
public int getPeriod () {
   return period;
}
```

Note that properties may take on any valid type or class.

One special case that is worth mentioning is **Indexed Properties**. These properties are arrays of objects (of any type). Additional (and optional) getter and setter methods may be defined to obtain individual elements following the signatures below:

```
public <type> getPropertyName (int i);
public void setPropertyName (int i, <type> name);
```

An example of an indexed property is shown below:

```
//...
private String[] names;
public void setName (int i, String n) {
  names[i] = name;
}
public String getName (int i) {
  return names[i];
}

public void setName (String[] n) {
  names = n;
}
public String[] getName () {
  return names;
}
```

Environment Support

Having rules is no fun unless the rules will provide some sort of tangible benefit. By exploring the environmental support in Java, we can see how powerful beans can become – but only if we follow the rules. Two mechanisms are worth mentioning – **Introspection** and **Reflection**.

In order to use beans with JSP, we don't *need* to know about the environment. However, we have found that it is helpful in giving the full picture of the behavior of beans.

Introspection

Introspection is the name of the process that occurs at runtime to discover what properties and methods are available for a given object (in our case, for a given bean). In order to provide reasonable efficiency, two different techniques are combined:

❏   The easy default case is to utilize reflection and design patterns (covered next)

❏   The more complex case (and beyond the scope of this book – see *Java Programmer's Reference*, ISBN 1-861004-22-2 for details) is for the beans designer to provide a java.beans.BeansInfo class with the bean to describe the key features (public methods and properties)

The java.beans.Introspector class defines resources that allow the programmatic construction of information on the bean using these two techniques.

Reflection

Reflection is a package of resources (java.lang.reflect) that allows any Java program to obtain information about classes and objects that are loaded (via the class loader). References to the fields, methods, and constructors are easily obtained. Those references can then be used to operate on the objects.

As we discussed above, the methods for getting and setting properties (getter/setter methods) in beans should follow the naming convention of get<PropertyName> and set<PropertyName>. Assuming this design pattern allows the reflection mechanism of Java to be efficiently used. By discovering all the getter and setter methods that fit our design pattern, the environment can quickly infer the set of properties that the object has.

This explains why we don't really need to be concerned with the actual variable names of the properties – they are private and only referenced by the corresponding getter/setter methods (the reflection mechanism doesn't need them to discover the getter/setter methods). But it's still good practice to follow the pattern when naming the variables for us humans that have to maintain the system.

JavaBeans Summary

When we tie the information in this section together, we have the following:

❑ A set of rules that designers must follow when creating beans (implement `Serializable` or `Externalizable`, naming conventions for getter/setter methods of properties, and a no-argument constructor)

❑ Java environment mechanisms for saving and restoring beans in a consistent fashion (the serialization mechanism)

❑ Java environment mechanisms for automatically discovering and using properties (via getter/setter methods) of beans (introspection, reflection, and design patterns)

We will shortly see how these features enable new JSP beans tags.

Example Bean

A full example of a Java bean that might be useful with JSPs is shown below:

```java
package com.wrox.projsp.ch05;

import java.io.Serializable;

public class Stock implements Serializable {

  Stock() {}

  private String name = null;
  private String tickerSymbol = null;
  private double tradingPrice = 0.0;
  private double sharesOwned = 0.0;

  public void setName(String n) {
    name = n;
  }
  public String getName() {
    return name;
  }

  public void setTickerSymbol(String s) {
    tickerSymbol = s;
  }
  public String getTickerSymbol() {
    return tickerSymbol;
  }

  public void setTradingPrice(double p) {
```

```
    tradingPrice = p;
  }
  public double getTradingPrice() {
    return tradingPrice;
  }

  public void setSharesOwned(double s) {
    sharesOwned = s;
  }
  public double getSharesOwned() {
    return sharesOwned;
  }
}
```

Remembering our rules, we can visually inspect this bean and declare it is a 'good bean'. The getter/setter methods follow the design pattern, we have implemented `java.io.Serializable`, and we have a no-argument constructor.

Further, upon inspection of all variables (`name`, `tickerSymbol`, `tradingPrice`, and `sharesOwned`), we can satisfy ourselves that this bean will be serializable since no variable holds an external reference (such as a file or socket reference).

Beans Tags Syntax Overview

There are three tags to support the use of beans:

❑   `<jsp:useBean>`

❑   `<jsp:setProperty>`

❑   `<jsp:getProperty>`

In this section we will formally define their capabilities and syntax. Just to review concepts introduced in previous chapters, let's talk about scope first. Then we will discuss each new tag.

Scope Revisited

In Chapters 3 and 4, we introduced the various values of scope and the corresponding objects that are available to each JSP file:

Scope	Object	Description
Page	pageContext	Visible only to the first Servlet or JSP that the request is mapped to
Request	request	Visible within the Servlet or JSP handling the request, as well as any other Servlet or page that is forwarded or included during the processing of that request
Session	session	Visible to all handlers (Servlets or JSPs) for requests of the same client session
Application	application	Visible to all handlers and sessions of the same webapp

These same four values apply to the scope (or life span) of beans when invoked via the beans tags. The default value in the beans tags is page scoped.

When we store an object into one of these scope objects (request, session, or application – it doesn't make much sense to store an object into the page scope since the page already has visibility to the object), what ends up happening is that the object reference is saved in a special data structure in the scope object (the scope's set of attributes). Because the object reference is stored, the object stays resident in memory. Thus, updates to the object itself do not require any additional action relative to the scope.

In this chapter, the objects we are interested in storing into a scope object are beans.

For example, if we start processing a request and create a session scoped object (say, via the `session.setAttribute()` method), the object's reference gets stored in the session. If we then set some properties of the object, we don't have to take any additional action. The object reference is preserved in the session, and as long as the session is active, the reference is still valid and the object will be preserved (not reclaimed by the garbage collection utility).

In the processing of subsequent requests, we can obtain the saved object reference (via the `session.getAttribute()` method). Once this page has the reference, if it makes any updates to the object they are automatically preserved in the session.

We can use the same analogy with objects in the request or application scope.

The <jsp:useBean> Tag

The `<jsp:useBean>` tag performs the following logic:

❑ If the specified object is found within the specified scope, it is retrieved and assigned to the object (in other words, via a `getAttribute()` method).

❑ If the object is not found, it is instantiated (as long as the `class` or `beanName` attribute is supplied). If the `class` or `beanName` attribute is not provided, the object is not instantiated. This last case (without `class` or `beanName` specified) is useful only for retrieving known objects from the specified scope.

❑ If the object is newly instantiated, it executes the code specified in the body (typically one or more `<jsp:setProperty>` tags or a scriptlet). Refer to the `<jsp:setProperty>` tag description below for details.

❑ If the object is newly instantiated, it is saved into the specified scope as an attribute (via the `setAttribute()` method).

One other subtle task performed by the `<jsp:useBean>` tag is to make the object visible to the JSP file. Other objects that were put into the scope (for example, `session`) by another entity (a Servlet, say) are not visible to a JSP page without the use of the `<jsp:useBean>` tag.

The available attributes include the following:

❑ `id` – the name of the object. This attribute is required.

❑ `scope` – the scope of the object. It may be `page`, `request`, `session`, or `application`. This attribute is optional and defaults to `page`.

❏   `class` – the fully qualified class name of the object.

❏   `beanName` – the name of the bean. This value must be populated as defined by the Beans specification as valid for the argument for a `java.beans.Beans.instantiate()` method. That specification allows for two different types of values – a fully qualified class name of a bean (such as `com.wrox.projsp.ch05.MyBean`) or a fully qualified serialized object name (such as `com/wrox/projsp/ch05/MyBean.ser`). We will expand this when we describe this attribute's use below. This attribute may be populated with a JSP expression.

❏   `type` – the type of the object. This value can be equal to the `class`, a superclass of the `class`, or an interface implemented by the `class`. If not supplied, the object is of type `class`.

At first glance, it appears that some of the attributes are redundant. But a further look at the allowable combinations sheds light on the need for each of the attributes.

As mentioned previously, when we use the `<jsp:useBean>` tag, the `id` attribute is always required, and the `scope` attribute is optional (and defaults to `page`). In addition, one of the following combinations of attributes is also required (note that the comments in the examples ignore the possibility of the object existing in the specified scope unless otherwise noted):

❏   `class` – this is probably the most often used form. The object `id` is instantiated using the value of `class` and is of type `class`. Here's an example, where we instantiate a bean called `today`, of class `java.util.Date`:

```
<%-- the following tag effectively does the same as:
   java.util.Date today = new java.util.Date();
--%>
<jsp:useBean id="today" class="java.util.Date" />
```

❏   `type` **and** `class` – the object `id` is instantiated using the value of `class`, and is of type `type`. This `type` attribute must be equal to `class`, be a superclass of `class`, or be an interface that `class` implements. This allows the object to function more generally and to hold different types at different times. For example, if we needed to do processing with different types of numbers (integers and floating points, say), we might want to store the object as a `Number`. Then based on input criteria, we could then instantiate the object with a more specialized class – say as an `Integer` or `Float` – so we could take advantage of the specialized class's resources and safeguards. In the example below, we instantiate an object named `count` of class `java.lang.Integer` which has a `type` of the superclass `java.lang.Number`:

```
<%-- the following tag effectively does the same as:
   Number count;
   count = new Integer();
--%>
<jsp:useBean
   id="count" class="java.lang.Integer" type="java.lang.Number" />
```

❏   `beanName` **and** `type` – the `id` is instantiated using `java.beans.Bean.instantiate()` with a value of `beanName`, and is of type `type`. The `type` attribute must be equal to `beanName`, be a superclass of `beanName`, or be an interface that `beanName` implements. `beanName` may be populated at request-time (which is the only difference between this case and the previous case). The following example illustrates this:

```
<%-- the following tag effectively does the same as:
  Number count;
  count = java.beans.Beans.instantiate(
    request.getParameter("beanName"));
--%>
<jsp:useBean id="count"
  beanNameclass="<%= request.getParameter("beanName")%>"
  type="Number" />
```

❑   type – the object with the name specified by id must be present in the specified scope. No
     instantiation is performed – the object id is only assigned to the value retrieved from the
     scope. Note that if the object does not exist in the specified scope,
     java.lang.InstantiationException will be thrown (not shown in the effective code).

```
<%-- the following tag effectively does the same as:
  Number count = (Number) session.getAttribute("count");
--%>
<jsp:useBean id="count" scope="session" type="Number" />
```

To summarize these variations, the formal syntax can be described as follows – first with no body:

```
<jsp:useBean id="name" {scope="page|request|session|application"}
  {
    class="class name"  |
    class="class name" type="type name"  |
    beanName="bean name" type="type name"  |
    type="type name"
  }
/>
```

And with a body specified:

```
<jsp:useBean id="name" {scope=="page|request|session|application"}
  { attribute details as shown above }
>
  body
</jsp:useBean>
```

> **Remember that if the object is found in the specified scope, the `<jsp:useBean>` body is
> not executed. Basically the body is a one-time only initialization.**

The following errors may be generated or exceptions thrown while processing the `<jsp:useBean>` tag:

❑   Translation-time error – a vendor-specified error message is generated when neither the type
     nor the class attribute was specified, or if type and class are both present but class
     cannot be cast to type

❑   java.lang.InstantiationException – thrown when the object is not found in the
     specified scope and neither class nor beanName are given, or when the object was not
     found in the specified scope and the class can not be properly instantiated (for example, it
     was abstract, an interface, or no public no-arguments constructor exists)

❑ `java.lang.ClassCastException` – thrown when the object is found in the specified `scope` but unable to be cast properly (for example, the object stored in the scope was different from this object)

The <jsp:setProperty> Tag

The `<jsp:setProperty>` tag does as the name implies – it sets one or more properties of a known bean to specific values, or to parameter values from the `request`. The tag may exist within the body of a `<jsp:useBean>` tag, or on its own (after the `<jsp:useBean>` tag). The behavior is identical in either invocation.

The available attributes include the following:

❑ `name` – the name of the object. This object must have been previously defined (using a declaration, in a `<jsp:useBean>` tag, or via a custom tag and the associated `VariableInfo()` entry) in this page. Objects set into a scope (say the session) are not visible to the scripting language without some action on the page developer's part (for example, via a `<jsp:useBean>` tag or equivalent). This attribute is required.

❑ `property` – the name of the property being set. A wildcard of * may be used. If so, the `value` attribute is not used and any matching request parameters (except those with values of `null` or `" "` – an empty string) will be used to set the properties of the bean. This attribute is required.

❑ `param` – the name of the parameter in the request to use when setting the `property`. This attribute is optional.

❑ `value` – the value of the property being set. A `String` constant or expression (which gets evaluated at request-time) may be used to set this attribute. This attribute is optional.

In a similar way to the `<jsp:useBean>` tag, the `<jsp:setProperty>` tag has a few different flavors of valid attribute combinations. The `name` attribute plus one of the forms shown below are always required:

❑ `property="*"` – used to set all matching properties of the bean with parameters with the same name from the `request` (excluding any parameters with a value of `null` or an empty-string). Note that if the user blanks out a field in an HTML form, that field will not set the corresponding property of the bean. You will have to handle this case (usually by assigning the properties' appropriate default values in the bean itself):

```
<jsp:setProperty name="transaction" property="*" />
```

❑ `property="property name"` – the specific property name is set with the parameter of the same name from the `request`:

```
<%-- the following tag effectively does the same as:
   transaction.setTransactionType
      (request.getParameter("transactionType");
--%>
<jsp:setProperty name="transaction" property="transactionType" />
```

❑ `property="property name"` `param="parameter name"` – the specific property name is set with the `param` named "parameter name" from the `request`:

```
<%-- the following tag effectively does the same as:
  transaction.setTransactionType
    (request.getParameter("transType");
--%>
<jsp:setProperty
  name="transaction" property="transactionType" param="transType"/>
```

❑ property="property name" value="some value" – the specific property name is set with the supplied value.

```
<%-- the following tag effectively does the same as:
  transaction.setTransactionType(myTransType);
--%>
<jsp:setProperty
  name="transaction" property="transactionType" value="<%= myTransType %>"/>
```

When setting the properties, the following conversions will be automatically performed:

❑ When value is set to an expression, no automatic conversion will be performed.

❑ When dealing with an indexed parameter in the request, the property in the bean must be an array.

❑ When value is set using a String constant, or when a property is set from a corresponding parameter in the request, the conversion from a String to properties of type boolean, Boolean, byte, Byte, char, Character, double, Double, int, Integer, float, Float, long, and Long will be automatically performed. Remember that the parameter values in the request are always of type String.

To summarize, the formal syntax of <jsp:setProperty> can be described as follows:

```
<jsp:setProperty name="name"
  {
    property="*"                              |
    property="property name"          |
    property="property name" param="param name"   |
    property="property name" value="some value"
  }
/>
```

The <jsp:getProperty> Tag

The <jsp:getProperty> tag – yes, you've guessed it – gets a property value from a bean. The tag takes a name attribute that references a previously defined bean (say, via a previous <jsp:useBean> tag or equivalent operation in this page), and a property attribute that references the specific property within the bean. The tag retrieves the property, converts it to a String if necessary (via the toString() method), and puts it into the out stream.

The formal syntax is shown below:

```
<jsp:getProperty name="name" property="property name" />
```

This tag may be used in an expression. An example is shown below:

```
<%= someMethod(<jsp:getProperty name="whatever" property="whatever">) %>
```

Running Tomcat's Bean Examples

Now let's examine some of the JSP examples supplied with Tomcat that we skipped in the previous chapter. They all have one thing in common – they all use beans.

The JSP files for the examples are in `CATALINA_HOME\webapps\examples\jsp\` (typically in a separate subdirectory for each example).

The beans are in the `\webapps\examples\WEB-INF\classes` directory.

While the examples do a good job of illustrating the concepts, there are some style issues that should not be repeated in practice. Specifically:

❑ In HTML and JSP tags, quote all attributes

❑ Be consistent with quoting (single or double quotes are usually permissible – stick with one or the other where possible

❑ Be consistent with your use of URLs (relative or absolute are often permissible for most constructs – be consistent where possible)

Using the <jsp:getProperty> Tag

We will use the Date JSP example that comes with Tomcat to illustrate the use of the `<jsp:getProperty>` tag and how we can display properties of a bean in a page.

To execute the Date JSP Example, go to http://localhost:8080/examples/jsp/ and select the Date Execute link. You should see a display similar to the following screenshot:

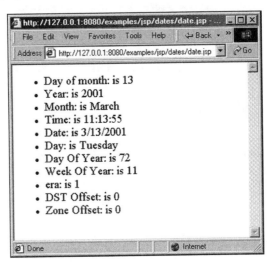

Nothing particularly exciting, but let's look at the code (found in
\webapps\examples\jsp\dates\date.jsp):

```
<html>
<!--
   Copyright (c) 1999 The Apache Software Foundation. All rights
   reserved.
-->

<%@ page session="false"%>

<body bgcolor="white">
<jsp:useBean id='clock' scope='page' class='dates.JspCalendar'
            type="dates.JspCalendar" />

<font size=4>
<ul>
<li>  Day of month: is
     <jsp:getProperty name="clock" property="dayOfMonth"/>
<li>  Year: is  <jsp:getProperty name="clock" property="year"/>
<li>  Month: is  <jsp:getProperty name="clock" property="month"/>
<li>  Time: is  <jsp:getProperty name="clock" property="time"/>
<li>  Date: is  <jsp:getProperty name="clock" property="date"/>
<li>  Day: is  <jsp:getProperty name="clock" property="day"/>
<li>  Day Of Year: is  <jsp:getProperty name="clock" property="dayOfYear"/>
<li>  Week Of Year: is  <jsp:getProperty name="clock"
                                        property="weekOfYear"/>
<li>  era: is  <jsp:getProperty name="clock" property="era"/>
<li>  DST Offset: is  <jsp:getProperty name="clock" property="DSTOffset"/>
<li>  Zone Offset: is  <jsp:getProperty name="clock" property="zoneOffset"/>
</ul>
</font>

</body>
</html>
```

This code uses two important tags. The first is the new `<jsp:useBean>` tag. This tag includes several attributes – an `id` with a value of `"clock"`, a `scope` of `"page"`, and a `class` and `type` that are both set to `"dates.JspCalendar"`.

```
<jsp:useBean id='clock' scope='page' class='dates.JspCalendar'
            type="dates.JspCalendar" />
```

If we look into the `classes/dates` directory, we find `JspCalendar.class` and `JspCalendar.java` files; a quick inspection of the Java file reveals that it is a bean.

What this tag is doing is defining a variable named `clock` of type `dates.JspCalendar`, and then instantiating it with the no-argument constructor of `dates.JspCalendar`. A look at the constructor for `JspCalendar` reveals the following:

```
Calendar  calendar = null;

public JspCalendar() {
```

```
        calendar = Calendar.getInstance();
        Date trialTime = new Date();
        calendar.setTime(trialTime);
    }
```

The constructor instantiated a new `Calendar` (into `calendar`) and set the time to the current `Date()`.

The next thing to note in the `date.jsp` code is the use of the `<jsp:getProperty>` tag:

```
<li>  Day of month:  is
    <jsp:getProperty name="clock" property="dayOfMonth"/>
```

This tag has two attributes – a `name` with a value of clock (note it is the same value as used in the id property of the `<jsp:useBean>` tag above – thus it references the same object), and a `property` with a value of `dayOfMonth`. Looking back at the `dates.JspCalendar`, we can find the getter method for the `dayOfMonth` property:

```
public int getDayOfMonth() {
    return calendar.get(Calendar.DAY_OF_MONTH);
}
```

The `<jsp:getProperty>` tag is within the `<li>` tag. A review of the display shows all of the calendar properties displayed in `<li>` format (that is, in an unnumbered, bulleted list). This behavior implies that the `<jsp:getProperty>` tag simply returned the requested property and placed it in the `out` stream. This is exactly what it did.

Summarizing this JSP file, we have utilized the following new concepts:

❑   Used the `<jsp:useBean>` tag to instantiate a new bean

❑   Used the `<jsp:getProperty>` tag to retrieve specific properties from that bean and display the value in the response

Using the <jsp:setProperty> Tag

We will use the Checkbox JSP example that comes with Tomcat to illustrate the use of the `<jsp:setProperty>` tag and how we can set properties of a bean with parameters in the request.

You can execute this from the JSP Examples page. You should see a display similar to the following screenshot:

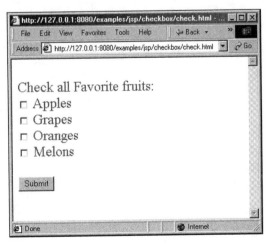

179

Go ahead and check some fruits and press Submit. We selected Apples and Oranges, and obtained the display shown in the following screenshot:

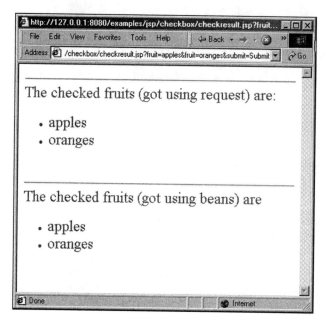

The display implies that the use of a request and bean technique yielded the same results.

Now let's take a look at the code. First, the \webapps\examples\jsp\checkbox\check.html file:

```
<HTML>
<!--
   Copyright (c) 1999 The Apache Software Foundation. All rights
   reserved.
-->

<BODY bgcolor="white">


<FORM TYPE=POST ACTION=checkresult.jsp>
<BR>
<font size=5 color="red">
Check all Favorite fruits: <br>

<input TYPE=checkbox name=fruit VALUE=apples> Apples <BR>
<input TYPE=checkbox name=fruit VALUE=grapes> Grapes <BR>
<input TYPE=checkbox name=fruit VALUE=oranges> Oranges <BR>
<input TYPE=checkbox name=fruit VALUE=melons> Melons <BR>


<br> <INPUT TYPE=submit name=submit Value="Submit">

</font>
</FORM>
</BODY>
</HTML>
```

Notice the use of the same name (fruit) for each checkbox. We'll explore this shortly. Also note that the ACTION attribute of the form points us to checkresult.jsp. Let's take a look at that file next:

```html
<html>
<!--
  Copyright (c) 1999 The Apache Software Foundation. All rights
  reserved.
-->

<body bgcolor="white">
<font size=5 color="red">
<%! String[] fruits; %>
<jsp:useBean id="foo" scope="page" class="checkbox.CheckTest" />

<jsp:setProperty name="foo" property="fruit" param="fruit" />
<hr>
The checked fruits (got using request) are: <br>
<%
  fruits = request.getParameterValues("fruit");
%>
<ul>
<%
    if (fruits != null) {
    for (int i = 0; i < fruits.length; i++) {
%>
<li>
<%
        out.println (fruits[i]);
    }
  } else out.println ("none selected");
%>
</ul>
<br>
<hr>

The checked fruits (got using beans) are <br>

<%
    fruits = foo.getFruit();
%>
<ul>
<%
    if (!fruits[0].equals("1")) {
    for (int i = 0; i < fruits.length; i++) {
%>
<li>
<%
        out.println (fruits[i]);
    }
  } else out.println ("none selected");
%>
</ul>
</font>
</body>
</html>
```

181

Now let's review the significant features of the file. First, an array of strings named `fruits` is declared.

```
<%! String[] fruits; %>
```

Next, the `<jsp:useBean>` tag is used to instantiate an object named `foo` of the class `checkbox.CheckTest` (a quick review of the `webapps\examples\WEB-INF\classes\checkbox\CheckTest.java` file reveals a simple bean with a basic `getFruit()` and `setFruit()` method for an array of strings):

```
<jsp:useBean id="foo" scope="page" class="checkbox.CheckTest" />
```

Then the `<jsp:setProperty>` tag is used to set the `fruit` property of `foo` to the `request` parameter named `fruit` (remember fruit was set to more than one value above in the HTML). Note the use of the `param` attribute is redundant since the parameter name and property name are the same (both are set to `fruit`):

```
<jsp:setProperty name="foo" property="fruit" param="fruit" />
```

Then we see the `fruits` object is set two different ways – first with the `request.getParameterValues()` method, and second, with the `foo.getFruits()` method. In both cases, a scriptlet then displays all values assigned to `fruits`. Since we know from the display that both techniques yielded the same result (apples and oranges), we can conclude that the `<jsp:setProperty>` tag set the array `foo` properly from the request parameter `fruit`.

Using Sessions

We will use the Carts JSP example that comes with Tomcat to illustrate the use of the sessions and how we can save a bean into the session and retrieve it in subsequent requests.

This example implements a simple shopping cart using sessions.

First let's execute it and see how it behaves. Go to http://localhost:8080/examples/jsp/sessions/carts.html. You should see the following display:

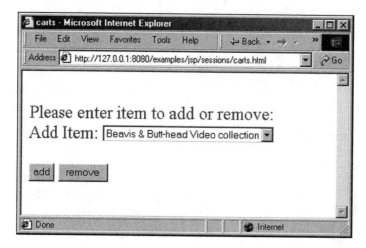

Select an item and press the **Add** button. Your display should indicate your selection:

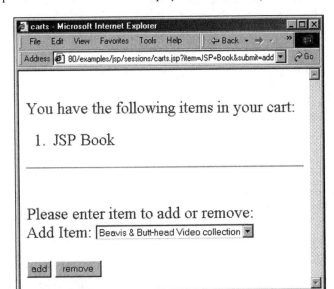

Experiment with the add and remove buttons to convince yourself of the example's consistency and preservation of the state of the shopping cart across the multiple requests. Then move on to look at the code below to see how it is implemented.

First look at the webapps\examples\jsp\sessions\carts.html file. You should note the definition of a <form> tag with an action of carts.jsp, a SELECT parameter named item, and a parameter named submit, which is set to either add or remove (<INPUT TYPE= ...> tag):

```
<html>
<!--
   Copyright (c) 1999 The Apache Software Foundation. All rights
   reserved.
-->

<head>
    <title>carts</title>
</head>

 <body bgcolor="white">
<font size = 5 color="#CC0000">

<form type=POST action=carts.jsp>
<BR>
Please enter item to add or remove:
<br>
Add Item:

<SELECT NAME="item">
```

```
<OPTION>Beavis & Butt-head Video collection
<OPTION>X-files movie
<OPTION>Twin peaks tapes
<OPTION>NIN CD
<OPTION>JSP Book
<OPTION>Concert tickets
<OPTION>Love life
<OPTION>Switch blade
<OPTION>Rex, Rugs & Rock n' Roll
</SELECT>


<br> <br>
<INPUT TYPE=submit name="submit" value="add">
<INPUT TYPE=submit name="submit" value="remove">

</form>

</FONT>
</body>
</html>
```

When the user selects the **add** or **remove** button, the `request` will be routed to `carts.jsp`, which appears below:

```
<html>
<!--
  Copyright (c) 1999 The Apache Software Foundation. All rights
  reserved.
-->

<jsp:useBean id="cart" scope="session" class="sessions.DummyCart" />

<jsp:setProperty name="cart" property="*" />
<%
  cart.processRequest(request);
%>


<FONT size = 5 COLOR="#CC0000">
<br> You have the following items in your cart:
<ol>
<%
  String[] items = cart.getItems();
  for (int i=0; i<items.length; i++) {
%>
<li> <%= items[i] %>
<%
  }
%>
```

```
</ol>

</FONT>

<hr>
<%@ include file ="/jsp/sessions/carts.html" %>
</html>
```

Let's move on to review the key tasks performed in carts.jsp. The <jsp:useBean> tag retrieves the cart object from the session if it exists. Otherwise, it is instantiated (using the sessions.DummyCart class) and stored in the session:

```
<jsp:useBean id="cart" scope="session" class="sessions.DummyCart" />
```

Then the <jsp:setProperty> tag is used to set the matching properties of cart to the non-null, non-empty string parameters in the request.

```
<jsp:setProperty name="cart" property="*" />
```

Remember that the <form> tag defined parameters named item and submit. We should expect to see item and submit as a property of the DummyCart class. The relevant code is shown below:

```
String submit = null;
String item = null;
. . .
public void setItem(String name) {
    item = name;
}

public void setSubmit(String s) {
    submit = s;
}
```

Next a scriptlet invokes a method to handle the request.

```
<%
  cart.processRequest(request);
%>
```

The relevant code from DummyCart class (webapps\examples\WEB-INF\classes\session\DummyCart.java) is shown below:

```
public void processRequest(HttpServletRequest request) {
    // null value for submit - user hit enter instead of clicking on
    // "add" or "remove"
    if (submit == null)
        addItem(item);
```

```
    if (submit.equals("add"))
        addItem(item);
    else if (submit.equals("remove"))
        removeItem(item);

    // reset at the end of the request
    reset();
}
```

Then a scriptlet displays all the items in the cart:

```
<ol>
<%
    String[] items = cart.getItems();
    for (int i=0; i<items.length; i++) {
%>
<li> <%= items[i] %>
<%
    }
%>
```

Finally, the `carts.html` file is included to allow additional selections.

```
<%@ include file ="/jsp/sessions/carts.html" %>
```

Note that this tag uses a fully qualified URL (`/jsp/sessions/carts.html`) where the action of the form used a relative URL (`carts.jsp`). It is usually bad practice to mix different methods like this and can lead to bugs or portability problems.

This example illustrated the ease with which we can use beans in conjunction with sessions. Most of the logic is hidden behind the implementation of the `<jsp:useBean>` tag.

A Day in the Life of a JSP-Invoked Bean

Let's now revisit the Cart JSP example, and look at some of the interaction that is happening.

Object Interaction

The following diagram illustrates the sequencing of events in a typical interaction with the Cart JSP example.

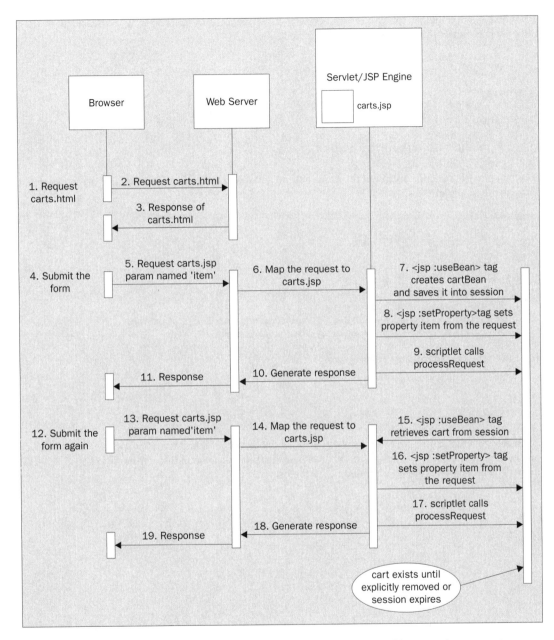

Notice that the `cart` object persists across multiple requests, as we would expect from a session-scoped object.

Indexed Parameters

A special case for parameter assignment called **Indexed Parameters** warrants an explanation and example. Indexed parameters allow the assignment of more than one value to a specified name – enabling the use of arrays as the recipient of the parameters. Indexed parameters can be used with checkboxes, and other data input scenarios such as the validation of a shopping cart on checkout.

Study the example below, for `ch05/jsp/indexedParameters.jsp`. The script passes an array of indexed parameters to itself, before displaying their values.

```
<%@ page import="java.util.Enumeration" %>

<html>

<body>

<h2>Indexed Parameter Test</h2>
```

The first part of the script prints out the names of the parameters stored in the `request` object, as well as the values of these parameters:

```
<ul>
  <li>Request Parameters:

  <ul>
<%
  Enumeration params = request.getParameterNames();
  while (params.hasMoreElements()) {
    String paramName = (String) params.nextElement();
    String paramValue = request.getParameter(paramName);
%>
    <li><%= paramName%>=<%=paramValue%>
<%
  }
%>
  </ul>
```

Then the JSP utilizes the `request.getParameterValues()` method to obtain an array of values from one of the parameters of `request`, in one line. This method takes the parameter name (`indexed` here) as input. The array values are then printed out to the browser:

```
  <li>Indexed Parameter Values:
  <ul>
<%
    String [] indexedParams = request.getParameterValues("indexed");
    if (indexedParams != null) {
      for (int i = 0; i < indexedParams.length; i++) {
        out.println("<li>" + indexedParams[i]);
      }
    }
%>
  </ul>
</ul>
```

In the final part of the script, multiple values are assigned to the same named parameter, `indexed`, using an HTML form. On `Submit`, the script calls itself:

```
<form action="indexedParameters.jsp" method="POST">
  <input type="hidden" name="indexed" value="1">
  <input type="hidden" name="indexed" value="2">
```

```
    <input type="hidden" name="indexed" value="3">
    <input type="submit">
</form>
</body>
</html>
```

Let's now consider what happens first time through the script. Try executing this file by accessing http://localhost:8080/ch05/jsp/indexedParamters.jsp. You should see this:

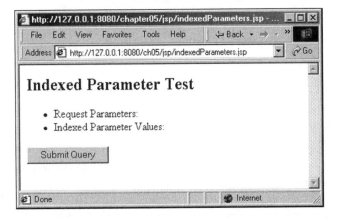

First time through the script, the `request` object (and therefore the `indexed` parameter too) is empty, so actually nothing is output to the browser. Eventually we reach the HTML form:

```
<form action="indexedParameters.jsp" method="POST">
  <input type="hidden" name="indexed" value="1">
  <input type="hidden" name="indexed" value="2">
  <input type="hidden" name="indexed" value="3">
  <input type="submit">
</form>
```

Here we see that the indexed parameter is filled with an array of values. The script calls itself when the user clicks on Submit Query, and we see the display as in the following screenshot:

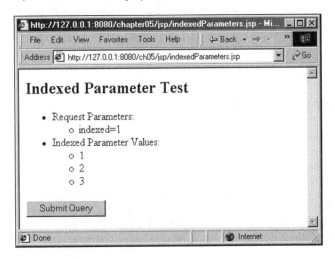

So what's happening here? This time through the script we encounter the
`request.getParameterNames()` method, which retrieves the names of the parameters present in the
request object. This time there is a parameter present – namely indexed. We then print out the name and
value of this parameter:

```
<%
   Enumeration params = request.getParameterNames();
   while (params.hasMoreElements()) {
     String paramName = (String) params.nextElement();
     String paramValue = request.getParameter(paramName);
%>
     <li><%= paramName%>=<%=paramValue%>
<%
   }
%>
```

You should note that even though the indexed parameter contains an array, the
`request.getParameter()` method returns just one value (the first member of the array), which is
subsequently printed out.

Next the JSP utilizes the `request.getParameterValues()` method to obtain the array of values for
indexed. The array values are then printed out to the browser:

```
String [] indexedParams = request.getParameterValues("indexed");
if (indexedParams != null) {
    for (int i = 0; i < indexedParams.length; i++) {
        out.println("<li>" + indexedParams[i]);
    }
}
```

Note that the recipient of the return value of the `getParameterValues()` method must be an array.

The example shows that only one parameter (indexed) is in the request, but this parameter actually
contains multiple values. In practice we should know which parameters are indexed and which parameters
are not indexed, and use the `getParameterValues()` or `getParameter()` methods appropriately.

Note that as of Servlet version 2.2, the value returned by `getParameter()` must always be equal to the first
value in the array of string values that `getParameterValues()` would have returned. Servlet engines that
do not fully support version 2.2 or 2.3 may not behave as expected – check the documentation for your
Servlet engine.

Using JSP and Beans

We will now revisit our Time Entry System that we have been building. This simplified system allows the
user to enter information (a charge record) for a project in order to charge their hours against it. The
information contains the user's name, the project name, the date, and the number of hours to charge.

In Chapter 3 we started with a Servlet design that utilized a Charge class to hold charge records. Problems with
that design included too much HTML embedded in the Servlet – difficult to maintain in the same code as
business logic. In Chapter 4, we redesigned it to utilize JSP. The HTML was easier to maintain but the scriptlet
code required to perform the business logic was at least as bad to maintain as the HTML in the Servlet.

In this chapter we will add beans to the JSP design. The result will eliminate a lot of scriptlet code – an improvement over the design in Chapter 4.

Integrating the Charge Bean

Here is our `Charge` bean, which is available in the Chapter 5 webapp `ch05.war`. When expanded, the file is in `ch05/WEB-INF/classes/com/wrox/projsp/time/beans/Charge.java`:

```java
package com.wrox.projsp.ch05.time.beans;

public class Charge implements java.io.Serializable {

  private String name;
  private String project;
  private String hours;
  private String date;

  public Charge() {}

  public void setName(String n) {
    name = n;
  }

  public String getName() {
    return name;
  }

  public String getProject() {
    return project;
  }
  public void setProject(String proj) {
    project = proj;
  }

  public String getHours() {
    return hours;
  }
  public void setHours(String h) {
    hours = h;
  }

  public String getDate() {
    return date;
  }
  public void setDate(String d) {
    date = d;
  }

}
```

The file from our design in Chapter 4 that deals with creating charge records is the `newRecord.jsp` file. We will try to remove as much Servlet code as possible and introduce our new beans tags into that file. It is available at `ch05/jsp/newRecord.jsp`:

```
<h3>Your Charge Record has been saved</h3>

<%@ page import="com.wrox.projsp.ch05.time.beans.Charge" %>
<%@ page import="java.util.Hashtable" %>

<jsp:useBean id="newCharge" class="com.wrox.projsp.ch05.time.beans.Charge" >
  <jsp:setProperty name="newCharge" property="*" />
</jsp:useBean>

<%
  Hashtable h = (Hashtable) session.getAttribute("charges");
  if (h == null) {
    h = new Hashtable();  // first charge
    session.setAttribute ("charges",  h);
  }
  String project = newCharge.getProject();
  h.put (newCharge.getProject(), newCharge);  // use project as the key
%>

Record Details: <p>
Name = <jsp:getProperty name="newCharge" property="name"/>,
Project = <jsp:getProperty name="newCharge" property="project"/>,
Hours = <jsp:getProperty name="newCharge" property="hours"/>,
Date = <jsp:getProperty name="newCharge" property="date"/>
```

Note the use of the `<jsp:useBean>` tag:

```
<jsp:useBean id="newCharge" class="com.wrox.projsp.ch05.time.beans.Charge" >
  <jsp:setProperty name="newCharge" property="*" />
</jsp:useBean>
```

Looking at the form in `enterRecord.jsp` that submits data to `newRecord.jsp`, we see the following parameters that will be extracted and used to set properties of the `newCharge` instance of the `Charge` bean:

```
<p>User Name<input type=text name=name>
<p>Project<input type=text name=project>
<p>Hours<input type=text name=hours>
<p>Date<input type=text name=date>
```

We replaced the scriptlet that instantiated a new object of `Charge` and set all of its properties with values from the request attributes with this straightforward tag. Here's the old scriptlet code that the `<jsp:useBean>` tag replaced:

```
String name = request.getParameter("name");
String project = request.getParameter("project");
String hours = request.getParameter("hours");
String date = request.getParameter("date");
Charge c = new Charge ();
c.setName(name);
c.setProject(project);
c.setHours(hours);
c.setDate(date);
```

We also replaced the following expressions:

```
Name = <%= name %>,
Project = <%= project %>,
Hours = <%= hours %>,
Date = <%=date %>
```

With the `<jsp:getProperty>` tags:

```
Name = <jsp:getProperty name="newCharge" property="name"/>,
Project = <jsp:getProperty name="newCharge" property="project"/>,
Hours = <jsp:getProperty name="newCharge" property="hours"/>,
Date = <jsp:getProperty name="newCharge" property="date"/>
```

This might not seem like a savings but consider that the tags allow the page designer to work entirely within the page scripting language and not intersperse references to scriptlet variables.

Note that once the `newCharge` object is created, it is available for access by other code within the page as shown here.

```
String project = newCharge.getProject();
h.put (newCharge.getProject(), newCharge);  // use project as the key
```

Once we have all the other JSP files from the Chapter 4 examples in our `ch05/jsp` directory, executing the http://localhost:8080/ch05/jsp/time.jsp URL, we get the following display:

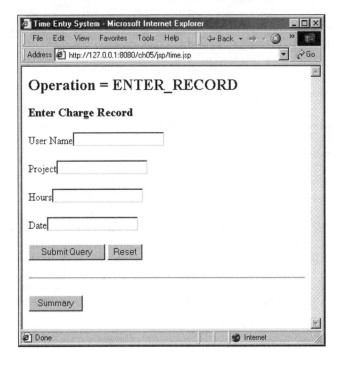

If we enter a record and submit, we are executing the `newRecord.jsp` file to pull the data off the form and save it into a `Charge` bean as shown in the following screenshot:

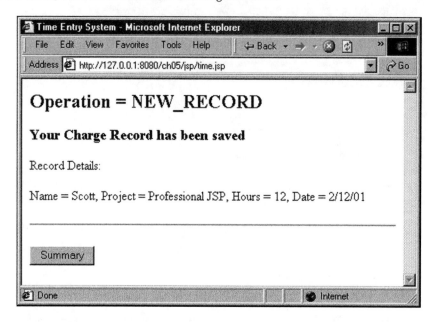

In summary, we have eliminated a substantial portion of the scriptlet code from the JSP file `newRecord.jsp`. It is now much easier to maintain.

We still have scriptlet code to manipulate the `Hashtable` object. When we discuss the use of custom tags in later chapters, we will be able to eliminate even that.

Summary

Summarizing the steps we have seen, we used built-in JSP tags to do the following, without any scriptlet code:

- ❏ Instantiate a bean
- ❏ Set properties in the bean from parameters in the request
- ❏ Get properties from the bean for display in an expression

Elimination of scriptlets from JSP files makes for better maintenance and allows the separation of tasks between programming (business logic to develop the beans) and page design (presentation code to use the bean resources in web pages).

However, we still have some messy scriptlet code that is required to provide control and sequencing. We will discuss how to eliminate that from our JSP files by combining JSP, beans, and Servlets in the next chapter.

6

Combining Servlets, JSP, and JavaBeans

As shown in Chapter 3, the use of Servlets allowed convenient management of events and program flow, but cumbersome ability to generate responses. Conversely in Chapter 4, the use of JSP provided excellent definition of response pages but gave maintenance concerns with scriptlets embedded in between HTML. Chapter 5 introduced beans as a way of eliminating some of that scriptlet code with easy yet powerful tags.

This chapter attempts to unite the three technologies (Servlets, JSP, and beans) by blending the best of all three approaches. This approach solves most of the above problems. When we add custom tags in later chapters, we will complete the picture.

In this chapter we will:

❑   Introduce the popular Model-View-Controller (MVC) architecture. In the development of Graphical User Interfaces, the MVC design pattern has emerged as a popular architecture for partitioning functionality.

❑   Explore the MVC architecture and apply it to our time entry system. This useful but limited example will also dramatize the importance of comprehensive frameworks such as Struts, which is discussed in depth in Chapter 21.

❑   Take a look at some advanced topics with Servlets and JSPs, such as HTTP Session Binding Events.

❑   Discuss some advanced techniques for combining Servlets and JSP, including the use of event listeners.

The Model View Controller Architecture

Originating with Smalltalk designs, the **MVC** pattern partitions functionality into three interacting components – the **Model**, the **View**, and the **Controller**. You may ask why do you care? Often it is not always apparent where in your design functionality should reside. For example, is a piece of functionality better served using a JSP, Servlet, or a bean? Writing out all of your HTML from a bean is surely not the appropriate solution, just as putting all your business logic in a JSP is not appropriate.

MVC is a design paradigm where each component easily and naturally maps to our three main implementation technologies – beans, JSP, and Servlets.

The Components of an MVC Architecture

At a simple level, the components of MVC architecture interact as shown below. The Model holds the data, the View retrieves the data and generates a dynamic display, and the Controller provides the logic processing layer and delegation to the Model and View:

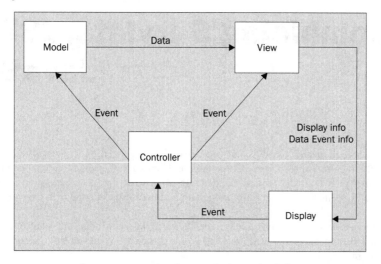

Tying the picture to our implementation technologies results in the following architecture:

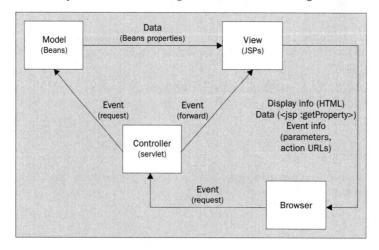

Let's now look at each of the major components of the MVC design pattern in turn. We'll look at what the component provides, and how it can be organized.

The Model

The Model represents the business logic of an application. Encapsulating business rules into components facilitates testing, improves quality, and promotes reuse.

The Model can be further partitioned into **State** and **Action** components.

State Components

The State defines the current set of values of the Model and includes methods to change those values. These methods are where some of the business logic is captured.

> **The State components are usually protocol independent. JavaBeans are a logical choice for implementing the State components.**

The reusable nature of beans allows for the somewhat independent construction of the State components. As far as being protocol independent, State components should be isolated enough so they can be accessed by applications that use HTTP, RMI, etc., that is, the protocol would be another layer on top of the component. Their construction should take into account current requirements and consider future growth and evolution. This independent construction facilitates sound design in these ways:

❑ **Reuse**
Elimination of presentation logic allows different applications (for different audiences or using different technology) to make use of the same business logic.

❑ **Quality**
By putting the business logic in one place, it can be reviewed and tested more thoroughly. Contrast this approach with the cost and less stringent test coverage if the business logic were embedded in each application that needs it.

❑ **Robustness**
The business logic is more easily enforced. Encapsulating the logic in one place can encourage its reuse, reducing room for errors to creep into the logic. For example, if every designer of a series of related applications (say time entry, expense reports, project budget requests, and salary planning) used the same `Approval` bean to route cost-related items (such as a time sheet charges to project budgets, expense reports for business trips, funding requests for pilot projects, and raise requests), the same business logic would be enforced across the entire suite of applications.

Action Components

The Actions define the allowable changes to the State in response to events. Business logic also dictates the construction of Action components.

In implementing the Action components, the choices get more complex. In simple systems, the Actions may actually get absorbed into the Controller, but this is generally not recommended. Typically a layer of Action beans is created to capture the requirements that govern interaction with the State components. As far as our time entry system, the 'Summary' action represents an example of an Action component.

Often Action components must be aware of the protocol in order to obtain information about the event. This is a dangerous situation, as it ties business logic to a specific protocol, limiting potential reuse.

Some simple rules of thumb are helpful when constructing your Action components. Adapt and add to this list for your particular set of requirements:

❑ Take a passive approach to Action components, only handling what each absolutely needs to handle. Create more State components if you need them. The Controller will manage all events and invoke the appropriate calls to Action methods.

❑ Partition the business logic to keep it separate from the implementation protocol (ideally in separate beans). As this book is focused on the HTTP browser based protocols, consider partitioning the use of resources from `javax.servlet.*` and `javax.servlet.http.*` packages into a separate layer from business rules (say, via an adapter design pattern). This allows the business rules to be reused in other architectures such as a GUI based and non-servlet architectures such as RMI or CORBA.

The View

The View represents the presentation logic of an application. The View components obtain the current state of the system from the Model and provide the user interface for the specific protocol involved. For the focus of this book, the protocol we are interested in is HTTP browser based systems.

As part of the generation of the user interface, the View is responsible for presenting the specific set of events that the user may enact at any given moment.

> **Separating the View from the Model enables the independent construction of user interfaces with different look and feel attributes. These different interfaces can all interact with the same Model. JSPs are a natural choice for implementing the View.**

As we have seen, JSPs are a convenient choice for generating HTTP browser based user interfaces. Interaction with the Model (beans) is easy via the built-in beans tags.

The Controller

The Controller provides the glue to the MVC architecture. It is responsible for receiving events, determining the appropriate handler, invoking the handler, and finally triggering the generation of the appropriate response.

> **With the full power of Java available to us, Servlets are an ideal selection for a Controller technology.**

In an MVC architecture, the Controller (servlet) acts as a dispatcher. This presents some challenges that must be addressed. Specifically, the controller must handle the following tasks:

❑ **Security**
Perform security related tasks such as ensuring authentication (you are who you say you are) and authorization (you are allowed to trigger this event). Some or all of these tasks might be delegated to the Servlet engine. We will defer a discussion of security until Chapter 16.

- ❏ **Event Identification**
  Identify the specific event that is to be executed. This can be as simple as through the use of a common parameter in the request or part of the request URL itself.

- ❏ **Prepare the Model**
  Ensure the availability of required Model components such as the instantiation of required JavaBeans.

- ❏ **Process the Event**
  Map the request to an appropriate event handler and invoke it. This may be implemented with a table lookup or with more advanced techniques.

- ❏ **Handle Errors**
  Handle any errors generated by the handler. This may be achieved through the use of exception handlers. The Controller can then forward control to an Error Page, as we have seen in previous chapters.

- ❏ **Trigger the Response**
  Forward control to the response generator. Typically this is implemented by invoking the `RequestDispatcher.forward()` method to pass control to a JSP.

Design Issues

Implementing MVC with Servlets, JSP, and beans introduces several technical and logistical hurdles. Ideally, we would like to reduce coupling between the components. Where we cannot reduce it, we would like to implement it in such a way as to remove any pain associated with the coupling.

For example, the View must provide event information to the display in such a manner as to allow the event generated by the display (say, a button push) to be uniquely identified by the Controller. The Controller must then decide on the appropriate handler and response generator for the event.

Thus the View is coupled to the Controller by the event information, and the Controller is coupled to both the Model (the Action components) and the View by the same information.

We can overcome most of the pain associated with this coupling through the use of an initialization file, by employing Java's built-in class mechanisms, Java's reflection capabilities, or some combination of the three. We will see an example of this strategy in the next section.

As you will see, through the use of these techniques, the Controller can become very efficient and elegant.

An Example of MVC

Returning to our time entry system from previous chapters, we will now apply the design principles of MVC. Our directory structure for this example will be as follows, all under `<webapps>`:

- ❏ HTML
  `ch06\`

- ❏ JSPs
  `ch06\jsp\`

- ❏ `web.xml`
  `ch06\WEB-INF\`

❑   Properties file
    ch06\WEB-INF\classes\

❑   Controller
    ch06\WEB-INF\classes\com\wrox\projsp\ch06\

❑   Event Handlers
    ch06\WEB-INF\classes\com\wrox\projsp\ch06\event

❑   Beans
    ch06\WEB-INF\classes\com\wrox\projsp\ch06\time\beans

The Controller

The Controller will be implemented as a Servlet. The `init()` method will be used to establish any configuration information needed to process requests. The `doGet()` method will call `doPost()`, so either HTTP method will produce the same response.

Design Overview

As discussed above, the Controller must employ an efficient technique to decouple itself and the rest of the system from the event identification and management. There are a variety of methods to use here, ranging from a simple table driven approach to quite complex techniques. For our example, we will choose something in the middle. The architecture is shown below:

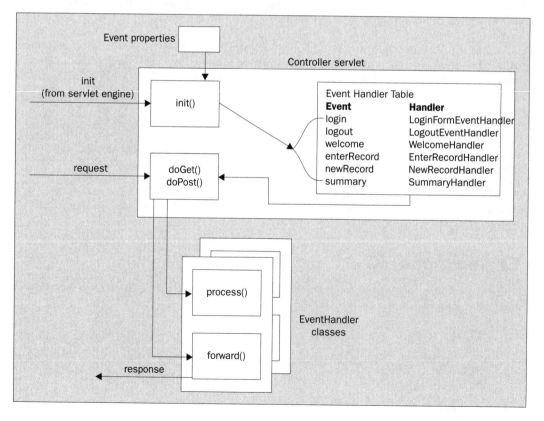

In our design we utilize a HashMap to hold all known event names (the key) and the associated handler class (the event). Each handler class must implement a process() and forward() method. We will revisit these methods when we discuss the Model in detail. For now we only need to know the following:

- The process() method takes a request and response parameter (of type HttpServletRequest and HttpServletResponse) and handles the event

- The forward() method takes a request and response parameter and produces the response

The Controller Class

The complete source code for our Controller example is shown here. Notice how little coupling there is with the other components of the system:

```
package com.wrox.projsp.ch06;

import com.wrox.projsp.ch06.Constants;
import com.wrox.projsp.ch06.event.EventHandlerBase;
import com.wrox.projsp.ch06.event.UnknownEventHandler;

import java.io.IOException;

import java.util.Enumeration;
import java.util.HashMap;
import java.util.ResourceBundle;

import javax.servlet.ServletContext;
import javax.servlet.ServletException;

import javax.servlet.http.HttpServlet;
import javax.servlet.http.HttpServletRequest;
import javax.servlet.http.HttpServletResponse;
import javax.servlet.http.HttpSession;

public class Controller extends HttpServlet {
```

The HashMap events is used to hold the event definitions:

```
protected HashMap events = new HashMap();
```

As shown in the above picture, the init() method reads the events from a properties file and inserts them into the event handler table. An event definition consists of an event name and the corresponding handler class:

```
public void init() throws ServletException {

  Debug.init();
```

The Event.properties file is read to determine the events that can be processed. This file is described after the source code:

```
      // get the event values and save them into events
      ResourceBundle bundle = ResourceBundle.getBundle("Event");

      Enumeration e = bundle.getKeys();
      while(e.hasMoreElements()) {
        String key = (String) e.nextElement();
        String value = bundle.getString(key);
```

It is worth taking a more detailed look at the mapping of an event to its associated handler class. Within the init() method of our example, we use the java.lang.Class class. Class has a forName() method that allows you to specify a class name. Then you can use the newInstance() method to instantiate a new object of the supplied class name. The newInstance() method assumes the existence of a no-argument constructor. The event object is then stored in the events HashMap, to be used during the processing of actions.

```
      try {
        EventHandlerBase event =
          (EventHandlerBase) Class.forName(value).newInstance();
        events.put(key, event);
        Debug.log this, "init", "event:" + key +
                          ", handler: " + event.getClass().getName());
      } catch(Exception exc) {
        Debug.log(this, "init", "event:" + key +
                          ", NO HANDLER FOUND! " + value);
      }
    }

    Enumeration servletParams = this.getInitParameterNames();
    while(servletParams.hasMoreElements()) {
      String sName = (String) servletParams.nextElement();
      String sValue = this.getInitParameter(sName);
      Debug.log(this, "init", "servlet param name: " + sName +
                  ", value:" + sValue);
    }

    ServletContext sc = getServletContext();
    Enumeration webappParams = sc.getInitParameterNames();
    while(webappParams.hasMoreElements()) {
      String wName = (String) webappParams.nextElement();
      String wValue = sc.getInitParameter(wName);
      Debug.log(this, "init", "webapp param name: " + wName +
                  ", value:" + wValue);
    }
  }
```

As mentioned earlier, doGet() simply calls doPost(), providing identical behavior for either HTTP method:

```
  public void doGet(HttpServletRequest request,
                    HttpServletResponse response)
                    throws ServletException, IOException {
    doPost(request, response);
  }
```

When a request is received, `doPost()` must determine the type of event and then extract the handler from the event handler table. Error checking must be performed (by the `validateEvent()` method) so an illegal or unknown event can be trapped and dealt with (usually with an error message):

```
public void doPost(HttpServletRequest request,
                   HttpServletResponse response)
                   throws ServletException, IOException {

  Debug.log(this, "doPost", "new request");

  String event = validateEvent(request);
```

Map the event to the appropriate handler and response generator (JSP). Note that this step is discussed in more detail in the next section:

```
EventHandlerBase handler = getEventHandler(event);
```

Once the handler is known, its `process()` method is called with the `request` and `response` parameters received by `doGet()` or `doPost()`:

```
try {
  handler.process(getServletContext(), request, response);
```

Any exceptions generated are caught and set an error message. Change the handler to the error handler for ERROR_EVENT:

```
} catch(Exception e) {
  request.setAttribute("error", e);
  handler = getEventHandler(Constants.ERROR_EVENT);
}
```

Once `process()` returns, the `forward()` method of the handler is called. At this point, control does not return to the Controller for this request, as the `forward()` method actually performs a `RequestDispatcher.forward()` operation:

```
  handler.forward(request, response);
}
```

The `validateEvent()` method, shown below, checks to see if a valid class has been mapped for this event, and returns the name of the class. If the event is not found, the UNKNOWN_EVENT string is returned:

```
protected String validateEvent(HttpServletRequest request) {
  String e = request.getParameter(Constants.EVENT);
  if (e == null || !events.containsKey(e)) {
    e = Constants.UNKNOWN_EVENT;
  }
  Debug.log(this, "validateEvent", "event=" + e);
  return e;
}
```

The event name e was passed into getEventHandler method and used to obtain the associated handler class via the HashMap events (with the code events.get(e)). Notice that if the runtime environment cannot find the class name, it throws an exception. The exception is caught and the UnknownEventHandler is substituted to process the event:

```
protected EventHandlerBase getEventHandler(String e) {
  EventHandlerBase h;
  try {
    h = (EventHandlerBase) events.get(e);
  } catch(Exception exc) {
    h = (EventHandlerBase) events.get(Constants.UNKNOWN_EVENT);
  }
  Debug.log(this, "getEventHandler",
            "handler=" + h.getClass().getName());
  return h;
}

}
```

Also notice the use of a Debug class for logging information. Consider building something like this in from the start to assist with the debugging process. Even if you have an interactive development environment (IDE) with a debugger, in a production system debuggers are typically not an option. Building in a flexible logging system can help in all phases of the project.

The Event.properties File

The Event.properties file is shown here:

```
LOGIN=com.wrox.projsp.ch06.event.LoginEventHandler
WELCOME=com.wrox.projsp.ch06.event.WelcomeHandler
LOGOUT=com.wrox.projsp.ch06.event.LogoutEventHandler
ENTER_RECORD=com.wrox.projsp.ch06.event.EnterRecordHandler
NEW_RECORD=com.wrox.projsp.ch06.event.NewRecordHandler
SUMMARY=com.wrox.projsp.ch06.event.SummaryHandler
ERROR_EVENT=com.wrox.projsp.ch06.event.ErrorEventHandler
UNKNOWN_EVENT=com.wrox.projsp.ch06.event.UnknownEventHandler
```

The Model

As relating to our time entry system, the business logic is contained in two different places. The events dispatched by the Controller are the Action components while the Charge bean is an example of a State component. Let us first examine the Actions.

Action Components

As described in the Controller architecture above, each event will have a handler class that implements the process() and forward() method. We decided that each handler class must extend the EventHandlerBase class, which defines a default process() and forward() method.

We chose a subclass approach versus an interface because we could provide a default implementation in the parent class. This allows the simplification of some subclasses by allowing methods to be defined in the parent and overridden only if necessary.

The EventHandlerBase Class

The `EventHandlerBase` class is responsible for the following processing:

- Implementing the `process()` method
- Defining the URL to forward control to
- Implementing the `forward()` method

The complete code for `EventHandlerBase` is shown below:

```
package com.wrox.projsp.ch06.event;

import com.wrox.projsp.ch06.Debug;

import java.io.IOException;

import javax.servlet.RequestDispatcher;
import javax.servlet.ServletContext;
import javax.servlet.ServletException;

import javax.servlet.http.HttpServletRequest;
import javax.servlet.http.HttpServletResponse;

public abstract class EventHandlerBase {
```

We use an abstract method that must be overridden. This allows the `forward()` method (and friends) to be more generic:

```
    protected abstract String getURL();
```

The `process()` method processes the request and updates the Model. Note that if any processing is required, the specific handler will override this method. Not all events will require processing – some will only require the generation of a response (such as displaying a form for data entry). In those cases, this method does not have to be overridden:

```
    public void process(HttpServletRequest request,
                        HttpServletResponse response)
                        throws IOException, ServletException {

      Debug.log(this, "process", "Using default process");
    }
```

The `forward()` method passes control to a JSP file to generate the response:

```
    public void forward(HttpServletRequest request,
                        HttpServletResponse response)
              throws IOException, ServletException {

      Debug.log(this, "forward", "Using default forward");
      dispatch(request, response);
    }
```

Note the use of the `RequestDispatcher` and the `getURL()` method in `dispatch()`. Breaking the `dispatch()` method off separately allows designers to focus on the business logic that `forward()` might have to perform. In addition, the `dispatch()` method shouldn't have to change at all. Making it separate removes any cut and paste errors that might occur if one had to preserve its functionality in an overridden `forward()` method:

```
protected void _dispatch(HttpServletRequest request,
                         HttpServletResponse response)
         throws IOException, ServletException {

  Debug.log(this, "_dispatch", "redirecting to " + getURL());

  RequestDispatcher rd = request.getRequestDispatcher(getURL());
  if(rd == null) {
    Debug.log(this, "_dispatch", "rd = null!");
  }
  rd.forward(request, response);
 }
}
```

The LogoutEventHandler Class

Now let's look at an example subclass. The code for the `LogoutEventHandler` is shown below:

```
package com.wrox.projsp.ch06.event;

import com.wrox.projsp.ch06.Debug;

import java.io.IOException;
import java.util.ResourceBundle;

import javax.servlet.RequestDispatcher;
import javax.servlet.ServletContext;
import javax.servlet.ServletException;

import javax.servlet.http.HttpServletRequest;
import javax.servlet.http.HttpServletResponse;
import javax.servlet.http.HttpSession;

public class LogoutEventHandler extends EventHandlerBase {
```

Note the `bundle` object used below. This is used in all of the `EventHandlerBase` objects, to avoid hard coding the value of the URL into this class. The `URL.properties` file is shown at the end of this section:

```
  private ResourceBundle bundle = ResourceBundle.getBundle("URL");

  protected String getURL () {
    return bundle.getString("LOGOUT");
  }

  public void forward (HttpServletRequest request,
                       HttpServletResponse response)
    throws IOException, ServletException {
```

```
      Debug.log (this, "forward", "invalidating session");

      HttpSession session = request.getSession();
      session.invalidate();
      super._dispatch (request, response);
   }
}
```

Notice how only the `getURL()` and `forward()` methods are overridden.

The NewRecordHandler Class

Let's look at another example. The `NewRecordHandler` contains specific business rules in the `process()` method and actually throws an exception if it uncovers a problem. Remember the `controller` will handle the exception and pass control to an error event handler, not back to the `forward()` method of the handler that generated the error.

```
package com.wrox.projsp.ch06.event;

import com.wrox.projsp.ch06.Debug;

import java.io.IOException;
import java.util.ResourceBundle;

import javax.servlet.ServletException;
import javax.servlet.ServletContext;
import javax.servlet.http.HttpServletRequest;
import javax.servlet.http.HttpServletResponse;

public class NewRecordHandler extends EventHandlerBase {

  private ResourceBundle bundle = ResourceBundle.getBundle("URL");

  protected String getURL () {
    return bundle.getString("NEW_RECORD");
  }

  public void process (ServletContext sc, HttpServletRequest request,
                       HttpServletResponse response)
                       throws IOException, ServletException {
    String project = request.getParameter("project");
    if (project.equals("")) {
      throw new IOException("Project must not be empty!");
    }
    String hours = request.getParameter("hours");
    try {
      Integer.parseInt(hours);
    } catch (NumberFormatException e) {
      e.printStackTrace();
      throw new IOException("Hours must be an Integer! hours = " + hours);
    }
    Debug.log (this, "process", "");
  }
}
```

Notice that business logic is represented in the protocol specific (that is, HTTP aware) `process()` and `forward()` methods. If your project has the potential for expanding to different audiences or architectures (especially non-HTTP architectures such as RMI, CORBA, or a messaging architecture), consider building another protocol independent layer that these methods can call. The protocol independent layer would capture the business logic in a reusable way.

The EnterRecordHandler Class

All the remaining event handlers follow a similar pattern to the `EnterRecordHandler` class, by retrieving the appropriate URL via the `bundle` object:

```
package com.wrox.projsp.ch06.event;

import java.util.ResourceBundle;
import javax.servlet.http.HttpServletRequest;

public class EnterRecordHandler extends EventHandlerBase {

  private ResourceBundle bundle = ResourceBundle.getBundle("URL");

  protected String getURL () {
    return bundle.getString("ENTER_RECORD");
  }
}
```

The ErrorEventHandler Class

```
package com.wrox.projsp.ch06.event;

import java.util.ResourceBundle;
import javax.servlet.http.HttpServletRequest;

public class ErrorEventHandler extends EventHandlerBase {

  private ResourceBundle bundle = ResourceBundle.getBundle("URL");

  protected String getURL () {
    return bundle.getString("ERROR_EVENT");
  }
}
```

The LoginEventHandler Class

```
package com.wrox.projsp.ch06.event;

import java.util.ResourceBundle;
import javax.servlet.http.HttpServletRequest;

public class LoginEventHandler extends EventHandlerBase {

  private ResourceBundle bundle = ResourceBundle.getBundle("URL");

  protected String getURL () {
    return bundle.getString("LOGIN");
  }
}
```

The SummaryHandler Class

```
package com.wrox.projsp.ch06.event;

import java.util.ResourceBundle;
import javax.servlet.http.HttpServletRequest;

public class SummaryHandler extends EventHandlerBase {

  private ResourceBundle bundle = ResourceBundle.getBundle("URL");

  protected String getURL () {
    return bundle.getString("SUMMARY");
  }
}
```

The UnknownEventHandler Class

```
package com.wrox.projsp.ch06.event;

import java.util.ResourceBundle;
import javax.servlet.http.HttpServletRequest;

public class UnknownEventHandler extends EventHandlerBase {

  private ResourceBundle bundle = ResourceBundle.getBundle("URL");

  protected String getURL () {
    return bundle.getString("UNKNOWN_EVENT");
  }
}
```

The WelcomeHandler Class

```
package com.wrox.projsp.ch06.event;

import java.util.ResourceBundle;
import javax.servlet.http.HttpServletRequest;

public class WelcomeHandler extends EventHandlerBase {

  private ResourceBundle bundle = ResourceBundle.getBundle("URL");

  protected String getURL () {
    return bundle.getString("WELCOME");
  }
}
```

The URL.properties File

All of the above event handlers use the following properties file to retrieved the corresponding URL to forward to:

```
LOGIN=/jsp/welcome.jsp
LOGOUT=/jsp/logout.jsp
ERROR_EVENT=/jsp/errorEvent.jsp
```

```
UNKNOWN_EVENT=/jsp/unknown.jsp
WELCOME=/jsp/welcome.jsp
ENTER_RECORD=/jsp/enterRecord.jsp
NEW_RECORD=/jsp/newRecord.jsp
SUMMARY=/jsp/summary.jsp
```

State Components

As discussed previously, JavaBeans technology is an excellent choice for the implementation of State components of the Model. In previous chapters, we already introduced the Charge bean for holding the attributes of a charge for a time sheet. The code is repeated here for clarity:

```java
package com.wrox.projsp.ch06.time.beans;

public class Charge implements java.io.Serializable {

    private String name;
    private String project;
    private String hours;
    private String date;

    public Charge() {
    }

    public void setName (String n) {
        name = n;
    }
    public String getName () {
        return name;
    }

    public String getProject () {
        return project;
    }
    public void setProject (String proj) {
        project = proj;
    }

    public String getHours () {
        return hours;
    }
    public void setHours (String h) {
        hours = h;
    }

    public String getDate () {
        return date;
    }
    public void setDate (String d) {
        date = d;
    }

}
```

The View

The View is easily represented by JSPs. The JSP files we introduced in previous sections are easily modified to work with the Controller. In most cases, we just needed to remove scriptlet code that the Controller is performing.

We also introduce a slight improvement in the user interface. The `time.html` file defines two frames – the top frame for the available options, and the bottom frame for the results:

```
<html>
<frameset frameborder=0 framespacing=0 border=0 rows=100,*>
    <frame name=top src=top.html scrolling=no marginheight=0 marginwidth=0>
    <frame name=bottom src=controller?event=WELCOME>
</frameset>
</html>
```

Notice how the URL for the bottom frame is `controller` (which is mapped to our `Controller.java` Servlet in the `web.xml` file):

```
<servlet>
    <servlet-name>Controller</servlet-name>
    <servlet-class>com.wrox.projsp.ch06.Controller</servlet-class>
</servlet>
<servlet-mapping>
    <servlet-name>Controller</servlet-name>
    <url-pattern>/controller</url-pattern>
</servlet-mapping>
```

The `event` parameter is set to `WELCOME`.

So when `time.html` is requested, thus the `controller` will map the `WELCOME` event to its appropriate handler and the response will go in the bottom frame.

The top frame is implemented by `top.html`:

```
<html>
<center>
<table width="50%">
<tr>
<td><a href="controller?event=WELCOME" target=bottom>WELCOME</a></td>
<td><a href="controller?event=ENTER_RECORD" target=bottom>ENTER RECORD</a></td>
<td><a href="controller?event=SUMMARY" target=bottom>SUMMARY</a></td>
<td><a href="controller?event=LOGOUT" target=bottom>LOGOUT</a></td>
</tr>
</table>
</center>
</html>
```

Notice how the `<a>` tags reference `controller` and set the appropriate `event` parameter.

The newRecord.JSP

The various JSP files invoked by the handlers are similar to ones we saw in previous chapters. Here is a typical example, the `newRecord.jsp` file:

```
<%@ page import="com.wrox.projsp.ch06.time.beans.Charge" %>
<%@ page import="java.util.Hashtable" %>

<jsp:useBean id="newCharge" class="com.wrox.projsp.ch06.time.beans.Charge" >
  <jsp:setProperty name="newCharge" property="*" />
</jsp:useBean>

<html>
<center>
<h3>Your Charge Record has been saved</h3>


<%
  Hashtable h = (Hashtable) session.getAttribute("charges");
  if (h == null) {
    h = new Hashtable();  // first charge
  }

  h.put (newCharge.getProject(), newCharge);  // use project as the key

  session.setAttribute ("charges", h);
%>

Record Details: <p>
Name = <%= newCharge.getName() %>, Project = <%= newCharge.getProject() %>,
Hours = <%= newCharge.getHours() %>, Date = <%= newCharge.getDate() %>

</center>
</html>
```

The enterRecord.JSP

The enterRecord.jsp file has a small change to make the input fields aligned in a table:

```
<html>
<form>
<center>
<h3>Enter Charge Record</h3>
<table>
<tr><td>User Name</td><td><input type=text name=name></td></tr>
<tr><td>Project</td><td><input type=text name=project></td></tr>
<tr><td>Hours</td><td><input type=text name=hours></td></tr>
<tr><td>Date</td><td><input type=text name=date></td></tr>
</table>
<input type=hidden name=event value=NEW_RECORD>
<p><input type=submit>
<input type=reset>
</center>
</form>
</html>
```

The errorEvent.JSP

The errorEvent.jsp file is called to display any errors encountered in the processing of the data (for example when an empty Project is entered). It retrieves the java.lang.Exception from the request object:

```
<html>
<center>
<h1>Error processing event:</h1>
<br>Error was: <%= request.getAttribute("error") %></br>
</center>
</html>
```

The logout.JSP

The `logout.jsp` file defines the html displayed after a user has logged out:

```
<html>
<center>
<h3>You have logged out.</h3>
</center>
</html>
```

The summary.JSP

The `summary.jsp` file survives fairly intact:

```
<%@ page import="com.wrox.projsp.ch06.time.beans.Charge" %>
<%@ page import="java.util.Enumeration" %>
<%@ page import="java.util.Hashtable" %>
<html>
<center>
<h3>Summary of your Charge Records</h3>

<%
  Hashtable h = (Hashtable) session.getAttribute("charges");
  if (h != null) {
%>
    <ul>

<%
    Enumeration charges = h.keys();
    while (charges.hasMoreElements()) {
      String proj = (String) charges.nextElement();
      Charge ch = (Charge) h.get(proj);
%>
      <li>
      name = <%= ch.getName() %>
      , project = <%= proj %>
      , hours = <%= ch.getHours() %>
      , date = <%= ch.getDate() %>
<%
    }
  }
%>
    </ul>
</center>
</html>
```

The unknown.JSP

The `unknown.jsp` file is returned invoked when the `Controller` cannot find a matching event:

```
<html>
<center>
```

```
<h1>Unknown Action</h1>
<br>Action was: <%= request.getParameter("event") %></br>
</center>
</html>
```

The welcome.JSP

The welcome.jsp file is displayed when the user first logs into the system:

```
<html>
<center>
<h3>Welcome!</h3>
</center>
</html>
```

Execution

If we execute http://localhost:8080/ch06, you should see the following display:

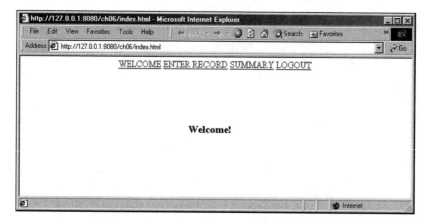

Selecting the **ENTER RECORD** link should result in the familiar charge record entry screen:

Now let's test our error handling capabilities. Enter a non-numeric value in the Hours field and submit the query. The result is the invocation of the `ErrorEventHandler`, which produces this screen:

The business logic for Summary is similar to what we saw in previous chapters.

The MVC Example: An Overview

This chapter ties together some design concepts into a solid architecture. The pros of this architecture include:

❑ **Loose Coupling**
The various design components interact with each other in flexible ways that don't impose maintenance problems.

❑ **Parallel Development**
New functionality can easily be partitioned to the different components and divided amongst different developers.

❑ **Excellent Scalability**
Since the Servlet engine spawns a new thread for each different request, the Controller can handle a substantial load (of course, for very heavy traffic, multiple servers will likely be involved which introduces a new set of problems). Threading or other asynchronous behavior can be introduced in the Model as appropriate.

❑ **Reusability**
The Controller can be a foundation for many different applications with little or no changes. Portions of the Model can be reused.

However, this architecture is not without its limitations. Some functional areas that are not supported include:

❑ **Forms Management and Internationalization**
Many applications will need to support internationalization. Virtually all HTTP based applications will have to deal with form data. Validation of form data, and preservation of that data for error screens are two of the main tasks that deal with form data. Frameworks such as Struts support internationalization and forms conveniently and easily.

217

❏ **Advanced User Interface Concepts**
Our architecture is very monolithic – one event, one event handler. If we try to introduce something like a Wizard to the design, where there are multiple requests to implement a function such as setting up a new account, our design will quickly get cumbersome. One quick solution to this would be to introduce the concept of dependencies between events, where one event could not be executed if the user had not already completed a dependent event. Some glue code (such as a bean) could be then used to make the handlers work together.

❏ **JSP files still include Scriptlets**
Notice how we still have some scriptlet code embedded in the JSP files. Available custom tag libraries provide support for many common tasks that designers must perform in JSP files.

Hopefully this example has provided you with a good foundation for simple applications, and a motivation to learn a more complete framework such as Struts for advanced applications.

HTTP Session Binding Events

Let's finish off the chapter by looking at one final, advanced topic: HTTP session binding events. These have long been part of the Servlet specification, and can enable highly dynamic applications. As the name implies, HTTP session binding events are points in time when something (an object) becomes bound or unbound to an HTTP session. Essentially, this amounts to the following triggers:

❏ `HttpSession.setAttribute()` – an object is bound to a session

❏ `HttpSession.removeAttribute()` – an object is unbound from a session

This event mechanism mimics other event mechanisms in Java. Two major objects are involved:

❏ `HttpSessionBindingEvent` – the event itself

❏ `HttpSessionBindingListener` – listener of the event (an interface)

However, the `HttpSessionBindingListener` interface works a little differently from other event mechanisms in Java. There are no `addListener()` or `removeListener()` methods. Instead, `HttpSessionBindingListeners` are added implicitly when bound to an `HttpSession` object via the `setAttribute()` method.

The listener needs to implement the following methods from the interface:

❏ `valueBound(HttpSessionBindingEvent event)` – the method that is called when an object is bound to a session (via `setAttribute()`).

❏ `valueUnbound(HttpSessionBindingEvent event)` – the method that is called when an object is unbound (removed) from a session. Note that an object is unbound via `removeAttribute()`, when a session is invalidated or session times out (via `session.invalidate()`).

The `HttpSessionBindingEvent` object defines the following methods:

❏ `getName()` – returns the name of the object (the name that was supplied in the `setAttribute()` call)

❑   getValue() – returns the actual object

❑   getSession() – returns the corresponding session object

If we remember the Servlet engine controlling the environment, these events are easier to visualize. Consider the following picture where a Servlet or JSP is setting, getting, and removing attributes. The events are generated as shown in the following diagram:

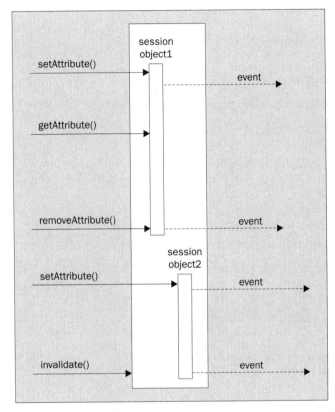

Let's discuss the removeAttribute() method. Notice how the event is generated before the object is unbound. This sequencing is vital and allows the event to identify the object that was removed.

Also notice that if the entire session is invalidated, any existing objects still bound to the session are unbound. Again, the binding event is generated before the object is unbound.

Now let's look at an example.

Extending the MVC Example

In our time entry system, we utilized a Hashtable stored in the session to represent all charge records entered by the user. Let's extend the functionality of the Hashtable to implement the listener. Our new class will need to implement the valueBound() and valueUnbound() methods.

When a new object is bound to the session we will read a serialized object from the file system and populate the Hashtable with it. When the object is unbound from the session, we will write the serialized object to the file system. Thus we will provide persistence in between sessions.

Add the following class to your `<webapps>\ch06\WEB-INF\classes\com\wrox\projsp\time\` directory.

The TimeHashtable Class

Here is the new `TimeHashTable` that implements the listener functionality. Note how the reading of the charges file (in `valueBound()`) and writing of the charges file (in `valueUnbound()`) achieves the persistence that we are looking for:

```
package com.wrox.projsp.ch06.time;

import java.util.Hashtable;
import java.io.*;
import javax.servlet.http.HttpSessionBindingListener;
import javax.servlet.http.HttpSessionBindingEvent;

public class TimeHashtable extends Hashtable
             implements HttpSessionBindingListener, Serializable {

  private String path;

  public TimeHashtable(String path) {
    this.path = path;
  }

  public void valueBound(HttpSessionBindingEvent event) {
    try {
      File file = new File(path);
      if (file.exists()) {
        FileInputStream in = new FileInputStream(path);
        ObjectInputStream s = new ObjectInputStream(in);
        TimeHashtable t = (TimeHashtable)s.readObject();
        this.putAll(t);
      }
    } catch (Exception e) {
      e.printStackTrace();
    }
  }

  public void valueUnbound(HttpSessionBindingEvent event) {
    try {
      FileOutputStream out = new FileOutputStream(path);
      ObjectOutputStream s = new ObjectOutputStream(out);
      s.writeObject(this);
      s.flush();
      s.close();
      out.close();
    } catch (Exception e) {
      e.printStackTrace();
    }
  }

}
```

Now all we have to do is replace our existing references to `Hashtable` with `TimeHashtable` and we will get this persistence functionality.

The URL.properties File

A couple of JSP files must be modified to incorporate the TimeHashtable object. As such, new JSP files are created, and update your URL.properties file as below:

```
LOGIN=/jsp/welcome.jsp
LOGOUT=/jsp/logout.jsp
ERROR_EVENT=/jsp/errorEvent.jsp
UNKNOWN_EVENT=/jsp/unknown.jsp
WELCOME=/jsp/welcome.jsp
ENTER_RECORD=/jsp/enterRecord.jsp
NEW_RECORD=/jsp/newRecordBind.jsp
SUMMARY=/jsp/summaryBind.jsp
```

The newRecordBind JSP

The file newRecordBind.jsp is slightly different from the newRecord.jsp file shown earlier. Instead of a Hashtable, the TimeHashtable object is used. TimeHashtable is instantiated with a filename to save and restore the TimeHashtable from. It also sets the attribute in the session if it doesn't already exist there:

```jsp
<%@ page import="com.wrox.projsp.ch06.time.beans.Charge" %>
<%@ page import="com.wrox.projsp.ch06.time.TimeHashtable" %>

<jsp:useBean id="newCharge" class="com.wrox.projsp.time.beans.Charge" >
  <jsp:setProperty name="newCharge" property="*" />
</jsp:useBean>

<html>
<center>
<h3>Your Charge Record has been saved</h3>

<%
  TimeHashtable h = (TimeHashtable) session.getAttribute("charges");
  if (h == null) {
    ServletContext context = config.getServletContext();
    h = new TimeHashtable(context.getRealPath("charges.bin")); //first
    session.setAttribute ("charges", h);
  }

  h.put(newCharge.getProject(), newCharge);  // use project as the key
%>

Record Details: <p>
Name = <%= newCharge.getName() %>, Project = <%= newCharge.getProject() %>, Hours
= <%= newCharge.getHours() %>, Date = <%= newCharge.getDate() %>

</center>
</html>
```

The summaryBind JSP

The file summaryBind.jsp performs the same operations relative to TimeHashtable:

```jsp
<%@ page import="com.wrox.projsp.ch06.time.beans.Charge" %>
<%@ page import="com.wrox.projsp.ch06.time.TimeHashtable" %>
<%@ page import="java.util.Enumeration" %>
<html>
<center>
<h3>Summary of your Charge Records</h3>
```

```jsp
<%
  TimeHashtable h = (TimeHashtable) session.getAttribute("charges");
  if (h == null) {
    ServletContext context = config.getServletContext();
    h = new TimeHashtable(context.getRealPath("charges.bin"));  // first
    session.setAttribute ("charges", h);
  }
%>
```

```jsp
    <ul>
```

```jsp
<%
    Enumeration charges = h.keys();
    while (charges.hasMoreElements()) {
      String proj = (String) charges.nextElement();
      Charge ch = (Charge) h.get(proj);
%>
      <li>
      name = <%= ch.getName() %>
      , project = <%= proj %>
      , hours = <%= ch.getHours() %>
      , date = <%= ch.getDate() %>
<%
    }
%>
    </ul>
</center>
</html>
```

Execution

If we execute http://localhost:8080/ch06, you should see the following display, just as before:

Selecting the **ENTER RECORD** link should result in the familiar charge record entry screen. Enter some values as shown below:

Now let's test our new persistence. Submit our charge record through the **Submit Query** button, and then click the **LOGOUT** link to show the screen below. Remember that this invalidates your session, so we lose all reference to our `TimeHashtable` object:

Now, click on **SUMMARY** to show that the `TimeHashtable` is read back in, and your data entered before is back!

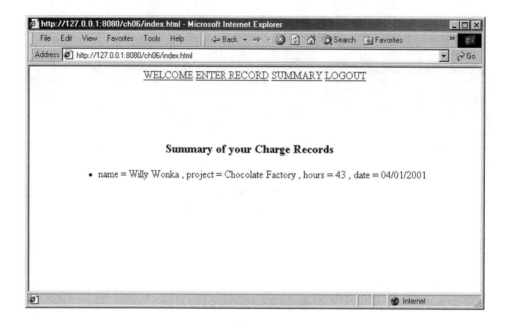

Summary

Let us examine some of the more important points covered in this chapter and what we hopefully can come away with.

We have spent a great deal of time at the beginning of this chapter explaining the intricacies of the MVC architecture. This is useful not only in our time entry application, but also in other more advanced frameworks such as Struts. The concepts are the same for any MVC based system:

- ❑ Model – Beans for the encapsulation the business logic.
- ❑ View – JSP for the presentation layer.
- ❑ Controller – Servlets for dispatching of events.

Our time entry system was then broken down and fit into the MVC architecture. This framework eases the maintainability and increases the ease at which we can expand our system. It became apparent how simple the mapping to MVC really is.

One advanced feature of the Servlet specification, HTTP Session Binding Events, was then introduced. Because of the MVC framework we used, adding new piece of functionality largely involved:

- ❑ Creating an additional bean for our Model (the `TimeHashtable`)
- ❑ Modifying two event handlers

As you can see, adding any functionality to an MVC framework is isolated to specific pieces of the application, with the rest of the system remaining relatively static.

In the next chapter, we'll be taking a more detailed look at web application architectures.

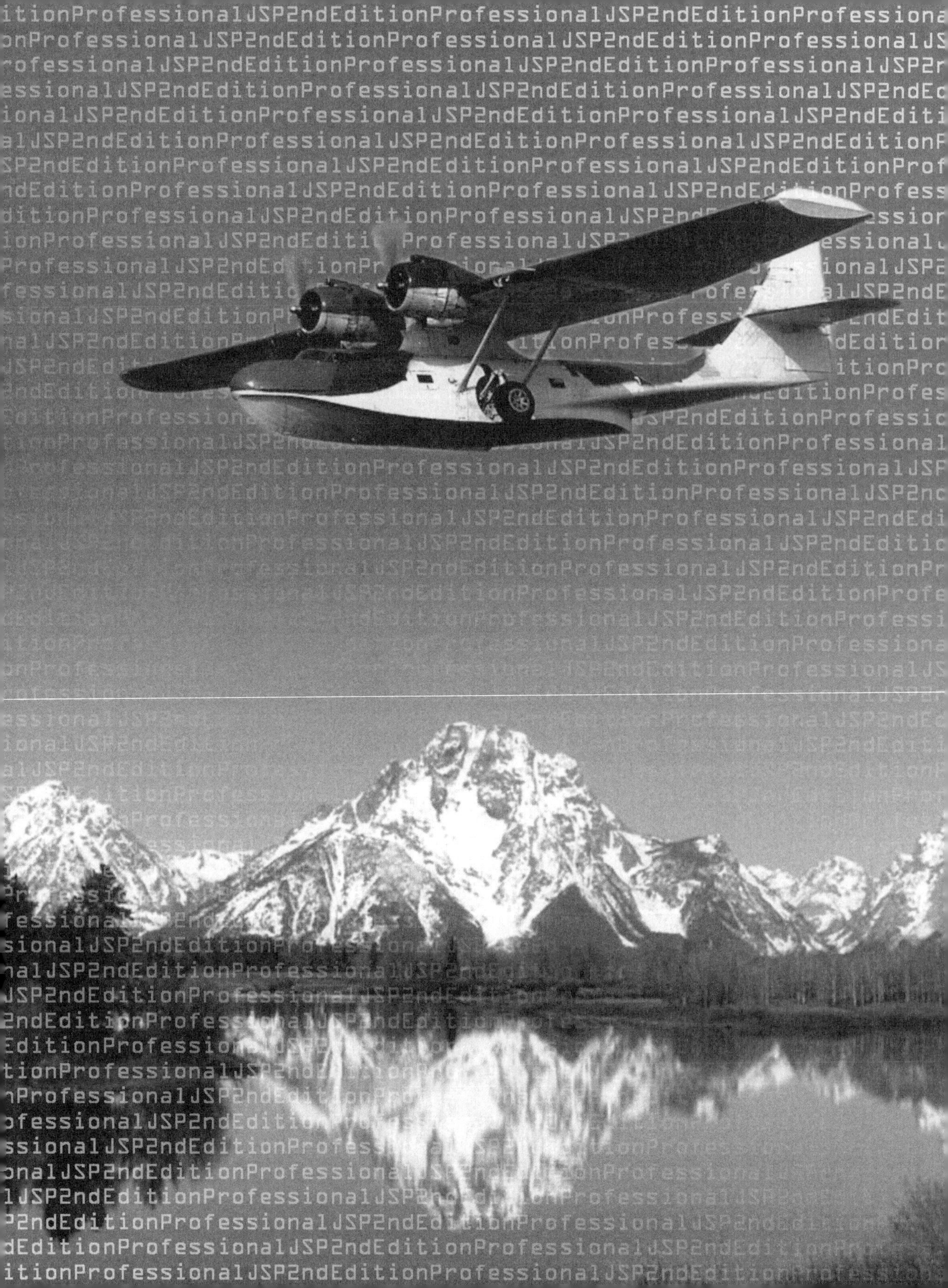
ProfessionalJSP2ndEdition

Web Application Architecture

So far we have examined the JSP and Servlet APIs in detail, and looked at ways in which they can be used together. In this chapter we will examine in more detail the ways in which we can architect a system with JavaServer Pages (JSP), Servlets, and JavaBeans, describing a series of related architectures and discuss benefits and drawbacks of each.

When Sun introduced JavaServer Pages, some were quick to claim that Servlets had been replaced as the preferred request handling mechanism in web-enabled enterprise architectures. Although JSP is a key component of the Java 2 Platform Enterprise Edition (J2EE) specification, serving as the preferred request handler and response mechanism, we must investigate further to understand its relationship with Servlets. For all the latest information on J2EE, including documentation relating to some of the issues discussed in this chapter, please refer to http://java.sun.com/j2ee/.

Other sections of this book explain the implementation details of JSP source translation and compilation into a Servlet. Understanding that JSP is built on top of the Servlet API, and utilizes Servlet semantics, raises some interesting questions: Should we no longer develop standalone Servlets in our web-enabled systems? How best can we combine Servlets and JSPs? Where do we place our Java code? Are there any other components involved in the request processing, such as JavaBeans? If so, where do they fit into the architecture and what type of role do they fulfill?

It is important to understand that, although JSP technology will be a powerful successor to basic Servlets, they have an evolutionary relationship and can be used in a cooperative and complementary manner.

Given this premise, we will:

- ❑ Investigate how these two technologies can be used co-operatively along with other components, such as JavaBeans, to create Java-based web-enabled systems

- ❑ Examine architectural issues as they relate to JSP and Servlets

❑   Discuss some effective designs, in the context of a simple example application, while looking
     at the tradeoffs of each

Before jumping directly into a discussion of specific architectures, though, we will briefly examine the need to
develop a variety of architectures.

Code Factoring and Role Separation

One of the main reasons why the Java Server Pages technology has evolved into what it is today (and it's still
evolving) is the overwhelming technical need to simplify application design by separating dynamic content
from static template display data. The foundation for JSP was laid down with the initial development of the
Java Web Server from Sun, which utilized page compilation and focused on embedding HTML inside Java
code. As applications came to be based more on business objects and n-tier architectures, the focus changed
to separating HTML from Java code, while still maintaining the integrity and flexibility the technology
provided.

In Chapter 5 we saw how beans and objects can be bound to different contexts just by defining a certain
scope. Good application design builds on this idea and tries to separate the objects, the presentation and the
manipulation of the objects into distinct, distinguishable layers.

Another benefit of utilizing JSP is that it allows us to more cleanly separate the roles of a web
production/HTML designer individual from a software developer. Remember that a common development
scenario with Servlets was to embed the HTML presentation markup within the Java code of the Servlet
itself, which can be troublesome. In our discussion, we will consider the Servlet solely as a container for Java
code, while our entire HTML presentation template is encapsulated within a JSP source page. The question
then arises as to how much Java code should remain embedded within our JSP source pages, and if it is taken
out of the JSP source page, where should it reside?

Let's investigate this further. On any web-based project, multiple roles and responsibilities will exist. For
example, an individual who designs HTML pages fulfills a web production role while someone who writes
software in the Java programming language fulfills a software development role.

On small-scale projects these roles might be filled by the same individual, or by two individuals working
closely together. On a larger project, they will likely be filled by multiple individuals, who might not have
overlapping skill sets, and are less productive if made too dependent on the workflow of the other.

If code that could be factored out to a mediating Servlet is included instead within HTML markup, then the
potential exists for individuals in the software development role and those in the web production role to
become more dependent than necessary on the progress and workflow of the other. Such dependencies may
create a more error-prone environment, where inadvertent changes to code by other team members become
more common.

This gives us some insight into one reason why we continue to develop basic Servlets: they are an
appropriate container for our common Java code that has been factored out of our JSP pages, giving our
software development team an area of focus that is as loosely coupled to our JSP pages as possible. Certainly,
there will be a need for these same individuals to work with the JSP source pages, but the dependency is
reduced, and these pages become the focus of the web-production team instead. Of course, if the same
individual fulfills both roles, as is typical on a smaller project, such dependencies are less of a concern.

So, we should try to minimize the Java code that we include within our JSP page, in order to uphold this cleaner separation of developer roles. As we have discussed, some of this Java code is appropriately factored to a mediating Servlet. Code that is common to multiple requests, such as authentication, is a good candidate for a mediating Servlet. Such code is included in one place, the Servlet, instead of potentially being cut and pasted into multiple JSPs.

We will also want to remove much of our business logic and data access code from our JSP page and encapsulate it within JavaBeans, called worker or helper beans. We start to see a pattern of code movement from our JSP into two areas: a Servlet (or JSP) that sits in front of the main JSP, and JavaBeans that sit behind. We refer to this common pattern as 'Factor Forward-Factor Back', as shown in the figure below:

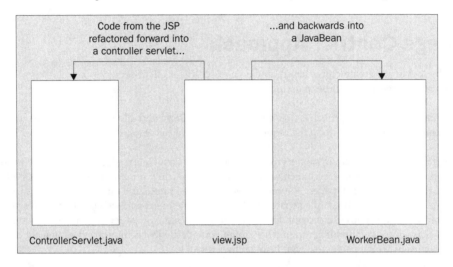

Another way to think about where code should be localized and encapsulated is that our JSP page should reveal as little as possible of our Java code implementation details.

Rather, the page should communicate our intent by revealing the delegating messages we send to worker beans, instructing them to get state from a model, or to complete some business processing.

Now, let's investigate how we build these systems.

Architectures

Before discussing specific architectures that we can use to build systems with Servlets and JSP, it is worth mentioning two basic ways of using the JSP technology. Each of the architectures discussed in this chapter will be based on one of these approaches.

- ❑ The first method is referred to here as the **page-centric** (or **Client-Server**) approach. This approach involves request invocations being made directly to JSP pages.

- ❑ In the second method, the **dispatcher** (or **N-tier**) approach, a basic Servlet or JSP acts as a mediator or controller, delegating requests to JSP pages and JavaBeans.

We will examine these approaches in light of a simple example, which will evolve to satisfy the requirements of various scenarios. The initial scenario involves providing a web interface for guessing statistics about a soon-to-be-born baby. The guesses are stored, and can be reviewed later by the parents, to see who has guessed the closest. As the requirement scenarios become more sophisticated, such as adding the desire for a persistence mechanism, the solution scenarios will become more sophisticated, as well. Thus, our example will evolve and we will gain an understanding of how the various architectures that we discuss will help us build a system that satisfies these requirements in an elegant and effective manner.

Let's look at some examples of architectures that utilize these approaches and discuss the tradeoffs and usage.

The 'Page-Centric' Approach

We start by looking at architectures based on the page-centric or client-server approach. We will look at the **page-view** and **page-view with bean** architectures.

The advantage of such an approach is that it is simple to program, and allows the page author to generate dynamic content easily, based upon the request and the state of the resources.

Unfortunately, as business requirements grow, relying on this architecture alone may become problematic. In this context, use of page-centric architectures may lead to significant amounts of Java scriptlet code being embedded directly within JSP pages. Not only does this reduce modularity and minimize opportunities for reuse, but also provides for poor role separation. Software developers and web production designers must contend for the same resource, although the aspects of the resource on which they work are entirely unrelated. This issue of embedding too much scriptlet code in the JSP is minimized somewhat by moving from the page-view to the page-view with bean architecture.

Page-View

This basic architecture involves direct request invocations to a server page with embedded Java code, and markup tags which dynamically generate output for substitution within the HTML.

This approach has many benefits. It is very easy to get started and is a low-overhead approach from a development standpoint. All of the Java code may be embedded within the HTML, so changes are confined to a limited area, reducing complexity. The figure below shows the architecture visually.

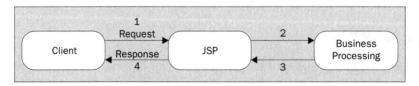

The big tradeoff here is in the level of sophistication. As the scale of the system grows, some limitations of this approach surface, such as including too much business logic in the page instead of factoring forward to a mediating Servlet, or factoring back to a worker bean. As we discussed earlier, utilizing a Servlet and helper beans allow us to separate developer roles more cleanly, and improves the potential for code reuse. Let's start with a fairly simple example JSP page that follows this model, handling requests directly and including all the Java code within the JSP source page.

We begin with a basic description of the example application. The user interface is shown below:

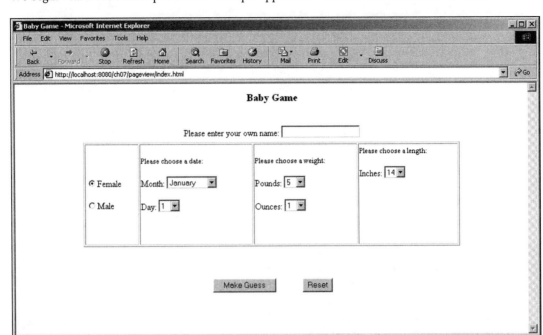

The HTML code for this page, `index.html`, should be placed in the `ch07/pageview/` directory inside the Tomcat `webapps` directory, and includes a form that prompts a user for selections. The user is asked to make some guesses about the statistics of a baby to be born in the near future. The HTML code is as follows:

```html
<html>
<head>
<title>Baby Game</title>
</head>
<body bgcolor="#FFFFFF">
<form method="post" action="BabyGame1.jsp" name="">
<center>
<h3>Baby Game</h3>
</center>

<center>
<br>
<table border cols=5 width="75%" >
<caption>Please enter your own name:
<input type="text" name="guesser"></caption>

<tr>

<td>
<br><input type="radio" name="gender" value="Female" checked>Female
<p><input type="radio" name="gender" value="Male">Male
<p></td>
```

```
<td><font size=-1>Please choose a date:</font>
<p>Month: <select name="month">
<option value="January">January</option>
<option value="February">February</option>
...
<option value="December">December</option>
<br></select>
<p>Day: <select name="day">
<option value="1">1</option>
<option value="2">2</option>
...
<option value="31">31</option>

<br></select>
<p> </td>


<td><font size=-1>Please choose a weight:</font>
<p>Pounds: <select name="pounds">
<option value="5">5</option>
<option value="6">6</option>
<option value="7">7</option>
<option value="8">8</option>
<option value="9">9</option>
<option value="10">10</option>
<option value="11">11</option>
<option value="12">12</option>
<br></select>
<p>Ounces: <select name="ounces">
<option value="1">1</option>
<option value="2">2</option>
...
<option value="15">15</option>

<br></select>
<p> </td>

<td><font size=-1>Please choose a length:</font>
<p>Inches: <select name="length">

<option value="14">14</option>
<option value="15">15</option>
...
<option value="25">25</option>


</select><p> <p> <p> </td>

</tr>
</table>
</center>

<br> 
<center>
```

```
<p><input type="submit" name="submit" value="Make Guess">
          
<input type="reset" name="reset" value="Reset">
</center>

<br></form>
</body>
</html>
```

This HTML form will POST the choices to our JSP, which is shown in source form below
(BabyGame1.jsp, again stored in directory ch07/pageview/). These choices are then stored and
displayed by our simple JSP, which has handled the request directly.

The resulting display looks like this:

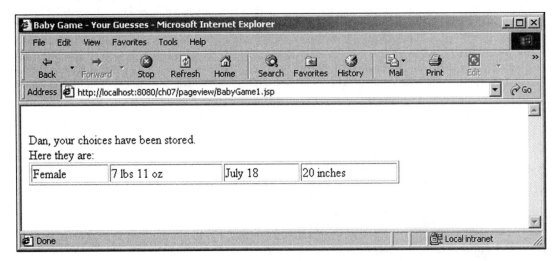

The first part of BabyGame1.jsp is responsible for extracting the values from each of the request
parameters and populating the state of the JSP. The name of the individual making the guess is contained in a
request parameter called guesser. Each of the statistics about the baby is stored in a request parameter with
an intuitive name, such as gender, length, etc.

```
<html>
<head><title>Baby Game - Your Guesses</title></head>
<body bgcolor="#FFFFFF">

<%@ page import="java.util.*,java.io.*" %>

<%
    String guesser = request.getParameter("guesser");

    String gender  = request.getParameter("gender");

    String pounds  = request.getParameter("pounds");
    String ounces  = request.getParameter("ounces");

    String month   = request.getParameter("month");
    String day     = request.getParameter("day");

    String length  = request.getParameter("length");
```

After this task is complete, there is a validation check on the data. If the validation is unsuccessful, then the JSP completes its processing by sending the user an appropriate message.

```
    if (guesser == null || gender == null || pounds == null || ounces == null
        || month == null || day == null || length == null)
  { %>

      <br>There were some choices that were not selected.<br><br>
      Sorry, but you must complete all selections to play.<br>
      <font size=-1>(Please hit the browser 'back' button to
      continue)</font><br>

  <% }
```

Otherwise, upon successful validation of the request parameters, the data is stored to disk and a table is generated using the JSP state, which corresponds to the user's guesses. The guesses are stored within a `java.util.Properties` object, which, for example purposes, is simply flattened to a text file in the directory from which Tomcat was run – typically the `%CATALINA_HOME%/bin` directory. The name of the text file corresponds to the name of the guesser, which was provided in the HTML form. One could easily imagine an even more basic example where the data was merely displayed but not stored. Such an example would differ only in that the storage code in `BabyGame1.jsp` would be omitted.

```
    else {

        //Store guess info and display to user
        Properties p = new Properties();
        p.setProperty("guesser", guesser);
        p.setProperty("gender", gender);
        p.setProperty("pounds", pounds);
        p.setProperty("ounces", ounces);
        p.setProperty("month", month);
        p.setProperty("day", day);
        p.setProperty("length", length);

        FileOutputStream outer = new FileOutputStream(guesser);
        p.store(outer, "Baby Game -- "+guesser+"'s guesses");
        outer.flush();
        outer.close();

    %>

        <br><%= guesser %>, your choices have been stored.<br>
        Here they are:<br>

        <table border cols=5 width="75%" >
          <caption></caption>
          <tr>
            <td><%= gender %></td>
            <td><%= pounds %> lbs <%= ounces %> oz</td>
            <td><%= month %> <%= day %></td>
            <td><%= length %> inches</td>
          </tr>
        </table>
```

```
        <br>
<% } %>

</body>
</html>
```

This JSP certainly was easy to build and is well suited to handling such simple needs. It is getting quite cluttered with Java code, though, and its processing requirements are extremely simple. More sophisticated business rules and data access code would require much more Java within the JSP and the source would become unwieldy quickly as it grows. Additionally, we are limited to mostly 'cut-and-paste' reuse, which means duplicate code and a more error-prone environment that is harder to maintain and debug.

In order to reduce the clutter of the current example and to provide a cleaner environment for future growth, we will look at another 'Page-Centric' architecture called 'Page-View with Bean' in the next section.

Page-View with Bean

This architecture is used when the 'Page-View' architecture becomes too cluttered with business-related code and data access code. The Baby Game example now evolves into a more sophisticated design, as shown in the figure below.

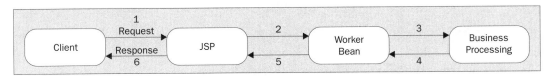

The modified JSP source page, `ch07/pageviewwithbean/BabyGame2.jsp`, is shown below, followed by the worker bean that works in tandem with the modified JSP in order to process the request. The HTML for the initial game interface remains unchanged. The resulting display to the user from the JSP is basically unchanged from that of the previous 'Page-View' example.

```
<html>
<head><title>Baby Game - Your Guesses</title></head>
<body bgcolor=FFFFFF>

<%@ page language="java" buffer="8k" %>

<jsp:useBean id="worker1" class="com.wrox.projsp.ch07.BabyGameWorker1"
 scope="request" />

<%-- Populate the JavaBean properties from the Request parameters. --%>
<%-- The semantics of the '*' wildcard is to copy all similarly-named --%>
<%-- request parameters into worker1 properties. --%>

<jsp:setProperty name="worker1" property="*" />

<% if(worker1.validate()) {
    worker1.store();
%>
    <br>
    <jsp:getProperty name="worker1" property="guesser" />, your choices
```

```
      have been stored.<br>  Here they are:<br>

      <table BORDER COLS=5 WIDTH="75%" >
        <caption></caption>
        <tr>
          <td><jsp:getProperty name="worker1" property="gender" /></td>
          <td><jsp:getProperty name="worker1" property="pounds" /> lbs
              <jsp:getProperty name="worker1" property="ounces" /> oz</td>
          <td><jsp:getProperty name="worker1" property="month" />
              <jsp:getProperty name="worker1" property="day" /></td>
          <td><jsp:getProperty name="worker1" property="length" />
              inches</td>
        </tr>
      </table>

      <br>

<% } else { %>

      <br> There were some choices that were not selected.<br><br>
      Sorry, but you must complete all selections to play.<br>
      <font size=-1>(Please hit the browser 'back' button to
      continue)</font><br>

%>

<% } %>
</body>
</html>
```

The source for the worker bean, BabyGameWorker1, is as follows:

```
package com.wrox.projsp.ch07;

import java.io.*;
import java.util.Properties;

public class BabyGameWorker1 {

  private Properties p = new Properties();

  public String getGuesser() {
    return p.getProperty("guesser");
  }

  public void setGuesser(String aString) {
    p.setProperty("guesser", aString);
  }

  // And similar "get" and "set" methods for Gender, Pounds, Ounces, Month,
  // Day, Length, and File.

  public Properties getProperties() {
    return p;
  }

  public void store() throws IOException {
    FileOutputStream outer = new FileOutputStream((String)p.get("guesser"));
    p.store(outer, "Baby Game -- "+p.get("guesser")+"'s guesses");
    outer.flush();
    outer.close();
```

```
    }

    public boolean validate() {
        return (getGuesser() != null && getGender() != null &&
                getPounds()  != null && getOunces() != null &&
                getMonth()   != null && getDay()    != null &&
                getLength()  != null);
    }

}
```

We see in these two listings that the Java code representing the business logic and simple data storage implementation has migrated from the JSP to the JavaBean worker. Since all major vendor implementations now support at least JSP version 1.1, we can also implement a worker as a Custom Tag to support View processing. This refactoring leaves a much cleaner JSP with limited Java code, which can be comfortably owned by an individual in a web-production role, since it encapsulates mostly markup tags.

Additionally, a less technical individual could be provided with a property sheet for the JavaBean workers, providing a listing of properties that are made available to the JSP page by the particular worker bean, and the desired property may simply be plugged into the `<jsp:getProperty>` action to obtain the attribute value. An example of a potential property sheet is shown below. Additionally, once a convention and format were agreed upon, an automated tool could be created to interrogate all JavaBeans of interest and generate property sheets automatically.

JavaBean Name:

```
examples.pageviewwithbean.BabyGameWorker1
```

Properties:

```
gender
ounces
pounds
guesser
day
length
month
```

Recommended Scope:

```
request
```

Template code to include in JSP code:

```
<jsp:useBean id="name" class="fully.qualified.name" scope="validScope" />
```

Example usage:

```
<jsp:useBean id="worker1" class="examples.pageviewwithbean.BabyGameWorker1"
    scope="request" />

<jsp:getProperty name="worker1" property="gender" />
```

237

Moreover, we now have created a bean that a software developer can own, such that functionality may be refined and modified without the need for changes to the HTML or markup within the JSP source page.

Another way to think about these changes is that we have created cleaner abstractions in our system by replacing implementation with intent. In other words, we have taken a bunch of code from our JSP source (the Java code that writes the guesses to a file on disk), encapsulated it within a bean, and replaced it with our intent, which is to store the data, `worker1.store()`.

Looping in JSP

So why might one choose to embed Java code in a JSP as opposed to using a predefined tag? An example would be in order to loop through some data and format HTML for output.

Earlier versions of the JSP specification included a tag syntax for looping through indexed properties of JavaBeans, so that no Java code was needed within the HTML for this purpose.

With the JSP software specification version 1.0, such tags have been removed in favor of the creation of an extensible custom tag markup mechanism that could be used for this purpose and much more. All the major vendor implementations currently support at least JSP 1.1, so looping and iterating code may now be encapsulated within a custom tag. This provides cleaner application partitioning and further reduces the amount of Java code embedded directly within the JSP. Custom tags are discussed in Chapters 8-11.

Further Refinements

After deploying this solution, our expectant family decides to limit the group of people who are able to access the system, deciding to include only their family and friends. To this end, they decide to add an authentication mechanism to their system so that each individual will have to provide proof of identity before accessing the system.

If a simple authentication mechanism is added to the top of our JSP page and we want to ensure that each JSP page is protected by this device, then we will need to add some code to each and every JSP page to execute this authentication check. Whenever there is a duplication of code such as this, it is beneficial to explore options for migrating the duplicated code to a common area, for example an include file or a custom tag.

In the previous example we 'factored back', as we moved business logic and data-access Java code from our JSP to our JavaBean, and in the next section we expand our example to 'factor forward' into a Servlet, continuing our efforts to minimize the amount of inline Java code in our JSPs.

The 'Dispatcher' Approach

We now move on to look at architectures based on the dispatcher approach, where a Servlet typically acts as a mediator or controller, delegating requests to JSP pages and JavaBeans. We will look at the **mediator-view**, **mediator-composite view**, and **service-to-workers** architectures.

In this approach, JSPs are used to generate the presentation layer, and Servlets to perform process-intensive tasks. The front end component acts as the controller and is in charge of the request processing and may manage the creation of any beans or objects used by the presentation JSP. Additionally, the controller manages navigation, deciding which JSP the request should be forwarded to next. There is no processing logic within the presentation JSP itself: it is simply responsible for retrieving any objects or beans that may have been previously populated with presentation data, and extracting the dynamic content for use within static templates.

Beans that are used by JSPs are not the same as Enterprise JavaBeans (EJBs), but are usually simple classes that serve as data wrappers to encapsulate information. They have simple get and set methods for each bean property. The properties further correspond by name to the HTML variables on the screen. This allows the bean properties to be set dynamically by the `<jsp:usebean>` tag without doing an individual `request.getParameter(parametername)` on the `request` object. See Chapter 5 for more about JavaBeans.

Mediator-View

Factoring common services, such as authentication out to a mediating Servlet allows us to remove potential duplication from our JSP pages. The code below is an example of a Servlet that provides us with central forwarding control for our game system, and includes a simple authentication check that will be reused across requests. A Bean could be used for this purpose, but you would have to add the same code to each page to perform the authentication checks. Instead, each request will be serviced by the Servlet, which now includes our authentication code.

The mediating Servlet, `BabyGameServlet.java`, is shown below. It is placed in the `ch07/WEB-INF/classes/com/wrox/projsp/ch07` directory.

```java
package com.wrox.projsp.ch07;

import javax.servlet.*;
import javax.servlet.http.*;
import java.io.*;


public class BabyGameServlet extends HttpServlet {

  public void doGet(HttpServletRequest request,
                    HttpServletResponse response) {
    processRequest(request, response);
  }

  public void doPost(HttpServletRequest request,
                     HttpServletResponse response) {
    processRequest(request, response);
  }

  protected void processRequest(HttpServletRequest request,
                                HttpServletResponse response) {

    try {

        // If we added actual authentication, this is where it would go
        // For example purposes, if the parameters exist, we consider the
        // auth successful.
```

239

```
        if (!(request.getParameter("guesser").equals("")) &&
            !(request.getParameter("password").equals("")))  {

            // Note: Based on the successful authentication of this user we may
            // want to consider writing something into the session state that
            // signifies that this is the case.  For example, if we wanted to
            // limit direct access to certain JSP pages only to authenticated
            // users, then we could include code that would check for this
            // session state before allowing such access.

            // In order to reuse this Servlet for multiple examples, we pass as
            // a request parameter the resource name to which we dispatch our
            // request.
            getServletContext()
              .getRequestDispatcher(request.getParameter("dispatchto"))
                .forward(request, response);
        } else {
            PrintWriter outy = response.getWriter();
            outy.println("Unable to authenticate, please try again.");
        }
    } catch (Exception ex) {
        ex.printStackTrace();
    }
  }
}
```

The `web.xml` file to use this Servlet is as follows:

```
<?xml version="1.0" encoding="ISO-8859-1"?>

<!DOCTYPE web-app
    PUBLIC "-//Sun Microsystems, Inc.//DTD Web Application 2.3//EN"
    "http://java.sun.com/j2ee/dtds/web-app_2.3.dtd">

<web-app>

  <servlet>
    <servlet-name>
      BabyGameServlet
    </servlet-name>
    <servlet-class>
      com.wrox.projsp.ch07.BabyGameServlet
    </servlet-class>
  </servlet>

  <servlet-mapping>
    <servlet-name>
      BabyGameServlet
    </servlet-name>
    <url-pattern>
      /BabyGameServlet/*
    </url-pattern>
  </servlet-mapping>

</web-app>
```

A new architecture is emerging, with the mediating Servlet working with a JSP page and worker bean pair to fulfill a service request. This 'Mediator-View' architecture is shown below, and illustrating how each service is partitioned. The Servlet initially handles the request and delegates to a JSP software page/worker bean combination. The JSP populates bean properties from the request parameters and then uses the bean to prepare the data for presentation.

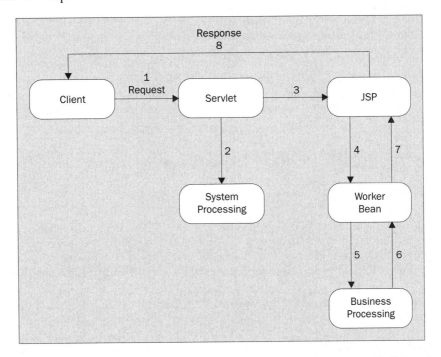

Continuing our attempts at creating the appropriate abstractions in our system, we shall consider how to better partition our business logic and data access code, attempting to reduce the coupling among the various parts of the system.

As we discussed, this request is handled first by a basic Servlet that dispatches to a JSP page for formatting and display. The JSP is responsible for delegating the processing of business functionality to a business delegate via a worker bean, which act as façades for the back-end resources. We call this component a **business delegate**, because it is a client-side (relative to the business processing itself) business abstraction used to complete the basic business processing by abstracting out the code that deals with the back-end communication. The worker beans might communicate through the business delegate with the back end via Enterprise JavaBeans components running in a scalable, load-balancing container.

In this case, we are able to decouple the EJB implementation from the JSP worker bean by moving the EJB-related code, such as the code relating to JNDI lookup, into the business delegate. If we include our EJB-related code in our worker beans, then we are closely coupling the bean to a specific underlying implementation, and if this implementation is modified or changed we must make modifications to our worker bean accordingly. So we have succeeded in creating abstractions that have reduced the coupling among the distinct pieces of our system. We can see how the worker bean and the business delegate reduce coupling between the client request and the ultimate back-end resource.

In other words, the public interfaces need not change even if the API to the underlying resource changes. The worker beans can be combined with different JSP pages in order to provide different views of the same underlying information. Also, the Servlet that initially handles each request, and is responsible for authenticating each user, may restrict direct access to our JSP pages, an added security mechanism. Once a user has been successfully authenticated, the Servlet might store certain information in that user's session, and access to certain JSP pages might only be allowed to users whose session state contained such information. The mechanism could be made more fine grained by including authorization information within this session state that would directly relate to which pages a user may view.

Our baby guessing game example will need to change, in order to adhere to this new design. The HTML user interface needs to change only slightly, adding an input field for each user to enter a password. The table caption in index.html is modified as shown below in order to add the password input field, and the revised file, is placed in ch07/mediatorview/.

```
<caption>Please enter your own name:
<input type="text" name="guesser"><br>
Please enter your Password:
<input type="password" name="password"></caption>
```

The other change to the HTML is to change the form and add a hidden input field called dispatchto. The Servlet uses this value to dispatch the request via the forward() method to the appropriate JSP, and the value is supplied simply to allow for easy modification of these examples. In this case we modify the value attribute to reference the JSP for our 'Mediator-View' example, and the modified lines look like this:

```
<form method="post" action="/ch07/BabyGameServlet/" name="">
<input type="hidden" name="dispatchto" value="/mediatorview/BabyGame3.jsp">
```

We have already seen the next piece of the puzzle in the Servlet, which handles each request, authenticating each user and dispatching the request appropriately. The Servlet and worker beans now contain Java code that is owned by an individual in the software development role, and the syntax and semantics of which may be modified without any changes to our JSP. The property sheets remain a simple contract between the web-production team and the software developers.

The benefit of a dispatcher approach is in the control the Servlet has on the request. Since the Servlet acts as the mediator, there is central forwarding control. As discussed, this also creates a nice role separation between the lower level coding in the Servlet and the JSP coding. A drawback of this architecture is that it involves more design work and more coding, since individual beans are created instead of code fragments. A very simple project might be overly burdened by this extra overhead, while more sophisticated efforts will benefit from the cleaner design.

Additionally, encapsulating as much Java code as possible into our Servlet and beans, and removing it from the JSP source, will also have the added benefit of encouraging more elegant and refined Java coding, because excessive Java code embedded within JSP source can quickly start to look like just another scripting language, and the cut-and-paste mentality tends to take over. Moreover, a software developer will be more inclined to refine code that he or she owns, without potential dependencies and conflicts with a web-production person. Of course the irony is that such unwieldy pages that are filled with Java code are in more need than any of refactoring.

Refining the Data Storage

Updating our example to include improvements based on these very forces, we add to our worker bean a factory that vends multiple storage implementations based on a parameterized factory method. Our actual storage process may be modified easily and dynamically, simply by providing an implementation that adheres to the `Store` interface:

```
package com.wrox.projsp.ch07;

import java.util.Properties;

public interface Store {
  public void store(Properties p) throws StoreException;
  public void store() throws StoreException;
  public Object load(String id) throws StoreException;
}
```

The `Store` operations can all throw a `StoreException`:

```
package com.wrox.projsp.ch07;

public class StoreException extends Exception {

  public StoreException() {}

  public StoreException(String string) {
    super(string);
  }

}
```

We move our basic file storage code into an implementation called `SimpleStore` that implements the `Store` interface:

```
package com.wrox.projsp.ch07;

import java.io.*;
import java.util.Properties;

public class SimpleStore implements Store {
  private Properties props;

  public SimpleStore() {}

  public SimpleStore(Properties p) {
    props = p;
  }

  public void store(Properties p) throws StoreException {
    props = p;
    store();
  }

  public void store() throws StoreException {
```

```
      if (props == null) {
        throw new StoreException("Problem.  store is null.");
      }

      try {
        FileOutputStream out = new FileOutputStream(
                                  (String)props.getProperty("guesser"));
        props.store(out, "Baby Game -- "+props.get("guesser")+"'s guesses");
        out.flush();
        out.close();
      }
      catch (IOException e) {
        throw new StoreException("Problem writing storage file: " +
                                 e.getMessage());
      }
    }

    public Object load(String id) throws StoreException {
      Properties props = new Properties();

      try {
        FileInputStream in = new FileInputStream(id);
        props.load(in);
        in.close();
      }
      catch (IOException e) {
        throw new StoreException("Problem reading storage file: " +
                                 e.getMessage());
      }

      return props;
    }

    public static void main(String[] args) throws Throwable {
      Properties p = new Properties();
      p.put("guesser", "abc");
      p.put("fish", "asdfasdfasdfasdfas");
      Store storer = StoreFactory.createStore();
      storer.store(p);
      System.out.println("LOADED SUCCESSFULLY  --->"+storer.load("abc"));
    }
}
```

An instance of `SimpleStore` is created by `StoreFactory`:

```
package com.wrox.projsp.ch07;

public class StoreFactory {

  public static final int SIMPLE = 0;

  public static Store createStore() {
    return createStore(SIMPLE);
  }
```

```
    public static Store createStore(int type) {
      if (type == SIMPLE) {
        return new SimpleStore();
      }

      return null;
    }

  }
```

We don't actually include 'real' data access code in this example, but it would reside in a worker bean and would reference the business delegate, which could then reference an EJB component. The `Store` interface also hides implementation details, in this case those of the storage mechanism behind it, exposing a well-defined interface instead.

The JavaBean that uses this store code, `BabyGameWorker2`, has this modified `store()` method:

```
  public void store() {
    try {
      Store storer = StoreFactory.createStore(StoreFactory.SIMPLE);
      storer.store(getProperties());
    } catch (StoreException e) {
      e.printStackTrace();
    }
  }
```

Reviewing the Mediator-View Architecture

The initial delegation point in this architecture is a JSP – we will see later another architecture in which the initial point of delegation is a worker bean ('Service-to-Workers'). The subtle difference between the two is worth discussing. In situations where there is ongoing workflow that is necessary for the generation of the data model, requiring multiple business calls, one needs to decide where to encapsulate these business calls.

❑ In one case, the JSP may contain the business calls that are required to obtain the necessary state for the intermediate model, which will be stored in the associated worker bean(s). The JSP is not only responsible for the presentation of the data, but additionally has some responsibility for coordinating the business calls, and may interact with different beans in order to present multiple views of the same underlying models.

❑ On the other hand, if the Servlet delegates initially to a worker bean, then the Servlet will need to adopt the responsibility for controlling these business calls, utilizing the worker beans to make its requests. If the required data can be gathered with a single business call, then dispatching this call to the worker bean directly from the Servlet allows the bean to populate the entire intermediate model. The Servlet is then able to forward the request to the JSP for presentation.

As you may have noticed, in the former scenario the JSP's responsibilities are increased as it fulfills part of the role of the controller in addition to the view. One needs to decide what is right for the job and move code forward or back based on the workflow and presentation needs. One issue to consider is that adding business calls to a JSP page allows for reuse of this code conditionally across requests simply by nesting pages, as in 'Mediator-Composite View', which we will discuss shortly. Adding business invocations to the Servlet means either that these calls will be invoked for each request the Servlet handles, limiting its potential for reuse, or that the Servlet may become cluttered with conditional logic dictating which code to execute for a particular request.

The elements of the current 'Mediator-View' example are:

- The HTML UI, which POSTs the request to the Servlet:
  `ch07/mediatorview/index.html`

- The Servlet, which dispatches to the JSP:
  `com.wrox.projsp.ch07.BabyGameServlet` in the `ch07/WEB-INF/classes/com/wrox/projsp/ch07/` directory.

- The JSP:
  `ch07/mediatorview/BabyGame3.jsp`

- The worker bean:
  `com.wrox.projsp.ch07.BabyGameWorker2`

- The supporting source code:
  `com.wrox.projsp.ch07.StoreFactory`, `com.wrox.projsp.ch07.Store`, `com.wrox.projsp.ch07.SimpleStore`, and `com.wrox.projsp.ch07.StoreException`

Mediator-Composite View

Sometimes we are building systems with dynamic template text as well as dynamic content. In other words, there is content being generated dynamically, and the template text that surrounds this data is also being constantly changed. Imagine that there are headers and footers in a page that are modified quite often, notifying individuals of status changes or information of special interest. If we simply type our header and footer text directly into our JSP source, then we will need to modify that source each time we want to change the template. Not only will we be duplicating our header and footer text in multiple places, making the changes harder to manage, we are reducing the modularity and reusability of the component pieces.

Moving the header and footer template text to external files provides us with one solution to this problem. We move a portion of the template text from our JSP source to another file, replacing it with the JSP `include` directive:

```
<%@ include file="gameheader.html" %>
```

Not only can we include resources such as static HTML template fragments within our JSP source, but we can also include other JSPs, creating a multiple-level nesting of pages. In this case, the presentation is built from numerous static and dynamic resources, which together make up the page presented to the user. Each of these resources is potentially composed of additional nested pages. Although the HTML template text is considered a static resource, meaning it is not generated dynamically at runtime, these template fragments are potentially a dynamic piece of the interface, since each can be modified continually with immediate updates occurring in the containing presentation. This type of structure can also be leveraged to create a central mechanism for handling page layout and modifications. This 'Mediator-Composite View' architecture is shown visually below.

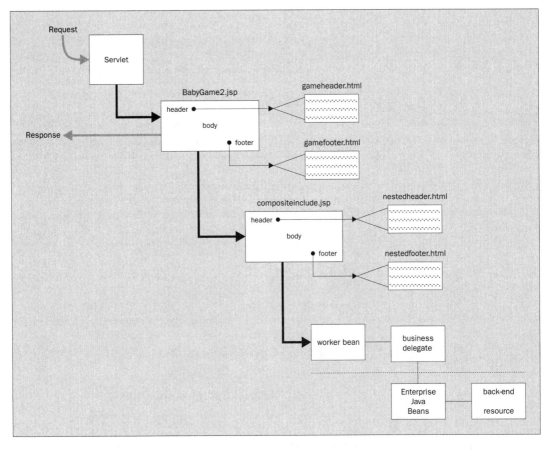

Each of these architectures builds on the previous ones in some way, and in this case we have modified the middle of the 'Mediator-View', while inheriting the front and back. As with the other dispatcher architectures, the Servlet mediator dispatches to a JSP, which imports the aforementioned static and dynamic resources. The figure above shows this nested JSP including dynamic content generated via an invocation on a helper bean, which gets to the business processing through a delegate which once again acts as a façade to the back-end resource that may be 'wrapped' in an Enterprise JavaBeans component.

As we have seen, the role of the delegate as a client-side business abstraction layer is to make business calls on the actual back-end resource, such as remote invocations on an Enterprise JavaBeans component. Once again, the role of the worker bean is to service the JSP page, preparing data for use and dynamic presentation by the page. The worker bean serves as an intermediate model for the JSP with which it is paired. Again, we are creating a more flexible architecture by abstracting out the worker bean and the business delegate, so that the model for the JSP is not actually responsible for remote invocations on business resources, and these two distinct parts of the system are more loosely coupled.

This architecture allows us to abstract out portions of our page, creating atomic pieces that can be plugged into a composite whole in different configurations. For example, a checkout page on a shopping site might present a user with the contents of a shopping cart. It is easy to imagine the shopping cart component as an atomic portion of the presentation that might be included by other pages, as well, such as a page that allows a user to survey, modify, or remove their current selections while still in 'shopping' mode, as shown in the next two figures.

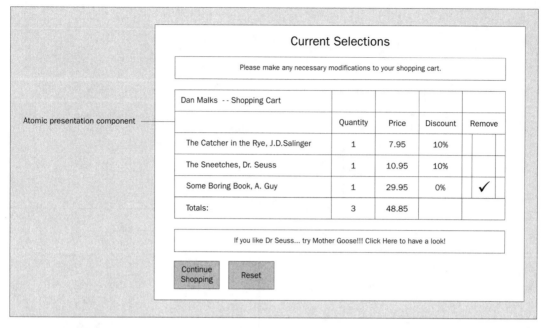

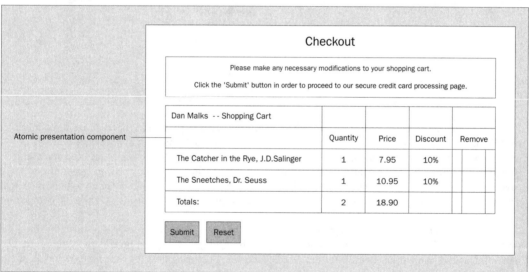

A presentation component that is nested within another page will often represent a fairly coarse-grained entity, such as the complete line-by-line inventory of the items in the aforementioned shopping cart, but may be decorated with different header and footer information based on the context of its usage within a page.

As an example, we will factor out the body of the presentation in our ongoing 'Baby Game' example, and decorate it with some headers and footers. So how has our code changed to support this architecture?

Our HTML simply requires a change to the hidden input field `dispatchto`.

Again, this value is used to dispatch to the appropriate JSP and is used simply to allow for easy modification of these examples. In this case we modify the value attribute to reference the JSP for our 'Mediator-Composite View' example. The modified line now looks like this:

```
<input type="hidden" name="dispatchto"
 value="/mediatorcompositeview/BabyGame4.jsp">
```

This modified user interface is now in `ch07/mediatorcompositeview/index.html`

The main JSP to which control is forwarded, `BabyGame4.jsp`, now looks like this:

```
<html>
<head><title>Baby Game - Your Guesses</title></head>
<body bgcolor="#FFFFFF">

<%@ include file="gameheader.html" %>

<jsp:useBean id="worker2" class="com.wrox.projsp.ch07.BabyGameWorker2"
 scope="request" />
<jsp:setProperty name="worker2" property="*" />

<jsp:include page="/mediatorcompositeview/compositeinclude.jsp"
 flush="true" />

<%@ include file="/mediatorcompositeview/gamefooter.html" %>

</body>
</html>
```

This performs a dynamic include on `compositeinclude.jsp`, which generates the main content of the page:

```
<jsp:useBean id="worker2" class="com.wrox.projsp.ch07.BabyGameWorker2"
 scope="request" />

<%@ include file="nestedheader.html" %>

<% if(worker2.validate()) {
    worker1.store();
%>
    <br>
    <jsp:getProperty name="worker2" property="guesser" />, your choices
    have been stored.<br>  Here they are:<br>

    <table border cols=5 width="75%" >
      <caption></caption>
      <tr>
        <td><jsp:getProperty name="worker1" property="gender" /></td>
        <td><jsp:getProperty name="worker1" property="pounds" /> lbs
            <jsp:getProperty name="worker1" property="ounces" /> oz</td>
        <td><jsp:getProperty name="worker1" property="month" />
            <jsp:getProperty name="worker1" property="day" /></td>
        <td><jsp:getProperty name="worker1" property="length" />
            inches</td>
      </tr>
    </table>
```

```
    <br>

<% } else { %>

    <br> There were some choices that were not selected.<br><br>
    Sorry, but you must complete all selections to play.<br>
    <font size=-1>(Please hit the browser 'back' button to
    continue)</font><br>

%>

<% } %>

<%@ include file="/mediatorcompositeview/nestedfooter.html" %>
```

Also, we have created some files containing the static header and footer template text to be included at runtime into our composite display. Here's an example of what one of these header files, gameheader.html, looks like:

```
<center>
<h3><b>Baby Game 2001! Fun for the whole family!</b></h3><br>
<hr>
</center>

<br>
<br>
```

This file includes the header template for the presentation that results from our 'Mediator-Composite View' example, as shown in the following screen shot:

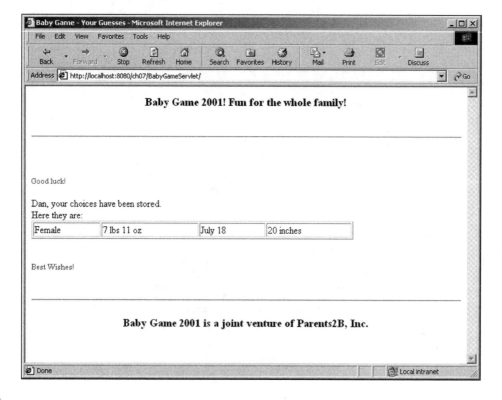

The elements of the current example are then:

- ❑ The HTML UI, which POSTs the request to the Servlet:
  `ch07/mediatorcompositeview/index.html`

- ❑ The Servlet, which dispatches to the JSP:
  `com.wrox.projsp.ch07.BabyGameServlet` in the `ch07/WEB-INF/classes/com/wrox/projsp/ch07/` directory

- ❑ The outermost JSP:
  `ch07/mediatorcompositeview/BabyGame4.jsp`

- ❑ The composite JSP, included within the outermost JSP:
  `ch07/mediatorcompositeview/compositeinclude.jsp`

- ❑ The worker bean:
  `com.wrox.projsp.ch07.BabyGameWorker2`

- ❑ The supporting source code:
  `com.wrox.projsp.ch07.StoreFactory`, `com.wrox.projsp.ch07.Store`, `com.wrox.projsp.ch07.SimpleStore`, and `com.wrox.projsp.ch07.StoreException`

- ❑ The static template text, which is included dynamically at runtime to create the composite display:
  `ch07/mediatorcompositeview/gameheader.html`, `ch07/mediatorcompositeview/gamefooter.html`, `ch07/mediatorcompositeview/nestedheader.html`, and `ch07/mediatorcompositeview/nestedfooter.html`

Service-to-Workers

The initial delegation point of the 'Service-to-Workers' architecture, shown visually below, is a worker bean that processes our business and data access code, once again via a client-side (relative to the business logic) business abstraction. As with each of the dispatcher architectures, the Servlet handles the request from the client, providing the opportunity for the processing of common services. After the worker bean has completed its responsibility of populating the intermediate model for the JSP, the Servlet dispatches to the JSP to generate the presentation.

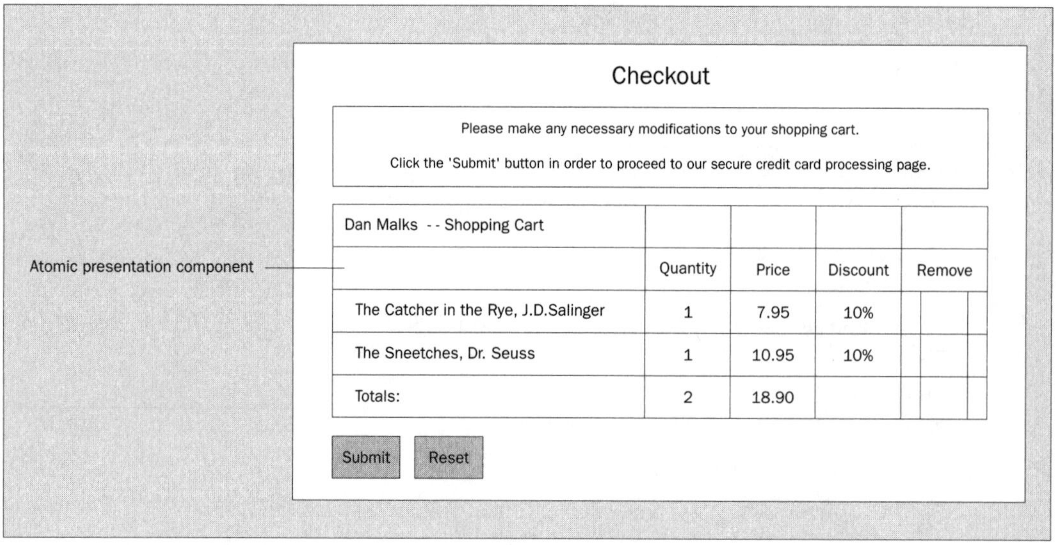

Checkout					
Please make any necessary modifications to your shopping cart.					
Click the 'Submit' button in order to proceed to our secure credit card processing page.					
Dan Malks - - Shopping Cart					
	Quantity	Price	Discount	Remove	
The Catcher in the Rye, J.D.Salinger	1	7.95	10%		
The Sneetches, Dr. Seuss	1	10.95	10%		
Totals:	2	18.90			

Atomic presentation component

Submit   Reset

This architecture provides a cleaner separation between the view and the controller, since the JSP page is no longer making business calls, but simply accessing the state of the pre-populated worker bean. Depending on the workflow needs of the system, a decision will have to be made about the suitability of this architecture versus one where the initial delegation point is a JSP, such as 'Mediator-View'. The cleaner separation of view and controller is indeed an important factor in the decision as well, and often an overriding one. Thus, 'Mediator-View' becomes a more appropriate choice as the processing logic that is necessary to handle a request is minimized. Likewise, as the amount of processing needed to handle a request increases, 'Service-to-Worker' will typically become a better choice. One obvious signal that can be used to help make this decision is the existence of too much scriptlet code in a JSP.

Our example will allow an authenticated user to examine his or her previously stored guesses. One could imagine this feature being expanded to allow modification of the previously stored data, as well.

The HTML for the user interface consists of a couple of input fields for the user to enter his or her id and password for authentication purposes. The `dispatchto` hidden field has been modified appropriately, and another hidden field, a flag called `delegatetobean`, has been added, and signals to the Servlet that we want to use our worker bean as the initial dispatch point in this scenario. It allows us to reuse the Servlet that we have been utilizing throughout our discussion with minor modifications. The screen shot opposite shows this HTML page:

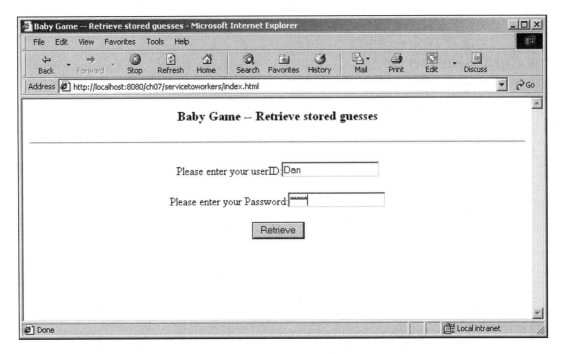

The HTML source for this page, ch07/servicetoworkers/index.html, is as follows:

```html
<html>
<head>
<title>Baby Game -- Retrieve stored guesses</title>
</head>
<body bgcolor="#FFFFFF">
<form method="post" action="/ch07/BabyGameServletSW" name="">
<center>
<h3>
Baby Game -- Retrieve stored guesses</h3></center>

<center>
<hr>
<br>

Please enter your userID:<input type="text" name="guesser"><br><br>Please enter
your Password:<input type="password" name="password">
<br><br>
<input type=hidden name="dispatchto" value="/servicetoworkers/BabyGameSW.jsp">
<input type=hidden name="delegatetobean" value="true">

<input type=submit value="Retrieve">

</form>
</body>
</html>
```

The Servlet has been modified to include a conditional check for the delegatetobean flag. If it is set, then the Servlet uses the worker bean as the initial delegation point. In previous examples, the Servlet uses the JSP as the initial delegation point.

Adding this condition, which will evaluate to `true` in this Service to Workers example only, allows us to reuse similar Servlet code throughout our discussion; the Servlet source is shown below. After successfully authenticating the user, the Servlet delegates to the worker bean (`BabyGameWorkerSW`), instructing it to load previously stored guesses based on the user's id. The worker bean is set as an attribute of the request object with the same bean id that is used in the presentation JSP (an `id` value of `"SWworker"`). This allows the JSP to share this previously instantiated and initialized bean, instead of creating a new one. In effect, we have passed the bean as an argument to the JSP.

The code for the Servlet is as follows, and is kept in `ch07/WEB-INF/classes/com/wrox/projsp/ch07/BabyGameServletSW.java`:

```
package com.wrox.projsp.ch07;

import javax.servlet.*;
import javax.servlet.http.*;
import java.io.*;


public class BabyGameServletSW extends HttpServlet {

  public void doGet(HttpServletRequest request,
                    HttpServletResponse response) {
    processRequest(request, response);
  }

  public void doPost(HttpServletRequest request,
                     HttpServletResponse response) {
    processRequest(request, response);
  }

  protected void processRequest(HttpServletRequest request,
                                HttpServletResponse response) {
    try {

      String guesser = request.getParameter("guesser");
      String password = request.getParameter("password");

      // Authenticate each request

      Authenticator auth =
        AuthenticatorFactory.create(AuthenticatorFactory.SIMPLE);
      AuthContext authContext =
        AuthenticatorFactory
          .createContext(AuthenticatorFactory.SIMPLE);
      authContext.addValue("guesser", guesser);
      authContext.addValue("password", password);

      auth.init(authContext);

      if (auth.authenticate()) {
        String dispatchto = request.getParameter("dispatchto");
        String delegateToBean = request.getParameter("delegatetobean");

        // Delegate to worker bean
        if (delegateToBean != null) {
```

```
                    BabyGameWorkerSW worker = new BabyGameWorkerSW();
                    worker.load(guesser);
                    request.setAttribute("SWworker", worker);
                  }

                  // In order to reuse this Servlet for multiple examples, we pass
                  // as a request parameter the resource name to which we dispatch
                  // our request
                  getServletConfig().getServletContext()
                    .getRequestDispatcher(dispatchto)
                      .forward(request, response);
              } else {
                PrintWriter outy = response.getWriter();
                outy.println("Unable to authenticate, please try again.");
              }
          } catch (Exception ex) {
            ex.printStackTrace();
          }
      }
  }
}
```

The web.xml file is modified to add this Servlet, as follows:

```
    ...

    <servlet>
      <servlet-name>
        BabyGameServletSW
      </servlet-name>
      <servlet-class>
        com.wrox.projsp.ch07.BabyGameServletSW
      </servlet-class>
    </servlet>

    ...

    <servlet-mapping>
      <servlet-name>
        BabyGameServletSW
      </servlet-name>
      <url-pattern>
        /BabyGameServletSW/*
      </url-pattern>
    </servlet-mapping>

    ...
```

In our earlier examples, we collected and stored a user's guesses to a text file. Now the example evolves such that the worker bean called com.wrox.projsp.ch07.BabyGameWorkerSW adds a method that loads our previously stored guesses from the store, based on an authenticated user's id. The class is defined as follows:

```
package com.wrox.projsp.ch07;

import java.io.*;
import java.util.Properties;


public class BabyGameWorkerSW {
```

```java
private Properties p = new Properties();

public String getGuesser() {
  return p.getProperty("guesser");
}

public void setGuesser(String aString) {
  p.setProperty("guesser", aString);
}

// And similarly for the gender, pounds, ounces, month, day, and
// length properties

public String getFile() {
  return p.getProperty("file");
}

public void setFile(String aString) {
  p.setProperty("file", aString);
}

public Properties getProperties() {
  return p;
}

public void setProperties(Properties props) {
  p = (Properties) props.clone();
}

public boolean validate() {
  return (getGuesser() != null && getGender() != null &&
          getPounds()  != null && getOunces() != null &&
          getMonth()   != null && getDay()       != null &&
          getLength()  != null);
}

public void store() {
  try {
    Store storer = StoreFactory.createStore(StoreFactory.SIMPLE);
    storer.store(getProperties());
  } catch (StoreException e) {
    e.printStackTrace();
  }
}

public void load(String id) {
  try {
    Store storer = StoreFactory.createStore(StoreFactory.SIMPLE);
    Properties props = (Properties) storer.load(id);
    setProperties(props);
  } catch (StoreException e) {
    e.printStackTrace();
  }
}
```

Additionally, the worker bean has a method that is included so that our example may make use of JSP error processing. The method is invoked as a guard clause from within the JSP in order to validate the accuracy of the data before it is presented to the user. The method throws an exception if the bean's state is incomplete, and is defined as follows:

```
public void validationGuard() throws Throwable {
  if (getGender() == null) {
    throw new Throwable("Error populating guess data.");
  }
}
}
```

The authentication mechanism is not described in detail here, but uses the same factory pattern as the data storage code we discussed earlier.

The JSP, ch07/servicetoworkers/BabyGameSW.jsp, is shown below. Notice that it includes an explicit reference to an error page.

```
<html>
<head><title>Baby Game - Your Guesses</title></head>
<body bgcolor="#FFFFFF">
<%@ page errorPage="errorPageSW.jsp" %>
```

If an uncaught exception occurs within a JSP, the flow of control immediately transfers to the referenced error page, in this case errorPageSW.jsp. As mentioned, the JSP includes a guard clause at the beginning, which checks for valid data. If valid data does not exist, then the worker bean will throw an exception, which will present the error page to the user, notifying him or her of the problem. In our example, if the client enters an id and password for a valid user who has not previously stored any guesses, then the bean state will be invalid and the bean's validationGuard() method will indeed throw an exception. The error page display could easily be made as informative as necessary for the user.

```
<jsp:useBean id="SWworker" class="com.wrox.projsp.ch07.BabyGameWorkerSW"
  scope="request" />
```

Notice also that the JSP has the same bean id that the Servlet previously included in its setAttribute() invocation. Thus, the JSP will reuse the existing bean, which was created in the Servlet:

```
<jsp:setProperty name="SWworker" property="*" />

<% SWworker.validationGuard(); %>

<br>
<jsp:getProperty name="SWworker" property="guesser" />, here are your
previously stored choices:<br>

<table border cols=4 width="75%" >
  <caption></caption>
  <tr>
    <td><jsp:getProperty name="SWworker" property="gender" /></td>
    <td><jsp:getProperty name="SWworker" property="pounds" /> lbs
        <jsp:getProperty name="SWworker" property="ounces" /> oz</td>
    <td><jsp:getProperty name="SWworker" property="month" />
```

```
        <jsp:getProperty name="SWworker" property="day" /></td>
    <td><jsp:getProperty name="SWworker" property="length" /> inches</td>
  </tr>
</table>

<br>

</body>
</html>
```

The full elements of the "Service-To-Workers" example are:

❑   The HTML UI, which POSTs the request to the Servlet:
    `ch07/servicetoworkers/index.html`

❑   The Servlet, which dispatches to the JSP:
    `ch07/WEB-INF/com/wrox/projsp/ch07/BabyGameServletSW.java`

❑   The JSP:
    `ch07/servicetoworkers/BabyGameSW.jsp`

❑   The ErrorPage:
    `ch07/servicetoworkers/errorpageSW.jsp`

❑   The worker bean: `com.wrox.projsp.ch07.BabyGameWorkerSW`

❑   The supporting code, much of which is reused from the previous examples:
    `com.wrox.projsp.ch07.StoreFactory`, `com.wrox.projsp.ch07.Store`,
    `com.wrox.projsp.ch07.SimpleStore`, `com.wrox.projsp.ch07.StoreException`,
    `com.wrox.projsp.ch07.AuthenticatorFactory`,
    `com.wrox.projsp.ch07.Authenticator`,
    `com.wrox.projsp.ch07.SimpleAuthenticator`,
    `com.wrox.projsp.ch07.AuthContext`, and
    `com.wrox.projsp.ch07.SimpleAuthContext`

Build versus Buy

Having described these architectures, it is worth pointing out that there are a number of frameworks available today that implement aspects of each. The traditional build versus buy decision must be considered, though in this case, it is less financially motivated than technical and philosophical. In the case of open-source frameworks, such as the one described in this section, the choice might be better termed 'Build versus Buy into'.

Since these frameworks and their source code are freely available, the question is more about whether they meet an organizations' requirements and whether the organization is willing to 'buy into' the design philosophies of the particular framework. Based on these considerations, an organization must decide whether they want to leverage a third-party framework as their starting point or build one themselves. Since everyone's needs are different, it is best to compile a matrix mapping your requirements against each feature of the framework being considered, in order to gauge how well each framework suits your organization. As these frameworks mature they will satisfy a broader range of requirements, and will become more popular and industry standard. Below we look at one of the options worth considering, the Struts framework.

The Jakarta Struts Framework

Part of the Jakarta project of the Apache Software Foundation (jakarta.apache.org), Struts is a framework for building web applications. It is an open-source project and supports Servlet and JSP development. Struts is patterned on the dispatcher architectures, such as Service to Worker, additionally utilizing the Command pattern for managing delegation of behavior. Also, Page View with Bean is supported, since Struts provides a set of workers in the form of a custom tag library and JavaBeans. These workers are used by the View to retrieve and adapt data, and format the data for display. As mentioned earlier, custom tags are an alternative to JavaBeans as helper objects, supporting the process of generating a view.

What are some of the benefits of using Struts?

- ❏ Enforces separation of business logic and presentation logic

- ❏ Enforces proper application partitioning, as suggested by the Service-to-Worker pattern.

- ❏ Provides xml-based configuration for mapping logical actions to concrete handler components and supporting views

- ❏ Provides support for form-based validation and error handling

- ❏ Provides support for Internationalization

- ❏ Provides numerous points for extensibility and customization

- ❏ Servlet and JSP spec compliant, thus compatible with numerous application servers

- ❏ Quick growth means its feature set is constantly being enhanced and refined

What are some of the drawbacks of using Struts?

- ❏ Still a relative newcomer

- ❏ Quick growth causes some compatibility and stability issues

- ❏ Layout mechanism for managing View is immature

- ❏ Validation and error-handling support is basic

The best way to gain a better understanding of any framework is to give it a quick test drive. One can often quickly get a feel for how well the design constraints imposed by the framework match one's own preferences. Struts is available from the Jakarta Project web site at http://jakarta.apache.org. Chapter 21 looks at Struts in more detail.

Summary

We have examined how to architect systems using JSPs, Servlets, JavaBeans, and Custom Tags, discussed benefits and limitations of various approaches and actually seen an example that evolves to satisfy the constraints of the various architectures.

We discussed a variety of architectures, each of which we categorized as either a Page-Centric or Dispatcher type of architecture. Page-Centric architectures have a JSP handling the request directly, while Dispatcher architectures include a Servlet that handles the request and delegates to a JSP.

The architectures we examined are:

- ❏ Page-View (Page-Centric)
- ❏ Page-View with Bean (Page-Centric)
- ❏ Mediator-View (Dispatcher)
- ❏ Mediator-Composite View (Dispatcher)
- ❏ Service-to-Workers (Dispatcher)

We also had a quick look at a framework that is built on these ideas, and outlined some of its benefits and drawbacks. As the maturity of this framework, and others like it, continue to evolve, we will see them used more commonly as a starting point for industry projects.

As we continue to investigate new ways to build our systems, we will continue to realize new architectures. Additionally, the specifications for these technologies continue to be refined and improved in ways that will potentially demand modifications to these architectures. This is certainly an exciting and important area of technology that continues to change at a rapid pace. Hopefully, this information will help you better understand the current state of affairs with respect to JSP architectures, and thus feel better positioned to follow the evolution of these architectural issues in the future.

In the next chapter we begin our exploration of JSP's powerful facility to define custom tag libraries.

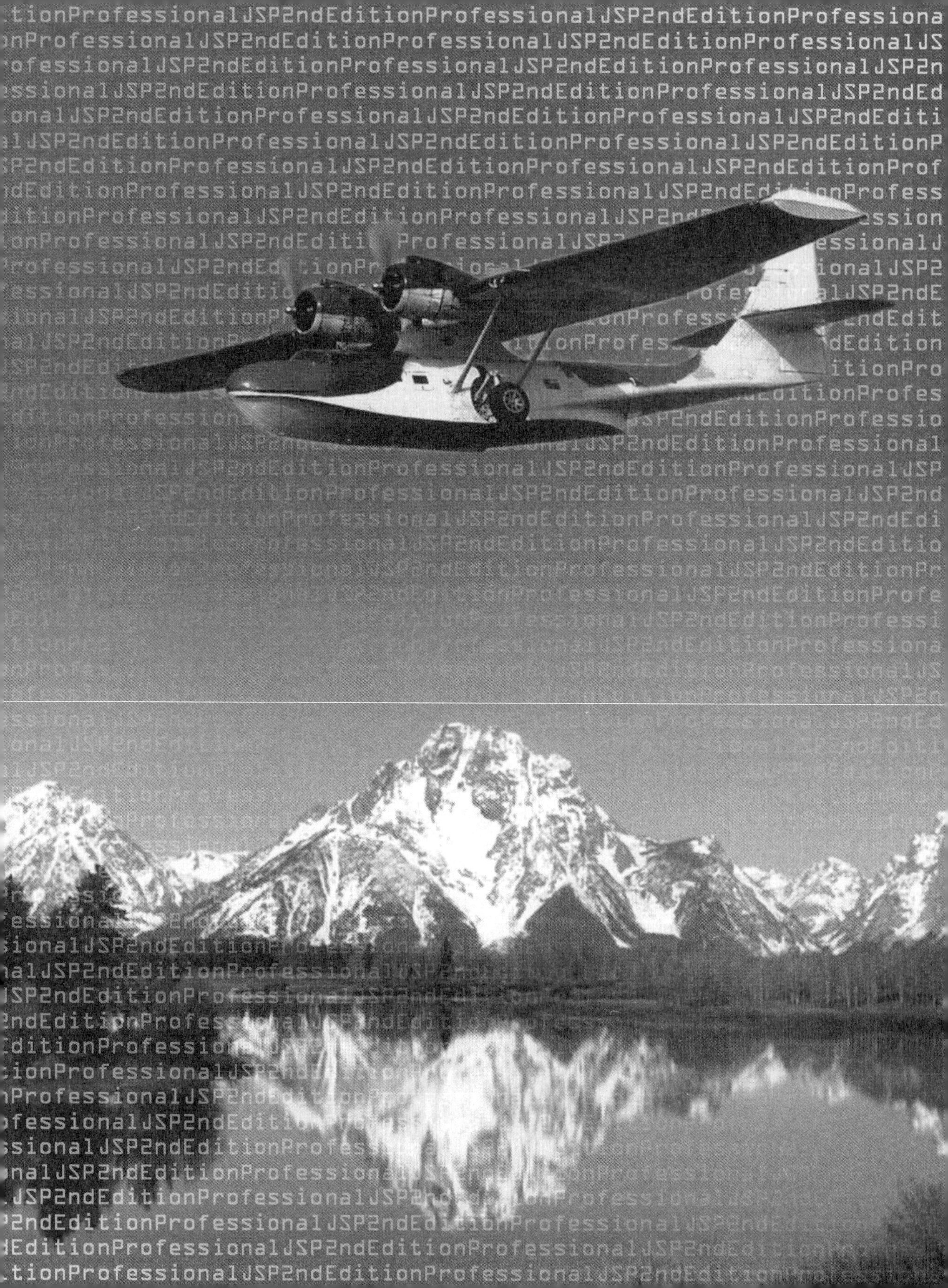

8

Introducing Custom Tags

JSP is a great solution for weaving together a web site. The structure of JSP is very similar to a central nervous system: it is a network of various interconnected languages that control the entire web application. As a technology it is a combination of many different languages, specifications, and events. It is this overall structure that gives JSP its tremendous power.

However, within this powerful structure of JSP lie two fundamental challenges.

JSP does so much that it can confuse a new programmer quite quickly. Maintaining everything within a JSP page can be a very complex undertaking for the typical web designer. In practice, server-side languages such as JSP, ASP or PHP require a very special type of programmer to build and maintain the web application. While any one piece of the server-side puzzle is easy to learn, the entire package requires a person who is capable of balancing the needs of all the tools used to build the web application. This means a traditional JSP web site requires an experienced JSP programmer to maintain and expand the web application.

This quickly leads to the second problem of JSP: in acting as the central nervous system it winds up *looking* like the central nervous system. This interconnected living code ends up being difficult for a team to build and maintain in a smooth manner.

So Sun developed **tag libraries** as a method to help solve both of these problems. A tag library allows programmers to package the central nervous system of JSP into easy reusable code libraries. Once built the actual code library provides a simple set of **custom tags** that even a non-Java programmer can use.

This chapter has three goals:

❑   To explain in depth why tag libraries are so important both for you and for JSP in general. It is surprising, but in examining the reasons why tag libraries exist you quickly discover that custom tag specification is one of the most critical features built into the JSP specification.

❑ To walk you through building a simple tag so you will feel comfortable with the basic mechanics of how tags work. The best way to understand a custom tag is to build one.

❑ To examine the disadvantages of tag libraries and look into how custom tags should be used within a JSP project.

Custom Tags

Custom tags can be defined as:

❑ A way for assembling reusable code in a JSP page

❑ An XML-like front end to access Java processing

❑ An extended JavaBean, which has a simple interface for using it within a JSP page

❑ An intersection where Java programmers and web designers meet to do business with each other

Now brief definitions don't show what a custom tag is or what it really does for both you as a programmer and the JSP language in general.

Advantages of Custom Tags

Before moving forward with tags it is necessary to clear up a common naming problem. Programmers will use the terms tag extension, tag library and custom tag seemingly interchangeably:

❑ **Custom Tag**
Refers to a single tag (defined and built by a JSP developer) being used on the JSP page and the associated code that drives the logic

❑ **Tag Library**
A collection of custom tags packaged together

❑ **Tag Extension**
A tag extension is the overall official term to define the specification of tag libraries. However, people use it interchangeably to stand for a custom tag or tag library

The Average Web Designer can now Maintain JSP Sites

A Java programmer could easily build a JSP page with intricate Java scriptlets. However, once built, this Java page will only be maintainable by another Java programmer. JSP pages are Servlets made easy for web application development. The problem is that JSP only made it simple for Java programmers to build web applications since the scripting engine is still Java. While this isn't a problem for the Java programmer, it *is* a problem for many companies who don't have the resources to have a Java programmer to maintain the code.

In JSP the goal has always been to use business objects to capture reusable code into one location. Business objects (JavaBeans), while powerful, almost always required some Java scripting to initialize the object and to modify conditions on the JSP page in order to best use these objects. The end result is that you still have Java scriptlets embedded within your JSP page.

With custom tags it is now simple to move all the scripting to a central hidden object which the Java programmer controls and the web designer accesses with simple XML tag like attributes. In fact, you could even expose the standard JSP implicit objects in the same manner. The advantage of this approach is being able to expose any object for the web designer to have easy access to without them ever having to learn one line of Java. This means an average web designer can have easy access to the Java objects within the web site.

Since tag libraries help to open JSP to non-Java programmers, this has a second benefit: it increases the number of people who can participate in building a JSP web application. Of course, Java programmers will also enjoy the benefit of JSP pages that are simpler to maintain.

Tags are Portable

While Java is an object-oriented language, JSP is not. Rather it is a specification that uses Java as a scripting language. In practice this means that the actual JSP page is a collection of scripting layers that gets converted to Java objects. This has many design implications. The major one is that the free standing scripts of a JSP page tend to be built for the specific task of creating a single page of output. The entire page itself can be considered to be a customized object, which is only reusable as a template for future pages. A template is not a reusable object but instead a coding guideline to assist in building a new script. Templates are not plug and play: you always have to initialize and customize a template to work within its new environment. While using a template is much faster than rebuilding your code from scratch, it still takes time and effort to modify your template to work in the new environment. Tags are an alternative to templates and are built to plug and play.

While a template never functions by itself, a custom tag can stand alone in a JSP page or in combination with other tags. This means you can pick up your custom tag, move it to any other JSP project and expect it to work as long as you call the tag properly.

You may wonder about reusability of JavaBeans. The problem with a JavaBean is that it doesn't have the same automatic interface with JSP that is built into the custom tag specification. As a result, a scriptlet is often required to interface with a JavaBean, meaning that additional code will be required to make the JavaBean work properly with the JSP. All in all a tag library will keep your code nicely encapsulated within Java objects and freely reusable across many JSP projects.

Tags Expand JSP

JSP is a great web application tool but was initially limited to its standard configuration. By creating tag libraries Sun has opened up a method that the whole developing community can use to expand JSP to meet any need. This means tag libraries allow JSP to become one of the most flexible server-side solutions in the market place. Sun doesn't have to rebuild new releases of JSP to meet new needs; rather, one developer can write a new tag library to address a future need. Since tag libraries are built according to the JSP specification's requirements, they can be shared with the entire JSP community.

The JSP 1.2 specification already has an example of this. The specification clearly states that the authors of JSP containers are allowed to create new implicit objects. Doing so requires the use of tag libraries to define the new implicit object. By using tag libraries to define the new object, the current JSP specification is able to account for new objects. In addition the specification states that it can then evolve to include any of these new objects that work out to the benefit of JSP.

Custom tags are also interesting for expanding JSP in ways you might not expect. For example, you can build special tags that extend and add prebuilt client-side scripting for your JSP page. So a JSP tag might generate the JavaScript for the validation of form fields or DHTML menu items for your HTML page. We will build a simple example of this later in the chapter to illustrate how custom tags can expand JSP in unexpected directions.

> **Overall, this one aspect of tag libraries makes JSP an extremely flexible development language with literally unlimited growth potential.**

Tags Speed up Web Development

The bottom line for many web sites is the speed at which they can be built. Using prebuilt tags can speed up the development of a web site by reducing the amount of time required in up front development of Java code. The largest speed increases come from the fact that custom tags are reusable. It is always faster to reuse existing code that to build new code from scratch.

Custom tags introduce a second major speed benefit in terms of both fixing and reducing bugs within your application. Each time you reuse a custom tag, the time spent debugging code is reduced. This is due to the fact that on average every time you use a custom tag you should be able to remove over 75% of the bugs present in that tag. It doesn't take much math to realize by the third time you use the custom tag that most of the bugs will have been removed in the testing. Also, since custom tags allow the JSP programmer to centralize scriptlet code to a single tag, a JSP programmer only needs to fix code in one spot versus many places.

Tags Make JSP Sites Easier to Maintain

Using tags gives you the power of code encapsulation to your project. While this can be performed using standard JavaBeans, the JSP tag interface makes it easier and adds extra flexibility. Since your code is encapsulated within the tag, you can update and improve your tags without breaking your final JSP page.

One problem with maintaining web sites is that a single change often times requires the fixing of many pages at once to implement revised logic. If your code resides within a tag, then you only need to update your central tag and every page will be updated automatically with the implementation of the revised tag. This not only makes it simple to maintain your code but also makes it easier to update your logic over time. You can even add new attributes and features to a tag so it remains compatible with older pages but creates extra functionality for new pages.

Finally, when used correctly tag libraries can make a JSP page easier to read. Clean and clear coding practices are a proven method of improving maintenance within any program. A custom tag simplifies code layout within your JSP page while giving a standard interface to contain server side logic. This has the direct benefit of making web sites easier to maintain. Clean and clearly laid out code is always easier to maintained over intertwined coding practices.

As an example of simplified maintenance we could create a custom tag to display the current server time:

```
<example:time />
```

The time tag is designed to produce output on our final HTML page that looks like this:

```
2:00 PM
```

Now let's look at what happens when we need to make a change. We have three options open to us:

- **We can change the way the tag works**
  We might decide to change the code within the tag to display time in military style. We only need to make one change to the central tag handler and then any JSP page using the tag will show the time in military fashion. This is great! Instead of updating every page, we only needed to fix the central tag itself.

- **We can add additional functionality**
  Instead of changing the way the tag works we may want to expand the tag. We can add attributes, which we can use to change what the tag does. So in this example we can add a 'style' attribute that sets the style to be either standard or military time:

  ```
  <example:time style="miltary" />
  ```

  So any existing tag will show time in standard format and we can now start using the new versions of the tag to also show time in military format.

- **We can change both the way the tag works and include expanded functionality**

This ability to change the way a custom tag works over time is incredibly powerful.

Other Benefits of Tags

A famous saying goes "But WAIT! There is MORE!" The same holds true here for tag libraries. Some additional benefits to using tag libraries should be mentioned:

- Tag libraries are a great way to group common functionality and methods spread across many JavaBeans and objects into a single interface for developers of a JSP page.

- Tag libraries will work on any JSP page no matter what the primary scripting language for the individual JSP page. While every JSP container supports Java, some support other languages such as server side JavaScript. So if you are planning on supporting JSP pages written in both Java and server side JavaScript then you should move your scriptlet logic into a tag library.

- A custom tag can perform actions that cannot be achieved using scriptlets. For example, it is possible to validate and perform post processing of JSP output.

- A custom tag can support event listeners. This is a new feature of JSP 1.2 and it will tremendously increase what is possible with a custom tag. Event listeners will be covered in Chapter 16.

- Tag libraries also help to set JSP apart from the other server side development environments. Tools such as ASP 3.0 have no similar functionality. Presently, the only other server side language that offers the ability to create and use a custom tag is ColdFusion.

Using a Custom Tag

In Chapter 10 we will go into quite some depth showing you how to use Java and JSP to parse XML data. Indeed, most web designers would not have the background in Java programming to write the Java code required to perform this work. However, with a single custom tag we can actually reduce all the code down to a few easy-to-use lines within the JSP page:

```
<%@ taglib uri="http://www.jspinsider.com/jspkit/JAXP" prefix="JAXP" %>

<JAXP:transformer>
  <JAXP:xmlFile>c:/xml/example.xml</JAXP:xmlFile>
  <JAXP:xslFile>c:/xml/example.xsl</JAXP:xslFile>
</JAXP:transformer>
```

With these 5 lines anyone can import an XML file, pick a style sheet and then have it produce a full report. This is one reason why tag libraries are so important to JSP. They create an easy front end, which opens JSP up to any user.

From this example you can see that using a tag library is just a simple two-step process.

Step 1: Import the Tag Library

Importing the tag library is simple and only requires that you use the `taglib` directive. This directive has two parameters:

❑ `uri`
This is the unique name which identifies the tag library. The URI (Uniform Resource Identifier) is often in the form of an URL. This name has been predefined for us in the JSP containers initialization file (`web.xml`) and we will cover how this is done later in this chapter.

❑ `prefix`
This attribute tells the JSP container which prefixed tags on the page are derived from this tag library. No rules exist for assigning this name. In this example we have called it `JAXP` since the tags were using the JAXP API. However, we could have called it `example` or any other name.

Step 2: Call the Custom Tag from the Tag Library

In this example:

```
<JAXP:transformer>
```

We are calling the tag library `JAXP` from the earlier `taglib` directive call. From the `JAXP` tag library we are specifically asking for the functionality of the `transformer` custom tag.

Examples Of Other Tags

Just like the example above there are many more pre-built tag libraries around. A resource devoted to listing JSP tag libraries is JSPtags.com, http://www.jsptags.com.

Another currently popular tag library site is http://jakarta.apache.org/taglibs/index.html, the Jakarta Taglibs subproject. This is an open-source taglib repository so it is possible to find free and low cost tags to use on a project. Even better, these custom tags are a solid source of information to help you learn how to build your own tags.

One example from this collection is the `datetime` tag library. With it you could use one tag to get the current time:

```
<%@ taglib uri="http://jakarta.apache.org/taglibs/datetime-1.0" prefix="dt" %>

<dt:format pattern="MM/dd/yyyy hh:mm"><dt:currenttime/></dt:format>
```

You can find tags that allow you to use regular expressions similar to Perl syntax regular expressions. Another tag library will permit you to introduce other scripting languages into your server side processing. Overall, this is a nice place to start your examination of what is possible with tag libraries.

Building a Custom Tag

As you saw above, using a custom tag is a very simple matter. Fortunately building custom tags is also a relatively simple task, provided the programmer is armed with a little guidance to understand the overall process. Without guidance, the learning experience for building a custom tag can be an exercise in frustration.

Programmers learning how to use tags encounter several common problems. The single most deadly mistake made by programmers is to think of custom tags as a single piece of code. Remember our first definition?

> **Custom tags are a way to assemble reusable code in a JSP page.**

Understanding this is critical for your success in building maintainable tag libraries. When you examine a tag you quickly find there is no single piece you can define as a tag. The closest you come to a central piece is the tag-handler, which is the core piece where your code and the JSP container meet to do business. However, even this 'heart' of your tag will not work without the whole framework that exists to run a tag. A custom tag is defined by its overall framework and building a tag is actually a six-step process that we will describe in a moment.

After this concept settles in, a new user then encounters the problem of trying to tie it all together to use on a JSP page. For most new JSP programmers getting everything correctly assembled is often the toughest part.

Our goal in this section will be to introduce you to the steps of building a custom tag. We don't expect that this will teach you exactly how to build a tag. Rather it will give you an overview of what needs to happen for a custom tag to work. We will talk about the basic steps within the methodology and introduce you to some of the technical syntax.

With this information you will be able to jump into the next chapters and really learn the details that comprise tags. Listed below is a quick step-by-step guide to give a programmer enough knowledge to prepare for the full glory of tags as presented in the later chapters of this book.

Getting Started

The best way to understand a custom tag is to walk through building a simple tag. Or you can download the source code for this chapter from http://www.wrox.com/.

The example is based on Java 1.3 using Tomcat 4.0 as the JSP container. To make this simple we will present this in a step-by-step manner. This example will build a custom tag that will let you display a JavaScript alert box on your client's browser.

Step 1: Laying the Ground Work

In many respects building a custom tag is like building a house. When you build the house the first thing you build is not the house but rather the foundation that the house sits upon. Reusable code modules are the foundation of the custom tag you will build. These reusable objects are not the custom tag, but rather are the business objects the custom tag will call to accomplish any generic action.

This foundation layer of objects is built because a custom tag should only be used from a JSP page. This means any code you place within the custom tag is then only accessible when the tag is called from your JSP page. As a result, any code that needs to be accessed from objects other than the custom tag should be built as a separate business object.

Keep in mind it is possible to roll all of the code into the custom tag. However, doing so will limit the flexibility of the final tag.

JavaScriptExample.java

We will build a simple Java object for this example. The object is a JavaBean that produces some JavaScript code to send down to a client page. The code is a function that takes an object, converts it to a string and finally produces an alert box to display the object as a string to the user viewing the JSP page.

This code is from the file JavaScriptExample.java. If you unpacked the code correctly this file can be found in the WEB-INF\classes\com\jspinsider\jspkit\javascript\ directory:

```
package com.jspinsider.jspkit.javascript;

public class JavaScriptExample extends java.lang.Object
        implements java.io.Serializable {

  public JavaScriptExample() {}

  private String start_script = "<script language=\"JavaScript\">";
  private String end_script = "</script>";

  public String alert(Object aobj_data) {
    return (start_script + " alert(\"" + aobj_data.toString() + "\");"
          + end_script);
  }

}
```

The code here is just a simple JavaBean. It has nothing directly to do with our tag, other than the fact our custom tag will use it to generate the script to produce a JavaScript alert.

There are no surprises here and we made no additional changes to make this code work with a custom tag.

Step 2: Building the Tag Handler

A tag handler is a special JavaBean, which contains the code the tag executes. For all practical purposes this is the step where we create the actual custom tag.

To be a tag handler, an object needs to implement Tag, IterationTag, or BodyTag. This means you could easily convert an existing class into a tag handler by just implementing the correct interface. In practice tag handlers usually extend the JSP TagSupport or BodyTagSupport classes. See Chapters 9 and 10 for details of these.

In this example we extend the BodyTagSupport class since we want to read in the data that is contained in the tag's body.

From a logical point of view building a tag handler is quite a bit different from building a JavaBean. When you build a JavaBean you think in terms of collecting all the common functions and placing them in the JavaBean. However, a tag handler is more focused than a JavaBean and it only has one purpose, to support the single tag for which it was built.

When you build a tag library you are actually building multiple tag handlers, one for each custom tag. For example, this tag handler builds an alert box but we might want to build another tag handler to create a special debugging alert box, and yet another tag handler to build a more robust javascript alert that can work with browser events. All these tags would belong to one JavaScript tag library but each custom tag has its own tag handler.

The other important fact to keep in mind is that a tag handler and the JSP page are tightly coupled with each other. As a result you have access to the PageContext object. This is critical since the tag handler has access to the same current data that is contained within your JSP page. For example, your tag can access anything from the session data to variables within the request object.

However, the most important thing we gain from the PageContext object is access to the JSP page's out object. We need this in order to write content back to the JSP page's output stream. There also exists a well-defined series of events, which are called from the JSP page to interact with the tag handler. This event model will be covered in the following two chapters, and gives fine control over how the tag will interact with the JSP page. Overall, it is this tight coupling that makes custom tags a JSP-only proposition and gives tags the power to interact with your JSP page.

JavaScriptExampleTag.java

This code is from the file JavaScriptExampleTag.java, which can be found in your WEB-INF\classes\com\jspinsider\jspkit\javascript\ directory:

```
package com.jspinsider.jspkit.javascript;

import java.io.IOException;
import javax.Servlet.jsp.*;
import javax.Servlet.jsp.tagext.*;
```

Just like all classes a normal declaration is needed, but notice we also extend `BodyTagSupport` as needed for the tag. We are using `BodyTagSupport` since we want to read the data contained with the tag body:

```
public class JavaScriptExampleTag extends BodyTagSupport {
```

The next logical step is to get the data meant for the display as an alert box. Since we want all the text within the body of our tag we will wait for the JSP page to process the entire tag first. The logic is placed within the `doEndTag()` function that gets triggered when the JSP page reaches the end of the tag:

```
public int doEndTag() throws JspTagException {
    String ls_alert = "";

    try {
```

We obtain our data from the `BodyContent` object and the `getBodyContent()` function:

```
        BodyContent lbc_bodycurrent = getBodyContent();
```

Once we have the data, we then call the `JavaScriptExample` object we created earlier to convert the string into a browser-side alert box call:

```
        if (lbc_bodycurrent != null) {
            String ls_message = lbc_bodycurrent.getString();
            JavaScriptExample JS = new JavaScriptExample();

            ls_alert = JS.alert(ls_message.trim());
        }
```

The resulting script needs to be written to the client, so the `pageContext` object is called to get a handle on the JSP page's output stream:

```
        pageContext.getOut().write(ls_alert);
```

Finally we close the tag and send our thread back to the JSP page to continue processing:

```
    } catch (IOException e) {
        throw new JspTagException("Error" + e.toString());
    }

    return EVAL_PAGE;
    }

}
```

This example brings a simple fact to mind. While coding a custom tag itself is easy, you still have to learn how to use the objects, timing and syntax that the tag extension specification introduces to JSP.

Step 3: Build a Tag Extra Info Class

This is an optional step. A TEI class is also referred to as a tag handler helper class, and building a TEI class is an advanced subject and is not required for building a simple custom tag. It is mentioned here to let you know that the TEI class represents a special interface you will have to build for more complicated custom tags.

The most important aspect of the TEI class is that it permits your tag handler to get direct access to scripting variables within the body of the tag. The custom tag can interact with these variables and you can set them from your tag handler class.

When building a TEI class it is standard to name it after the tag handler class with 'TEI' appended to the end of the name.

The TEI class will be covered in more detail in the following chapters.

Step 4: Build a Tag Library Descriptor

A Tag Library Descriptor (TLD) is an XML-based file that describes and defines a custom tag – an intersection between the JSP container and the tag handlers. For all practical purposes it is just an index file that tells the JSP container where to find and use each tag handler. This means that the TLD is where a tag library is defined within your JSP application.

When building a TLD file it is standard to name it after the tag handler class. This file must be saved with a `.tld` extension to the file name.

Since a TLD is an XML file it also has a Document Type Definition that defines its syntax. Keep in mind that the definition file has changed between JSP 1.1 and JSP 1.2 so you need to be careful to use the correct syntax within your TLD file when upgrading to the latest JSP specifications. The DTD is defined in Appendix D.

When placing a TLD directly in a web application it must be put in the `WEB-INF` directory.

JavaScriptExampleTag.tld

For this example our TLD file will tell Tomcat (from the `web.xml` file) where to find our tag handler.

Save this file as `JavaScriptExampleTag.tld` in the `WEB-INF` directory. Note that this TLD file is based on the JSP 1.1 DTD specification, but is compatible with JSP 1.2.

```
<?xml version="1.0" encoding="ISO-8859-1" ?>
<!DOCTYPE taglib
    PUBLIC "-//Sun Microsystems, Inc.//DTD JSP Tag Library 1.1//EN"
    "http://java.sun.com/j2ee/dtds/web-jsptaglibrary_1_1.dtd">
```

In this example, the TLD file has three important sections. The first section describes our overall tag library. We let the system know which version of JSP this tag library uses and more importantly we assign a unique URI to our tag library so we can reference it later:

```
<taglib>
  <tlibversion>1.0</tlibversion>
  <jspversion>1.1</jspversion>
  <shortname>JavaScriptExampleTag</shortname>
  <uri> http://www.jspinsider.com/jspkit/javascript </uri>
  <info>A simple tag library for making a JavaScript alert   </info>
```

Notice the use of the term tag library here since the TLD file is the file that defines the overall tag library being built. Inside the TLD file are all of the individual tag declarations. A simple tag call would look like:

```
<tag>
  <name>message</name>
  <tagclass>com.jspinsider.jspkit.javascript.JavaScriptExampleTag</tagclass>
  <info>Display Alert Box</info>
</tag>
</taglib>
```

The most important aspect of the <tag> element is that it represents the tag handler. So if you were including six custom tags, you would have to create six tag references. We define which tag handler (<tagclass>) is being used by what name (<name>). This <name> element is what you reference when calling the tag handler within the JSP page.

Step 5: Tell the JSP Container the Location of the Tag Library

The JSP container must be informed where the TLD file resides in order for it to process a tag handler. Three methods are available to inform a JSP container of the location of a TLD file.

The first method is to provide a unique path to the TLD file when the taglib declaration is used on a JSP page. Here's an example:

```
<%@ taglib uri="/your_tags.tld" prefix="tagexample" %>
```

In this example the JSP container will look for the TLD file within the path given in the URI. You can specify either a relative path or an absolute path. Of course, the big problem with using this syntax is that it isn't very portable among JSP projects: for each project you will have to verify the path is correct. In addition, if the TLD file was relocated or had a name change you would have to update every page that had referenced it by this method. For these reasons it is preferable to use one of the other methods for identification of the TLD location.

The second method requires that you package the tag library as a JAR file. Then this JAR file is referenced by the taglib declaration. For example:

```
<%@ taglib uri="/your_tags.jar" prefix="tagexample" %>
```

In this example the JSP container will look for the JAR file within the path given in the URI. You may specify either a relative path or an absolute path. While this has the same pathing issues as the first method, this style has the advantage that the entire tag library has been packaged within the JAR file. When using this method, a TLD file still exists but it is packaged with the JAR file and stored within the JAR file's META-INF directory.

Finally the third method is to directly edit the web.xml file (found in the WEB-INF directory) to include an entry describing the information required to run the tag library. It should be noted if you are using a WAR file to distribute the tag library, you must also update the web.xml file associated with the WAR file. When you use the web.xml file to identify the tag library, you must use the URI provided in the TLD file. We show you this method in our example.

web.xml

In this example we are editing our web.xml file. This tells the JSP container where to look for the TLD file.

Create a web.xml file and save it to your WEB-INF directory:

```
<?xml version="1.0" encoding="ISO-8859-1"?>
<!DOCTYPE web-app
    PUBLIC "-//Sun Microsystems, Inc.//DTD Web Application  2.2//EN"
    "http://java.sun.com/j2ee/dtds/web-app_2.2.dtd">
```

The <taglib-uri> parameter is where the unique name for our tag library is defined. In this example not only do we get a unique name but we get a second benefit of the URI acting as a pointer to get additional information:

```
<web-app>
  <taglib>
    <taglib-uri>
      http://www.jspinsider.com/jspkit/javascript
    </taglib-uri>
```

The <taglib-location> parameter tells your JSP container where it can find the TLD file:

```
    <taglib-location>
      /WEB-INF/JavaScriptExampleTag.tld
    </taglib-location>
  </taglib>
</web-app>
```

Before running the next step you will need to restart your JSP container since we updated its initialization file. A restart is required so Tomcat will read in the new changes made within the web.xml file.

In this example we only added the <taglib> section to the <web-app> section of the web.xml. It should be noted that we would add a new <taglib> section for each tag library we are defining for our project.

Step 6: Build a JSP Page

Using a tag library is the best part of the whole process and it's simple. Only two steps are needed to access the tag library. The first step is to use a taglib directive to tell the JSP page that you will be accessing a tag library. Here's an example:

```
<%@ taglib uri="http://www.jspinsider.com/jspkit/javascript"
           prefix="JavaScript"
%>
```

The `taglib` directive has two attributes:

❑ `uri`
   This is the unique name which identifies the tag library. The URI often consists of the URL of the organization maintaining the tag library. By using a URL we help to document where the tag originated and ensure a unique name. Note that the system doesn't try to actually access the URL listed in the URI attribute; the only thing special about the URI is that it needs to be unique. This uniqueness is important so that more than one tag library doesn't get associated with the same call. One confusing thing about the URI is that it can be a pathname with an appended file name (which the system assumes is your TLD file). In this case the JSP container will use the pathname to try to search for the TLD file. If the name doesn't map to an actual TLD file then the JSP container will search through the application WAR file (if one exists) or the `web.xml` configuration file to locate the TLD document.

❑ `prefix`
   This attribute tells the JSP container which prefixed tags on the page are derived from this tag library. No rules exist for assigning this name, except that certain names (`jsp`, `jspx`, `java`, `javax`, `servlet`, `sun`, and `sunw`) are reserved.

The second step in building a JSP page with custom tags is the easiest. Just plug the tag into the page and begin using it. After the `taglib` directive imports your tag library you are free to use your tag at will within the JSP page. Here's an example:

```
<your_prefix:Tag_Function> The Tag Body </ your_prefix:Tag_Function>
```

Or, if you are not using the tag body then:

```
<your_prefix:Tag_Function/>
```

JavaScriptTag_Example.jsp

Save this file as `JavaScriptTag_Example.jsp`, which can be saved anywhere within your JSP application:

```
<%@ taglib uri="http://www.jspinsider.com/jspkit/javascript"
           prefix="JavaScript"
%>
<html>
  <head>
  </head>
  <body>

    <p>This is a simple test page</p>

    <JavaScript:message >
      This is a simple java alert message
    </JavaScript:message>

  </body>
</html>
```

Running this example produces the following JSP page on your browser:

Reviewing the Example

Building a tag library was actually quick and easy. The work required to build a tag follows this flow:

❑ Use JavaBeans as a repository for any reusable code

❑ Build the tag handler where the actual custom tag performs its logical processing

❑ Create a TEI file to define any special processing that occurs between the custom tag and the JSP page

❑ Create a TLD file, which defines the tag so the outside world knows how to use the tag, and which functions as the spot where we collect all the tag handlers together to form a tag library

❑ Initialize the JSP container to alert it to where the custom tag is stored

❑ Call the tag from our JSP page

Technically you don't have to perform the first step, but it is included since the majority of the time you should separate your logic to get maximum benefit for reusability within your project.

There are several questions raised by this example.

Why Build a Tag to Produce JavaScript?

As a general rule it isn't recommended to mix client side and server side code such as JavaScript and Java together, unless the programmer is very familiar with the overall picture. The reason for the rule is that it can be confusing and the interaction between the server side and client scripts can be complex. However, every rule is made to be broken and we have a very good reason to do so here.

The overall example itself shows that it is easy to expand JSP to have functionality it doesn't normally have. In this case we added the ability to pop up an alert box to the user from within the browser.

The JavaScript example was also chosen to show that you could use a tag to produce any sort of output. This example illustrates that a custom tag can encapsulate the logic for many different processes, including processes that may not be directly associated with server side activities. For example, a custom tag could generate client side validation scripts for form fields.

Why are There so Many Steps to Building a Single Custom Tag?

It comes down to an issue of portability and flexibility. These extra up front steps of the TEI and TLD files are actually what make custom tags easier to modify and expand. In fact the TLD file is the central piece that actually helps make custom tags portable. Overall the TLD and TEI are the layering of the logic and the definition files that gives tags their inherent power.

Also if you look more closely at what we just did, you will notice a good portion of the work is just building simple files and creating pointers so the JSP container can find everything. The good news is that much of this work for building a tag can be automated. JSP editors are being released with solid custom tag support to ease the task of building tags. While it might seem like some extra work to connect all the parts, they are all needed to keep the solid structure of a tag library.

Extending the Example

As mentioned earlier, custom tags can expand JSP, but sometimes this expansion can occur in surprising directions. One of these is that we can time the alert boxes to be triggered by events within the client side window. Now we could pop up a special box when the window is loaded or pop up a warning box when a browser window closes.

JavaScript.java

First of all we will use the `JavaScript.java` file to generate the JavaScript code. Below is the relevant code that we will use to display our closing message. The constructor for this class reads the browser type and sets this in a variable, which is used later in the alert box code:

```
public JavaScript() {
  broswer_validation =
    "var isIE = (navigator.appName == \"Microsoft Internet Explorer\") ? 1 : 0;";
  broswer_validation +=
    "var isNS = (navigator.appName == \"Netscape\") ? 1 : 0;";
  broswer_validation +=
    "var isNS4 = (navigator.appName == \"Netscape\" &&
parseInt(navigator.appVersion) < 5);";
  }
```

This new `alert()` method overloads the `alert()` method we have already seen above:

```
public String alert(Object aobj_data, String as_name, String as_element,
                    String as_event) {
```

Netscape 6.0 doesn't use "on" prefixes for events, so strip it out if we find it:

```
        String ls_test = as_event.trim().substring(0, 2).toLowerCase();

        if (ls_test.equals("on")) {
          as_event = as_event.substring(2, as_event.length());
        }
```

The alert box is filled with JavaScript that creates a function based on the name of the event:

```
        String ls_start_alert = start_script + broswer_validation;
        String ls_event_alert = "function " + as_name + "(){alert(\""
                            + aobj_data.toString() + "\");}";
        String ls_end_alert = end_script;
        String ls_alert = ls_start_alert;
```

As we shall see in a moment, the tag is given an event (on_unload) with a name (goodbye) and an element to use (window). These are passed up in a function that is dependent on the client's browser:

```
        ls_alert += "if (isIE)   " + as_element + ".on" + as_event + " = "
                + as_name + "; ";
        ls_alert += "if (isNS && !isNS4) " + as_element
                + ".addEventListener(\"" + as_event + "\"," + as_name
                + ", true);";
        ls_alert += ls_event_alert;
        ls_alert += ls_end_alert;

        return (ls_alert);
      }
```

JavaScriptTag.java

The JavaScriptTag.java tag handler is similar to the JavaScriptExampleTag.java example we saw above. Only those lines that have been altered are shown below.

The setEvent() method is used to indicate which event triggers the alert box. An event could be a page loading (the onload event) or a page closing (the onunload event):

```
      private String event = "";

      public void setEvent(String as_event) {
          this.event = as_event;
      }
```

The setElement() method is used to indicate which element the event is associated with. In this example, the only element used is the window element:

```
      private String element = "";

      public void setElement(String as_element) {
        this.element = as_element;
      }
```

The setName() element is used to give the newly created alert function a unique name. For example, an alert triggered by an onload event could be called "welcome":

```
private String name = "";

public void setName(String as_name) {
  this.name = as_name;
}
```

The doEndTag() method is similar to that in the JavaScriptExampleTag.java with a few alterations:

```
public int doEndTag() throws JspTagException {
  String ls_alert   = "";
  String ls_display = "";

  try {
    BodyContent lbc_bodycurrent = getBodyContent();

    if(lbc_bodycurrent != null) {
      JavaScript  JS = new JavaScript();
      String ls_message = lbc_bodycurrent.getString() + ls_display;
      if (event.length() > 0 && event.length() >0) {
        ls_alert = JS.alert(ls_message.trim(),name,element,event);
      } else {
        ls_alert = JS.alert(ls_message.trim());
      }
    }
    pageContext.getOut().write(ls_alert);
  }
  catch (IOException e) {
    throw new JspTagException("JSP Kit JavaScriptTag Error:" + e.toString());
  }

  // Have the JSP Container continue processing the JSP page as normal.
  return EVAL_PAGE;
}
```

JavaScriptTag.tld

The TLD for this example describes the tag and attributes from above:

```
<?xml version="1.0" encoding="ISO-8859-1" ?>
<!DOCTYPE taglib
    PUBLIC "-//Sun Microsystems, Inc.//DTD JSP Tag Library 1.1//EN"
    "http://java.sun.com/j2ee/dtds/web-jsptaglibrary_1_1.dtd">

<taglib>

  <tlibversion>1.0</tlibversion>
  <jspversion>1.1</jspversion>
  <shortname>JavaScriptTag</shortname>
  <uri></uri>
  <info>
      A simple tab library for making JavaScript
```

```
    </info>

    <tag>
      <name>alert</name>
      <tagclass>com.jspinsider.jspkit.javascript.JavaScriptTag</tagclass>
      <info> Display Alert Box</info>
      <attribute>
        <name>name</name>
        <required>false</required>
        <rtexprvalue>true</rtexprvalue>
      </attribute>
      <attribute>
        <name>element</name>
        <required>false</required>
        <rtexprvalue>true</rtexprvalue>
      </attribute>
      <attribute>
          name>event</name>
          required>false</required>
          rtexprvalue>true</rtexprvalue>
      </attribute>

    </tag>

</taglib>
```

web.xml

The web.xml file looks like this:

```
<?xml version="1.0" encoding="ISO-8859-1"?>
<!DOCTYPE web-app
    PUBLIC "-//Sun Microsystems, Inc.//DTD Web Application  2.2//EN"
    "http://java.sun.com/j2ee/dtds/web-app_2.2.dtd">

<web-app>
  <taglib>
    <taglib-uri>
      http://www.jspinsider.com/jspkit/JavaScriptTags
    </taglib-uri>
    <taglib-location>
      /WEB-INF/JavaScriptTag.tld
    </taglib-location>
  </taglib>

</web-app>
```

Kit_JavaScript.jsp

The final piece of this example is the JSP page:

```
<%@ taglib uri="http://www.jspinsider.com/jspkit/JavaScriptTags"
    prefix="JavaScript" %>
```

```
<html>
  <head>

    <JavaScript:alert name="welcome" element="window" event="onload">
      Welcome to our JavaScript Test.
    </JavaScript:alert>

    <JavaScript:alert name="goodbye" element="window" event="onunload">
      Good Bye thanks for testing this!
    </JavaScript:alert>

    <title> Custom Tag Example </title>
  </head>

  <body>

    <p>This is a simple test page</p>

  </body>
</html>
```

A Debug Extension

Now that we can trigger an alert, there are a number of possibilities. One of these that we will explore is the ability to display an alert box containing debugging information. This will provide us with a useful tool to see the data within the `request` object when submitting a form, or to track what is in the `session` object as we move from page to page.

JavaScriptDebugTag.java

The tag handler for the debug tag utilises the `JavaScript.java` file to create the alert box:

```
package com.jspinsider.jspkit.javascript;

import java.io.IOException;
import javax.Servlet.jsp.*;
import javax.Servlet.jsp.tagext.*;
import java.util.*;
import javax.Servlet.jsp.PageContext.*;
import javax.Servlet.*;


public class JavaScriptDebugTag extends BodyTagSupport {
```

In a similar manner to the `JavaScriptTag.java` tag handler the tag attributes we will use are defined in the methods `setView()` (what scope we are interested in, be it session, or application) and `setDisplay()` (whether we want the alert to display or not):

```
private String view = "";

public void setView(String as_object) {
  this.view = as_object.trim().toLowerCase();
}
```

```
/* Prevent alert from displaying */
private boolean display = true;

public void setDisplay(boolean ab_display) {
 this.display = ab_display;
}
```

The `doEndTag()` method is called once the entire tag has been processed by the browser:

```
public int doEndTag() throws JspTagException {
  /* Don't do anything if user prevents alert */
  if (display == false) {
    return EVAL_PAGE;
  }

  /* initialize our variables */
  String ls_alert = "";
  String ls_message = "";
  String ls_data = "";
  String ls_current = "";
  int    li_scope = 0;
```

The next step is to determine which implicit objects attributes the user wants to see:

```
  if (view.equals("session")) {
    li_scope = PageContext.SESSION_SCOPE;
  }

  if (view.equals("request")) {
    li_scope = PageContext.REQUEST_SCOPE;
  }

  if (view.equals("application")) {
    li_scope = PageContext.APPLICATION_SCOPE;
  }

  if (view.equals("page")) {
    li_scope = PageContext.PAGE_SCOPE;
```

If the user requested to see an implicit object, loop through and build list of variables stashed in the object:

```
  if (li_scope > 0) {
    Enumeration enum_app =
    pageContext.getAttributeNamesInScope(li_scope);

    ls_data += " Data stored within " + view;

    for (; enum_app.hasMoreElements(); ) {
      ls_current = enum_app.nextElement().toString();

      if (ls_current != null) {
        ls_data += "\\n Attribute: " + ls_current + "  = ";

        Object results = pageContext.getAttribute(ls_current, li_scope);
```

```
          if (results != null) {
            ls_data += results.toString().trim();
          }
        }
      }
```

If it's a `request` object then we also get all its passed parameters. This simple loop won't catch multi-element data elements:

```
        if (li_scope == PageContext.REQUEST_SCOPE) {
          ServletRequest lparms = pageContext.getRequest();
          Enumeration    req_data = lparms.getParameterNames();

          ls_data += "\\n Parameters within Request ";

          for (; req_data.hasMoreElements(); ) {
            ls_current = req_data.nextElement().toString();

            if (ls_current != null) {
              ls_data += "\\n element: " + ls_current + " = ";

              Object results = lparms.getParameter(ls_current);

              if (results != null) {
                ls_data += results.toString().trim();
              }
            }
          }
        }
      }
```

Any data in the tag body is collected and used to build a JavaScript alert box:

```
      try {
        BodyContent lbc_bodycurrent = getBodyContent();

        /* Create our JavaScript object which will build the alert */
        JavaScript  JS = new JavaScript();

        if (lbc_bodycurrent != null) {
          ls_message = lbc_bodycurrent.getString().trim();
        }

        /* Create our alert box */
        ls_alert = JS.alert(ls_message + "\\n" + ls_data);

        /* print out the alert box to the JSP Page */
        pageContext.getOut().write(ls_alert);
      } catch (IOException e) {
        throw new JspTagException("JavaScriptDebugTag Error:"
                                  + e.toString());
      }

      return EVAL_PAGE;
    }

  }
```

JavaScriptTag.tld

In order for us to utilise the new tag, we must make additions to the TLD file to point the JSP container to the correct specification. However, the web.xml file does not need to be changed – it already points to this TLD file:

```
<tag>
  <name>debug</name>
  <tagclass>com.jspinsider.jspkit.javascript.JavaScriptDebugTag</tagclass>
  <info> Display Debugging Alert Box</info>
  <attribute>
    <name>view</name>
    <required>false</required>
    <rtexprvalue>true</rtexprvalue>
  </attribute>
  <attribute>
    <name>display</name>
    <required>false</required>
    <rtexprvalue>true</rtexprvalue>
  </attribute>
</tag>
```

Kit_JavaScript.jsp

The final addition to this example is the actual tag in the JSP page:

```
<JavaScript:debug view="application">
    This is a Test
</JavaScript:debug>
```

Running this example produces the following JSP page on your browser:

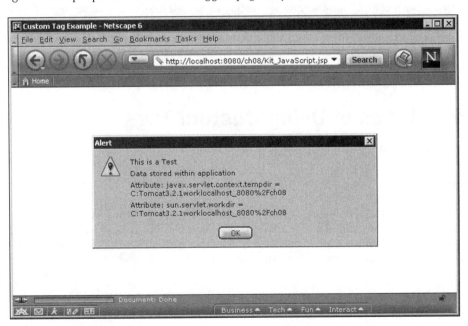

Final Examination of the Example

Our example tags also illustrate some additional advantages of custom tags.

Tags Speed Up the Learning Curve of JSP

Building JSP is much more than knowing how to program Java – it requires learning many different skills. The main problem with scriptlets is the requirement that the programmer understands a minimum of three technologies at once:

❑   You must know Java

❑   You must understand the scripting syntax and JSP objects

❑   You need to understand the client output you are producing (JavaScript/HTML, XML/XSL, etc.)

When you use a custom tag, someone else has already dealt with a good portion of the logic. In this example we handled and encapsulated JavaScript within our tags. A person using this tag doesn't need to understand how JavaScript works to display an alert box to the user. We also dealt with the Java code to produce the alert box. This means we have just cut the learning curve by over 50% since the user only needs to concentrate on the JSP page and how the tag results interact with the browser.

Simple Tags Lead to Unexpected Improvements

This example is a simple JavaScript alert. We quickly realized we could add two additional features. We could time the alert boxes to be triggered by events within the client side window. Now we could pop up a special box when the window is loaded or pop up a warning box when a browser window closes. However, this led to the second realization that an immediate practical use for this is to help to debug JSP pages.

So taking the same code as our example we quickly expanded it to have a debug tag. This tag pops up an alert box to display the contents of the implicit objects. Now we have a useful tool to see the data within the `request` object when submitting a form, or to track what is in the `session` object as we move from page to page. So even simple tags can form the building blocks for many possible uses within your project.

Disadvantages of Using Custom Tags

While they are extremely useful, tags do have some drawbacks in their use.

Performance

Accomplishing reusability within tag libraries comes at the price of adding extra layers into your web application, which means additional processing is required. For the average web sites this *will not* be a problem and you will not see a performance hit. However, for web applications where the design demands each drop of performance, you will want to closely examine your tag usage.

Overuse

Tags have many clear benefits in their use. These benefits are so overwhelming in many cases that for the 1.2 release of JSP there probably will be a tendency to overuse custom tags. Custom tags are a new methodology for doing business, and the common sense boundaries of where, when and how they should be used have not been fully determined yet. By the time JSP 2.0 is released the proper balance of using custom tags relative to scriptlets will be understood and documented. Until this time, as developers, we need to watch how Sun and the larger open source projects such as Struts are deploying custom tags.

Currently, it seems the old 80/20 rule is in effect in determining the right balance: 80% of a JSP project should be based upon custom tags and 20% on scriptlets. However, the problem with setting a rule like this is that the rule is too simple. This brings us back to the real problem of how to determine the right balance for your current project. For new projects it is easy to jump into custom tags for the easy sections and as the project gains experience to ramp up the use of tag libraries. For existing projects, it would be wise to leave code that is working alone and to upgrade as the new sections of the project are built.

The wonderful thing about tags is that we have time to implement them properly; JSP does not rely on tags to function. Take a deep breath and don't feel pressured to implement tag libraries. You have the time to understand tags before rushing out to use them on your mission critical project. Start small and develop a solid understanding before jumping in to tag libraries.

Tags can be Awkward

There is a line of thought in the Java community that tags are not the best solution, since at times the syntax can be awkward and clumsy. This is true to some extent; no language is ever perfect. The fact of the matter is that tags solve many problems but will introduce a few new ones.

Many times it will come down to personal preferences. When this is the case and it is felt that scriptlets would be easier to maintain, then use scriptlets. Always remember you are a JSP programmer and that tag libraries are merely one tool in the overall JSP specifications. The old saying, "Use the right tool for the right job" is alive and well within the JSP specifications.

Performance Costs of Third Party Tags

Using prebuilt tags is a wonderful way to speed up development. In fact, it is one of the best ways to give your project a boost in speed. While the current selection of third party tags is limited, over time a whole industry will grow to support building custom tags.

However, it should be noted that using a prebuilt tag may have hidden costs. The third party tag may not meet the performance requirements for your project. As a result, if you plan on using third party tags in any mission critical aspect, it is always prudent to have a back up plan or tag ready in case your first choice doesn't meet expectations.

JSP Only

Custom tags are meant only for JSP. They don't port over to Servlets or other Java-based solutions. This really isn't a problem since tags primarily replace scriptlets, which are also a JSP-only solution. The biggest impact for programmers is to remember to embed reusable logic within JavaBeans, which will be reusable in other Java solutions.

As an example of this you could build a report tag to output a report into an HTML table. If you are generating the report from the database, then much of your logic is reusable for other database-generated work. As a result any generic Java code used to access the database should be placed within a JavaBean. Later your tag can easily access this bean to get to its data. In practice, there are other design reasons to partition your logic. Especially since it will help you maintain and organize complicated tag handlers. Once you have your JavaBean you can then base your custom tag on the JavaBean.

When to use Custom Tags In JSP

When building custom tags several basic design considerations must be addressed. These topics will be fully discussed in the later chapters. However, it is important to point out several facts early.

Accessing your Java Objects

Within JSP you often use JavaBeans to package your logic into independent code packages. However, when you need to kick these objects into action you will often use a tag library to do so. This is something we are already used to doing with the `<jsp:useBean>` tag. The only difference is that now, when the `<useBean>` tag is not enough we can create our own tag to handle the situation.

General Design Practices

A successful JSP site is a reflection of a successful design model. There are many different schools of thought on how to best implement a JSP site. The majority of the Java community believes that reducing dependence on inline JSP scripting is of critical importance. This helps to place custom tags as a central part of many JSP implementations.

However, there are many developers who feel there are times when heavy JSP scripting is a perfectly legitimate design model. The correct design model actually varies from project to project and in the end it is not the model that matters as much as having a successful maintainable product. As a result there are times when you may decide not to use custom tags.

For example, in the future as the role of JSP grows, JSP will also be used to build web applications that deliver XML based content to other systems rather than the typical HTML site we normally see today. Java programmers rather than a web designer will maintain these JSP/XML systems.

On this style of application a Java programmer might be more comfortable using embedded Java rather than the custom tags. On average, the majority of Java programmers would still want to use tags in this situation, but again it is a decision that should be based on successful practical experience and personal preferences as much as the benefits that using custom tags bring to the project.

Threading Issues

Many JSP programmers will use custom tags just because of the easy threading model that they present. JSP containers handle tags differently from other objects within a JSP page.

Among other aspects, JSP containers maintain an active pool of custom tag objects to reuse. This helps performance and under certain circumstances it may be faster to use a tag over a standard JavaBean for this reason. More importantly this means a custom tag will always be thread-safe since the container will only let one thread use an active tag object at a time.

However, while the tag itself is thread-safe, the objects that the tags are referencing may not be. For example, three tags could reference and modify the same session or application object attribute. The effects of this can be quite unexpected. Consider, what would happen if two developers built different tags, which by chance happened to create and modify an attribute of the same name in the `session` object. In this case one tag would clobber the results of the other tag. This means extreme care must be used when modifying objects which are outside of the tag.

Tag Scope

A custom tag has page scope, and this must be taken into consideration when designing tags. However, while the tag has page scope you can still access data and objects stored in any scope. To accomplish this, it is a simple matter of using the `getAttribute()` method of the `PageContext` object. For example, retrieving an object from the `session` object:

```
myObject = pageContext.getAttribute("The_Key", PageContext.SESSION_SCOPE);
```

Since the scope of a tag is page level, a tag should only be designed to last as long as the calling request requires.

When to Build a Custom Tag

While tags offer the benefit of reusability, they come at the cost of some extra development time up front to actually build the tag. After you decide that building a custom tag is the right technical solution, you also must decide if it is the right choice for your project's timeline.

Generally, the ease of reuse and reduced debugging over the long-term counterbalances the initial up front development costs of the tag. However, you can look at this as a relatively simple equation of time: does the extra time used to initially build and test a tag library get counter balanced by the timesaving from having the reusable object? To find the answer you can ask two questions to help you decide when a custom tag is worth the extra time.

Will the Code be Used on More than Two JSPs?

The simple fact is that there is no economy of scale from reusing scriptlets. When you cut and paste scriptlets from page to page, you are not maintaining a single scriptlet but are instead creating more unique code that spreads across your JSP site, creating more code that needs maintenance.

While this might sound more like a fungus than a scriptlet, from a maintenance point of view it isn't much better than fungus. In fact, the official technical term 'spaghetti code' pretty well describes the end result of cut and paste scriptlet reuse. As a direct result, it only takes a few times of reuse to make a custom tag a project time saver.

The magical rule of three is actually an ancient object-oriented rule used for reusable objects in general. Once you find you need to use a single piece of code more than two times you almost always save development time when you place the logic in a centralized reusable module.

If you answer yes to this question then it's time to move your code to a custom tag.

Do you Expect the Scriptlet to Change over Time?

This rule is not as obvious as the first rule. After all, if the code isn't being reused in other places wouldn't a scriptlet actually be easier to maintain than a custom tag? This rule is more a choice of personal preferences of the programmer. By moving the code into a tag you are effectively moving code from the JSP scripting matrix into objects.

The true benefit comes from placing the logic into a more structured environment. This added structure can be of great benefit in helping a programmer make sense of complicated code that is subject to many changes. The other major benefit comes from the fact that complicated scriptlets can be broken down into several tags. The advantage is the ability to partition the work more logically and in smaller sections that makes debugging and changing logic simpler.

If you answer yes here, then it's a matter of your personal preference on which solution you think will be easier to maintain.

Acceptance of Custom Tags

Newer JSP programmers may wonder at the slow adoption rate of custom tags. After all, if tags are so great why has the JSP community been slow to use them within projects? This reticence was due to two main reasons:

❑　The major brand name JSP containers are upgraded slowly to the latest JSP standards. As a result it took a while before a sizeable segment of the JSP community even had a chance to use custom tags.

❑　Custom tags are a new concept for Java unique to JSP. More importantly, tag libraries are a fundamental shift in the way JSP pages are built. It just takes time for the developing community to understand the changes enough so they can be reflected in standard practices. In other words, JSP programmers had to ponder tags a bit before embracing them in their standard tool kit.

Ironically the slow adoption has been beneficial since it has given time for JSP developers to learn more about custom tags. This also means the JSP standard has had time to polish and improve custom tags with relatively minor impact to the overall marketplace. Custom tags are quickly increasing in use and with the release of JSP 1.2 they will become a standard part of most JSP projects. For the long term, custom tags will be one of the main features that will drive the market to build JSP projects.

Summary

In studying custom tags we find an exciting technology that improves JSP on all fronts. There are quite a few benefits that custom tags bring to the JSP specification:

❑　Tags allow JSP to be easily expanded

❑　Using tags gives easy access to JSP for non-Java programmers

❑　It is easier than ever to reuse code between projects

❑　Tags open up JSP to unexpected improvements by the whole JSP community

❑　Development and maintenance time are decreased

Using a custom tag is extremely easy and this ease of use is what will cause many projects to adopt custom tags as a standard way to do business. While building a tag isn't very hard, there is still a learning curve that is associated with custom tags.

As a result, using tags will be a gradual process for many programmers as they get used to building them within their projects. With time the JSP developer community will get more proficient at using tags and using of tags will become commonplace for JSP programmers. Eventually tags will become the standard method for implementing code within a JSP page.

As with any product there are performance and implementation issues associated with using custom tags. However, custom tags are still new enough that the optimal way to implement tag libraries within a project is still being determined by the user community. Overall, custom tags are a powerful feature of JSP that will drive JSP to new directions as the user community embraces this exciting technology.

More importantly from a project point of view custom tags are probably the single most important feature that JSP has to offer the developer community and, as a result, a central part of any JSP developer's bag of tricks. However, JSP developers should not view custom tags as a replacement for any current JSP feature, but rather as a new and additional tool for our use to build better JSP applications. The JSP community can look to products such as Struts to offer an indication of the importance of custom tags and what many projects will look like where tag libraries form the core of the JSP logic.

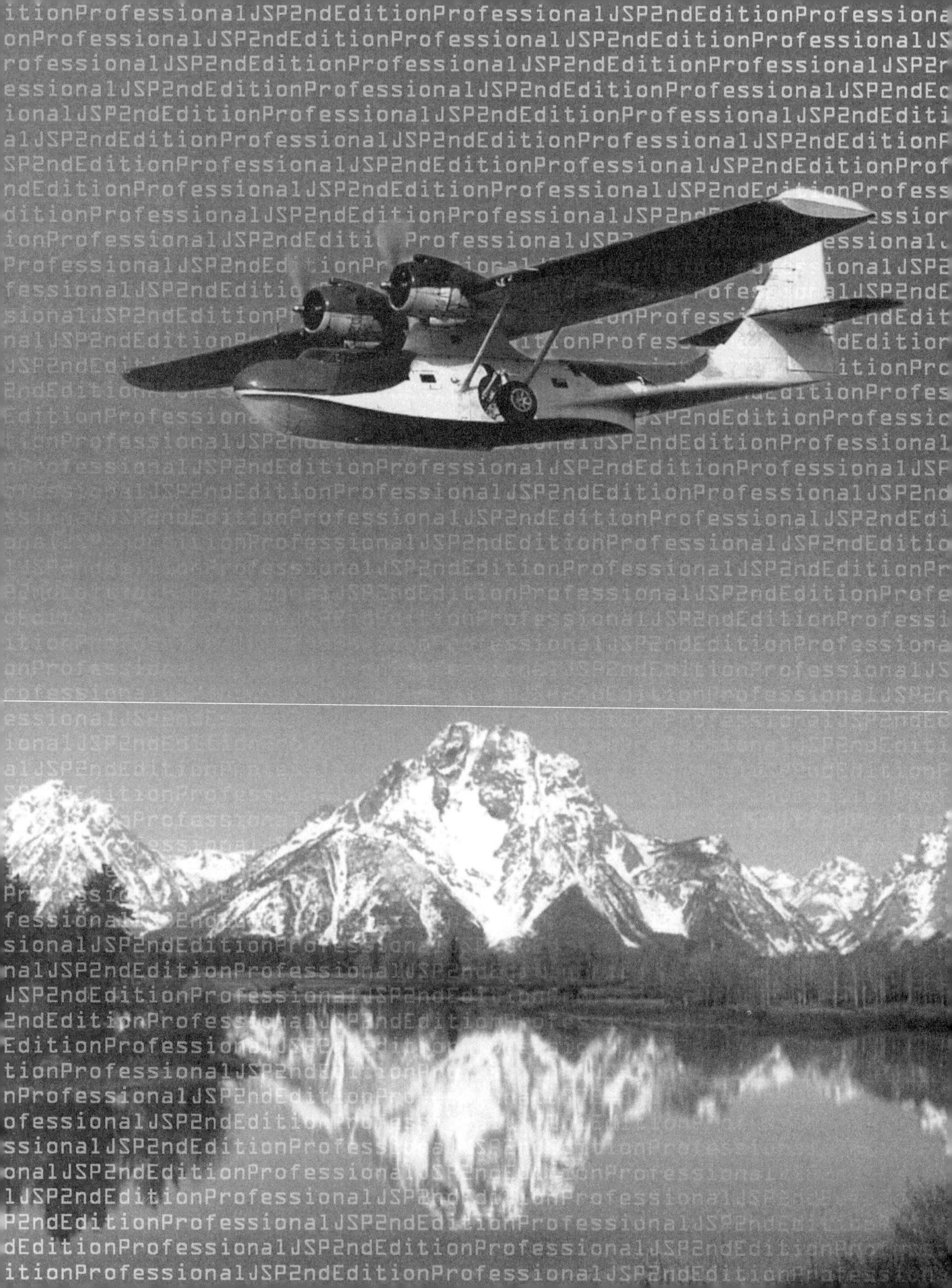
ProfessionalJSP2ndEdition

Creating Simple Custom Tags

As we have seen, at its most basic a custom tag is just a Java class written to a specific interface that the web server can use. The mechanism itself is designed to be simple to understand and program, yet powerful and flexible enough to be used in a wide variety of situations. Even though Java is the only scripting language currently supported by JSP, the custom tag mechanism is independent of the choice of page scripting language and so is to an extent future-proofed.

There are already servers such as Caucho's Resin server (http://www.caucho.com) which can use server-side Javascript as an 'unofficial' second scripting language, but you will be able to use your custom tags in your JSP pages no matter which scripting language is actually used on the page itself.

The simplest tags are ones that just 'do something', such as output some constant or computed text. This can be useful if, for instance, you wanted to create a 'copyright' tag that could be put on every page that would display "© 2001 AnyCorp. All Rights Reserved." Then when the year changes and AnyCorp is taken over by MegaCorp, you can easily change every page's copyright notice to display "© 2001, 2002 MegaCorp. All Rights Reserved." just by changing the tag class. These simple tags can be a great help in maintaining large sites.

In this chapter, we'll be covering the basics of creating custom tags. Specifically, we'll be looking at:

- ❑ What we need to create our custom tags
- ❑ The `Tag` interface
- ❑ The `PageContext` object
- ❑ Handling tag attributes
- ❑ Processing a closing tag

❑ Storing objects in the page attributes

❑ Introducing scripting variables from a tag, and from the TLD

❑ Loops

What do you Need to use a Custom Tag?

As we saw in Chapter 8, there are four things you need to use a custom tag:

❑ The Java file that does the processing

❑ The Tag Library Descriptor (TLD) file that points from the JSP to the Java file

❑ The web.xml file that tells the server where to find the TLD

❑ The JSP file that contains the tag being used

In order to understand how these things fit together, we'll start with a simple "Hello World" example.

Hello World Tag

Here's the code for a small Java class that will print "Hello JSP World" on a web page when called as part of a tag.

There are some important things to note about the code. First of all is the superclass, TagSupport. This class is a helper class defined in the JSP specification to simplify the creation of tags. It's not essential that it's used but it saves you from the pain of having to implement all of the Tag interface's methods when you really just want to use one or two of them. What is important is that all tag extensions must implement the Tag interface.

The Tag interface requires a number of methods be implemented for server actions, even if the actions themselves aren't relevant to that particular tag. The TagSupport base class we use implements simple default versions of these methods, freeing us from having to implement methods we don't need:

```
package com.wrox.projsp.ch09;

import javax.servlet.jsp.*;
import javax.servlet.jsp.tagext.*;

public class HelloWorld extends TagSupport {
```

Our HelloWorld class only implements one method, called doStartTag(). This is one of the Tag interface's methods, and it is called by the server at the point in the page where the server finds one of our opening tags:

```
public int doStartTag() throws JspException {
    try {
```

The next important section to note is the following line. This is the line that actually does the work of writing "Hello JSP World" to the JSP page. The call to PageContext.getOut() returns the current JspWriter object, out. This is the same out object that is used in JSP scriptlets to write to the output stream:

```
                pageContext.getOut().print("Hello JSP World!");
```

It's possible that the `print()` call may throw an `IOException`. In this case we rethrow the `IOException` as a `JspException`, which is the only type of exception `doStartTag()` can throw. Rethrowing the exception means the error page specified in the `errorPage` directive will be shown to the user, hopefully with some useful debugging for developers or a friendly error message for visitors:

```
        } catch (Exception ioException) {
            System.err.println("IO Exception thrown in HelloWorld.doStartTag():");
            System.err.println(ioException.toString());

            throw new JspException(ioException);
        }
```

Finally, our `doStartTag()` method returns the `Tag.SKIP_BODY` constant. This can be used by any tag handler to tell the server that it is not required to process the text enclosed between the start tag and end tag. We'll get to other possible return values later:

```
        return SKIP_BODY;
    }

}
```

Our `HelloWorld` tag doesn't need to do anything when an end tag is found, so we don't implement the `doEndTag()` method. By leaving the `doEndTag()` method unimplemented in the `HelloWorld` class, the `doEndTag()` method in the `TagSupport` class is called instead when an end tag is processed. All the methods in `TagSupport` are designed to provide a default 'do-nothing' action when called. This allows the derived classes such as `HelloWorld` to provide only the behavior that is non-default.

In fact, `TagSupport` implements the `IterationTag` interface that we'll see later in the chapter; since `IterationTag` extends `Tag`, you can use `TagSupport` as a base class for either 'normal' or iteration tags.

The PageContext Object

The `PageContext` object is used to provide convenient access to implicit JSP objects, as well as provide a simple object store for passing objects within a JSP page. You can see this in the following line from the above `HelloWorld` source code:

```
    pageContext.getOut().print("Hello JSP World!");
```

We'll cover use of the `PageContext` as an object store later in this chapter, but for now it's worth noting that it has the following useful methods:

❑   `getOut()`

❑   `getPage()`

❑   `getRequest()`

❑   `getResponse()`

❏   `getServletConfig()`

❏   `getServletContext()`

❏   `getSession()`

The above methods provide quick access to the JSP implicit objects. These objects (and in fact the `PageContext` object itself) are all the same objects that you use in scriptlets. The `PageContext` object here is just providing an easy interface for tags to get a handle on the implicit objects.

Making the HelloWorld Class Available to the Server

Once we have the Java class ready, we need to tell the web server about it and how it should be used. This is done through an XML document called a **Tag Library Descriptor**, or **TLD**. The TLD gives the server structured information on the tag library itself, as well as details of the individual tags in the library. The TLD for our `HelloWorld` class is as follows, which we'll save as `helloworldtags.tld`:

```
<?xml version="1.0" encoding="ISO-8859-1" ?>
<!DOCTYPE taglib
   PUBLIC "-//Sun Microsystems, Inc.//DTD JSP Tag Library 1.2//EN"
   "http://java.sun.com/j2ee/dtds/web-jsptaglibrary_1_2.dtd

<taglib>
  <tlib-version>1.0</tlib-version>
  <jsp-version>1.2</jsp-version>
  <short-name>Hello World</short-name>
  <description>
    A simple Hello World tag library.
  </description>

  <tag>
    <name>helloworld</name>
    <tag-class>com.wrox.projsp.ch09.HelloWorld</tag-class>
    <body-content>empty</body-content>
  </tag>
</taglib>
```

> **The Document Type Definition for the XML Tag Library Descriptor file has changed significantly from the one used in the JSP 1.1 standard. New tags have been added and many tags are now hyphenated. For example `<tlibversion>` has become `<tlib-version>` in the JSP 1.2 DTD. Old TLDs based on the JSP 1.1 DTD will continue to work as long as they reference the 1.1 DTD in their DOCTYPE directive.**

The preliminary information within the `taglib` directive is simply to specify which version of the tag library is in use, and which version of the JSP specification it was written for. Also included is a friendly name for the library and a brief summary of the tag's purpose.

After that `taglib` information, the individual tags themselves are specified. Our library contains just one tag, `helloworld`, so there is only one `<tag>...</tag>` structure. Within that structure, the tag is given a `name`, and a `tag-class` is specified.

The `tag-class` is the actual Java class that will be used when the tag is encountered in a JSP page, and so is the same as that of our `HelloWorld` class shown above.

> The name given in the `<tag>`...`</tag>` structure is the name you must use to specify the tag in the JSP page. The actual class name itself is only ever referenced in the TLD file, not in the JSP page. This makes the tag name act like an alias for referring to the class.

Our class is simple and doesn't need to enclose any body text. We let the server know this by specifying:

```
<body-content>empty</body-content>
```

If the tag is accidentally used to enclose some body text, this will cause a translation-time error when the JSP page is first compiled. This is a good thing. Remember – it's always better to catch errors sooner rather than later. We'll cover tags that enclose body text later in this chapter, and tags that can manipulate their body will be discussed in the next chapter.

Making the Tag Visible to the Server

The server itself needs to be told the location of this TLD, and this is done via a `web.xml` file. All our examples in this chapter are contained within one web application, so we only need one `web.xml` for all our tag libraries. If the examples were to be split across several web applications, each application would require its own `web.xml` file. Here's the start of the `web.xml` we'll use throughout this chapter – as we add extra examples, we'll add to this file:

```
<!DOCTYPE web-app
   PUBLIC "-//Sun Microsystems, Inc.//DTD Web Application 2.2//EN"
   "http://java.sun.com/j2ee/dtds/web-app_2_2.dtd">

<web-app>
   <display-name>Chapter 9 examples</display-name>
   <description>
     This is the collection of sample tag libraries used in
     chapter 9 of Professional JSP, 2nd edition.
   </description>

   <taglib>
      <taglib-uri>/helloworldtags.tld</taglib-uri>
      <taglib-location>/WEB-INF/helloworldtags.tld</taglib-location>
   </taglib>

</web-app>
```

Both the `web.xml` file and the `helloworldtags.tld` file go in the `WEB-INF` directory. We also have a simple error page, `error.jsp`:

```
<%@ page import="java.io.*" isErrorPage="true" %>
<html>
<head>
   <title>Error!</title>
</head>
<body>

<h1>Error: <%=exception%></h1>
   <%
   StringWriter errorWriter = new StringWriter ();
```

```
    PrintWriter errorStream = new PrintWriter (errorWriter);
    exception.printStackTrace (errorStream);
    %>
    <p>Stack trace:
    <blockquote>
      <pre><%=errorWriter%></pre>
    </blockquote>
  </body>
  </html>
```

This error page prints out any exception followed by the complete stack trace. We'll use this same error page for all our examples.

The structure of our web application is now as follows, where <webapps> is the path to the Tomcat standard webapps folder for holding installed web applications:

- ❑   <webapps>\ch09\HelloWorld.jsp

- ❑   <webapps>\ch09\error.jsp

- ❑   <webapps>\ch09\WEB-INF\helloworldtags.tld

- ❑   <webapps>\ch09\WEB-INF\web.xml

- ❑   <webapps>\ch09\WEB-INF\classes\< Java tag handler classes>

All our examples will follow this standard layout. Each example will have its own JSP file and TLD file, but the rest of the structure will remain the same for all examples. We'll only use the one web.xml file, and it will just map the TLD resource names used in the JSP pages onto the files in the WEB-INF directory.

Using the HelloWorld Tag in a JSP

Now we get to actually use the tag. Here's our simple JSP that uses the tag:

```
<%@ page errorPage="error.jsp" %>
<HTML>
<HEAD>
  <TITLE>Hello World Example</TITLE>
</HEAD>
<BODY>
  <%@ taglib uri="/helloworldtags.tld" prefix="chap09" %>
  <chap09:helloworld/>
</BODY>
</HTML>
```

The TLD is specified in the taglib directive, and this library is given a prefix of "chap09". This prefix is used to avoid name clashes between custom JSP tags and standard HTML tags, and between custom JSP tags from different vendors. The prefix used in the taglib directive is the responsibility of the page author, not the tag author, so page authors can choose any prefix they want here to avoid name clashes as long as they use the prefix consistently. It's probably better to use a name that's unique to that tag vendor, such as the name of the tag library or the organization.

The actual tag itself is:

```
<chap09:helloworld/>
```

> Note that unlike HTML tags such as **
** and **<img...>**, custom tags in JSP must be closed, or must be self-closed, such as: **<tag/>**

This call uses the same prefix specified in the `taglib` directive, and the name of the tag as specified in the TLD. This way the server knows which TLD to refer to (from the prefix) and then which tag within the TLD (from the tag name).

And finally, loading the page in your browser should show you the following:

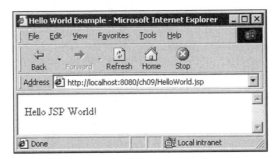

Notice how all that's actually sent to the browser is the phrase "Hello JSP World!". Only the tag's output is sent to the client – the tag itself is never sent. This allows you to produce pages that are dynamically generated but independent of any particular client features.

The Tag Interface

All tag handler classes are Java classes that implement one of the `Tag`, `IterationTag`, or `BodyTag` interfaces. Interfaces are used to simplify the process of adapting an existing Java class to make it a tag handler. If an existing class already inherits from a base class, we could not make it inherit from a required tag-handling base class as Java doesn't support multiple inheritance. We would have to remove the object from its existing hierarchy or use a wrapper object. Instead the JSP standard provides a more elegant solution based on interfaces. Classes can still only inherit from one base class, but they can implement as many interfaces as they choose.

The `Tag` interface is the simplest, and is the one used by the `HelloWorld` example. Its main features are summarized below:

Description

This is the simplest interface for JSP tag handlers. Classes that implement this interface can perform custom actions at their start tag and at their end tag, but have no control over body content and cannot perform iterations.

Fields

First we will look at the fields that are defined in the `Tag` interface.

```
public final static int EVAL_BODY_INCLUDE
```

This Field tells the server to evaluate the body content and places it in the out stream. Note: this is the value returned by `TagSupport.doStartTag()` if it is not over-ridden.

299

```
public final static int SKIP_BODY
```

This field tells the server explicitly not to process any body content. Returned by doStartTag().

```
public final static int EVAL_PAGE
```

This field tells the server to continue evaluating the page. Note: this is the value returned by TagSupport.doEndTag() if it is not over-ridden.

```
public final static int SKIP_PAGE
```

This field tells the server explicitly not to process the rest of the page. Returned by doEndTag().

Methods

Next we will look at the methods that are defined in the Tag interface.

```
public abstract int doEndTag()throws javax.servlet.jsp.jspException
```

The server invokes this method on all tag handlers when it encounters a closing tag for this handler instance. A call to doStartTag() will already have been made, and the body content may or may not have been processed. If SKIP_PAGE is returned, no more evaluation is done on the page and the request is completed. If EVAL_PAGE is returned, the page evaluation continues as normal.

```
public abstract int doStartTag()throws javax.servlet.jsp.jspException
```

The server invokes this method on all tag handlers when it encounters an opening tag for this handler instance. If SKIP_BODY is returned, no body content is evaluated and doEndTag() is called. If EVAL_BODY is returned, the body content is evaluated as normal and placed in the out stream.

```
public abstract javax.servlet.jsp.tagext.Tag getParent()
```

This method gets the closest tag handler that encloses this tag handler, or null if one can't be found.

```
public abstract void release()
```

This method is called by the server to allow the tag handler to release any resources it has acquired throughout its life. The JSP standard states that the server must call the release() method for each tag handler object it creates, but it also states that tag handling objects may be re-used if the same tag is used in several places on the same page.

```
public abstract void setPageContext(javax.servlet.jsp.PageContext pc)
```

This method sets the current PageContext for the tag handler, and is called by the server before any calls to doStartTag().

```
public abstract void setParent(javax.servlet.jsp.tagext.Tag param1)
```

This method sets the parent tag handler that will be returned by getParent(). It is called by the server before any call to doStartTag(), so that doStartTag() will have access to its parent should it need it.

> The **javax.servlet.jsp.tagext.TagSupport** class implements the **javax.servlet.jsp.tagext.Tag** interface and provides a simple way to create tag handlers. If you create a tag handler based on **TagSupport**, you only need to create methods for actions you actually want to carry out. For example, our **HelloWorld** class is based on **TagSupport** and only implements one method – **doStartTag()**.

Here's a brief flowchart that shows when the Tag interface's methods are called:

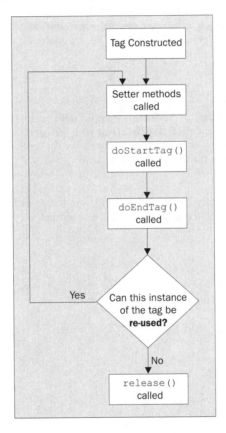

> The server can re-use instances of the tag object to represent the same tag in several places on the same page. Don't count on always getting a newly constructed object. This is something the server has complete control over, and it is free to take an existing tag handler instance and, if **doEndTag()** has been called, re-use it by setting only those attributes which have changed from the first tag instance. There's no way to guarantee the re-use of an existing instance, or guarantee a new instance is created.

Handling Tag Attributes

Most HTML tags can take attributes of some sort to modify the default tag behavior. For instance, one common use of an HTML attribute is to change the background color of a web page. You would change the background of a web page to black by changing the page's BODY tag so it had a BGCOLOR attribute:

```
<body bgcolor="black">
```

An attribute is basically a name/value pair included inside a tag. Custom JSP tags can handle such attributes just as well as HTML tags can, and in advanced use can even accept non-String values.

Handling attributes is done in a simple and elegant way, by taking advantage of the JavaBean specification. Attributes in the tag are mapped on to bean properties, where the JSP server calls the appropriate property setter methods for any attributes included in the page. For example:

```
<mytags:tag1 attr="Springfield"/>
```

> As with JavaBean properties, an attribute is mapped onto get and set methods by capitalizing its first letter and prefixing the result with 'get' and 'set'. For example, our 'username' attribute maps on to getUsername() for the 'read' method and setUsername(String) for the 'write' method.

In the above snippet, the object tag1 is instantiated and then has its setAttr() method called with the parameter Springfield. Only after all the appropriate setter methods have been called is the doStartTag() method called.

The HelloUser Class

To demonstrate this, let's personalize the HelloWorld class. This version takes a username attribute and outputs "Hello <username>!" on the page:

```
package com.wrox.projsp.ch09;

import javax.servlet.jsp.*;
import javax.servlet.jsp.tagext.*;

public class HelloUser extends TagSupport {
  private String username = "";

  public String getUsername() {
    return this.username;
  }

  public void setUsername(String newUsername) {
    this.username = newUsername;
  }

  public int doStartTag() throws JspException {
    try {
      pageContext.getOut().print("Hello " + this.getUsername() + "!");
```

```
      } catch (Exception ioException) {
        System.err.println("IO Exception thrown in HelloUser.doStartTag():");
        System.err.println(ioException.toString());

        throw new JspException(ioException);
      }

      return SKIP_BODY;
    }

  }
```

Notice the addition of get and set methods for the `username` property. The `setUsername()` method is used by the server to set the property to the value contained in the tag, **before** `doStartTag()` is called.

The hellouser1tags TLD

Naturally the server needs to know the names of all the permitted attributes. It can derive a list of setter methods by introspection on the JavaBean, but this tells it all bean properties that are writeable rather than just those properties that can be used as attributes. Because of this a definitive list of tag attributes must be listed in the tag definition in the TLD file. Here's our TLD for the `HelloUser` bean, which we'll save as `hellouser1tags.tld`:

```
<?xml version="1.0" encoding="ISO-8859-1" ?>
<!DOCTYPE taglib
  PUBLIC "-//Sun Microsystems, Inc.//DTD JSP Tag Library 1.2//EN"
  "http://java.sun.com/j2ee/dtds/web-jsptaglibrary_1_2.dtd">

<taglib>
  <tlib-version>1.0</tlib-version>
  <jsp-version>1.2</jsp-version>
  <short-name>Hello User</short-name>
  <description>
    This is a simple Hello User tag library.
  </description>

  <tag>
    <name>hellouser</name>
    <tag-class>com.wrox.projsp.ch09.HelloUser</tag-class>
    <body-content>empty</body-content>
    <attribute>
      <name>username</name>
    </attribute>
  </tag>
</taglib>
```

As you can see, the attribute `username` is listed explicitly as part of the tag definition.

Addition to web.xml

Here is the addition to the `web.xml` file, which will let the server know where to find the TLD file:

```
<taglib>
  <taglib-uri>/hellouser1tags.tld</taglib-uri>
  <taglib-location>/WEB-INF/hellouser1tags.tld</taglib-location>
</taglib>
```

The HelloUser1 JSP

We can then set the username attribute as in the following JSP file:

```
<%@ page errorPage="error.jsp" %>
<html>
<head>
  <title>Hello User Example</title>
</head>
<body>
  <%@ taglib uri="/hellouser1tags.tld" prefix="chap09" %>
  <chap09:hellouser username="Homer"/>
</body>
</html>
```

When this page is processed by the server, the following things happen:

❑ The TLD file is loaded

❑ The custom tag `<chap09:hellouser username="Homer"/>` is found

❑ The class indicated by that tag is located via the TLD file

❑ A new instance of that class is created, since there is no existing class to re-use

❑ That tag object's username attribute is set to Homer in the `setAttribute()` call

❑ `doStartTag()` is called, which gets the username attribute and outputs the "Hello..." text

❑ `doEndTag()` is called, which, by default, does nothing

Viewing `HelloUser1.jsp` gives us the following output:

One important thing to note about the example is that the string itself is hard-coded into the attribute. Other web programming systems such as ASP don't differentiate between hard-coded expressions and runtime expressions, but in this case JSP does. This enables JSP to perform optimizations where it doesn't have to calculate the attribute value every time the page is loaded.

However, this means that if you try and put a runtime expression in the attribute without telling the server to expect runtime expressions, the expression won't be evaluated.

The HelloUser2 JSP

For instance, the following `HelloUser2.jsp` won't work as expected:

```
<%@ page errorPage="error.jsp" %>
<html>
<head>
  <title>Hello User 2 Example</title>
</head>
<body>
  <%@ taglib uri="/hellouser2tags.tld" prefix="chap09" %>
  <%
    String user = "Marge";
  %>
  <chap09:hellouser2 username="<%=user%>"/>
</body>
</html>
```

This will output "Hello <%=user%>!" to your browser, rather than "Hello Marge", although the
<%=user%> string probably won't be visible in your browser window.

The hellouser2tags TLD

To fix this, you need to explicitly mark each attribute that can accept a runtime expression as such in the
`<attribute>` structure in the TLD. This forces the evaluation of the attribute to be delayed until run-time,
whether it truly is a run-time-evaluated scriptlet or not, so overusing this feature may result in a performance
penalty. You mark an attribute as accepting run-time expressions by adding
`<rtexprvalue>true</rtexprvalue>` to the tag's details in the `hellouser2tags.tld`, as follows:

```
<?xml version="1.0" encoding="ISO-8859-1" ?>
<!DOCTYPE taglib
   PUBLIC "-//Sun Microsystems, Inc.//DTD JSP Tag Library 1.2//EN"
   "http://java.sun.com/j2ee/dtds/web-jsptaglibrary_1_2.dtd">

<taglib>
  <tlib-version>1.0</tlib-version>
  <jsp-version>1.2</jsp-version>
  <short-name>Hello User</short-name>
  <description>
    This is a simple Hello User tag library.
  </description>

  <tag>
    <name>hellouser2</name>
    <tag-class>com.wrox.projsp.ch09.HelloUser</tag-class>
    <body-content>empty</body-content>
    <attribute>
      <name>username</name>
      <rtexprvalue>true</rtexprvalue>
    </attribute>
  </tag>
</taglib>
```

Addition to web.xml

Once you've changed the TLD, you'll also need to add something to `web.xml`:

```
<taglib>
  <taglib-uri>/hellouser2tags.tld</taglib-uri>
  <taglib-location>/WEB-INF/hellouser2tags.tld</taglib-location>
</taglib>
```

This gives the correct "Hello Marge!" output in the browser window.

The <attribute> structure

The full list of elements you can put in the `<attribute>` structure are:

❑ `name`
The canonical name of the attribute, which must be used to refer to it in tags in JSPs. This must map on to a setter method in the tag bean. This element is required.

❑ `required`
States whether this attribute must be present in the tag on the JSP for the tag to be well formed. Possible values: `true`, `false`, `yes`, `no`. This element is optional and defaults to `false`.

❑ `rtexprvalue`
States whether this attribute values can be dynamically calculated at runtime (via a scriptlet expression) or must instead be a static value determined at translation time. Possible values: `true`, `false`, `yes`, `no`. This element is optional and defaults to `false`.

❑ `type`
Defines the Java type of the attribute value. Static values are always of type `String`, but runtime expressions can be of any type. This element is optional and defaults to `String`. It ensures that the correct setter method is found, and if not specified the setter method that takes one `String` parameter is used.

The `required` element ensures that an attribute is always supplied, which can be a useful guarantee in some circumstances. For instance, a tag that accesses a database may not work properly unless it is given a JDBC connection string as an attribute. By making that element 'required', you can ensure that pages that use the tag will not compile if the page designer tries to use the tag without supplying the JDBC connection string attribute. Naturally you always need to ensure that the supplied connection string is usable. We'll come across more ways tags can be validated in the next chapter.

Declining Body Processing

The `HelloWorld` bean above didn't need to work with any page text enclosed between the beginning and end tags, so `doStartTag()` just returned the value `SKIP_BODY`. There's a similar return value for tags that want to enclose some body text and allow it to be processed, and that value is `EVAL_BODY_INCLUDE`. In fact, a tag can decide at runtime whether or not it wants to process its body, and can return `SKIP_BODY` to decline body processing or `EVAL_BODY_INCLUDE` to require it.

How can this be useful? Take the example of a site that needs to show certain information to administrators, such as the number of active sessions, or an edit button for a form. In this circumstance we need to process the enclosed body text if the person is logged in as an administrator, and 'hide' or decline body processing if the user is not logged in or is logged in as a regular user.

The AdminOnly Class

Here's the code for a tag to make this work. This is just example code for the tag though – we're not going to delve into the murky waters of user authentication here:

```java
package com.wrox.projsp.ch09;

import javax.servlet.jsp.*;
import javax.servlet.jsp.tagext.*;

public class AdminOnly extends TagSupport {
  private String username = "";

  public String getUsername() {
    return this.username;
  }

  public void setUsername(String newUsername) {
    this.username = newUsername;
  }

  public int doStartTag() throws JspException {
    int processBodyOrNot = SKIP_BODY;

    if (this.getUsername().equals("Lisa")) {
      processBodyOrNot = EVAL_BODY_INCLUDE;
    }

    return processBodyOrNot;
  }

}
```

The important part of the code to note is that doStartTag() returns EVAL_BODY_INCLUDE if and only if username is 'Lisa'.

The adminonlytags TLD

The adminonlytags.tld file for this example is as follows:

```xml
<?xml version="1.0" encoding="ISO-8859-1" ?>
<!DOCTYPE taglib
  PUBLIC "-//Sun Microsystems, Inc.//DTD JSP Tag Library 1.2//EN"
  "http://java.sun.com/j2ee/dtds/web-jsptaglibrary_1_2.dtd">

<taglib>
  <tlib-version>1.0</tlib-version>
  <jsp-version>1.2</jsp-version>
  <short-name>Admin Only</short-name>
  <description>
    A simple tag that will show HTML to an administrator
    but not a regular user.
  </description>

  <tag>
```

```
      <name>adminonly</name>
      <tag-class>com.wrox.projsp.ch09.AdminOnly</tag-class>
      <attribute>
        <name>username</name>
        <rtexprvalue>true</rtexprvalue>
      </attribute>
    </tag>
</taglib>
```

Addition to web.xml

```
    <taglib>
      <taglib-uri>/adminonlytags.tld</taglib-uri>
      <taglib-location>/WEB-INF/adminonlytags.tld</taglib-location>
    </taglib>
```

The AdminOnly JSP

We'll use the following AdminOnly.jsp file to demonstrate this tag is as follows:

```
<%@ page errorPage="error.jsp" %>
<html>
<head>
  <title>Admin Only Example</title>
</head>
<body>
  <%@ taglib uri="/adminonlytags.tld" prefix="chap09" %>
  <p>
  Some text that everyone can see.
  </p>

  <p>
  <%String username = "Bart";%>
  Using username 'Bart'.
  </p>

  <chap09:adminonly username="<%=username%>">
    <blockquote>
      <I>Some text that only administrators can see.</I>
    </blockquote>
  </chap09:adminonly>

  <p>
  <%username = "Lisa";%>
  Using username 'Lisa'.
  </p>

  <chap09:adminonly username="<%=username%>">
    <blockquote>
      <I>Some text that only administrators can see.</I>
    </blockquote>
  </chap09:adminonly>

  <p>
```

```
    <%username = "Maggie";%>
    Using username 'Maggie'.
    </p>

    <chap09:adminonly username="<%=username%>">
      <blockquote>
        <I>Some text that only administrators can see.</I>
      </blockquote>
    </chap09:adminonly>
  </body>
</html>
```

In this JSP page, the tag is being used three times with three different usernames. Here's where the use of SKIP_BODY works for us, by allowing us to ignore the enclosed lines. Since only Lisa is defined as an administrator in the AdminOnly class, the tag 'hides' the enclosed text when Bart and Maggie are given as the usernames, and 'shows' the text only when Lisa is the username.

We can see this in action in the following screenshot:

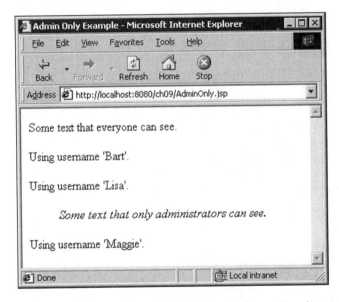

Again it's worth reiterating that the text isn't just 'hidden' if the username doesn't match an administrator's username – the enclosed text isn't sent to the client at all. The text enclosed by the adminonly tag is only ever sent to the client browser if the doStartTag() method returns EVAL_BODY_INCLUDE.

Processing a Closing Tag

You can also have your code perform an action at the closing tag. As mentioned earlier, this is done by implementing the doEndTag() method. This works the same way as doStartTag() but uses two different possible return values: SKIP_PAGE and EVAL_PAGE. Using a doEndTag() method allows you to close any HTML tags you opened in doStartTag() or to clean up any objects you created in doStartTag() that had to be available while the tag was open.

As a demonstration of this, we shall create a `Footnote` tag. A major problem facing large sites is maintaining consistency between page styles, and updating the styles when site redesigns happen. One of the great benefits of custom JSP tags is that they allow site-specific tags to be created for site-specific elements, allowing page designers to create pages using the custom styles and update the tag bean when the style needs to change. All the pages will then use the new style without needing to be re-edited.

This is one of the main reasons that sites use custom tags – to provide a simple way for different HTML authors to use a consistent, easily updated style throughout a site. Our example here is used to enclose footnote text to make it stand out as separate from regular body text. Cascading Style Sheets could be used instead, but they are still not supported widely enough in browsers for some sites to make them the exclusive mechanism for page styles. By using custom tags we have a flexible arrangement where all that's output is pure HTML accessible to a wide range of browsers, from handheld PDAs to desktop clients.

The Footnote Class

```java
package com.wrox.projsp.ch09;

import javax.servlet.jsp.*;
import javax.servlet.jsp.tagext.*;

public class Footnote extends TagSupport {

  public int doStartTag() throws JspException {
    try {
      JspWriter out = pageContext.getOut();

      out.print("<TABLE ALIGN=\"right\" BGCOLOR=\"#CCCCCC\">");
      out.print("<TR><TD><I>");
    } catch (Exception ioException) {
      System.err.println("Exception thrown in Footnote.doStartTag():");
      System.err.println(ioException.toString());

      throw new JspException(ioException);
    }

    return EVAL_BODY_INCLUDE;
  }

  public int doEndTag() throws JspException {
    try {
      pageContext.getOut().print("</I></TD></TR></TABLE>");
    } catch (Exception ioException) {
      System.err.println("Exception thrown in Footnote.doEndTag():");
      System.err.println(ioException.toString());

      throw new JspException(ioException);
    }

    return EVAL_PAGE;
  }
}
```

The footnotetags TLD

The `footnotetags.tld` for this tag handler is:

```xml
<?xml version="1.0" encoding="ISO-8859-1" ?>
<!DOCTYPE taglib
  PUBLIC "-//Sun Microsystems, Inc.//DTD JSP Tag Library 1.2//EN"
  "http://java.sun.com/j2ee/dtds/web-jsptaglibrary_1_2.dtd">

<taglib>
  <tlib-version>1.0</tlib-version>
  <jsp-version>1.2</jsp-version>
  <short-name>Footnote</short-name>
  <description>
    This is a simple footnote tag, to show how to use both doStartTag () and
doEndTag ().
  </description>

  <tag>
    <name>footnote</name>
    <tag-class>com.wrox.projsp.ch09.Footnote</tag-class>
  </tag>
</taglib>
```

Addition to web.xml

```xml
<taglib>
    <taglib-uri>/footnotetags.tld</taglib-uri>
    <taglib-location>/WEB-INF/footnotetags.tld</taglib-location>
</taglib>
```

The footnote JSP

Our sample `footnote.jsp` to show this in action is:

```jsp
<%@ page errorPage="error.jsp" %>
<html>
<head>
  <title>Footnote Example</title>
</head>
<body>
  <%@ taglib uri="/footnotetags.tld" prefix="chap09" %>
  <p>
  Some text. Some text. Some text. Some text. Some text. Some text.
  Some text. Some text. Some text. Some text. Some text. Some text.
  Some text. Some text. Some text. Some text. Some text. Some text.
  <chap09:footnote>Footnote goes here</chap09:footnote>
  Some text. Some text. Some text. Some text. Some text. Some text.
  </p>

  <p>
  Some text. Some text. Some text. Some text. Some text. Some text.
  Some text. Some text. Some text. Some text. Some text. Some text.
  Some text. Some text. Some text. Some text. Some text. Some text.
  </p>
</body>
</html>
```

Here we have some sample text with a footnote placed in the middle of it. This footnote is placed in the text where a standard footnote marker would appear. When used, this page gives us the following output:

As you can see, when the tag is used it encloses the body text in an HTML table with a gray background, aligned with the right margin with text flowing on the left. If the site is redesigned and you need all footnotes to appear on a purple background aligned with the left margin, you only need to change this Footnote bean instead of all the pages in the site.

Storing Objects in Page Attributes

A common practice in JSP development is to encapsulate the creation of important objects so they can be easily created on JSPs. For instance you might need an easy way for page designers to retrieve the currently-selected record from a database so that some fields can be shown later on the page without each requiring their own lookup. One of the conventions advocated in the JSP standard is that such implicit objects are created via a defineObjects tag. This has the advantage of making explicit any dependencies on the object creation, while also fitting in well with the JSP standard.

Here we'll look at a simpler version of the above. The following tag library creates a five-element array in one tag and prints out those five elements in a second tag. As usual, we'll start by looking at the JavaBean for the tag.

One of the uses of the PageContext object is to allow storage of objects for use later. In this way the PageContext acts as an object store for any objects page designers and tag authors care to place there. These objects are essentially kept in a Hashtable object internal to the PageContext, and can be stored and retrieved via calls to PageContext.setAttribute() and PageContext.getAttribute(). The object is given a name in the defineObjects tag, and this is the name that is used as the key for storing the array in the attribute Hashtable.

The CreateAttArray Class

The Java code for the `CreateAttArray` class used for the `defineObjects` tag is as follows:

```
package com.wrox.projsp.ch09;

import javax.servlet.jsp.*;
import javax.servlet.jsp.tagext.*;

public class CreateAttArray extends TagSupport {
  private String arrayName = "";
```

Note how we don't need to check that getName() actually returns a name. We already know that setName() will have been called beforehand since name is a required attribute in the TLD. If the page author tries to use the defineObjects tag without a name attribute, the server will generate a page compilation error at translation time. It won't let the defineObjects tag be used on a page without the name attribute being supplied:

```
public String getName() {
  return this.arrayName;
}

public void setName(String newArrayName) {
  this.arrayName = newArrayName;
}

public int doStartTag() throws JspException {
  String[] myArray = new String[5];

  myArray[0] = "Homer";
  myArray[1] = "Marge";
  myArray[2] = "Bart";
  myArray[3] = "Lisa";
  myArray[4] = "Maggie";
```

Most of the code is straightforward, and the only really new line is the setAttribute() call. We don't specify any scope in the setAttribute() call, so the array is stored with the default 'page' scope. If we wanted, we could instead store it with application scope, session scope or request scope:

```
  pageContext.setAttribute(this.getName(), myArray);

  return SKIP_BODY;
  }

}
```

The ShowAttArray Class

The tag that retrieves the array and prints out its contents is similarly straightforward:

```
package com.wrox.projsp.ch09;

import javax.servlet.jsp.*;
import javax.servlet.jsp.tagext.*;
```

```
public class ShowAttArray extends TagSupport {
  private String arrayName;

  public String getName() {
    return this.arrayName;
  }

  public void setName(String newArrayName) {
    this.arrayName = newArrayName;
  }

  public int doStartTag() throws JspException {
    String[] myArray;
```

Again the most interesting line is the one that deals with the `pageContext`. Note the cast to `String[]`. As with other `Hashtable` objects, the get method returns an object of class `Object`. It is up to the calling function to know the type of object returned, or to be prepared to deal with an object of unknown type:

```
myArray = (String[]) pageContext.getAttribute(this.getName());
```

Once the array is retrieved, a loop steps through it and prints out the individual values in an HTML unordered list. The `html` variable is our string that will later be output to the final page. It is instantiated with a title and the opening tag of the unordered list, before each value of the array is concatenated on to it. Finally the unordered list tag is closed:

```
String html = "<H1>Array values from page attributes</H1><UL>";

for (int counter = 0; counter < myArray.length; counter++) {

  // Naturally a StringBuffer.append () would be used in
  // production code for improved performance.
  html += "<LI>" + myArray[counter];
}

html += "</UL>";

try {
```

This code is then output by:

```
  pageContext.getOut().print(html);
} catch (Exception ioException) {
  System.err.println("IO Exception thrown in doStartTag():");
  System.err.println(ioException.toString());

  throw new JspException(ioException);
}

  return SKIP_BODY;
}

}
```

The attarraytags TLD

Here's the `attarraytags.tld` for these two tags:

```xml
<?xml version="1.0" encoding="ISO-8859-1" ?>
<!DOCTYPE taglib
  PUBLIC "-//Sun Microsystems, Inc.//DTD JSP Tag Library 1.2//EN"
  "http://java.sun.com/j2ee/dtds/web-jsptaglibrary_1_2.dtd">

<taglib>
  <tlib-version>1.0</tlib-version>
  <jsp-version>1.2</jsp-version>
  <short-name>AttArray</short-name>
  <description>
    This is a simple application that creates an array in one tag
    and displays it in another.
  </description>

  <tag>
    <name>defineObjects</name>
    <tag-class>com.wrox.projsp.ch09.CreateAttArray</tag-class>
    <attribute>
      <name>name</name>
      <required>true</required>
    </attribute>
  </tag>

  <tag>
    <name>showarray</name>
    <tag-class>com.wrox.projsp.ch09.ShowAttArray</tag-class>
    <attribute>
      <name>name</name>
      <required>true</required>
    </attribute>
  </tag>
</taglib>
```

Addition to web.xml

```xml
<taglib>
  <taglib-uri>/attarraytags.tld</taglib-uri>
  <taglib-location>/WEB-INF/attarraytags.tld</taglib-location>
</taglib>
```

The ArrayInPageAttributes JSP

And finally, the following `ArrayInPageAttributes.jsp` file shows how this example can be used:

```jsp
<%@ page errorPage="error.jsp" %>
<html>
<head>
  <title>Creating A Variable In One Tag And Showing It In Another</title>
</head>
<body>
  <%@ taglib uri="/attarraytags.tld" prefix="chap09" %>
```

315

```
    <chap09:defineObjects name="myArray"/>
    <chap09:showarray name="myArray"/>
  </body>
  </html>
```

Running this JSP page gives us the following output:

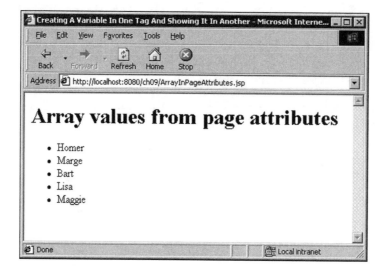

Introducing Scripting Variables from a Tag

What if you wanted to manipulate the array in a scriptlet? The above example doesn't allow this directly, since it doesn't place the array object on the page. You can still use PageContext.getAttribute() within a JSP scriptlet to get a handle on the object, but that may not be type-safe since it relies on the page designer correctly casting the object type.

A better, cleaner way would be for the tag to explicitly create the object within the page's scripting scope, so that the page author has a correctly-typed variable to work with. This requires some additional work on the tag author's part, but it can be well worth it from the page designer's perspective.

Creating a variable within the page's scope requires a new class that is derived from another standard JSP object. The object in question is the TagExtraInfo class, and as well as allowing you to create scripting variables it allows you to validate tags at translation time. We'll get to that in the next chapter.

> The **TagExtraInfo** class only makes items available that have already been stored in the **PageContext** via **setAttribute()**. It doesn't create items in isolation – they must already exist in the **PageContext**.

To create a script variable, you create both your Tag class and a TagExtraInfo class and tell the server about them in the TLD file. Following on from the previous example, we'll create a defineObjects tag that will create an array and store it in a variable whose name is passed as an attribute to the defineObjects tag. We'll then print out the values of that array using a scriptlet.

The only new line of code is the `<tei-class>` tag, which defines the `TagExtraInfo` class. In fact, the main tag class is still `CreateAttArray`, the tag class from the previous example. All our `ArrayExtraInfo` class does is make the objects stored in the `PageContext` attributes available to the page scripting.

Our `ArrayExtraInfo` class contains only one method, `getVariableInfo()`, which overrides the same method in the abstract base class. It takes a `TagData` object as its one parameter, and it returns an array of `VariableInfo` objects. Both of these are explained below. The `TagData` object is a very simple object that is only available at translation time. It just provides a way to access tag attributes and attribute values. The most commonly used methods of the `TagData` object are `getAttribute(String)` and `getAttributes()`.

The TagData Object

The `TagData` object is a translation-time only class that provides access to attribute name/value information for a given tag instance.

Fields

First we will look at the fields that are defined in `TagData` objects.

```
public final static Object REQUEST_TIME_VALUE
```

Although the standard defines this constant as part of the object, it is not yet used anywhere since `TagData` objects are only used at page translation-time. Later versions of the JSP standard may extend this object for use at request-time, and then this constant will be used to differentiate translation-time and request-time instances.

Constructors

Next we will look at the constructors for `TagData` objects.

```
public TagData(Object[][] atts)
```

This constructor takes a collection of name/value pairs. All elements must be a `String` except for those using REQUEST_TIME_VALUE.

```
public TagData(Hashtable attrs)
```

Alternatively, this constructor just stores all the elements in a `Hashtable` and passes it as the sole construction parameter.

Methods

Next we will look at the methods that are associated with `TagData` objects.

```
public Object getAttribute(String attName)
```

This method returns the attribute value stored under the key `attName`, or `null` if it is not set.

```
public Enumeration getAttributes()
```

This method returns all the attributes the `TagData` has stored, as an enumeration.

`public String getAttributeString(String attName)`

This method returns the attribute value stored under the key `attName` as a `String`, or `null` if it is not set.

`public String getId()`

This method returns the value of the `id` attribute if it is available, or `null` if it is not.

`public void setAttribute(String attName, Object attValue)`

This method sets the value of key `attName` using value `attValue`.

The VariableInfo Class

The `VariableInfo` class is really the key to the way variables are made available. It contains all the necessary information to declare and define the variable, as well as limit its scope. It takes four parameters in its constructor:

`VariableInfo(String varName, String className, boolean declare, int scope)`

The `varName` is simply the name under which the variable will be known in the page scripting. `className` is the type of the variable we're making available – not necessarily just its class name, as we'll see. The `declare` flag states whether the script variable should be declared here or if it is just to be set from the `PageContext` attributes. The `scope` parameter tells the server whether it should be defined at the beginning of the tag scope (just after the end of the opening tag), at the end of the tag scope (just after the end of the closing tag), or if it should have a 'nested' scope, available between the end of the opening tag and the beginning of the closing tag.

These three possible scopes are defined as `VariableInfo.AT_BEGIN`, `VariableInfo.AT_END`, and `VariableInfo.NESTED`.

`VariableInfo.AT_BEGIN` creates the variable immediately after the end of the opening tag, before any of the enclosed body. It is then available to the end of the page. Here's a typical invocation of a tag:

```
<myTag:myCustomAction>
   ...enclosed body...
</myTag:myCustomAction>
```

If we use `VariableInfo.AT_BEGIN`, our script variable is declared at the following point:

```
<myTag:myCustomAction>
   <!-- variable declared here -->
   ...enclosed body...
</myTag:myCustomAction>
<!-- variable still available here -->
```

`VariableInfo.AT_END` creates the variable immediately after the end of the closing tag, and it is in scope until the end of the page:

```
<myTag:myCustomAction>
  ...enclosed body...
</myTag:myCustomAction>
<!-- variable declared here and available until the end of the page -->
```

`VariableInfo.NESTED` declares the variable so that it is available **only** between the end of the opening tag and the beginning of the closing tag.

```
<myTag:myCustomAction>
  <!-- variable declared here -->
  ...enclosed body...
  <!-- variable goes out of scope here -->
</myTag:myCustomAction>
<!-- variable not available here -->
```

Since `NESTED` scope is the most restricted scope, and the one that least pollutes the page attributes, it is probably best to use it as your first choice unless you know you need otherwise. In our example though, we want the variable to be available for use after our tag is closed so we use `AT_END` scope for our variable's declaration.

There's not much more to the `VariableInfo` class apart from some methods to provide simple access to construction parameters, so we won't list the full class reference.

The ArrayExtraInfo Class

Here's all the code for our `ArrayExtraInfo` class:

```
package com.wrox.projsp.ch09;

import javax.servlet.jsp.tagext.*;

public class ArrayExtraInfo extends TagExtraInfo {

  public VariableInfo[] getVariableInfo(TagData data) {
```

This line gets the name of the array from the tag data. This is the name under which the tag was stored in the `PageContext` attributes by our `CreateAttArray` object:

```
String myArrayName = (String) data.getAttribute("name");
```

Next we create our `VariableInfo` object. Note that the name used in the `VariableInfo` constructor is important because it is used to store the value in the `pageAttributes` as well being the name of the scripting variable:

```
VariableInfo myArrayInfo = new VariableInfo(myArrayName, "String []",
                                   true, VariableInfo.AT_END);
```

We use the array name we just retrieved, we state the type of the variable as an array of `Strings`, we tell the server to declare the variable, and we say we want the resultant variable to be in scope from the end of the closing tag. Note how the second parameter is a variable type ('array of `Strings`') rather than a pure class name.

When we have this `VariableInfo`, we create an array of `VariableInfos` of size 1:

```
VariableInfo[] myTagVariables = new VariableInfo[1];
```

This matches the return type – an array is returned so you can create as many script variables as you need instead of being limited to just one variable. In our case however we're only creating one variable, so our array only contains one element. We set this element to the `TagVariable` object we created earlier:

```
myTagVariables[0] = myArrayInfo;
```

And finally we return the array:

```
        return myTagVariables;
    }

}
```

The arrayinscripttags TLD

Now that we have our `TagExtraInfo` class set up, let's look at our `arrayinscripttags.tld` for our `defineObjects` tag:

```
<?xml version="1.0" encoding="ISO-8859-1" ?>
<!DOCTYPE taglib
  PUBLIC "-//Sun Microsystems, Inc.//DTD JSP Tag Library 1.2//EN"
  "http://java.sun.com/j2ee/dtds/web-jsptaglibrary_1_2.dtd">

<taglib>
  <tlib-version>1.0</tlib-version>
  <jsp-version>1.2</jsp-version>
  <short-name>ScriptArray</short-name>
  <description>
    This is a simple application which creates an array in the tag and
    makes it available to page scripting.
  </description>

  <tag>
    <name>defineObjects</name>
    <tag-class>com.wrox.projsp.ch09.CreateAttArray</tag-class>
    <tei-class>com.wrox.projsp.ch09.ArrayExtraInfo</tei-class>
    <attribute>
      <name>name</name>
    </attribute>
  </tag>
</taglib>
```

Addition to web.xml

```
<taglib>
  <taglib-uri>/arrayinscripttags.tld</taglib-uri>
  <taglib-location>/WEB-INF/arrayinscripttags.tld</taglib-location>
</taglib>
```

The ArrayInScript JSP

The last bit of code we need for this example is our `ArrayInscript.jsp`:

```
<%@ page errorPage="error.jsp" %>
<html>
<head>
  <title>Making A Tag Variable Available To Page Scripting</title>
</head>
<body>
  <%@ taglib uri="/arrayinscripttags.tld" prefix="chap09" %>
  <chap09:defineObjects name="myArray"/>

  <h1>Array values handled in script</h1>
  <ul>
    <%
    String html = "";
    for (int counter = 0; counter < myArray.length; counter++) {
      html += "<LI>" + myArray [counter];
    }
    %>
    <%=html%>

  </ul>
</body>
</html>
```

Here we see our `defineObjects` tag, followed by a scriptlet that loops through an array outputting values. The array itself is called `myArray`, but there's no declaration for it in the JSP page and nor is it set to anything. In fact, the declaration and setting of this array is handled at translation time, by the server inserting something like the following into the Java code to be compiled into the servlet:

```
String [] myArray = null;
myArray = (String []) pageContext.findAttribute("myArray");
```

These lines show the actual insertion of the `myArray` variable into the page. It is declared (since the declaration parameter in the `VariableInfo` constructor was set to `true`) and then its value is retrieved from the `PageContext`.

> The **scope** parameter to the **VariableInfo** constructor is used to determine the placement of the above code snippet. If the scope parameter is **VariableInfo.AT_BEGIN**, the above setting of the variable occurs just after the end of the opening tag. If it is **VariableInfo.AT_END**, the variable is set just after the end of the closing tag. If the scope is **VariableInfo.NESTED**, the variable is set just after the end of the opening tag and it goes out of scope just before the start of the closing tag.

Finally running this JSP page gives us the following output:

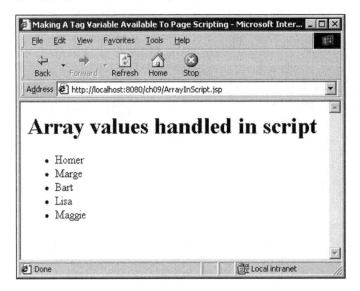

So the same `defineObjects` tag is used to create the array, but it's made accessible to the page scripting language by the addition of a `TagExtraInfo` class.

Creating Variables via the TLD file

In simple cases like the one above you can take a shortcut. Instead of having to create a separate class based on `TagExtraInfo`, you can specify a variable in the TLD file. This method isn't as flexible or as powerful as creating it in the `TagExtraInfo` class, but it's quick and simple.

The information passed in the constructor of the `VariableInfo` class in the `ArrayExtraInfo` class above was simply:

❏ The variable's name

❏ The variable's type

❏ Whether the variable should be declared or not – you may have already created the variable in a previous tag, or you may be relying on the page author creating the variable for you

❏ The scope of the variable

All this information can instead be included in a `<variable>...</variable>` tag within the `<tag>...</tag>` tags. Here's the equivalent `arrayinscriptviatldtags.tld` for the above example, but which creates the variable through the TLD settings instead of through the `TagExtraInfo` class:

```
<?xml version="1.0" encoding="ISO-8859-1" ?>
<!DOCTYPE taglib
  PUBLIC "-//Sun Microsystems, Inc.//DTD JSP Tag Library 1.2//EN"
  "http://java.sun.com/j2ee/dtds/web-jsptaglibrary_1_2.dtd">

<taglib>
  <tlib-version>1.0</tlib-version>
```

```
        <jsp-version>1.2</jsp-version>
        <short-name>ScriptArrayViaTLD</short-name>
        <description>
          This is a simple application which creates an array in the tag and
          makes it available to page scripting, via the variable tag in the TLD.
        </description>

        <tag>
          <name>defineObjects</name>
          <tag-class>com.wrox.projsp.ch09.CreateAttArray</tag-class>
          <variable>
            <name-from-attribute>name</name-from-attribute>
            <variable-class>String []</variable-class>
            <declare>true</declare>
            <scope>AT_END</scope>
          </variable>
          <attribute>
            <name>name</name>
          </attribute>
        </tag>
      </taglib>
```

You'll also need to make the following addition to web.xml:

```
    <taglib>
      <taglib-uri>/arrayinscriptviatldtags.tld</taglib-uri>
      <taglib-location>/WEB-INF/arrayinscriptviatldtags.tld</taglib-location>
    </taglib>
```

The output of this example is identical to the previous one; it's just the method of setting up the variable that's different.

> Like in the **VariableInfo** constructor, the name used in the variable tags is also used to store the value in the **pageAttributes**.

There are two ways to set the name of the variable. The first option is the easiest – just specify the name explicitly in the TLD using `<name-given>myVariableName</name-given>` tags. This will use the name 'myVariableName' as the name of the variable.

The second way is a little more complicated. Instead of explicitly saying what the name of the variable is, you can specify an attribute of the tag that will contain the name of the variable. This way uses a `<name-from-attribute>...</name-from-attribute>` tag instead of a `<name-given>myVariableName</name-given>` tag. This is the way used above. In the TLD we specify:

```
    <name-from-attribute>name</name-from-attribute>
```

This means we're using the 'name' attribute of the defineObjects tag to allow the page author to set the name used for the variable. This process only accepts static strings for the attribute, since the mechanism for creating the variables is a translation-time one and scriptlets are only evaluated at request-time.

> You are free to choose either **<name-given>...</name-given>** or **<name-from-attribute>...</name-from-attribute>** tags when creating your variable. You must however choose one and only one method for each variable. If you try to specify both **<name-given>...</name-given>** and **<name-from-attribute>...</name-from-attribute>** tags within the same **<variable>...</variable>** structure, you'll get a translation-time error.

Loops

One issue that has bugged JSP since before version 1.0 is the ability that tags have to process their body more than once. It has proved to be a particularly difficult area to implement cleanly without disagreement, but finally version 1.2 appears to have solved the problems with the `IterationTag` interface.

The `IterationTag` interface contains just one new method, `doAfterBody()`. This method is called just after processing of the enclosed body, to determine whether to loop back to the start of the body or to continue on and process the closing tag. If you want to loop back to the beginning of the body processing your `doAfterBody()` should return `EVAL_BODY_AGAIN`.

When you've looped enough, your `doAfterBody()` should return `SKIP_BODY` to signal the end of looping. Since, as we noted earlier, the `TagSupport` class implements `IterationTag` rather than just `Tag`, we can carry on using `TagSupport` as the superclass for our iterating tag handler.

The IterationTag Interface

This interface extends the `Tag` interface by adding one method that allows the tag to repeat evaluation of the tag's enclosed body.

Fields

First we will look at the fields that are defined in the `IterationTag` interface.

```
public final static int EVAL_BODY_AGAIN
```

When returned by `doAfterBody()` this tells the server to re-evaluate the tag's enclosed body. Note it is only a valid return value for `doAfterBody()`.

Methods

Next we will look at the single method that is defined in the `IterationTag` interface.

```
public abstract int doAfterBody() throws javax.servlet.jsp.JspException
```

The server invokes this method after every evaluation of the body, to determine whether to repeat the evaluation or to continue with the rest of the page evaluation. This method is not invoked if there is no body to evaluate.

Calls to the `IterationTag` interface are made as in the following flowchart:

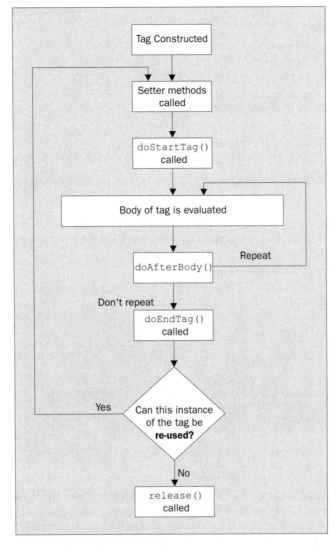

As an example of iteration, we'll use the same `defineObjects` tag we used earlier and we'll create a new tag that prints out an element of the array on each iteration and stops when there are no more elements.

The IterateAttArray Class

Here's our iterating tag class:

```
package com.wrox.projsp.ch09;

import java.lang.*;
import javax.servlet.jsp.*;
import javax.servlet.jsp.tagext.*;
```

```
public class IterateAttArray extends TagSupport {
  private String[] array = null;
  private int      arrayCounter = 0;
  private String   arrayName;

  public String getName() {
    return this.arrayName;
  }

  public void setName(String newArrayName) {
    this.arrayName = newArrayName;
  }

  public int doStartTag() throws JspException {
    this.array = (String[]) pageContext.getAttribute(this.getName());

    return EVAL_BODY_INCLUDE;
  }
```

Of particular importance here is the doAfterBody() method. The first part of this method gets a handle on the JspWriter for the page, and then outputs the one element of the array in the following format:

[<loop-counter>]: <element-value>

It does this as follows:

```
public int doAfterBody() throws JspException {
  try {
    JspWriter out = pageContext.getOut();

    out.print(" [" + this.arrayCounter + "]: ");
    out.print(this.array[this.arrayCounter] + "<BR>");
  } catch (Exception ioException) {
    System.err.println("Exception thrown in doAfterBody():");
    System.err.println(ioException.toString());

    throw new JspException(ioException);
  }
```

Next it makes the decision about whether to loop again or to finish. This simply checks to see if the current value of the loop counter is less than the length of the array. If it is, repeatOrSkip is set to EVAL_BODY_AGAIN and the tag loops. If the current value of the loop counter is equal to or greater than the length of the array, SKIP_BODY is returned and no more iterations are performed. This is done by the following code:

```
    int repeatOrSkip = SKIP_BODY;

    if (this.arrayCounter < (this.array.length - 1)) {
      repeatOrSkip = EVAL_BODY_AGAIN;
      this.arrayCounter++;
    }

    return repeatOrSkip;
  }

}
```

The iteratearraytags TLD

The `iteratearraytags.tld` for this example should contain no surprises:

```xml
<?xml version="1.0" encoding="ISO-8859-1" ?>
<!DOCTYPE taglib
   PUBLIC "-//Sun Microsystems, Inc.//DTD JSP Tag Library 1.2//EN"
   "http://java.sun.com/j2ee/dtds/web-jsptaglibrary_1_2.dtd">

<taglib>
   <tlib-version>1.0</tlib-version>
   <jsp-version>1.2</jsp-version>
   <short-name>IterateArray</short-name>
   <description>
     This is a simple application that creates an array in one tag
     and iterates through it in another.
   </description>

   <tag>
     <name>createarray</name>
     <tag-class>com.wrox.projsp.ch09.CreateAttArray</tag-class>
     <attribute>
       <name>name</name>
     </attribute>
   </tag>

   <tag>
     <name>iteratearray</name>
     <tag-class>com.wrox.projsp.ch09.IterateAttArray</tag-class>
     <attribute>
       <name>name</name>
     </attribute>
   </tag>
</taglib>
```

Addition to web.xml

```xml
<taglib>
  <taglib-uri>/iteratearraytags.tld</taglib-uri>
  <taglib-location>/WEB-INF/iteratearraytags.tld</taglib-location>
</taglib>
```

The IterateArray JSP

The `IterateArray.jsp` we're using to demonstrate this example is equally simple:

```jsp
<%@ page errorPage="error.jsp" %>
<html>
<head>
  <title>Iterator Example Using Page Attributes And An Iterating Tag</title>
</head>
<body>
  <h1>Array values iterated in a tag</h1>

  <%@ taglib uri="/iteratearraytags.tld" prefix="chap09" %>
```

327

```
    <chap09:createarray name="myArray"/>

    <chap09:iteratearray name="myArray">
      Array value
    </chap09:iteratearray>
  </body>
</html>
```

However, note the text 'Array value' in the body of the iteratearray tag. This will be output as part of the body processing. Since we're writing out the array values in doAfterBody(), they will appear **after** this text on each iteration. To make the order in which things happen clearer, here's the output of running this example:

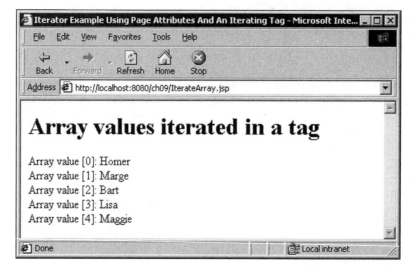

This shows that the phrase 'Array value' from the body text on the JSP page is output together with the [<loop-counter>]: <element-value> from doAfterBody(), once per iteration. When doAfterBody() returns EVAL_BODY_AGAIN, the body is processed once more and the body content 'Array value' is output again.

Summary

In this chapter we've taken a look at the basics of creating custom tags. We've talked about how useful they can be, and then we looked at several examples:

- ❏ We produced some simple text in HelloWorld.java

- ❏ We passed an argument to a tag via a tag attribute in HelloUser.java

- ❏ We performed actions at both the start tag and end tag in Footnote.java

- ❏ We saw how to optionally show or hide the enclosed body content based on a decision made at run-time, in AdminOnly.java

- ❏ We created an array in a defineObjects tag using CreateAttArray.java and accessing it in another tag handler using ShowAttArray.java

❑ We created an array in a `defineObjects` tag using `CreateAttArray.java` and making that array available to the rest of enclosed body as a script variable, using `ArrayExtraInfo.java`

❑ We iterated through an array by looping over a tag's enclosed body, in `IterateAttArray.java`

In the next chapter, we will look in more depth at how tags can manipulate their enclosed body. We'll also look in more depth at validating tags at translation time and at the process of packaging tag libraries for distribution and use.

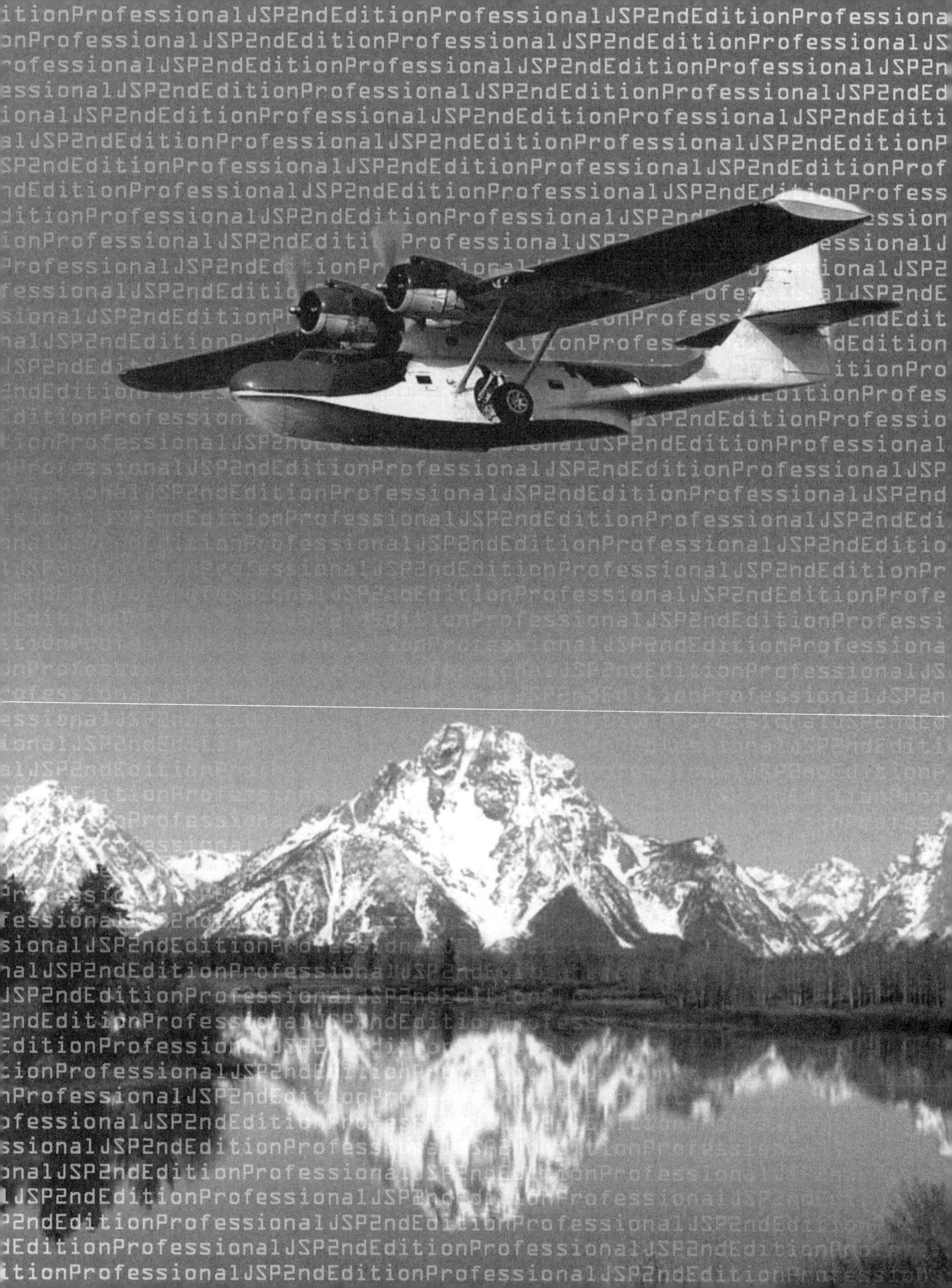
ProfessionalJSP2ndEdition

10

More Complicated Custom Tags

Having now seen the basics of creating custom tags in the previous chapter, we can move on to create more complicated tags that can process their bodies and work cooperatively; in order to do this, we need to know about some more complicated class structures. We'll also cover the important subject of validating the use of your tags, making sure that all your custom tags have been nested properly, if appropriate, and that all necessary attributes have been supplied and are correct. We'll then look at what you need to do to package a library for other people to use.

In this chapter we'll be looking at:

- ❑ The `BodyTag` interface
- ❑ Filtering content
- ❑ The lifecycle of tags
- ❑ Cooperating tags
- ❑ Validation
- ❑ Handling errors
- ❑ Common pitfalls in developing tag libraries
- ❑ Tag Library Descriptor file reference
- ❑ Potential tools
- ❑ Documenting tag libraries
- ❑ Distributing tag libraries

The BodyTag Interface

The final type of tag we need to look at are those that implement the BodyTag interface; BodyTag is the largest and most complete of the tag interfaces, allowing use of its own methods as well as those of Tag and IterationTag. (See Appendix C for more details on the JSP interfaces and classes.) It has its own support class, BodyTagSupport, which extends TagSupport. BodyTag's additional field and methods are:

Fields

There is only one field in the BodyTag interface:

```
public final static int EVAL_BODY_BUFFERED
```

When returned by doStartTag() this tells the server to create a new BodyContent buffer in which to evaluate the body content of this tag. Note it is only a valid return value for doStartTag().

Methods

We will look at two of the methods in the BodyTag interface:

```
public abstract int doInitBody() throws javax.servlet.jsp.JspException
```

This method is invoked by the server after setBodyContent() has been called but before evaluation of the body itself starts. It is not invoked if there is no body to evaluate:

```
public abstract int setBodyContent()
```

This method is invoked by the server before doInitBody() and will be called at most once per tag. If there is to be no body processing (for instance if doStartTag() returns SKIP_BODY) this method is not called.

Web Application Structure

The structure of the web application we will build in this chapter is very similar to the one from the previous chapter:

- Classes
  <tomcat_home>\webapps\ch10\WEB-INF\classes\com\wrox\projsp\ch10\

- web.xml
  <tomcat_home>\webapps\ch10\WEB-INF\

- TLDs
  <tomcat_home>\webapps\ch10\WEB-INF\

- JSPs
  <tomcat_home>\webapps\ch10\

A Profanity Filter Tag

So what can you do with a `BodyTag` that you can't do with an iteration tag? When is it useful? Well, one common situation facing webmasters is the problem of filtering content provided by someone else. This can take the form of information pulled from another company's servers, or text input by site visitors in a guest book or discussion forum.

One great use of a body tag is to provide a simple way of filtering all such text, irrespective of where it came from or what application is used to gather and process it.

For example, say a discussion forum message is shown on the JSP page using the following tag:

```
<forum:showmessage>
```

Using a filtering body tag, you can process all the output generated by this call by wrapping the forum tag within a filtering body tag:

```
<tags:profanityfilter>
  <forum:showmessage>
</tags:profanityfilter>
```

This filtering works at runtime, so even dynamically generated content is filtered. The following scriptlet would also work:

```
<tags:profanityfilter>
  <%= forum.showmessage() %>
<tags:profanityfilter>
```

The ProfanityFilter Class

Let's look at the Java code to make this work. In order to protect those with delicate sensibilities, we're not going to include any real naughty words. Instead we'll filter out the words "D'oh" and "D'uh" wherever they occur in the tag body. You'll easily be able to extend this to filter an arbitrary list of words:

```java
package com.wrox.projsp.ch10;

import javax.servlet.jsp.*;
import javax.servlet.jsp.tagext.*;

public class ProfanityFilter extends BodyTagSupport {
```

The core of this class is the `filterWord()` method. This method processes the enclosed body text (passed as the first argument, `bodyToFilter`), searching for a specific word to filter (the second parameter, `wordToRemove`). If that word is found, it is replaced by the substitution word passed as the third and final parameter, `wordToUse`. The actual `filterWord()` method is:

```java
private String filterWord(String bodyToFilter, String wordToRemove,
                          String wordToUse) {
  StringBuffer filteredContent = new StringBuffer();
  int previousMarker = 0;
```

An important point to note is the use of `indexOf()` to find occurrences of the initial string. This is what actually does the searching, and so performance of this method is very dependent on the implementation of `indexOf()`. It's also very dependent on the size of the enclosed body text – the more body text, or the more words being filtered, the longer the searching and replacing will take.

Note that the `indexOf()` search only looks for the exact characters passed in the search parameter. The `filterWord()` method could usefully be extended to be case insensitive or to use regular expressions to provide a more general solution:

```
int foundWordAt = bodyToFilter.indexOf(wordToRemove, previousMarker);

while (foundWordAt != -1) {
```

Every time the word to filter is found, all the text up to that point (from the last occurrence if there was one, or from the start if there wasn't) to the filter word is copied to our `filteredContent StringBuffer`:

```
filteredContent.append(bodyToFilter.substring(previousMarker,
                                              foundWordAt));
```

The replacement word is then appended to our `filteredContent`, and another search is performed on the remainder of the body content:

```
filteredContent.append(wordToUse);

previousMarker = foundWordAt + wordToRemove.length();
foundWordAt = bodyToFilter.indexOf(wordToRemove, previousMarker);
}

filteredContent.append(bodyToFilter.substring(previousMarker));
```

This repeats until the end of the string is reached. Finally the filtered content is returned:

```
    return filteredContent.toString();
}
```

The `doEndTag()` call is not quite as straightforward as in other tags we've seen, and needs a little explanation. One result of allowing processing of body content is that the body content itself isn't finalized until all enclosing body-processing tags have had their chance to process the content. This means that the `out` object used within a body-processing tag can't just write directly to the Servlet output stream, it must write to a buffer that body-processing tags can access and change. Only after the body processing is complete can the content finally be written to the output stream.

This is a subtle point, but it's important to get right. In a JSP, or in a custom tag, you can access the `out` object. It may be the real `out` object, or it may be a buffer-writing object masquerading as an `out` object, but in any case it doesn't matter. You just use `out` and it works, as you'd expect:

```
public int doEndTag() throws JspException {
  try {
```

First of all, the current body content is retrieved as a `String`:

```
String currentContent = this.getBodyContent().getString();
String filteredContent;
```

It's then filtered using the filter methods we discussed earlier. Once that is done we want to use our filtered string as the body content instead of the existing body content. To do that we first of all `clear()` the existing body and then write our filtered content by using the `print()` method. The final line of that block is what's actually used to place our processed body in the `out` stream:

```
filteredContent = this.filterWord(currentContent, "D'oh", "****");
filteredContent = this.filterWord(filteredContent, "D'uh", "****");

this.getBodyContent().clear();
this.getBodyContent().print(filteredContent);
this.getBodyContent().writeOut(pageContext.getOut());
} catch (Exception ioException) {
System.err.println("Exception thrown in ProfanityFilter.doEndTag()");
System.err.println(ioException.toString());

throw new JspException(ioException);
}

return EVAL_PAGE;
}

}
```

So that's how the actual words are replaced. The `doEndTag()` method calls the `filterWord()` method once for each word it needs to replace. It's worth bearing in mind that each call to `filterWord()` will require a search of the whole body content.

This repeated searching may bring a large performance penalty on tags with large bodies. One method that may prove to be more efficient for long lists of search terms is the use of regular expressions to match words. The Jakarta project at Apache has one such regular expression package – visit http://jakarta.apache.org/regexp/ for more information.

> You could even extend this tag to provide request-time substitutions of specific keywords, to insert the current date and time, or the logged-in username. This could take the code beyond simple censorship of words, maybe even as far as your own macro language.

When your tag has processed its body, it's necessary for it to explicitly write the body content out to the `out` object. This may be direct, or it may go through the buffer – what matters is that you use it to write out the processed body content.

The profanityfiltertags TLD

Our Tag Library Descriptor for our `ProfanityFilter` example is straightforward:

```
<?xml version="1.0" encoding="ISO-8859-1" ?>
<!DOCTYPE taglib
   PUBLIC "-//Sun Microsystems, Inc.//DTD JSP Tag Library 1.2//EN"
```

```
    "http://java.sun.com/j2ee/dtds/web-jsptaglibrary_1_2.dtd">

<taglib>
  <tlib-version>1.0</tlib-version>
  <jsp-version>1.2</jsp-version>
  <short-name>ProfanityFilter</short-name>
  <description>
    This is a simple tag that filters all its body text to remove
    profanities.
  </description>

  <tag>
    <name>profanityfilter</name>
    <tag-class>com.wrox.projsp.ch10.ProfanityFilter</tag-class>
  </tag>
</taglib>
```

The web.xml file

All the examples in this chapter (except for the last example on packaging tag libraries) are part of the same web application. The web.xml file for this application, which contains the TLD mappings for all this chapter's tags, is as follows:

```
<!DOCTYPE web-app
    PUBLIC "-//Sun Microsystems, Inc.//DTD Web Application 2.2//EN"
    "http://java.sun.com/j2ee/dtds/web-app_2_2.dtd">

<web-app>
  <display-name>Chapter 10 examples</display-name>
  <description>
    This is the collection of sample tag libraries used in
    chapter 10 of Professional JSP, 2nd edition.
  </description>

  <taglib>
    <taglib-uri>/profanityfiltertags.tld</taglib-uri>
    <taglib-location>/WEB-INF/profanityfiltertags.tld</taglib-location>
  </taglib>

</web-app>
```

The ProfanityFilter JSP

The example JSP contains just one line of real text to filter, but it could easily be much bigger if it was deriving the body content from a database or from user-input text:

```
<%@ page errorPage="error.jsp" %>
<html>
<head>
  <title>Profanity Filter Example</title>
</head>
<body>
  <h1>Profanity Filter</h1>

  <%@ taglib uri="/profanityfiltertags.tld" prefix="chap10" %>
```

```
    <chap10:profanityfilter>
      <p>
      Some text to filter: D'oh!
      </p>
      <p>
      With a D'uh and another D'uh!
      </p>
      <p>
      D'oh, a deer, a female deer.
      </p>
    </chap10:profanityfilter>
  </body>
  </html>
```

When the page is viewed, the filtering tag has replaced the "D'oh" with "****":

So if you buy a JSP application to store user-input text (for example a discussion forum) and it doesn't provide filtering, you can add your own without needing any knowledge of the internal structure of the forum program or how it stores its data. Tag handlers' ability to process the body content irrespective of where it came from is one of the most powerful aspects of custom tags.

> One consequence of the `out` stream potentially being a tag's buffer is that as of JSP 1.2 you can use the `<jsp:include .../>` tag within a custom tag that manipulates its body. The `include` tag's behavior has been changed so that it no longer automatically flushes the output before processing the included file.

The Tag Lifecycle

We've covered all the main methods of all the tag interfaces, so now let's review just when each method is called. Here's the complete code for a simple Java tag class, `CallTrace`, which outputs a message when each of the tag methods are called.

The CallTrace Class

```
package com.wrox.projsp.ch10;

import javax.servlet.jsp.*;
import javax.servlet.jsp.tagext.*;

public class CallTrace extends BodyTagSupport {
  private int iterationCounter = 0;
```

Even though it looks like there's a lot of code there, the class itself is really doing very little. It just outputs some HTML in each method and traps any potential exceptions. It loops through the body content a number of times, just to show how this is done. This is controlled through the NUMBER_OF_ITERATIONS constant which is set to 3 in the code but you can change that if you want it to iterate more times.

The tag itself has one attribute, name. This attribute is included to show at what point the attribute setter methods are called by the server:

```
  private static final int NUMBER_OF_ITERATIONS = 3;
  private String name = "";

  public String getName() throws JspException {
    try {
      pageContext.getOut().print("<h6>getName() called.</h6>");
    } catch (Exception ioException) {
      System.err.println("IO Exception thrown in CallTrace.getName():");
      System.err.println(ioException.toString());

      throw new JspException(ioException);
    }

    return name;
  }

  public void setName(String newName) throws JspException {
    name = newName;

    try {
      pageContext.getOut().print("<h6>setName() called.</h6>");
    } catch (Exception ioException) {
      System.err.println("IO Exception thrown in CallTrace.setName():");
      System.err.println(ioException.toString());

      throw new JspException(ioException);
    }
  }

  public int doStartTag() throws JspException {
    try {
      JspWriter out = pageContext.getOut();

      out.print("<h2>doStartTag() called - ");
      out.print("iterating " + NUMBER_OF_ITERATIONS + " times</h2>");
    } catch (Exception ioException) {
```

```
        System.err.println("IO Exception thrown in CallTrace.doStartTag():");
        System.err.println(ioException.toString());

        throw new JspException(ioException);
    }

    return EVAL_BODY_BUFFERED;
}
```

One other point worth noting is that the call to setBodyContent() calls the superclass' version first, otherwise the BodyContent object won't be initialized properly and calls to getBodyContent() will return null:

```
public void setBodyContent(BodyContent body) {
    super.setBodyContent(body);

    try {
        pageContext.getOut().print("<h3>setBodyContent() called</h3>");
    } catch (Exception ioException) {
        System.err.println("Exception thrown in CallTrace.setBodyContent()");
        System.err.println(ioException.toString());

        // Can't throw JspException from this method - it's not part of
        // the method signature.
    }
}

public void doInitBody() throws JspException {
    try {
        pageContext.getOut().print("<h4>doInitBody() called</h4>");
    } catch (Exception ioException) {
        System.err.println("IO Exception thrown in CallTrace.doInitBody():");
        System.err.println(ioException.toString());

        throw new JspException(ioException);
    }
}

public int doAfterBody() throws JspException {
    int repeatBody = SKIP_BODY;

    try {
        JspWriter out = pageContext.getOut();

        out.print("<h5>doAfterBody() called - ");
        out.print("iteration " + iterationCounter);

        if (iterationCounter < NUMBER_OF_ITERATIONS) {
            repeatBody = EVAL_BODY_AGAIN;
            iterationCounter++;
        } else {
            out.print(", stopping.");
        }

        out.print("</h5>");
```

```
      } catch (Exception ioException) {
        System.err.println(
              "IO Exception thrown in CallTrace.doAfterBody():");
        System.err.println(ioException.toString());

        throw new JspException(ioException);
      }

    return repeatBody;
  }

  public int doEndTag() throws JspException {
    try {
      JspWriter out = pageContext.getOut();

      this.getBodyContent().writeOut(out);
      out.print("<h2>doEndTag() called</h2>");
    } catch (Exception ioException) {
      System.err.println("IO Exception thrown in CallTrace.doEndTag():");
      System.err.println(ioException.toString());

      throw new JspException(ioException);
    }

    return EVAL_PAGE;
  }

}
```

The calltrace1tags TLD

The TLD for this tag library is simple:

```xml
<?xml version="1.0" encoding="ISO-8859-1" ?>
<!DOCTYPE taglib
  PUBLIC "-//Sun Microsystems, Inc.//DTD JSP Tag Library 1.2//EN"
  "http://java.sun.com/j2ee/dtds/web-jsptaglibrary_1_2.dtd">

<taglib>
  <tlib-version>1.0</tlib-version>
  <jsp-version>1.2</jsp-version>
  <short-name>CallTrace</short-name>
  <description>
    This is a simple application that prints out methods
    in the order in which they are called.
  </description>

  <tag>
    <name>calltrace</name>
    <tag-class>com.wrox.projsp.ch10.CallTrace</tag-class>
    <body-content>empty</body-content>
    <attribute>
      <name>name</name>
    </attribute>
  </tag>
</taglib>
```

Addition to web.xml

```
<taglib>
  <taglib-uri>/calltrace1tags.tld</taglib-uri>
  <taglib-location>/WEB-INF/calltrace1tags.tld</taglib-location>
</taglib>
```

The CallTrace1 JSP

First we'll look at what is called when the tag is self-closing. There's no body content to process in this JSP:

```
<%@ page errorPage="error.jsp" %>
<html>
<head>
  <title>Call Trace</title>
</head>
<body>
  <%@ taglib uri="/calltrace1tags.tld" prefix="chap10" %>
  <h1>Test 1 - a self-closing tag.</h1>
    <chap10:calltrace name="name1"/>
</body>
</html>
```

Viewing this JSP page shows the following output:

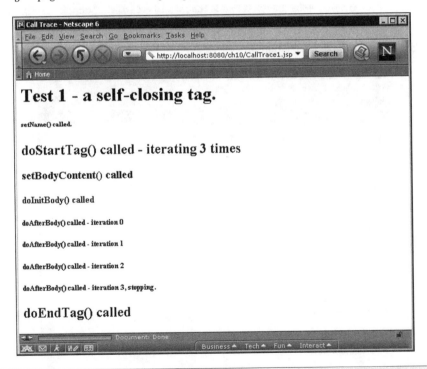

Note that the body content methods (`doInitBody()` and `setBodyContent()`) are both called even though the tag self-closes and the `<body-content>` in the TLD is set to `empty`. The JSP 1.2 standard says only that they are not called if there is no body evaluation by, for example, `doStartTag()` returning `SKIP_BODY`.

341

The CallTrace2 JSP

A more complete example is one that contains body text:

```
<%@ page errorPage="error.jsp" %>
<html>
<head>
  <title>Call Trace</title>
</head>
<body>
  <%@ taglib uri="/calltrace2tags.tld" prefix="chap10" %>
  <h1>Test 2 - with enclosed body text</h2>
  <chap10:calltrace name="name2">
    <blockquote>Body text here.</blockquote>
  </chap10:calltrace>
</body>
</html>
```

The TLD for this example has of course had the `<body-content>empty</body-content>` removed.
Therefore, we need another addition to the `web.xml` file:

```
<taglib>
  <taglib-uri>/calltrace2tags.tld</taglib-uri>
  <taglib-location>/WEB-INF/calltrace2tags.tld</taglib-location>
</taglib>
```

Viewing this page shows the following output:

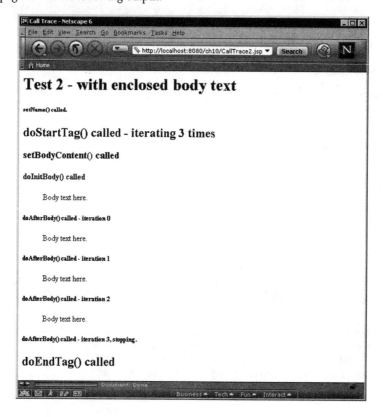

As you can see, the body content is always output **before** the call to doAfterBody().

We can summarize the calls with this flowchart:

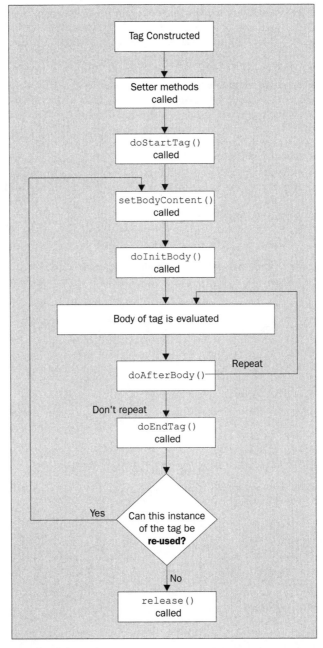

Remember that the decision on whether to repeat the body is made within doAfterBody() which is called once per iteration. There is no need to prescribe the number of iterations in advance – it can be decided at request-time once your termination condition or conditions are met. This can happen when you have reached the end of the file you're processing, or when you have no more records in your result set.

Cooperating Tags

We've already seen several cooperating tags in the last chapter. In particular, the CreateAttArray tag class took an attribute name that was used as the key for storing the array in the page attributes. This attribute was also used in the ShowAttArray and IterateAttArray tag classes as the key for them to access the array that CreateAttArray had stored. In many cases, this level of cooperation is all that's necessary.

One disadvantage of the above method is that it is dependent on both tags being given the same name attribute in the JSP page, and unfortunately this can't be guaranteed since it is the page author's responsibility to make sure they match, not the tag library developer's. Also it involves storing the object within the PageContext, where it could potentially conflict with other tags storage (if they try and use the same key), or where page authors could access and even replace it, knowingly or unknowingly. The system would be much improved if there were a way around these limitations.

Of course there is a way around it, based on **nested tags**. This approach allows you to create a shared object in one main enclosing tag, and have that class store and manage it while the tag itself is open. Cooperating tags can go to the parent enclosing tag when they need access to the object. This way is both well scoped and quite separate from any reliance on unique keys.

The Parent Class

Let's look at the Java code behind this. The Parent class is quite straightforward – it just creates an array in doStartTag() and deletes it in doEndTag(). It also provides get and set methods for accessing the array object:

```
package com.wrox.projsp.ch10;

import javax.servlet.jsp.*;
import javax.servlet.jsp.tagext.*;

public class Parent extends TagSupport {
  private String[] array = null;

  public String[] getArray() {
    return array;
  }

  public void setArray(String[] newArray) {
    this.array = newArray;
  }

  public int doStartTag() throws JspException {
    this.array = new String[5];
    this.array[0] = "Homer";
    this.array[1] = "Marge";
    this.array[2] = "Bart";
    this.array[3] = "Lisa";
    this.array[4] = "Maggie";

    return EVAL_BODY_INCLUDE;
  }

  public int doEndTag() throws JspException {
    this.array = null;
```

```
        return EVAL_PAGE;
    }

}
```

The Child Class

The `Child` class is a bit more interesting:

```
package com.wrox.projsp.ch10;

import javax.servlet.jsp.*;
import javax.servlet.jsp.tagext.*;

public class Child extends BodyTagSupport {
    private int        arrayCounter = 0;
    private String[]   array = null;
```

The `doAfterBody()` and `doEndTag()` methods are both straightforward and don't do anything that hasn't already been covered. The interesting code is in the `doStartTag()` method, where the `Child` class actually gets a handle on the array object.

The first line calls `findAncestorWithClass()`, which uses `getParent()` to step through all the enclosing tag handlers until it finds one with the required class, `Parent`. Calls to `getParent()` are used recursively – if the parent tag handler isn't the correct class, its `getParent()` method is called and checked, and so on up the chain of tags, until a tag handler of the correct class is found or `getParent()` returns `null` to indicate no enclosing tag handler.

In our example case, there is no need for recursion – the tag immediately enclosing our `Child` class is our `Parent` class. In the real world, of course, we couldn't make these assumptions about how the page author will use the code:

```
public int doStartTag() throws JspException {
    Parent parentTag = (Parent) this.findAncestorWithClass(this,
                                                 Parent.class);
```

Once we have our enclosing tag handler we call its `getArray()` method to access the tag's internal array object. We store it for use later in `doAfterBody()`:

```
    this.array = parentTag.getArray();

    return EVAL_BODY_BUFFERED;
}

public int doAfterBody() throws JspException {
    try {
        JspWriter out = pageContext.getOut();

        out.print(" [" + this.arrayCounter + "]: ");
        out.print(this.array[this.arrayCounter] + "<br>");
    } catch (Exception ioException) {
```

```
        System.err.println("IO Exception thrown in Child.doAfterBody():");
        System.err.println(ioException.toString());

        throw new JspException(ioException);
    }

    int repeatOrSkip = SKIP_BODY;

    if (this.arrayCounter < (this.array.length - 1)) {
      repeatOrSkip = EVAL_BODY_AGAIN;
      this.arrayCounter++;
    }

    return repeatOrSkip;
  }

  public int doEndTag() throws JspException {
    try {
      this.getBodyContent().writeOut(pageContext.getOut());
    } catch (Exception ioException) {
      System.err.println("IO Exception thrown in Child.doEndTag():");
      System.err.println(ioException.toString());

      throw new JspException(ioException);
    }

    return EVAL_PAGE;
  }
}
```

> Remember – if an exception is thrown from any of your tag methods (such as
> `doStartTag()`, `doAfterBody()` or `doEndTag()`), the processing of the page stops
> and the user is directed to the error page. A tag based on `IterationTag` won't keep
> iterating if an exception is thrown.

The cooperatingtags TLD

Our TLD file for these tags is:

```xml
<?xml version="1.0" encoding="ISO-8859-1" ?>
<!DOCTYPE taglib
  PUBLIC "-//Sun Microsystems, Inc.//DTD JSP Tag Library 1.2//EN"
  "http://java.sun.com/j2ee/dtds/web-jsptaglibrary_1_2.dtd">

<taglib>
  <tlib-version>1.0</tlib-version>
  <jsp-version>1.2</jsp-version>
  <short-name>CooperatingTags</short-name>
  <description>
    This is a demonstration of cooperating tags. Information is
    created/maintained in one tag and accessed in a nested tag.
  </description>
```

```
    <tag>
      <name>parent</name>
      <tag-class>com.wrox.projsp.ch10.Parent</tag-class>
    </tag>

    <tag>
      <name>child</name>
      <tag-class>com.wrox.projsp.ch10.Child</tag-class>
    </tag>
</taglib>
```

Addition to web.xml

```
<taglib>
  <taglib-uri>/cooperatingtags.tld</taglib-uri>
  <taglib-location>/WEB-INF/cooperatingtags.tld</taglib-location>
</taglib>
```

The Cooperating JSP

Our JSP page for this example is broadly similar to the one for the `IterateArray` example. The exception is that the tag that iterates over the array (the `child` tag in this example) is now nested within a `parent` tag:

```
<%@ page errorPage="error.jsp" %>
<html>
<head>
  <title>Cooperating Tags</title>
</head>
<body>
  <h1>Cooperating tags</h1>

  <%@ taglib uri="/cooperatingtags.tld" prefix="chap10" %>
  <chap10:parent>
    <chap10:child>
      Array value
    </chap10:child>
  </chap10:parent>
</body>
</html>
```

In the above page, it is the `parent` tag that creates and manages the array. The `child` tag goes to the parent tag when it needs to access the array to display the next array value. It does this by calling the `TagSupport.findAncestorWithClass()` method. This method steps through the enclosing tag handler hierarchy via calls to `getParent()`, searching for an enclosing tag of the type passed as a parameter.

When we run this example with `Cooperating.jsp`, we see exactly what we expect:

Although the output is little different from previous examples, what's happening behind the scenes is different in several important ways:

❑ The object itself is only available through the `Parent` tag class. It's not available from the page attributes, so you can be assured that it isn't being manipulated via a JSP scriptlet.

❑ You have control over what sort of access is allowed on the object. We have both `getArray()` and `setArray()` methods, but if you wanted to enable read access but not write access you just wouldn't implement the `setArray()` method (or you'd make it a private method).

❑ The object is only available within the body of the `Parent` tag. It's created in `doStartTag()` and removed in `doEndTag()`.

❑ Accessing the object is type-safe. There's no cast necessary on calls to `getArray()`, since it was written specifically to return an array. More general methods which return objects from the page attributes require a cast because they work with the lowest common denominator object, the `java.lang.Object`.

❑ The dependency is clear to page authors. The whole idea of tags only being valid within certain other tags is a common concept in HTML. For instance a `<td>...</td>` tag pair is only available within a `<tr>...<tr>` pair, which themselves are only valid within a `<table>...</table>` pair. Since page authors are familiar with the concept of nesting tags, it should be easier for them to understand how your custom tags should be used. Of course this is no reason not to provide appropriate examples in your documentation, something we'll be looking at later in this chapter.

Of course introducing the dependency that one custom tag must be nested within another also introduces the possibility that the page author will mistakenly use it without the proper nesting. How can we check at page translation-time that the tag has been used properly?

Tag Validation

The whole idea of requiring that certain tags be placed within a specific enclosing tag brings up the question of validation. What happens if the tag isn't placed properly? What happens if a mandatory attribute is left out? What happens if one attribute is only mandatory under certain circumstances – can tags be checked using finer granularity than just mandatory/non-mandatory?

Fortunately there are several ways of checking to see if a tag is being used appropriately. These methods all happen at translation-time, when the JSP is compiled into Java. This gives a better experience for the user, since all pages will likely be compiled before the site is released and so all translation-time errors should be caught and fixed before the user ever gets to see the pages. However, it also means that new problems can still occur at run-time, and they too must be handled appropriately within the tag handling classes.

With custom tag libraries, you not only need to validate each user-input field value (as with any web programming), but you also need to verify each attribute specified by the page author. If the page author specifies a JDBC connection URL in an attribute, you need to be prepared for a connection URL that doesn't work. If the page author has to place a child tag within the body of a co-operating parent tag, you need to be prepared for the page author using the child tag on its own, or using it outside the parent tag, or using the parent tag on its own.

> Remember, while you control everything your tag library does, you have no control over the JSP page on which it is used. You need to ensure your tags handle all of the incorrect ways a page author can use them.

We'll look at a couple of different situations based on the same tag, just to show a variety of validating methods and what happens when such validation fails. Our tag handling class is quite simple: a tag based on TagSupport, it takes one attribute, firstName, which can be one of "Homer", "Marge", "Bart", "Lisa", or "Maggie". If no firstName attribute is set, or if firstName is set to a value other than one of those five, then the tag is invalid. If all is well, doStartTag() just prints out the firstName attribute.

The Validation Class

Here's our tag handler:

```
package com.wrox.projsp.ch10;

import javax.servlet.jsp.*;
import javax.servlet.jsp.tagext.*;

public class Validation extends TagSupport {
  String firstName = "";

  public String getFirstName() {
    return this.firstName;
  }

  public void setFirstName(String newFirstName) {
    this.firstName = newFirstName;
  }

  public int doStartTag() throws JspException {
    try {
      pageContext.getOut().print("First name is: " + this.firstName);
    } catch (Exception ioException) {
      System.err.println(
              "IO Exception thrown in Validation.doStartTag():");
      System.err.println(ioException.toString());

      throw new JspException(ioException);
```

```
      }

      return SKIP_BODY;
    }

  }
```

Notice how there's no validation in the above class. Translation-time validation is dealt with separately from the tag handling class.

The validationfailure1tags TLD

The simplest approach to ensuring that an attribute is always set is to mark it as mandatory in that tag's TLD file. This is done by specifying `<required>true</required>` within the `<tag>...</tag>` tags, as in the following TLD:

```
<?xml version="1.0" encoding="ISO-8859-1" ?>
<!DOCTYPE taglib
    PUBLIC "-//Sun Microsystems, Inc.//DTD JSP Tag Library 1.2//EN"
    "http://java.sun.com/j2ee/dtds/web-jsptaglibrary_1_2.dtd">

<taglib>
  <tlib-version>1.0</tlib-version>
  <jsp-version>1.2</jsp-version>
  <short-name>ValidatingTags</short-name>
  <description>
    This is a demonstration of failed validation. The tag
    requires a firstName attribute of either "Homer", "Marge",
    "Bart", "Lisa" or "Maggie".
  </description>

  <tag>
    <name>validation</name>
    <tag-class>com.wrox.projsp.ch10.Validation</tag-class>
    <attribute>
      <name>firstName</name>
      <required>true</required>
    </attribute>
  </tag>
</taglib>
```

A complete reference to the tags available within a TLD file is available later in this chapter.

Addition to web.xml

```
<taglib>
  <taglib-uri>/validationfailure1tags.tld</taglib-uri>
  <taglib-location>/WEB-INF/validationfailure1tags.tld</taglib-location>
</taglib>
```

The ValidationFailure1 JSP

If we use the following JSP page, no attribute is set and the tag is invalid:

```
<%@ page errorPage="error.jsp" %>
<html>
<head>
  <title>Validating Tags</title>
```

```
  </head>
  <body>
    <h1>Validating tags (no attribute supplied)</h1>

    <%@ taglib uri="/validationfailure1tags.tld" prefix="chap10" %>
    <chap10:validation/>
  </body>
</html>
```

As you'd expect, this gives a translation-time error:

> ValidationFailure1.jsp(9,2) According to the TLD attribute firstName is mandatory for tag validation

However, this isn't a very fine-grained validation. For instance, it is perfectly happy with the following **invalid** JSP page.

The ValidationFailure2 JSP

```
<%@ page errorPage="error.jsp" %>
<html>
<head>
  <title>Validating Tags</title>
</head>
<body>
  <h1>Validating tags (invalid attribute supplied)</h1>

  <%@ taglib uri="/validationfailure1tags.tld" prefix="chap10" %>
  <chap10:validation firstName="Barney"/>
</body>
</html>
```

This time an attribute has been supplied, but it is "Barney", not one of the five valid attributes: "Homer", "Marge", "Bart", "Lisa", and "Maggie". Since an attribute has been supplied, it passes the simple validation by the TLD. This type of validation failure can be caught in two ways. One way is available in JSP 1.1, and a second, more complete way is available in JSP 1.2.

Validating tags the JSP 1.1 way

Tags can be validated at translation-time by their own `TagExtraInfo` class. One of the methods available in `TagExtraInfo` is the `isValid()` method. If such a method is defined in the `TagExtraInfo` class specified for a tag handler in its TLD file, it is called when the page is being translated and passed a `TagData` parameter which includes details of the tag's attributes.

> **This method of validation was introduced in version 1.1 of the JSP standard, but it's also available in JSP 1.2. If you use this validation mechanism it will work in both JSP 1.1 and JSP 1.2 compliant servers, giving your tags a wider potential audience.**

The ValidationExtraInfo Class

We can see this in action with a `TagExtraInfo` class `ValidationExtraInfo`, written for our `Validation` class:

```java
package com.wrox.projsp.ch10;

import javax.servlet.jsp.tagext.*;

public class ValidationExtraInfo extends TagExtraInfo {

  public boolean isValid(TagData data) {
    String  myFirstNameAtt = (String) data.getAttribute("firstName");
    boolean isASimpson = false;

    if (myFirstNameAtt.equals("Homer") ||
        myFirstNameAtt.equals("Marge") ||
        myFirstNameAtt.equals("Bart") ||
        myFirstNameAtt.equals("Lisa") ||
        myFirstNameAtt.equals("Maggie")) {
      isASimpson = true;
    }

    return isASimpson;
  }

}
```

All the class does is get the value of the `firstName` attribute from the `TagData` passed as a parameter, and compares it with the five allowed values. If the attribute is one of those values, `isValid()` returns `true`. If not, `false` is returned.

The validationfailure2tags TLD

Our TLD has to be modified to include the `ValidationExtraInfo` class:

```xml
<?xml version="1.0" encoding="ISO-8859-1" ?>
<!DOCTYPE taglib
  PUBLIC "-//Sun Microsystems, Inc.//DTD JSP Tag Library 1.2//EN"
  "http://java.sun.com/j2ee/dtds/web-jsptaglibrary_1_2.dtd">

<taglib>
  <tlib-version>1.0</tlib-version>
  <jsp-version>1.2</jsp-version>
  <short-name>ValidatingTags</short-name>
  <description>
    This is a demonstration of failed validation. The tag
    requires a firstName attribute of either "Homer", "Marge",
    "Bart", "Lisa" or "Maggie", but the attribute supplied
    is "Barney".
  </description>

  <tag>
    <name>validation</name>
    <tag-class>com.wrox.projsp.ch10.Validation</tag-class>
    <tei-class>com.wrox.projsp.ch10.ValidationExtraInfo</tei-class>
    <attribute>
      <name>firstName</name>
      <required>true</required>
    </attribute>
  </tag>
</taglib>
```

Addition to web.xml

```
<taglib>
  <taglib-uri>/validationfailure2tags.tld</taglib-uri>
  <taglib-location>/WEB-INF/validationfailure2tags.tld</taglib-location>
</taglib>
```

Finally change the following line in `ValidationFailure2.jsp`:

```
<%@ taglib uri="/validationfailure2tags.tld" prefix="chap10" %>
```

When we try and show the JSP that has "Barney" as an attribute (`ValidationFailure2.jsp`), the server returns the following error:

ValidationFailure2.jsp(9,2) Attributes are invalid according to TagInfo

This is great – we have specific validation based on the attributes supplied, using an algorithm of our choosing. Naturally this could be extended to cover attributes that are only valid if other attributes are certain values, since the information about all the attributes is supplied in the `TagData` parameter.

However, this poor error message doesn't give much of a clue to the page author about **why** the attributes are invalid, or even **which** attributes are causing the problem. Since it's just a general message that indicates validation failed, there's no way to tailor it either, so even though your validation code knows the reason validation failed, it can't share that with the page author except by printing to `System.err`. Not only that, but this validation mechanism provides no way of checking the context of a tag. There's no way to be sure at translation time if the tag is properly nested inside, for example, a parent `defineObjects` tag, although you'll obviously get a request-time error when you try to view the page.

The TagLibraryValidator Class

The latest version of the JSP standard, JSP 1.2, introduces a new, more complete mechanism for controlling tag validation. It defines a new class, `TagLibraryValidator`, from which you derive classes specifically to validate the use of a tag in a page. This `TagLibraryValidator` class has several methods, but most of the time only the `validate()` method will be used.

Constructors

The constructor for the `TagLibraryValidator` class is as follows:

```
public void TagLibraryValidator()
```

Each validator class must provide a no-argument constructor.

Methods

The `TagLibraryValidator` class has four methods:

```
public java.util.Map getInitParameters()
```

This method returns the initialization parameters which should have already been set by a call to `setInitParameters()`. Initialization data is stored as key-value pairs in the map with the parameter name as the 'key' and the parameter value as the 'value'.

```
public void release()
```

This method is called by the server once the class isn't needed any more. This allows the class to free up any resources it required while performing the validation.

```
public void setInitParameters(java.util.Map map)
```

The server can use this method to pass the validator initialization data from the TLD file to the validator class.

```
public String validate(String prefix, String uri, Pagedate page)
```

This method is the main reason for the class' existence, and it is called to validate the use of the tag library on the page. It takes three parameters:

❑ prefix
The prefix the page author defined in the taglib directive for use with this tag library

❑ uri
The URI of the TLD file used in the taglib directive

❑ page
The PageData XML rendition of the JSP page

Using the three parameters allows the validate() method to verify the use of the tag in the context of the page itself, not just as a standalone tag. If only the page data were passed, there would be no way for the validating class to differentiate between someone else's custom tag <someoneelseslib:tag/> and <mylib:tag/>.

Since the page author and not the tag library author chooses the particular prefix on the JSP, the validation class cannot know the prefix in advance. Even if the tag names were chosen more sensibly, there is always the possibility of a name collision and so the validation class must be informed of the unique tag prefix used for **this** tag library on **this** page.

The ValidationValidator Class

Our validation class looks a bit unpleasant:

```
package com.wrox.projsp.ch10;

import java.io.*;
import javax.servlet.jsp.*;
import javax.servlet.jsp.tagext.*;

public class ValidationValidator extends TagLibraryValidator {
  private int PAGE_BUFFER_SIZE = 8192;
```

Really the ValidationValidator class has just two methods. The first method is a private one, getAttributeValue(), that does not exist in the TagLibraryValidator superclass. It just parses the XML version of the JSP page and returns the value of the attribute whose name is passed as its first parameter. In our case, we use 'firstName' as the parameter and getAttributeValue() returns the value of that attribute.

It's a straightforward method, but it's not the recommended approach for creating a full validation class. A more appropriate way would be to use JAXP to parse the whole JSP page first, allowing more comprehensive processing on the tag and its position on the page. That however would likely distract from the actual validation code itself, so we've gone for the simple approach here to focus on the validation:

```
    private String getAttributeValue(String attribute, String tag,
                                     PageData page)
         throws IOException, JspException {

  String attValue = null;
  InputStream pageStream = page.getInputStream();
  byte[]pageText = new byte[PAGE_BUFFER_SIZE];

  pageStream.read(pageText, 0, PAGE_BUFFER_SIZE);

  String pageString = new String(pageText);
  int foundAt = pageString.indexOf(tag);

  if (foundAt < 0) {
    throw new JspException("Could not locate tag " + tag +
                             " in XML document.");
  }

  int attFoundAt = pageString.indexOf(attribute + "=\"", foundAt);

  if (attFoundAt < 0) {
    throw new JspException("Tag " + tag + " contained no \"" +
                             attribute + "\" attribute.");
  }

  int closingDelimiterFoundAt = pageString.indexOf(">", foundAt);

  if (closingDelimiterFoundAt < attFoundAt) {
    throw new JspException("Tag " + tag + " closed before finding \"" +
                             attribute + "\" attribute.");
  }

  int startAt = attFoundAt + attribute.length() + "=\"".length();
  int endAt = pageString.indexOf("\"", startAt);

  attValue = pageString.substring(startAt, endAt);

  return attValue;
}
```

The important part of the class is really the `validate()` method. First of all it builds up the complete tag name, including the prefix given to the library by the page author. It then calls `getAttributeValue()` using this complete tag name to retrieve the value of the `firstName` attribute. This value is then compared with the five acceptable values and if it matches one of them then the value `null` is returned. If it doesn't match one of these values, a string containing a useful error message is returned.

Note that `null` returned by `validate()` indicates success. If a `String` is returned instead it is taken to be an error message and validation is deemed to have failed:

```
    public String validate(String prefix, String uri, PageData page) {
      String returnedErrorOrSuccess;

      try {
        String tag = prefix + ":validation";
        String firstName = this.getAttributeValue("firstName", tag, page);

        if (firstName.equals("Homer") || firstName.equals("Marge") ||
            firstName.equals("Bart") || firstName.equals("Lisa") ||
            firstName.equals("Maggie")) {
          returnedErrorOrSuccess = null;
        } else {
          returnedErrorOrSuccess = "firstName attribute value \"" +
                                   firstName + "\" is not a valid value.";
        }
      } catch (Exception ioException) {
        System.err.println("IO Exception thrown in " +
                           "ValidationValidator.validate():");
        System.err.println(ioException.toString());

        returnedErrorOrSuccess = ioException.toString();
      }

      return returnedErrorOrSuccess;
    }

}
```

Note that our `ValidationValidator` class has some serious limitations that would make it inappropriate for real-world use. It only reads in the first 8k of the XML version of the page, it only checks the attribute in the first matching tag it encounters, and it's not very good at finding the tag within the XML document. Full use of an XML parser is really the best approach.

> One such parser is JAXP, the Java API for XML Parsing. This is an optional Java package from Sun, and you can get it at **http://java.sun.com/xml/**. (Chapter 12 covers the use of XML in your web applications in depth.)

The validationfailure3tags TLD

We include our validation class in the `validationfailure3tags.tld` as follows:

```
<?xml version="1.0" encoding="ISO-8859-1" ?>
<!DOCTYPE taglib
  PUBLIC "-//Sun Microsystems, Inc.//DTD JSP Tag Library 1.2//EN"
  "http://java.sun.com/j2ee/dtds/web-jsptaglibrary_1_2.dtd">

<taglib>
  <tlib-version>1.0</tlib-version>
  <jsp-version>1.2</jsp-version>
  <short-name>ValidatingTags</short-name>
  <description>
    This is a demonstration of failed validation. The tag
    requires a firstName attribute of either "Homer", "Marge",
```

```
      "Bart", "Lisa" or "Maggie", but the attribute supplied
      is "Barney".
    </description>

    <validator>
      <validator-class>
        com.wrox.projsp.ch10.ValidationValidator
      </validator-class>
    </validator>

    <tag>
      <name>validation</name>
      <tag-class>com.wrox.projsp.ch10.Validation</tag-class>
      <attribute>
        <name>firstName</name>
        <required>true</required>
      </attribute>
    </tag>
</taglib>
```

> The `<validator>` tag exists outside the `<tag>` class since it is used to validate the use of all tags in the library, not just a specific tag.

Addition to web.xml

```
    <taglib>
      <taglib-uri>/validationfailure3tags.tld</taglib-uri>
      <taglib-location>/WEB-INF/validationfailure2tags.tld</taglib-location>
    </taglib>
```

The ValidationFailure3 JSP

Change the following line in `ValidationFailure2.jsp`:

```
    <%@ taglib uri="/validationfailure3tags.tld" prefix="chap10" %>
```

When this is used to validate the JSP page that uses Barney as the `firstName` attribute, Tomcat gives the following error:

> org.apache.jasper.JasperException: TagLibraryValidator in ValidatingTags library – invalid page: firstName attribute value "Barney" is not a valid value.

If we try passing a value for the `firstName` attribute that matches one of the valid names (say, "Maggie"), then we get the page we expect, showing the name.

The ValidationSuccess JSP

```
    <%@ page errorPage="error.jsp" %>
    <html>
    <head>
      <title>Validating Tags</title>
    </head>
    <body>
```

```
        <h1>Validating tags (valid attribute supplied)</h1>

        <%@ taglib uri="/validationsuccesstags.tld" prefix="chap10" %>
        <chap10:validation firstName="Maggie"/>
    </body>
    </html>
```

Note that `validationsuccesstags.tld` is identical to `validationfailure3tags.tld`. Remember to add the appropriate entry to your `web.xml` file if you implement the `validationsuccesstags` TLD.

Viewing `ValidationSuccess.jsp` gives us the following page:

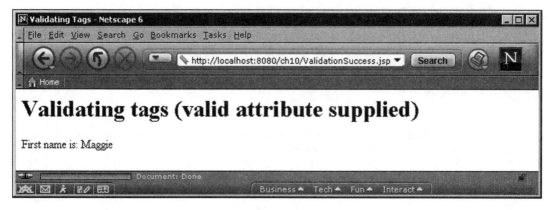

The `TagLibraryValidation` mechanism for validating tag libraries is much more comprehensive than the `isValid()` mechanism in JSP 1.1, for the following reasons:

❑   It allows you to validate the whole page, not just the tag and its attributes. This means if you use a cooperating-tags model like the one demonstrated earlier, you can use your `TagLibraryValidation` class to ensure that tags that **must** be enclosed within parent tags **are** enclosed.

❑   It allows you to use a custom error message to indicate what particular validation rule is being broken. It's all very well having lots of rules that tags and attributes must follow, but `isValid()` just gives one error that says "Something's wrong". `TagLibraryValidation` allows you to tell the page author exactly what's wrong, and even how to fix it.

`TagLibraryValidation` classes can be much more complicated to implement than in the `isValid()` method in a `TagExtraInfo` class. They require stepping through the XML version of the JSP page, or using a full-blown XML parser to do that, and this can dramatically increase the amount of time it takes to write a simple validation class. Even so, validation classes are now the preferred way of handling tag validation as of JSP 1.2, and they can be worth the extra effort involved.

Although this tag validation mechanism can take longer to run, the performance penalty should not be an issue since it is done at translation-time rather than at request-time. Ideally all validation and translation will be done before the pages are released for use.

Handling Errors in Tag Libraries

Validating as much as possible at translation time is incredibly important. No webmaster ever wants users to see the bare white page saying "A Servlet Exception Has Occurred". Ever. Even if the webmaster has done something silly with your tags, they're not going to be happy with your library if it displays their errors to the world. By validating as much as possible at translation time, you catch errors as early as possible and hopefully before those pages are made available to users. Strict validation and a formal release procedure are an important part of any serious site – there are enough broken web sites out there.

Sometimes you just can't validate everything at translation-time though. No matter how good your tags are, sometimes they just have to depend on data input by users (or other dynamic data) and that means potential run-time problems. So even though translation-time validation is important, it's essential that **everything** is checked at request-time. People can enter the strangest values for things that seem obvious, and particularly nefarious users have been known to change the values of IDs passed in the query string or even in hidden form data.

An error reporting strategy that's common to all tags in your library, maybe even common to all your tag libraries is a good idea. It should be simple, consistent, and shouldn't break a webmaster's carefully laid-out pages. You could even store all your messages in a property file – that would mean you could supply your tag library in different languages, just by including a different property file in the distribution.

The first main question to be sorted out by an error handling strategy is when, if ever, your tag library should throw an exception to the calling Servlet. This is important because it has such an impact on what the user sees and what the webmaster can do. On one hand the default error page is often used by inexperienced JSP webmasters, but it's not something you'd ever want to show users. On the other hand a custom error page is a useful way for advanced webmasters to track problems in pages – for example to e-mail a stack trace or log it to a special file.

In the main you should separate recoverable and unrecoverable errors, and should do your best to deal with recoverable errors within your tag library while throwing an exception for unrecoverable errors. Some simple examples are:

❑   If your tags form part of a database-driven web application and you can't connect to the database, throw an exception with a good explanation of what's wrong.

❑   If some user-input data fails validation (for example if the user didn't fill out a mandatory field), redisplay the form with all the fields already filled out, along with a simple, clear error message telling the user what field is invalid and what information it should contain. This is a bit better than relying on the user pressing the 'back' button, and much, much better than making the user complete the whole form again. The example application in Chapter 21 demonstrates this method of interaction.

The situation becomes more complicated when you encounter invalid data that **should** be correct. Passing a database record's ID as a hidden form field is common practice, but what if someone creates their own form that masquerades as a valid form from your site, but with an invalid ID? Or worse, what if it's the ID of a record that user shouldn't be able to access? Obviously your library shouldn't allow the edit, but should it handle it internally and display an error message, or should it throw an exception to the webmaster's error page?

On balance it's probably best to throw an exception in this kind of situation. That allows the webmaster of the site (and the user of your tag library) to define their own mechanism for handling such things. Vigilant administrators will want to be notified of any suspicious activity at the earliest moment, and a good custom error page can still provide a good end-user experience if the cause isn't malicious.

Webmasters will only follow this structured approach if they have confidence that your tag library will **never** normally throw an exception. If your library throws exceptions in anything other than exceptional circumstances then you increase the risk that all your exception reports will be ignored.

The TryCatchFinally Interface

What happens if you need to perform some cleanup after your tag has run? Naturally you can clean up after any exceptions **your** class throws, but what if an exception is thrown within the body of one of your tags? This would result in doStartTag() being successfully called, and doEndTag() never being called. Any cleanup code you had in doEndTag() would never be processed, potentially leaving database connections open and other resources locked.

JSP 1.2 introduces another interface to fix this problem. This interface, javax.servlet.jsp.tagext.TryCatchFinally, introduces two new methods, doCatch() and doFinally(). This is a simple interface to allows you to hook into the Java exception handling mechanism. The doCatch() and doFinally() methods allow your tag to catch and process exceptions thrown between invocations of its tag-handling methods.

Methods

The TryCatchFinally Interface defines two methods:

public void doCatch(Throwable t)

The server invokes this method if an exception is thrown while a tag handler is in scope. Specifically it is invoked if an uncaught exception is thrown in doStartTag(), doInitBody(), doAfterBody(), or doEndTag(), or if one is thrown while evaluating the body of a tag. It is not invoked if an exception is thrown by a tag's setter methods.

public void doFinally()

This method is invoked by the server in all circumstances, after doEndTag() has been called, even if an exception has been thrown. In that sense it is just like a finally block inside a method – it is always executed to allow you to clean up resources. It should not throw an exception.

How this works is really quite straightforward. We can see that by looking at the way the tag handlers themselves are invoked. Here's a very simple tag-handling class that implements the TryCatchFinally interface.

The ExceptionHandler Class

```
package com.wrox.projsp.ch10;

import javax.servlet.jsp.*;
import javax.servlet.jsp.tagext.*;

public class ExceptionHandler extends TagSupport implements TryCatchFinally {

  public void doCatch(Throwable t) {

    // Do nothing
  }
```

```
    public void doFinally() {

      // Do nothing
    }

}
```

As you can see, this class doesn't do anything. It just implements the required interface methods with do-nothing stubs, and relies on the `TagSupport` base class to implement default methods for the tag handling. We set this up as follows.

The exceptionhandlingtags TLD

```
<?xml version="1.0" encoding="ISO-8859-1" ?>
<!DOCTYPE taglib
   PUBLIC "-//Sun Microsystems, Inc.//DTD JSP Tag Library 1.2//EN"
   "http://java.sun.com/j2ee/dtds/web-jsptaglibrary_1_2.dtd">

<taglib>
   <tlib-version>1.0</tlib-version>
   <jsp-version>1.2</jsp-version>
   <short-name>ExceptionHandlingTags</short-name>
   <description>
     This is a demonstration of exception handling within tags.
     It doesn't do anything, it's just used to generate the servlet
     code to show what's going on.
   </description>

   <tag>
     <name>exceptionhandler</name>
     <tag-class>com.wrox.projsp.ch10.ExceptionHandler</tag-class>
   </tag>

</taglib>
```

Additions to web.xml

```
<taglib>
   <taglib-uri>/exceptionhandlingtags.tld</taglib-uri>
   <taglib-location>/WEB-INF/exceptionhandlingtags.tld</taglib-location>
</taglib>
```

The ExceptionHandler JSP

```
<%@ page errorPage="error.jsp" %>
<html>
<head>
   <title>Exception Handling Within Tags</title>
</head>
<body>
   <h1>Exception handling within tags</h1>

   <%@ taglib uri="/exceptionhandlingtags.tld" prefix="chap10" %>
   <chap10:exceptionhandler>
```

```
     Enclosed body text
   </chap10:exceptionhandler>
 </body>
 </html>
```

What's interesting about this tag is how it is called. When the JSP page is compiled into a servlet, we get some fairly ugly code. Remember, this is Java code generated by the server, and it's not meant for human eyes to see. You can find the servlet in your %CATALINA_HOME%\work\localhost\ch10 directory. The key part of this servlet, as far as we're concerned, is the try-catch-finally block:

```
            try {
                    int _jspx_eval_chap10_exceptionhandler_0 =
_jspx_th_chap10_exceptionhandler_0.doStartTag();
                    if (_jspx_eval_chap10_exceptionhandler_0 ==
BodyTag.EVAL_BODY_BUFFERED)
                        throw new JspTagException("Since tag handler class
com.wrox.projsp.ch10.ExceptionHandler does not implement BodyTag, it can't return
BodyTag.EVAL_BODY_TAG");
                    if (_jspx_eval_chap10_exceptionhandler_0 != Tag.SKIP_BODY) {
                        do {
                        // end
                        // HTML // begin
[file="C:\\tomcat4.0\\webapps\\ch10\\ExceptionHandler.jsp";from=(9,27);to=(11,2)]
                            out.write("\r\n    Enclosed body text\r\n   ");

                        // end
                        // begin
[file="C:\\tomcat4.0\\webapps\\ch10\\ExceptionHandler.jsp";from=(11,2);to=(11,28)]
                        } while (_jspx_th_chap10_exceptionhandler_0.doAfterBody()
== BodyTag.EVAL_BODY_AGAIN);
                    }
                    if (_jspx_th_chap10_exceptionhandler_0.doEndTag() ==
Tag.SKIP_PAGE)
                        return;
```

As you can see, the doCatch() and doFinally() methods simply 'plug in' to the existing Java exception framework, to be called when the Java keywords they are named after are entered:

```
            } catch (Throwable t) {
                _jspx_th_chap10_exceptionhandler_0.doCatch(t);
            } finally {
                _jspx_th_chap10_exceptionhandler_0.doFinally();
                _jspx_th_chap10_exceptionhandler_0.release();
            }
        // end
        // HTML // begin
[file="C:\\tomcat4.0\\webapps\\ch10\\ExceptionHandler.jsp";from=(11,28);to=(14,0)]
            out.write("\r\n</body>\r\n</html>\r\n");

        // end

    } catch (Throwable t) {
        if (out != null && out.getBufferSize() != 0)
            out.clearBuffer();
```

```
            if (pageContext != null) pageContext.handlePageException(t);
        } finally {
            if (_jspxFactory != null)
_jspxFactory.releasePageContext(pageContext);
        }
    }
}
```

Common Pitfalls

Custom tags are a really great feature of JSP, and they are incredibly powerful if done properly. There are a number of fairly common mistakes people make when first trying to create their own tags though, and we'll try to clear up some of them here:

❑ **Tag names versus class names**
There's no need for the name of the tag you create to be the same as the name of the class that it calls. Obviously they will probably be related, but remember that you are dealing with two different audiences. The page designers will want a nice simple tag name that clearly indicates what it's for. The people who maintain the tag classes will be happier with more descriptive class names that are consistent throughout the package and describe the purpose of the class. For instance, you may want all the classes in your library that implement a custom tag to have class names that end with a tag suffix.

We saw this in action in the previous chapter where the tag class com.wrox.projsp.ch09.CreateAttArray was used. Although this class does indeed create an array and store it in the page attributes, the tag for this class was named defineObjects. This gives the page designers a familiar paradigm – a defineObjects tag is the recommended way of setting up any objects needed for use later on the page – while not restricting what the class is called or circumventing any standard naming conventions for classes.

❑ **Not throwing exceptions properly**
No-one likes being on the receiving end of the default error page, but exceptions have an important part to play in the JSP architecture. A good rule of thumb is that if the problem is recoverable (for example failed validation) your tag should try to recover as best it can. If the problem is unrecoverable (for example you can't connect to a data source that was specified in an attribute) you should probably throw an exception. Throwing an exception means the site administrator has a chance to log the problem and handle it in a site-specific way (perhaps sending themselves an e-mail or an SMS message). It wouldn't be a good idea to force a specific error reporting path on administrators (by making them give you an address for SMS messages as a tag attribute); it would be better to leave it open so they can define any reporting path they wish.

❑ **Not knowing what happens at translation-time and what happens at request-time**
Some things only happen when a page is being translated into the servlet, and some things happen every time the page is loaded. Tag validation, for example, happens only when the page is being compiled into a servlet. This makes sense because you can do a lot of checks on a tag to see if it is placed properly but it would be pointless to do this every time – the tag's placement isn't going to change unless the page is changed, and if the page is changed it must be re-compiled. It also means that the delay that comes from performing validation only happens once, and ideally that will be before users ever see it.

❑ **Not validating the use of the tag**

You wouldn't believe the weird and wonderful ways page authors will try and use your tag library. Make sure that it's easy for them to find out why their page won't compile, and how they can fix it.

❑ **Not performing request-time checks**

Just because your page passed validation doesn't mean that everything is correct. Some attributes may be request-time values (if you set `<rtexprvalue>true</rtexprvalue>` in your TLD), and you'll need to verify that they are acceptable every time you try and use them. Or worse, you might be relying on user-input data to perform actions, so you'll need to normalize **and** validate that data before you can reliably use it.

❑ **Not separating the page design from the program logic**

Every time you hard-code HTML into your custom tag's output, you're making it harder for the page designer to use them. You're also storing up problems for yourself later when it's time to change the design of the site. So instead of writing one tag like:

```
<mysite:shownewsitem/>
```

Instead try using the parent/child dependency with a group of tags that just output the individual data items:

```
<mynews:newsitem>
  <table>
    <tr>
      <td><mynews:title></td>
    </tr>
    <tr>
      <td><mynews:story></td>
    </tr>
  </table>
</mynews:newsitem>
```

That way, you won't have to change your code when they want to put the title on a yellow background.

❑ **Not knowing just how much a tag can do**

Tags that can manipulate their body content are incredibly powerful. Not only can they do lots of things as part of an application, they can also do great things on top of existing or bought-in applications. Earlier in the chapter we looked at a profanity filter – remember, this filtering tag could enclose a bought-in piece of software, for example a user forum, and you can filter the output of the forum without changing the forum code. This could be essential, because if you bought in the forum program you may not have received the source code. Custom tags mean it simply isn't an issue – you can filter the output of the program before it gets to the browser, no matter what source it came from.

❑ **Not having a formal release mechanism for your site**

Including custom tags on a JSP page slows down their initial compilation. It's a fact of life. It slows down even more if you perform validation on the tags (which you really, really should). There are enough problems with pages being slow to load because of bandwidth without adding to the delay by expecting your visitors to sit around while they trigger the compilation process. Compile your pages in advance so they'll be amazed at how fast your site is!

TLD Reference

As we've already seen the Tag Library Descriptor file is the XML file used to describe a tag library. A JSP 1.2 TLD file must start with the following:

```
<?xml version="1.0" encoding="ISO-8859-1" ?>
<!DOCTYPE taglib
    PUBLIC "-//Sun Microsystems, Inc.//DTD JSP Tag Library 1.2//EN"
    "http://java.sun.com/j2ee/dtds/web-jsptaglibrary_1_2.dtd">
```

Next comes the XML document root for the file, which in this case is the `<taglib>` tag. The following tags are valid within `<taglib>`...`</taglib>` tags:

Element	Mandatory	Description
tlib-version	Yes	The version of the tag library.
jsp-version	Yes	The version of JSP that the library needs.
short-name	Yes	A simple default short name for the tag library. This may be used by JSP authoring tools to create a mnemonic for the tag library, or to create a default prefix for the tags.
uri	Yes	A unique URI for this tag library.
display-name	Yes	The name of the tag library that is to be displayed by JSP authoring tools.
small-icon	No	A small icon to be used by authoring tools to represent the tag library.
large-icon	No	A large icon to be used by authoring tools to represent the tag library.
description	Yes	A string describing the tag library's purpose and how it should be used.
validator	No	Information on the validator class for the library.
listener	No	Information on event listeners for the library.
tag	Yes	Information on one of the custom tags in the library.

Many of these tags were designed with page authoring tools in mind. The idea behind this is that these tools will be able to, for instance, put an icon for the tag library on the toolbar (using the icon file pointed to by `<large-icon>` within the `<taglib>`...`</taglib>` tags). The same library could also, for instance, be represented on property pages by the icon pointed to by `<small-icon>`, together with the `<display-name>` and maybe even with the `<description>` available when you hover over the icon.

This same principle applies to the elements for the tags themselves – the icons can be used to represent them on the page itself, perhaps with attributes being set via a property sheet which uses the display name and description. We'll cover page authoring tools a little later in this chapter, but so far none of the tools available take advantage of these facilities.

The `<validator>`...`</validator>` requires some sub-elements of its own:

Element	Mandatory	Description
validator-class	Yes	The class written for the tag library which implements `TagLibraryValidator` and can perform validation for the library
init-param	No	Initialization parameters for the validator class
descriptor	No	A simple description of the validator

The `<init-param>`...`</init-param>` itself requires some sub-elements:

Element	Mandatory	Description
param-name	Yes	The name of the parameter
param-value	Yes	The value of the parameter
description	No	A simple description of the parameter

There are a lot of sub-elements to the `<tag>`...`</tag>` tag:

Element	Mandatory	Description
name	Yes	A name for the tag that is unique within this library.
tag-class	Yes	The tag-handler class that implements the `Tag`, `BodyTag`, or `IterationTag` interface.
tei-class	No	An optional class that subclasses `TagExtraInfo`, used to provide extra translation-time information on the tag.
body-content	No	States what the content of the body will be. Can be one of the following three values: `tagdependent`, `JSP` or `empty`. The default value is `JSP`.
display-name	Yes	A short name that should be used by JSP authoring tools to refer to the tag.
small-icon	No	A small icon to be used by authoring tools to represent the tag.
large-icon	No	A large icon to be used by authoring tools to represent the tag.
description	No	A simple description of the tag and how it should be used.
variable	No	Information on any scripting variable the tag introduces.
attribute	No	Mechanism for listing all attributes of this tag.
example	No	A simple example of using the tag.

The sub-elements required to define a variable via `<variable>...</variable>` tags are as follows:

Element	Mandatory	Description
name-given	No	The variable's name, given as a constant. Although this element is not mandatory, it is a requirement that either name-given or name-from-attribute is specified.
name-from-attribute	No	The name of an attribute whose value is to be used as the variable name.
variable-class	No	The class of the variable. java.lang.String is the default.
declare	No	States whether the variable is to be declared or not. true is the default.
scope	No	The scope the variable is to have. NESTED is the default value, and AT_BEGIN and AT_END are the other possible values.
description	No	A simple description of the variable

Sub-elements that are valid within `<attribute>...</attribute>` tags are:

Element	Mandatory	Description
name	Yes	The name of the attribute.
required	No	States whether the attribute must be present or if it is optional. Possible values are true and yes, indicating the attribute must be present, and false and no, indicating the attribute is not mandatory. The default is false.
rtexprvalue	No	States whether the attribute can accept scriptlet expressions evaluated at request-time as the value of the attribute, or if they must be static values instead. Possible values are true and yes, indicating the attribute can use a scriptlet expression to generate its value, and false and no, indicating the attribute has a static value. The default is false.
type	No	Defines the Java type of attribute value. The default value is java.lang.String, and that is also the value for any static expression used as a value.
description	No	A simple description of the attribute

Event Listeners

As you might have noticed from the above tables, TLDs provide an easy way for tag libraries to introduce event listeners to the system. Event listeners, which are a new feature of the Servlet 2.3 and JSP 1.2 specifications, will be covered in more detail in Chapter 16, but essentially they provide a way for library classes to hook into important server objects and be notified certain things happen to them; they can be registered either in the web.xml file, or by a tag library via the `<listener>` element in the TLD.

The most useful type of listener for a tag library is likely to be that which is notified when the web application is started up or shut down; this could be useful for setting up resources that your tags will need and storing them in the `ServletContext`.

Once they have been loaded, the server does not differentiate between event listeners defined for the server in the `web.xml` configuration file and those defined for a tag library in a TLD.

Tool Support

In this section, we'll take a look at some of the different tools you can use to help you work with custom tags.

Authoring Tools

One of the more exciting areas of JSP authoring is the way the standard has built-in hooks for page-authoring tools. As well as the standard bean introspection that's available on all classes, the TLD file introduces short-names and display-names for tags and tag libraries, along with small and large icons.

Authoring tools could read in this information and use it to show an appropriate icon in an otherwise-WYSIWYG page and right-clicking on the icon would bring up a property sheet for the tag allowing you to find and set attributes. Since the XML format of the `web.xml` and TLD files are well known, the authoring tools could verify that all tags have mandatory attributes, that none of the attributes contain scriptlet expressions if that's not permitted in the TLD, and it could even instantiate any `TagExtraInformation` and `TagLibraryValidator` classes to verify that the tags being entered are valid.

Unfortunately there are no such tools at the minute. The JSP 1.2 standard is just too new for the tool support to have caught up yet. Hopefully JSP page authoring tools will embrace the custom tag paradigm soon, so that custom tags will be just as well served as regular HTML tags.

Jakarta Taglib

The Taglib project at Jakarta, the Apache project that develops the Tomcat server, aims to provide an open-source repository for tag libraries. Current tag libraries include ones for performing XSL transformations, simplifying the use of HTML form fields, and running SQL queries and updates. These tags have been developed by volunteers, and the Apache group actively encourages participation in such projects. Involvement in the Taglib project can be as simple as answering questions on the Taglib-users mailing list, right up to checking in and out code from the Taglib source control system.

You can find out more information and download the complete repository at http://jakarta.apache.org/taglibs/.

Jakarta Struts

The Struts project at Jakarta is aimed at developing an open-source framework useful to the development of Servlet and JSP web applications. Based on the Model-View-Controller paradigm, it is comprised of a **controller mechanism** that dispatches requests to the appropriate action handlers, a **collection of tag libraries** to create form-based applications, and a **set of utility classes** for XML parsing, internationalization, and bean manipulation.

Participation in the Struts project is open to all, the same as the Taglib project. You can read all about it and download the framework at http://jakarta.apache.org/struts/. Struts is also covered in Chapter 21 of this book.

Documenting Tag Libraries

The most important thing to realize when writing tag library documentation is that there are two distinct audiences. The first audience is the page authors who will use your tags, and the second audience is the programmers who will maintain the Java code and XML files that constitute the tags. Since both groups have very distinct goals, it's probably best to deal with them separately.

Documentation for Page Authors

Page authors need to know how to use your tags properly. That means for each tag they need to know:

❏ The tag name, what it does, and in some cases how it works

❏ The runtime environment the tag needs, including any additional libraries, packages and resources it needs if they are different from those of the tag library in general

❏ What mandatory attributes the tag requires, what their purpose is, and what values are acceptable

❏ What optional attributes the tag can take, what their purpose is, and what values are acceptable

❏ What dependencies this tag has. For example, whether it must be nested within another tag, or whether it must come after another particular tag that defines objects for this tag to use

❏ What tags in turn depend on this tag

❏ What exceptions this tag may throw, and under what circumstances

❏ At least one good, realistic example of how to use the tag, and ideally more examples covering all the main ways the tag and its attributes can be used

❏ Anything else the tag may do that could affect page formatting

❏ Where to turn for help if things go wrong, for example a help area for this library or an e-mail address for support

That's a lot of information to put together even for a small tag library. Good documentation can sometimes be the largest part of a product. However, it's only by being clear and explicit about such information that page authors will have enough confidence in the tag library to trust it on their sites. Good documentation is important simply because no-one will use your tags if they don't know how. The Jakarta Struts and Taglibs projects have both developed documentation systems for their tag libraries which may repay further investigation.

Documentation for Tag Maintainers

The programmers who will actually maintain your work have significantly different needs and would not be well served by the above documentation alone. The above documentation would give some guidance on what the tag **should** do, but it would probably not sufficiently cover the internal data structures and algorithms employed by the library.

Documentation for programmers is becoming a well understood topic and Java is particularly good in that it allows programmers to put the documentation for the code in along with the code itself, and use the Javadoc tool to extract and format it.

In general, good Javadoc comments will work well for programmers and maintainers. Sun already has a useful article on the subject called "How To Write Doc Comments For Javadoc", and is available online at http://java.sun.com/j2se/javadoc/writingdoccomments/index.html.

In addition to regular programming comments, it is also worth emphasizing which version of the JSP standard you used when developing the library, and also which version of Java you used. Standards change, and knowing which standard to refer to can be a big help.

Distributing your Tag Libraries

Tag libraries can easily be included in a WAR file as part of any web application, just as Servlets and JSPs can. However, tag libraries themselves bring their own unique problems that often mean distributing them in a WAR file might not be the best way.

The main issue with using WAR files is that tag libraries themselves tend to be produced for page authors to use on their own pages, or they come with bare-bones JSPs that are designed for the webmaster to customize to the site's look and feel. Creating and editing JSPs within a WAR file is more work than necessary, so it's often best to distribute the tag library itself as part of a JAR file that can just be dropped in to the site's `WEB-INF/lib` directory.

There are three ways to map the TLD file specified in the `taglib` directive on the JSP page to the real TLD file. The easiest method, the default, is to simply use the real path to the TLD file. For example, you could keep all your TLD files in a separate folder called `/TLDs/`, and then you'd use the following directive to refer to the file `mytags.tld`:

```
<%@ taglib uri="/TLDs/mytags.tld" prefix="mytags" %>
```

Although this method is quick and easy, it's really only designed as a simple mechanism for when you're developing the library.

The second method is the one we've used in this chapter and the last, and is based on an explicit mapping in the application's `web.xml` file.

The third method is the best one for packaging tag libraries, and can only be used when you distribute a tab library in a JAR file. Each JAR file stored in the `WEB-INF/lib` folder of a web application is automatically processed, and any TLD files contained in those JAR files are *automatically* read in. If the `<taglib>...</taglib>` contains a `<uri>...</uri>` sub-element, it is used as the mapping for that TLD file. This allows us to package up all the tag library Java classes with the required TLD file, and distribute just that package without needing to install any new tags in the site's (or application's) `web.xml` file.

For example, to distribute the `ProfanityFilter` as a JAR package, we need to add a `<uri>...</uri>` mapping to the TLD file:

```
<taglib>
  <tlib-version>1.0</tlib-version>
  <jsp-version>1.2</jsp-version>
  <short-name>ProfanityFilter</short-name>
  <uri>/profanityfiltertags.tld</uri>
  <description>
    This is a simple tag that filters all its body text to remove
    profanities.
  </description>
```

We then put that file in our `META-INF` directory along with a `Manifest.mf` file, and package that in a JAR with the `ProfanityFilter.class` file. The directory structure within the JAR file is:

- ❏ `META-INF\profanityfiltertags.tld`
- ❏ `META-INF\Manifest.mf`
- ❏ `com\wrox\projsp\ch10\ProfanityFilter.class`

We can then distribute this JAR file for webmasters to drop into their own `WEB-INF\lib` directory, and tell them to use `\profanityfiltertags.tld` in their `taglib` directive, along with the documentation on what tags are available and how to use them. This is much simpler for webmasters and page authors to install than distributing the tag library as a WAR package with embedded JSP pages.

> *The ability of a JAR file to contain more than one tag library, and the automatic mapping of URIs to TLD files, is a new feature of JSP 1.2. In JSP 1.1, when a tag library was packaged as a JAR the TLD file had to be called `taglib.tld` and located in the JAR's `META-INF` directory.*

Summary

In this chapter we've seen beyond the basics of creating customer tags. Not only have we seen more details on what we can use them for, but we've looked at the important issues surrounding other people using our tag libraries. Specifically, we've seen:

- ❏ How a tag can modify the text it encloses, in `ProfanityFilter.java`. Also, how this happens at request-time, not translation-time, so it doesn't matter if the body is static text or generated dynamically from a database query – it's all modifiable via a tag.

- ❏ The full tag lifecycle, displayed using `CallTrace.java`, showing when each method is called.

- ❏ How to use cooperating tags, and how nesting one tag within another allows you to cleanly illustrate dependencies, using `Parent.java` and `Child.java`.

- ❏ How to validate tags, firstly just by specifying required attributes in the TLD, then by the JSP 1.1 method of using the `TagExtraInfo` class, and finally by the JSP 1.2 method using the `TagValidator` class.

- ❏ How you can recover from exceptions thrown both in your own tag methods and by code enclosed within your tags.

- ❏ What minimal tool support is currently available for custom tags, and how hopefully that will grow in the near future.

- ❏ How to document and distribute your tag libraries so that others can use them.

In the next chapter, we'll be looking at how best to design our tag libraries to make them as widely useful as possible, and some common tag library idioms.

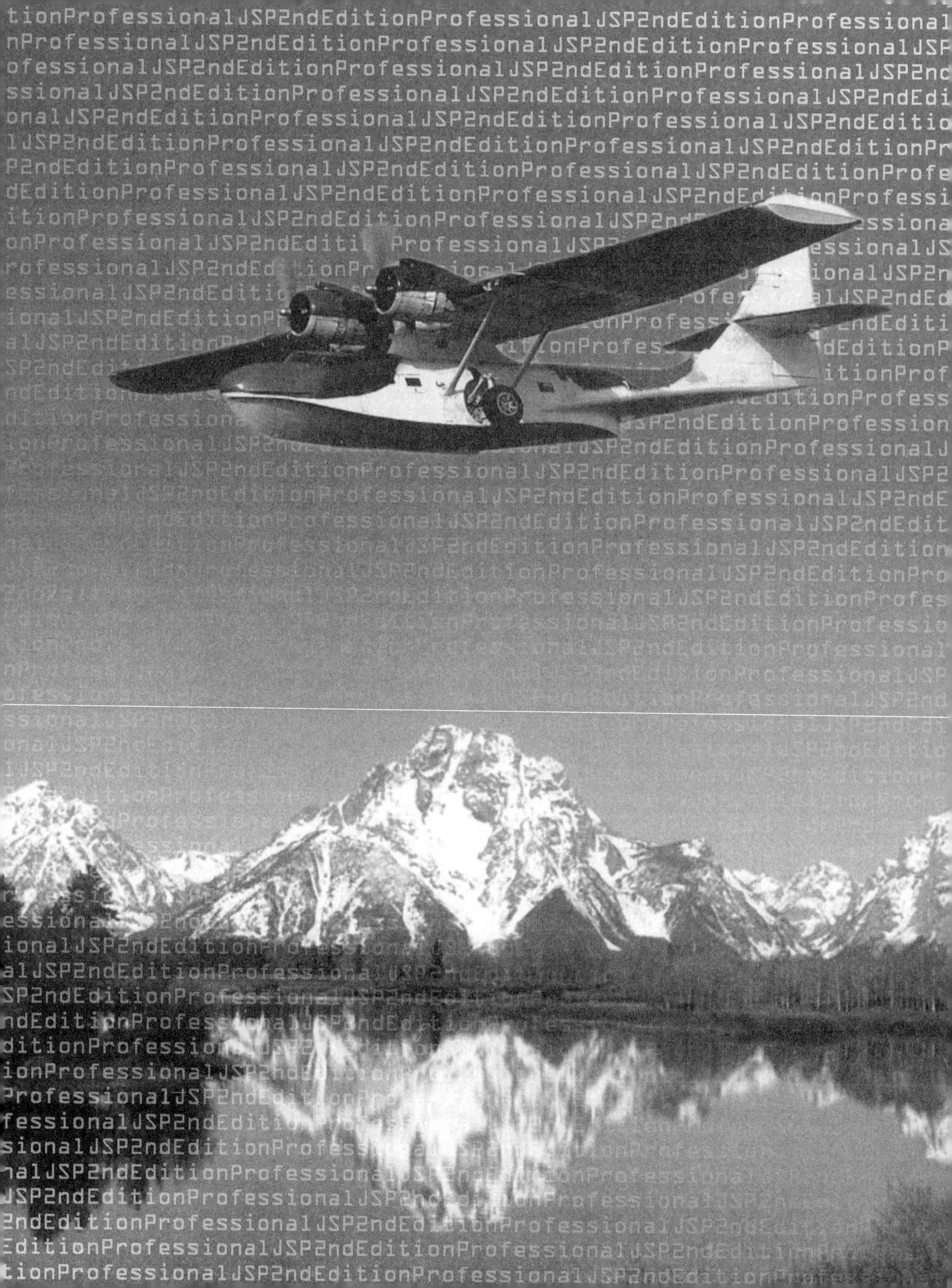
ProfessionalJSP2ndEdition

11

Custom Tag Idioms

In the last three chapters we've explored the JSP tag library model in some detail – we've seen what custom tags are for, how to use them in a JSP, and how to code the various types of custom tag. But what sorts of custom tag should we be writing and using? There are many, many possible tag libraries that we could create, employing all manner of different idioms, but they will vary in their usability and reusability, and the degree to which they promote good practice and the writing of maintainable JSPs.

In this chapter we will explore some of the ways to use custom tags, discuss what justifies writing them, and give some ideas on suitable idioms. We will look in turn at:

❑ General guidelines for designing tag libraries

❑ Using scripting variables

❑ How best to design sets of cooperating tags

❑ The various problem domains to which custom tags are commonly applied

Tag libraries can be thought of as falling into two broad categories: **horizontal** tag libraries, which aim to be very general and of wide applicability, and **vertical** tag libraries, which address application- or domain-specific concerns. This chapter in general addresses the developer of horizontal tag libraries, though many of the topics are more broadly relevant to both categories.

At the end of the chapter we will develop a tag library to take advantage of the power of XPath (a language for addressing parts of an XML document) and then use these tags to build a threaded discussion forum where readers can vote on individual messages, and adjust their view so that only messages with a certain number of votes will appear initially open.

Tag Library Design

Custom tags are components, and writing components tends to be a bit different from writing 'production' code. The two main reasons for this are:

❑   **The audience is different**
    The component is being written for component users, not for 'developers like us'. As authoring tools become more sophisticated, it is increasingly likely that JSPs will be written by people who are much more attuned to web page design than to the intricacies of Java coding. Obviously we need to take the needs of the machine and the code's maintainers into account, but the primary audience we're aiming at is the person making use of our component.

❑   **We need to look to the future**
    Whilst we may be looking primarily at a particular application of our tags, the component writer is always looking into the future, trying to grasp as much functionality as possible to make the component more generic and more widely applicable. We need to take care to divide functionality in a meaningful way between our components, making sure that they work with and complement other components.

General Guidelines

Given these constraints, we can draw out some basic points that are worth bearing in mind when designing custom tags:

❑   **Have a good reason**
    When should we write a custom tag – should we encapsulate every function likely to be called from a JavaServer Page? It is possible to write tags for all manner of types of functionality, possibly in a very application-specific way. There is a danger that the proliferation of diverse tag libraries, each covering a corner of the environment and having it's own conventions and idiosyncrasies, is likely to diminish the benefit of custom tags to the point where it will be easier for the page designer just to learn how to make method calls. Closely-integrated tag libraries from a single vendor are likely to be much more productive for the page designer. Closely related to this is the next point:

❑   **Don't duplicate effort**
    Over the last six months the number of available third-party tag libraries has expanded dramatically. Many are available for free download from sites such as http://jsptags.com/; the Jakarta project includes a 'taglibs' subproject that acts as a repository for contributed tag libraries. Check that there isn't already a tag library that provides the functionality you require.

    An effort to create a definitive JSP tag library is making its way through the Java Community Process but, as of this writing, no draft specification has yet emerged. Keep an eye on http://java.sun.com/aboutJava/communityprocess/jsr/jsr_052_jsptaglib.html for the latest news.

❑   **Choose descriptive names**
    The component nature of custom tags makes it even more important to choose good names. Fortunately Java has helped spread some good naming practices, which are worth following. Make names clear and obvious, yet sufficiently generic that when you find yourself extending your `<mytags:arrayiterator>` tag so that it can iterate over a collection instead of an array, you don't find yourself burdened with an attribute whose name still contains `array`.

❑ **Write reusable tools**
Aim to solve a class of problems, not just the one at hand, thus making the library of much wider applicability. It is of course possible to aim too high and spend time solving problems that never show up, but (depending on the problem area) a slight increase in effort can often greatly increase the reach of the solution.

❑ **Write code, not content**
Respect the separation of code and content – in general, you should try to avoid generating HTML within custom tags, as this reduces the generality of the tags. If you need to format some data in an HTML table, write the tags in such a way that the particular HTML code used isn't dictated to the page designer but can be specified within the JSP. The **views** tag library used in Chapter 18 is a good example of such a design. Avoid at all cost making page design decisions in your Java code where they will be out of the page designers' reach.

Sometimes generating HTML from a custom tag *is* justifiable though. An example is form-handling tags, such as those in the Struts framework (see Chapter 21 for a sample application using the Struts tags), as it allows us to remove a lot of the intricacy of our business logic from the JSP itself. For example, if we're sending the user back to a form to fill in missing values we can arrange for form fields to be pre-filled with the original values.

❑ **Stay away from business logic**
We've looked at web application architecture in detail in Chapters 6 and 7, and will return to the subject in Chapter 17. The basic point, from a custom tags point of view, is that JSPs are best used as a presentation layer, not for doing complex business logic. It can be tempting to use custom tags to access enterprise resources (such as your database) directly, and in some simple cases (often when searching, rather than updating, the database) this approach may suffice. But putting workflow actions into the page, such as sending confirmation e-mail in response to an order will eventually make the application difficult to maintain. For this reason, although we do discuss idioms for writing custom tag interfaces to various APIs later in the chapter, such an approach is often *not* the best way forward.

❑ **Avoid creating a new language**
Writing a system of interdependent tags may seem like a good idea, but if it requires the user to read through long documentation it may become a failure. Think of your audience: it already knows HTML; don't make them learn a new formatting language too. Whilst using cooperating tags is a very powerful idiom, where possible you should aim to work with existing tags rather than inventing your own domain-specific ones. We'll see an example of this shortly.

❑ **Use scripting variables**
The ability to introduce new scripting variables from a custom tag is extremely powerful, and intelligent use of scripting variables is crucial for effective tag library design. We will look at scripting variables next.

Using Scripting Variables

How you use scripting variables in connection with your custom tags is the key to making your tags generic and easy to integrate into an application. Whilst the value of exposing data from a tag in this way is obvious, there are many possible ways of doing this – as tag designers, we need to decide not only what data to expose but also how to expose it.

Three good rules of thumb to remember are:

❑ Allow the page designer to set the name of the scripting variables

❏   Minimize the number of scripting variables

❏   Use a composite scripting variable, with accessor methods

We'll look at each of these in turn.

Allow the Page Designer to Set the Variable Name

Allowing the page developer to name his own variables will allow him to write clear code. It is also a way to avoid name clashing, especially when nesting instances of the same tag. For example, if we have a tag that iterates over a `Collection` and exposes the current item via the `item` scripting variable:

```
<flow:iterate data="<%= variable %>" >
  <%-- The item scripting variable is available here --%>
</flow:iterate>
```

then we are going to run into problems once we have to iterate over a `Collection` of `Collections`. But if we allow the page designer to specify the name of the scripting variable:

```
<flow:iterate id="myItem" data="<%= variable %>" >
  <%-- The myItem scripting variable is available here --%>
</flow:iterate>
```

then we can easily nest `<flow:iterate>` tags:

```
<flow:iterate id="outerItem" data="<%= theData %>" >
  <flow:iterate id="innerItem" data="<%= outerItem %>" >
    <%-- The outerItem and innerItem scripting variables
         are available here --%>
  </flow:iterate>
</flow:iterate>
```

Naming also helps the reader to see where the variable comes from – without naming it may not be obvious which tag the variable belongs to.

Minimize the Number of Scripting Variables

Whilst scripting variables are a great idea, it is generally best to try and minimize the number of variables declared by a particular tag, particularly if you are requiring the page designer to name the variable. There are two main reasons for this:

Performance

The first is a performance concern: there is an overhead for each scripting variable declared by a custom tag, and their values must be evaluated by the tag handler and placed in the `PageContext`, whether or not they will actually be accessed later. On a busy site, this could amount to a significant performance hit.

Presentation

Secondly, while allowing the user to name scripting variables is a good practice, if we have many scripting variables the necessary attributes in the start tag will tend to clutter the code. For example, we could hypothetically write a custom tag that perform a database lookup for a particular book in a library management system based on its ISBN, and makes available via scripting variables the book's title, author, and publisher, along with an `Iterator` holding `Strings` representing the shelfmark of each copy of the book:

```
<library:lookupISBN isbn="<%= theIsbn %>" titleVar="title"
 authorVar="author" publisherVar="publisher" shelfmarksVar="shelfmarks" >

  <%-- The title, author, publisher, and shelfmarks scripting variables are
       available within the tag body --%>
  <p>Title: <%= title %><br>
     Author: <%= author %><br>
     Publisher: <%= publisher %></p>

</library:lookupISBN>
```

Whilst this would certainly work, the `<library:lookupISBN>` tag is getting rather cumbersome, and if we decided that we additionally needed to add a new scripting variable this would be a complex process involving changes in many places. The solution involves creating a composite scripting variable, which neatly brings us on to the final point in this section.

Use Composite Scripting Variables

A good compromise is to create a composite scripting variable – create a single JavaBean that encapsulates all the data that the tag needs to expose, and makes it available through its methods and the objects they return. The page designer can name this root object, which is enough to show which tag it comes from, but does not have to clutter up the start tag naming a host of variables. This methodology is conceptually very similar, but at a different level in the application architecture to MVC architectures (as discussed in Chapters 6 and 7) where the business logic code, in the model component, creates a JavaBean containing the data necessary for populating a JSP view.

This approach also allows you to add new functionality without the performance penalty of an additional scripting variable, simply by adding new accessor methods to the bean. Adding a new method is also a lot simpler than adding a new scripting variable. Let's revise our ISBN lookup tag:

```
<library:lookupISBN isbn="<%= theIsbn %>" id="book" >

  <%-- The book scripting variables is available within the tag body,
       encapsulating all the data about this book

       ...
  --%>

</library:lookupISBN>
```

The code for our bean might look something like the following:

```
package com.wrox.librarymanagement;

public class BookInfo {

  // Constructor and setter methods ...

  public String getIsbn() {
    // ...
  }

  public String getTitle() {
    // ...
  }

  public String getAuthor() {
    // ...
  }

  public String getPublisher() {
    // ...
  }

  public Iterator getShelfmarks() {
    // ...
  }
}
```

But the question remains of how to access the properties of this type of composite bean. There is certainly a temptation here for the page designer to use function calls to manipulate the bean:

```
<library:lookupISBN isbn="<%= theIsbn %>" id="book" >

  <p>Shelfmarks for this book:</p>
  <%-- Iterate over the array of shelfmarks --%>
  <ul>
    <flow:foreach id="item" group="<%= book.getShelfmarks() %>" >
      <li><%= item %></li>
    </flow:foreach>
  </ul>

</library:lookupISBN>
```

The more data the bean contains, and the more nested properties it acquires, the larger this problem becomes. However, the Struts **bean** tag library, which we'll discuss a little more later in the chapter, provides a range of tags for bean manipulation, including defining new beans based on existing bean properties, and writing out nested bean properties. Using these tags, and the Struts logic library, our example above could become:

```
<library:lookupISBN isbn="<%= theIsbn %>" id="book" >

  <p>Shelfmarks for this book:</p>
  <%-- Iterate over the array of shelfmarks --%>
  <bean:define id="marks" name="book" property="shelfmarks"
   type="java.util.Iterator" />
```

```
  <ul>
    <logic:iterate id="item" collection="marks" >
      <li><%= item %></li>
    </flow:foreach>
  </ul>

</library:lookupISBN>
```

Expect similar functionality to be included in the standard JSP tag library, when that becomes available.

Designing Cooperating Tags

We mentioned that, when designing a set of cooperating tags, we must take care to avoid inventing a whole new language. Careful design of the set of tags, and use of scripting variables, can be a great help.

Models of Tag Cooperation

The JSP specification draws out two different models for tag cooperation:

Using Scripting Variables

As we have already seen, one custom tag can make data available to another by creating a scripting variable. All that is necessary for the tags to cooperate is for them to agree on the name of the scripting variables, for example:

```
<vars:define id="myVariable" />
<vars:use name="myVariable" />
```

Using Tag Nesting

An alternative method involves nesting one custom tag within the body of another, and using the BodyTagSupport method findAncestorWithClass() to obtain a reference to an enclosing tag handler. The nested tag can then call methods on the enclosing tag, either to *obtain* data from it, or to *manipulate or configure* that tag. For example:

```
<nesting:outer>
  <nesting:configureOuter value="3" />
  <nesting:useData />
</nesting:outer>
```

The best ways to use these models are still being explored by tag implementers; each has advantages. Using scripting variables, as we have seen, makes the interaction very explicit and thus makes the page easy to follow. Using nested tags works well when a complex tag needs to be configured, particularly as it is not possible to use a custom tag within a tag attribute:

```
<mytags:configuration name="<othertags:name/>"/> <%-- ILLEGAL SYNTAX --%>
```

In this sort of circumstance, using nested tags to configure an outer tag can add a lot of flexibility:

```
<mytags:configuration>
  <mytags:configName>
```

```
          <othertags:name/>
        </mytags:configName>
      </mytags:configure>
```

On the other hand, this syntax is rather over-the-top in some cases. For instance, why use...

```
  <mytags:configuration>
    <mytags:configName>
      Wrox Press
    </mytags:configName>
  </mytags:configure>
```

...if all you need to do is:

```
  <mytags:configuration name="Wrox Press>"/>
```

Consider designing your tags so that page designers can use either idiom.

An Example

Consider the system of tags below (the pager tag library) that we might use as part of a URL database application. The <pager:page> splits a set of search results, here specified by the myResults scripting variable, into individual pages:

```
  <%-- Get the search results ... --%>

  <pager:page group="<%= myResults %>" perpage="20">
    <pager:foreachresult>
      <pager:currentLink>
        <pager:currentText/>
      </pager:currentLink>
    </pager:foreachresult>
    <pager:previouspage>previous page</pager:previouspage>
    <pager:nextpage>next page</pager:nextpage>
  <pager:page>
```

At first glance this looks neat, but on closer examination there are three problems:

❑   First, it is a bit hard to fathom. By reading only this fragment one can *guess* that the
    <pager:foreachresult> tag loops through twenty results, that the
    <pager:currentLink> tag hyperlinks a piece of text to another page, and that
    <pager:previouspage> and <pager:nextpage> will provide hyperlinks to the previous
    and next batch of results. But it remains guesswork. To fully understand what is happening
    one would have to read the taglib documentation or, worse, the tag handler code.

❑   Second, to write this construct would be almost impossible without the documentation or at
    least an example.

❑   Third, and most importantly, this set of tags has frozen some design decisions that are really
    the realm of the page designers: <pager:currentLink>, <pager:previouspage>, and
    <pager:nextpage> might well generate textual hyperlinks, whereas we may change our
    mind and prefer buttons or images instead.

Let's see what happens if we instead design the `<pager:page>` tag so that it exposes a scripting variable encapsulating the current set of results, and use a pre-existing `flow` tag library to provide an iteration tag. We might then be able to write something like the following:

```
<pager:page id="pager" group="<%= myResults %>" perpage="20">
  <flow:foreach id="result" group="<%= pager.getResults() %>" >
    <a href="<%= result.getHrefCurrent() %>">
      <%= result.getText() %>
    </a>
  </flow:foreach>
  <a href="<%= pager.getHrefPrevious() %>previous page</a>
  <a href="<%= pager.getHrefNext() %>next page</a>
</pager:page>
```

This is a good example of the techniques we discussed earlier about using scripting variables. Here the `pager` scripting variable is exposed; `pager` has three pertinent methods:

❏ `getResults()`, which returns an `Iterator` containing the twenty results themselves. This allows us to use our pre-existing `<flow:foreach>` tag to iterate over these results.

❏ `getHrefPrevious()`, which returns the URL of the page containing the previous twenty results. Exposing the information in this way, rather than creating a tag that renders the link, allows us to use the information in a variety of ways, to create a text link, an image link, or a form button as we see fit.

❏ `getHrefNext()` similarly returns the URL of the page containing the next twenty results.

Similarly, each element within the `Iterator` returned by `getResults()`, which we expose as the result scripting variable within the `<flow:foreach>` tag, is a bean with `getHrefCurrent()` and `getText()` methods that return the URL and description of each link. Again, we can use these properties as we choose to construct the final HTML page.

At first glance the revised code above might look like the footprints of a flock of crows (though judicious use of the Struts **bean** tag library could reduce the number of scriptlets), but closer examination reveals that it eliminates the three problems in the previous attempt:

❏ It is quite readable by anyone who knows HTML and is familiar with the general syntax of custom tags

❏ It requires far less knowledge to write: only one specific tag plus one general tag for looping, and there is no fragile interdependence of tags

❏ Last, but not least, the design decisions are back in the hands of the designer

Problem Domains for Custom Tags

Having looked at the ways in which we can design custom tags, let's move on to consider what problem domains we might want our tag libraries to address. We'll look in turn at:

❏ Display logic

❏ Generating markup

❑ Accessing the JSP environment

❑ Adapting APIs

❑ Postprocessing body content

Remember that this chapter is being written before the standard JSP tag library becomes available; it is likely that the standard library will address many of these areas.

Display Logic

The first obvious category of custom tags we might want are those to embed logic within the JSP. Page display logic – controlling the flow of execution during the production of the response stream – is one area where JSP designers have traditionally had to resort to the use of scriptlets, but custom tags allow us to encapsulate logic in a simple way.

Flow Control

The most obvious use of custom tags is to provide basic flow control within a page, notably iteration and conditional logic. This is definitely an area where we can expect to see the standard tag library make an impact; the absence of flow control tags has been a real problem for JSP since version 1.0.

Many third-party tag libraries contain flow-control tags. The Struts **logic** tags, for example, contain a `<logic:iterate>` tag that will process its body content for each element in an `Iterator`, a `Collection`, a `Map`, or an array of objects. It also contains a wide range of conditional tags that will compare beans, bean properties, and request parameters, headers, and cookies.

Other slightly less obvious flow control tags include login checks (such as that which we use in Chapter 21), or framework-specific tags like certain of those included in the Struts **logic** tag library.

Pagers and Site Navigation

One step up from flow control is to design more specific custom tags that make it easier to produce specific page design effects from within a JSP. A good example, which we saw earlier, is a set of tags to split a long set of results into manageable chunks and generate suitable navigation links, in the manner of well-known web search engines. A full example of such a tag library can be found at http://jsptags.com/tags/navigation/pager/.

An interesting category of tag library assists the page designer with page composition – a sort of enhanced `<jsp:include>` tag. Once again the Struts team have an offering: their `template` tag library allows content to be plugged into page design templates in an easily-configurable manner. Consider this JSP, which uses a template, `maintemplate.jsp`, and specifies that the given pages and content are to be plugged into the template:

```
<%@ taglib uri='/WEB-INF/tlds/struts-template.tld' prefix='template' %>
<template:insert template='/maintemplate.jsp'>
   <template:put name='title' content='Example' direct='true'/>
   <template:put name='heading' content='/heading.html' />
   <template:put name='contents' content='/contents.jsp' />
   <template:put name='body' content='/body.html'/>
   <template:put name='footer' content='/footer.html' />
</template:insert>
```

`maintemplate.jsp` reads very much like a standard HTML page, except that the actual page content is mysteriously absent. The `<template:get>` tags are replaced at runtime with the content specified by the `<template:put>` tags above.

```
<%@ taglib uri='/WEB-INF/tlds/struts-template.tld' prefix='template' %>
<html><head><title><template:get name='title'/></title></head>
<body>
  <table>
    <tr valign='top'>
      <td><template:get name='contents'/></td>
      <td>
        <table>
          <tr><td><template:get name='heading'/></td></tr>
          <tr><td><template:get name='body'/></td></tr>
          <tr><td><template:get name='footer'/></td></tr>
        </table>
      </td>
    </tr>
  </table>
</body></html>
```

It is likely that the template tag library will be significantly enhanced in future Struts releases – keep an eye on http://jakarta.apache.org/struts/.

Presentation of Complex Data

Whilst the generic flow control tags mentioned above may suffice for some purposes, we often have complex data structures that need to be traversed within a JSP; tabular and tree-based data are common examples. In Chapter 18 we shall see an example of a tag library that can (among other things) iterate over tabular data in an intelligent, configurable manner.

The case study at the end of this chapter presents an example of custom tags to construct a threaded discussion forum – the tags allow us to traverse tree-like data easily.

Generating Markup

As we discussed earlier, while it is generally frowned upon there *are* cases where it can be helpful to generate markup from using a custom tag. The classic example of this is form tags, which can help automate the round trip of bean property values to the user (via field values in the HTML) and back to the server (via request parameters). In typical usage, the user is presented with a set of initial values, which he can then change and submit; if he makes errors his previous entries can be shown to him accompanied by error messages. Such tags can also help automate validation on the server side, or output JavaScript code to do client-side validation.

Various form tag libraries are available, including those from Gefion, JRun, and libraries from the Jakarta Taglibs and Struts projects. We will look at the Struts tags in detail in Chapter 21.

Accessing the JSP Environment

The environment available to JSPs through the implicit objects is very rich, but until recently scriptlets have generally been required to make full use of their facilities. However, many tag libraries are becoming available that make it easier to access the JSP runtime environment.

The Jakarta Taglibs project provides tag libraries based on the `request`, `response`, `page`, `session`, and `application` objects. The **application** library, for example, has custom tags that allow the page designer to work with `ServletContext` attributes and application initialization parameters: querying, setting, and removing them, looping through them, performing comparisons, and so on. The **request** tag library provides access to information in the `request` implicit object: attributes, query parameters, session information, headers, cookies, and so on. Work is now underway to integrate these into a new composite tag library.

The Struts **bean** library has already been mentioned as an example of a tag library that makes manipulation of the JSP environment much easier. An interesting facet of the Struts tag libraries is the way they use tag attributes. For example, using the **html** library we could do the following:

```
<html:text name="profileBean" property="userName">
```

The tag-handler will attempt to call a `getUserName()` method on the `profileBean` object and write the result as the value of the `value` attribute of the final `input` tag. If the user name was `John` the final output looks like this:

```
<input type="text" value="John">
```

In effect, Struts has defined a mini-language to use within attributes, extending beyond what has been shown here to encompass nested and indexed bean properties. So, for example, specifying `property="user.name.firstName"` above would result in a call to `profileBean.getUser().getName().getFirstName()`, while `property="emailAddress[2]"` would call `profileBean.getEmailAddress(2)`. This pattern is implemented consistently across the Struts tag libraries, and provides an intuitive extension to the basic JSP syntax. Such a language is of course more valuable if it is widely used across tag libraries.

A similar approach is used by Gefion Software's InstantOnline Basic 3.0 beta release (http://www.gefionsoftware.com/InstantOnline/TP/) where, for example, to use the value of a cookie called `loginName` as an initial value on a login form, you can write:

```
<iob:input type="text" value="$cookie|loginName$">
```

The variables provide access to the `page`, `request`, `session`, and `application` objects; to cookies, and headers, and to information traditionally available to CGI handlers as environment variables such as `remote_address` and `remote_host`.

Adapting APIs

Our discussions of web application architecture so far, in Chapters 6 and 7, suggest that the place to perform data access is generally *not* in the JSP, but in business logic classes accessed from a controller servlet. However, tag libraries have been written encapsulating access to various APIs, including the core J2EE APIs, and this model should not be written off for simple applications, such as pages that simply perform a database query. In other cases the use of the APIs is tightly bound to the business rules of the application and their use within the JSP itself is almost certainly a bad idea.

- ❑ **JDBC, SQL** – JRUN, Gefion, and Jakarta Taglibs project tag libraries all provide tags to construct and execute SQL queries and to iterate through the result-set. JRUN also provides a custom tag to convert the result of an SQL query to XML.

❑ **JNDI** – JRUN and Jakarta Taglibs provide tags that search for and lookup JNDI references and make the result available as scripting variables. Using JNDI might be a nice way to specify beans in a future version of JSP, instead of the `<jsp:useBean>` tag.

❑ **JMS** – Sending JMS messages from various places can serve as a foundation of an event driven mechanism, with various backend processes being notified of user actions in a consistent manner.

❑ **Mail** – It can be argued that sending mail from a JSP is putting business logic in the presentation layer. On the other hand, JSP is well suited to provide templates for mail messages, whether in plain text, HTML, or something else. Gefion and JRUN provide custom tags to send mail; JRUN also has a tag to fetch mail from POP3 and IMAP servers.

❑ **XML** – Various tag libraries provide XML functionality. JRUN provides a `<query2xml>` tag that maps any query to a simple XML document, where each field represents an XML tag and the body of the tag is the value of the field. Tags are also available to process XML documents with an XSL stylesheet (see Chapter 8 for an example), but remember that XSLT tends to be slow and it may be necessary to build in some kind of caching. XPath is a convenient syntax to navigate a parsed XML tree – the case study in the end of this chapter implements several tags that use XPath syntax to traverse an XML document.

❑ **Regular Expressions** – The Jakarta Taglibs project includes the **RegExp** library, a comprehensive tag library that encapsulates Perl-style regular expressions. The tags can check whether a `String` matches a regular expression pattern, perform substitutions within a `String`, and split a `String` into its component parts according to the pattern you specify.

❑ **HTTP** – Performing HTTP requests from within a JSP is another potentially powerful operation. The Jakarta Taglibs project includes the **Utility** Taglib, which provides an `<utility:include>` tag which includes in-line the output of the specified URL. As of this writing, further work in this field is ongoing within the project with proposals for an extensive tag library including the ability to specify request headers and parameters easily, and to perform SOAP requests.

Postprocessing Body Content

The final common idiom is custom tags that capture and transform their body content in some way as we saw in the last chapter. Here the possibilities (and the dangers) are almost endless, but we will mention a couple of possibilities here.

Caching the Body Content

As we mentioned a moment ago, it would be very useful in some circumstances to be able to cache JSP-generated content when it is not going to change with great frequency, but it is too expensive to perform the whole operation each time the page is requested. A tag that caches its body content, using a key as an attribute to store the content under, would be very useful with (for example) XSL transformations. The OpenSymphony OSCache tag library (http://www.opensymphony.com/oscache/) provides such a facility along with the ability to specify how long to retain the cached content for, to use the cached content if an error occurs evaluating the tag body, and to programmatically dispose of cached content.

Scripting in the Body Content

One final possibility is to use the tag body for a purpose other than plain content generation. The Jakarta Taglibs **BSF** library encapsulates IBM's Bean Scripting Framework, making various scripting languages such as JavaScript, VBScript, Perl, Tcl, Python, NetRexx and Rexx available within a JSP:

```
<bsf:scriptlet language="tcl">
    $out println "Hello world"
</bsf:scriptlet>

<bsf:expression language="perlscript">
    CreateBean("java.util.Date")
</bsf:expression>
```

The SQL tags covered earlier also fall under this category.

Tag Library Resources

There are many web sites about tag libraries; this brief listing can only scratch the surface. However, some of the most useful ones are:

- ❑ Jakarta Taglibs project: http://jakarta.apache.org/taglibs/

- ❑ Jakarta Struts project: http://jakarta.apache.org/struts/

- ❑ JRun tag library: http://www.allaire.com/

- ❑ JSPTags.com: http://jsptags.com/

- ❑ The standard JSP tag library:
  http://java.sun.com/aboutJava/communityprocess/jsr/jsr_052_jsptaglib.html

Case Study: XPath Tags

In this section we will write a couple of tags to take advantage of the power of XPath, and to show how powerful a small set of very generic tags can be. XPath is a specification designed to enable addressing a part or parts of an XML document.

We will then use this tag to implement a threaded discussion where the participants can vote on each other's messages (voting is intended to build consensus on which messages are interesting, allowing other readers to concentrate on those) and specify the number of votes a message has to have to appear initially open. Remember that the code for this case study is present in the code download for the book, from http://www.wrox.com.

The Discussion XML File

The syntax of the XML file (discussion.xml) that holds a discussion is simple. The root <discussion> element can contain zero or more <message> elements. Each <message> contains a <subject>, a <body>, and a <responses> element. The <subject> and <body> elements contain text while the <responses> element contains further messages:

```
<discussion>
    <message id="0" author="" date="" votes="-1" level="0">
      <subject>template to clone new messages</subject><body></body>
    </message>
    <message id="1" author="Ann" date="28/10/2000 19:45"
```

```
               votes="2" level="0" >
          <subject>
              Hello discussion
          </subject>
          <body>
              This is Ann's message.
          </body>
          <responses>
            <message id="2" author="Brian" date="28/10/2000 19:45"
               votes="1" level="1" >
            <subject>
                Re: Hello discussion
            </subject>
            <body>
                This is Brian's reply to Ann.
            </body>
            <responses>
                <message id="3" author="Ann" date="28/10/2000 19:55"
                   votes="1" level="2" >
                <subject>
                    Re: Hello discussion
                </subject>
                <body>
                    This is Ann's reply to Bryan's reply
                </body>
                <responses>
                </responses>
                </message>
                <message id="4" author="Cecil" date="28/10/2000 20:15"
                   votes="3"  level="2">
                <subject>
                    Re: Hello discussion
                </subject>
                <body>
                    This is Cecil's comment on Brian's reply
                </body>
                <responses>
                    <message id="5" author="Ann" date="28/10/2000 20:18"
                       votes="0" level="3" >
                    <subject>
                        Re: Hello discussion
                    </subject>
                    <body>
                        This is Ann's reply to Cecils comment.
                    </body>
                    <responses>
                    </responses>
                    </message>
                </responses>
                </message>
            </responses>
            </message>
          </responses>
      </message>
      </responses>
  </message>
</discussion>
```

Only the <message> element has attributes. They are id (the message identifier), author, (the author of the message), votes (the number of votes the message has received), and level (how deeply the message is nested within other messages).

Introduction to XPath Syntax

Obviously, in order to retrieve a particular message from the discussion.xml document, we do not want to have to retrieve *all* of the information contained in the XML document. We need a way to specify which parts of the document tree to retrieve. Thankfully, there's a W3C language specification for doing just that, called **XPath**.

An XPath expression addresses a specific part of a document tree, by specifying a **location path**. This path is a series of steps to take throughout the document (like giving directions from one street to another: 'turn first right, then second left...'). So the question becomes: what format do these location path addresses take in XPath?

Before we deal with this, there are a couple of issues of notation we should deal with. First, XPath uses the term **node** to mean a particular location in an XML document; this node may be an element, attribute, comment, processing instruction – anything within the document.

Second, before it can start searching for a path through an XML document, XPath needs to know where to begin. This starting position for XPath is known as the **context node**. This may be the document root (the conceptual root of the document), in which case we get an *absolute* XPath expression. Or, it can be any node within the document, which yields a *relative* XPath expression (note the similarity here to relative and absolute directory paths).

Let's throw in a few examples here, so you start to get the idea. We'll base the examples around the document tree of discussion.xml. First, if we wanted to retrieve the contents of all of the <message> nodes, we could use the following absolute XPath:

```
"/discussion/message"
```

The slash (/) at the start of the expression indicates that the path starts at the document root. So XPath moves from the document root, to the <discussion> element, and then to its child <message> elements. If we removed the first slash , the path would begin at the context node, whatever that has been defined to be, instead.

If we wished to retrieve all of the author attributes of the <message> elements within the document, we could use the following notation:

```
"message/@author"
```

Note the use of the @... notation to indicate an attribute. Actually, there is an easier way to do this, using the recursive descent operator "//":

```
"//@author"
```

This simply means 'get all author attributes within the document'. Of course, there will be times when we will want to retrieve just one message or one author, and there are several ways of doing this. First, say we wanted an XPath to a message authored by Cecil. To specify this, we would use the expression:

```
"message[@author = 'Cecil']"
```

Note the use of the `[@...]` notation to indicate 'with an attribute of'. If we wanted to retrieve all of the `<message>` elements with `author` attributes (all of them!), we would just use:

```
"message[@author]"
```

Next, if we only wanted messages that had been responded to, we would write:

```
"message[response]"
```

Here, we are essentially saying 'find only the `<message>` elements which have child `<response>` elements'. And, finally, we can also specify which `<message>` element to find by position, as in:

```
"/discussion/message[2]"
```

Here we are retrieving the second child `<message>` of `<discussion>` (Ann's first message).

Finally, we can also incorporate node functions into an XPath; these return information about nodes, or return a specific type of node. For example, the `text()` function returns the contents of an element (although not the contents of any child elements of that element). For instance:

```
"/discussion/message[2]/subject/text()"
```

This will return the contents of the `<subject>` element of the second `<message>` element:
Hello discussion.

There is obviously a lot more than this to XPath, but this introduction should be enough to understand the case study.

Designing the XPath Tags

The objective of the XPath tags is to facilitate working with XML files inside JSPs without having to use XSL stylesheets. The tag or tags should give us access to the list of nodes corresponding to a particular expression, and any of these nodes should be able to act as the context node for another instance of the tag too. We have two tag design aspects to consider at this point.

Our first important question is whether the tag that gives access to the list of nodes should be an iterator. The advantage of an iterator is that it can make a correctly-typed variable available on each iteration: if we used a generic `foreach` tag we would have to use type casting. The disadvantage is that body tags are more complicated to write and maintain. However, in this case study, we will go all the way and write an iterating tag.

The second question is whether we should create a subtag to access values relative to the current node. For example:

```
<xpath:value xpath='@author' />
```

Alternatively we could use an expression like:

```
<%= node.getValue("@author") %>
```

Although it can be argued that the former is easier for non-programmers to understand, the benefit of using a subtag is obviously rather small. However, we will write one anyway because it is instructive.

Implementing the XPath Tags

In this section, we will review the code relevant to the tags used by our discussion forum. We will focus mainly on the three tag-related classes:

❑   XPathForEachNodeTag

❑   XPathForEachNodeTei

❑   XPathValueTag

Before we start walking through these classes it is worth noting how incoming requests are handled. The miniature web comprising this case study is fronted by a simple dispatching servlet (DispatchServlet). This Servlet associates any incoming request with a bean of certain name, class and scope and a response JSP. An internal mapping object specifies the association. In the interest of brevity, the mapping is hard-coded inside the servlet, although a production version would obviously read it from a configuration file.

The mapping associates the request reply.do with a session-scoped bean of class com.wrox.projsp.ch11.jsp.DiscussionBean, named discussion, which we access from inside the page by using the <jsp:usebean> tag.

The request parameters are mapped to properties of the bean. Request parameters that don't have any corresponding set methods in the bean are stored, along with their value, in a special property map. This alleviates the need to create getters and setters of each parameter. Furthermore, if the bean has a method called doX() where X is the name of some request parameter, then doX() is called with the value of this parameter. This automates the calling of action methods.

This arrangement is similar to the one used by Struts (covered in Chapter 21), and in fact borrows its property-setter method. When all this is done, control is transferred to the response JSP associated with the request, unless the bean has set its forward property to another page, which then gets called instead.

The XPathForEachNodeTag Class

The XPathForEachNodeTag class deals with the XPath tag attribute properties, scripting variables, and tag lifecycle. Let's take a look.

```
package com.wrox.projsp.ch11.jsp;

import java.io.*;
import java.lang.reflect.*;
import javax.servlet.jsp.*;
import javax.servlet.jsp.tagext.*;
import org.w3c.dom.*;
import org.xml.sax.*;
import org.apache.xalan.xpath.*;
import org.apache.xalan.xpath.xml.*;
import org.apache.xerces.parsers.*;
import com.wrox.projsp.ch11.utils.*;
```

Note that the implementation uses the Xerces XML parser and the Xalan XPath processor.

```
public class XPathForEachNodeTag extends BodyTagSupport {
```

First we define getter and setter methods for tag attribute properties such as xpath, id, document, and context:

```
    private String xpath;

    public void setXpath(String xpath) {
      this.xpath = xpath;
    }
    public String getXpath() { return xpath; }

    private String id;

    public void setId(String id) {
      this.id = id;
    }
    public String getId() {
      return id;
    }

    private String document;

    public void setDocument(String document) {
      this.document = document;
    }

    private Node context;

    public void setContext(Node context) {
      this.context = context;
    }

    public Node getContext() {
      return context;
    }
```

The second category of methods provides functionality to use in the page. The tag exports itself as a scripting variable, named by value of the id attribute. If the name is xptag, these methods are accessed as, for example <%= xptag.getNode() %>. The attribute properties are of course also accessible.

```
    private NodeList nodes;

    public NodeList getNodes() {
      return nodes;
    }

    private int index;

    public int getIndex() {
      return index;
    }
```

```
public Node getNode() {
  return nodes.item(index);
}

public String getPathValue(String xpath)
throws org.xml.sax.SAXException {
    return XPathUtil.getValue(getNode(), xpath);
}
```

The rest of the methods are the lifecycle methods of the tag:

```
XMLParserLiaison xpathSupport =  new XMLParserLiaisonDefault();
XPathProcessor xpathParser = new XPathProcessorImpl(xpathSupport);

public int doStartTag() throws JspException {
  try {
    if(document != null) {
      DOMParser parser = new DOMParser();
      parser.parse(new InputSource(new FileInputStream(document)));
      context = parser.getDocument().getDocumentElement();
    }
    PrefixResolver prefixResolver = new PrefixResolverDefault(context);
    XPath xp = new XPath();
    xpathParser.initXPath(xp, xpath, prefixResolver);
    XObject list = xp.execute(xpathSupport, context, prefixResolver);
    nodes = list.nodeset();
    index = 0;
  } catch(SAXException e) {
    e.printStackTrace();
  } catch(IOException e) {
    e.printStackTrace();
  }
  if (nodes.getLength() > 0) {
    pageContext.setAttribute(id, this);
    return (EVAL_BODY_TAG);
  } else
    return (SKIP_BODY);
}

public int doAfterBody() throws JspException {
  if (++index < nodes.getLength()) {
    pageContext.setAttribute(id, this);
    return (EVAL_BODY_TAG);
  } else
    return (SKIP_BODY);
}

public int doEndTag() throws JspException {
  if (bodyContent != null) {
    try {
      JspWriter out = getPreviousOut();
      out.print(bodyContent.getString());
    } catch (IOException e) {
      throw new JspException(getClass().getName() + ".doEndTag(): " + e);
```

```
        }
      }
      return (EVAL_PAGE);
    }

    public void release() {
      xpath = null;
      id = null;
      document = null;
      context = null;
      nodes = null;
      index = 0;
      xpathSupport = null;
      xpathParser = null;
    }

  }
```

The TagExtraInfoClass

The TagExtraInfo class, listed below, communicates to the page compiler which objects should be exported as scripting variables, the class of these objects and the name under which they should be available to the page developer:

```
package com.wrox.projsp.ch11.jsp;

import javax.servlet.jsp.tagext.*;

public class XPathForEachNodeTei extends TagExtraInfo {
    public VariableInfo[] getVariableInfo(TagData data) {
        return new VariableInfo[]{
            new VariableInfo(data.getAttributeString("id"),
            "com.wrox.projsp.ch11.jsp.XPathForEachNodeTag",
            true,
            VariableInfo.NESTED)};
    }
}
```

In our case we export a single variable, which is the tag handler itself. The first parameter in the constructor for the VariableInfo class specifies under which name the variable should be exported; we allow the user of the tag to specify this name in the value to the id attribute. The second parameter gives the class for the exported variable, which in our case is the class of the tag itself. The third parameter specifies whether the JSP translator should create a declaration for the variable, which is what we want, so we give this parameter a value of true. The fourth parameter specifies that the variable should only be visible within the body of the tag.

The XPathValueTag class

The XPathValueTag class is simpler. Since it doesn't export any variable there is no TagExtraInfo class to write. The attributes are fewer and the lifecycle methods to implement are also fewer:

```
package com.wrox.projsp.ch11.jsp;

import java.io.*;
import java.lang.reflect.*;
import javax.servlet.jsp.*;
```

```
import javax.servlet.jsp.tagext.*;
import org.w3c.dom.*;
import com.wrox.projsp.ch11.utils.*;

public final class XPathValueTag extends BodyTagSupport {

  private String xpath;
  public void setXpath(String xpath) { this.xpath = xpath; }
  public String getXpath() { return xpath; }

  public int doStartTag() throws JspException, JspTagException {
    try {
      XPathForEachNodeTag parent =
      (XPathForEachNodeTag) findAncestorWithClass(this,
                            XPathForEachNodeTag.class);
      if(parent == null)
        throw new JspTagException("XPathValueTag outside of
                                  XPathForEachNodeTag");
```

As we don't want the tag to be used outside of the XPathForEachNode, we throw an exception if that occurs. Otherwise we retrieve the parent tag's context node and write the value of the XPath expression relative to it.

```
      Node context = parent.getNode();
      JspWriter out = pageContext.getOut();
      out.print(XPathUtil.getValue(context, xpath));
    } catch(IOException e) {
      System.out.println("XPathValueTag.doStartTag(): exeception" + e);
    } catch(org.xml.sax.SAXException e) {
      System.out.println("XPathValueTag.doStartTag(): exeception" + e);
    }
    return SKIP_BODY;
  }

  public void release() {
    xpath = null;
  }
}
```

The Tag Library Definition

The tag library definition (TLD) file informs the JSP container about the available custom tags and their syntax:

```
<?xml version="1.0" encoding="ISO-8859-1" ?>
<!DOCTYPE taglib
  PUBLIC "-//Sun Microsystems, Inc.//DTD JSP Tag Library 1.1//EN"
  "http://java.sun.com/j2ee/dtds/web-jsptaglibrary_1_1.dtd">

<taglib>

  <tlibversion>1.0</tlibversion>
  <jspversion>1.1</jspversion>
  <shortname>XPath Tags</shortname>
```

```
<uri>http://www.wrox.com/projsp/chapter11/taglibs/xpath</uri>
<info>
</info>

<tag>
  <name>nodes</name>
  <tagclass>com.wrox.projsp2.ch11.jsp.XPathForEachNodeTag</tagclass>
  <teiclass>com.wrox.projsp2.ch11.jsp.XPathForEachNodeTei</teiclass>
  <bodycontent>JSP</bodycontent>
  <attribute>
    <name>document</name>
    <required>false</required>
    <rtexprvalue>true</rtexprvalue>
  </attribute>
  <attribute>
    <name>context</name>
    <required>false</required>
    <rtexprvalue>true</rtexprvalue>
  </attribute>
  <attribute>
    <name>xpath</name>
    <required>true</required>
    <rtexprvalue>true</rtexprvalue>
  </attribute>
  <attribute>
    <name>id</name>
    <required>false</required>
    <rtexprvalue>true</rtexprvalue>
  </attribute>
</tag>

<tag>
  <name>value</name>
  <tagclass>com.wrox.projsp2.ch11.jsp.XPathValueTag</tagclass>
  <attribute>
    <name>xpath</name>
    <required>true</required>
    <rtexprvalue>true</rtexprvalue>
  </attribute>
</tag>

</taglib>
```

Since the user of the tag can give either a document or a context node from an enclosing tag, neither of these attributes can be required, although the tag will not work unless one of them is specified. All other attributes are mandatory and all strings can be specified using JSP expressions.

Using the XPath Tags to Implement the Discussion Forum

Now we can use the tags to implement a discussion forum where the users can vote on the messages they find interesting and where they can specify the minimum number of votes a message must have to appear initially open. The code for the forum, discuss.jsp, is listed below. We'll walk through it, step by step.

The discuss.jsp Page

Let's examine the `discuss.jsp` code. First, after declaring the taglib, a session scoped bean (`discussion`) is introduced which holds user information and implements the actions of voting, replying, and setting the visibility threshold:

```
<%@ taglib uri="/WEB-INF/xpath.tld" prefix="xpath" %>
<jsp:useBean id="discussion" scope="session"
  class="com.wrox.projsp.ch11.jsp.DiscussionBean"/>
```

Next we have a small form so the user can change the minimum number of votes necessary for a message to appear open initially. The value of the `action` attribute (`"discuss.do"`) of the form tag is the JSP itself. Since the request generated by this form includes a parameter called `changeMinVote`, the `dispatchServlet` will take care of calling `discussionBean.doChangeMinVote()` to change the minimum number of votes needed to have a message open initially.

```
<html>
  <head>
    <title> Discussion </title>
  </head>
  <body>

    <%-- a form to specify min no of nodes for messages to appear open --%>
    <form name="discussion" action="discuss.do" method="post">
        Pre-open messages with
        <input type="text" name="minVotes"
            value=" <%= discussion.get("minVotes") %>"
            size="3"> or more votes
        <input type="submit" name="changeMinVote" value="ok">
    </form>
```

Next, a `nodes` tag iterates through all the messages.

Its `id` attribute gives an identifier by which to refer to the only scripting variable exported by the tag, which is in fact the tag itself. It is called `message` because a single message is formatted within the body of the tag.

The `context` attribute says which document contains the current state of the discussion. The parsed document is a static member of the tag-handler, which means all instances will see the same instance. If this document has already been parsed, the tag handler will simply use the existing parsed copy.

The third attribute of the `nodes` tag, `xpath`, specifies the actual document nodes to look at. The XPath expression is very simple: `"//message"`. This will result in one node for each message in the file. Note that this doesn't cut the discussion neatly into distinct parts. This is because some messages are included in others, but there is a node in the result set for each message and they are in the order of the messages in the file. All messages contain subject, author, and date, but only some of them contain responses.

```
    <%-- the messages --%>
    <xpath:nodes
        id='message'
        context='<%= discussion.getDiscussion() %>'
        xpath='<%= "//message[@id > 0]" %>'>
```

Next, a variable is declared to store the unique identifier for the message because it will be used in a couple of places later in the code.

```
<% String id = message.getPathValue("@id"); %>
```

Then it's time to start writing some output. First we indent the message headline with non-breaking spaces to represent the depth of the message within the discussion.

```
<%-- the header line --%>
<% int level = Integer.parseInt(message.getPathValue("@level")); %>
<% while(level-- > 0){ %>
        
<% } %>
```

Then the `<xpath:value>` subtag is used to write the parts of the headline: these are the author, the subject, the number of votes the message has received, and its time-stamp. The `reply` link contains the `id` of the message as a URL parameter, which will indicate to the application which message the user is responding to when he clicks on it.

```
<xpath:value xpath='@author' /> :
<a href='discuss.do?openMessage="<%= id %>"'>
    <xpath:value xpath='<%= "subject/text()" %>' />
</a> ·
<xpath:value xpath='@votes'/> votes ·
<xpath:value xpath='@date' /><br>
```

Next we encounter a second `nodes` tag, which functions as an `if` statement. Its purpose is to display the body of the message only if it has the minimum number of votes associated with it, or if it is the currently open message. The context (the starting point) of the expression is the current node of the enclosing `xpath` tag:

```
<%-- the conditional body --%>
<xpath:nodes
    id='body'
    context='<%= message.getNode() %>'
    xpath='<%=
        "self::node()[" +
            "@votes >= " + discussion.get("minVotes") +
            " or @id = " + discussion.get("openMessage") +
        "]/body" %>'>
```

Let's walk through the expression in detail. When the page has been compiled and the porridge of quotes is a bit less thick, it looks like this:

```
"self::node()[@votes >= " + discussion.get("minVotes") + " or @id = " +
                    discussion.get("openMessage") + "]/body"
```

When this expression is evaluated the actual XPath expression emerges. Let's assume that `minVotes` is 5 and `openMessage` is 26. This would result in the expression:

```
self::node()[@votes >= 5 or @id = 26]/body
```

397

The axis of the first location step in the `xpath` expression is the current node itself. The expression in brackets limits one element result set to those that have an attribute called `votes` with the value of 5 or higher or `id` equal to 26. In other words, if the bracketed expression doesn't evaluate to `true`, the result set is empty and the body of the tag is never evaluated. The second location step specifies the `<body>` XML tag of the current node, which represents the body of the message.

Inside the second `nodes` tag the `value` tag is used next to output the text of the body of the message, and to output links which the reader can click to reply to the message and to vote for it. The two links use the variable `id`, established earlier, to communicate the message identifier to the server.

```
<table bgColor="yellow" width="70%" align="center"> <tr><td><br>
  <xpath:value xpath='<%= "text()" %>' /><p>
  <a href='discuss.do?requestReplyForm=<%= id %>'>reply</a> |
  <a href='discuss.do?vote=<%= id %>' >vote!</a>
<br></td></tr></table>
```

As you can see, the rest of the code closes all open tags:

```
      </xpath:nodes>
    </xpath:nodes>
  </body>
</html>
```

So, what happens when the user votes for a message? The anchor specifies `discuss.do` with the parameter vote set to the `id` of the message. This results in a call to the `discussion.doVote(id)` method in `DiscussionBean`, which appears below:

```
public static synchronized void doVote(String id)
throws org.xml.sax.SAXException {
  String votes = XPathUtil.getValue(discussion,
                            "//message[@id='" + id + "']/@votes");
  XPathUtil.setValue(discussion,
                  "//message[@id='" + id + "']/@votes",
                  Integer.parseInt(votes) + 1 + "");
}
```

This method simply uses the utility methods `getValue()` and `setValue()` to alter the value of the `votes` attribute of the in-memory DOM representation of the XML file.

A similar sequence of events occurs when a user clicks the reply link. The anchor requests `discuss.do` with the parameter `requestReplyForm` set to the message id. The `DispatchServlet` turns this into a call to the method `doRequestReplyForm()` in `DiscussionBean`, which is shown below:

```
public void doRequestReplyForm(String id) {
  set("forward", "/reply.jsp");
}
```

This does nothing but set the `forward` property to the `reply` page. The `dispatchServlet` then uses this instead of the page specified in the mapping (`discuss.jsp`). Note that the property `requestReplyForm` is set to the value of `id`. This property is used on the reply page.

The reply.jsp

The reply page is very simple, little more than a form with input fields for the authors name and e-mail address, and the subject and the body of the message. The code for this is present in `reply.jsp`:

```
<%@ taglib uri="/WEB-INF/xpath.tld" prefix="xpath" %>
<jsp:useBean id="discussion" scope="session"
class="com.wrox.projsp.ch11.jsp.DiscussionBean"/>
<html>
<head> <title> Discussion - Reply </title> </head>
<body>
  <form name="discussion" action="discuss.do" method="post">
    <input
      type="hidden"
      name="submitReplyForm"
      value="<%= discussion.get("requestReplyForm") %>" >
    author:
    <input
        type="text" name="author"
        value=" <%= discussion.get("author") %>"><br>
    email:
    <input
        type="text"
        name="email"
        value=" <%= discussion.get("email") %>"><br>
    subject:
    <input
        type="text"
        name="subject"
        value=" <%= discussion.get("subject") %>"><br>
    message:
    <input
        type="text"
        name="body"
        value=" <%= discussion.get("body") %>"><br>
    <input
        type="submit"
        name="perform"
        value="submit">
  </form>
</body>
<html>
```

This page uses the same session-scoped bean as `discuss.jsp`. The `discussion.get()` calls will assign empty strings to the value attributes on the first submission of this form but thereafter these calls pre-fill the form with the values entered last time.

The hidden field, `submitReplyForm`, will result in a call to `DiscussionBean`'s `doSubmitReplyForm()` on submission. Since the reply anchor on the discussion page specifies the parameter `requestReplyForm` with the value of the message id, the property of the same name now contains the id. The `doSubmitReplyForm()` method is reproduced below:

```
public void doSubmitReplyForm(String id)
throws org.xml.sax.SAXException {
  NodeList nodes = XPathUtil.getNodes(discussion,
```

399

```
                                           "//message[@id='" + id + "']");
  if(nodes.getLength()==0) {
    set("forward", "/error.jsp");
    return;
  }
  Node message = nodes.item(0);
  Node reply = messageTemplate.cloneNode(true);
  int level = 1 + Integer.parseInt(XPathUtil.getValue(
      discussion, "//message[@id='" + id + "']/@level"));
  XPathUtil.setValue(reply, "subject/text()", get("subject"));
  XPathUtil.setValue(reply, "body/text()", get("body"));
  XPathUtil.setValue(reply, "@author", get("author"));
  XPathUtil.setValue(reply, "@email", get("email"));
  XPathUtil.setValue(reply, "@id", "" + ++maxId);
  XPathUtil.setValue(reply, "@level", "" + level);
  synchronized(discussion) {
    message.appendChild(reply);
  }
  set("forward", "/discuss.jsp");
}
```

The method proceeds to retrieve the message with the given `id`. Then it creates the node structure representing the response. To avoid having to build the reply message node by node, the first message in the XML file is taken to be a template for new messages. We give it the vote of -1 to keep it from showing up on the page. The `cloneNode()` method returns a deep clone (copy) of the node. Next the various attributes and text values of the message are set and finally the reply is appended as the last child node to the message.

Deploying the Discussion Forum

Before we start up Tomcat and run the application, we need to install the `DispatchServlet` by specifying it in `web.xml`:

```xml
<?xml version="1.0" encoding="ISO-8859-1"?>

<!DOCTYPE web-app
    PUBLIC "-//Sun Microsystems, Inc.//DTD Web Application 2.3//EN"
    "http://java.sun.com/j2ee/dtds/web-app_2_3.dtd">

<web-app>
  <servlet>
    <servlet-name>dispatcher</servlet-name>
    <servlet-class>com.wrox.projsp.ch11.jsp.DispatchServlet</servlet-class>
    <load-on-startup>1</load-on-startup>
  </servlet>
  <servlet-mapping>
    <servlet-name>dispatcher</servlet-name>
    <url-pattern>*.do</url-pattern>
  </servlet-mapping>

  <taglib>
    <taglib-uri>http://www.wrox.com/projsp/chapter11/taglibs/xpath</taglib-uri>
    <taglib-location>/WEB-INF/xpath.tld</taglib-location>
  </taglib>

</web-app>
```

Using the Discussion Forum

Place the webapp for this case study in your webapps directory, and fire up Tomcat. Then access the following URL in your browser: http://localhost:8080/ch11/discuss.jsp. You should see the following page:

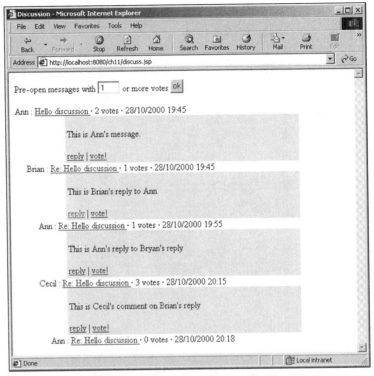

If you click on reply, you can add a response to any of the messages:

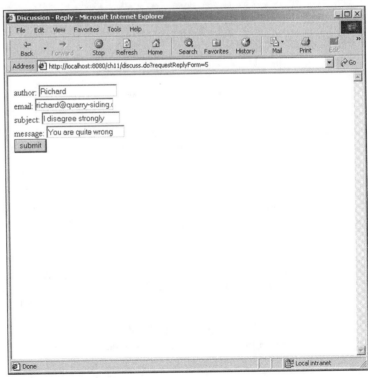

401

We can also change the number of votes required for a message to be seen when we open the forum:

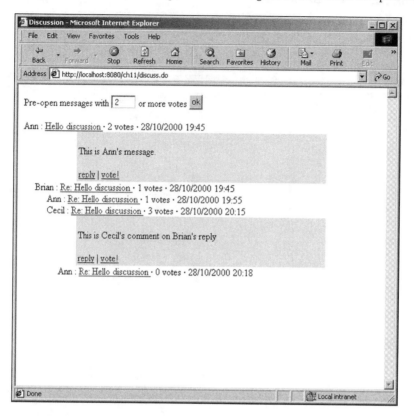

Refining the Forum

While the forum has interesting qualities it also has some limitations:

- ❑ Firstly it has scalability and performance issues: it is non-scalable, it must run on a single server, and it cannot be too big or too frequently updated.

- ❑ Secondly the voting mechanism is open to fraud. We should allow only one vote per user per session; and at best the users should get only one vote each per message.

- ❑ Thirdly the action of voting is disruptive; the page is refreshed and the user is taken away from the message he was reading to the top of the page.

  Possible solutions to this include having a tiny frame which is the target of the vote link. We could use JavaScript to pop up a small window saying "thank you for voting", and use that window as target. Alternatively, we could use #messageId at the end of the voting URL to take the user back to the message.

- ❑ Finally, we allow only one specifically open message in addition to those automatically opened by the vote threshold. While greatly simplifying the implementation, this is an arbitrary limitation. A remedy to that might be to construct a separate session-scoped view component that would interact with the global-scoped discussion component to construct the users view of the discussion. The easiest way to do that is probably by taking advantage of the extension function mechanism provided by XPath.

Summary

In this chapter we have provided you with guidelines for writing your own custom tags. Let's first reiterate the points you should consider before writing your own tag libraries:

- ❑ **Have a good reason, and don't duplicate effort** – don't write tags that have the same functionality as tags already in existence.

- ❑ **Choose descriptive tag names** – so that you can easily extend the functionality of your tag without having to rename it.

- ❑ **Write reusable tools** – aim to solve a class of problems, not just one.

- ❑ **Write code, not content** – avoid generating HTML within custom tags because this reduces the generality of the tags.

- ❑ **Stay away from business logic** – putting workflow actions into the page will eventually make the application difficult to maintain.

- ❑ **Avoid creating a new language** – your audience already knows HTML; don't make them learn a new formatting language too by overusing tags.

- ❑ **Use scripting variables** – these are the key to making tags generic. Allow the page designer to set the name of the scripting variables. Minimize the number of them that you use – if possible, create a composite scripting variable, for instance a single JavaBean, that encapsulates all the data that the tag needs to expose, and makes it available through its methods.

We also saw that there are five main application areas for tags:

- ❑ **Accessing the JSP environment** – working with `request` objects, `servletContext`, and so on

- ❑ **Generating markup** – for instance, form tags

- ❑ **Accessing APIs** – such as JDBC, JNDI, JMS

- ❑ **Postprocessing body content** – caching body content, and incorporating scripting

- ❑ **Display logic** – examples include: controlling flow within the page, login checks, using page design templates, and traversing tree-like data

We finished the chapter with a case study of a discussion forum, in which we built some tag classes that use XPath expressions to extract discussion data from an XML file. Our case study highlighted the versatility and power of custom tags.

In the next chapter we will continue this XML theme, by looking more closely at how we can profit from combining XML with JSP.

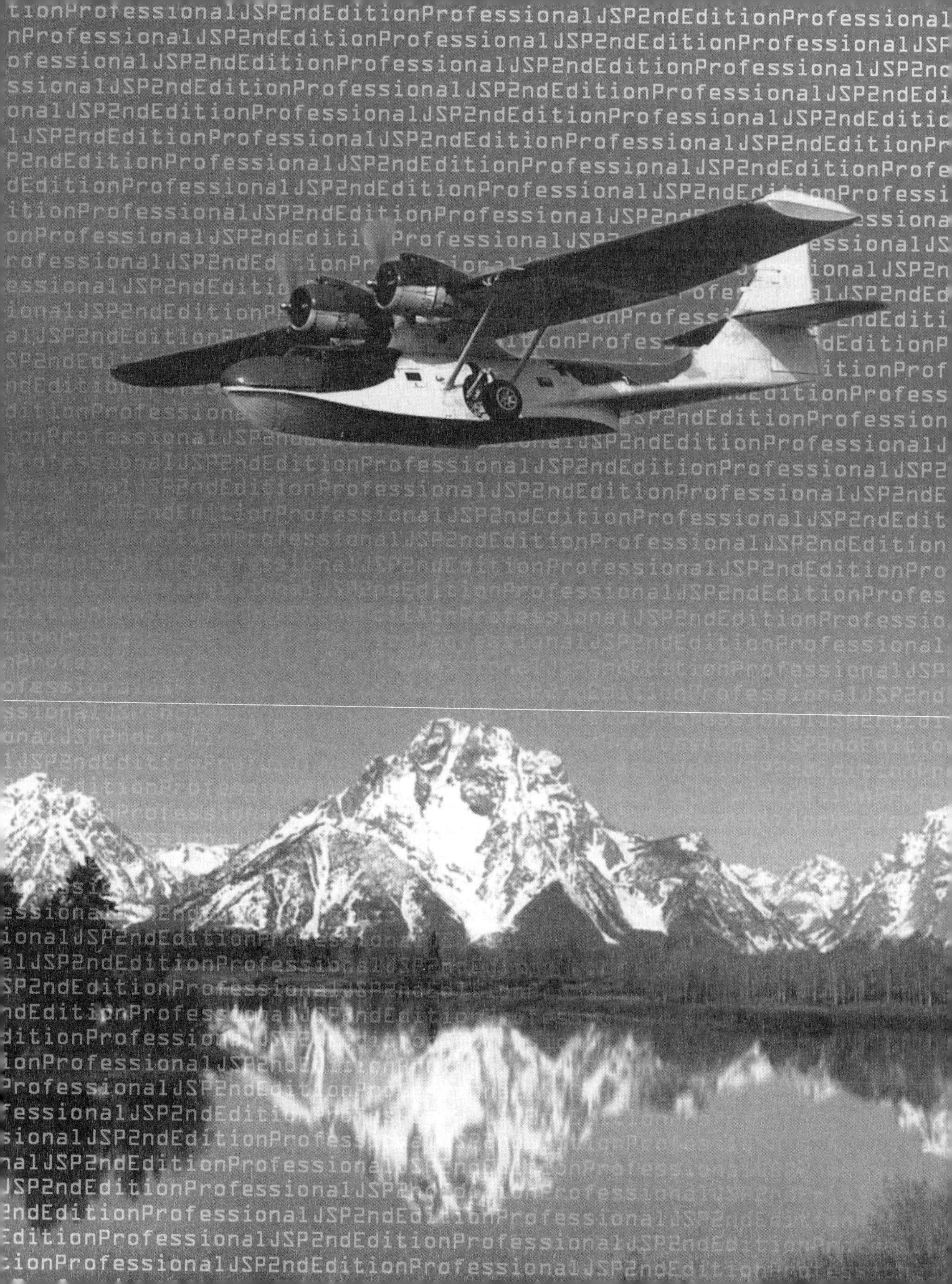

12

JSP and XML

XML and JSP are two important tools available in producing a web application. This chapter examines the potential of mixing these two technologies in order to enhance the capabilities of JSP. While this chapter will cover many things about XML, this chapter will not attempt to teach XML. Instead it focuses on how JSP and XML can be used together as a highly flexible and powerful tool. In general the usage of XML in these examples will be kept simple and should cause no problems for users who are starting XML.

In short the chapter will be broken down into five main sections:

❑   **A quick look at XML**
     Why is XML valuable? Before even dealing with XML combined with JSP we need to
     understand why it would be beneficial to do so. As mentioned this is not going to be a tutorial
     on how to write your own XML and XSLT. Instead the first section will be dealing with
     concepts of XML and its implementation in your project.

❑   **An overview of Java-XML tools**
     Using XML with JSP is much easier if you have the right tools. Before diving right in to
     some examples this section will give a brief overview of some of the most popular Java-
     XML tools. Along with overviews we will also cover which tools this chapter requires and
     where to get them.

❑   **Focus on the DOM, JDOM and SAX**
     Several pre-built Java based code libraries are available to access XML. This section will go
     more in depth about dealing with the Document Object Model, Java Document Object Model
     and Simple API for XML. While DOM, JDOM, and SAX can be of great aid to a developer,
     the reader should understand the benefits and drawbacks for each API. This section will cover
     the DOM in the greatest detail as it can be considered to be the baseline standard for working
     with XML.

❏ **A Step By Step Tutorial**

The best way to learn is to walk through and build some useful code. This section will show you a practical example on how JSP and XML can be combined to work together on a project. The best part is the code will be reusable for any project. The tutorial will help you create a JSP tag library to use with XML.

❏ **JSP Documents**

A review of the merging of XML and JSP in the JSP 1.2 Specification. All of the examples up to this point are implemented using the JSP 1.1 specifications simply because most developers are already familiar with them. JSP 1.2 shows great promise in allowing JSP to be authored in a fully XML compliant syntax. This section is devoted to understanding the new XML based JSP syntax.

What Is XML?

Besides being a common buzzword, what exactly is XML? Before diving right in to the code let's take some time to examine what exactly XML is and what it is good for. For those of you that are already quite familiar with XML this section should only need a skim. However, if XML is completely new to you then this section will explain why XML is so important and give a brief introduction to XML.

XML stands for Extensible Markup Language. The official XML recommendation is made by the W3C and is publicly available at the W3C's website, http://www.w3.org/XML/. Reading through the entire XML recommendation can be quite tedious so we will summarize some of the most important points:

❏ XML is a markup language that is designed for easy use over the Internet. XML is compatible with the SGML (Standard Generalized Markup Language) specifications and can be easily created, edited or viewed by a simple text editor.

❏ XML markup gives data a logical structure that is both easily human-legible and easily processed by applications. While XML markup may resemble other markup languages, such as HTML, here is where a big difference can be seen. An application using XML can verify a document's structure before using the document's content, via either a Document Type Definition (DTD), or a schema. If an XML document is malformed then an application can identify the error before producing an undesired result. However, this doesn't concern us in this chapter.

❏ Optional features in XML are kept to an absolute minimum, currently zero. This means that an XML document will be universally accepted by any XML compliant parser or application. Porting an XML document between operating systems or projects will not require a syntax change for compatibility.

❏ XML is a syntax for defining data and meta-data. It allows you to self describe and serialize information in a universal method. This is one of the most important features of the XML specification. Consider the fact that literally everything can be described in terms of data.

As an example, even a programming language could have its rules and definitions defined with XML. This means you could use XML to form and describe any programming language. In fact the JSP 1.2 spec allows for just that and your JSP can now be coded as XML. Why is this important? This means we will be able to apply the tools we use in XML to many new tasks which would have been harder to perform in the past. We will examine this idea a little more towards the end of the chapter.

So the critical word is 'data'. XML doesn't change the data we use, it merely gives us a way to store and describe it more easily. XML gives us a way to store items that in the past we might not have thought of as data, but now can express in XML as a collection of data. It is this standard way of defining data and storing data that empowers XML. This means over time as programmers, we will use XML to replace other methods of storing and using data. Many of the techniques we have honed over the years are still applicable, it is just we have a new format to apply these skills against.

While XML has many benefits it can still be difficult to understand these benefits especially if you have never used XML. To clarify let's examine a mock case where initially using an XML compatible language saved a lot of work later on.

The Value of XML: An Example

Imagine you are the webmaster of an online publication. The publication has been around for years and consists of thousands of HTML pages. Since you are quite the HTML guru, each HTML page has been crafted to look perfect for the average computer screen. Then one day you walk in and are told every page needs to be changed so they could appear in a paper based book.

The new format poses quite a problem. When constructing the site it was satisfactory to make each page look good on the average web browser. Now each page needs to have its content extracted and reformatted for the book. If all the pages share an identical layout a custom built utility to change the formatting might be a solution, however no fore thought was given to strictly following a standard structure.

While all the pages are coded in a similar fashion they still have enough difference to toss out a custom code-changing tool. The only working solution is to manually go through each page and copy the content. Not only is this inefficient but also the amount of work would easily overburden a single webmaster.

The importance of a common format should now be fairly easy to recognize, but one could still argue that the project above did use a common HTML structure for all of the documents. There is no fault in this argument. Only a misunderstanding of what we are defining as a strictly followed and standard format. For our definition a standard format should allow for clear and easy understanding for both a person and a program.

HTML falls short of our standard format because it does not enforce a common coding syntax throughout a document. HTML tag attributes can be surrounded by quotes or not. Some HTML tags have optional ending tags. HTML even allows for markup syntax to be intermixed with content to be displayed. All of these little allowances work for what HTML was intended for; however, they make it much more difficult for a program to work with the markup correctly.

With a few changes HTML could easily be made in to a format that is easier on a program. The changes might require all attribute values to be surrounded by quotes, all tags to have a clear start and end and markup to be clearly separated from content.

By requiring all of these little changes HTML would provide the same functionality but have a more clearly defined format. Because of the more clearly defined format a program to read HTML would need to do less guessing at optional rules and could display content correctly following the strict rules. In fact this is exactly where XML comes in to play. Don't think of XML as some totally new and different technology. Instead think of XML as enforcing a strict format on markup that does not require a loss of functionality.

One of the most powerful aspects of XML is its ability to define a language that follows these strict formatting rules. In fact XML has already been used to do this for the above issues with HTML. XHTML almost identically resembles normal HTML, but is made using XML for a strict format and structure. Since XHTML also complies with XML standards it may also easily be used by any utility built to support XML. The official XHTML recommendation is hosted publicly at the W3C's website, http://www.w3.org/TR/xhtml1/.

If the troubled webmaster from above had used XHTML he would have a much easier job changing the pages in to new formats. Keep in mind XML is a markup language for easy reading and understanding. XML does not restrict what a program does with the information after it is read. The webmaster could design a custom utility that followed XML rules and performed the format conversion automatically, or the webmaster could go out in search utilities already built to read XML and change its format.

Here is where XML shines some more and the next section proves its worth. The above webmaster would not have to search far for utilities that work with XML. Many developers, companies and other individuals have already decided to support XML and have created software to use its functionality. Some of the most current and popular free software will be reviewed in the next section. We will also take a look at what software will be required to use the XML examples from this chapter.

Useful Tools for XML and JSP

Objects are used to represent data in Java. XML is a mark-up language, but by itself it does nothing, so it must be parsed into a Java object before it is useful to a Java programmer. Fortunately many fine free implementations of Java XML parsers already exist.

Here is an overview of some of the tools used in the examples of this chapter. Each overview includes a location on the Internet where you can find the tool. Most of the tools listed are open-source and all the tools are freely available for your use.

XSLT

XSLT is an XML defined language for performing transformations of XML documents from one form in to another. XSLT by itself does not do much, but relies on other software to perform its transformations.

XSLT is very flexible and becoming quite popular; however, it does not have the same level of support as XML. A few good utilities are available for XSLT and will be listed below. For the XSLT examples in this chapter we are using the default XSLT support that is packaged with the JAXP 1.1 release.

The official XSLT recommendations are made by the W3C and are publicly available at the W3C's website, http://www.w3.org/Style/XSL/.

JAXP

JAXP is meant to be an API to simplify using XML within Java. The JAXP isn't built to be an XML parser. Instead, it is set up with a solid interface with which you can use any XML parser. To further aid developers it does also include a default XML parser.

The JAXP supports XSL transformations and by default uses the Apache Group's Xalan and part of Sun's Project X, renamed to Crimson, for XSLT. Sun and the Apache Group are cooperating for Java XML functionality and because of this Crimson was donated to the Apache Group for future integration with XML projects.

Just about every example in this chapter requires that you have the JAXP resource files available to your JSP container. If you do not have the JAXP 1.1 release installed we recommend you do so now before trying out any code examples.

To download or learn more about JAXP you can visit the Sun web site, http://java.sun.com/xml/download.html.

JDOM

JDOM is an XML utility designed to create a simple and logical Java Document Object Model representation of XML information. The W3C DOM, which we will cover more in depth later, creates a fully accurate representation of a document and is sometimes thought of as too complex.

JDOM simplifies the DOM by only covering the most important and commonly used aspects of the DOM. By taking this approach JDOM is both faster and easier to use but at the cost of limited functionality compared to the standard W3C DOM. While JDOM doesn't have all the features of DOM it does have more then enough features to be a solid tool for a Java-XML developer.

JDOM is only required for the JDOM specific section and the final example of this chapter. You will need to download at least JDOM beta 5 to try those examples, but you do not need it for the rest of the chapter.

To download or learn more about JDOM you can visit the JDOM organization site, http://www.jdom.org/.

Xerces

Xerces is the Apache Group's open-source XML parser. Xerces is 100% W3C standards compliant and represents the closest thing to a reference implementation of a Java parser for the XML DOM and SAX.

JAXP comes with packaged support for XML parsing by Crimson. Crimson does not have the widespread support and documentation of Xerces, but if you would like to try another XML parser with JAXP then Xerces is recommended. The JDOM portion of the chapter use Xerces and it is included within the JDOM package.

To download or learn more about Xerces you can visit the Apache XML site, http://xml.apache.org/xerces-j/index.html.

Xalan

Xalan is the Apache Group's open-source XSLT processor for transforming XML documents into HTML, text or other XML document types. Xalan implements the W3C Recommendations for XSL Transformations. It can be used from the command line, in an applet or a Servlet or as a module for other programs.

Xalan is packaged with the normal JAXP 1.1 so you will not need to download it separately for use with examples in this chapter.

To download Xalan or learn more about it visit the Apache Group's Xalan webpage, http://xml.apache.org/xalan-j/index.html.

Other Software

All of the examples in this chapter are built using the Tomcat 4 beta release. Earlier versions of Tomcat will work for all the examples except the ones found in the JSP in XML syntax section.

If you do not have a JSP container or would like to download Tomcat visit the Apache Group's Jakarta project website; here is the address, http://jakarta.apache.org/tomcat/index.html.

Before continuing on we feel there is need for a word of caution. Tomcat already uses some of the same tools we listed above. Chapter 19 and Appendix A discuss in some detail how classloading works in Tomcat; the easiest way around any potential problems is to just dump all of the JAR files from the JAXP 1.1 release into each web applications's WEB-INF\lib directory.

If you do continue and get a 'sealing violation' error, it probably means you have conflicting JAR files. Double check your environment resources and fix any duplications of JAR or class files.

Extracting and Manipulating XML Data With Java

There is not one be all and end all way of accessing XML data with Java. The JAXP supports two of the most commonly used methods know as the Document Object Model (DOM) and the Simple API for XML (SAX). In addition to the support found in the JAXP the Java Document Object Model (JDOM) is also becoming a commonly used and popular method. At the writing of this material only the DOM is a formal recommendation by the W3C.

This section will briefly give an introduction to these three methods and then compare the advantages and disadvantages of using each.

Extracting XML Data with the DOM

The first example is fast and easy to code. In this example we will examine how to a parse and expose XML information using the JAXP with a JSP page. This example is only geared towards showing how to construct a Java object from an XML document. In a production system you would use a set of JavaBeans to perform most of the work being done within this JSP page. We are keeping the first example simple on purpose to illustrate the much-repeated process of parsing XML to Java. In future examples we will incorporate this code into a JavaBean for repeated use in our JSP pages.

We first need a sample XML document and some code to parse it. The sample XML document will be a simple message. All XML files required for this chapter are referenced as being in the C:/xml/ directory. If you are copying examples verbatim place all XML files in this directory.

Here is message.xml:

```
<?xml version="1.0" encoding="UTF-8"?>
<messages>
  <message>Good-bye serialization, hello Java!</message>
</messages>
```

Next we need to parse the XML file into a Java object. The JAXP makes this easy requiring only three lines of code. Define a factory API that allows our application to obtain a Java XML parser:

```
DocumentBuilderFactory dbf   = DocumentBuilderFactory.newInstance();
```

Create a `DocumentBuilder` object to parse an `org.w3c.dom.Document` from XML:

```
DocumentBuilder db = dbf.newDocumentBuilder();
```

Call the `parse` method to actually parse the XML file to create our `Document` object:

```
Document doc = db.parse("c:/xml/message.xml");
```

As noted in the JAXP API documentation, the `Document` object supports the Document Object Model Level 2 recommendations of the W3C. If you are a W3C standard savvy individual the above three lines of code are all that is needed to place this Java object into your field of experience. If you are not familiar with the W3C's recommendation don't worry. Later in the chapter we will spend some time getting acquainted with the standard DOM as well as some of the other options available for using XML with JSP.

For now it is important to understand that the DOM is a model to describe your data. The whole and only purpose of the DOM is to be a tool for manipulating data. The DOM comes with methods and properties with which you can read, modify and describe the data that the DOM models.

The model the DOM uses is a tree structure of nodes. These nodes are the placeholders for the data and everything else contained in the DOM. For example, if you wanted to reference the overall data tree you would reference the document node, but if you wanted to reference some comments about the data file you could check the comment nodes.

Keeping that brief introduction of the DOM in mind let's finish retrieving our example message. From the `Document` object we can get a `NodeList` object that represents all of the elements in our XML document named `message`. Each slot in the `NodeList` is a single node that represents a message element:

```
NodeList nl = doc.getElementsByTagName("message");
```

A `NodeList` can be thought of as an array starting from 0 and going up to the length of the array. We know this example only has one message element so the list should have only one node for the message element. To return a node from a `NodeList` the `item()` method is used with the index of the node wanted. In this case `item(0)` of the `Nodelist` representing the message element would return the first message in the example XML file:

```
Node my_node = nl.item(0);
```

Once the first node is retrieved it is possible to query it to get more information about that node. In this case we would like to get the message stored within the node. Fortunately convenient self-named methods such as `getNodeValue()` are available for extracting this data:

```
String message = my_node.getFirstChild().getNodeValue();
```

Some readers may ask why we have to use the `getFirstChild()` method when our example node has no attributes or another node besides the text. The reason for this comes from the fact that with the W3C DOM data representation of the node really has more sub-nodes in its tree-like structure. The one sub-node we are interested in contains the message text. After calling `getFirstChild()` the desired text node is returned and we can use `getNodeValue()` for our message.

Here is where a difference can be seen between the various parsers. In this simple example the DOM is tracking many pieces of information we really don't need. JDOM creates a simpler representation of the XML file. This means JDOM uses less memory to represent the XML file and the function calls would be easier.

Since we know no other sub-nodes are present in the message node why even bother with the text node? JDOM would let us concentrate on a simpler model. The standard W3C DOM provides these sub-nodes for extra flexibility regardless of the programming language or situation. JDOM on the other hand is built specifically for Java and ease of use. However, the ease JDOM provides comes at the loss of some of the standards such as these sub-nodes. In the long run either API would accomplish the same goal.

Putting all of the above together gives us a JSP that will read in our XML document and display the message. Here is the code for `dom_message.jsp`:

```
<%@ page contentType="text/html"%>
<%@ page import="javax.xml.parsers.DocumentBuilderFactory,
        javax.xml.parsers.DocumentBuilder,
        org.w3c.dom.*"
%>
<%
DocumentBuilderFactory dbf = DocumentBuilderFactory.newInstance();
DocumentBuilder db = dbf.newDocumentBuilder();
Document doc = db.parse("c:/xml/message.xml");
NodeList nl = doc.getElementsByTagName("message");
%>
<html>
<body>
<%= nl.item(0).getFirstChild().getNodeValue() %>
</body>
</html>
```

The output for this example should be a plain HTML page that says the example message. Here is a screenshot of our results:

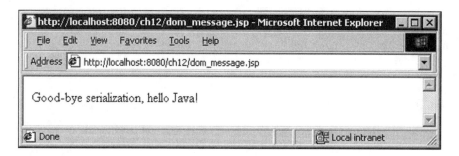

The above example should help illustrate what an XML parser does and what exactly a DOM is, but don't think the DOM is restricted to the above example. Let's look a little closer at the Document Object Model and the flexibility it provides.

Focusing on the DOM

The Document Object Model is an important and commonly used object when dealing with XML. Remember how earlier we mentioned the DOM is a tool for creating a structure to represent data. Having a complete and well-defined structure is what allows us to both manipulate the data and the structure itself. Now let's learn a little more about the DOM and how it is used.

A document never starts off as a DOM object for use with Java. Instead a data source must be processed and converted into a DOM object. For practical purposes in Java, the DOM object is the intersection of a data object, such as an XML file, and your Java. The intersection formed provides a JSP programmer's interface to the XML document.

Over the years several different DOM objects have been created to handle different document types. This can make it confusing to understand the exact nature of a DOM object. When we use the term DOM we are referencing the standard W3C DOM built to support an XML structured document.

> *The W3C Document Object Model Level 2 Core Specification can be found at,* http://www.w3.org/DOM/.

For the next example we will continue to use the W3C standard DOM object in the JAXP. Keep in mind while the DOM is based upon a recommendation and is a specification, we are also using Java-based libraries to create a DOM representation. This can be confusing since we are referring to the DOM as both the specification and the Java representation.

In the next section we are reviewing the objects that comprise the Java representation of the DOM. We will present a brief overview for some of the most commonly used objects and methods. Keep in mind this is not a complete listing by any means. This list will serve to make these objects familiar for a future example. For a complete list, reference the documentation with your JAXP download or visit Sun's web site for the online version, http://java.sun.com/xml/docs/api/.

Common DOM Objects

Below are some of the commonly used DOM objects found in the `org.w3c.dom` package. Each object has a short description along with a list of relative method information for our examples.

Node

A node is the primary data type of the DOM tree. An object with the `Node` interface implements methods needed to deal with children objects but is not required to have children. Some common objects with the `Node` interface are `Document` and `Element`:

Method	Description
`appendChild(org.w3c.dom.Node)`	Adds a child node to this node and returns the node added
`getFirstChild()`	Returns the first child of the node if it exists
`getNextSibling()`	Returns the node immediately after this node
`getNodeName()`	Returns the name of the node depending on its type (see API)
`getNodeType()`	Returns the node's type (see API)
`getNodeValue()`	Returns the value of the node

Element

Elements are an extension of the `Node` interface and provide additional methods similar to the `Document` object. When retrieving nodes by using the `getElementsByTagName()` method often times a cast to the element type is needed for further manipulation of sub-trees:

413

Method	Description
getElementsByTagName(String)	Returns a NodeList of all of the elements with the specified tag name.
getTagName()	Returns a String representing the tag name of the element.
getAttribute(String)	Returns a String value of the attribute. Caution should be used because XML allows for entity references in attributes. In such cases the attribute should be retrieved as an object and further examined.
getAttributeNode(String)	Returns the attribute as an Attr object. This Attr may contain nodes of type Text or EntityReference. See API.

Document

The document object represents the complete DOM tree of the XML source:

Method	Description
appendChild(org.w3c.dom.Node)	Adds a node to the DOM tree
createAttribute(String)	Create an Attr named by the given String
createElement(String)	Creates an element with a name specified by the given String
createTextNode(String)	Creates a node of type Text that contains the given String as data
getElementsByTagName(String)	Returns a NodeList of all of the elements with the specified tag name
getDocumentElement()	Returns the node that is the root element of the document

NodeList

The NodeList interface acts as an abstraction for a collection of nodes. A NodeList can be though of much like an array. Any item in the NodeList may be manipulated by making reference to its index in the list:

Method	Description
getLength()	Returns the number of nodes in the list
Item(int)	Returns the specified node from the collection

Putting the DOM to Work

With the next example we will use some of the above objects and methods. Instead of explaining the syntax for each bit of code we will focus on what exactly the code is doing. If you get lost on syntax just reference the above section.

For the next example we will create a JSP to verify the status of a DOM full of URLs. The JSP page will have a small form for adding or clearing the URLs from our DOM. Ideally for this example we would like to stash a Document object throughout the session. In the Java API the Document object is only an interface. We will need an object implementing the Document interface for this example to work. In the JAXP the XmlDocument is an ideal object to use and it can be found within the `org.apache.crimson.tree` package.

Before going farther we should warn you the Crimson documentation isn't easily found. The JAXP 1.1 does not bind a specific XML parser or XSLT processor to itself. As a result the documentation for these two parts of the JAXP is found from the suppliers of the XML and XSLT tool sets used within JAXP.

The Apache Group happens to be the owner of the XML parser and XSLT processor that comes packaged by default with the JAXP 1.1. At the time of writing the Apache web site lacks pre-built documentation for the Crimson package. If you would like to make your own documentation you can download the Crimson source files from the Apache Group and run the javadoc utility yourself. For your aid we will also javadoc the Crimson source files and include the documentation files with this chapter's download. Xalan, the default XSLT processor with the JAXP 1.1, has excellent documentation but we will get to that later.

As mentioned at the start of this section, the first part of this example stashes a DOM tree to the session context. See if you can pick out where the `XmlDocument` object is used.

The dom_links JSP

Here is the code for `dom_links.jsp`. The three lines of code below use the `XmlDocument` object and are the same three we have been using throughout the chapter. Because the Crimson package is being used `db.newDocument()` creates an `XmlDocument` object even though we treat it as a W3C compliant Document object:

```
<%@ page
 import=" org.w3c.dom.*,
 javax.xml.parsers.*" %>
<%
DocumentBuilderFactory dbf = DocumentBuilderFactory.newInstance();
DocumentBuilder db = dbf.newDocumentBuilder();
Document doc = db.newDocument();
```

The new code below places our DOM tree within the session and then creates a root node so we can add URLs:

```
session.setAttribute("doc", doc);

Element newLink = doc.createElement("root");
doc.appendChild(newLink);
%>
<jsp:forward page="dom_links_checker.jsp" />
```

With our object stashed in the session the request is forwarded to a JSP that will check and modify our DOM.

The dom_links_checker JSP

Here is the code for dom_links_checker.jsp:

```
<%@ page
 import="org.w3c.dom.*,
 javax.xml.parsers.*,
 java.net.*"%>
<html>
```

The easy part comes first; two simple HTML forms. One form will add the URL submitted while the other will clear all the set of URLs:

```
<table>
  <tr>
    <td colspan="2">
      <form action="dom_links_checker.jsp" method="post">
      Add a url: <INPUT name="add" size="25">
    </td>
  </tr>
  <tr>
    <td align="center"><INPUT type="submit" value=" Send "></form></td>
    <td align="center">
     <form action="dom_links_checker.jsp" method="post">
     <INPUT name="clear" type="hidden" value="true">
     <INPUT type="submit" value=" Clear List">
     </form>
    </td>
  </tr>
</table>
<%
```

After the forms we need to add the functionality in our JSP. In order to manipulate our tree of URLs it must first be snagged from the session:

```
org.w3c.dom.Document doc = (org.w3c.dom.Document)session.getAttribute("doc");
```

Next we need some code for adding URLs from the form. For adding a URL we must first make a new element in our DOM. After a url element is created we then toss a text node in with the URL. You can see we name each of these elements "url" for convenience. Later on we will retrieve every url element to check the actual URL:

```
if (request.getParameter("add") != null)
{
  Element newLink = doc.createElement("url");
  org.w3c.dom.Text linkText =
  (org.w3c.dom.Text)doc.createTextNode(request.getParameter("add"));
  newLink.appendChild(linkText);
  doc.getDocumentElement().appendChild(newLink);
}
```

When the clear button is clicked our tree of URLs will be reset. Removing all the URLs from our DOM is as easy as looping through and taking out each url element:

```
if (request.getParameter("clear") != null)
{
  int count = doc.getElementsByTagName("url").getLength();
  for(int i = 0; i< count; i++)
  doc.getDocumentElement().removeChild(doc.getElementsByTagName("url").item(0));
}
```

After making our changes to the DOM object, we still need to verify the URLs stored within the DOM object are valid. The following code loops through all our `url` elements and performs a quick connection to see if they are available over the Internet. The only addition from above is that a URL is created and checked for each `url` element. As the URLs are validated the code returns the name of the URL, and the response code for the URL connection attempt is sent back to the user:

```
for(int i = 0; i < doc.getElementsByTagName("url").getLength(); i++)
  {
    URL url = new
    URL(doc.getElementsByTagName("url").item(i).getFirstChild().getNodeValue());
    HttpURLConnection link = (HttpURLConnection)url.openConnection();
%>
<font color="blue">
<%= doc.getElementsByTagName("url").item(i).getFirstChild().getNodeValue() %>
</font>
<font color="red"><%= link.getResponseCode() %></font><br />
<% } %>
</html>
```

Just about everyone knows that a 404 response-code means trouble, however you should expect to see the "OK" 200 code if you typed in a real URL. Here is a screen shot after we typed in a few URLs:

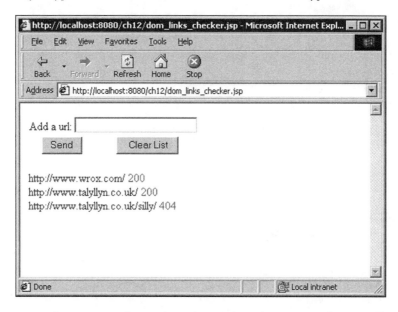

Now the above example seems easy, but we haven't gained much over a simple array. The power of a tool based on a DOM would be that it could read any XML source. If we were maintaining a web site with all the links in XML compatible format we could use a JSP page to check the entire site.

Following that thought let's create an XML file of URLs to plug in with `dom_links.jsp`. The XML source will not only be helpful to this example but later we will reuse it to generate things like an HTML page for a web browser and a WML page for WAP devices.

The URL File

Here is the code for `links.xml`:

```
<?xml version="1.0" encoding="ISO-8859-1" standalone="yes"?>
<links>
```

The document is a set of links. Each link element represents a URL and some important information pertaining to it. The first link is for Wrox publishing:

```
<link>
  <text>Wrox publishing</text>
  <url newWindow="no">http://www.wrox.com</url>
  <author>Wrox</author>
  <date>
    <day>1</day>
    <month>1</month>
    <year>2001</year>
  </date>
    <description>Check out Wrox for more books.</description>
</link>
```

The next link is structured identically but with information for JSP Insider:

```
<link>
  <text>JSP Insider</text>
  <url newWindow="no">http://www.jspinsider.com</url>
  <author>JSP Insider</author>
  <date>
    <day>2</day>
    <month>1</month>
    <year>2001</year>
  </date>
  <description>A JSP information site.</description>
</link>
```

Another link, but this time for Sun Microsystems main Java page:

```
<link>
  <text>The makers of Java</text>
  <url newWindow="no">http://java.sun.com</url>
  <author>Sun Microsystems</author>
  <date>
    <day>3</day>
    <month>1</month>
    <year>2001</year>
  </date>
  <description>Sun Microsystem's website.</description>
</link>
```

A final link to the JSP container reference implementation:

```
    <link>
      <text>The standard JSP container</text>
      <url newWindow="no">http://jakarta.apache.org</url>
      <author>Apache Group</author>
      <date>
        <day>4</day>
        <month>1</month>
        <year>2001</year>
      </date>
      <description>Some great software.</description>
    </link>
  </links>
```

To plug the XML source in to our dom_links.jsp we need to change three lines of code. Here is the new code for dom_links2.jsp:

```
<%@ page
 import=" org.w3c.dom.*,
 javax.xml.parsers.*" %>
<%
DocumentBuilderFactory dbf = DocumentBuilderFactory.newInstance();
DocumentBuilder db = dbf.newDocumentBuilder();
Document doc = db.parse("c:/xml/links.xml");

session.setAttribute("doc", doc);
%>
<jsp:forward page="dom_links_checker.jsp" />
```

With that fix here is the screen shot after running dom_links2.jsp:

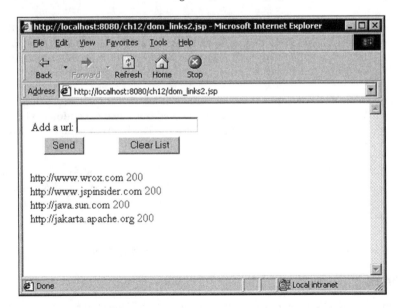

Now the value of a DOM in dom_links2.jsp can be seen over a simple array. Instead of reading a file we could tweak dom_links2.jsp one more time to accept request parameter specifying an XML compatible source. The source could then be from a client, database or just about anything else.

DOM: Pros and Cons

After the above example you should know enough to start working on your own with the DOM; however remember what we said in the beginning: there is not one be all and end all way of accessing XML data with Java.

With that in mind, let's look at a few reasons to use the DOM as well as some of the limitations of the DOM:

❑ The DOM is very flexible and generic. The W3C DOM can describe many different documents, including anything in XML syntax. Since the DOM provides such broad support it can be thought of as a generic tool, especially when dealing with XML.

❑ By gaining skills with the standard W3C DOM you can apply them wherever a W3C DOM might appear. For example, many browsers are now supporting the W3C DOM. Currently Mozilla and Opera both have excellent support for the W3C DOM and IE has fairly good support as well. Using client-side scripting such as JavaScript you can use the same DOM manipulating methods described in the previous section.

❑ A DOM is not customized for any one type of project. The memory requirements of a standard DOM and processing time are greater then a customized object. For large XML resources a DOM will have a very noticeable speed difference.

Moving away from the W3C DOM, let's take a look at a tool aimed at solving the third of these issues.

Focusing on the JDOM

DOM issues such as memory requirements and a desire to create a simpler model for working with XML data has prompted several Java developers to create an API called JDOM. JDOM is a Java specific Document Object Model.

The most important fact we must make clear is that JDOM is not a layer that sits over the DOM. JDOM takes a different approach by taking an XML document and creating a Java object representation of the XML file. In addition JDOM takes a simplified approach in comparison to what the DOM object implements. JDOM has 80% to 90% of the DOM functionality.

However, JDOM steers clear on some of the less used but highly complex areas of the DOM. This means JDOM will accomplish most things you would need but a few exceptions exist where you still might need to use DOM. The other good thing about the JDOM design is that it is easy to integrate JDOM and SAX together.

As JDOM is still a new and evolving product you should check in at the JDOM site to get the latest specifications. Popular open-source projects like the Apache Group's Xerces are also working JDOM support in to future releases. Another big bonus to JDOM is that it is starting the Java Community Process. Overall JDOM appears to have a bright future.

For more information on JDOM, visit the official website, http://www.jdom.org/.

Installing JDOM

You will want to install JDOM to work with your container. With Tomcat this means copying the `jdom.jar` and `xerces.jar` files into the web application's `WEB-INF\lib` directory.

Now this introduces a slight problem, many versions of xerces.jar are in existence and it is possible you will have several copies from different programs using Xerces. So this means you need to be careful on managing your JAR files. If you are getting strange results make sure you have the version of xerces.jar that comes bundled with JDOM. With all of the different versions of Java parsing tools floating around it is easy to get confused by using the wrong JAR file.

Revisiting the dom_message JSP

Remember the slight difficulty we had getting the message from message.xml with dom_message.jsp? Let's now take a look at how to accomplish the same simple task with JDOM.

The jdom_message JSP

This example uses the message.xml within the C:/xml directory from the earlier example:

```
<%@ page contentType="text/html"%>
<%@ page import="java.io.File, org.jdom.*, org.jdom.input.SAXBuilder" %>
<%
SAXBuilder builder = new SAXBuilder("org.apache.xerces.parsers.SAXParser");

Document l_doc = builder.build(new File("c:/xml/message.xml"));
%>
<html>
<body>
   <%= l_doc.getRootElement().getChild("message").getText() %>
</body>
</html>
```

This produces the exact same output as the dom_message.jsp example. As you can see the code actually appears to be a bit simpler. Some programmers feel the syntax within JDOM is easier to use than the DOM syntax.

For example, getText() vs. getFirstChild().getNodeValue().

However, this is a matter of personal preference, and usually depends on which style one is exposed to first as a programmer. In fact many programmers will have experienced DOM-like syntax from other tools.

In this example, you will notice the use of SAXBuilder. A nice feature of JDOM is the great integration with SAX it offers. The code illustrates the ease of creating a SAXBuilder object and directly importing an XML file into our JSP code. In fact since JDOM uses builders to import an XML file it is easy to choose which builder fits your needs the best.

Currently JDOM has two builders, one for SAX and one for DOM. Usually it is best to use the SAX builder over the DOM builder. It usually doesn't make sense to use the DOM builder unless you are using a DOM that is already created. This is due to the fact you are already using the tree structure of JDOM. The act of creating a DOM would be redundant in most cases ending up being an inefficient use of resources. The SAX builder is the quickest method to use in importing an XML file.

A Different Example of Using JDOM

This next example will read in the links.xml file from the DOM example, modify data within it, and then display the modified results. The actual change performed will be to simply change the year, but this will show how to access and modify multiple records several layers down within the XML file.

The jdom_example JSP

The links.xml file saved within the C:/xml directory is also required for this example:

```
<%@ page contentType="text/html"%>
<%@ page import="java.io.File,
                java.util.*,
                org.jdom.*,
                org.jdom.input.SAXBuilder,
                org.jdom.output.*" %>
```

We will need to import the XML file. As stated earlier, JDOM uses builders to actually create the document object and for speed purposes we will use SAX to import the XML file into memory:

```
<%
String ls_xml_file = "c:/xml/links.xml";

SAXBuilder builder = new SAXBuilder("org.apache.xerces.parsers.SAXParser");

Document l_doc = builder.build(new File(ls_xml_file));
```

Now that a JDOM document has been created we can perform queries upon it and modify the data. We will need to get a handle on the root element of the document. Once we have the root, it is possible to ask JDOM to give us an iterator. The iterator permits us to generically loop through all elements under the root. Using this technique we can access any element under the root:

```
Element root = l_doc.getRootElement();

/* get a list of all the links in our XML document */
List l_pages = root.getChildren("link");

    Iterator l_loop =  l_pages.iterator();
```

Now the code will loop through each link record. Since the year element is actually an element under the date tag, some additional drilling down must be performed by the code. Once we get the child record for the year we can reset the data with a quick setText() function call:

```
        while ( l_loop.hasNext())
        {
          Element l_link = (Element) l_loop.next();
          Element l_year = l_link.getChild("date").getChild("year");
          l_year.setText("2002");
        }
```

Finally, we can take the JDOM document and create a string representation of the XML data. In this case we are left with data that is formatted as an XML file:

```
    XMLOutputter l_format = new XMLOutputter();
    String ls_result = l_format.outputString(l_doc);
```

Since we want to display our data in an HTML file we must format our data to display correctly. This means we have to encode all of the < and > characters as < and >. However, we will use a special feature of JDOM to illustrate the difference between plain text and XML.

When you use the setText() function in JDOM, two things happen. The first is that it replaces everything within the tag with the text you supply. If you wanted to insert text and XML into a tag then you would use the setMixedContent() function. The second thing setText() does is to encode all of the < and > characters for us:

```
    root.setText(ls_result);

    ls_result = l_format.outputString(l_doc);
%>

<html><head><title></title></head>
  <body>
    <pre>
      <%=ls_result%>
    </pre>
  </body>
</html>
```

So in the last step, the call root.setText(ls_result) replaces everything within the JDOM object under the root element with a string representation of the XML object. The important point to realize is a string of XML data is not always treated as XML data, it might be treated as a simple string, depending on the functions you use.

This example will produce a result that looks like this:

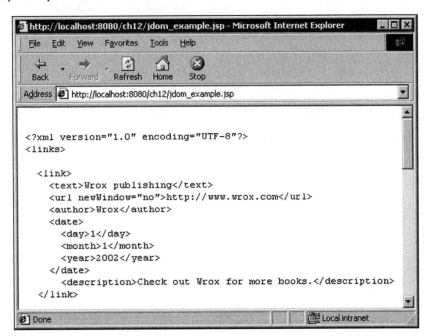

This example shows several things:

- ❑   One thing to keep in mind is that when accessing an element you are only dealing with that level of data. To access sub-elements you need to drill down to that sub-elements level. This means you have to drill down to get to your final destination. This actual drill down is relatively simple as shown in the code above.

❏ JDOM is merely a tool to represent and access an XML data source as a collection of Java objects. In many respects using JDOM doesn't change the way we approach programming and using data. From a practical viewpoint the only change is reducing the dependence of using string logic and switching to using elements and nodes to store and change your data. This will become clearer in the last example of the chapter.

Now that we have used JDOM a little let's examine the benefits of JDOM.

JDOM: Pros and Cons

Just like we highlighted in the DOM section, there is no be all and end all way for accessing XML information with Java. Here are some good points to help decide if JDOM is meant for your project:

❏ JDOM is specific for Java and has smaller memory requirements then a generic DOM.

❏ JDOM has a simpler and more logically based set of methods for accessing its information. This difference can be both a blessing and a curse. What JDOM trades off for ease is some flexibility.

❏ JDOM currently does not have support for XSLT. To drive an XSLT processor you would have to use the XMLOutputter class to get XML from your JDOM. Hopefully in the future Java XSLT processors and APIs like the JAXP will have native support for JDOM and XSLT transformations.

❏ JDOM can suffer memory problems when dealing with large files. The issue boils down to the fact that you can only use JDOM if the final document it generates fits within RAM memory. Future releases of JDOM should address this issue.

❏ JDOM is Java specific and can offer support to access other data from sources other than XML. For example classes are being built to access data from SQL queries.

Focusing on the SAX

And now for something completely different. The Simple API for XML is a valuable tool for accessing XML; however, it is not similar at all to its Document Object Model counterparts. Instead the SAX is made for quickly reading through a stream of XML and appropriately firing off events to a listener object. We will cover some of these SAX parsing events later. By using parsing events and having an event handler object SAX is very efficient for handling even large XML sources. You may ask why does this make SAX efficient? Unlike the DOM, which handles everything, events within SAX let us get selective in what our code processes.

JAXP 1.1 supports the SAX 2 API and SAX 2 Extensions developed cooperatively by the XML-DEV mailing list hosted by XML.org. Here are the links for the official information. We will give a brief example of using the SAX next:

❏ SAX 2 API
http://www.megginson.com/SAX/index.html

❏ SAX 2 Extensions
http://www.megginson.com/Software/sax2-ext-1.0.zip

❏ XML-DEV mailing list
http://www.xml.org/xml-dev/index.shtml

Before creating an object to handle SAX events we must use a few lines of code to create a `SAXParser`. Similar to `DocumentBuilderFactory` for a DOM there is a `SAXParserFactory` for making `SAXParsers`:

```
SAXParserFactory spf = SAXParserFactory.newInstance();
```

By calling the `newSAXParser()` method we can now get a `SAXParser` object:

```
SAXParser sp = spf.newSAXParser();
```

The only thing left to do is call the `parse()` method on our `SAXParser`. When calling the `parse()` method we must pass in the source to be parsed and an object that listens to SAX events as parameters. From the DOM section we still have `links.xml` to use as our XML source. The only thing left for us to do is create our SAX event listener object.

A SAX event listener object must implement the correct interface for the appropriate SAX events. Interfaces such as `ContentHandler`, `DTDHandler` and `ErrorHandler` all exist in the SAX API for listening to events.

As you might have guessed all of these interfaces are named after the type of event they handle. `ContentHandler` deals with events such as the start of a document or the beginning of an element. `DTDHandler` handles events associated with the Document Type Definition such as notation declarations. `ErrorHandler` deals with any sort of error encountered when parsing through the XML document.

The `DocumentHandler` interface also exists; however, it is only around for legacy support of SAX 1.0 utilities. `ContentHandler` should be used for SAX 2.0 applications because it also supports namespaces.

For our example object we will use the `ContentHandler` interface. In the `org.xml.sax.helpers` package a `DefaultHandler` object already implements the `ContentHandler` interface. Our example will extend this object to ease the amount of code required for the example. The goal of our SAX utility will be to parse through `links.xml` and notify us of a few events as well as counting the number of URLs in the file.

The SAXExample Class

Save this file to WEB-INF/classes/com/jspinsider/jspkit/examples:

```
package com.jspinsider.jspkit.examples;

import org.xml.sax.helpers.*;
import org.xml.sax.*;
import javax.xml.parsers.*;
import javax.servlet.jsp.*;
import java.io.*;
```

First we must extend the `DefaultHandler` object so that we can implement the `ContentHandler` interface. Next some objects are declared that will be used throughout the code. One of these is a `Writer` object. We will use this to stash a reference to our JSP out implicit object:

```
public class SAXExample extends DefaultHandler{
   private Writer w;
   String currentElement;
```

```
int urlCount = 0;

public SAXExample(java.io.Writer new_w){
  w = new_w;
}
```

Here is the first of the SAX events we are overriding. At the start of each document a `startDocument()` event is called. Any relevant task should be placed in this method that needs to be dealt with each time a document begins to parse:

```
public void startDocument() throws SAXException{
  try{
    w.write(new String("<b>Document Started</b>\n"));
  }
  catch(Exception e){throw new SAXException(e.toString());}
}
```

The counterpart to `startDocument()` is the `endDocument()` method. If you have a task that needs to be done at the end of a document parsing this is the place it should go:

```
public void endDocument() throws SAXException{
  try{
    w.write(new String("<br><b>Document Finished:</b> Total URLs = " +
                    urlCount));
  }
  catch(Exception e){throw new SAXException(e.toString());}
}
```

Whenever an element is encountered the `startElement()` method is called. Anything needing to get accomplished when an element is encountered should be placed here. Relevant information is passed in to the method describing things such as the element's name and attributes. An `endElement()` method also exists and is called when the ending of an element is encountered.

The code in our `startElement()` method will check to see if the element is a URL. If it is, the `urlCount` object is incremented and some information about the attributes is displayed:

```
public void startElement(String uri, String localName, String qName,
                    Attributes attributes) throws SAXException{
  currentElement = localName;
  if(0 == localName.compareTo("url"))
  {
  urlCount++;
  try{
    w.write(new String("<br><font color=\"blue\">URL Element.</font> Open in new
window? <font color=\"red\">" + attributes.getValue(0) +
"</font><br>   "));
  }
  catch(Exception e){throw new SAXException(e.toString());}
  }
}
```

For the most part SAX events are intuitive with the exception of the characters method. The `characters()` method is called whenever character data is encountered in your XML source. Unfortunately, the parameters passed in to this function don't describe from what element the character data came from. If needed you will have to keep track of this information yourself. For this example, you can see we track this information by having the `currentElement` object updated each time an element is encountered. If the `currentElement` is a URL we will display the URL:

```
public void characters(char[] ch, int start, int length) throws SAXException{
  try{
    if (0 == currentElement.compareTo("url")){
      int count = 0;
      while(count < length)
        {
          w.write(ch[start + count]);
          count++;
        }
      w.write("\n");
    }
  }
  catch(Exception e){throw new SAXException(e.toString());}
  }
}
```

This example doesn't require any further events; however, there are many other different types of event you can track within SAX. Depending on your need different events are available to use in your own custom event handling objects. SAX 2 provides support for every logical event that occurs when parsing an XML document. Consult the JAXP 1.1 documentation to see all of the available SAX events supported.

Now that we have an object ready to listen to SAX events let's tie it in to a JSP.

The sax_example JSP

Here is the code for `sax_example.jsp`:

```
<%@ page
  import="org.xml.sax.helpers.*,
  javax.xml.parsers.*,
  com.jspinsider.jspkit.examples.*,
  org.xml.sax.*" %>
<html>
<%
  SAXParserFactory spf = SAXParserFactory.newInstance();
  SAXParser sp = spf.newSAXParser();
  SAXExample se = new SAXExample(out);

  sp.parse(new java.io.File("c:/xml/links.xml"), se);
%>
</html>
```

The only new code that was required is the parse method telling our SAXParser to parse links.xml and notify our SAXExample object of events. The output for this JSP looks like this:

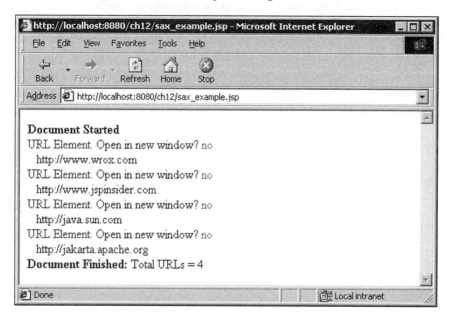

As you can see SAX-style and DOM-style handling of XML is very different. Both can be used effectively for different purposes and should be used as needed. Compared to the example we used in the DOM section you can see we could have used the SAX to verify each of the links in our XML; however, we could not have allowed for the links to be manipulated similarly by stashing a SAX object in the client's session. On the other hand if we wanted to use DOM-style manipulation on a 20mb XML file it would most certainly cause trouble for our system whereas a SAX-style would work.

SAX: Pros and Cons

To conclude the final of our three main Java XML accessing methods we will give a similar list as in the DOM and JDOM example. After this we will give one final reminder on the key differences of the DOM, JDOM, and SAX all at the same time. We will also mention when it might be appropriate to use each:

❏ SAX is sequential event based XML parsing. SAX represents an XML document by providing a method to transform the XML as a stream of data, which then can be processed by the programmer.

❏ SAX cannot directly modify the streaming document it creates. You can consider SAX to be a read only process. Once the programmer has received a parsed bit of data from SAX , it is then up to the programmer to decide what to do with this received data.

❏ SAX is the hardest method to use when performing parsing in non-sequential order. Jumping around in a SAX stream removes any efficency gain you achieved over a DOM and will usually cause a headache.

DOM / JDOM / SAX: A Final Comparison

Do we really need all of these tools to handle XML? The short answer is yes. While XML is simple it is being used in countless different ways on different projects. The simple fact is that XML represents data and in dealing with data it is important to have several different ways to handle and process this data. This guarantees that no single XML API will ever meet everyone's needs.

These API's all have one thing in common as they all present methods to represent XML data. The strange aspect of these API's is that you might think they share more in common, but in reality what each tool offers is something distinct and unique relative to their specifications.

All the talk about DOM, JDOM and SAX can be a bit confusing to someone encountering these beasts for the first time. In conclusion of this section we would like to give a summary of key points regarding each API along with when each API might be appropriate to use:

❑ The streaming nature of SAX makes it generally the fastest way to work through an XML source. When speed is a key issue with your XML SAX is a good place to start.

❑ SAX requires the least memory requirements and you can start working with the results as the parser processes the XML stream. For very large XML sources SAX is usually the only viable option.

❑ JDOM relies on other processors to actually perform the first step transformation of the XML data into the JDOM model. Of course if you are not using an XML source in the first place this is not an issue.

❑ JDOM is usually faster then a DOM and offers a simple Java interface to use in working with an XML document. JDOM also slightly simplifies the syntax required within your Java code.

❑ Both the DOM and JDOM have a tree-like structure. The tree-like structure is usually preferred when representing an entire XML document or when needing to access any part of the tree at will.

❑ DOM is based on recommendations from W3C and as such is the closest to being a 'standard' of the three systems listed here. SAX and JDOM are not standards, but rather are open source projects that were created to resolve problems that exist within the DOM recommendations. However, while not official standards, both SAX and JDOM have become unofficial standards to address XML parsing issues. At the writing of this book JDOM has started the official JSR process at Sun to become a standard under the Java code umbrella.

In all the above sections we have been describing each of these XML tools separately. Keep in mind there are no restrictions keeping you from mixing and matching the DOM, JDOM and SAX. Use what works best for you.

JSP and XML: A Step By Step Tutorial

The first part of this chapter was a gentle introduction to using XML with Java and the various methods with JSP. Now let's work on a more practical example that will illustrate using the JAXP and JSP together to produce many different formats from the same XML content. For styling XML to different formats we will use something called XSLT (eXtensible Styling Language Transformations).

Styling XML with XSLT

We introduced XSLT when describing some of the XML tools available for use with JSP. XSLT is used to transform an XML document into another form such as HTML, plain text, or even a different XML layout. XSLT is a very rich and comprehensive language. Like the XML in this chapter, for brevity's sake we will not attempt to give a tutorial on XSLT.

> *The XSLT examples we do use should be fairly easy to follow even without XSLT experience; however, if you would like to read more on XSLT here is the link once more, http://www.w3.org/Style/XSL/. Also see XSLT Programmer's Reference 2nd Edition from Wrox Press, ISBN 1861005067.*

Before explaining XSLT further let's explain why we are using it at all. A series of JSP templates could be constructed in place of an XSLT transformation sheet; however, a JSP template approach has a few disadvantages:

❑ A JSP template would be project specific and would tend to be cumbersome and impractical for reuse amongst projects. XSLT documents are natively authored in XML and in comparison are extremely portable between projects.

❑ A JSP template system would have a higher training cost since each developer has to learn the rules of the unique JSP templates. XSLT already exists for styling XML and is becoming a standard format that many developers are learning.

To be fair XSLT has its own drawbacks. The major disadvantage of XSLT is ironically its biggest advantage. XSLT and the supporting standards form a large and rich environment. As a result fully mastering XSLT is something that can take a while for a programmer.

From a JSP programmer's perspective XSLT also brings a valuable new resource to the programming mix because web browsers are beginning to support it. Client-side XSLT support gives the option to transfer work to the client instead of keeping it on the server. Reducing a server's workload is key in scalability.

As more client-side tools besides web-browsers begin to support XML and XSLT this option could be much more heavily used by web applications. As a result XSLT should spark interest because of its flexibility and be regarded as a powerful tool to watch for a JSP developer. Here are some points to be aware of when choosing between client-side and server-side XSLT.

Some benefits of server-side XSL transformations:

❑ Simply put, the client doesn't have to support XML or XSLT. This is the factor that often determines the decision on where you apply the XSLT.

❑ Higher degree of data security. You can control the data before it is sent to a client. This means each user will only receive their specific data. This is a great security tool as you can finely control both the data being sent to the client and what client can see the data. Of course with security there are many other factors involved, however, having central control of the data is an important first step.

❑ Since you apply the style sheet on the server-side, there is 100% control over the format the user is given. (Of course different client tools could still change the way the final data appears). Keeping tight control over format is helpful when you use one dataset to drive presentations for different users. So on the server you could use one set of data and upon request of the data apply different style sheets depending on the user.

❑ Extending on the previous point, for large datasets you can reduce the amount of data sent to the client. Formatting can be conscious of bandwidth issues as well.

However, client-side XSL transformations also have some benefits:

❑ Most importantly, client-side transformations distribute the workload so the server doesn't have as much processing to perform. For high load systems this could be a major reason to use client-side XSLT.

❑ An XML data island is downloaded to the user. Since the user has local access to the raw data, it is possible to apply many different XSL transformations to the same data without having to go back to the web server. The major benefit is the data only needs to be downloaded once. Once the user has the data, then they are free to apply an infinite amount of different transformations on the same dataset. This reason is often a factor when your users have consistently low bandwidth or limited connection times.

Currently, performing the XSL transformation within the server environment is the most popular method of using XSLT. The major reason is that XSLT is still very new and client-side support is limited. Over the next few years as client-side support increases there will be more applications porting XSLT support to the client.

For our example we will keep all the XSLT on the server-side because of limited support in current web-browsers.

Step 1: Build the XML Source

Before styling we do need some XML content. Again we will reuse `links.xml` from the DOM example. If you have `links.xml` saved from the previous examples this step is already done. If not head back up and snag it from the DOM section.

Next we will work on the XSLT documents that will be needed to perform each of the transformations.

Step 2: The XSLT File

To transform the XML file we will need a few XSLT documents, one XSLT document for each desired output format. Each of these XSLT documents will need to be saved locally on your hard drive for use in the later steps. In our examples we will use the `C:\xml\` directory but you may use anything as long as the URI matches appropriately.

The first XSLT document will be for making the commonly known format of HTML. This first example will have many comments with the code to aid understanding of what exactly is going on. The rest of the XSLT documents will follow the same format so they will have much less explanation. In brief, this XSLT is going to make an HTML document with links to each of our 'link' elements in the original XML source.

The links_html XSL

Here is our XSLT document for `links_html.xsl`:

```
<?xml version="1.0"?>
<xsl:stylesheet
  xmlns:xsl="http://www.w3.org/1999/XSL/Transform"
  version="1.0">
<xsl:output method="html" indent="yes"/>
```

The header for XSLT documents is the default XML header. Remember XSLT is 100% XML compatible. Like the rest of the XML in this chapter you can manipulate XSLT documents in Java with tools such as the DOM, JDOM or SAX.

After the header is the XSLT namespace declaration along with a special `xsl` prefixed tag named output. The output tag will remove the default XML header from the output and also convert some XML syntax tags to HTML 4.0 tags. Since HTML is commonly used XSLT inherently provides support.

Next is the first template match on our XML document. This match will process every element titled `links` in our XML document. All tags inside a template without the `xsl` namespace will be sent directly to the output. Notice that all the tags without the `xsl` namespace are simply the HTML:

```
<xsl:template match="links">
<HTML>
  <HEAD>
    <TITLE>Fun with XSL</TITLE>
  </HEAD>
  <BODY>
    <table cellspacing="0" width="100%">
      <tr>
        <td class="clear" align="center">
        <table width="95%">
        <xsl:apply-templates select="link"/>
        </table>
        </td>
      </tr>
    </table>
  </BODY>
</HTML>
</xsl:template>
```

The first template has a call to another template for each element named `link` in our main links element. In our source XML document each link element describes an actual link to a resource. Here is where we add the appropriate HTML for each specific link:

```
<xsl:template match="link">
   <tr>
    <td class="clear">
     <table cellpadding="0" cellspacing="0" width="100%">
      <tr>
        <td style=" font-family: verdana; font-size: 10pt; background: #aabbbb;
border-style: groove; border-width:2px; border-color:#ffffff; padding:2px;">
```

Two xsl namespace tags called `use-attribute-sets` and `value-of` are new here. The xsl tag `use-attribute-sets` will call another set of tags similar to the xsl template tag. Instead of sending more tags to the output the `use-attribute-sets` will add attributes to the tag it was called in. The xsl `value-of` tag does exactly what it says. The value of our element named `text` will be inserted in the XSLT template:

```
      <A xsl:use-attribute-sets="a"><xsl:value-of select="text"/></A><br />
      </td>
     </tr>
     <tr>
      <td style=" font-family: verdana; font-size: 10pt; border-style: groove;
border-width:2px; border-color:#ffffff; padding:2px; background: #f5f5f5; border-
top-width:0px; padding-left:10px; padding-top:0px; margin-top:0px;">
```

Here the `value-of` tag is seen again. This time the author's name will be used from our XML document:

```
        <xsl:value-of select="author"/><br />
        </td>
      </tr>
      <tr>
        <td style=" font-family: verdana; font-size: 10pt; border-style: groove;
  border-width:2px; border-color:#ffffff; padding:2px; background: #eeeeee; border-
  top-width:0px; padding-left:10px; padding-top:0px; margin-top:0px;">
```

One last time the `value-of` tag is used for the description of the link:

```
        <xsl:value-of select="description"/><br />
        </td>
      </tr>
    </table>
   </td>
  </tr>
</xsl:template>
```

After the end of our template a description is needed for the `attribute-set` we called earlier. Inside this attribute set a name and value is placed for each attribute tag. We only have one attribute named `href` for our link and its value is set as the URL in our XML document:

```
<xsl:attribute-set name="a">
  <xsl:attribute name="href"><xsl:value-of select="url"/></xsl:attribute>
</xsl:attribute-set>
```

With all the templates and attribute sets done this XSLT is finished:

```
</xsl:stylesheet>
```

That is it for the first template. The above might be a little confusing if you are unfamiliar with XML and XSLT. The key point to remember with each of these templates is that they will transform our XML source into a new format. For this template the result will be basic HTML. The benefit of using XSLT for this is that we can add support for a new format by adding a new template.

The links_wml XSL

Here is the next template for supporting WML. WML is the Wireless Markup Language and is used on smaller devices such as web-enabled cell phones. WML is not the only markup for wireless devices but is currently popular. WML is fully XML compliant and has many similar tags to HTML. The WAP Forum standardizes WML.

The current WML specification can be found in pdf format at:
http://www.wapforum.org/what/technical.htm.

With no more delay here is the template (`links_wml.xsl`) for creating WML. Again this template is the same as the previous with the HTML tags swapped to WML:

```
<?xml version="1.0"?>

<xsl:stylesheet
  xmlns:xsl="http://www.w3.org/1999/XSL/Transform"
  version="1.0">
<xsl:output method="xml" indent="yes"/>
```

Again the default XML header is seen and the xsl output tag is called. This time the output will be XML compatible.

Next the same set of templates will be used substituting WML for the HTML. Don't worry about understanding the WML syntax; we will give a screen shot of what the result looks like on a WAP device:

```
<xsl:template match="links">
<xsl:text disable-output-escaping="yes">&lt;!DOCTYPE wml PUBLIC "-//WAPFORUM//DTD
WML 1.1//EN" "http://www.wapforum.org/DTD/wml_1.1.xml"&gt;</xsl:text>
<wml>
  <card id="card0" title="JSPInsider.com">
    <do type="prev" label="Back"><prev/></do>
    <p>
      <table columns="1">
        <xsl:apply-templates select="link"/>
      </table>
    </p>
  </card>
</wml>
</xsl:template>
```

The same link template is here as well. Each link from our XML is used when creating the WML output:

```
<xsl:template match="link">
<tr>
  <td class="clear"></td>
</tr>
<tr>
  <td>
    <a xsl:use-attribute-sets="a"><xsl:value-of select="text"/></a><br />
  </td>
</tr>
<tr>
  <td>
    <xsl:value-of select="author"/><br />
  </td>
</tr>
<tr>
  <td>
    <xsl:value-of select="description"/><br />
  </td>
</tr>
</xsl:template>
```

The identical attribute set is being reused from the first template. Since many of the markup languages have similar syntax, it is possible to reuse much of the XSLT templates for these various examples:

```
<xsl:attribute-set name="a">
  <xsl:attribute name="href"><xsl:value-of select="url"/></xsl:attribute>
</xsl:attribute-set>
```

The document is now done so we end it:

```
</xsl:stylesheet>
```

WML support is now available for our XML source. Once we create the JSP to combine these XSLT documents with our XML we will be in business. Let's make one more template before moving on to the JSP.

The final XSLT document will be for sending out a simplified XML tree. XSLT is often used to reformat XML data itself so different systems can use the same data. To show how this is done, we will take the original XML file and create a new one with only a subset of the data we need for our code.

The new XML file created is what we are calling the simplified tree. The simplified tree will contain nothing more than what is needed for the link check example in the DOM section of this chapter. We could use this method to simplify what our DOM in `dom_links.jsp` will represent. After all why have the DOM use memory to represent information we are not even using?

The links_xml XSL

Here is the XSLT document for `links_xml.xsl`:

```
<?xml version="1.0"?>
<xsl:stylesheet
  xmlns:xsl="http://www.w3.org/1999/XSL/Transform"
  version="1.0">
<xsl:output method="xml" indent="yes"/>

<xsl:template match="links">
<links>
  <xsl:apply-templates select="link"/>
</links>
</xsl:template>

<xsl:template match="link">
  <url>
  <xsl:value-of select="url"/>
  </url>
</xsl:template>

</xsl:stylesheet>
```

That is it for the XSLT templates. As we mentioned previously all of the example transformations will be done on the server-side using JSP. If you would like to try out a client-side transformations use the latest Internet Explorer or Mozilla browser.

For extra XSLT help for IE 5.5 see, http://www.netcrucible.com/xslt/msxml-faq.htm, or for Mozilla XSLT information see, http://www.mozilla.org/projects/xslt/.

Step 3: Build a Source Object

Source objects represent the XML data that will be used to create a final formatted output from our XSLT. Combining the source with our XSLT is done in the JAXP with a transformation. Do not confuse what we are calling a JAXP transformation with the 'T' at the end of XSLT. XSLT defines what a transformation should do. A JAXP transformation does what the XSLT document defines.

In JAXP a source is an actual interface. To define a source for a transformation we need to use an object that implements the source interface. Three objects in the JAXP 1.1 release implement the source interface and they are called StreamSource, DOMSource and SAXSource.

StreamSource

A StreamSource is a placeholder for a transformation source in the form of an XML stream. A StreamSource is a convenient object when you have an XML file or a string that you will be using as a source.

Here is code you would use for creating a StreamSource object from an XML file:

```
StreamSource ss = new StreamSource(new File("Your_xml_file.xml"));
```

Turning a String object in to a StreamSource object can be done similarly:

```
StreamSource ss = new StreamSource(new StringReader(new String()));
```

DOMSource

A DOMSource represents a node from a DOM object. The node could be as small as one data element or it could be the entire document the DOM is representing. You create the DOMSource to represent the piece of the DOM you would like to modify or work with. Once you have the DOMSource you can then use it to perform a transformation.

Here is some code showing how a Document object can be used as a DOMSource:

```
DocumentBuilderFactory dbf = DocumentBuilderFactory.newInstance();
DocumentBuilder db = dbf.newDocumentBuilder();
Document d = db.parse("Your_xml_file.xml");
DOMSource ds = new DOMSource(d);
```

SAXSource

A SAXSource object represents a SAX-style source. SAXSource objects can be constructed out of an XMLReader object or any InputSource object. Check the JAXP 1.1 javadocs for more information about XMLReader and InputSource.

Here is some code showing how a SAXSource can be created from a FileReader object:

```
SAXSource ss = new SAXSource(
  new InputSource(new FileReader("Your_xml_file.xml")));
```

Creating a StreamSource

For step five in this tutorial we will need an XML source and an XSLT source for a JAXP transformation. The sources we will use are two `StreamSource` objects made from `links.xml` and `links_html.xsl`.

Here is the code for our XML source:

```
StreamSource xml = new StreamSource(new File("c:/xml/links.xml"));
```

Here is the code for our XSLT source:

```
StreamSource xsl =
  new StreamSource(new File("c:/xml/links_html.xsl"));
```

Step 4: Build a Result Object

`Result` objects are the output of a JAXP transformation. The result does not have to be in XML format, it can be in many different forms such as HTML, XML, WML or even plain text. The result object is actually an interface and should not be declared as an object itself. In the JAXP 1.1 three objects use the `Result` interface: `StreamResult`, `DOMResult` and `SAXResult`.

StreamResult

A `StreamResult` acts as a holder for a transformation result that is a stream. `StreamResult` is commonly used when writing the transformation result to a file or the JSP output stream.

Here is some code for writing a JAXP transformation to a file:

```
StreamResult sr = new StreamResult(new File("example.out"));
```

Here is some code for writing a JAXP transformation to output of a JSP:

```
StreamResult sr = new StreamResult(out);
```

DOMResult

A `DOMResult` holds the result of a transformation in a DOM tree object. The object can then be further manipulated as a `Document` object. When it is convenient to pass a `Document` object between applications this type of result should be used:

```
DocumentBuilderFactory dbf = DocumentBuilderFactory.newInstance();
DocumentBuilder db = dbf.newDocumentBuilder();
Document d = db.newDocument();
DOMResult dr = new DOMResult(d);
```

SAXResult

A `SAXResult` is a holder for a JAXP transformation in an object that implements the `ContentHandler` interface for handling SAX events. These objects can be customized to a great extent for working with SAX.

For an example snippet we will use the basic `DefaultHandler` object. In a practical situation you would use an object customized to accept SAX events and do whatever task you were trying to accomplish:

```
SAXResult sr = new SAXResult(new DefaultHandler());
```

Displaying the Results

For this step-by-step tutorial we will use the `out` implicit object to display the result of our JAXP transformations. The code from the second `StreamSource` example is exactly what we need.

Here is the code for our `StreamResult`:

```
StreamResult result = new StreamResult(out);
```

Step 5: Transform the Data

Taking steps one through four we now have enough information to do a sample JAXP transformation. Using scriptlets we will make a JSP that performs a transformation using our sources from step three and our result from step four.

Here is the code for `example_transformation.jsp`:

```
<%@ page
   import="javax.xml.parsers.*,
            org.w3c.dom.*,
            javax.xml.transform.*,
            javax.xml.transform.stream.*,
            java.io.*"%>
<%
StreamSource xml = new StreamSource(new File("c:/xml/links.xml"));
StreamSource xsl = new StreamSource(new File("c:/xml/links_html.xsl"));

StreamResult result = new StreamResult(out);
```

For a transformation a `TransformerFactory` is required so we can then produce a transformer object. When constructing a `Transformer` object we will take advantage of the option to associate an XSLT source. For this example we will use the `StreamSource` representing `links_html.xsl`:

```
TransformerFactory tFactory = TransformerFactory.newInstance();
Transformer transformer = tFactory.newTransformer(xsl);
```

Once we have a `Transformer` object it is possible to perform a JAXP transformation. For the transformation we need to provide a parameter specifying the XML source and where we want the destination of the transformation result:

```
transformer.transform(xml, result);
%>
```

The result will be an HTML page with links and descriptions to the resources in our XML file:

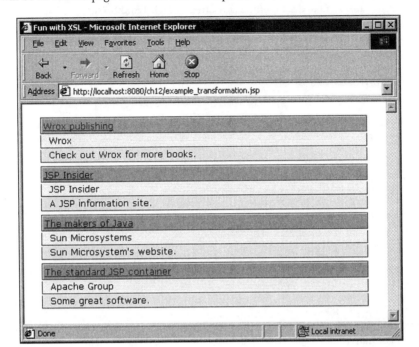

We will not end the tutorial here. As mentioned in the beginning we are trying to create a generic tag library providing easy access to the functionality of the JAXP. For this tag library we will need some custom JavaBeans and some tags.

Step 6: Build a JavaBean to Access XML Data

Now that the basic mechanics have been explained it is now possible to begin writing reusable code. The first step is to build a JavaBean for specifying sources and the result for a transformation. The Bean will be very useful so that we may specify information for the transformation anywhere and then pass it along as needed. To keep all of the flexibility of the JAXP this Bean will need to allow each of the various `Source` and `Result` objects. To implement this flexibility three main objects will be created and named `XMLSource`, `XSLSource` and `transformationResult` and be used as follows:

❑ `XMLSource`
Holds the XML resource to be used in the transformation. Since this could be either a `StreamSource`, `DOMSource` or `SAXSource` initially it will be declared as an object and later cast into the appropriate type.

❑ `XSLSource`
Holds the XSL resource to be used in the transformation. Exactly like the `XMLSource`, `XSLSource` will initially be declared as an object and later cast into the appropriate type at transformation.

❑ `transformationResult`
Represents the output of the transformation. Since the JAXP is capable of `StreamResult`, `DOMResult` and `SAXResult` this will also initially be declared as an object and later cast as needed.

All of the above objects will also have get and set methods for each type of possible cast. This means that each object will have three get and set methods for Stream, DOM and SAX.

With the above said here is our code that does exactly that. The next section will cover creating the JAXP transformer.

The JAXPTransformerResources Class

Save this file to `WEB-INF/classes/com/jspinsider/jspkit/jaxp`:

```
package com.jspinsider.jspkit.jaxp;

import javax.xml.transform.dom.DOMSource;
import javax.xml.transform.dom.DOMResult;
import javax.xml.transform.stream.StreamSource;
import javax.xml.transform.stream.StreamResult;
import javax.xml.transform.sax.SAXResult;
import javax.xml.transform.sax.SAXSource;
import java.lang.Object;

public class JAXPTransformerResources extends java.lang.Object implements
java.io.Serializable
{
```

Here are the three main objects of the Bean. Each of these resources is kept as an object to allow for the DOM, SAX and Stream sources:

```
private Object XMLSource;
private Object XSLSource;
private Object transformResult;

public JAXPTransformerResources(){}
```

Each resource needs the appropriate get method:

```
public Object getXMLSource(){ return XMLSource; }
public Object getXSLSource(){ return XSLSource; }
public Object getTransformResult(){ return transformResult; }
```

Next each resource has the appropriate set method to complement the gets:

```
public void setXMLStreamSource(StreamSource newXMLStreamSource)
    { XMLSource = newXMLStreamSource; }
public void setXMLDOMSource(DOMSource newXMLDOMSource)
    { XMLSource = newXMLDOMSource; }
public void setXMLSAXSource(SAXSource newXMLSAXSource)
    { XMLSource = newXMLSAXSource; }
public void setXSLStreamSource(StreamSource newXSLStreamSource)
    { XSLSource = newXSLStreamSource; }
public void setXSLDOMSource(DOMSource newXSLDOMSource)
    { XSLSource = newXSLDOMSource; }
public void setXSLSAXSource(SAXSource newXSLSAXSource)
    { XSLSource = newXSLSAXSource; }
public void setStreamResult(StreamResult newStreamResult)
```

```
    { transformResult = newStreamResult; }
  public void setDOMResult(DOMResult newDOMResult)
    { transformResult = newDOMResult; }
  public void setSAXResult(SAXResult newSAXResult)
    { transformResult = newSAXResult; }
}
```

Step 7: Build an XML JavaBean to Transform the XML Data

The next object we require is one that does the actual transformation. All that is needed for this object is a few constructors and a method calling for a JAXP transformation using the above resource object. The next step will be to make this Bean into a custom tag for easy use with a JSP.

The JAXPTransformer Class

Save the file to WEB-INF/classes/com/jspinsider/jspkit/jaxp:

```
package com.jspinsider.jspkit.jaxp;

import java.lang.Object;
import javax.xml.transform.TransformerFactory;
import javax.xml.transform.Transformer;
import javax.xml.transform.dom.DOMSource;
import javax.xml.transform.dom.DOMResult;
import javax.xml.transform.stream.StreamSource;
import javax.xml.transform.stream.StreamResult;
import javax.xml.transform.sax.SAXResult;
import javax.xml.transform.sax.SAXSource;
import javax.xml.transform.TransformerException;

public class JAXPTransformer extends java.lang.Object
        implements java.io.Serializable {
```

First an object is declared for holding our JAXPTransformerResources object. Next the default public constructor made along with a constructor that will take a JAXPTransformerResources object:

```
JAXPTransformerResources source;

public JAXPTransformer(){}

public JAXPTransformer(JAXPTransformerResources source)
        throws TransformerException {
  transform(source);
}
```

The transform method of this object will do the actual JAXP transformation. If the resources are not set properly then an error will be thrown to reflect that:

```
public void transform (JAXPTransformerResources source)
        throws TransformerException {
```

Inside the transform method our three requirements for a JAXP transformation are extracted from the JAXPTransformationResources object:

```
Object XMLSource = source.getXMLSource();
Object XSLSource = source.getXSLSource();
Object transformResult = source.getTransformResult();

TransformerFactory tFactory = TransformerFactory.newInstance();
Transformer transformer = tFactory.newTransformer();
```

The code for the JAXP transformation is the same as seen in step five except that we now need to determine what type of source is being used from our main objects. The XSLSource object is compared against its three possibilities and set when correct:

```
if(XSLSource.getClass().getName().compareTo
           ("javax.xml.transform.stream.StreamSource") == 0)
  transformer = tFactory.newTransformer((StreamSource)XSLSource);

if(XSLSource.getClass().getName().compareTo
           ("javax.xml.transform.dom.DOMSource") == 0)
  transformer = tFactory.newTransformer((DOMSource)XSLSource);

if(XSLSource.getClass().getName().compareTo
           ("javax.xml.transform.sax.SAXSource") == 0)
  transformer = tFactory.newTransformer((SAXSource)XSLSource);
```

The last step in the transformation is accomplished in the same fashion as the previous example. To determine what class XMLSource and transformResult are they are compared against the possibilities. When the correct two matches are found the transformation is finally called and our method is complete:

```
if(XMLSource.getClass().getName().compareTo
           ("javax.xml.transform.stream.StreamSource") == 0) {
    if(transformResult.getClass().getName().compareTo
           ("javax.xml.transform.stream.StreamResult") == 0)
      transformer.transform((StreamSource)XMLSource,
                             (StreamResult)transformResult);
    if(transformResult.getClass().getName().compareTo
                     ("javax.xml.transform.dom.DOMResult") == 0)
      transformer.transform((StreamSource)XMLSource, (DOMResult)transformResult);
    if(transformResult.getClass().getName().compareTo
                     ("javax.xml.transform.sax.SAXResult") == 0)
      transformer.transform((StreamSource)XMLSource, (SAXResult)transformResult);
}

if(XMLSource.getClass().getName().compareTo
           ("javax.xml.transform.dom.DOMSource") == 0) {
    if(transformResult.getClass().getName().compareTo
           ("javax.xml.transform.stream.StreamResult") == 0)
      transformer.transform((DOMSource)XMLSource, (StreamResult)transformResult);
    if(transformResult.getClass().getName().compareTo
           ("javax.xml.transform.dom.DOMResult") == 0)
      transformer.transform((DOMSource)XMLSource, (DOMResult)transformResult);
    if(transformResult.getClass().getName().compareTo
           ("javax.xml.transform.sax.SAXResult") == 0)
      transformer.transform((DOMSource)XMLSource, (SAXResult)transformResult);
}
if(XMLSource.getClass().getName().compareTo
```

```
                  ("javax.xml.transform.sax.SAXSource") == 0) {
       if(transformResult.getClass().getName().compareTo
               ("javax.xml.transform.stream.StreamResult") == 0)
        transformer.transform((SAXSource)XMLSource,(StreamResult)transformResult);
       if(transformResult.getClass().getName().compareTo
               ("javax.xml.transform.dom.DOMResult") == 0)
        transformer.transform((SAXSource)XMLSource, (DOMResult)transformResult);
       if(transformResult.getClass().getName().compareTo
               ("javax.xml.transform.sax.SAXResult") == 0)
        transformer.transform((SAXSource)XMLSource, (SAXResult)transformResult);
   }
 }
```

The last two methods are the simple get and set for the `JAXPTransformerResources` object:

```
public void setTransformerResources(JAXPTransformerResources new_resources) {
  source = new_resources;
}

public JAXPTransformerResources getTransformerResources() {
  return source;
}
}
```

Step 8: Create a JAXP Tag Library Interface

Finally let's put all of the code into an easy and reusable tag library. By doing this we can use a few tags in our JSP to accomplish a complete JAXP transformation. To picture what we are talking about, imagine using the simple tags below instead of steps one through four. That is what we are building here:

```
<transform>
    <xmlFile>c:/xml/links.xml</xmlFile>
    <xslFile>c:/xml/links_html.xsl</xslFile>
</transform>
```

In Chapters 8 to 11 tag libraries are extensively covered. For now, the important thing to know about tag libraries is that they are a method of making your code easy to use. They do this by moving scriptlets from your JSP page and enclosing them within special tag handler objects. The intersection of these tag handler objects and your JSP container are some special XML configuration files that describe your tag library. As we build the JAXP tags we will walk you through where to place everything.

The first thing needed for our tag library are some custom tag handler objects. The first of these tag handler objects will be the transformer tag seen surrounding the `xslFile` and `xmlFile` tags above.

The JAXPTransformerTag Class

Save the file to `WEB-INF/classes/com/jspinsider/jspkit/jaxp`:

```
package com.jspinsider.jspkit.jaxp;

import java.io.IOException;
import java.io.File;
import javax.xml.transform.dom.DOMSource;
```

```
import javax.xml.transform.dom.DOMResult;
import javax.xml.transform.stream.StreamSource;
import javax.xml.transform.stream.StreamResult;
import javax.xml.transform.sax.SAXResult;
import javax.xml.transform.sax.SAXSource;
import javax.servlet.jsp.*;
import javax.servlet.jsp.tagext.*;
import javax.servlet.*;

public class JAXPTransformerTag extends BodyTagSupport {
  JAXPTransformer transformer = new JAXPTransformer();
  JAXPTransformerResources resources = new JAXPTransformerResources();
  boolean isResources = false;

  public void setTransformerResources(String new_resources) {
    resources = (JAXPTransformerResources)pageContext.getAttribute
            (new_resources, pageContext.getAttributesScope(new_resources));
    isResources = true;
  }
```

Set methods are available in this tag for each of the three types of the two `Source` objects. Without these we could not preserve the flexibility the JAXP offers for source types:

```
public void setXSLStreamSource(StreamSource new_XSLStreamSource)
  { resources.setXSLStreamSource(new_XSLStreamSource); }
public void setXSLSAXSource(SAXSource new_XSLSAXSource)
  { resources.setXSLSAXSource(new_XSLSAXSource); }
public void setXSLDOMSource(DOMSource new_XSLDOMSource)
  { resources.setXSLDOMSource(new_XSLDOMSource); }
public void setXMLStreamSource(StreamSource new_XMLStreamSource)
  { resources.setXMLStreamSource(new_XMLStreamSource); }
public void setXMLSAXSource(SAXSource new_XMLSAXSource)
  { resources.setXMLSAXSource(new_XMLSAXSource); }
public void setXMLDOMSource(DOMSource new_XMLDOMSource)
  { resources.setXMLDOMSource(new_XMLDOMSource); }
```

Set methods are also made available for all of the result types in the JAXP:

```
public void setStreamResult(StreamResult new_StreamResult)
  { resources.setStreamResult(new_StreamResult); }
public void setSAXResult(SAXResult new_SAXResult)
  { resources.setSAXResult(new_SAXResult); }
public void setDOMResult(DOMResult new_DOMResult)
  { resources.setDOMResult(new_DOMResult); }
```

When the first `transformer` tag is used in a JSP page the output of our transformation will default to the JSP implicit `out` object. Later on this can be changed at will:

```
public int doStartTag() throws JspTagException {
  if (!isResources) resources.setStreamResult
        (new StreamResult(pageContext.getOut()));
    // Have the JSP Container continue processing the JSP page as normal.
    return EVAL_PAGE;
}
```

When the end `transform` tag is encountered a JAXP transformation will then take place:

```
public int doEndTag() throws JspTagException {
  try {
    transformer.transform(resources);
  }
  catch (Exception e) {
    throw new JspTagException("JSP Kit JAXPTransformerTag Error:" +
                                  e.toString());
  }
  // Have the JSP Container continue processing the JSP page as normal.
  return EVAL_PAGE;
  }
}
```

The above tag definitely has a lot of code but does nothing without having the resources needed in a transformation. For this tag two different mechanisms exist to allow resources to get set for our transformation. A `JAXPTransformationResources` Bean could be initialized for the process, but this would only work for experienced Java programmers because scriptlets would be needed to complement the Bean. Instead let's create some more custom tags for setting resources by simply typing in the resource or result URI.

If you wish to make some of your own custom tags these next two sections of code will serve as a good template. The only thing you will need to change is what gets done with the `BodyContent`, the text that is placed inside your custom tag. The next two pieces of code will be used for the tags named `xmlFile` and `xslFile` seen at the beginning of this step.

The JAXPTransformerXMLFileTag Class

Save this file to `WEB-INF/classes/com/jspinsider/jspkit/jaxp`:

```
package com.jspinsider.jspkit.jaxp;

import java.io.IOException;
import java.io.File;
import javax.xml.transform.stream.StreamSource;
import javax.xml.transform.stream.StreamResult;
import javax.servlet.jsp.*;
import javax.servlet.jsp.tagext.*;
import javax.servlet.*;
import java.io.StringReader;
import java.io.StringWriter;

public class JAXPTransformerXMLFileTag extends BodyTagSupport
{
  /* The JSP container calls this function when it encounters the
     end of the Tag. */
  public int doEndTag() throws JspTagException {
    try {
```

The only part of this code that we will comment on is this section including the `BodyContent` object. The `BodyContent` contains what is typed in between the start and end of our custom tag. You can see here that we use this text as the URI to the XML source file:

```
        BodyContent lbc_bodycurrent = getBodyContent();
        StringWriter sw = new StringWriter();
        lbc_bodycurrent.writeOut(sw);
        File f = new File(sw.toString());
        JAXPTransformerTag tag =
                (JAXPTransformerTag)findAncestorWithClass(this,
                        com.jspinsider.jspkit.jaxp.JAXPTransformerTag.class);
        tag.setXMLStreamSource(new StreamSource(f));
    }
    catch (Exception e) {
      throw new JspTagException("JSP Kit JAXPTransformerXMLFileTag Error:" +
                                e.toString());
    }

    // Have the JSP Container continue processing the JSP page as normal.
    return EVAL_PAGE;
  }
}
```

Next comes the code for the xslFile tag seen at the beginning of this step. As you might have guessed the code for this tag is almost identical to the above except for its name and one function call.

The JAXPTransformerXSLFileTag Class

Save this file to WEB-INF/classes/com/jspinsider/jspkit/jaxp:

```
package com.jspinsider.jspkit.jaxp;

import java.io.IOException;
import java.io.File;
import javax.xml.transform.stream.StreamSource;
import javax.xml.transform.stream.StreamResult;
import javax.servlet.jsp.*;
import javax.servlet.jsp.tagext.*;
import javax.servlet.*;
import java.io.StringReader;
import java.io.StringWriter;

public class JAXPTransformerXSLFileTag extends BodyTagSupport {
  public int doEndTag() throws JspTagException {
    try {
      /* Gather up the contents between the start and end of our tag */
      BodyContent lbc_bodycurrent = getBodyContent();
      StringWriter sw = new StringWriter();
      lbc_bodycurrent.writeOut(sw);
      File f = new File(sw.toString());
      JAXPTransformerTag tag = (JAXPTransformerTag)findAncestorWithClass(this,
                      com.jspinsider.jspkit.jaxp.JAXPTransformerTag.class);
```

Please note the one difference from the previous object is that the setXSLStreamSource() method is called instead of the setXMLStreamSource():

```
      tag.setXSLStreamSource(new StreamSource(f));
    }
    catch (Exception e) {
      throw new JspTagException("JSP Kit JAXPTransformerXSLFileTag Error:" +
                                e.toString());
    }
    // Have the JSP Container continue processing the JSP page as normal.
```

```
            return EVAL_PAGE;
    }
}
```

Now that we have built our custom tag objects to perform the work, we need to tell our JSP container about them, so we can use them.

Step 9: Using the JAXP Tag Library in a JSP Page

Finally we can actually use the tags seen in step eight. The JSP for this example will actually be quite small since all of our code is in the above Beans and tags. This is good because now just about anyone can use the transformer tag. Even if the page editors have no experience with Java they can now specify a few simple tags and everything will work. Of course your page editors will still need to be able to match up a URI to what they type between tags. So if your editors are smart enough to know about what a URI is then you are set, other wise you might have to help in the set up a little.

To get this tag to work we need to do two more simple steps. First we need to insert into the web.xml some XML to tell the JSP container about the tags. The second step is to include a special file called a tag library descriptor (TLD) that describes the custom tag.

Both the XML file fragment to be inserted within web.xml and the TLD file are included with the code for this book.

Additions to web.xml

To let your JSP container know about these new custom tags you must edit the web.xml file in your JSP project's WEB_INF directory to include the code below:

```
<?xml version="1.0" encoding="ISO-8859-1"?>

<!DOCTYPE web-app
    PUBLIC "-//Sun Microsystems, Inc.//DTD Web Application 2.2//EN"
    "http://java.sun.com/j2ee/dtds/web-app_2.2.dtd">

<web-app>
    <taglib>
        <taglib-uri>
        http://www.jspinsider.com/jspkit/JAXP
        </taglib-uri>
        <taglib-location>
            /WEB-INF/JAXP.tld
        </taglib-location>
    </taglib>
</web-app>
```

Next you will need to add the JAXP.tld file in your WEB-INF folder for this JSP project. The TLD just tells the system where to find our tags and what attributes are within the tag on the JSP page. Once you have installed this file and updated the web.xml file, restart Tomcat so it can learn about the JAXP tag and then everything is set to go.

The JAXP TLD

```xml
<?xml version="1.0" encoding="ISO-8859-1" ?>
<!DOCTYPE taglib
        PUBLIC "-//Sun Microsystems, Inc.//DTD JSP Tag Library 1.1//EN"
        "http://java.sun.com/j2ee/dtds/web-jsptaglibrary_1_1.dtd">
<taglib>
  <tlibversion>1.0</tlibversion>
  <jspversion>1.1</jspversion>
  <shortname>JAXPTransformerTag</shortname>
  <uri></uri>
  <info>
    A tag for XML transformations using XSL via Sun's JAXP.
  </info>

  <tag>
    <name>transformer</name>
    <tagclass>com.jspinsider.jspkit.jaxp.JAXPTransformerTag</tagclass>
    <info>Uses Sun's JAXP to do a transformation given an XML source, XSL source
and output result.</info>
    <attribute>
        <name>transformerResources</name>
        <required>false</required>
    </attribute>
  </tag>
  <tag>
    <name>xmlFile</name>
    <tagclass>com.jspinsider.jspkit.jaxp.JAXPTransformerXMLFileTag</tagclass>
    <info>XML file Source tag for the JAXPTransformerTag</info>
  </tag>
  <tag>
    <name>xslFile</name>
    <tagclass>com.jspinsider.jspkit.jaxp.JAXPTransformerXSLFileTag</tagclass>
    <info>XSL file Source tag for the JAXPTransformerTag</info>
  </tag>
</taglib>
```

Here is an example JSP page that uses the transformer tag. Notice it looks very much like the example we mentioned in step eight:

```jsp
<%@ taglib uri="http://www.jspinsider.com/jspkit/JAXP" prefix="JAXP"%>
<JAXP:transformer>
  <JAXP:xmlFile>Your_XML_File.xml</JAXP:xmlFile>
  <JAXP:xslFile>Your_XSL_File.xsl</JAXP:xslFile>
</JAXP:transformer>
```

Using the XSLT documents built in step three we can now have some real fun. Everything is now set and all we need to do is use our templates. Let's start by again demonstrating the HTML example but this time using the custom tags.

The links_html JSP

```jsp
<%@ taglib uri="http://www.jspinsider.com/jspkit/JAXP" prefix="JAXP"%>
<JAXP:transformer>
  <JAXP:xmlFile>c:/xml/links.xml</JAXP:xmlFile>
  <JAXP:xslFile>c:/xml/links_html.xsl</JAXP:xslFile>
</JAXP:transformer>
```

448

We encourage you to actually run these examples mostly because they are fun. Since this is a book we will also show you a screenshot of the output. The output looks the same as before.

For our WML JSP we use the same tags but change the XSLT sheet to be `links_wml.xsl`.

The links_wml JSP

```
<%@ page contentType="text/vnd.wap.wml" %>
<%@ taglib uri="http://www.jspinsider.com/jspkit/JAXP" prefix="JAXP"%>
<JAXP:transformer>
  <JAXP:xmlFile>c:/xml/links.xml</JAXP:xmlFile>
  <JAXP:xslFile>c:/xml/links_wml.xsl</JAXP:xslFile>
</JAXP:transformer>
```

And here is what the phone displays (if you have the Opera web browser you can also view this page with it):

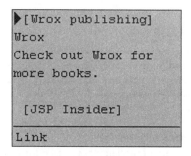

Setting up an actual WAP server to serve the WML to real WAP devices is a completely different story. If you noticed we actually just used a WAP emulator to show our WML. You can download this WAP browser yourself from http://developer.openwave.com/download/license_41.html and test the output.

The links_xml JSP

```
<%@ taglib uri="http://www.jspinsider.com/jspkit/JAXP" prefix="JAXP"%>
<JAXP:transformer>
  <JAXP:xmlFile>c:/xml/links.xml</JAXP:xmlFile>
  <JAXP:xslFile>c:/xml/links_xml.xsl</JAXP:xslFile>
</JAXP:transformer>
```

And the simplified XML tree ends up like this:

```
<?xml version="1.0" encoding="UTF-8"?>
<links>
<url>http://www.wrox.com</url>
<url>http://www.jspinsider.com</url>
<url>http://java.sun.com</url>
<url>http://jakarta.apache.org</url>
</links>
```

Fine Points of JAXP

Be sure to try the above examples when you get a chance. The combination of XML, XSLT and JSP permits a developer to accomplish quite a bit of work with relative ease. Now is the time to become creative. The output and input can be from any sort of resource.

In building JSP applications, developers tend to think of a traditional web application delivering data to human clients on the web. However, this is rapidly changing and many web applications are dealing with other applications. One of the fastest growing markets is getting application servers to share data with each other. The marketplace of SOAP and inter-application communication should be one of the hot areas of development over the next few years. Code like JAXP will be one of the tools needed to build these new systems.

If anything the above example should illustrate some of the benefits of using XML in general. For JSP we have just constructed a very flexible and generic tool that links our XML to Java. Just about anything could be tied into this process. Using a database? No problem, many databases can now produce pure XML result sets. If not just add another step to the chain that converts your database results to XML and pump it through your new custom tags.

As mentioned before the above tag library will be available from Wrox with this book.

XML Syntax for JSP 1.2

All of the above sections have focused on using content described by XML with your JSP. Now we will briefly look at an XML related enhancement promised with the JSP 1.2 specification. The enhancement we are talking about is JSP code that is 100% compatible XML syntax.

With JSP compliant in XML syntax we will be able to use JSP code with any XML utility. Keep in mind we mentioned XML based JSP is promised with the JSP 1.2 specification. As of publication of this book the JSP 1.2 specs are not official and have plenty of disclaimers in place for change. However, it is highly doubtful that these specs will significantly change before being finished so we will give a little preview. Tomcat 4.0 is geared towards supporting all the JSP1.2 specs.

Goodbye Normal JSP Syntax?

No, in the proposed final draft the original syntax for JSP is not being deprecated. Just because JSP will be XML compliant in its new syntax does not mean it is the best solution. The new XML JSP syntax has both advantages:

- ❑ JSP code can now be authored in an XML compatible syntax. Tools designed to work with XML can be used with JSP code.

- ❑ XML content can be natively added in to a JSP document using the new XML syntax.

- ❑ A container that follows the JSP 1.2 specifications will automatically validate XML syntax JSP. Same as every other XML compatible language you will be forced to use correct XML syntax when using XML syntax JSP code.

- ❑ JSP can now be 100% dynamic in XML syntax. Complete applications can be produced on the fly using already existing XML tools. The usefulness of this will have to be seen as more developers have time to work with the JSP 1.2 specification.

and disadvantages:

- ❑ Full support for JSP 1.2 specifications will take time to implement. First generation utilities will not truly show all the impacts of XML syntax JSP.

- ❑ Projects using JSP documents will require everyone coding to know basic XML syntax. XML does have a learning curve regardless if it is an easy one.

❑ A web designer using JSP as HTML with custom tags will not be able to use JSP in the same method if the XML syntax is being used.

Making JSP Compatible with XML

XML syntax JSP is not a very difficult transition from traditional JSP. Since parts of JSP were already XML based some tags had no need for a change. Here is a summary of some of the important features of JSP in XML syntax and a chart for some of the easy changes:

❑ XML syntax JSP works the same as JSP always has and uses a JSP 1.2 compliant container. If you are already using a JSP 1.2 compliant container you will not have to install any new software.

❑ When using an include directive it is valid to have the included fragment be in either syntax; however, the same fragment cannot intermix syntax styles.

❑ If a tag is already XML compliant, the syntax is unchanged.

❑ Request-time attributes are in the form of '%= text %' with optional white space around the argument.

❑ Plain text may not be outside a tag because it breaks XML rules. New 'cdata' tags are used for this.

A lot of JSP syntax is already XML compliant including any custom tag library. For the tags that did need a change of syntax it was usually intuitive. Here is a chart of XML versus traditional JSP syntax from the JSP 1.2 proposed final draft specification. After the chart we will give a more in depth explanation of some of the more significant changes:

Traditional JSP Syntax	XML JSP Syntax
`<% page ... %>`	`<jsp:directive.page ... />`
`<%@ taglib ... %>`	See `<jsp:root>` element
`<%@ include ... %>`	`<jsp:directive.include ... />`
`<%! ...%>`	`<jsp:declaration> ... </jsp:declaration>`
`<% ...%>`	`<jsp:scriptlet> ... </jsp:scriptlet>`
`<%= ...%>`	`<jsp:expression> ... </jsp:expression>`

As you can see we were not lying when saying most of the changes were intuitive. Scriptlets, expressions, declarations and directives are now just placed in a self-named XML tag. Only the `taglib` directive is left as a slight mystery in the above chart. Below we will cover the `taglib` directive mystery as well as some of the new additions needed for JSP in XML syntax.

<jsp:root> ... </jsp:root>

The root element for all XML syntax JSP documents is `jsp:root`. Inside this element is an attribute `xmlns` that allows for all of the standard JSP 1.2 XML tags to be used as well as any custom taglibs. The `xmlns` attribute follows the syntax of `xmlns:prefix="uri"`.

Here is an example given in the JSP 1.2 proposed final draft:

```
<jsp:root
  xmlns:jsp="http://java.sun.com/jsp_1_2"
  xmlns:prefix1="URE-fortaglib1"
  xmlns:prefix2="URI-for-taglib2" ... >
    JSP Page
</jsp:root>
```

This example shows how the required first `xmlns` attribute is used to enable the standard JSP document tags. The next prefix declarations would be for other taglibs being used in the JSP document. No other attributes should be declared inside the `jsp:root` element.

<jsp:cdata> ... </jsp:cdata>

Something new with JSP but familiar in XML is CDATA. CDATA is information that does not pertain to the XML structure but needs to be included in your document. You can think of this as the plain text you normally would write outside of tags in HTML. This plain text is referred to as the template data stored within your `jsp:cdata` tags.

Here is the example given in the JSP 1.2 proposed final draft:

```
<jsp:cdata> template data </jsp:cdata>
```

`template data` would be passed to the current value of `out`.

`jsp:cdata` tags have no attributes and are allowed anywhere that template data may appear. In your final JSP document template data should only appear inside a `jsp:cdata` element. If you want to use XML compliant tags outside of `jsp` namespace tags you may. Content used in a JSP document outside of `jsp` namespace tags is called an XML fragment.

XML Fragments

XML fragments are allowed anywhere that a `jsp:cdata` is allowed in a JSP document. The interpretation of the XML fragment gets passed to the current output of the JSP page with the fragment's white space preserved. A key difference between `jsp:cdata` and XML fragments is that an XSL transformation will see an XML fragment; however, it will not see the content of a `jsp:cdata` tag. Remember anything inside a `cdata` section is considered content of the `cdata` tag.

An Example JSP Document

Now let's look at a real example of a JSP page in the older style syntax and then the same page converted to XML syntax JSP. Earlier in the chapter we created a tag library for a web site using XML content. For this example we will take that same page and rewrite it in to a JSP document.

Here is the previous example:

```
<%@ taglib uri="http://www.jspinsider.com/jspkit/JAXP" prefix="JAXP"%>
<JAXP:transformer>
  <JAXP:xmlFile>c:/xml/links.xml</JAXP:xmlFile>
  <JAXP:xslFile>c:/xml/links_html.xsl</JAXP:xslFile>
</JAXP:transformer>
```

And now here would be the equivalent in XML syntax. Keep in mind not all JSP containers yet support the JSP 1.2 specifications, though our examples work on Tomcat 4.0:

```
<jsp:root
   xmlns:jsp="http://java.sun.com/jsp_1_2"
   xmlns:JAXP="http://www.jspinsider.com/jspkit/JAXP">
<JAXP:transformer>
   <JAXP:xmlFile><jsp:cdata>c:/xml/links.xml</jsp:cdata></JAXP:xmlFile>
   <JAXP:xslFile><jsp:cdata>c:/xml/links_html.xsl</jsp:cdata></JAXP:xslFile>
</JAXP:transformer>
</jsp:root>
```

The above was rather easy and it should not be much of a shock. While XML syntax JSP is new it is not a totally different beast. Both of the above examples will work identically in a JSP 1.2 container.

The decision to use XML syntax JSP should be based on your needs. Not all projects will benefit from using XML syntax. Along with the benefits of XML specifications also comes the drawback of well-formed coding rules. Sometimes it will just be easier to write your JSP in the normal syntax and allow for non-XML programmers to edit away. Also XML syntax can dramatically increase the size of a simple JSP page. Overall the new syntax for JSP should be seen as an additional tool to be used as needed. The original syntax of JSP can still be a blessing.

Dynamic JSP Made Easy with XML

To end the chapter we wanted to show you one of the most powerful aspects of JSP in XML syntax.

With JSP in XML syntax we can now use all the already existing XML tools to make dynamic JSP. In the past this was rarely done since parsing a JSP page would be a difficult and slow task. Now with the combination of the XML, JSP syntax and XML tools, new doors of opportunity have been opened to the programmer.

It should be noted right away that this is not a technique you will want to use everywhere since it comes at the high price of interpreting your JSP page every time you modify it. However, in certain circumstances there can be practical purposes for this technique. Some of the ways this technique can be useful are:

❑　JSP sites can be self-updating. At first glance this doesn't seem like a big issue, after all, database sites already change when you update the database. However, changing the database doesn't change the internal logic of the JSP pages that drives the site. With JSP you now have easy access to the code stored on your page. This opens up the possibility for a web site to grow and expand itself driven by its own logic.

❑　It is common to see an IDE tool generically build a site quickly for a user. What these tools usually don't do would be to go back and change a site once the tool has generated the initial version. Since a JSP site can be 100% XML compatible, it becomes easy for the tool to go back and re-modify the site. Over the next few years some extremely advanced JSP site management tools might appear.

We will build a simple example which will show you how to dynamically modify an XML based JSP. This example uses JDOM and we will also expand your knowledge of how to use JDOM.

An Example Dynamic JSP

This example consists of three parts. The first page is `dynamic_test.jsp`, which is the JSP page we will dynamically modify with another JSP page. The second page is `dynamic_link.jsp` which when called modifies `dynamic_test.jsp`. Finally you will need the `links.xml` from the previous examples. This XML file will provide the data which we will use to add links to our `dynamic_test.jsp` page.

The dynamic_test JSP

Keep in mind your JSP container must support JSP 1.2 to run this example:

```
<?xml version="1.0" encoding="UTF-8"?>
<jsp:root xmlns:jsp="http://java.sun.com/jsp_1_2">
  <html>
    <head><title> Dynamic Test Page </title>
      <ExampleCount views="0">
      <jsp:scriptlet> String ls_Display = ""; </jsp:scriptlet>
      </ExampleCount>
    </head>
    <body>
      <ExampleLinks>
        <table border="1">
          <tr><th> Great Sites </th></tr>
          <tr>
            <td align="center">
            <a href="http://www.wrox.com">wrox</a>
            </td>
          </tr>
        </table>
      </ExampleLinks>
      <p><jsp:expression>ls_Display</jsp:expression></p>
      <p><a href="dynamic_links.jsp">Update This Page</a></p>
    </body>
  </html>
</jsp:root>
```

The first thing you will notice in this example is that it uses the new XML based JSP syntax. The actual XML syntax isn't that strange; however, you will notice two tags `<ExampleCount>` and `<ExampleLinks>`. These tags are just XML tags we added to the page to make it easier to perform our modifications. We could have called the tags anything we wanted as long as we followed the rules of XML.

The `<ExampleCount>` tag is used to keep track of how many times this page gets modified and also to store our simple JSP logic that we want to modify. The `<ExampleLinks>` tag is where we are storing the data for the links we dynamically add to the page. We didn't need to create these tags; however, by using these tags we now have extremely convenient markers within our page to help us both navigate the JDOM model and to insert our modified code within.

The first time you run this page it will look like this:

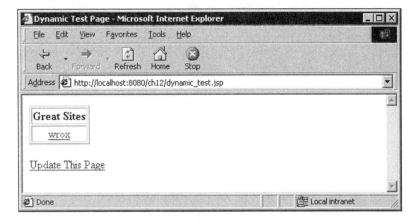

To make life simple we added a link on the first page to execute the second page. The second file is where we will perform all of our work that will update the `dynamic_test.jsp` page.

The dynamic_links JSP

This file is saved to the same directory in which you saved the `dynamic_test.jsp` file:

```
<%@page contentType="text/html"%>
<%@ page import="java.io.*,
                 java.util.*,
                 org.jdom.*,
                 org.jdom.input.SAXBuilder,
                 org.jdom.output.*" %>

<%

/* determine where all our files are located */
String ls_path = request.getServletPath();
```

The first logical step is to load in our XML file, in this case our first JSP page:

```
ls_path = ls_path.substring(0,ls_path.indexOf("dynamic_links.jsp")) ;

String ls_Jsp_Template = application.getRealPath(ls_path + "dynamic_test.jsp");
String ls_XML_Links = "c:/xml/links.xml";

SAXBuilder builder = new SAXBuilder("org.apache.xerces.parsers.SAXParser");
Document  l_jspdoc = builder.build(new File(ls_Jsp_Template));
```

Once we have our JSP page represented as a JDOM structure we will define the base HTML element of our page for a common reference point. It should be noted that within JDOM if you 'drill down' through the XML with the wrong path you would receive a `NullPointerException` error.

So if you are getting a mysterious `NullPointerException` check the syntax in the code matches to the actual XML layout. So for example if in this code if we had used `getChild("HTML")` it would have caused a `NullPointerException` since XML is case sensitive and "HTML" is considered to be a different node from "html":

```
Element l_page = l_jspdoc.getRootElement().getChild("html");
```

We then determine how many times we have modified the page and increment the count. The actual count is saved within the <ExampleCount> element stored in the attribute views. Retrieving and saving an attribute is similar to working with an element (or node). The main difference is in using the Attribute object associated with the Element object rather than just the Element object:

```
Element l_count = l_page.getChild("head").getChild("ExampleCount");
String ls_number = l_count.getAttributeValue("views");
int li_modcount = Integer.parseInt(ls_number) + 1;

ls_number = Integer.toString(li_modcount);
l_count.getAttribute("views").setValue(ls_number);
```

After updating the modify count the next step is to update the JSP scriptlet. This means we must get the data from within the <jsp:scriptlet> tag. This tag is using a namespace (the jsp portion of jsp:scriptlet). Working with namespaces is a little more complicated than working with a plain tag. It requires defining a Namespace object and then using this Namespace object as part of the key for determining the element:

```
Namespace jsp = Namespace.getNamespace("jsp", "http://java.sun.com/jsp_1_2");
Element l_change = l_page.getChild("head").getChild("ExampleCount")
                        .getChild("scriptlet",jsp);

String ls_message = "This page has been modified : " + ls_number + " times.";
l_change.setText("String ls_Display =\"" + ls_message + "\";");
```

Now we are ready to import the links.xml file. The code here is similar to previous code. The file is imported and we create a Document object. Once we have a document, it is possible to get a reference to the basic XML structure. In addition, a handle to the <ExampleLinks> tag is created so we can update our JSP page:

```
Document l_doc = builder.build(new File(ls_XML_Links));

Element root = l_doc.getRootElement();
Element example_links = l_page.getChild("body").getChild("ExampleLinks");

List l_links = root.getChildren("link");
```

The setText() function is used to set the <ExampleLinks> element to null. This effectively clears the element and all of its children, letting us start with a clean slate:

```
example_links.setText(null);
```

Now for the fun part. In the past, the task of modifying HTML consisted of appending many strings together. This style of coding has the problem of being not very readable and difficult to debug at times. We are modifying an XML file and the table we are adding is an XML data structure.

So instead of appending many strings, we create the elements we need, loop through the data, populate the elements with data and finally add the elements to our node (in our case the <ExampleLinks> node). The code is much cleaner and easier to automate than the older append string methodology:

```
Element l_table = new Element("Table");
Element l_tr = new Element("tr");
Element l_th = new Element("th");
Element l_td = new Element("td");
Element l_anchor= new Element("a");

l_th.setText(" Great Sites ");
l_tr.addContent(l_th);
l_table.addContent(l_tr);
l_table.addAttribute("border","1");

Iterator l_loop =  l_links.iterator();
while ( l_loop.hasNext()) {
  Element l_link   = (Element) l_loop.next();
  l_tr     = new Element("tr");
  l_td     = new Element("td");
  l_anchor = new Element("a");
  l_anchor.addContent(l_link.getChild("author").getText());
  l_anchor.addAttribute("href",l_link.getChild("url").getText());
  l_td.addContent(l_anchor);
  l_tr.addContent(l_td);
  l_table.addContent(l_tr);
}

example_links.addContent(l_table);
```

After we are done modifying our JSP page we need to rewrite the results back to the original file:

```
try {
  FileOutputStream l_write_file = new FileOutputStream(ls_Jsp_Template);
  XMLOutputter l_format = new XMLOutputter();
  l_format.output(l_jspdoc, l_write_file);
}
catch (IOException e) {
  out.print(e.toString());
}
%>
```

Finally when done, a simple HTML page will be displayed to indicate we have processed the first JSP page:

```
<html><head><title>Dynamic JSP</title></head>
  <body>
    We have finished processing your JSP Page <br>
    <p><a href="dynamic_test.jsp">View the Changes</a></p>
  </body>
</html>
```

When you run this page it will produce a screen indicating when it gets done processing which will look like:

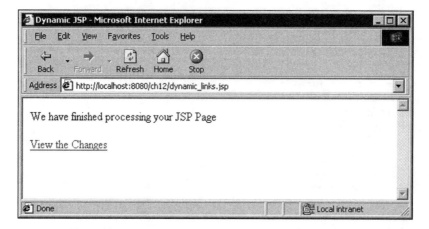

So at this point you go back to our first page to find it has indeed been modified to look like this:

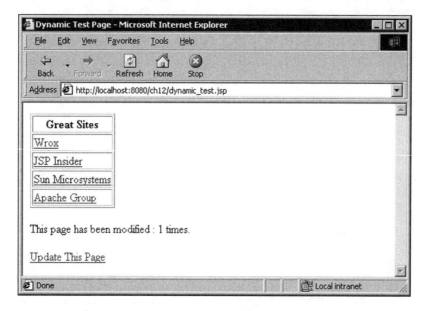

And more importantly our JSP page has now been changed to be a totally new page.

The following code is from dynamic_test.jsp after being modified by the dynamic_link.jsp page. This code has been reformatted to fit in this page. The actual output is identical but without the line breaks. The presence or non-presence of line breaks has no effect on the functionality of the code:

```
<?xml version="1.0" encoding="UTF-8"?><jsp:root
xmlns:jsp="http://java.sun.com/jsp_1_2">
<html>
  <head><title> Dynamic Test Page </title>
    <ExampleCount views="1">
      <jsp:scriptlet>
        String ls_Display ="This page has been modified : 1 times.";
```

```
        </jsp:scriptlet>
      </ExampleCount>
  </head>
  <body>
    <ExampleLinks>
      <Table border="1"><tr><th> Great Sites </th></tr>
        <tr><td><a href="http://www.wrox.com">Wrox</a></td></tr>
        <tr><td><a href="http://www.jspinsider.com">JSP Insider</a></td></tr>
        <tr><td><a href="http://java.sun.com">Sun Microsystems</a></td></tr>
        <tr><td><a href="http://jakarta.apache.org">Apache Group</a></td></tr>
      </Table>
    </ExampleLinks>

    <p><jsp:expression>ls_Display</jsp:expression></p>

    <p><a href="dynamic_links.jsp">Update This Page</a></p>

  </body>
</html>
</jsp:root>
```

Keep in mind this is a simple example. Use your creativity to expand it. For example, we could have modified this JSP page to keep track of the last time it was modified by the server. Then it would become possible to set a time when the page would automatically run the update process on its own. So you could fine-tune your JSP page to run its own scheduler to update on the first of every month, or any time period you specify.

Summary

Using JSP with XML can add a lot of flexibility and functionality to your JSP. Some of the important points we covered are:

❑ XML allows for information to be dealt with in a manner that is easily used by both people and machines. Content stored in XML syntax can easily be reused and changed into many different formats. The only downside to XML is that it will never be optimised for speed on a specific project.

❑ To use XML with JSP you need to have a parsing utility to create a Java object from serialized XML. The W3C makes the official recommendations for XML and many open-source parsers are available that follow these specifications.

❑ There is no one best way for using XML with JSP. The DOM, JDOM and SAX are all excellent tools and should be used when best suited for your project.

❑ XSLT is an XML syntax language used for XML transformations. Many browsers are starting to integrate support for these transformations and many Java utilities exist for these transformations. Using XSL to style XML has many benefits such as reusability and spreading your server workload to your clients.

❑ JSP 1.2 specification allows for fully compatible XML syntax JSP. Since JSP is already semi-compliant with XML syntax the new format is not hard to use. Since XML based JSP syntax is new it will take a little time before the full power of this development can be taken for best advantage.

Even though we covered quite a bit of ground, this chapter only gives a brief glimpse of using XML with JSP. If this entire book focused on using JSP with XML even then it would not have been enough to fully document all the possibilities. Remember the examples from this chapter but don't be limited by them. With JSP and XML together you have a very powerful tool to work with.

The next chapter examines how we can use the JDBC API to access relational databases.

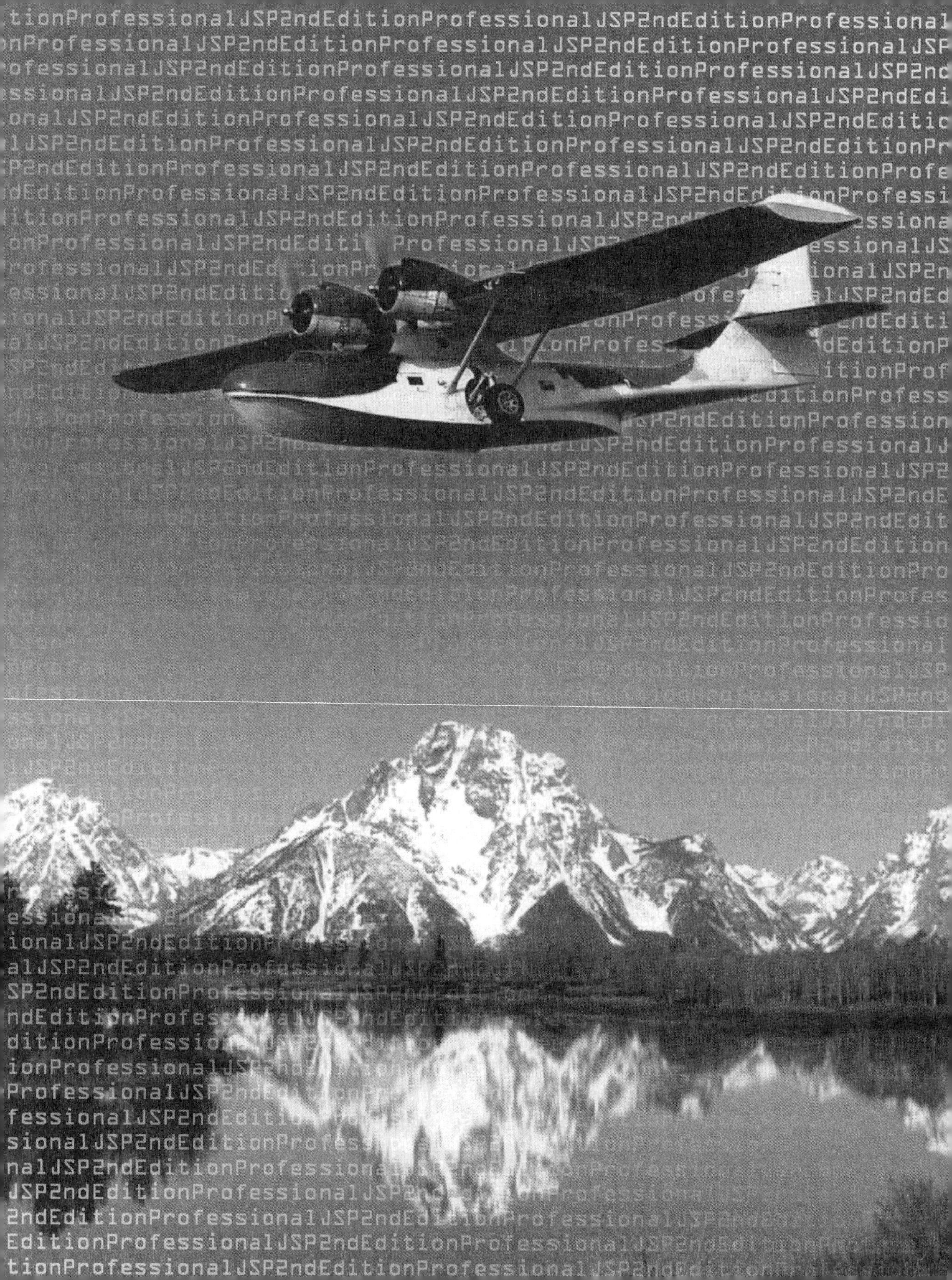

13

Data Access and JDBC

It is difficult to imagine an interactive company web-presence that does not employ considerable database interaction. Most of the most popular web-applications, including message boards, and auction sites, rely on back-end relational databases. JDBC is Java's solution to providing programmatic access for retrieving and storing relational data from within any Java program. Using the JDBC API, it is possible to access different relational databases using consistent syntax, thus making it possible to port an application component across different underlying relational databases with relative ease.

JDBC is a very large API, and an integral part of the Java platform, including both the Java 2 Standard Edition (J2SE) and the Java 2 Enterprise Edition (J2EE). At the time of writing the JDBC 1.0 core API (contained in the `java.sql` package), a basic set of classes and interfaces for interacting with a database, is part of the J2SE. The JDBC 2.1 Optional Package (contained in the `javax.sql` package, formerly known as the Standard Extension), a higher-level data-access abstraction built on top of the JDBC 1.0 core API, is part of the J2EE. All of this will change after the release of the JDBC 3.0 consisting of even newer `java.sql` and `javax.sql` packages, currently available as a proposed final draft. When the JDBC 3.0 specification is finalized, it is expected that the complete JDBC API v.3.0 packages will be included in the next releases of both the J2SE and J2EE platforms.

This chapter will provide an in-depth coverage of the JDBC specifically as it relates to JSP, including web-based data access models, strategies, optimizations, and debugging tips. We will cover:

- ❑ The JDBC 1.0 core API, containing the most fundamental concepts required for achieving simple database connectivity from JavaServer Pages

- ❑ As an example, a web-based voting application is presented

- ❑ We will also cover certain aspects of the JDBC 2.1 Optional Package API, including a discussion of how and when to use the new interfaces as opposed to using the core 1.0 API

Relational Databases

Building an interactive JSP application requires fetching and saving data from a database – for example, an e-commerce shopping application will require that data including a customer's profile, and order details be persisted into a database. JDBC abstracts away the details of interfacing with a database, in particular, relational databases.

The relational model represents data as tables consisting of **rows** (often called **records**) and **columns** (also called **attributes**), with each column holding data of a pre-defined type (for instance text, numbers, dates, and so on). A special column that uniquely identifies every row within a table is called a **primary key**; for example, in the US a social security number (or taxpayer identification number) could uniquely identify a person in a voter registration database.

The tabular data in a relational database is accessed via a standardized data-access language called the **Structured Query Language (SQL)**, which is to some extent supported by all major database vendors. SQL is a declarative language used in querying, updating, and managing relational databases. SQL statements (typically queries or updates) may be used to retrieve, sort, and filter specific data to be extracted from the database. An SQL query is a declarative expression; those rows that satisfy the declared criterion are included in the results. A typical SQL query will involve **joining** two or more relational database tables to extract the required data. A join of two tables is an operation that matches records in two tables, which have at least one common field – in other words, the join field is a member of both tables.

When E.F. Codd published his paper on the relational model and relational calculus in 1970, he made the claim that a declarative language was preferable over traditional navigational-based data access paradigms because a database engine could optimize queries, which would later become extremely important for very large enterprise data stores. Over a decade later, he was proved to be correct and relational databases are today by far the most widely adopted data storage model employed by industry today. There are many commercial and open-source Relational Database Management Systems (RDBMS) all widely used by industry today. Some of the popular commercial database vendors include Oracle, Microsoft, IBM, Sybase, and Informix, and popular open-source products include PostgreSQL and MySQL. These products vary in size from small simple installs to massive multi-CD 1.3 Gb installs, and vary in price from free to tens of thousands of dollars. When estimating the requirements of your application you should consider issues such as the availability of JDBC drivers, support for advanced functionality including distributed transactions (transactions involving multiple resources across a network), as well as stability and scalability requirements.

Throughout this book we will assume basic familiarity with SQL syntax and the relational data model. For more a complete coverage of ANSI standard SQL-92 as well as database theory and normalization we recommend *Instant SQL programming* (ISBN 1-874416-50-8). In this chapter the sample application has setup notes for Microsoft Access 2000 as well as MySQL, both of which have JDBC drivers freely available for download.

JSP and JDBC: A Historical Perspective

HTTP and the World Wide Web were initially designed as a simple means for sharing documents across a wide area network, but are now being employed as a preferred front end for any distributed application. Some of the original approaches to building web applications included writing server-side scripts with database hooks using CGI or other proprietary scripting languages such as Allaire's ColdFusion or Microsoft's Active Server Pages (ASP); these ideas were built-upon and extended by the Java Servlets specification in 1998, and subsequently JSP in 1999. The combination of Servlets and JSP to provide presentation logic and JDBC to access databases became an overnight success! In many ways, JSP & JDBC together represented the first big win for Java and were largely responsible for Java's re-invention as a popular server-side programming platform. Java specifications continue to evolve in time, with considerable changes in what exactly constitutes the middle-tier; regardless, JSP and JDBC remain respectively the required front and back-end of any J2EE application architecture.

JDBC Drivers

Data access in JDBC is accomplished via a **driver**, which implements the `java.sql.Driver` interface. Generally speaking, the driver can be thought as a layer of interposition between your Java application and the underlying database, accepting SQL commands from your application, forwarding them to a database, obtaining the results and returning them to the calling application. The exact details of how communication between application and database is conducted depend on the type of the driver.

The JDBC core API is found in the `java.sql` package, and additional optional extensions for JDBC v.2.1 are found in the `javax.sql` package. These packages contain only a few concrete classes; the remainder is left as database-neutral interfaces that specify method signatures without any implementation. This is because the details of interacting with a database are entirely dependent on the underlying database, so virtually all implementation details are left to the database product companies or third-party software vendors who typically either bundle drivers with their product or sell drivers as a stand-alone product. Broadly speaking, JDBC driver implementations generally fall into one of four different categories, which meet the demands of different applications.

Type I: JDBC-ODBC Bridge plus ODBC Driver

This is JDBC over ODBC. As the similar-sounding acronym suggests, Open Database Connectivity (ODBC) is a closely related predecessor to JDBC. ODBC is a Microsoft-touted technology to provide programmatic access to relational databases, which was later enhanced by Visigenic and Intersolve to provide ODBC SDKs for non-Windows platforms. JDBC builds on all of the concepts and features of ODBC, but differs in that it provides a higher-level abstraction of interacting with a database in Java, as opposed to invoking methods in C libraries. ODBC enjoys good support from all of the leading database product companies.

The most common implementation is the JDBC-ODBC bridge, freely distributed with the JDK. The bridge driver works with products such as Microsoft Access and Microsoft SQL Server. The bridge driver delegates all data access methods to an underlying ODBC implementation, which requires that every client has access to the native binary code that implements the ODBC functionality. Although the bridge driver is excellent for prototyping and development, it is not recommended for your production environment because it is not thread safe, and could potentially crash an entire server.

Type II: Native-API, Partly-Java Driver

This type of driver wraps a thin layer of Java around database-specific native code. For example, with an Oracle database, the JDBC calls would be converted into calls based on the Oracle Call Interface (OCI), which were designed for C/C++ programmers. A native type-II driver sometimes has better performance than an all-Java counterpart. Again, like the bridge driver, this requires that the database's client code (native binary code) be loaded on every machine that directly accesses the database.

Type III: JDBC-Net Pure Java Driver

This is a flexible driver, ideal for Internet based applications. The driver translates JDBC calls on a client into a RDBMS-independent network protocol (for example HTTP), and sends the request to a custom middleware server. The middleware server translates the network protocol request into an RDBMS-specific protocol to provide access to the underlying database. The networked middleware server is thus able to connect its Java clients to many different databases.

Type IV: Native Protocol Pure Java Driver

This all-Java driver is the smallest and usually the most efficient driver available because it works directly with a particular DBMS. This implementation is a 2-tier driver because it has nothing intervening between the driver and the underlying data source. In contrast, all other JDBC drivers require some kind of intermediate component. A type-IV driver communicates directly to a database using the database vendor's proprietary network protocol. An application using a type-IV driver must be able to resolve the database URL and open the appropriate port; which could potentially be problematic in network topologies involving firewalls beyond your control; in all other situations the type-IV driver is an excellent solution.

Sun Microsystems maintains a searchable listing of JDBC driver implementations at http://industry.java.sun.com/products/jdbc/drivers. Additionally, many application server or database vendors bundle JDBC drivers with their respective products as a matter of convenience. Consult your vendor's documentation before purchasing a driver.

Using JDBC:

To use JDBC, we must perform the following steps:

1. Load the JDBC Driver

2. Obtain a connection

3. Obtain a statement to execute a query or update

4. Process the results

5. Close the connection

Each of these steps will now be discussed as smaller code fragments, and in the next section we will bring it all together in a worked-out example. Keep in mind that all JDBC method calls must be enclosed by a try/catch block, which must handle SQLExceptions appropriately. However, we will omit the try/catch blocks in the following section for improved readability.

Loading the JDBC Driver

The first step to make use of a JDBC driver is to load the driver class into the application's Java Virtual Machine (JVM), which makes the driver available for opening a connection. As part of its initialization, the `DriverManager` class will attempt to load all of the driver classes referenced in the `jdbc.drivers` system property. This allows a user to customize the JDBC drivers used by their applications. Alternatively, a program can also explicitly load JDBC drivers at any time using the `Class.forName()` method. The following code fragment shows how you would load either a JDBC-ODBC bridge driver or a MySQL type-4 driver:

```
// Load the JDBC-ODBC bridge driver
Class.forName("sun.jdbc.odbc.JdbcOdbcDriver");
```

```
// Load the MySql Type-4 driver
Class.forName("org.gjt.mm.mysql.Driver");
```

If the class-loader fails to load the specified driver a `ClassNotFoundException` is thrown, which must be caught and dealt with appropriately. Ensure that your JDBC driver is in your server's `CLASSPATH`, or simply copy it into your web-application's `WEB-INF/lib` directory.

Obtaining a Database Connection

Whenever a driver is loaded into memory, it is registered as an available driver with the `java.sql.DriverManager` class, which is a basic service for managing a set of JDBC drivers. The next step is to ask the `DriverManager` for a connection to a database as specified in a specially formatted string or URL. The method used to open the connection is `DriverManager.getConnection()`. It returns a class that implements the `java.sql.Connection` interface. Here we show several examples for connecting to various databases:

```
// Example 1: Get connection using the JDBC-ODBC bridge
Connection con = DriverManager.getConnection("jdbc:odbc:datasourcename",
                                              "user", "pass");
```

```
// Example 2: Connecting to MySQL DB.
Connection con = DriverManager.getConnection("jdbc:mysql:///databasename",
                                              "user", "pass");
```

```
// Example 3: Connecting to an Oracle DB.
Connection con = DriverManager.getConnection
                        ("jdbc:oracle:thin:@dbhost:port:sid",
                         "user", "pass");
```

The database URL identifies a database in a driver specific manner. Different drivers require different information in the URL string in order to specify the database being connected to.

> The URL to specify a data source using the JDBC-ODBC bridge is of the form `jdbc:odbc:datasource`; other JDBC drivers such as MySQL or Oracle have similar though slightly-different URL patterns. Consult the driver documentation for the exact semantics of the connection URL.

The driver manager inquires if a registered driver recognizes the URL string, and if so, it will use that driver to create a `Connection` object. The following code fragment demonstrates how to obtain a connection.

```
Connection con = null;
// Use this line instead for MySQL:
// Class.forName("org.gjt.mm.mysql.Driver");

Class.forName("sun.jdbc.odbc.JdbcOdbcDriver");

// Open connection to the database
con = DriverManager.getConnection("jdbc:odbc:somedb", "user", "password");

// Do something interesting with the database connection
```

The `javax.sql.DataSource` interface, new in the JDBC 2.1 API, provides another way to connect to a data source for more advanced applications. Later in this chapter we'll show how to use a `DataSource` and explain when you would use it.

Executing SQL Commands Using Statements

Now that a connection has been established with the database, we will want to interact with it by means of invoking operations on the underlying relational data – querying, inserting, updating, and deleting the data contained in the database. The `java.sql.Statement` interface is the means by which SQL commands are sent to the database. `Statement` objects are not instantiated directly; rather your application calls a factory method on the `Connection` object, which is the root of all remote objects returned from the JDBC driver. Here is how you would create a `Statement` object:

```
Statement stmt = con.createStatement();
```

A `Statement` object's `executeQuery()` method is used to execute any query that is expected to return data. The `executeQuery()` method returns a `java.sql.ResultSet` which represents the data from the database which satisfied the search criteria.

For example, consider the following statement:

```
ResultSet rs = stmt.executeQuery("SELECT * FROM MYTABLE");
```

Here, the `ResultSet` object `rs` represents the contents of `MYTABLE`. SQL also includes means to define and modify data, using UPDATE, INSERT, and DELETE commands. To execute commands like these, which intuitively do not return a `ResultSet`, you would instead use the `executeUpdate()` method of a `Statement`. Unlike the `executeQuery()` method, `executeUpdate()` returns an integer, corresponding to the number of rows modified by the statement, as shown in the following code fragment:

```
int count = stmt.executeUpdate("DELETE FROM USER WHERE USERID = 'lkim');
```

In this case the count would correspond to the number of rows that were actually deleted as a result of invoking this command.

Finally, suppose your program dynamically accepts arbitrary SQL commands (perhaps entered by a user), and as such, you have no idea of the nature of the commands being executed. In this case your last alternative is to use the generic `execute()` method which returns a `boolean` whose value is `true` if the `Statement` returned one or more `ResultSet` objects, or `false` if the `Statement` returned an update count:

```
boolean outcome = stmt.execute(userSuppliedSqlString);
```

Access to the `ResultSet` or update `count` is obtained by invoking either the `getResultSet()` or the `getUpdateCount()` methods of `Statement`.

Prepared and Callable Statements

SQL statements intended to be executed multiple times are more efficiently done by using `java.sql.PreparedStatement`. A `PreparedStatement` differs from a regular `Statement` in that it specifies a parameterized, fill-in-the-blanks SQL template. For example, in the statement `"INSERT INTO mytable values (?, ?)"` there are two unknown parameters (the question marks) which are set at run-time by your application. The `PreparedStatement` is sent to the database for compilation before actually being used, and the question marks are used as placeholders for data supplied at run-time.

A `PreparedStatement` is obtained from the `Connection` object by invoking the `prepareStatement()` factory method. Every time you use the `PreparedStatement`, simply set the parameterized parameters using a `setXXX()` method call corresponding to the parameter you wish to set (the place-holder index starts from 1). You then call `executeUpdate()` or `executeQuery()` as you would on a normal `Statement` object.

One example where this could be useful is in performing multiple updates. For example, saving a listing of company stock symbols into your profile, in which case you might do the following:

```
Connection con = DriverManager.getConnection(url, user, pass);

String template = "INSERT INTO stocks values (?, ?)";
PreparedStatement ps = con.prepareStatement(template);

String customer = session.getAttribute("customer");
String[] stockList = getParameterValues("stocks");

// userId only needs to be set once.
ps.setString(1, customer);

for (int i = 0; i < stockList.length; i++) {
  ps.setString(2, stockList[i]);
  ps.executeUpdate();
}

// close the prepared statement and connection.
```

In this case, an array of stock symbols are retrieved from the `request` object and the `PreparedStatement`'s parameters are set and subsequently executed once for every stock supplied by the user. As a reminder, be mindful of the rules for object synchronization and threading in Java; for example, if the `PreparedStatement` is a member variable, there could potentially be hundreds of threads of execution zipping through your Servlet and if one thread was setting parameters while a different thread was executing the `PreparedStatement`, the results would be totally unpredictable and disastrous. In the case above the `PreparedStatement` is assumed to be a local variable so we are okay.

If the user entered many stocks then recycling the same statement, as opposed to creating new ones from scratch each time, results in considerable performance improvements. Unfortunately there are performance penalties associated with object synchronization. It is hard to say exactly what kind of performance increases you would expect to see from using a `PreparedStatement`. This is because the underlying database might not support precompiled queries and, even if does support them, the JDBC drivers might not take advantage of it. The Java programming philosophy has always been to standardize an interface and compete on implementation; from a vendor's perspective, a `PreparedStatement` is a logical place for performance optimizations.

The `PreparedStatement` has one other very important possible use in conjunction with JSP, involving data submitted by a user from a form. You must always ensure that the user-supplied data does not introduce any special control characters (for example ' or ") without escaping them in the proper manner as required by your database. Suppose in the previous stock-saving application that we were using regular `Statements` and that the customer's name was "Bill O'Reilly". In this case, the SQL statement becomes:

```
String template = "INSERT INTO stocks values (Bill O'Reilly', 'SUNW')";
```

This would cause an `SQLException` because the SQL statement is invalid. (The apostrophe in O'Reilly mistakenly acts as a control character). A possible solution to this problem is to manually escape the input at run-time but this is could lead to some portability problems if underlying databases have different control characters and escape sequences. An alternative solution would be to use the `PreparedStatement` and the `setString(1, customer)` method as illustrated previously, which automatically escapes any control characters in the customer string in the correct format as required by the underlying database.

JDBC also provides a stored procedure SQL escape syntax that allows stored procedures to be called in a standard way for all RDBMSs. Stored procedures are programs that you can write, which are stored and executed in the database's process; typically these stored procedures are written in a vendor-proprietary language such as Oracle's Procedural Language extension to SQL (PL/SQL). Stored procedures allow data in the DB engine to be customized to the needs of your application and have extremely fast access to the data by virtue of executing within the DB engine.

A `CallableStatement` is used to call into stored procedures for DB engines which support them. `CallableStatement` extends `PreparedStatement`, so they are quite similar in terms of their usage. A `CallableStatement` is obtained from the `Connection`'s `prepareCall()` factory method, and the stored procedure's required parameters are set using the `setXXX()` methods. Finally, a `CallableStatement` is typically executed using the `execute()` method. Since stored procedures are written in a proprietary language internal to the database, the database is free to define calling and data return conventions.

Using ResultSets

A `ResultSet` is a collection of rows corresponding to the results of a query. A default `ResultSet` object has a built-in forwards-moving cursor (or iterator); using the default cursor, it is possible to iterate through a `ResultSet` only once, from the first row to the last row. To extract specific data values contained in the `ResultSet` we iterate through the collection, retrieving column values row-by-row, according to their types. The built-in cursor keeps track of the current row, and is initially placed right before the first row. A call to the `ResultSet`'s `next()` method advances the cursor to the next row, making it the current row. Successive invocations of `next()` move the cursor forward, moving through the results from the first to the last row. The `next()` method can be invoked from within a `while` statement because it returns `true` so long as the cursor is on a valid row. When the cursor falls off the end of the `ResultSet`, the call to `next()` returns `false`, terminating the `while` loop. The following code fragment illustrates iteration through a `ResultSet`:

```
while(rs.next()) {
  out.println(rs.getString("name"));
  out.println(rs.getInt("age"));
  out.println("<br>");
}
```

The ResultSet's getString() and getInt() methods are discussed in more detail in the next section, but for now, note that an instance of a ResultSet object is usually a remote reference (a stub) closely related to its parent Statement object (depending on the vendor implementation). This is because the results of a query could potentially be extremely large, and copying it into memory could potentially crash a system. Instead, using the cursor, the required information is initialized on demand. If the Statement is closed or used to execute a different query, all data in the ResultSet is also closed automatically.

Therefore, if you need access to the ResultSet data after closing the connection, you will need to have made a local copy all of the data; be warned that the amount of data contained in a ResultSet (and the work required to copy it all) could potentially be enormous. Another possibility here is to create a disconnected JDBC 2.1 RowSet (extends ResultSet), which is a scrollable (forwards/backwards or to any relative/absolute position), offline-yet-updateable object which contains an actual copy of all the data. The trade-off here is that this typically requires saving a reference to RowSet across client calls (perhaps in the user's session), which consumes more memory, and might not meet the scalability requirements of certain web-applications.

For maximum portability when using a ResultSet, columns within each row should be read only once, in left-to-right order (so try to avoid using "SELECT * ..." queries), and each column should be read only once because some drivers are limited to this behavior.

Data Types in JDBC

In order to understand a ResultSet's getString() and getInt() methods from the code fragment above, we need to understand data-types in JDBC. Although SQL is technically a standard, in practice you will find that every database supports its own set of internal data-types, which vary among vendors. JDBC provides a layer of abstraction between Java data types and the underlying database type, an important feature for achieving application portability. Therefore JDBC defines a mapping of Java data types to JDBC types, which in turn logically map to native database types. The JDBC types themselves are modeled after standard SQL data types. This is illustrated in the figure below:

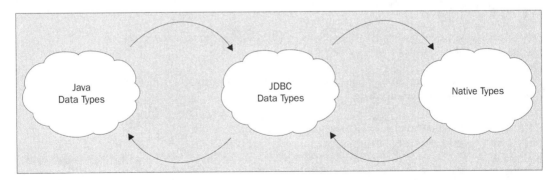

As Java developers, we need only concern ourselves with the Java-to-JDBC and consequently, the reverse, JDBC-to-Java mappings, since the JDBC driver provider implements the mappings between SQL data types and native data types. Our interaction is typically limited to the java.sql.ResultSet interface, which among other things has dozens of helper methods to retrieve data from the ResultSet as a particular type.

The following table lists the most common data types and the recommended methods that should be used to extract their values from a `ResultSet`:

Java Data-type	JDBC Data-type	Retrieval Method on `ResultSet`
Short	SMALLINT	getShort()
Int	INTEGER	getInt()
Double	DOUBLE	getDouble()
java.lang.String	CHAR	getString()
java.lang.String	VARCHAR	getString()
java.util.Date	DATE	getDate()
java.sql.Time	TIME	getTime()
java.sql.Timestamp	TIMESTAMP	getTimeStamp()

In addition to the recommended retrieval methods you can always call `getObject()` and do type-casting yourself (this is often helpful for dealing with `null` values). Finally there are many other legal (but not recommended) `getXXX()` methods for retrieving data as a specified type. For example, you could retrieve a date column value as a `String` by calling:

```
// a query that returns a column of type date
ResultSet rs = stmt.executeQuery
                    ("SELECT birthdate from USERS where userid ='lkim'");
String birthday = rs.getString("birthdate");
```

Here, the call to `getString()` would return a `String` representation of the date rather than a `java.util.Date` representation of the JDBC `Date` object.

The ResultSetMetaData Interface

The `ResultSetMetaData` interface provides information about the properties of a `ResultSet`, including the column names and data-types. A `ResultSetMetaData` object is created using the `getMetaData()` factory method on `ResultSet`, as shown here:

```
ResultSet rs = statement.executeQuery("SELECT a, b, c FROM MyTable");
ResultSetMetaData rsmd = rs.getMetaData();
```

Using the `ResultSetMetaData` object it is possible to then obtain useful information about the `ResultSet`'s schema as shown here:

```
int numberOfColumns = rsmd.getColumnCount();

for (int i=1; i <= numberOfColumns; i++) {
  out.println("Column " rsmd.getColumnName(i) + " is of type "+
  rsmd.getColumnType(i));
}
```

The output of the above code fragment might look something like the following:

Column name is of type VARCHAR
Column age is of type INTEGER

The ResultSetMetaData is particularly useful when the schema of the ResultSet is unknown in advance. For example, if we execute queries supplied by a user at run-time, it makes it possible to ascertain which ResultSet.getXXX() method to use to retrieve data.

Closing the Database Connection

Finally database–related objects are expensive in terms of memory utilization and have substantial impact on overall system performance. It is therefore important to clean up after yourself by closing the Connection as well as anything returned from the Connection, including Statement and ResultSet objects. It's a good idea to place the clean-up code in the finally block immediately following your data access code, to ensure that clean-up takes place regardless of the outcome as shown here:

```
finally {
  // Close everything returned from the
  // connection no matter what!
  try {
    if (rs!=null) rs.close();
    if (stmt!=null) stmt.close();
    if (con!=null) con.close();
  }
  catch(SQLException ignored) {}
}
```

In the above code fragment, we explicitly closed everything returned from the Connection, as well as the Connection itself. Note the order in which they were closed. In theory closing the connection should close all associated Statement and ResultSet objects; however, a poorly-implemented driver could potentially omit that step so it doesn't hurt to be sure. Remember that these are essentially remote objects (stubs), and it is not a good idea to rely on the distributed garbage collector since the drivers might be implemented natively.

A Bird's Eye View of the JDBC

The figure overleaf recaps our discussion of the JDBC thus far, illustrating how applications can use JDBC to interact with almost any underlying database:

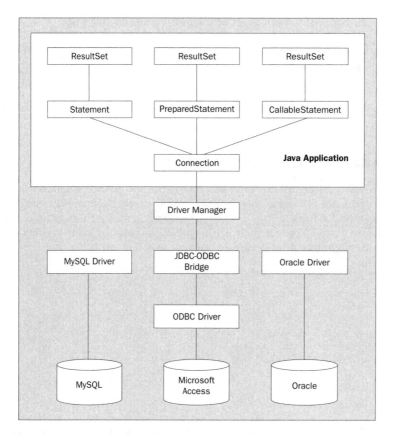

The figure shows how the `Connection` is the root of all objects returned from the `DriverManager`, and also that there are other ways of executing statements and obtaining `ResultSet` objects, namely the `PreparedStatement`, which is precompiled by the database for faster execution, and the `CallableStatement`, which can be used to access stored procedures.

A JDBC-Based Voting Application

Up until now we have been for the most part presenting code snippets so now we'll bring it all together with a sample voting application. Most books on JSP and JDBC contain some sample application typically involving a shopping cart of some kind, with customers, products, and categories. At the time of this writing, the dot-com economy seems to be slowing down and it's possible that the demand for electronic shopping carts might diminish... in fact, Internet Consultants are even being laid-off.

Therefore we really need to innovate here. The sample application for this chapter is an online voting application, which has some really great selling points! For example, you can register and vote from anywhere in the world, the ballot is a straightforward HTML form, and there would certainly be no dimpled-chads. We'll have setup and deployment notes to get you up and running for both Microsoft Access 2000 and MySQL. The application has been tested using both Allaire JRun and Jakarta-Tomcat.

Disclaimer: This application couldn't be used for a real presidential election – it has virtually no security. It would probably be better to use an EJB server and database with better support for distributed transactions.

Voting Application Architecture

The easiest way to explain the voting application is to examine the sequence of page views that a user encounters when going through the voting process. The sequence is displayed in the figure below:

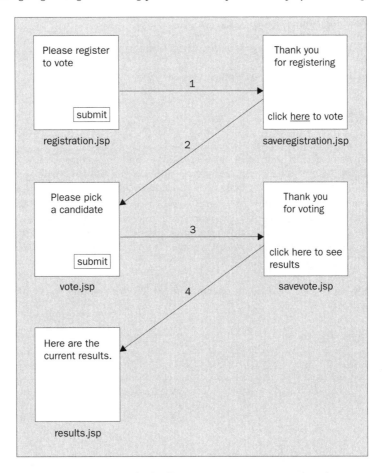

It is a simple page-centric architecture, which allows a user to register, vote, and view current election results. Most of the application logic occurs upon transition from one page to the next; all of these transitions will be discussed later when the JSP pages are presented in detail.

> *Elsewhere in this book, in Chapters 6-7 and 17, we talk about more advanced programming paradigms, including the Model-View-Controller (MVC) architecture.*

A JSP/Servlet engine (such as Tomcat or JRun) services all client requests; the server process loads a JDBC driver and handles all operations with the database; therefore a client never directly establishes a connection with the database. The JSPs contain all application logic and data-access code, recording the voter registrations and votes, as well as displaying the results. This architecture could be made into a complete J2EE application architecture if we added Enterprise JavaBeans, which could be modeled as an additional layer of interposition between the Servlet/JSP engine and the database, removing practically all Java code out of the JSP file. We'll have more on this later on in the chapter, but for now be aware that there are many ways to access a database!

The proposed application architecture has some great selling points:

❑ The client doesn't need to download any client code, and the browser doesn't have to support Java at all

❑ The client never directly accesses the database, and HTTP traffic could be secured using a digital certificate (Secure Sockets Layer)

❑ This application shouldn't have trouble navigating through firewalls

Let's now move on to look at the structure of the database – the schema.

Database Schema

Proper data and object modeling is the most important part of building enterprise applications. This is often easy for these smaller (and somewhat contrived) sample applications, but enterprise applications can potentially involve hundreds of tables in databases physically located across the world. It is important, for example, that you **normalize** your table data to protect the integrity of your data and achieve a happy medium between maximizing application performance and minimizing data redundancy. There are many other interesting considerations and we highly recommend some great books which cover these topics in depth including *Professional Oracle 8i Application Programming with Java, PL/SQL and XML* (ISBN 1-861004-84-2, and *Instant UML* (ISBN 1-861000-87-1).

In this application, we will keep the database schema simple. We will use only four tables, which should be pretty self-explanatory.

VoterRegistration Table

Column Name	JDBC Data-type	Notes
SSN	INTEGER	VoterRegistration Table Social Security Number, primary key.
FIRSTNAME	VARCHAR(32)	
LASTNAME	VARCHAR(32)	
COUNTYNUMBER	INTEGER	Foreign key, references County table.

County Table

Column Name	JDBC Data-type	Notes
COUNTYNUMBER	INTEGER	Primary Key, auto_increment
COUNTYNAME	VARCHAR(32)	
STATE	VARCHAR(32)	

Candidate Table

Column Name	JDBC Data-type	Notes
CANDIDATENUMBER	INTEGER	Primary Key, auto_increment
FIRSTNAME	VARCHAR(32)	
LASTNAME	VARCHAR(32)	
POLITICALPARTY	VARCHAR(32)	

Votes Table

Column Name	JDBC Data-type	Notes
VOTENUMBER	INTEGER	Primary Key, auto_increment
CANDIDATENUMBER	INTEGER	Foreign key, references Candidate table
COUNTYNUMBER	INTEGER	Foreign key, references County table

Every table has a **primary key**, which uniquely identifies each record in a table. For example, a social security number (tax-payer identification number) uniquely identifies a voter. There are relationships between some of the tables; for instance, a vote record contains both a CANDIDATENUMBER attribute, which refers to the primary key of the candidate table, as well as a COUNTYNUMBER attribute, which refers to the primary key of the county table. Using these relationships, it's possible to do some complex join operations to obtain just about any result set we want.

Configuring the Voting Application

In this section we present complete database and database driver set-up notes for Microsoft Access and MySQL.

Configuring Access 2000 and the JDBC:ODBC Bridge

Copy the OnlineVotingApp.mdb file to your computer (it doesn't matter where, just remember where you copied it to) from the code that accompanies this book. All source code for this chapter is available at http://www.wrox.com. The tables have all been created and populated with sample data. Data types in Microsoft Access aren't exactly the same as JDBC data types; in fact, even though SQL is a standard, you will find that databases have all sorts of different primitive data-type definitions. Thankfully this is not a problem because JDBC was designed with this in mind. Here are examples of the type substitutions that we will be using:

JDBC Type	Microsoft Access 2000 Type
VARCHAR	TEXT
Bit	YES/NO
Integer	Number

In the case of the JDBC-ODBC Bridge, we need to perform some additional ODBC setup to get it up and running, since the bridge driver relies on the underlying ODBC implementation. This step is usually not required of any other drivers.

On Windows 2000:

❑ On Windows 2000, click Start/Programs/Administrative Tools/Data Sources (ODBC); on Windows 98, click Start/Settings/Control Panel then choose ODBC Data Sources (32 bit). This should bring up the ODBC Data Source Administrator panel as shown below:

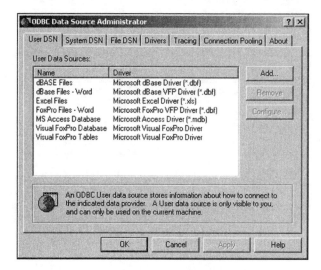

❑ We need to add a new ODBC data source for the online presidential voting application. Click Add. This will bring up the Create New Data Source panel, shown below:

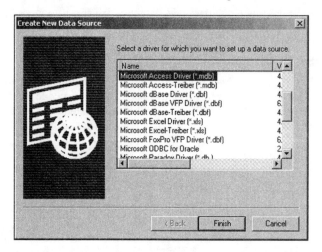

❑ As you can see, ODBC can connect to a variety of different underlying data sources. Select Microsoft Access Driver (*.mdb).

❑ Now click Finish. This should bring up the ODBC Microsoft Access Setup panel:

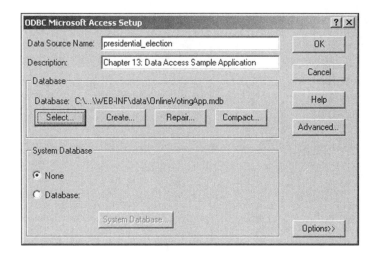

- ❏ Enter `presidential_election` as the **Data Source Name**.

- ❏ If you wish, enter a brief **Description** for the data source.

- ❏ Click **Select...**

- ❏ Using the file chooser, select the `OnlineVotingApp.mdb` file from the source code that accompanies this book.

- ❏ Click **OK**.

You have now successfully configured an ODBC data source!

Configuring MySQL and the Type IV JDBC Driver

MySQL is a free, open source, relational database management system, available under the GPL (GNU General Public License). MySQL is very easy to get up and running, and has builds available for nearly every platform. At the time of writing, the most recent stable build is the 3.23 version available for download from: http://www.mysql.com/downloads/mysql-3.23.html. For Windows platforms, the file name is `mysql-3.23.33-win.zip` (binaries only). After downloading, unzip the files to a temporary directory and run the installer.

We will be using an open-source MySQL Type-4 JDBC driver called `mm.mySQL`, available for download at http://mmmysql.sourceforge.net/. Specifically, you should download `mm.mysql-2.0.1-bin.jar` (binaries only – the source files aren't required) and place the JAR file where it will be found by anything that needs to use the driver including your web application's `WEB-INF/lib` directory, and your IDE if necessary.

To create the database, open a command shell, go to the `mysql/bin` directory, and type:

```
>mysqladmin create presidential_election
```

This requires that you have administrative privileges. Next we need to create the tables required for the voting application. We need to run the `createtables.sql` script included with the source code that accompanies this book. The following command will execute the SQL script:

```
>mysql -u <userid> -p presidential_election < createtables.sql
```

The default administrator username is `admin`; you will also be prompted to enter a password, and the default password is also `admin`. Here's the `createtables.sql` script:

```
create table county (
countynumber integer not null auto_increment,
countyname varchar(32),
state varchar(32),
primary key(countynumber));

create table candidate (
candidatenumber integer not null auto_increment,
firstname varchar(32) not null,
lastname varchar(32) not null,
politicalparty varchar(32) not null,
primary key(candidatenumber));

create table voterregistration (
ssn integer not null,
firstname varchar(32) not null,
lastname varchar(32) not null,
countynumber integer not null,
primary key(SSN),
foreign key(countynumber) references county);

create table votes (
votenumber integer not null auto_increment,
candidatenumber integer,
countynumber integer,
primary key(votenumber),
foreign key(candidatenumber) references candidate,
foreign key(countynumber) references county);
```

Finally, we'll insert some sample data to the tables to get up and running. Run the `populatetables.sql` script, which populates the tables that were just created:

```
insert into candidate(firstname, lastname, politicalparty) VALUES('George'
,'Bush', 'Republican Party');
insert into candidate(firstname, lastname, politicalparty) VALUES('Al' ,'Gore',
'Democratic Party');
insert into candidate(firstname, lastname, politicalparty) VALUES('Ralph'
,'Nader', 'Green Party');
insert into candidate(firstname, lastname, politicalparty) VALUES('Pat' ,'
Buchanan', 'Reform Party');

insert into county(countyname, state) VALUES('Broward' ,'Florida');
insert into county(countyname, state) VALUES('Miami-Dade' ,'Florida');
insert into county(countyname, state) VALUES('West Palm Beach' ,'Florida');
insert into county(countyname, state) VALUES('Duval' ,'Florida');
insert into county(countyname, state) VALUES('Pensacola' ,'Florida');
insert into county(countyname, state) VALUES('Seminole' ,'Florida');
insert into county(countyname, state) VALUES('Martin' ,'Florida');
```

```
insert into voterregistration values(123456789, 'William','Renquist', 4);
insert into voterregistration values(226541846, 'Jesse','Jackson', 2);
insert into voterregistration values(238940238, 'Winona','LaDuke', 5);
insert into voterregistration values(456187950, 'James','Baker', 6);
insert into voterregistration values(798456455, 'Ross','Perrot', 3);
insert into voterregistration values(808975464, 'Warren','Christopher', 1);
insert into voterregistration values(987654321, 'Jeb','Bush', 4);
insert into voterregistration values(111222333, 'David','Boise', 5);
```

Building the Voting Application

We now turn our attention to the individual JSPs required to built the voting application. Earlier in this section we mentioned that we were using a page-centric approach to building this web application, with server-side processing occurring on transition from one page to the next. A more generalized way of thinking about this loading and unloading of form data, and interaction between pages, is illustrated below:

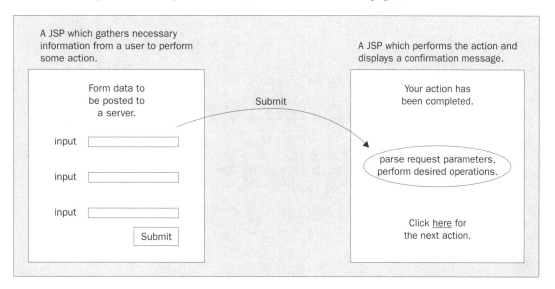

On the left side of the figure, we have a form with input fields, required for executing some business process such as posting a message, placing an online order, placing a stock trade; or in our case, registering and voting for a candidate. The form is submitted to the workhorse JSP on the right side of the figure, which executes the required JDBC logic to process the action. Typically the workhorse JSP prints out some kind of confirmation – for example, "Your order has been placed" or "Your trade has been executed". Finally, it hyperlinks to the next page in the application.

This works well in basic cases, although a potential problem with this simple approach arises when users start book-marking pages, using the Back browser button, or hitting the Reload button. Again we would like to emphasize that data-access code doesn't usually go directly into a JSP, typically we would use Servlets, session beans, or other layered architectures which are the subject of several case studies later in this book. In this chapter, for the sake of clarity we will use this simple web architecture in order to focus on the JDBC data access code. We now turn our attention to the individual JSPs, which make up the online voting application.

The registration.jsp Page

The first requirement of the sample application is to provide an easy way for voters to register their information. The registration page, registration.jsp, is illustrated below:

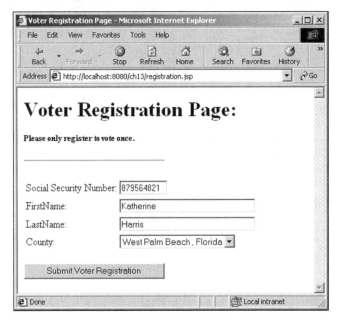

The source code for registration.jsp is shown below. We start with a pretty standard header; if an exception occurs anytime while processing this page, the user gets forwarded to error.jsp, which is a standard JSP error page. We then make a start on the form. There are input fields corresponding to Social Security Number (required to vote in the US), as well as first and last name, and county:

```
<!DOCTYPE HTML PUBLIC "-//W3C//DTD HTML 4.0 Transitional//EN">
<%@ page import="java.sql.*" errorPage="error.jsp" %>
<html>
<head>
  <title>Voter Registration Page</title>
</head>
<body>
<h1>Voter Registration Page:</h1>
<h5>Please only register to vote once.</h5>
<hr align="left" width="50%">
<form action="saveregistration.jsp" method="post">
<p>
<table>
  <tr>
    <td>Social Security Number:</td>
    <td><input type="text" name="ssn" maxlength="9" size="9"></td>
  </tr>
  <tr>
    <td>FirstName:</td>
    <td><input type="text" name="firstname" maxlength="32" size="32"></td>
  </tr>
  <tr>
```

```
    <td>LastName:</td>
    <td><input type="text" name="lastname" maxlength="32" size="32"></td>
  </tr>
  <tr>
    <td>County:</td>
    <td>
```

Next, we connect to a database in order to dynamically populate the data in the county drop-down box:

```
    <select name="county">
<%  Class.forName("sun.jdbc.odbc.JdbcOdbcDriver");
    Connection con = DriverManager.getConnection
                            ("jdbc:odbc:presidential_election", "", "");

    // Class.forName("org.gjt.mm.mysql.Driver");
    // Connection con =
    // DriverManager.getConnection
    //              ("jdbc:mysql:///presidential_election", "admin", "admin");

    Statement stmt = con.createStatement();
    ResultSet rs = stmt.executeQuery
                    ("SELECT countynumber, countyname, state FROM COUNTY");
    while(rs.next()) {
%>

<option value="<%= rs.getString("countynumber") %>">
  <%= rs.getString("countyname") %>,
  <%= rs.getString("state") %>
</option>

<%  } // end while()

    // clean up.
    if (rs!=null) rs.close();
    if (stmt!=null) stmt.close();
    if (con!=null) con.close();
%>

    </select>
    </td>
  </tr>
</table>
</p>
<input type="submit" value="Submit Voter Registration">
</form>
</body>
</html>
```

Throughout this application, you will need to comment and uncomment the section pertaining to loading a database driver and establishing a connection, depending on which database you are using.

The voting application has a very simple design. The idea is to obtain a connection, populate the drop-down box (corresponding to the counties) then release the connection. There will be no form validation performed here for the sake of clarity. When the form is posted to the server, the saveregistration.jsp page is invoked, which fetches the form inputs and saves the results to a database.

The saveregistration.jsp Page

Let's take a look at the interaction with the `saveregistration.jsp` file, which is the workhorse behind this step of the application, and is illustrated below:

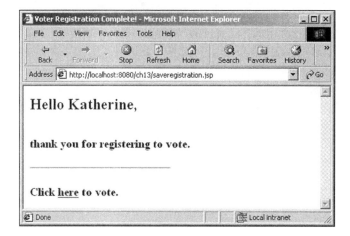

The `saveregistration.jsp` file performs four main tasks:

❏ Fetching the voter registration parameters

❏ Saving a new record into the `voterregistration` table

❏ Displaying a thank-you note as a confirmation message

❏ Providing a hyperlink to get to the voting area

`saveregistration.jsp` starts by fetching the request parameters and saving them into local variables. We also save the data into the user's session, which are later invalidated after the user votes, as a cheap way of discouraging fraud:

```
<!DOCTYPE HTML PUBLIC "-//W3C//DTD HTML 4.0 Transitional//EN">
<%@ page import="java.sql.*" errorPage="error.jsp" %>
<html>
<head>
  <title>Voter Registration Complete!!</title>
</head>

<body>

<%
    // Fetch the form data
    String ssn = request.getParameter("ssn");
    String firstName = request.getParameter("firstname");
    String lastName = request.getParameter("lastname");
    String county = request.getParameter("county");

    // save info into the user's session
    session.setAttribute("ssn",  ssn);
    session.setAttribute("firstname",  firstName);
    session.setAttribute("lastname",  lastName);
    session.setAttribute("county",  county);
```

A connection to the database is established and we use a `PreparedStatement` to insert the data, rather than a regular `Statement`, since the input might contain control characters such as an apostrophe:

```
        Class.forName("sun.jdbc.odbc.JdbcOdbcDriver");
        Connection con = DriverManager.getConnection
                            ("jdbc:odbc:presidential_election", "", "");

        // Class.forName("org.gjt.mm.mysql.Driver");
        // Connection con = DriverManager.getConnection
        //             ("jdbc:mysql:///presidential_election", "admin", "admin");

        String template = "INSERT INTO VOTERREGISTRATION (SSN, FIRSTNAME, " +
                            "LASTNAME, COUNTYNUMBER) VALUES( ?, ?, ?, ? )";
        PreparedStatement pstmt = con.prepareStatement(template);
        pstmt.setInt(1, Integer.parseInt(ssn));
        pstmt.setString(2, firstName);
        pstmt.setString(3, lastName);
        pstmt.setInt(4, Integer.parseInt(county));
        pstmt.executeUpdate();

        if (pstmt!=null) pstmt.close();
        if (con!=null) con.close();
%>

<h2>Hello <%= firstName %>, </h2><br>
<h3>thank you for registering to vote.</h3>
<hr align="left" width="50%">
<h3>Click <a href="vote.jsp">here</a> to vote.</h3>

</body>
</html>
```

The vote.jsp Page

The `vote.jsp` file produces a voting ballot form, as shown here:

`vote.jsp` is just a form, although it is dynamically generated by iterating through all of the entries in the candidate table, and making a radio button input corresponding to each candidate.

485

```
<!DOCTYPE HTML PUBLIC "-//W3C//DTD HTML 4.0 Transitional//EN">
<%@ page import="java.sql.*" errorPage="error.jsp" %>
<html>
<head>
  <title>Pick a presidential candidate!</title>
</head>

<body>

<h1>Please pick a candidate:</h1>

<form method="post" action="savevote.jsp">
<table border="1" cellpadding="2" cellspacing="0">
<%  Class.forName("sun.jdbc.odbc.JdbcOdbcDriver");
    Connection con = DriverManager.getConnection
                          ("jdbc:odbc:presidential_election", "", "");

    // Class.forName("org.gjt.mm.mysql.Driver");
    // Connection con = DriverManager.getConnection
    //            ("jdbc:mysql:///presidential_election", "admin", "admin");

    Statement stmt = con.createStatement();
    String queryStr = "SELECT CANDIDATENUMBER, FIRSTNAME, LASTNAME, " +
                      "POLITICALPARTY FROM CANDIDATE";

    ResultSet rs = stmt.executeQuery(queryStr);
    while(rs.next()) {
%>

<tr>
  <td><input type="radio" name="candidate"
            value="<%= rs.getString("CANDIDATENUMBER") %>"></td>
  <td><%= rs.getString("FIRSTNAME")%>
      <%= rs.getString("LASTNAME")%></td>
  <td><%= rs.getString("POLITICALPARTY") %></td>
</tr>

<%  } // end while()

    // clean up.
    if (rs!=null) rs.close();
    if (stmt!=null) stmt.close();
    if (con!=null) con.close();
%>
</table>
<p><input type="submit" value="Record your vote!"></p>
</form>
</body>
</html>
```

Note how the `vote.jsp` page posts its form data to `savevote.jsp`. We'll take a look at this file next.

The savevote.jsp Page

This is a workhorse JSP that fetches the voting information and records it into a database, and displays a confirmation message as well as a hyperlink to the next page in the application. The savevote.jsp page is shown in the screenshot below.

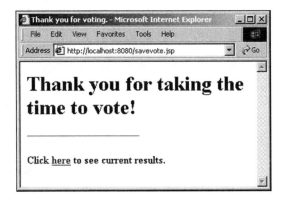

The code for savevote.jsp is shown here:

```
<%-- savevote.jsp
     records the vote into a database and invalidates the current user's session.
--%>
<!DOCTYPE HTML PUBLIC "-//W3C//DTD HTML 4.0 Transitional//EN">
<%@ page import="java.sql.*" errorPage="error.jsp" %>
<html>
<head>
  <title>Thank you for voting.</title>
</head>

<body>

<h1>Thank you for taking the time to vote!</h1>
<hr align="left" width="50%">
<h4>Click <a href="results.jsp">here</a> to see current results.</h4>
<%  // Fetch the form data
    int candidate = Integer.parseInt
                           ((String)request.getParameter("candidate"));
    int county = Integer.parseInt((String)session.getAttribute("county"));
    int ssn = Integer.parseInt((String)session.getAttribute("ssn"));

    // connect to database.

    Class.forName("sun.jdbc.odbc.JdbcOdbcDriver");
    Connection con = DriverManager.getConnection
                           ("jdbc:odbc:presidential_election", "", "");

    // Class.forName("org.gjt.mm.mysql.Driver");
    // Connection con = DriverManager.getConnection
    //           ("jdbc:mysql:///presidential_election", "admin", "admin");

    // record the vote (just the vote and county information)
    String template = "INSERT INTO VOTES(CANDIDATENUMBER, COUNTYNUMBER) " +
```

```
                         "VALUES( ?, ?)";
        PreparedStatement pstmt = con.prepareStatement(template);
        pstmt.setInt(1, candidate);
        pstmt.setInt(2, county);
        pstmt.executeUpdate();

        // invalidate the session.
        session.invalidate();

        // clean up
        if (pstmt!=null) pstmt.close();
        if (con!=null) con.close();
    %>

    </body>
    </html>
```

This JSP simply fetches some session data saved earlier on, as well as information from the ballot. The vote is recorded as an entry in the vote table, and the session is invalidated so that hitting Reload will result in failure as opposed to recording more votes. (Although in theory, a user could simply register again...)

A final controversial feature of this application is the ability to view election results in real-time. You probably are thinking that this is not supposed to happen, because it could affect the election outcome, but this is a great way to demonstrate more advanced queries! Besides, all the major television networks have a tendency to project winners before the polls close, so viewing official election results in real-time would at least be more objective! The Click here to see current results hyperlink on the savevote.jsp file brings up the results.jsp file.

The results.jsp Page

The results.jsp page is shown in the following screenshot:

The results.jsp page is a snapshot of the votes table at a particular instance of time. In the above screenshot, there have been 15 votes cast thus far, and it looks like the final results could be really close! Here is the JSP code for generating the results:

```
<!DOCTYPE HTML PUBLIC "-//W3C//DTD HTML 4.0 Transitional//EN">
<%@ page import="java.sql.*, java.util.*" errorPage="error.jsp" %>
<html>
<head>
  <title>Current Election Results:</title>
</head>

<body>
<h2>Here are the latest voting results... </h2>
<%  Class.forName("sun.jdbc.odbc.JdbcOdbcDriver");
    Connection con = DriverManager.getConnection
                            ("jdbc:odbc:presidential_election", "", "");

    // Class.forName("org.gjt.mm.mysql.Driver");
    // Connection con = DriverManager.getConnection
    //            ("jdbc:mysql:///presidential_election", "admin", "admin");

    Statement stmt = con.createStatement();
    String queryStr = "SELECT Candidate.FIRSTNAME, Candidate.LASTNAME, " +
            "Count(Votes.VOTENUMBER) AS CountOfVoteID FROM Candidate " +
            "LEFT JOIN Votes ON Candidate.CANDIDATENUMBER = " +
            "Votes.CANDIDATENUMBER GROUP BY Candidate.FIRSTNAME, " +
            "Candidate.LASTNAME";
    ResultSet rs = stmt.executeQuery(queryStr);
%>
<table border="0" cellspacing="0" cellpadding="2">
<tr bgcolor="lightgrey">
<th align="left">Candidate</th>
<th align="right">Total Votes</th>
</tr>

<%  while (rs.next()) {
        String firstname = rs.getString(1);
        String lastname = rs.getString(2);
        int votes = rs.getInt(3);
%>

<tr>
<td><%= firstname %> <%= lastname %></td>
<td align="right"><%= votes %></td>
</tr>
<%
    }  // end while()

    // clean up.
    if (rs!=null) rs.close();
    if (stmt!=null) stmt.close();
    if (con!=null) con.close();
%>
</table>
</body>
</html>
```

There is the possibility that a candidate could potentially have no votes, but if that happened, we would still want that candidate's name to show up in the output of the query; therefore we use an outer join to deal with this possibility. In a left outer join, all rows in the table on the left (in this case, the Candidate table) participate in the join, and are joined with any matching rows on the right (in this case, the Votes table). All of the rows on the left table appear in the output, even if no matching row can be found on the right side can be found; null values are inserted in columns where no matching row could be found. Thus, the voting information for every candidate is then printed out.

489

The error.jsp Page

Finally here is the code listing for `error.jsp`, the error page, which catches any uncaught exceptions. The error page prints out a simple message, and the name of the exception that was thrown.

```
<!DOCTYPE HTML PUBLIC "-//W3C//DTD HTML 4.0 Transitional//EN">
<%@ page isErrorPage="true" %>
<html>
<head>
  <title>Error Page:</title>
</head>

<body>

<h1>Something has gone wrong.</h1>
<%= exception %>

</body>
</html>
```

That concludes the sample application!

Transaction Management

Every SQL command that we have executed up until now only involved single actions where a statement was executed and then we were finished. It is often desirable to group together a series of statements that need to either succeed in its entirety, or else not be done at all – this is the notion of a transaction. As an example, an electronic money transfer transaction requires debiting one account and crediting another; it is not acceptable to update one account and not the other. The debit and credit operations that together constitute one unit of work (the transaction) and are either executed as a single unit of work, or if one of the operations fails, the transaction is rolled back (undone) in order to preserve the integrity of the underlying data.

By default, when a new `Connection` object is created, it is set to **commit** every database update as it is executed (every operation is a transaction), and therefore cannot be undone. The `Connection` interface, however, also has several methods to demarcate transaction boundaries, and either rollback or commit them to the database.

To begin a transaction, we call `setAutoCommit(false)`, which gives us control over what gets committed and when. A call to `commit()` will commit everything that was done since the last time `commit()` was issued. Conversely, a `rollback()` call will undo any changes since the last time `commit()` was called. In keeping with the tradition of using bank-account examples to explain transactions, the following code snippet illustrates how you would use the JDBC to transfer funds from one account to another:

```
// begin transaction
con.setAutoCommit(false);
try {
  Statement stmt = con.CreateStatement();
  // withdraw from savings account
  stmt.executeUpdate("UPDATE SAVINGS SET BALANCE = " +
                     "(BALANCE - 100) WHERE ACCOUNTNO = ...)";
```

```
    // make payment to visa card
    stmt.executeUpdate("UPDATE VISA SET BALANCE = " +
                        "(BALANCE + 100) WHERE ACCOUNTNO = ...");
    con.commit();
}
catch(SQLException sqle) {
    // perhaps an insufficient balance or invalid account number
    con.rollback();
}
finally {
    // return to default settings
    con.setAutoCommit(true);
}
```

In this example we require a withdrawal of 100 credits from a savings account to make a credit card payment. A partial failure will result in either an unhappy customer or unhappy credit card company. The UPDATE statements are wrapped in a try/catch block, and the transaction is rolled back if anything goes wrong. For example we may have provided invalid account numbers, had insufficient funds, the Visa payment systems could have been down temporarily, and so on. By wrapping both SQL operations into a single transaction we ensure consistency of the underlying data – either the whole thing completes, or everything fails – not something in-between.

> **Please note that MySQL not a transactional database in the traditional sense. MySQL has made a conscious decision to support another paradigm for data integrity called atomic operations. For the above code to work you would need to install the Berkeley Database support files and change the CREATE TABLE ... data definition commands to specify transaction-safe tables. For more information consult the MySQL documentation (mysql/docs directory), section 5.4.3 on Transactions.**

Connection Pooling and the Optional 2.x API

Up to this point we have been using the Core JDBC 1.0 API, which includes all classes and interfaces contained within the java.sql package provided with the J2SE, which is typically sufficient for basic web applications. In this section we will discuss the JDBC 2.x API, which consists of classes and interfaces in the javax.sql package, currently included with the J2EE. In order to build more robust distributed enterprise applications you should be looking at EJB application server technologies that support or have similar functionality to the JDBC 2.x Optional Package API. The optional package is a higher-level abstraction to the JDBC, implemented by application server, database, or database-driver companies, designed to relieve you of the more mundane tasks of developing your application by implementing some of the most common functionality in a standardized manner. Here are some of the key features provided by the JDBC 2.x Optional Package API.

❑ **Connection Pooling**: A connection pool is a cache of database connections that is maintained in memory, so that the connections may be reused, rather than created and destroyed after every subsequent use. In JDBC 2.x, the responsibility of implementing connection pools rests with application server, database, or driver vendors, freeing individual developers from rolling out their own custom connection pooling solutions, resulting in less work, easier portability, and (hopefully) better overall performance.

❑ **JNDI-based lookup of databases**: Rather than having every client load a driver into their respective machine and try to connect to a specific database URL, the Java Naming and Directory Interface (JNDI)-based look-up service allows us to access database resources using logical names, insulating clients from possible changes in the underlying data store.

❑ **Distributed Transaction Support**: The optional package API specifies a standardized means for an application server or driver to support distributed transactions, that is, transactions involving multiple databases or other resources across the network.

❑ **RowSets**: A lightweight JavaBeans-compliant object (complete with event sources and listeners) that encapsulates database result sets and all data access methods. Unlike a ResultSet, a RowSet can be optionally **disconnected**; in other words, the connection to the database need not be open for the RowSet to exist. RowSets can also be optionally updateable, meaning that any changes to the RowSet will be propagated back to the underlying database. A RowSet has different concurrency and transaction-isolation levels which determines what to do in the event that changes occur to the underlying database while the RowSet was offline.

As previously mentioned, application server and database vendors implement most of the code in the optional java.sql package, which in turn requires willingness on the part of vendors to buy into supporting these APIs. This is often a slow process, however the JDBC drivers listing at http://industry.java.sun.com/products/jdbc/drivers shows numerous JDBC drivers that implement the JDBC 2.x API. It is not very difficult to integrate JDBC 2.x into your application code because most of the work is implemented for you behind-the-scenes; you will see shortly that you get a ton of advanced functionality in just a few lines of code! It is most important to understand the concepts and so in this section we will present some more code snippets to illustrate them. In practice most application servers will offer support for connection pooling and distributed transactions, but the syntax for accessing those features (although very similar conceptually) may differ slightly – you will probably need to consult your server documentation. To test the concepts illustrated in this chapter you will require either the J2EE reference implementation from Sun Microsystems (freely available for download at http://java.sun.com/j2ee) or any commercial implementation with support for the JDBC optional package.

In this section we will cover various interfaces in the JDBC 2.x API for connecting to an underlying data source, and explain how to use them to obtain a connection with optional support for connection pooling and even distributed transactions.

The javax.sql.DataSource Interface

As the name suggests, a DataSource is an object-oriented abstraction of an underlying data source and is the interface through which we connect to and interact with a data source. DataSource objects can provide transparent connection pooling and distributed transactions behind the scenes, both of which are essential for enterprise-class applications.

To use a DataSource it is necessary to:

1. Create an instance of the DataSource class

2. Set its properties

3. Register the DataSource with a registry or naming service that uses the Java Naming and Directory Service (JNDI)

When using a `DataSource`, there are three general cases to be considered:

- ❑ A `DataSource` that is neither pooled nor used in a distributed transaction environment
- ❑ A `DataSource` that supports connection pooling
- ❑ A `DataSource` that is used in a distributed transaction, meaning that it produces connections which can be used in a transaction involving multiple database servers or resources

The first case is the easiest. Assuming that we are using a database for which you have purchased a database driver which supports the optional package, and that the class that implements the `DataSource` interface is called `com.dbcompany.BasicDataSource`, here's how you would make it available to your clients:

```
import javax.sql.*;   // import optional package
import javax.naming.*;   // import JNDI

com.dbcompany.BasicDataSource ds = new com.dbCompany.BasicDataSource();
dataSource.setServerName("decartes");   // a DB server
db.setDatabaseName("presidential_election");
```

Here, the `DataSource` variable's properties have been set to refer to the `presidential_election` database on the `decartes` database server. This `DataSource` object is then registered with a JNDI naming service to be discovered by clients on the network. The registration process might look something like this:

```
Context context = new InitialContext();
context.bind("jdbc/election", dataSource);
```

Here we are using JNDI to create an `InitialContext` object as a starting point and then binding the `DataSource` object into a registry under the sub-context `jdbc` and name `election`. We could have picked any name here; however, this is the preferred naming convention for JDBC data sources. Once the `DataSource` is bound to the registry, any client on the network can locate the data source using its full logical-name as follows:

```
Context ctx = new InitialContext();
DataSource ds = (DataSource)ctx.lookup("jdbc/election");
```

Again, we create an `InitialContext` object on the client as a starting point, then use the `lookup()` method to find the object bound to the logical name `"jdbc/election"`. The `lookup()` method returns an object of type `Object`, which must be cast into a `DataSource`. The `javax.sql.DataSource` interface eliminates details of the database connection information from your code, and instead you refer to your database sources by a logical name such as `ELECTION` or `EMPLOYEES`. If a new driver class becomes available, or the database server moves, or the login information changes, only the resource description needs to be reconfigured. Compare this with changing every JSP in your web application and it becomes easy to understand the benefits. Any components or code referencing this named resource will not have to be modified, thanks to JNDI.

Now that we have a reference to an underlying data source (the `DataSource` object created above), we can obtain a connection to the data source by calling `DataSource`'s `getConnection()` method:

```
Connection con = ds.getConnection("admin","pass");
```

Here the username and password need to be supplied as arguments to the `getConnection()` method. Contrast this to the JDBC 1.0 core API's way of connecting to a data source by manually loading a driver then hard-coding the URL of the database as an argument to the `DriverManager.getConnection()` method. Clearly the latter method of connecting to a database suffers from portability problems since the driver and URL information is hard-coded into every JSP or Java file that accesses a database.

In addition the use of the `DataSource.getConnection()` method simplifies code maintenance in the event that there is a change in the underlying database's configuration; you would only need to change one property on the `DataSource` object as opposed to modifying every JSP or Java class that accessed the database. Aside from this `DataSource` offers to additional benefits, in particular the ability to produce connections that implement connection pooling or distributed transactions support automatically. We now take a look at how this is accomplished.

Connection Pooling using the JDBC 2.x API

The vast majority (typically over 80%) of the time taken to service an HTTP request for dynamic data is spent at the database. Opening a connection to a database (usually) requires crossing process boundaries (possibly several times), network latencies, as well as expensive operations like synchronization and object instantiation. All of this makes obtaining database connections a very costly operation, and therefore also an obvious target for potential optimization. Connection pooling refers to pre-allocating database connections and recycling them across different client requests. Most books have an example of how to implement some homegrown connection pooling classes. The idea is quite simple:

- ❏ Create a handful of database connections upon startup (perhaps in the `jspInit()` method, or in an event listener)
- ❏ Save references to the connections in a collection accessible from all your servlets/JSPs (perhaps by placing them in the application context)
- ❏ When client requests come in, locate a database connection, use it to perform the required operations, then release the connection back to the pool

J2EE specifications have evolved considerably over the past few months to the point where it is no longer advisable to roll out your own custom database connection pooling classes, but rather to using the `javax.sql.DataSource` interface from the JDBC 2.x API to obtain connections with built in connection pooling.

To summarize, there are several major reasons why we would recommend against using custom pooling classes:

- ❏ If your web application needs to be fine-tuned to the point where it requires the use of connection pools, then you should automatically start thinking about moving this code out of your JSPs (or even Servlets) and consider using an EJB container.
- ❏ At the time of this writing, most application servers have built-in connection pooling which can be retrieved from a JNDI registry. Different vendors have slightly different means of looking-up a connection pool, but we will show how to do this later in this section.
- ❏ Even if you don't want to use an EJB server or `DataSource`, various web application frameworks (such as Apache Struts) and other third party JSP tag libraries implement data access paradigms with built-in connection pooling saving you the trouble of rolling out your own code. (Why re-invent the wheel?)

❑ The most important reason why the use of a DataSource object is Sun's preferred means of connecting to a data source is because, in addition to providing transparent connection pooling, it also supports distributed transactions – the idea that a transaction might involve different tables across different databases; however, in order for this to work it really requires that all clients access the underlying data source in a consistent manner. This functionality, part of the JDBC 2.0 Standard Extension API, is essential for enterprise database computing, and is used throughout Enterprise JavaBeans technology.

Connection pooling using the JDBC 2.x API is accomplished by deploying a javax.sql.ConnectionPoolDataSource object in a manner very similar to the regular javax.sql.DataSource object that was discussed earlier, with one additional step. Assume that your database/server/driver vendor's JDBC 2.x classes are named as follows:

JDBC 2.x Interface	Implementing Ilass
javax.sql.ConnectionPoolDataSource	com.dbcompany.ConnectionPoolDS
javax.sql.DataSource	com.dbcompany.PooledDataSource

First, the ConnectionPoolDataSource object needs to be deployed. It involves creating an instance of an object which implements the javax.sql.ConnectionPoolDataSource interface (in this case, com.dbcompany.ConnectionPoolDS), then setting its properties and binding it into the JNDI name service as follows:

```
import javax.sql.*;  // import optional package
import javax.naming.*;  // import JNDI


...


// ConnectionPoolDS implements javax.sql.ConnectionPoolDataSource
com.dbcompany.ConnectionPoolDS cpds = new com.dbcompany.ConnectionPoolDS();

// Set the properties
cpds.setServerName("decartes");  // a DB server
cpds.setDatabaseName("presidential_election");
cpds.setPortNumber(1433);
cpds.setDescription("Presidential Election Results in Florida");

// ...

// Bind to JNDI naming service
Context ctx = new InitialContext();
ctx.bind("jdbc/pool/connection_pool_ds", cpds);
```

The ConnectionPoolDataSource is bound in the registry under the sub-context (similar to a directory structure) of "jdbc/pool/conection_pool_ds" which is a recommended naming convention for pooled data sources. The ConnectionPoolDataSource, cpds, represents the object that implements all of the connection pooling behind the scenes. Once it is deployed, there is one additional step. We must deploy the DataSource object which is configured to interact with cpds, as follows:

```
com.dbcompany.PooledDataSource = new com.dbcompany.PooledDataSource();
ds.setDescription
        ("produces pooled connections for the online voting application");
```

```
// This is the javax.sql.CConnectionPoolDataSource that we just deployed
ds.setDataSourceName("jdbc/pool/connection_pool_ds");

Context ctx = new InitialContext();
ctx.bind("jdbc/election", cpds);
```

And finally, for a client to obtain and use a pooled connection it is the same as in the case of a regular `DataSource` as shown below:

```
import javax.sql.*;
import javax.ejb.*;
import javax.naming.*;
import java.sql.*;

// ...

try {
  Context ctx = new InitialContext();
  DataSource ds = (DataSource) ctx.lookup("jdbc/election");
  Connection con = ds.getConnection("admin", "pass");
  // Do something with the connection

  // ...
}
catch (Exception e) {
  // handle the exceptions
}
finally {
  if (con!=null) con.close();
}
```

Note that this is identical to the code that was used in the case of a non-pooled `DataSource` object except that we closed the connection in the `finally` statement, returning the connection to the pool. In summary, here were the steps required to set up and use connection pooling in the JDBC 2.x API:

❑   Create an instance of a class that implements `javax.sql.ConnectionPoolDataSource` (this is the class that implements the connection pooling functionality), set its properties and deploy it using JNDI.

❑   Create an instance of a class that implements the `javax.sql.DataSource`, set its `dataSourceName` property to the logical name that was bound to the `ConnectionPoolDataSource` object created in the first step; deploy the `DataSource` using JNDI.

❑   Have your clients look up the `DataSource` deployed in the second step using JNDI, obtain a pooled connection simply by calling `getConnection()`, and close the connection when finished.

Distributed Transactions using the JDBC 2.x API

A distributed transaction is a transaction involving multiple participants located across the network. Suppose a transaction for ordering a book from an online bookstore involved checking to see if the bookstore's supplier had that book in stock and if so ordering a copy, as well as debiting your credit card and crediting the bookstore's account for the amount of the purchase. Just like a regular transaction, we would like all of theses operations to succeed or fail as a single unit; however, what makes this more difficult is the fact that there are multiple databases (or other resources) acting as participants here and they each must communicate their progress to a central location (called a transaction coordinator). If any one database fails, then all work on all databases must be rolled-back.

Most enterprise-class applications require support for distributed transactions. This is a much harder problem than in the case of a regular transaction involving only one database, yet the use of JDBC 2.0 `DataSource` objects completely abstracts away all of the details of managing a distributed transaction. This is perhaps the most compelling reason to use a `DataSource` rather than trying to roll out your own database infrastructure code.

The use of a `DataSource` object for getting connections that can be used in distributed transactions is virtually the same as in the case of using a `DataSource` that supports connection pooling. Two different classes must be deployed, a `javax.sql.XADataSource` and a `javax.sql.DataSource` object that is implemented to work with it. Lets make the following assumptions concerning the names of your database/server/driver vendor's JDBC 2.x class names:

JDBC 2.x Interface	Implementing Class
`javax.sql.XADataSource`	`com.dbcompany.XATransactionalDS`
`javax.sql.DataSource`	`com.dbcompany.TransactionalDS`

Once the `javax.sql.XADataSource` and `javax.sql.DataSource` objects have been deployed, any connections obtained from the `DataSource` will be able to participate in a distributed transaction. Here's how you would create and deploy an instance of `com.dbcompany.XATransactionalDS` and set its properties:

```
com.dbcompany.XATransactionalDS xads =
        new com.dbcompany.XATransactionalDS();
xads.setServerName("neo"); // a database server
xads.setDatabaseName("presidential_election");
xads.setPortNumber(1433);
xads.setDescription("Provide distributed transaction support for
presidential_election");

// ...

// Deploy using JNDI
Context ctx = new InitialContext();
ctx.bind("jdbc/xa/xa_data_source", xads);
```

Here the `jdbc/xa/` sub-context is the preferred naming convention for distributed transactional data sources, and `xads` is the object that is providing the distributed transaction support. This must be associated with a `DataSource`, as follows:

```
com.dbcompany.TransactionalDS ds = new com.dbcompany.TransactionalDS();
ds.setDescription
        ("Produces distributed transaction connections for US election");
ds.setDataSourceName("jdbc/xa/xa_data_source");

// ...

// Deploy using JNDI
Context ctx = new InitialContext();
ctx.bind("jdbc/election", ds);
```

Now that we have deployed classes that implement the required `javax.sql.XADataSource` and `javax.sql.DataSource` interfaces, any connections obtained from `ds` in the above code fragment will produce a connection which can be used in distributed transactions.

Finally, for a client to obtain and use a connection with support for distributed transactions it is the same as in the case of a regular or pooled `DataSource` as shown below:

```
import javax.sql.*;
import javax.ejb.*;
import javax.naming.*;
import java.sql.*;

// ...

try {
  Context ctx = new InitialContext();
  DataSource ds = (DataSource) ctx.lookup("jdbc/election");
  Connection con = ds.getConnection("admin", "pass");
  // Do something with the connection, updating different tables across
  // different databases

  // ...

}
catch (Exception e) {
  // handle the exceptions
}
finally {
  if (con!=null) con.close();
}
```

Again this is identical to the code that was used in the case of a non-pooled `DataSource` object as well as the pooled `DataSource`. (We are beginning to sound like a broken record player!) A few notes worthy of mention when using a `DataSource` that creates connections capable of participating in distributed transactions: a transaction manager is controlling demarcation of transaction boundaries and when to commit/rollback a transaction in progress – you must not call `con.commit()` or `con.rollback()`, nor should you call `con.setAutoCommit(true)` since all of this would interfere with the transaction manager's control over the distributed transaction. Again note that we closed the connection in the `finally` statement, returning the connection to the pool.

In summary, the steps required to set up and use distributed transactions in the JDBC 2.x API were:

❑ Create an instance of a class that implements `javax.sql.XADataSource` (this is the class that implements the connection pooling functionality) set its properties and deploy it using JNDI.

❑ Create an instance of a class that implements the `javax.sql.DataSource`, set its `dataSourceName` property to the logical name that was bound to the `XADataSource` object created in the first step; deploy the `DataSource` using JNDI.

❑ Have your clients look up the `DataSource` from the second step using JNDI, obtain a connection (with support for distributed transactions) by calling `getConnection()`, and close the connection when finished.

Data Access Strategies

We have now looked at many different ways to use JSP and JDBC together to build interactive data driven web applications, all of which work fine, but in some cases one methodology is better suited than others. There are many considerations and trade-offs that need to be taken into account when architecting different applications, including code maintenance, scalability, portability, and much more. These issues are not so clear-cut, and there is considerable debate over the middle–tier and where to put JDBC code.

Understanding the data access debate is really like trying to nail down a moving target. If you look back at old best practices, or API documentation from Sun, you will see that data access recommendations vary considerably over time. For example, initially we didn't even have JSPs, so everything was placed inside servlets. Further, custom tags were only introduced in 1999, so data access tags only recently became a new possibility. The initial EJB 1.0 specification didn't make Entity Beans mandatory; Entity Beans using Container Managed Persistence (CMP) in the EJB 1.1 specification work only for contrived examples where an object maps directly to a table (no support for dependent objects), and the EJB 2.0 specification, currently in proposed final draft at the time of this writing, will likely undergo significant change by the time it is finalized. The key is to recognize that specifications are continuously evolving through an iterative community process.

In this section we present/review the most common data access strategies and explain some of the trade-offs, to help you choose one that best fits your application requirements.

Using Scriptlets

Embedding scriptlets into your JSP files is obviously a very tempting solution for an easy way to get an application up and running in a hurry. That is its only advantage. We know from experience that tight coupling of presentation and application leads to code maintenance problems down the road; conversely using more layered architectures can isolate, reduce, or eliminate effects felt throughout the application due to changes to one specific part of the system.

Using JavaBeans

In Chapter 6 we talked about using JavaBeans as a means to separate business and presentation logic. We could easily envision a database access bean with methods such as `connect()` and `disconnect()`, which we would then invoke at the beginning and end of every JSP in our application, like a pair of bookends on a bookshelf. Additionally we could expand on this idea by writing a `getData()` method which would execute the required SQL command, and return a `ResultSet` to the caller. In this case the JSP would only need to handle formatting of the results.

The advantages of using JavaBeans to hide data access code include:

❑ Significant reduction of Java code in your JSP files, resulting in better readability, particularly for the front-end user-interface people.

❑ Promotes encapsulation of common tasks resulting in code re-use at a class-level. Contrast this to using similar-looking scriptlets in each of your JSPs and re-using them by cutting-and pasting them onto new pages. This is of course more error prone.

❑ After the initial investment to create JavaBeans encapsulating the various actions performed by JSPs, subsequent development time is accelerated considerably.

❑ A degree of decoupling and isolation of business and presentation logic, resulting in lower code maintenance requirements in the long run.

Using Tag Extensions

Custom tags (see Chapters 8-11) are closely related to the JavaBeans solution. Many templating or scripting systems offer tag-based abstractions to data access – for example the `<cfquery>` tag in ColdFusion. The introduction of tag extensions into the JSP 1.1 allows for the development of tags that can do just about anything, including providing tag-based abstractions to the JDBC API. There are numerous open source and vendor tag libraries available which showcase such tags. For instance, the following example is from the JRun tag library, which is bundled with their server (available for download at http://commerce.allaire.com/download/):

```
<%@ taglib uri="jruntags" prefix="jrun" %>

<jrun:sql datasrc="source" id="x">
  SELECT Date, StartTime, EndTime, Name
  FROM Appointments
  Where UserName = '<%= request.getParameter("username") %>'
</jrun:sql>
<jrun:param id="x" type="allaire.taglib.QueryTable"/>
<table>
  <jrun:foreach group="<%= x %>">
    <tr>
      <td><%= x.get("Date") %></td>
      <td><%= x.get("StartTime") %></td>
      <td><%= x.get("EndTime") %></td>
      <td><%= x.get("Name") %></td>
    </tr>
  </jrun:foreach>
</table>
```

In this code fragment we import the tag library, and execute a `<jrun:sql>` tag, which has attributes corresponding to the data source and variable name identifying the results of the query. The body of the `<jrun:sql>` tag is the SQL query to be executed. The results are processed using an iteration tag, which takes as an attribute the collection to be iterated over. We will talk more about writing and using tag extensions in a later chapter, but for now just remember that this is a possible solution.

The Jakarta Taglibs subproject (http://jakarta.apache.org/taglibs/) has recently released a `jdbc` tag library, which provides rich access to JDBC databases including the ability to connect directly using a JDBC URL, by being passed a `DataSource` object, or using JNDI. The `jdbc` taglib also provides tags that use both `Statements` and `PreparedStatements`, iterate over a `ResultSet`, and retrieve column values. For example, the JSP below uses this tag library to display a list of the candidates in our voting application:

```
<%@ taglib uri="http://jakarta.apache.org/taglibs/jdbc" prefix="jdbc" %>
<html>
<head><title>The Candidates</title></head>
<body>
<h1>The Candidates</h1>

<%-- Open a connection --%>
<jdbc:connection id="conn">
  <jdbc:url>jdbc:odbc:presidential_election</jdbc:url>
  <jdbc:driver>sun.jdbc.odbc.JdbcOdbcDriver</jdbc:driver>
</jdbc:connection>

<%-- Create a query --%>
<table border="1" cellpadding="2" cellspacing="0">
  <tr>
    <th>Name</th>
    <th>Party</th>
  <tr>

  <jdbc:statement id="candidates" conn="conn">
    <jdbc:query>
      SELECT FIRSTNAME, LASTNAME, POLITICALPARTY FROM CANDIDATE
    </jdbc:query>

    <%-- Iterate through the candidates --%>
    <jdbc:resultSet id="results">
      <tr>
        <td><jdbc:getColumn position="1"/>
            <jdbc:getColumn position="2"/></td>
        <td><jdbc:getColumn position="3"/>
            <jdbc:wasNull><i>Not specified</i></jdbc:wasNull></td>
      </tr>
    </jdbc:resultSet>
  </jdbc:statement>
</table>

<%-- Close connection --%>
<jdbc:closeConnection conn="conn"/>

</body>
</html>
```

The advantages of using data-access tag extensions are the same as using JavaBeans, except that the use of tag extensions are typically more familiar to somebody not familiar with Java syntax. The disadvantages of data-access tag extensions include:

❑ Less obvious separation of presentation and business logic since the query is set on the JSP

❑ Appearing to go against the spirit of J2EE which advocates a much more layered approach for data access using entity and session beans

❑ Lack of third-party web authoring tools

The last point is probably the most serious shortcoming of using tag extensions. If the premise of using tag extensions in the first place is to make life easier for the user-interface design team, but they use a product that cannot properly render these new tags and subsequently ignores them, or if the tags are too complicated for the design team to read, then we haven't really made their job any easier. Often designing a page using an editor screen cluttered with unrecognized tags is like navigating a minefield, with code very susceptible to being broken.

501

However, tag extensions are a better solution than using scriptlets and are a great solution for smaller (and less graphics intense) projects such as intranets or personal web pages.

Using Enterprise JavaBeans (EJBs)

All of the above methodologies are probably not appropriate for large scale distributed transactional applications, such as airline reservation or financial systems, and presidential election voting applications too.

In its entirety, EJB is a framework for building component-based, transactional, distributed applications. Just like all other Java API, EJB is a specification, not limited to any particular company, server implementation, communication protocol, or platform. Once you decide to write EJBs, this is essentially nothing more than writing several Java classes and an XML file bundled into a single unit, and deploying them to an application server. The Java classes that you write adhere to certain rules and implement some required methods, and are managed by the application server. The current EJB 1.1 specification defines **entity beans**, which are meant to model persistent data and encapsulate all data access code; and **session beans**, which model business processes, and often act as facades to access or perform operations on entity beans.

Contrast this to what we have been doing up until now – essentially coding all business logic and representing business objects (for example, a vote or candidate in the sample application) in your JSPs or servlets. In order to make the sample application into an EJB application, you would move code out of the JSPs. Code that checks to see if a person already voted, and queries to see who won the election, both represent business processes, and would be represented as session beans. The persistent entities, like voting records, candidates, and eligible voters would all be modeled as entity beans.

EJB is the other extreme of the data access debate, representing the most layered architecture to solving the common problem of where to place data access and business logic code. Many web software developers with backgrounds in scripting languages such as JSP, PHP, ColdFusion, or Perl, will have difficulty understanding why EJBs are necessary; after all, numerous web sites have demonstrated that it is possible to provide dynamic content using servlets or JSPs alone, making this additional layer of interposition seem like unnecessary complexity. It is also difficult to distill the true value of EJB from all of the marketing hype surrounding EJB. We'll return to the subject of EJBs in Chapter 24. For more on this subject, see *Professional Java Server Programming, J2EE Edition* (ISBN 1-861004-65-6).

So Which One To Choose?

There isn't consensus here, and best practices are always evolving. The best advice is to get a good understanding of the trade-offs between different data access strategies. You must then determine the scalability and long-term code maintenance requirements of your application, as well as the competency of your team of developers. As a rule of thumb, as you move from scriptlets towards EJBs, the scalability and support for other advanced functionality increases, the complexity and flexibility of the overall application increases, and the long term code maintenance requirements decreases.

JDBC/JSP Debugging Tips

JDBC debugging can be tricky by itself; when combined with JSP it can become frustrating. This may be due to poor error messages, the relative absence of JSP debuggers in the marketplace, and so on. The following are the common-sense tips for troubleshooting JDBC/JSP errors.

SQLException

All JDBC code must be wrapped in a `try/catch` block that catches `SQLException`, potentially thrown by any JDBC method. `SQLException` provides useful debugging information. In addition to a `String` describing the error, available via the method `getMessage()`, there is also the `getErrorCode()` method which returns the database vendor-specific integer error code, typically corresponding to the actual error code returned by the underlying database (you will need to consult your database documentation to figure out what the error code means). Finally, `SQLExceptions` can be chained together; the following code fragment shows how to print out all nested exceptions using the `getNextException()` method:

```
catch (SQLException sqle) {
  out.println(sqle.getMessage());
  while((e = e.getNextException()) != null) {
    out.println(e.getMessage);
  }
}
```

Null Pointer Exceptions

Remember that the `Connection` object is the root of all other remote objects being returned including `Statements` and `ResultSets`, and that these objects are no longer available once the `Connection` is closed. Possible solutions to this would be to copy the data or use disconnected `RowSets`.

If a column in a database record is not assigned a value it will be set to `null`. Unfortunately, there is no such thing in Java as `null` values for primitive types. For example, a call to `getInt()` might return 0 or −1 to indicate a `null` value; but this is misleading because they are both valid integer values. In addition, if `getString()` is called on a `null` entry some drivers will return `null`, whereas others will return the empty string (`" "`). This leads to potentially dangerous problems with application portability. There are two possible solutions to dealing with this situation:

❑   Use the `ResultSet`'s `wasNull()` method, which returns `true` or `false` depending on whether or not the last row access method corresponded to a `null` value in the database

❑   Use the `getObject()` method, which always returns `null` if a particular column value is `null`

Some `ResultSet` implementations impose the restriction that you can only read a column value for a particular row once, and that the failure to do so results in a null-pointer exception.

Integrity Constraints

Don't forget the fundamentals of the relational model. Often during the development or testing, errors result from, say, running the same test twice.

Perhaps you are inserting data that already exists in the database, which would be a violation of the primary key uniqueness constraint. Another common error is violating the referential integrity constraint – inserting data for which a foreign key has no corresponding entry in the table that it references.

Limitations of JDBC

As we have seen throughout this chapter, the JDBC API makes it possible to achieve application-database portability across many underlying data stores, making good on Java's *write once, run anywhere* marketing mantra. While JDBC represents an excellent technology offering, it is important to realize that there are several limitations to JDBC that one should be aware of:

❑　JDBC standardizes the mechanism for connecting to a database, and the syntax for sending queries and committing transactions. It also defines data structures that encapsulate the result of a query. However, JDBC does not try to enforce the standardization of the SQL language itself: you can execute any query using any syntax, so long as the underlying database understands that syntax.

　　In practice, SQL syntax can vary between databases; for example, some databases allow for the use of proprietary SQL extensions, or might have slightly varying syntax for specifying inner or outer joins, or likely have some support for other proprietary hooks. Therefore, while using JDBC greatly simplifies achieving application-database portability, and generally works 100% in simple cases, it does not in any way make any guarantees, nor does it relieve you of the responsibility to run QA or testing when porting an application to a different database.

❑　As seen throughout the chapter, data access code could be placed in scriptlets, JavaBeans, tag-extensions, or entity beans, all of which have different trade-offs. JDBC does not specify where to place data access code within an application, nor does it make any recommendations about data-access style, and indeed this is the source of considerable confusion and debate in the Java community.

❑　JDBC relies entirely on the availability of JDBC drivers (although at this point in time drivers are available for virtually all popular databases).

❑　There are many other types of databases are used in the industry today, some of which are non-relational in nature, for example, object or other heretical databases like XML data stores, as well as proprietary data models used by Enterprise Resource Planning systems. JDBC currently has a strong relational assumption, so it is probably not the right solution if your enterprise data warehouse falls into the non-relational category. Note that the J2EE connector architecture specification (a separate standards initiative) tries to address this issue by abstracting away the underlying data storage model, allowing one to access data from any enterprise data store (relational or otherwise); however, this is outside the scope of this chapter.

Summary

In this chapter we have seen that JSP and JDBC working together represent the front and back-end of the J2EE architecture, and are possibly the most important APIs for building interactive web applications. In particular, we covered:

❑　An overview of the JDBC standard APIs and an overview of the relational model

❑　The concept of a JDBC driver, and their varying types

❑　How JSP and JDBC can be used to create, read, update and delete data from a relational database, all from a web application

❑   A sample web application with setup notes for both Microsoft Access and MySQL

❑   User-demarcated transaction management

We also touched on some of the advanced functionality of JDBC 2.x optional package, including using data sources to transparently provide connection pooling and support for distributed transactions. We looked at some of the trade-offs involved with different data access strategies, and finished off with some tips for troubleshooting the most common JDBC programming errors.In the next chapter we will take a first look at a new and exciting feature of the Servlet 2.3 API: filtering.

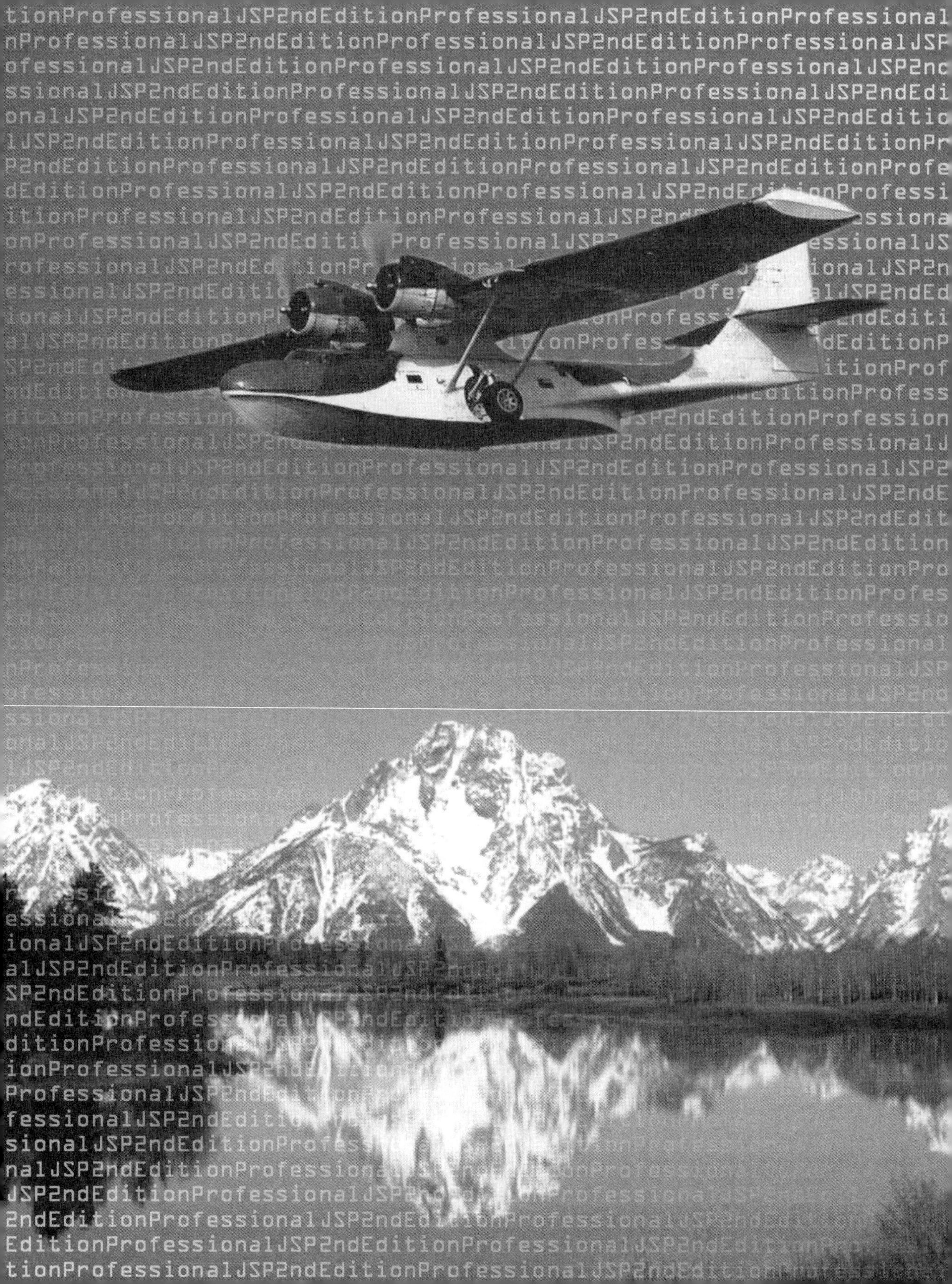
ProfessionalJSP2ndEdition

14

Introduction to Filtering

One very important new feature of the Servlet 2.3 specification is filtering, which has the potential to rapidly become one of the most used value-added features across most J2EE containers compatible with Servlet 2.3 specifications. The immediate application areas for filtering include authentication, auditing, compression, encryption and on-the-fly format transformation, to name but a few. For the very first time, an application level programmer can tap into the request processing pipeline of the container – in a portable, non server-specific manner.

The unique positioning of filters in the processing pipeline, the relative ease with which they can be written and designed, and the versatile way these filters can be configured will make them the idea design choices for a wide range of web application features that were formerly impossible, difficult, or awkward to implement.

This chapter will introduce filtering. We will show via conceptual diagrams, discussion, and code fragments:

- ❑ What a filter is, what it can do, and why it is needed

- ❑ How filters fit in with the rest of the Servlets/JSP machinery

- ❑ The container-managed lifecycle of filters

- ❑ The power of filter mapping

- ❑ The importance of filter chaining

- ❑ Then, walking through three complete code samples of filters, we will gain hands on experience working through the development procedure and the requirements for filters

- ❑ Finally, we will conclude with some words of wisdom on filter design and coding, and we will contrast filters with two common filter-like mechanisms – interceptors and valves – that often get confused with Servlet 2.3 filters

The material covered in this chapter will provide a basic understanding of what Servlet 2.3 filtering is all about. We will dive into the important concepts, and illustrate them with simple, easy to understand code wherever necessary. We have purposely deferred advanced concepts in filtering, together with detailed design of more complex filters, to the next chapter.

This chapter is concept heavy and code light, while the next one will be both concept and code heavy. In fact, the next chapter will provide an insight into the design and coding of many typical filters. It will focus on the techniques in programming filters, and will serve as a 'cookbook' for the practising JSP programmer – adding filters to their repertoire of tools.

Potential Filter Applications

Before we take a technical look at what a filter really is, we will briefly discuss a few potential applications for filters in the real world.

Since a filter can examine request header information ahead of the resource in the processing pipeline, filters can be used to create customized authentication schemes. For example, a filter can be written to authenticate a user against an external legacy system before allowing access to a resource. Having 'wide open' exposure to all the request headers, filters can be written to perform sophisticated logging and auditing. Combining the use of filters with URL pattern-based filter mapping, we can have fine grained control on the set of resources to protect, or to audit.

Filters are also useful in data transformation. For example, we can use filters to present an XML document as HTML via an XSLT transform filter on-the-fly. Another form of data transformation filter might perform encryption or compression. For example, a filter can first detect if a user agent (browser) supports compressed stream of data. If the browser can handle compression, the filter can then compress the response from the resource on-the-fly.

Filters can pre-empt the serving of the associated resource altogether, and generate its own response. One example of such a filter could be a time-sensitive filter that will block game resource access during official office hours. Yet another interesting application in this category is customized caching. A filter can maintain a cache of most frequently requested (static) resources based on pre-specified criterion, and serve a cached copy instead of accessing the real resource whenever possible.

The Big Picture of Filtering

The middle tier of the J2EE architecture typically consists of a web/application server (or a combination of them). This server will serve web content and execute Servlet/JSPs in response to incoming client requests. The Tomcat standalone server is an example of such a server. The figure below illustrates how client requests flow through such a server:

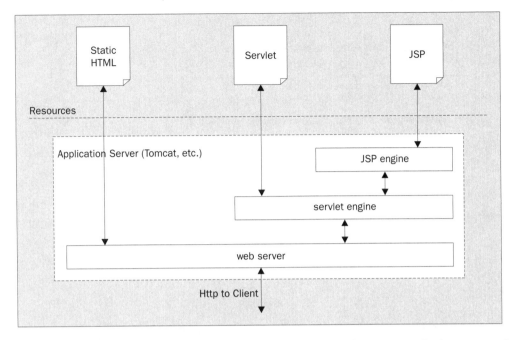

One way of looking at the above figure is to view it as a server for resource requests. In this view, we do not differentiate between static and dynamically generated resources. Therefore, our middle tier server becomes a server that serves one of three different types of resources based on incoming requests:

❑   Static content (web pages)

❑   A Servlet

❑   A JSP (which may be considered as a specialized case of a Servlet)

> **We will make reference again and again throughout this chapter and the next to this resource based view of request processing. It is the way a filter designer/programmer looks at the container.**

The figure overleaf illustrates this simplified view of the middle-tier server, emphasizing the request/response flow. It also shows where filters fit into the picture:

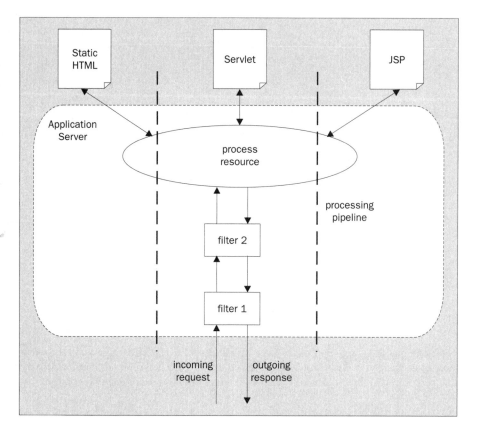

You can see from the diagram that the filters are positioned in the **processing pipeline**, between the application server and the client.

> **A filter provides application level access into the request handling pipeline of the container.**

Before the advent of filters, there was no way for web applications to participate in the processing being performed along the request-handling path. A web application can only supply and define the resources that are being served. If an application required access to the processing pipeline, we had to resort to non-portable server level extensions (interceptors, valves, etc. which are explained later) to accomplish the task.

Due to the strategic position of filters in the request-processing pipeline, they can easily handle the pre- and post-processing of requests for potentially a heterogeneous set of resources (a mix of static HTML pages, JSPs, and Servlets). The specialized construction of filters, as we shall discover later, will actually allow them to participate in the processing of the request or response throughout the processing path.

We also have the option of chaining several filters together dynamically to process each incoming request. This allows the filter deployer to combine the action of two or more filters together at deployment time. At runtime, the container uses filter mappings to determine the filter that each request or response will pass through.

Filtering the Pipeline

Filters enable a developer to tap into the pipeline of request and response processing. A filter can do its work just before the resource is fetched (or executed in the case of dynamic output), or immediately after the resource is fetched and/or executed. It is even possible to inject custom behavior **while** the request is being processed by the resource.

More specifically, when we apply the above to the HTTP based request/response that is serviced by the middle tier servers of today, filters can be used to:

❑ Take a look at the request header and data **before** it reaches the resource

❑ Take a look at the response header and data **after** it has been sent to the resource

❑ Provide a modified version of the request to the resource being processed by the container

❑ Access and modify the response from the resource before returning it

❑ Stop a request from reaching a resource altogether

This behavior is depicted in the diagram below:

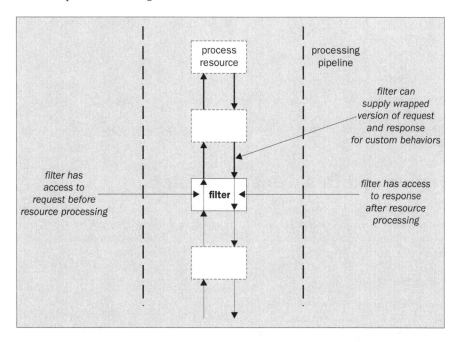

We will be examining the implementation of filters that perform each of these actions within this chapter and the next. You should note that code implemented in filters can have the same power, if not more, as the code implemented in the resources (in other words Servlets and JSP) when it comes to request processing. In some ways, one can view the Servlet engine and the JSP engine simply as end-point filters in this processing pipeline.

Filters in Depth

We will now take a more concrete, technical look at what filters really are. First, we will become intimately acquainted with the single interface that defines a filter: the `Filter` interface.

The Filter Interface

On a concrete level, a filter is simply a class that implements the `javax.servlet.Filter` interface. Here are the three methods that the class must implement:

doFilter(ServletRequest, ServletResponse, FilterChain)

This is the key method of a filter. It is where almost all of the work of a filter is done. The container will call this method each time an applicable request is being handled. We will see how to associate filters with types of requests in the next section.

init(FilterConfig)

The container is responsible for setting the `FilterConfig` object before the `doFilter()` method is called for the first time. The `FilterConfig` object provides the initialization parameters for the filter, and also allows access to the associated `ServletContext`.

destroy()

The container calls `destroy()` when the filter is being taken out of service.

Any class that implements this interface is officially a filter, and can then be included as a component of a web application.

Configuration and Deployment of Filters

In the deployment phase, filters are an integral part of a web application, at the same level as Servlets, JSPs, or static resources with the web application. Filters are typically created by developers, and delivered as bytecode classes within a web application. The filter user – the web application deployer – will configure filters at deployment time by specifying:

❑ Which filter(s) to use

❑ Any initialization parameters to the filter

❑ Where to apply the filter

❑ The order to chain several filters together (if applicable) for processing requests

All of the above are specified within the 'standard' J2EE web application deployment descriptor (WEB-INF/web.xml). New automated J2EE IDE and tools will have user-friendly configuration screens for entry of this descriptor information.

In this way, filters are configured and deployed in a similar fashion as Servlets in a web application. The Servlet container supporting filters will parse two types of filter related declarations present within this file:

❑   The **filter definition**
Tells the container the textual name associated with the filter

❑   The **filter mapping**
Tells the container which resources the filter will be applied to

We will cover these in more detail shortly when we examine filter definition and configuration.

Now that we know what a filter is, we need to take a look at the interactions that occur between a container and the filter, and specifically the lifecycle of a filter.

The Lifecycle of a Filter

Just like Servlets and JSPs, the container manages the lifecycle of a filter. We will describe:

❑   When the container instantiates a filter

❑   How initialization parameters are passed into a filter

❑   How the container determines how many instances of the filter to create

❑   When the `doFilter()` method is called

❑   How filters can cleanup on application shutdown

The figure below illustrates the lifecycle of a filter. Each block in the diagram represents a state that the filter can be in. In fact, there are only three explicit states:

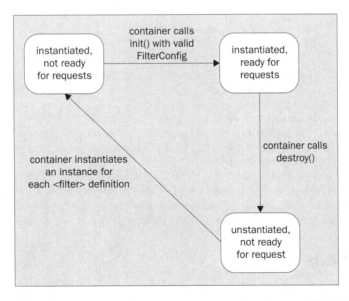

For each filter definition in the web application (as specified in the `web.xml` file), the container will create a filter instance and initialize it. That single filter instance, with its initial parameters, will service all requests that correspond to its filter mapping specified within the deployment descriptor. The only exception to this occurs when the engine consists of multiple Java VMs servicing requests. In this case, the container mechanism will create one instance in each VM – allowing all participating VMs to service filtered resources equally.

The initialization must occur before the first request is mapped through the filter instance. During initialization, the container passes a `FilterConfig` object (an object that implements the `FilterConfig` interface) via the `init()` method of the `javax.servlet.Filter` interface.

The `FilterConfig` can be used by the filter to obtain initialization parameters of the filter, the textual name of the filter, or the `ServletContext` that the application is running under.

FilterConfig Interface

The FilterConfig interface declares four methods:

`getFilterName()`

This method obtains the textual name of the filter, as defined in the `web.xml` file deployment descriptor.

`getInitParameter(String paramName)`

This method obtains the string value of a specific initialization parameter by name. Returns `null` if not found.

`getInitParameterNames()`

This method obtains a `java.util.Enumeration` consisting of all the names of the initialization parameters for this instance. These parameters are specified in the `web.xml` deployment descriptor within the `<filter>` definitions. Returns `null` if no parameter is set.

`getServletContext()`

This method obtains the `ServletContext` that the filter is executing within. This context is typically specified in the `server.xml` file of the server.

In all cases, once a filter is instantiated and initialized, the container will fire all requests that it maps to through its `doFilter()` method. For most static page, JSP, and Servlet resources, this means that many threads of execution may be executing the `doFilter()` method at the same time. Because of this, one must take care to write filters that are thread-safe.

The filter instance will be kept alive to process a request, until the container (or a VM in the container) shuts down or the associated web application is no longer deployed. Before this happens, the container calls `destroy()` to give the filter a chance to perform any cleanup work that may be necessary.

Filter Definitions

Filters are defined per web application. Their definition appears in the deployment descriptor `web.xml` file using the `<filter>` element. Each `<filter>` element must have a `<filter-name>` sub-element, a `<filter-class>` sub-element, and optionally one or more `<init-param>` sub-elements. Here is a brief description of each:

❑ `<filter-name>`
  Textual name to associate with the filter. Used in filter mapping. This is a mandatory sub-element.

❑ `<filter-class>`
The actual class that implements a filter. Should be a fully qualified class name with package prefix. This is a mandatory sub-element.

❑ `<init-param>`
Specifies the initial parameters to supply to this instance of the filter. Contains `<param-name>` and `<param-value>` sub-elements, specifying the name and value of the parameter respectively. Note that `<init-param>` is an optional sub-element of `<filter>`, and can also appear multiple times, one for each initialization parameter for the filter.

For an example, consider an audit filter. Such a filter may log all accesses to certain pre-specified resources. The `AuditFilter` class can be specified in the application's `web.xml` file as:

```
<filter>
  <filter-name>Wrox Audit Filter</filter-name>
  <filter-class>filters.AuditFilter</filter-class>
</filter>
```

The segment above associates the name "`Wrox Audit Filter`" with the filter implementation in `AuditFilter.class`.

In Tomcat 4, the default path to store the filter is in the `WEB-INF/classes` directory of the web application, together with the Servlet and supporting classes. `AuditFilter` would reside in a `filters` subdirectory under this default path.

Here's an example of how to specify initial parameters for filter initialization. This `web.xml` file segment controls the hours that a 'games playing blocking' filter may operate:

```
<filter>
  <filter-name>Wrox Stop Games Filter</filter-name>
  <filter-class>filters.StopGamesFilter</filter-class>
  <init-param>
    <param-name>starthour</param-name>
    <param-value>10</param-value>
  </init-param>
  <init-param>
    <param-name>stophour</param-name>
    <param-value>11</param-value>
  </init-param>
</filter>
```

The container will associate the textual name "`Wrox Stop Games Filter`", with `StopGamesFilter.class`, under the `filters` subdirectory. The parameters are accessed within the filter, and will restrict gaming activities only between 10:00 and 11:00 am. The `starthour` and `stophour` will be accessible within the filter via a call to the `FilterConfig` object, similar to:

```
String startHour = filterConfig.getInitParameter("starthour");
String stopHour = filterConfig.getInitParameter("stophour");
```

Multiple Filter Instances

Note that a container will create an instance of a filter for each `<filter>` declaration encountered within the application. It is possible, therefore, to define two instances of the same filter within the same application – each with different initialization parameters. Of course, the two instances should have different textual names. For example, we may want to set up an instance of a `StopGamesFilter` to block games access from 8 am to 10 pm for access to the Engineering department resources; while another instance of the same filter to block games access from 8 am to 10 am for the Administrative department.

Filter Mapping

We've seen how to define a filter in the `web.xml` deployment descriptor file. Now let's move on to look at how to map a filter. Filter mapping allows us to specify resources that the filter will be applied to within our application, on a by-request basis. Applying a filter to a resource literally means adding the filter to the processing pipeline when accessing the resource.

Filter mappings are XML based entries, specified per web application, within the `web.xml` file. The 'mapping' that is performed is between the filter's textual name and one or more resources that the filter will be applied to. Since the filter mapping uses the filter's textual name, the corresponding `<filter>` declaration must precede a filter mapping within the `web.xml` file.

This is what the filter mapping for our audit filter may look like:

```
<filter-mapping>
  <filter-name>Wrox Visual Audit Filter</filter-name>
  <servlet-name>FindProd</servlet-name>
</filter-mapping>
```

Here, the mapping specifies that the filter declared as "`Wrox Visual Audit Filter`" (in a previous `<filter>` declaration) will be applied only when an incoming request is accessing a Servlet resource called `FindProd`. It is assumed, of course, that the Servlet is declared properly (in a `<servlet>` declaration for this application) within the same `web.xml` file – for example:

```
<servlet>
  <servlet-name>Findprod</servlet-name>
  <servlet-class>FindProd</servlet-class>
</servlet>
```

To map a filter to more than one resource, we need to either create multiple mapping entries, or create a filter mapping that uses a URL pattern. Now let's take a look at how to make use of URL patterns.

Matching URL Patterns

The real power of filter mapping becomes evident when one considers mappings containing URL patterns. URL patterns allow users to apply a filter to a group of resources with some commonality in their URL. We can also use wild card characters (such as *) within the URL to match multiple URLs.

Depending on how the URL pattern is specified, one can apply a filter to a set of homogeneous resources (in other words only Servlets), a set of heterogeneous resources (a mix of static HTML files, Servlets and JSPs). Here are some samples of URL patterns:

URL Pattern	Matches
/*	Everything that is served by this engine, including static pages, Servlets and JSPs
/servlet/*	All Servlets
/jsp/*.jsp	All JSPs
/dept/accounting/*	All resources in the accounting department branch of the web

The following is an example of filter mapping that uses a URL pattern:

```
<filter-mapping>
  <filter-name>Wrox Audit Filter</filter-name>
  <url-pattern>/*</url-pattern>
</filter-mapping>
```

This declaration applies the "Wrox Audit Filter" filter to all the resources served within the application. Here's another example:

```
<filter-mapping>
  <filter-name>Wrox Stop Games Filter</filter-name>
  <url-pattern>/servlet/*</url-pattern>
</filter-mapping>
```

As you can see, this mapping will apply the "Wrox Stop Games Filter" to all Servlets in the application.

Filter Chaining

Chaining is the action of passing a request through multiple filters in sequence, before accessing the resource requested. For example, we may want an authentication filter on an XML based resource that is also processed by an XSLT transformation filter. The good news is that all Servlet 2.3 filters are inherently chainable. Unlike most other chaining mechanisms, however, filter chaining in Servlet 2.3 also means passing the response (headers) from the resource back through the chains of filters in the reverse order. This is a very important concept, and is an essential component in the versatility of Servlet 2.3 filters.

The FilterChain Interface

The interface that enables every filter to be chainable is the javax.servlet.FilterChain interface. An object that implements this FilterChain interface is passed into the core doFilter() method of a filter by the container. This object allows the filter to directly call the next filter in the chain after its own processing. Here is what the interface contains:

doFilter(ServletRequest, ServletResponse)

Calling this method will invoke the doFilter() method of the next filter in the chain. If the filter is the very last filter in the chain, the actual resource processing will occur. This method does not return until all downstream filters have returned from their doFilter() calls.

All Filters are Chainable

Compatibility with filter chaining is an integral requirement of every filter. In action, filter chaining is provided by a series of interactions between the container and the filter. The diagram below shows this interaction:

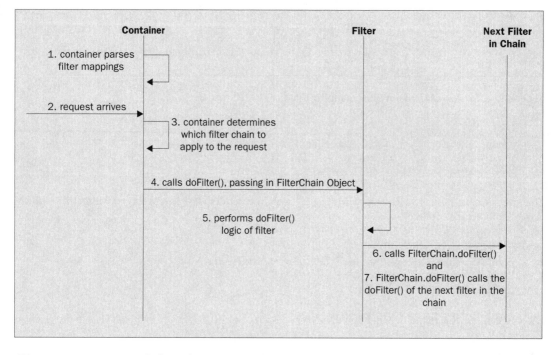

Here is an examination of what is happening in the figure:

❑ The container parses the `<filter-mappings>` defined in the `web.xml` file of the application.

❑ A request arrives accessing a resource in the application.

❑ The container determines the filter chain that will be applied to this request.

❑ The container invokes the `doFilter()` method of the first filter in the chain, passing in the request, a response (holder), and a `FilterChain` object reference. The container has loaded the filter chain information into the `FilterChain` object that is passed in.

❑ The filter performs its `doFilter()` logic.

❑ The filter completes its filter logic, and calls the `doFilter()` method of the `FilterChain` object reference, passing in the request and response. All filters are required to do this, since all filters are intrinsically chainable.

❑ Logic in the `doFilter()` method of `FilterChain` object calls the `doFilter()` method of the next filter chain to be called. Repeat from step 4, until the last filter in the chain has completed its work. The `FilterChain.doFilter()` call on the last filter in chain will actually cause the access of the resource to occur.

Note that the mechanism of chaining is inherently different from most other conventional filtering or server extension mechanism (such Apache Modules and IIS ISAPI). The next section will expand on this.

Unique Properties of Servlet 2.3 Filter Chaining

Note the following interesting properties regarding this approach to extending server functionality:

❑ Each of the `FilterChain.doFilter()` method calls are stacked upon one another, so program flow is blocked in a nested fashion across all the filters involved.

❑ After the actual resource access, the `FilterChain.doFilter()` method on the last filter on the chain returns. At this point, the response object is filled with header and content from the actual resource access. This last filter now has the freedom to examine and modify the response header and (remaining) contents at will. When it finishes, it will return from `doFilter()`. The next filter up the chain then gets a chance to process the response, and so on.

❑ The logic in a filter's `doFilter()` method has full access to the request in its incoming flow, prior to the `FilterChain.doFilter()` call. The logic in a filter's `doFilter()` method has full access to the response in its outgoing flow, after the `FilterChain.doFilter()` call.

❑ The local variables declared within the `doFilter()` method are consistent and available to both the incoming flow processing logic and the outgoing flow processing logic. In fact, the very same thread will be executing both pieces of the logic.

These properties of the chaining mechanism are perhaps the hardest concepts to understand with respect to Servlet 2.3 filters.

> In essence, filter chaining in Servlet 2.3 is not a 'call and forget' mechanism provided by container intervention; but rather a 'nested call' mechanism assisted by the container.

Of course, we must realize that even though filter chaining is built into every single filter, the processing logic within the filter is not obliged to chain to the next filter. In fact, this is one major application area for filters – blocking access to the actual resource. For example, an authorization filter can determine that the client is not allowed to access a resource and generate a refusal response all on its own, without further chaining.

A Fly in the Filtering Ointment

The avid reader (and indeed experienced JSP/Servlet programmers) will realize that not all containers buffer their resource response in the response object after the resource completes processing. More specifically, JSPs and Servlets may write and flush their output stream as the response is being generated on-the-fly. This places dubious value on the processing window that each filter gets during a response's return trip through the filter chain. Although this processing window is perfect for resources and containers that **do** encapsulate the entire output in the response object; we must also deal with the reality of those that don't.

The way that Servlet 2.3 filters deal with processing resources that generate output on-the-fly is via a customized wrapped response object. That is, the filter will pass into the `FilterChain.doFilter()` method a specialized version of the response object instead of the one that it receives as invocation parameter.

This wrapped response object can then provide its own version of `OutputStream` and/or `Printwriter` to downstream filter or resource to work on. We will not go into any further depth on this topic since it is out of the scope of this chapter. However, rest assured that we will delve into these 'wrapped response' and 'wrapped request' mechanisms in great depth within the next chapter.

Mapping Requests Through a Filter Chain

The order of `<filter-mapping>` declarations in the `web.xml` file is significant. This is the order that the container will build filter chains. Therefore, filter declarations within the `web.xml` file should be in the order that you want them to be applied to a resource – whenever filter chaining is used.

When the order of chaining for the same set of filters is changed, the final result can be completely different. This typically happens when a downstream filter depends on the result of an upstream filter for proper operations. For example, imagine a filter that transforms XML data from a resource to HTML via an XSLT (a stylesheet language for XML), and another filter that translates the HTML document via CSS1 (another stylesheet language, typically for HTML). If we place the XSLT filter first in the chain, the XML resource will be translated to HTML, and subsequently formatted by the CSS1 filter. If we place the CSS1 filter first, however, it will not work on the XML data. As a result, only the XSLT transformation will be applied in this chain. The figure below depicts this situation:

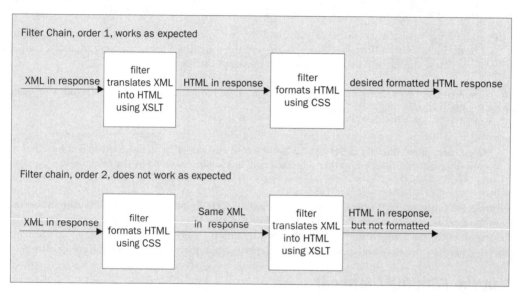

Filter application order in a chain is determined by the order that the `<filter-mappings>` declarations are defined in within the `web.xml` file. For example, consider the following set of filter mappings:

```
<filter-mapping>
  <filter-name>Wrox Audit Filter</filter-name>
  <url-pattern>/*</url-pattern>
</filter-mapping>

<filter-mapping>
  <filter-name>Wrox Authentication Filter</filter-name>
  <url-pattern>/*</url-pattern>
</filter-mapping>
```

In this case, both `"Wrox Audit Filter"` and `"Wrox Authentication Filter"` are mapped to all resources served by this server. This means that both filters will be applied to all resources. The order of application will be `"Wrox Audit Filter"` followed by `"Wrox Authentication Filter"` (unless `"Wrox Audit Filter"` blocks access to subsequent resources, but audit filters in general do not do this). Remember that the order of chained filter execution on the incoming request is **down** the filter stack, while the order of chained filter execution on the outgoing path is **up** the filter stack.

Given an incoming request, the container will go through the list of filter mappings to determine which filter to apply on a per-request basis. For example, if we have the following filters mapping defined in order:

```
<filter-mapping>
  <filter-name>Wrox Audit Filter</filter-name>
  <url-pattern>/*</url-pattern>
</filter-mapping>

<filter-mapping>
  <filter-name>Wrox Authentication Filter</filter-name>
  <url-pattern>/servlet/*</url-pattern>
</filter-mapping>

<filter-mapping>
  <filter-name>Wrox Visual Audit Filter</filter-name>
  <servlet-name>FindProd</servlet-name>
</filter-mapping>
```

An incoming request for http://tomcathost/myapp/index.html will have the following filter applied:

❑   Wrox Audit Filter

While an incoming request for http://tomcathost/myapp/servlet/listprod will have the following filters applied in order:

❑   Wrox Audit Filter

❑   Wrox Authentication Filter

Finally, an incoming request for http://tomcathost/myapp/servlet/findprod will have the following filters applied in order:

❑   Wrox Audit Filter

❑   Wrox Authentication Filter

❑   Wrox Visual Audit Filter

This concludes our initial conceptual coverage of filters.

Hands-On Filter Development

Now it's time to get our hands on some code, and implement our very own filter. In this section, we will discover how to set up a development and testing environment for filters. We will also code, configure, and test several simple filters in this environment.

The very first version of Tomcat that will support Servlet 2.3 specification (required to support filters) is Tomcat 4. Currently, according to jakarta.apache.org announcements, it is anticipated that Tomcat 3.2 may be the last 3.x release available.

One interesting thing about Tomcat 3 versus Tomcat 4 is that fact that Tomcat 4 has a completely overhauled internal architecture: it is not an incremental upgrade from Tomcat 3.x. This is reflective of the combined effort between the former Apache JServ group, and the Tomcat team working with Sun's donated version of the Servlet /JSP engine under the auspices of the Jakarta project. The new architecture promises to deliver a highly customizable, higher performance, and more scalable solution to Tomcat.

Setting up a Context for Our Web Application

This section assumes that you have already installed and tested the Tomcat 4.x level container that supports Servlet 2.3 filters.

First, we must setup Tomcat 4 with a context for our web application. To do this, you will need to edit the `conf/server.xml` file under the Tomcat 4 distribution. Add the following `<context>`, within the default `<host>`, after the `<context>` for the "`/examples`" application:

```
<Context path="/ch14" docBase="ch14" debug="0" reloadable="true">
  <Logger className="org.apache.catalina.logger.FileLogger"
  prefix="localhost_ch14_log." suffix=".txt"
  timestamp="true"/>
</Context>
```

You will need to change the path in the `docBase` attribute, making it point to where you have unarchived the source code directory. This addition sets up the `/ch14` context to point to our web application.

Note that we have configured a logger, this will allow us to see the action of our `AuditFilter` a little later. It will create log files under the `logs` directory of the Tomcat installation directory. The log files will have file names similar to: `localhost_ch14_log.09-22-01.txt`. Obviously the timestamp on the file name will reflect today's date though.

Our First Filter: SimpleFilter

Before coding our first filter, let us take a quick look at one additional interface that we will be using within the filters sample.

The ServletContext interface

Using the `javax.servlet.FilterConfig` object (object that implements the interface), the filter can obtain a reference to the current `ServletContext` that it is executing under. There is a `ServletContext` for each running web application. Because of this single instance nature, the `ServletContext` is frequently used for sharing information globally.

Using this reference, the filter can utilize the context's logger service. It can also use this interface to attach arbitrary attributes to the context during runtime. An attribute can be an arbitrary object associated with a `String` name. Attaching attributes to `ServletContext` is a popular way to pass information between processing agents during runtime. For example, state information can be passed between filter instances using these attributes. Here are several of the most frequently used methods by filter writers:

❑   `log(String)`

This writes a string to the currently active logging facility associated with the context.

❑   `log(String, Throwable)`

This writes a string and a stack trace to the log.

❑   `getAttribute(String)`

This obtains the value of a named attribute.

❑   `setAttribute(String, Object)`

This attaches a named attribute to the `ServletContext`.

❑   `removeAttribute(String)`

This removes a previously attached attribute.

❑   `getAttributeNames()`

This returns a `java.util.Enumeration` consisting of the names of all the currently attached attributes.

Coding the Filter

Our very first filter is one called `SimpleFilter`. Place the source code to `SimpleFilter` in the `webapps/ch14/WEB-INF/classes/com/wrox/projsp/ch14/filters` directory. This simple filter will not do anything useful for now. It will simply make a log entry before calling `FilterChain.doFilter()`, and another one right after it. Here is the source code line by line:

```
package com.wrox.projsp.ch14.filters;
import java.io.*;
import javax.servlet.*;
import javax.servlet.http.*;
```

As we mentioned before, all filters must implement the `javax.servlet.Filter` interface, and our `SimpleFilter` is no exception:

```
public final class SimpleFilter implements Filter {
  private FilterConfig filterConfig = null;
```

Here's the essential `doFilter()` method. Note the parameters: a `request`, `response`, and a `FilterChain` object:

```
public void doFilter(ServletRequest request, ServletResponse response,
                  FilterChain chain)
          throws IOException, ServletException {
```

The container will set our `filterConfig` to a `null` before taking itself down. `doFilter()` should never be called before the `filterConfig` is set by the container:

```
if (filterConfig == null)
  return;
```

To write to the log, we access the `ServletContext` from the `filterConfig` given by the container. The `log()` method will write a line out using the logger that we have set up earlier for this context:

```
        filterConfig.getServletContext().log("in SimpleFilter");
        chain.doFilter(request, response);
        filterConfig.getServletContext().log("Getting out of SimpleFilter");
    }
```

The rest of the methods are standard trivial implementations to comply with the `Filter` interface:

```
    public void init(FilterConfig filterConfig) {
        this.filterConfig = filterConfig;
    }

    public void destroy() {}
```

Defining `toString()` allows us to write out the filter instance for debugging purposes:

```
    public String toString() {
      if (filterConfig == null)
        return ("SimpleFilter()");
      StringBuffer sb = new StringBuffer("SimpleFilter(");
      sb.append(filterConfig);
      sb.append(")");
      return (sb.toString());

    }

}
```

Declaring the Filter and Configuring Filter Mapping

Now, we need to add a `<filter>` declaration to our `web.xml` file, the deployment descriptor for our web application. Create the `web.xml` file and save it to `webapps/ch14/WEB-INF`:

```
<?xml version="1.0" encoding="ISO-8859-1"?>

<!DOCTYPE web-app
    PUBLIC "-//Sun Microsystems, Inc.//DTD Web Application 2.3//EN"
    "http://java.sun.com/j2ee/dtds/web-app_2_3.dtd">

<web-app>

  <filter>
    <filter-name>Wrox Simple Filter</filter-name>
    <filter-class>com.wrox.projsp.ch14.filters.SimpleFilter</filter-class>
  </filter>
```

Add the following filter mapping immediately after the filter declaration:

```
<filter-mapping>
  <filter-name>Wrox Simple Filter</filter-name>
  <url-pattern>/*</url-pattern>
</filter-mapping>

</web-app>
```

This will configure the "Wrox Simple Filter" to filter every resource within this web application.

> **If you're working with the downloaded source code, these filter definitions and mappings would already be included – but commented out. You should uncomment the set that you need as we move along in the example.**

Now, all that is left to do is to create a resource for access. We'll simply create a static HTML page. Add the following web page to the code/webapps/ch14 directory as index.html:

```
<html>
<head></head>
<body>
  <h1>Welcome to Wrox Filtering Demo Application!</h1>
</body>
</html>
```

Testing the Filter

We are now ready to test the filter. Assuming that Tomcat is not currently running, perform the following steps:

❑ Go to the logs directory underneath the Tomcat installation, and delete all files

❑ Start Tomcat using startup script in the bin directory of Tomcat

❑ Start a browser and enter URL http://localhost:8080/ch14/

❑ After the web page has loaded in the browser, shutdown Tomcat using the shutdown script in the bin directory

Your browser display should be similar to the screenshot below, just the simple HTML resource page being served:

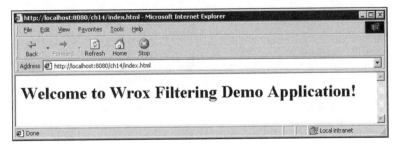

Now, to see that the filter has actually worked, even on this simple access of the static page, we should change directory to `logs` under the Tomcat installation directory. Find the ch14 application log file. In our case, it is named: `localhost_ch14_log.2001-03-14.txt`.

Inside, we find the two log entries written by our filter, one in the processing window **before** the web page is accessed, and the other one **after**:

```
...
2001-09-11 23:01:27 StandardWrapper[/ch14:default]: Loading container servlet
default
2001-09-11 23:01:27 default: init
2001-09-11 23:01:27 StandardWrapper[/ch14:invoker]: Loading container servlet
invoker
2001-09-11 23:01:27 invoker: init
2001-09-11 23:01:27 jsp: init
2001-09-11 23:01:51 in SimpleFilter
2001-09-11 23:01:51 Getting out of SimpleFilter
```

Experimentation with Filter Chaining

We will now create a second filter, called the `WroxSkeletonFilter`. Like the `WroxSimpleFilter`, it does not do anything other than logging an entry in the log file. By chaining these filters together, it will give us some insight into the action of filter chaining under Tomcat 4 (Servlet 2.3 specifications). You will find very minor differences between `WroxSkeletonFilter.java` and `SimpleFilter.java`. Most of them deal with renaming the filter. Here is a brief summary.

Of course, the class name has changed:

```
import javax.servlet.*;
import javax.servlet.http.*;
public final class SkeletonFilter implements Filter {
    private FilterConfig filterConfig = null;
```

The output to the log now reflects the new filter name:

```
    filterConfig.getServletContext().log("in SkeletonFilter");
    chain.doFilter(request, response);
    filterConfig.getServletContext().log("Getting out of SkeletonFilter");
```

And finally, the `toString()` method has the filter name changed as well:

```
public String toString() {

    if (filterConfig == null)
      return ("SkeletonFilter()");
    StringBuffer sb = new StringBuffer("SkeletonFilter(");
    sb.append(filterConfig);
    sb.append(")");
    return (sb.toString());
}
```

Additions to web.xml

We can now add the `SkeletonFilter` to the chain. Add the following entries to the `webapps/ch14/WEB-INF/web.xml` file, making sure the ordering of `<filter-mapping>` entries is followed exactly:

```
...

<filter>
  <filter-name>Wrox Simple Filter</filter-name>
  <filter-class>com.wrox.projsp.ch14.filters.SimpleFilter</filter-class>
</filter>
<filter>
  <filter-name>Wrox Skeleton Filter</filter-name>
  <filter-class>com.wrox.projsp.ch14.filters.SkeletonFilter</filter-class>
</filter>

<filter-mapping>
  <filter-name>Wrox Simple Filter</filter-name>
  <url-pattern>/*</url-pattern>
</filter-mapping>
<filter-mapping>
  <filter-name>Wrox Skeleton Filter</filter-name>
  <url-pattern>/*</url-pattern>
</filter-mapping>

...
```

This mapping now maps both the `"Wrox Simple Filter"` and the `"Wrox Skeleton Filter"` to all resources being accessed. This effectively chains them for all resources.

Clear the log files, start Tomcat, access the URL http://localhost:8080/ch14/ again, then shutdown Tomcat.

Now, look into the `ch14` log file again, you should see something similar to:

```
...
2001-09-12 23:06:35 default: init
2001-09-12 23:06:35 StandardWrapper[/ch14:invoker]: Loading container servlet
invoker
2001-09-12 23:06:35 invoker: init
2001-09-12 23:06:35 jsp: init
2001-09-12 23:07:31 in SimpleFilter
2001-09-12 23:07:31 in SkeletonFilter
2001-09-12 23:07:31 Getting out of SkeletonFilter
2001-09-12 23:07:31 Getting out of SimpleFilter
```

Notice the nesting of the log entries, clearly showing that the filter chaining mechanism consists of a series of nested `doFilter()` calls on the two participating filters. The chaining order is the order of `<filter-mapping>` declaration within the `web.xml` file, as expected.

Creating an AuditFilter

Both `SimpleFilter` and `SkeletonFilter` already write to the log. However, they do little else. We will now create our first filter that delivers some added value. This filter will audit and log resource access. The information logged includes the time of access, the IP address of the client, the resource being accessed, and the time used in accessing the resource.

For brevity, we will only show the code for the `doFilter()` method from the `AuditFilter` class here; the rest of the code is identical to the two filters above, taking into account any name changes. This filter takes advantage of access to the request to obtain the required information. It also times the access to the resource by keeping the system time before the `FilterChain.doFilter()` call. After the resource processing, it creates the log entry containing all the information:

```
public void doFilter(ServletRequest request, ServletResponse response,
                     FilterChain chain)
        throws IOException, ServletException {

  if (filterConfig == null)
    return;

  long startTime = System.currentTimeMillis();
  String remoteAddress =  request.getRemoteAddr();
  String remoteHost = request.getRemoteHost();
  HttpServletRequest myReq = (HttpServletRequest) request;
  String reqURI = myReq.getRequestURI();
  chain.doFilter(request, response);
  filterConfig.getServletContext().log("User at IP " + remoteAddress +
        "(" + remoteHost + ") accessed resource " + reqURI +
        " and used " + (System.currentTimeMillis() - startTime) + " ms");
}
```

Note the ease with which this summary information is maintained and written. They are simply local variables in the `doFilter()` method itself. Thanks to the nested call nature of Servlet 2.3 filters, maintaining states across the two processing windows before and after resource access is simple.

Edit the `web.xml` file, removing the `<filter>` and `<filter-mapping>` entries for `SimpleFilter` and `SkeletonFilter` from our last example. Instead, add the following declarations to the file:

```
<filter>
  <filter-name>Wrox Audit Filter</filter-name>
  <filter-class>com.wrox.projsp.ch14.filters.AuditFilter</filter-class>
</filter>

<filter-mapping>
  <filter-name>Wrox Audit Filter</filter-name>
  <url-pattern>/*</url-pattern>
</filter-mapping>
```

To make things more interesting, we will add a JSP resource and a Servlet resource to do this test. They are located at `webapps/ch14/jsp/FindProd.jsp`, and at `webapps/ch14/WEB-INF/classes/FindProd.class` respectively.

The FindProd.jsp

This JSP is very straightforward. It simple reads the request parameter DEPT and displays it on screen:

```
<html>
<%@ page language="java"  %>
<head></head>
<body>
  <h1>You have submitted as <%= request.getParameter("DEPT") %>
      department!</h1>
</body>
</html>
```

The FindProd Class

The Servlet performs exactly the same function as the above JSP:

```
import javax.servlet.*;
import javax.servlet.http.*;
import java.io.*;

public class FindProd extends HttpServlet {

  public void doGet(HttpServletRequest req, HttpServletResponse res)
          throws java.io.IOException {
    res.setContentType("text/html");
    PrintWriter out = res.getWriter();
    out.println("<html><head></head>");
    out.println("<body><h1>You have called from the " +
            req.getParameter("DEPT"));
    out.println(" department!</h1></body></html>");
    out.close();
  }
}
```

Additions to web.xml

Add the following Servlet declaration in the web.xml file as well:

```
<servlet>
  <servlet-name>findprod</servlet-name>
  <servlet-class>FindProd</servlet-class>
</servlet>
```

We're ready to test. Follow these procedures:

❑   Clean up the Tomcat logs directory

❑   Start Tomcat

❑   Access the URL http://localhost:8080/ch14/jsp/FindProd.jsp?DEPT=Engineering

❑   Access the URL http://localhost:8080/ch14/jsp/FindProd.jsp?DEPT=Accounting

❑   Access the URL http://localhost:8080/ch14/

529

❏ Here, we'll try a Servlet resource instead of the JSP; access the URL
http://localhost:8080/ch14/servlet/findprod?DEPT=Engineering

❏ Access the URL http://localhost:8080/ch14/servlet/findprod?DEPT=Accounting

❏ Shutdown Tomcat

Now, if we examine the ch14 log file, we will see the audit trail left behind by the AuditFilter. Here is a segment of our log file:

```
. . .
2001-03-14 13:14:31 StandardWrapper[/ch14:invoker]: Loading container servlet
invoker
2001-03-14 13:14:31 invoker: init
2001-03-14 13:14:31 jsp: init
2001-03-14 13:15:37 jsp: init
2001-03-14 13:15:37 User at IP 127.0.0.1(127.0.0.1) accessed resource
/ch14/jsp/FindProd.jsp and used 1452 ms
2001-03-14 13:15:59 User at IP 127.0.0.1(127.0.0.1) accessed resource
/ch14/jsp/FindProd.jsp and used 0 ms
2001-03-14 13:16:10 User at IP 127.0.0.1(127.0.0.1) accessed resource /ch14 and
used 70 ms
2001-03-14 13:16:10 User at IP 127.0.0.1(127.0.0.1) accessed resource /ch14/ and
used 0 ms
2001-03-14 13:16:10 User at IP 127.0.0.1(127.0.0.1) accessed resource
/ch14/index.html and used 0 ms
2001-03-14 13:16:27 findprod: init
2001-03-14 13:16:27 User at IP 127.0.0.1(127.0.0.1) accessed resource
/ch14/servlet/findprod and used 70 ms
2001-03-14 13:16:44 User at IP 127.0.0.1(127.0.0.1) accessed resource
/ch14/servlet/findprod and used 0 ms
2001-03-14 13:34:57 findprod: destroy
```

We can glean some very interesting data from this. The initial compile and load of the JSP took 1452 ms to complete, while subsequent access required negligible time. We can also see that initial Servlet access took about 70 ms, while subsequent access to the same instance again required negligible time.

If you want to experiment with url-patterns, repeat the experiment with the following <filter-mapping> in the web.xml file instead:

```
<filter-mapping>
   <filter-name>Wrox Audit Filter</filter-name>
   <url-pattern>/servlet/*</url-pattern>
</filter-mapping>
```

Try the experiment again, and you'll see that only access to the Servlet resource will be logged now.

Writing this useful auditing filter is really quite painless. We will find in general that, once we are familiar with the model of operation of the Servlet 2.3 filter, writing highly functional filters can be quite an easy task.

Other Filter-like Technologies

Prior to Servlet 2.3 filters, there had been many server extension mechanisms based on similar concepts to filtering. In fact, **interceptors** form a key server extension mechanism that is used quite heavily in many Tomcat 3.x based containers. However, there are fundamental differences between filters and these mechanisms: **they are not the same**. The following section will briefly describe the essential differences between the technologies.

Filters are not Conventional Interceptors

Interceptors are a server-level extension mechanism for servers that support them. It is not an application level technology. Being a server extension technology, it is specific to Tomcat. Furthermore, effects of interceptors are typically global to the server – filter effects are local to the web application that the filters belong to.

The general architecture of interceptors and filters are completely different. Interceptors are 'hooked in' modules that are called during different pre-specified points in the processing pipeline by the container. There are different types of interceptors for different access points. Filters, however, rely on nested chain calling (and custom wrapping of request/response) to get its work done. There is only one 'type' of filter. All filters implement the same `javax.servlet.Filter` interface.

Filters are not Valves

Valves are a system level mechanism used extensively within the design of Tomcat 4.x. On an architectural level, they are almost identical to filters. But that's where the similarity ends.

Valves are Tomcat specific and are typically not portable to other Servlet 2.3 compatible servers. On the other hand, filters are portable. Valves are also internal to the Tomcat server and have privileged access to many structures and resources that application level filters cannot access.

Writing Well Behaved Filters

There are a few 'rules of thumb' guidelines that one should apply when designing and writing filters. Following these guidelines may save significant debugging time during the development cycle. Here is an encapsulation of four. We will see several more in the next chapter when we explore the design and coding of more involved filters.

Make Code Thread-Safe

This cannot be stressed enough. Remember that there is typically only one instance of a filter per Java VM (unless the same filter is declared multiple times with different names or initial parameters). This literally guarantees that the `doFilter()` method will be re-entered by many threads simultaneously. Therefore, filter code must be thread-safe. This means:

❑ Local variables in `doFilter()` are typically fine (unless it is a complex object that may hold reference to instance variables in which case the next bullet applies)

❑ Instance variables in the filter class scope should be read-only, or its access must be synchronized

❏   Beware of calling methods that may modify instance variables indirectly, or outside of synchronization

The figure below provides a spatial representation of this approach:

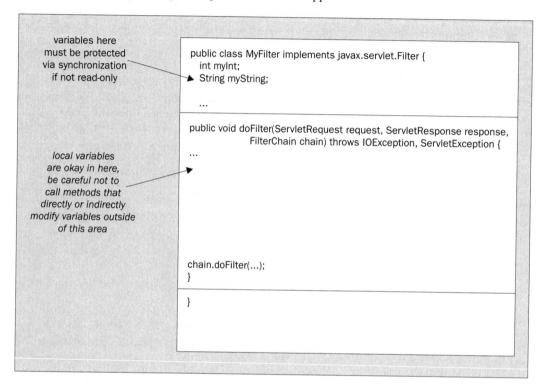

Handle States Carefully

State information can be readily maintained via local variables in doFilter(). The pre-request and post-response processing window within the doFilter() method has full access to this state information. To pass state information between filters on the same chain, one can associate attributes with the ServletContext, obtainable through the FilterConfig.getServletContext() method. The reason why ServletContext attributes can be used rather than request attributes will be clear when we examine request/response wrapping in the next chapter.

You should note that, in general, filters should not maintain state across multiple requests – since the very same instance of filter can be servicing a very large number of requests over time. Logic requiring this style of state maintenance is best served by Servlets or JSPs.

Make Filters Chainable

Break up your filter processing work into reusable, independent, chainable filters whenever possible. This will enhance the reuse potential of the filters, and also allow users to use your filters in new and innovative ways.

Avoid Duplicating System Features

Many problems addressed by filters can be readily solved via configuration of standard server features. This is especially true with Tomcat 4.x releases, where logging, authentication, and authorization support is built-in. Encrypted sessions via TLS (Transport Level Security, or more commonly known as secured socket (https)) is also supported natively.

You should avoid duplicating system features in your filter design: investigate all the server features first, to see if your filter application can be accommodated by simple server configuration. Write your filter only after you determine that is the only appropriate solution, given project requirements and constraints.

Summary

In this chapter, we have introduced the new filtering feature of Servlet 2.3 containers (such as Tomcat 4). We have discovered that:

- ❑ Filters enable web application programmers to tap into the request processing pipeline of the container

- ❑ Filters are packaged code components in a web application, at the same level as Servlet and JSPs

- ❑ Filters are deployed in the same way as Servlets and JSPs, through the deployment descriptor for the application

- ❑ The filter has access to incoming requests before they reach the final resource, and to the outgoing response immediately after the resource processing

- ❑ Filters can also substitute their own version of the request and response (typically wrapped) for consumption of the resource

We have explored the lifecycle of a filter, as managed by the container. We have seen how to define filters in deployment descriptors, and how to define filter mappings. The subtle relationship between filter mapping and filter chaining was also explored.

Next, we discussed the very important concept of filter chaining. We learnt that Servlet 2.3 filter chaining actually makes use of a nested call mechanism, unlike most other filtering schemes. One major advantage of this approach is the preservation of thread state throughout the filter invocation.

Working with actual code, we have created two simple filters and practiced deploying them. We have also experimented with filter chaining and observed its effect using log files. We have also created a useful audit filter to show how easily it can be constructed.

Finally, we provided some guidelines in programming filters, and contrasted two other filter-like mechanisms (valves and interceptors) with filters – noting their differences in approach and level of abstraction.

This provides us with a sound foundation to proceed with the next chapter, where we will go code-intensive and explore a large variety of filter design (and coding). Along the way, we will take a more in depth look at how to create wrapped requests and responses to offer customized dynamic behavior throughout the request processing pipeline.

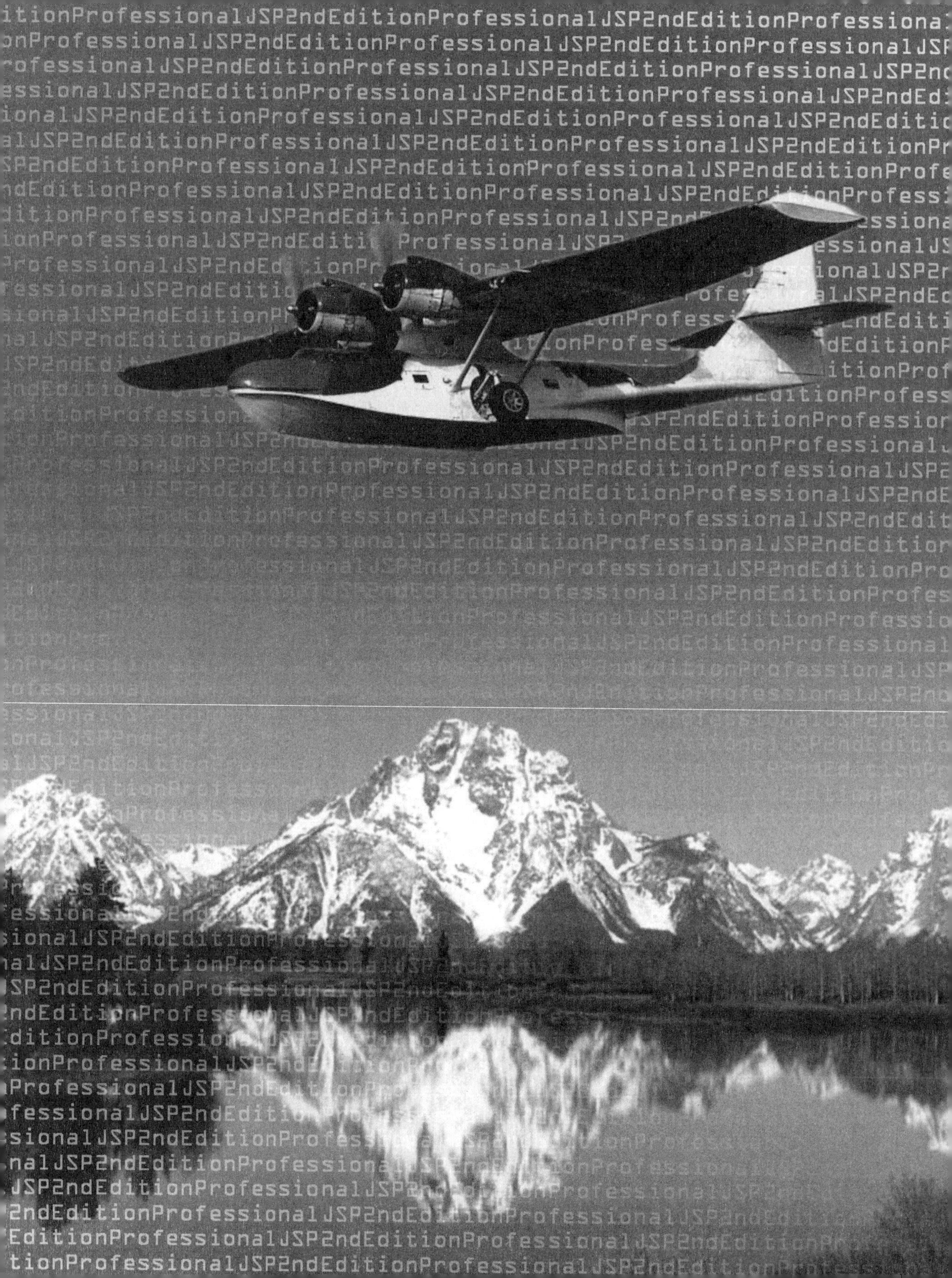
ProfessionalJSP2ndEdition

15

Advanced Filtering Techniques

In the previous chapter we discovered what Servlet 2.3 filtering involves. Filtering offers us the ability to intercept and process requests and responses before and after processing by the underlying resource (Servlet, JSP, etc.). Filters can add great value to any J2EE web application by transforming the behavior of existing Servlets, JSPs, or even static pages.

Chaining multiple filters together combines their transformations in most cases, and can offer the application assembler/deployer great flexibility in configuring the final behavior of the web application. We've even built and configured several simple filters in the last chapter to experiment with many of the concepts. In this chapter we will turn our attention to the more advanced techniques involved in applied filter programming.

This chapter is a cookbook for the various application areas of filters. The goal is to deliver sample code that covers a broad spectrum of the most frequently applied areas for Servlet filters. Each sample is also designed to illustrate several subtleties or important points to consider when programming each type of filter.

Filters for Six Problem Domains

We will build, test, and deploy a total of six filters in this chapter:

Application Domain	Filter Sample
Auditing	A visual auditing filter that includes audit information in-line with every resource that it services
Authorization	A stop games filter that disallows gaming access on the server during certain hours of the day

Table continued on following page

Application Domain	Filter Sample
Adapter (Legacy)	An adapter filter that allows newly-formatted queries to work with an old legacy set of resources
Authentication	An ad-hoc authentication filter that can add simple login protection to any (group) of resources
Compression/Encryption	A filter that automatically detects a client's ability to accept compressed streams, and compresses the resource using GZIP compression before sending it over the network to the client
Output Format Transformation	A filter that provides on-the-fly XSLT transformation to an existing XML-generating JSP resource

We will first present the functionality and design considerations for each filter. This will be followed by a presentation of the actual code, annotated with detailed comment highlighting the design issues addressed. Finally, we will give detailed deployment, configuration and testing information for each filter.

Most filter applications fall into one or more of the above application domains, so the code we will present can serve as a base for your own filter development.

Furthermore, during the development of several of the above filters, we will pause for coverage of conventional techniques used in filter programming. These are the very same 'filter application patterns' that we will see again and again when designing filters: they are an encapsulation of the type of work that a filter can perform – on a high level. An understanding of these patterns can prove to be very helpful in your own experimentation and application of Servlet 2.3 filters. This is a tabulation of the techniques we will cover, and the filter example that they appear in:

Technique Illustrated	Filter
Transforming incoming request headers	Adapter filter
Stopping downstream request flow	Stop game filter Authentication filter
Generating response	Stop game filter Authentication filter
Transforming outgoing response content	Visual auditing filter Compression filter XSLT filter
Dynamically adapting filter behavior based on incoming requests	Authentication filter Compression filter
Wrapping request objects	Adapter filter
Wrapping response objects	Visual auditing filter Compression filter XSLT filter

Be forewarned that this chapter is extremely code intensive. By the end of the chapter, you will be fluent in Servlet 2.3 filter concepts, design and programming. To boot, you will even have an extensive code framework and library to start your filter projects immediately.

Setting Up the Development Environment

The first thing we need to do is to edit the CATALINA_HOME\conf\server.xml file to include a new context. Bring up this file now, and add the context for the code in this chapter:

```
<Context path="/ch15" docBase="ch15" debug="0" reloadable="true">
  <Logger className="org.apache.catalina.logger.FileLogger"
          prefix="localhost_ch15_log." suffix=".txt" timestamp="true"/>
</Context>
```

Of course, you should modify the docBase attribute above to reflect where you have installed the distribution source code from this chapter. Most of the code for the filters in this chapter is in a package called com.wrox.projsp.ch15.filters, and the classes are located as usual under the webapps\ch15\WEB-INF\classes directory.

Now, in the webapps\ch15\WEB-INF\web.xml file, add this Servlet definition:

```
<?xml version="1.0" encoding="ISO-8859-1"?>

<!DOCTYPE web-app
  PUBLIC "-//Sun Microsystems, Inc.//DTD Web Application 2.3//EN"
  "http://java.sun.com/j2ee/dtds/web-app_2_3.dtd">

<web-app>

<servlet>
  <servlet-name>findprod</servlet-name>
  <servlet-class>FindProd</servlet-class>
</servlet>

</web-app>
```

The FindProd Class

This includes a very simple "findprod" Servlet, which you may have already seen in the previous chapter. This Servlet emulates the legacy resource being accessed by a user. It is hard-coded to use a DEPT parameter (department information). Later on, we will create a filter that automatically provides this parameter, even though the client system accessing the legacy resource does not know how to supply it. Save this code in the webapps\ch15\WEB-INF\classes directory:

```
import javax.servlet.*;
import javax.servlet.http.*;
import java.io.*;

public class FindProd extends HttpServlet {

  public void doGet(HttpServletRequest req, HttpServletResponse res)
          throws java.io.IOException {
    res.setContentType("text/html");
    PrintWriter out = res.getWriter();
    out.println("<html><head></head>");
    out.println("<body><h1>You have called from the " +
                req.getParameter("DEPT"));
```

```
    out.println(" department!</h1></body></html>");
    out.close();
  }
}
```

The FindProd JSP

A similar JSP has been included in webapps\ch15\jsp\FindProd.jsp (again, you may have seen this file in the previous chapter). This JSP is used in filter testing, to test against the handling of JSP resources. The JSP trivially contains:

```
<html>
<%@ page language="java"  %>
<head></head>
<body>
<h1>You have submitted as the <%= request.getParameter("DEPT") %> department!</h1>
</body>
</html>
```

Like the findprod Servlet, this legacy emulation JSP prints out a message, and expects the client to supply the DEPT parameter. This completes our preparation for filter testing.

A Brief Word on Terminology

Before we go any further, take a look at the figure below:

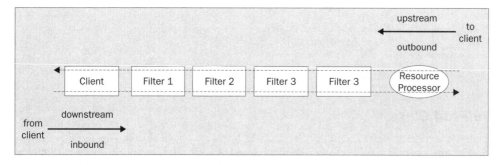

We will clarify some terminology that is used throughout this chapter. The request originates from the client and goes through a **chain of filters** before reaching the final **resource processor** in this figure. As the request travels from the client, through the first filter, through the second filter, and so on, we call this the **downstream**, or **inbound** trip. The downstream trip is always towards the final goal – the resource processor. Once the resource processor has finished with the request, a response then will travel **upstream**, or **outbound**, back through all the filters, and head towards the client. Upstream trips are always away from the resource processor and towards the client.

Visual Auditing Filter: Wrapping the Response Object

The first filter that we will tackle is similar to the WroxAuditFilter that we developed towards the end of the previous chapter. Instead of quietly writing the audit information into the log, as the old WroxAuditFilter does, this one will include the auditing information in the output of the resource. The screenshot below shows an example of this filter being applied to a web page; note the audit information at the bottom of the page. This information is inserted by the filter, and changes with every access to the page:

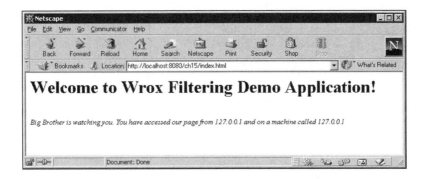

Wrapping the Response Object for Content Modification

The important concept to understand from this example is custom response wrapping. This is also one of the most difficult techniques to grasp for novice Servlet 2.3 programmers. In custom response wrapping, we provide our own implementation of a custom response object to downstream filters/resources – with the response object that was passed to us wrapped inside. This means that we can modify the response content (inside our custom response wrapper object) after the resource has completed processing the request. The figure below shows this interception:

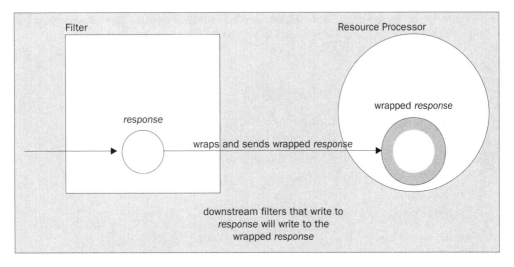

Note that we must wrap the response with our own custom version during the request's inbound trip, before we call Chain.doFilter(). In fact, the following happens:

- ❑ The filter supplies a custom wrapped version of the response to downstream filters when it calls the Chain.doFilter() method

- ❑ This custom wrapped response object will hand down a custom OutputStream or PrintWriter object that is actually a byte array managed in our own code

- ❑ When downstream filters, or the resource processor, write to our custom OutputStream or PrintWriter, we are buffering all the output

- ❑ When downstream filters, or the resource processor, flush or close our custom OutputStream or PrintWriter, we examine the buffered output for the closing </body> tag, and insert our auditing information just before it (if found)

Therefore, any downstream filters on the inbound (including the actual resource processor) are actually writing their data into our custom stream. Of course, it is foreseeable that some other downstream filters may perform further wrapping (of our custom response with one of their own). The filter chaining mechanism supports this successive nested wrapping of response (and requests) as a means of multiple layers of content interception. In our case, our custom response wrapper object will add the "Big Brother is watching..." visual audit message to all resources that are accessed through this filter. The end user will see this auditing message at the bottom of every resource that he/she access, and will not be able to tell that the output originates from a filter.

Now let us examine the source code for this filter. Save it as `VisAuditFilter.java`, under the `webapps\ch15\WEB-INF\classes\com\wrox\projsp\filters` directory. We will highlight the important portions of the code here.

The VisAuditFilter Class

Our custom stream is called `VisAuditOutStream`, and it inherits from a class called `ReplaceContentOutputStream`. `ReplaceContentOutputStream` is a utility library (abstract) class for creating custom streams to be used in response wrapping. It takes care of buffer management, and intercepting the write, close, and flush calls by the downstream filters/processors. We will examine the source code for `ReplaceContentOutputStream` a little later.

The constructor of our `VisAuditOutStream` takes the output stream to wrap as the first parameter. The second and third parameters contain the IP address and host name of the client accessing the page, and are passed directly from the filter when the custom stream is created:

```
package com.wrox.projsp.ch15.filters;

import java.io.*;
import javax.servlet.*;
import javax.servlet.http.*;


class VisAuditOutStream extends ReplaceContentOutputStream {
  String Addr;
  String Host;

  public VisAuditOutStream(OutputStream outStream, String inAddr,
                           String inHost) {
    super(outStream);
    Addr = inAddr;
    Host = inHost;
  }
}
```

The single method that a child class must override, since the method is declared abstract in `ReplaceContentOutputStream`, is the `replaceContent()` method. This method takes a byte array as input – this is the content that is written into the buffer by the downstream filters/processors. The return value is another byte array, which is the content that you wish to write to the client. In our case, we look for the `</BODY>` or `</body>` tag.

```
public byte [] replaceContent(byte [] inBytes) {
  String retVal ="";
  String firstPart="";

  String tpString = new String(inBytes);
```

```
                  String srchString = (new String(inBytes)).toLowerCase();

                  int endBody = srchString.indexOf("</body>");
```

Once we find the `</body>` tag, we insert a line that adds the auditing information just before the end of the document:

```
      if (endBody != -1) {
        firstPart = tpString.substring(0, endBody);
        retVal = firstPart + "<br><small><i>Big Brother is watching you. " +
                "You have accessed our page from " + Addr +
                " and on a machine called " + Host + "</i></small></br>" +
                tpString.substring(endBody);

      } else {
        retVal=tpString;
      }

      return retVal.getBytes();
    }
  }
```

The Customized Response Wrapper Class

The next class we will define is the response wrapper called `VisAuditResponseWrapper`. It conveniently inherits from `javax.servlet.http.HttpServletResponseWrapper`. This wrapper class allow us to readily wrap any `HttpServletResponse` object, and override only the methods that we want to customize. The `HttpServletResponseWrapper` class has provided trivial implementations of all the methods of the `HttpServletResponse` interface – they all call the corresponding method of the class being wrapped:

```
    class VisAuditResponseWrapper extends HttpServletResponseWrapper {
      private PrintWriter tpWriter;
      private VisAuditOutStream tpStream;
```

The constructor passes the IP address and host name of client, in addition to the response that will be wrapped. Note that we create our customized stream in the constructor, and pass the IP address and host name right through. We also create a `PrintWriter` object based on the stream:

```
    public VisAuditResponseWrapper(ServletResponse inResp, String inAddr,
                                   String inHost)
            throws java.io.IOException {
      super((HttpServletResponse) inResp);
      tpStream = new VisAuditOutStream(inResp.getOutputStream(), inAddr,
                                   inHost);
      tpWriter = new PrintWriter(tpStream);
    }
```

The two other methods that we override are the `getOutputStream()` and `getPrintWriter()` methods. These methods hand out our customized stream instead of the response's actual stream:

541

```
      public ServletOutputStream getOutputStream() throws java.io.IOException {
        return tpStream;
      }

      public PrintWriter getWriter() throws java.io.IOException {
        return tpWriter;
      }
    }
```

The Filter Logic

Finally, we get to the actual filter class, `VisAuditFilter`. You will recognize the general organization from last chapter's samples. We focus our attention on the `doFilter()` method:

```
public final class VisAuditFilter implements Filter {
  private FilterConfig filterConfig = null;

  public void doFilter(ServletRequest request, ServletResponse response,
                      FilterChain chain)
          throws IOException, ServletException {
    if (filterConfig == null)
      return;
```

This code is executed on the inbound request. Here, we find out the client's IP address and the host name. This information will be passed down to the custom stream:

```
      String clientAddr = request.getRemoteAddr();
      String clientHost = request.getRemoteHost();
      filterConfig.getServletContext().log("in VisAuditFilter");
```

Here, we create a new customized wrapped response, passing in the actual response as well as the IP and host name:

```
      VisAuditResponseWrapper myWrappedResp =
              new VisAuditResponseWrapper(response, clientAddr, clientHost);
```

And then we pass the wrapped response downstream to other filters and the resource processor:

```
      chain.doFilter(request,  myWrappedResp);
```

Some resource processor and downstream filter combinations do not close the output stream properly, so here we force a close. You will see shortly that the implementation of the `ReplaceContentOutputStream` class is guarded against multiple closes, so this is safe even if the stream is already closed previously:

```
      myWrappedResp.getOutputStream().close();
      filterConfig.getServletContext().log("Getting out of VisAuditFilter");
    }
```

The rest of the methods implement the filter interface, and are standard implementations that we have seen within the samples of the previous chapter. After this example, we will not repeat them for brevity's sake, unless we change them significantly:

```
    public void init(FilterConfig filterConfig) {
      this.filterConfig = filterConfig;
    }

    public void destroy() {}

    public String toString() {

      if (filterConfig == null)
        return ("VisAuditFilter()");

      StringBuffer sb = new StringBuffer("VisAuditFilter(");
      sb.append(filterConfig);
      sb.append(")");
      return (sb.toString());
    }

}
```

The ReplaceContentOutputStream Class

The custom stream, `VisAuditOutStream`, depends on the `ReplaceContentOutputStream` class to do a lot of its magic. This class wraps an `OutputStream`, as well as:

❑   Supplying its own byte array based stream for the `write()` method, called by downstream filters and the resource processor

❑   Handling the `close()` or `flush()` methods by calling a child's `ReplaceContent()` method to transform the byte array stream

❑   Taking the transformed content, and writing it to the `OutputStream`

This class can be used for any filter that transforms or replaces the response content. Save the source code in the `webapps\ch15\WEB-INF\classes\com\wrox\projsp\filters` directory:

```
    package com.wrox.projsp.ch15.filters;
    import java.io.*;
    import javax.servlet.*;
```

This abstract class extends another abstract class, called `ServletOutputStream`. `ServletOutputStream` is the base class of the `OutputStream` returned by `getOutputStream` on a response. `ServletOutputStream` requires the `write(int)` method to be implemented by its subclass. It implements all the rest of the `write()` variants based on this method. Our own `ReplaceContentOutputStream` requires the `ReplaceContent()` method to be implemented by all its subclasses:

```
    public abstract class ReplaceContentOutputStream
            extends ServletOutputStream {

      private OutputStream intStream;
      private ByteArrayOutputStream baStream;
      private boolean closed = false;
      private boolean transformOnCloseOnly = false;
```

Note the use of two flag variables here:

❑ closed
   Initially false, is used to ensure that the wrapped stream is closed only once, regardless of how many times the close() method may be called.

❑ transformOnCloseOnly
   Controls when the ReplaceContent() method will be called; default is false, and the ReplaceContent() method will be called on every flush() as well as the close() method call. Setting this to true will ensure that stream transformation is only done once, when the close() method is called for the first time.

The constructor simply hides a reference to the stream being wrapped, and creates the memory based ByteArrayOutputStream() for the downstream processors:

```
public ReplaceContentOutputStream(OutputStream outStream) {
   intStream = outStream;
   baStream = new ByteArrayOutputStream();
}
```

We implement the required write(int) method which writes to our in-memory stream called baStream. This ensures that all writes on this stream write to baStream (essentially a buffer):

```
public void write(int i) throws java.io.IOException {
   baStream.write(i);
}
```

When close() is called for the first time, we will transform the output in the in-memory stream. After the transformation, we will write the results to the actual wrapped stream. Multiple calls to close() will not cause a problem in this case:

```
public void close() throws java.io.IOException {
   if (!closed) {
      processStream();
      intStream.close();
      closed = true;
   }
}
```

When flush() is called, the action that occurs will depend on the flag called transformOnCloseOnly. If this flag is set to true, the method does nothing. If this flag is set to false, the default, a stream transformation and write will occur to the underlying wrapped stream. A new ByteArrayStream is then created to catch any additional output after the flush(), and before close() or the next flush():

```
public void flush() throws java.io.IOException {
   if (baStream.size() != 0) {
      if (!transformOnCloseOnly) {
         processStream();
         baStream = new ByteArrayOutputStream();
      }
   }
}
```

Here is the definition of the abstract method. It transforms the `inBytes` byte array and returns the transformed byte array as the return value:

```
public abstract byte []  replaceContent(byte [] inBytes)
            throws java.io.IOException;
```

The `processStream()` method calls the `replaceContent()` method to transform the in-memory stream, and write the transformed output to the wrapped output stream:

```
public void processStream() throws java.io.IOException {

   intStream.write(replaceContent(baStream.toByteArray()));
   intStream.flush();
}
```

The `setTransformOnCloseOnly()` method is used by the subclass to control the `close()` and `flush()` behavior as described above:

```
public void setTransformOnCloseOnly() {
   transformOnCloseOnly = true;
}
}
```

This is the end of the code analysis for the `ReplaceContentOutputStream` abstract class. We will be relying on this class for two subsequent filters that transform their outgoing response's content.

Filter Configuration and Testing

To deploy the filter, add the filter definition and filter mapping to the `webapps\ch15\WEB-INF\web.xml` file:

```
<filter>
   <filter-name>Wrox VisAudit Filter</filter-name>
   <filter-class>com.wrox.projsp.ch15.filters.VisAuditFilter</filter-class>
</filter>

<filter-mapping>
   <filter-name>Wrox VisAudit Filter</filter-name>
   <url-pattern>/*</url-pattern>
</filter-mapping>
```

This mapping will apply the filter to every resource served within the application. Now, we can start Tomcat 4. Use a browser, and access the following URL, http://localhost:8080/ch15/index.html.

The output should be similar to the screenshot that we saw earlier in this section. Note that the resource here is a static HTML file. Now, let us try a JSP resource, http://localhost:8080/ch15/jsp/FindProd.jsp.

The page should look like the figure below, showing that the filter applies equally to a JSP resource:

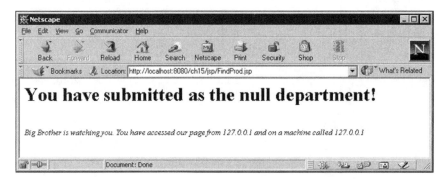

Next we will try a Servlet resource instead. Access the URL, http://localhost:8080/ch15/servlet/findprod.

The Servlet output, shown in the screenshot below, has once again been intercepted and the auditing information embedded:

At this point, some readers may question the necessity to test all three types of resources (static HTML, JSP, and Servlet). However, if you're creating filters that must work across many types of resources, you **must** test against each type of resource. This is necessary because each type of resource is passed through a different resource processor, each of which potentially has different assumptions and behavior from the others (Servlets are passed to Catalina, JSPs are passed to Jasper first, and so on).

Authorization Filter: Generating Our Own Response

One action that a filter can perform is to generate its own output, and deprive the downstream filters and resource processor of a chance to see the request altogether. Obviously, there is very little application for a filter that does this all the time. However, a filter that does this based on some dynamic criterion can be very useful. An example may be a filter that blocks resource access based on the time of day. We will create such a filter in this section.

The filter we are going to create falls into the authorization filter application domain. More specifically, it allows or disallows an incoming request to reach its destined resource processor, depending on the time of day. The actual application is intended to stop users from accessing game playing resources during certain office hours of the day. The figure opposite illustrates the action of the filter:

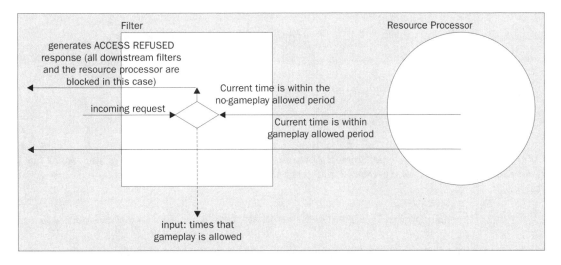

input: times that
gameplay is allowed

If a request arrives during the allowed time window, the user will be allowed through to the resource processor to play games. If a request arrives outside of the allowed time window, the filter generates a response of its own, depriving the downstream resource processor of a chance to see the request. This effectively blocks the use of the game resources.

The way the filter is designed allows us to make the range of allowable hours a configurable parameter. This will provide the web application assembler/deployer with flexibility when using the filter in his/her specific environment. It will also give us a chance to see how to access and work with initial parameters in filters.

The StopGamesFilter Class

Save the source code to this filter in the `webapps\ch15\WEB-INF\classes\com\wrox\projsp\filters`. Here is a brief code analysis of this filter:

```
package com.wrox.projsp.ch15.filters;

import java.io.*;
import javax.servlet.*;
import javax.servlet.http.*;
import java.util.Calendar;

public final class StopGamesFilter implements Filter {
```

There are no wrapper or customized stream classes, since we will not be transforming the response or modifying requests:

```
private FilterConfig filterConfig = null;
```

First, we set up the default hours of operation, which allows game playing all the time. These parameters are used if the filter is configured without initial parameters, or if the access to the initial parameters failed. It is always a good idea to set some usable default value for the filter. Note the instance scope of these private variables:

```
private int starthour = 0;
private int stophour = 24;  // default is to allow all the time

public void doFilter(ServletRequest request, ServletResponse response,
                 FilterChain chain)
        throws IOException, ServletException {
  if (filterConfig == null) {
    return;
  }
```

We obtain the current hour, depending on a 24 hours clock to make things simple. We also assume that the start and stop hour does not cross the 12 midnight boundary to keep the logic simple:

```
Calendar myCal = Calendar.getInstance();
int curhour = myCal.get(Calendar.HOUR_OF_DAY);
```

Next we make a log entry to show the various values, which is useful for auditing or debugging purposes:

```
filterConfig.getServletContext().log("in StopGamesFilter cur:" +
        curhour + ", start: " + starthour + ", end: " + stophour );
```

If the incoming request arrives outside of the allowed time range, we simply generate the content of the response ourselves. The generated content lets the user know that access to the game resource page is disallowed. The content generation is simple, and uses the same call as most Servlets:

```
if (( curhour >= stophour)|| (curhour <= starthour)) {
  PrintWriter out = response.getWriter();
  out.println("<html><head></head><body>");
  out.println
        ("<h1>Sorry, game playing is not allowed at this time!</h1>");
  out.println("</body></html>");
  out.flush();
  filterConfig.getServletContext().log("Access to game page denied");
  return;
}
```

Finally, we let the request through to access the game resource, and log an entry to indicate so:

```
filterConfig.getServletContext().log("Access to game page granted");

chain.doFilter(request, response);
filterConfig.getServletContext().log("Getting out of StopGamesFilter");

  }
}
```

Thread-safety Considerations

One question that the alert reader may have is: where do we access the initialization parameters? The answer is: generally **not** in the doFilter() method. This goes back to our discussion in the last chapter of thread-safe programming. The starthour and stophour variables are instance scope variables. Modifying the value of instance scoped variables in doFilter() requires careful synchronization, because doFilter() **will** be accessed in multiple threads at the same time.

Therefore, the only reasonable and safe place to read the value from the web.xml file, and modify the instance variables, is in the init() method for the filter. But a filter does not have an init() method. A reasonable approximation is available however, if we remember the filter lifecycle.

Taking Advantage of the Filter Lifecycle

After an instance of a filter has been created, and before the very first doFilter() is called, the container calls the init() method to set the FilterConfig object for the filter. This is a natural point to perform any initialization required, and is conceptually equivalent to the init() method of a Servlet.

In our case, we will take advantage of it by setting our instance variables with values from the filter definition. The container always calls init() in a single thread when it sets up the filter instance. In the init() method below, the filterConfig.getInitParameter() method reads the actual web.xml file for initialization parameters:

```
public void init(FilterConfig filterConfig) {
  String tpString;
  if ((tpString = filterConfig.getInitParameter("starthour")) != null)
    starthour = Integer.parseInt(tpString, 10);
  if ((tpString = filterConfig.getInitParameter("stophour")) != null)
    stophour = Integer.parseInt(tpString, 10);

  this.filterConfig = filterConfig;
}

public String toString() {
  // ...
}
}
```

Installing and Configuring the StopGamesFilter

To install and configure the filter, add the following entries to the web.xml file:

```
<filter>
  <filter-name>Wrox VisAudit Filter</filter-name>
  <filter-class>com.wrox.pjsp2.filters.VisAuditFilter</filter-class>
</filter>

<filter>
  <filter-name>Wrox Stop Games Filter</filter-name>
  <filter-class>com.wrox.projsp.ch15.filters.StopGamesFilter</filter-class>
  <init-param>
    <param-name>starthour</param-name>
    <param-value>8</param-value>
  </init-param>
  <init-param>
    <param-name>stophour</param-name>
    <param-value>9</param-value>
  </init-param>
</filter>

<filter-mapping>
  <filter-name>Wrox Stop Games Filter</filter-name>
  <url-pattern>/games/*</url-pattern>
```

```
  </filter-mapping>

<filter-mapping>
  <filter-name>Wrox VisAudit Filter</filter-name>
  <url-pattern>/*</url-pattern>
</filter-mapping>
```

Make sure that you have configured the `starthour` and `stophour` variables to make the current time outside of the allowable range, and create a `games` directory in your current webapp that contains an appropriate `index.html` file. Start Tomcat, and try to access the following URL through a browser, http://localhost:8080/ch15/games/index.html.

You should see an "access denied" message similar to the screenshot below:

This is our custom generated response, right from the filter. Now, shutdown Tomcat. Modify the `<filter>` definition in the `web.xml` file to include the current time within the range. Start Tomcat again, and try to access the same URL. You should now see the game-playing page, shown below:

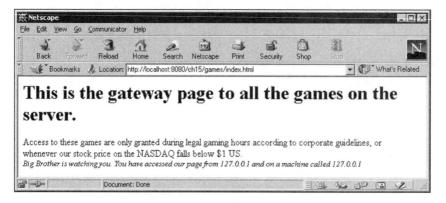

That's great, everything is working as expected. Or is it? We can see the effect of the chained `VisAuditFilter` on the games resource page above. But why did the `VisAuditFilter` auditing information not show up in the "access denied" page that was generated by the filter? We will see why in the next section.

Importance of Chaining Order: A Visual Demonstration

Here is a great demonstration of the side effect of ordering on filter chaining. If you examine the `web.xml` file again, you will see the `<filter-mapping>` of "Wrox Stop Games Filter" before that for the "Wrox Visual Audit Filter". This is the quintessential difference.

The `Stop Games` filter is applied to the request first as it travels inbound towards the resource. Since it blocks and generate its own response, the `VisAudit` filter did not even have a chance to see the request. To prove this, shutdown Tomcat and modify the filter mapping order to:

```
<filter-mapping>
    <filter-name>Wrox VisAudit Filter</filter-name>
    <url-pattern>/*</url-pattern>
</filter-mapping>

<filter-mapping>
    <filter-name>Wrox Stop Games Filter</filter-name>
    <url-pattern>/games/*</url-pattern>
</filter-mapping>
```

With this ordering, the `VisAudit` filter will be called first with the inbound request and last with the outbound response – giving it a chance to transform the output with its auditing information. Before restarting Tomcat, make sure you reset the allowed range to disallow the current time in the `web.xml` file as well. The screenshot below illustrates the result:

You should be able to see that Big Brother is back.

A Filter for Adapting to Legacy Resources

The next filter we will examine addresses a very common problem that occurs in the real world. You have two independent systems that refer to each other through hyperlinks. Over time, the requirement and access has changed because of independent evolution. Due to the size of the independent projects, or due to political situations, you cannot change the links to either one of the systems. In order to keep them working, we will need to create a filter that adapts one system to another, without modifying a single line of code in either system. The figure overleaf shows the action of just such an 'adapter' filter within an example system:

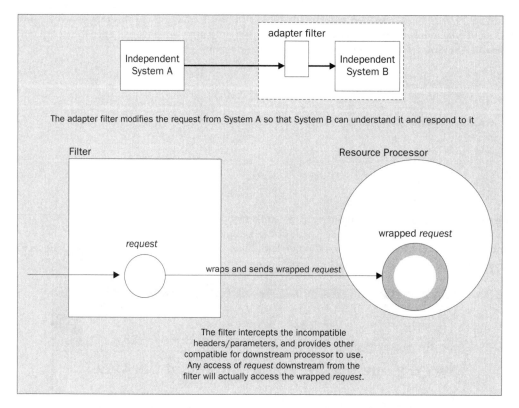

The adapter filter modifies the request from System A so that System B can understand it and respond to it

The filter intercepts the incompatible
headers/parameters, and provides other
compatible for downstream processor to use.
Any access of *request* downstream from the
filter will actually access the wrapped *request*.

In our example, a JSP page represents the legacy resource. A centralized administrative server that is accessed by multiple departments in a company services this JSP. This legacy system requires the originating department information (supplied in the form of a DEPT parameter) in order to work properly. Unfortunately, due to political situations, the links coming into this server do not and will not contain the originating department information (the DEPT parameter). Therefore, we will design a filter to adapt the two systems.

This filter, by design, will intercept the request, examine where it is from, and generate the required DEPT parameter for the JSP resource so that it can function properly. In fact, it determines the department of the incoming client by examining its subnet portion of the IP address corresponding to the client (assuming it has the subnet IP to department mapping knowledge). Therefore, this adapter translates an incoming IP address to a required DEPT parameter, adapting two incompatible systems and allowing them to work together.

One can easily imagine many more involved examples from the real world that may require significantly more adaptation code. However, the general structure and technique for creating such adapter filters will remain the same.

For this example we will be revisiting FindProd.jsp. We have already seen the effect of accessing this page before, when we tried out the VisAudit filter:

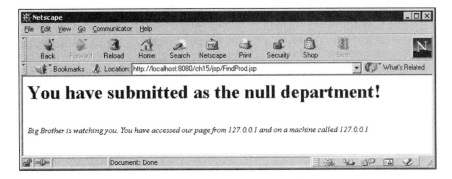

The reason why it says null department is due to the missing DEPT parameter when the URL is accessed. We will fix this by creating a filter that will adapt any incoming requests by detecting the department information and providing the missing parameter.

Wrapping an Incoming Request

We will now analyse the code of the LegacyAdapter filter. The filter:

- ❑ Determines the incoming IP address
- ❑ Finds out which department the request originates from, by examining the IP address
- ❑ Adds the DEPT parameter to the request before it reaches the underlying JSP resource

The LegacyAdapterFilter Class

Save the code in the webapps\ch15\WEB-INF\classes\com\wrox\projsp\filters directory. We will now review the partial source code:

```
package com.wrox.projsp.ch15.filters;

import java.io.*;
import javax.servlet.*;
import javax.servlet.http.*;
import java.util.*;
```

In this example, we must wrap the incoming request – unlike the VisAudit filter where we wrapped the outgoing response. We will actually be modifying header information associated with the incoming request.

The wrapper class here extends the useful HttpServletRequestWrapper class. HttpServletRequestWrapper will take as argument for its constructor the actual HttpServletRequest to wrap. It trivially implements all of its methods by calling the methods of the wrapped request. By inheriting from this class, we can choose to override only the methods that we are interested in:

```
class LegacyAdapterRequestWrapper extends HttpServletRequestWrapper {
    String myDept = null;
```

Note that we take the department as an argument for the constructor of our custom wrapper class:

```
    public LegacyAdapterRequestWrapper(HttpServletRequest inReq,
                                       String deptString) {
      super(inReq);
      myDept = deptString;
    }
```

The methods that we provide custom implementation for are `getParameterMap()`,
`getParameterValues()`, and `getParameter()`. This will ensure that we can work with most of the
resources that may access parameters. In fact, for our specific JSP case, we only had to override the
`getParameter()` method since this is the only method it uses. In each override below, you will see how we
add the DEPT parameter. The downstream filter/processor accessing the headers will have no way of
knowing that the DEPT parameter was actually added by our filter, and not from the original request –
demonstrating the beauty of filter chaining:

```
    public Map getParameterMap() {
      Map tmpMap = super.getParameterMap();
      tmpMap.put("DEPT",myDept);
      return tmpMap;
    }

    public String [] getParameterValues(String paramName) {
      if (paramName.equalsIgnoreCase("DEPT")) {
        String [] tpAry = new String[1];
        tpAry[0] = myDept;
        return tpAry;
      }
      else
        return super.getParameterValues(paramName);
    }

    public String getParameter(String paramName) {
      if (paramName.equalsIgnoreCase("DEPT")) {
        return myDept;
      }
      else
        return super.getParameter(paramName);
    }
  }
```

The actual filter class starts here:

```
  public final class LegacyAdapterFilter implements Filter {

    private FilterConfig filterConfig = null;

    public void doFilter(ServletRequest request, ServletResponse response,
             FilterChain chain)
          throws IOException, ServletException {
      LegacyAdapterRequestWrapper aCustomReq;
      if (filterConfig == null)
        return;
```

The code first determines the department that the request is coming from. It does so by mapping the subnet
of the IP address to a department. In this case, it trivially examines the subnet – if it is zero,
DEPT=Accounting is used, otherwise DEPT=Engineering is used:

```
String clientAddr = request.getRemoteAddr();
System.out.println("the addr is " + clientAddr);
int idx = clientAddr.indexOf(".");
clientAddr = clientAddr.substring(idx + 1);
idx = clientAddr.indexOf(".");
clientAddr = clientAddr.substring(idx + 1);
idx = clientAddr.indexOf(".");
clientAddr = clientAddr.substring(0, idx);
System.out.println("the subnet is " + clientAddr);
String dept = null;
if (clientAddr.equals("0"))
  dept = "Engineering";
else
  dept = "Accounting";
```

Next, it creates a wrapper request, passing in the `dept`, and calling downstream filters/processor via filter chaining:

```
aCustomReq = new LegacyAdapterRequestWrapper
                    ((HttpServletRequest) request, dept);

filterConfig.getServletContext().log("in LegacyAdapterFilter");

chain.doFilter(aCustomReq, response);
filterConfig.getServletContext().log
        ("Getting out of LegacyAdapterFilter");

}

public void init(FilterConfig filterConfig) {
  // ...
}

public FilterConfig destroy() {}

public String toString() {
  // ...
}
}
```

Installing and Configuring the LegacyAdapterFilter

To install and configure the filter, first make sure all other `<filter>` and `<filter-mapping>` definitions are removed or commented out (we want to reduce the side-effect of chaining other sample filters). Then, add the following entries to the `web.xml` file:

```
<filter>
  <filter-name>Wrox VisAudit Filter</filter-name>
  <filter-class>com.wrox.projsp.ch15.filters.VisAuditFilter</filter-class>
</filter>
```

```
<filter>
  <filter-name>Wrox Legacy Adapter Filter</filter-name>
  <filter-class>
```

```
        com.wrox.projsp.ch15.filters.LegacyAdapterFilter
     </filter-class>
  </filter>

  <filter-mapping>
    <filter-name>Wrox Legacy Adapter Filter</filter-name>
    <url-pattern>/jsp/FindProd.jsp</url-pattern>
  </filter-mapping>


  <filter-mapping>
    <filter-name>Wrox VisAudit Filter</filter-name>
    <url-pattern>/*</url-pattern>
  </filter-mapping>
```

This will specifically apply the filter to the FindProd.jsp resource. Note that we are chaining with the VisAudit filter. Start Tomcat, and try accessing the URL, http://localhost:8080/ch15/jsp/FindProd.jsp.

You should see a page similar to:

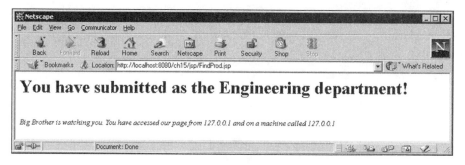

Note that it no longer indicates a null department as it had when we accessed the page in the VisAudit filter example. The JSP is picking up the DEPT parameter from our wrapped request. If possible, you may want to access the JSP from another subnet to see the automatic department detection at work.

Authentication – An Ad Hoc AuthenticateFilter

Tomcat 4 and almost all Servlet 2.3 compliant containers come with extensive authentication and authorization support. Therefore, in theory, there is very little need to implement one's own authentication filter. In practice however, there is almost always room to apply an ad-hoc authentication filter on a selected resource – without affecting the rest of the application, or involving the overhead of setting up, say, JDBC realms.

One should always analyze the problem at hand to see if it would be better solved by the native authentication support of the server. However, in those cases where we need simple temporary protection of selected resources, the AdHocAuthenticate filter can be the best choice for the problem.

The action of this filter is straightforward. It triggers basic authentication on the client browser. Almost all known browsers, including even the earliest versions, support basic authentication. It works like this:

❑ Client attempts to access a protected resource

❑ The server examines the client's request, to determine if there is any authorization data in the 'Authorization' header

❑ If authorization data is not found, the server sends back HTTP status code 401 – unauthorized access – and a header with `"WWW-authenticate:   BASIC realm=<realm>"` where the `realm` is a text string that will be displayed to the client

❑ The client pops up a login screen, for the user to enter a username and password

❑ The client encodes the username and password using simple base64 encoding, and sends both to server

❑ The server examines the client request to determine if there is any authorization data, decoding the base64 encoded password if necessary; if there is no authorization data it goes back to step 3

❑ The server verifies the username and password, and either allows or rejects access

Basic authentication is not very secure, since the base64 encoding can easily be decoded. However, for applications that just need to protect resources from casual access, it is more than sufficient. For more details on different kinds of authentication, see the next chapter.

The `AdHocAuthenticate` filter that we examine now will perform this simple protection. It will check the authorization data against a global password that is configured as an initial parameter for the filter.

The AdHocAuthenticateFilter Class

Save the filter's source code in the `webapps\ch15\WEB-INF\classes\com\wrox\projsp\ch15\filters` directory. Here is a brief analysis:

```
package com.wrox.projsp.ch15.filters;

import java.io.*;
import javax.servlet.*;
import javax.servlet.http.*;
import java.util.Map;
import sun.misc.*;
```

There is no need to wrap the response or request in this filter. Note the instance variable that will be used to hold the single, read-only, `adhocPassword`. This variable is initialized from the `web.xml` value from the `setConfig()` method:

```
public final class AdHocAuthenticateFilter implements Filter {

  private FilterConfig filterConfig = null;
  private String adhocPassword = null;

  public void doFilter(ServletRequest request, ServletResponse response,
                       FilterChain chain)
        throws IOException, ServletException {
    if (filterConfig == null)
      return;
```

We cast the request and response to their HTTP Servlet version, in order to access and manipulate the headers associated with them:

```
    HttpServletRequest myReq = (HttpServletRequest) request;
    HttpServletResponse myResp = (HttpServletResponse) response;
```

Here we perform the basic authentication request if we do not find authorization data:

```
String authString = myReq.getHeader("Authorization");
if (authString == null) {
  myResp.addHeader("WWW-Authenticate", "BASIC realm=\"Wrox PJSP2\"");
  myResp.setStatus(HttpServletResponse.SC_UNAUTHORIZED);
  return;
}
else { // authenticate
```

If we find authorization data, we decode the username and password. The substring(6) below skips over the constant string "Basic " of the authorization header, getting to the beginning of the base64 encoded username and password:

```
BASE64Decoder decoder =new BASE64Decoder();
String enString = authString.substring(6);
String decString = new String(decoder.decodeBuffer(enString));
int idx = decString.indexOf(":");
String uid = decString.substring(0, idx);
String pwd = decString.substring(idx + 1);
```

We call a method named externalAuthenticate() to do the actual authentication. In production, authentication via an external server may be implemented here. Failed authentication will cause the login dialog to pop up again on the client's browser:

```
if (!externalAuthenticate(uid,pwd)) {
   myResp.addHeader("WWW-Authenticate", "BASIC realm=\"Wrox PJSP2\"");
   myResp.setStatus(HttpServletResponse.SC_UNAUTHORIZED);
   return;
  }
}
```

If we reach this point, everything has been authenticated properly, and access of the resource can begin:

```
filterConfig.getServletContext().log("in AdHocAuthenticateFilter");
chain.doFilter(request, response);
filterConfig.getServletContext().log
        ("Getting out of AdHocAuthenticateFilter");
}
```

The externalAuthenticate() method encapsulates the authentication mechanism. In our case, we authenticate against a single password from the initial parameters. We can modify it to perform any type of authentication we desire, including authentication against some physically external servers:

```
private  boolean externalAuthenticate(String user, String password) {
  if (adhocPassword == null)
    return false;
  return adhocPassword.equals(password);
}

public void destroy() {}
```

It is in the `init()` method that the initial parameter is read and handed to the filter.

```
public void init(FilterConfig filterConfig) {
  if (adhocPassword == null)
    adhocPassword = filterConfig.getInitParameter("adhocpassword");
    this.filterConfig = filterConfig;
}

public String toString() {
  if (filterConfig == null)
    return ("AdHocAuthenticateFilter()");
  StringBuffer sb = new  StringBuffer("AdHocAuthenticateFilter(");
  sb.append(filterConfig);
  sb.append(")");
  return (sb.toString());

}
}
```

Installing and Configuring the AdHocAuthenticateAdapterFilter

To install and configure the filter, first make sure all other `<filter>` and `<filter-mapping>` definitions are removed or commented out. Then, add the following entries to the `web.xml` file.

```
<filter>
  <filter-name>Wrox Legacy Adapter Filter</filter-name>
  <filter-class>
    com.wrox.projsp.ch15.filters.LegacyAdapterFilter
  </filter-class>
</filter>

<filter>
  <filter-name>Wrox AdHoc Authentication Filter</filter-name>
  <filter-class>
    com.wrox.projsp.ch15.filters.AdHocAuthenticateFilter
  </filter-class>
  <init-param>
    <param-name>adhocpassword</param-name>
    <param-value>bestofbreed</param-value>
  </init-param>
</filter>

<filter-mapping>
  <filter-name>Wrox AdHoc Authentication Filter</filter-name>
  <url-pattern>/jsp/*</url-pattern>
</filter-mapping>

<filter-mapping>
  <filter-name>Wrox Legacy Adapter Filter</filter-name>
  <url-pattern>/jsp/FindProd.jsp</url-pattern>
</filter-mapping>
```

Note that we have chained with the legacy adapter filter in order to supply the missing originating department information for the JSP.

This will protect all JSP access with the password "bestofbreed". Now, start Tomcat, and access the URL, http://localhost:8080/ch15/jsp/FindProd.jsp.

You should be prompted with a login dialog box, shown in the screenshot below:

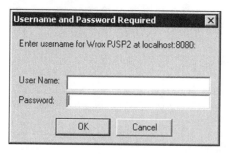

Enter any user name, and an invalid password. You will see that it bars access to the protected resource until we enter the correct password.

Compression/Encryption – An On-The-Fly Zipping Filter

Our original intention was to create an encryption filter. It was quickly rejected for two reasons:

❑ Tomcat 4 provides full TLS security (SSL) support, rendering additional encryption filters largely unnecessary

❑ Most encryption algorithms are complex to implement, detracting from our topic of filters

Instead, we are going to create a filter that zips content on-the-fly. It will only do this if it detects a client that can handle the GZIP format (this includes almost all modern browsers). The current versions of both the Microsoft Internet Explorer and Netscape browsers support this format. Aside from being pretty useful for zipping on-the-fly, this compression filter has two advantages:

❑ The GZIP algorithm has been implemented by the JDK library, freeing us to focus on the filtering aspect of design and coding

❑ The method of incorporating encryption and compression functionality in a GZIP filter is identical to that in an encryption filter

The figure below shows the action of this filter:

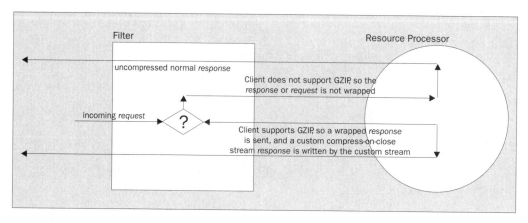

We can see the need to wrap the response in order to intercept the content. In this case, we also need to modify the response header to notify the client of the GZIP content being returned.

The KryptPressFilter Class

We can detect if a client supports an encoding format by examining the "Accept-Encoding" header of the incoming request. Then, when we actually serve the response, we must intercept and set the outgoing response header called "Content-Encoding" to "gzip" in order to signal the client that the content is actually compressed.

Save the code for this filter in webapps\ch15\WEB-INF\classes\com\wrox\projsp\filters:

```
package com.wrox.projsp.ch15.filters;

import java.io.*;
import javax.servlet.*;
import javax.servlet.http.*;
import java.util.zip.*;
```

Not surprisingly, we are using the ReplaceContentOutputStream to intercept the downstream output and compress it before sending it upstream. The setTransformOnCloseOnly() call here in the constructor is not strictly necessary since GZIP can perform compression on the stream byte-by-byte. It is possible, however, that there are certain compression or encryption algorithms that must work on the entire content at one time (or on fixed size blocks):

```
class KryptOutStream extends ReplaceContentOutputStream {
    public KryptOutStream(OutputStream outStream) {
        super(outStream);
        setTransformOnCloseOnly();
    }
```

The replaceContent() method is where the work is done. Here we simply pass whatever is in the incoming in-memory stream through the GZIPOutputStream and out to the return value byte array. The base class will take care of writing the data out back to the client:

```
public byte [] replaceContent(byte [] inBytes)
        throws java.io.IOException {
    ByteArrayOutputStream tpBaStream = new ByteArrayOutputStream();
    GZIPOutputStream tpZipStream = new GZIPOutputStream(tpBaStream);

    tpZipStream.write(inBytes, 0, inBytes.length);
    tpZipStream.close();
    tpBaStream.close();
    return tpBaStream.toByteArray();
}

}
```

The ResponseWrapper class shares a common structure with the class in the VisAudit filter example:

```
class ResponseWrapper extends HttpServletResponseWrapper {
    private PrintWriter tpWriter;
    private KryptOutStream tpStream;
```

```
    public ResponseWrapper(ServletResponse inResp)
            throws java.io.IOException {
      super((HttpServletResponse) inResp);
      tpStream = new KryptOutStream(inResp.getOutputStream());
      tpWriter = new PrintWriter(tpStream);
    }

    public ServletOutputStream getOutputStream() throws java.io.IOException {
      return  tpStream;
    }

    public PrintWriter getWriter() throws java.io.IOException {
      return tpWriter;
    }
  }
}
```

The actual filter logic begins now. We need to determine if the client issuing the incoming request will support GZIP encoding format:

```
public final class KryptPressFilter implements Filter {
  private FilterConfig filterConfig = null;

  public void doFilter(ServletRequest request, ServletResponse response,
          FilterChain chain) throws IOException, ServletException {
    if (filterConfig == null)
      return;
```

The default is that GZIP is not supported. The filter will examine the request header called "Accept-Encoding" for "gzip". This is the indication that the client will support GZIP content. Once this is determined, we also set the actual response header, called "Content-Encoding", to indicate that the response is in GZIP format:

```
    boolean gzipSupportedByClient = false;
    String allowedEncoding =
            ((HttpServletRequest) request).getHeader("Accept-Encoding");
    if (allowedEncoding != null) {
      if (allowedEncoding.indexOf("gzip") != -1) {
        gzipSupportedByClient = true;
        ((HttpServletResponse) response).addHeader
                ("Content-Encoding","gzip");
      }
    }
```

If the client supports GZIP, we create a wrapper response to compress the outgoing content. Otherwise, we just pass through the request/response and do no processing of our own:

```
    filterConfig.getServletContext().log("in KryptPressFilter");

    if (gzipSupportedByClient) {
      ResponseWrapper myWrappedResp = new ResponseWrapper( response);
      chain.doFilter(request,  myWrappedResp);
      myWrappedResp.getOutputStream().close();
```

```
    }
    else
      chain.doFilter(request, response);

    filterConfig.getServletContext().log("Getting out of KryptPressFilter");
  }

  public void init(FilterConfig filterConfig) {
    // ...
  }

  public void destroy() {}

  public String toString() {
    // ...
  }
}
```

Installing and Configuring the KryptPressFilter

To install and configure the filter, first make sure all other `<filter>` and `<filter-mapping>` definitions are removed or commented out, except for the `LegacyAdapter` filter. Then, add the following entries to the `web.xml` file:

```xml
<filter>
  <filter-name>Wrox Encrypt Compress Filter</filter-name>
  <filter-class>com.wrox.projsp.ch15.filters.KryptPressFilter</filter-class>
</filter>

<filter-mapping>
  <filter-name>Wrox Encrypt Compress Filter</filter-name>
  <url-pattern>/servlet/*</url-pattern>
</filter-mapping>

<filter-mapping>
  <filter-name>Wrox Legacy Adapter Filter</filter-name>
  <url-pattern>/servlet/*</url-pattern>
</filter-mapping>
```

This will configure the filter to act on any Servlets being served. Start Tomcat, and try the URL, http://localhost:8080/ch15/servlet/findprod.

You will see the page show up as in the screenshot below:

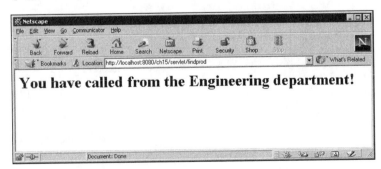

563

In fact it doesn't look any different from direct access. If you have a very old browser that does not support GZIP content, you can try the URL with it. With such a browser, you will be able to see the compressed page in 'gerbish' form. Otherwise, you need to take our word for it: that the page was compressed before transmission, and that the browser has dynamically decompressed it before showing it to you.

An Aside

Just before the entrepreneurial reader runs out and markets this filter as the bandwidth-saving miracle of the decade, we need to make a few comments concerning the practicality of this filter.

The general perception from the developer community is that it would be useful. However, the general consensus from system administrators and ISPs is that the cost would not justify the marginal benefit that it provides, due to the following non-intuitive, but very practical reasons:

❑   Compression is typically 5x more expensive than decompression, therefore loading up the typically already heavily-loaded server

❑   Compressed streams are difficult to cache, wiping out the benefit of many high performance caching systems

❑   Most ironic of all, users who are on slow links where this may matter are already using modems that support high compression ratios on hardware – rendering the actual bandwidth savings over these lines with zipped data marginal

Nevertheless, the `KryptPressFilter` makes for a great filter example (and conversation piece).

An XSLT Filter for Dynamically Transforming XML Content

This is the last filter we will cover in this already code-intensive chapter. It also happens to be the most difficult filter to set up and test. Ironically, coding it is rather simple. By now, we are very familiar with wrapped response, and the use of the `ContentReplacementOutputStream`. This is yet another filter that uses the wrapped response mechanism to get its work done. The figure below shows the action of the filter. It also shows the filter in a wider context of a travel agency web application:

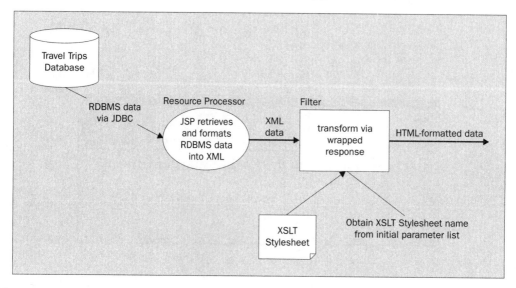

The application does the following:

- ❑ xTrips.jsp extracts trip (holiday) records for the travel agency from a database via JDBC, and formats the output as an XML document

- ❑ The XSLTFilter transforms this XML output, via a pre-configured XSLT stylesheet, to HTML for the user to view

As the data in the database changes (in other words trips get added or sold), the user will have a customized live view of the data.

Before we examine the code of the filter, we must first obtain an XSLT parser and see how to make it work within our code.

Applying the Xalan XSLT Processor

One of the most popular XSLT parsers for Java is available from the Apache XML group. It is called **Xalan**. You can download Xalan from http://xml.apache.org/xalan-j/index.html. Our example here uses the 2.0.0 version of the processor. The figure below shows how Xalan will work in our case:

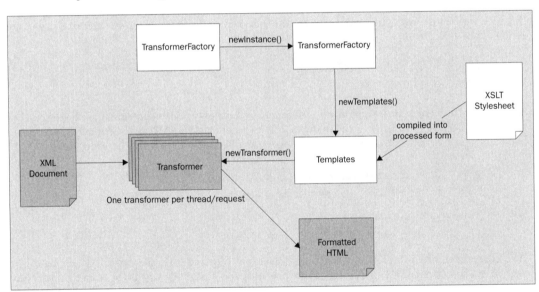

As you can see from the diagram, we need to:

- ❑ Use the TransformerFactory class' static method newInstance() to obtain an instance of a TranformerFactory

- ❑ Use the newTemplates() method of the TransformerFactory to pre-process and XSLT stylesheet, and create a Templates instance associated with the stylesheet

- ❑ For every request, we use the Templates instance's newTransformer() method to create a transformer instance that can be used to transform the XML document input

By design, thanks to the intermediate Templates instance, the XSLT stylesheet needs to be processed only once per filter instance – and not once per request.

Note that out of the three steps above, the `Transformer` instance in the third step is not thread-safe. Therefore, one must create a new `Transformer` (from the templates) for processing each request. Fortunately, the Xalan library designers have made sure this is a very efficient operation. For more on XSLT and XML in JSP, see Chapter 12.

The XSLTFilter Class

Save the source code for the `XSLTFilter` in the `webapps\ch15\WEB-INF\classes\com\wrox\projsp\ch15\filters` directory. Here is a brief code analysis:

```
package com.wrox.projsp.ch15.filters;

import java.io.*;
import javax.servlet.*;
import javax.servlet.http.*;
import javax.xml.transform.stream.*;
import javax.xml.transform.*;
import org.apache.xalan.transformer.*;
import org.apache.xalan.templates.*;
import java.util.zip.*;
```

Since we will be transforming response content, we inherit from `ReplaceContentOutputStream` and create our custom stream:

```
class XSLTXformStream extends ReplaceContentOutputStream {
  private Templates templatesXSLT = null;
```

This time, we do want to make sure that transformation occurs only once upon closing of the document. This is important because the `flush()` call in the middle of generating an XML document may create partial buffers that are not valid XML documents – breaking the operation of the XSLT transformer:

```
public XSLTXformStream(OutputStream outStream, Templates inTp)  {
  super(outStream);
  setTransformOnCloseOnly();
  templatesXSLT = inTp;
}
```

When the custom stream is created, a `Templates` instance is passed in. In the `replaceContent()` method, we simply create a `Transformer` instance using the `Templates` and transform the byte array using it:

```
public byte [] replaceContent(byte [] inBytes)
          throws java.io.IOException {
  ByteArrayOutputStream outBaStream = new ByteArrayOutputStream();
  ByteArrayInputStream inBaStream = new ByteArrayInputStream(inBytes);

  try {
    Transformer transformerXSLT = templatesXSLT.newTransformer();
    transformerXSLT.transform(new StreamSource(inBaStream),
    new StreamResult(outBaStream));
  } catch (Exception ex) {
    throw (new java.io.IOException());
  }
```

```
        inBaStream.close();
        outBaStream.close();
        return outBaStream.toByteArray();
    }
}
```

Our `XSLTResponseWrapper` class follows the classic structure used in both `VisAuditFilter` and `KryptPressFilter`. The constructor here takes the `Templates` instance and passes it right through to the `XSLTXformStream`, our custom stream, being created:

```
class XSLTResponseWrapper extends HttpServletResponseWrapper {
  private PrintWriter tpWriter;
  private XSLTXformStream tpStream;

  public XSLTResponseWrapper(ServletResponse inResp, Templates inTp)
          throws java.io.IOException {
    super((HttpServletResponse) inResp);
    tpStream = new XSLTXformStream(inResp.getOutputStream(), inTp);
    tpWriter = new PrintWriter(tpStream);
  }

  public ServletOutputStream getOutputStream() throws java.io.IOException {
    return  tpStream;
  }

  public PrintWriter getWriter() throws java.io.IOException {
    return tpWriter;
  }
}
```

The actual filter logic begins here:

```
public final class XSLTFilter implements Filter {
  private FilterConfig filterConfig = null;
  private TransformerFactory xsltFactory = null;
  private Templates xsltTemplates = null;

  public void doFilter(ServletRequest request, ServletResponse response,
                    FilterChain chain)
          throws IOException, ServletException {
    if (filterConfig == null)
      return;
```

Below, we do something that we normally shouldn't, because we have no choice. We modify two instance variables `xsltFactory` and `xsltTemplates` right in the `doFilter()` method where highly multi-threaded access can cause big problems. We need to do it here because the code involves loading a resource – the XSLT stylesheet via a URL (and hence through a URL loader).

This code causes a security exception if we place it in the `init()` method where it should belong. Later versions of Tomcat 4 may fix this problem; however, since we only need to initialize once, we can legitimately place the code here – given that the user must access the URL once (thus initializing the values) before turning it over to public multi-threaded access:

```
      if (xsltFactory == null) {
        try {
          xsltFactory = TransformerFactory.newInstance();
          String xsltfile = filterConfig.getInitParameter("xsltfile");
          if (xsltfile != null)
            xsltTemplates = xsltFactory.newTemplates(new StreamSource
                                  (filterConfig.getServletContext()
                                      .getResourceAsStream(xsltfile)));
        } catch (Exception ex) { ex.printStackTrace(); }
      }
```

As usual, we create a wrapped response, and use it to call the downstream filters/processor via the `chain.doFilter()` call. If the `Templates` instance is not initialized, this filter does nothing and passes the request/response through untouched:

```
      filterConfig.getServletContext().log("in XSLTFilter");

      if (xsltTemplates != null) {
        XSLTResponseWrapper myWrappedResp = null;
        try {
          myWrappedResp = new XSLTResponseWrapper( response, xsltTemplates);
        } catch (Exception ex) { ex.printStackTrace(); }

        chain.doFilter(request,  myWrappedResp);
        myWrappedResp.getOutputStream().close();

      }
      else {
        chain.doFilter(request, response);
      }
      filterConfig.getServletContext().log("Getting out of XSLTFilter");
    }

  public void init(FilterConfig filterConfig) {
    // ...
  }

  public void destroy() {}

  public String toString() {
    // ...
  }

}
```

Installing and Configuring the XSLTFilter

To install and configure the filter, first make sure all other `<filter>` and `<filter-mapping>` definitions are removed or commented out. Then, add the following entries to the `web.xml` file:

```
<filter>
  <filter-name>Wrox XSLT Transform Filter</filter-name>
  <filter-class>com.wrox.projsp.ch15.filters.XSLTFilter</filter-class>
  <init-param>
    <param-name>xsltfile</param-name>
```

```
    <param-value>/xslt/cust.xsl</param-value>
  </init-param>
</filter>

<filter-mapping>
  <filter-name>Wrox XSLT Transform Filter</filter-name>
  <url-pattern>/jsp/* </url-pattern>
</filter-mapping>
```

This sets the filter to use an XSLT stylesheet called /xslt/cust.xsl. It also only applies the filter to any JSP resource in this application. Save the following as xTrips.jsp in your jsp directory:

```
<?xml version="1.0" ?>
<%@ page language="java" import="com.wrox.projsp.ch15.travelbase.*"  %>

<%!
public DealsFinder myFinder;

public void jspInit() {
  myFinder = new DealsFinder();
  myFinder.init();
}
%>

<%
   String myStr = myFinder.locateDealsXML();
 %>
<selloff>
<%= myStr %>
</selloff>
```

This JSP generates an XML document with a root element called <selloff>. We see that it uses a library package called com.wrox.projsp.ch15.travelbase to do its work. More specifically, it creates an instance of DealsFinder and calls its locateDealsXML() method to generate most of the XML.

The com.wrox.projsp.ch15.travelbase Library Package

Save the following source code to DealsFinder in the webapps\ch15\WEB-INF\classes\com\wrox\pjrosp\travelbase directory:

```
package com.wrox.projsp.ch15.travelbase;

import java.io.*;

public class DealsFinder {
  queryBean myQuery;

  public DealsFinder() {
  }
```

The init() method is used to make the connection to the DB once only during the initialization of the JSP:

```
public void init() {
  try {
    myQuery = new queryBean();
    myQuery.makeConnection();
  } catch (Exception e) {
  }
}
```

locateDealsXML uses a JDBC helper class, called queryBean, to traverse through the records in the database. It then generates an XML element for each record found:

```
public String locateDealsXML() {
  String retVal = "";
  try {
    myQuery.getDeals("" + 0 );

    while (myQuery.getNextTrip()) {
      retVal += "<trip number=\"" + myQuery.getColumn("tripno") +
                "\" region=\"" + myQuery.getColumn("region") +
                "\"><startdate>" + myQuery.getColumn("startdate") +
                "</startdate><duration>" + myQuery.getColumn("duration") +
                "</duration><location>"+ myQuery.getColumn("location") +
                "</location><price commission=\"" +
                myQuery.getColumn("commission") +
                "\">" + myQuery.getColumn("price") + "</price></trip>\n";
    }

  } catch (Exception ex) {
    retVal = "";
  }

  return retVal;
  }
}
```

We will not analyze the code in the queryBean or sqlBean classes here, since they include basic JDBC helper code, and are not pertinent to our filter discussion. However, we will list them here for completeness.

The queryBean Class

```
package com.wrox.projsp.ch15.travelbase;

import java.sql.*;
import java.io.*;

public class queryBean extends sqlBean {
  String myTripQuery = "select * from hotdeals where tripno > ";

  ResultSet myResultSet = null;
  public queryBean() {super();}

  public boolean getDeals(String tripNo) throws Exception {
    String myQuery = myTripQuery + tripNo;
    Statement stmt = myConn.createStatement();
    myResultSet = stmt.executeQuery(myQuery);

    return (myResultSet != null);
  }

  public boolean getNextTrip() throws Exception {
    return myResultSet.next();
  }

  public String getColumn( String inCol) throws Exception {
    return myResultSet.getString(inCol);
  }

}
```

The sqlBean Class

```
package com.wrox.projsp.ch15.travelbase;

import java.sql.*;
import java.io.*;

public class sqlBean {
  private String myDriver = "sun.jdbc.odbc.JdbcOdbcDriver";
  private String myURL = "jdbc:odbc:travel";

  protected Connection myConn;

  public sqlBean() {}

  public void makeConnection() throws Exception {
   Class.forName( myDriver);
   myConn = DriverManager.getConnection(myURL);
  }

  public void takeDown() throws Exception {
   myConn.close();
  }

}
```

The XSLT Stylesheet

One final piece of code we will examine is the XSLT stylesheet that is used. Save the following code to webapps\ch15\xslt\cust.xsl:

```
<?xml version="1.0" ?>
<xsl:stylesheet xmlns:xsl="http://www.w3.org/1999/XSL/Transform" version="1.0">
  <xsl:template match="/">
    <html>
      <body>
        <table width="600">
         <tr><td><h1>Wrox Vacations Center</h1></td></tr>
         <tr><td><h2>Server-side XSLT Filtering - JSP Generated XML
                   Data</h2></td></tr>
        </table>
        <table border="1">
          <tr>
            <td><b>Trip Number</b></td>
            <td><b>Region</b></td>
            <td><b>Location</b></td>
            <td><b>Start</b></td>
            <td><b>Duration</b></td>
            <td><b>Price</b></td>
          </tr>
          <xsl:for-each select="selloff/trip">
            <tr>
              <td><xsl:value-of select="@number"/></td>
              <td><xsl:value-of select="@region"/></td>
              <td><xsl:value-of select="location"/></td>
              <td><xsl:value-of select="startdate"/></td>
```

```
                    <td><xsl:value-of select="duration"/></td>
                    <td><xsl:value-of select="price"/></td>
                </tr>
            </xsl:for-each>
        </table>
      </body>
    </html>
  </xsl:template>
</xsl:stylesheet>
```

It basically formats the XML document into an HTML table, with one row for each <trip> element in the document.

Setting Up the ODBC Datasource

In order for our web application to work properly, we must create a JDBC database. We have included an MSACCESS MDB file in the download for you to try the application out using the JDBC to ODBC bridge. The database should be put in the CATALINA_HOME\db directory, and called traveldeals.mdb.

You should use the ODBC wizard in the Control Panel. To reach this, if you are using Microsoft Windows 2000, go to Control Panel/Administrative Tools/Data Sources (ODBC). You will see the ODBC Data Source Administrator dialog. Click on the Add button on the right, which brings up the Create New Data Source dialog. Select Microsoft Access Driver (*.mdb) from the menu, click on Finish, and you will see the ODBC Microsoft Access Setup dialog shown below:

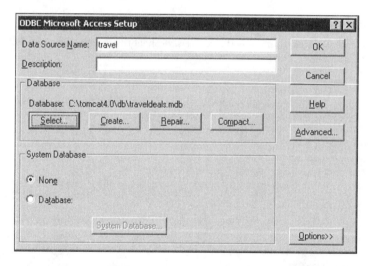

Select the db\traveldeals.mdb database, and give it a Data Source Name of travel.

Setting Up the Xalan Processor

To install Xalan, simply unarchive the distribution in a convenient directory, for instance directly under the JDK directory. Next, make sure that your CLASSPATH environment variable points to the two library files in this order:

❑   xerces.jar

❑   xalan.jar

They are both located under the `bin` directory of the Xalan installation. Xerces is the Apache XML group's XML processor – a library that Xalan depends on.

Since the filter will perform parsing inside Tomcat, we must also add these JAR files to our `webapp\WEB-INF\lib` directory. This is preferred over placing them in `CATALINA_HOME\lib`, as other web applications may prefer to use different XML-processing libraries.

Testing XSLTFilter

Finally you can start testing. Start Tomcat, and access the URL, http://localhost:8080/ch15/jsp/xTrips.jsp.

You should see the `XSLTFilter` at work, because you will see the transformed HTML output instead of XML – as shown in the screenshot below:

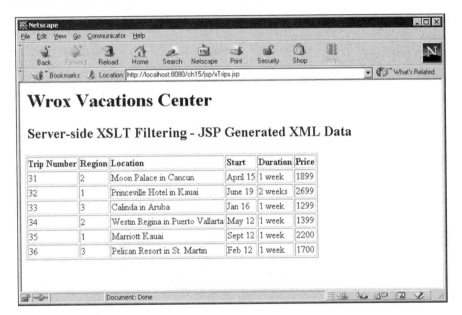

Now, if you remove the filter and try to access the URL again, you will get the (less exciting) XML document:

```xml
<?xml version="1.0" ?>
<selloff>
<trip number="31" region="2"><startdate>April 15</startdate><duration>1
week</duration><location>Moon Palace in Cancun</location><price
commission="400">1899</price></trip>
<trip number="32" region="1"><startdate>June 19</startdate><duration>2
weeks</duration><location>Princeville Hotel in Kauai</location><price
commission="700">2699</price></trip>
<trip number="33" region="3"><startdate>Jan 16</startdate><duration>1
week</duration><location>Calinda in Aruba</location><price
commission="300">1299</price></trip>
<trip number="34" region="2"><startdate>May 12</startdate><duration>1
week</duration><location>Westin Regina in Puerto Vallarta</location><price
commission="300">1399</price></trip>
<trip number="35" region="1"><startdate>Sept 12</startdate><duration>1
week</duration><location>Marriott Kauai</location><price
commission="600">2200</price></trip>
```

```
<trip number="36" region="3"><startdate>Feb 12</startdate><duration>1
week</duration><location>Pelican Resort in St. Martin</location><price
commission="400">1700</price></trip>
</selloff>
```

Enhancing the XSLTFilter

There are lots of practical uses for a filter like the XSLTFilter. With some simple modification, a reader should be able to adapt it to the scenario illustrated in the figure below:

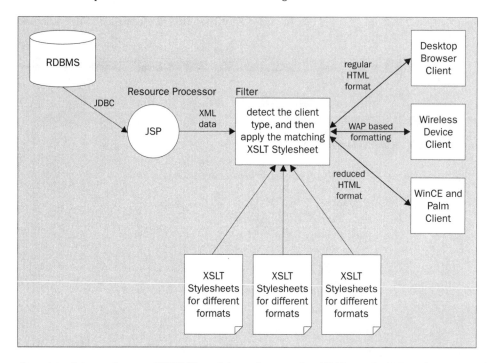

Here, the original data is from an RDBMS, and this is formatted to XML via the JSP and associated libraries. Now, depending on the client that is used to access the JSP, the XSLTFilter will select from one of three stylesheets (initialized from the initial parameters) – one for conventional browsers through the Internet, one for WAP browsers using the wireless network, and one for a small format WindowsCE styled browser. The idea of dynamically adapting the filter's behavior depending on the incoming request is a very powerful one. Filtering enables us to do this detection and adaptation easily, and customize both pre- and post-processing of the request accordingly.

Another 'thought application' that we will leave with the reader is to imagine a version of an XSLTFilter being used in an EDI (or B2B) application where the filter detects the IP of the incoming request and uses it to determine the business partner that the request originates from. The filter will then process the resource according to the format that is required by that particular trading partner. This is what used to take multiple man-years to implement, only a few short years ago. The figure opposite illustrates this system:

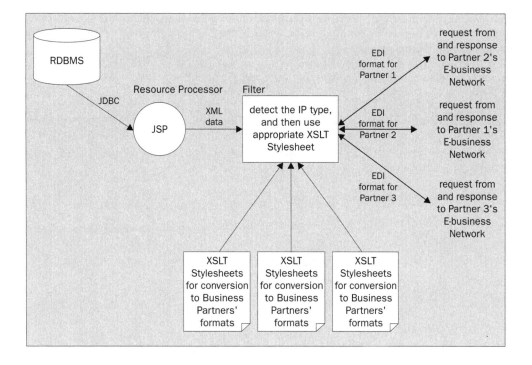

Summary

In this chapter, we have painstakingly worked through six complete filter examples. These examples have covered the application domains:

- ❑ Auditing
- ❑ Authorization
- ❑ Adapting Legacy Resources
- ❑ Authentication
- ❑ Compression/Encryption
- ❑ XML Content Transformation

Working through the code to these filters, we have discovered how to:

- ❑ Generate our own response, and block downstream processing
- ❑ Wrap a response to transform or replace its content
- ❑ Wrap a response to change its headers
- ❑ Wrap a request to modify headers
- ❑ Access initialization parameters
- ❑ Dynamically alter filter behavior based on the incoming request

We now have six examples that we can use as basis for our own filter implementation. We also have one versatile class, called `ReplaceContentOutputStream` that can be used whenever we need to wrap a response to modify its content.

We are now fluent in Servlet 2.3 filtering technology, and will be able to apply them to many challenges that the real world may throw at us.

In the next chapter we will look at some further aspects of the Servlet API: application events (new in Servlet 2.3), and the declarative security features.

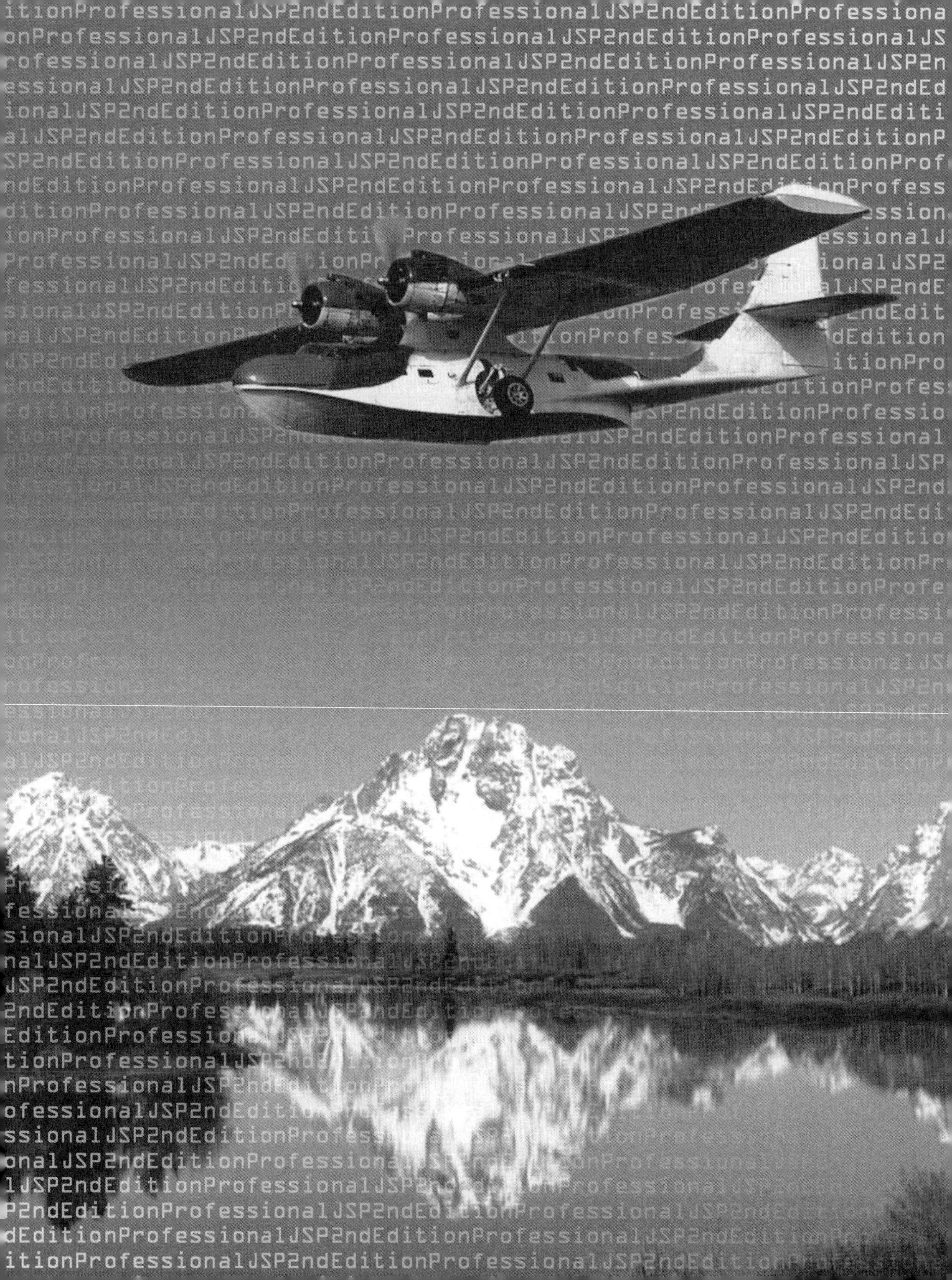

16

Application Events and Web Application Security

Amongst the facilities provided by a Servlet container, there are two that we have not yet touched upon: **application events**, which are new to the Servlet 2.3 specification, and **security**.

Application events give greater flexibility and control over the lifecycle of web applications, by allowing applications to listen for events associated with the application environment (or context) and state (or session).

The J2EE security model provides both **declarative** and **programmatic** security control. Declarative security allows the application deployer to specify the application's security policy (roles, access control, etc.) without changing the application's internal structure or code. This is achieved by different elements in the XML based deployment descriptor (web.xml) for the web application. When deploying and executing the application the container enforces these specified details. Programmatic security is used internally by the applications to enforce this model at the code level where methods can check specific permissions in the code itself.

In this chapter we'll begin by looking at application events, starting with a brief look at the Java event model, followed by:

❑ Session listeners, including both the HttpSessionBindingListener interface and the new Servlet 2.3 listeners

❑ How listeners are configured

❑ The new Context listener interfaces

❑ An example of using context and session listeners to build a phone directory application

We'll then move on to consider the J2EE security mechanism. These can be broadly categorized into:

- Authentication – who users are
- Authorization – what the authenticated users are allowed to do
- Encryption – ensuring that communication with the users is secure
- Signing – checking that we know where our code came from
- Auditing – keeping track of what has been happening within our application

Application Events

Two critical resources in the Servlet API are the `ServletContext`, which represents a logical view of the Web Application to the resources and serves as an interface between the resources and the container, and the `HttpSession`, used to preserve user state on the server between different stateless HTTP requests.

In the Servlet 2.2 specification, the `HttpSessionBindingListener` interface allowed a JavaBean to be notified when it was bound to or unbound from a session. The new event listeners in the Servlet 2.3 specification additionally allow applications to listen for:

- Session creation and invalidation
- New, changed, or removed session attributes
- Application startup and shutdown
- New, changed, or removed application attributes

The Java Event Model

Before we look at session listeners, let's look briefly at the Java event model introduced in Java 1.1. Each broad category of event that might require processing (for example, events involving the `ServletContext`, or events involving `HttpSession` attributes) is represented by an **event object** that is an instance of `java.util.EventObject` or a subclass.

Listeners are objects that wish to be notified of events; a listener is **registered** with the relevant object that generates the events. Just as each type of event has an appropriate `java.util.EventObject` subclass, each listener is an instance of a class that implements the appropriate listener interface. The listener interface defines a method for each specific event (for example, a new `HttpSession` was created) that will be called when that particular event occurs. Each of these listener methods is passed an instance of the appropriate `EventObject` subclass, which contains further information about the event (such as a reference to the newly-created `HttpSession`).

What is different about the way event handling is implemented in web containers, as opposed to the 'classical' Java event handling in, for example, GUI programming with AWT or Swing, is that event listener instantiation and registration is done by the web container, based on settings declared in the `web.xml` deployment descriptor, rather than by the web application code itself. We shall return to this topic later in the chapter.

The Session Listeners

We'll start our tour of the event listeners with those that listen for session-based events.

The HttpSessionEvent Class

The relevant `EventObject` subclass is `javax.servlet.http.HttpSessionEvent`, which has a single method that returns a reference to the event's encapsulating session object:

```
public HttpSession getSession()
```

Events for Notifying Bound Objects

Until Servlet 2.3, the only session-based listener was the `javax.servlet.http.HttpSessionBindingListener`. Objects could implement this listener interface and its associated methods to receive notifications from the container when *the object itself* was either bound or unbound to a session.

The HttpSessionBindingListener Interface

The `HttpSessionBindingListener` methods are:

```
public void valueBound(HttpSessionBindingEvent evt)
```

This method notifies the object that it is being bound to a session. The event object can be used to access the session object as well as the associated name-value of the object itself in the session.

```
public void valueUnbound(HttpSessionBindingEvent evt)
```

This is the same as above, only difference is this method is invoked by the container when the object is being unbound from the session.

The HttpSessionBindingEvent Class

The event class passed as an argument to the methods of `HttpSessionBindingListener` is an instance of `HttpSessionBindingEvent`, a subclass of `HttpSessionEvent`. This encapsulates the attributes via the three methods below, as well as the session:

```
public String getName()
```

This method returns the name with which the object is bound too in the session.

```
public HttpSession getSession()
```

This method returns a reference to the session.

```
public Object getValue()
```

This method returns the value of the attribute being added, removed or replaced.

The HttpSessionActivationListener Interface

Implementing this listener is particularly useful when objects that are being bound to a session need to perform some sort of initialization or cleanup in their state. However, there was one shortcoming in this listener interface, particularly for containers that managed sessions in a cluster across different JVMs or containers that persisted sessions (to a database for example) across container recycles: there was no clean and clear way for objects bound to a particular session to know if the container had passivated or activated the session.

For example consider this (rather contrived) scenario: an object that was holding on to other resources (remote resources, connections, etc.) was bound to the session in a clustered application server environment that used sticky load balancing (meaning a user request would be routed to a same instance in the cluster). Suppose this application server using persistent sessions was to suffer a crash and was restarted automatically by some means: there was no way for the object to refresh and re-acquire the resources, even though it held references to them.

The Servlet 2.3 specification introduces the `javax.servlet.http.HttpSessionActivationListener` interface; objects that implement this interface and are bound to the `HttpSession` will be notified of the session's activation or passivation. The methods that the container will call when the session the object is bound to undergoes such a change in its state are:

```
public void sessionDidActivate(HttpSessionEvent evt)
```

This method notifies the listener that the session has just been activated.

```
public void sessionWillPassivate(HttpSessionEvent evt)
```

This method notifies the listener that the session is about to be passivated.

Events for Monitoring Session State

The Servlet 2.3 specifications also introduces two new listener interfaces that can be used to actually monitor the state of the session itself to a very fine grained level:

- ❑   `javax.servlet.http.HttpSessionListener`
- ❑   `javax.servlet.HttpSessionAttributeListener`

The HttpSessionListener Interface

Objects implementing the `HttpSessionListener` interface are notified by the container if a new session has been created or a session within the container has been destroyed. This is particularly useful when an application needs to keep track of a single session's life, create objects on a per-session basis, and clean up when the session is destroyed.

Before the introduction of this listener, developers had to write elaborate session managers to keep track of user sessions or just to determine when a particular session was invalidated (even though the containers were doing this internally). Now the onus of keeping track and notification is on the container.

`HttpSessionListener` has two methods:

```
public void sessionCreated(HttpSessionEvent evt)
```

This method notifies the listener that a session was created.

```
public void sessionDestroyed(HttpSessionEvent evt)
```

This method notifies the listener that a session was destroyed (either due to invalidation or due to a timeout).

In Chapter 24, we will see a more detailed example of how this listener can be useful when interfacing EJBs into a web application. An HttpSessionListener is used to create a session EJB when a new user session starts; this bean is then used throughout that user's interaction with our system, and is destroyed when the session ends.

Counting the Number of Active Sessions

For now we'll look at a simpler example, that shows how we can use an HttpSessionListener to count the number of active users of a web application, and the total. We do this by counting sessions, rather than page hits.

The listener code is shown below:

```
package com.wrox.projsp.ch16;

import java.util.Date;
import javax.servlet.http.HttpSessionEvent;
import javax.servlet.http.HttpSessionListener;

public class CounterListenerExample implements HttpSessionListener {

    // Hold the counters for number of vistors
    // and number of active sessions, starting with 0
    private static int counter = 0;
    private static int activeCount = 0;

    // Methods of the HttpSessionListener Interface
    public void sessionCreated(HttpSessionEvent evt) {
        long time = evt.getSession().getCreationTime();
        System.out.println("A new session was created at " +
                        new Date(time));
        counter++;
        activeCount++;
    }

    public void sessionDestroyed(HttpSessionEvent evt) {
        activeCount--;
    }

    // Return an informative String about counter values
    public static String getCounterInfo() {
        return "Number of active sessions on server = " + activeCount + "\n" +
                "Number of total vistors to date = " + counter;
    }
}
```

The JSP used, `counter.jsp`, is also very simple:

```
<%@ page import="com.wrox.projsp.ch16.CounterListenerExample" %>
<html><head>
<title>Example Session Counter For Application Listeners</title>
</head>
<body bgcolor="#FFFFCC">
<h3 align="center">Counter Example: </h3>
<hr size="1">
  <%= CounterListenerExample.getCounterInfo() %>
</body>
</html>
```

Listener Configuration

All that remains is to ensure that the container knows about our listener; as we mentioned earlier, this is done via the XML deployment descriptor for the web application, `web.xml`.

In fact, configuring listeners is extremely straightforward: all that is needed is to add a `<listener>` element to `web.xml` (see Appendix D for full details of where in the file it should be placed). The `<listener>` element has a `<listener-class>` element nested inside, which contains the name of the listener class.

> *We'll see later that event listeners can also be declared within a tag library descriptor file.*

```
<?xml version="1.0" encoding="ISO-8859-1"?>

<!DOCTYPE web-app
    PUBLIC "-//Sun Microsystems, Inc.//DTD Web Application 2.3//EN"
    "http://java.sun.com/j2ee/dtds/web-app_2_3.dtd">

<web-app>

  <listener>
    <listener-class>
      com.wrox.projsp.ch16.CounterListenerExample
    </listener-class>
  </listener>

  <session-config>
    <session-timeout>
      1
    </session-timeout>
  </session-config>

</web-app>
```

> *Note that we also set the session timeout value to only one minute, to help us exercise the example without getting bored waiting for sessions to time out.*

The container instantiates these listeners, in the order they are listed in `web.xml`, when the application is loaded and before any user requests are serviced. It then holds a reference to each listener for the life of the web application, ensuring that the listeners are not garbage collected, and when the application shuts down the listeners are notified in reverse order.

To maintain integrity, when the application shuts down the session listeners are notified first of the session invalidations, and subsequently the Servlet context listeners are notified. This allows the session listeners to deal with individual user state before the entire application state is shut down.

> Note that there is no explicit definition of the type of the listener (for example, session or context) in the descriptor; the container does this automatically by determining which of the event listener interfaces are implemented). In a clustered or distributed environment, the container implementations are not required by the specifications to propagate any of the listeners beyond a single container.

So, returning to our example, after opening a number of browser windows over a period of time and requesting `counter.jsp` in each, the output should be something like that below:

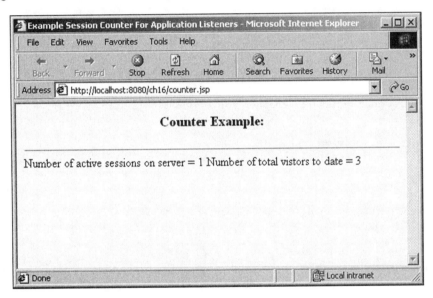

Better Control over Session Contents

Fine-grained control over the contents of the session, and keeping track of when certain objects or attributes are bound, removed or replaced from a session in the web application, can be obtained by a listener that implements the `javax.servlet.HttpSessionAttributeListener` interface.

The HttpSessionAttributeListener Interface

`HttpSessionAttributeListener` declares the following methods:

```
public void attributeAdded(HttpSessionBindingEvent se)
```

This method notifies the listener that an attribute has been added to a session.

```
public void attributeRemoved(HttpSessionBindingEvent se)
```

This method notifies the listener that an attribute has been removed from a session.

```
public void attributeReplaced(HttpSessionBindingEvent se)
```

This method notifies the listener that an existing attribute has been replaced with a new value in a session.

Extending the Counter Example

As an example, the previous CounterListenerExample could be modified to count total page hits. We create a modified JSP, counter2.jsp, that sets a session attribute "pagehit" each time the page is accessed:

```
<%@ page import="com.wrox.projsp.ch16.CounterListenerExample2" %>

<%
    session.setAttribute("pagehit","xxx");    // value doesn't matter
%>


<html>
  <head>
    <title>Example Session Counter For Application Listeners</title>
  </head>

  <body bgcolor="#FFFFCC">
    <h3 align="center">Counter Example:</h3>

    <hr size="1">

    <%= CounterListenerExample2.getCounterInfo() %>
  </body>
</html>
```

A new listener class, CounterListenerExample2, implements HttpSessionAttributeListener and is notified when this session attribute is added or replaced:

```
package com.wrox.projsp.ch16;

import java.util.Date;
import javax.servlet.http.*;

public class CounterListenerExample2 implements HttpSessionAttributeListener {

  // Hold the counters for number of vistors
  private static int counter = 0;

  // Increment the counter if we add a "pagehit" attribute...
  public void attributeAdded(HttpSessionBindingEvent se) {
    if(se.getName().equals("pagehit")) {
      counter++;
    }
  }

  // ...or replace it
```

```
public void attributeReplaced(HttpSessionBindingEvent se) {
  if(se.getName().equals("pagehit")) {
    counter++;
  }
}

// Not interested in attributes being removed
public void attributeRemoved(HttpSessionBindingEvent se) {}

public static String getCounterInfo() {
  return "Number of total vistors to date = " + counter;
}
}
```

Finally, we have to register this new listener in `web.xml`:

```
...

<listener>
  <listener-class>
    com.wrox.projsp.ch16.CounterListenerExample2
  </listener-class>
</listener>

...
```

and restart the application (so that `web.xml` is re-read). Accessing `counter2.jsp` now gives us a running count of page accesses:

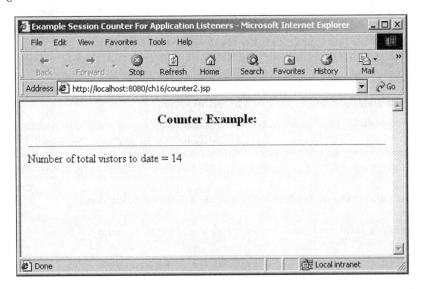

This will of course have a performance hit, as the listener is trapping all attribute additions from all sessions. In real use, an attribute listener would be more likely to be used to catch very specific and infrequent events.

The Context Listeners

In addition to the new `HttpSession` listeners we have just discussed, the Servlet 2.3 specification also provides analogous listeners for `ServletContext`-related events (web application startup and shutdown, and the binding, replacement, and removal of `ServletContext` attributes):

❑   `javax.servlet.ServletContextListener`

❑   `javax.servlet.ServletContextAttributeListener`

The javax.servlet.ServletContextEvent Class

Just as session listeners have `HttpSessionEvent` objects, servlet context listeners have `javax.servlet.ServletContextEvent` objects. `ServletContextEvent` is a subclass of java.util.EventObject, and has one method that returns a reference to the events encapsulating context object:

```
public ServletContext getServletContext()
```

This method returns the `ServletContext` that caused the event to be triggered.

The javax.servlet.ServletContextListener Interface

Much like its counterpart `HttpSessionListener`, the `ServletContextListener` is an interface that can be implemented to monitor the state of a Servlet context. An object of the class will be instantiated and receive notifications from the container via the two methods of the interface:

```
public void contextDestroyed(ServletContextEvent evt)
```

This method notifies the listener that the Servlet context (web application) is about to be shut down.

```
public void contextInitialized(ServletContextEvent evt)
```

This method notifies the listener that the web application is ready to process requests.

The javax.servlet.ServletContextAttributeListener Interface

Just as the `HttpSessionAttributeListener` can monitor attributes of a single session, the `ServletContextAttributeListener` is an interface that can be implemented to monitor the attributes of the context as a whole and keep track of when certain attributes are bound, unbound or replaced from a context. The implementing class will receive notifications from the container via the three methods of the interface:

```
public void attributeAdded(ServletContextAttributeEvent evt)
```

This method notifies the listener that a new attribute was added to the Servlet context.

```
public void attributeRemoved(ServletContextAttributeEvent evt)
```

This method notifies the listener that an existing attribute has been removed from the Servlet context.

```
public void attributeReplaced(ServletContextAttributeEvent evt)
```

This method notifies the listener that an existing attribute in the Servlet context has been replaced with a new value.

The javax.servlet.ServletContextAttributeEvent Class

The event class for `javax.servlet.ServletContextAttributeListener`, `javax.servlet.ServletContextAttributeEvent`, is a subclass of `ServletContextEvent` and encapsulates the attributes that cause the events. It has the following methods:

```
public String getName()
```

This method return the name of the attribute that changed on the `ServletContext`.

```
public Object getValue()
```

This method returns the value of the attribute being added removed or replaced.

Applications of Event Listeners

We've seen how session and context listeners work, and how they give developer greater flexibility. But an obvious question is where do these fit in the real world?

❑ The most obvious use of event listeners is initializing application-wide resources. For example, if our application needs to use a database connection pool (and we are not running in an environment where this is provided for us), a `ServletContextListener` could be used to create connections and initialize the connection pool at startup, and store it in the `ServletContext`, from where connections can conveniently be obtained by any Servlet or JSP needing one. Similarly, the connections can be closed and the pool disposed of tidily when the application is shut down.

❑ In a similar way, and as we shall see in Chapter 24, an `HttpSessionListener` can be used to instantiate per-session resources such as session EJBs and store them in the `HttpSession`.

❑ In some application designs it can be critical to keep track of when certain beans are instantiated, bound, and when clean-up needs to be performed. In such cases, code can be abstracted to a common listener that is invoked by the container asynchronously to handle the state of these beans. It will be interesting to see the ways in which event listeners are used to this end.

A Simple Example

Let's look at an example: a small application that provides a directory of names and numbers that can be listed, inserted, and searched, much like a phone book. The directory is stored as a set of name-value pairs stored in a `Properties` object, and displayed using a JSP.

We use a `ServletContextListener` to initialize the web application by reading the data from file into a `Properties` object, and binding to the `ServletContext` under the name `"directory"` for use in the JSP. During application shutdown, it serializes the data and saves them back to the file, for use later. The name of the file is read from the deployment descriptor as a `ServletContext` initialization parameter.

The code below explains this in detail:

```
package com.wrox.projsp.ch16;

import javax.servlet.*;
```

```
import javax.servlet.http.*;
import java.io.*;
import java.util.*;

// This listener is a simple ServletContext listener
public class FirstListenerExample implements ServletContextListener {

  private String FILENAME;

  public void contextInitialized(ServletContextEvent evt) {
    ServletContext ctx = evt.getServletContext();
    FILENAME = (String) ctx.getInitParameter("FILENAME");
    Properties props;
    try {
      ObjectInputStream oin =
        new ObjectInputStream(new FileInputStream(FILENAME));
      Object obj = oin.readObject();
      props = (Properties) obj;
      oin.close();
    } catch (Exception e) {
      props = new Properties();
      System.err.println("Initialization failed for database file "
                     + FILENAME + " " + e);
      System.err.println("If this is the fist time the listener " +
                     "example is being run, this exception " +
                     "is normal, it will cause the db to be created " +
                     "when the server is gracefully shutdown");
    }

    // set the directory as an attribute of the context so that its
    // available thoughout the Web App.
    ctx.setAttribute("directory", props);
  }


  // Methods of the ServletContextLisener interface
  public void contextDestroyed(ServletContextEvent evt) {
    Properties props =
      (Properties) evt.getServletContext().getAttribute("directory");
    if (props == null) {
      props = new Properties();
    }
    try {
      ObjectOutputStream os =
        new ObjectOutputStream(new FileOutputStream(FILENAME));
      os.writeObject(props);
      os.flush();
      os.close();
    } catch (Exception e) {
      System.err.println("Object serialization failed for database file "
                     + FILENAME + " " + e);
    }
  }
}
```

The listener code above traps the `contextDestroyed()` event of the `ServletContext` to store the serialized object. (In order to successfully trap this event, the web container must be gracefully shut down with its shut down command and not be killed abruptly.)

In this example, the file with the serialized object will be created in Tomcat's working directory – typically the `%CATALINA_HOME%/bin` directory.

`directory.jsp` uses the `<jsp:useBean>` standard action to locate the bean. Notice that the scope "application" makes it look for the attribute in the `ServletContext`, which we had bound at application startup by trapping the appropriate event.

The same JSP is used to insert, list, and update the directory based on the request parameters:

❑ If the request contains a parameter `"insert"` it updates the directory with the values of the parameters `"new_name"` and `"new_tel"`

❑ If the request contains a parameter called `"person_name"`, it looks up the directory for that specific name

❑ If no parameter is found in the request the entire directory is displayed

```jsp
<%@ page import="java.util.*" %>
<jsp:useBean id="directory" scope="application"
            class="java.util.Properties"/>

<html>
  <head>
    <title>Wrox Directory Example For Application Listeners</title>
  </head>

  <body bgcolor="#FFFFCC">
    <h3 align="center">Thank you for using the Wrox directory ! </h3>
    <table width="100%" border="1" cellspacing="0" cellpadding="0"
          bgcolor="#CCCCFF" bordercolor="#000000">
      <tr>
        <td>
          <form action="directory.jsp" >
            <input type="submit"value="List Directory">
          </form>
        </td>
        <td>
          <form action="directory.jsp">
            <input type="text" name="person_name">
            <input type="submit" value="Lookup">
          </form>
        </td>
        <td>
          <form action="directory.jsp" >
            <b>Name</b>
            <input type="text" name="new_name">
            <br>
            <b>Number</b>
            <input type="text" name="new_tel">
            <input type="submit" value="Insert In Directory">
          </form>
        </td>
      </tr>
    </table>
    <hr size="1">


<%
  // The request object contains the HttpRequest parameters
  // This JSP checks for a parameter called 'name' ie the name to lookup
  // Or checks for the parameter 'insert' which contains the entry to insert

  String name = request.getParameter("person_name");
```

```
    String newname= request.getParameter("new_name");

    if ((name != null) && (!name.equals(""))) {
      // Try to return the phone number for the specified
      // 'person_name' parameter
      String phone= directory.getProperty(name.trim());
      if (phone == null)
        out.println("<h2>" +name + " is not listed in the directory </h2>");
      else
        out.println("<h2>" +name +  " can  be reached at " + phone +"</h2>");
      return;
    }


    if ((newname != null) && (!newname.equals(""))) {
      directory.setProperty(newname,request.getParameter("new_tel").trim());
      out.println(" <h2>Your entry has been inserted in the directory </h2>");
      return;
    }


    // if the above returns have not been processed
    // then just list the directory
%>
    <hr>
    <table width="100%" border="1" cellspacing="0"
           cellpadding="0"bgcolor="#CCCCFF" bordercolor="#000000">
      <tr>
        <td><h3>Name</h3></td>
        <td><h3>Phone number</h3></td>
      </tr>

      <% Enumeration enum = directory.propertyNames();
         while(enum.hasMoreElements()) {
           String propname= (String)enum.nextElement();
           out.println("<tr> <td><b>" + propname+ "</b></td><td>" +
                       directory.getProperty(propname) + " </td></tr>");
      }
      %>

    </table>
    <hr>
  </body>
</html>
```

The `web.xml` file requires a configuration as shown below:

```
...

  <context-param>
    <param-name>FILENAME</param-name>
    <param-value>directory.db</param-value>
  </context-param>

...


  <listener>
    <listener-class>
      com.wrox.projsp.ch16.FirstListenerExamples
```

```
    </listener-class>
  </listener>

...
```

Pointing your browser at `directory.jsp` will produce a similar result to that shown below. Here, we have already added some people to the directory and have then clicked List Directory. Since no parameter was passed with the URL request the complete directory is displayed:

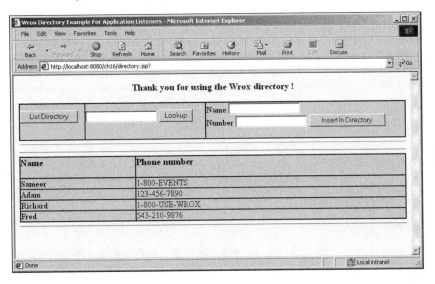

The second screenshot shows the result of entering the name of someone in the directory and clicking Lookup. The single request parameter `person_name` is passed with the name to be looked up:

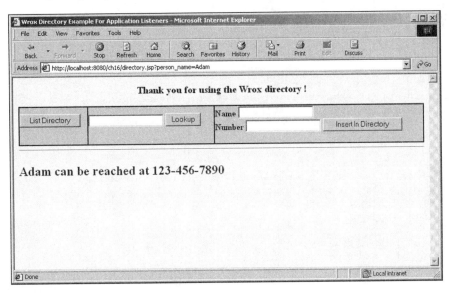

Notice in the above example that the same `Properties` object is being referenced in multiple places. Multiple JSP or user invocations on the same JSP could be changing the state of the same object. The container will provide no guarantees on synchronization on this object. It is up to us to make sure that this synchronization occurs. The same is true for objects being shared between multiple listeners; the onus for synchronization is on the developers.

Extending the Example

Let's modify this example somewhat. The code below shows the same listener, but modified to implement the `HttpSessionAttributeListener` interface as well as `ServletContextListener`. To insert a new entry now, instead of doing the simple `setProperty()` method call on the `Properties` object directly in the JSP, we do it another way, to look at one possible use of `HttpSessionAttributeListener`. When the **Insert In Directory** button is clicked and the form submitted, our JSP will update the session with a variable called `"DO_INSERT"`, whose value is a `String` of the form `"name@number"`. The session attribute listener will pick up this attribute change and insert the value in the directory.

The modified listener code is shown below; some variable names have been changed to prevent clashing with the previous example (the `Properties` object is referenced by `directory_two` instead of `directory`):

```
package com.wrox.projsp.ch16;

import javax.servlet.*;
import javax.servlet.http.*;
import java.io.*;
import java.util.*;


// This listener is a combination of ServletContext and HttpSession
// listeners

public class SecondListenerExample
        implements ServletContextListener, HttpSessionAttributeListener {

  private String FILENAME;
  private ServletContext ctx;


  // Methods of the ServletContextListener interface

  public void contextInitialized(ServletContextEvent evt) {
    ctx = evt.getServletContext();
    FILENAME = (String) ctx.getInitParameter("FILENAME_TWO");
    Properties props;
    try {
      ObjectInputStream oin =
        new ObjectInputStream(new FileInputStream(FILENAME));
      Object obj = oin.readObject();
      props = (Properties) obj;
      oin.close();

    } catch (Exception e) {
      props = new Properties();
      System.err.println("Initialization failed for database file "
```

```
                            + FILENAME + e);
      System.err.println("If this is the fist time the listener example " +
                         "is being run, this exception is normal,it will " +
                         "cause the db to be created when the server is " +
                         "gracefully shutdown");
    }

    // set the directory as an attribute of the context so that it's
    // available thoughout the Web App.
    ctx.setAttribute("directory_two", props);
  }


  public void contextDestroyed(ServletContextEvent evt) {
    Properties props = (Properties) ctx.getAttribute("directory_two");
    if (props == null) {
      props = new Properties();
    }
    try {
      ObjectOutputStream os =
        new ObjectOutputStream(new FileOutputStream(FILENAME));
      os.writeObject(props);
      os.flush();
      os.close();
    } catch (Exception e) {
      System.err.println("Object serialization failed for database file "
                         + FILENAME + e);
    }
  }



  // Methods of the HttpSessionAttributeListener interface

  // A session attribute was added... was it "DO_INSERT"? If so, parse
  // the attribute value and store in the application-scope Properties
  // object
  public void attributeAdded(HttpSessionBindingEvent evt) {
    if (evt.getName().equalsIgnoreCase("DO_INSERT")) {
      StringTokenizer st = new StringTokenizer((String) evt.getValue(),
                                               "@");
      Properties props = (Properties) ctx.getAttribute("directory_two");
      props.setProperty(st.nextToken(), st.nextToken());
    }
  }


  // Same as above
  public void attributeReplaced(HttpSessionBindingEvent evt) {
    if (evt.getName().equalsIgnoreCase("DO_INSERT")) {
      StringTokenizer st = new StringTokenizer((String) evt.getValue(),
                                               "@");
      Properties props = (Properties) ctx.getAttribute("directory_two");
      props.setProperty(st.nextToken(), st.nextToken());
    }
  }


  // No need to deal with attributes being removed
  public void attributeRemoved(HttpSessionBindingEvent evt) {}
}
```

Notice in the above example, we either need to hold a reference to `ServletContext` (or the `Properties` object) as an instance variable, in order to update the same properties from an `HttpSessionAttributeListener` listening to multiple sessions.

The JSP, `directory2.jsp`, is the same as the one before, except for the portions highlighted below.

```jsp
<%@ page import="java.util.*" %>
<jsp:useBean id="directory_two" scope="application"
             class="java.util.Properties"/>

<html>
  <head>
    <title>Wrox Directory Example For Application Listeners</title>
  </head>

  <body bgcolor="#FFFFCC">
    <h3 align="center">Thank you for using the Wrox directory ! </h3>
    <table width="100%" border="1" cellspacing="0" cellpadding="0"
           bgcolor="#CCCCFF" bordercolor="#000000">
      <tr>
        <td>
          <form action="directory2.jsp" >
            <input type="submit"value="List Directory">
          </form>
        </td>
        <td>
          <form action="directory2.jsp">
            <input type="text" name="person_name">
            <input type="submit" value="Lookup">
          </form>
        </td>
        <td>
          <form action="directory2.jsp" >
            <b>Name</b>
            <input type="text" name="new_name">
            <br>
            <b>Number</b>
            <input type="text" name="new_tel">
            <input type="submit" value="Insert In Directory">
          </form>
        </td>
      </tr>
    </table>
    <hr size="1">


<%
    // The request object contains the HttpRequest parameters
    // This JSP checks for a parameter called 'name' ie the name to lookup
    // Or checks for the parameter 'insert' which contains the entry to insert

    String name = request.getParameter("person_name");
    String newname= request.getParameter("new_name");

    if ((name != null) && (!name.equals(""))) {
```

```
    // Try to return the phone number for the specified
    // 'person_name' parameter
    String phone= directory_two.getProperty(name.trim());
    if (phone == null)
      out.println("<h2>" +name + " is not listed in the directory </h2>");
    else
      out.println("<h2>" +name +  " can  be reached at " + phone +"</h2>");
    return;
  }


  if ((newname != null) && (!newname.equals(""))) {
    String str = newname.trim() +"@" +
                 request.getParameter("new_tel").trim();
    session.putValue("DO_INSERT",str);
    out.println(" <h2>Your entry has been inserted in the directory </h2>");
    return;
  }

  // if the above returns have not been processed
  // then just list the directory
%>
    <hr>
    <table width="100%" border="1" cellspacing="0"
           cellpadding="0"bgcolor="#CCCCFF" bordercolor="#000000">
      <tr>
        <td><h3>Name</h3></td>
        <td><h3>Phone number</h3></td>
      </tr>

      <% Enumeration enum = directory_two.propertyNames();
         while(enum.hasMoreElements()) {
            String propname= (String)enum.nextElement();
            out.println("<tr> <td><b>" + propname+ "</b></td><td>" +
                        directory_two.getProperty(propname) + " </td></tr>");
         }
      %>

    </table>
    <hr>
  </body>
</html>
```

Finally we again need to add some entries to web.xml:

```
...

  <context-param>
    <param-name>FILENAME_TWO</param-name>
    <param-value>directory2.db</param-value>
  </context-param>


...

  <listener>
```

```
        <listener-class>
          com.wrox.projsp.ch16.SecondListenerExample
        </listener-class>
      </listener>

  ...
```

This example works in exactly the same manner as the example we did before; it just uses a different approach to demonstrate the use of the `HttpSessionAttributeListener`.

> **Attribute listeners are cool. They allow developers to asynchronously trigger specific actions within the container by simply adding or modifying session or Servlet context attributes.**

Event Listeners and Tag Libraries

As we mentioned earlier, the event listeners described above can also be packaged with reusable tag libraries (described in Chapters 8-11) allowing application component providers to use and package listeners specific to their components. In this case, the listeners specific to the tag library are listed in the tag library descriptor (TLD) file rather than in `web.xml` to minimize the steps necessary to deploy the tag library. Listeners declared in a tag library are handled just like those in `web.xml`; however, unlike those declared in `web.xml` where the listeners are loaded in the order they were defined, for tag libraries the order is not defined.

Full details of the relevant TLD elements are given in Appendix D; briefly, `<listener>` elements, each containing a `<listener-class>` element, are included in the `.tld` file before the `<tag>` elements.

The most obvious use of this facility will be when a tag library requires application- or session-wide resources to be made available to its custom tags. For example, a tag library might require a configuration file to be read at application startup, and use a `ServletContextListener` to do this and store the necessary details in the `ServletContext`, ready for access by the tag handlers. One example of a tag library that already makes use of event listeners (although it does not as yet use the TLD elements provided for the purpose) is the OpenSymphony OSCache tags (http://www.opensymphony.com/oscache/), which provide the ability to cache JSP-generated content and uses a `ServletContextListener` to instantiate a repository for the cached content.

Listeners: A Brief Summary

The list below summarizes the session and context listeners that we have discussed in the preceding sections:

❑ **For beans and objects:**
   Listener interface: `HttpSessionBindingListener`
   Event class: `HttpSessionBindingEvent`
   Invoked when the implementing object is bound to or unbound from the session

❑ **For session activity:**
   Listener interface: `HttpSessionListener`
   Event class: `HttpSessionEvent`
   Invoked when a session is created or destroyed

❑ **For session activity:**
Listener interface: `HttpSessionActivationListener`
Event class: `HttpSessionEvent`
Invoked when the session the implementing object is bound to is persisted or activated

❑ **For session attributes:**
Listener interface: `HttpSessionAttributeListener`
Event class: `HttpSessionBindingEvent`
Invoked when a session attribute is modified (added, removed, or replaced)

❑ **For context activity:**
Listener interface: `ServletContextListener`
Event class: `ServletContextEvent`
Invoked when the context is created or destroyed

❑ **For context attributes:**
Listener interface: `ServletContextAttributeListener`
Event class: `ServletContextAttributeEvent`
Invoked when context attributes are modified (added, removed or replaced)

Web Application Security

Security is a critical aspect for enterprise applications and compromise of an application due to any threat can have disastrous consequences. The J2EE specifications detail an application security model and mechanisms spanning multiple application tiers that distributed applications can leverage to avert such compromise.

The J2EE security model provides both **declarative** and **programmatic** security control. Declarative security allows the application deployer to specify the applications security policy (roles, access control, etc.) without changing the applications internal structure or code. This is achieved by different elements in the XML based deployment descriptor (`web.xml`) for the web application. When deploying and executing the application the container enforces these specified details. Programmatic security is used internally by the applications to enforce this model at the code level where methods can check specific permissions in the code itself.

> *In Chapter 21 we will see an application where authentication is performed by the application code, rather than by the web container. This chapter focuses on the security provisions built into the J2EE platform.*

As we saw at the start of this chapter, the J2EE security mechanisms can be broken down into authentication, authorization, encryption, signing, and auditing. In this chapter we will concentrate on the relevance and implementation of these mechanisms within the Web (JSP/Servlet) tier, rather than the details of J2SE or Java's general security architecture.

J2SE security architecture uses a security policy to decide the granting of individual access permissions to running code. When the protected resource is accessed, the granted permissions are checked against the permissions actually needed to utilize that resource. This makes sense because it is up to the developer (or application) to control **what** code it trusts and this is where the J2SE policy based security model comes in. The other aspect: **who** to trust is what authentication and authorization is all about.

User Authentication

Simply put, authentication is the process of verifying that the user is who they claim to be. The *users* may be physical users, or other applications, services, or even external systems.

More specifically, a **principal** is any entity that can be authenticated based on an **identity**. Once authenticated the principal acquires credentials that contain information or attributes legitimizing the principal. (Sometimes the terms **authentication-context** and **credential** are used interchangeably.) Further, the principal has a **role** in the application and can perform actions based on the privileges granted to that role. Sometimes a principal may want to perform actions on behalf of another that allows its credentials to be delegated; for example, EJB-1 might invoke methods on another EJB-2, which needs to invoke a method on EJB-3.

The concept of a principal is a part of the core Java security API and is represented by the `java.security.Principal` interface. In the J2EE, model entities may communicate without actually requiring any authentication as long as they are a part of a **protection-domain**. A protection-domain (or realm) is a set of entities that are assumed or known to trust each other.

> The J2EE v1.2 specifications mandate the web container to support the JSP 1.1 and Servlet 2.2 specifications as well as the J2SE 1.2 APIs. The newer J2EE v1.3 specifications update the support to JSP 1.2 and Servlet 2.3 specifications and support for J2SE 1.3 APIs.

The Servlet 2.3 specifications details four mechanisms which browsers can use for authentication:

❑ HTTP basic authentication

❑ HTTP digest authentication

❑ Form based authentication

❑ HTTPS client authentication

HTTP Basic Authentication

This mechanism is covered in the HTTP1.1 and 1.0 protocols and web containers implementing HTTP 1.1 and 1.0 support this.

> HTTP based authentication is detailed in RFC 2617 available at
> **http://www.ietf.org/rfc/rfc2617.txt**

When a user requests a protected resource such as a JSP or HTML file, the web server or container prompts the web client for a username and password. The client responds by sending the username and password as a Base64 encoded string. Once the server verifies these it allows the client to access the resource.

The internal details of this working are described below:

❑ The browser requests a protected resource.

❑ The server responds with a 401 (Unauthorized) response to challenge the authorization of the user agent. As a part of the 401 response, the server returns a "WWW-Authenticate" header, such as WWW-Authenticate: Basic realm="MyRealm".

❑ The browser reacts to this by popping up a dialog asking the user to input these values. The browsers typically cache the user-id and password in memory (cache is lost after browser is closed) after the first prompt for a particular realm in a session. On subsequent requests, the user is not prompted again.

❑ Upon submission, the browser takes these values and Base64 encodes the `User:Password` string and sends it to the server along with an authorization header, for example, `Authorization: Basic QABhxGRpbjpvcGVuIHNlc2FtZQ==`.

❑ If the username-password pair is valid, an HTTP 200 code is returned along with the resource.

❑ For resources below the requested path, the browser automatically sends the Authorization header without prompting the user.

It is important to note that the HTTP realm does not have to reflect any particular J2EE protected domain (which, confusingly, can also be referred to as a realm). The HTTP realm can be used by the web server to logically separate resources.

Basic authentication is often referred to as plain text, clear text, or shallow authentication because the Base64 encoded string can be captured and decoded. (A malicious user can capture data packets on the network.) The authentication mechanism is configured using the `<login-config>` element of the Web application's deployment descriptor:

```
<web-app>
<!-other elements here ->
  <login-config>
     <auth-method>BASIC|DIGEST|FORM</auth-method>
     <realm-name>HTTP Realm Name on the Server</realm-name>
  </login-config>
</web-app>
```

A Basic Authentication Example

Having talked about how it works, let's now look at an example. There are three files we need for the example to work:

❑   `index.jsp`

❑   `web.xml`

❑   `tomcat-users.xml`

Each of the three files plays it's own part in the example, so we'll show you what you need for each of them.

index.jsp

Here is the `index.jsp` file that we wish to access, but is protected by a password:

```
<html>
<head>
<title>Protected Area Page</title>
</head>
<body>
<%
  out.println("<H2>Authentication Mechanism "+ request.getAuthType() +" </H2>" );
%>
</body>
</html>
```

web.xml

As with most web applications, we need a web.xml file. In this one, we define a <security-constraint>. The /* for <url-pattern> means all contexts under the specified context, or the whole application. The <login-config> tag defines, as you would expect, the login configuration. For this example, we use the BASIC method, and give it an HTTP realm name, which is the realm that will also be shown in the pop up box in most browsers:

```xml
<?xml version="1.0" encoding="ISO-8859-1"?>

<!DOCTYPE web-app
    PUBLIC "-//Sun Microsystems, Inc.//DTD Web Application 2.3//EN"
    "http://java.sun.com/j2ee/dtds/web-app_2_3.dtd">

<web-app>

  <security-constraint>
    <web-resource-collection>
      <web-resource-name>Entire Application</web-resource-name>
      <url-pattern>/*</url-pattern>
    </web-resource-collection>
  </security-constraint>

  <login-config>
    <auth-method>BASIC</auth-method>
    <realm-name>ProJSP Authentication Example</realm-name>
  </login-config>
</web-app>
```

The tomcat-users.xml File

Along with the by now familiar web.xml file, and the broader-scoped server.xml, Tomcat uses another XML file to specify settings. The tomcat-users.xml file (located in CATALINA_HOME\conf) is used to specify users and passwords – any user-password combination specified in this file will be accepted and allowed to access the resources since we have not explicitly specified a role.

The tomcat-users.xml file is specific to Tomcat – other web containers and application servers will provide their own means of authenticating users. Later we will see how Tomcat can be configured to use a different mechanism to store usernames passwords and roles.

The user declaration to add to tomcat-users.xml in this case is:

```xml
<tomcat-users>

  ...

  <user name="projsp" password="projsp" roles="superuser" />
</tomcat-users>
```

Execution

Having got our index.jsp file in place (in the <webapps>/chapter16-basic directory), along with our suitably amended tomcat-users.xml (in<TOMCAT_HOME>\conf) and our web.xml file, we point our browser at the file:

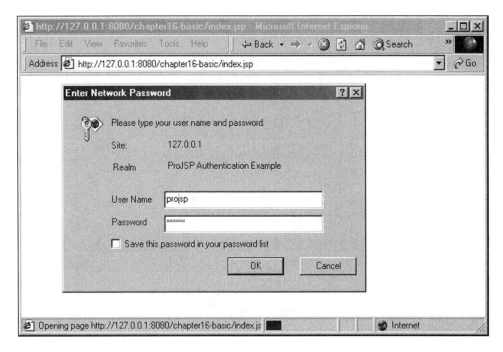

After logging in, we get the following screenshot:

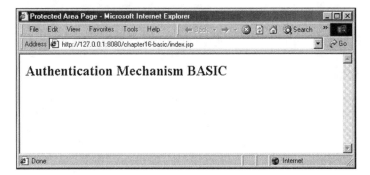

HTTP Digest Authentication

This is a more secure form of the Basic authentication. Along with the 401 reply, the server sends a generated/random string (called a **nonce**). The browser creates a one-way hash (MD-5) of the username, the password, the URL, the HTTP method, and the nonce it received. In order to verify the user, the server creates its own checksum and compares the two.

Many of the semantics for creating the digest lie on the web client. The digest authentication mechanism at present is supported by IE 5.X only. Support for this mechanism is not mandatory for containers.

> **Throughout this chapter, there are references to the XML deployment descriptor and its elements. Most commercial Web container and J2EE container providers supply a graphic deployment tool to do this and generate the XML descriptor.**

A Digest Authentication Example

We will repeat the basic authentication example, using digest authentication. The only changes to be made are in the web.xml file. Remember this example will only work in IE 5.x.

Additions to web.xml

```
<login-config>
  <auth-method>DIGEST</auth-method>
  <realm-name>ProJSP Authentication Example</realm-name>
</login-config>
```

Execution

Much like the last example, we have a changed web.xml file, along with the index.jsp file, at which we point our browser. After we log in, we should see the following screenshot:

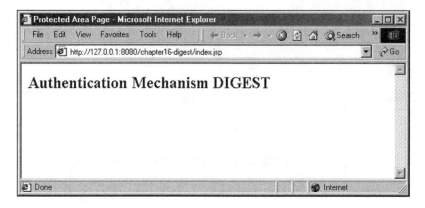

Form Based Authentication

Form based authentication is used to describe the mechanism where developers can write their custom login/error screens containing HTML forms. Unlike basic authentication where the web client is responsible for accepting the username and password and transmitting it to the container, form based authentication gives greater flexibility in controlling the appearance of the screens to the developers by specifying a custom login and error page.

When a user accesses a protected resource, the process is as follows:

❑ An HTML page containing the login form is returned and the path to the resource stored by the container, in the session or in a cookie.

❑ The user then fills out the form, including the username and password fields, which is returned to the server via the POST method. This is where the authentication is sent.

❑ The container processes the form fields and like basic authentication verifies the user.

❑ If authentication fails, the error page is returned.

❑ If not, the authenticated principal is checked to see if it is in an authorized role for accessing the original web request.

❑ If the principal is authenticated, the client is redirected to the original resource using the stored path. If not the error page is returned to the client.

A Form Based Authentication Example

We will repeat the above examples, using form based authentication. The only changes to be made are in the web.xml file. However, we will have to provide a login form page and a login failed error page.

The loginpage JSP

The login form must contain fields for the user to specify username and password. These fields must be named j_username and j_password, respectively and the form action must always be j_security_check.

The code below shows a login.jsp:

```
<html>
<body>
<h2>Login page </h2>
<form method="POST" action="j_security_check">
<input type="text" name="j_username">
<input type="password" name="j_password">
<input type="sumbit" value="Login Now">
</form>
</body>
</html>
```

The errorpage JSP

```
<html>
<head>
<title>Authentication Error</title>
</head>
<body>
You entered an invalid username/password.<br>
Please <a href="login.jsp">try again</a> or contact the administrator at
admin@wrox.com
</body>
</html>
```

Additions to web.xml

Just like the basic and digest methods, the form based authentication is also configured in the Web application deployment descriptor with the addition of the <form-login-config> element that specifies the login and error pages to display when the resource is accessed:

```
<login-config>
  <auth-method>FORM</auth-method>
    <form-login-config>
      <form-login-page>/loginpage.jsp</form-login-page>
      <form-error-page>/errorpage.jsp</form-error-page>
    </form-login-config>
</login-config>
```

Execution

As before, once we have out new JSP files in place, and have made the changes to the web.xml file, we point our browser at the index.jsp file, and are presented with a display similar to the following screenshot:

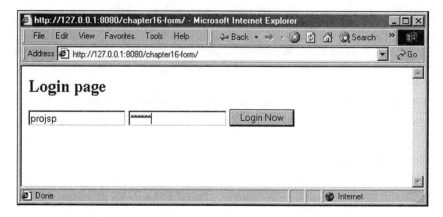

After we log in successfully, we get the following display:

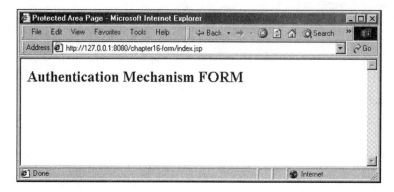

HTTPS Client Authentication

Secure Sockets Layer (SSL) is the leading security protocol on the Internet. The SSL uses TCP/IP on behalf of the higher-level protocols, meaning it runs above TCP/IP and below higher-level application protocols such as HTTP, LDAP, RMI, etc. The SSL protocol uses a combination of public-key and symmetric key encryption to establish a secure session and transmit data between the client and the server.

J2EE containers must support SSL 3.0 and certificate based authentication.

SSL has two security aims:

❑ To authenticate the server and (optionally) the client using public-key signatures

❑ To provide an encrypted connection for the client and server to exchange messages

An SSL session begins with an exchange of messages called the **SSL handshake**. The handshake allows the server to authenticate itself to the client using public-key techniques (and the client to the server if needed), and then allows the client and the server to cooperate in the creation of symmetric keys. These keys are then used for encryption, decryption, and tamper detection of any data transmitted during the session. HTTPS (HTTP Secure) describes the usage of HTTP over an SSL session to access resources on the web server. The URLs are prefixed with https:// and servers usually listen on the default port number 443.

> Developed by Netscape, SSL has been merged with other protocols and authentication methods by the IETF into a new protocol known as Transport Layer Security (TLS) http://www.ietf.org/rfc/rfc2818.txt. The original SSLv3 specifications can be found at http://home.netscape.com/eng/ssl3/ssl-toc.html and a good introduction to SSL can be found at http://www.iplanet.com/developer/docs/articles/security/ssl.html.

At any point in time it has a set of parameters, known as a cipher suite, associated with it, which define the cryptographic methods being used. There are a number of cipher suites defined by the SSL standard, but J2EE containers are required to support two cipher suites: SSL_RSA_EXPORT_WITH_RC4_40_MD5 (RSA public key encryption for key exchange, RC4 cipher for bulk data encryption, MD5 hashing to ensure data integrity) and SSL_DHE_DSS_EXPORT_WITH_DES40_CBC_SHA (encrypt data with DES in CBC mode). Both these suites use 40 bit keys, are exportable under US laws and widely used.

When the SSL session is first established it has a default cipher suite of SSL_NULL_WITH_NULL_NULL (no encryption at all). This is where the SSL handshake protocol comes in. It defines a series of messages in which the client and server negotiate the type of connection that they can support, perform authentication, and generate a bulk encryption key. At the end of the handshake, they exchange *ChangeCipherSpec* messages, which switches the current cipher suite of the protocol to the one they negotiated. The following diagram depicts the sequence of exchanges between the browser and server:

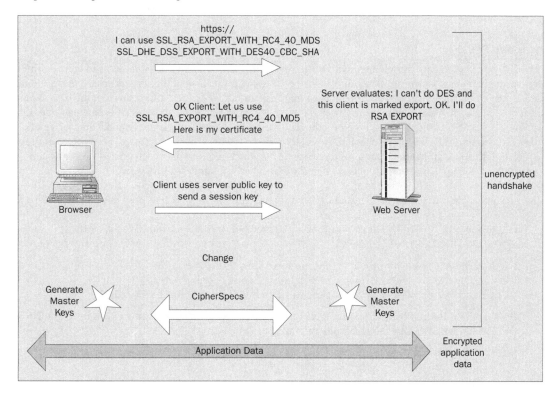

Note that only the server is authenticated, so the client does not need to provide a certificate. If client authentication were required by the server, the handshake would be a little longer.

The `<security-constraint>` element in the Web application's deployment descriptor is used to control access to Web resources at deployment time. These constraints can be applied to the entire Web application or logical collection of resources in the Web application. Among other things, the encryption to be used in the communication between clients and the server is also specified here via the `<transport-guarantee>` element. The descriptor below shows the outline for form-based authentication over SSL:

```
<web-app>
  <security-constraint>
    <web-resource-collection>
      <web-resource-name>Logical name for group</web-resource-name>

      <!--Other details such as path and HTTP methods supported by group can
          be configured here if necessary -->

    </web-resource-collection>

    <user-data-constraint>
      <transport-guarantee>NONE|INTEGRAL|CONFIDENTIAL</transport-guarantee>
    </user-data-constraint>
  </security-constraint>
</web-app>
```

Tomcat and SSL

`<transport-guarantee>` element with NONE means that the container does not have to enforce any transport guarantees for the application. A value of INTEGRAL means that the servers ensure that the data sent between the client and server is not altered in transit and CONFIDENTIAL means that the data cannot be observed in transit. Most containers use both the INTEGRAL and CONFIDENTIAL values to mean that SSL is required since SSL ensures both. Therefore, the data cannot be altered and is encrypted.Tomcat by default does not come with SSL support enabled. In order to use SSL with Tomcat 4, the SSL connector needs to be enabled. In J2EE a **connector** represents an endpoint by which requests are received and responses are returned. Each connector passes requests on to the associated container for processing.

In order to enable SSL you need to install the security provider in the JDK that provides SSL. The steps are:

❑ Install SSL libraries. (Download JSSE 1.0.2, see below, and put the JAR files into `<JAVA_HOME>\jre\lib\ext`)

❑ Add the new security provider that supports SSL. (Edit `<JAVA_HOME>\jre\lib\security\java.security` and set `security.provider.2=com.sun.net.ssl.internal.ssl.Provider`

❑ Generate the public and private keys for the alias "tomcat" (this is the alias name that Tomcat uses internally). Use the JDK tool `keytool` to execute:

```
keytool -genkey -alias tomcat -keyalg RSA
```

The default keystore password is `"changeit"`. When prompted to Enter key password for <tomcat>, press *Return*.

❑ Also enable the SSL connector by un-commenting the following lines in the server configuration file (`server.xml`):

```
<Connector className="org.apache.catalina.connector.http.HttpConnector"
           port="8443" minProcessors="5" maxProcessors="75"
           acceptCount="10" debug="0" scheme="https" secure="true">
   <Factory className="org.apache.catalina.net.SSLServerSocketFactory"
           clientAuth="false" protocol="TLS"/>
</Connector>
```

Of course, the above mechanism is specific to Tomcat. Other container providers may choose a different mechanism.

> **JSSE is the** Java Secure Sockets Extension **and is implemented by a Java Cryptography Architecture (JCA) security provider class. It can be downloaded from http://java.sun.com/products/jsse/. Containers are required to support SSL, not a particular security provider. There are others also available, for a cost. JSSE is a freely available and exportable package from Sun, although you will have to fill in a simple registration form.**

An HTTPS Authentication Example

We will repeat the first example, but using HTTPS as the transport protocol. The only additions will be to the `web.xml` file.

Additions to web.xml

HTTPS can be used in combination with the basic, digest or form based authentication. The descriptor below configures the application to use basic authentication over SSL:

```
<web-app>
  <security-constraint>
    <!-Other web resource collection configuration ->
    <user-data-constraint>
      <transport-guarantee>CONFIDENTIAL</transport-guarantee>
    </user-data-constraint>
  </security-constraint>

  <login-config>
    <auth-method>BASIC</auth-method>
      <form-login-config>
        <form-login-page>loginpage.jsp</form-login-page>
        <form-error-page>errorpage.jsp</form-error-page>
      </form-login-config>
  </login-config>

</web-app>
```

Execution

Having setup everything we've already discussed (in a new webapp, chapter16-HTTPSform), we point the browser at the index.jsp file using URL https://localhost:8443/chapter16-HTTPSforms/index.jsp.

Note the URL starts with https://, and we're telling the browser to direct the request to port 8443 (instead of the usual 8080 for Tomcat).

The figures below show the screenshots when the JSP is accessed over SSL. Since we generated our own certificate and were not issued one by a publicly trusted certifying authority (CA) the browser will pop up a box similar to the one shown below for IE (we see a Netscape example later):

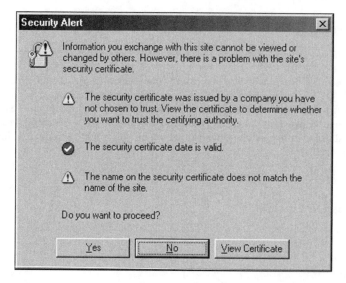

In the following screenshot, after we have clicked Yes to proceed, we can see the differences (circled) between HTTP and HTTPS in the browser screen:

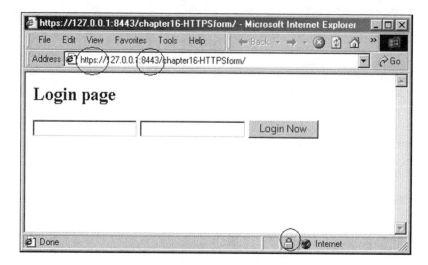

Programmatic Security

We mentioned programmatic and declarative security earlier and what we've seen up until now is declarative in nature. Programmatic security can be enforced in JSPs and Servlets at the code level to make business decisions and enforce business logic rules by using three methods in the `javax.servlet.http.HttpServletRequest` interface:

- ❏ `getRemoteUser()`
- ❏ `isUserInRole(String role)`
- ❏ `getUserPrincipal()`

The `getRemoteUser()` method returns the user name that the client authenticated with, the `isUserInRole(String role)` queries the container if the user has a particular role and the `getUserPrincipal()` method returns a `java.security.Principal` object.

For unauthenticated users `getRemoteUser()` returns `null`, `isUserInRole()` method will always return `false` and the `getUserPrincipal()` will always return `null`.

> These methods are particularly useful while writing reusable custom tag libraries. Tag libraries have access to the **PageContext** object and the same tag library can be used to provide different functionality based on the user role and principal.

EJBs have a similar set of methods in the `javax.ejb.EJBContext`:

- ❏ `isCallerInRole(String role)`
- ❏ `getCallerPrincipal()`

So for example if the Servlet was invoking an EJB, the `Principal` would be propagated.

Application developers should not hard code the role name in the code or in invocations to the `isUserInRole()` method, but rather use security role references (parameters). This gives application assemblers greater flexibility, allowing them to dynamically change roles at deployment without recompiling the application. The `<security-role-ref>` element in the deployment descriptor defines a mapping between the security role reference coded in the servlet and the actual role as decided by the application deployer. The actual role names are always specified with the `<security-role>` element.

Consider the following Servlet code:

```
if(isUserInRole("XXX")){
  operation1();
  operation2();
}
else if(isUserInRole("YYY")){
  operation3();
}
```

The web application's deployment descriptor can then contain the following element:

```
<web-app>
  <servlet>

    <servlet-name>catalog</servlet-name>
    <servlet-class>com.wrox.projsp.MyServlet</servlet-class>
      <!--OR  <jsp-file>/MyJSP </jsp-file> -->

    <security-role-ref>
      <role-name>XXX</role-name>
      <role-link>administrator</role-link>
    </security-role-ref>

    <security-role-ref>
      <role-name>YYY</role-name>
      <role-link>customerservice</role-link>
    </security-role-ref>
  </servlet>

  <security-role>
    <role-name>administrator</role-name>
    <role-name>customerservice</role-name>
  </security-role>
</web-app>
```

In the Servlet code shown earlier, if a user belonging to the administrator security role calls the Servlet only the `if` block will be executed. If no `<security-role-ref>` has been specified, the container will default to checking the argument to `isUserInRole()` against the list of role names specified in the `<security-role>` element.

Single Sign On

J2EE requires containers to support **single sign on**, due to the stateless nature of the HTTP protocol. The Servlet containers already maintain session state, and single sign on allows the user to access different applications in the same session. The container keeps track of the security policy across different web applications and prompts the user to re-authenticate if the boundary between applications is crossed. When a user successfully authenticates, the container maintains the credentials stored in the session for successive use until the session is invalidated.

In the previous form based example, if the protected page was linked to another application which required different credentials, the container would prompt the user to login again if needed, perhaps using a different mechanism, depending on the application descriptor for the second application.

In Tomcat 4.0, single sign on support is enabled by uncommenting an entry in the `server.xml` file; the appropriate entry is clearly indicated by comments in the file.

User Authorization

Authorization mechanisms limit user (or application) manipulation of resources and allow only authenticated caller identities with the required privileges to do so. The J2SE security model focuses on authorization by using policy and permission based control of a code-base (only certain identities are allowed to execute certain pieces of code, if they have the permissions to do so, which is verified at runtime by the JVM).

The J2EE component model takes this a step further by controlling to what functionality or capabilities of a component a given identity has access. The capabilities of an identity are specified at deployment time by the application deployer, who maps the permissions model of the component to the identity roles. This is what the container enforces.

For example, the application developer can develop a set of EJBs, JSPs and Servlets. The application deployer can define roles and decide what roles can control access what part of these resources, including specific sets of JSPs, Servlets, EJBs and specific methods in the EJBs. The J2EE container has to enforce these rules.

The authorization criteria for the web application are specified in the deployment descriptor along with the other security constraints using the `<auth-constraint>` element. The `<auth-constraint>` element specifies the user roles that are permitted to access the resource collection. The role defined in `<auth-constraint>` must either appear in a `<security-role-ref>` for a Servlet or JSP as shown earlier, or appear in the `<security-role>` element. The role-name `"*"` refers to all roles in the web application.

The sample below shows how only the supervisor is allowed access to the `/orders/` resources and the customer service role is allowed to access the `/accounts/` resource collection:

```
<web-app>
  <security-constraint>
    <web-resource-name>ProJSP1 </web-resource-name>
    <url-pattern>/orders/</url-pattern>
    <auth-constraint>
      <role-name>supervisor</role-name>
    </auth-constraint>
  </security-constraint>

  <security-constraint>
    <web-resource-name>ProJSP2 </web-resource-name>
    <url-pattern>/accounts/</url-pattern>
    <auth-constraint>
      <role-name>customerservice</role-name>
    </auth-constraint>
  </security-constraint>

  <security-role>
    <role-name>supervisor</role-name>
    <role-name>customerservice</role-name>
  </security-role>
</web-app>
```

During application deployment, the deployer can map roles to a user or a user group but containers are allowed the flexibility to choose the implementation mechanism to specify username and passwords for users. Tomcat for example uses an XML file (`tomcat-users.xml`). Most commercial application servers, such as WebLogic, provide a graphical interface.

> **The J2EE 1.3 specs (now in draft) require that J2EE application servers support the Java Authentication and Authorization Service (JAAS). JAAS (http://java.sun.com/products/jaas) provides a transparent interface like other enterprise API (JDBC, JNDI, etc.) to developers.**

Even though Tomcat uses the `tomcat-users.xml` file for storing usernames and passwords by default, it can also be configured to store them in a database. (Storing information in a file isn't ideal from a security perspective but is the default configuration for most containers due to its simplicity.) This is done by replacing the standard 'realm' component (specified in `server.xml`) by one called JDBCRealm. The Tomcat 4.0 documentation includes detailed documentation on how to set up the necessary database tables and configure `server.xml` – see http://localhost:8080/docs/JDBCRealm-howto.html and the comments in `server.xml`. It is even possible to construct your own authentication and authorization component for Tomcat by extending `org.apache.catalina.realm.RealmBase` – for example, you could write a realm that interrogates an LDAP directory.

Signing and Auditing

The concept of **signing** is an integral part of J2SE and there are tools and API level interfaces exposed for this purpose (this includes signing code and establishing identity based on the signatures). In enterprise applications it is important to provide security on the basis of who is the originator of a given call; more importantly, we should also be able to verify that in some manner. It is also very important for application deployers to verify that the component or JAR file that they are deploying has not been tampered with. **Auditing** is the practice of capturing the occurrences of security related events (a similar process to logging), and is valuable to understand the damage done when security is breached.

> The J2EE specifications do not place any specific requirements on containers for auditing APIs for application components to generate audit records.

Adding Security to the Phone Directory

Let us look at the previous example that we covered earlier in this chapter where users could add and lookup users from a phone directory (implemented via a `java.util.Properties` object). We will define a role – users – and only visitors in this role can access the resources. We will use form based authentication over SSL. The three main steps are:

❑ Configure the users and roles. We will add 2 users to the `tomcat-users.xml` file

❑ Make the appropriate entries in the web applications descriptor (`web.xml`) file, as shown below.

❑ Access the secure URL https://localhost:8443/chapter16-HTTPSdirectory/directory.jsp

JSP Pages

We will use the pages from the previous examples (`loginpage.jsp`, `errorpage.jsp`, and `directory.jsp` from the earlier listener example).

Additions to web.xml

```
<web-app>

<!--This is the same as the last chapter. Nothing new here -->
<context-param>
  <param-name>FILENAME</param-name>
  <param-value>directory.db</param-value>
```

```
  </context-param>
  <listener>
    <listener-class>com.wrox.projsp.ch16.FirstListenerExample</listener-class>
  </listener>
  <!--End configuration for example from previous chapter -->

  <!- define all the constraints ->
  <!- We will use SSL, FORM based authentication for the entire Web Application ->

  <security-constraint>
    <web-resource-collection>
      <web-resource-name>Entire Application</web-resource-name>
      <url-pattern>/*</url-pattern>
    </web-resource-collection>

    <auth-constraint>
      <role-name>user</role-name>
    </auth-constraint>

  <!- Specify that we will use SSL from the browser ->
    <user-data-constraint>
      <transport-guarantee>CONFIDENTIAL</transport-guarantee>
    </user-data-constraint>
  </security-constraint>

  <!- define the login configuration for form based authentication ->

  <login-config>
    <auth-method>FORM</auth-method>
    <realm-name>Secure Area</realm-name>
    <form-login-config>
      <form-login-page>/loginpage.jsp</form-login-page>
      <form-error-page>/errorpage.jsp</form-error-page>
    </form-login-config>
  </login-config>
</web-app>
```

Additions to tomcat-users.xml

This contains the same information as earlier, the username, password and role:

```
<tomcat-users>
  <user name="justin" password="justin" roles="user" />
</tomcat-users>
```

Alternatively, you can create your own realm by storing this information in the database or LDAP or some other place. This part is specific to the container you are using and involves using container specific classes.

Execution

Please ensure that you have enabled SSL as described earlier.

Because the certificate we are using is self-generated and not verified by a known Certifying Authority, the first time the URL is accessed a dialog similar to the one below will show up (this one is from Netscape):

615

> **Regarding certificates and certifying authorities, unless you're happy to have visitors to your site jump through certificate installation hoops in order to get at the content, you'll need to get your certificates signed by a certificate authority.**

Once the certificate is accepted the visitor will be prompted to login by redirection to our login page, `loginpage.jsp`. When the valid username and password (`justin`/`justin` from the server's configuration file) for the role `user` are entered, the browser will be redirected to the `directory.jsp` page:

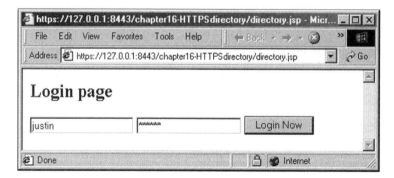

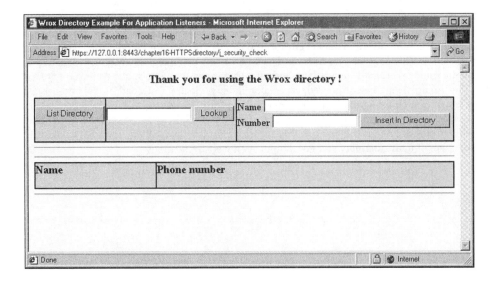

Summary

In this chapter, we have talked about the new context and session event listeners in the Servlet 2.3 API, and security within the web tier.

Servlet 2.3 introduces a new level of flexibility in handling events associated with web applications. We looked at:

- ❑ The `HttpSessionBindingListener` interface
- ❑ Session listeners: How to track individual session state changes
- ❑ Context listeners: How to track application state changes
- ❑ Listener configuration: How to configure listeners in a Web Container
- ❑ And wrapped them up with a couple of examples

We then saw some of the different J2EE security mechanisms, as applied to the Web containers and JSPs. In particular, we examined the different elements of the deployment descriptor and how to use SSL with Form based authentication:

- ❑ Basic authentication, specified in the `web.xml` file, and the `tomcat-users.xml` file, with a browser created pop up for the log in.
- ❑ HTTP Digest authentication. Like basic authentication using `web.xml`, `tomcat-users.xml`, a browser pop up, but with the authentication transferred to the browser.
- ❑ Form based authentication. Here we specified in the `web.xml` file that requests for our `index.jsp` were to be redirected to a login form, from where the authentication was sent to the server.
- ❑ HTTPS client authentication. For this, we used Secure Sockets Layer to encrypt and protect the authentication details as they are passed from the form to the browser.

Balancing security and performance always involves a trade-off. Authentication, authorization, and encryption use processing time and resources. Authenticating users once per session may not be a big overhead; however, authorization may occur for every object invocation (Servlet, EJB, JMS, JTS, JDBC, etc.). Web containers serving content over SSL need to do CPU intensive key generation and encryption for every HTTPS request they receive. (Interestingly, Sun offers a hardware card to speed this up on Solaris!) Trade-offs like this should always be considered, especially under projected workload model and this evaluation is an important step in choosing the right container and platform for your application.

In the next chapter, we'll start to draw together the different APIs and architectures we've discussed by looking at issues of maintainability and good practice in web applications.

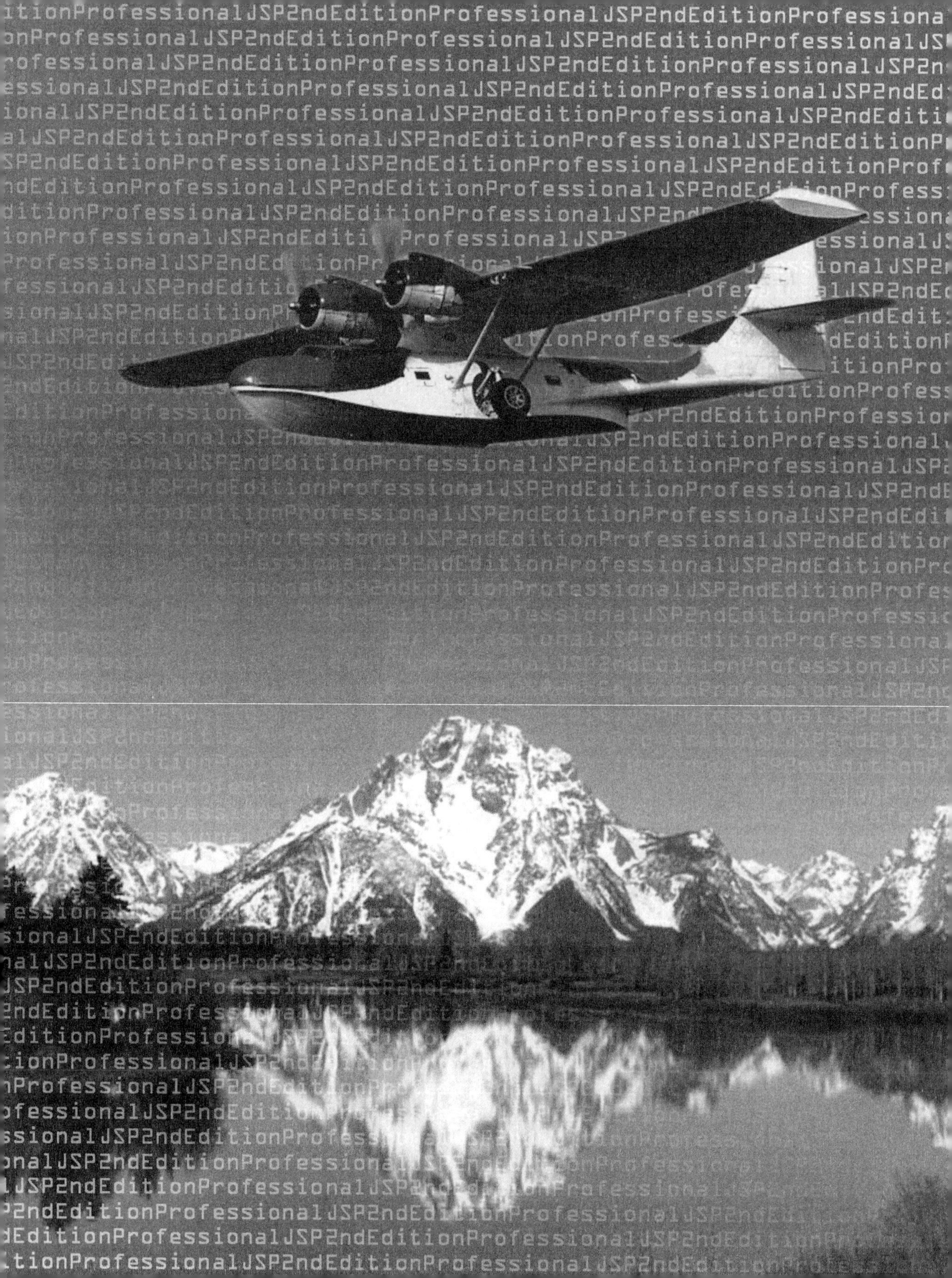
ProfessionalJSP2ndEdition

Maintainability and Good Practice

Exciting as JSPs are, they do not solve all the problems of designing web interfaces. Presentation and content are not automatically cleanly separated, and HTML generation code often sits uneasily on OO middleware. Whether or not we use JSPs, the HTTP request-response punctuation of the work of web applications fits poorly with the need for an application's objects to cooperate. The problem of representing the state of Java objects on web pages and updating them using HTML forms is surprisingly awkward.

Many JSPs in production systems are hard to read and maintain. Too often they consist of a mish-mash of Java code in scriptlets and HTML markup, with jarring transitions between levels of abstraction that no experienced developer would tolerate in a Java application. Writing maintainable JSPs is not easy. While the Java language itself does a good job of helping developers to write maintainable code, JSP provides little help and much temptation to write messy code that does not support even procedural reuse.

The enthusiasm that greeted the early release of JSP caused far too many developers to assume that Servlets were outmoded. This is a misconception: JSPs may be compiled into Servlets at translation time, but JSPs and Servlets have very different strengths and weaknesses from an authoring perspective. JSPs *are* far superior to Servlets at text-oriented presentation; they are inferior at handling control flow. Well-written web applications of any complexity will use both JSPs and Servlets.

There is a scarcity of resources on writing good JSPs, as opposed to mastering JSP syntax. This is in marked contrast to the discipline of OO design, where any good bookstore carries a shelf of books at every level from novice to expert.

This chapter is an effort to address this gap. We will:

❑ Describe approaches to JSP authoring that overcome the major pitfalls

❑ Discuss some of the practical challenges involved

❑ Look at using the Model View Controller design pattern in Java web applications

❑ Look at using JSPs in conjunction with Servlets

❑ Present guidelines for good practice

> **In this chapter we assume that JSPs are being used primarily to generate HTML or XHTML. Of course this is not always the case. However, the concepts are generic enough to translate to any text based content generation. (If a binary or non human-readable format like PDF is to be generated, a Servlet is the correct choice – see Chapter 23 for examples.)**

The Goal

Most experienced JSP developers will share a basic rule:

> **A JSP should look like a readable HTML page with a little dynamic content, rather than a Java program with embedded markup, or even a balance of scriptlets and markup. A JSP is a view.**

There are many justifications for this rule. Perhaps the most important relates to the division of roles in web development teams. The HTML on today's web sites can be very complex. Unless the page generation approach in use is understandable by page designers, it will be impossible for them to contribute their skills to maintaining and enhancing presentation on a site. Programmers, on the other hand, will always be required if the application logic changes. They will find it difficult to make such changes if the application workflow is obscured by complex markup. JSPs containing lots of Java code and lots of markup will create problems for both designers and programmers.

Two further rules follow from this basic premise. Together, they amount to *a clear separation of presentation and content*:

❑ **Ensure that business logic is where it belongs**
This is emphatically not in JSPs. Not only do scriptlets (fragments of Java code embedded in JSPs) obscure the markup generation that is the main role of JSPs, but they are not reusable and do not fit into an OO model. In fact, business logic is not usually web specific, and can often be captured in classes below the web tier.

❑ **Ensure that presentation is centralized where it belongs**
Presentation belongs in JSPs, assuming pages contain some dynamic content. (There is nothing wrong with static HTML.) Don't generate HTML from Java code. Since the early days of Servlets, developers have realized that Java code is poor at generating HTML. (The issues in escaping double quotes alone tend to make Java code generating raw HTML unreadable.)

Having Servlets read markup from properties files or templates is an improvement, or as an alternative we can use OO HTML generation libraries such as Weblogic's proprietary **htmlKona**, or the Jakarta **ECS** (**Element Construction Set**) API available from http://jakarta.apache.org/ecs/. The result, however, tends to be a web interface that is hard to understand. Each dynamic page is built from scattered building blocks that make little sense on their own. For example, tracking down a browser error that may be due to unbalanced or crossed tags is often difficult, as may be an attempt to understand the behavior of JavaScript on a generated page.

Developers who have worked throughout the lifecycle of systems with JSP interfaces realize how important it is to create JSPs that can be manipulated by HTML designers. This usually amounts to ensuring that Java content (scriptlets) are limited, of easily manageable complexity, and clearly demarcated from HTML content.

The potential for JSPs to be refined by non-programmers is particularly important, as a clear division of roles between Java developers and HTML coders is crucial to the success of web development using JSPs. Lack of such a division is one of the reasons JSP development tends to fall down a gap in development teams, without being subject to any real development methodology. There is much to be gained by empowering HTML specialists to work on JSPs; Java developers tend to lack design flair, and find HTML coding unrewarding.

Developers should always consider the future of the JSPs they write. Are they likely to want to be interrupted while working on a new project to change the fonts and colors in a JSP-generated table? But can they expect anyone else to do it if their JSPs are really Java classes escaping into HTML to simplify the syntax of generating markup? The presentational requirements of real-world systems change with surprising frequency, and developers have a responsibility to create interfaces that permit rapid response to business needs.

These aims are surprisingly difficult to achieve in practice. To do so, we must visualize JSPs in the context of an n-tiered architecture, maximize our use of those features of JSP that enable the separation of presentation and content, and be aware of the pitfalls that must be avoided.

The Web Tier in a Multi-Tier Architecture

Unless we have a well-designed middleware layer exposing data at the appropriate level of abstraction and handling core application workflow, our JSPs will inevitably be complicated by business logic, which will soon become a nightmare to keep up to date. Before moving on to more practical coding issues, we must consider the place of the web tier in a well-designed J2EE system.

The J2EE model is based on the assumption that the presentation of data changes frequently, while the structure of the data being presented changes infrequently. (Note the distinction between change in data *values*, which occurs constantly in any system, and change in data *structure*. The latter will generally occur only with each major application rollout.) It is also important to remember that the J2EE model supports a variety of client types, not merely JSPs.

Multi-tier architectures are now a 'given' in large-scale web design. The following diagram tries to put more detail into the presentational tiers of a J2EE application:

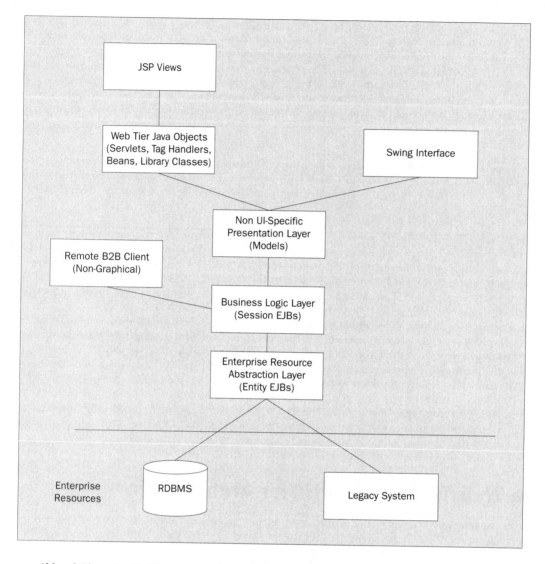

Although I have described this in terms of J2EE architecture, EJBs are not always necessary. There are applications where the robustness and scalability of an enterprise application server is not required; however, the need for a clean architecture remains. In such applications, a similar tiering can be implemented using layers of Java classes with clearly defined contracts, rather than EJBs. Preserving the distinction between business logic layer and enterprise resource abstraction layer (implemented in EJB systems by session and entity beans respectively) is still advisable; if a system is separated into tiers with clearly defined interfaces, it will be easier to modify and maintain. If greater robustness and scalability come to be required, such a cleanly designed system can easily be modified to take advantage of EJB.

This is not the place for an in-depth look at J2EE architecture, but let us briefly consider each of these tiers in turn, from the bottom. The top three tiers will be of most interest to us. They are also the most often neglected in architectural discussions:

❏ **Enterprise resources**
Non-Java resources offering raw data without the business logic necessary for a particular application. Most commonly this tier will consist of one or more relational databases, but other possibilities are legacy systems and distributed resources accessed by JNDI.

❏ **Enterprise resource abstraction layer**
This is a relatively thin object abstraction layer wrapping the enterprise resources. In an EJB model, entity beans will often be used to implement this layer.

❏ **Business logic layer**
This is not concerned with presentation, but will implement most of the application's workflow. This layer will provide the logic required to support the system's use cases. In an EJB architecture, it will be comprised of session beans. The design of this layer is crucial in underpinning a cleanly implemented JSP interface. This layer tends to be among the hardest to design.

❏ **Non UI-specific presentation layer**
This layer is not always necessary, and often overlooked, but in more complex systems it will have an important role. The key question should be: *Is this presentation logic specific to a JSP interface, or would it be common to all interfaces?* I find it helpful to think of a Swing interface as an alternative. (Swing is the client-side GUI library provided by the Java 2 platform.) Swing UI components use abstract data models that are a good example of non UI-specific presentation code: although they hook directly into Swing view components, they provide an abstraction that is usable by any kind of GUI.

❏ **Web tier Java objects: Servlets, custom tag classes, JSP beans, web-specific library classes, and those parts of the web tier that handle logic or data acquisition**
These objects will perform any complex request parsing, cookie handling, encryption, or other functions specific to a web interface. They will provide a bridge between JSPs and the business objects they use.

❏ **JSP views**
A long way from the data and main business logic layer, aren't they? If we get this layering right, the JSPs will contain little, if any, Java code, but will be *views* of data provided by the supporting tiers of the application.

To get a more practical insight into how such architectures work in practice, imagine we are working on a new version of the user registration system on a large web site. The core functionality of this system will be the logic applied when users attempt to log in by entering a username and password. Due to database changes, there are a number of rules that must be applied to logins: for example, some existing usernames are now illegal, and such users must be allowed to log in and then prompted to choose new usernames. Users from certain countries should be shown a special offer the first time they log in to the new version of the site. When users log in successfully, cookie values must be generated to integrate with third party web sites. This cookie generation requires complex algorithms. Where should each piece of functionality required fit into a J2EE architecture?

❏ The new rules on usernames and the need to force some users to change their usernames should be implemented in the business logic layer. This is not specific to a JSP interface. It is not even specific to a graphical interface: the session EJBs implementing it could allow a remote CORBA client to support a command-line interface. The business logic layer will not only implement such special cases, but also provide an abstraction for all data access. UI code should not be tied to the schema of the database in use, but should only access (and be able to access) objects and methods helping to realize the use cases.

❑ The special offer is specific to presentation, but not to JSP. There might be a URL associated with the special offer, but a Swing client might present a hyperlink to this while supporting the same login functionality as the JSP. The implementation of this belongs in the non UI-specific presentation layer.

❑ The cookie generation requirement is, however, specific to HTTP. The classes involved in implementing the cookie generation algorithms would be of no interest to a remote CORBA client or a Swing applet. Their implementation should fit into the layer of web-tier Java objects.

None of this functionality belongs in the JSPs themselves. The JSPs will be concerned with how the system *looks*, rather than how it works, and will use JSP beans, and custom tags if necessary, to access data from the lower architectural layers.

Techniques for Writing Maintainable JSPs

Moving from the theoretical to the practical, let's consider some of the most important issues in designing the JSP layer. It is assumed that the underlying middleware appropriately abstracts the business logic, and that we're not merely moving the deckchairs on the Titanic.

This discussion reflects a desire to leverage proven design patterns as far as possible within the HTTP request-response paradigm. Fortunately, we can still make effective use of what is perhaps the most successful of all architectural patterns: the model view controller pattern.

Request Controller Architecture: Dividing Logic and Presentation

JSP design is often complicated by the need for JSPs both to perform request processing and to present content. These tasks are quite distinct for many pages, and request processing may be complicated.

If a JSP is a view, the idea that it should handle incoming requests to the application it belongs to is clearly flawed. How do we know that this JSP is the correct view in all cases? How should it react to recoverable errors? (Presenting an error page may be an over-reaction.) Some JSPs may need to manipulate session or application-wide resources or state before the response can be generated. Others may need to examine request values to check whether to redirect the request. Simply mapping request properties onto a bean (see the discussion of JSP beans below) is not a universal solution, especially if redirection may be required.

Encountering such problems while writing JSPs is a clear indication that the application's design needs to be revisited. Fortunately, there is an elegant solution, often called the "**JSP Model 2 Architecture**". I prefer to call it **request controller architecture**. This is an attempt to apply the model view controller pattern to web applications. It involves having one JSP or Servlet as a single point of entry into a whole application or group of pages. The entry point produces no output itself but processes the request, optionally manipulates session and application state, and redirects requests to the appropriate JSP view. Complex applications may consist of a number of request-controller page groups.

Request-controller implementations often include an `action` or similarly named parameter in each request. The value of this parameter is examined by the controller, which uses it to decide how to process the request. Alternatively, the controller JSP or Servlet can intercept all incoming requests, and determine the appropriate processing strategy based on the request URL.

Request controller architecture is one of the most valuable approaches to building maintainable JSP systems. It is a true design pattern for JSPs. Systems built using it tend to be more flexible and extensible than those using a page-centric approach, and tend also to achieve a better separation of presentation and content.

Request controller architecture promotes thinking of a web application as being in a well-defined state at any time, due to the controller nature of the architecture. (This can easily be made explicit by holding a state variable in the request-controller.) A state-oriented approach can be helpful in understanding and documenting web applications. (See the case study in the next chapter for an example of a state machine describing a web application.)

Request controller architecture is widely advocated (for example in Sun's J2EE Blueprints), and goes under a variety of names. IBM refers to it as "Structured Web Interactions" (see the excellent discussion at http://www-4.ibm.com/software/ebusiness/pm.html). This IBM article and a number of authors recommend using Servlets as controllers. This has the benefit of making explicit the distinction between logic processing (which will be in Servlets and helper classes), and presentation (which will be in JSPs). In complex applications, the Servlet approach is usually preferable. However, it tends to be slightly harder to comprehend and implement. The following discussion considers Servlet controllers; the sample application in the next chapter will use a JSP controller. The discussion below focuses on using a single controller servlet for the entire application: it is also possible to divide an application into logically distinct subsystems, each with their own controller. The approach described below would then be applied to each subsystem.

Implementing a Request Controller Architecture

The request controller pattern can be implemented in one JSP consisting of a long scriptlet and no HTML generation, but this is inelegant. Java classes, not JSPs, are the correct place for control logic. Compare, for example, the definition of methods in JSPs and Java classes. JSP declaration syntax is inelegant, and allows no opportunity to use Javadoc, or to expose methods to other objects. A better alternative is to use a Servlet controller, or make a JSP controller delegate control logic to a controller class.

Let's consider a simple implementation of request controller architecture using a controller Servlet. The minimal requirements will be:

- ❏ One controller Servlet to handle all incoming requests and delegate processing to 'request handler' helper classes. Note that the controller shouldn't do the processing itself, as this would make the application hard to extend.

- ❏ One request handler helper class to do the processing for each type of request. (A 'type of request' will be defined by its URL within the application, or the value of a particular parameter.) The RequestHandler interface will define a single method, handleRequest(), that will do any necessary processing in response to a request and return the URL of the JSP view that should render the response. This will enable the controller to forward the response to this view, without knowing how the processing is implemented.

- ❏ A number of page beans (also known as 'View beans'), to provide model data for JSP views.

- ❏ Many view JSPs.

In more complex applications, a session object might be required. This would be created and accessed by request handler classes, and would not be manipulated by JSPs. (Remember that a view shouldn't change the state of a system.)

627

There will be more view JSPs than request handlers (one request handler may forward the response to different views, depending on the result of logic processing). There will be at most the same number of page beans as views.

At first sight this may look unnecessarily complex in comparison with a Model 1 approach. There *are* more individual components; the virtue is that each component has clearly defined responsibilities, and Java classes and JSPs are used where they are most appropriate. The greater conceptual complexity will prove far more manageable than the JSP code complexity that tends to result from adopting a less sophisticated approach. (In contrast, JSP Model 1 is the obvious, and rather naïve, way to use JSPs. In JSP Model 1, or 'JSP-centric', design, requests are directly handled by JSPs, and the norm is for the JSP that receives a request to generate the necessary response content.)

Let's see how this might fit together by examining each component in turn.

Controller Servlet

There will be one instance of the application's controller Servlet, which will handle all incoming requests. We can map all application URLs onto the controller Servlet in a WAR's web.xml file, meaning that the application's public URLs will not correspond to physical JSPs, but will be virtual.

The controller Servlet won't know how to handle each individual request. Its main responsibility will be to decide which request handler helper class should handle each request, and delegate request processing to it. If we put all our application logic in the controller, we'd end up with a monolithic, procedural class, and, most likely, un-maintainable chains of if/else statements. It would be hard to add new functionality. By using delegation, we can add new functionality very easily: new types of requests can be handled by additional request handlers.

The controller will choose a request handler for each request based on a set of mappings from request type to the request handler instances it maintains. These mappings might be based on request URL or the value of a special 'action' parameter. Although we won't try to implement this in the simple example code here, these mappings should be defined outside Java code. A .properties file or XML configuration document will be ideal.

Delegating request processing to helper classes and using mappings will mean that the controller Servlet will be generic. With different mappings, the same controller Servlet could be used for many applications.

Request Handlers

Unlike the controller Servlet, implementations of the RequestHandler interface (which we'll look at shortly) will be application specific. Each request handler will perform the following steps:

- ❑ Examine the parameters of incoming requests
- ❑ Update application state if necessary
- ❑ Obtain any necessary data to display and make it available to views
- ❑ Choose a JSP view to which the controller will forward the response

Because RequestHandler implementations are Java classes, they can take full advantage of Java's object orientation. For example, an application might include an abstract RequestHandler implementation that retrieves the user's session state and calls a protected abstract method to be defined by subclasses to handle the request given the session state.

Like the controller Servlet, RequestHandler implementations must be thread-safe, as they will be shared between many users.

Page Beans

These will be simple Java objects, constructed by request handlers and set as attributes in the request to make them accessible to view JSPs using the `<jsp:useBean>` tag. Page beans won't do markup generation or execute any logic. They will be treated as read-only objects by JSP views.

JSP Views

The JSP views in this architecture will contain no workflow logic. They will be given beans containing the data they need, and will simply display it, possibly using custom tags if the data is complex. They will have no need to examine request parameters; all choices will have been made before the JSP is called. They will not change the state of the system.

Note that we'll need two sets of names in the cases where a request URL matches the natural view name. For example, let's suppose we have a login form, and the view for the form is `login.jsp`. If we map the URL `login.jsp` onto the controller Servlet, we'll never be able to display the JSP view. My preferred solution to this problem is to use `<pagename>.html` as the public URL, mapped onto the controller, and leave the `.jsp` URL as a view. There is no need to expose `.jsp` URLs publicly: if a resource generates HTML, it's best to make that clear in the URL. (Also, why share your technology choice with the world?)

Implementation

Now let's look at how we might implement this approach. First, let's consider the complete listing of the `RequestHandler` interface. This contains a single method, which will be called by the controller:

```
package com.wrox.projsp.ch17;
/**
 * Interface to be implemented by application-specific helper classes
 * to which a controller Servlet will delegate request processing.
 */
public interface RequestHandler {

    /**
     * Given an HTTP request, perform any necessary processing,
     * set any required page beans as request attributes,
     * and return the URL of the view that should render the response.
     * @return the URL of the view that should render the response
     * (probably a JSP), or null to indicate that the response has been
     * output already and processing is complete.
     */
    String handleRequest(HttpServletRequest request,
                    HttpServletResponse response) throws ServletException,
                    IOException;

}
```

The implementations of this interface will be the core of the web tier of our application and enable the controller to delegate application-specific logic. The return value of the `handleRequest()` method will probably be the URL within our application of a view JSP; in some cases it could be the URL of a static HTML page. A return value of `null` will have a special meaning, indicating to the controller that the RequestHandler implementation built the response itself. This is necessary to support those cases when a JSP view *isn't* appropriate: for example, if we need to generate binary data.

The controller will examine incoming requests, and call one of its registered request handlers for each. Let's choose the request handler to use based on the request's URL within the web application, as returned by calling the `HttpServletRequest.getServletPath()` method. The controller's `init()` method, which is not implemented in this listing, would build a hash table of `RequestHandler` instances, keyed by request URL. If the controller doesn't find a handler for a particular request, it will send an HTTP response code 404 ("Not Found").

Of course, in real applications we might want to be more helpful to the user in this situation. For example, a more sophisticated controller with access to the user's session state might call a non application-specific method asking the session state for the most appropriate view to prompt the user to continue her session.

A partial listing of the controller Servlet will look like this:

```java
package com.wrox.projsp.ch17;
/**
 * Simple fragment of a controller Servlet using
 * mappings from application URL to a number of
 * RequestHandler helper classes.
 */
public class ControllerServlet extends HttpServlet {

    /**
     * Hash table of RequestHandler instances, keyed by request URL
     */
    private Map handlerHash = new HashMap();

    /**
     * Initialize mappings: not implemented here
     */
    public void init() throws ServletException {

        // This will read mapping definitions
        // and populate handlerHash
    }

    /**
     * Based on the URL within our application, choose a RequestHandler
     * to handle the request and delegate processing to it.
     * Return an HTTP error code 404 (not found) if there's no RequestHandler
     * mapped to this URL.
     */
    public void doGet(HttpServletRequest request,
                      HttpServletResponse response) throws ServletException,
                      IOException {
        RequestHandler rh =
          (RequestHandler) handlerHash.get(request.getServletPath());
        if (rh == null) {
          response.sendError(HttpServletResponse.SC_NOT_FOUND);

          // If we get to here, we have a handler for this request
        }
        String viewURL = rh.handleRequest(request, response);
        if (viewURL == null) {
```

```
            // The RequestHandler has finished output: do nothing
        } else {

            // The RequestHandler told us the view to use
            // Forward the response to it
            request.getRequestDispatcher(viewURL).forward(request, response);
        }
    }   // doGet

}       // class ControllerServlet
```

Note that nothing in this class is specific to a particular application.

The Java code for our application will reside in its request handler implementations. To illustrate what it might look like, imagine we're building a simple application that displays the data we hold about users in our data store (probably a relational database, but we won't make the web tier dependent on such a low level detail).

The entry point to our application will be showInfo.html, which will prompt the user to enter their name if it isn't known, and display their record if it is. There will be a page allowing the user to correct their name if no data is found for the submitted name.

The URL showInfo.html will be handled by one RequestHandler implementation. Each of these cases (username not submitted, data found for username, and username not found) will require a separate view. This is a good example of a crucial aspect of the request controller architecture: one URL (and hence one request handler) may produce different views under different circumstances.

Let's call the required RequestHandler implementation ShowRecordRequestHandler. Because data retrieval isn't web specific, ShowRecordRequestHandler will use a helper class outside the web tier to perform the data lookup. A complete listing of the ShowRecordRequestHandler will look like this:

```
package com.wrox.projsp.ch17;
/**
 * Will show the data we hold about the user,
 * or force the user to enter their name so that we can
 * look them up
 */
public class ShowRecordRequestHandler implements RequestHandler {

    ApplicationDataSource dataSource = new ApplicationDataSource();

    /**
     * Given an HTTP request, perform any necessary processing,
     * set any required page beans as request attributes,
     * and return the URL of the view that should render the response.
     * @return the the URL of the view that should render the response
     * (probably a JSP), or null to indicate that the response has been
     * output already and processing is complete.
     */
    public String handleRequest(HttpServletRequest request,
                                HttpServletResponse response)
                         throws ServletException,
                                IOException {
```

```
      String name = request.getParameter("name");
      if (name == null) {
        return "enterName.jsp";
      } else {

        // Do database lookup for the user
        DataObject dataObject = dataSource.lookupUser(name);
        if (dataObject == null) {
          return "sorryNotFound.jsp";
        } else {

          // We have data for this user
          DataInfoBean dib = new DataInfoBean();
          dib.setDataObject(dataObject);
          request.setAttribute("dataInfoBean", dib);
          return "showInfo.jsp";
        }
      }
    }   // handleRequest

}       // class ShowRecordRequestHandler
```

The first task of this class is to examine the request and look for a name parameter. If no name parameter is found, `ShowRecordRequestHandler` will send the user to the 'enter name' view. If a name parameter is present, `ShowRecordRequestHandler` will use a helper class to look up the data. If no data is found, it will send the user to the "not found" view.

The most interesting case is when data is retrieved for a user. In this case, we need to make this data available to the view JSP before returning its URL. We do this by creating a page bean to hold the data, and adding it to the request as an attribute. This will enable a JSP view to retrieve it using the `<jsp:useBean>` tag.

> **Don't feel that you need to use the `<jsp:useBean>` tag to instantiate JSP beans. There is a very useful form of this tag that does not specify an implementing class, and which throws an exception if no such object is defined in the HTTP session or request. Simply omit the class attribute of the useBean tag, and specify only the type, like this:**
>
> ```
> <jsp:useBean id="dataInfoBean" scope="request"
>  type="DataInfoBean"/>
> ```
>
> **Beans used in such pages can be instantiated through a complete `<jsp:useBean>` tag in another JSP, or can be placed in the session by a controller.**

The `DataInfoBean` is a very simple object:

```
package com.wrox.projsp.ch17;
/**
 * Simpe JSP bean to expose the data
 * we hold for a user. This is web specific
 */
class DataInfoBean implements java.io.Serializable {
```

```
    private DataObject dataObject;

    /**
     * A bean should have an empty constructor
     */
    public DataInfoBean() {}

    /**
     * Setter for DataObject property
     */
    public void setDataObject(DataObject dataObject) {
      this.dataObject = dataObject;
    }

    /**
     * Getter for DataObject property
     */
    public DataObject getDataObject() {
      return dataObject;
    }

    // Possibly some web-specific properties
}
```

The data lookup helper and the data objects it returns aren't part of the web tier, so we don't need to consider them here. The data lookup helper, `ApplicationDataSource`, might obtain data from EJBs, or, in a simpler application, do SQL queries itself. The data objects could also be used to provide data for a Swing interface. Note that it is advisable to retrieve all data before invoking any JSP views; a view shouldn't access data that is lazily loaded, as this might cause unexpected failures that cannot be handled by a controller. It is also important for views to avoid being dependent on data-source specific code.

The JSPs views will contain no logic. Because each JSP view represents a particular outcome of the processing of a request, request controller architectures will typically require more JSPs than JSP Model 1 designs.

Here are listings for simple JSPs for the three views. Of course, the HTML would be much more complex in a real application. But because these JSPs contain no logic, a page designer could update them without altering application functionality:

```
<%-- showInfo.jsp --%>

<%-- Access bean placed in the request by ShowInfoRequestHandler --%>
<jsp:useBean id="dataInfoBean"
  scope="request"
  type="DataInfoBean" />

Hello <%=dataInfoBean.getDataObject().getName()%>

<br />Show other information...if it's complex, use a tag library


<%-- enterName.jsp --%>

<%-- Doesn't need a bean: in fact could be a static page --%>

<form method="GET" action="showInfo.html">
```

```
Enter your name:
<input type="text" name="name" value="" />

</form>
```

```
<%-- sorryNotFound.jsp --%>

<%-- We could use a bean here to hold the name the user submitted,
       which we couldn't look up --%>

Sorry, we couldn't find you in our database.
Maybe you entered your name incorrectly.
Please try again.
<p/>

<form method="GET" action="showInfo.html">

Enter your name:
<input type="text" name="name" value="" />

</form>
```

Events

An interesting refinement to request controller architecture introduces the notion of web application "events," and the Observer design pattern.

The controller Servlet (or possibly a singleton object in the web tier) might maintain a set of listeners, and publish events such as 'URL requested,' 'page rendered,' or 'request handler error'. It might also offer an API for request handlers to publish application-specific events (for example, 'user logged in' or 'search performed'), which might contain information such as the time the operation took to complete. Like the concept of delegating events to request handlers, this is a powerful means of designing extensible applications.

The designers of the application might not envisage all the listeners that may later be added: for example, a listener might be added that e-mails a warning to an administrator if more than five successive logins to a site each take more than one second, without any need to modify the existing code of the application. This is also a powerful approach to handling logging and performance monitoring.

If events and listeners are used, it is a good idea to follow JavaBean conventions for listener naming and deriving events from `java.util.EventObject`. (See *Professional Java Programming*, Wrox Press, 2000, ISBN 1-861003-82-x for further details.)

One important caveat applies to writing event listeners. If they are to be called by the thread handling the request, they must be thread safe and must not risk blocking the caller (perhaps starting a new thread to perform any lengthy processing). A rogue listener might destroy the performance and reliability of an application.

Benefits

JSPs produced using a request controller architecture will have the right level of responsibility, and scriptlets will only be necessary if they are genuinely concerned with presentation.

There are further benefits in running all application URLs through a single point of entry. For example, it is easy to implement consistent performance monitoring, logging, error reporting and security.

Since contributing a chapter on this subject to *Professional Java Server Programming: J2EE Edition* (Wrox Press, 2000, ISBN 1-861004-65-6), I have led a team implementing a request controller architecture at a complex, high-volume web site. Our proprietary controller framework offers much richer functionality than that we've just seen, but the basic concepts are the same. The presentation of complex data in JSP views is handled by a library of custom tags. A hierarchy of request handlers abstracts common functionality, while the framework offers sophisticated management of session state. (Following the principle that views shouldn't manipulate application state, session objects are not accessible to JSPs.) Through careful J2EE design, only web-specific application logic is included in the web tier.

The benefits have been substantial. All our applications use the same controller framework and basic structure; almost all JSPs can be maintained by the design team; security is handled by the controller and is transparent to JSP views; detailed performance and usage statistics are available for all applications without the need to write application-specific code; and error reporting is handled transparently by the controller Servlet in a consistent manner.

Using a Generic Request Controller Framework

While it is vital to understand the design involved and how to go about implementing it, a good option may be a generic request controller framework. An exciting open source possibility is Struts, from the Apache Project (see http://jakarta.apache.org/struts/index.html for more details).

The aim of Struts is to provide a flexible model view controller approach for Java web development. The most important component is a generic controller Servlet, which is configured outside Java code, and which dispatches requests to `Action` classes provided by the application developer. (This approach is very similar to that we've just discussed.) Struts also provides handy custom tags, and support for data binding using Java reflection.

Struts is still in its early days, but if it gains the interest (and contribution!) it deserves from Java web developers, it may deliver substantial benefits in productivity and maintainability. For more information on Struts, see Chapter 21.

When Not to Use a Request Controller Architecture

Some web applications fit well with the notion of every page handling its own request parameters (probably using a bean). This approach can work well for simple applications that maintain no session state – for example, relying on query strings for communication between pages. In such cases, a request controller architecture will deliver little benefit, and will probably not justify the complexity it introduces. But more often than not, the investment in a slightly more complex design will be handsomely repaid in producing a cleaner and more maintainable application.

Using Includes in JSP

Adopting request controller architecture is a design-level choice that will ensure that an application's JSPs have the correct responsibilities. There are many techniques we can use inside JSPs themselves to make them more maintainable. Adopting MVC is about writing the right JSPs; we'll now look at some techniques to write JSPs right. One of the most important issues to understand is how includes are supported in JSP.

There is a real danger of code and markup duplication in JSP interfaces. Including common JSPs or JSP fragments where necessary can minimize this. This does not help to move code out of JSPs, or to achieve a true OO solution, but it can significantly enhance system maintainability. It is analogous to procedural code reuse.

Two Types of Includes

JSP supports two types of include: **static**, and **dynamic**. In a static include, the content of the included JSP fragment is inserted into the including JSP at translation time, and used along with that file's own content to build the Java source file that will be compiled. In a dynamic include, the request is passed to the specified URL, with its response being inserted into the page response. This means that the contents of a statically included file must be legal in the including file at the point at which it is included. Dynamic includes, however, need not even be JSPs; static HTML or Servlet output can also be included.

Static includes are performed using the `include` **directive**:

```
<%@ include file="pickList.jsp" %>
```

Dynamic includes are performed using the `include` **action**:

```
<jsp:include page="include.jsp" flush="true" />
```

The `flush` parameter is optional (although Tomcat 3.1 wrongly insists on it). In JSP 1.1 the default, and only legal, value for the `flush` parameter is `true` (we'll discuss this further shortly). The `<jsp:param>` element can be used as a subtag of `<jsp:include>` to pass data to the included page, as in the following JSP fragment:

```
<jsp:include page="include.jsp" flush="true" >
  <jsp:param name="newParam" value="extra" />
  <jsp:param name="existingParam" value="new value" />
</jsp:include>
```

The additional data will be available to the included page in the form of additional or overridden request parameters. In the example above, assume that the `newParam` parameter was not part of the request to the original page, while the `existingParam` parameter was. The included page will see the additional parameter, `newParam`, and the new value for `existingParam`. The scope of the new parameters will be the `<jsp:include>` call only; the new parameters will not be available after the include.

Because of limitations in the way dynamic includes work in JSP 1.1, static includes are the more useful of the two include types in practice. The main problem with dynamic includes is that the `<jsp:include>` action always causes a flush before the include.

> **This means that dynamically included pages can't cause redirection to an error page on an uncaught exception – a very serious problem.**

Dynamically included pages also have limited access to the response object; they cannot set headers (including cookies). Dynamic inclusion is also a performance overhead; static inclusion isn't really inclusion at all once the translation unit has been generated, so it has no performance penalty.

Another serious drawback with dynamic includes is that the means of communication between including and included page cannot be enforced at translation time, except for primitive types for which we can use <jsp:param>. Objects can only be communicated using a mechanism like setAttribute(), meaning that if an include is used incorrectly, the problem will show up as a null pointer exception at runtime. Static includes don't have this problem. If an included JSP fragment accesses one or more variables, pages including it won't compile unless those variables are in scope at the time of the include.

> **JSP 1.2 (as of the Proposed Final Draft) rectifies the flush problem of the dynamic include mechanism, by mandating that JSP engines respect the value of the flush attribute. Once implementations of JSP 1.2 become widely available, dynamic includes may become much more attractive.**

Using Static Includes

Because communication between including and included pages is checked at translation time, it is useful and acceptable to parameterize static includes using scripting variables. The scripting variables required should be documented in a hidden header comment in the statically included JSP fragments, as should any dependencies on session beans. Static includes are unlikely to be reusable outside a particular application, so such dependencies are not usually problematic.

Static includes are not complete JSPs in their own right. This should be reflected through a naming convention (the JSP 1.2 Proposed Final Draft suggests using a .jsf or .jspf extension) or a location convention. Perhaps best of all, static includes may be gathered together in a directory not made publicly accessible by the Servlet engine, ensuring that no requests are directed to them. Directories under /WEB-INF in a WAR are ideal. I gather static includes in the /WEB-INF/includes directory.

One potential drawback to using static includes must be noted. JSP defines no mechanism for letting pages know when static content they've included has changed. After translation, this content is compiled into self-contained implementation classes. So, when a statically included page fragment changes, remember to "touch" all the pages that include it (that is, update their last modification time), unless you are using a JSP engine that provides more sophisticated content management than the specification mandates. JRun 3.0 does reliably take care of this important piece of housekeeping.

Using JSP Beans

Request controller architecture removes **logic** from JSPs. We must also consider the problem of **data acquisition**.

The most obvious way to reduce the amount of Java code in a JSP is to use one or more **JSP beans**. This has been possible since the early days of JSP.

How best to use beans is not entirely clear-cut, and they are not the panacea one might at first think. There is some confusion in the way in which beans are supported in the JSP specification. A bean should really be a resource for the presentation of the page, but much emphasis has been given to mapping request parameters onto bean properties. This is essentially a JSP Model 1 approach, incompatible with a request controller architecture, and works poorly in complex applications.

Request parameters can be mapped onto JSP beans in two ways. Individual request parameters can be mapped onto a bean property using a <jsp:setProperty> action like this:

```
<jsp:setProperty name="bean" property="propertyName" param="paramName" />
```

Alternatively, all request properties can be mapped onto a bean in a single `<jsp:setProperty>` action like this:

```
<jsp:setProperty name="bean" property="*" />
```

In the latter case, remember that no exception will be thrown if there are request parameters that do not have matching bean properties. The bean will also need to check that all required attributes have been set by the mapping. Beans that process request parameters do not aspire to wide reusability, so tailoring them to handle a particular request structure using the `property="*"` syntax is generally best.

Although the `<jsp:setProperty>` action is annoyingly ignorant of its context, and doesn't automatically act on the current bean if it is invoked within a `<jsp:useBean>` action, it is good practice to limit use of `<jsp:setProperty>` to `<jsp:useBean>` actions.

> **However, remember that the contents of a `<jsp:useBean>` action are only executed if the bean is instantiated. If the bean already existed in the JSP's `PageContext`, scriptlets or `<jsp:setProperty>`, actions within the `<jsp:useBean>` action will be ignored.**

Beans in a well-engineered JSP interface usually fall into two types: **page beans**, which help in the presentation of a particular page and may process requests to it; and **session beans**, which provide common state across a user's session. These are entirely different in purpose, and should be considered separately. There is a third bean type: **application beans**, which are shared between all users of a web application to maintain global state. These are less commonly used, but can produce significant efficiency gains if used appropriately (for example, to maintain read-only data loaded only once on behalf of all users).

Both page beans and session beans are necessary when implementing non-trivial systems. Most systems will use one session bean to hold state, and one page bean for each page that presents a view of complex data.

Page Beans

A page bean is a model, with the JSP being a view. Page beans are closely integrated with the JSPs that use them. They will only be used on multiple pages if the same content must be presented in different formats. (This is, however, a frequent requirement.) Typically, page beans will define 'getter' methods for each piece of dynamic content displayed by the corresponding JSP. These getters may return primitive types, or more complex object types, which the JSPs will be responsible for displaying (possibly through the use of custom tags).

Page model beans may occasionally perform some request processing (usually the simple mapping of request parameters onto their attributes before exposing a model) but should not be used to handle complex page flow logic. (For example, they are not suited to handling redirection.) The approach I prefer is for page beans to be outputs of a controller, and merely hold data for JSPs, rather than play an active part in an application's workflow.

Session Beans

Session beans belong to a user's session within an application, not a page. They are not tied to presentation, but help hold references to enterprise resources and other data allowing a user session to maintain and cache state. For example, a session bean might be used to hold a user's real name and email address through a session, and a reference to a session EJB that could be used to obtain more information. Session beans should never be used to process requests.

Developers new to J2EE often confuse JSP session beans with stateful session EJBs. These are different in purpose, although there may be a one-to-one correspondence between JSP session beans and stateful session EJBs in many systems. Although JSP session beans are not directly concerned with page production, they should be *views* of or proxies for enterprise middleware, not enterprise middleware themselves. Stateful session EJBs *are* part of the enterprise middleware, although they perform processing for a particular client.

Application Beans

Application beans are still wider in scope than session beans. They maintain state for all users of an application. They are used less often than session beans, but can be useful to minimize memory usage and enhance performance, especially when many users require access to some data that is expensive to retrieve or compute.

Application beans are best used for read-only data. Using them to hold read-write data is a recipe for concurrency problems or synchronization bottlenecks. There is little need to use application beans to hold constant data for the application: this can be placed in the `web.xml` file of a web application and accessed using JNDI, or placed in `.properties` files following established Java convention. If the data to be held in an application bean is not web-specific, a singleton object will be more appropriate, and will ensure that the necessary data is available anywhere in the application without the need for extracting values from the `PageContext`.

> **Although the benefits of maintaining server-side state are well worthwhile, don't be tempted to cram large amounts of data into session objects. Any respectable application server or Servlet engine will provide server clustering, and cluster-wide preservation of HTTP session state. This allows successive requests to be directed to different servers in the event of the failure of a particular server, or network congestion, without loss of session state.**
>
> **Implementing this will mean capturing the state of all session objects (probably using Java serialization) and constantly passing it over the wire to ensure synchronization. Thus session objects should only hold data that is modest in storage demands and constantly in use, together with references to enterprise objects or keys that can be used to retrieve other data as required.**
>
> **If an application can be made stateless without severely impacting its design, it should be; this will improve performance and scalability. In some cases, session state (if it doesn't contain an excessive volume of data) can be held in a cookie. This approach is also highly scalable.**

Bean Configuration

Remember that JSP beans *are* beans. One way to add flexibility to a running system is to write GUI property editors for JSP beans. This can empower the business owners of the system and free developers from the need to perform minor maintenance.

JSP beans can be instantiated from a serialized file by setting the `beanName` attribute of the `<jsp:useBean>` tag to a value supported by the `java.beans.Beans.instantiate()` method, such as the following, which tries to instantiate the bean `mypackage.TestBean`:

```
<jsp:useBean id="test" scope="page" beanName="mypackage.TestBean" >
```

The Beans class will check for a serialized file of the form mypackage/TestBean.ser, and instantiate a bean from the CLASSPATH using new only if this fails.

For property editing to produce useful results, it is vital to make JSP beans as generic as possible. They should expose properties that control their behavior.

Dos and Don'ts

The most important rule with beans is that they shouldn't be used to generate HTML. Nor should they handle business logic that isn't specific to JSP presentation.

Because they get first shot at processing the values in the requests, page beans can be useful to provide data to custom tags. If request processing is really complicated, it is better centralized using the request controller pattern than handled by each JSP bean.

Using Custom Tags

The custom tag mechanism is a powerful feature of JSP introduced with version 1.1 that greatly increases our ability to keep logic in Java, while most markup generation remains in JSPs. Custom tags are particularly valuable in enabling JSP views to present complex data without being complicated by iteration and conditional logic.

Although custom tags are also implemented by Java classes, they differ significantly from beans:

❑ Tag handlers can create scripting variables that can be accessed by JSPs that use the tags they implement.

❑ Custom tags are usually intended for use in multiple JSPs. They are standard building blocks, not resources for one or two JSPs.

❑ Although they can access them, custom tags should not normally be concerned with the parameters to the JSPs that call them. Custom tags should have local context. Their behavior is controlled by the XML attributes they are given each time they appear, which may be dynamic.

The following example shows three different uses of one tag, which implements simple search functionality. In the first case, all parameters to the tag are static, so it will always perform the same search (although, of course, the results of its search may change over time):

```
<chap17:search query="whale" format="html"  maxResults="5"
               firstResult="0" />
```

In the second case, the query is obtained from the request to the current JSP:

```
<chap17:search query="<%=request.getParameter("query")%>"
               format="html"  maxResults="5" firstResult="0" />
```

This approach is questionable, as no validation is performed on the request parameter before it is passed to the tag.

In the third case, the tag is configured by parameters obtained from two beans: a page bean placed in the request by a controller, and a session bean holding the user's preferences:

```
<chap17:search
   query="<%=searchBean.getQuery()%>"
   format="<%=sessionBean.getFormat()%>"
   maxResults="<%=sessionBean.getMaxResults()%>"
   firstResult="<%=searchBean.getResultOffset()%>"
/>
```

The developer of the search tag may not have envisaged all these scenarios, but they all honor the contract between JSP and tag.

Custom tags are discussed in detail in Chapters 9 and 10. The following discussion assumes familiarity with their use, so please refer back to those chapters if necessary.

Categories of Tags

Custom tags usually fall into two categories: **generic**, and **application-specific**.

The difference is significant, and relates to implementation as well as usage. In general, since tag handlers are Java classes, we prefer not to generate HTML within them. However, a blanket ban is inappropriate.

Generic custom tags should be usable in a variety of contexts. Because markup generation tends to limit reusability, generic custom tags should not normally generate HTML. The actual markup they are used to produce may differ widely. Generic custom tags may increasingly come to be provided by specialists in custom tags. Examples include custom tags to access enterprise resources, such as databases, and custom tags that interpret their body content as a language more appropriate to a particular problem than JSP code.

Application-specific custom tags do not aspire to such wide reusability. They are the building blocks of one particular application. It may be appropriate for application-specific custom tags to generate HTML. The benefits of having all your HTML in the one place, so that a number of pages will change after a change to a single tag, can outweigh the problems of markup generation in tag handlers. My experience has also shown that it is simply unrealistic to ban markup generation from application-specific tag handlers. Generating markup from within Java code remains inelegant; unless the markup is trivial, a better solution is to read in a template file and substitute variables into it. (An abstract superclass could make this behavior available in a consistent way to a number of application-specific tags.)

Examples of application-specific tags include application-wide headers and footers with some dynamic content specified using attributes, and the formatting of complex objects unique to the application. Application-specific custom tags should still be made as generic as possible, through maximizing their potential for configuration at runtime.

Let's now look at some important uses of custom tags.

Model Tags

Generic custom tags are particularly well suited to making JSPs cleanly implement the model view controller pattern. This is an important and flexible use of custom tags that justifies detailed discussion.

Typically, such view tags will obtain the models they require from page beans. They will use the model data to provide values and control flow to JSP views, concealing access to the model and iteration over the model's contents. The standard data models defined in Swing are particularly useful, as they facilitate the sharing of UI code between Swing and JSP interfaces.

JSP tags providing views for the Swing `ListModel` and `TableModel` play a major role in the case study in the next chapter.

Translation Tags

Translation tags take their body content (the JSP or other content that appears between their start and end tags) and filter, translate, or interpret it. The variety of end results is almost limitless: typical examples are replacing the original content with a filtered version and writing it into the page output; or processing their body content multiple times. Translation tags are usually generic tags.

Another example of this type of tag suggested in the JSP 1.1 specification is a tag that executes SQL content and displays the results. This is a good indication of the power of translation tags, but it's not a good design approach. As we have seen, JSPs should be far removed from SQL in J2EE architecture.

Other examples include tags interpreting another language themselves (perhaps ASP, to incorporate fragments of a legacy system), and tags that might suppress their body content depending on context (for example, if a user had insufficient system privileges).

A particularly useful tag of this type is a tag to take XML body content and render it using an XSLT stylesheet specified as an attribute.

Tags as Application Building Blocks

Application building block tags are application specific, and may generate HTML. Such tags vary widely in character, and don't tend to fall easily into standard patterns.

Consider implementing personalization on a complex web site. One approach would be to use dynamic includes, and build up an interface using small, reusable JSPs. This is viable in JSP 1.2 (but not JSP 1.1, due to its flushing issues with dynamic includes). However, a better alternative might be to use custom tags as the building blocks of the interface. Communication with them, using attributes of any type, is more sophisticated and type-safe than communication between JSPs using dynamic includes, and the advantage of modularity remains.

Third Party Tag Libraries

Significant effort is going into developing standard tag libraries. Leveraging standard code benefits everyone. Monitor the availability of standard tag libraries for your industry or application type; http://www.jsptags.com is a good starting point. Alternatively, there's Taglibs from Apache: http://jakarta.apache.org/taglibs/index.html.

Dos and Don'ts

Elegant as custom tags often are, they can still be abused. Using too many custom tags can produce JSPs that are incomprehensible to a reader first viewing a system who may understand JSP, but not the ways in which a complex tag library works. This is justifiable only if it is demonstrably more effective than any alternative.

As we have seen, deciding whether or not it is appropriate for a particular tag to generate HTML (or XHTML) is a thorny issue. Avoid it if possible, but don't be rigid.

Tag handlers, like all objects, should be coded to be as generic as possible. A well-designed tag will provide a single solution for a requirement that appears in many JSPs. Experience shows that further uses are likely to suggest themselves once a tag is in use. By designing a tag to address too narrow an interpretation of the initial requirement and not carefully considering how to make it useful in as wide a variety of contexts as is reasonably possible, much of the tag's potential may be lost, and the effort put into developing it not fully leveraged. The analysis phase should try to establish common ground between problems. Otherwise, you'll end up trying to merge three different approaches to the same problem, and you're likely to end up with code duplication.

Try to make tags configurable by attributes (which may be optional) and, possibly, by descendant tags that provide additional output depending on their context. When designing a tag, as when designing a library class, try to envisage all its likely uses and allow for them. If a number of tag handlers have significant commonality in their implementation, define an abstract base class implementing the common functionality.

Tag handlers can be made generic in four main ways:

❑   Using tag attributes to configure the tag

❑   Making the tag process its body content

❑   Using nested tags to configure the outer tag (for an example, see the `<views:jspTable>` tag in the next chapter)

❑   Having the tag read and customize an HTML template

Choosing between these mechanisms is the trickiest (and most rewarding) issue in designing reusable tags. Nesting can be very powerful, but can make your tags harder to use. If you use an HTML template, you will probably need to define a means of substituting variables. However, you can then get different behavior from the same tag without modifying its implementation by passing in the template reference as an attribute.

The abilities of tag handlers to play havoc with the host page's `request` and `response` objects (for example, to cause the response to be redirected), and to return values causing the JSP engine to skip evaluation of the remainder of the page, should be used with extreme caution. Will this behavior be obvious to readers of your JSPs? Although legitimate at times (for example in a tag handler that checks if users are logged in and redirects to a login page if they are not), it resembles the dreaded `goto`, exhibiting irrational behavior.

Handling Iteration

JSPs often need to iterate over data. It is acceptable to use scriptlets to do this. However, if the iteration involves not merely access to multiple items of data to render the page, but other processing logic, one of the two following approaches may be preferable:

❑   Define a custom tag that handles the iteration. The tag handler will then perform the processing logic with each iteration, before processing its body content.

❑   Wrap the access to each element of the iteration in a bean, and make the bean perform the processing logic required before returning the result.

For example, consider the following code:

```
<% for (int i = 0; i < bean.getFields(); i++) {
    if (bean.isSpecialField(i)) {
```

```
        response.setCookie...
        LogHandler.Log(...
        // Several more lines of code setting application state
    } %>
    <input type="text" name="<%=bean.getName(i)%>"
            value="<%=bean.getValue(i)%>" />
<% } %>
```

The handling of the special case is not concerned with presentation, but cookie generation and auditing. It doesn't belong in the JSP. A better solution is to modify the bean so that one of the methods takes any additional parameters required to handle the special case. I've modified the beans `getValue()` method to take the JSPs response object as a parameter. Now the special case can be implemented by the bean, and is transparent to the JSP:

```
<% for (int i = 0; i < bean.getFields(); i++) { %>
    <input type="text" name="<%=bean.getName(i)%>"
            value="<%=bean.getValue(i, response)%>" />
<% } %>
```

Handling Conditional Logic

The obvious way to handle conditional logic in JSPs is using scriptlets. For example, the following code will pre-populate a form field with a user's name if it is already held by the application, and distinguishes between unregistered users who arrived at this page by different routes:

```
<% String name = ""; %>
<% if (pageBean.getUserWasInvited ()) { %>
    Please enter your name as it appeared on your letter of invitation
<% } else if (pageBean.getUserIsRegistered()) { %>
    Please verify that your name appears correctly below
    <% name = pageBean.getName(); %>
<% } else { %>
    Please enter your name
<% } %>
<input type="text" name="name" value="<%=name%>" />
```

Sometimes, expressions can be used to handle simple conditionals, through use of the ternary operator. For example, the following expression is used in the case study in the next chapter to output commas only in between columns in a table, and not at the end of each row:

```
<%=(column < tableModel.getColumnCount() - 1) ? "," : "" %>
```

The ability of scriptlets and expressions to handle conditional logic is too useful to ignore. However, a mass of conditionals can quickly make a JSP verbose and hard to maintain. Even the simple `if`/`else` example above already requires a few seconds to comprehend. If the conditional statements are broken up by lengthy blocks of HTML (a common occurrence without careful design), or if there was a longer chain of `if-else` statements, it could quickly become unreadable.

If conditional logic is bloating scriptlets, consider the following alternative approaches:

❑ Use more JSPs. If a JSP produces two or more very different page structures, move the conditional logic out of the JSP into a controller and replace it with two or more simple JSPs.

- ❑ If the bodies of conditional statements are large, making the whole page hard to follow, consider replacing the bodies with static includes.

- ❑ Expose content as XML, using XSLT stylesheets determined by the conditional logic (see *Using Styled XML* below).

- ❑ Handle the conditional logic in a page-view bean. The getter methods of the bean may return different values depending on the page's context.

It can be easy to get results using these techniques. For example, consider code that performs the following logic for every form field, obtaining it from a session object if that object is non-null, otherwise assigning the field no value:

```
<% if (object != null && object.getFieldValue(fieldName) != null) %>
  <input type="text"
    name="<%=fieldName%>"
    value="<%=object.getFieldValue(fieldName)%>" />
<% } else { %>
  <input type="text" name="<%=fieldName%>" />
<% } %>
```

Although this looks relatively harmless, in a form with many fields it can pose a major problem to page maintainability. An easy and effective solution is to define a page bean that acts as a proxy for the object that may be null. The bean can then perform the test and return the appropriate value without the JSP performing any tests.

The necessary method in the bean will look like this:

```
public String getFieldValue(String fieldName) {
  if (object != null)
    return object.getFieldValue(fieldName);
  return "";
}
```

Every occurrence of the conditional expression in the JSP is now replaced by the following:

```
<input type="text"
       name="<%=fieldName%>"
       value="<%=bean.getFieldValue(fieldName)%>" />
```

This is both more readable and more maintainable. The conditional logic can be altered in one place without the need for repeated editing. This is, of course, a very simple example, but this pattern can be used in many contexts.

Using Styled XML

It's important to recognize when JSP is *not* the ideal means of rendering content. We have already considered the alternative of a Servlet, which is preferable where the generated output is not human-readable. Another alternative is to present XML data as HTML using XSLT. This is a particularly good approach for rendering non-HTML content such as WML. A custom tag can perform the transform in an elegant way.

This use of islands of XML is a tradeoff between elegance and pragmatism. Despite its appeal, there are still performance issues in presenting *all* content as XML and performing server-side transforms on it. (The alternative of performing the transforms on the client presently works only in Internet Explorer, which is not fully compliant with XSLT standards.) XSLT is still difficult for non-programmers to write, and no satisfactory authoring tools are available as yet. Using XML and XSLT for those parts of the document that are most easily expressed as XML, however, can reduce, rather than increase, complexity, and will have little impact on performance.

> See the XSLT Programmer's Reference *by Michael Kay (Wrox ISBN 1-861-003-12-9) for detailed discussion of what can be achieved using XML and XSLT.*

When to Use Custom Superclasses for JSPs

JSPs have always had the ability to extend a class of their own choice, rather than the container's. This custom superclass can perform any kind of functionality behind the scenes.

Common uses of custom superclasses are to handle the request before the code in JSPs extending them is invoked, and to define additional implicit objects (although this is usually better done through custom tags).

Imagine an implementation of data binding. Form fields with special names could be bound to properties of objects in the HTTP session. A custom superclass, `DataBoundHttpJspPage`, could look in the request for such fields and attempt to map them to the relevant objects using reflection. This would be transparent to JSPs extending it. They would sacrifice none of their functionality to use this feature.

Custom superclasses must fulfill the following requirements:

❑ They should implement the `HttpJspPage interface`.

❑ They should declare all of the methods in the `Servlet` interface to be `final`.

❑ They should invoke the `_jspService()` method in their `service()` method.

❑ Their `init(ServletConfig)` method should store the configuration, make it available via the `getServletConfig()` method, then invoke `jspInit()`. This enables JSPs to perform custom initialization if necessary.

❑ Their destroy method should invoke `jspDestroy()`. This enables JSPs to perform custom cleanup if necessary.

Custom superclasses should not be used if there is a simpler alternative. Using them can make the behavior of pages harder to understand and may interfere with the ability of the JSP engine to perform optimization. Remember that by telling the JSP engine that a particular JSP should be derived from your superclass, you deprive it of the power to derive the JSP from an optimized superclass of its own. In my experience, it is usually better to use a request controller architecture than to rely on JSP superclasses.

Standard Abstractions for Common Objects

The JSP expression mechanism is geared towards string content, and objects for which the `toString()` method will produce a desirable representation of their state, such as `Integer` objects.

Some objects are more complex, but nevertheless standard: consider hyperlinks. In fact, they're not even specific to JSP presentation; a Swing GUI could present a hyperlink in its interface.

Often it makes sense to define reusable objects for such common concepts. For example, if we define a `Link` object with `getTitle()` and `getURL()` methods, we can return it in a single call to a page view bean, and use it as a parameter to an object such as a tag handler.

Other candidate objects for such standard classes include images and checkboxes. The `NameValueModel` introduced in the case study in the next chapter is an example of a very general model that is useful in many situations.

Handling Exceptions

Perhaps the easiest way to complicate the code and confuse an HTML designer trying to manipulate a working JSP is to use JSPs to perform exception handling. Fortunately, this is seldom a good idea.

Of the many good features introduced in JSP 1.0, the error page mechanism was perhaps the most welcome. (This is the mechanism that allows an error page to be specified, to which the request will be redirected in the event of an uncaught exception.) There are two types of exceptions that JSP developers will be concerned with:

- ❑ Application exceptions that are possible in normal operation and do not cause a fatal error conditions

- ❑ Unrecoverable exceptions reflecting an unexpected system failure such as inability to contact a database or a remote object such as an EJB

Application exceptions should be concealed from JSPs through being handled in request controllers or JSP beans or tag handlers.

Unrecoverable exceptions can and should be ignored by JSP developers (so long as developers remember to declare error pages to handle them and display appropriate user-oriented information about the system failure). Suppose a session JSP bean cannot connect to an underlying session EJB. There is nothing the JSP can reasonably do to handle this situation: the best approach is to redirect the response to a page apologizing for an internal system error. This behavior can be achieved simply by declaring the affected methods in JSP beans and tag handlers to re-throw the underlying `RemoteException`.

Documenting the JSP Layer

All experienced Java developers use Javadoc, and know just how helpful it is as projects grow in size and require collaboration among a significant number of developers. Unfortunately, JSPs offer no such built-in documentation support.

The first step to a well-documented JSP system is to place Java code in Servlets, beans, and tag handlers rather than JSPs. This will enable us to use Javadoc to generate documentation for most of our interface logic. However, we require strict documentation standards to fill the inevitable gaps.

Each of the components of a JSP interface requires a different type of documentation:

- ❑ **JSPs**
  JSPs require code-level documentation in the form of hidden comments. These use the special syntax:

647

```
<%-- text of comment
     which can be on several lines
--%>
```

Unlike HTML comments (delimited by `<!--` and `-->`), they will not be included in generated pages. A technical specification for the system should also discuss the parameters required by each JSP and page transitions. Any required parameters should be listed in a header in each JSP.

❑ **JSP beans**

JSP beans can be documented with Javadoc.

❑ **Custom tags**

Custom tags require several types of documentation, most of which will be outside the files that implement them:

❑ Javadoc for the tag handler classes.

❑ Documentation of any scripting variables they define.

❑ Documentation of any 'side effects' they may have. These include redirection of the response, and causing the remainder of the page to be skipped in some circumstances.

❑ Documentation of the attributes they require. XML tag library descriptors (TLDs) are too verbose for this purpose, and are not ideal reading matter for page designers.

❑ Example JSPs can be very useful in showing the potential of custom tags.

Tool Support

Given the level of interest in JSP authoring, present authoring tools are disappointingly immature. A number of Java IDEs provide useful, but limited, assistance in writing JSPs. For example, Sun's free Forte for Java Community Edition 2.0 has a JSP editor that clearly delimits scriptlet content from markup, and can even compile JSP code (see http://www.sun.com/forte/ffj/index.html). This is very handy in avoiding frustrating syntax errors (such as failure to terminate a scriptlet). But integration with HTML editors and more sophisticated functionality is still lacking.

However, many vendors are working hard on the problem, and in the next generation of tools we can hope for major progress. Areas in which tool support could make JSP development easier and promote good practice include:

❑ Support for writing JSP beans in conjunctions with JSPs. Some vendors are already providing a rudimentary form of this.

❑ Support for request controller architectures.

❑ Sophisticated support for using custom tags.

Watch the major Java IDEs such as Forte, JBuilder, Visual Café, and Visual Age for further progress. Much better vertical integration for developing J2EE applications can also be expected from initiatives such as WebGain Studio (http://www.webgain.com/). This is a new product supported by BEA Systems, which is built on existing 'best of breed' tools such as DreamWeaver and Visual Café, and aims to provide a suite of tools to facilitate EJB and JSP development. Although it integrates most easily with the WebLogic application server, it is intended to support J2EE standards, rather than tie in to any one deployment environment.

Whether using sophisticated tools or not, it is usually a good idea to design and test the desired HTML code before beginning the final phase of JSP coding. It is *much* easier to resolve issues such as browser incompatibilities by editing static pages than by editing JSPs, however well designed they may be.

Coding Standards for Maintainable JSPs

This section attempts to take the techniques already discussed and distill them into a set of guidelines for JSP authoring. These guidelines do *not* aim to be hard and fast rules.

Design Principles and Coding Style

- ❑ The whole of the JSP/JSP-bean presentation tier should be as thin and simple as possible. If it is impossible to achieve a thin JSP tier, it indicates shortcomings in the overall design. The business logic layer probably does not provide a consistent level of abstraction, or rich enough functionality.

- ❑ Remember that most JSPs should be read-only views, with a page bean providing the model. The way in which content is presented in a JSP may change as the desired HTML changes; the structure of the content itself changes more rarely, and it is acceptable for such changes to require updates to a bean.

- ❑ Think vertically. First identify the data that must be presented by a JSP, then design the appropriate bean to provide a model for the data. JSPs and JSP beans should be designed together.

- ❑ Business logic should be removed from JSPs as far as is reasonably possible. Business logic not specific to HTML presentation should live in the business logic layer or a non UI-specific presentation layer. Although such logic could easily be placed in JSP beans, this would be poor design as such business logic should be available to *all* clients, not merely JSPs. HTTP-specific logic (for example, cookie manipulation) belongs in beans or support classes, not JSPs.

- ❑ For non-trivial sets of pages, think and design in terms of *groups* of JSPs collaborating to provide a discrete piece of functionality, rather than treating each JSP as an individual piece of work. This will help in identifying session beans and whether the request controller design pattern may be appropriate.

- ❑ Try to place conditional logic in controllers rather than in views. For example, if a substantial part of a JSP varies according to a condition, the JSP is a candidate for refactoring, with a controller forwarding requests to two separate pages, each of which includes the common parts. (See *Refactoring: Improving the Design of Existing Code,* by Martin Fowler (Addison-Wesley, 1999, ISBN: 0201485672) for an excellent introduction to the aims and benefits of refactoring.)

- ❑ Follow standard naming and location conventions for JSPs, included files, JSP beans, and classes implementing custom tags. I use the following conventions:

  - ❑ JSP controller: xxxxController.jsp.

  - ❑ Included JSPs: gathered together in the /WEB-INF/includes directory. Note also the JSP 1.2 Proposed Final Draft suggestion of using a .jsf or .jspf extension.

  - ❑ JSP page model beans: <pagename>Bean.

  - ❑ JSP session beans: xxxxSessionBean.

❏ Tag handlers and related classes: xxxxTag, xxxxTagExtraInfo.

❏ Page import directives should be avoided in JSPs. The use of imports encourages the instantiation of classes other than JSP beans. The more verbose fully qualified syntax serves as a deterrent to this. Instead of issuing a directive like this:

```
<%@ page import="com.java.util.*" %>
```

refer to each class in the required package by its fully qualified name: for example

```
<% java.util.List l = new java.util.LinkedList (); %>
```

❏ JSPs should not directly access request parameters. Request controllers or beans should perform such processing and expose processed model data. Accessing request parameters requires careful error checking; this is likely to be overlooked in JSPs, and will complicate them if it is not.

❏ JSPs should not access properties files, or use JNDI. JSP beans may access properties (for example, to support internationalization).

❏ If a JSP bean cannot have all its properties mapped from the page request, try to set properties within the <jsp:useBean> tag. This ensures that the bean will be appropriately initialized before it is used, and maximizes readability. Include also within the <jsp:useBean> tag any scriptlets required to initialize the bean.

❏ Avoid designing pages that both present a form and process its results. This tends to lead to confusing conditionals depending on the page's purpose in its context. Extra JSPs are cheap.

❏ Avoid code duplication in JSPs. The need for code duplication is an indication of poor design. Refactor the duplicated functionality into an included JSP, bean, or custom tag to make it reusable. Favor static includes over dynamic includes.

❏ JSP beans should never generate HTML. Java is not well suited to HTML generation, and JSPs were designed to avoid this central drawback of Servlets. Tag extension classes should not generate HTML without good reason.

❏ Using out.println() to generate page content should be avoided in JSPs. Using this syntax encourages thinking of JSPs as programs rather than web pages, and is likely to confuse an HTML designer editing a JSP.

❏ The JSP tier should *not* access data directly; this includes JDBC database access and EJB access. Beans used in the JSPs may access session EJBs or other objects in the business logic layer, although it's usually better to obtain the necessary data before constructing the beans. However, even JSP beans should not access entity EJBs or use JDBC directly to access system data sources. It's best to retrieve all data required to display a JSP view *before* the view is rendered: otherwise there is a risk that a data access problem might break page generation mysteriously.

❏ Scriptlets should not exceed 5 lines in length. There are situations in which scriptlets cannot be avoided; accept these, but only after considering all genuine alternatives.

❏ JSPs should not instantiate complex read-write objects other than JSP beans. This risks giving JSPs the ability to perform inappropriate business logic.

❏ JSP session beans should not contain excessive amounts of data. This is a performance issue.

❑ If `<jsp:forward>` or `<jsp:include>` is used, and primitive values must be communicated to the external page, use one or more `<jsp:param>` subelements. If this is not possible, consider using a static include instead of communicating objects via `setAttribute()`, which risks unpleasant surprises at runtime.

❑ Custom tags should be used where appropriate to remove logic from JSPs.

❑ `<jsp:forward>` should be used with caution. It amounts to a JSP equivalent of a `goto`, and can make page behavior hard to comprehend. A controller page is an exception to this rule. Forwarding from pages other than controllers also violates the principle that a JSP is a view; if the JSP does not know how to respond to the request it was passed, there is probably an error in the design of the system.

❑ In general, declarations or scriptlets should *not* be used to create variables referred to throughout a JSP. State within a JSP should be held within beans. Custom tags may, however, legitimately declare scripting variables.

❑ Hidden comments should be used to prevent comments bloating HTML output. Document not only the handling of dynamic content, but also any complex markup. This is likely to cause more confusion to readers than appropriately used expressions and custom tags.

❑ Avoid exception handling in the JSP that causes the exception.

❑ Each JSP should use an error page to handle exceptions that it cannot recover from. Exceptions should be caught in the JSP tier (but *not* the JSP itself) if it is still possible to produce a valid page. `RemoteExceptions` and other system errors are examples of exceptions that should simply propagate to an error page.

❑ In JSP error pages, use HTML comments to display a stack trace of the exception passed to the page. This is very helpful in debugging, and, if a custom tag is developed to display the stack trace, a single configuration option can be used to suppress the logging in production. Of course, the most important action to take on an error condition is to log it, and perhaps publish it as an event. This will enable a listener to perform any required action, such as e-mail the operations team if the error indicates an urgent, rectifiable, problem such as a network failure, or e-mail the development team if the cause is more likely a software bug. Of course such logging and event publishing should occur well below the JSP layer.

❑ `jspInit()` and `jspDestroy()` should only be overridden in a JSP if they produce significant performance gains. Using these methods makes a JSP more like a Servlet (a program) and less like a web page. Acquiring and relinquishing resources is the business of Servlets, JSP beans, and tag handlers, not JSPs, so there should be no need for cleanup. However, if necessary, it is possible to cordon off these methods so that they don't affect designers subsequently working on the JSP.

❑ Although it seems obvious, **hacking must be strictly avoided**. Hacking is bad enough in Java code, but quick hacks to JSPs are a maintenance nightmare, and quickly lead to an excessive amount of Java code in JSPs. The correct approach is to ensure that throughout the product life-cycle, the architecture and the functionality evolve together. To ensure this it is preferable to make changes to JSP beans (and even the business logic layer) rather than do a quick fix to JSPs that compromises the division between presentation and content, and correct location of business logic.

❑ Methods and inner classes should not be defined in JSPs without very good reason. The kind of logic behind a method is better placed in a JSP bean.

Formatting JSPs

The most important rule is to think of JSPs as HTML or XHTML documents. Follow the standards for markup formatting in use within your organization; these will probably include guidelines for indentation and overall layout (for example, using a blank line in the source file to mirror the use of a <p/> tag).

Format code with <% and %> on every line of scriptlets, except for lengthy scriptlets (say to perform initialization). This reduces the likelihood of frustrating errors with unbalanced escaping, avoids excessive white space, and helps reinforce the crucial point that JSPs are markup, not Java. This formatting style works best with Sun's recommended Java coding conventions, with the opening { of a compound statement on the same line as the conditional or other control flow expression that requires it.

The following looks verbose, and is hard to follow:

```
<%
if (condition)
{
%>
  Condition was true<br/>
<%
}
else
{
%>
  Condition was false<br/>
<%
}
%>
```

This is much more readable (and produces an identical compiled page):

```
<% if (condition) { %>
  Condition was true<br/>
<% } else { %>
  Condition was false<br/>
<% } %>
```

Note that the else keyword is on the same line as the close of the if compound statement:

```
<% } else { %>
```

You *must* use this condensed style for if/else statements and try/catch blocks. JSPs containing code like this will fail to compile:

```
<% try { %>
  ...
<% } %>
<% catch (Exception ex) { %>
  ...
<% } %>
```

If the catch statement and the close of the try block are consolidated like this, the code will compile:

```
<% } catch(Exception ex) { %>
```

The reason for this is that JSP engines will translate this JSP into a Java source file with an `out.println()` statement to preserve white space between the closing brace of the `try` block and the `catch` statement. This is a syntax error, as it means that the `try` and `catch` blocks are separated from each other. This affects all JSP engines I have seen. The following is the output from this code in JRun 3.0:

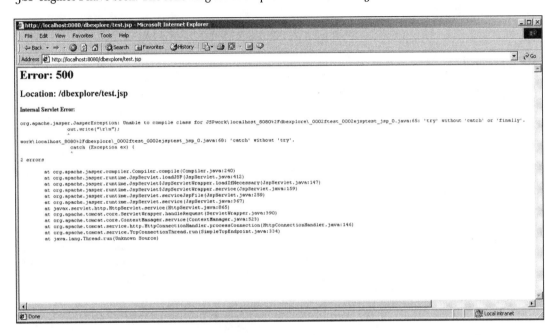

Fortunately, this error message almost makes sense: the output of many engines processing this page fragment will not.

Indent code within compound statements, as in the examples above. The following, without indentation, is hard to read:

```
<% if (condition) { %>
Condition was true
<% } else { %>
Condition was false
<% } %>
```

Using normal Java indentation (as in the earlier examples above) makes the code far more readable. Since JSPs should normally preserve HTML indentation, deeply nested Java indentation may create a conflict. The solution to this dilemma is to avoid using scriptlets to perform complex conditional logic and nested iteration.

Indent subelements of custom tags, and custom tag content if it would otherwise create a long line. Compare these two fragments. Which is the more readable?

```
<mytags:outer>
   <mytags:inner>
```

```
        This is inner content
    </mytags:inner>
  </mytags:outer>
```

```
  <mytags:outer>
  <mytags:inner>
  This is inner content
  </mytags:inner>
  </mytags:outer>
```

Summary

Writing maintainable JSPs is hard, but the effort involved is well worthwhile. Poorly designed JSP interfaces are costly to maintain and insufficiently responsive to business needs; well designed JSP interfaces cleanly separate presentation and content.

We've seen in this chapter that there are several requirements and best practices for developing maintainable JSPs:

❑ The first requirement is a well-engineered J2EE architecture, and an understanding of how the web tier fits into it. It's impossible to write a clean web interface without a solid underlying implementation of the necessary business logic.

❑ In the web tier itself, consider using the model view controller design pattern, so that your JSPs can cleanly handle the presentation of data without being complicated with control logic. Consider using technologies such as XML/XSLT to complement JSPs if they are more appropriate to render your content.

❑ Another key requirement is an understanding of how to leverage features of JSP that enable us to separate presentation and context: most importantly, JSP beans and tag handlers.

❑ With this understanding, we are in a position to enforce strict coding standards. The key goal is to minimize the amount of Java code used in JSPs. JSP is dangerously powerful, and discipline is required if we are to avoid producing un-maintainable mixes of markup and Java scriptlets. This chapter attempts to provide coding standards for writing maintainable JSPs that provide this discipline.

❑ Finally, we must allow for the entire product lifecycle. Throughout the product lifecycle, the architecture and the functionality should remain in sync. If changes are required to JSP beans (and even session EJBs) to ensure this, this is preferable to a quick fix to JSPs that compromises the division between presentation and content and correct location of business logic.

In the next chapter, we'll be applying these guidelines as we go through an example application.

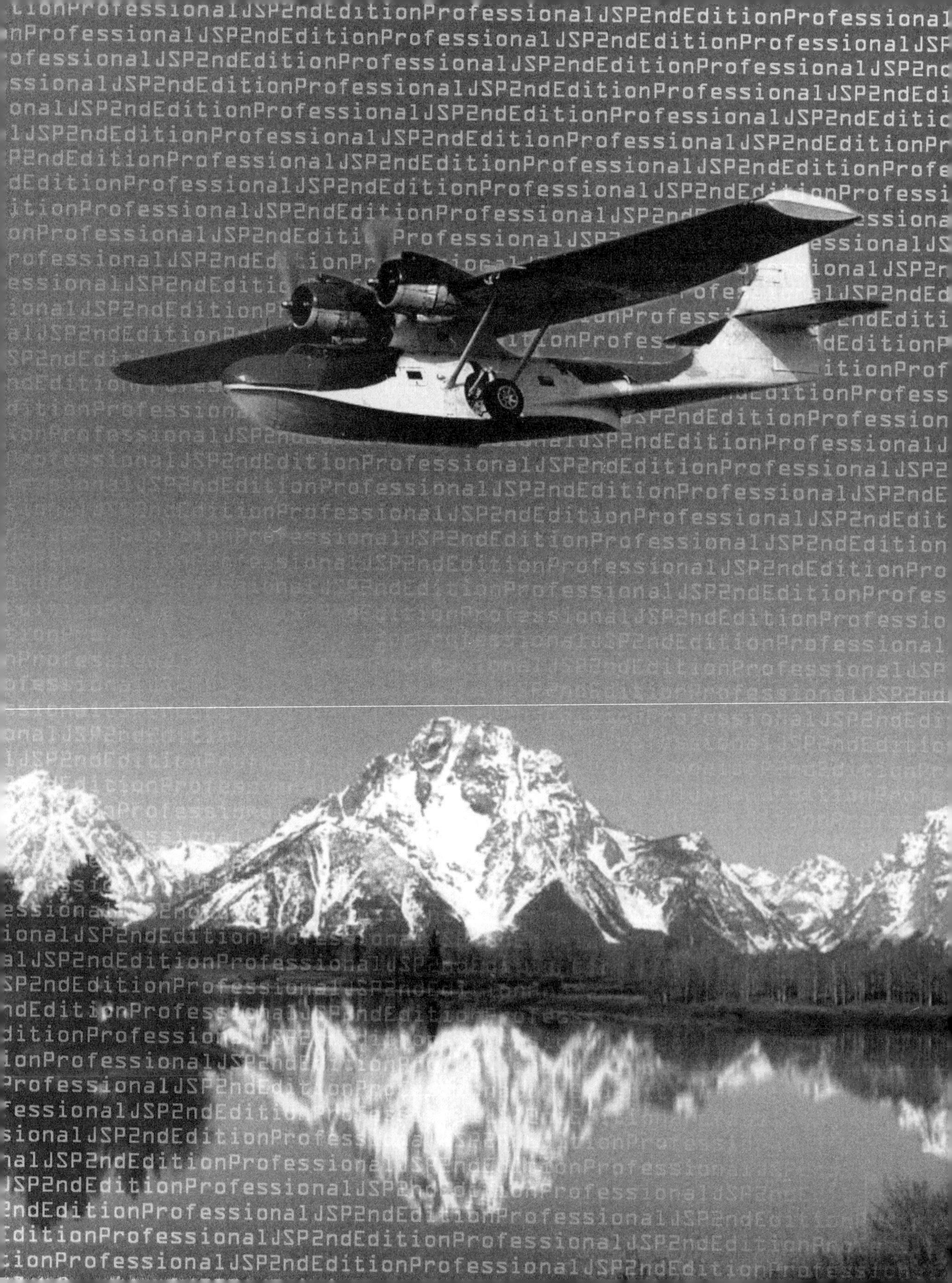
ProfessionalJSP2ndEdition

Case Study: A Maintainable Database Explorer

In the previous chapter, we looked at how to develop maintainable JSPs. Let us now take this advice on board, and present a practical example.

The application I have chosen to implement is a database explorer: a JSP view of a relational database that enables the viewing of any table and the results of any query in a number of different formats.

Although this is a simple application, the challenge is to implement it to be both maintainable and extensible.

For this example, we used the example database `music1.mdb` file provided with j2sdkee1.2.1 with the JDBC-ODBC bridge and a system DSN of `music`; however any database with JDBC support will do. You'll have to set up the DSN yourself, or use an existing one. Full deployment details follow the code.

Requirements

The requirement is for a web interface to allow users to browse the contents of relational databases. It will enable a user to connect to a database by specifying a JDBC driver and URL. The application will then allow users to see all the tables defined in the database, choose any table, and work with its data. It will also be possible for the user to enter SQL queries and see the tabular data they produce. It must be easy at any point during a user session for the user to disconnect from one database and connect to another.

Users will be allowed to choose the way in which they view data. Three views will be required in the first phase of development:

❑ A tabular view showing the table's content in a clear, read-only format

❑ A CSV (comma-separated variable) view allowing data to be cut and pasted into a spreadsheet or text file

❑ An editable view, allowing any row to be updated

Initially, functionality will be more important than presentation, but it is essential that it is easy to improve the presentation of the JSP views without requiring heavy technical input.

It is likely that there will be future requirements for additional views: a number of XML views, and a Microsoft Excel format view which will enable the user to download content without viewing it in her browser. Each view page must allow the user to navigate to any other available view of the same data. Until a new view is selected, the current view will be the default during all browsing.

There may also be a requirement in the next phase of development for a Swing applet to allow a more responsive interface, so it is important that the data objects are not tied to JSP presentation.

The first phase of the system need not persist user preferences between sessions, although this will be a later requirement.

Another long-term requirement is support for data sources other than relational databases. These might include directories accessed using JNDI.

The following is a sample walk through of the required functionality.

On first accessing the application, the user will be asked to provide information about the required database connection:

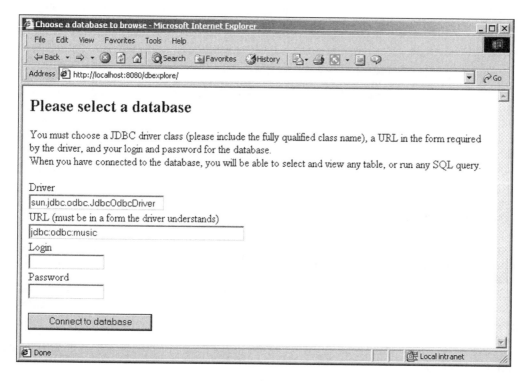

Once valid input is submitted, the user will be prompted to choose a table or enter an SQL query before viewing actual data:

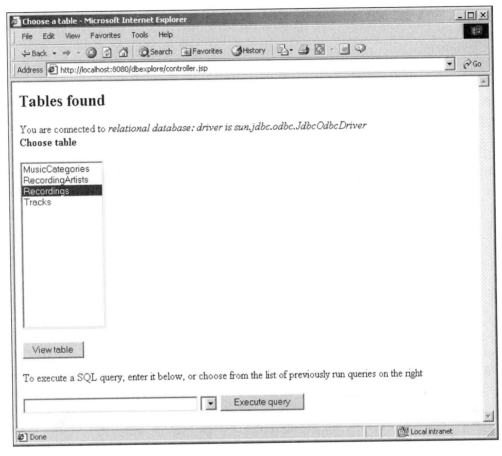

After choosing a table, the user will be able to navigate between different views of data, with the ability to choose different tables or queries at any point. The following is a typical data view, and includes the navigation links that will be available throughout the application:

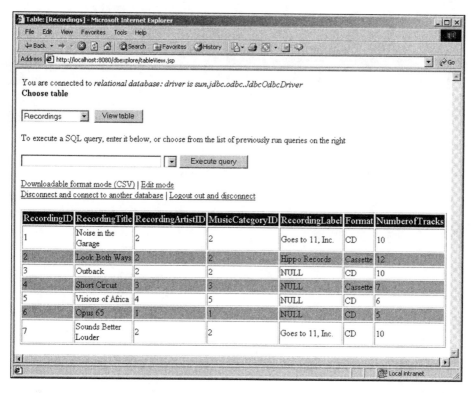

When users have finished browsing this or any other database they wish to connect to, they will be able to log out of the system, which will close any open resources and produce a confirmation page:

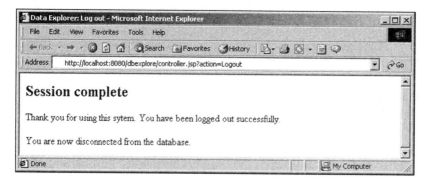

Design

The first step in the development cycle is for the JSP/Java developer to ask the business to produce a walkthrough of the pages: something similar but more detailed than these screenshots. This walkthrough will also define the required error handling. This will enable the developer to produce a proof of concept early in the project. Real world applications have risks. How difficult will it be to develop the most complex parts of their functionality? Will performance be satisfactory? Early proof of concept development enables these risks to be attacked and measured early in the project lifecycle, and is an important step in an iterative development process.

Complementing an understanding of page flow is the use of a state diagram, a very useful way of understanding and documenting the behavior of web applications. (Note that a state diagram is distinct from a page flow diagram. An application's state transitions may not correspond to the page flow of a user session.) The following state diagram shows the states the database explorer transitions through, and the legal transitions from each state:

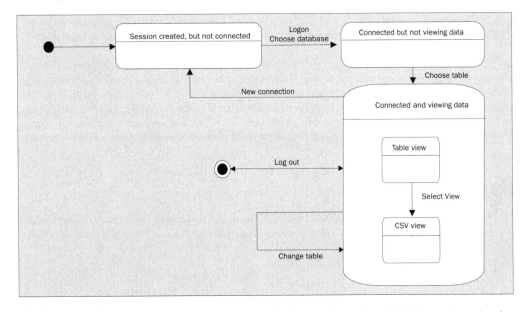

Working in parallel with the programmers, a web designer will produce HTML templates for the pages. Once the page flow is agreed and correctly implemented, these HTML templates will be made dynamic by the addition of the necessary JSP code. It is vital that the resulting JSPs contain a minimum of logic, so that they will be intelligible to page designers required to make ongoing changes to the rendering of the data. (The actual HTML I've written is very simple, as it is a side issue here. Imagine it's the output of the proof of concept phase.)

The first important technical design decision is to identify the application objects. (In a real project an architect rather than a JSP developer will probably take this decision.) We will need a data source object and one or more views that make it available to a GUI, and a number of JSPs to present the data. We will take the view that the JSPs are merely views of data exposed by middleware components; JSPs will not directly access the system data objects.

We must take a vertical view of the architecture and decide where each component belongs. The data source object clearly belongs in the enterprise resource abstraction layer. There is little workflow logic in this application beyond the required page flow, so the business logic layer doesn't have a major role. However, this is not to say that the JSPs will contain much of the application's logic. There is a clear need for a non UI-specific presentation layer. Remember that the requirements call for a Swing interface to be supported in the future, and some views of the data (such as the Excel view) that cannot be rendered by JSPs. This layer will not merely provide data for JSPs, but may service any GUI. It will consist of a number of models of the system's data.

We will use the `views` tag library, described shortly, to enable us to use Swing data models where possible. This will enable us to generate markup dynamically without heavy use of scriptlets, and will ensure that as much of the system's implementation as possible is independent of JSP technology.

661

User preferences will be held in a session bean. This will also hold a copy of the required data model for each user. Because the session bean can hold data models that change with the session state, there is no requirement for page beans. (Usually, a page bean would hold the model data for each view.) This reflects the fact that all the application's views display the same data structure, which is therefore part of the application rather than unique to any page.

Due to the likelihood of additional views being added, using the request controller pattern maximizes flexibility. It means that when additional views are required, no page flow logic needs to be included in them.

Unlike the code examples shown when we first introduced the request controller pattern, this application is implemented using a JSP controller. (This is both to illustrate an alternative approach, and because an application using a JSP controller is a little easier to implement and deploy.) It also uses a special `action` parameter, rather than its mapped URL, to determine the handler for each request. The controller loads handler classes dynamically, based on the value of the action parameter, ensuring that application functionality can be extended by adding new request handlers.

Implementation

Because of the decoupling of presentation from data source, it is possible to consider presentation (JSP and supporting classes) and data sources separately. Once the interfaces are established, it will be possible for different developers (in a complex real-world application, different teams) to work in parallel on these two main divisions of the system.

Since we are primarily concerned with JSP here, let's start with the presentation code. This involves cooperating JSPs and Java classes, which we'll look at in turn as we follow a typical page flow through the application. We can assume that a `DataSource` interface will expose information about the current data source, including a `NameValueModel` (a type of `ListModel`) of available tables, and the ability to retrieve the data in any table as a Swing `TableModel`. Details specific to the implementation of the data source will not be available to the presentation objects.

Presentation Tier – The views Tag Library

As previously mentioned, the `views` tag library provides several sets of custom tags to present data stored in the Swing data models described in Chapter 17.

The `<views:jspList>` tag iterates over a `javax.swing.ListModel` (an instance of `javax.swing.DefaultListModel`). Within the tag, each item in turn is made available via the `value` scripting variable:

```
<ul>
   <views:jspList model="<%=listModel%>" >
     <li><%=value%>
   </views:jspList>
</ul>
```

The `jspstyle.NameValueModel` interface extends `ListModel` to provide name-value mappings:

```
package jspstyle;

import javax.swing.ListModel;
```

```
/**
 * Extension of Swing ListModel interface to support
 * name-value mappings. The new getName() method will provide
 * the String name, while the ListModel getElementAt() method will
 * provide the object value.
 */
public interface NameValueModel extends ListModel {

  String getName(int i);

}
```

`<views:jspNameValue>` iterates over an instance of a class implementing `NameValueModel`, and for each entry makes its name and value available via the `name` and `value` scripting variables:

```
<select name="sel3">
  <views:jspNameValue model="<%=nvModel%>">
    <option value="<%=value%>"><%=name%>
  </views:jspNameValue>
</select>
```

Finally, a set of custom tags is provided to render the contents of a `javax.swing.table.TableModel`. To make this as generic and reusable as possible, six values must be parameterized:

❑ The opening and closing of the table header

❑ The format of each header cell

❑ The opening and closing of each table row

❑ The format of each table cell

Separate tags are provided to customize each of these, nested within the `<views:jspTable>` tag. This is more suitable than specifying these values via tag attributes, as it allows us to specify markup that is illegal in a tag attribute. For example:

```
<table>
  <views:jspTable model="<%=tableModel %>" >
    <views:headingOpen><tr bgcolor="black"></views:headingOpen>
    <views:headingClose></tr></views:headingClose>
    <views:headingCell><td><%=heading%></td></views:headingCell>
    <views:rows>
      <views:rowOpen><tr></views:rowOpen>
      <views:rowClose></tr></views:rowClose>
      <views:cell><td><%=value%></td></views:cell>
    </views:rows>
  </views:jspTable>
</table>
```

The tags are:

- ❏ `<views:jspTable>` – saves the `TableModel`, making it available to subtags. Holds header open and header close properties.

- ❏ `<views:headingOpen>` – configures the `TableModel`'s header open property.

- ❏ `<views:headerClose>` – configures the `TableModel`'s header close property.

- ❏ `<views:headingCell>` – corresponds to the `<headerCell>` tag. Handles iteration over the table headings, and outputs content including header open and close values. Defines `heading` (header value) and `column` (column index) scripting variables.

- ❏ `<views:rows>` – handles iteration over the table's rows. Defines the `row` (row index) scripting variable.

- ❏ `<views:rowOpen>` – configures `RowsTag`'s row open property.

- ❏ `<views:rowClose>` – configures `RowsTag`'s row close property.

- ❏ `<views:cell>` – implements the `<cell>` tag in the example; analogous to `HeaderTag`. Handles the iteration over a table row, including output of row open and close markup and each cell's value. Defines `column` (column index) and `value` (model value) scripting variables.

If we don't want a heading and are happy with the HTML default values we can omit most of these tags, merely providing the elements required to support iteration over the table's content:

```
<table>
  <views:jspTable model="<%=model%>">

  <views:rows><views:cell><td><%=value%></td></views:cell></views:rows>
  </views:jspTable>
</table>
```

views Tag Library Descriptor

Here is the complete tag library descriptor for the `views` tag library; the full source code for the library is included in the code download for this chapter:

```
<?xml version="1.0" encoding="ISO-8859-1" ?>
<!DOCTYPE taglib
        PUBLIC "-//Sun Microsystems, Inc.//DTD JSP Tag Library 1.1//EN"
        "http://java.sun.com/j2ee/dtds/web-jsptaglibrary_1_1.dtd">
<taglib>
  <tlibversion>1.0</tlibversion>
  <jspversion>1.1</jspversion>
  <shortname>views</shortname>

  <info>MVC tag library. Author: Rod Johnson</info>

  <tag>
    <name>jspTable</name>
    <tagclass>jspstyle.TableTag</tagclass>
    <bodycontent>JSP</bodycontent>
    <info>JSP table view</info>
    <attribute>
```

```
      <name>model</name>
      <required>true</required>
      <rtexprvalue>true</rtexprvalue>
    </attribute>
    <attribute>
      <name>headerOpen</name>
      <required>false</required>
      <rtexprvalue>true</rtexprvalue>
    </attribute>
    <attribute>
      <name>headerClose</name>
      <required>false</required>
      <rtexprvalue>true</rtexprvalue>
    </attribute>
  </tag>

  <tag>
    <name>rows</name>
    <tagclass>jspstyle.RowsTag</tagclass>
    <teiclass>jspstyle.RowsTagExtraInfo</teiclass>
    <bodycontent>JSP</bodycontent>
    <info>JSP table tag</info>
  </tag>

  <tag>
    <name>headingCell</name>
    <tagclass>jspstyle.HeadingTag</tagclass>
    <teiclass>jspstyle.HeadingTagExtraInfo</teiclass>
    <bodycontent>JSP</bodycontent>
    <info>JSP table tag</info>
  </tag>

  <tag>
    <name>cell</name>
    <tagclass>jspstyle.CellTag</tagclass>
    <teiclass>jspstyle.CellTagExtraInfo</teiclass>
    <bodycontent>JSP</bodycontent>
    <info>JSP table tag</info>
  </tag>

  <tag>
    <name>rowOpen</name>
    <tagclass>jspstyle.RowOpenTag</tagclass>
    <bodycontent>JSP</bodycontent>
    <info>JSP table tag</info>
  </tag>
  <tag>
    <name>rowClose</name>
    <tagclass>jspstyle.RowCloseTag</tagclass>
    <bodycontent>JSP</bodycontent>
    <info>JSP table tag</info>
  </tag>

  <tag>
    <name>headingOpen</name>
```

```
      <tagclass>jspstyle.HeadingOpenTag</tagclass>
      <bodycontent>JSP</bodycontent>
      <info>JSP table tag</info>
    </tag>
    <tag>
      <name>headingClose</name>
      <tagclass>jspstyle.HeadingCloseTag</tagclass>
      <bodycontent>JSP</bodycontent>
      <info>JSP table tag</info>
    </tag>

    <!-- List tag -->
    <tag>
      <name>jspList</name>
      <tagclass>jspstyle.ListTag</tagclass>
      <teiclass>jspstyle.ListTagExtraInfo</teiclass>
      <bodycontent>JSP</bodycontent>
      <info>JSP list MVC tag</info>
      <attribute>
        <name>model</name>
        <required>true</required>
        <rtexprvalue>true</rtexprvalue>
      </attribute>
    </tag>

    <!-- Name value tag -->
    <tag>
      <name>jspNameValue</name>
      <tagclass>jspstyle.NameValueTag</tagclass>
      <teiclass>jspstyle.NameValueTagExtraInfo</teiclass>
      <bodycontent>JSP</bodycontent>
      <info>JSP Name-Value MVC tag</info>
      <attribute>
        <name>model</name>
        <required>true</required>
        <rtexprvalue>true</rtexprvalue>
      </attribute>
    </tag>
  </taglib>
```

Presentation Tier – The ui and ui.requesthandlers Packages

The core of the presentation tier is the request controller, `controller.jsp`. This is a very simple JSP that instantiates a `RequestController` session bean that implements page flow logic, and forwards the response to each request to the JSP view determined by the controller:

```
<%--
    JSP controller for the data explorer application.
    This page produces no output, but redirects each request
    to the appropriate JSP view.
    The logic required to make this choice
    is supplied by the RequestController session bean.
--%>
```

```
<%@page session="true" errorPage="systemError.jsp" %>

<%-- The controller object will be instantiated by a session's first
    call to this page --%>
<jsp:useBean id="controller" scope="session" class="ui.RequestController" />

<%-- Each request to this page will be forwarded to the appropriate view,
    as determined by the controller and its helper classes. These classes
    will set the session state appropriately before returning the URL of
    a view, to which this page will forward the response. --%>
<jsp:forward page="<%=controller.getNextPage(pageContext, request)%>"/>
```

This JSP is the entry point for the application. (Later we will see how to specify this in the application's web.xml file.)

Logic

The RequestController class handles all page flow in the application, yet manages to avoid being limited to the page flow possibilities initially envisaged. To achieve this, it requires a number of RequestHandler objects to help it choose the required view. It loads the necessary class dynamically (by name), and instantiates an object of each type as required.

RequestController.java

The task of the RequestController itself is to examine the action parameter, call the appropriate RequestHandler instance to determine the required JSP view, and return the URL of this view to controller.jsp. The RequestController determines the class of the required RequestHandler by a simple mapping from the action parameter value onto a value classname. For example, DBConnect (the first action required by the application) is mapped onto a Java class named ui.requesthandlers.DBConnect, which must implement the RequestHandler interface. For efficiency reasons, the RequestController class keeps instantiated request handlers in a hash table and uses them to handle future requests of the same type. This will ensure that the use of reflection does not degrade the application's performance significantly.

If the action parameter is not passed to this page (for example at the time of the initial request to the application), the user is forwarded to the login page. Note the imports:

```
package ui;

import java.io.Serializable;
import javax.swing.*;
import javax.servlet.http.*;
import javax.servlet.jsp.*;

// Import the NameValueModel
import jspstyle.*;

import java.util.HashMap;
```

All requests go to the RequestController class; the class is responsible for instantiating the beans required by the system and uses reflection to instantiate request handlers as required. Notice that we specify a login page for users who don't have a connection:

```
public class RequestController implements Serializable {

  public static final String LOGIN_PAGE = "login.html";

  // Package from which to attempt to load RequestHandler objects
  private static final String REQUEST_HANDLER_PACKAGE =
    "ui.requesthandlers";

  // Name of the session bean used for this application.
  // This must be matched by the useBean actions in the JSPs.
  private static final String SESSION_BEAN_NAME = "browseSession";

  /**
   * Convenience method for RequestHandler implementations, allowing Java
   * classes to access the session bean easily. Unlike
   * checkSessionBeanIsAvailable(), this method will throw an exception if
   * the bean has not already been instantiated.
   * @return the session bean, which must have been instantiated already.
   */
  public static BrowseSession FindSessionBean(PageContext pageContext,
                                              RequestHandler rh)
                                          throws BrowseException {
    BrowseSession session =
      (BrowseSession) pageContext
        .getAttribute(RequestController.SESSION_BEAN_NAME,
                  PageContext.SESSION_SCOPE);

    if (session == null) {
      throw new BrowseException("Internal error: illegal state. " +
                                "Session bean shouldn't be null " +
                                "handling action " + rh.getClass());
// In a real system, the error messages would be more user-friendly,
// specifying an error code and any necessary information
// to help a support team
    }
    return session;
}

  // Hash table to hold instantiated classes for optimization
  private HashMap handlerHash = new HashMap();
```

RequestController.getNextPage()

getNextPage() is the method through which all requests to the application are sent. The method processes the request, updating the session and returning the URL of the resulting JSP view. This method will first check if the action parameter contains a value and if not will direct the user to the login page. Otherwise, if there is a value the method tries to instantiate the handler associated with the action, throwing a BrowseException if there is no handler associated with the action. Finally, we end by creating the session bean if it does not already exist through checkSessionBeanIsAvailable() method and return the URL of the view chosen by the handler:

```
public String getNextPage(PageContext pageContext,
                          HttpServletRequest request) throws BrowseException {
  String action = request.getParameter("action");
```

```
                // If no action was specified, the user must first log in
                if (action == null || action.equals("")) {
                  return LOGIN_PAGE;


                }
                RequestHandler requestHandler = getHandlerInstance(action);

                // Create the session bean if it doesn't exist
                checkSessionBeanIsAvailable(pageContext);

                return requestHandler.handleRequest(pageContext, request);
              }
```

RequestController.getHandlerInstance()

As we have discussed, getHandlerInstance() stores instances of classes in a hash table so that after they are initially loaded (using forName()) they no longer need reloading, improving its speed and resource cost.

```
              private RequestHandler getHandlerInstance(String action)
                     throws BrowseException {
                String handlerName = REQUEST_HANDLER_PACKAGE + "." + action;

                RequestHandler requestHandler =
                  (RequestHandler) handlerHash.get(handlerName);

                if (requestHandler == null) {

                  // We don't have a handler instance associated with this action,
                  // so we need to instantiate one and put it in our hash table

                  try {
                    System.out.println("Loading handler instance...");

                    // Use reflection to load the class by name
                    Class handlerClass = Class.forName(handlerName);

                    // Check the class we obtained implements RequestHandler interface
                    if (!RequestHandler.class.isAssignableFrom(handlerClass)) {
                      throw new BrowseException("Class " + handlerName + " does not "+
                                    "implement the RequestHandler interface ");

                      // Instantiate the request handler object
                    }
                    requestHandler = (RequestHandler) handlerClass.newInstance();

                    // Save the instance so we don't have to load it dynamically to
                    // process further requests from this user
                    handlerHash.put(handlerName, requestHandler);
                  } catch (ClassNotFoundException ex) {
                    throw new BrowseException("No handler for action [" + handlerName
                                      + "]: class " + handlerName
                                      + " could not be loaded. " + ex);
                  } catch (InstantiationException ex) {
```

```
            // It probably doesn't have a no-argument constructor
            throw new BrowseException("Class " + handlerName
                                    + " could not be instantiated. "
                                    + " Is it a bean? " + ex);
        } catch (IllegalAccessException ex) {
            throw new BrowseException("Class " + handlerName
                                    + " could not be instantiated. "
                                    + "Does it have a public constructor? "
                                    + ex);
        }
    }

    // If we get to here, we have a valid RequestHandler instance,
    // whether it came from the hash table or from dynamical class loading
    return requestHandler;
}
```

RequestController.checkSessionBeanIsAvailable()

checkSessionBeanIsAvailable() checks for a session bean in the user session and returns it. If none can be found it will instantiate a new bean:

```
private void checkSessionBeanIsAvailable(PageContext pageContext) {
    BrowseSession session =
        (BrowseSession) pageContext.getAttribute(SESSION_BEAN_NAME,
                                        PageContext.SESSION_SCOPE);
    if (session == null) {
        System.out.println("RequestController: creating session object");
        session = new BrowseSession();

        // Place the session in the PageContext, so it will be accessible
        // to JSPs as a session bean
        pageContext.setAttribute(SESSION_BEAN_NAME, session,
                            PageContext.SESSION_SCOPE);
    }
}
```

RequestHandler Interface

The RequestHandler interface, which each action class must implement, is very simple. It is slightly more JSP-oriented than the RequestHandler interface shown in the previous chapter. It contains a single method, handleRequest(), which returns the URL of the required JSP view after performing any necessary updates to the session:

```
package ui;

import javax.servlet.http.*;
import javax.servlet.jsp.*;

// Interface to be implemented by objects that can process requests
public interface RequestHandler {

    /**
```

```
     * Perform any processing requiring to support this request, and
     * return the URL of the JSP view that should display the results
     * of the request.
     * @return the URL within the web application of the JSP view to which
     * the controller should redirect the response
     */
    String handleRequest(PageContext pageContext,
                         HttpServletRequest request) throws BrowseException;
}
```

We can extend the application's functionality indefinitely without modifying the `RequestController` class by adding more action parameter values, corresponding `RequestHandler` parameters, and the necessary JSP views. To emphasize the decoupling between the framework of `RequestController` and `RequestHandler` interface (in the `ui` package) and the application's set of actions, we group installed request handlers in a separate package, `ui.requesthandlers`.

BrowseSession.java

Before we look at the implementations of the `RequestHandler` interface, let's look at how they will communicate with the application's JSP views. This will be through the session bean, which will hold the current data source and information about the user's session (any current table selection, the history of user-typed SQL queries, and the current JSP view). Each JSP view will declare this session bean, which, however, will be instantiated in only one place, in the `RequestController` class. Although the session bean isn't concerned with presentation, it is slightly unusual in that it exposes models used by JSP views. This is normally the job of page beans:

```java
package ui;

import java.io.Serializable;
import javax.servlet.http.*;
import javax.swing.AbstractListModel;
import javax.swing.table.TableModel;
import java.util.*;
import jspstyle.NameValueModel;

import datasources.*;
import datasources.db.DatabaseDataSource;

/**
 * JSP session bean to contain information about user
 * view preferences and models exposing user input history.
 * Implements HttpSessionBindingListener interface to
 * ensure that data source resources are freed
 * when the session terminates.
 * This bean allows the RequestHandler objects to communicate
 * with the JSP views in the system.
 */

public class BrowseSession implements Serializable,
                                      HttpSessionBindingListener {

    // Current view page.
    private String viewPage = "tableView.jsp";
```

```java
// Current data source.
// This object can change data source during the life of the application
private DataSource dataSource;

// Index of the current table the user is viewing
// -1 if they haven't selected a table
private int currentTableIndex;

// Current table model.
private TableModel tableModel;
private String lastQuery;

// List of SQL queries the user has typed in
// This will back a NameValueModel of query history
private List queries = new LinkedList();

private NameValueModel queryModel = new QueryNameValueModel();

// -------------------------------------------------------------------
// Public methods
// -------------------------------------------------------------------

// @return the JSP view the user presently wants to use for viewing data
public String getTableViewJSP() {
  return viewPage;
}

// Change the current view JSP
public void setTableViewJSP(String viewPage) {
  this.viewPage = viewPage;
}

// Set the DataSource behind this session
public void setDataSource(DataSource dataSource) {
  this.dataSource = dataSource;
}

public DataSource getDataSource()
        throws DataSourceException, BrowseException {
  if (dataSource == null) {
    throw new BrowseException("No connection");

  }
  return dataSource;
}

// Choose a table index in the DataSource
public void setTableIndex(int index) {
  currentTableIndex = index;

  // Throw away any table model based on a query:
  // the user wants to see a table from the data source
  tableModel = null;
}

// Return the currently selected table index, -1 if no table index has
```

```java
  // been selected
  public int getTableIndex() {
    return currentTableIndex;
  }

  // Return the name of the current table. If no table name is selected,
  // the user must have typed in a query: return the query
  public String getTableName() throws DataSourceException, BrowseException {
    if (currentTableIndex < 0) {
      return lastQuery;

    }
    return getDataSource().getName(currentTableIndex);
  }

  // Return the current table model.
  public TableModel getTableModel()
          throws DataSourceException, BrowseException {

    // If we hold a table model in this class, the user typed in a query
    // and isn't looking at one of the tables in the data source
    if (tableModel != null) {
      return tableModel;

    }
    return getDataSource().getTableModel(currentTableIndex);
  }

  // Return current data source support for SQL?
  public boolean getDataSourceSupportsSQL()
          throws DataSourceException, BrowseException {
    return getDataSource() instanceof DatabaseDataSource;
  }

  // If the current data source supports SQL queries, obtain and save a
  // table model built from an SQL query
  public TableModel getTableModelForSQL(String query)
          throws DataSourceException, BrowseException {
    if (!getDataSourceSupportsSQL()) {
      throw new BrowseException("The current data source does not"
                                + " support SQL queries");
    }
    lastQuery = query;

    // Save this query in the history list if it's new
    if (!queries.contains(query)) {
      queries.add(query);

      // The user isn't looking at a table in the data source, so
      // unset any table index value
    }
    currentTableIndex = -1;
    tableModel =
      ((DatabaseDataSource) getDataSource()).getTableModelForSQL(query);

    return tableModel;
```

```
  }

  // Return a NameValueModel exposing this session's query history.
  // This model is implemented by an inner class.
  public NameValueModel getQueryModel() {
    return queryModel;
  }

  public boolean isTableEditable()
          throws DataSourceException, BrowseException {
    return currentTableIndex >= 0
          && getDataSource().isTableEditable(currentTableIndex);
  }
```

The last few methods make up the isXXX, getXXX and setXXX methods for the class. The remaining methods are the valueBound() and valueUnbound() methods and the inner class QueryNameValueModel that implements jspstyle.NameValueModel to expose the query history:

```
  // Implemention of HttpSessionBindingListener
  public void valueBound(HttpSessionBindingEvent event) {
    System.out.println("OperatorSession object bound to a session");
  }

  /**
   * Use this callback from the JSP engine (issued when this object
   * is being removed from the session when the session ends)
   * to ensure that the data source cleans up after itself
   */
  public void valueUnbound(HttpSessionBindingEvent event) {
    try {
      System.out.println("OperatorSession object unbound to a session:"
                         + " will cleanup data source");
      getDataSource().cleanup();
    } catch (Exception ex) {

      // It won't do anyone much good to throw this:
      // simply produce console output. In a real application,
      // this would go to a proper log
      ex.printStackTrace();
    }
  }

  private class QueryNameValueModel extends AbstractListModel
      implements NameValueModel {
    public int getSize() {
      return queries.size();
    }

    public Object getElementAt(int i) {
      return queries.get(i);
    }

    public String getName(int i) {
      return queries.get(i).toString();
    }
  }
}
```

Application Walk Through

Now let's start a walk through of the application. Let's return to the first page the user sees when entering the application, the login page. Like all external requests to the application, this goes to the controller JSP, which detects the absence of an action and forwards the response to the form:

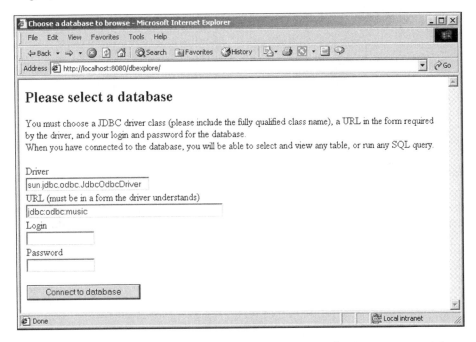

This page is `login.html`, and contains a form that, in addition to the driver name, url, login, and password fields, contains a hidden `action` field with a value of `DBConnect`. This value will be used by the `RequestController` class to establish that the user should be directed to the `ui.requesthandlers.DBConnect RequestHandler` implementation:

```
<html>
  <head>
    <title>Choose a database to browse</title>
  </head>
  <body>

    <h2>Please select a database</h2>
    You must choose a JDBC driver class (please include the fully
    qualified class name), a URL
    in the form required by the driver, and your login and password for
    the database.
    <br/>
    When you have connected to the database, you will be able to select
    and view any table, or run any SQL query.
    <p/>

    <form method="post" action="controller.jsp">
      Driver<br/>
      <input type="text" name="driver" size="30"
             value="sun.jdbc.odbc.JdbcOdbcDriver" /> <br />
```

```
                URL (must be in a form the driver understands)<br/>
                <input type="text" name="url" size="50"
                        value="jdbc:odbc:music" /><br />
                Login<br/>
                <input type="text" name="login" size="15" /><br />
                Password<br/>
                <input type="password" name="password"  size="15" /><br />
                <p/>

                <!-- Hidden field to provide correct action
                    The value corresponds to a RequestHandler implementation -->
                <input type="hidden" name="action" value="DBConnect"/>
                <input type="submit" value="Connect to database" />
            </form>
        </body>
    </html>
```

DBConnect.java

The DBConnect class must attempt to instantiate a data source object and, if the attempt succeeds, return the URL of another form that will allow the user to select a table to view or enter a query. (Note that the application could easily be extended to support non-JDBC data sources by the addition of another login form defining another action parameter leading to another RequestHandler that instantiated a different data source.) The DBConnect class instantiates a DatabaseDataSource. We'll meet the DataSource interface and this implementation of it later:

```
package ui.requesthandlers;

import javax.servlet.http.*;
import javax.servlet.jsp.*;

import ui.*;

import datasources.*;
import datasources.db.*;

public class DBConnect implements RequestHandler {

  private static final String TABLE_CHOICE_PAGE = "chooseTable.jsp";

  public String handleRequest(PageContext pageContext,
                              HttpServletRequest request)
                              throws BrowseException {
    System.out.println(getClass() + ".handleRequest");
    String url = request.getParameter("url");
    String driver = request.getParameter("driver");

    if (url == null || driver == null || url.equals("")
            || driver.equals("")) {

      // Throw an exception that will land us on the system error page
      // with a link back to the login form to allow the user to try again
      throw new InvalidInputException("Both URL and driver must be supplied"
                                        , RequestController.LOGIN_PAGE);
```

```
    // Some databases (like Access) allow null or empty authentication
    // information. Others, like Oracle, won't. We leave it to the driver
    // to throw an exception if necessary.
  }
  String login = request.getParameter("login");
  String password = request.getParameter("password");
  BrowseSession session = RequestController.FindSessionBean(pageContext,
          this);

  try {
    DataSource dbDataSource = new DatabaseDataSource(url, driver, login,
                                                    password);

    session.setDataSource(dbDataSource);
  } catch (DataSourceException ex) {
    throw new BrowseException("Cannot connect to database: "
                             + ex.getMessage());
  }

  // If we get to here, everything is fine, and the session state is ready
  // to underpin the table choice view JSP
  return TABLE_CHOICE_PAGE;
  }
}
```

If the connection parameters were valid, the user will now see a page offering a choice of tables in the database:

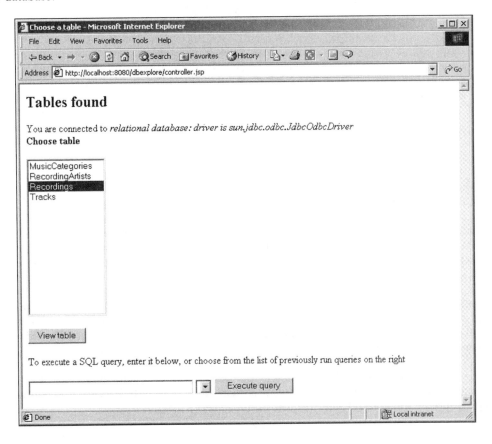

chooseTable.jsp

This page is dynamic, implemented by `chooseTable.jsp`. Since we will need to offer a choice of table from every view in the application, we will factor out the actual form into an included JSP:

```
<%--
    JSP to allow the user to choose a table from
        the database. The user will be connected to a database
        and the session bean available before this view is invoked.
--%>

<%@page session="true" errorPage="systemError.jsp" %>

<%@ taglib uri="/views" prefix="views" %>

<%--
    The request controller will instantiate this bean
    This page will throw an exception here if the bean is not
    already in the PageContext
--%>
<jsp:useBean id="browseSession" scope="session" type="ui.BrowseSession" />

<html>
<head>
  <title>Choose a table</title>
</head>

  <body>
    <h2>Tables found</h2>

<%-- Parameter to _chooseTable.jspf: this value will ensure that
    the drop down is expanded on this page --%>
<% boolean multiSelect = true; %>

<%-- Include the actual form. We want to share this code
    with other pages --%>
<%@ include file="_chooseTable.jspf" %>

  </body>
</html>
```

The included JSP, `_chooseTable.jspf`, generates the form. It is parameterized by a `boolean` variable (`multiSelect`) that must be defined in JSPs that include it, and which controls whether the table select will be a dropdown, or a multi line select. The data comes from the data source added to the session object by the `DBConnect` request handler.

Data source objects expose a `NameValueModel` of the tables they contain, and we can use the `<views:jspNameValue>` tag to display this data. This is a body tag, which iterates over its body content based on the size and the content of the model it takes as an XML attribute. The JSP content of the name value tag will be evaluated for every element in the model.

A second name value model will be exposed by the session bean to contain the history of any previous SQL queries, if the data source is known by the session bean to support SQL. A separate form will be used to display this model and allow the user to run a query.

_chooseTable.jspf

```
<%--
    JSP fragment to allow the user to choose which table to view, and to
    allow SQL query input if we are connected to a relational database.
    There must be a valid connection before a JSP can include this fragment.
    Including JSPs must define a boolean variable named multiSelect. If this
    is true, the list of database tables will be expanded; otherwise it will
    appear as a drop down.
--%>

  You are connected to <i><%=browseSession.getDataSource()%></i>
  <br/>
  <b>Choose table</b><br/>
  <form method="post" action="controller.jsp">
    <select name="tableIndex"
      <% if (multiSelect) { %>
        size="15"
      <% } %>
    >

<%-- Use the NameValueModel exposed by the DataSource object
     to display the list of tables
--%>
      <views:jspNameValue model="<%=browseSession.getDataSource()%>">
        <option value="<%=value%>"
          <% if (index.intValue() == browseSession.getTableIndex()) { %>
            selected="true"
          <% } %>
        >
          <%=name%>
        </option>
      </views:jspNameValue>
    </select>

<%-- Hidden parameter setting the actual action --%>
    <input type="hidden" name="action" value="ChooseTable"/>
    <% if (multiSelect) { %>
      <br />
      <p />
    <% } %>
    <input type="submit" value="View table" />
</form>

<%-- Only show the SQL query input form if we're connected to a
     relational database
--%>
  <% if (browseSession.getDataSourceSupportsSQL()) { %>
    To execute a SQL query, enter it below, or choose from the list
    of previously run queries on the right
    <form method="post" action="controller.jsp">
      <input type="hidden" name="action" value="RunQuery"/>
      <input type="text" name="query" size="40" />

<%-- The select box allows the user to choose from previously run queries
--%>
```

```
      <select name="oldquery">
        <views:jspNameValue model="<%=browseSession.getQueryModel()%>">
          <option value="<%=value%>">
              <%=name%>
          </option>
        </views:jspNameValue>
      </select>
      <input type="submit" value="Execute query" />
    </form>
  <% } %>
```

ChooseTable.java

The hidden action field of ChooseTable will cause the RequestController class to use the ChooseTable request handler class to process the request produced by submitting this form:

```java
package ui.requesthandlers;

import javax.servlet.http.*;
import javax.servlet.jsp.*;

import ui.*;

/**
 * Implementation of the RequestHandler interface to handle
 * table choice. The user will have submitted a form
 * selecting the index of the table the user would like to view
 * before being directed to this RequestHandler. We need to update
 * the user's session to record this selection, and forward to the
 * table view JSP of the user's current view mode,
 */
public class ChooseTable implements RequestHandler {

  public String handleRequest(PageContext pageContext,
                              HttpServletRequest request)
                              throws BrowseException {
    System.out.println(getClass() + ".handleRequest");
    String tableIndex = request.getParameter("tableIndex");
    if (tableIndex == null) {

      // This shouldn't happen, but we'll check anyway
      throw new InvalidInputException("Please choose a table",
                                      "chooseTable.jsp");

    }
    BrowseSession session = RequestController.FindSessionBean(pageContext,
                                                             this);

    session.setTableIndex(Integer.parseInt(tableIndex));

    // Using a method here rather than hard coding the page name
    // means that the user can continue in his or her current view mode.
    return session.getTableViewJSP();
  }
}
```

The user, having chosen a table or entered an SQL query, will now see the default view of the tabular data. This is a simple HTML table, with a minimum of aesthetic refinement to make it readable by alternating the color of rows:

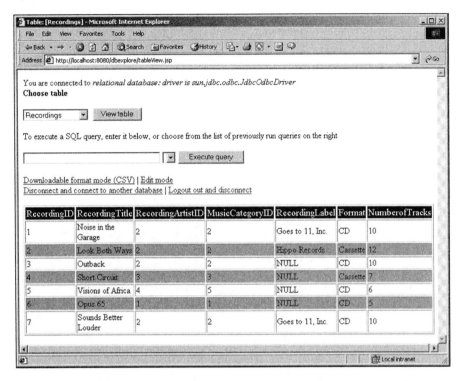

This page is produced by `tableView.jsp`. This JSP view finds what data should back the table by calling the session bean's `getTableModel()` method. The appropriate table model will have been set in the session bean by the `ChooseTable` request handler's call to the session bean's `setTableIndex()` method. The table choice and text input for SQL queries at the top of the page are produced by the same `_chooseTable.jspf` page fragment that we used in `chooseTable.jsp`.

As the requirement is for each view to remain the default until the user chooses to change it, this JSP calls the session bean's `setTableViewJSP()` method with its Servlet path to ensure that it is now the default view.

tableView.jsp

The actual table is produced by the `<views:jspTable>` tag, which handles iteration over the table model it is passed as an XML attribute. This tag requires a number of descendant tags such as `<views:headingOpen>`, `<views:headingClose>`, and `<views:rows>`, which make it possible to control all the generated markup:

```
<%--
   Default table view of data. Read only. Uses some simple color banding.
--%>

<%@page session="true" errorPage="systemError.jsp" %>
```

```
<%@ taglib uri="/views" prefix="views" %>

<%-- The request controller will instantiate this bean --%>
<jsp:useBean id="browseSession" scope="session" type="ui.BrowseSession" />

<%--
  Make this the default view page until the user chooses another page
--%>
<% browseSession.setTableViewJSP(request.getServletPath()); %>

<html>
  <head>
    <title>Table: [<%=browseSession.getTableName()%>]</title>
  </head>
  <body>

<%-- We only want a drop down, not an expanded list --%>
<% boolean multiSelect = false; %>
<%@ include file="_chooseTable.jspf" %>

<% javax.swing.table.TableModel tableModel =
                                    browseSession.getTableModel(); %>

<%@ include file="_chooseMode.jspf" %>

<% String color="white"; %>
<table border="1">
  <views:jspTable model="<%=tableModel %>" >
    <views:headingOpen>
      <tr bgcolor="black">
    </views:headingOpen>
    <views:headingCell>
        <td>
          <font size=4 color="white"><%=heading%></font>
        </td>
    </views:headingCell>
    <views:rows>
      <views:rowOpen>
        <%-- Use a scriptlet to achieve color banding for readability --%>
        <% color = (row.intValue() % 2 == 0) ? "white" : "cyan"; %>
        <tr bgColor="<%=color%>">
      </views:rowOpen>
      <views:rowClose></tr></views:rowClose>
      <views:cell><td><%=value%></td></views:cell>
    </views:rows>
  </views:jspTable>
</table>

  </body>
</html>
```

We need an additional page fragment to implement this page, _chooseMode.jspf. This provides the links to alternative views. It excludes the present view by checking the name of the page in which it is used. Note that additional links to new views can be added by modifying this single JSP fragment. These links are the only links within the application that do not pass through the controller JSP. This is legitimate because all views occur with the application in the same state, and render the same data.

_chooseMode.jspf

```
<%--
  JSP fragment to offer a choice of mode, depending on the user's
  location in the system.
--%>

<% if (request.getServletPath().indexOf("tableView") == -1) { %>
  <a href="tableView.jsp">View mode</a> |
<% } %>

<% if (request.getServletPath().indexOf("csvView") == -1) { %>
  <a href="csvView.jsp">Downloadable format mode (CSV)</a> |
<% } %>

<% if (request.getServletPath().indexOf("editTable") == -1 &&
       browseSession.isTableEditable()) { %>
  <a href="editTable.jsp">Edit mode</a>
<% } %>


<br/>

<a href="controller.jsp?action=NewConnection">
  Disconnect and connect to another database
</a> |
<a href="controller.jsp?action=Logout">
  Logout out and disconnect
</a>
<p/>
```

The CSV view

Let's consider another view, the CSV view we were required to implement to allow users to cut and paste data into other applications. This looks quite different from the previous table, apart from sharing the common navigational controls at the top of the page:

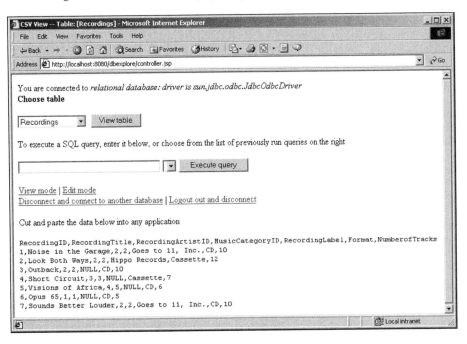

csvView.jsp

This view also uses the `<views:jspTable>` tag. This is possible because this tag enables JSPs to control all aspects of the markup it produces, and so is not limited to generating HTML table code:

```jsp
<%--  CSV table view of data. --%>

<%@page session="true" errorPage="systemError.jsp" %>
<%@ taglib uri="/views" prefix="views" %>

<%-- The request controller will instantiate this bean --%>
<jsp:useBean id="browseSession" scope="session" type="ui.BrowseSession" />

<%-- Make this the default view page --%>
<% browseSession.setTableViewJSP(request.getServletPath()); %>

<%
   javax.swing.table.TableModel tableModel = browseSession.getTableModel();
%>
<html>
  <head>
    <title>CSV View -- Table: [<%=browseSession.getTableName()%>]</title>
  </head>
  <body>

<% boolean multiSelect = false; %>
<%@ include file="_chooseTable.jspf" %>
<%@ include file="_chooseMode.jspf" %>

  Cut and paste the data below into any application
  </p>
  <code>
    <views:jspTable model="<%=tableModel %>" >
      <views:headingOpen></views:headingOpen>
      <views:headingClose><br/></views:headingClose>
<%-- We use the ternary operator to ensure that we don't place a comma
    after the last entry on each line
--%>
    <views:headingCell><%=heading%><%=(column.intValue()
    <tableModel.getColumnCount() - 1) ? "," : ""%></views:headingCell>
    <views:rows>
      <views:rowOpen></views:rowOpen>
      <views:rowClose><br/></views:rowClose>
      <views:cell><%=value%>
        <%=(column.intValue() <
                          tableModel.getColumnCount() - 1) ? "," : ""%>
      </views:cell>
    </views:rows>
    </views:jspTable>
  </code>
  </body>
</html>
```

The Edit View

The third and final view we need to implement in the first phase of development is the edit view, allowing the user to update each row of the table. It will look like this:

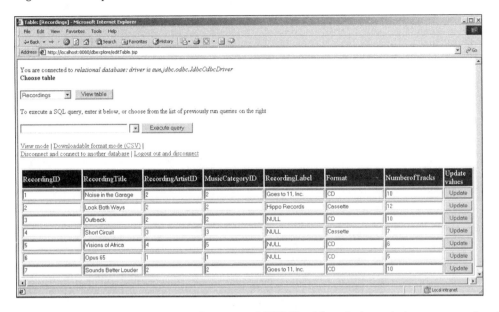

Again the `<jsp:table>` tag generates the required HTML, although the code is more complex. We further test the flexibility of the table tag by adding an additional header field (Update values) and column to the data values returned by the table model. Each row of the table is a form, with the usual hidden action value for the request controller (UpdateTable), and an additional hidden value containing the index of the row that the user wishes to update. The additional column will contain the submit button for each row.

editTable.jsp

```
<%-- Editable table view. This will contain a form for each row of data.
--%>

<%@page session="true" errorPage="systemError.jsp" %>
<%@ taglib uri="/views" prefix="views" %>

<%-- The request controller will instantiate this bean --%>
<jsp:useBean id="browseSession" scope="session" type="ui.BrowseSession" />

<%-- Make this the default view page until the user chooses another page
--%>
<% browseSession.setTableViewJSP(request.getServletPath()); %>
<html>
  <head>
    <title>Table: [<%=browseSession.getTableName()%>]</title>
  </head>
  <body>
    <% boolean multiSelect = false; %>

<%@ include file="_chooseTable.jspf" %>
```

```
<%@ include file="_chooseMode.jspf" %>

<%
  javax.swing.table.TableModel tableModel =
                                      browseSession.getTableModel(); %>

<% String color="white"; %>
<table border="1">
  <views:jspTable model="<%=tableModel %>" >
    <views:headingOpen>
      <tr bgcolor="black"></views:headingOpen>
        <views:headingClose>
        <%-- We can use this to add an extra column --%>
        <td><font size=4 color="white">Update values</font></td>
      </tr>
    </views:headingClose>
    <views:headingCell>
        <td><font size=4 color="white"><%=heading%></font></td>
    </views:headingCell>
    <views:rows>
      <views:rowOpen>
        <%-- Each row of the table is a form --%>
        <form method="post" action="controller.jsp">

        <%-- As always, we need a hidden field containing the required
             RequestHandler's name --%>
        <input type="hidden" name="action" value="UpdateTable"/>
        <input type="hidden" name="row" value="<%=row.intValue()%>" />
        <%-- Use the ternary operator to implement color banding --%>
        <% color = (row.intValue() % 2 == 0) ? "gray" : "white"; %>
      <tr bgColor="<%=color%>">
      </views:rowOpen>
      <views:rowClose>
        <%--
          We need to provide the extra column we promised in the heading.
          We need to provide a variable containing the current alert's
          id for the included form
        --%>
        <td><input type="submit" value="Update" /></td>
      </form>
    </tr>
      </views:rowClose>
    <views:cell><td>

<% if (!tableModel.isCellEditable(row.intValue(), column.intValue())) { %>
 <%-- The primary key is not editable: don't use a form field --%>
   <b><%=value%></b>
 <% } else { %>
   <input type="text" name="<%=column.intValue()%>" value="<%=value%>" />
 <% } %>

    </td></views:cell>
    </views:rows>
  </views:jspTable>
</table>

  </body>
</html>
```

We need a confirmation page (updateOK.jsp) to let users know if their update request succeeded. The code for this is pleasingly simple:

```
<html>
  <head><title>Update succeeded!</title></head>
  <body>
    <a href="editTable.jsp">Continue editing table</a><br/>
    <a href="tableView.jsp">View table</a><br/>
  </body>
</html>
```

Dealing with Errors

Before we look at the implementation of the `UpdateTable` request handler, let's consider what would have happened if the update didn't succeed. Here, as anywhere else in the application, if we encounter an error we will be forwarded to the system error page, `systemError.jsp`. This page makes some attempt to tailor the error message depending on what we can learn from the exception passed to it, although a real application would need more sophisticated and user-friendly error handling. To support diagnostics, this page includes the exception's stack trace in an HTML comment:

```
<%@page isErrorPage="true" %>
<html>
  <head>
    <title>Data Browser: Error</title>
  </head>
  <body>
    <% if (exception instanceof ui.InvalidInputException) { %>
      <%-- Provide a link to allow the user to retry --%>
      Sorry. Your input was invalid.<br/>
      <i><%=exception.getMessage()%></i><br/>
      Please
      <a href="<%=((ui.InvalidInputException) exception).getRetryURL()%>">
        try again
      </a>.

    <% } else { %>
      Sorry. Your request could not be processed.<br/>
      <i><%=exception.getMessage()%></i><br/>
    <% } %>

  <%-- Include the actual exception in a hidden comment --%>
  <!--
    <% exception.printStackTrace(new java.io.PrintWriter(out)); %>
  -->
  </body>
</html>
```

The following screenshot shows the output of the error page following an unsuccessful update, along with a source listing (courtesy of the **Show Source** command) displaying the generated stack trace. (Since the simple implementation of JDBC data access behind this application doesn't support updates, attempts to update tables will always produce this result.)

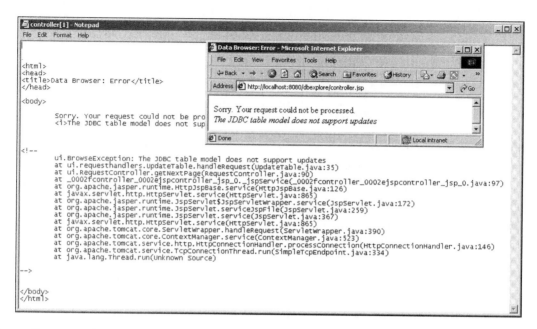

More RequestHandlers

Now let's return to the RequestHandlers required to implement the remaining views. Remember the application's ability to run SQL queries, producing output like this:

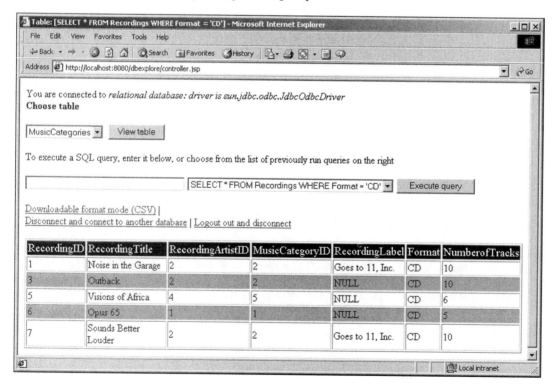

This functionality is implemented by the RunQuery request handler. (However, the page may be rendered by any of the three view JSPs we have seen.)

RunQuery.java

RunQuery needs to check two parameters: query (which would have resulted from the user typing a new query), and oldquery, which may have resulted from the user choosing a previously run query from the drop down on the right of the query entry text field. If neither of these parameters contains data, the user's input was invalid, and this object should throw an exception causing the user to be sent to the error page, with a link back to a page allowing another try to enter a query:

```java
package ui.requesthandlers;

import java.sql.SQLException;
import javax.servlet.http.*;
import javax.servlet.jsp.*;
import javax.swing.table.TableModel;

import datasources.*;
import ui.*;

public class RunQuery implements RequestHandler {

  public String handleRequest(PageContext pageContext,
                              HttpServletRequest request)
                              throws BrowseException {
    System.out.println(getClass() + ".handleRequest");
    String query = request.getParameter("query");

    if (query == null || "".equals(query)) {

      // We need to look at the value passed from the dropdown
      query = request.getParameter("oldquery");

    }
    if (query == null || "".equals(query)) {
      throw new InvalidInputException("A query must be supplied",
                                      "chooseTable.jsp");
    }
    System.out.println("RunQuery will execute query " + query);
    try {

      // Update the session bean appropriately
      BrowseSession session = RequestController.FindSessionBean(pageContext,
                                                               this);

      session.getTableModelForSQL(query);
      return session.getTableViewJSP();
    } catch (DataSourceException ex) {
      throw new BrowseException(ex.getMessage());
    }
  }
}
```

We also need to allow the user to return to the login page at any point and choose to connect to a new database. This is implemented by the NewConnection request handler.

NewConnection.java

To ensure that the data source cleans up after itself, we invalidate the current session. As the current `BrowseSession` object is unbound from the session, it will call the `cleanup()` method of its `DataSource` object. This is why the `BrowseSession` bean implements the `HttpSessionBindingListener` interface, meaning that the JSP engine will notify instances as they are bound to or unbound from a session. The next request to `controller.jsp` will result in the instantiation of a fresh session object:

```java
package ui.requesthandlers;

import javax.servlet.http.*;
import javax.servlet.jsp.*;

import ui.*;

public class NewConnection implements RequestHandler {

  public String handleRequest(PageContext pageContext,
                              HttpServletRequest request) {

    // We can rely on the session object to clean up after itself:
    // all we need to do is invalidate the session
    pageContext.getSession().invalidate();
    return RequestController.LOGIN_PAGE;
  }
}
```

The `Logout` request handler is almost identical.

Logout.java

It invalidates the session and forwards the response to a static page, `logout.html`:

```java
package ui.requesthandlers;

import javax.servlet.http.*;
import javax.servlet.jsp.*;

import ui.*;

public class Logout implements RequestHandler {

  private static final String LOGOUT_PAGE = "logout.html";

  public String handleRequest(PageContext pageContext,
                              HttpServletRequest request) {

    // We can rely on the session object to clean up after itself:
    // all we need to do is invalidate the session
    pageContext.getSession().invalidate();
    return LOGOUT_PAGE;
  }
}
```

Making `logout.html` a static page helps avoid the temptation of trying to access session information; this has now been invalidated, and is unavailable:

```html
<html>
  <head>
    <title>Data Explorer: Log out</title>
  </head>

  <body>
    <h2>Session complete</h2>
      Thank you for using this system.
      You have been logged out successfully.
    <p/>
    You are now disconnected from the database.
  </body>
</html>
```

UpdateTable.java

Finally, there is `UpdateTable`, the request handler to handle the update action resulting from form submissions from `editTable.jsp`:

```java
package ui.requesthandlers;

import java.sql.SQLException;
import javax.servlet.http.*;
import javax.servlet.jsp.*;
import javax.swing.table.TableModel;

import datasources.*;
import ui.*;

public class UpdateTable implements RequestHandler {

  public String handleRequest(PageContext pageContext,
                              HttpServletRequest request)
                              throws BrowseException {
    System.out.println(getClass() + ".handleRequest");
    try {
      BrowseSession session = RequestController.FindSessionBean(pageContext,
                                                               this);

      TableModel model = session.getTableModel();
      String row = request.getParameter("row");
      if (row == null) {
        throw new InvalidInputException("Invalid or missing table index",
                                        "login.html");


      }
      for (int col = 0; col < model.getColumnCount(); col++) {

        // Look for parameter value for this column
        String colval = request.getParameter("" + col);
        if (colval != null) {
          System.out.println("Value of " + col + " is " + colval);
          model.setValueAt(colval, Integer.parseInt(row), col);
```

```
          // The following method will throw an exception
          // if the last update failed
          session.getDataSource().checkLastUpdate();
        }
      }
    } catch (DataSourceException ex) {
      throw new BrowseException(ex.getMessage());
    }

    return "/updateOK.jsp";
  }
}
```

Two simple Java classes complete the support for the JSP interface. BrowseException is a subclass of JSPException that is thrown when the request handlers or the RequestController encounter errors. Having a custom exception hierarchy is useful in JSP systems as elsewhere: it enables us to include additional information with exceptions in more complex systems, and enables the applications to determine between types of error. (Little use is made of this capability in this example.)

BrowseException.java

```
package ui;

import javax.servlet.jsp.JspException;

public class BrowseException extends JspException {

  // Constructs a <code>BrowseException</code> with the specified detail
  // message.
  // @param msg the detail message.
  public BrowseException(String msg) {
    super(msg);
  }
}
```

A subclass of BrowseException is used for those cases when we know which page the user needs to return to correct invalid input.

InvalidInoutExcpetion.java

An InvalidInputException is thrown by RequestHandlers that detect that the user has submitted invalid data:

```
package ui;

/** Extension of BrowseException to handle recoverable errors. This
 * exception can tell the error page where the user can go to resubmit
 * the invalid data.
 */
public class InvalidInputException extends BrowseException {
  private String retryURL;

  /** Constructs an <code>InvalidInputException</code> with the specified
```

```
        * detail message.
        * @param msg the detail message.
        * @param retryURL the location a user can go to
        * in order to resubmit the invalid data
        */
       public InvalidInputException(String msg, String retryURL) {
         super(msg);
         this.retryURL = retryURL;
       }

       public String getRetryURL() {
         return retryURL;
       }
     }
```

Note that none of these classes or JSPs is closely tied to the data tier. This means that the application is not inextricably linked to relational database concepts. Even the support for SQL is a supplement to the application's basic functionality, not a fixed requirement. (If the BrowseSession bean detects that the current data source does not support SQL, the _chooseTable.jspf page fragment won't generate the form allowing SQL input.)

Data Tier – The datasources and datasources.db Packages

Remembering the likelihood that the interface may be used for data sources other than relational databases, let's begin by abstracting the common requirements of a data source into an interface. We'll consider a data source to be an object that consists of a number of tables, each with a name. A more sophisticated extension might have a getChildDataSources() method to allow hierarchical browsing of data sources. This functionality is not required in working with relational databases, but would be if we wished to expose JNDI directory contents.

DataSource Interface

A DataSource object exposes a NameValueModel of the tables it contains, and a method allowing the retrieval of a particular table:

```
package datasources;

import javax.swing.table.TableModel;

import jspstyle.NameValueModel;

public interface DataSource extends NameValueModel {

    TableModel getTableModel(int i) throws DataSourceException;
    boolean isTableEditable(int i) throws DataSourceException;

    // Ensure resources associated with the data source are freed
    void cleanup() throws DataSourceException;

    // check last update was successful
    // necessary as the TableModel, setValueAt() cannot be overridden
    public void checkLastUpdate() throws DataSourceException;

    // Additional methods could support hierarchical retrieval

}
```

We will also define an exception class that can be thrown by `DataSource` implementations, regardless of the data source-specific exceptions they may encounter:

```
package datasources;

public class DataSourceException extends Exception {

  /** Construct a new DataSourceException
  * @param msg the detail message.
  */
  public DataSourceException(String msg) {
    super(msg);
  }
}
```

The only implementation of `DataSource` we include in the sample application is `DatabaseDataSource`, which uses JDBC to access a database.

DatabaseDataSource.java

This implementation does not run queries itself (leaving this to `JDBCTableModel` objects), but obtains a connection to a database and retrieves database meta-data to allow it to expose the list of tables as a `NameValueModel`. To emphasize the separation between common data source concepts and this particular implementation, we place `DatabaseDataSource` and the classes that support it in a separate package, `datasources.db`:

```
package datasources.db;

import datasources.*;
import java.sql.*;
import java.util.*;

import javax.swing.AbstractListModel;
import javax.swing.table.TableModel;

// Implementation of DatabaseDataSource exposing a relational database.
// Extends the Swing AbstractListModel for a partial implementation of
// the Swing ListModel, which NameValueModel extends.

public class DatabaseDataSource extends AbstractListModel
                            implements DataSource, ConnectionFactory {

  // Connection parameters
  private String url;
  private String driverName;
  private String user;
  private String passwd;

  // List of tables found in the database
  private List tableList;

  // The object that will perform the actual data retrieval
  JDBCTableModel model;

  // constructor
```

```java
public DatabaseDataSource(String url, String driverName, String user,
                          String passwd) throws DataSourceException {
  this.url = url;
  this.driverName = driverName;
  this.user = user;
  this.passwd = passwd;

  try {

    // load the driver
    Class.forName(driverName);

    // Test the connection
    Connection connection = getConnection();
    loadMetaData(connection);
    connection.close();
    model = new JDBCTableModel(this);
  } catch (ClassNotFoundException ex) {
    throw new DataSourceException("Driver class " + driverName
                                 + " cannot be loaded");
  } catch (SQLException ex) {
    throw new DataSourceException("Unable to connect to database: " + ex);
  }
}

public String toString() {
  return "relational database: driver is " + driverName + " url is "
                                          + url;
}


// Methods from DataSource interface
public boolean isTableEditable(int i) throws DataSourceException {
  return ((JDBCTableModel) getTableModel(i)).isEditable();
}

public TableModel getTableModel(int i) throws DataSourceException {
  String sql = "SELECT * FROM " + getName(i);
  return getTableModelForSQL(sql);
}

public TableModel getTableModelForSQL(String sql)
      throws DataSourceException {
  try {
    model.executeSQL(sql);
    return model;
  } catch (SQLException ex) {
    throw new DataSourceException("getTableModelForSQL with SQL=[" + sql
                                  + "] threw SQLException :" + ex);
  }
}

public void cleanup() throws DataSourceException {

  // The JDBCTableModel closes all resources,
```

```
        // So we don't need to do anything more
    }

    public void checkLastUpdate() throws DataSourceException {

        // Since our simple JDBCTableModel doesn't implement the setValueAt()
        // method, we always tell the user the update failed
        throw new DataSourceException("The JDBC table model does not support"
                                      + "updates");
    }

    // Methods from NameValueModel interface

    // Return the name of the i -th table (indexed from 0)
    public String getName(int i) {
      return tableList.get(i).toString();
    }

    // Return the number of tables we found
    public int getSize() {
      return tableList.size();
    }

    // Return the index of the table:
    // this will be a parameter to this class's getXXXX(int) methods
    public Object getElementAt(int i) {
      return new Integer(i);
    }

    // Methods from ConnectionFactory interface that JDBCTableModel uses
    public Connection getConnection() throws SQLException {

        // If this application were guaranteed to run in a J2EE-compliant
        // JSP engine, this connection could be obtained from a connection
        // pool specified in the application's web.xml file and accessed
        // via JNDI
        return DriverManager.getConnection(url, user, passwd);
    }
```

The loadMetaData() method loads and stores information about the tables within the database. This information will be retrieved once during the life of the class. The information is returned by JDBC as a ResultSet. Each table description row has the following columns:

❑ String value giving the table catalog, TABLE_CAT. Value returned may be null.

❑ String value giving table schema, TABLE_SCHEM. Again value returned may be null.

❑ TABLE_NAME as a String.

❑ TABLE_TYPE as a String.

❑ REMARKS as a String. Explanatory comment on the table.

DatabaseDataSource.loadMetaData()

Common types are TABLE, VIEW and SYSTEM TABLE. In this case we only want the table name and table type, columns 3 and 4.

```java
private void loadMetaData(Connection connection) throws SQLException {
  DatabaseMetaData dbmd = connection.getMetaData();

  // Change the second parameter below to retrieve information
  // about a particular schema in the database
  ResultSet rs = dbmd.getTables(null, null, "%", null);

  tableList = new LinkedList();
  while (rs.next()) {
    String tableName = rs.getString(3);
    String tableType = rs.getString(4);

    // NB: this check may not work for all databases
    // With Oracle, it successfully excludes views and the many
    // strange system tables that would otherwise appear
    if (tableType.toUpperCase().equals("TABLE")) {
      tableList.add(tableName);
    }
  }

  // sort the table list by name
  Collections.sort(tableList);

  }
}
```

Note that DatabaseDataSource implements a simple interface, ConnectionFactory, unique to JDBC. This is used to enable DatabaseDataSource objects to communicate with the JDBCTableModel helper class without exposing their structure:

```java
package datasources.db;

import java.sql.*;

public interface ConnectionFactory {
  Connection getConnection() throws SQLException;
}
```

The core of the JDBC functionality is contained in the JDBCTableModel class.

JDBCTableModel.java

This class runs SQL queries and maintains an internal data structure built from the ResultSets:

```java
package datasources.db;

import java.util.*;
import java.sql.*;
import javax.swing.table.*;
```

697

```java
/**
 * Class to present JDBC query results as Swing table models.
 * Thanks to Gary Watson for the code on which this is based.
 */
class JDBCTableModel extends AbstractTableModel {

  /**
   * Names of the current columns
   */
  private List columnNames;

  /**
   * Types of the current columns (contains Class objects)
   */
  private List columnTypes;

  /**
   * Data in current table. Each entry is a List of cell value objects.
   */
  private List rowList;

  /**
   * Object used to obtain JDBC connections
   */
  private ConnectionFactory connectionFactory;

  // Constructor using a DatabaseDataSource object to obtain connections to
  // the database
  public JDBCTableModel(ConnectionFactory connectionFactory) {
    this.connectionFactory = connectionFactory;
  }

  // Update the table's structure based on this query
  public void executeSQL(String query) throws SQLException {

    // Clear any data already in the table
    rowList = new LinkedList();
    columnTypes = new LinkedList();
    columnNames = new LinkedList();

    Connection connection = null;
    Statement statement = null;

    try {
      System.out.println("** About to execute: " + query);
      connection = connectionFactory.getConnection();
      statement = connection.createStatement();
      ResultSet resultSet = statement.executeQuery(query);
      updateFromResultSet(resultSet);
      resultSet.close();
    }

    // We don't need to catch SQL exceptions: let this method throw them
    // We do need to ensure that we clean up, however
    finally {
```

```
    try {
      if (statement != null) {
        statement.close();
      }
    } catch (SQLException ex) {

      // Ignore this exception, but catch it so that we can
      // try to close the connection anyway
    }

    try {
      if (connection != null) {
        connection.close();
      }
    } catch (SQLException ex) {
      throw new SQLException("JDBCTableModel threw SQLException in"
                             + "cleanup:" + ex);
    }
  }
}

// This is a simple-minded implementation to check if table is editable
public boolean isEditable() {
  return true;
}

// This is backed by the ResultSetMetaData that our query generated
public String getColumnName(int col) {
  String retVal;
  retVal = (String) columnNames.get(col);
  if (retVal == null) {
    retVal = "";
  }
  return retVal;
}

public Class getColumnClass(int col) {
  Class retVal;
  retVal = (Class) columnTypes.get(col);
  if (retVal == null) {
    retVal = Object.class;
  }
  return retVal;
}

public boolean isCellEditable(int row, int col) {

  // Should really check here whether the column is part of the primary
  // key. If it is, it shouldn't be editable
  return true;
}

public int getColumnCount() {
  return columnNames.size();
}
```

```java
public int getRowCount() {
  return rowList.size();
}

public Object getValueAt(int row, int col) {

  // Find the object for the correct row and look in
  // it for the value
  List rowData = (List) rowList.get(row);
  return rowData.get(col);
}

// Note that Swing models index from 0, JDBC ResultSets from 1
public void setValueAt(Object value, int row, int col) {

  // Not implemented
  // This might be implemented by giving this class the ability to
  // execute an update, or by using a JDBC 2.0 updateable ResultSet
}

// Set the table's contents based on this ResultSet
private void updateFromResultSet(ResultSet rs) throws SQLException {
  int curType;

  // We need the ResultSetMetaData to find out the number of
  // columns in this ResultSet and the column types and names
  ResultSetMetaData metaData = rs.getMetaData();
  int columns = metaData.getColumnCount();

  for (int col = 0; col < columns; col++) {
    columnNames.add(metaData.getColumnLabel(col + 1));
    try {
      curType = metaData.getColumnType(col + 1);
    } catch (SQLException e) {

      // This will go to the default case in the switch below
      curType = -1;
    }

    switch (curType) {
    case Types.CHAR:
    case Types.VARCHAR:
    case Types.LONGVARCHAR:
      columnTypes.add(String.class);
      break;

    case Types.TINYINT:
    case Types.SMALLINT:
    case Types.INTEGER:
      columnTypes.add(Integer.class);
      break;

    case Types.BIGINT:
      columnTypes.add(Long.class);
```

```
        break;

    case Types.FLOAT:
    case Types.DOUBLE:
      columnTypes.add(Double.class);
      break;

    case Types.DATE:
      columnTypes.add(java.sql.Date.class);
      break;

    default:
      columnTypes.add(Object.class);
      break;
    }    // switch
  }      // for each column

  // Load the actual data
  while (rs.next()) {

    // We hold each row of data in a list
    List rowData = new LinkedList();
    for (int col = 0; col < columns; col++) {

      // Remember that ResultSet columns are indexed from 1!
      rowData.add(rs.getObject(col + 1));
    }
    rowList.add(rowData);
  }

  // Remember to let any listeners know the table has changed.
  // This table may be used to support Swing clients as well as
  // web applications
  fireTableChanged(null);
  }
}
```

A more complex implementation of JDBCTableModel would implement table update functionality, possibly through JDBC 2.0 updateable ResultSets. To retain focus on JSPs, I have left this task as an exercise for the reader.

Another interesting possibility would be to supplement the JDBCTableModel with an EntityBeanTableModel, and the DatabaseDataSource with an EntityDataSource. EntityDataSource could use JNDI to locate entity EJBs, and EntityBeanTableModel could return their state and allow it to be updated.

Reviewing the Application

Several things could be done to improve this sample application. The error handling should be more sophisticated. Logging could be done using a third-party logging package or the logging methods of the Servlet API, rather than using System.out. (A good open-source logging package is Log4j, from the Apache Project, at http://jakarta.apache.org/log4j/. There is also a JSR for an official Java logging API: see http://java.sun.com/aboutJava/communityprocess/jsr/jsr_047_log.html.)

701

The HTML contained in the JSPs could be made more sophisticated, producing more attractive pages. Additional database information could be supplied: the schema to which each table belongs would be useful in large databases. A model could be used to populate a dropdown of available JDBC drivers, to spare users the need to type them in. The `JDBCTableModel` could be enhanced to support updates. Sharing controllers between many users would be likely to significantly improve performance if scalability is a major issue.

However, the soundness of the basic approach is proven by the ease with which some significant functional enhancements could be made.

The HTML contained in the existing JSP views could be improved easily by a page designer with a minimum of exposure to JSP concepts. No changes to these views could compromise the application's page flow, or produce a worse result than a JSP that temporarily wouldn't compile.

Consider adding the downloadable Excel data view: JSPs are not suited to generating such non-text formats, but a Servlet could be added to the application to access the session state and generate this content. The Servlet would obtain data from the same models as the JSP views. Adding additional HTML or XHTML views would be even easier: it would simply be necessary to write more JSP views. Each JSP view in this application is equivalent to an implementation of a single interface: the session bean will always expose the same data at the point when the controller forwards a request to a JSP view. (No such guarantee would be possible were the view pages to be public entry points for the application.)

Likewise, XML could be produced by the data tier or an additional view JSP, and transformed using an XSLT stylesheet tag. This could result in the addition of many views without further JSP coding, through the authoring of additional XSLT stylesheets.

Extending the application to handle JNDI directory data would require minimal changes to the front end: simply the provision of additional `DataSource` implementations, perhaps in a `datasources.jndi` package.

Importantly, the interface design used for the data explorer is not predicated on using JSP. Most of the code could be reused in a Swing interface.

Deploying the Application

The last remaining file required to implement the application is the WAR's `web.xml` file. This has two important jobs: it must let the JSP engine know where to locate the tag library descriptor required to describe the views tab library; and it must set the application's 'welcome page' to be `controller.jsp`. The context for the application is set as `dbexplore`:

```xml
<?xml version="1.0" encoding="UTF-8"?>

<!DOCTYPE web-app PUBLIC '-//Sun Microsystems, Inc.//DTD
   Web Application 2.2//EN' 'http://java.sun.com/j2ee/dtds/web-app_2.2.dtd'>

<web-app>
  <display-name>dbexplore</display-name>
  <description>Database Explorer</description>

  <session-config>
    <session-timeout>100</session-timeout>
```

```
    </session-config>

    <welcome-file-list>
      <welcome-file>controller.jsp</welcome-file>
    </welcome-file-list>

    <taglib>
      <taglib-uri>/views</taglib-uri>
      <taglib-location>/WEB-INF/lib/taglib.tld</taglib-location>
    </taglib>

  </web-app>
```

I developed this web application as an expanded WAR, testing it in both Tomcat and JRun. My expanded WAR had the following directory structure:

```
dbexplore/
          controller.jsp
          systemError.jsp
          editTable.jsp
          login.html
          chooseTable.jsp
          tableView.jsp
          csvView.jsp
          _chooseTable.jspf
          updateOK.jsp
          _chooseMode.jspf
          logout.html
          WEB-INF/
                  web.xml
                  lib/
                      taglib.tld
                      viewsclasses.jar
                  classes/
                          ui/
                              InvalidInputException.class
                              RequestController.class
                              RequestHandler.class
                              BrowseSession$QueryNameValueModel.class
                              BrowseSession.class
                              BrowseException.class
                              requesthandlers/
                                              NewConnection.class
                                              RunQuery.class
                                              DBConnect.class
                                              ChooseTable.class
                                              Logout.class
                                              UpdateTable.class
                          datasources/
                                      DataSource.class
                                      DataSourceException.class
                                      db/
                                          ConnectionFactory.class
                                          DatabaseDataSource.class
                                          JDBCTableModel.class
```

Note the inclusion of two files that include the implementation of the views tag library, both in the WEB-INF/lib directory: taglib.tld and viewsclasses.jar. The JSP engine automatically loads the classes in JARs placed in this directory, enabling the classes required to implement existing tag libraries to be packaged as a single distribution unit.

Before running the application, ensure that the JDBC drivers you wish to use are available to the JSP engine at runtime. The means of achieving this will differ between JSP engines. Although WARs are normally self-contained, it is impractical for this WAR to contain all the JDBC drivers it may be used with.

Summary

The sample application in this chapter illustrates one way in which the model view controller pattern discussed in Chapter 17 can be implemented using JSP. The core of this approach is the use of a 'controller' to handle incoming requests, ensuring that control flow is not handled by JSP views.

Although the concepts are those introduced in Chapter 17, the example in this chapter complements rather than builds directly on the code examples in that chapter. It uses JSPs and helper classes to implement the controller, rather than a Servlet controller. Rather than the request handler registration mechanism shown in Chapter 17, this example uses Java reflection to load additional request handlers at runtime. Like the registration mechanism, this delivers the key benefit of avoiding the necessity for complex conditional statements to determine how to handle a request. Compared with the approach implied by the code examples in the previous chapter, that shown in this chapter is simpler to implement and deploy, but is less suited to complex applications, in which the power of Servlet controllers can be fully leveraged.

This example shows an application of the coding standards for maintainable JSPs introduced in the last chapter. Most importantly:

❏   It achieves a clean separation of presentation, data and logic. Presentation is centralized in the JSP views; data is held in non UI-specific models, and logic is handled by request handler classes.

❏   It uses Java beans as models for the data presented on each JSP, rather than allowing JSP views to access request parameters themselves.

❏   It uses custom tags to help in the presentation of tabular data, avoiding the necessity for JSPs to perform nested iteration.

❏   It uses static includes to avoid code duplication and make conditional logic easier to follow.

The example is not a true J2EE architecture (it doesn't make use of EJB), but it does attempt to establish a clean separation between presentation and data layers, enabling the underlying data source to be changed without affecting the JSPs or helper classes.

Finally, the example is deployed as a WAR, showing the recommended approach to J2EE web deployment.

However well your application is designed, some bugs will always creep in. In the next chapter, we look at debugging web applications, and how we can make this task easier.

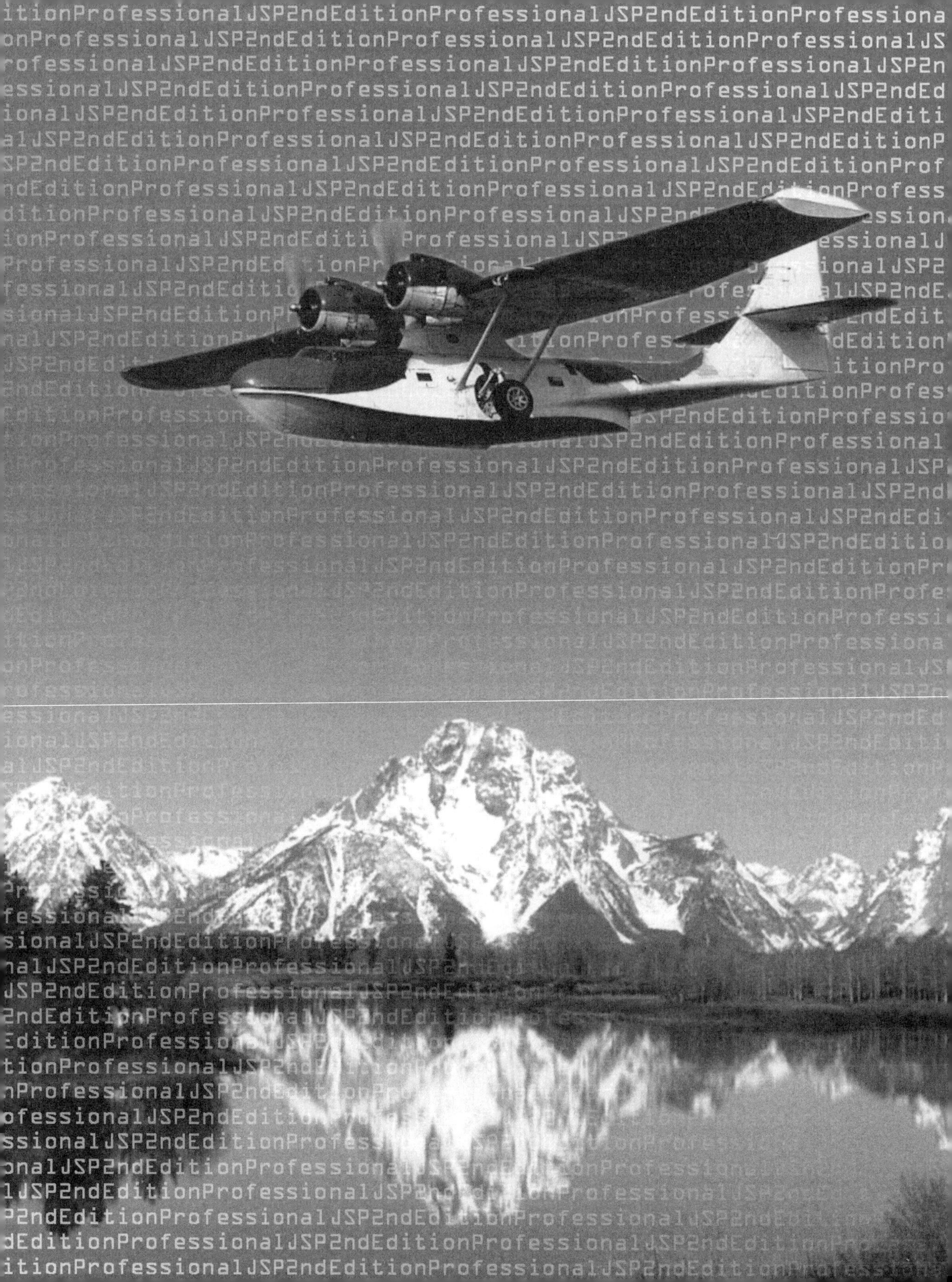

19

Debugging JSP and Servlets

Debugging web-based applications using JSP and Servlets is hard work – harder, in many ways, than debugging other Java-based systems. Why?

❑   The separation between the client (typically a web browser such as Internet Explorer) and our server-based code causes newcomers conceptual difficulties, something not assisted by 'helpful' browser caching (HTTP headers related to caching are discussed in Appendix F).

❑   The inherent concurrency of a web application leads to many potential problems with synchronization and thread-safety.

❑   Java Web containers and application servers provide their very own directory structures and class-loading rules, which can be extremely confusing at first. This also makes using a conventional debugger such as `jdb` hard, as you in effect have to debug the server itself.

❑   With JSP in particular, there's a lot going on 'under the surface'. Despite the best intentions of JSP's designers, a thorough understanding of both Servlets and the JSP execution model (discussed in Chapters 3 and 4) is essential for effective debugging.

❑   Intermixing of various languages (JSP, Java, HTML, JavaScript) and their syntax and escaping rules can make reading and understanding the code very tricky.

The key to making it easy to debug your web applications is to design them well in the first place. A well-designed application (as described in Chapter 17) will be divided into a clearly demarcated multi-tier architecture. Because this will mean it has distinct, easily testable components, the application will avoid many of the potential pitfalls.

This chapter will not give you a simple, foolproof method of debugging your code, because there's no such thing. Debugging is as much a mental issue as a strict computational one. A bug is a part of a program that doesn't exactly do what it's supposed to – an error in our mapping between the system's requirements and its implementation. In a strict sense, debugging can be seen as locating and fixing the 'bad' code, but will only be truly effective when your application has been carefully designed in a modular and testable manner.

The easiest bug to fix is the one that never existed, and a lot of debugging frustration can be saved by taking more care and time over the design and development of the application. Chapter 17 discusses best practices in writing well-structured, maintainable (and hence debuggable) web applications with the Java code where it belongs, in JavaBeans and Servlets.

In this chapter we'll look in turn at:

❑ Understanding error messages you receive when running JSP pages

❑ Tools and techniques for debugging our web applications

❑ Ways of using debuggers with Java web applications

❑ Common problems that occur, and how we can address them

Debugging Techniques and Tools

Let's start by looking at some of the more common techniques that are used when debugging the web tier.

Understanding JSP Errors

Since JSP is in fact a layer on top of Servlets and combines different languages, bugs can come from any one of these layers and in any language. The first step in debugging is to understand the error, get an idea where it comes from, and know where to look for it.

Compilation Errors

The first errors you typically encounter are compilation errors. When you request a page for the first time, the JSP is first transformed into a Servlet, which is compiled to a `.class` file and used by the web container to create the page. In general, compiling the `.jsp` file into a Servlet doesn't often go wrong. When it does, the error message can be recognized in Tomcat 4.0 since it throws an `org.apache.jasper.compiler.ParseException` referring to the original `.jsp` file.

For example, if we start a page with:

```
<%@ page impot="java.sql.*" %>
```

(misspelling `impot` instead of `import`), we get this error message from Tomcat 4.0:

The error reporting comes from the JSP engine (Jasper is Tomcat's JSP engine) and can be different for other implementations. As you can see, the error message includes the filename, the line and column number at which the error was found (0, 0 in this case), and some more information about the type of error; other JSP engines may differ in the information they provide.

Most compilation errors come from the second stage, where the Java compiler transforms the .java file into a .classfile. In this case, the error report comes from the Java compiler. Since that compiler doesn't know anything about JSP, but is just compiling the automatically generated Servlet code, interpreting this error report is much more difficult.

How do you know it's a compilation error?

❑ It doesn't work at all; you only get a bunch of errors in your browser.

❑ There will probably be some information about the compilation error (see screenshot below).

❑ If you check the work directory the JSP engine uses to put its .java and .class files, you'll notice that it did generate a new .java file but no new .class file.

❑ Some containers allow you to compile the JSP off-line (like Tomcat's jspc command). This can also be used to trap compilation errors before putting the files on a server.

For example, if we include a line of the form:

```
<%= results %>
```

when the scripting variable results is not defined, the error in Tomcat 4.0 looks like this:

The error reporting shows the type of error, line number, and a piece of code where the error is located; but here the line number refers to the line in the generated Servlet; you'll have to go and dig out that code from the server's work directory to figure out where the error is in your JSP. Note that at present Tomcat conveniently hides the useful bit of the error message (Undefined variable: results) off the screen. Hopefully the formatting of the error messages will improve soon.

The most common compilation errors are just small Java syntax mistakes like missing semicolons, non-matching quotes, or typos in variable or class names, but sometimes it isn't easy to understand the messages. The following table gives you some examples of error messages encountered with Tomcat 4.0 and what they really mean. Again, this isn't always the same for every setup and can vary depending on which JSP engine and java compiler you use. I found that the JServ error reporting is easier to read than Tomcat, for example:

Java compiler error	Possible causes	Example
')' expected	When you put a ';' at the end of an expression.	`<%=getValue(i);%>` is translated into `out.println(getvalue(i););`

try without catch, or catch without try, with line numbers pointing to the end of the file	Missing { or }.
	
	The JSP engine puts all your code from the JSP page in one big try – catch block. When the curly brackets in your code are not balanced, this error is thrown.
		`try{`
		`    ... your code ...`
		`} catch (exception e) {`
		`    ...`
		`}`

useBean tag must begin and end in the same physical file	The / at the end of the `<jsp:useBean>` tag is missing.	`<jsp:useBean id="theID"` `  class="theClass" >`

If it really isn't clear what the error means, it can be good to look at the generated `.java` file. (Some JSP engines require you to explicitly enable an option to retain the generated source files.) The directory where these files are stored depends on the JSP engine; for Tomcat, look inside the subdirectories of the `<CATALINA_HOME>\work` directory (`<TOMCAT_HOME>\work` on Tomcat 3.x). Overall, system generated code is difficult to read, but most JSP engines produce code that's easy to understand. Normally you have a standard header that stays more or less the same for all generated servlets. In the middle you find your entire HTML code translated into strings that are printed to the `out` stream. Scriptlets are just copied.

> *Some JSP engines (like that from ServletExec) don't copy the HTML code but use a function to extract the HTML portions from the original JSP file. Luckily, they also add comments to specify the link between the generated servlet code and the position in the JSP file.*

When you start using a newly installed JSP setup or when you use new packages, a 'class not found' compilation error is very likely a missing `import` statement or a class loading problem. These are easy to detect, but it's not always easy to solve them. Whilst standardization is improving, every Servlet engine has its own particular way for you to specify classes to load; we'll return to this shortly.

Runtime Errors

When your code makes it through the compiler, the Servlet is run and, if you're unlucky, the runtime errors start to appear. The first type of runtime error is where an exception is thrown. Runtime errors aren't always 'all-or-nothing' like compilation errors. An error occurring might depend on the input parameters, the value of some variables, the user that's logged in, etc. If you specified an `errorPage`, the request is redirected to that page; otherwise, you get the JSP engine's default error. Normally this is a printout of the error type (`NullPointerException` being one of my favorites), error message, and a stack trace.

> **If the stacktrace shows '(Compiled code)' instead of line numbers, you should try to start your Servlet engine with JIT compilation disabled. You can do this by specifying –Djava.compiler=NONE as a start option for the web container.**

We said that for compilation errors the line number might not be that informative, but with runtime errors it's about the only information shown, and in this case it almost always refers to the underlying Servlet and not to the JSP source.

We already mentioned that your JSP code is put inside one big `try – catch` block in the Servlet. Since this block catches `Exception`, we never get the compilation error about not catching a particular type of exception. This `try – catch` block catches all the `RuntimeExceptions` and the `Exceptions` we should have caught in our code like `SQLException`. When an exception is thrown, the output that was not yet flushed will be cleared; in most cases, this means that we get an empty page with the error message but hardly any information about whether the first part of the code did work out fine. There are two possibilities:

❑ Insert `out.flush();` after crucial places in your code: everything before the `flush()` is sent to the browser. This might very likely result in a bad HTML page, but it helps locating the error.

❑ Temporarily enclose your entire `.jsp` file in a `try – catch` block yourself. Looking at the resulting HTML code gives you a very precise hint on where to look for the bug.

One particularly unintuitive message produced by Tomcat is java.lang.IllegalStateException: Response has already been committed. At face value, this means that an attempt has been made to forward the request after at least a partial response has been sent to the client; this is illegal, hence this error. What is less intuitive is that with some versions this error occurs when an exception within the page causes an error page to be accessed.

If the response to the client has already been 'committed' (in other words, the output buffer has been flushed) when the exception occurs, the attempt to forward control to the error page will fail in this manner. This often happens when an exception is thrown after a `<jsp:include>` action with `flush="true"` has been performed.

Another type of runtime error is where there are no exceptions thrown and, from a Java point of view, everything is working fine. However, the resulting file is not what it should be. It can be wrong data that's being displayed or incorrect HTML formatting. It is particularly for these types of errors that the debugging techniques we'll explain later can be helpful.

HTML and JavaScript Errors

When part of the HTML formatting or even JavaScript functions are dynamically generated, this can easily result in incorrect HTML pages. Some browsers are more susceptible than others to these errors, so you might not immediately notice that there is a problem. In most cases, the errors can be located by comparing the generated output to a static HTML page that has correct formatting.

There are several utilities available that can check if your HTML syntax is correct. Some, like NetMechanics (http://www.netmechanics.com), even allow you to have your page checked online. In general, these problems are not difficult but they might require some concentration for a more complex page. If you dynamically create JavaScript the complexity increases.

Other tools like SiteScope (http://www.freshwater.com) allow you to periodically request a specific URL and alert you if an error occurs or if something is missing on the page. Normally these tools are used to guarantee that a server is still running, but they could be just as well be used to find out if a certain JSP is still displaying the correct content.

Debugging Techniques for the Web Tier

So, our JSP runs after a fashion, but we're getting the wrong result or an exception is being thrown somewhere. What can be done to isolate the problem? Running a conventional debugger is certainly an option that we'll look at presently, but there are other, simpler approaches to take.

Eyeballing

As simple as it may seem, eyeballing or code walkthrough – just looking at the code – is one of the most important and most used techniques for finding bugs. In fact eyeballing is almost always part of the total debugging process. It happens quite often that we're using JDB-type debugging, and while stepping through the code we suddenly see the bug in one of the lines that is not processed yet.

This mechanism can be extended to what we may call 'peer eyeballing', the ability of someone not involved in the code development to instantly pick out an error you have been spending hours trying to find. We can become so consumed by the project that we can develop a forest-and-trees syndrome that only a fresh set of eyeballs can overcome. Formal inspection of the code can be a highly effective technique for complex or error-prone code.

In order to enhance the visual inspection, we should keep our code clean and adhere to good standards and practices whether widely accepted good practices or those set by our organization. (I can recommend *Essential Java Style* by Jeff Langr, from Prentice Hall, ISBN:0-13-085086-1.) Here are a few guidelines:

- ❑ Keep methods small and clear.
- ❑ Try to make the code self-explanatory. Use intuitive variable and method names.
- ❑ Use proper indentation. Whatever style we use for aligning braces, be consistent, and use plenty of whitespace. (Indenting JSP code neatly is particularly difficult.)
- ❑ A nice list of how not to do it can be found at http://mindprod.com/unmain.html .

The success of eyeballing depends very much on the expertise of our developer and how familiar they are with the code.

Although it appears that this is just a technique, there are also tools that can make the eyeballing easier. A good code editor has features like syntax coloring, bookmarks, and commands for locating matching braces. Use these options and take some time to learn or install the necessary shortcuts. (Unfortunately, the combination of HTML, JSP tags, Java code, and client-side JavaScript may well be too much for the syntax highlighter of your favorite editor.)

System.out.println()

Using the standard output or error stream is an obvious and often used debugging technique. It doesn't look very sophisticated at first, but its simplicity is also its power; it is often much simpler to insert a `System.out.println()` statement than to go through the rigmarole of starting up a debugger.

In most server components, it's very unlikely that the standard output will be used in the core processing of the object. This leaves it available for outputting debug messages:

- ❑ Since the `System` object is part of the core Java objects, it can be used everywhere without the need to install any extra classes. This includes Servlets, JSP, RMI, EJB's, ordinary Beans and classes, and standalone applications.
- ❑ Compared to stopping at breakpoints, writing to `System.out` doesn't interfere much with the normal execution flow of the application, which makes it very valuable when timing is crucial; for example, when debugging concurrency issues, or when stopping at a breakpoint could cause a timeout in other components.

`System.out.println()` is easy to use as a marker to test whether a certain piece of code is being executed or not. Of course, we can print out variable values as well, but then its inflexibility becomes more apparent. I personally use it mostly with `String` constants such as `System.out.println("debug: end of calculate method")`. If we print out variables appended to a `String` message like in `System.out.println("debug: loop counter=" + i);` frequently, we're using a relatively expensive string concatenation just for debugging. Since the debugging overhead should be as low as possible, it might be better to use two statements if we are concerned about this:

```
System.out.print("debug: loop counter=");
System.out.println(i);
```

The most important problem is that it isn't always clear where the information is printed. Depending on the application server, our messages might be written to a file, a terminal window on the server, or they might just vanish altogether. Later in the chapter, we'll look at a monitoring tool that can be used to get around this problem.

As an alternative to printing to `System.out`, debugging information of this sort can be directed into the JSP output stream itself using `out.println()` in a scriptlet. Another useful technique is to dump all the information available to the JSP – request parameters, cookies, session ID, etc. – in this way. Tomcat 4.0 also provides a 'request dumper' facility (enabled via a setting in `server.xml`) that provides similar functionality.

Logging

The Servlet API provides a simple way of outputting information by using the `log()` method. Both `GenericServlet` and `ServletContext` provide `log()` methods, the `GenericServlet` method prepending the Servlet's name to the log entry. In both cases, `log()` takes either a single `String` argument or a `String` and a `Throwable`. The file to which the logging information is sent to depends on the Servlet container you're using and on its configuration.

While we can use this function to record debug information, strictly speaking the log isn't meant for this type of debugging purposes. The log should really be used to keep an eye on what happens in a production environment – when you start debugging, making small changes and requesting the pages again and again, it's not very convenient to keep opening the log files and scrolling to the bottom every time to see what happened.

The log files do give an indication of new emerging bugs or the frequency of problems. For that reason it's good to use the `log()` function in the `catch` clause of exceptions which should normally not occur.

Home-Made Logging Helper Classes

Creating your own `Debug` class, like in Alan R. Williamson's *Java Servlets By Example*, (Manning Publications, ISBN 188477766X) is a more flexible approach. A singleton class, or a class with only static functions, can be easily called from anywhere in your code. You can direct the output to whatever suits you best and there's the possibility to have a central switch to start and stop debugging mode.

The debug information can be rather easily directed to:

❑ A file

❑ A console-like window

❑ A network socket

❑ A buffer in memory

❑ The `out` PrintWriter

To do this you need to create you own `Debug` class that has an outline like the following:

```
public final class Debug {

    private Debug() {}

    public static void println(String logValue) {
```

```
        // put the code to output the
        // logValue to whatever you like here
        // (keep in mind that you can only use static class variables)
    }

}
```

The nice thing about the static `println()` method is that sending debug information is as easy as `Debug.println("my debug info");` and outputting information is not restricted to the Servlet environment, but is also possible in other classes and JavaBeans you want to use in your JSP pages.

Since you create this class yourself, you can keep extending the possibilities as you need them, such as:

❑ Printing the date and time, and session ID, when debugging in a situation where multiple clients are sending requests

❑ Printing out the stack trace when needed

❑ Dump variables of a specific bean by using introspection

❑ Using a threshold level in order to use different debug levels

❑ Showing which class/method the debugging info came from

A minor disadvantage of this technique is that it creates a tight coupling between all your code and the `Debug` class itself, which may limit the portability of your JavaBeans.

> **Instead of creating your own logging classes, you may prefer to use a ready-made logging library. The Apache Jakarta project's `log4j` is an open-source logging library that allows logging behavior to be controlled by editing a configuration file, without any need to recompile. Logging messages can be categorized, and categories organized in a hierarchy, allowing fine control of which log messages are output. See http://jakarta.apache.org/log4j/ for more information.**

Using Comments

Comments in your code can help the debugging process in various ways – I'm not only talking about the obvious advantage of having your code well documented. Comments can be used in lots of other ways in the debugging process.

Since we're mixing different languages, we also have different types of comments.

Java Comments

The Java single line (`// ...`) and multiple line (`/* ... */`) comments can be used to temporarily remove parts of your Java code. If the bug disappears, take a closer look at the code you just commented. The nice thing about the multi-line comment is that it can be used across HTML section in a JSP page so you can remove large parts very easily. The following code shows a part of a JSP file where we extract database data from a `ResultSet` object:

```
<TABLE>
  <% while (rs.next()) { %>
```

```
            <TR>
              <TD><%=rs.getString("first_name")%></TD>
              <TD><%=rs.getString("last_name")%></TD>
              <TD><%=rs.getString("order_date")%></TD>
            </TR>
          <% } %>
        </TABLE>
```

To check whether the error occurs when filling the table you can remove the retrieval of the data from the `ResultSet` by using the multi-line comments like this:

```
  <TABLE>
    <% /* while (rs.next()) { %>
        <TR>
          <TD><%=rs.getString("first_name")%></TD>
          <TD><%=rs.getString("last_name")%></TD>
          <TD><%=rs.getString("order_date")%></TD>
        </TR>
      <% } */ %>
  </TABLE>
```

The resulting HTML page will contain `<TABLE></TABLE>`, which will not ruin the normal HTML layout. Of course, you should pay attention as to where to put the comments, and to close the multi-line comment properly or you will get compilation errors again.

JSP Comments

JSP comments (`<%-- ... --%>`) can be used more or less like the Java multi-line comment but they should appear in the template portions of the JSP file. One important difference is that the code between the JSP comments isn't compiled into the Servlet, so it can be used to remove code that would produce an error when the JSP file is compiled into a Java file:

```
  <TABLE>
    <%-- <%while (rs.next()){%>
        <TR><TD><%=rs.getString("first_name")%></TD>
        <TD><%=rs.getString("last_name")%></TD>
        <TD><%=rs.getString("order_date")%></TD></TR>
      <%}%> --%>
  </TABLE>
```

HTML Comments

HTML comments (`<!-- ... -->`) are fundamentally different from Java and JSP comments. HTML comments are processed like any other code in the JSP file and included in the output, but the browser hides what is inside the comments. Therefore, HTML comments cannot be used to temporarily remove incorrect code like the previous types.

What these comments can be used for is to find out the value of a variable during processing, without having this output interfere with the page layout. In our previous example, it might be good to know the internal ID number of the client:

```
  <TABLE>
    <%while (rs.next()){%>
      <!--client ID: <%=rs.getString("client_id")%>-->
        <TR><TD><%=rs.getString("first_name")%></TD>
```

```
        <TD><%=rs.getString("last_name")%></TD>
        <TD><%=rs.getString("order_date")%></TD></TR>
    <%}%>
</TABLE>
```

The browser shows a page that's identical to the original one, but selecting View Source gives you the ID numbers right between the rest of the output. You should be careful about leaving too much debugging information like this in your final code – the HTML comment can be easily changed into a JSP comment to hide the debugging information in a production environment.

> **Remember that as well as always considering any input from a client suspect, you should view all text sent to a browser as being sent to someone with hostile purposes who will seek to exploit any potential security loopholes made evident.**

Invoking Debuggers

The time may well come when these simple debugging tips and tricks fail us, and we have to resort to a 'conventional' debugger, and the tools we should use for this depend on several factors. Some companies standardize on a single product or vendor and expect us to use the tools they provide for debugging. A more important factor is the developer's attitude and habits.

Some developers like working with a slick editor that does a lot behind the scenes and lets us focus on the real programming issues. Others will argue that these editors mean that we lose control over vital parameters and that 'real programmers' prefer a simple text editor and use the command line to compile their classes. Most probably, both approaches are correct in their own way. The same attitudes determine the tools and techniques a developer will use for debugging.

Integrated Debuggers

Most of the popular Java IDE's (IBM's VisualAge for Java, JBuilder, Visual Café, Forté for Java, etc.) have debugging facilities for server-side Java that integrate nicely with the rest of the development environment. Other tools like JProbe offer additional debugging facilities. These debuggers can be helpful, and some of them offer extremely useful facilities; Forté for Java Internet Edition, for example, offers the ability to step through a JSP side-by-side with the Servlet generated from it. However, they're not always the perfect and complete solution they often seem to suggest:

❑ The debugging process is mostly reduced to setting breakpoints, stepping through the code, and inspecting variables at runtime. However, debugging is much more than that, and many problems (like concurrency bugs) cannot be caught by this type of debugging. In fact, integrated IDE debuggers often introduce problems that either mask real application bugs, or introduce their own complexities that make their results unreliable when compared with real runtime behavior.

❑ If we can run everything on our development machine, debugging is rather more straightforward, but this doesn't always resolve errors. Even if the debugger is capable of doing 'remote debugging' this is always more difficult. The virtual machines (VMs) on the different servers need to be started in some sort of 'debug mode'. This isn't always easy and sometimes even impossible. The effort and impact of restarting servers makes it much harder to switch to debug mode, so should only be used for errors that are difficult to find.

❑ The debugger is often linked to a specific application server and even to a certain platform. In OO-terminology: the lack of encapsulation creates a tight coupling between the development/debugging practices and the deployment possibilities. Independence and 'Write Once, Run Anywhere' is one of the most important features of Java.

❑ No matter how fancy and advanced our tool is, debugging a server-side application will never be easy. Saying "debugging is no problem because we use an advanced integrated debugger" is like saying "we don't have to bother with security anymore, because we use Java". In reality, keeping track of a distributed system with multiple threads on multiple systems will always be a complex task.

❑ Some of these tools aren't bug free themselves, and the bigger the tool, the more bugs they have. Even if the tool is working fine, some developers don't like to depend on them and feel that they don't have total control over what's happening.

❑ These tools can be rather expensive, especially when they force us to use specific Servlet engines or web servers.

Do-It-Yourself: Using JDB

Although it's more low-level and doesn't have a point-and-click interface, the standard Java debugger, JDB, also allows remote debugging. In a standard debugging session, an application is started with the JDB command instead of java; as a rule, we should try to debug our applications on our local machine whenever possible. Most server components can be started on our development computer, like Tomcat, or have a standalone counterpart that can be used to simulate the server version.

In the case of Tomcat, the server is started with a batch file or Unix shell script. Open a copy of this startup script in a text editor and look for the line where the server itself is started. In Tomcat 4.0 on a Windows platform, the file is catalina.bat, which contains these lines:

```
...

if not "%OS%" == "Windows_NT" goto noTitle
set _STARTJAVA=start "Catalina" "%JAVA_HOME%\bin\java"
set _RUNJAVA="%JAVA_HOME%\bin\java"
goto gotTitle
:noTitle
set _STARTJAVA=start "%JAVA_HOME%\bin\java"
set _RUNJAVA="%JAVA_HOME%\bin\java"
:gotTitle

...

%_RUNJAVA% %CATALINA_OPTS% -Dcatalina.home="%CATALINA_HOME%"
    org.apache.catalina.startup.Bootstrap %2 %3 %4 %5 %6 %7 %8 %9

...
```

Changing java to jdb, we have an alternative startup script that starts the server in debug mode.

In earlier versions of Tomcat, the file was instead called tomcat.bat. *Note that this sort of experimentation with the Tomcat startup script is actually encouraged by the Tomcat developers; as the Tomcat 3.2 User Guide says "Do not hesitate, just do it." However, it would be prudent to make your changes to a **copy** of the file rather than to the original, indeed it is possible to assemble a good-sized collection of Tomcat startup scripts that each address a different debugging configuration.*

Other application servers allow us to specify a JVM startup path and additional options to achieve the same results. It might take some time to figure out how to start a particular Servlet engine in debug mode, but in most cases it is possible.

An important feature of jdb is that it allows us the option to connect to an already running JVM, which may be on another computer. This might be easier than the normal JDB use we just described, especially in a server environment. For details of how to do this, see the jdb documentation: the VM we want to debug must be started in debug mode, and we have to disable the JIT compiler by adding - Djava.compiler=NONE to the command line, and make a few extra classes available to the debugger. The JVM starts as usual but displays a password on the screen that we need to supply to jdb in order to connect to this VM.

This password is necessary to correctly identify the VM, since there can be more than one running on the same server. Also, because you can connect to this debug VM from another host, the password provides additional security. The biggest problem is that it's not always possible to start the JVM visually in order to get the password.

This is a very narrow interpretation of the debugging concept. As we said before, debugging is much more than setting breakpoints and stepping through the code. Most of the remarks mentioned, regarding the fancy integrated IDE's are also valid with this low level JDB approach. But if you are the kind of developer who edits their code with notepad or vi and uses the command line to compile their classes, you might prefer this JDB command-line technique.

Monitoring Tools

Monitoring tools, whether generic or developed especially for a particular application, can provide a valuable further weapon in our debugging arsenal. We'll look at a couple of potential tools.

Redirecting Standard Output

Most application servers and Servlet engines start the JVM without a visual presence, like a console window. However, even if we have the option of displaying a terminal window, (for example, by using java instead of javaw), the messages still show up on the server instead of on our PC.

Luckily, System.setOut() lets us change the OutputStream that is used by System at runtime. The following Debug class uses that technique to redirect the standard out to a ServerSocket at a specified port. The class extends OutputStream and registers itself as the standard output. It also starts a thread that listens to incoming connections. When a client connects, the standard out is redirected to that client socket. Since we keep a reference to the previous standard output, we can keep sending all messages to the old OutputStream as well. To keep things simple, this class only supports a single connection:

```
import java.io.*;
import java.util.*;
import java.net.*;

public class Debug extends OutputStream implements Runnable {

    // Instance variables
    int          port;      // The port we listen on
    ServerSocket server;    // ServerSocket listening on the port
    boolean      active;    // Are we actively awaiting connections?
```

```
Socket        client;          // Our debugging client
OutputStream clientStream;      // The OutputStream to the client
Thread        listener;         // The thread used to listen for connections
PrintStream  old;              // The original System.out

// Create a Debug OutputStream listening on the specified port

public Debug(int port) {
  this.port = port;

  try {
    server = new ServerSocket(port);
  } catch (IOException e) {
    System.out.println("could not create server");
  }
}
```

The `isActive()` method returns true if the debug stream is currently active:

```
public boolean isActive() {
  return active;
}
```

The `startServer()` method activates the debug stream by redirecting `System.out`:

```
public void startServer() {
  if (!active) {
    old = System.out;

    System.setOut(new PrintStream(this));

    active = true;
    listener = new Thread(this);

    listener.start();
    System.out.println("debug server started");
  }
}
```

The `stopServer()` method stops the debug stream by directing System.out back to the original stream:

```
public void stopServer() {
  active = false;

  System.setOut(old);
  System.out.println("debug server stopping");

  if (client != null) {
    try {
      client.close();
    } catch (IOException e) {}
  }
}
```

The Debug class implements Runnable and run() listens for socket connections and if no-one is already connected directs debugging output to the client:

```java
public void run() {
  Socket localSocket = null;

  try {
    while (active) {
      localSocket = server.accept();

      if (client == null) {
        client = localSocket;
        clientStream = client.getOutputStream();

        new PrintStream(clientStream).println("Welcome to the Debug Server");
      } else {
        PrintWriter second = new PrintWriter(localSocket.getOutputStream());

        second.print("already connected");
        localSocket.close();
      }
    }

    System.out.println("debug server stopped");
  } catch (IOException e) {
    System.out.println("debug server crashed");
    System.out.println(e.getMessage());

    active = false;
  }
  finally {
    if (server != null) {
      try {
        server.close();
      } catch (IOException e) {}
    }
  }
}
```

A client is disconnected if communication with it goes wrong. This method is called from write() below in the event of an IOException:

```java
protected void clearClient() {
  if (client != null) {
    try {
      client.close();
    } catch (IOException ioe) {}
  }

  client = null;
  clientStream = null;
}
```

The following method overrides OutputStream.write() to direct output to both any remote debugging client and the old System.out:

```
public void write(byte[] b) throws IOException {
    if (old != null) {
        old.write(b);
    }

    if (clientStream != null) {
        try {
            clientStream.write(b);
        } catch (IOException e) {
            clearClient();
        }
    }
}

public void write(byte[] b, int off, int len) throws IOException {
    if (old != null) {
        old.write(b, off, len);
    }

    if (clientStream != null) {
        try {
            clientStream.write(b, off, len);
        } catch (IOException e) {
            clearClient();
        }
    }
}

public void write(int b) throws IOException {
    if (old != null) {
        old.write(b);
    }

    if (clientStream != null) {
        try {
            clientStream.write(b);
        } catch (IOException e) {
            clearClient();
        }
    }
}

}
```

So how do we use this Debug class? We simply use System.out.println() to send debug messages. The nice thing is that there is no direct connection between the class we want to debug and this Debug server. We don't have to additionally import anything. The Debug server makes sure that these messages are sent to the developer's machine.

To use this class to debug servlets and JSP, we can create a DebugServlet:

```
import java.io.*;
import javax.servlet.*;
import javax.servlet.http.*;
```

```
public class DebugServlet extends HttpServlet {
  Debug debugger ;

  public void service(HttpServletRequest req, HttpServletResponse res)
          throws ServletException, IOException {

    String option = req.getParameter("option");
    res.setContentType("text/html");
    PrintWriter out = res.getWriter();
    out.println("<html><head><title>Debug servlet</title></head><body>");
    out.println("<h1>Debug servlet</h1>");
```

Debugging is switched on and off like this:

```
    if ("socket".equals(option)) {
      if (debugger == null) {
        debugger = new Debug(9999);
      }
      debugger.startServer();
    }
    if ("closesocket".equals(option)) {
      if (debugger != null) {
        debugger.stopServer();
      }
    }
    String testValue = req.getParameter("test");
    if (testValue != null) {
      System.out.println("Debug test: " +testValue);
    }

    if ((debugger != null) && (debugger.isActive())) {
      out.print("<a href=\"telnet://");
      out.print(req.getServerName());
      out.println(":9999\" target=\"_blank\"> Connect to the debugger </a><p>");

      out.print("<a href=");
      out.print(req.getRequestURI());
      out.println("?option=closesocket> Shut down debugger </a ><p>");
    } else {
      out.print("<a href=\"");
      out.print(req.getRequestURI());
      out.println("?option=socket\"> Start remote debugger </A><p>");
    }
    out.println("<form method=\"post\" >");
    out.println("Test <input type=\"text\" name=\"test\">");
    out.println("<input type=\"submit\">");
    out.println("</form> </body> </html>");
  }
}
```

By specifying the `option` parameter, the Servlet controls starting and stopping of the remote debugger. The servlet itself shows the correct hyperlinks to perform these commands. We could create a 'debug client' as an application or an applet that opens a socket connection to our debug server. However, the only thing this client has to do is display to the user what was sent over the socket connection.

723

On most Operating Systems there is already a tool that does exactly that. It's called Telnet, and it's mostly used to control a server or interact with a certain service, but in our case, we just use it as an ultra thin client solution to connect to port 9999 and see the debug messages. To make this even more convenient, the Servlet presents us with a hyperlink that tries to open Telnet with the correct host and port. Any string that's entered into the form is printed to System.out, so this immediately allows us to check if everything is working, as is shown in the next screenshot.

> *Some versions of Windows have rather limited Telnet programs that lack the ability to scroll back up the screen; in this case, a third-party Telnet client may be of use.*

The Telnet window not only shows the messages sent by Servlets or JSP, but also those from any other object or Bean that runs in the same VM:

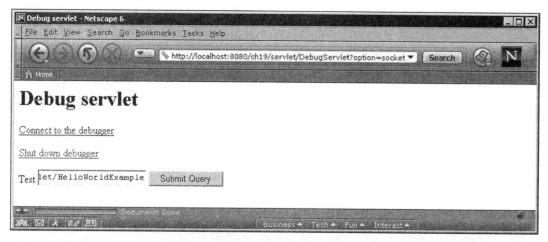

This Debug class is already very powerful, but there are many potential enhancements:

- ❑ Add security like asking for a password or restricting access to certain IP addresses.
- ❑ Allow multiple Telnet sessions to connect to a single server.
- ❑ Allow the client to specify filters. When there are lots of debugging messages, it might be better to only send the messages that contain a specified 'filter' string.
- ❑ Add an optional timestamp to each message.
- ❑ Allow the client to enter certain commands, like asking for memory usage, or shutting down the debug server through the Telnet session.
- ❑ The JDBC DriverManager has a method SetLogWriter that works just like System.setOut. We could try to change the Debug class so that this JDBC log information is sent over the network instead of System.out.

Session Monitoring

The following servlet allows us to check out all objects stored in the session. We might also provide mechanisms to change the values of the objects or to delete them from the session:

```
import java.io.*;
import java.util.*;
import java.lang.reflect.*;
import javax.servlet.*;
import javax.servlet.http.*;

public class SessionMonitor extends HttpServlet {
```

doGet() processes a client request. An option is given to add a TestBean to the session. Then, if a Bean name was specified display that Bean's details, otherwise list all Beans in the session:

```
public void doGet(HttpServletRequest req, HttpServletResponse res)
        throws ServletException, IOException {
  res.setContentType("text/html");
  PrintWriter out = res.getWriter();
  HttpSession session = req.getSession(true);
  out.println("<HTML><HEAD><TITLE>session monitor</title></head>");
  out.println("<BODY><H1>SessionMonitor</H1>");
  out.println("This form allows us to add new string values to the ");
  out.println("current session to check out this servlet");
  out.println("<FORM>add string key <INPUT TYPE=\"text\" ");
  out.println("NAME=\"key\"><br/>");
  out.println("add string value<INPUT TYPE=\"text\" NAME=\"value\"><br/>");
  out.println("<INPUT TYPE=\"submit\"></FORM><P>");

  testInit(req,session);
  String beanName = req.getParameter("name");
  if (beanName == null) {
    showBeanList(req, session, out);
  } else {
    showSingleInstance(beanName, session, out);
  }
  out.println("</BODY></HTML>");
}
```

A TestBean is stored in the session with the specified name and first value:

```
private void testInit(HttpServletRequest req, HttpSession session) {
  String newKey = req.getParameter("key");
  String newValue = req.getParameter("value");
  if ((newKey !=null) && (newValue != null)){
    TestBean test= new TestBean();
    test.setValue1(newValue);
    test.setValue2("fixed text");
    test.setValue3(newKey+"-->"+newValue);
    session.setAttribute(newKey, test);
  }
}
```

The showBeanList() method displays a list of beans stored in the session, and links back to this Servlet to give details of each one:

```
private void showBeanList(HttpServletRequest req, HttpSession session,
                          PrintWriter out) {
  String URI = req.getRequestURI();
  Enumeration names = session.getAttributeNames();

  while (names.hasMoreElements()) {
    String attributeName= (String) names.nextElement();
    out.print("<A HREF=");
    out.print(URI);
    out.print("?name=");
    out.print(attributeName);
    out.print(">");
    out.println(attributeName);
    out.print("</A><BR />");
  }
}
```

The following method displays the details of the bean stored in the session under the name beanName. Introspection is used to display each of its fields:

```
private void showSingleInstance(String beanName, HttpSession session,
                                PrintWriter out) {
  Object check = session.getAttribute(beanName);
  out.println("<H2> Checking object ");
  out.println(beanName);
  out.println("</H2><UL>");
  try {
    Class checkClass = check.getClass();
    Field[] fields = checkClass.getFields();
    for (int i = 0; i < fields.length; i++) {
      out.println("<LI>");
      out.println(fields[i].getName());
      out.println(" (");
      out.println(fields[i].getType().toString());
      out.println("): ");
      try {
        out.println(fields[i].get(check).toString());
      } catch (Exception e) {
        out.println(" ! Cannot be displayed !");
      }
    }
  } catch (NullPointerException e) {
    out.println("null pointer Exception");
  }
}
```

TestBean is a sample bean we can put into the session to test this Servlet:

```
private class TestBean {
  public String value1;
  public String value2;
  public String value3;
  public String getValue1() {
    return value1;
  }
  public void setValue1(String value) {
```

```
      value1 = value;
    }
    public String getValue2() {
      return value2;
    }
    public void setValue2(String value) {
      value2 = value;
    }
    public String getValue3() {
      return value3;
    }
    public void setValue3(String value) {
      value3 = value;
    }
  }
}
```

The application event listeners introduced in the new Servlet 2.3 specification introduce further possibilities for monitoring the status of an application. Running the Servlet gives us the following output:

Once we add a key and a string value, they are stored in the session and can be viewed by clicking on the key's name. For example, if we add a key named shoppingCart and give it the value empty we would see the following screen if we clicked on the appropriate link:

Avoiding Common Problems

Having reviewed the debugging tools and techniques that will be of use when dealing with Java-based web applications, let's look at some of the more specifically problematic areas that often cause problems.

Long Running Processes

Server-side Java processes typically run for a long time when compared to CGI scripts, as they don't start a new process with every request; therefore, some problems might never occur in an application/applet context, just because these are typically stopped and restarted quite often. This is obviously not something normally done on server-side applications.

One of the potential problems caused by long running processes is running out of system memory resources. Java's garbage collector takes care of many potential memory leaks; compared to C++ this saves the Java developer from some problems that are otherwise hard to debug. However, this doesn't mean that we can forget about memory issues altogether. The garbage collector destroys all objects that are no longer referenced, yet we can still have object instances that are no longer required but somehow still have a reference to them, and they cannot be cleaned. Since these objects can keep references to other objects, we might keep a lot of memory space occupied.

These objects are called 'loiterers'. (See http://www.ddj.com/articles/2000/0002/0002l/0002l.htm *for some more details on memory leaks in Java.)*

Firstly, we can use our OS to monitor the memory usage of the JVM. JDK 1.3 comes with a somewhat unfriendly profiler, or there are also tools like JProbe profiler (http://www.sitraka.com) and OptimizeIt (http://www.optimizeit.com) that give us a very detailed overview of how much memory our objects occupy and can help debugging these problems. The implementation of the garbage collector depends on the JVM. Some are better than others, which might lead to bugs or problems that only occur on a certain OS.

Most server-side applications use caching on several layers to speed up processing. In long running processes, it's important that this cache doesn't grow to unlimited size. Since there's no 'sizeOf' in Java to measure how much memory an object uses, it's not easy to create a cache that is strictly memory limited.

Most caches simply allow a fixed number of objects, regardless of their size. Although not very sophisticated, this might give good results, provided we base our cache size on tests and not on some wild guess. Also, keep in mind that an object in the cache might keep a reference to other objects, preventing these instances from being garbage collected. In which case, a cache with a rather small number of objects can still occupy a lot of memory.

Even when resources are container managed it is important to hold on to resources for as little time as possible and to clean up other resources. We often see code like this:

```
try {
    FileInputStream in = new FileInputStream(filename);
    // Do something that can throw an IOException
    in.close();
} catch (IOException e) {
    // We don't have a handle here to the InputStream
}
```

When an error occurs, the `InputStream` isn't properly closed. We might just rely on the garbage collector to close the file, but the correct code should declare the `FileInputStream` outside the `try` block and close the `FileInputStream` in a `finally` block. In any case, the OS will close the file when the program finishes. Therefore, this code might not be a big problem for normal applications. Server-side applications, however, are meant to run for days or even months without restarting, so proper cleanup becomes much more important.

The situation is even more complex in the case of JDBC connections, especially when we use connection pooling. Some JDBC drivers not only keep resources occupied when a connection isn't closed, but also with an open `Statement` or `ResultSet`. Normally we could expect the closing connection to take care of closing a `Statement` or a `ResultSet`, but this isn't always the case. Besides, when we use connection pooling, we don't close the connection at all, and therefore the garbage collector cannot help us in any way:

```
try {
   Connection conn = // Get a connection from the pool
   Statement stmt = conn.createStatement();
   ResultSet rs = stmt.executeQuery("SELECT COLUMNS FROM TABLE");
   // Get the values
   // or update the database
   rs.close();
   stmt.close();
   // Return connection to the pool
} catch (SQLException e) {
   System.out.println(e.getMessage());
}
```

If we use JDBC code like this, there are several potential problems:

❑   If something goes wrong the `Connection` is never returned to the pool, but also the `ResultSet` and `Statement` aren't closed properly and could keep open resources on the database.

❑   If we don't use auto-commit, we should do a rollback in case of failure.

❑   Another thing that's often forgotten, we only use the first `SQLException`. `SQLExceptions` have a special feature that allows them to have several error messages linked to a single exception. We'll come back to this feature later. In our example, valuable information that's contained in the errors that are chained to the first exception is lost.

To avoid these problems, we should code it like this:

```
Connection conn = null;
Statement stmt = null;
ResultSet rs = null;
try {
   conn = // Get a connection from the pool
   conn.setAutoCommit(false);
   Statement stmt = conn.createStatement();
   ResultSet rs = stmt.executeQuery("SELECT COLUMNS FROM TABLE");
   // Get the values
   // or update the database
   conn.commit();

} catch (SQLException e) {
```

If we're handling the exception at this level, deal with it. Otherwise let this method throw a
`java.sql.SQLException` and get the next level up to deal with the consequences:

```
System.out.println(e.getMessage());
while ((e=e.getNextException()) != null) {
  System.out.println(" next "+ e.getMessage());
}

} finally {
```

In the `finally` block, close the `ResultSet`, `Statement`, and `Connection`. Do each inside its own `try`
`- catch` block, to help ensure that they all get called even if one of the `close()` calls throws an exception:

```
try {
  if (rs != null) {
    rs.close();
  }
} catch (SQLException e) {
  System.out.println(e.getMessage());
  while ((e = e.getNextException ()) != null){
    System.out.println("  next "+ e.getMessage());
  }
}

try {
  if (stmt != null) {
    stmt.close();
  }
} catch (SQLException e) {
  System.out.println(e.getMessage());
  while ((e = e.getNextException ()) != null){
    System.out.println("  next "+ e.getMessage());
  }
}

try {
  if (conn != null) {
    conn.rollback();
    // Return the connection to the pool
  }
} catch (SQLException e) {
  System.out.println(e.getMessage());
  while ((e = e.getNextException ()) != null){
    System.out.println("  next "+ e.getMessage());
  }
}

}
```

Even this code isn't 100% bullet proof, but it certainly becomes ugly. OK, we might choose to ignore
handling the exceptions that are thrown by the closing and rollback statements, but we still have more error
handling than actual database code. Do we really write code like this everywhere we access the database?
Probably not, unless we're a very disciplined programmer, but we ought to.

The difficulty with these memory- or resource-related bugs is that they only show up after a certain time and
they are difficult to reproduce, especially on our development computer.

Robustness and Stability

Server-side applications should not fail, but when they do, they should do so gracefully with minimal impact on other components and the server. A server application crashing due to component failure can affect many users in addition to other applications running in the same VM.

Built-in range checking, memory management, and exception handling plus the absence of pointers prevent Java code from producing the types of system crashes associated with languages such as C++. It remains the developers' responsibility to follow the specifications for API's carefully to avoid threading issues and other programmatic failure.

Whilst the only real way around these issues is to design the system from the outset to avoid concurrency problems, we can use tools such as Apache JMeter (http://java.apache.org/jmeter/) that simulate a number of concurrent users requesting information – normally used to measure performance – to test the robustness of our setup under heavy load. Such tools will be covered in Chapter 20.

Stress testing the system can highlight weaknesses and look for performance bottlenecks. To provide stability at the hardware level, an application might be deployed on multiple servers. When one of them goes down, the others take over. Such a fail-over setup adds complexity to the total system.

Due to this complexity using a fail-over backup server might, curiously, introduce new bugs. For example, if we store non-`Serializable` objects in a session or if the application server doesn't support distributed sessions we could lose session state information while switching over to the backup server. (With distributed sessions, a session can be serialized and transferred bodily across to a different server.) The same problem can arise if we use multiple servers in parallel to provide better performance (known as load balancing) – the only solution here is to read your server documentation carefully.

Nesting Exceptions

In a typical setup, the interface to the user is made up of JSPs and Servlets. This is an appropriate place to use an error page to inform the user about the error. Exceptions move up the call stack to the point where they are caught. Eventually they reach the `try – catch` block around the body of the JSP-Servlet (the Servlet that's automatically created by the JSP engine) and the user is redirected to the error page.

In complex systems, the exception can originate from a distant low-level component. The end user shouldn't be bothered with these low-level details. A user should be shown an error like "user registration failed" instead of "SQLError: X03805: Primary key for table reg_usr is not unique", although for debugging purposes the latter is very useful.

In a clean setup, the higher-level components should catch exceptions (like `IOExceptions` or `SQLExceptions`) thrown by the components they use, and in turn, throw a higher-level exception (like `LoginException` or `EmployeeException`) themselves. If these higher-level components just pass on the low-level exceptions, all possible exceptions would have to be specified in the interface. This not only looks bad, but it also means our classes aren't properly encapsulated.

Of course, it would be ideal if we could somehow show the higher-level error messages to the end user, but still have the option of recording all the details of the original errors for debugging/maintenance purposes. To achieve this we can use nested (or chained) exceptions. Using nested exceptions means that an exception contains a handle to another exception (which might in turn have a reference to another, creating a chain of exceptions). This is a technique that's used in the JDK classes too, such as in `java.sql.SQLException` or `java.rmi.RemoteException`. Unfortunately, this isn't always implemented in the same way and it might have been better if this chaining mechanism were provided by the root exception object.

Exceptions normally have two constructors: the default constructor, and one where we can specify a `String` error message. In order to create nested exceptions, we make a third constructor that takes the message `String` and another object of type `Exception` that's stored in a member variable:

```java
public class NestedException extends Exception {
  private Exception nested;

  public NestedException(){}

  public NestedException(String msg) {
    super(msg);
  }

  public NestedException(String msg, Exception nested) {
    super(msg);
    this.nested=nested;
  }

  public Exception getNestedException() {
    return nested;
  }
}
```

To use this technique, we must inherit our own custom exceptions from `NestedException` instead of from the root `Exception` class.

In our components that throw the higher-level exceptions and catch the lower-level ones, we typically use code like this:

```java
public boolean login(String userid, String password) throws LoginException {
  try {
    // Here we have code to validate the login
    // say, by looking it up in the database
  } catch (SQLException e) {
    // Log the error
    throw new LoginException("Could not validate login", e);
    // Constructor type 3 from NestedException
  }
}
```

Since we inherited our `LoginException` from `NestedException`, we can use the `LoginException` information to show the user what happened, and recursively check all exceptions that are chained to this `LoginException` to provide a more detailed error message for the developer. Since the chaining mechanism isn't built into the standard exception object, probably the safest way to recursively get all the information from a `NestedException` is to override the `getMessage()` method:

```java
public String getMessage() {
  StringBuffer msg = new StringBuffer (super.getMessage());
  if (nested !=null) {
    msg.append("\r\n"); // or <BR /> for display in browser
    msg.append(nested.getMessage());
  }
  return msg.toString();
}
```

The standard SQLException doesn't use this technique to show the messages of the contained exceptions automatically in their getMessage() method. As a result, most nested exceptions in SQLexceptions are never used and the information is just thrown away.

The article at http://www.javaworld.com/javatips/jw-javatip91-2.html gives a more detailed explanation of nested exceptions and shows how to get the stack trace from the nested exception, even if that exception is thrown on a remote RMI server.

Concurrency

Unlike some other technologies, web applications are inherently multi-threaded. Every request uses a unique thread that executes the service() method of a single Servlet instance. While this technique offers good performance and easy solutions to some specific problems, it also introduces a certain complexity. Developers not familiar with multi-threaded systems might miss code that is not thread-safe. The Java keyword synchronized is the key to making sure a piece of code is only executed by one thread at a time, and a thorough understanding of its use and related threading issues is crucial in writing thread-safe web applications.

We emphasized at the beginning of this chapter that a good design is the best way to reduce time spent debugging, and this applies particularly when considering concurrency. The way to prevent concurrency problems is to think about it very carefully before starting to code, rather than discovering the problems while debugging and trying to fix them at that stage.

Let's give an example of a Servlet that is not thread safe. We first create a very simple hit counter like this:

```
import java.io.*;
import javax.servlet.*;
import javax.servlet.http.*;

public class HitCounter extends HttpServlet {
  int hits = 0;

  public void doGet(HttpServletRequest req, HttpServletResponse res)
              throws ServletException, IOException {
    PrintWriter out = res.getWriter();
    res.setContentType("text/html");
    hits++;

    out.println("<html><head><title>Run command</title></head>");
    out.println("<body><h1>You are visitor # ");
    out.println(hits);
    out.println("</h1></body></html>");
  }
}
```

At first we might see nothing wrong with this code. However, consider two requests at almost exactly the same moment. Assume the current number of hits is 78. The first thread starts executing the doGet() method but when it reaches line 11 (hits is now 79), the OS switches to the second request and this new thread processes the complete method and displays "You are visitor # 80". Immediately after that the first thread can continue and will also show "You are visitor # 80". The following table clearly shows the execution of the two concurrent requests:

Thread 1	Thread 2	Hits
res.setContentType("text...		78
hits++;		79
out.println("<html><head>...		79
	res.setContentType("text...	79
	hits++;	**80**
	out.println("<html><head>...	80
	out.println("<body><h1>...	80
	out.println(hits);	80
	out.println("</h1></body>...	80
out.println("<body><h1>...		80
out.println(hits);		**80**
out.println("</h1></body>...		80

There's never been a number 79 and we have two number 80s. Of course, if it's only a hit counter, we don't really care much about this. However, the same problem can occur in code that is more critical as well.

Think about the consequences if we want to give a prize for the 1000th visitor. We run the risk of having zero or two winners.

In our hit counter example, we might try to combine lines 11 and 15 to:

```
out.println(++hits);
```

The probability of still having the concurrency problem will be much lower, but it still exists. Besides, it isn't always possible to put the related lines that close together.

That's where we would need to synchronize to make sure no two threads will execute a single block of lines at the same time:

```
public void doGet(HttpServletRequest req, HttpServletResponse res)
        throws ServletException, IOException {

  PrintWriter out = res.getWriter();
  res.setContentType("text/html");

  out.println("<html><head><title>Run command</title></head>");
  out.println("<body><h1>Number of hits: ");

  synchronized(this){
    hits++;
    out.println(hits);
  }

  out.println("</h1></body></html>");
}
```

However, synchronizing can have a serious impact on execution speed. First of all, the action of locking an object itself takes some time, but obviously, when a thread has to wait on another thread to finish a piece of code, that time is just wasted. That's why we had better not synchronize the complete doGet() method by using:

```
public synchronized void doGet(HttpServletRequest req, HttpServletResponse res)
        throws ServletException, IOException {
```

In this case, the chances of having one thread waiting for another would become much higher.

If it weren't for this performance penalty, the easiest solution would be to just synchronize every method. It's also not easy to decide what parts to synchronize. If the question, "What to synchronize?" could be answered easily, this would most probably be done automatically for you by the Java compiler. Instead, we need to carefully decide ourselves, as part of our system design, how we are going to prevent problems arising from concurrent access to shared objects.

Performance isn't the only issue in considering where to use synchronization. In fact, not designing your synchronization carefully can cause deadlock problems. Especially in a distributed environment, this can become quite complicated. If we have an RMI server that calls back to the original calling object and both methods are synchronized, we end up with two servers waiting for each other and the system hangs.

Where can we expect concurrency problems?

- ❑ Objects stored in the ServletContext (the JSP application scope). It should be obvious that these objects can be used by several threads at the same time.

- ❑ Objects stored in a session. Although at first, it might seem strange to have multiple concurrent requests using an object in a session. We might imagine a screen with several browser windows and a user clicking the mouse as fast as he can, but it's less spectacular. A single request for a page that uses frames can easily cause multiple requests that result in concurrent threads on the server. The fact that these multiple threads originate from a single user doesn't make it less problematic.

- ❑ To speed up our application, we often implement a caching mechanism. Instead of recreating certain objects every time we need them, we could put objects that take some time to be instantiated in a cache and use the same instance again later. An instance stored in such a cache can be retrieved and used by multiple requests at the same time. Ideally, the decision whether you're using a cache or not should be transparent to the programmer that uses the beans. Performance optimizations should be done near the end of the development cycle, once the code is working, though it is important to have eventual optimization in mind during the design phase. However, by simply starting to use a cache, new concurrency bugs can suddenly appear in code that always ran fine.

- ❑ Singleton patterns and static methods which access static variables. The reason to use a Singleton pattern and static methods is to have a single instance of an object available to the whole VM, so obviously, we can have concurrent requests.

- ❑ Servlet member variables like in the HitCounter example. Since there's normally only one instance of a Servlet and every request uses that same Servlet instance, every method that changes member variables should use synchronized blocks. The same is true for variable declarations between <%! %> JSP tags, that results in an instance variable in the generated Servlet. We often see code where people use <%! %> to declare variables, where a thread safe <% %> scriptlet (which generates a local variable within the _jspService() method) would give the same results. In fact, you hardly ever need to use <%! %> declarations in JSP.

Consider the final point above. We could write the following code to declare the `myPage` variable and instantiate it:

```
<%! String myPage; %>
<% myPage = request.getParameter ("target"); %>
<jsp:include page="<%=myPage%>" />
```

However, a simpler, thread safe way of doing the same thing would be:

```
<% String myPage = request.getParameter ("target"); %>
<jsp:include page="<%=myPage%>" />
```

This at first sight does exactly the same thing, and if you try it out, gives exactly the same results. However, with the first code, the requested page might be mixed up when two users try this at the same moment.

Once again, we must conclude that concurrency errors are hard to debug. The bugs are difficult to reproduce on a development server and almost impossible to isolate properly. It's very likely that they show up only when the application is being used at full speed. Step debugging (JDB-like) probably won't help very much in locating the problem since the timing of the different threads is so crucial for the error to occur. This is where logging is very important, as it may be the only way to locate these errors.

Some multi-threading issues like deadlocks and race conditions can be investigated with tools like JProbe ThreadAnalyzer (http://www.sitraka.com).

The Stress-test tools we mentioned before, like JMeter, can help us reproduce concurrency problems.

Class Loading

One final area that seems to cause particular difficulty when deploying JSP and Servlet-based applications is class loading: getting Tomcat to recognize the classes you need for your application. You know the classes are there; it looks as though Tomcat ought to be able to see them, but still you get the dreaded "Class java.wibble not found" message.

In Java, classes are loaded into the virtual machine by a `ClassLoader`, and Tomcat 4.0 uses a hierarchy of such `ClassLoaders` to load all relevant classes (including its own). The locations from which Tomcat 4.0 loads classes are many and various. The Tomcat documentation provides full details, but to summarize the relevant points for our purposes, the classes visible to web applications come from:

❑ The Java system classes, located in `rt.jar` and `i18n.jar` in the Java Runtime Environment's `jre/lib` directory.

❑ Any Java extensions found in the `jre/lib/ext` directory.

❑ All directories and JAR files listed in the CLASSPATH environment variable. Note that Tomcat 4.0's startup script, `catalina.bat`, deliberately **ignores** any system-wide CLASSPATH environment variable you may have set and constructs its own CLASSPATH containing only `bootstrap.jar` from the $CATALINA_HOME/bin directory.

❑ Any JAR files located in the $CATALINA_HOME/lib directory. This contains further Tomcat 4.0 components, and can be used to make available any sets of classes (like JDBC drivers) that are required by a number of web applications.

❑ Within each web application, the classes in its `WEB-INF/classes` directory and any JAR files in the `WEB-INF/lib` directory are made available to that application only.

That sounds quite straightforward, but to fully understand the implications remember that these `ClassLoaders` form an inverted tree-like hierarchy. The full picture, including Tomcat implementation classes not visible to web applications, looks like this:

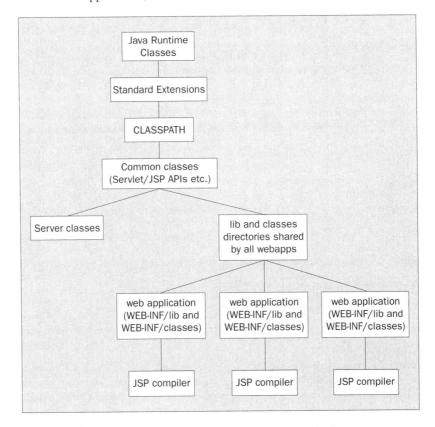

There are therefore three things to bear in mind about how classes will be located:

❑ A class will be loaded by the highest `ClassLoader` that can locate it. Therefore, if a given JAR file is placed in both the `jre/lib/ext` directory and a web application's own `WEB-INF/lib` directory, its classes will be loaded from `jre/lib/ext`.

❑ When one class is trying to load another, this is possible if the class to be loaded and the loading class are in the same `ClassLoader`.

❑ However, a class cannot be loaded if it is only available in a `ClassLoader` lower down the hierarchy than the class attempting to load it.

This has important implications when using frameworks such as Struts (see Chapter 21) that need to load application-specific classes such as those implementing the Struts `Action` interface. If `struts.jar` is placed in the `$CATALINA_HOME/lib` directory, and the application-specific classes in that application's `WEB-INF/classes` or `WEB-INF/lib` directory, then the `Action` classes will not be found as they are in a lower `ClassLoader`. Therefore, `struts.jar` must **only** occur within that application's `WEB-INF/lib` directory.

> **In general, even if a JAR file is required by more than one application, it is best to make it available by placing a copy in *each* application's WEB-INF/lib directory.**

Tomcat 4.0 Beta 1 had problems loading XML parsers other than the version of JAXP 1.1 release it came with, failing with a 'sealing violation' exception. This problem has been overcome, and the rules for using an XML parser within your web application are now that you should either:

❏ Place the JAR files for your choice of XML parser in the application's WEB-INF\lib directory

❏ If you want JAXP 1.1 to be available to every web application, move the JAXP 1.1 JAR files from the $CATALINA_HOME\jasper directory to the $CATALINA_HOME\lib directory

Alternatively, if you do not require JSP, you can place the JAR files for your choice of XML parser directly in $CATALINA_HOME\lib, but this is likely to cause the JSP engine to fail with 'sealing violation' exceptions.

Summary

In this chapter, we've covered:

❏ Understanding error messages you receive when running JSP pages

❏ Techniques for tracking down and isolating bugs, including logging, printing, and using comments

❏ Ways of using debuggers with Java web applications

❏ Building tools to help with debugging and monitoring applications

❏ Potential problem areas that you will often run into: robustness, concurrency, and class loading

Even after reading this chapter, debugging JSP/Servlet applications will still be hard. Hopefully some of the techniques and tools that we've shown will help you to get started, and you'll be able to avoid some of the more common pitfalls, but most importantly you'll need to acquire the special debugging mindset.

The next chapter looks at techniques for getting good performance from our web applications.

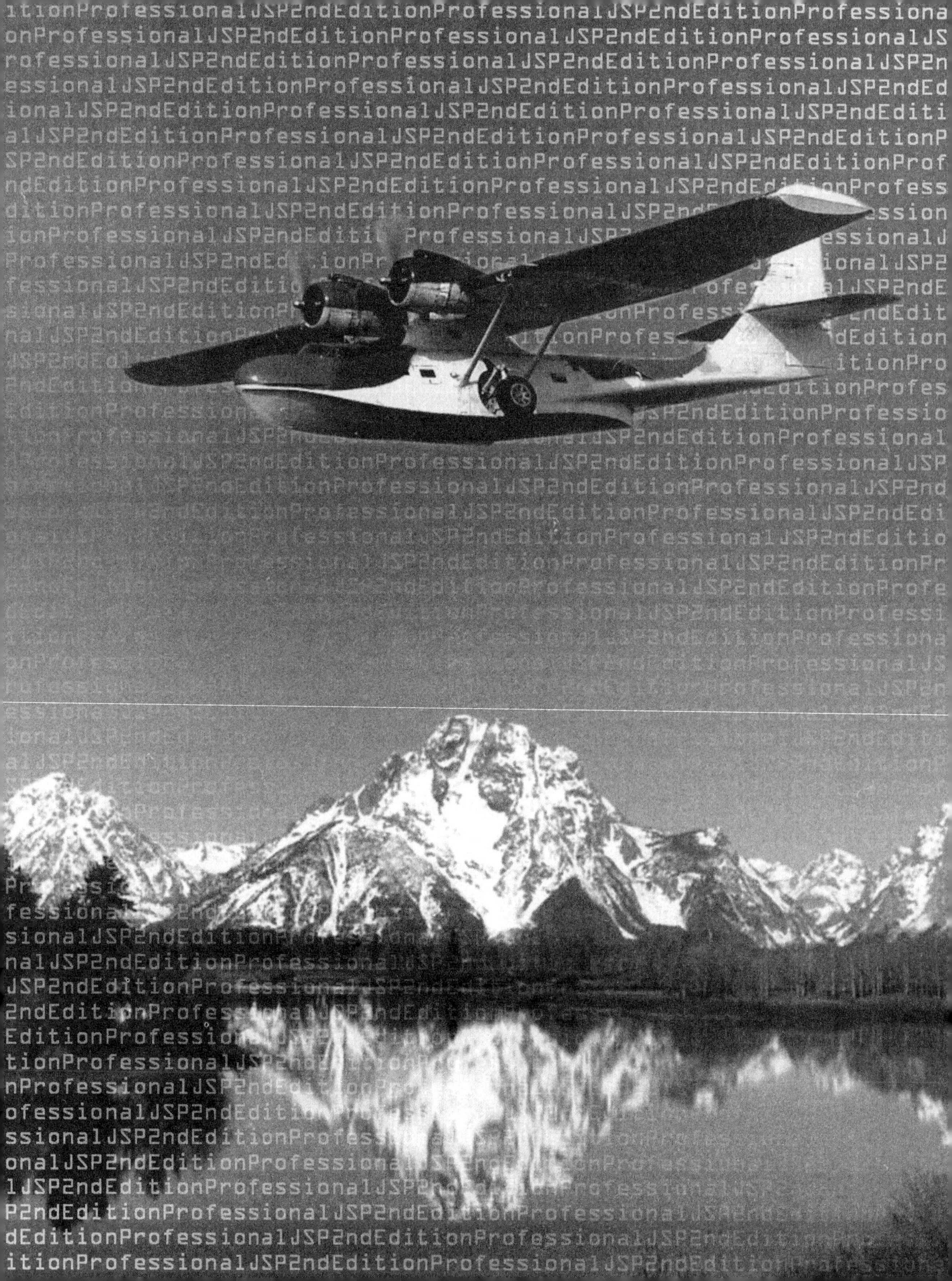
ProfessionalJSP2ndEdition

20

Performance

Getting your web applications to do what you want is one thing; getting them to do it fast and efficiently is often another. This chapter will explore some general strategies and specific techniques for optimizing Servlets and JavaServer Pages.

Critical to optimizing a web application for high performance is establishing what 'high performance' actually means. Two common metrics are used to establish an objective measurement of a web application's performance: **speed** and **scalability**.

'Speed' in the context of web applications has at least two meanings. For the average user browsing the web at home on a dial-up connection, the speed of a website is closely related to the number of graphics required to render the web page in a usable manner. A poorly-designed highly graphical dynamic website would be measured as 'slow' in this sense, although the web application serving the web pages might be performing extremely 'fast'. This sense of speed is controlled by the presentation technology, which is typically HTML. This topic is outside the scope of this book, but it's worth reviewing from other sources to ensure that your presentation layer doesn't spoil the backend performance of your web application.

Another meaning of a web application's speed is how fast it is able to respond to a request. Home-based users with broadband technology or work-based intranet users are likely to associate a website's speed with this measurement. Nearly all of the optimization techniques in this chapter relate to this measurement of speed, as it is directly related to the efficiency of the Java code and other server-side factors.

Along with speed, **scalability** is an important measure of a web application's performance. While speed focuses on the amount of time that passes between the client's request and the server's response, scalability measures how many simultaneous requests a web application can process before its speed deteriorates to unacceptable levels.

No web application can handle an unlimited number of requests; the trick in optimization is to anticipate the likely user demand and ensure that the web site can gracefully scale up to the demand while maintaining acceptable levels of speed. **Stress testing** is a common process for determining the scalability of a web application. Stress testing simulates a high volume of users, measuring the deterioration of the web application's speed until it is no longer within acceptable tolerances, or simply melts down.

Stress testing identifies the general areas of the web application that require optimization. With this information, **profiling** techniques can be used to determine what specific portions of the web application's code are the best candidates for optimization. Profiling tools and techniques develop a performance 'profile' of a Java class, paying special attention to the speed of each specific method.

In this chapter, we'll examine the following means for improving the performance of our web applications:

- ❑ Various methods available to developers for stress testing and profiling their web applications (discovering the limitations and inefficiencies of the web application)

- ❑ Next, we'll discuss some specific techniques for optimizing web applications (resolving the discovered inefficiencies)

- ❑ We'll also discuss alternative Java Virtual Machines (JVMs) as an effective optimization technique

Example Application: Widget Industries

To better illustrate how some of the performance techniques outlined in this chapter can be used in real-world situations, I've created an example web-enabled application that could benefit from some optimizations. **Widget Industries** is a fictional widget manufacturing plant in the business of making and selling its own widgets and distributing widgets from a foreign firm in its own catalog. The company has developed a web application to ease its way into the e-commerce field; it allows Widget Industries' various customers to view its inventory on-line, but no e-commerce functionality is in place.

Before Widget Industries deploys the application, it wants to ensure that its web platform will support the anticipated demand. The marketing and distribution departments anticipate that in the first month's launch, as many as twenty-five web clients may hit the web application *simultaneously* on a daily, recurring basis. It has been decided by Widget Industries management that no user should have to wait more than three seconds to view any web page. It should be noted that nearly 100% of the targeted audience for the web application has broadband connectivity. As we move through the elements of this chapter, we'll apply some of the concepts to this application and optimize it as necessary to meet these demands.

The Widget Industries web application is quite simple; it's just two JSPs: index.jsp, and catalog.jsp. The former provides a simple entry page to the latter, which queries against two separate databases to produce a consolidated listing of the widgets that Widget Industries sells. If you review the code, you'll notice some glaring inefficiencies. These are present intentionally, to help illustrate the examples. As the chapter progresses, this web application will migrate to a Model 2 (MVC) architecture.

Here is the code for index.jsp, which would be a simple static HTML page, were it not for a few JSP elements, which we've highlighted. Note that this HTML has been optimized for Internet Explorer:

```
<%@page import="java.text.*,java.util.*"%>
<html>
  <head>
```

```
    <title>Widget Industries</title>
    <link rel="stylesheet" media="all" title="Default Styles"
          href="widget.css">
</head>
<body leftmargin="0" topmargin="0" rightmargin="0" bottommargin="0">

    <%
      DateFormat df = DateFormat.getDateInstance(DateFormat.FULL);
    %>

    <table width="100%" height="100%" border="0"
           cellpadding="10" cellspacing="0">
      <tr>
        <td class="sidebar" align="left" valign="top">
           
          <br>
          <b>ABOUT US</b><br>
          <hr>
          <b>Widget Industries</b> was
          founded by J. Kennedy Ault in
          1855, when he and life-long friends
          Russell Newman and Mark Walter discovered
          the famous "Lost Norseman" widget mine
          in central Texas.
          <p>
          While today's widgets are artificially
          made, the founders' attention to detail
          and quality are very much present in
          our manufacturing facilities. <i>Our
          widget quality is unimpeachable.</i>
          <p>
          In recent years, Widget Industries
          has supplemented their leading position
          in widget sales with outsourcing
          and distribution services. Do you need
          some custom widgets made? We'll make them
          for you. Do you need a distribution
          channel for your own widgets? We'll
          put them in front of the top
          widget buyers in the world.
          <p>
          We hope you enjoy your stay here
          at our virtual headquarters!

        </td>
        <td align="center" width="100%" height="100%"
                           valign="top" class="normal">
          <span class="title">Welcome to Widget Industries!</span>
          <br>
          <span class="quote">"If it can be fabricated,
                              we'll make it up, honest!"
          <p>
          <%= df.format(new Date()) %></span>
          <p>
          <hr>
```

```
            <br>
            This website has been created for our channel partners
            to view our current widget availability and ID numbers.
            <p>
            In subsequent months, we'll be upgrading our website
            to enable on-line ordering of widgets ("e-commerce")
            and two-way support messaging.
            <p>
            To order widgets, call us: <b>1-800-WIDGETS</b>
            <p>
            For technical inquiries, e-mail us:
               <a href="mailto:webmaster@widgets.com">webmaster@widgets.com</a>
            <p>
            <table border="2" width="200" height="50"><tr><td align="center">
            <a href="catalog.jsp"><b>Browse Our Catalog</b></a>
            </td>
            </tr>
            </table>
         </td>
      </tr>
   </table>

   </body>
</html>
```

The following screenshot shows the output for `index.jsp`:

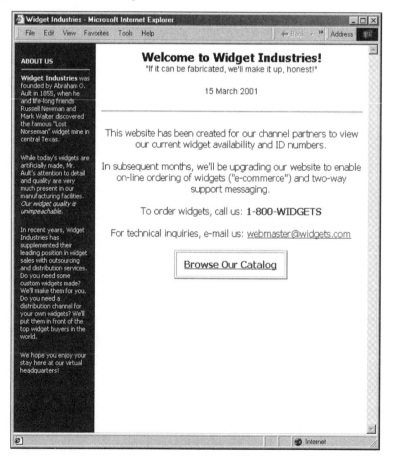

`catalog.jsp` involves much more dynamic content than `index.jsp`. In this JSP, we open two connections to two different databases, execute a simple select statement against each connection, and display the results in an HTML table. I use two different Oracle databases to add complexity to the application, and from my experience combining information from two entirely different data sources onto a single page is common. Together, the two databases contain 680 records. For readability, we've highlighted all the dynamic elements:

```jsp
<%@page import="java.sql.*,java.text.*"%>
<html>
  <head>
    <title>Widget Industries</title>
    <link rel="stylesheet" media="all" title="Default Styles"
          href="widget.css">
  </head>
  <body>

    <%
      String cs = "jdbc:oracle:thin:@db.widget.com:1521:WIDGET";
      String cs2 = "jdbc:oracle:thin:@foreign.widget.com:1521:FWIDGET";
      Class.forName("oracle.jdbc.driver.OracleDriver");
      Connection con = DriverManager.getConnection(cs, "wteam", "wteam");
      Statement stmt = con.createStatement();
      ResultSet rs = stmt.executeQuery("select * from WIDGETS");
    %>
    <p align="center" class="title">
    Here are the widgets we produce and distribute:
    </p>

    <p align="center">
    <table class="catalog_table" cellspacing="1" cellpadding="4">
      <tr class="catalog_header">
        <th>
          Widget ID
        </th>
        <th>
          Widget Name
        </th>
        <th>
          Widget Description
        </th>
        <th>
          Date Available
        </th>
      </tr>
    <% while (rs.next()) { %>
      <tr class="catalog_items">
        <td>
          D<%= rs.getString("WIDGET_ID") %>
        </td>
        <td>
          <%= rs.getString("NAME") %>
        </td>
        <td>
          <%= rs.getString("WIDGET_DESC") %>
        </td>
        <td>
          <%= DateFormat.getDateInstance(DateFormat.SHORT).format(
                                   rs.getDate("DATE_AVAILABLE")) %>
        </td>
      </tr>
    <% }
```

```
      stmt.close();
      con.close();
      con = DriverManager.getConnection(cs2, "fwteam", "fwteam");
      stmt = con.createStatement();
      rs = stmt.executeQuery("select * from FOREIGN_WIDGETS");
  %>
  <% while (rs.next()) { %>
    <tr class="catalog_items">
      <td>
        F<%= rs.getString("F_W_ID") %>
      </td>
      <td>
        <%= rs.getString("F_WIDGET") %>
      </td>
      <td>
        <%= rs.getString("F_WIDGET_DESC") %>
      </td>
      <td>
        <%= DateFormat.getDateInstance(DateFormat.SHORT).format(
                            rs.getDate("DATE_AVAIL")) %>
      </td>
    </tr>
  <% }
  stmt.close();
  con.close();
  %>
  </table>
  </p>

  </body>
</html>
```

Again, the adjacent screenshot shows the output from this code:

Here are the widgets we produce and distribute:

Widget ID	Widget Name	Widget Description	Date Available
D767	Our Widget 268	This is the description of our quality widget 268	06/26/01
D768	Our Widget 269	This is the description of our quality widget 269	08/06/01
D769	Our Widget 270	This is the description of our quality widget 270	08/05/01
D770	Our Widget 271	This is the description of our quality widget 271	10/02/01
D771	Our Widget 272	This is the description of our quality widget 272	08/14/01
D772	Our Widget 273	This is the description of our quality widget 273	07/20/01
D773	Our Widget 274	This is the description of our quality widget 274	09/05/01
D774	Our Widget 275	This is the description of our quality widget 275	06/10/01
D775	Our Widget 276	This is the description of our quality widget 276	09/08/01
D776	Our Widget 277	This is the description of our quality widget 277	11/12/01
D777	Our Widget 278	This is the description of our quality widget 278	07/02/01
D778	Our Widget 279	This is the description of our quality widget 279	09/20/01
D779	Our Widget 280	This is the description of our quality widget 280	03/03/01
D780	Our Widget 281	This is the description of our quality widget 281	06/17/01
D781	Our Widget 282	This is the description of our quality widget 282	04/16/01
D782	Our Widget 283	This is the description of our quality widget 283	09/26/01
D783	Our Widget 284	This is the description of our quality widget 284	04/24/01
D784	Our Widget 285	This is the description of our quality widget 285	07/08/01
D785	Our Widget 286	This is the description of our quality widget 286	12/13/01
D786	Our Widget 287	This is the description of our quality widget 287	10/05/01
D787	Our Widget 288	This is the description of our quality widget 288	05/06/01
D788	Our Widget 289	This is the description of our quality widget 289	05/06/01

Finally in this section, the source code for `widget.css`, a simple cascading stylesheet used by both JSPs to format the HTML:

```css
.sidebar {
  font-family : Tahoma, Arial, Helvetica, sans-serif;
  font-size : 11px;
  background-color : navy;
  color : white;
}
.title {
  font-family : Tahoma, Arial, Helvetica, sans-serif;
  font-size : 20px;
  font-weight : bold;
}
.quote {
  font-family : Arial, Helvetica, sans-serif;
  font-size : 14px;
}
.normal {
  font-family : Tahoma, Arial, Helvetica, sans-serif;
  font-size : 16px;
}
.catalog_table {
  background-color : black;
}
.catalog_header {
  background-color : navy;
  color : white;
  font-size : 14px;
}
.catalog_items {
  background-color : white;
  color : black;
  font-size : 12px;
  text-align : center;
}
```

Stress Testing

The objective of stress testing is to produce a request load on a web server sufficient to determine under what conditions the speed of the web server deteriorates past acceptable levels. An effective methodology for performing a stress test is:

❑ Determine the maximum acceptable **delay** from the receipt of the request to the complete sending of the response

❑ Estimate the maximum likely number of simultaneous **users** of your web application

❑ Simulate user requests against the web application, starting with a light **load** and gradually adding simulated users until the web application response delay becomes greater than **delay**

❑ If **load** is less than **users**, it's time to optimize the web application; otherwise, you may or may not perform optimizations, based on how soon and by how much **users** is expected to increase, and if **delay** is likely to decrease

Simulating the user requests is the most complicated step in this simple methodology. While you could actually sit down in a room with ten computers and refresh the browser to create your simulated user load, this is obviously not very efficient.

At first sight, creating a program to simulate web requests might seem simple: just create a program that opens a socket and sends a whole bunch of GET requests, logging the amount of time elapsed before the response is received, and if you're feeling really fancy, make it multi-threaded. However, modern web applications require a much more complicated tool. Consider some of the features that you'll be likely to require of a stress testing tool to get meaningful results:

- ❑ Send GET and POST requests
- ❑ 'Record' GET and POST requests sent from a browser (as opposed to requiring the developer to hand write the appropriate requests)
- ❑ Retrieve and send cookies
- ❑ Spawn multiple threads
- ❑ Simulate user delays
- ❑ Log performance data
- ❑ Throttle bandwidth

Fortunately, there are some free tools available for simulating these loads. Here are a few I've come across:

- ❑ **Web Application Stress Tool** by Microsoft, http://homer.rte.microsoft.com/
- ❑ **JMeter** by the Java Apache Project, http://java.apache.org/
- ❑ **LoadItUp** by BroadGun Software, http://www.broadgun.com/

My favorite is the Microsoft's Web Application Stress Tool (WAS). WAS supports all the features I've mentioned, plus many more, including the ability to coordinate with multiple computers on your network to simulate additional web clients. If you're on a Win32 platform, I recommend it. JMeter is a 100% pure Java (GUI Swing) load tester and, unlike WAS, it is user extensible. LoadItUp isn't in the same class as the previous two utilities; it's a simple command-line driven load tester and offers very few features. If you're looking for something simple, it may be exactly what you need. Here's a screenshot of the WAS tool:

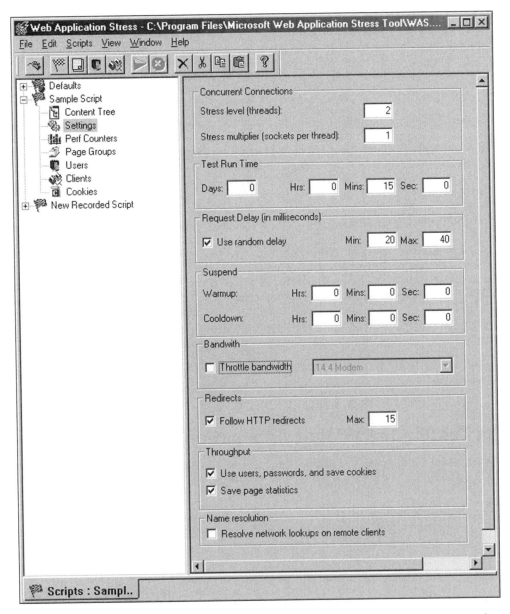

There are also a number of commercial load testers available, but hold on to your hats: they cost $10,000 or more. A few options:

❑ **WebLoad** by RadView Software, http://www.radview.com/

❑ **SilkPerformer** by Segue Software, http://www.segue.com/

❑ **Benchmark Factory** by Quest Software, http://www.benchmarkfactory.com/

❑ **LoadRunner** by Mercury Interactive, http://www.mercuryinteractive.com/

Regardless of which tool is used, to effectively stress test, the following data should be collected:

❑ Number of simulated clients

❑ Minimum, average, and maximum delay for each resource

❑ Refused connections or errors

One machine alone can simulate several hundred simultaneous web clients by opening multiple sockets and sending and receiving requests much faster than a normal user would. However, if you need to simulate thousands of simultaneous web clients, you'll need to involve many physical machines in your stress testing process, and compiling all the raw performance data collected by each web client involved in the process can be somewhat time consuming. The WAS tool I use takes care of this step automatically, compiling in one place all of the data collected by various WAS clients that participate in the test. Since you may well wind up tweaking your web application and re-running stress tests over and over again, as I do, you'll want to acquire a tool like WAS that has this feature.

Pay special attention to any refused connections that have occurred during your stress test. A refused connection indicates that the Servlet container has become overwhelmed and can no longer queue up pending requests intended for your web application. While this problem could be resolved indirectly by optimizing your web application and thus reducing the amount of time each request is queued up, often optimizing your hardware configuration and/or your Servlet container will yield better results. Regardless of which path you choose, whenever you see refused connections occurring within the web client tolerances your web application is required to support, take care of the problem immediately.

If any errors occur during the process, determine whether the error has occurred in your web application or the Servlet container itself. If it's the former, time to start debugging. If it's the later, it may be a good idea to contact the vendor of the container to determine the cause of the error.

Stress Testing the Widget Application

The Widget Applications is required to support twenty-five simultaneous web clients and service each request within three seconds. Using the WAS utility, I tested its performance under one, ten, and twenty-five users.

The web server for these tests is a Pentium II 400 96 MB RAM running Tomcat 4.0B1 and Apache 1.3.14 on Windows 2000. The database is Oracle 8.1.7 running on a dual CPU Pentium II 450 512 MB RAM, also on Windows 2000. Tests run for 4 minutes.

This data is a summary of the test results:

One Web Client

Resource	Average response time (in seconds)
index.jsp	0.197
widget.css	0.139
catalog.jsp	0.862

Ten Web Clients

Resource	Average response time
index.jsp	0.339
widget.css	0.209
catalog.jsp	1.763

Twenty-Five Web Clients

Resource	Average response time
index.jsp	0.203
widget.css	0.250
catalog.jsp	6.889

While the initial benchmarks of the Widget web application were promising, performance clearly begins to deteriorate once multiple users are thrown into the fray. This example illustrates the necessity of stress testing! If you don't ever test, you'll discover the limitations of your application at the worst possible time. Since the only portion of the application that degraded beyond acceptable limits was catalog.jsp, we'll focus our optimization efforts on that resource.

Profiling

If stress testing reveals that the web application's performance isn't acceptable, as is the case in our example, profiling techniques can now be used to find out which methods should be optimized. Some developers often skip the step of profiling and review their code without any granular performance data, looking for obvious inefficiencies. While such developers can find some areas that do need optimization, profiling helps save a developer's time by showing him exactly where the *greatest* performance gains can be realized. It may surprise you which objects and methods in Java are most expensive, especially if you're new to the language.

Many profiling applications (profilers) are available which work with the JVM to record performance information, though I've yet to find a freeware version. These three profilers are front-runners in the Java development community:

- ❑ **Quantify** by Rational Software, http://www.rational.com/
- ❑ **Optimizeit** by Intuitive Systems, http://www.optimizeit.com/
- ❑ **JProbe** by Sitraka Software, http://www.jprobe.com/

Configuring a profiler is simple: you point it at your JVM and the startup class file, and the profiler does the rest, ultimately producing a performance matrix for your Java code. In the case of profiling Servlets (and JSP), the profiler can be configured to integrate with the Servlet container or application server.

To illustrate how easy the process is with modern profilers, let's examine the process of using JProbe to profile the Widget Industries web application:

❑ Configure JProbe to integrate with our application server, which in this case is Tomcat:

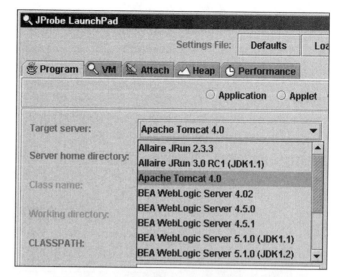

❑ Choose your desired JVM:

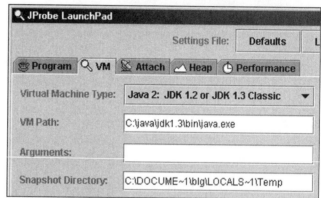

❑ Run Tomcat through JProbe:

To generate performance data, I'll request the `catalog.jsp`. After Tomcat has finished serving up the JSP, I can view a report summarizing the performance of the individual methods executed during the test. Here's what that report looks like:

JProbe records the number of times each method is called, the average amount of time spent in the method, the average amount of time spent in the method *and* all of the methods that it launches, and the number of objects that each method creates. Because each method we've explicitly called in the JSP creates a large number of methods behind the scenes, this list is rather long.

The following table summarizes the performance of the methods that are explicitly called in the JSP:

Method	Calls	Cumulative Time	Method Time	Cumulative Objects
DriverManager.getConnection()	2	6.455	0.005	48944
DateFormat.getDateInstance()	670	1.976	1.976	29720
Class.forName()	26	1.355	1.341	12086
OracleConnection.createStatement()	4	1.157	0.155	5648
DateFormat.format()	670	0.887	0.887	11791
OracleResultSet.getString()	2010	0.689	0.009	8878
OracleStatement.executeQuery()	4	0.593	0.009	5987

While the resolution of the time measurement is somewhat high, it is important to note that these numbers are not precision measurements of how the application will perform; by recording its metrics, the profiler always slows the execution speed of the code it measures. Rather, use the numbers as relative indications of which methods are slowest.

Sorted by cumulative time, it's readily apparent which methods are causing the largest inefficiencies. Take particular note of Class.forName(): it is called 26 times by our web application, yet we've only called it once in our JSP code. This indicates that other methods that we do not explicitly control call this method, and thus it's not clear what impact an optimization of that method in our JSP code will be.

Profilers clearly are essential to efficiently optimize code. Yet at $500 to $1,000 per license, profilers may not be for everyone, especially the casual programmer. Also, at times a developer may be obligated to optimize code without having access to a profiler. For various reasons, it may be desirable to employ an alternate profiling technique that doesn't require a third-party application.

Profiling without a Profiler

The core objective of code profiling is determining the execution duration of each method; the remaining data collected by profilers is also very useful but this first datum is the key to code optimization. This information can be measured easily in Java by implementing something like the following code snippet:

```
long beforeMethod = System.currentTimeMillis();

/* the method to measure */
ExpensiveObject gucciShoes = FancyClothier.purchase(GUCCI_SHOES);

long afterMethod = System.currentTimeMillis();
System.out.print("FancyClothier.purchase() - ");
System.out.println(afterMethod - beforeMethod);
```

The resulting output of this code would of course be the duration of the `purchase()` method, in milliseconds.

How does this method compare to our profiler? Only one way to find out. After adding lines similar to the ones used in the code snippet to the `catalog.jsp` file, I received the following results:

Method	Calls	Cumulative Time
DriverManager.getConnection()	2	410
Table Loop	2	301
OracleStatement.executeQuery()	2	10
Class.forName()	1	0
OracleConnection.createStatement()	2	0

Comparing this table with the previous one, we can see that although the performance was significantly faster here than with the profiler, the relative speeds are very similar. However, there are a number of disadvantages with this method of profiling, not least of which is having to wrap the profiling lines around each method. In addition, by slowing down the execution of the Java code, intentionally or not, the profiler was able to measure the performance of the application with greater precision. With the manual profiling, it's not at all clear how the last three methods in this table will perform under stressful conditions.

It is clear that a commercial profiler adds significant value to the optimization process. While profiling with `System.out.print()` is straightforward and easy, it is tedious and impractical to incorporate as a methodology, to say nothing of being feature-poor in comparison to profilers.

Optimizing Java Code

Now that we've determined which methods in the application need improvement, it's time to get down the code and start speeding it up. The optimization techniques we'll cover fit into four categories:

- ❑   J2SE Optimizations
- ❑   J2EE Optimizations (Servlet and JSP)
- ❑   Resource Pooling
- ❑   Servlet Container Configuration

Because speed optimization can often involve concessions in terms of code maintainability, be sure that all speed optimizations you perform are truly necessary by measuring the performance gains.

J2SE Optimizations

In the years since Java has been introduced, techniques for optimizing the core Java 2 Standard Edition features have been covered by a multitude of different sources, and new articles continue to be published regularly. Searches on www.javaworld.com, www.jguru.com, and even www.google.com for "java performance" and other related topics turn up a slew of J2SE optimization articles. I'm not going to spend too much time discussing this particular topic, but we will take a look at one J2SE optimization technique that our application needs.

In catalog.jsp from our example application, two of the methods we identified for optimization are J2SE related:

- ❑   DateFormat.getDateInstance()
- ❑   DateFormat.format()

Let's take a look at these methods in their context (from catalog.jsp) and determine if we can apply a J2SE optimization to them:

```
<% while (rs.next()) { %>
  <tr class="catalog_items">
    <td>
      D<%= rs.getString("WIDGET_ID") %>
    </td>
    <td>
      <%= rs.getString("NAME") %>
    </td>
    <td>
      <%= rs.getString("WIDGET_DESC") %>
    </td>
    <td>
      <%= DateFormat.getDateInstance(DateFormat.SHORT).
          format(rs.getDate("DATE_AVAILABLE")) %>
    </td>
    </tr>
  <% }
```

Because these two methods are called from within a loop with a relatively large number of iterations (due to the size of the database), any improvements we make to these two methods will likely be rather effective. Notice that in each loop iteration, a new `DateFormat` object is being instantiated, and then immediately orphaned. Let's pull `DateFormat` out of the loop and reuse the same object, revising the code to look like this:

```
<% DateFormat df = DateFormat.getDateInstance(DateFormat.SHORT);
    while (rs.next()) { %>
  <tr class="catalog_items">
    <td>
      D<%= rs.getString("WIDGET_ID") %>
    </td>
    <td>
      <%= rs.getString("NAME") %>
    </td>
    <td>
      <%= rs.getString("WIDGET_DESC") %>
    </td>
    <td>
      <%= df.format(rs.getDate("DATE_AVAILABLE") %>
    </td>
  </tr>
<% } %>
```

Alternately, we could push the date formatting off to the database entirely. Enterprise RDBMS systems are *very* well tuned for maximum performance, so it's possible that a SQL-based date formatting function might speed our web application. The drawback is that we pay a penalty for portability: we no longer benefit from Java's date localization. Here's how we'd modify the code for this scenario:

```
ResultSet rs = stmt.executeQuery("select WIDGET_ID, NAME, WIDGET_DESC,
                        TO_CHAR(DATE_AVAILABLE, 'MM/DD/YY')
                        STR_DATE_AVAILABLE from BEN_WIDGETS");
...

<% while (rs.next()) { %>
  <tr class="catalog_items">
    <td>
      D<%= rs.getString("WIDGET_ID") %>
    </td>
    <td>
      <%= rs.getString("NAME") %>
    </td>
    <td>
      <%= rs.getString("WIDGET_DESC") %>
    </td>
    <td>
      <%= rs.getString("STR_DATE_AVAILABLE") %>
    </td>
  </tr>
<% } %>
```

Now that we've seen two possibilities for increasing the speed of this page, let's stress test the page again and see which of the two gives us the greatest performance.

Twenty-Five Web Clients

Resource	Average response time
un-optimized `catalog.jsp`	6889
Java date format `catalog.jsp` (`catalog_2.jsp`)	5757
Oracle date format `catalog.jsp` (`catalog_3.jsp`)	5544

Both the SQL and the recycled `DateFormat` object solutions deliver superior performance to the web applications original configuration, but one does not appear to be markedly superior to the other. In a real-world situation, you may not want to push the date formatting off to the SQL level for such a small speed gain, especially if you are developing RDBMS-agnostic solutions. Our example web application will move forward with the SQL date formatting.

J2EE Optimizations

Up to this point, our example application has performed its intended function, but it's hardly been an example of good system design. Notice that all of the revisions to `catalog.jsp` have employed scriptlets that contain business logic. While technically legal, such an approach is not advisable, as it is:

- ❏ inflexible
- ❏ poorly extensible
- ❏ difficult to maintain
- ❏ barely reusable

The preferred way to implement a web application is the Model 2, or MVC (Model-View-Controller), architecture. Does the overhead of adding a controller Servlet and moving the business logic out to a JavaBean impose a measurable performance penalty on an application? Let's find out.

I've rewritten the Widget web application as a Model 2 web application. I've created a controller Servlet called `Controller.java` and a JavaBean that encapsulates the database transactions called `WidgetData.java`. The JSP has been modified and renamed `catalog_4.jsp`.

The following diagram illustrates the differences between the two architectures:

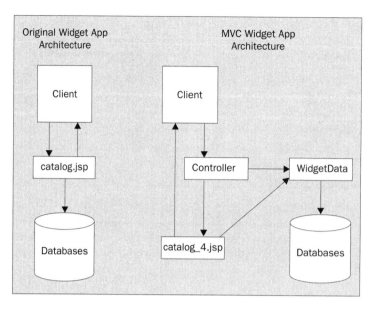

The catalog_4.jsp Page

First, let's take a look at the revised catalog_4.jsp. The most striking difference is the absence of any data access code; in fact, I no longer import the "java.sql" package:

```
<%@page import="java.text.*"%>
<html>
  <head>
    <title>Widget Industries</title>
    <link rel="stylesheet" media="all" title="Default Styles"
          href="widget.css">
  </head>
  <body>

<p align="center" class="title">
Here are the widgets we produce and distribute:
</p>

<p align="center">
<table class="catalog_table" cellspacing="1" cellpadding="4">
  <tr class="catalog_header">
    <th>
      Widget ID
    </th>
    <th>
      Widget Name
    </th>
    <th>
      Widget Description
    </th>
    <th>
      Date Available
    </th>
  </tr>
```

Next, note that I retrieve a `WidgetData` object from the `HttpRequest` object. The `Controller` Servlet takes care of initializing the object for me; all I have to do is call some get methods and close it when I'm done:

```
<jsp:useBean id="localWidgets" class="com.wrox.projsp.ch20.WidgetData"
             scope="request"/>
<% while (localWidgets.next()) { %>
e<tr class="catalog_items">
  <td>
    D<%= localWidgets.getWidgetID() %>
  </td>
  <td>
    <%= localWidgets.getWidgetName() %>
  </td>
  <td>
    <%= localWidgets.getWidgetDescription() %>
  </td>
  <td>
    <%= localWidgets.getWidgetDate() %>
  </td>
</tr>
<% } localWidgets.closeWidget(); %>

<jsp:useBean id="foreignWidgets" class="com.wrox.projsp.ch20.WidgetData"
             scope="request"/>
<% while (foreignWidgets.next()) { %>
<tr class="catalog_items">
  <td>
    F<%= foreignWidgets.getWidgetID() %>
  </td>
  <td>              .
    <%= foreignWidgets.getWidgetName() %>
  </td>
  <td>
    <%= foreignWidgets.getWidgetDescription() %>
  </td>
  <td>
    <%= foreignWidgets.getWidgetDate() %>
  </td>
</tr>
<% } foreignWidgets.closeWidget(); %>

  </table>
  </p>

  </body>
</html>
```

Controller.java

This next file is `Controller.java`, our simple MVC controller. The Servlet parses the resource requested in the URL, and if it's `catalog_4.jsp`, our new JSP, we'll initialize two `WidgetData` beans representing the two different databases and send them to `catalog_4.jsp` in the `HttpRequest` object:

```
package com.wrox.projsp.ch20;

import javax.servlet.*;
import javax.servlet.http.*;
import java.sql.*;
```

```java
public class Controller extends HttpServlet {
  private static final String PARAM_POOL_SIZE = "poolSize";
  private static final String CATALOG_JSP = "/catalog_4.jsp";
  private static final String JDBC_DRIVER =
    "oracle.jdbc.driver.OracleDriver";

  private static final String WIDGET_CONN =
    "jdbc:oracle:thin:@db.widget.com:1521:WIDGET";
  private static final String WIDGET_NAME = "wteam";
  private static final String WIDGET_PW = "wteam";

  private static final String FOREIGN_CONN =
    "jdbc:oracle:thin:@foreign.widget.com:1521:FWIDGET";
  private static final String FOREIGN_NAME = "fwteam";
  private static final String FOREIGN_PW = "fwteam";

  private Connection con;
  private Connection con2;

  public void init() throws ServletException {
    try {
      Class.forName(JDBC_DRIVER);
    } catch (Exception e) {
      throw new ServletException(e.getMessage());
    }
  }

  public void doGet(HttpServletRequest req,
                    HttpServletResponse resp) throws ServletException {

    // determine which resource is requested
    String resourceName = getResourceName(req);

    // if resource requires bean, add it to request
    if (resourceName.equalsIgnoreCase(CATALOG_JSP)) {
      try {
        con = DriverManager.getConnection(WIDGET_CONN, WIDGET_NAME,
                                          WIDGET_PW);
        WidgetData localWidgets = new WidgetData(con,
                                          WidgetData.LOCAL_WIDGETS);
        localWidgets.getWidgets();

        con2 = DriverManager.getConnection(FOREIGN_CONN, FOREIGN_NAME,
                                           FOREIGN_PW);
        WidgetData foreignWidgets =
          new WidgetData(con2, WidgetData.FOREIGN_WIDGETS);
        foreignWidgets.getWidgets();

        req.setAttribute("localWidgets", localWidgets);
        req.setAttribute("foreignWidgets", foreignWidgets);
      } catch (SQLException e) {
        throw new ServletException(e.getMessage());
      }
    }
```

```
    // forward request to resource
    try {
      req.getRequestDispatcher(resourceName).forward(req, resp);
    } catch (java.io.IOException e) {}
  }

  public void doPost(HttpServletRequest req,
                     HttpServletResponse resp) throws ServletException {
    doGet(req, resp);
  }

  private String getResourceName(HttpServletRequest req) {
    return req.getPathInfo();
  }

}
```

WidgetData.java

WidgetData.java is a simple JavaBean that is initialized via its constructor with a Connection object and a SQL statement. It wraps the appropriate ResultSet methods to iterate through each record in the table, and then it closes the Statement and Connection objects via the close() method called in catalog_4.jsp (it's not necessary to explicitly close ResultSet objects):

```
package com.wrox.projsp.ch20;

import java.sql.*;

public class WidgetData {
  private Connection con;
  private Statement stmt;
  private ResultSet rs = null;
  private String query;

  public static final String LOCAL_WIDGETS =
    "select WIDGET_ID, NAME, WIDGET_DESC, TO_CHAR(DATE_AVAILABLE, " +
    "'MM/DD/YY') STR_DATE_AVAILABLE from BEN_WIDGETS";
  public static final String FOREIGN_WIDGETS =
    "select F_W_ID, F_WIDGET, F_WIDGET_DESC, TO_CHAR(DATE_AVAIL, " +
    "'MM/DD/YY') STR_DATE_AVAIL from FOREIGN_WIDGETS";

  private static final String ERROR_NO_RESULTSET =
    "ResultSet not initialized.";

  public WidgetData(Connection con, String query) {
    this.con = con;
    this.query = query;
  }

  public void getWidgets() throws SQLException {
    stmt = con.createStatement();
    rs = stmt.executeQuery(query);
  }

  public boolean next() throws SQLException {
```

```
  if (rs == null) {
    throw new SQLException(this.ERROR_NO_RESULTSET);
  }

  return rs.next();
}

public String getWidgetID() throws SQLException {
  return rs.getString(1);
}

public String getWidgetName() throws SQLException {
  return rs.getString(2);
}

public String getWidgetDescription() throws SQLException {
  return rs.getString(3);
}

public String getWidgetDate() throws SQLException {
  return rs.getString(4);
}

public void closeWidget() {
  try {
    stmt.close();
    con.close();
  } catch (SQLException e) {}
}
}
```

Addition to web.xml

One last thing we need to add – declare and map our `Controller` Servlet in `web.xml` for the web application:

```xml
<servlet>
  <servlet-name>
    Controller
  </servlet-name>
  <servlet-class>
    com.wrox.projsp.ch20.Controller
  </servlet-class>
  <load-on-startup>
    -1
  </load-on-startup>
  </servlet>
  <servlet-mapping>
    <servlet-name>
      Controller
    </servlet-name>
    <url-pattern>
      /widget/*
    </url-pattern>
  </servlet-mapping>
```

```
<session-config>
  <session-timeout>
    600
  </session-timeout>
</session-config>
```

Once we've got everything in place, we should be able to point our browser at index.jsp, follow the link to the catalog, and get the same results as last time. We'll see if it's any faster as we measure its performance.

Twenty-Five Web Clients

Resource	Average response time
catalog_3.jsp	5544
catalog_4.jsp	5619
(MVC version of catalog.jsp)	

Developers should consider Model 2 architecture for any web application of more than a trivial nature. The advantages of an object-oriented distributed model come with little inherent performance penalty, and Model 2 applications are able to scale much further up than single-tiered or Model 1 approaches.

Resource Pooling

Instantiating some objects can be a very time expensive process. Note that in the profiling results from our example application, obtaining the database connections (the DriverManager.getConnection() method) was the single most time-consuming operation recorded, even more expensive that the ResultSet iteration loops.

To avoid the performance hit of repeatedly instantiating expensive objects, such objects should be instantiated once and then reused whenever possible. We accomplished this in catalog_2.jsp by reusing a DateFormat object.

Often, it is desirable to reuse objects across multiple classes. Mechanisms to accomplish this are called **resource pools**. Reusable pools of java.sql.Connection objects, called **connection pools**, are one of the most common implementations of resource pools in J2EE applications.

Web applications commonly implement connection pooling using the Model 2 (MVC) architecture. The controller Servlet manages the connection pool from which the various JavaBeans obtain their connections. However, JDBC 2.0 drivers and some application servers provide connection pool functionality. If you are using either of these technologies, you may want to consider using their native connection pooling.

To illustrate the performance gains of connection pooling, we'll implement a basic connection pooling system into our application. I've created a new class, ConnectionPool.java, which implements a very rudimentary connection pooling system adequate for our testing and modified Controller.java, WidgetData.java, and catalog_4.jsp to use the new class, renaming those files to ControllerPool, WidgetDataPool, and catalog_5.jsp, respectively.

ConnectionPool.java

The code to `ConnectionPool.java` follows. The code simply opens *x* connections and keeps them open until the `closePool()` method is called:

```java
package com.wrox.projsp.ch20;

import java.sql.*;

public class ConnectionPool {
  private static final String NO_CONNECTIONS =
    "No connections available in pool.";

  private Connection pool[];
  private long timeout = 10000;

  public ConnectionPool(String driver, String connection, String username,
                        String pw, int connections) throws SQLException {
    pool = new Connection[connections];

    initializePool(driver, connection, username, pw);
  }

  private void initializePool(String driver, String connection,
                              String username,
                              String pw) throws SQLException {
    try {
      Class.forName(driver);

      for (int i = 0; i < pool.length; i++) {
        pool[i] = DriverManager.getConnection(connection, username, pw);
      }

    } catch (ClassNotFoundException ce) {
      throw new SQLException(ce.getMessage());
    }
  }

  public synchronized Connection getConnection() throws SQLException {
    Connection con = null;
    long timeStart;

    timeStart = System.currentTimeMillis();
    while ((System.currentTimeMillis() - timeStart) < timeout) {
      for (int i = 0; i < pool.length; i++) {
        if (pool[i] != null) {
          con = pool[i];
          pool[i] = null;
          break;
        }
      }
      if (con != null) {
        break;
      }
    }
```

```
        if (con == null) {
          throw new SQLException(NO_CONNECTIONS);
        }

        return con;
      }

      public synchronized void returnConnection(Connection con) {
        for (int i = 0; i < pool.length; i++) {
          if (pool[i] == null) {
            pool[i] = con;
            break;
          }
        }
      }

      public void closePool() {
        for (int i = 0; i < pool.length; i++) {
          try {
            pool[i].close();
          } catch (SQLException e) {}
        }
      }
    }
```

ControllerPool.java

ControllerPool.java is not much different from its predecessor; we've highlighted the differences:

```
    package com.wrox.projsp.ch20;

    import javax.servlet.*;
    import javax.servlet.http.*;
    import java.sql.*;

    public class ControllerPool extends HttpServlet {
      private static final String PARAM_POOL_SIZE = "poolSize";
      private static final String CATALOG_JSP = "/catalog_4.jsp";
      private static final String JDBC_DRIVER =
        "oracle.jdbc.driver.OracleDriver";

      private static final String WIDGET_CONN =
        "jdbc:oracle:thin:@db.widget.com:1521:WIDGET";
      private static final String WIDGET_NAME = "wteam";
      private static final String WIDGET_PW = "wteam";

      private static final String FOREIGN_CONN =
        "jdbc:oracle:thin:@foreign.widget.com:1521:FWIDGET";
      private static final String FOREIGN_NAME = "fwteam";
      private static final String FOREIGN_PW = "fwteam";

      private static final int DEFAULT_POOL_SIZE = 10;

      private ConnectionPool widgetPool;
      private ConnectionPool foreignPool;
```

```
    private int poolSize;

    public void init(ServletConfig config) throws ServletException {
      super.init(config);

      /* retrieve pool size */
      this.poolSize = getPoolSize(config);

      // initialize connection pools
      try {
        widgetPool = new ConnectionPool(JDBC_DRIVER, WIDGET_CONN,
                                        WIDGET_NAME, WIDGET_PW, poolSize);
        foreignPool = new ConnectionPool(JDBC_DRIVER, FOREIGN_CONN,
                                         FOREIGN_NAME, FOREIGN_PW, poolSize);
      } catch (SQLException e) {
        throw new ServletException(e.getMessage());
      }
    }

    public void doGet(HttpServletRequest req,
                      HttpServletResponse resp) throws ServletException {

      // determine which resource is requested
      String resourceName = getResourceName(req);

      // if resource requires bean, add it to request
      if (resourceName.equalsIgnoreCase(CATALOG_JSP)) {
        try {
          WidgetDataPool localWidgets = new WidgetDataPool(widgetPool,
                  WidgetData.LOCAL_WIDGETS);
          localWidgets.getWidgets();
          WidgetDataPool foreignWidgets = new WidgetDataPool(foreignPool,
                  WidgetData.FOREIGN_WIDGETS);
          foreignWidgets.getWidgets();
          req.setAttribute("localWidgets", localWidgets);
          req.setAttribute("foreignWidgets", foreignWidgets);
        } catch (SQLException e) {
          throw new ServletException(e.getMessage());
        }
      }

      // forward request to resource
      try {
        req.getRequestDispatcher(resourceName).forward(req, resp);
      } catch (java.io.IOException e) {}
    }

    public void doPost(HttpServletRequest req,
                       HttpServletResponse resp) throws ServletException {
      doGet(req, resp);
    }

    public void destroy() {

      // deinitialize pool
      widgetPool.closePool();
```

```
        foreignPool.closePool();
    }

    private String getResourceName(HttpServletRequest req) {
      String name = req.getPathInfo();
      return name;
    }

    private int getPoolSize(ServletConfig config) {
      int paramPoolSize;

      String sps = config.getInitParameter(PARAM_POOL_SIZE);
      try {
        paramPoolSize = Integer.parseInt(sps);
      } catch (Exception e) {
        paramPoolSize = DEFAULT_POOL_SIZE;
      }

      return paramPoolSize;
    }
}
```

WidgetDataPool.java

WidgetDataPool.java also required very few changes, which we've also highlighted. Instead of being passed a Connection object, WidgetDataPool is passed a ConnectionPool object and retrieves the Connection object from the ConnectionPool object:

```
package com.wrox.projsp.ch20;

import java.sql.*;

public class WidgetDataPool {
  private ConnectionPool cp;
  private Connection con;
  private Statement stmt;
  private ResultSet rs = null;
  private String query;

  public static final String LOCAL_WIDGETS =
     "select WIDGET_ID, NAME, WIDGET_DESC, TO_CHAR(DATE_AVAILABLE, " +
     "'MM/DD/YY') STR_DATE_AVAILABLE from BEN_WIDGETS";
  public static final String FOREIGN_WIDGETS =
     "select F_W_ID, F_WIDGET, F_WIDGET_DESC, TO_CHAR(DATE_AVAIL, " +
     "'MM/DD/YY') STR_DATE_AVAIL from FOREIGN_WIDGETS";

  private static final String ERROR_NO_RESULTSET =
     "ResultSet not initialized.";

  public WidgetDataPool(ConnectionPool cp, String query) {
    this.cp = cp;
    this.query = query;
  }

  public void getWidgets() throws SQLException {
```

```
    con = cp.getConnection();
    stmt = con.createStatement();
    rs = stmt.executeQuery(query);
  }

  public boolean next() throws SQLException {
    if (rs == null) {
      throw new SQLException(this.ERROR_NO_RESULTSET);
    }

    return rs.next();
  }

  public String getWidgetID() throws SQLException {
    return rs.getString(1);
  }

  public String getWidgetName() throws SQLException {
    return rs.getString(2);
  }

  public String getWidgetDescription() throws SQLException {
    return rs.getString(3);
  }

  public String getWidgetDate() throws SQLException {
    return rs.getString(4);
  }

  public void closeWidget() {
    try {
      stmt.close();
      cp.returnConnection(con);
    } catch (SQLException e) {}
  }
}
```

The catalog_5.jsp Page

Finally, `catalog_5.jsp` had lines changed from `catalog_4.jsp`, and again they're highlighted:

```
<%@page import="java.text.*"%>
<html>
  <head>
    <title>Widget Industries</title>
    <link rel="stylesheet" media="all" title="Default Styles" href="widget.css">
  </head>
  <body>

  <p align="center" class="title">
  Here are the widgets we produce and distribute:
  </p>

  <p align="center">
  <table class="catalog_table" cellspacing="1" cellpadding="4">
```

```
      <tr class="catalog_header">
        <th>
          Widget ID
        </th>
        <th>
          Widget Name
        </th>
        <th>
          Widget Description
        </th>
        <th>
          Date Available
        </th>
      </tr>

      <jsp:useBean id="localWidgets"
            class="com.wrox.projsp.ch20.WidgetDataPool" scope="request"/>
      <% while (localWidgets.next()) { %>
      <tr class="catalog_items">
        <td>
          D<%= localWidgets.getWidgetID() %>
        </td>
        <td>
          <%= localWidgets.getWidgetName() %>
        </td>
        <td>
          <%= localWidgets.getWidgetDescription() %>
        </td>
        <td>
          <%= localWidgets.getWidgetDate() %>
        </td>
      </tr>
      <% } localWidgets.closeWidget(); %>

      <jsp:useBean id="foreignWidgets"
            class="com.wrox.projsp.ch20.WidgetDataPool" scope="request"/>
      <% while (foreignWidgets.next()) { %>
      <tr class="catalog_items">
        <td>
          F<%= foreignWidgets.getWidgetID() %>
        </td>
        <td>
          <%= foreignWidgets.getWidgetName() %>
        </td>
        <td>
          <%= foreignWidgets.getWidgetDescription() %>
        </td>
        <td>
          <%= foreignWidgets.getWidgetDate() %>
        </td>
      </tr>
      <% } foreignWidgets.closeWidget(); %>

    </table>
    </p>

    </body>
</html>
```

769

Additions to web.xml

As with the previous example, we'll have to amend the `web.xml` file, although this time it's a lot smaller change:

```
<servlet>
  <servlet-name>
    Controller
  </servlet-name>
  <servlet-class>
    com.wrox.projsp.ch20.ControllerPool
  </servlet-class>
  <load-on-startup>
    -1
  </load-on-startup>
</servlet>


<servlet-mapping>
  <servlet-name>
    ControllerPool
  </servlet-name>
  <url-pattern>
    /widgetpool/*
  </url-pattern>
</servlet-mapping>
```

Twenty-Five Web Clients

Resource	Average response time
catalog_4.jsp	5627
catalog_5.jsp	669

Pooling connections has delivered the biggest performance gains of any of our other optimizations. Clearly, finding ways to recycle expensive objects within a class and pooling expensive objects across an application can offer large performance gains.

Tomcat vs. Apache: Static and Dynamic

The Apache web server is highly optimized for serving up static resources. Tomcat, like most other application servers, is optimized for serving up dynamic content. How much of a performance gain is realized by mating Tomcat with Apache to leverage their combined strengths? Let's find out by testing the performance of Tomcat serving up static HTML and comparing it with Apache. I've modified `index.jsp` to be a static page, and we'll first see how well the two servers fare:

Fifty Web Clients

Server	Average response time
index.html via Apache	5
index.html via Tomcat	201

One-Hundred Web Clients

Server	Average response time
`index.html` via Apache	6
`index.html` via Tomcat*	210

* Tomcat failed to complete 3% of its requests

Apache is clearly significantly faster at static content than Tomcat, yet Tomcat performs well until placed under considerable stress. Stand-alone Tomcat appears sufficient for small- to medium-sized web applications, but when the hits start stacking up, Tomcat should be mated with Apache to serve up all static content. It's a good idea to mate Tomcat with Apache from the start if there's any chance that you will need the performance boost in the future.

Note also from the example that Tomcat did fail to complete 3% of its requests. At press time, the only stable version of Tomcat 4.0 available for testing was Beta 1, so I'm not going to worry too much about this inefficiency.

Once Apache is mated with Tomcat, how much slower are Servlets than equivalent static content? Let's now compare the Apache numbers with `index.jsp` served up by Tomcat:

Fifty Web Clients

Server	Average response time
`index.html` via Apache	5
`index.jsp` via Tomcat	71

One-Hundred Web Clients

Server	Average response time
`index.html` via Apache	6
`index.jsp` via Tomcat*	71

* Tomcat failed to complete 2% of its requests

As the numbers show, Tomcat serving dynamic content is only slightly slower than Apache. However, because at high loads Tomcat starts to fail on completing its requests, developers facing high loads should consider substituting static content for dynamic content where practical to increase the scalability of the web application.

Filters

What speed impact do filters have on a web application? Let's implement a simple filter in the Widget web application and find out. Widget Industries have decided that they want to restrict those who can view their web application on an IP basis, thus ensuring that only specific clients with static broadband IP addresses can view what they consider to be protected and proprietary information. We'll modify `catalog_5.jsp` to use the filter and compare it with the previous `catalog_5.jsp` benchmarks.

Using the `Filter` interface that is discussed in Chapters 14 and 15, `SecurityFilter.java` checks to see if the client has a certain IP address which is specified in the deployment descriptor. If it does not, access to the requested resource is denied:

```java
package com.wrox.projsp.ch20;

import javax.servlet.*;
import javax.servlet.http.*;
import java.io.*;

public class SecurityFilter implements Filter {
  public static final String PARAM_VALID_IP = "validIP";
  private static final String ERROR_PAGE = "/error.html";

  private FilterConfig filterConfig;
  private String strIP;

  public void doFilter(ServletRequest req, ServletResponse res,
                       FilterChain chain)
          throws java.io.IOException, ServletException {
    boolean allowed;

    allowed = checkIP(req);
    if (allowed) {
      chain.doFilter(req, res);
    } else {
      RequestDispatcher rd = req.getRequestDispatcher(ERROR_PAGE);
      rd.forward(req, res);
    }
  }

  public void init(FilterConfig filterConfig) {
    this.filterConfig = filterConfig;
    strIP = filterConfig.getInitParameter(this.PARAM_VALID_IP);
  }

  public void destroy() {}

  /*
   * In a real-world implementation, we'd take into account a collection of
   * IP addresses for this type of restriction, or allow in a group of IP
   * addresses. For our example, blocking all but one address will suffice.
   */
  private boolean checkIP(ServletRequest req) {
    boolean validIP = true;

    if (this.strIP != null) {
      String ip = req.getRemoteAddr();
      if (!ip.equals(this.strIP)) {
        validIP = false;
      }
    }

    return validIP;
  }
}
```

In order to have the filter applied to our webapp, as you will remember from Chapter 14, we need to make some additions to web.xml:

```
<filter>
  <filter-name>SecurityFilter</filter-name>
  <filter-class>com.wrox.projsp.ch20.SecurityFilter</filter-class>
  <init-param>
    <param-name>validIP</param-name>
    <param-value>198.69.99.01</param-value>
  </init-param>
</filter>

<filter-mapping>
  <filter-name>SecurityFilter</filter-name>
  <url-pattern>/widgetpool/*</url-pattern>
</filter-mapping>
```

Note that for this web.xml example, only browsers with the IP address 198.69.99.01 will be allowed to visit the latest version of our catalog.

Twenty-Five Web Clients

Resource	Average response time
catalog_5.jsp	545
catalog_5.jsp w/ Filter	731

The filter in this example imposed roughly a 20% average speed penalty, which is somewhat steep considering the filter doesn't do many actual calculations. Remember that I'm only using a beta of Tomcat 4.0, so this may be a sign of un-optimized Servlet container code. Regardless, as you develop your filters, test your model early to ensure that you aren't negatively impacting your scalability in significant ways. If a needed filter is hampering performance, try switching Servlet containers.

Servlet Container Configuration

Each Servlet container has vendor-specific configuration options that can greatly affect performance.

> Be sure to take the time to review all available documentation you can get your hands on.

Having said that, there are a few general tips that apply to all Servlet containers.

First, ensure that you have enough sockets listening for HTTP requests. Tomcat's term for a socket is a "processor". You can define a minimum ("minProcessors") and maximum ("maxProcessors") number of processors for each connector (in other words, listening services) in Tomcat's server.xml file. Make sure that you have enough processors allocated to meet your estimated number of simultaneous clients otherwise performance will deteriorate greatly.

Next, as you configure and stress test your Servlet container, monitor the physical server's memory and CPU usage. If either or both of those two resources are constantly at the edge of their capacity, and you aren't aware of any glaring software inefficiencies, it's time to upgrade your hardware.

Third, consider disabling your Servlet container's access log. Statistics are invaluable to many organizations, but if you're not one of them, and you're pushing the envelope of your server, disable the access log and save the expense of repeated disk I/O, buffered though it may be.

JVMs Compared

Perhaps the easiest of all of the optimizations we've talked about is replacing your Java Virtual Machine (JVM). Sun's latest JVM, HotSpot 1.3 (http://java.sun.com/j2se), is significantly faster than any previous Sun JVM. However, Sun is the first to admit that there's still a lot of progress to be made with JVM technology.

Over the years, many other vendors have created their own Java Virtual Machine. A short list of possible Sun JVM substitutes includes:

❑   **TowerJ** by Tower Technology, http://www.towerj.com/

❑   **Oracle JVM**, http://www.oracle.com/

❑   **IBM JVM**, http://www.ibm.com/developerworks/index.html

Let's compare the performance of Sun's HotSpot JVM versus IBM's JVM 1.3. For the benchmark, we'll send 25 requests to the MVC version of the Widget web application.

Twenty-Five Web Clients

Server	Average response time
catalog_5.jsp on Sun	0.731
catalog_5.jsp on IBM	0.438

As you can see, the IBM JVM significantly increased our performance. Talk about easy; once installed, changing the JVM with Tomcat is as simple as changing a single environment variable. Only resource pooling provides a comparable return on investment of development time for optimization. It's worth your time as a developer to experiment with new JVMs as you come across them; you may want to verify that the JVMs have passed Sun's compatibility tests, however, if only to preserve your own sanity.

As we close this chapter, let's compare the applications initial performance with 25 web clients with it's final performance having applied all the optimizations we've discussed in this chapter (and with filtering turned on):

Twenty-Five Web Clients

Server	Average response time
catalog.jsp on Sun	6.889
catalog_5.jsp on IBM	0.438

After optimizing the example Widget web application, we've seen a 1500% speed increase without adjusting a single hardware setting, and our final performance is within the parameters established in the beginning of the chapter: 25 simultaneous users with no greater than a three second delay.

Summary

The Java platform is constantly evolving. As new Java Virtual Machines become available and the various J2EE APIs improve, specific techniques and measurements will become obsolete. While I'm hopeful that the benchmarks in this chapter will serve as a good reference for some time, you should take them with a grain of salt and learn what works for you in your environment.

Here are the things we've seen from this chapter:

❑ Never assume that your web applications will automatically scale. As you develop your web applications, establish the performance requirements. Using stress-testing techniques, validate that your application meets those requirements. If it does not, use a profiler to identify those areas of your application that need improvement.

Next, apply specific optimizations to those areas. Resource pooling and upgrading your JVM have the best potential for realizing large, quick speed gains. Repeat the stress test/profile/optimize cycle as often as necessary until your application meets its performance requirements.

Of course, if software optimization doesn't give you the performance you need, you should consider buying more hardware.

❑ As you optimize, always consider your **return on investment**. Object recycling and resource pooling tend to deliver the most significant improvements to application performance.

❑ Study the configuration options of your application server or Servlet container, and spend time monitoring its resource usage to ensure that your hardware is adequately supporting your software infrastructure. *Make sure you have enough sockets allocated to support your simultaneous client requests.*

❑ Finally, remember that replacing the JVM for your web applications can make a significant improvement in their performance. If you're using a Sun JVM earlier than HotSpot, you should upgrade immediately. Otherwise, benchmark other JVM's and consider your options. IBM's JVM appears to be an excellent performer.

In the next chapter, we'll be taking a look at the Struts framework, and how it can make producing a Model 2 web application that bit easier.

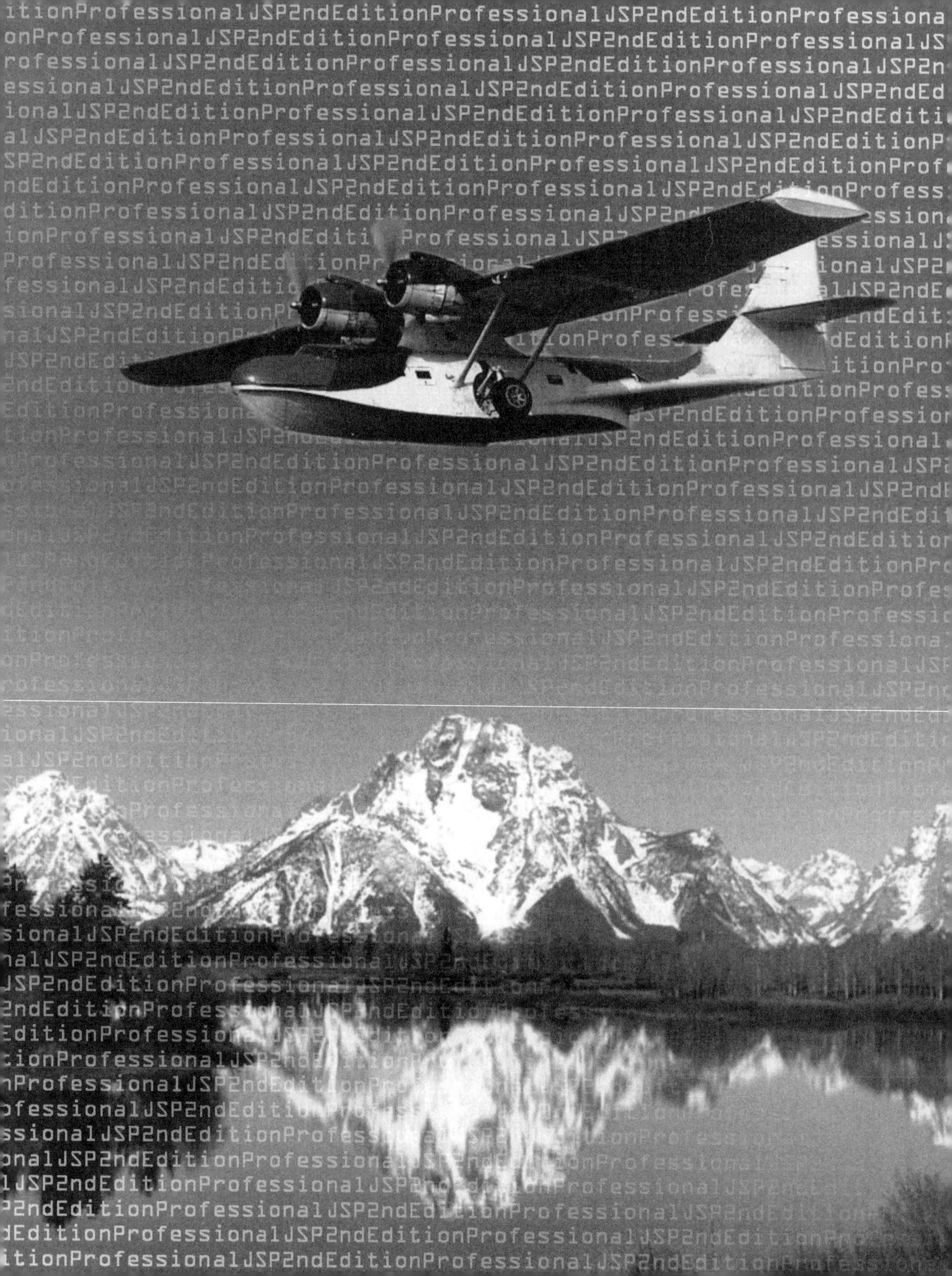
ProfessionalJSP2ndEdition

21

The Jakarta Struts Framework

This chapter introduces the first open source framework that encapsulates best software design practices along with the power of the JSP Custom Tags. This framework, called **Struts**, is the culmination of a web development methodology that has been discussed for over three years in mail lists, JSP specifications, and Servlet and JSP development books.

The Struts framework takes what was discussed in a general sense from these various sources and implements it in a practical and extendable fashion that highlights good software design and good use of the Servlet and JSP technologies. There are many people who believe that this framework will become very popular in web development circles.

This chapter introduces the framework's architecture and provides a sample application that is not simply a spin on the sample application found in the framework's distribution. The chapter encapsulates various design strategies and implementation details that are sprinkled throughout the Struts documentation, and teaches some subtleties of using the framework.

More specifically, the chapter covers the following topics:

❑   What is Struts, and why should we use it?

❑   A description of the example, including a run-through to demonstrate its functions

❑   An explanation of the chapter example, including the component parts

❑   A look at the Struts components

❑   Some design considerations for using Struts, plus what the future holds for Struts

The chapter covers a lot of information in a small amount of space. It is recommended that the reader download the source code for the chapter example, along with the framework itself. Instructions for doing so are contained within the chapter.

What is Struts?

Struts is an open source framework useful for building web applications in Java Servlets and JavaServer Pages (JSP) technologies, architected by Craig R. McClanahan and donated by him to the Apache Software Foundation. Craig, who works as the team lead on the Tomcat project for Sun Microsystems, still leads the Struts project and is often found responding to e-mail on both the struts-dev and struts-user mail lists. The Struts web site can be found at http://jakarta.apache.org/struts/index.html.

Struts implements a Model 2 JSP web application architecture (which we referred to in Chapter 7 as the 'dispatcher' approach) that uses a Servlet as a request dispatcher, a JavaBean that contains data for the request, and a JSP that presents a view of the data to the user. The UML component diagram in the following figure represents the Model 2 approach:

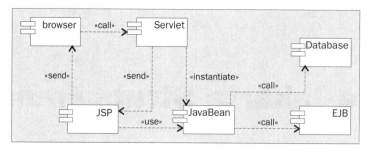

The Model 2 architecture utilizes a Servlet to receive the request. The Servlet delegates the collection of data for the request to a JavaBean. The JavaBean collects the needed data to satisfy the request, by making calls to enterprise components like EJBs and databases, and when it is finished collecting the needed data returns control back to the Servlet. The Servlet then forwards the request to the JSP, which constructs the HTML response using the data from the JavaBean and its own HTML code. After construction, the response is sent to the browser for display.

The architecture allows for decoupling of the business logic that collects the data from both the JSP and the Servlet. The decoupling of control, business logic and presentation is what differentiates the Model 2 architecture from the Model 1 (or, in the terminology of Chapter 7, 'page-centric') architecture that predominated in many early JSP projects. Model 1 is still used today, but most developers that have experienced problems with this approach have migrated to a Model 2 approach. The diagram below illustrates the Model 1 architecture:

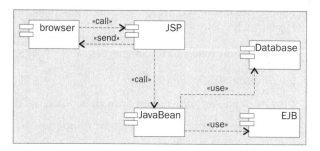

In the Model 1 architecture, the JSP acts upon the request by calling a JavaBean. The JavaBean can make requests to EJBs and the Database to collect the needed data to satisfy the request, and once the information is collected control returns to the JSP. The JSP then extracts the data from the JavaBean and the response is sent to the browser. This model is JSP-centric because the JSP controls the collection of data and the construction of the response, and typically results in large amounts of scriptlet code within the JSP. Larger web applications tend to have maintenance issues with this architecture.

Given the maintenance issues of the Model 1 approach, current web architectures have gravitated to the Model 2 approach, which is commonly associated with the **Model-View-Controller** (**MVC**) architectural software design pattern. To facilitate discussion we will look at the design of a system that would benefit from an MVC type software solution: an interactive application that needs to present multiple views of the same model data to multiple users. An example is illustrated in the following figure:

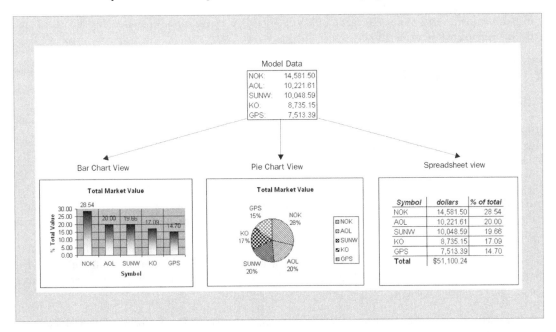

In this system, the model data has a Bar Chart View, a Pie Chart View, and a Spreadsheet View that rely on the model data. There can be multiple users looking at each view simultaneously. In this case, the application must keep each active view up to date whenever the model data changes. The MVC pattern facilitates this update by allowing each view to register with the model as a listener. The model is a **publisher** of information and each view is a **subscriber** of the data. When the data changes, the publisher sends notice to all of its subscribers that the data has changed and each subscriber must request the new data to keep its view updated.

This is known as the **publisher-subscriber pattern** because it helps to keep the subscribers synchronized with the publisher. In our example, the views subscribe to the model data and are notified by an event that the model has changed. This example represents a 'classic' solution using the MVC software architecture pattern. In the Java Platform, the Swing classes support this classic implementation of the MVC pattern. However, the use of the MVC pattern in a web application usually results in a variant of the classic MVC pattern.

In the web application realm, the view does not typically subscribe to the model because of the nature of the browser client, which connects to the web server to make its request and disconnects when it receives the response. While there are web applications that require a refresh of data that is not initiated by the user, this is not the typical implementation. Thus in the web application space the MVC pattern is implemented without the publisher-subscriber pattern. It's a hair splitting issue as to whether the web variant can technically be classified as an MVC pattern.

Since the decoupling feature of the MVC pattern is considered the 'heart' of the pattern, most web application developers take creative license and call Model 2 an MVC pattern. Some software design pattern purists will be quick to argue this classification. However, as is always the case with software design patterns, variants exist; sometimes they are referred to as the same as the 'classical' pattern, and sometimes they encounter a name change. Rather than justifying the naming convention we will refer to the architecture as an MVC variant. Thus we will discuss the Struts component in an MVC-type language, even though technically it is a variant implementation of MVC. The MVC classification is used in this chapter to highlight the decoupling nature of the framework.

Why use Struts?

The adoption of a framework like Struts allows the decoupling of the business logic, control, and presentation, such that each can change in implementation without forcing the others to change. Adoption of the framework also speeds the development time for the web application developer, because the developer can concentrate on business logic, application control, and presentation, and not have to worry about ensuring that they are decoupled from one another.

The adoption of the Struts framework reduces the amount of code that needs to be generated for a web application, since much has already been produced and debugged. However Struts is still in its infancy, and does sometimes require some debugging. This would also be true for an application that developed its own method of decoupling business logic, control, and presentation.

Another benefit to Struts is the extensive JSP Custom Tag library. The custom tags significantly reduce the amount of scriptlet coding in the JSPs. Scriptlet coding sometimes has to exist, but the smaller the amount the easier it is to change the look and feel without re-coding the JSP.

Lastly, Struts provides the ability to internationalize your application. The explosion of the web has lead to the need to support multiple languages yet maintain the same server-side logic. Struts relies on the internationalization features of the Java 2 Platform to change the content of a web page based on the locale of the user.

Overview of the Struts Components

Before we delve too deeply into either Struts or our example application, it's worth taking a broad overview of the components that make up a Struts-based application – both components of Struts itself and the application-specific components. Typically we will have:

❑ HTML forms, generated by JSPs using the Struts `html` tag library.

❑ The Struts `ActionServlet` controller, to which the form data is posted. `ActionServlet` is configured by an XML file, `struts-config.xml`.

❑ Application-specific subclasses of the Struts `ActionForm` class, which are JavaBeans with properties corresponding to the form fields. `ActionServlet` automatically instantiates the form bean, populates its properties with the form data, and stores it in the specified scope (typically `request` or `session`).

   `ActionServlet` will then optionally ask the `ActionForm` subclass to validate its contents to check that valid data was received from the user. If not, `ActionServlet` can forward control back to the original JSP form; the `html` tag library includes the ability for the JSP to display appropriate error messages and to populate the form with the previous values.

❑ Application-specific subclasses of the Struts `Action` class. `Action` subclasses contain (or call) your application's business logic, in the `perform()` method. In this method you can examine the form data, perform the appropriate processing, and store any necessary data in the request or session that will be needed by the JSP to produce the response.

`perform()` returns an `ActionForward`, a Struts class representing the JSP that should be used to render the response. Mappings between logical names and the actual JSPs are established in the `struts-config.xml` file.

❑ `ActionMapping` is a Struts-defined class representing the mapping between a URL pattern used in a client request and the `ActionForm` and `Action` subclasses to be used. `ActionMappings` are defined in `struts-config.xml`.

The component diagram below shows these main Struts components, relative to the MVC pattern:

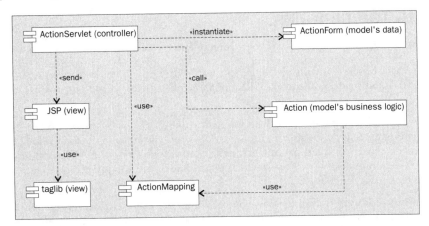

Let's look at these components in a little more detail:

❑ `ActionServlet` – This is an MVC Controller component that acts as a request dispatcher. There is only one instance of this Servlet running in the Struts framework. `ActionServlet`, and indeed all of the core classes in this diagram, may be extended to provide additional functionality; however, this has not been done in this chapter's example application.

❑ `ActionMapping` – This class represents a mapping between a URL pattern and a business logic component (`Action`). It defines input, output, and specific 'forward' targets based on the business logic. This class may be extended, but has not been in the example in this chapter.

❑ `ActionForm` – This is an MVC Model component; in Struts it operates as a JavaBean that represents the input from the MVC View component. The `ActionServlet` automatically populates the properties of the bean after it is instantiated, and if the bean has a `validate()` method it is called before the user implemented `Action` class is called. The `ActionForm` is extended to represent a JSP View component.

To illustrate a naming practice used in the example application, given a JSP called `logon.jsp` and a corresponding request URI of `/logon`, the user implemented `ActionForm` class will typically be named `LogonActionForm`.

❑ `Action` – This class represents the business logic and is part of the MVC Model component; it is extended to implement business logic for a particular request. As an example, the `Action` for the `/logon` URI would typically be called `LogonAction`.

The developer-implemented `Action` must be designed and coded to operate in a thread-safe manner, because the controller will share the same instance for multiple simultaneous requests. There are two ways to do this: make sure that each request works independently of the others without sharing data, or use synchronization to protect shared resources. A good rule of thumb in `Action` design is:

❑ *Don't* store state for a particular request within the Action in instance or static variables.

❑ *Do* protect shared resources like files and database connections with synchronized access.

❑ `taglib` – This component represents all the tag libraries in the Struts 1.0 release: `bean`, `html`, `logic`, and `template`.

Later we will review the classes in the figure above individually, with a diagram of the class and an explanation of key attributes and operations of the class.

The Struts Tag Libraries

The Struts tag libraries are used by the JSP view components; there are four libraries in Struts 1.0:

❑ The `html` library contains tags to generate HTML, display values from an `ActionForm` in HTML input fields, and encode URL links with the session id so that cookies are not required by the client browser.

❑ The `bean` library is concerned with the manipulation of JavaBeans within the JSP, and contains tags that define new scripting variables based on properties of existing beans, HTTP headers, cookies, request parameters, write out bean properties into the response, as well as a tag that automatically recognizes which `Locale` is in use and selects message strings in the corresponding language.

❑ The `logic` library is used for flow control within the JSP view; various comparison tags are provided, along with the ability to iterate over an `Iterator`, `Collection`, `Map`, or array, and facilities to further forward or redirect the request.

❑ The `template` tag library is not used in the chapter example, but provides the ability to construct from individual JSP components pages that use a common format using dynamic templates. This library will undergo significant enhancement in the next release of the framework, at which time the author will use it. (I have not found any other items subject to this kind of change – to stay informed of changes to Struts you should visit the mail list described at the end of the chapter.)

The tag libraries will be discussed in more detail as part of the example application; a comprehensive list of and documentation for the custom tags is contained within the Struts documentation. (Unfortunately space does not permit their listing here.)

Installing Struts

Various Struts distributions are available. As of this writing the latest 'milestone' (stable, but not formally released) version is Struts 1.0 Beta 1; alternatively there are also nightly builds of the very latest code, or for the brave of heart there is anonymous CVS access to the code repository.

Note that the nightly builds may not always compile, but you can always select another build that will. However, the nice thing about using nightly builds is that you know what the last one was that worked. If there is a problem with the latest download, simply re-install an older version.

Both source and binary distributions are available, depending on whether or not you want to build Struts yourself. To download Struts, go to:

❑ http://jakarta.apache.org/builds/jakarta-struts/nightly/ for nightly binary distributions

❑ http://jakarta.apache.org/builds/jakarta-struts/nightly/src/ for nightly source distributions

❑ Subdirectories of http://jakarta.apache.org/builds/jakarta-struts/release/ for release builds; as of this writing the latest is 1.0 Beta 1 in http://jakarta.apache.org/builds/jakarta-struts/release/v1.0-b1/

Download the appropriate archive for your development environment, and then check http://jakarta.apache.org/struts/installation.html for the most up-to-date instructions for installing both source and binary distributions, including directions for installing the needed components into your own web application. (These files are included in the chapter example source code.)

Struts comes with a number of web applications, including its documentation (`struts-documentation.war`), an example application (`struts-example.war`), demonstrations of its template tag library and file upload features (`struts-template.war` and `struts-upload.war`), and a 'blank' web application (`struts-blank.war`) you can use as the basis of your own Struts applications.

The installation page also highlights the prerequisite software and environment variables that you need for both the source and binary distributions to work fully. The version of Java 2 Platform Standard Edition you have must be 1.2 (JDK1.2) or later; if you have version 1.3 (JDK1.3) less effort is required since you don't need to install the JDBC 2.0 standard extensions library.

To build from a source distribution, assuming you have all the prerequisites already installed, change to the directory where you unpacked Struts (hereafter called `<struts-home>`) and compile the source code using the appropriate `build.bat` or `build.sh` script file. This script uses Ant 1.2 (another Jakarta subproject located at http://jakarta.apache.org/ant/) to compile the source.

Next you need to execute the build script with the `dist` argument so it will create everything needed to install on Tomcat 4.0, resulting in all the code and support files being placed in the `<struts-home>/dist` directory. It's a good idea to build the framework from the source if you plan on using an IDE to debug your code within the Struts framework.

> Note that when using the nightly distributions you will need to delete your entire directory structure from the `<struts-home>` level before installing a new source distribution. This ensures that any deleted files or directories will be removed and won't cause compile errors.

The Struts committers have been very good about providing backward compatibility by deprecating old functionality before they remove it. The first release 0.5 has significantly different syntax to version 1.0; this syntax is supported in 1.0, but has been deprecated and will not be in subsequent releases. The amount of deprecation prior to the 1.0 release is to make the framework a stable, long-term base for development; there should be a smaller number of deprecations in future releases.

The Example Application

The example application in this chapter implements an online CD store, the CDs Galore Web Store. Users can register with the web store to receive an account; once they have registered, they can view and order CDs from the three categories in the store. The store features a shopping cart that displays the number of unique items selected for purchase and the total price of these items.

The web store runs as a web application under Tomcat, and does not require a database. Instead, it emulates a database with the same technique used in the `struts-example` application in the 1.0 version of the framework, namely using a Servlet that is loaded on startup, and defines objects in the Servlet context by reading them from a `database.xml` file.

The following UML Activity Diagram describes a typical visit to the web store:

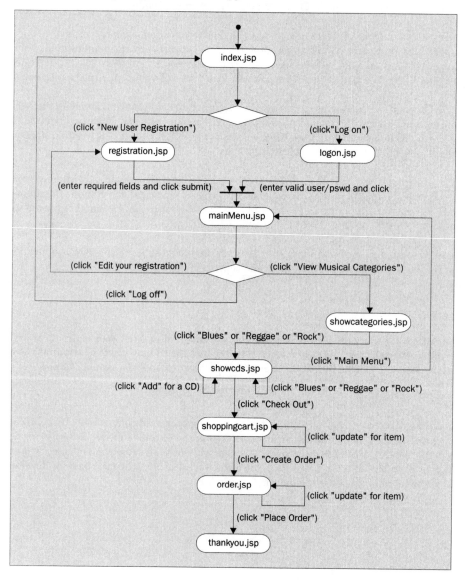

Installing the Example Application

Download the example application for this chapter, either from the Wrox Press web site (http://www.wrox.com/), or from the New Particles web site (http://www.newparticles.com/struts/). The New Particles Corporation has graciously volunteered to provide access to the chapter example and host a series of web pages dedicated to the use of Struts; this site will always contain any bug fixes to the chapter example, and will provide new versions of the example as Struts provides new versions.

The chapter example is based on the Tomcat 4.0 reference implementation of the Servlet 2.3 and JSP 1.2 specification. However, the application will run on most Servlet/JSP containers that implement the Servlet 2.2 and JSP 1.1 specification. Some commercial implementations of the Servlet/JSP container do not conform to the specification entirely, and thus there are install notes within the Struts distribution that attempt to assist the reader in implementing the framework on specific containers. At the time of this writing there are sections for iPlanet application server, Tomcat, Weblogic, Resin, Bluestone Universal Business Server, iPlanet web server, JRUN, Orion Application Server, Silverstream, and Webshere.

Tomcat is the recommended Servlet/JSP engine for the reader to use for the chapter example, since it conforms more closely to the specification than many of the other containers, and the reader can be assured that Struts will stay current with Tomcat, since the architect of the framework works on the Tomcat 4.0 team. This has propelled Struts into position as a kind of 'litmus test' for containers; customers of the various commercial containers want to use the Struts framework too, and have prompted their vendors to produce service packs to address the non-compliance issues and give them ability to use Struts framework in the container.

The example application is provided with an Ant 1.2 build script from which the reader can build the class files and deploy the application to the Tomcat server. Once you have downloaded the source archive for the example you will need to extract it into the Tomcat webapps directory, creating the following directory structure:

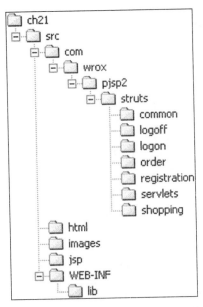

In the ch21 directory there is an Ant build.xml file that will compile the code and set up the web application. Execute the build from the wrox-struts directory by calling ant.bat or ant.sh, depending on your development environment. After executing this script your directory structure should be like that illustrated in the following figure, where the src directory is collapsed to limit the size of the image:

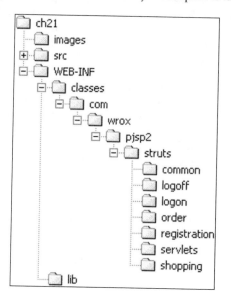

The build.xml script contains an options target that lists possible targets and explains their purpose; the default target is the all target, which is automatically called when you execute the ant.bat or ant.sh script from the ch21 directory. The relevant section from build.xml for the all target is as follows:

```
<!-- used to build all and copy jsp pages. -->
<target name="all" depends="dist,compile">
</target>
```

The all target depends on the dist and compile targets. These are provided in the next listing:

```
<!-- compiles application classes -->
<target name="compile" depends="init">
  <javac srcdir="src" destdir="${classes.dest.dir}"
    classpath="${struts.jar}"
    debug="true" optimize="false" deprecation="true"/>
</target>

<!-- used to build all and copy jsp pages. -->
<target name="dist"
  depends="dist.def.files,dist.html,dist.images,dist.jsp,dist.prop">
</target>
```

The compile target compiles the source code under the ch21/src directory, putting the .class files into the WEB-INF/classes directory. The classes are compiled with debug on, optimization off, and deprecation notification on. The dist target copies the tag library files, the application resource file, and other required XML documents into the WEB-INF directory. It also copies the HTML pages, JSP pages, and the images to their location under the ch21 directory (the web application root directory).

The reader is encouraged to execute this target when building the application, since it accomplishes all tasks needed to deploy the application on Tomcat. If you download the example and forget to compile it, you will receive a Servlet exception with a root cause of:

```
java.lang.NoClassDefFoundError: org/apache/struts/taglib/html/HtmlTag
```

If you compile the source code you should not see this error.

A Walk Through the Application

Let's take a tour through the application, following Sally Byalot as she logs on and orders a CD. Here's the first page we see as we point our browser at the website:

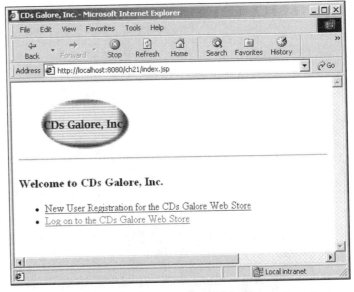

From now on, we're going to be using Sally's account, so we'll click on the **Log on to the CDs Galore Web Store** link, which takes us to the following page:

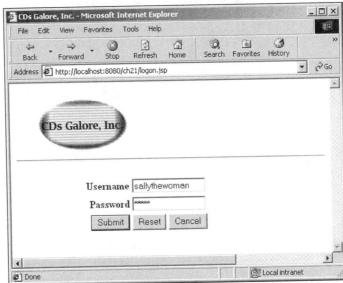

As you see, Sally has logged on with her username `sallythewoman` and input her password (for which she has rather insecurely chosen `sally`), so clicking on the Submit button takes us on to the next page:

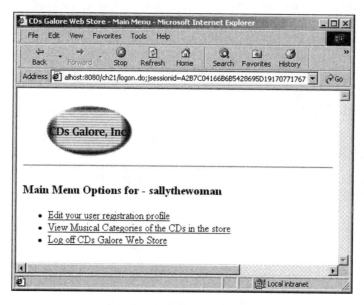

This is a fairly standard main menu, with enough functionality to get us around the site. At the moment Sally is only interested in buying music, so we click on the middle link, which takes us to the following page:

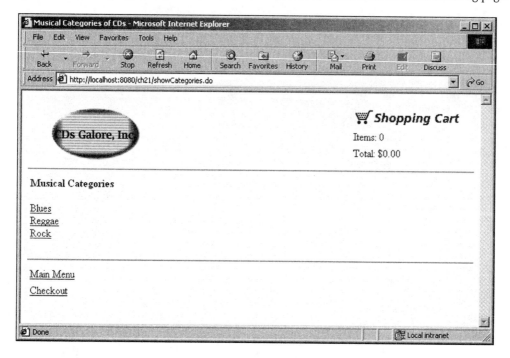

Again, a functional page, with links to take us to where we want to go – in this case, straight to the Reggae section:

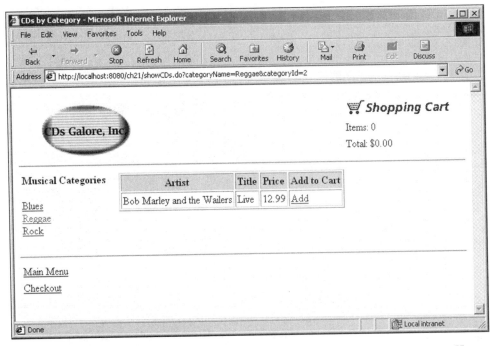

Well, the store is only just starting up, so we can't expect them to have every album we want. However, Sally is in luck, since she has been looking for a live Bob Marley CD for a while. A click on the Add link results in the CD being added to the shopping cart, as can be seen in the next screenshot:

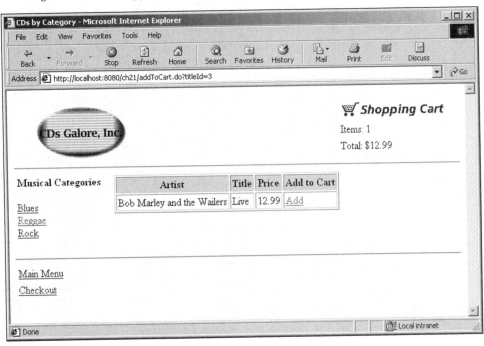

One click, and we have one
item in the shopping cart.
Sally doesn't want anything
else today, so let's head for
the Checkout:

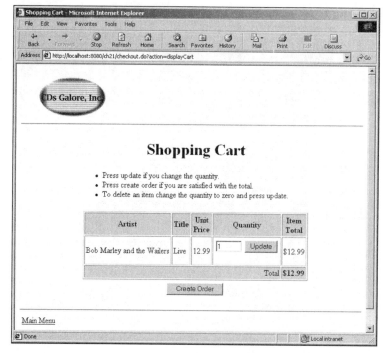

Since Sally doesn't want
anything else, we'll click on
the Create Order button,
which will take us to the
next page:

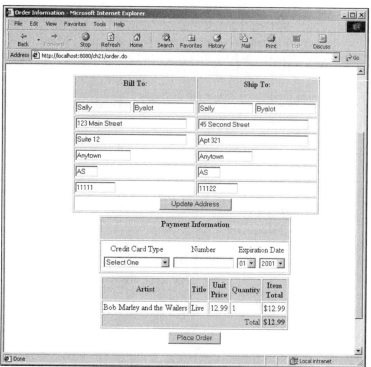

Sally checks that the billing and shipping address are correct, and clicks on Place Order:

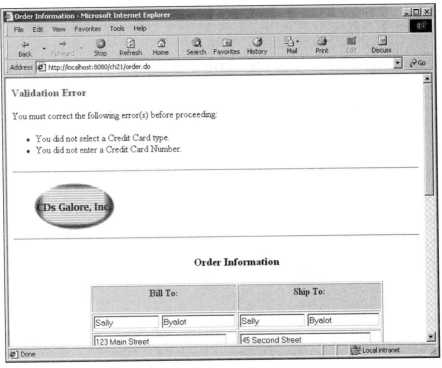

Oops! We got distracted and forgot to specify a credit card and number. We'll fill those in, and pass swiftly on to the next page:

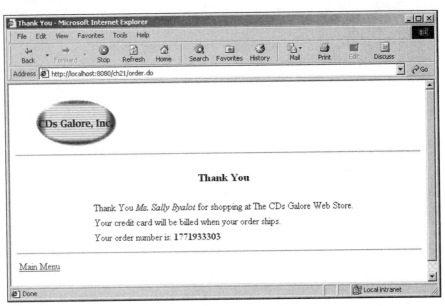

Finally, we're there! We've purchased a CD online, and we can sit back in the knowledge that it will come to us at home. Well, we could if this was a real online store; since it's only an example of how the Struts framework can be harnessed to produce dynamic websites, we'll have to find somewhere else to buy our music from.

Understanding the Example Application

Having seen the example Struts-based application in action, let's now take a closer look at how it works. At this point, we'll be looking at the specific implementation for the example. We'll look at the Struts framework itself in a more general light in the section *What are the Key Struts Components?*

The parts of the chapter example we'll be looking closely at are:

❑ The web.xml file

❑ The DatabaseServlet and its database.xml file

❑ The index.jsp page

❑ The struts-config.xml file

❑ The example application components from the logon, registration, and shopping packages

The web.xml File

The first item to understand about the chapter example is the web.xml file. After executing the build.xml script the web.xml file is located in the ch21/WEB-INF directory. This establishes the web application configuration for our example:

```xml
<?xml version="1.0" encoding="ISO-8859-1"?>
<!DOCTYPE web-app
  PUBLIC "-//Sun Microsystems, Inc.//DTD Web Application 2.2//EN"
  "http://java.sun.com/j2ee/dtds/web-app_2_2.dtd">
<web-app>

  <!-- Action Servlet Configuration -->
  <servlet>
    <servlet-name>action</servlet-name>
    <servlet-class>org.apache.struts.action.ActionServlet</servlet-class>
    <init-param>
      <param-name>application</param-name>
      <param-value>com.wrox.pjsp2.struts.ApplicationResources</param-value>
    </init-param>
    <init-param>
      <param-name>config</param-name>
      <param-value>/WEB-INF/struts-config.xml</param-value>
    </init-param>
    <init-param>
      <param-name>debug</param-name>
      <param-value>4</param-value>
    </init-param>
    <init-param>
      <param-name>detail</param-name>
      <param-value>9</param-value>
    </init-param>
```

```xml
    <init-param>
      <param-name>validate</param-name>
      <param-value>true</param-value>
    </init-param>
    <load-on-startup>1</load-on-startup>
  </servlet>

  <!-- Database Initialization Servlet (must load after ActionServlet) -->
  <servlet>
    <servlet-name>database</servlet-name>
    <servlet-class>
      com.wrox.pjsp2.struts.servlets.DatabaseServlet
    </servlet-class>
    <init-param>
      <param-name>debug</param-name>
      <param-value>2</param-value>
    </init-param>
    <load-on-startup>2</load-on-startup>
  </servlet>

  <!-- Action Servlet Mapping -->
  <servlet-mapping>
    <servlet-name>action</servlet-name>
    <url-pattern>*.do</url-pattern>
  </servlet-mapping>

  <!-- The Welcome File List -->
  <welcome-file-list>
    <welcome-file>index.jsp</welcome-file>
  </welcome-file-list>

  <!-- Application Tag Library Descriptor -->
  <taglib>
    <taglib-uri>/WEB-INF/app.tld</taglib-uri>
    <taglib-location>/WEB-INF/app.tld</taglib-location>
  </taglib>

  <!-- Start: Struts Tag Library Descriptors -->
  <taglib>
    <taglib-uri>/WEB-INF/struts-bean.tld</taglib-uri>
    <taglib-location>/WEB-INF/struts-bean.tld</taglib-location>
  </taglib>
  <taglib>
    <taglib-uri>/WEB-INF/struts-html.tld</taglib-uri>
    <taglib-location>/WEB-INF/struts-html.tld</taglib-location>
  </taglib>
  <taglib>
    <taglib-uri>/WEB-INF/struts-logic.tld</taglib-uri>
    <taglib-location>/WEB-INF/struts-logic.tld</taglib-location>
  </taglib>
  <taglib>
    <taglib-uri>/WEB-INF/struts-template.tld</taglib-uri>
    <taglib-location>/WEB-INF/struts-template.tld</taglib-location>
  </taglib>
  <!-- End: Struts Tag Library Descriptors -->

</web-app>
```

The first Servlet loaded in the web application is the `ActionServlet`. It is loaded first because the `DatabaseServlet`, which is loaded second, requires that the `ApplicationResources.properties` file (which contains the default-locale messages for this application – `ActionServlet` loads this and stores it in the `ServletContext`) be already loaded when it starts up.

The DatabaseServlet

The `DatabaseServlet` emulates a database for our application, and is similar to the `DatabaseServlet.java` contained in the `struts-example` web application. Our `DatabaseServlet` uses its `init()` method to load two users of the web store, the musical categories of our CDs, the credit card types, the month values, the year values, and the title values:

```java
public void init() throws ServletException {

    // Process our servlet initialization parameters
    String value = getServletConfig().getInitParameter("debug");

    servletContext = getServletContext();

    // Get MessageResources from the Servlet Context
    // returns null if ActionServlet not loaded first, see web.xml file.
    messages = (MessageResources)
                    servletContext.getAttribute(Action.MESSAGES_KEY);

    try {
      debug = Integer.parseInt(value);
    } catch (Throwable t) {
      debug = 0;
    }
    if(debug >= 1) {
      log("Initializing database servlet");
    }

    // Load our database from persistent storage
    try {
      load();
    } catch(Exception ex) {
      log("Database load exception", ex);
      throw new UnavailableException("Cannot load database from '" +
                          pathname + "'");
    }
    setCreditCardTypes();
    setMonthValues();
    setYearValues();
    setTitleValues();
} //end init
```

The first thing the `init()` method does is load the `ApplicationResources` from the Servlet context. The `ApplicationResources` are used for all text that will be displayed to the user; you would have one for each language that your application supported; the `ActionServlet` places the `ApplicatonResources` in the `ServletContext` when it starts up. Next, `init()` makes calls to five methods within the `DatabaseServlet`. The first call is to the `load()` method, as seen below.

The DatabaseServlet.load() Method

The `load()` method makes use of one of the `org.apache.struts.util` classes called the `Digester`. The `Digester` class provides an abstracted interface to SAX parsing of an XML document, and is used within Struts to parse the `struts-config.xml` file. Given a set of patterns-matching rules, it can read and parse an XML file, and will instantiate Java objects and call methods on them to populate them with the data from the file. The `Digester` is used in the `load()` method below.

The `load()` method first opens a `BufferedInputStream` to the `database.xml` file, then adds parsing rules to the `Digester`. This will permit the class to load the `database.xml` file, parse it and create instance objects that represent the data in the file:

```
private synchronized void load() throws Exception {

  // Initialize our tables
  userTable = new HashMap();
  categoryTable = new HashMap();
  cdTable = new HashMap();

  // Acquire an input stream to our database file
  if(debug >= 1) {
    log("Loading database from '" + pathname() + "'");
  }
  FileInputStream fis = null;
  try {
    fis = new FileInputStream(pathname());
  } catch (FileNotFoundException e) {
    log("No persistent database to be loaded");
    return;
  }
  BufferedInputStream bis = new BufferedInputStream(fis);

  // Construct a digester to use for parsing
  Digester digester = new Digester();
  digester.push(this);
  digester.setDebug(debug);
  digester.setValidating(false);

  // rule to create instance of User class
  digester.addObjectCreate("database/user",
                           "com.wrox.pjsp2.struts.common.User");
  // rule to get properties attributes on user tag
  digeSester.addSetProperties("database/user");
  // rule to call addUser method on this class
  digester.addSetNext("database/user", "addUser");

  // rule to create instance of Address class for userAddress data
  digester.addObjectCreate("database/user/userAddress",
                           "com.wrox.pjsp2.struts.common.Address",
                           "userAddress");
  // rule to get properties from attributes on userAddress tag
  digester.addSetProperties("database/user/userAddress");
  // rule to call setUserAddress method on the User class
  digester.addSetNext("database/user/userAddress",
                  "setUserAddress",
```

```
                          "com.wrox.pjsp2.struts.common.Address");

        // rule to create instance of Address class for billingAddress data
        digester.addObjectCreate("database/user/billingAddress",
                              "com.wrox.pjsp2.struts.common.Address",
                              "billingAddress");
        // rule to get properties from attributes on billingAddress tag
        digester.addSetProperties("database/user/billingAddress");
        // rule to call setBillingAddress method on the User class
        digester.addSetNext("database/user/billingAddress",
                          "setBillingAddress",
                          "com.wrox.pjsp2.struts.common.Address");

        // rule to create instance of Category class
        digester.addObjectCreate("database/category",
                              "com.wrox.pjsp2.struts.common.Category");
        // rule to get properties from attributes on category tag
        digester.addSetProperties("database/category");

        // rule to call addCategory method on this class
        digester.addSetNext("database/category", "addCategory");

        // rule to create instance of CD class
        digester.addObjectCreate("database/CD",
                              "com.wrox.pjsp2.struts.common.CD");
        // rule to get properties from attributes on cd tag
        digester.addSetProperties("database/CD");

        // rule to call addCD method on this class
        digester.addSetNext("database/CD", "addCD",
                          "com.wrox.pjsp2.struts.common.CD");

        // Parse the input stream to populate hashMaps within this servlet.
        digester.parse(bis);
        bis.close();

        servletContext.setAttribute(Constants.CATEGORY_TABLE_KEY, categoryTable);
        servletContext.setAttribute(Constants.CD_TABLE_KEY, cdTable);
        servletContext.setAttribute(Constants.USER_TABLE_KEY, userTable);

    } //end load
```

The database.xml File

Next we will look at the database.xml file, which represents the data to be loaded. <database> is the root element, within which are <user>, <category>, and <CD> elements:

```
<database>

  <user firstName="Sam" lastName="Byalot" userName="samtheman"
        password="tunes" passwordHint="first" title="Mr."
        e-mail="samtheman@aol.com">
    <userAddress address1="45 Second Street" address2="Apt 321"
               city="Anytown" state="AS" zip="11122"/>
    <billingAddress address1="123 Main Street" address2="Suite 12"
```

```
                                    city="Anytown" state="AS" zip="11111"/>
        </user>
        <user firstName="Sally" lastName="Byalot" userName="sallythewoman"
              password="sally" passwordHint="first" title="Ms."
              e-mail="sallythewoman@aol.com">
          <userAddress address1="45 Second Street" address2="Apt 321"
                      city="Anytown" state="AS" zip="11122"/>
          <billingAddress address1="123 Main Street" address2="Suite 12"
                      city="Anytown" state="AS" zip="11111"/>
        </user>

        <category categoryId="1" categoryName="Blues"/>
        <category categoryId="2" categoryName="Reggie"/>
        <category categoryId="3" categoryName="Rock"/>
        <CD titleId="1" titleName="Live On" artist="Kenny Wayne Shepherd"
            price="16.99" categoryId="1"/>
        <CD titleId="2" titleName="Trouble Is" artist="Kenny Wayne Shepherd"
            price="16.99" categoryId="1"/>
        <CD titleId="3" titleName="Live" artist="Bob Marley and the Wailers"
            price="12.99" categoryId="2"/>
        <CD titleId="4" titleName="Razorblade Suitcase" artist="Bush"
            price="14.99" categoryId="3"/>
        <CD titleId="5" titleName="Sixteen Stone" artist="Bush"
            price="13.99" categoryId="3"/>
        <CD titleId="6" titleName="The Science of Things" artist="Bush"
            price="15.99" categoryId="3"/>

    </database>
```

Creating the Users

The first set of rules for the `Digester` creates `User` object instances, populates them from the attributes on the all <user> XML tags, and sends the `User` object instances to the `addUser()` method within this Servlet. The three rules that accomplish this are picked out from `DatabaseServlet` in the following code listing:

```
// rule to create instance of User class
digester.addObjectCreate("database/user",
                         "com.wrox.pjsp2.struts.common.User");
// rule to get properties attributes on user tag
digester.addSetProperties("database/user");
// rule to call addUser method on this class
digester.addSetNext("database/user", "addUser");
```

The `addObjectCreate()` method creates a parsing rule for the `Digester` saying that when a <user> tag in encountered in the XML stream, it is to create a `User` object instance. The next rule is to set the newly created `User` object's properties to the values of the <user> tag attributes. The next rule, `addSetNext()`, registers the `addUser()` method on the `DatabaseServlet` as the recipient of the newly create and populated `User` objects.

These rules will apply to all XML <user> entries within the `database.xml` file. Using our file, the `DatabaseServlet` loads the two users of the web application. These sets of rules are processing the data within the following section of the `database.xml` file:

```
<user firstName="Sam" lastName="Byalot" userName="samtheman"
      password="tunes" passwordHint="first" title="Mr."
      e-mail="samtheman@aol.com">
  <userAddress address1="45 Second Street" address2="Apt 321"
              city="Anytown" state="AS" zip="11122"/>
```

```
        <billingAddress address1="123 Main Street" address2="Suite 12"
                        city="Anytown" state="AS" zip="11111"/>
    </user>
    <user firstName="Sally" lastName="Byalot" userName="sallythewoman"
          password="sally" passwordHint="first" title="Ms."
          e-mail="sallythewoman@aol.com">
      <userAddress address1="45 Second Street" address2="Apt 321"
                   city="Anytown" state="AS" zip="11122"/>
      <billingAddress address1="123 Main Street" address2="Suite 12"
                      city="Anytown" state="AS" zip="11111"/>
    </user>
```

You will notice that the <userAddress> and <billingAddress> tags are not mentioned in the previous rules. This is because the addresses are body elements of the <user> tag and not attributes. They represent class instances that are stored inside the User object. Thus, we have to tell the Digester to create an Address class instance for both the <userAddress> and the <billingAddress> tags, populate the objects from their respective attributes, and add them to the User object.

Adding the User's Addresses

The following code listing accomplishes this task:

```
    // rule to create instance of Address class for userAddress data
    digester.addObjectCreate("database/user/userAddress",
                             "com.wrox.pjsp2.struts.common.Address",
                             "userAddress");
    // rule to get properties from attributes on userAddress tag
    digester.addSetProperties("database/user/userAddress");
    // rule to call setUserAddress method on the User class
    digester.addSetNext("database/user/userAddress",
                "setUserAddress",
                "com.wrox.pjsp2.struts.common.Address");
```

This says that the <userAddress> is a sub-element to the <user> element, and is of the type com.wrox.pjsp2.struts.Address. Next the addSetProperties() rule is added to copy the attributes of the <userAddress> tag into the Address instance that represents the user address. The last rule instructs the Digester to call the setUserAddress() method on the User object and passes the instance of the Address object that represents the UserAddress. The last rule for the <user> element is in the following code listing:

```
    // rule to create instance of Address class for billingAddress data
    digester.addObjectCreate("database/user/billingAddress",
                             "com.wrox.pjsp2.struts.common.Address",
                             "billingAddress");
    // rule to get properties from attributes on billingAddress tag
    digester.addSetProperties("database/user/billingAddress");
    // rule to call setBillingAddress method on the User class
    digester.addSetNext("database/user/billingAddress",
                "setBillingAddress",
                "com.wrox.pjsp2.struts.common.Address");
```

This does the same as the last set of rules, except it calls the setBillingAddress() method on the User object. Since we were calling two different methods on the User object we had to create two separate rules.

> As you can see, the `Digester` is a very useful class, and can be used as a simple way to create instances of classes and populate them with instance data.

The <category> Element

The next element in the `database.xml` file is the `<category>` element, for distinguishing types of music, so we must use an `addObjectCreate()` rule as below:

```
// rule to create instance of Category class
digester.addObjectCreate("database/category",
                         "com.wrox.pjsp2.struts.common.Category");
// rule to get properties from attributes on category tag
digester.addSetProperties("database/category");

// rule to call addCategory method on this class
digester.addSetNext("database/category", "addCategory");
```

Then we add an `addSetProperties()` rule and an `addSetNext()` rule; this time the `addCategory()` method is in the `DatabaseServlet`. These three rules are all that is needed for processing multiple category elements within the `database.xml` file.

The last set of rules for the `<CD>` entries is similar to the category section.

The digester.parse() Method

The `digester.parse()` method is called in within the last few statements of the `init()` method, to perform the parse of the XML input stream that was read from `database.xml`. The parse will follow the rules that were added when parsing the file:

```
// Parse the input stream to initialize our database
digester.parse(bis);
bis.close();

servletContext.setAttribute(Constants.CATEGORY_TABLE_KEY, categoryTable);
servletContext.setAttribute(Constants.CD_TABLE_KEY, cdTable);
servletContext.setAttribute(Constants.USER_TABLE_KEY, userTable);
```

Lastly, `init()` puts these objects in the `ServletContext` so they can be accessed from `Action` classes and from JSPs.

Using the ApplicationResources Bundle

The last few methods of the `DatabaseServlet` use the `ApplicationResources` to generate drop downs for JSPs, and these too are added to the `ServletContext`. We will review the `setCreditCardTypes()` method as an illustration:

```
public void setCreditCardTypes() {
  ArrayList ccTypes = new ArrayList(5);
  ccTypes.add(
        new OptionLabelValue(messages.getMessage("title.option.selectOne"),
                             messages.getMessage("option.unknown")))
```

```
                         );

        String i8nLabelValue = messages.getMessage("cc.option.visa");
        ccTypes.add(new OptionLabelValue(i8nLabelValue,i8nLabelValue));

        i8nLabelValue = messages.getMessage("cc.option.mc");
        ccTypes.add(new OptionLabelValue(i8nLabelValue,i8nLabelValue));

        i8nLabelValue = messages.getMessage("cc.option.amex");
        ccTypes.add(new OptionLabelValue(i8nLabelValue,i8nLabelValue));

        i8nLabelValue = messages.getMessage("cc.option.discover");
        ccTypes.add(new OptionLabelValue(i8nLabelValue,i8nLabelValue));

        servletContext.setAttribute(Constants.CCTYPES_ARRAY_KEY, ccTypes);
    } //end setCreditCardTypes
```

You will notice that the elements within the `ArrayList` are first placed into the `OptionLabelValue` class, and the credit card types are then placed in the `ServletContext`. Using the `OptionLabelValue` class to store the credit card information facilitates the use of the Struts custom tags in the JSP, as we will see later.

This completes the explanation of the `DatabaseServlet` class. The next item to cover in the example is the `struts-config.xml` file.

The struts-config.xml File

The `struts-config.xml` file is used to configure Struts. You register **form-beans**, **global-forwards**, **action-mappings**, and **actions** in this file. For the example application it resides in the `ch21/WEB-INF` directory.

The <form-beans> Element

In Struts, form beans represent HTML input data that is collected from a JSP; the Struts controller Servlet populates a bean with the values from the form before sending the request on to our business logic classes.

The `<form-beans>` tag is used to register all of your application's form-bean mappings; in the example application, we have the following form beans registered in `struts-config.xml`:

```
<form-beans>
  <form-bean name="registrationForm"
             type="com.wrox.pjsp2.struts.registration.RegistrationForm"/>
  <form-bean name="logonForm"
             type="com.wrox.pjsp2.struts.logon.LogonForm"/>
  <form-bean name="checkoutForm"
             type="com.wrox.pjsp2.struts.shopping.CheckoutForm"/>
  <form-bean name="orderForm"
             type="com.wrox.pjsp2.struts.order.OrderForm"/>
</form-beans>
```

In this application, the `registrationForm` holds input values from `registration.jsp`, the `logonForm` is from the `logon.jsp` page, the `checkoutForm` is from the `checkout.jsp` page, and the `orderForm` is from `order.jsp`. In each `<form-bean>` element, the `name` attribute is the name of the form bean in its associated scope, while the `type` attribute specifies the Java package qualified class of the form bean. For example, for the `logonForm` the bean class is `LogonForm`, contained in the `com.wrox.pjsp2.struts.logon` package.

The <action-mappings> and <action> Elements

Once we have registered our form beans, we then register the application's actions using the <action-mappings> element. An action is defined by a URI path, and must specify the name of the Action class that will process the user request. An action is also optionally assigned a form bean, with the name attribute.

The example application defines the following actions and illustrates the use of the previously defined form beans:

```
<action-mappings>

  <!-- Edit user registration -->
  <action path="/editRegistration"
          type="com.wrox.pjsp2.struts.registration.EditRegistrationAction"
          name="registrationForm"
          scope="request"
          validate="false">
    <forward name="success" path="/registration.jsp"/>
  </action>

  <!-- Save user registration -->
  <action path="/saveRegistration"
          type="com.wrox.pjsp2.struts.registration.SaveRegistrationAction"
          name="registrationForm"
          scope="request"
          input="/registration.jsp">
  </action>

  <!-- Process a user logon -->
  <action path="/logon"
          type="com.wrox.pjsp2.struts.logon.LogonAction"
          name="logonForm"
          scope="request"
          input="/logon.jsp">
  </action>

  <!-- Process a user logoff -->
  <action path="/logoff"
          type="com.wrox.pjsp2.struts.logoff.LogoffAction">
    <forward name="success" path="/index.jsp"/>
  </action>

  <!-- Process showCategories request -->
  <action path="/showCategories"
          type="com.wrox.pjsp2.struts.shopping.ShowCategoriesAction">
    <forward name="success" path="/showcategories.jsp"/>
  </action>

  <!-- Process showCDs request -->
  <action path="/showCDs"
          type="com.wrox.pjsp2.struts.shopping.ShowCDsAction">
    <forward name="success" path="/showcds.jsp"/>
  </action>

  <!-- Process addToCart request -->
  <action path="/addToCart"
```

```
            type="com.wrox.pjsp2.struts.shopping.AddToCartAction">
        <forward name="success" path="/showcds.jsp"/>
    </action>

    <!-- Process checkout request -->
    <action path="/checkout"
            type="com.wrox.pjsp2.struts.shopping.CheckoutAction"
            name="checkoutForm"
            scope="request"
            validate="false">
        <forward name="success" path="/shoppingcart.jsp"/>
    </action>

    <!-- Process order request -->
    <action path="/order"
            type="com.wrox.pjsp2.struts.order.OrderAction"
            name="orderForm"
            scope="session"
            validate="false"
            input="/order.jsp">
        <forward name="success" path="/order.jsp"/>
        <forward name="thankyou" path="/thankyou.jsp"/>
    </action>

</action-mappings>
```

In our example, this says for a request path of /logon the associated Action class is LogonAction in the com.wrox.pjsp2.struts package. The associated form can be retrieved using the key name logonForm. The scope in which the form is located is the request scope. The input page from which the data is collected is the /logon.jsp.

The <action-mappings> tag also allows you to define local 'forward' targets, as illustrated for the /order URI. A <forward> element maps a logical name to an actual page to which control should be forwarded after the user request has been processed. For the /order action we define success as pointing to /order.jsp. As we shall see below, forwards can also be defined globally; the success forward defined here overrides the global definition.

The <global-forwards> Element

The last XML element that we are concerned with in the configuration file is the <global-forwards> element, defined in the example as follows:

```
<global-forwards>
    <forward name="logon"      path="/logon.jsp"/>
    <forward name="success"    path="/mainMenu.jsp"/>
    <forward name="emptycart"  path="/showcategories.jsp"/>
    <forward name="cancel"     path="/index.jsp"/>
</global-forwards>
```

The <global-forwards> tags specify application-wide forwards and are available to each Action defined in the configuration file. An individual Action can define its own local-scoped <forward> tags that can override the global settings, as we saw above.

The index.jsp Page

Now that we have covered the configuration file, we will proceed with the first page of the application, `index.jsp`, which is the default page for the ch21 web application. The first few lines in `index.jsp` establish that the page will use Java for its scripting language (nothing new) and set up the definitions of the Struts tab libraries:

```
<%@ page language="java" %>
<%@ taglib uri="/WEB-INF/struts-bean.tld" prefix="bean" %>
<%@ taglib uri="/WEB-INF/struts-html.tld" prefix="html" %>
<%@ taglib uri="/WEB-INF/struts-logic.tld" prefix="logic" %>
```

Within Struts, a JSP generally just contains a mixture of HTML and JSP custom tags. The first custom tag is `<html:html locale="true">`, which sets a locale based on the user's request headers within the request, and generates an HTML tag of the form `<html lang="en">`:

```
<html:html locale="true">
<head>
```

The next tag uses the `<bean:message>` tag to display an internationalized message in the HTML page:

```
<title><bean:message key="index.title"/></title>
```

This generates an HTML `<title>` tag based on the default locale. To do this it retrieves the message from the default locale properties file, called `ApplicationResources.properties`. The result is that the title displayed comes from the value of the `index.title` entry within `ApplicationResources.properties`:

```
index.title=CDs Galore, Inc.
```

The HTML produced is then:

```
<title>CDs Galore, Inc.</title>
```

The next tag is again from the `struts-html` tag library:

```
<html:base/>
```

This establishes a base reference in the HTML page, rendering the following HTML:

```
<base href="http://localhost:8080/wrox-struts/index.jsp">
```

The output of this will depend on the web configuration, but does not change in the source JSP – the dynamic generation automatically inserts the proper values when the tag is expanded. The next few entries within the JSP are HTML and JSP tags:

```
</head>
<body bgcolor="white">
<%@ include file="header.html" %>
```

The JSP include directive includes a static HTML version of the page header. The next series of tags uses the struts-logic library's <logic:notPresent> tag:

```
<logic:notPresent name="org.apache.struts.action.MESSAGE"
                  scope="application">
  <font color="red">
    ERROR:  Application resources not loaded -- check servlet container
    logs for error messages.
  </font>
</logic:notPresent>
```

This checks in the application scope for the <org.apache.struts.action.MESSAGE> tag. This is the name of the key that holds the application resources object in the application scope, and is present if the ActionServlet loaded the application resources for this locale. If not, the application was not configured properly and an error message will be displayed to the user.

The rest of the tags in index.jsp are listed below:

```
<bean:message key="index.heading"/>
<ul>
  <li>
    <html:link page="/editRegistration.do?action=Create">
      <bean:message key="index.registration"/>
    </html:link>
  </li>
  <li>
    <html:link page="/logon.jsp">
      <bean:message key="index.logon"/>
    </html:link>
  </li>
</ul>
</body>
</html:html>
```

The first tag outputs an internationalized message with the value associated with the key index.heading. The next tag is for the html library's link tag, which will encode the URL provided with an href that corresponds to the ActionMapping called editRegistration, which will allow a new user to be established with the application. (The action editRegistration is used for both editing a user's settings and for creating a user's settings.) If the user selects this link, they will be asked to enter registration data and a logon will be performed for them. The generated HTML is as follows:

```
<li><a href="http://localhost:8080/wrox-
struts/editRegistration.do;jsessionid=5003A4D4E081E030104000F1A3549324?action=Crea
te">New User Registration for the CDs Galore Web Store</a></li>
<li><a href="http://localhost:8080/wrox-
struts/logon.jsp;jsessionid=5003A4D4E081E030104000F1A3549324">Log on to the CDs
Galore Web Store</a></li>
</ul>
</body>
</html>
```

;jsessionid=<value> allows the session to be established without cookies being set on the client browser. The second link is for logon.jsp, which is used if the user already knows their username and password. The output of index.jsp is shown in the following screenshot:

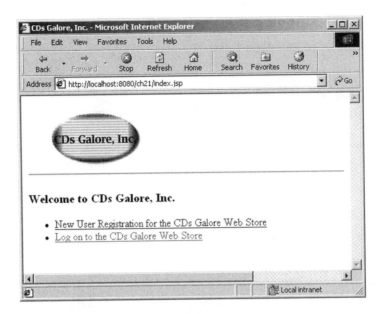

Example Application Components

The remainder of the example application is broken up into package components under `com.wrox.pjsp2.struts`, as shown in the component diagram below:

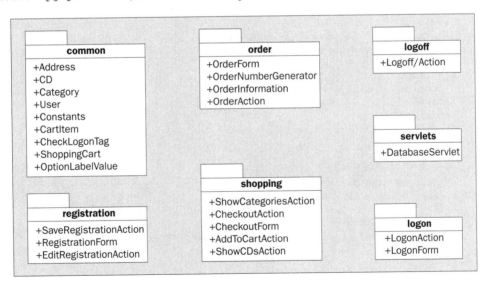

We will discuss the `logon`, `registration`, and `shopping` packages. The other packages are straightforward and are left to the reader to understand by looking at the source code.

Logon Package Components

The components of the `logon` are shown below:

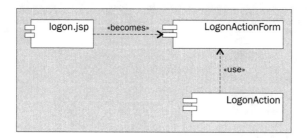

The logon.jsp Page

We will look at the `logon.jsp` component first:

```
<%@ page language="java" %>
<%@ taglib uri="/WEB-INF/struts-bean.tld" prefix="bean" %>
<%@ taglib uri="/WEB-INF/struts-html.tld" prefix="html" %>
<html:html locale="true">
<head>
<title><bean:message key="logon.title"/></title>
<html:base/>
</head>
<body bgcolor="white">
<%@ include file="header.html" %>
<html:errors/>
<html:form action="/logon.do" focus="userName">
<table border="0" width="100%">
  <tr>
    <th align="right">
      <bean:message key="prompt.userName"/>
    </th>
    <td align="left">
      <html:text property="userName" size="16" maxlength="16"/>
    </td>
  </tr>
  <tr>
    <th align="right">
      <bean:message key="prompt.password"/>
    </th>
    <td align="left">
      <html:password property="password" size="16" maxlength="16"/>
    </td>
  </tr>
  <tr>
    <td align="right">
      <html:submit>
        <bean:message key="button.submit"/>
      </html:submit>
    </td>
    <td align="left">
      <html:reset>
        <bean:message key="button.reset"/>
```

```
        </html:reset>
        <html:cancel>
          <bean:message key="button.cancel"/>
        </html:cancel>
      </td>
    </tr>
  </table>
  </html:form>
  </body>
  </html:html>
```

This page utilizes the `<html:form>` tag to generate the correct HTML code to reference our Action class. The `action` attribute generates the following HTML:

```
<form name="logonForm" method="POST"
 action="/wrox-struts/logon.do;jsessionid=A2105639D48039B0F8F6A1B170039450">
```

The `name` attribute in the HTML `<form>` tag is the key to use when retrieving the `LogonActionForm` from the specified scope when processing the request. This is defined in the `action` tag for the URI `/logon.do`. The action is automatically URL encoded to provide session access without the need to have cookies turned on in the browser. When you use the `<html:form>` tag you must be consistent and use it in the whole application to ensure access to the session.

The `focus` attribute of the `<html:form>` tag generates a JavaScript function in the HTML page that sets the focus of the browser on the username input field when the page is displayed. You can see this at the bottom of the generated HTML for the logon page:

```
<script language="JavaScript" type="text/javascript">
  <!--
    document.logonForm.userName.focus()
  // -->
</script>
```

There are other JavaScript capabilities within the `struts-html` tag library, but as yet Struts has no client-side validation facility. This is because Struts can be used to generate different types of content (XML, WML, etc.) and server-side validation is best when it comes to supporting multiple interfaces to the server-side Java. However, for those interested in client-side validation this is on the TODO list for release 1.1. Therefore, for now you will have to code around this by adding the JavaScript directly into your JSPs, but when client-side validation support becomes available within Struts you can pull your own code and use the custom tags that will produce the JavaScript.

The login page uses the `<html:text>` input field to generate HTML input fields:

```
        <html:text property="userName" size="16" maxlength="16"/>
```

The property, `userName`, is an attribute of the `LogonActionForm` class, which therefore must provide `getUserName()` and `setUserName()` methods. The generated HTML for this input field is:

```
<input type="text" name="userName" maxlength="16" size="16" value="">
```

When the `logon.jsp` page is displayed the `<input>` tag's `value` attribute is set to the value of the corresponding `LogonActionForm` attribute; since the `userName` attribute is `null`, the `value` attribute in this case is empty.

The last part of the `logon.jsp` page defines buttons using the `struts-html` tag library:

```
<td align="right">
  <html:submit>
    <bean:message key="button.submit"/>
  </html:submit>
</td>
<td align="left">
  <html:reset>
    <bean:message key="button.reset"/>
  </html:reset>
  <html:cancel>
    <bean:message key="button.cancel"/>
  </html:cancel>
</td>
```

There are tags for submit, reset, and cancel buttons. The generated HTML is as follows:

```
<td align="right">
  <input type="submit" name="submit" value="Submit">
</td>
<td align="left">
  <input type="reset" name="reset" value="Reset">
  <input type="submit" name="org.apache.struts.taglib.html.CANCEL"
   value="Cancel">
</td>
```

The button values are retrieved from the `ApplicationResources` file, and the tag library determines the `<input>` tag's name attribute. The three buttons act as follows:

❏   The Reset button calls the reset within the browser.

❏   The Cancel button uses a name value from the tag library, permitting the `ActionServlet` to check for this parameter in the request. When this parameter exists, the `ActionServlet` does not call the `validate()` method on the `LogonActionForm` class but instead calls the `LogonAction`'s `isCancelled()` method to detect the cancel and return the appropriate `ActionMapping` to the `ActionServlet`.

❏   The Submit button submits the form to the designated target. The request is sent to the `ActionServlet`, and the `LogonActionForm` is populated with the input values from the `logon.jsp` page. The `ActionServlet` then calls the `validate()` method on the newly populated `LogonActionForm` and if the return value is `true`, the `ActionServlet` calls the `perform()` method on the `LogonAction`.

The LogonAction Class

The `LogonAction` class contains the `perform()` method that is called to process the client request:

```
// Import statements...

public class LogonAction extends Action {
  public ActionForward perform(ActionMapping mapping,
```

```
                              ActionForm form,
                              HttpServletRequest request,
                              HttpServletResponse response)
              throws IOException, ServletException {
```

The `ActionServlet` sends an `ActionMapping` attribute to the `LogonAction`, for use in returning the appropriate `ActionForward` value. It also sends an `ActionForm`, in this case a `LogonActionForm`, and a reference to the request and response. The first thing the `LogonAction` does is set up its local variables:

```
    HttpSession session = request.getSession();
    ServletContext servletContext = servlet.getServletContext();
    int debugLevel = servlet.getDebug();
    User user = null;
    ActionErrors errors = new ActionErrors();
```

The `ActionServlet` is a protected attribute stored in the `Action` base class and accessed by the variable `servlet`. The debug level is set for the `ActionServlet` on startup by a parameter in the `web.xml` file. The `ActionErrors` instance is created for reporting errors to the user.

Next, the `LogonAction` retrieves the input values from the `LogonForm`:

```
    String userName = ((LogonForm)form).getUserName();
    String password = ((LogonForm)form).getPassword();
```

Since the `LogonForm` is passed as an `ActionForm`, a class cast is required to retrieve the input values. Next the `LogonAction` obtains a list of known users to the application:

```
    HashMap userTable =
            (HashMap)servletContext.getAttribute(Constants.USER_TABLE_KEY);
```

Since our example uses a `DatabaseServlet` rather than a real database, we obtain the list from the `ServletContext`. If you have a database you would obtain the data source from the `ActionServlet` and make a call to the database to obtain a list of users known to the application. This is beyond the scope of this chapter. However, you should watch the Struts source code for a Struts database example and the New Particles web site for one from the author.

The following code listing illustrates accessing the list of users from the `ServletContext`:

```
    if(userTable == null) {
      errors.add(ActionErrors.GLOBAL_ERROR,
                  new ActionError("error.userTable.missing"));
    } else {
      user = (User)userTable.get(userName);
      if((user != null) && !user.getPassword().equals(password)) {
        user = null;
      }
      if(user == null) {
        errors.add(ActionErrors.GLOBAL_ERROR,
                    new ActionError("error.password.mismatch"));
      }
    }
```

If the userName was not in the userTable or if the password did not match the User object's password attribute, then a generic message is added to the ActionErrors collection. The next section of code will return an ActionForward to the logon.jsp:

```
if(!errors.empty()) {
   saveErrors(request, errors);
   return (new ActionForward(mapping.getInput()));
}
```

As you will recall, the input was an attribute for the logon action in the struts-config.xml. The action definition for the logon request is as follows:

```
<action path="/logon"
        type="com.wrox.pjsp2.struts.logon.LogonAction"
        name="logonForm"
        scope="request"
        input="/logon.jsp">
</action>
```

Thus the call to mapping.getInput() returns "/logon.jsp" and this is set into an ActionForward and returned to the ActionServlet so that the user will be presented the logon.jsp page with a list of the errors. The display of an error in the logon.jsp page is shown below:

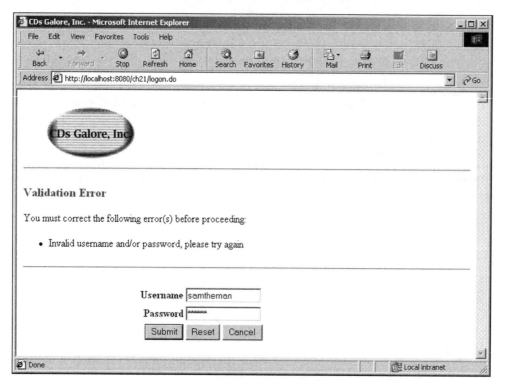

The last section of code within the LogonAction class is as follows:

```
      // Save our logged-in user in the session
      session.setAttribute(Constants.USER_KEY, user);
      if(debugLevel >= 1) {
        servlet.log("LogonAction: User '" + user.getUserName() +
                    "' logged on in session " + session.getId());
      }
      // Remove the obsolete form bean
      if(mapping.getAttribute() != null) {
        if("request".equals(mapping.getScope())) {
          request.removeAttribute(mapping.getAttribute());
        } else {
          session.removeAttribute(mapping.getAttribute());
        }
      }
      // Forward control to the specified success URI
      return mapping.findForward("success");
    }
}
```

The `LogonAction` places the user in the session, because at this point we have a valid user, then removes the object that represents the `LogonForm` from the scope in which it was stored. It returns the `ActionForward` mapping for success. Since we did not have a `success` mapping for the `/logon` action, this is the `ActionForward` that was defined in the `<global-forwards>` tag in our `struts-config.xml` file:

```
<global-forwards>
   <forward name="logon"       path="/logon.jsp"/>
   <forward name="success"     path="/mainMenu.jsp"/>
   <forward name="emptycart"   path="/showcategories.jsp"/>
   <forward name="cancel"      path="/index.jsp"/>
</global-forwards>
```

This displays the `mainMenu.jsp` page to the user and completes the `/logon` request.

The mainMenu.jsp Page

The `mainMenu.jsp` is the last page to discuss in the logon process. The first thing the page does after making the Struts tags available, is make a call to the custom tag `<app:checkLogon/>`:

```
<%@ page language="java" %>
<%@ taglib uri="/WEB-INF/app.tld" prefix="app" %>
<%@ taglib uri="/WEB-INF/struts-bean.tld" prefix="bean" %>
<%@ taglib uri="/WEB-INF/struts-html.tld" prefix="html" %>
<app:checkLogon/>
```

This makes a call to the `com.wrox.pjsp2.struts.common.CheckLogonTag` class. This is borrowed from the `struts-example` application, and simply checks for a `User` object in the session. If it's not present it will forward to the `logon.jsp` page.

The rest of the `mainMenu.jsp` page is in the following code listing:

```
<jsp:useBean id="user" scope="session"
             type="com.wrox.pjsp2.struts.common.User"/>
```

```
<html:html locale="true">
<head>
<title><bean:message key="mainMenu.title"/></title>
<html:base/>
</head>
<body bgcolor="white">
<%@ include file="header.html" %>
<h3>
  <bean:message key="mainMenu.heading"/>
  <jsp:getProperty name="user" property="userName"/>
</h3>
<ul>
  <li>
    <html:link page="/editRegistration.do?action=Edit">
      <bean:message key="mainMenu.registration"/>
    </html:link>
  </li>
  <li>
    <html:link page="/showCategories.do">
      <bean:message key="mainMenu.showcategories"/>
    </html:link>
  </li>
  <li>
    <html:link page="/logoff.do">
      <bean:message key="mainMenu.logoff"/>
    </html:link>
  </li>
</ul>
</body>
</html:html>
```

This page uses some standard JSP directives like `<jsp:useBean>` and `<jsp:getProperty>`, and also the `<html:link>` tag which is used to encode the URLs for all of the links so the session can be accessed without cookies. From the main menu we click on the **Edit your user registration profile** link, which displays the `editRegistration.jsp` page, and leads us into a discussion of the registration components.

Registration Package Components

The components of the registration package are shown in the following diagram:

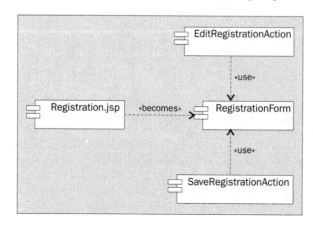

The Registration components all use the same input page, registration.jsp, and the EditRegistrationAction class is used for both creating and editing a user's registration information.

EditRegistrationAction

There are two paths to get to the EditRegistrationAction:

- ❑ From index.jsp, using the **New User Registration** link
- ❑ From mainMenu.jsp, using the **Edit your registration** link.

We will review the **Edit your registration** link, which uses the /editRegistration URI to call the perform() method on the EditRegistrationAction class. The first thing the doPerform() method does is set the method variables:

```
public ActionForward perform(ActionMapping mapping,
                             ActionForm form,
                             HttpServletRequest request,
                             HttpServletResponse response)
        throws IOException, ServletException {

// setup method variables
HttpSession session = request.getSession();
String action = request.getParameter("action");
int debugLevel = servlet.getDebug();

if(action == null) {
  action = "Create";
}
if(debugLevel >= 1) {
  servlet.log("EditRegistrationAction:  Processing " + action +
              " action");
}
```

The session is used to store the modified user registration information, and the String action determines if this is a 'Create' or an 'Edit' action. The 'Create' action would be called from the **New User Registration** link on index.jsp, but since we have called this action from mainMenu.jsp the action is 'Edit'. This was established as a query parameter on the link in mainMenu.jsp. The next section of code checks to make sure we have an established User object in the session:

```
// Is there a currently logged on user?
User user = null;
if(!"Create".equals(action)) {
  user = (User) session.getAttribute(Constants.USER_KEY);
  if(user == null) {
    if(debugLevel >= 1) {
      servlet.log(" User is not logged on in session " + session.getId());
    }
    return servlet.findForward("logon");
  }
}
```

This ensures that the user of the web application has not book marked the page. After the user is retrieved from the session, we cast the ActionForm to the RegistrationForm:

```
        RegistrationForm regform = (RegistrationForm)form;
```

The `form` attributes are set to their initialized state, because we reached this `Action` class from a link and not from an input JSP.

The next section of code will populate the `RegistrationForm` if the `User` object is not `null`. Since we are looking at the editing of a user's registration, the following code is relevant to our discussion:

```
    // Populate the user if one exists
    if(user != null) {
      if(debugLevel >= 1) {
        servlet.log(" Populating form from " + user);
      }
      regform.setAction(action);
      regform.setUser(user);
      if("request".equals(mapping.getScope())) {
        request.setAttribute(mapping.getAttribute(), regform);
        // Tell the receiving page which option is to be selected
        String title = user.getTitle();
        request.setAttribute(Constants.SELECTED_OPTION_KEY, title);
      }
    } //end if(user != null)
```

The `RegistrationForm` contains only two attributes:

```
    private String action = "Create";
    private User user = null;
```

However, before the `RegistrationForm` is passed to the `EditRegistrationAction` the `reset()` method is called and an empty `User` object is created. Note though that this is not the `User` that we will use.

We will obtain the `User` object we want to use from the session, and set this on the `RegistrationForm`. This `User` object represents the user that is currently logged. Populating this `User` object in the `RegistrationForm` will allow the target `registration.jsp` to populate its input fields with the values contained in the `User` object. Lastly, the `EditRegistrationAction` informs the `ActionServlet` to display the target JSP that was defined in the `struts-config.xml` file:

```
    // Forward control to the edit user registration page
    if(debugLevel >= 1) {
      servlet.log(" Forwarding to 'success' page");
    }
    return (mapping.findForward("success"));

  }
```

As you will recall from the `struts-config.xml` file the `"success"` mapping points to the `registration.jsp` page:

```
  <action path="/editRegistration"
          type="com.wrox.pjsp2.struts.registration.EditRegistrationAction"
          name="registrationForm"
          scope="request"
```

```
              validate="false">
        <forward name="success" path="/registration.jsp"/>
     </action>
```

The registration.jsp Page

The `registration.jsp` page is used both for new user creation and editing of a logged in user's registration information. It accomplishes this by conditionally displaying information, based on the `action` variable within the `RegistrationForm`.

The `registration.jsp` page is one of the more important demonstrations of the power of using the Struts framework. This discussion will be lengthy, so we will discuss it in sections with small listings of code. The first portion of `registration.jsp` uses the Struts `logic` tag library to decide if this is an edit or a create action:

```
<%@ page language="java" import="com.wrox.pjsp2.struts.common.Constants" %>
<%@ taglib uri="/WEB-INF/app.tld" prefix="app" %>
<%@ taglib uri="/WEB-INF/struts-bean.tld" prefix="bean" %>
<%@ taglib uri="/WEB-INF/struts-html.tld" prefix="html" %>
<%@ taglib uri="/WEB-INF/struts-logic.tld" prefix="logic" %>
<logic:equal name="registrationForm" property="action"
             scope="request" value="Edit">
  <app:checkLogon/>
</logic:equal>
```

The `<logic:equal>` tag takes `name`, `property`, `scope`, and `value` attributes:

❑ The `name` is a `String` key under which the object is stored in the specified `scope`

❑ The `property` is an attribute within the retrieved object

❑ The `value` is the constant value that the `property` is compared against

The nested body content of the tag is evaluated if the value of the `property` equals the constant `value`. Here we're using this conditional logic tag to perform a logic check if we're going to be editing an existing registration, but not if we're registering a new user.

The next section of code selects a title within the `<head>` portion of the generated HTML page:

```
<%@ include file="header.html" %>
<html:html locale="true">
<head>
<logic:equal name="registrationForm" property="action"
             scope="request" value="Create">
  <title><bean:message key="registration.title.create"/></title>
</logic:equal>
<logic:equal name="registrationForm" property="action"
             scope="request" value="Edit">
  <title><bean:message key="registration.title.edit"/></title>
</logic:equal>
</head>
```

This is a typical use of the `<logic:equal>` tag within this page, using the tag to help eliminate scriptlet coding within the JSP. This conditional behavior allows the same JSP to be used both for creating a new user registration and for editing an existing user registration. The `action` property is available for use within other Struts tags, as illustrated in the next section of the listing:

```
<html:base/>
<body>
<html:errors/>
<!-- save is needed for both Create and Edit -->
<html:form action="/saveRegistration.do">
  <table align="center" cellspacing="0" cellpadding="0" border="0"
    width="480">
  <html:hidden property="action"/>
```

This sets a hidden property called `"action"` that has the value that was in the `registrationForm` page. Access to this variable is by name, since it was exposed within the logic tag. There are other conditional logic tags within the `registration.jsp` page to control the display based on the value of the action attribute. We will investigate only the tags that have not been covered so far, rather than discussing the whole document. The next new tag is the `<html:select>` tag in the following listing:

```
<html:select property="user.title" size="1">
  <html:options collection="<%= Constants.TITLE_ARRAY_KEY %>"
                property="value"
                labelProperty="label"/>
</html:select>
```

The `property` attribute of this tag specifies the name of the selected attribute when the form is posted. The `<html:options>` tag is used as a nested tag within the `select` tag. This particular version of the `options` tag takes a collection of objects, which we pre-loaded in `DatabaseServlet`. The `property` and `labelProperty` correspond to the label and value in the HTML `option` tag, and the collection is an array of `OptionLabelValue` objects.

Each HTML `option` tag is generated using the value and label, as you would in standard HTML, and the number of tags generated depends on the length of the array. The next interesting use of the Struts tag libraries is shown in the following code:

```
<tr>
  <td width="120"><bean:message key="prompt.address"/></td>
  <td colspan="2">
  <html:text property="user.userAddress.address1" size="34" maxlength="50"/>
  </td>
</tr>
```

The `<html:text>` tags can traverse nested attributes within a `Form` class; in this code listing the nested `address1` attribute of the `Address` class will be the `property` for the input tag. Thus when a user types the value into the form field the nested attribute is set, and when using this tag for display the nested attributes are displayed. To further illustrate this we'll look at the nested classes.

The Nested Classes

The first nested class is the `User` class, used within the `RegistrationForm` class:

```
public final class RegistrationForm extends ActionForm {

  private String action = "Create";
  private User user = null;

  // setters/getters omitted
  // ...
}
```

The `User` class also contains two different nested `Address` classes:

```
public final class User implements Serializable {
    private String firstName = null;
    private String lastName = null;
    private String title = null;
    private String userName = null;
    private String password = null;
    private String confirmPassword = null;
    private String passwordHint = null;
    private Address userAddress = new Address();
    private Address billingAddress = new Address();
    private String e-mail = null;

    // setters/getters omitted
}
```

The `Address` class is the last nested class used within the `RegistrationForm`:

```
public class Address implements Serializable {
    private String address1 = null;
    private String address2 = null;
    private String city = null;
    private String state = null;
    private String zip = null;

    // setters/getters omitted
}
```

When the `ActionServlet` receives the request from the JSP, it calls a series of utilities to traverse nested classes and sets the `address1` attribute; the utilities know to traverse the classes because of the dot operator '.' within the `property` value. This is a very powerful attribute of the Struts framework, which eliminates the need for duplicate setter and getter of the `address1` field within the `RegistrationForm` page and the `Address` class.

The utilities that perform this nested feature are contained within the `BeanUtils` and the `PropertyUtils` classes in the `org.apache.struts.util` package. The framework also supports the concept of index properties. This feature is not used in the chapter example, but with a form attribute holding an array of objects, like this:

```
private String address[] = new String[2];
```

an indexed property could be used like this within the JSP:

```
<html:text property="city[0]"/>
<html:text property="city[1]"/>
```

This completes the discussion of the registration package; the last package we will discuss is the shopping package.

Shopping Package Components

The shopping package components are responsible for displaying the categories of music that the web store has to offer, the individual CDs within a particular category, maintenance of the shopping cart, and processing of a checkout request. The components in this package are shown in the diagram below:

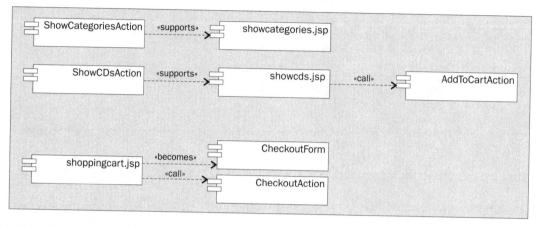

The ShowCategoriesAction Class

ShowCategoriesAction's perform() method builds an array of Category objects that represent the musical categories within the web store:

```
HashMap categoryTable = (HashMap)
  servletContext.getAttribute(Constants.CATEGORY_TABLE_KEY);

if(categoryTable == null) {
  errors.add(ActionErrors.GLOBAL_ERROR,
           new ActionError("error.categoryTable.missing"));
} else {
  int size = categoryTable.size();
  if(size > 0) {
    Iterator iterator = categoryTable.values().iterator();
    Category[] categoryArray = new Category[size];
    Category aCategory = null;
    Object aObject = null;
    int position = 0;
    while(iterator.hasNext()) {
      aCategory = (Category)iterator.next();
      // Set the mapping for the html:link tag
      aCategory.setMapping();
      position = aCategory.getCategoryId() - 1;
      categoryArray[position] = aCategory;
    }
    servlet.log("setting categoryArray in the application scope.");
    servlet.log("number of categories = " + size);
    servletContext.setAttribute(Constants.CATEGORIES_ARRAY_KEY,
                          categoryArray);

  } //end if(size > 0)
}
```

You may recall that the musical categories are in a `HashMap` in the `ServletContext`, where they were stored by the `DatabaseServlet` on startup of the web application. The job of the `ShowCategoriesAction` is to package the categories into an array of `Category` objects and set up a mapping for the Struts `<html:link>` tag. Once constructed the `Category` array is stored in the `ServletContext`, and is ready to be used by `showcategories.jsp`.

The showcategories.jsp Page

`showcategories.jsp` uses the `<logic:iterate>` tag to display all the categories on the left of the screen for navigation of the musical categories.

```
<logic:iterate id="category" type="com.wrox.pjsp2.struts.common.Category"
                name="<%= Constants.CATEGORIES_ARRAY_KEY %>">
  <tr>
    <td>
      <html:link page="/showCDs.do" name="category" property="mapping">
        <bean:write name="category" property="categoryName" filter="true"/>
      </html:link>
    </td>
  </tr>
</logic:iterate>
```

In the body of the `<logic:iterate>` tag, links are constructed for each of the musical categories. The `<html:link>` tag has a special capability to generate a query string in the link from a `java.util.Map` object; the `Category` object's mapping attribute is constructed in the `ShowCategoriesAction` class. The link will inform the next `Action` class of the selected musical category and its corresponding `categoryId`. These values are used to construct the next page, `showcds.jsp`. The HTML anchor tags generated are of the following form:

```
<a href="http://localhost:8080/ch21/showCDs.do?categoryName=Rock&amp;categor
yId=3">Rock</a>
```

The `showcategories.jsp` page also performs two includes. The first is of `headerWithCart.jsp`, which displays the number of items in the shopping cart and the total price of all the items in the shopping cart; the second is for the bottom navigation menu and is contained in the `footer.jsp` page.

When the user clicks on the **Rock** link, the `ShowCDsAction` is called.

The ShowCDsAction Class

This action generates an array of CD objects, based on the selected `categoryId` within the query string:

```
// Probably should handle the case if it's not present.
int requestedCategoryId =
        Integer.parseInt(request.getParameter("categoryId"));

HashMap cdTable = (HashMap)
        servlet.getServletContext().getAttribute(Constants.CD_TABLE_KEY);

if(cdTable == null) {
  errors.add(ActionErrors.GLOBAL_ERROR,
             new ActionError("error.cdTable.missing"));
} else {
  int size = cdTable.size();
```

```
    if(size > 0) {
      // Generate list of cds based on request parameters
      Iterator iterator = cdTable.values().iterator();
      ArrayList cdArrayList = new ArrayList();

      CD aCD = null;
      Object aObject = null;
      int categoryId = 0;
      while(iterator.hasNext()) {
        aObject = iterator.next();
        aCD = (CD)aObject;
        categoryId = aCD.getCategoryId();
        if(requestedCategoryId == categoryId) {
          cdArrayList.add(aCD);
        }
        // Set the mapping for the form:link tag
        aCD.setMapping();
      }
      CD[] cdArray = new CD[0];
      cdArray = (CD[])cdArrayList.toArray(cdArray);
      session.setAttribute(Constants.CD_ARRAY_KEY, cdArray);
    }
  }
  // ...
```

The CD Array contains only the CDs that have the same `categoryId` as the selected musical category. Once constructed the array is placed in the session, and sent to `showcds.jsp` for display. The CD object also contains a `mapping` attribute, which is to generate the Add link in the page.

The showcds.jsp Page

The `showcds.jsp` page generates the CDs with their links using the `iterate` tag:

```
<%
  int num = 0;
  String SLATE = "#C0C0C0";
  String WHITE = "#FFFFFF";
  String bgColor = null;
%>
<logic:iterate id="cd" type="com.wrox.pjsp2.struts.common.CD"
                name="<%= Constants.CD_ARRAY_KEY %>">
<%
  num++;
  if((num % 2) == 0) {
    bgColor = SLATE;
  } else {
    bgColor = WHITE;
  }
%>
  <tr bgcolor="<%= bgColor %>">
    <td><bean:write name="cd" property="artist" filter="true"/></td>
    <td><bean:write name="cd" property="titleName" filter="true"/></td>
    <td><bean:write name="cd" property="price" filter="true"/></td>
    <td>
      <html:link page="/addToCart.do" name="cd" property="mapping">
```

```
        <bean:message key="cds.add"/>
      </html:link>
    </td>
  </tr>
</logic:iterate>
```

The loop scriptlet is used to change the color for each row of the table, as we saw in the walkthrough of the application. The `<logic:iterate>` tag exposes each CD object in turn as a bean, and within the loop the `<bean:write>` tag is used to display its `artist`, `titleName`, and `price` attributes. This code sample illustrates a very important feature of some of the Struts tags: the 'filter' attribute, which causes the data to be filtered before sending it to the browser. We will digress briefly and take a quick look at what this is.

Filtering Data

When the `filter` attribute of the `<bean:write>` tag is set to `true`, bean property values will be filtered for characters that are 'sensitive' in HTML, which are replaced with their associated character entity reference to permit the characters to be displayed appropriately in the browser. These sensitive characters are listed in the table below:

Appearance	Name	Entity Reference	Description
<	lt	&lt;	Less than sign
>	gt	&gt;	Greater than sign
&	amp	&amp;	Ampersand
"	quote	&quote;	Double quote sign

This filtering is disabled by default for the `<bean:write>` tag, but is set to `"true"` in this example because the attributes of a CD could contain HTML sensitive characters. Now let's return to the examination of the `showcds.jsp` page.

The showcds.jsp Page (continued)

The JSP also presents a link within the HTML table row that the user can click on to add the CD to the shopping cart. The `mapping` attribute is used to provide the `AddToCartAction` class with the ability to add the appropriate CD into the shopping cart. The link for the first CD in the table has this HTML:

```
<a href="http://localhost:8080/ch21/addToCart.do?titleId=6">Add</a>
```

When the user selects one of the **Add** links, the item is added to the shopping cart. The `ShoppingCart` maintains a `HashMap` containing `CartItem` objects representing the items that have been added to the users's cart. Each `CartItem` stores the number of that item contained in the cart, and the cart itself also maintains a count of the total number of unique items it contains.

The shopping cart is presented to the user in the included `headerWithCart.jsp`, which we turn to next.

The headerWithCart.jsp Page

The following listing shows how the cart is displayed:

```
<table width="700" border="0" cellspacing="2" cellpadding="2">
  <tr>
    <td width="470"><IMG src="images/cdsgalore.gif"></td>
```

```
<td width="120">
  <table cellspacing="2" cellpadding="2" border="0">
    <tr>
      <td><IMG src="images/cart.gif"></td>
    </tr>
    <tr>
<%
Locale locale = (Locale) session.getAttribute(Action.LOCALE_KEY);
if (locale == null) {
  locale = java.util.Locale.getDefault();
}

ShoppingCart cart = (ShoppingCart)
        session.getAttribute(Constants.SHOPPING_CART_KEY);
if(cart == null) {
  log("cart was null.");
  cart = new ShoppingCart();
}
cart.setLocale(locale);
%>
      <td>Items: <%= cart.getItemCount() %></td>
    </tr>
    <tr>
      <td>Total: <%= cart.getTotal() %></td>
    </tr>
  </table>
</td>
</tr>
</table>
<hr>
```

The `ShoppingCart` class also provides a `getTotalPrice()` method which will yield the cost of the items in the shopping cart, and maintains a `Locale` attribute to be able to display the currency according to the particular locale required. The scriptlet code sets the locale for the `ShoppingCart` based on the `Locale` that was set in the session when the user entered the application, which was done for us free of charge by the `ActionServlet`, by examining the HTML headers.

If the user clicks the **Add** link for first CD twice and the second CD once, it will render a unique item count of two and a total price of $45.97 as illustrated in the following screenshot:

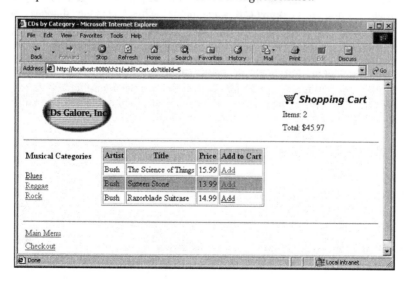

The item count represents unique items within the shopping cart. An individual item may have a quantity greater than one, but will still count only once in the shopping cart item count.

Once the user has selected all the CDs he wants to buy, he will click the **Checkout** link in the footer portion of the page:

```
<a href="http://localhost:8080/ch21/checkout.do?action=displayCart">Checkout
</a>
```

The link passes an action tag with a value of `displayCart` to the `CheckoutAction` class. This action, when called from this link, simply ensures that there is a cart in the session and forwards to `shoppingcart.jsp`:

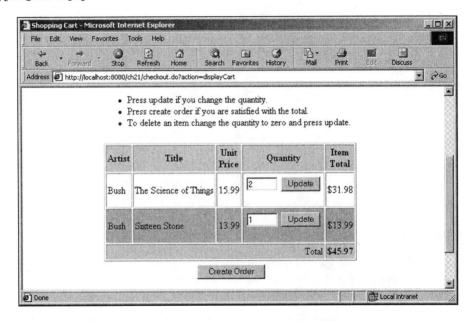

The shoppingcart.jsp Page

`shoppingcart.jsp` allows the user to modify the quantity of each item in the shopping cart, through an **Update** button on each item's line. The page uses the `<logic:iterate>` tag to display the HTML table of shopping cart items:

```
<logic:iterate id="cartItem"
               type="com.wrox.pjsp2.struts.common.CartItem"
               name="<%= Constants.SHOPPING_CART_KEY %>"
               property="cartItems">
<%
  num++;
  if((num % 2) == 0) {
    bgColor = SLATE;
  } else {
    bgColor = WHITE;
  }
%>
  <bean:define id="cd" name="cartItem" property="cd"
```

```
                  type="com.wrox.pjsp2.struts.common.CD"/>
    <tr bgcolor="<%= bgColor %>">
      <td><jsp:getProperty name="cd" property="artist"/></td>
      <td><jsp:getProperty name="cd" property="titleName"/></td>
      <td><jsp:getProperty name="cd" property="price"/></td>
      <td valign="middle">
        <html:form action="/checkout.do">
          <html:hidden property="action" value="update" />
          <bean:define id="titleId" name="cd" property="titleId"/>
          <html:hidden property="<%= Constants.TITLE_ID %>"
                       value="<%= String.valueOf(titleId) %>" />
          <table cellspacing="2" cellpadding="2" border="0">
            <tr>
              <td>
                <bean:define id="quantity" name="cartItem"
                             property="quantity"/>
                <html:text property="quantity"
                           value="<%= String.valueOf(quantity) %>"
                           size="5" maxlength="5"/>
              </td>
              <td>
                <html:submit>
                  <bean:message key="button.update"/>
                </html:submit>
              </td>
            </tr>
          </table>
        </html:form>
      </td>
      <td><jsp:getProperty name="cartItem" property="total"/></td>
    </tr>
</logic:iterate>
```

Each item is contained within its own HTML form; each form has a submit button to update the quantity of the line item, and a hidden set of parameters that represent the item (by the `titleId`) and the new quantity. The `CheckoutAction` form is passed a hidden action value of `update`, which changes the quantity of the `titleId` in the shopping cart and recalculates the total prices of the shopping cart, updates the shopping cart, and redisplays the shopping cart to the user.

The following screenshot shows the results of changing the quantity of the first CD from 2 to 1 and clicking its Update button:

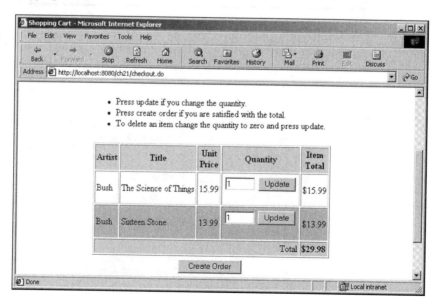

This demonstrates the multi-form aspect that is often employed in web store applications; Struts does not limit web applications to a single form per page.

The last form on the `shoppingcart.jsp` page creates an order from the shopping cart, and has a button labeled **Create Order**. The form calls the `com.wrox.pjsp2.struts.OrderAction` class.

The OrderAction Class

The `OrderAction` pre-populates the `OrderForm` object with the user's shipping and billing addresses:

```
servlet.log("create the order.");
User user = (User)session.getAttribute(Constants.USER_KEY);
if(user == null) {
  servlet.log("User was not logged on.");
  return mapping.findForward("logon");
}
ShoppingCart cart =
        (ShoppingCart)session.getAttribute(Constants.SHOPPING_CART_KEY);
if(cart == null || cart.getItemCount() < 1) {
  servlet.log("empty cart.");
  errors.add("empty cart", new ActionError("error.emptycart"));
  return mapping.findForward("emptycart");
}
// populate billing information from user
OrderInformation billing = new OrderInformation();
billing.setFirstName(user.getFirstName());
billing.setLastName(user.getLastName());
billing.setAddress(user.getUserAddress());

// populate shipping information from user
OrderInformation shipping = new OrderInformation();
shipping.setFirstName(user.getFirstName());
shipping.setLastName(user.getLastName());
shipping.setAddress(user.getBillingAddress());

// pre-populate the orderForm
orderForm.setBillingInformation(billing);
orderForm.setShippingInformation(shipping);
// add pre-populated orderForm to the request
servlet.log("setting form with key=" + mapping.getAttribute());
session.setAttribute(mapping.getAttribute(), orderForm);
```

The address information is obtained from the user's registration information and displayed to the user to allow updates for a different shipping address. The `order.jsp` page displays the information in a table, with its own action to process address updates.

The order.jsp Page

The `order.jsp` page also has another form that allows the user to enter credit card information and place the order:

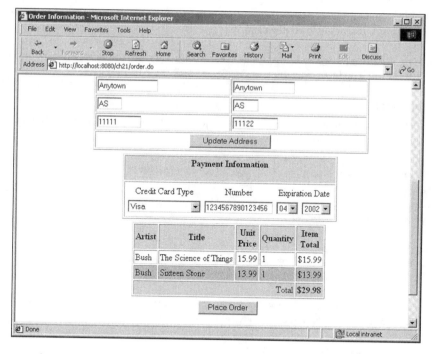

The user can update the address information if needed and place the order. When the user places the order an order number is generated for the user as a purchase reference number, and is shown in `thankyou.jsp`:

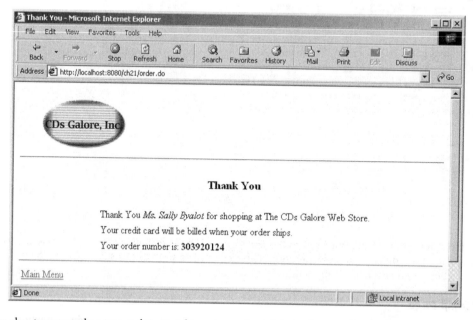

In our chapter example a true order record is not saved, and the order number is simply a random number that is generated for example purposes. In an actual online store, the order would be persisted for billing and inventory purposes.

Unfortunately, space does not permit the full listing of the application's code, so it's left to the reader to download the code from the aforementioned web sites to understand its details. Please watch the Struts site and the New Particles site for further examples using the Struts framework; the New Particles site will continue to adapt this example to enhance the web application and take advantage of new Struts capabilities.

Key Struts Components

Having seen our sample application in detail, we can now start reviewing the Struts components. In this section, we take a closer look at the following components of the Struts framework:

- ❏ ActionServlet
- ❏ ActionMapping
- ❏ ActionForm
- ❏ Action
- ❏ ActionForward

The following section attempts to describe how each component works. This is a very detailed discussion, looking at code and diagrams to explain the interaction and function of the components; it will be something that you will want to re-read after using the framework.

Class Diagrams

There are two things to note about the class diagrams we're going to look at in this chapter.

First, the following diagrams are not 'true' class diagrams, because they don't show the relationships between other classes in the system. However, they will be referred to as class diagrams for simplicity. A complete class diagram would not fit within a page of this book if all classes contained their attributes, operations, and interaction with one another. Given these issues, the following diagrams are for single classes.

Second, the modeling tool used to create the diagrams provides a shorthand notation for communicating properties that exhibit JavaBean qualities. The symbol is a box in the left corner of the box, which indicates that the diagram is using shorthand notation for attributes that have getters and setters according to the JavaBeans specification, as we shall see in a moment.

The Sample1 class below provides a range of methods and properties, for illustration:

```
public class Sample1 implements Serializable {

    private int state;
    protected String MY_STRING = "MY_STRING_CONSTANT";
    private String value;

    public String getValue(){
        return value;
    }

    public void setValue(String value){
        this.value = value;
```

```
    }

    public String toString() {
      StringBuffer tmp = new StringBuffer();
      tmp.append("value = " + value);
      return tmp.toString();
    }

    protected void updateState(int state) {
      this.state = state;
    }
  }
}
```

The diagram for this class is shown below:

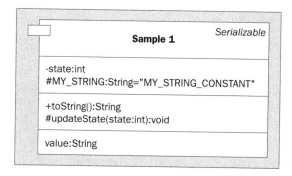

Notice also that the `value` attribute is in the lower portion of the diagram rather than the top portion of the diagram; this communicates that there are corresponding getters and setters for this attribute, but they are not listed in the operations section of the diagram. This shorthand notation is not standard UML, but a communication enhancement used by the modeling tool that saves space within the diagram.

The diagram uses a UML notation for attributes and operations. Attributes will have their name listed first, then their type; operations will list their name, parameters, and return type. As you can see, there are some symbols next to the attributes and methods in the previous diagram:

❑ The minus sign (–) beside an attribute or operation indicates that it is `private` as is the case with the `state` attribute in the previous diagram.

❑ The hash sign (#) beside an attribute or operation designates its exposure as `protected`, like the `updateState()` method and the `MY_STRING` constant.

❑ The plus symbol (+) indicates a `public` attribute or operation as illustrated by the `toString()` method.

Secondly let's look at an abstract class, `Sample2`:

```
abstract public class Sample2 extends Object {

  private String property;

  public String getProperty(){
      return property;
```

```
        }

    public void setProperty(String property){
        this.property = property;
    }
}
```

The class diagram for `Sample2` looks like this; the italicized class name ***Sample2*** designates that the class is abstract:

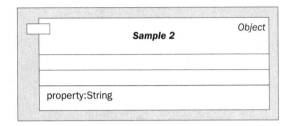

ActionServlet

The first component of the Struts framework we'll discuss is the `ActionServlet` class. `org.apache.struts.action.ActionServlet` extends the abstract class `javax.Servlet.http.HttpServlet`; to see a full listing of `ActionServlet`'s methods, please consult the Struts Documentation. `ActionServlet` overrides the `init()`, `doGet()`, and `doPost()` methods of the `HttpServlet`; the `init()` method executes other initialization methods – `initApplication()`, `initMapping()`, `initDigester()`, and `initOther()` – which we will consider later.

The process() Method

The `ActionServlet` receives requests from the JSP view component through both the `doGet()` and the `doPost()` methods. Both methods pass the request and response objects to the `process()` method.

The sequence diagram for the `process()` method is illustrated below:

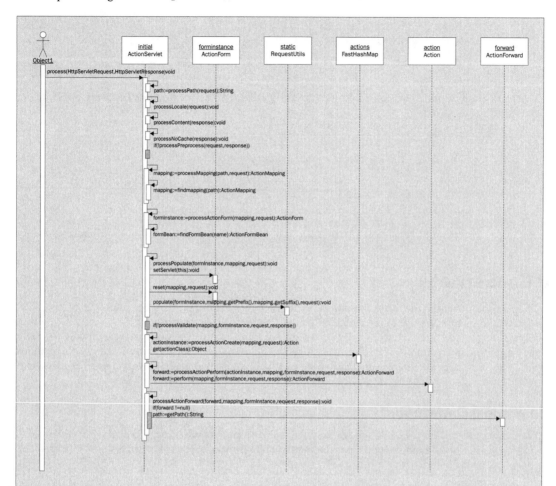

The `process()` method makes several calls to other methods within the `ActionServlet` to process the request. In this sequence diagram we will review nine of those method calls; the others perform local variable initialization for the request thread. (Consult the `ActionServlet.java` class for details.) Here are the methods, in the order they are called:

❏ `processPath()` extracts the URI from the request instance and eliminates the suffix or prefix of the request URI parameter. For example, if the request was `/logon.do` the path is returned as `/logon`.

❏ Then the `processLocale()` method is called. This checks to see if a `Locale` has been established for the request. If not it creates one and stores it in the session.

❏ Then `processMapping()` is called. This uses its `path` parameter as key to retrieve the `ActionMapping` object; if there is an `ActionMapping` object in the `ActionMappings` collection matching the path it is returned to the `process()` method.

❏ The request object is also passed to `processMapping()`. This is not used in the standard implementation of `processMapping()`, but if you extend the `ActionServlet` to implement your own `processMapping()` method you can use it to store data representing a user's application permissions.

For example, in a role based user application, your code could determine whether the user has permission to request a particular `ActionMapping`, and if not you could return an `ActionMapping` to display an error to the user.

❏ Next in line is the `processActionForm()` method. This uses the `ActionMapping`'s name attribute to determine if an `ActionForm` of this type has already been created. If so, the `ActionForm` is returned to the `process()` method, otherwise it creates and returns a new `ActionForm` of the type specified in the `ActionMapping`. Though the `ActionForm` instance may be recycled, its values are reset before it is used, as we shall see next.

❏ After this the `processPopulate()` method is called. This method sets a reference to the `ActionServlet` in the `ActionForm`, calls `reset()` on the `ActionForm` to set the attributes to their default values, populates the `ActionForm` attributes from the request attributes, and sets a request attribute whose key is the `ActionForm` name and whose value is the `ActionForm` itself. This method returns `void`.

❏ `processValidate()` comes next, and checks to see if there is validation for this `ActionForm`. If so it calls the `validate()` method on the `ActionForm`, and if it returns `false`, the `ActionServlet` returns to the calling JSP. (At this point, the `validate()` method would have set any errors and they would be displayed to the user.) If the `validate()` method returns `true`, the `process()` method continues to the next method call below.

❏ Then `processActionCreate()` is called. This method returns the `Action` class associated with the `ActionMapping`. The method looks for an existing instance of the desired `Action` class in the `Actions` collection and returns it if found, but otherwise creates an object of the `Action` class, stores it in the `Actions` collection, and returns a reference to it. The returned `Action` class is specifically mapped to the request URI, and contains the business logic to handle the request.

❏ After this the next method call is to `processActionPerform()`, which calls the `perform()` method on the `Action` object that was returned by `processActionCreate()`. After executing its business logic the `Action` object returns an `ActionMapping` which contains a target for the `ActionServlet` to forward the request to.

❏ The ninth and last method called is `processActionForward()`. This method uses either a `RequestDispatcher` or the `Request.sendRedirect()` method to render the desired view, completing the processing of the request by the `ActionServlet`.

The purpose of this flow is to show how each component gets accessed or called from a request thread within the `ActionServlet`. The flow can be altered by any method – consult the `ActionServlet.java` source for details.

The initApplication() Method

This method loads the `MessageResources` for the application; these are properties files for the different locales that the application supports and is part of Struts' use of Java's internationalization features.

> *For further details on internationalization, please consult your Java 2 SDK Platform documentation. The link, if you have installed the JDK documentation, is located on the `<JAVA_HOME>/docs/index.html` page under Basic Features and is titled Internationalization.*

In Struts, this is backed by a `.properties` file. The one used in the sample application is for the default locale and is called `ApplicationResources.properties`; if your site supported French, the properties file that contained the French text would be in the file named `ApplicationResources_fr.properties`. The location of these files is passed to the `ActionServlet` on startup in the `web.xml` file:

```
<servlet>
  <servlet-name>action</servlet-name>
  <servlet-class>org.apache.struts.action.ActionServlet</servlet-class>
  <init-param>
    <param-name>application</param-name>
    <param-value>com.wrox.pjsp2.struts.ApplicationResources</param-value>
  </init-param>
  <init-param>
    <param-name>config</param-name>
    <param-value>/WEB-INF/struts-config.xml</param-value>
  </init-param>
  <init-param>
    <param-name>debug</param-name>
    <param-value>4</param-value>
  </init-param>
  <init-param>
    <param-name>detail</param-name>
    <param-value>9</param-value>
  </init-param>
  <init-param>
    <param-name>validate</param-name>
    <param-value>true</param-value>
  </init-param>
  <load-on-startup>1</load-on-startup>
</servlet>
```

In addition to the `ApplicationResources` file, the `ActionServlet` uses a configuration file called `struts-config.xml`, which is used to register `Actions`, `ActionMappings`, `ActionForwards`, etc.

The initMapping() Method

This method allows you to provide `package.ClassName` registrations to the `ActionServlet`, instructing `ActionServlet` to use the extended rather than the default classes. The default class for the `formBean` is `org.apache.struts.action.ActionFormBean`; if you extend `ActionFormBean` you will need to add an `<init-param>` to the `web.xml` for the `ActionServlet`, for example:

```
<init-param>
  <param-name>formBean</param-name>
  <param-value>com.wrox.pjsp2.struts.MyActionFormBean</param-value>
</init-param>
```

If the entry above is added in the `ActionServlet` definition previously shown, the `ActionServlet` knows to use `MyActionFormBean` for all form beans; the `ActionForward` class can be overridden in the same fashion. Similarly, the `ActionMapping` can be overridden with an initialziation parameter `config` and a package qualified class.

The initDigester() Method

This method uses the `org.apache.struts.digester.Digester` class to read in the configuration of the web application from the `struts-config.xml` file. The digester allows the developer to establish parsing rules for an XML file; after establishing the rules, the file is read into an XML input stream and parsed, and objects created that contain the data from the configuration file. This was explained previously when we looked at the database servlet.

> *Note that if the value of the `<init-param>` `validate` is set to `true`, this tells the Servlet to call the `initDigester()` method to parse the `struts-config.xml` file. In the 0.5 release of Struts, there is an `action.xml` file that contains the configuration information; the developer can tell `ActionServlet` to use the `initOldDigester()` method by providing a `false` attribute for the `validate` parameter. If set to `true`, the `ActionServlet` will perform validation against the `struts-config_1_0.dtd`.*

> *If the parameter is set to `false` the `ActionServlet` assumes the `action.xml` file is used to configure the application and will not validate it against the DTD. Since the 1.0 release, use of the `action.xml` file has been deprecated, and applications that use the `action.xml` file need to convert to the `struts-config.xml` file to ensure the ability to use future releases of Struts.*

The initOther() Method

This is yet another initialization method; it has a strange name, but it is catch all for the other things that need to be initialized. `initOther()` looks for parameters with the name of `content`, `locale`, and `nocache` in the `struts-config.xml` file:

- ❑ The default `content` is `text/html`.

- ❑ The `locale` parameter is used to decide if the Servlet should use the HTTP request headers to create a `java.util.Locale` object representing the user's locale if one is not already present. If the parameter value is `true` or `yes` the request headers are used, which is the default, otherwise the Locale must be explicitly set for the request.

- ❑ The `nocache` parameter determines whether the `nocache` header entry is sent with each response. The default is `false`; a parameter value of `true` or `yes` will set the nocache header.

ActionServlet Design Note

We need to mention a design note about `ActionServlet` before we move on: `ActionServlet` does maintain local instance variables, of type `org.apache.struts.util.FastHashMap`, containing configuration information that the `ActionServlet` uses to service a request. The `FastHashMap` is a special 'thread safe' `HashMap` that has non-synchronized access for reads and implements the following steps for a write:

- ❑ Clone the existing collection
- ❑ Perform the modification on the clone
- ❑ Replace the existing collection with the (modified) clone

Since the `ActionServlet` is multi-threaded, this collection provides controlled access to the instance variables. The use of the read-only access to the instance variables helps to ensure that the `ActionServlet` will not become a bottleneck in the request process with over-synchronization. It should also be noted that if you choose to implement the `SingleThreadModel` within the Servlet architecture, these collections should be changed to a `HashMap`. This will remove all synchronization and provide a performance increase in this model.

The ActionMapping Class

The ActionMapping class is illustrated here:

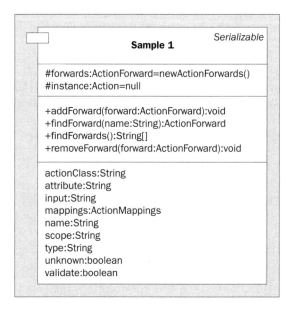

```
                                          Serializable
                      Sample 1

  #forwards:ActionForward=newActionForwards()
  #instance:Action=null

  +addForward(forward:ActionForward):void
  +findForward(name:String):ActionForward
  +findForwards():String[]
  +removeForward(forward:ActionForward):void

  actionClass:String
  attribute:String
  input:String
  mappings:ActionMappings
  name:String
  scope:String
  type:String
  unknown:boolean
  validate:boolean
```

org.apache.struts.action.ActionMapping contains the processing information that the ActionServlet needs to pass the request to the Action class that will execute the business logic. ActionMappings are created based on <action> entries in the struts-config.xml file, within the <action-mappings> element, for example:

```
<action-mappings>
    ...
    <!-- Process a user logon -->
    <action path="/logon"
            type="com.wrox.pjsp2.struts.LogonAction"
            name="logonForm"
            scope="request"
            input="/logon.jsp">
    </action>
    ...
</action-mappings>
```

This entry says that when we receive a request with the path of /logon, the action class is LogonAction, and the name of the form that represents the input is 'logonForm', the scope in which the form will be set is the request and the input form path is '/logon.jsp'.

<action> has the following attributes:

❑ path – The request URI path that is matched to select this mapping. The URI must begin with the '/' character. If extension mapping is used any extensions will be stripped. For example, /login.do will be mapped to /login. Extension mapping is defined in the web.xml file, for example:

```
<!-- Action Servlet Mapping -->
<servlet-mapping>
  <servlet-name>action</servlet-name>
  <url-pattern>*.do</url-pattern>
</servlet-mapping>
```

This informs Tomcat that a URL request like `/login.do` will be sent to the Servlet with the name of `action`.

The `ActionServlet`, using the Servlet name `action`, receives the `/login.do` from our example. The `ActionServlet` automatically strips the `.do` off the request, and looks for an `ActionMapping` of `/login` to send the request.

❑ `type` – Fully qualified Java class name of the `Action` implementation class used by this mapping.

❑ `name` – The name of the form bean defined in the `struts-config.xml` file that this action will use.

❑ `scope` – This determines where the `ActionForm` will be stored: request, application, session, or page.

❑ `input` – This is the mapping to the input page. When the `ActionServlet` calls the validation method on the `ActionForm`, if there is an error the input variable becomes the target of the `forward` or `sendRedirect`.

❑ `unknown` – Set to `true` if this action should be configured as the default for this application, to handle all requests not handled by another action. Only one `Action` can be defined as a default within a single application.

❑ `validate` – Set to `true` if the `validate()` method of the `Action` associated with this mapping should be called.

The ActionForm Class

The `ActionForm` class is illustrated in the following diagram:

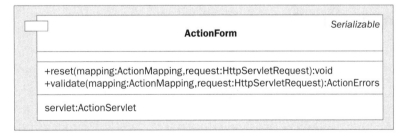

The `ActionForm` classes are defined in the `struts-config.xml` file. An example of such a listing is provided following:

```
<form-beans>
  <form-bean name="logonForm"
             type="com.wrox.pjsp2.struts.LogonForm"/>
</form-beans>
```

All `ActionForm` implementations are registered as in the body of the `<form-beans>` tag. Since the `ActionForm` is abstract, you, the developer, extend it to implement the class that will hold the user input data. The `name` attribute of the `<form-bean>` tag is used to retrieve it from the scope defined in the `ActionMapping` as described previously. The `type` attribute is a package qualified reference to the user implemented `ActionForm`. This is used to instantiate the `ActionForm` via the `java.lang.Class` object within the `ActionServlet`.

The Action Class

The `Action` class is illustrated in the following diagram:

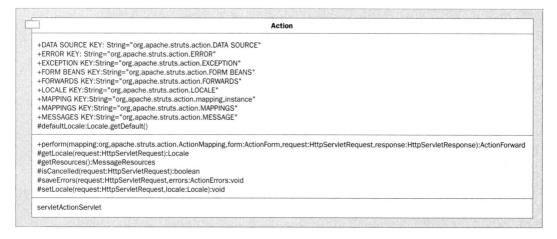

The `Action` class, as stated previously, is extended to provide a specific action for a URI request. Its purpose is to execute the business logic for the request. The `Action` class is instantiated by the `ActionSerlvet`. The `Action` class provides storage for the default `Locale`, and a reference to the `MessageResources` for the application. It provides an `isCancelled()` method that can determine if the cancel button was pressed on the input page. It also contains a reference to the `ActionServlet` in the instance variable `servlet`. This is used to gain access to standard Servlet resources such as the `ServletContext`.

The ActionForward Class

The `ActionForward` class is illustrated in the following diagram:

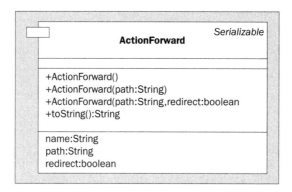

The `ActionForward` classes are configured in the `struts-config.xml` file. There are two kinds of `ActionForward`s: global forwards and `Action`-specific forwards. Both are shown in the following listing:

```
<global-forwards>
  <forward name="success" path="/mainMenu.jsp"/>
</global-forwards>

<action-mappings>
  <action path="/editRegistration"
          type="com.wrox.pjsp2.struts.EditRegistrationAction"
          name="registrationForm"
          scope="request"
          validate="false">
    <forward name="success"  path="/registration.jsp"/>
  </action>
</action-mappings>
```

The first `ActionForward` is defined in a global sense. Any `Action` class can return it as a target for the `ActionServlet` to send the request and response. The second `ActionForward` is specific to the action, and is contained in its `<action>` element. The example says that for a success, the target for the `ActionServlet` is `registration.jsp`.

This completes the high level discussion of the components within the Struts framework. The `taglib` component was discussed in the chapter example.

Design Considerations with Struts

As stated earlier, the Struts framework provides the web developer with components to rapidly develop a web application without having to focus on the web infrastructure: the web developer can concentrate on writing JSPs and business logic, and the interaction with external data sources.

The Struts framework does require that the web developer design his `Action` classes to work in a multi-threaded environment. As the framework continues to mature, new functionality will appear to help developers to create a robust web application. Developers using the Struts framework should stay tuned in to the evolution of the framework, and look for examples on how to implement the new capabilities.

It is the author's belief that the Struts framework will revolutionize the 'Model 2' development of web applications. The Struts example, provided with the framework, will be a continual source for a reference implementation of the framework, as will the New Particles site. Future examples will utilize a database and EJB components that are called within the `Action` classes.

Current Design Focus

The current design focus of the Struts framework emphasizes server-side validation of form information, because of the belief that the client may include non-browser interfaces. The server-side validation approach allows the interface to vary, yet maintain the server-side validation of user information.

Future Design Focus

Some future design considerations within the Struts framework include an improved template mechanism that will provide more flexibility than the current implementation. There are plans to introduce a 'workflow' processing model. Watch the Struts home page and the New Particles Struts pages for examples of these new features.

The best way to stay informed about the Struts framework is to subscribe to the struts-user and struts-dev mail lists. On these you can interact with other developers who are implementing systems with Struts and providing additional functionality to the framework. If you have a request for future development you can post it to the struts-dev mail list, on which the Struts committers often discuss new features planned for future releases on this mail list.

Application Servers and Struts

The chapter example is implemented on Tomcat, the JSP and Servlet reference implementation. Many web developers will want to implement their web application on another application server. There are often workarounds that are required when doing this, since most application servers do not fully implement the Servlet and JSP specifications.

In the Struts distribution there are files that provide assistance on using Struts with various application servers; you may also post questions about using Struts with your desired application server in the struts-user mail list. At the time of this writing, Struts has been implemented on the following application servers:

- ❏ Bluestone Universal Business Server
- ❏ iPlanet Application Server
- ❏ iPlanet Web Server
- ❏ iPortal Application Server
- ❏ JRUN
- ❏ Orion Application Server
- ❏ Resin 2.1+ "standalone"
- ❏ Silverstream
- ❏ Tomcat 3.2.1+
- ❏ Weblogic
- ❏ WebLogic 6.0
- ❏ WebSphere

Where Do We Go From Here?

Now that you have seen an application built with Struts you are probably interested in building your own web application using Struts. So, where do you go from here?

The best approach is it to try your own implementation. When doing this you will undoubtedly need to ask questions and seek help in solving problems. The primary resources for questions are the struts-user and struts-dev mail lists. You can either subscribe to each one from the Struts home page, or use the mail archives at http://www.mail-archive.com/ to search for answers to your question. The author suggests subscribing to the struts-user list if you are serious about using Struts. You can ask questions here and receive a lot of help. Craig answers questions on the list, along with the other committers and Struts enthusiasts like myself.

If you subscribe to the mail list, be sure to save the welcome messages, because they tell you how to unsubscribe. You can't unsubscribe by posting an unsubscribe message to the list. If you forget how to unsubscribe send an e-mail to struts-user-unsubscribe@jakarta.apache.org; the content doesn't matter.

How You Can Help the Struts Framework

Since Struts is an open source framework, it needs people to help make it a success. Some view this as a high risk in commercial software development. However, the author would like to point out that the majority of the XML technologies that are used in J2EE development rely on open source software from the Apache Software Foundation – popular XML sub-projects like Xerces, Xalan, and SOAP.

The open source effort survives and thrives as long as people contribute to the effort. The simplest way to contribute is to use the software. After using the software you can make suggestions for improvements, provide bug fixes or new functionality, help others by answering e-mail on the mail lists, and report your success stories.

Summary

The Struts framework has created the first open source 'Model 2' framework that utilizes Servlet 2.2 and JSP 1.1 technologies. The framework takes advantage of the JSP 1.1 custom tags feature to reduce scriptlet coding in JSP pages. As the Servlet and the JSP specifications continue to evolve you will see Struts introduce new functionality to support them.

Using a framework like Struts provides the web developer with the ability to concentrate on implementing a web application without writing infrastructure code that allows for separation of content from the business logic. Struts is built upon the 'Model 2' design concept, which is also classified as a web variant of the MVC design pattern. Utilizing an existing framework like 'Struts' provides rapid development of new web applications.

We looked at the following aspects of Struts:

- ❏ The importance of the framework to the web developer
- ❏ The development history of the framework
- ❏ Downloading and installing the framework
- ❏ How the framework is maintained and contributed to
- ❏ The architecture of Struts
- ❏ The key components of Struts: `Action`, `ActionForm`, `ActionForward`, `ActionServlet`, and `ActionMapping`
- ❏ The design considerations for an `Action` class

❑   The importance of the `Digester` class and how it can be used to create Java object instances from XML documents

❑   How to develop a web application using the framework

❑   The `struts-config.xml` file in the framework

❑   The power of the Struts tag libraries

We also looked at design considerations for a web application based on the framework, how to get involved in the Struts effort, future design focus of the framework, and how you can help determine its future.

In the next chapter, we'll see a practical application of JSP technology to target content at both HTML and WAP clients.

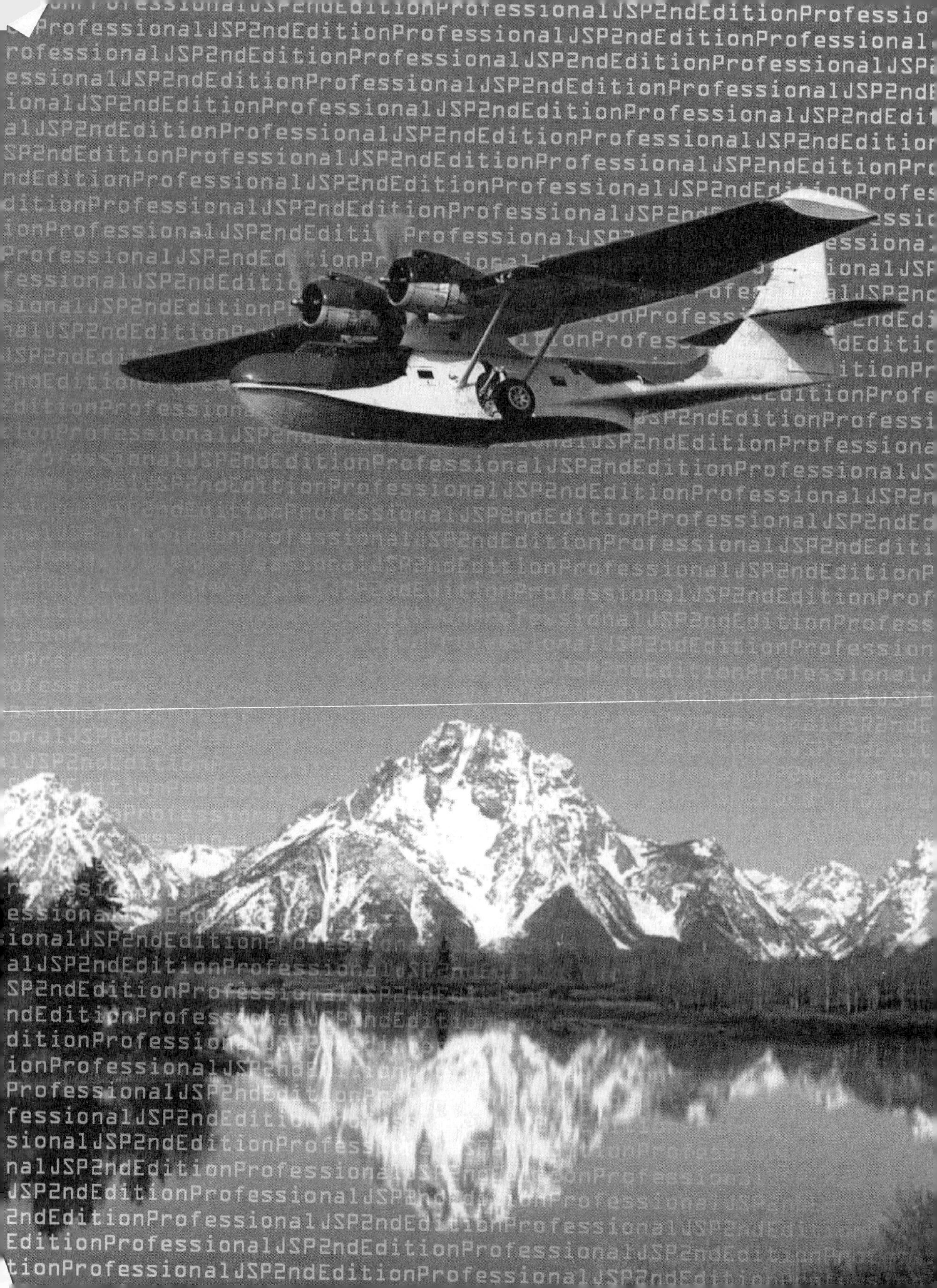

22

WAP Programming with JSP

The Internet is no longer restricted to the confines of the bulky, static computer. A wide variety of mobile devices, ranging from personal digital assistants to cellular telephones, are now capable of connecting to the Internet without wires.

One of the prevalent wireless Internet protocols is the **Wireless Application Protocol**, or **WAP** as it is more commonly called. WAP is designed as a modest bandwidth protocol, suitable for data communication at rates of between 5 and 10 kilobits per second. A number of carriers now support WAP, opening the market for Internet applications to a huge number of wireless device users.

As we will see, programming applications for the WAP environment is surprisingly similar to writing traditional Internet applications. Software developers can leverage their knowledge of standard Internet programming technologies, such as Java Servlets, JSP, XML, and XSLT, to rapidly build and deploy WAP applications.

So, in this chapter we'll take a look at:

- ❑ The Wireless Application Protocol in brief
- ❑ Wireless Markup Language and WMLScript
- ❑ An example application using XML, and WML, and JSPs
- ❑ How to make WML and HTML from the same XML source
- ❑ Making the XML with JSP

For more details about the history of WAP and its architectural details, you should visit the WAP Forum at http://www.wapforum.org. For a wealth of WAP programming resources, see the Openwave Systems web site at http://www.openwave.com. Remember that the code examples from this chapter (and all of the others too) can be obtained from http://www.wrox.com.

The WAP Programming Model

The WAP programming model is not too different from that of the traditional wired Internet. In fact, much of the network infrastructure used for WAP is the same as the wired Internet. Requests for wireless web content and data are made from a browser embedded in a WAP-enabled cellular phone or other mobile device, and the responses are generated by web servers (such as those which typically serve content to browsers on a desktop PC). Furthermore, the protocol used by a web server that generates WAP content is HTTP.

The difference between WAP networks and the wired Internet is the presence of a **WAP gateway** between the WAP browser and the web server. The figure below shows such a WAP gateway in a WAP network.

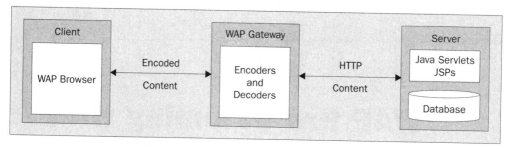

Since WAP is a low bandwidth protocol, WAP enabled devices send and receive signals in a compressed, encoded format. The job of the WAP gateway is to encode and decode information in this compressed format.

For example, requests made by a WAP phone are decoded by the WAP gateway into HTTP requests and forwarded to the appropriate web server computer. Similarly, the WAP gateway encodes HTTP responses from the server into the compressed format that is sent over the air to the WAP phone.

Fortunately for the WAP application programmer, the details of WAP network architecture have little impact on application development. In fact, writing WAP applications is fundamentally the same as writing more traditional web applications.

This allows programmers to apply all of their content server programming experience to WAP application programming. Since WAP content is served by HTTP based networks, content server programming technologies such as Java Servlets and JavaServer Pages can be used to generate WAP content. However, as we see in the next section, the client's side of the story is different.

The WAP Application Programming Environment

Another major difference between WAP application programming and traditional web application programming is the WAP application programming environment. Although the WAP application programming environment has the same types of components as those used for programming applications for traditional browsers, the details of these components are quite different.

First, WAP specifies a markup language for creating WAP application content. This language is called the **Wireless Markup Language**, or **WML**, and WML is an XML document type. Everything from the tags defined by WML to the WML concept of a document is different from the corresponding parts of HTML. Perhaps the most significant difference between WML and HTML is that WML supports far fewer language tags than HTML. Because it is delivered over relatively-low bandwidth networks, WML content must be described much more succinctly than HTML content.

Next, WAP specifies a scripting language for adding procedural logic to WAP applications. This language, **WMLScript**, is the WAP analogue of JavaScript.

Finally, each of these WAP application programming components must be interpreted by a microbrowser that displays WAP content on the device screen.

We next discuss WML and WMLScript in greater detail. Describing these two languages in complete detail is beyond the scope of this chapter. However, we will provide enough information to allow you to write and understand the most common types of WAP applications.

> *For further information on WAP, WML and WMLScript, take a look at* 'Beginning WAP: WML and WMLScript', *ISBN 1-861004-58-3, or* 'Professional WAP', *ISBN 1-861004-04-4, both from Wrox Press.*

The UP.Simulator

Openwave Systems, Inc. (formerly Phone.com) is the primary vendor of WAP gateways. They also provide a free WAP programming SDK for writing WAP applications. A significant component of this SDK is the **UP.Simulator**, a WAP phone browser simulation environment. With this simulator, WAP programmers can write and debug applications without having access to a real WAP phone. The Openwave UP.SDK4.1 is available for free download from http://developer.phone.com/download/index.html. You should note that this UP.SDK4.1 release only supports WML 1.1, not the latest version of WML, 1.2. Strangely, the UP.SDK4.0 can be used to run WML 1.2 instead! You can download this from ftp://dload.phone.com/developer/. The file you need from this site is upsdkW40e.exe. An example of the UP.Simulator, from this UP.SDK4.0, is shown in the figure below:

Using the UP.Simulator is simple. It can display WML files stored locally on a computer as well as displaying WML files on a remote web server. Local files are specified by entering file:// followed by the full path to the local file in the UP.Simulator address bar. Files on a web server are accessed by entering http:// followed by the URL of the desired file.

The Wireless Markup Language – WML

Despite the differences between HTML and WML, readers who are familiar with HTML will have little difficulty mastering the basics of the WML language. Since WML is an XML document type, it follows all of the XML syntax rules. This makes learning WML even easier for programmers familiar with XML, and not particularly difficult for those not familiar.

In the next few sections, we present a brief introduction to WML and some of the most important and common features of the language. This is by no means meant to be a complete introduction to WML. There are entire books detailing the WML and WMLScript languages, and readers interested in a deeper understanding of WAP programming are encouraged to take a look at them. Perhaps the best place to start is the Openwave Systems WAP developer website at http://updev.phone.com.

WML Decks and Cards

To a traditional web application, a document is a single HTML page. In WML, a document is called a **deck**. A WML deck is composed of one or more **cards**. Each card corresponds to a screen of information rendered on a WAP browser.

A deck is the smallest unit of WML information that can be transmitted to a WAP device from a WAP gateway. Since WAP is designed to be a modest bandwidth protocol, operating at transfer rates on the order of 1 kilobit per second, it is generally recommended that WML decks be no greater than 1KB in size.

A WML deck (or document if you prefer) is defined with the following syntax:

```
<?xml version="1.0"?>
  <!DOCTYPE wml PUBLIC  "-//WAPFORUM//DTD WML 1.1//EN"
    "http://www.wapforum.org/DTD/wml_1.1.xml">

<wml>

  <head>
    <!-- Head Information. This is used to specify optional access
         privileges with the <access> tag, and meta information (such as
         cache control) with the <meta> tag
    -->
  </head>

  <template>
    <!-- Deck-level event definitions -->
  </template>

  <card>
    <!-- One or more cards -->
  </card>

</wml>
```

The XML header, specifying the XML version as well as the WML document type definition, will be left out of the rest of our WML code for simplicity. Unfortunately, we can't do this with anything we want to be used by a WML browser.

WML cards are defined with the `<card>` element. Here is an example of a WML deck with a single card:

```
<wml>
  <card id="HelloWAP">
    <p>
      Hello WAP!!
    </p>
  </card>
</wml>
```

The `id` attribute gives a name to the card so that the card can be referred to in other WML code. This will be useful, for example, when linking between cards. The WML sample above looks like this when displayed in the UP.Browser:

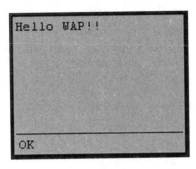

Although the UP.Browser will have a mobile phone skin surrounding the LCD screen representation, for ease of presentation, we'll only be showing the LCD portion. In addition, there are several skins or masks available for the phone, some of which have smaller screen sizes.

Text Formatting

> **WML requires that all text in any WML card be enclosed within paragraph tags:**
> `<p>...</p>`.

Like HTML, the WML language defines a number of elements for formatting text. For example, WML can specify that text be displayed in bold using the `<b>` tag, or in italic using the `<i>` tag. Line breaks can be specified with the `<br/>` tag.

WML also supports a basic table formatting feature. The `<table>` tag defines a table, and the `columns` attribute specifies the number of columns in the table. Table rows are specified with the `<tr>` tag, and table columns are specified with the `<td>` tag. For example, the following WML card defines a simple table with two columns:

```
<wml>
  <card id="Menu">
```

```
      <p align="center">
      <b>Lunch Menu</b>
      </p>

      <p align="left">
        <table columns="2">
          <tr> <td>Burger:</td> <td>4.95</td> </tr>
          <tr> <td>Salad:</td> <td>2.50</td> </tr>
        </table>
      </p>

      </card>
   </wml>
```

Here is what this WML deck looks like when rendered:

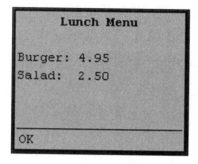

WML Hyperlinks

An important feature of any browser markup language is the ability to link from one page or document to another. WML allows linking between cards with the <a> anchor tag. This tag has an `href` attribute like HTML. In WML, the `href` specifies the card to display when the link is selected. Hyperlinks are indicated by placing the corresponding text in brackets. For example:

```
<wml>

  <card id="HelloWAP">
  <p>
    Hello WAP!! <br/>
    <a title="Menu" href="#Menu">Click for the Lunch Menu</a>
  </p>
  </card>

  <card id="Menu">
  <p align="center">
  <b>Lunch Menu</b>
  </p>

  <p align="left">
    <table columns="2">
      <tr> <td>Burger:</td> <td>4.95</td> </tr>
      <tr> <td>Salad:</td> <td>2.50</td> </tr>
    </table>
```

```
        </p>
      </card>

    </wml>
```

In this example, moving the arrow on the screen by pressing the browser down-arrow key selects the hyperlink. Once selected, it can be invoked by pressing the Menu button, and the browser navigates to the lunch menu card shown previously.

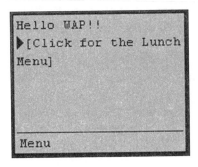

WML Events

A WML **event** is defined as some action (such as the user pressing a WAP phone button) that makes the WAP browser do something interesting. Events and event processing can be thought of as the WML equivalent of HTML form processing.

WML events are tied to **tasks**, such as submitting a request to a JSP on a web server. Such a task is specified with the <go> tag, as in this example:

```
<card id="JSPGet">
  <do type="accept" label="Go!" >
    <go href="http://localhost:8080/ch25/Hangman.jsp" method="get"/>
  </do>

  <p>Submit HTTP GET Request</p>
</card>
```

Displaying this WML code looks like this:

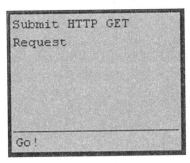

Selecting the Go! button in the bottom left corner of the screen causes the browser to navigate to the location specified in the `<go>` tag `href` attribute. In this case, that means submitting an HTTP GET request to the specified JSP, as indicated by the `"get"` value of the `method` attribute. The POST method is also supported. To specify an HTTP POST, set the `method` attribute to `"post"`.

WML events are the primary mechanism linking WAP programming and JavaServer Pages. JSP requests will always be made in response to WML events.

The events we have been discussing so far have been **card-level events**. In other words, the event defined by the `<do>` element is only valid within the context of the WML card that contains it. Some applications require events that are valid for all cards within a WML deck. To specify a **deck-level event**, use the `<template>` tag:

```
<wml>
  <template>
    <do type="accept" label="Help">
      <go href="#Help" />
    </do>
  </template>
  ...
</wml>
```

With this code, each card is given an event that displays the Help card when the phone's OK button is pressed. The browser indicates this option by placing the text Help under the right-hand hardware button.

WML Variables

The WML language includes the concept of variables. A WML variable has *deck scope*, meaning that a variable value set in one card is available to all cards in the same deck. Variables in WML are untyped. Their values are either strings or `null`. To get numeric results in WMLScript, string variables are converted to integers or floats by calling the WMLScript Lang library `parseInt()` or `parseFloat()` functions. Note that the names of the variables are case sensitive, just as in the C++ or Java programming languages.

WML variables are defined with the `<setvar>` tag. For example:

```
<setvar name="occupation" value ="engineer" />
<setvar name="age" value="35" />
```

Be aware that the `<setvar>` tag cannot appear by itself – it must appear inside of a task tag such as `<go>` or `<refresh>`.

To reference a WML variable's value, use the variable name preceded by the $ character. For example, to display the value of the variable named `word` in a WML card, you could use the following code:

```
<card id="vardisplay">
  <p>
    The variable word = $word
  </p>
</card>
```

User Input

WML defines an `<input>` tag for adding text input to WML content:

```
<input name="username" type="text" size="30" />
```

This tag is the analogue of the HTML `<input>` tag. In WML, however, the only types supported are `text` and `password`. The name attribute specifies the name of a WML variable. This variable's value gets set to the value entered by the user in the input field. In this way, WML cards can send named parameter values to JSPs, as in this example, which sends names to a JSP called `HelloWAP.jsp` (which we will define a little later):

```
<wml>
  <card id="login">

    <do type="accept" label="OK" >
      <go href="http://localhost:8080/ch25/HelloWAP.jsp" method="get" >
        <postfield name="firstname" value="$_firstname"/>
        <postfield name="lastname" value="$_lastname"/>
      </go>
    </do>
    <p>
      First Name:
      <input name="_firstname" maxlength="15" emptyok="false" /><br/>
      Last Name:
      <input name="_lastname" maxlength="15" emptyok="false" /><br/>
    </p>
  </card>
</wml>
```

Here, the `<postfield>` tag defines a named parameter value to submit to the JSP. The `<postfield>` name attribute specifies the name of the JSP parameter. The `value` attribute specifies the value of the corresponding JSP parameter.

As you can see, in this example there are two `input` fields. They are used to enter the values of the WML variables `_firstname` and `_lastname`. The card-level event specified by the `<do>` tag submits these variable values as the JSP parameters `firstname` and `lastname`.

Assume the user enters the first name "Joe" and the last name "Smith" and then presses the OK button on his WAP phone. The web server machine (via the WAP gateway) receives the HTTP GET request:
http://localhost:8080/ch25/HelloWAP.jsp?firstname=Joe&lastname=Smith.

WMLScript

We mentioned earlier that, in addition to the Wireless Markup Language, WAP applications can include procedural logic via **WMLScript**. WMLScript is the WAP counterpart of the more familiar JavaScript language. Since most WMLScript code looks a lot like JavaScript, we will spend less time on this subject than we did introducing WML. Most of our WMLScript examples will be presented as we work through our 'Hangman' application implementation later.

WMLScript code must live within code files separate from your WML code. This is different from JavaScript, which can be embedded directly into HTML documents. WMLScript files generally have the `.wmls` extension. A `.wmls` file consists of one or more WMLScript functions. A typical WMLScript function looks like this:

```
extern function getAverage(num1, num2) {
  var _result;

  _result = (num1+num2)/2;
  WMLBrowser.setVar("result", _result);
  WMLBrowser.go("#ResultCard");
}
```

Here, the `extern` keyword indicates that the function can be referenced from outside its `.wmls` file, for example, from WML code. WMLScript does not include a return statement; instead WMLScript functions give results to their callers by setting WML variable values. This is done using the `WMLBrowser.setVar()` function call.

The `WMLBrowser.setVar()` function is an example of a WMLScript **standard library** function. The `WMLBrowser.go()` call is another example. This function causes the WAP browser to link to the specified WML card.

WMLScript functions are called from WML with `<go>` tasks. For example, the `getAverage()` function above could be called as follows:

```
<do type="accept" label="CallFunction">
  <go href="functions.wmls#getAverage($val1, $val2)" />
</do>
```

The `href` indicates the name of the WMLScript file containing the function. The fragment (indicated by the # character) specifies the name of the function to call and the arguments.

WMLScript Standard Libraries

There are six libraries of commonly used WMLScript functions that are part of the WAP specification. These libraries are analogous to Java packages that implement a set of standard programming functions and utilities used in most WAP applications.

The six standard libraries and their contents are described in the following table:

Library Name	Contents
Lang	Arithmetic functions, type conversion, etc.
Float	Floating point functions
String	String functions
URL	Functions for managing URLs
WMLBrowser	Functions for accessing WML variables, navigation, etc.
Dialogs	Functions for displaying common WML dialogs

We will look at some WMLScript functions specific to the Hangman application later in this chapter. We will use these functions to demonstrate basic WMLScript programming as well as the use of the standard libraries.

WAP MIME Types

Another important difference between WAP application programming and traditional web application programming are the MIME types defining the content delivered by the web server to the WAP browser through the WAP gateway.

As most WAP applications are composed primarily of WML and WMLScript content, the MIME types corresponding to these content types are most important. (WAP does support other types, such as a simple graphics format called **WBMP**, and an **alert** type, but we will not be discussing these other types here.) The WML MIME type is `text/vnd.wap.wml`, and the WMLScript MIME type is `text/vnd.wap.wmlscript`. Any web server that wants to deliver these WAP content types must be configured to support these MIME types. For example, under the configuration directory for my installation of the Apache web server for Linux, the `mime.types` file specifies the following MIME types:

```
text/vnd.wap.wml
text/vnd.wap.wmlscript
image/vnd.wap.wbmp
```

The way to configure our JSP WAP applications to recognize the WAP mime types is to add `<mime-mapping>` elements to the `web.xml` file in the `/webapps/ch22/WEB-INF` folder:

```xml
<?xml version="1.0" encoding="ISO-8859-1"?>
<!DOCTYPE web-app
    PUBLIC "-//Sun Microsystems, Inc.//DTD Web Application  2.2//EN"
    "http://java.sun.com/j2ee/dtds/web-app_2.2.dtd">

<web-app>

  <mime-mapping>
    <extension>wml</extension>
    <mime-type>text/vnd.wap.wml</mime-type>
  </mime-mapping>

  <mime-mapping>
    <extension>wmlc</extension>
    <mime-type>application/vnd.wap.wmlc</mime-type>
  </mime-mapping>

  <mime-mapping>
    <extension>wmls</extension>
    <mime-type>text/vnd.wap.wmlscript</mime-type>
  </mime-mapping>

  <mime-mapping>
    <extension>wmlsc</extension>
    <mime-type>application/vnd.wap.wmlscriptc</mime-type>
  </mime-mapping>

  <mime-mapping>
    <extension>wbmp</extension>
    <mime-type>image/vnd.wap.wbmp</mime-type>
  </mime-mapping>

</web-app>
```

The `web.xml` file in the code download for this chapter (from http://www.wrox.com) already contains these `<mime-mapping>` elements.

Setting WAP Content Type in a JSP

The fact that WAP applications rely on different content types implies that content server code, such as JSPs, written for WAP must specify their content type differently. To deliver WML from a JSP, for example, the JSP code must specify its content type.

As an example, consider the following `HelloWAP.jsp` file, which gets the `firstname` and `lastname` parameters from an HTTP request and generates a WML response greeting the user:

```
<% response.setContentType("text/vnd.wap.wml"); %>
    <?xml version="1.0"?>
  <!DOCTYPE wml PUBLIC "-//WAPFORUM//DTD WML 1.1//EN"
     "http://www.wapforum.org/DTD/wml_1.1.xml">
<wml>
  <card id="res">
    <p>
      Hello, <b><%= request.getParameter("firstname") %>
      <%= request.getParameter("lastname") %> </b>
      <br />
      This is your first dynamic WML application!
    </p>
  </card>
</wml>
```

This JSP can be invoked with an HTTP GET request like this:

```
HelloWAP.jsp?_firstname=Robert&_lastname=Burdick
```

The `response.setContentType()` call must come before any content is delivered to the client. Alternatively, if the JSP will always generate the same content type, you can use:

```
<%@ page contentType="text/vnd.wap.wml" %>
```

Creating a JSP/WAP-based Hangman Game

To demonstrate the application of JSP technology to WAP programming, we will write a simple game for the WAP platform. Since the WAP platform is not very graphics intensive, we will write a game that focuses more on words and letters than action.

Hangman is thus a perfect game for the WAP environment. In the classic two-player game of Hangman, generally played with pencil and paper instead of state of the art electronics, a secret word is selected by one player. The other player must guess the letters in the hidden word until he is able to guess the entire hidden word. For each incorrect guess, a part of a line drawing of a person is added. If the guesser makes so many guesses that the entire stick figure is drawn, that player loses the game. The other player delivers the coup de grace by drawing a noose around his opponent's stick figure, indisputably indicating that the game is over.

In our WAP version of the game, we will dispense with drawing stick figures. Our version of Hangman will be greatly simplified to include only the selection of a secret word, the guessing of individual letters in the word, and the option to guess the secret word. Additionally, we will keep track of the score, where each letter guess, correct or not, counts as one point. If the player guesses the secret word correctly, a WML card is displayed showing how many tries it took to get the answer.

Making a Platform-Independent Implementation

We could very easily implement our game with WML and WMLScript, using JSPs to generate WAP-specific content, and then call it a day. But our Hangman game would be much more flexible, not to mention more instructional, if we implemented it in such a way that it could be run from a variety of browser platforms.

We will therefore write our WAP application such that it can be used from both WAP enabled devices and traditional HTML based browsers. Specifically, we will design the Hangman game so that it can run on both the UP.Browser and Internet Explorer.

Hangman, XML, and XSLT

The technologies of choice in the web programming community for building platform independent applications are the **Extensible Markup Language** (**XML**) and the **Extensible Stylesheet Language** Transformations (**XSLT**).

We will represent the various Hangman screens with an XML document, and then use XSL stylesheets to convert the XML to the appropriate browser-specific presentation code (WML or HTML). The Hangman application will randomly select hidden words from another XML document stored on the web server.

JavaServer Pages will be used to generate the XML document representing a session of the Hangman game, as well as to select a word from the secret word XML document. We will look at these two XML document types later when we begin implementing the application.

Hangman WML Deck

To start with, let's get an overall picture of how the game works in WML. We have shown below what the WML deck code looks like after starting the game and requesting a new secret word. Bear in mind that this WML content is not going to be delivered by our JSP code. As described above, the application will be written using XML and XSLT so that it can easily be run on a variety of browser platforms. However, this look at the basic structure of the WML and WMLScript code generated by the application will help us understand the overall operation of the application.

This WML deck consists of three WML cards. The first is called `Hangman`. This card sets the value of four WML variables: `result`, `word`, `answer`, and `score`. These variables are used throughout the application to keep track of the secret word, the word with correctly guessed letters revealed, and the player's score; the variables are then used in WMLScript code to check for the occurrence of letters in the secret word, update the score, and so on.

```
<?xml version="1.0" encoding="UTF-8"?>
<wml>
  <template>
    <do label="Answer" type="options">
    <go href="#Answer"/>
  </do>
  </template>

  <!-- *** The Main Hangman Card *** -->
  <card id="Hangman">
    <onevent type="onenterforward">
      <refresh>
        <setvar value="********" name="result"/>
```

```
            <setvar value="internet" name="word"/>
            <setvar value="" name="answer"/>
            <setvar value="0" name="score"/>
        </refresh>
    </onevent>


    <p>
      <select multiple="false">
        <option
            onpick="http://localhost:8080/ch22/Hangman.jsp?action=getword">
          New Word
        </option>
        <option onpick="#Play">Play the Game!</option>
      </select>
    </p>
  </card>
```

Next, the Play WML card gives the user the option of guessing a letter (Guess) or guessing the entire word (by means of the Answer option generated with the deck-level event defined in the <template> block above).

```
<!-- The Play Options Card *** -->
<card id="Play">
  <onevent type="onenterforward">
    <refresh>
      <setvar value="" name="guess"/>
      <setvar value="" name="answer"/>
    </refresh>
  </onevent>

  <do label="Guess" type="accept">
    <go href="./../wmls/hangman.wmls#matchChar()"/>
  </do>

  <p>
    $result<br/>
    Guess a Letter:

    <input emptyok="false" maxlength="1" size="1" name="guess"/>
  </p>

</card>

<!-- *** The Answer Card *** -->
<card id="Answer">
  <do label="Guess Word" type="accept">
    <go href="./../wmls/hangman.wmls#guessWord('$(answer)')"/>
  </do>
  <p>

    Guess the Word:
    <input type="text" name="answer"/>
  </p>
</card>

</wml>
```

Having whizzed through all of the code, let's now go back over it in more depth. The Hangman card looks like this when rendered on a WAP browser:

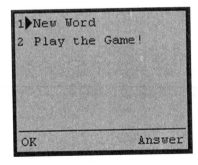

The Hangman deck also defines a deck-level event via the `<template>` element at the top of the code. This code adds the Answer option to the Menu button on the WAP browser for every card in the WML deck. In other words, the user can choose to guess the entire secret word from any card without requiring us to add WML code to this effect explicitly in each Hangman card.

The Hangman card contains a `select` element with two options:

```
<select multiple="false">
  <option
      onpick="http://localhost:8080/ch22/Hangman.jsp?action=getword">
    New Word
  </option>
  <option onpick="#Play">Play the Game!</option>
</select>
```

The simplest option is the second. It simply navigates the WAP browser to the Play card shown in the figure below. The first option is more interesting. Selecting this option sends an HTTP GET request to the Hangman.jsp JavaServer Page. The request includes the getword value for the action parameter, telling the web server to randomly select a new secret word for the game player to guess. We will examine the role of this JSP in detail later (in the section *Hangman.jsp*).

Now let's look more closely at the Play WML card. The browser screen produced by this card is shown below:

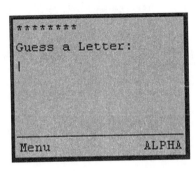

(Note that the ALPHA in the bottom right of the screen indicates whether the caps lock is on or off.) The first thing this code does is to define a new variable, guess, which will store the player's letter guess. The answer variable defined previously is cleared for a new guess:

```
<card id="Play">
  <onevent type="onenterforward">
    <refresh>
      <setvar value="" name="guess"/>
      <setvar value="" name="answer"/>
    </refresh>
  </onevent>
```

The `Play` card shows the player's guesses so far by rendering the current value of the `result` variable. As we will see shortly, this variable is updated after each letter guess with some simple WMLScript code to reveal each correctly-guessed letter:

```
<p>
  $result<br/>
  Guess a Letter:

  <input emptyok="false" maxlength="1" size="1" name="guess"/>
</p>
```

To guess a letter, the user enters his guess in the input field and chooses the **Guess** option. The `Play` card submits the guess to a WMLScript function which checks to see if the guessed letter is in the secret word with the following WML code:

```
<do label="Guess" type="accept">
  <go href="./../wmls/hangman.wmls#matchChar()"/>
</do>
```

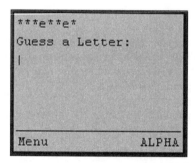

In a similar fashion, the `Answer` card (shown below) tests to see if the player has guessed the secret word. The player's word guess is stored in the `answer` variable and passed to the WMLScript `guessWord()` function:

```
<card id="Answer">
  <do label="Guess Word" type="accept">
    <go href="./../wmls/hangman.wmls#guessWord('$(answer)')"/>
  </do>
  <p>

    Guess the Word:
    <input type="text" name="answer"/>
  </p>
</card>
```

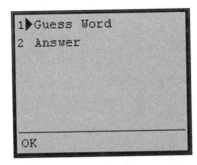

Submitting the answer requires pressing the WAP browser **Menu** button, which brings up the options shown in the figure below:

The player then selects the **Guess Word** option, corresponding to the `GuessWord` `<do>` event shown in the last piece of WML code we discussed above. The extra step of pressing the **Menu** button is required because every card in the Hangman WML deck has at least two options. Recall that the option to guess the secret word is added to every card by the deck-level event defined in the `<template>` code at the top of the WML deck.

Hangman WMLScript Code

We have yet to discuss the WMLScript code referred to in the previous section. The Hangman application includes a WMLScript file, `Hangman.wmls`, which contains all of the WMLScript code used in the application. This file contains two functions, `matchChar()` and `guessWord()`.

The `matchChar()` function compares a guessed letter to all of the letters in the secret word. If the guessed letter appears in the word, the function replaces the asterisk hiding that letter with the actual letter. Each guess updates the score variable. As we discussed in the previous section, the `Play` card uses the `matchChar()` function to update the result variable that keeps a visual record of the player's guesses.

```
extern function matchChar(){
    var _guess = WMLBrowser.getVar("guess");
    var _word =  WMLBrowser.getVar("word");
    var _score = Lang.parseInt(WMLBrowser.getVar("score"));
    var _resultold = WMLBrowser.getVar("result");
    var _result;

    for (var i = 0; i < String.length(_word); i++) {
      if (_guess == String.charAt(_word, i)) {
        _result = _result + _guess;
```

```
      }
    else {
       _result = _result + String.charAt(_resultold, i);
    }
  }
  _score += 1;
  WMLBrowser.setVar("result", _result);
  WMLBrowser.setVar("score", _score);
  WMLBrowser.go("#Play");
}
```

The calls to the getVar() function of the WMLBrowser WMLScript library assign the various WML variables to local copies to simplify the comparison code. The function simply loops through the entire secret word, comparing each letter to the guessed letter. If the guessed letter matches the letter at the current character location in the secret word, the asterisk occupying that location in the result variable is replaced with the actual character:

```
if (_guess == String.charAt(_word, i)) {
  _result = _result + _guess;
}
```

The guessWord() function is called when the player guesses the secret word. His guess is passed to the function and compared to the _word WML variable:

```
extern function guessWord (guess) {
  var _word = WMLBrowser.getVar("word");
  var _score = WMLBrowser.getVar("score");

  if (String.compare(_word, guess) == 0) {   //User wins!
    Dialogs.alert("You Won!  You guessed the word in " + _score +
                  " tries");
    WMLBrowser.go("#Hangman");   //Return user to start of game
  }
  else {
    Dialogs.alert("Your guess " + guess + " is incorrect!");
    WMLBrowser.go("#Play");
  }
}
```

The guessed word is passed as the function argument. The WMLScript library String.compare() call compares the guessed word to the secret answer word. If the guess is correct, a WMLScript Dialog is displayed announcing that the user won the game and displaying his score. When the dialog is dismissed, the function automatically navigates the player's browser to the Hangman card to let him start a new game. This dialog is shown in the following screenshot:

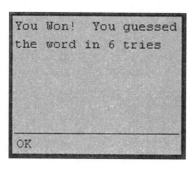

If the guessed word is incorrect, a dialog to this effect is displayed (with the guessed word intelligence), and the player is returned to the Play card to let him keep guessing:

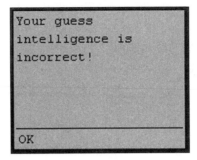

Hangman XML Documents

There are two document types used by the Hangman application. The simpler of the two contains a set of words used as the secret words in the game. This XML document, called words.xml, looks like this (for the sake of brevity, document type definitions in this file and the XML document representing the Hangman screens have been left out):

```
<hangman_words>
   <word>internet</word>
   <word>network</word>
   <word>microbrowser</word>
   <word>servlet</word>
   <word>tomcat</word>
   <word>apache</word>
   <word>Wrox</word>
   <word>client</word>
   <word>gateway</word>
   <word>programmer</word>
</hangman_words>
```

The <word> tag is used to indicate a word that can be used by the Hangman application. This XML file is parsed by our JSP code whenever the player requests a new word. A random integer between 1 and 10 is selected, and the word corresponding to that number is then parsed from the words.xml file.

Note that throughout this chapter, it is assumed that the actual words in the words.xml file do not contain any characters that might be construed as XML syntax, such as < or >.

The other XML document type used by our application is called hangman.xml. This document type is used to represent the various browser screens that get displayed while playing the game:

```
<?xml version="1.0"?>
<hangman>

  <Screen_Hangman>
    <Screen_Hangman_Enter>
        <Screen_Hangman_Vars>
           <result>********</result>
```

```
            <word>internet</word>
            <answer></answer>
            <score>0</score>
        </Screen_Hangman_Vars>

    </Screen_Hangman_Enter>

    <Screen_Hangman_Options />
  </Screen_Hangman>

  <Screen_Play>
    <Screen_Play_Enter>
      <Screen_Play_OnGuess>
        <Screen_Play_Content
      </Screen_Play_OnGuess>
    </Screen_Play_Enter>
  </Screen_Play>

  <Screen_Answer>
      <Screen_Answer_OnGuess>
        <Screen_Answer_Content />        </Screen_Answer_OnGuess>
    </Screen_Answer>

</hangman>
```

This document type can be broken down into three sections. The first section, represented by the
<Screen_Hangman> tag, models the main game screen. This corresponds to the WML card containing the
New Word and **Play the Game** options.

The next section, indicated by the <Screen_Play> tag, represents the screens used to guess letters. This
section also represents the screen containing the **Guess** and **Answer** menu options.

Finally, the <Screen_Answer> tag defines the screen used for guessing the entire word.

The most interesting part of this document type is the part of the first section defined by the
<Screen_Hangman_Vars> tag:

```
      <Screen_Hangman_Vars>
        <result>********</result>
        <word>internet</word>
        <answer></answer>
        <score>0</score>
      </Screen_Hangman_Vars>
```

This section contains four other elements that represent the current state of the game:

❑   <result> is used to display the number of letters correctly guessed by the player so far

❑   <word> contains the secret word

❑   <answer> contains the last complete word guessed by the player

❑   <score> contains his current score

These elements are used by the application to keep track of the status of the game.

Our JSP code generates XML based on this document format whenever the user requests a new word. This generated XML is in turn interpreted by the appropriate XSLT stylesheet and converted into either WML or HTML. You have probably noticed that this XML document type does not explicitly describe all of the game screens shown back in the section '*Hangman WML*'. This is because some of these screens are created by WMLScript code that is generated by the XSLT transformation. We will look at this process in detail a bit later.

Transforming the Hangman XML to WML

The `hangman.xml` document type just described is used as a model of the Hangman game screens that are presented while the Hangman application user plays the game. As a model, it describes the screens independent of any browser presentation language.

To be useful, we need a way to transform the XML representation of our Hangman game into WML, the language understood by a WAP browser. The natural choice for transforming XML into WML is XSLT, Extensible Stylesheet Language Transformations. With XSLT, an object called a processor takes the XML document to transform as input. It also takes another XML document, called an XSLT stylesheet, which tells the processor how to map the various XML elements in the input document into the desired presentation language.

To render the Hangman application screens on a WAP phone, we therefore require an XSLT stylesheet describing how to transform the `hangman.xml` XML format into WML. For this job, we implement the file `Hangman-WML.xsl`. Like almost any XSLT file, this file consists of a set of `<xsl:template>` tags indicating which XML tag to match in the input document. These template matching tags then contain the WML with which the input XML tag should be replaced.

The first `<xsl:template>` element in the `Hangman-WML.xsl` file matches the `<hangman>` tag:

```
<?xml version="1.0"?>

<xsl:stylesheet version="1.0"
                xmlns:xsl="http://www.w3.org/1999/XSL/Transform">

    <xsl:template match="hangman">
      <wml>
        <template>
          <do type="options" label="Answer">
            <go href="#Answer" />
          </do>
        </template>
        <xsl:apply-templates/>
      </wml>
    </xsl:template>
```

The only WML code specific to this tag to add is the opening and closing `<wml>` tags and the deck-level `Answer` event. The rest of the WML code to be generated corresponds to other Hangman XML tags, so we simply insert an `<xsl:apply-templates>` tag to tell the XSLT processor to apply any other XSL templates that are encountered relative to the `<hangman>` tag.

At this point, our XSLT stylesheet can specify the transformations for each of the individual Hangman screen tags. Here is how the WML card `Hangman` is generated. The most interesting part of this code is the `<xsl:template>` tag that matches the `<Screen_Hangman_Vars>` input tag:

```
<xsl:template match="Screen_Hangman">
  <card id="Hangman">
    <xsl:apply-templates />
  </card>
</xsl:template>

<xsl:template match="Screen_Hangman_Enter">
  <onevent type="onenterforward">
    <refresh>
      <xsl:apply-templates />
    </refresh>
  </onevent>
</xsl:template>

<xsl:template match="Screen_Hangman_Vars">
  <setvar name="result" value="{result}" />
  <setvar name="word" value="{word}" />
  <setvar name="answer" value="{answer}" />
  <setvar name="score" value="{score}" />
</xsl:template>

<xsl:template match="Screen_Hangman_Options">
  <p>
  <select multiple="false" >
  <option
      onpick="http://localhost:8080/ch22/Hangman.jsp?action=getword">
      New Word
  </option>
  <option onpick="#Play">Play the Game!</option>
  </select>
  </p>
</xsl:template>
```

The contents of each Hangman XML tag representing one of the variables is used to set the `value` attribute of the WML `<setvar>` tag, thus setting the initial value of each of these WML variables.

The Hangman `Play` and `Answer` cards are similarly generated. Note that the WMLScript code references are added as part of the `<Screen_Play_OnGuess>` and `<Screen_Answer_OnGuess>` XML tags:

```
<xsl:template match="Screen_Play">
  <card id="Play">
    <xsl:apply-templates />
  </card>
</xsl:template>

<xsl:template match="Screen_Play_Enter">
  <onevent type="onenterforward">
    <refresh>
      <setvar name="guess" value ="" />
```

```
        <setvar name="answer" value="" />
      </refresh>
    </onevent>
      <xsl:apply-templates />
  </xsl:template>

  <xsl:template match="Screen_Play_OnGuess">
    <do type="accept" label="Guess">
      <go href="./wmls/hangman.wmls#matchChar()" />
    </do>
    <p>
      <xsl:apply-templates />
        <input name="guess" size="1" maxlength="1" emptyok="false" />
    </p>
  </xsl:template>

  <xsl:template match="Screen_Play_Content">
    $(result)<br />
    Guess a Letter:
  </xsl:template>

  <xsl:template match="Screen_Answer">
    <card id="Answer">
      <xsl:apply-templates />
    </card>
  </xsl:template>

  <xsl:template match="Screen_Answer_OnGuess">
    <do type="accept" label="Guess Word">
      <go href="./wmls/hangman.wmls#guessWord('$(answer)')" />
    </do>
    <p>
    <xsl:apply-templates />
      <input name="answer" type="text" />
    </p>
  </xsl:template>

  <xsl:template match="Screen_Answer_Content">
    Guess the Word:
  </xsl:template>

</xsl:stylesheet>
```

We will see how this XSLT stylesheet is used when we look at the Hangman.jsp code.

Parsing the Hangman words.xml File

Next, we look at how to parse our secret word file words.xml in order to select a word at random. This operation will be used whether we are creating WML or HTML content.

Parsing XML is a very standard requirement of many web applications. Therefore there are a number of freely available XML parsers that application developers can use. In the spirit of free open source software, our Hangman application will use the Apache Xerces parser (available from http://xml.apache.org). Xerces contains a SAX (Simple API for XML) XML parser implementation in the org.apache.xerces.parsers.SAXParser package. This SAX parser in turn implements the XMLParser interface that defines the parsing operations.

At this point, when you download Xerces from http://xml.apache.org, it is a good idea to download the Apache Xalan XSLT package too. Xalan is the XSLT counterpart of the Xerces XML parser we will use for parsing the `words.xml` file; it is an XSLT processor, which we will use later for performing XSLT transformations.

The `xerces.jar` file should be placed in your `webapps/ch22/WEB-INF/lib` folder, along with the `xalan.jar` file, and the paths to these files should be added to your `CLASSPATH` when compiling the Java source files.

In order to parse our `words.xml` file, we will implement a Java class called `Hangman_WordFileParser`, that we walk through below. The `Hangman_WordFileParser` class constructor takes an `int` argument containing a random integer between 1 and 10. This is the random index of the word to extract from the `words.xml` file. This value is stored in the public `index` data member for later use. The class also defines a `String` data member called `word`. This member contains the randomly selected word after the `words.xml` file has been successfully parsed.

```java
import java.io.IOException;
import java.io.InputStream;

import org.xml.sax.Attributes;
import org.xml.sax.ContentHandler;
import org.xml.sax.ErrorHandler;
import org.xml.sax.Locator;
import org.xml.sax.SAXException;
import org.xml.sax.SAXParseException;
import org.xml.sax.InputSource;
import org.xml.sax.XMLReader;
import org.xml.sax.helpers.XMLReaderFactory;

public class Hangman_WordFileParser {

  public String word;    // Randomly selected word
  public int index;      // Random index of word to select


  public Hangman_WordFileParser(int _index) {

    index = _index;
  }

  // Accessor method for returning randomly selected word
  public String getWord() {
    return (word);
  }
```

The class also implements a method called `parseWordFile()`. The string argument contains the name of the XML file to parse. `parseWordFile()` creates an instance of the `SAXParser` class, and then registers a content handler and an error handler for the parser to use. The parse method then calls the `XMLReader` parse method that performs the actual XML file parsing.

```java
public void parseWordFile(InputStream uri) {

  ContentHandler contentHandler = new WordContentHandler();
  ErrorHandler errorHandler = new WordErrorHandler();

  try {
```

```
        // Instantiate a parser
        XMLReader parser =
          XMLReaderFactory
            .createXMLReader("org.apache.xerces.parsers.SAXParser");

        // Register the content handler
        parser.setContentHandler(contentHandler);

        // Register the error handler
        parser.setErrorHandler(errorHandler);

        // Parse the document
        word = null;
        parser.parse(new InputSource(uri));

      } catch (IOException e) {
        System.out.println("IOException: " + e.getMessage());

      } catch (SAXException e) {
        System.out.println("Error in parsing: " + e.getMessage());
      }
    }
```

For the SAX parser to do any useful parsing for us, it must register a content handler. This content handler defines a number of callback methods that get called whenever the various XML elements and attributes in the `words.xml` file are encountered. Our content handler is implemented in the `WordContentHandler` class. This class is nested within the `Hangman_WordFileParser` class so that the public `Hangman_WordFileParser` data members are readily accessible to the content handler class. We will see why this is important shortly.

The `WordContentHandler` class is implemented as follows. (Note that the error handler implementation has been left out for simplicity.) You should also notice that some of the methods, such as `startPrefixMapping()` and `endPrefixMapping()`, are empty. This is because the base class, `ContentHandler()`, is abstract. All methods founded on the base class must therefore be defined.

```
    class WordContentHandler implements ContentHandler {
      /**
       * Hold onto the locator for location information
       * (not used in Hangman)
       */
      private Locator locator;
      private int currentIndex;    // Index of word being parsed
      private boolean bExtract;

      /**
       * Provide reference to <code>Locator</code> which provides
       * information about where in a document callbacks occur.
       */
      public void setDocumentLocator(Locator locator) {
        this.locator = locator;
      }

      // Start of document
```

```
      public void startDocument() throws SAXException {
        currentIndex = 0;
      }

      // End of document...

      public void endDocument() throws SAXException {}

      // Processing instruction callback....

      public void processingInstruction(String target,
                                        String data) throws SAXException {}

      // Start of a namespace prefix mapping...

      public void startPrefixMapping(String prefix, String uri) {}

      // End of a namespace prefix mapping...

      public void endPrefixMapping(String prefix) {}
```

Most of the `WordContentHandler` class is not of much interest to us for the purposes of the Hangman application. Like any SAX content handler implementation, most of the class methods are callbacks that get called at, before, and after the various XML parsing steps. The `words.xml` document is fairly simple, and we are only interested in the contents of the <word> tags. Selecting the randomly selected word is the job of the `startElement()` method:

```
      // Start of a document element / tag...

      public void startElement(String namespaceURI, String localName,
                               String rawName,
                               Attributes atts) throws SAXException {

        if ((localName.equals("word")) && (currentIndex == index)) {
          bExtract = true;
        } else {
          bExtract = false;
          currentIndex++;
        }
      }

      // End of a document element / tag...

      public void endElement(String namespaceURI, String localName,
                             String rawName) throws SAXException {}
```

The `startElement()` method is called whenever the SAX parser detects the beginning of an XML element. The `localName` argument of this method is a string that contains the name of the detected tag, not including namespace identifiers.

Since the `WordContentHandler` class is nested within the `Hangman_WordFileParser` class, our content handler has access to the public members of `Hangman_WordFileParser`. This means that the random integer passed to the `Hangman_WordFileParser()` constructor is accessible. This random integer is stored in the containing class's `index` member.

So, to select the word corresponding to the random index passed to the `Hangman_WordFileParser()` constructor, we simply maintain a count of the number of times the `startElement()` method has been called. This count is the `WordContentHandler` member `currentIndex`. If the tag being parsed (as indicated by the `localName` argument) equals `"word"`, `currentIndex` is compared to `index`. If `currentIndex` and `index` are equal, the Boolean member `bExtract` is set to `true`.

Once `bExtract` is true, the contents of the parsed `<word>` tag can be extracted and returned as the secret Hangman word. This is the role of the `WordContentHandler.characters()` method. This callback method is called to report the character data contents of XML tags. Therefore, after the random `<word>` tag has been detected, the content handler needs to tell the `characters()` method to save the parsed characters as the secret Hangman word:

```
// Element / tag content characters...

public void characters(char[] ch, int start,
                       int end) throws SAXException {

  if (bExtract) {
    if ((word == null) && (ch != null)) {
      word = new String(ch, start, end);
      bExtract = false;
    }
  }
}
```

The `characters()` method is called to parse the character data contained by any XML tag in the document. In order to know which characters to save as our desired word, the `bExtract` member is tested. It will only be `true` after the correct random number of `<word>` tags has been parsed. `bExtract` is set back to false after the correct word has been parsed. This must be done since the parser will finish parsing the entire `words.xml` file even after the correct random word has been found.

The secret word is stored in the `Hangman_WordFileParser` class `word` data member. The JSP code that invokes our parser will therefore have access to the randomly selected word by calling the `Hangman_WordFileParser.getWord()` accessor method. We will see how the `words.xml` file parser is used by our application a little later. Meanwhile, here's the rest of the `WordContentHandler` class:

```
// Skip over whitespace...

public void ignorableWhitespace(char[] ch, int start,
                                int end) throws SAXException {

  String s = new String(ch, start, end);
}

// report any skipped elements, attributes, etc...

public void skippedEntity(String name) throws SAXException {}
```

```
   }

   class WordErrorHandler implements ErrorHandler {

     // This reports a warning that has occurred...

     public void warning(SAXParseException exception) throws SAXException {

       throw new SAXException("Warning encountered");
     }

     // This will report an error that has occurred...

     public void error(SAXParseException exception) throws SAXException {

       throw new SAXException("Error encountered");
     }

     // This reports fatal errors...

     public void fatalError(SAXParseException exception)
             throws SAXException {

       throw new SAXException("Fatal Error encountered");
     }
   }
```

Generating the Hangman XML Using A JSP

We now look at how to generate the Hangman XML data from a JavaServer Page. The JSP file
Hangman_XMLGen.jsp generates the XML data for the Hangman game:

```
<%@ page import="java.io.*" %>
<%@ page import="java.util.*" %>
<%@ page import="Hangman_WordFileParser" %>

<%
  String fileName = "xml/words.xml";
    String action = request.getParameter("action");
    String word = null;
    StringBuffer encWord = new StringBuffer();
    int nWordIndex;
```

Note that this JSP first sets the content type returned by the HTTP response to text/plain. This is because
the response is plain text XML, not WML or HTML:

```
      response.setContentType("text/plain");

      //Parse words.xml file and extract a word at random
      if ( (action != null) && (action.equals("getword")) ){
        nWordIndex = (int)(java.lang.Math.random()*10)+1;
```

```
Hangman_WordFileParser parser = new Hangman_WordFileParser(nWordIndex);
InputStream ios = application.getResourceAsStream(fileName);
parser.parseWordFile(ios);
  word = parser.getWord();
  if ( (word == null) || (word.equals("")) ){
    return;
  }
  for (int i = 0; i < word.length(); i++) {
    encWord.append("*");
  }
}
%>
```

This JSP supports only one named parameter, called `action`. This only recognized value for this parameter is `getword`. As the name suggests, this named value combination is used to ask the web server to select a secret word at random from the `words.xml` document. A random `int` between 1 and 10 is generated, and that value is then passed into an instance of our `Hangman_WordFileParser` java class.

The selected word is stored in the `word` variable. The string variable `encWord` stores the word with each letter replaced by an asterisk. This is used as the contents of the `<result>` tag that provides a visual representation of the number of letters the player has guessed correctly. The rest of `Hangman_XMLGen.jsp` outputs the Hangman XML back to the entity that invoked this JSP:

```
<hangman>
  <heading/>

    <Screen_Hangman>
      <Screen_Hangman_Enter>

        <Screen_Hangman_Vars>
          <%
            out.println("<result>" + encWord + "</result>\r\n");
            if (word != null)
              out.println("<word>" + word + "</word>\r\n");
            else
              out.println("<word></word>\r\n");
          %>
          <answer></answer>
          <score>0</score>
        </Screen_Hangman_Vars>

      </Screen_Hangman_Enter>

      <Screen_Hangman_Options />
    </Screen_Hangman>

    <Screen_Play>
      <Screen_Play_Enter>
        <Screen_Play_OnGuess>
          <Screen_Play_Content />
        </Screen_Play_OnGuess>
      </Screen_Play_Enter>
    </Screen_Play>

    <Screen_Answer>
```

```
        <Screen_Answer_OnGuess>
          <Screen_Answer_Content />
        </Screen_Answer_OnGuess>
      </Screen_Answer>

  </hangman>
```

Hangman.jsp

The code that invokes `Hangman_XMLGen.jsp` is the JSP file `Hangman.jsp`. Users start the Hangman application by browsing to this JSP file. The primary purpose of `Hangman.jsp` is to ask `Hangman_XMLGen.jsp` to generate the XML associated with the Hangman game, and then transform that XML content into the appropriate browser presentation language via XSLT.

Just like `Hangman_XMLGen.jsp`, `Hangman.jsp` recognizes only the `action` parameter. In this case, as with `Hangman_XMLGen.jsp`, the only parameter value used is `getword`. Since `Hangman.jsp` is the user's only entry point into the Hangman application, this JSP file must initiate any request that the server select a hidden word. As we will see shortly, the action parameter value is simply passed on to `Hangman_XMLGen.jsp`.

`Hangman.jsp` uses the Apache Xalan XSLT package for its XSLT transformations. Xalan is the XSLT counterpart of the Xerces XML parser used by the `Hangman_WordFileParser` class for parsing the `words.xml` file we saw earlier.

The complete `Hangman.jsp` file is shown below:

```
<%@ page import="java.io.InputStream" %>
<%@ page import="java.io.IOException" %>
<%@ page import="java.net.URL" %>

<%@ page import="org.apache.xalan.xslt.XSLTInputSource" %>
<%@ page import="org.apache.xalan.xslt.XSLTProcessor" %>
<%@ page import="org.apache.xalan.xslt.XSLTProcessorFactory" %>
<%@ page import="org.apache.xalan.xslt.XSLTResultTarget" %>

<%
    /* The hostname variable may need to be changed depending on
     * where you're running Hangman.jsp from. In this case, we
     * assume the hostname is localhost this could also be 127.0.0.1
     */
    String hostname = "localhost";
    int portNumber = 8080;
    String wml_stylesheet = "xsl/Hangman-WML.xsl";
    String htm_stylesheet = "xsl/Hangman-HTML.xsl";

    XSLTInputSource stylesheet = null;
    String userAgent = request.getHeader("User-Agent");
    String action = request.getParameter("action");
    String file = "/ch22/Hangman_XMLGen.jsp";
    URL Hangman_XMLGenURL;
```

Hangman.jsp first determines the requesting browser type by examining the HTTP request User-Agent header. For the UP.Browser, this header contains the substring UP.Browser. The User-Agent header for HTTP requests originating from Internet Explorer contains the substring MSIE.

Testing for these substrings is how Hangman.jsp is able to decide which XSLT stylesheet to assign to the variable stylesheet. This variable is an instance of the Xalan XSLTInputSource class. Instances of this class are used to represent XSLT stylesheets.

```
/* Select the XSL stylesheet appropriate for the client's browser
 * by examining the HTTP request User-Agent header.
 */
  if (userAgent.indexOf("UP.Browser")>=0){
  //Requesting browser is UP.Browser
    response.setContentType("text/vnd.wap.wml");
    InputStream ios = application.getResourceAsStream(wml_stylesheet);
    stylesheet = new XSLTInputSource(ios);
  }
  else if (userAgent.indexOf("MSIE")>=0){
  // Requesting browser is Internet Explorer
    response.setContentType("text/html");
    InputStream ios = application.getResourceAsStream(htm_stylesheet);
    stylesheet = new XSLTInputSource(ios);
  }
```

After determining the correct XSLT stylesheet to use for transforming the Hangman XML, Hangman.jsp opens an HTTP connection to Hangman_XMLGen.jsp. Any action parameter value that may have accompanied the original Hangman.jsp request is forwarded to Hangman_XMLGen.jsp. The InputStream that results from this connection contains the generated XML for the Hangman game.

```
Hangman_XMLGenURL = new URL("http", hostname, portNumber,
                          file+"?action="+action);

InputStream in = Hangman_XMLGenURL.openStream();
```

As an alternative to retrieving Hangman_XMLGen.jsp using an HTTP connection, we could use Custom Tags to perform the transformation (see Chapter 8), or a filter (see Chapters 14-15).

The final and perhaps most important part of Hangman.jsp is the code that transforms the XML into the appropriate browser presentation language:

```
try {
  XSLTProcessor processor = XSLTProcessorFactory.getProcessor();
  //Transform XML into HTML with the appropriate style sheet
  processor.process(new XSLTInputSource(in),
                  stylesheet, new XSLTResultTarget (out));
} catch (Exception ignored){}
%>
```

We obtain a Xalan XSLTProcessor instance through the XSLTProcessorFactory, which, like the rest of the Xalan classes, is part of the org.apache.xalan.xslt package. The XSLTProcessor method which transforms XML is called process(), and has the following definition:

```
void process(
    XSLTInputSource xmlSource,
    XSLTInputSource xslStylesheet,
    XSLTResultTarget target
);
```

The `xmlSource` and `xslStylesheet` arguments are the input XML stream and the XSLT stylesheet to use when transforming that XML, respectively. The `target` argument tells the processor where to write the result of the XSLT transformation.

In the case of `hangman.jsp`, the transformation result is written directly to the JSP output stream, meaning that the transformed XML is directly sent as the `hangman.jsp` HTTP response. For requests made by WAP browsers, this response will therefore contain the WML deck representation of the Hangman game screens.

Finally, have a play with the Hangman application by accessing http://localhost:8080/ch22/Hangman.jsp in the UP.Simulator browser.

A Small Leap: Making Hangman Work for HTML Browsers

Our discussion of the Hangman application has focused on how it works with the Wireless Application Protocol and WML based browser. But after all of this work designing and implementing the Hangman application such that it works with XML instead of a specific browser markup language, it should be a simple task to get the Hangman game to work for an HTML based browser such as Internet Explorer.

This is indeed the case. The beauty of our XML based implementation of the hidden word file `words.xml` and the XML structure of the Hangman game screens is that it can be used as a model for a variety of content-specific application environments. All that needs to be done to make the application work for an HTML base environment is to implement a new XSLT stylesheet for generating HTML.

Since the XSLT stylesheet for HTML is similar in structure to that for transforming our XML format into WML, we will not spend a lot of time explaining the details of this file. However, there is one major issue to point out here. As we have seen, in WAP applications every screen is implemented as a separate WML card. This is the case in the WAP version of the Hangman application as well. Each screen is a separate card, and these cards are sent from the web server to the WAP browser as a single WML document called a deck.

The HTML document model is different, though. A single HTML document does not contain multiple screens. So in an attempt to preserve the interaction model of the WML version of the application, the HTML version of Hangman will rely heavily on alert dialog screens implemented with JavaScript.

For example, the screen with which the user guesses a letter looks like this:

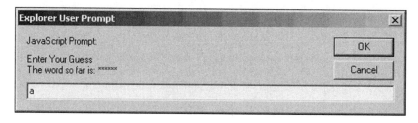

As in the WML version of the application, this screen displays the letters guessed so far in the game. One call to the JavaScript `prompt()` function creates this screen. A similar JavaScript function call creates the input screen used to guess the Hangman word:

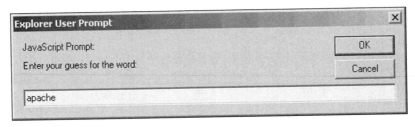

When run in Internet Explorer 5.0, the HTML version of the main Hangman screen looks like this:

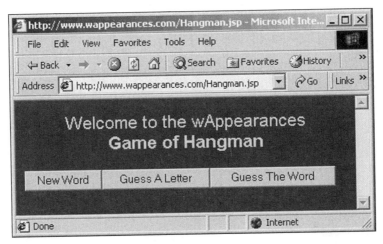

The Hangman-HTML.xsl File

This section presents the XSLT stylesheet used to transform the Hangman XML document format into HTML and JavaScript. Since it is assumed that the reader is more familiar with HTML and JavaScript than WML and WMLScript, this code is presented for your perusal and study without further discussion:

```
<?xml version="1.0"?>
<xsl:stylesheet version="1.0" xmlns:xsl="http://www.w3.org/1999/XSL/Transform">
  <xsl:template match="hangman">
   <HTML>

   <BODY BGCOLOR="#202080" TEXT="YELLOW" LINK="YELLOW">

    <FONT FACE="Lucida,San-Serif,Arial,Helvetica" SIZE="5">
    <CENTER>
    Welcome to the wAppearances
    <BR />
    <STRONG>Game of Hangman</STRONG>
    </CENTER>
      </FONT>
      <xsl:apply-templates/>
   </BODY>
```

```
    </HTML>
  </xsl:template>
  " "
  <xsl:template match="Screen_Hangman">
     <SCRIPT LANGUAGE="JavaScript">
        <xsl:apply-templates />
     </SCRIPT>
  </xsl:template>
  <xsl:template match="Screen_Hangman_Enter">
        <xsl:apply-templates />
  </xsl:template>
```

The following XSLT template fills the `result`, `word`, `answer`, and `score` variables with the appropriate values:

```
  <xsl:template match="Screen_Hangman_Vars">
    var result="<xsl:value-of select="result" />";
    var word="<xsl:value-of select="word" />";
    var answer="<xsl:value-of select="answer" />";
    var score=0;
  </xsl:template>
```

This template generates the JavaScript for event handling within the page:

```
  <xsl:template match="Screen_Hangman_Options">
  <![CDATA [
```

The next function enables the user to select a new word to guess:

```
  function NewWord() {
  window.navigate("http://localhost:8080/ch22/Hangman.jsp?action=getword");
    }
```

The `matchChar()` function checks to see if the guessed letter is present in the hidden word:

```
  function matchChar(guess) {
     var resultold = result;
    var _result = "";

    for (var i = 0; i < word.length; i++) {
    if (guess == word.charAt(i)) {
      _result = _result + guess;
    }
    else {
      _result = _result + resultold.charAt(i);
    }
    }
    score += 1;
  result = _result;
  }
```

The following functions allow a user to guess a word and a letter, respectively:

```
function Guess(){
  var _answer;
  _answer = prompt("Enter your guess for the word:", "");

  if (_answer != null) { //i.e., if the cancel button is pressed
    if (_answer == word){
      alert("You Won! You guessed the word in " + score + " tries!");
    }else{
      alert("Your guess " + _answer + " is incorrect. Keep playing...");
    }
  }
}

function GuessLetter(){
  var guess;

  guess = prompt("Enter Your Guess\nThe word so far is: "+result, "");
  if (guess != null){ //i.e., user did not Cancel
    matchChar(guess);
  }
}
]]>

</xsl:template>
```

The final section of XSLT code processes the rest of the Hangman XML document:

```
<xsl:template match="Screen_Play">
    <xsl:apply-templates />
</xsl:template>
<xsl:template match="Screen_Play_Enter">
    <xsl:apply-templates />
</xsl:template>
<xsl:template match="Screen_Play_OnGuess">
    <xsl:apply-templates />
</xsl:template>
<xsl:template match="Screen_Play_Content">
  <P>
    <CENTER>
    <INPUT TYPE="BUTTON" VALUE="New Word" onclick="NewWord()"></INPUT>
    <INPUT TYPE="BUTTON" VALUE="Guess A Letter" onclick="GuessLetter()"></INPUT>
    <INPUT TYPE="BUTTON" VALUE="Guess The Word" onclick="Guess()">
      </INPUT>
      </CENTER>
    </P>
</xsl:template>
<xsl:template match="Screen_Answer">
    <xsl:apply-templates />
</xsl:template>
<xsl:template match="Screen_Answer_OnGuess">
    <xsl:apply-templates />
</xsl:template>
</xsl:stylesheet>
```

Summary

In this chapter, we have taken a quick look at how to write WAP applications using JSP, XML and XSLT. We looked specifically at these areas:

❑ The WAP application programming model and environment, and WAP MIME types.

❑ Our example used JSPs to create an XML document, which was then transformed into WML or HTML depending on the browser it was being accessed from.

Using these standard Internet programming technologies, you are now well on your way to delivering your Internet applications to a variety of WAP enabled mobile devices.

The next chapter looks at another aspect of dynamically creating non-HTML content: generating binary content types.

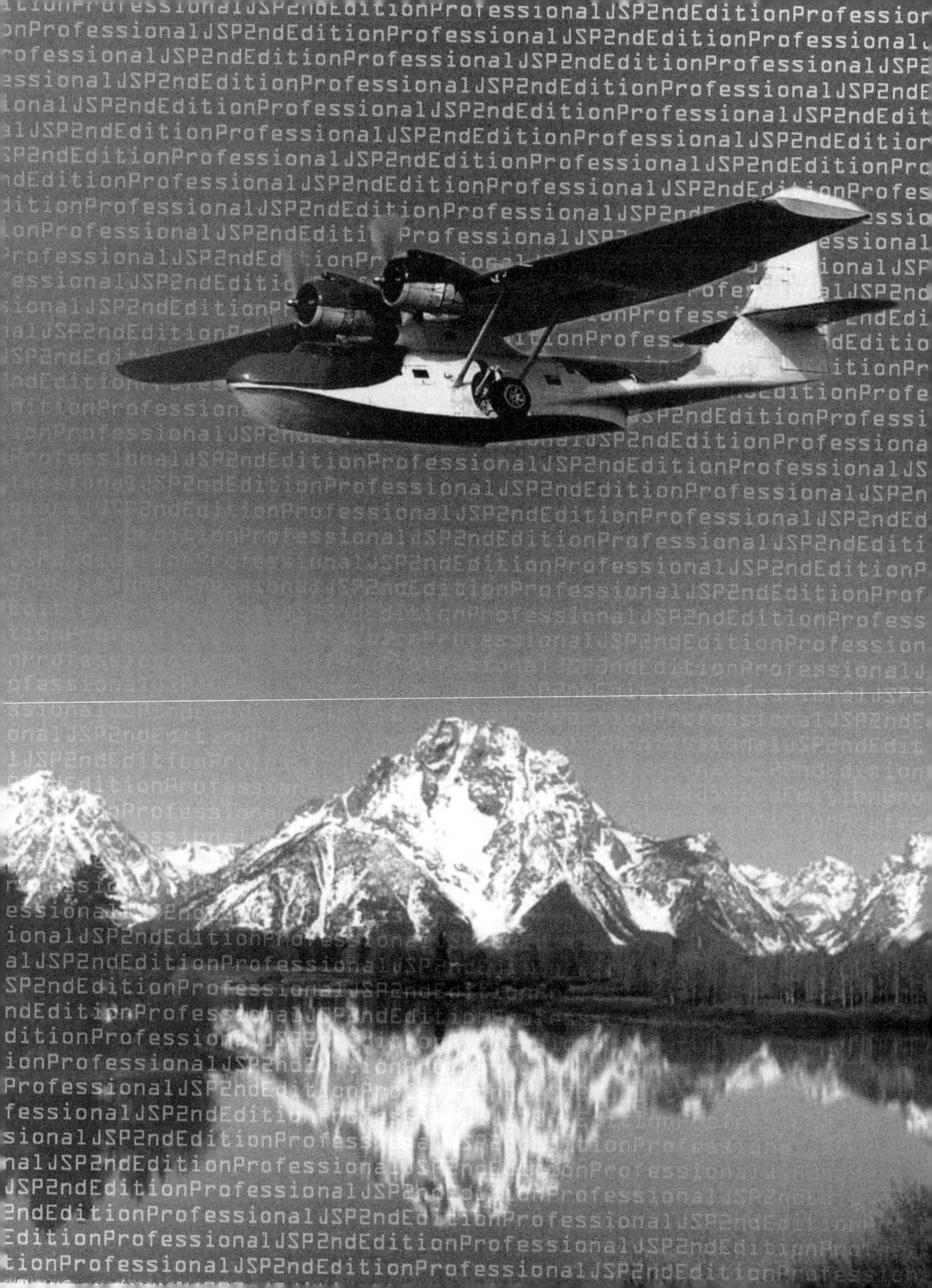
ProfessionalJSP2ndEdition

Generating Binary Content

Up to this point, we have covered the process of generating textual content from a Servlet or JSP extensively, but what about the generation of binary content? Servlets and JSP are not limited to returning HTML; they can dynamically generate images and other binary content quite easily. The benefits of creating content on-the-fly include increased flexibility and functionality of web applications. Dynamically creating binary content has never been easier – a direct result of publicly available tools such as Xerces, Xalan, FOP, and Batik. In this chapter we will focus on:

- ❑ Returning binary content from Servlets and JSPs
- ❑ Generating bitmap or pixel based images (JPG, PNG, and so on)
- ❑ Generating Scalable Vector Graphics (SVG) images
- ❑ Creating Adobe's Portable Document Format (PDF) files

Returning Binary Content

The process of returning binary content from a Servlet is fairly simple. The first step is to use the `setContentType()` method of the `HttpServletResponse` object to set the appropriate MIME content type. The second step is to write the bytes of the binary content to the appropriate `ServletOutputStream`. Returning binary data from JSP can be a problem, which we will discuss later. So the first item for discussion is: what exactly are the various MIME content types?

MIME Content Types

The format of data returned by a Servlet is specified by a MIME (Multipurpose Internet Mail Extension) Content Type. All content types are of the form `media-type/sub-type`. Five top level media types are defined by RFC2046. See: http://info.internet.isi.edu/in-notes/rfc/files/rfc2046.txt for more detail about this.

The top-level media types are:

MIME type	Purpose
text	For content types that return textual information. For example, the default content type for a JSP page is text/html. XML data is normally formatted as text/xml. Plain text is formatted as text/plain.
image	For content types that return graphical data. image/jpeg, image/gif, image/png are common. These types are ones we will be concerned with in the chapter.
audio	For returning audio data. One common format is audio/wav which is used for wav files.
video	For returning video data. AVI and MPEG files are represented by video/avi and video/mpeg respectively.
application	For data that requires an application external to the browser. Some common content types are application/msword for Microsoft Word documents, and application/pdf for Adobe's Portable Document Format documents.

All types except for text represent binary content, as far as generation from Servlets and JSP is concerned. The focus here will be on the image and application media types.

Using Content Types

In this section we will examine how to set the content type, both in Servlets and JSP. We will also examine why Servlets are the preferred method of generating binary content.

Servlets

When using Servlets, the content type is specified using the setContentType() method of the ServletResponse object. The following snippet shows how to set the content type to image/gif for returning a GIF image:

```
response.setContentType("image/gif");
```

The next step for returning binary data is to write the data back to the client.

> When using binary data, it is important to remember that you should use the
> ServletOutputStream from the response.getOutputStream() method, and not
> the PrintWriter object returned from the response.getWriter() method. This is
> because a PrintWriter translates the data from the internal Unicode representation to
> the character encoding that the client accepts.

The ServletOutputStream is retrieved as follows:

```
ServletOutputStream out = response.getOutputStream();
```

The RetrieveFile Class

The last step is to actually write the data back to the client. To demonstrate, the following `RetrieveFile` Servlet takes two parameters:

❑ `file` – the file to return to the client. This file is relative to the web application directory

❑ `contentType` – the content type to set as the return type

```java
import java.io.*;
import java.net.*;
import java.util.*;
import javax.servlet.*;
import javax.servlet.http.*;

public class RetrieveFile extends HttpServlet {

    protected void doGet(HttpServletRequest request,
                         HttpServletResponse response) throws
                         ServletException, IOException {
    ServletOutputStream out = response.getOutputStream();
    ServletContext      context =
        this.getServletConfig().getServletContext();

        try {

            // set the content type to the parameter passed.
            response.setContentType(request.getParameter("contentType"));

            // read the "file" request parameter. This should be a file
            // relative to the web application directory.
            String file = request.getParameter("file");
```

Next, note the use of `context.getResourceAsStream()`. This returns an `InputStream` that is opened to the file located relative to the `ServletContext` (in other words in the webapp directory):

```java
            InputStream istream = context.getResourceAsStream(file);
            BufferedInputStream bis = new BufferedInputStream(istream);
            BufferedOutputStream bos = new BufferedOutputStream(out);
```

Also, be aware of the use of the `BufferedOutputStream`. Many Servlet engines do not use buffered streams when writing the data back to the client, so it is a good idea to check your particular implementation. For example, early versions of JRun and JServ do not use buffered streams. If your Servlet engine does not provide buffering, you should make sure to use a `BufferedOutputStream` to return data to the client. If the Servlet engine does provide buffering, the `ServletOutputStream` should be used:

```java
            // stream the file back to the client
            byte[]buffer = new byte[4096];
            int size;

            size = bis.read(buffer);

            while (size != -1) {
              bos.write(buffer, 0, size);
```

```
            size = bis.read(buffer);
        }

        bis.close();
        bos.flush();
    } catch (Exception e) {
        e.printStackTrace();
        }
    }

}
```

The following screenshot illustrates the use of the `RetrieveFile` Servlet to retrieve the `wroxlogo.gif` file at: http://localhost:8080/ch23/servlet/RetrieveFile?file=/wroxlogo.gif&contentType=image/gif:

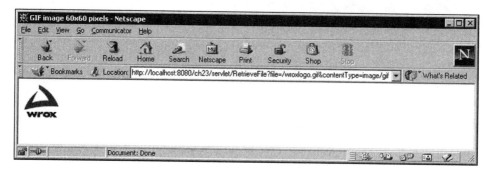

JSP

Returning binary content from JSP can be a problem. The reason is that the implicit `out` object is an instance of `JspWriter`, and `JspWriter` converts the internal Unicode representation of the data into a character set specified by the client. So, although it is possible to do so, JSPs should not be used when sending binary content.

Bitmap Image Generation

The previous section examined how to return binary content to the browser, but we want to actually generate content. As part of this chapter, we will be creating a web application that charts stock performance over a period of time.

Web Application Setup

All of the examples in this chapter are available in the code download as part of the `ch23` webapp. Let's start off by explaining the components and requirements for the examples now. The directory structure for the web application is shown below:

File(s)	Description
`/*.jsp`	JSP files used throughout the chapter.
`/welcome.svg`	Example SVG file.

File(s)	Description
/wroxlogo.gif	Example GIF file for RetrieveFile example.
/xml/*.xml	Input XML files containing stock data.
/xml/*.xsl	XSLT stylesheets used to transform XML files.
/xml/*.fo	XSL FO stylesheets.
/WEB-INF/fop.tld	Tag Library Descriptor for PDF file generation.
/WEB-INF/xsl.tld	Tag Library Descriptor for XSL transformer.
/WEB-INF/classes/*	Servlet and tag library class files.
/WEB-INF/lib/batik-awt-util.jar	Needed for the g2d_2_svg class. From http://xml.apache.org/batik, v.1.0 Beta.
/WEB-INF/lib/batik-util.jar	Needed for the g2d_2_svg class. From http://xml.apache.org/batik, v.1.0 Beta.
/WEB-INF/lib/fop.jar	Needed for PDF generation. From http://xml.apache.org/fop, v.0.16.
/WEB-INF/lib/w3c.jar	Needed for PDF generation. From http://xml.apache.org/fop, v.0.16.
/WEB-INF/lib/xalan.jar	Needed for XSL transformation. From http://xml.apache.org/xalan, v.1.2.2.
/WEB-INF/lib/xerces.jar	Needed for XML parsing. From http://xml.apache.org/xerces, v.1.2.2.

An example of a stock performance chart is shown below. The chart is drawn from the stock closing prices for a mythical dot com company, AnyDot.com, from January 1999 to December 2000:

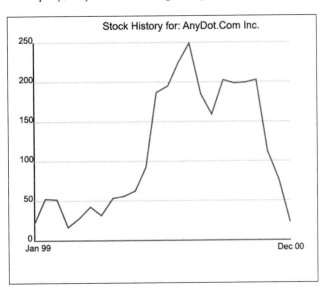

What are the steps needed to produce a chart like this one? The major points that need to be addressed are:

- ❑ Retrieve values from the source data

- ❑ Calculate the maximum closing price, to properly scale the Y axis values

- ❑ Calculate the offset between X axis values, to use the entire width of the chart

- ❑ Draw the X and Y axes, scaled appropriately

- ❑ Draw the closing price line

- ❑ Render the image back to the browser

The chart above was generated from an XML file, dotcom.xml (in the /xml directory). The format of this file will be used for all of the examples in this chapter:

```xml
<?xml version="1.0" encoding="UTF-8"?>
<StockHistory company="AnyDot.Com Inc.">
    <Period>
        <Date>Jan 99</Date>
        <Open>12.0938</Open>
        <High>25.6875</High>
        <Low>12.50</Low>
        <Close>21.8125</Close>
        <Volume>768200</Volume>
    </Period>
    <Period>
        <Date>Feb 99</Date>
        <Open>67.1875</Open>
        <High>72.175</High>
        <Low>48.375</Low>
        <Close>52.50</Close>
        <Volume>1635500</Volume>
    </Period>

    . . .

</StockHistory>
```

The dotcom.xml file contains a root <StockHistory> element, followed by <Period> elements for each month. Let's assume for now that the XML has already been parsed and we have an org.w3c.dom.Element object for the root <StockHistory> element, called root. We now need to build a class to create the image from the data in the XML file.

Creating the Image

In this section we will review a class, HistoryFrame, which we will use to create the image of the stock performance chart. This class makes use of the Abstract Windowing Toolkit and Graphics2D objects to generate images, so let's take a closer look at these first.

AWT and Graphics2D Objects

One method of generating images in Servlets is using the Abstract Windowing Toolkit (AWT). Although mostly associated with applications and applets, AWT components can be used in Servlets. The key is the concept of **double-buffering**. Double-buffering is the process of drawing complex graphics off-screen, and then copying the entire buffer to a viewable AWT component. Double-buffering speeds up drawing because block memory operations can be used to copy the entire 'buffered' image to the screen. Otherwise, each drawing operation will be executed one at a time, at a much slower pace. The same can be done in Servlets, but the buffered image is never copied to a viewable component. Thus the same code that creates a chart for an applet can be reused to generate the chart from a Servlet.

> Note that the use of AWT components requires an available display, even though the components will never be rendered to the screen. Why does this matter? Most production servers operate without displays, in 'headless' mode. For Unix boxes, this means a DISPLAY variable must be set to a machine with a display, or a 'virtual' X server must be run. This requirement should disappear in JDK 1.4, when a headless mode for Java is introduced.

Normal AWT methods can be used to create the image. Graphics2D object rendering is used to create the proper lines and text for our chart. More information on using the 2D Graphics objects can be found at http://java.sun.com/docs/books/tutorial/2d/index.html.

The steps involved in drawing any shape (line, text, path) involve setting rendering attributes in the Graphics2D object. Attributes pertinent to this example are:

❑ **Paint** – using setPaint(Paint paint) to set the color of the shape

❑ **Font** – using setFont(Font font) to set what font is used if text is being drawn

❑ **Stroke** – using setStroke(Stroke stroke) to set the line width used to draw the shape

The shapes needed for our example are represented by classes from the java.awt.geom package. The stock history chart requires the use of the following:

❑ java.awt.geom.Line2D.Double – for the axis

❑ java.awt.geom.GeneralPath – for the closing price line

The HistoryFrame Class

We will now examine the HistoryFrame class from the beginning. We need to import various AWT classes, as well as XML DOM classes (for more information on the org.w3c.dom.Node object and the DOM API, refer to Chapter 12). Note that the HistoryFrame object extends the Swing component javax.swing.JFrame, so this class could be reused for an applet or application.

```
import java.awt.*;
import java.awt.geom.*;
import java.awt.image.*;
import javax.swing.JFrame;

import org.w3c.dom.*;

public class HistoryFrame extends JFrame {
```

Next, we have the `HistoryFrame()` constructor, which takes the XML document root as an argument:

```
private Element root;

public HistoryFrame(Element root) {
  this.root = root;
}
```

Since all of the price data is stored as text nodes of the XML, a small helper function would be appropriate to retrieve the values from the XML: `getValue()`. This is merely a convenience method to extract values of text nodes from the XML, making sure the text is normalized into a single element before retrieving it:

```
private String getValue(Node node) {
  node.normalize();
  String value = node.getFirstChild().getNodeValue();
  return value;
}
}
```

Another necessary function is provided by the `findMax()` method. In order to scale the values properly, the maximum stock price must be found. `findMax()` takes an `org.w3c.dom.Element` object, and a `String` object. It uses the `getElementsByTagName()` method to retrieve all of the `<Close>` nodes from the root element, and then uses the `getValue()` procedure to access the closing stock prices:

```
private double findMax(Element element, String name) {
  double max = 0.0;

  NodeList nl = element.getElementsByTagName(name);

  double current;
  for (int i = 0; i < nl.getLength(); i++) {
    try {
      current = Double.parseDouble(getValue(nl.item(i)));
      if (current > max) {
        max = current;
      }
    } catch (NumberFormatException nfe) {
      System.out.println ("Error converting to double: " +
                          nl.item(i).getNodeValue());
    }
  }
  return max;
}
```

The `paint()` method is the heart of `HistoryFrame`. The structure is similar to most applet or application `paint` methods. One item to note is that the background color must be set, or none of the remaining drawing operations will be visible:

```
public void paint(Graphics g) {

  // cast to a Graphics2D object and get size
```

```
Graphics2D g2 = (Graphics2D) g;
Dimension dim = this.getSize();

// make sure to fill in the background color
g2.setColor(Color.white);
g2.fillRect(0,0,dim.width,dim.height);
```

The findmax() method we saw earlier in the code is not all that is required to properly scale the Y axis. How would it look if the maximum closing price was 36.50? Scaling the Y axis to multiples of 50 will allow the minor grid lines to be placed on the chart easily. For example, the Y axis will range from 0 to 50 when the maximum is 36.50, but be 250 when it is 236.50. The X axis is scaled in a similar way; based on the number of <Period> nodes, the offset between X values is calculated based on the total width of the chart. The RenderingHints are added to remove the aliasing effect when lines are drawn diagonally:

```
// find the largest y value, to make the scale properly
double maxClose = findMax(root, "Close");

// calculate the max Y, multiple of 50.
long yMax = maxClose==0 ? 50 : Math.round((maxClose+25.0)/50.0) * 50;

// calculate the X offset.
int numberPeriods = root.getElementsByTagName("Period").getLength();
double xOffset = numberPeriods<2 ? 0 : (dim.width - 80.0)
                / (numberPeriods - 1.0);

g2.setRenderingHint(RenderingHints.KEY_ANTIALIASING,
                    RenderingHints.VALUE_ANTIALIAS_ON);
```

The X and Y axes lines are drawn black, with a stroke width of 2 pixels. The minor Y divisions are drawn in light gray, with a stroke width of 1 pixel. The code assumes you never want to draw too close to the edge (at least 40 pixels), and calculates the end of the lines based on the width and height of the Graphics2D object itself:

```
// draw the x and y axis
g2.setPaint(Color.black);
g2.setStroke(new BasicStroke(2.0f));
g2.draw(new Line2D.Double(40,40, 40,dim.height-60));
g2.draw(new Line2D.Double(40,dim.height-60,
                          dim.width-40,dim.height-60));

// draw the y axis scale
g2.setPaint(Color.lightGray);
g2.setStroke(new BasicStroke(1.0f));
for (int i=0; i <= 5; i++) {
   g2.draw(new Line2D.Double(40,dim.height-60-(i*60),
                             dim.width-40, dim.height-60-(i*60)));
}
```

The title of the chart is made using the company attribute of the StockHistory node. The FontMetric object is used to help decide where the title should start, in order to appear in the center of the chart. The drawString() method is then called to write the title:

```
//draw the title
g2.setPaint(Color.black);
String title = "Stock History for: " + root.getAttribute("company");
Font font = g2.getFont().deriveFont(12.0f);
g2.setFont(font);
FontMetrics metrics = g2.getFontMetrics();
g2.drawString(title, dim.width/2-metrics.stringWidth(title)/2, 20);
```

The labels for the X and Y axes are then drawn:

```
//draw the y axis labels
font = g2.getFont().deriveFont(10.0f);
g2.setFont(font);
metrics = g2.getFontMetrics();
long yDivisions = yMax / 5;
for (int i = 0; i <= 5; i++) {
  // calculate the x position based on width of label
  String ylabel = String.valueOf(yDivisions*i);
  g2.drawString(ylabel, 35-metrics.stringWidth(ylabel),
                dim.height-60-(i*60));
}

//draw the x axis labels
NodeList nl = root.getElementsByTagName("Date");
g2.drawString(getValue(nl.item(0)),
              25, dim.height-45);
g2.drawString(getValue(nl.item(nl.getLength()-1)),
              dim.width-60, dim.height-45);
```

The closing price line is drawn using a `GeneralPath` object, made by moving to the first point in the series, and then drawing lines to the next point in the series. The line is drawn red, with a stroke width of 2 pixels:

```
//draw the graph
g2.setPaint(Color.red);
g2.setStroke(new BasicStroke(2.0f));
GeneralPath path = new GeneralPath(GeneralPath.WIND_EVEN_ODD,
                                   numberPeriods);

// loop through all of the "Close" elements, filling
// in path, scaling in relation to yMax
nl = root.getElementsByTagName("Close");
for (int i = 0; i < nl.getLength(); i++) {
  double yValue = Double.parseDouble(getValue(nl.item(i)));
  if (i == 0) {
    // if first item, do a moveTo, not a lineTo
    path.moveTo(40, Math.round(dim.height-60 -
                       ((yValue / yMax) * (dim.height-100))));
  } else {
    path.lineTo(Math.round(i * xOffset)+40,
                Math.round(dim.height-60 -
                       ((yValue / yMax) * (dim.height-100))));
  }
}
g2.draw(path);
}
```

The calculations for the X locations of the `lineTo()` methods move the appropriate distance from left to right, based on the `xOffset` calculated earlier. The Y location of the `lineTo()` methods is calculated as a percentage of the maximum Y value, `yMax`.

Image Encoding

We now have the chart drawn using `Graphics2D`, but how do we get the image back to the client? We need to encode it into some browser recognizable format, `.gif`, `.jpg`, `.png`, etc. One problem has been that Java does not include any image encoders as part of the core API. This has led to a proliferation of many encoders from various sources, even multiple entries from within Sun. The major ones in use are:

- **ACME GIF Encoder** – at http://www.acme.com/java/software
- **JIMI Software Development Kit** – at http://java.sun.com/products/jimi
- **Java Advanced Imaging API** – at http://java.sun.com/products/java-media/jai
- **Java Image I/O API** – at http://java.sun.com/aboutJava/communityprocess/jsr/jsr_015_iio.html
- **JDK 1.2 and JDK 1.3** – see `com.sun.image.codec.jpeg`

The good news is that the next major release of the JDK (v1.4, 'Merlin') will include the Java Image I/O API as part of the JAI framework.

Although the `com.sun.image.codec.jpeg` package is an internal Sun API included as of JDK 1.2, it is still used due to the fluctuating nature of the current Image I/O Early Access versions.

Encoding images to an `OutputStream` is easy using `com.sun.image.codec.jpeg`, as shown below:

```
// encode the output back to the client
JPEGImageEncoder encoder = JPEGCodec.createJPEGEncoder(out);
encoder.encode(image);
out.flush();
```

The g2d_2_jpg Class

Now that we know how we are going to encode the image back to the client, we can discuss the transition from a `Graphics2D` object to a JPG file. We will use the `g2d_2_jpg` Servlet to do this; this Servlet performs the following operations:

- Sets the content type to `image/jpeg`
- Parses the XML with a DOM parser
- Creates the `HistoryFrame`, `BufferedImage` and `Graphics2D` objects
- Paints the chart onto the `Graphics2D` object
- Encodes the resulting image and streams it back to the browser

Let's now have a look at the source code. The `g2d_2_jpg` Servlet starts by importing the necessary Servlet and AWT classes. Also needed are the Xerces XML classes used to parse the stock history XML file (so remember to include the path to the `xerces.jar` file in your `CLASSPATH`). The width and height of the resulting image are declared as `final` constants.

```
import java.io.*;
import javax.servlet.*;
import javax.servlet.http.*;
```

```
import java.awt.*;
import java.awt.image.*;

import org.w3c.dom.*;
import org.apache.xerces.parsers.DOMParser;
import org.xml.sax.InputSource;

import com.sun.image.codec.jpeg.*;

public class g2d_2_jpg extends HttpServlet {

   private static final int WIDTH = 480;
   private static final int HEIGHT = 400;
```

The doGet() method performs the Servlet processing. The context method is used to acquire the XML file represented by the xml parameter passed to the Servlet.

```
protected void doGet(HttpServletRequest request,
                     HttpServletResponse response)
              throws ServletException, IOException {

   ServletOutputStream out = response.getOutputStream();
   ServletContext context = this.getServletConfig().getServletContext();

   try {
     response.setContentType("image/jpeg");

     // read and parse the file specified by xml parameter
     InputStream xmlStream = context.getResourceAsStream
                                 (request.getParameter("xml"));
```

Xerces' DOMParser object is used to parse the XML, and the root element is passed to the HistoryFrame object, set to the proper size.

```
     DOMParser parser = new DOMParser();
     parser.parse(new InputSource(xmlStream));

     Document doc = parser.getDocument();
     Element root = doc.getDocumentElement();

     // create a proper size Frame object
     HistoryFrame dummy = new HistoryFrame(root);
     dummy.setSize(new Dimension(WIDTH, HEIGHT));
```

The most important step is next. A Graphics2D object is created from the BufferedImage object. The HistoryFrame.paint() method is used to construct the chart.

```
     BufferedImage image = new BufferedImage(WIDTH, HEIGHT,
                                          BufferedImage.TYPE_INT_RGB);
     Graphics2D g2 = image.createGraphics();

     // draw the graph onto the image
     dummy.paint(g2);
```

The last step is to use the `JPEGImageEncoder`, discussed earlier, to render the `BufferedImage` to the `ServletOutputStream`:

```
        // encode the output back to the client
        JPEGImageEncoder encoder = JPEGCodec.createJPEGEncoder(out);
        encoder.encode(image);
        out.flush();

    } catch (Exception e) {
        e.printStackTrace();
    }
  }

}
```

By using the `g2d_2_jpg` Servlet, and the `HistoryFrame` object, we now have all the pieces of the puzzle required to create an image of the stock history in the browser. Type the address http://localhost:8080/ch23/servlet/g2d_2_jpg?xml=/xml/dotcom.xml into your browser, and you should get the following display:

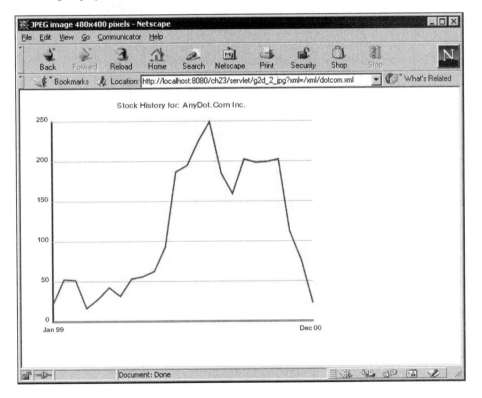

Vector Image Generation

The image that we generated earlier is a 15Kb JPG image. That is because each pixel in the image must be described. If we could describe the shapes required and have the browser render it to the screen, the size of the transferred image would be much smaller. Did you notice how the JPG image from the previous section is somewhat fuzzy? That is what happens when you take a vector command and rasterize it to a pixel based image. If we wanted to resize the image, the JPG would be even more distorted. The answer to this is to use vector based images.

Until recently, the predominant vector format has been Macromedia's Flash; being a proprietary format, it has not been easy to create Flash graphics from any type of web application. That is why Scalable Vector Graphics (SVG) were created.

SVG

SVG is currently a candidate recommendation from the World Wide Web Consortium (W3C). The major advantage that SVG holds over Flash is that **SVG files are entirely XML**. Since XML parsers and XSL translators are freely available, dynamic creation of SVG graphics is very easy. Companies such as Adobe, Sun and IBM are promoting SVG as the answer for creating high quality graphics for the web. Many drawing tools, such as Adobe's Illustrator 9, are exporting SVG XML files directly from their products. For more information about SVG go to http://www.w3c.org/Graphics/SVG.

However, SVG does present one problem because the current dominant browsers on the market today do not yet support SVG natively. For Internet Explorer and Netscape, Adobe provides a plugin that serves this need. Mozilla is also currently building in native support for SVG.

> The examples presented in this section require some type of browser SVG support.
> Adobe's SVG Viewer 2.0 (beta) is currently available for IE and Netscape at:
> http://www.adobe.com/svg/viewer/install/beta.html, and you should download
> this if you wish to run the examples. For a tutorial on SVG see:
> http://www.adobe.com/svg/tutorial/intro.html, and for a reference on SVG see:
> http://www.zvon.org/xxl/svgReference/Output/index.html.

A Simple SVG File

Complex graphics are possible with SVG. Gradients, transformation, animation, mouse and keyboard interactions are all available. We will create a simple SVG file called `welcome.svg` to give you an idea of what an SVG file looks like:

```
<?xml version="1.0"?>
<svg width="200" height="200" viewBox="0 0 200 200">
  <rect style="fill:gray;stroke:black" x="20" y="20" width="160" height="160"/>
```

As you can see, the `<svg>` node is the root XML element. The `"Welcome to SVG!"` text is drawn using the `<text>` element:

```
<text style="font-size:14pt;text-anchor:middle" x="100" y="105">
   Welcome to SVG!
</text>
```

We can draw lines using <path> elements. Also note the <g> element. This element is used to set default information for the two path elements below it, setting the color (stroke) to blue, and the stroke-width to 2 pixels. The points that make up the blue lines are described by the d attribute of the path nodes. The phrase "M40,60 L160,60" specifies to move to the point (40,60) and draw a line to point (160,60):

```
<g style="stroke:blue;stroke-width:2">
    <path d="M40,60 L160,60"/>
    <path d="M40,140 L160,140"/>
</g>
</svg>
```

Let's examine the simple elements that make up welcome.svg at:
http://localhost:8080/ch23/servlet/RetrieveFile?file=welcome.svg&contentType=image/svg-xml. Note that for IE you should add &fakeIE=usethis.svg to the end of the URL too (we'll explain this in a moment). Here's what you should get:

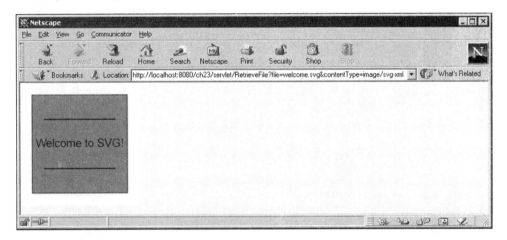

Internet Explorer Idiosyncrasies

At this point it is worth mentioning a quirk of the Microsoft Internet Explorer browser – *IE does not always use the MIME content type set by the server.* Depending on whether IE recognizes the type or not, it handles the content differently, and sometimes not intuitively.

For example, when the Adobe SVG Viewer is installed, the plugin registers image/svg+xml, image/svg-xml, and image/svg as types the Adobe SVG plugin uses. When handling SVG XML files, IE treats the returned image/svg-xml as only a **suggestion**, and tries to examine the content to determine what type of data is being returned. It cannot determine the type from the content, and then relies on the last four characters of the URL to determine the content type. If your URL does not end in ".svg", the Adobe SVG plugin *will not be invoked!*

> To get around this problem, if you are using IE, you should add
> "&fakeIE=usethis.svg" to the end of ALL of the URLs in this chapter.

For more information on how Internet Explorer handles content types, go to
http://msdn.microsoft.com/workshop/networking/moniker/overview/appendix_a.asp.

The g2d_2_svg Class

A great deal of effort has been put forth by many programmers to generate their charts and other binary images using the Graphics2D method used in the previous section. Fortunately, the advantages of SVG can still be realized with only a small amount of change. Sun has been gracious enough to donate an SVGGraphics2D class to Apache's Batik project. SVGGraphics2D extends Graphics2D, and adds functions to output SVG directly.

> The Batik project is available at: **http://xml.apache.org/batik**. The following example requires both the **batik-awt-util.jar** and the **batik-util.jar** file from the Batik 1.0 Beta distribution.

Using the org.apache.batik.util.awt.svg.SVGGraphics2D class, our changes to the g2d_2_jpg class are as follows (note that the following source code can be found in the g2d_2_svg.java file):

```java
import java.io.*;
import javax.servlet.*;
import javax.servlet.http.*;

import java.awt.*;
import java.awt.image.*;
import org.w3c.dom.*;
import org.apache.xerces.parsers.DOMParser;
import org.apache.xerces.dom.DocumentImpl;
import org.xml.sax.InputSource;

//import com.sun.image.codec.jpeg.*;
import org.apache.batik.util.awt.svg.SVGGraphics2D;

//public class g2d_2_jpg extends HttpServlet {
public class g2d_2_svg extends HttpServlet {

  private static final int WIDTH = 480;
  private static final int HEIGHT = 400;

  protected void doGet(HttpServletRequest request,
                       HttpServletResponse response)
                 throws ServletException, IOException {

    ServletOutputStream out = response.getOutputStream();
    ServletContext context = this.getServletConfig().getServletContext();
```

The content type for SVG images is image/svg-xml. Although all SVG files are XML files, text/xml is not used for the content type, as the image/svg-xml type is needed for the Adobe SVG plugin to be invoked:

```java
    try {
      //response.setContentType("image/jpeg");
```

```
                    response.setContentType("image/svg-xml");

                // read and parse the file specified by xml parameter
                InputStream xmlStream = context.getResourceAsStream
                                            (request.getParameter("xml"));
                DOMParser parser = new DOMParser();
                parser.parse(new InputSource(xmlStream));

                Document doc = parser.getDocument();
                Element root = doc.getDocumentElement();

                // create a proper size Frame object
                HistoryFrame dummy = new HistoryFrame(root);
                dummy.setSize(new Dimension(WIDTH, HEIGHT));
                BufferedImage image = new BufferedImage(WIDTH, HEIGHT,
                                            BufferedImage.TYPE_INT_RGB);
                //Graphics2D g2 = image.createGraphics();

                // create the SVGGraphics2D object, remember to set the size!
                Document svgDoc = new DocumentImpl();
                SVGGraphics2D g2 = new SVGGraphics2D(svgDoc);
                g2.setSVGCanvasSize(dummy.getSize());
```

The `SVGGraphics2D` object takes an `org.w3c.dom.Document` object in its constructor, where it keeps the DOM tree representing the graphic. `SVGGraphics2D` also adds the ability to stream the DOM tree to a `Writer` object.

```
                // draw the graph onto the image
                dummy.paint(g2);

                // encode the output back to the client
                //JPEGImageEncoder encoder = JPEGCodec.createJPEGEncoder(out);
                //encoder.encode(image);
                Writer writer = new java.io.StringWriter();
                g2.stream(writer, false);
                out.print(writer.toString());
                out.flush();
            } catch (Exception e) {
                e.printStackTrace();
            }
        }

    }
```

By pointing your SVG enabled browser to
http://localhost:8080/ch23/servlet/g2d_2_svg?xml=/xml/nasdaq.xml (for IE add &fakeIE=usethis.svg),
you can see a chart of the performance of the Nasdaq Stock Market over the same period:

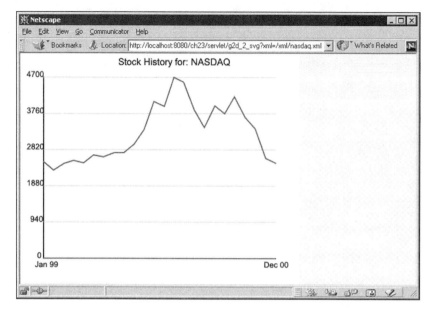

By saving the file to your local disk, you can see that the 15Kb JPG chart has been reduced in size to a 3.5Kb SVG file. We can also zoom in and out, pan and resize the image without any loss of quality.

XML to SVG

As SVG is represented in XML, and our input data originally came from an XML document, it seems sensible to consider XSLT for transforming between these two formats. In doing so, all of the drawing logic in the `HistoryFrame` object will get moved to an XSLT stylesheet.

Recall the steps we followed to create the chart using a `Graphics2D` object:

❑ Retrieve values from the source data

❑ Calculate the maximum closing price, in order to scale the Y axis values properly

❑ Calculate the offset between X axis values, in order to use the entire width of the chart

❑ Draw the X and Y axes, scaled appropriately

❑ Draw the closing price line

❑ Render the image back to the browser

XSLT can accomplish most of these, and with SVG, the rendering takes place at the browser. For further information on the use of XSLT, refer to Chapter 12.

The svgHistory XSL

This section introduces the `svgHistory.xsl` stylesheet. Found in the `/xml` directory of the ch23 webapp, `svgHistory.xsl` uses similar convenience methods to the `HistoryFrame` object discussed earlier.

Let's start by deriving the maximum closing price. This is slightly trickier to do in XSLT, but not too difficult. Adapting the max XSLT template from Chapter 4 of the *XSLT Programmer's Reference* (Michael Kay, Wrox Press, ISBN 1-861003-12-9) results in the following:

```
<xsl:template name="max">
<xsl:param name="list"/>
<xsl:choose>
<xsl:when test="$list">
    <xsl:variable name="first" select="$list[1]/Close"/>
    <xsl:variable name="max-of-rest">
       <xsl:call-template name="max">
          <xsl:with-param name="list" select="$list[position()!=1]"/>
       </xsl:call-template>
    </xsl:variable>
    <xsl:choose>
    <xsl:when test="$first &gt; $max-of-rest">
       <xsl:value-of select="$first"/>
    </xsl:when>
    <xsl:otherwise>
       <xsl:value-of select="$max-of-rest"/>
    </xsl:otherwise>
    </xsl:choose>
</xsl:when>
<xsl:otherwise>0</xsl:otherwise>
</xsl:choose>
</xsl:template>
```

The max template takes the list of Period nodes as a parameter, and recursively calls itself until the list is empty. At each recursion, max compares the value of the current period node's Close element, first, with the maximum from the rest of the list, max-of-rest.

This max template is placed at the end of the svgHistory.xsl stylesheet. Let's now go back to the start of the svgHistory.xsl stylesheet, and examine the remaining code. The first step is to match the StockHistory, or root element of the XML. The result of the max template is stored in the variable maxClose:

```
<?xml version="1.0"?>
<xsl:stylesheet version="1.0" xmlns:xsl="http://www.w3.org/1999/XSL/Transform"
xmlns:svg="http://www.w3.org/2000/svg">
<xsl:template match="StockHistory" name="makeSVG">

  <xsl:variable name="maxClose">
     <xsl:call-template name="max">
        <xsl:with-param name="list" select="Period"/>
     </xsl:call-template>
  </xsl:variable>
```

The offset between values on the X axis is calculated and stored in the xOffset variable:

```
<xsl:variable name="xOffset">
  <xsl:choose>
     <xsl:when test="count(Period) &lt; 2">0</xsl:when>
     <xsl:otherwise>
```

```
            <xsl:value-of select="400 div (count(Period)-1)"/>
          </xsl:otherwise>
      </xsl:choose>
  </xsl:variable>
```

The top of our Y axis is then calculated and stored in the `yMax` variable:

```
<xsl:variable name="yMax">
    <xsl:choose>
        <xsl:when test="$maxClose=0">50</xsl:when>
        <xsl:otherwise>
       <xsl:value-of select="round(($maxClose+25) div 50) * 50"/>
          </xsl:otherwise>
      </xsl:choose>
  </xsl:variable>
```

Let's now look at how we draw paths. By contrasting these with the same section of code from the Graphics2D section, we can see remarkable similarities.

The next step in the Graphics2D example was to draw the path representing the closing price line. In this case, we have made an XSL template to construct the d attribute of the path. The `makePath` template makes use of the `xsl:for-each` instruction to loop through the `Close` nodes and construct the required line:

```
<xsl:template name="makePath">
  <xsl:param name="closes"/>
  <xsl:param name="xOffset"/>
  <xsl:param name="yMax"/>
  <xsl:for-each select="$closes">
    <xsl:choose>
        <xsl:when test="position()=1">M</xsl:when>
        <xsl:otherwise>L</xsl:otherwise>
      </xsl:choose>
      <xsl:value-of select="concat(round((position()-1) * $xOffset)+40,',',
                              round(340 - ((. div $yMax) * 300)),' ')"/>
  </xsl:for-each>
</xsl:template>
```

The `makePath` template is called when processing the `StockHistory` node, and stored in the `svgPath` variable:

```
<xsl:variable name="svgPath">
    <xsl:call-template name="makePath">
      <xsl:with-param name="closes" select="Period/Close"/>
      <xsl:with-param name="xOffset" select="$xOffset"/>
      <xsl:with-param name="yMax" select="$yMax"/>
    </xsl:call-template>
  </xsl:variable>
```

In the `Graphics2D`-based example, we used the DOM API and the `getValue()` procedure to retrieve the data from the XML. In XSLT, we will use the `<xsl:value-of>` method instead. For example, to retrieve the company name for the title of the chart, we use:

```
<svg:svg width="460" height="380">
  <!-- draw the title -->
  <svg:text style="font-size:12pt;text-anchor:middle" x="230" y="20">
    Stock History for: <xsl:value-of select="@company"/>
  </svg:text>
```

Lines and paths are represented in SVG via the path element. The process is similar to the `GeneralPath()` method used in the Graphics2D section, moving to a point and drawing a line to other points. In the example below, the `svg` namespace has been used to easily identify SVG entities from the other XSL entities:

```
<!-- draw the x and y axis -->
<svg:path style="fill:none;stroke:black;stroke-width:2"
    d="M40,40 L40,340 L440,340"/>
<!-- draw the y axis scale -->
<svg:g style="fill:none;stroke:grey;stroke-width:1">
  <svg:path d="M40,280 L440,280"/>
  <svg:path d="M40,220 L440,220"/>
  <svg:path d="M40,160 L440,160"/>
  <svg:path d="M40,100 L440,100"/>
  <svg:path d="M40,40 L440,40"/>
</svg:g>
<!-- draw the y axis labels -->
<xsl:variable name="yDivisions" select="$yMax div 5"/>
<svg:g style="font-size:10pt;text-anchor:end">
  <svg:text x="35" y="40"><xsl:value-of select="$yMax"/></svg:text>
  <svg:text x="35" y="100">
    <xsl:value-of select="$yDivisions * 4"/></svg:text>
  <svg:text x="35" y="160">
    <xsl:value-of select="$yDivisions * 3"/></svg:text>
  <svg:text x="35" y="220">
    <xsl:value-of select="$yDivisions * 2"/></svg:text>
  <svg:text x="35" y="280">
    <xsl:value-of select="$yDivisions * 1"/></svg:text>
  <svg:text x="35" y="340">0</svg:text>
</svg:g>
<!-- draw the x axis labels... -->
<svg:g style="font-size:10pt;text-anchor:middle">
  <svg:text x="40" y="355"><xsl:value-of
select="Period[1]/Date"/></svg:text>
  <svg:text x="440" y="355"><xsl:value-of
select="Period[last()]/Date"/></svg:text>
</svg:g>
```

The path itself is then drawn with the following:

```
<svg:path style="fill:none;stroke:red;stroke-width:2">
  <xsl:attribute name="d">
    <xsl:value-of select="$svgPath"/>
  </xsl:attribute>
</svg:path>
  </svg:svg>
</xsl:template>
```

This stylesheet can also be found in `svgHistory.xsl` from the download.

An XSL Tag Library

As SVG is XML and not a binary file, we can use JSP in a way that we could not for the bitmap images. In order to do XSL transformations from within JSP, a custom tag that provides this functionality is useful. Many custom tag libraries exist for XSL transformation, but we will provide one here using the Xalan processor, as it leads into other customs tags needed for PDF generation. For more information on custom tags, see Chapters 8-10.

The UseXSLTag class

The first step is to construct the class to perform the transformations. Found in the file `UseXSLTag.java`, the `UseXSLTag` class extends `BodyTagSupport`, as it might be useful to have JSP generate the XML for transformation. `UseXSLTag` imports the required JSP tag classes, as well as the needed XSLT classes from Xalan.

```
package xsl;

import java.io.*;
import javax.servlet.jsp.*;
import javax.servlet.jsp.tagext.*;

import org.apache.xalan.xslt.*;

public class UseXSLTag extends BodyTagSupport {
```

The first item needed to perform XSL transformations is the input XML itself. In our case, the XML may appear either as a URL in the `xml` attribute, or in the `body` of the tag.

```
private String body = null;

private String xml = null;

public String getXml() {
  return (this.xml);
}

public void setXml(String xml) {
  this.xml = xml;
}
```

The second item required is the XSLT stylesheet that will be used to transform the data. The URL to the resource is stored in the private `xsl` variable:

```
private String xsl = null;

public String getXsl() {
  return (this.xsl);
}

public void setXsl(String xsl) {
  this.xsl = xsl;
}
```

Since the `xsl` attribute is mandatory, the format of the tag is validated in the `doStartTag()` method. (The `xml` attribute is not mandatory, as the XML may appear in the body of the tag). Note that the body of the tag is only evaluated if the `xml` attribute is not present.

```
public int doStartTag() throws JspException {

  if (xsl == null) {
    throw new JspException("Must have an xsl property");
  }

  if (xml == null) {
    return (EVAL_BODY_AGAIN);
  } else {
    return (SKIP_BODY);
  }

}
```

If the body of the tag actually contain content, it is saved in the private body variable in the `doAfterBody()` method:

```
public int doAfterBody() throws JspException {

  if (bodyContent == null)
    body = "";
  else
    body = bodyContent.getString().trim();
  return (SKIP_BODY);

}
```

The `doEndTag()` method contains the actual processing of the XSLT stylesheet. First, an `XSLTInputSource` needs to be constructed from either the `body` or `xml` attribute:

```
public int doEndTag() throws JspException {

  // Make an XSLTInputSource from either the body or the xsl attribute
  XSLTInputSource data;
  if (body != null) {
    data = new XSLTInputSource(new StringReader(body));
  } else {
    data = new XSLTInputSource(
              pageContext.getServletContext().getResourceAsStream(xml));
  }
```

An `XSLTInputSource` is then created for the XSLT stylesheet (from the `xsl` attribute):

```
XSLTInputSource style = new XSLTInputSource(
            pageContext.getServletContext().getResourceAsStream(xsl));
```

The target of the transformation is then created from the current `JspWriter` (acquired via `pageContext.getOut()`):

```
        XSLTResultTarget result = new XSLTResultTarget(pageContext.getOut());
```

The last step is to create the `XSLTProcessor` and perform the transformation:

```
        XSLTProcessor processor;
        try {
           // Create a XSLTProcessor and transform the xml.
           processor = XSLTProcessorFactory.getProcessor();
           processor.process(data, style, result);
        } catch (Exception e) {
           throw new JspException(e.toString());
        }

        return (EVAL_PAGE);

     }
```

Finally, the `release()` method shown below is used to clear out any variables we may have used during the processing of this tag:

```
     public void release() {
        this.body = null;
        this.xml = null;
        this.xsl = null;
     }

  }
```

The XSL Tag Library Descriptor

Now that we have a class for the tag, we need a Tag Library Descriptor (or tld) that describes the tag to the JSP engine. The tld file, `xsl.tld` shown below, declares the `usexsl` tag to be a body content tag, with an optional `xml` attribute and a mandatory `xsl` attribute:

```
<?xml version="1.0" encoding="ISO-8859-1" ?>
<!DOCTYPE taglib
        PUBLIC "-//Sun Microsystems, Inc.//DTD JSP Tag Library 1.1//EN"
        "http://java.sun.com/j2ee/dtds/web-jsptaglibrary_1_1.dtd">

<taglib>
  <tlibversion>1.0</tlibversion>
  <jspversion>1.2</jspversion>
  <shortname>Simple XSL Tag Library</shortname>

  <info>
    A tag library for transforming XML via XSLT.
    The usexsl tag translates XML input data via XSLT and
    writes the resultant XML to the JspWriter object.
  </info>

  <tag>
    <name>usexsl</name>
    <tagclass>xsl.UseXSLTag</tagclass>
    <bodycontent>JSP</bodycontent>
    <info>
      Applies the specified XSL stylesheet to the XML input,
      and writes the output to the JspWriter. If no "xml" attribute
      is specified, it reads the XML from the body of the tag.
    </info>
```

```
      <attribute>
        <name>xml</name>
        <required>false</required>
        <rtexprvalue>true</rtexprvalue>
      </attribute>
      <attribute>
        <name>xsl</name>
        <required>true</required>
        <rtexprvalue>true</rtexprvalue>
      </attribute>
    </tag>
  </taglib>
```

Returning SVG to the Browser

We now have all of the pieces required to use XSLT in a JSP page. XML, however, can also be tricky to return from JSP. For valid XML, the `<?xml?>` line must be the first line of an XML file. That means that any spaces, tabs, and newline characters cannot be returned before the XML processing instruction. Therefore your JSP file must either appear all on one line, or you must trick the JSP interpreter into leaving the whitespace out by encoding it within JSP scriptlet tags:

```
<%@taglib uri="/WEB-INF/xsl.tld" prefix="xsl" %><%
%><%@page contentType="image/svg-xml"%><%
   String xmlFile = request.getParameter("xml");
%><xsl:usexsl xml="<%= xmlFile %>" xsl="/xml/svgHistory.xsl"/>
```

The file above, `xml_2_svg.jsp`, uses this trick. Note that the `<%` and `%>` tags encircle all of the whitespace in the file. The JSP `page` directive sets the content type of the response to the SVG MIME type, `image/svg-xml`.

Entering http://localhost:8080/ch23/xml_2_svg.jsp?xml=/xml/bluechip.xml (for IE, remember to add &fakeIE=usethis.svg too) into your browser should show the following output:

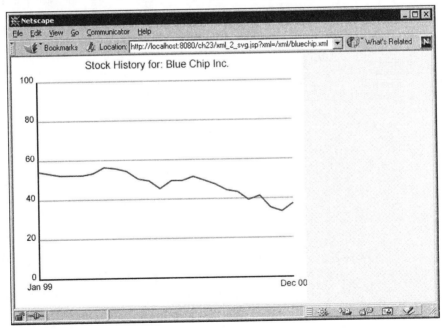

905

Decision Time

We have now successfully generated the stock history chart as a JPG file, and also as an SVG file from both the `Graphics2D` object and an XSLT stylesheet. Now we must make a decision about which method is most appropriate. Here are some considerations.

❑   Until SVG support in browsers is more readily available, rendering the chart to a JPG should be the first choice. However, if you can tolerate the user having to download a plugin, SVG provides more legible graphics and greater flexibility.

❑   If an applet or application is also used, then generation from a `Graphics2D` object is preferred. In our case, this would allow the same `HistoryFrame` object to be used in both the Servlet and applet. If legacy code already creates the `Graphics2D` object, it is an easy conversion to the `SVGGraphics2D` object, so SVG could be used instead of rendering to a JPG file.

❑   XSLT may be easier for some programmers not familiar with the use of AWT components in Java. As browser support increases, and XSLT becomes entrenched, this approach will grow in popularity.

PDF Generation

The W3C has also created a specification for dealing with the layout of objects on a page. As one half of the XSL specification, it is known as the XSL Formatting Objects (XSL FO) specification. XSL FO is currently a Candidate Recommendation, with the review period ending on February 28, 2001, so it should soon become a Recommendation (the final product for the W3C). XSLT 1.0, the other part of the XSL specification is already a Recommendation, with XSLT 1.1 in the working draft state.

With XSL FO, it is possible to control where objects occur on a page, how pagination is handled, and how text is styled. It is also possible to embed SVG graphics or other pixel based images into an XSL FO file. XSL FO, like XSLT, is XML-based, so the creation of XSL FO files can easily be accomplished using Servlets and JSP. A simple XSL FO file is shown below (`simple.fo`):

```
<?xml version="1.0"?>
<fo:root xmlns:fo="http://www.w3.org/1999/XSL/Format">
  <fo:layout-master-set>
    <fo:simple-page-master master-name="simple"
        page-height="11in"
        page-width="8.5in"
        margin-top="1in"
        margin-bottom="1in"
        margin-left="1in"
        margin-right="1in">
      <fo:region-body/>
    </fo:simple-page-master>
  </fo:layout-master-set>

  <fo:page-sequence master-name="simple">
    <fo:flow flow-name="xsl-region-body" text-align="center">
      <fo:block font-size="24pt">
        Welcome to XSL FO!
      </fo:block>
```

```
        <fo:block font-size="18pt" color="blue">
          Welcome, Welcome, Welcome
        </fo:block>
      </fo:flow>
    </fo:page-sequence>
  </fo:root>
```

All of the elements use the xsl:fo namespace. Pages in XSL FO are split into 5 basic regions:

- ❏ region-before – where the header information would appear
- ❏ region-after – where footer information is displayed
- ❏ region-start – the left margin of the page
- ❏ region-body – where the actual page content is displayed
- ❏ region-end – the right margin of the page

All of the content in the simple.fo file is part of the region-body section. The page layout is described by the layout-master-set, which sets the page size to US letter with 1 inch margins.

Note that the text on the page is inside of a block element. All word-wrap and pagination is handled for you (although you can override it). Another thing to note is that each block element will start on a new line. This is the normal way of achieving breaks between paragraphs and other items. The other types of elements are called *inline* elements. These elements appear inside block elements, and do not start a new line. Here's a summary of some useful FO elements:

- ❏ block – for basic text, paragraphs, titles, and so on
- ❏ block-container – to group block elements that use similar styles
- ❏ table – for drawing tables; child elements include table-body, table-row, table-column
- ❏ external-graphic (inline) – for referencing external image files (jpg, gif)
- ❏ instream-foreign-object (inline) – for non-FO XML elements, like SVG
- ❏ inline (inline) – for applying attributes to text within a block

> **For more information on XSL FO, go to:**
> **http://www.w3.org/TR/2000/CR-xsl-20001121/.**

Using XSL FO, complete control over the page layout is possible. But something is still needed to turn the XSL FO file into a recognizable format. Once again, the Apache Group has a solution for this – the Formatting Object Parser (FOP). FOP reads XSL FO format files and generates PDF files of the result. There are various commercial products that serve the same purpose, such as the XEP Rendering Engine from RenderX.

> **The FOP Project is available from: http://xml.apache.org/fop/.**
> **The XEP Rendering Engine is available at: http://www.renderx.com/.**

FO to PDF

The process of translating the FO XML file to a PDF file is accomplished using the FOP processor. We have a choice of using a Servlet to accomplish this task, or using JSP as we did for the SVG transformation shown previously. In the interest of re-usability, a custom tag would be appropriate to invoke FOP from a JSP page.

The FO2PDFTag class

The FO2PDFTag class is a custom tag that extends the BodyTagSupport class. Similar to the UseXSLTag class, it uses the fo attribute or the body of the tag as the input XML, and uses the FOP processor in the doEndTag() method to transform the input XSL FO into a PDF file.

Let's take a look at the source code for the FO2PDFTag class. As we move through the code, we'll highlight the differences in FO2PDFTag from UseXSLTag.

Starting at the beginning of the FO2PDFTag.java file, we see the additional import of the FOP classes (instead of the XSL packages in the UseXMLTag.java):

```
package fop;

import java.io.*;
import javax.servlet.jsp.*;
import javax.servlet.jsp.tagext.*;

import org.apache.xalan.xslt.*;

import org.apache.fop.apps.*;

public class FO2PDFTag extends BodyTagSupport {
```

Instead of an xml attribute as in UseXMLTag, this tag has an fo attribute:

```
/**
 * If no fo attribute is specified, the body contains the
 * fo XML. Store it here.
 */
private String body = null;

/**
 * The fo attribute is the resource where the
 * fo XML is, if it's not in the body.
 */
private String fo = null;

public String getFo() {
  return (this.fo);
}

public void setFo(String fo) {
  this.fo = fo;
}
```

As in the case of the `UseXSLTag`, the body of the tag is only evaluated if the `fo` attribute is not present:

```
/**
 * Evaluate the body of the tag only if no fo attribute
 * is specified.
 */
public int doStartTag() throws JspException {
    if (fo == null) {
        return (EVAL_BODY_AGAIN);
    } else {
        return (SKIP_BODY);
    }
}
```

If the body of the tag actually contain content, it is saved in the private `body` variable in the `doAfterBody()` method:

```
/**
 * Save the body content in the body private variable.
 */
public int doAfterBody() throws JspException {
    if (bodyContent == null) {
        body = "";
    } else {
        body = bodyContent.getString().trim();
    }
    return (SKIP_BODY);
}
```

The `doEndTag()` method contains the actual processing. The input XSL FO, whether from the `fo` attribute, or the body of the tag, is read into the `XSLTInputSource`:

```
/**
 * Render the PDF using FOP. This is where all the
 * work of the tag takes place.
 */
public int doEndTag() throws JspException {

    // Make an XSLTInputSource from either the body or the fo attribute
    XSLTInputSource data;
    if (body != null) {
        data = new XSLTInputSource(new StringReader(body));
    } else {
        data = new XSLTInputSource(
                pageContext.getServletContext().getResourceAsStream(fo));
    }
```

The `ElementMapping` and `PropertyList` items instruct the FOP `Driver` object to expect standard XSL FO, as well as SVG objects in the input `fo` XML. The `FOTree` is then built and formatted by the `org.apache.fop.apps.Driver` object, using the SAX parser from Xerces:

```
try {
    Driver driver = new Driver();
    driver.setRenderer("org.apache.fop.render.pdf.PDFRenderer",
                Version.getVersion());
    driver.addElementMapping("org.apache.fop.fo.StandardElementMapping");
    driver.addElementMapping("org.apache.fop.svg.SVGElementMapping");
```

```
        driver.addPropertyList(
                        "org.apache.fop.fo.StandardPropertyListMapping");
        driver.addPropertyList("org.apache.fop.svg.SVGPropertyListMapping");
        driver.buildFOTree(new org.apache.xerces.parsers.SAXParser(),
                        new XSLTInputSource(data));
        driver.format();
```

The last step is to render the resultant PDF file to an OutputStream. One problem solved here is that the org.apache.fop.apps.Driver object only renders to an OutputStream. From our custom tag, we only have access to a JspWriter object (from the pageContext.getOut() method). The solution is to create a temporary ByteArrayOutputStream and print the ByteArrayOutputStream to the JspWriter:

```
        // create a ByteArrayOutputStream to store the PDF data in
        ByteArrayOutputStream ostr = new ByteArrayOutputStream();
        driver.setOutputStream(ostr);

        // render the PDF to the ByteArrayOutputStream
        driver.render();

        // print the PDF bytes in the ByteArrayOutputStream to the JspWriter.
        pageContext.getOut().print(ostr);
    } catch (Exception e) {
        throw new JspException(e.toString());
    }

    return (EVAL_PAGE);

}
```

> One caveat is that the **ByteArrayOutputStream** trick cannot be used to return binary files, as translation from Unicode would occur. Luckily, the FOP processor by default does not generate binary PDF files, instead encoding the PDF objects as ASCII streams.

Finally, the release method show below is used to clear out any variables we may have used during the processing of this tag:

```
/**
 * Release any allocated resources.
 */
public void release() {
    this.body = null;
    this.fo = null;
}

}
```

The fop.tld Tag Library Descriptor

The fop.tld Tag Library Descriptor describes the use of the FO2PDFTag class to the JSP engine. A body content tag, fo2pdf, is declared, with an optional fo attribute:

```
<?xml version="1.0" encoding="ISO-8859-1" ?>
<!DOCTYPE taglib
        PUBLIC "-//Sun Microsystems, Inc.//DTD JSP Tag Library 1.1//EN"
        "http://java.sun.com/j2ee/dtds/web-jsptaglibrary_1_1.dtd">

<taglib>
  <tlibversion>1.0</tlibversion>
  <jspversion>1.2</jspversion>
  <shortname>Simple FOP Tag Library</shortname>

  <info>
      A tag library for turning XML into PDF documents
      via XSLT. The xml2pdf tag translates XML input data
      to FO XML via XSLT, and then renders that to PDF using
      FOP. The fo2pdf tag renders FO XML into PDFs using FOP.
  </info>

  <tag>
    <name>fo2pdf</name>
    <tagclass>fop.FO2PDFTag</tagclass>
    <bodycontent>JSP</bodycontent>
    <info>
      Applies the specified XSL stylesheet to the XML input,
      and writes the output to the JspWriter. If no "fo" attribute
      is specified, it reads the FO XML from the body of the tag.
    </info>
    <attribute>
      <name>fo</name>
      <required>false</required>
      <rtexprvalue>true</rtexprvalue>
    </attribute>
  </tag>
</taglib>
```

The fo_2_pdf.jsp JSP

We are now ready to use the usexsl tag in a JSP page. The fo_2_pdf.jsp is shown below. First, the corresponding tag library is referenced by the taglib directive. Then, the content type of the page is set to application/pdf, the MIME content type for PDF documents. The fo2pdf custom tag is used to transform the fo parameter using FOP.

```
<%@taglib uri="/WEB-INF/fop.tld" prefix="fop" %><%
%><%@page contentType="application/pdf"%><%
   String foFile = request.getParameter("fo");
%><fop:fo2pdf fo="<%= foFile %>"/>
```

It should be noted that this JSP also 'encircles' the whitespace, to make sure that no extra whitespace is added to the beginning of the generated PDF file.

The result of invoking the JSP with this custom tag on the simple.fo at http://localhost:8080/ch23/fo_2_pdf.jsp?fo=/xml/simple.fo is shown below (remember that Internet Explorer will require the same 'trick' as with SVG files, this time with the URL ending with &fakeIE=usethis.pdf).

XML to PDF

The preceding section demonstrated how we could generate PDF files using JSP and the FOP processor, but how does this help us with our stock history charts? Fortunately, the FOP processor supports the inclusion of SVG files as the `instream-foreign-object` element. It should be noted that support is still somewhat limited (for FOP version 0.16), but mostly functional. To make our PDF file more useful, we will also include a table of the actual stock prices.

Here are the actions we need to perform to create this stock history report:

❑   Create an XSLT stylesheet that transforms the stock history XML into XSL FO XML

❑   Create a custom tag that executes XSLT, and feeds that into FOP

❑   Make a JSP file to run the custom tag and display the PDF file

The pdfHistory Stylesheet

`pdfHistory.xsl` is the XSLT stylesheet that we will use to generate our PDF report. As SVG can be embedded directly into XSL FO, we will re-use the code from the XSLT stylesheet that generates the chart. It would be normal to think we could use `xsl:include` to reference the `svgHistory.xsl` stylesheet, and use `xsl:call-template` to call the `makeSVG` template. However, this would require that we reference the file using the full URL:

```
<xsl:include href=http://localhost:8080/ch23/xml/svgHistory.xsl
```

This is not very portable, as every time we move our webapp, or change the server port number, we must edit the `pdfHistory.xsl` file and change the include. For this reason, I have chosen to append a copy of the `svgHistory.xsl` file to the end of the `pdfHistory.xsl` file. Also, some SVG features are not yet functional in FOP version 0.16, like the `text-align` attribute for SVG `text` elements. This requires that some pixel locations for the text are changed, but the logic for creating the chart is the same.

Below we see the first section of the `pdfHistory.xsl` file. Since this XSL FO file includes an SVG graphic we also include a reference to the `xmlns:svg` namespace. Note that the page setup is the same as with `simple.fo`:

```
<?xml version="1.0"?>

<xsl:stylesheet
     xmlns:xsl="http://www.w3.org/1999/XSL/Transform" version="1.0"
     xmlns:fo="http://www.w3.org/1999/XSL/Format"
     xmlns:svg="http://www.w3.org/2000/svg">

<xsl:output indent="yes"/>

<xsl:template match ="StockHistory">
<fo:root xmlns:fo="http://www.w3.org/1999/XSL/Format">

  <fo:layout-master-set>
    <fo:simple-page-master master-name="simple"
            page-height="11in"
            page-width="8.5in"
            margin-top="1in"
            margin-bottom="1in"
            margin-left="1in"
            margin-right="1in">
      <fo:region-body/>
    </fo:simple-page-master>
  </fo:layout-master-set>
```

The next section describes the inclusion of the SVG as an `instream-foreign-object`. The `white-space-collapse` attribute is set to `false`, and a space appears before the `instream-foreign-object` due to a bug in FOP that will not display an `instream` object if the surrounding block is empty:

```
<fo:page-sequence master-name="simple">
  <fo:flow flow-name="xsl-region-body">
    <fo:block white-space-collapse="false"> <fo:instream-foreign-object>
      <xsl:call-template name="makeSVG"/>
      </fo:instream-foreign-object>
    </fo:block>
```

The next section will create a table of the stock values within the PDF. An `xsl:for-each` element is used to loop through all of the children of the first `Period` node, creating columns for each of them:

```
<fo:table text-align="center">
  <xsl:for-each select="Period[1]/*">
    <fo:table-column column-width="2.77cm"/>
  </xsl:for-each>
```

A `fo:table-body` is then created, with the first row in the table being the node names of the children of the first `Period` node. This is the method used to create the header row for the table. Note that each name occurs within `fo:table-cell` and `fo:block` elements. Although the XSL FO spec does not require `fo:block` elements within `fo:table-cell` elements, a limitation in FOP does:

```
<fo:table-body>
  <fo:table-row>
    <xsl:for-each select="Period[1]/*">
      <fo:table-cell border-width="0.5mm">
```

```
                <fo:block>
                    <xsl:value-of select="name()"/>
                </fo:block>
            </fo:table-cell>
        </xsl:for-each>
    </fo:table-row>
    <xsl:apply-templates/>
  </fo:table-body>
  </fo:table>
  </fo:flow>
  </fo:page-sequence>
 </fo:root>
</xsl:template>
```

The `xsl:apply-templates` element above is used to call the template below for each `Period` node in the XML. For each `Period`, a new row in the table is created (`fo:table-row`). An `xsl:for-each` loop then loops through the children (`Date`, `Open`, `High`, `Low`, `Close` and `Volume`), and enters the value in a `fo:table-cell`:

```
<xsl:template match ="Period">
    <fo:table-row>
        <xsl:for-each select="*">
            <fo:table-cell border-width="0.3mm">
                <fo:block>
                    <xsl:value-of select="."/>
                </fo:block>
            </fo:table-cell>
        </xsl:for-each>
    </fo:table-row>
</xsl:template>
```

And that's all we need in our XSLT stylesheet to transform our input stock price XML into XSL FO.

The XML2PDFTag Class

We now need a custom tag that takes our input stock history XML, and an XSLT stylesheet to produce XSL FO format XML, and creates a PDF from the result. The `XML2PDFTag` class is a combination of the `FO2PDFTag` and `UseXSLTag` classes described earlier. The difference is that this tag first invokes the Xalan XSLT processor to transform the input XML, and feeds the resulting XSL FO into FOP.

```
package fop;

import java.io.*;
import javax.servlet.jsp.*;
import javax.servlet.jsp.tagext.*;

import org.apache.xalan.xslt.*;

import org.apache.fop.apps.*;

public class XML2PDFTag extends BodyTagSupport {
```

The next section is largely a straight copy of the same section in the `UseXSLTag`:

```
/**
 * If no xml attribute is specified, the body contains the
 * XML. Store it here.
 */
private String body = null;

/**
 * The xml attribute is the resource where the
 * XML is, if it's not in the body.
 */
private String xml = null;

public String getXml() {
  return (this.xml);
}

public void setXml(String xml) {
  this.xml = xml;
}


/**
 * The xsl attribute is the resource to where the
 * XSL stylesheet is, it is mandatory.
 */
private String xsl = null;

public String getXsl() {
  return (this.xsl);
}

public void setXsl(String xsl) {
  this.xsl = xsl;
}


/**
 * Make sure the XSL attribute is specified.
 * Evaluate the body of the tag only if no xml attribute
 * is specified.
 */
public int doStartTag() throws JspException {

  if (xsl == null) {
    throw new JspException("Must have an xsl property");
  }

  if (xml == null) {
    return (EVAL_BODY_AGAIN);
  } else {
    return (SKIP_BODY);
  }

}
```

```
/**
 * Save the body content in the body private variable.
 */
public int doAfterBody() throws JspException {

  if (bodyContent == null)
    body = "";
  else
    body = bodyContent.getString().trim();
  return (SKIP_BODY);

}
```

The doEndTag() method contains the most of the changes needed:

```
/**
 * Transform the XML via XSL, and render to PDF.
 */
public int doEndTag() throws JspException {

  // Make an XSLTInputSource from either the body or the fo attribute
  XSLTInputSource data;
  if (body != null) {
    data = new XSLTInputSource(new StringReader(body));
  } else {
    data = new XSLTInputSource(pageContext.getServletContext()
                                    .getResourceAsStream(xml));
  }

  // Make an XSLTInputSource from the xsl attribute.
  XSLTInputSource style = new XSLTInputSource
          (pageContext.getServletContext().getResourceAsStream(xsl));
```

Now instead of returning the output of Xalan directly (via pageContext.getOut()), we use a java.io.StringWriter object to hold the output of the transformation:

```
  // Make a Writer to store the resulting fo XML in.
  java.io.Writer writer = new java.io.StringWriter();
  XSLTResultTarget result = new XSLTResultTarget(writer);

  // Create an XSLT processor and use it to perform the transformation
  XSLTProcessor processor;
  try {
    // Create a XSLTProcessor and transform the xml.
    processor = XSLTProcessorFactory.getProcessor();
    processor.process(data, style, result);
```

We then create a java.io.StringReader object, for the FOP Driver to read from:

```
  // Create a Reader object to hold the fo xml.
  java.io.Reader reader = new java.io.StringReader(writer.toString());
  writer.flush();
  writer.close();
```

The `Driver` is invoked as before ...

```
Driver driver = new Driver();
driver.setRenderer("org.apache.fop.render.pdf.PDFRenderer",
                   Version.getVersion());
driver.addElementMapping("org.apache.fop.fo.StandardElementMapping");
driver.addElementMapping("org.apache.fop.svg.SVGElementMapping");
driver.addPropertyList(
               "org.apache.fop.fo.StandardPropertyListMapping");
driver.addPropertyList("org.apache.fop.svg.SVGPropertyListMapping");
```

... but this time the `XSLTInputSource` is from the `reader` object, not an input FO file:

```
// build the FOTree from the Reader object.
driver.buildFOTree(new org.apache.xerces.parsers.SAXParser(),
                   new XSLTInputSource(reader));
driver.format();

// create a ByteArrayOutputStream to store the PDF data in
ByteArrayOutputStream ostr = new ByteArrayOutputStream();
driver.setOutputStream(ostr);

// render the PDF to the ByteArrayOutputStream
driver.render();

// print the PDF bytes in the ByteArrayOutputStream to the JspWriter.
pageContext.getOut().print(ostr);
} catch (Exception e) {
throw new JspException(e.toString());
}

return (EVAL_PAGE);

}
}
```

The tag library descriptor, `fop.tld`, also needs to be amended for the new `xml2pdf` custom tag. The `xml2pdf` tag has one mandatory attribute, `xsl`, for the XSLT stylesheet to transform the XML into XSL FO. The second attribute is the optional `xml` attribute. If the `xml` attribute is not specified, the input XML is retrieved from the body of the tag:

```
<?xml version="1.0" encoding="ISO-8859-1" ?>
<!DOCTYPE taglib
        PUBLIC "-//Sun Microsystems, Inc.//DTD JSP Tag Library 1.1//EN"
        "http://java.sun.com/j2ee/dtds/web-jsptaglibrary_1_1.dtd">

<taglib>
  <tlibversion>1.0</tlibversion>
  <jspversion>1.2</jspversion>
  <shortname>Simple FOP Tag Library</shortname>

  <info>
    A tag library for turning XML into PDF documents
    via XSLT. The xml2pdf tag translates XML input data
```

```
      to FO XML via XSLT, and then renders that to PDF using
      FOP. The fo2pdf tag renders FO XML into PDFs using FOP.
   </info>

   <tag>
     <name>fo2pdf</name>
     <tagclass>fop.FO2PDFTag</tagclass>
     <bodycontent>JSP</bodycontent>
     <info>
       Applies the specified XSL stylesheet to the XML input,
       and writes the output to the JspWriter. If no "fo" attribute
       is specified, it reads the FO XML from the body of the tag.
     </info>
     <attribute>
       <name>fo</name>
       <required>false</required>
       <rtexprvalue>true</rtexprvalue>
     </attribute>
   </tag>
   <tag>
     <name>xml2pdf</name>
     <tagclass>fop.XML2PDFTag</tagclass>
     <bodycontent>JSP</bodycontent>
     <info>
       Applies the specified XSL stylesheet to the XML input,
       and writes the output to the JspWriter. If no "xml" attribute
       is specified, it reads the XML from the body of the tag.
     </info>
     <attribute>
       <name>xml</name>
       <required>false</required>
       <rtexprvalue>true</rtexprvalue>
     </attribute>
     <attribute>
       <name>xsl</name>
       <required>true</required>
       <rtexprvalue>true</rtexprvalue>
     </attribute>
   </tag>
</taglib>
```

The last step is to create the JSP file, xml_2_pdf.jsp, that executes the xml2pdf tag. Note that the value of the xsl attribute is the pdfHistory.xsl stylesheet constructed earlier.

```
<%@taglib uri="/WEB-INF/fop.tld" prefix="fop" %><%
%><%@page contentType="application/pdf"%><%
  String xmlFile = request.getParameter("xml");
%><fop:xml2pdf xml="<%= xmlFile %>" xsl="/xml/pdfHistory.xsl"/>
```

The results can be seen at http://localhost:8080/ch23/xml_2_pdf.jsp?xml=/xml/dotcom.xml (for IE remember to add &fakeIE=usethis.pdf):

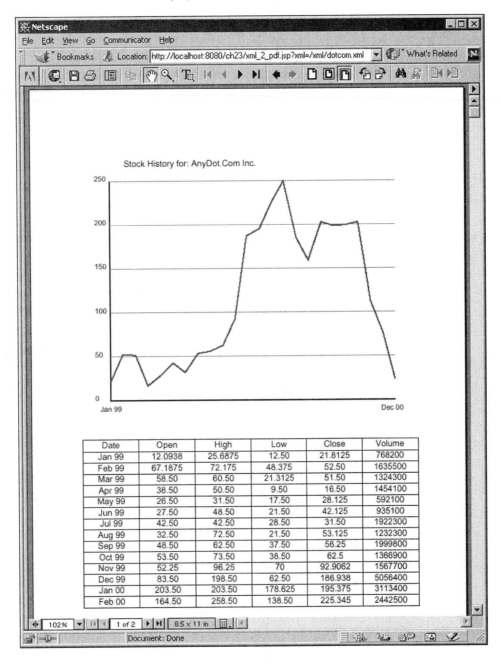

Summary

A tremendous amount of ground has been covered in this chapter, illustrating the various techniques used to generate binary content. Here are some of the more salient points:

❑ Servlets are the appropriate method of returning true binary content. JSP has some inadequacies that can be addressed if the content is not truly binary (like XML).

❑ Programmers with AWT experience should have an relatively easy time generating JPG or SVG files from `Graphics2D` objects.

❑ Scalable Vector Graphics represent the next wave in web image content. Its advanced features make this a smart choice for any new projects when the client browser environment is considered.

❑ Microsoft's Internet Explorer has some idiosyncrasies regarding MIME content types that any Servlet or JSP developer should be aware of when returning binary content.

❑ The combination of XML, XSLT and SVG can be used to create a powerful system for generating content. We created a `UseXSL` custom tag that can be reused to perform any XML transformation needed from a JSP.

❑ The addition of the XSL FO specification, and the FOP processor, make the creation of PDF files possible. We introduced a set of FOP custom tags (FO2PDF and XML2PDF) that allow the creation of PDF files from both XSL FO format XML, and from using an XSLT stylesheet.

A group that deserves a special mention is the Apache Group. All of the examples in this chapter rely on the hard work of those individuals creating the open source software used here. Tomcat, Xerces, Xalan, Batik and FOP represent a tremendous investment of people's time and energy. Without these products, this chapter would have been so much more complicated.

In the final chapter, we will move on to look at JSP within the context of the J2EE platform.

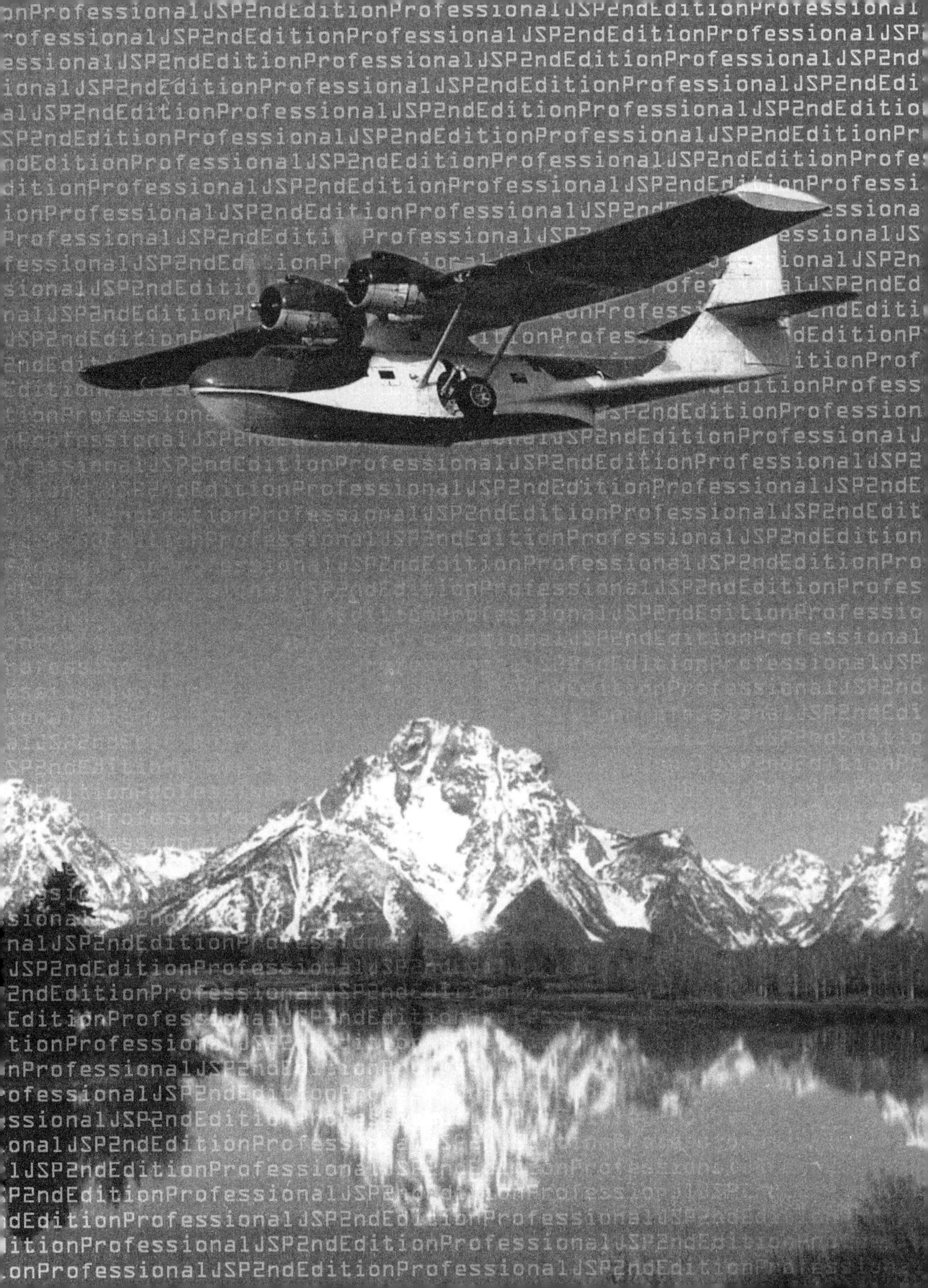

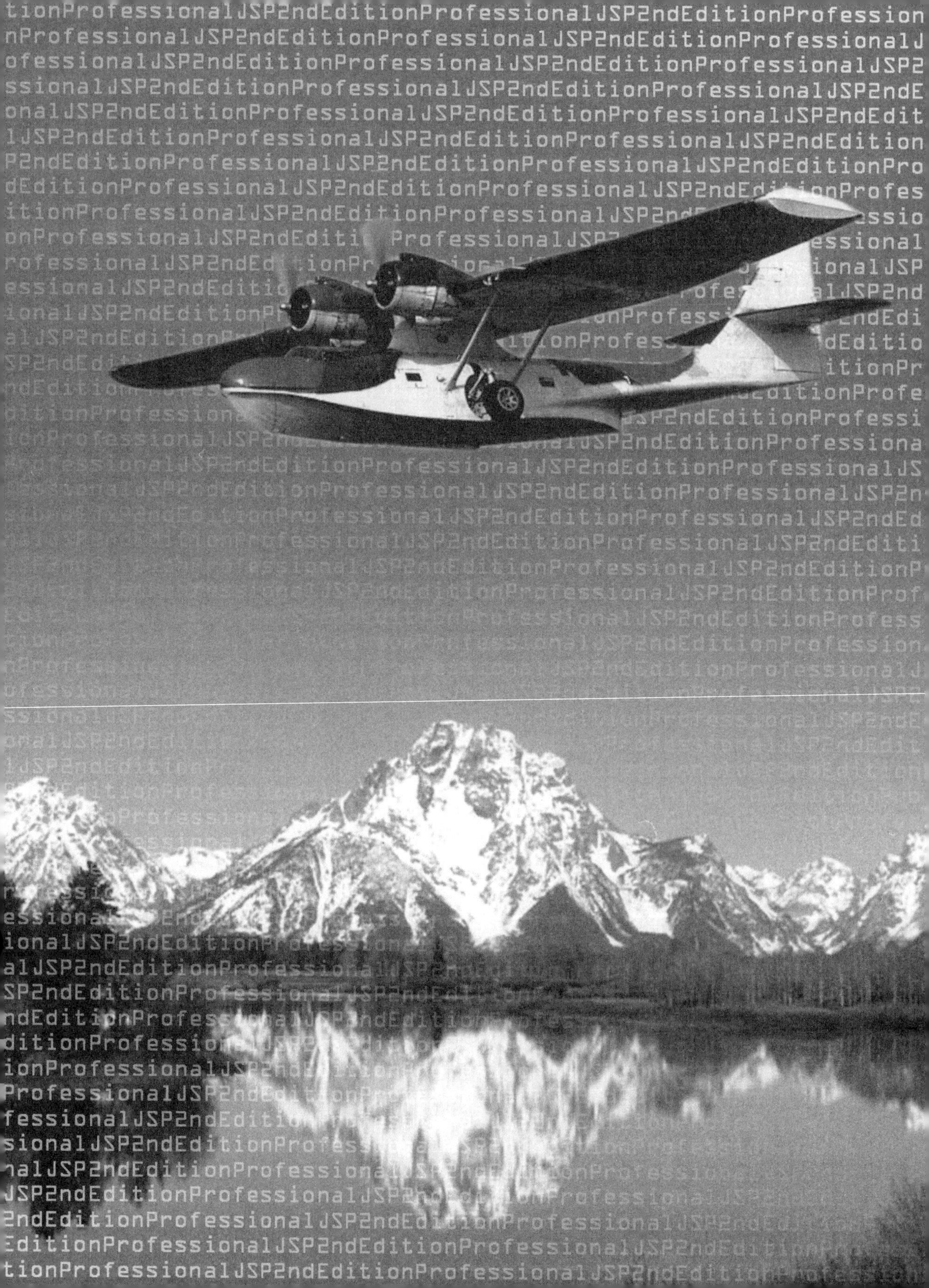
ProfessionalJSP2ndEdition

24

JSP Within the Java 2 Enterprise Edition

In Chapter 13 we saw how JSPs can use relational databases through JDBC directly, and by encapsulating the data access logic in JavaBeans. Accessing the database from the web tier is useful in a number of circumstances. However, JSPs and Servlets are part of a much larger platform from which to build enterprise applications – the Java 2 Enterprise Edition (J2EE). In this chapter, we will introduce J2EE and show how web applications can be designed and implemented using some of the major APIs.

In this chapter we'll see:

- ❑ J2EE's constituent parts
- ❑ How we can use the component APIs in conjunction with JSPs
- ❑ How we can access data
- ❑ How we can use Enterprise JavaBeans
- ❑ How we access them from JSPs

Introducing J2EE

The Java 2 Enterprise Edition (J2EE) is essentially a collection of APIs that can be used to build large scale, distributed, component based, multi-tier applications. However, saying that the J2EE is a collection of APIs is only half of the picture. The J2EE is also a standard for building and deploying enterprise applications, held together by the specifications of the APIs that it encompasses and the services that J2EE compliant application servers must provide.

What this means is that the 'write once, run anywhere' promises of Java apply for enterprise applications too:

❑   Enterprise applications can be run on different platforms supporting the Java 2 platform

❑   Enterprise applications are portable between application servers supporting the J2EE specification

There are of course a couple of caveats to the second point. For applications to be portable, they should not make use of any proprietary features offered by the application server on which they are developed. This is not to say that they shouldn't, but to remain truly portable, they should only use the standard features provided by the J2EE platform.

What it also means is that when you design and develop an application for the J2EE platform, you can be sure that the services you require will be available to any J2EE compliant server that you choose. For example, writing an EJB based system requires an EJB container for the beans to live in, a JNDI server for registering the beans, JDBC for accessing/persisting data and transactions to ensure the integrity of the system.

How the chosen server implements all of this is irrelevant. What is important though is that you can be sure that any J2EE compliant server will provide these services and that your application will behave as expected. As the J2EE specification and its APIs are refined and enhanced over time, we'll not only see more and more services being provided, but also the way in which we interact with and use those services will become more standardized. This will not only reduce the learning curve associated with each server offering, but will also reduce the time taken to build and deploy enterprise applications even further.

The APIs

So we've established that J2EE is a platform for building enterprise scale applications, but what are the building blocks, the APIs, that it provides? In no particular order, they are as follows:

❑   JavaServer Pages (JSP)

❑   Java Servlets

❑   Enterprise JavaBeans (EJB)

❑   Java Naming and Directory Interface (JNDI)

❑   JavaMail

❑   Java Message Service (JMS)

❑   Java Transaction API (JTA)

❑   JavaIDL

❑   JDBC

As this chapter is concerned with the role that JavaServer Pages have in the J2EE, we're not going to go into detail about the majority of the APIs listed above. Instead, a good point of reference is the J2EE home page on the Sun Microsystems website (http://java.sun.com/products/j2ee/) and one of the other books in the Wrox Professional series, *Professional Java Server Programming J2EE Edition*, ISBN 1861004656.

What we are going to do is introduce some of the primary APIs within the J2EE, and explain what they do and why they may be useful when building web-based applications in conjunction with JSP.

JavaServer Pages and Java Servlets

The role of JSPs and Servlets in J2EE is that of the presentation layer, or more accurately and conceptually, the web tier. They are very important building blocks for developing enterprise scale applications, and don't have to be confined to generating dynamic content for displaying in a web browser. In fact, there are many uses as we've already seen earlier in the book such as the MVC pattern and JSP model 2 architectures.

What's important here is that JSPs and Servlets are web technologies and as such, are confined to the web tier of your application. All but the simplest applications are more than likely to require business logic to manipulate data and present it to the user. If JSPs are the web tier, where can this come from?

Chapter 13 demonstrated the use of JDBC from within JSPs, both directly and by using JavaBeans to encapsulate the data access logic. However, the J2EE features an API for building server-side components to encapsulate business functionality and provide an abstraction for accessing enterprise datasources – Enterprise JavaBeans.

Enterprise JavaBeans

Enterprise JavaBeans are a major part of J2EE and an important technology in allowing Java to be used for building scalable, distributed applications. EJB is a framework for building server-side components for use inside application servers.

One of the real benefits of EJBs is that bean developers don't have to worry about system level features such as security and managing transactions. These are provided by the application server and are part of the contract that J2EE compliant products must provide. The EJB specification provides a standard interface to all this infrastructure so that bean developers can concentrate on building the beans. The task of defining how the beans are secured and the transactions managed is performed when the beans are deployed into the application server.

Another big benefit is that application servers can manage the instances of beans to improve performance of the application. For example, if a bean hasn't been used for a certain period of time, the container could choose to passivate (shutdown) the bean to free up memory and resources. A container could also choose to create multiple instances of the same bean with which to service multiple requests and improve scalability.

At the time of writing, the EJB 2.0 specification is at Proposed Final Draft stage (available at http://java.sun.com/products/ejb/docs.html) and there are now three different types of EJB available – **entity**, **session** and **message driven**.

Entity Beans

An entity bean essentially represents a row in a database and provides a structured way to access and manipulate that data in a distributed environment. The persistence of this data, in this case how it is kept in synchronization with the database, can be managed by the container, or by the bean itself:

❑ **Container Managed Persistence (CMP)**
The container takes care of accessing the database. At the time of deployment, each entity bean is mapped onto a table, with each of its persistent properties mapped onto a specific column. CMP is easy to set up, maintainable and means that the application server can choose the way in which it performs the persistence.

❑ **Bean Managed Persistence (BMP)**
The bean developer writes the database code for the bean using JDBC calls. BMP is useful when the object-relational mapping is complex or the bean developer just wants more control over how the data is persisted.

Session Beans

Session beans, of which there are two types (stateful and stateless), can be viewed as extensions to the client application. **Stateful** session beans are used to store information related to the client between requests. For example, in an online store, a stateful session may be used to store the contents of the customer's shopping cart. When marked as stateful, conceptually that bean represents state that belongs to a specific client.

On the other hand, **stateless** session beans may be shared between client requests and are typically used as a mediator or façade to services provided by other EJBs in the system. For example, imagine a method that manipulates a handful of entity beans on the server. Implementing this on the client would mean a high number of remote method calls. Instead, this logic could be placed in a session bean giving a reduction in the number of remote method calls from the client, and the ability to reuse the logic from various types of client application.

Message Driven Beans

Message driven beans are new for the EJB 2.0 specification and are a special type of session bean. Their purpose is to listen for Java Message Service (JMS) based messages and act upon those messages in some way. For example, this means that an application can have a bean listening for messages from some external system. Once the message comes in, the bean can process and respond to it in some way. The reason message driven beans are a welcome addition to the EJB 2.0 specification is that the only way to do this beforehand was to have the messaging framework consume the messages and call the appropriate methods on the EJBs.

Java Naming and Directory Interface

This provides an abstraction from which to look up hierarchical information from directory servers such as those provided by LDAP. JNDI is the standard method for binding Enterprise JavaBeans and other resources to the application server's naming service, and is looked up by clients, and is supported by all J2EE compliant products.

This is an important API when building applications that make use of Enterprise JavaBeans, whether they are web-based or not. As we'll see shortly, the examples in this chapter make extensive use of JNDI to lookup references to our remote objects.

JavaMail

The ability to send e-mail is taken for granted on the Internet now and is becoming more and more essential to people in and outside of work. JavaMail provides a standard way of accessing recognized mail services such as POP3 and SMTP.

So why would JavaMail be a useful API to access from the web-tier? There are all sorts of uses for JavaMail. For example, sending questions/comments, sending order confirmations from an online store and of course web-based mail services such as those provided by Yahoo! and Hotmail. How you access JavaMail is a discussion for later in the chapter.

Java Message Service

Like JavaMail, JMS is a standard way to send and receive messages from JMS compliant messaging services. Two types of messages are available – Point-to-Point and Publish/Subscribe, both being guaranteed to reach their destinations.

The possibilities for using JMS in the context of a web-based application are limitless. In an online store for example, messages (possibly in XML) could be sent to a credit card processing server to obtain authorization of a credit card in real-time, and afterwards, an asynchronous message could be sent to the third party fulfillment house that is actually going to ship your order. Provided that the fulfillment house receives the message containing the order details, sending this message asynchronously means that the server is immediately free to process other orders.

An Online Store Example

With our whistle stop tour of the J2EE over, we're now going to move on to discuss how the enterprise APIs mentioned above can be incorporated into web-based applications in a number of different ways. To help explain the techniques and concepts used in the rest of the chapter, we're going to use the now famous example of an online store. Because this chapter is about how JSP fits into the J2EE, the store will be a very simple one. We're going to explore how this sort of application can be designed and present a number of different ways of integrating with some of the other J2EE components. In doing so, we'll look at how this affects the design, the benefits and drawbacks.

To set the scene, our online store will be selling books. When the user visits the site, they'll be presented with a list of books from which they can purchase one or more. After clicking the button to order the books, the user will be asked to enter all of their details (name, address, e-mail, credit card), following which, these details will be sent back to the server. At this point, the credit card number will be authorized by a third party and if successful, the order details will be sent to the third party fulfillment house. The user will be given a confirmation page and sent an e-mail containing the details of their order.

Although this chapter shows the source code used in the examples, the full application, including all source code and deployment instructions for jBOSS 2.1, is available to download from http://www.wrox.com.

We'll now move on to discuss some of the ways in which this application can be designed, starting with the most basic (direct data access) and moving on to various designs based around EJBs.

Directly Accessing the Data

The first way of designing the application would be to have the presentation layer directly accessing the data layer. As discussed earlier, there are several ways to implement this, including:

❏   Embedding the data access code in the JSPs

❏   Encapsulating the data access code in JavaBeans

Whichever we choose, the web tier is still talking to the database in some way. We may have cleaned up the JSPs and made the code more maintainable, but at the end of the day, the presentation layer (our JSPs) are accessing the database directly.

If we were to draw an architecture diagram of this solution, it would probably look something like this:

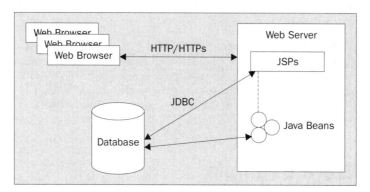

As hinted, directly accessing the database from the web tier is useful in a number of circumstances. For small applications with a limited number of concurrent users, this architecture may prove to be ideal because of the rapid development time and cost to deploy. Another situation where this type of application is suited is prototyping where you need to demonstrate the concepts of manipulating data on the web quickly.

With this architecture come some drawbacks:

Performance and Scalability

Imagine a system where all of the JDBC code and SQL statements were embedded in the JSP. This would mean that every time a page was requested from the web server, a database connection would be opened, SQL fired across the network, run on the database, sent back as a result set and processed in some way before being returned to the user. If we had several thousand people browsing our online store, imagine the amount of network traffic and the number of database connections that would be used up, along with all the other resources of the web server.

Of course, you could pool the database connections on the web tier in some way and although this would reduce the number of database connections being opened, the SQL statements would still have to be fired across the network and processed. This still means the web server doing more work than it need be doing.

The next logical step is to start caching the results, maybe using JavaBeans to store the data. Well this would certainly reduce the number of database accesses for reads but what about writes – the database updates? Rolling back transactions on the server would probably also mean rolling back any updates made to local JavaBeans, essentially reverting them back to their previous state. Once this type of functionality is involved, thread safety starts to become an issue with multiple threads all trying to access/update the state of the beans.

Security

Having JDBC code in the web tier poses a few questions. Firstly, could sensitive information such as database logons become available either accidentally through a system crash or from attacks by hackers? And secondly, has the database been adequately secured so that it can't be accessed from the web itself? If the database is on the same hardware as the web server then this is obviously cause for concern. Likewise, if the database server is not placed behind a firewall for example, the data is open to attacks.

Maintainability

In the first scenario, maintainability of the system could also become an issue as JDBC connection code and SQL statements are spread throughout the JSPs. In fact, even in the example where the JDBC code is encapsulated in JavaBeans, maintainability could still be an issue if code such as opening connections is duplicated between beans. The usual guidelines for not putting too much code in the JSP apply.

To wrap up our discussion of directly accessing the data from the web tier, this architecture certainly has its uses. But for more scalable systems, a different approach is required – Enterprise JavaBeans.

Using Enterprise JavaBeans

Now let's repeat the exercise by bringing EJB into the picture. Instead of directly accessing the database from the web tier (our web server), we're using remote method calls to access the Enterprise JavaBeans running in the middle tier (our application server), which will in turn provide us with our access to the data. If we also introduce the links to the mail server and fulfillment house, an architecture diagram of the application would now look something like this:

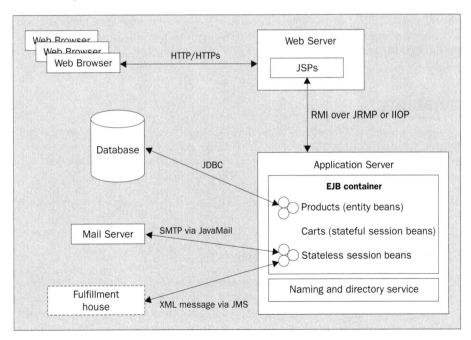

As you can see from the diagram, we now have our JSPs talking to the database via the middle-tier and our Enterprise JavaBeans. We have three different types of EJBs, breaking down as follows:

❑ Entity beans representing the products in the database

❑ Stateful session beans in which to store the contents of the customer's cart

❑ Stateless session beans for sending confirmation e-mails and messages to the third party fulfillment center, wrapping up calls to the JavaMail and JMS APIs respectively

Now that we've redesigned our system using J2EE, we solve some of the problems associated with the two-tier architecture that we outlined earlier:

Performance and Scalability

Application servers in general provide various features to improve the performance and scalability of your enterprise applications. These include passivating those beans that aren't accessed regularly, optimizing CMP based entity beans, and cloning instances to service high numbers of concurrent requests. A good example of this is when the container creates more than one instance of a stateless session bean. As there is no state involved, it doesn't matter if a client actually uses a different stateless session bean for each request.

In addition to this, application (like web) servers can be clustered and load balanced for those applications expected to have a high load.

Security

By moving the database so that it is no longer directly accessible from the web tier, we help to ensure that the data in the database stays intact and secure. But how secure are the objects running on the application server?

One of the benefits of EJB is that developers do not have to concern themselves with writing massive amounts of code to secure the beans that they write. The infrastructure is there to help and provide some of those services, with parts of the security taken care of at deployment time by the assignment of roles to beans and their methods.

Maintainability

With large systems, maintainability is very important. Most application servers now provide various mechanisms for building maintainable systems including the ability to hot-deploy new versions of beans. In addition to this, entity beans can make use of Container Managed Persistence (as discussed earlier) meaning that changes in the data model are easy to reflect in the middle tier.

Now that we've seen some of the benefits of using an EJB approach, let's take a closer look at the example and the various ways it can be implemented.

Building Enterprise JavaBeans

We'll use three different types of EJBs in our design and each one is useful in various situations. As this chapter is not about EJBs specifically, we're not going to go into great depth about the intricacies of designing, developing and deploying EJBs. Instead, we'll give a brief overview of how each could be designed and implemented.

The Product Bean

In our application, we can assume that our product information is stored in some type of database, and assume that there is a row for every product. Each instance of an entity bean wraps up one row in a database table and it's for this reason that we're using entity beans to represent the products. The product bean wraps up the data in the table containing product information, there being one instance for every unique product.

To implement our product bean, we must first decide upon the business interface, or the services that our bean will provide. The products in our application are very simple, only consisting of a unique ID (a `String` in this simple example), name and price.

The Product Interface

The interface must extend `javax.ejb.EJBObject`, with each method declaring that it throws `java.rmi.RemoteException` should the remote method call fail for any reason. The code for the `Product` interface is therefore as follows:

```
package com.wrox.store.ejb.product;

import java.rmi.RemoteException;

import javax.ejb.EJBObject;

public interface Product extends EJBObject {

  public String getId() throws RemoteException;

  public String getName() throws RemoteException;
  public void setName(String newName) throws RemoteException;

  public double getPrice() throws RemoteException;
  public void setPrice(double newPrice) throws RemoteException;

}
```

The ProductBean Class

The next class we need to write is an implementation of the interface and because we're writing an entity bean, our implementation will implement the `javax.ejb.EntityBean` interface. For clarity, our implementation will actually extend a class called `AbstractEntityBean`. This is much like the adapter classes in the AWT and just provides a default (in this case empty) implementation of the entity bean lifecycle methods that are defined in the `javax.ejb.EntityBean` interface. Our implementation is as follows:

```
package com.wrox.store.ejb.product;

import java.rmi.RemoteException;

public class ProductBean extends com.wrox.store.ejb.AbstractEntityBean {

  public String id;
  public String name;
  public double price;
```

Notice that our `ProductBean` has `ejbCreate(String id)` and `ejbPostCreate(String id)` methods. These are again required by the EJB specification and are called before and after the bean is created respectively:

```
public String ejbCreate(String id) {
  this.id = id;

  // return null as creation is performed by the container
  return null;
}

public void ejbPostCreate(String id) {

  // do nothing here
}

public String getId() throws RemoteException {
  return this.id;
}

public String getName() throws RemoteException {
  return this.name;
}

public void setName(String newName) throws RemoteException {
  this.name = newName;
}

public double getPrice() throws RemoteException {
  return this.price;
}

public void setPrice(double newPrice) throws RemoteException {
  this.price = newPrice;
}

}
```

What you've probably noticed is that our `ProductBean` class is not actually implementing the `Product` interface. This is to stop remote beans passing local references to themselves to other remote beans. All beans should be passed through their remote reference because there is no guarantee that the remote object is on the same server. What you should ensure though is that the methods match up exactly.

The ProductHome Interface

Although not shown on the diagram, instances of entity beans (in fact all enterprise beans) are looked up through an appropriate 'home' – an interface containing methods to lookup one or more instances. Ours is no different and our `ProductHome` interface contains a method to lookup `Product` instances based upon their primary key (unique database table identifier), a method to find all products in the application and finally, a method to create a new product with a specified ID:

```
package com.wrox.store.ejb.product;

import java.rmi.RemoteException;
import java.util.Collection;
```

```
import javax.ejb.CreateException;
import javax.ejb.FinderException;

public interface ProductHome extends javax.ejb.EJBHome {

  public Product create(String id) throws CreateException, RemoteException;

  public Product findByPrimaryKey(String id)
          throws FinderException, RemoteException;

  public Collection findAll() throws RemoteException, FinderException;

}
```

In our example, the implementation of the home interface is provided for us automatically by the EJB container. When we deploy the Product, ProductBean and ProductHome classes, we will also provide a configuration file associating these classes with the various roles that they play. The deployment is discussed shortly.

The AbstractEntityBean Class

This abstract class is much like the adapter classes in AWT and just provides a default (in this case empty) implementation of the entity bean lifecycle methods that are defined in the javax.ejb.EntityBean interface:

```
package com.wrox.store.ejb;

import javax.ejb.EntityBean;
import javax.ejb.EntityContext;

public abstract class AbstractEntityBean implements EntityBean {

  protected EntityContext entityContext;

  public void setEntityContext(EntityContext ctx) {
    this.entityContext = ctx;
  }

  public void unsetEntityContext() {
    this.entityContext = null;
  }

  public void ejbActivate() {
    // do nothing
  }

  public void ejbPassivate() {
    // do nothing
  }

  public void ejbLoad() {
    // do nothing
  }
```

```
    public void ejbStore() {
      // do nothing
    }

    public void ejbRemove() {
      // do nothing
    }

}
```

The Cart Bean

The customer's shopping cart does not represent data in the database and therefore it is not an entity bean. For this reason, the cart will be implemented as a session bean. Of course it could be argued that the data in the shopping cart does eventually make its way into the database, but it will be stored by some other means and is out of the scope of this chapter. Session beans can be viewed as an extension of the client and in this case, the bean stores information about those products that the customer has selected for purchase. Because we need to keep track of this state, the cart is a stateful session bean.

So why store the contents of the customer's cart in a stateful session bean and not in the HTTP session? We could do this, but moving this information into the middle-tier means that the same mechanism can be reused for non web-based clients, such as a point-of-sale terminal in a traditional brick and mortar store. Although this information is directly related to the client manipulating it, the information is located elsewhere in the architecture.

The other point to mention here is that session beans don't just have to be used to store information; they can also contain functionality that would usually be implemented at the client. For instance, our cart bean has a method for submitting the order. It already has much of the information that it requires, and in this case can also act as a mediator for controlling the interactions between the various objects required to perform this operation. This not only simplifies development of the client, but also reduces the number of remote method calls that need to be made to perform a specific task.

Although only briefly mentioned, this is an important design principle for partitioning the business logic and optimizing performance. Further details can be found in the references listed in the further reading section at the end of this chapter.

The Cart Interface

Moving back to the implementation, session beans are implemented in a similar way to entity beans, having an interface, an implementation, and a home. We'll start with the Cart interface. Note that some of these methods throw an AuthorizationException, which we will define later:

```
package com.wrox.store.ejb.cart;

import java.rmi.RemoteException;
import java.util.*;

import com.wrox.store.ejb.customer.Customer;
import com.wrox.store.ejb.product.Product;
import com.wrox.store.exception.*;

public interface Cart extends javax.ejb.EJBObject {
```

```
    public void add(Product product, int newQuantity) throws RemoteException;

    public Collection products() throws RemoteException;

    public int getQuantity(Product product) throws RemoteException;

    public double getTotal() throws RemoteException;

    public void submitOrder(Customer customer)
            throws AuthorizationException, RemoteException;

}
```

The CartBean Class

As with the `ProductBean`, our implementation extends an adapter class called `AbstractSessionBean` to aid clarity of the code shown below. This abstract class just provides default implementations of the lifecycle methods, this time defined in the `javax.ejb.SessionBean` interface. Here's the `CartBean`:

```
package com.wrox.store.ejb.cart;

import java.rmi.RemoteException;
import java.util.*;

import com.wrox.store.ejb.customer.Customer;
import com.wrox.store.ejb.product.Product;
import com.wrox.store.exception.*;

public class CartBean extends com.wrox.store.ejb.AbstractSessionBean {

  // the collection of products in the cart
  public HashMap products = new HashMap();

  // Adds the specified quantity of the supplied product to the cart.

  public void add(Product product, int newQuantity) throws RemoteException {
    int existingQuantity = getQuantity(product);

    products.put(product, new Integer(existingQuantity + newQuantity));
  }

  // Gets a reference to the collection of products in the cart.

  public Collection products() throws RemoteException {
    return new ArrayList(products.keySet());
  }

    // Determines how many of the specified product are in the cart -
    // if any

  public int getQuantity(Product product) throws RemoteException {
    Integer quantity = (Integer)products.get(product);

    if (quantity == null) {
```

```
            return 0;
        } else {
            return quantity.intValue();
        }
    }
```

The `submitOrder()` method submits the contents of this cart that are to be purchased. This involves a number of steps, including: authorising the credit card, sending a message to the fulfillment center and sending a confirmation e-mail to the customer. The e-mail function of our online store will be implemented later in the chapter:

```
    public void submitOrder(Customer customer)
            throws AuthorizationException, RemoteException {
        products.clear();
    }

}
```

The CartHome Interface

And finally we have our cart home with one method allowing clients to create new carts:

```
    package com.wrox.store.ejb.cart;

    import java.rmi.RemoteException;

    import javax.ejb.CreateException;

    public interface CartHome extends javax.ejb.EJBHome {

        public Cart create() throws CreateException, RemoteException;

    }
```

The AbstractSessionBean Class

Like `AbstractEntityBean`, this abstract class is much like the adapter classes in AWT and just provides a default (in this case empty) implementation of the entity bean lifecycle methods that are defined in the `javax.ejb.SessionBean` interface:

```
    package com.wrox.store.ejb;

    import javax.ejb.SessionBean;
    import javax.ejb.SessionContext;

    public abstract class AbstractSessionBean implements SessionBean {

        protected SessionContext sessionContext;

        public void setSessionContext(SessionContext ctx) {
            this.sessionContext = ctx;
        }

        public void ejbActivate() {
```

```
    // do nothing
  }

  public void ejbPassivate() {
    // do nothing
  }

  public void ejbCreate() {
    // do nothing
  }

  public void ejbRemove() {
    // do nothing
  }

}
```

The Customer Bean

You may have noticed that the submitOrder() method in out CartBean shown above makes use of a class called Customer. This is just another bean in which to store the details of the customer, such as their name, address, e-mail address and credit card details.

The Customer Interface

In a real system, the customer would more than likely be an entity bean as we would probably like to store the details of our customers. In this case, our customer bean would certainly have a primary key property and may have a unique login for the system. For the simplicity of the example though, the customer is another stateful session bean, the remote interface being as follows:

```
package com.wrox.store.ejb.customer;

import java.rmi.RemoteException;

import com.wrox.store.exception.*;

public interface Customer extends javax.ejb.EJBObject {

  public String getName() throws RemoteException;
  public void setName(String newName) throws RemoteException;

  public String getAddress() throws RemoteException;
  public void setAddress(String newAddress) throws RemoteException;

  public String getZipCode() throws RemoteException;
  public void setZipCode(String newZipCode) throws RemoteException;

  public String getEmailAddress() throws RemoteException;
  public void setEmailAddress(String newEmailAddress)
          throws RemoteException;

  public String getCreditCardNumber() throws RemoteException;
  public void setCreditCardNumber(String newCreditCardNumber)
          throws RemoteException;

}
```

The CustomerBean Class

```
package com.wrox.store.ejb.customer;

import java.rmi.RemoteException;
import com.wrox.store.exception.*;

public class CustomerBean extends com.wrox.store.ejb.AbstractSessionBean {

  public String name;
  public String address;
  public String zipCode;
  public String emailAddress;
  public String creditCardNumber;

  /** Gets the name of the customer */
  public String getName() throws RemoteException {
    return this.name;
  }

  /** Sets the name of the customer */
  public void setName(String newName) throws RemoteException {
    this.name = newName;
  }

  /** Gets the address of the customer */
  public String getAddress() throws RemoteException {
    return this.address;
  }

  /** Sets the address of the customer */
  public void setAddress(String newAddress) throws RemoteException {
    this.address = newAddress;
  }

  /** Gets the zip code of the customer */
  public String getZipCode() throws RemoteException {
    return this.zipCode;
  }

  /** Sets the zip code for the customer */
  public void setZipCode(String newZipCode) throws RemoteException {
    this.zipCode = newZipCode;
  }

  /** Gets the e-mail address of the customer */
  public String getEmailAddress() throws RemoteException {
    return this.emailAddress;
  }

  /** Sets the e-mail address of the customer */
  public void setEmailAddress(String newEmailAddress)
          throws RemoteException {
    this.emailAddress = newEmailAddress;
  }

  /** Gets the credit card number of the customer */
```

```
    public String getCreditCardNumber() throws RemoteException {
      return this.creditCardNumber;
    }

    /** Sets the credit card number of the customer */
    public void setCreditCardNumber(String newCreditCardNumber)
            throws RemoteException {
      this.creditCardNumber = newCreditCardNumber;
    }

  }
```

The CustomerHome Interface

```
    package com.wrox.store.ejb.customer;

    import java.rmi.RemoteException;

    import javax.ejb.CreateException;

    public interface CustomerHome extends javax.ejb.EJBHome {

      public Customer create() throws CreateException, RemoteException;

    }
```

The AuthorizeException Class

A simple exception that might be thrown when credit card authorization fails:

```
    package com.wrox.store.exception;

    public class AuthorizationException extends Exception {

      public AuthorizationException(String message) {
        super(message);
      }

    }
```

The Other Beans

As for the other session beans in our application, these are just convenient wrappers with which to send the messages to the external systems and e-mails to the customer. These beans don't need to store any state between requests and are therefore stateless session beans. These will be discussed a little later on.

Deploying Enterprise JavaBeans

Now that we've seen how our beans are built, let's look at how they're deployed. Deploying EJB's is fairly straight forward, although not entirely standard between the various application servers on the market. The way that the core features of enterprise beans are defined is the same; however, each application server has a slightly different way of configuring additional details such as the JNDI names for the home interfaces for example.

For the purposes of this example, we'll be deploying our EJBs into jBOSS – an open-source EJB server written in 100% in pure Java, complete with a database called Hypersonic.

Download jBoss 2.1 from http://www.jboss.org and unzip it into C:\jBoss-2.1_FINAL or /jBoss-2.1_FINAL directory (%JBOSS_HOME% from now on). Set the environment variable JBOSS_HOME to this directory. Finally, start jBoss by running run.bat (run.sh in Unix) in the %JBOSS_HOME%\bin directory. jBoss can be stopped at any time by pressing Ctrl-C in the jBoss window.

The Deployment Descriptor

The first step is to write the deployment descriptor – a configuration file that specifies the details of our EJBs. This is written in XML and is named ejb-jar.xml. Full details on the format of this file can be found in the references listed in the further reading section; however let's take a look at how the beans themselves are defined.

First of all, each EJB must be defined within an <entity> or <session> tag (as appropriate), and we need to define some properties that are common to both entity and session beans:

- ❑ ejb-name
- ❑ home
- ❑ remote
- ❑ ejb-class

The ejb-name is just a name with which to refer to all of the various parts of which our EJB consists – the remote interface, bean class and home interface. This name is used in another configuration file shown shortly. The home, remote and ejb-class properties are the fully qualified class names of the home interface, remote interface and bean classes respectively:

```
<?xml version="1.0"?>
  <ejb-jar>
    <enterprise-beans>

      <entity>
        <ejb-name>Product</ejb-name>
        <home>com.wrox.store.ejb.product.ProductHome</home>
        <remote>com.wrox.store.ejb.product.Product</remote>
        <ejb-class>com.wrox.store.ejb.product.ProductBean</ejb-class>
```

For our product entity bean, we then need to indicate the fully qualified class name of the primary key and whether re-entrant calls are allowed to the bean. Re-entrant calls mean that bean A calls a method on bean B, which subsequently calls a method on bean A. This is discouraged when writing EJBs because of issues surrounding multiple threads operating on single instances of entity beans. While out of scope of this chapter, this is an important topic to consider when designing EJB based systems, more information on which may be found in the references listed in the further reading section. For the sake of our small example, we'll say that our beans are not re-entrant:

```
<prim-key-class>java.lang.String</prim-key-class>
<reentrant>False</reentrant>
```

The final part in defining our product bean is to say how the persistence is going to be managed. Because we are using container managed persistence, we must specify the names of those properties that we wish to persist, and which one is the primary key. For simplicity, the names of our bean properties match the field names in the database and behind the scenes; jBOSS also uses a table matching the name of the EJB that we defined earlier:

```
            <persistence-type>Container</persistence-type>
            <cmp-field><field-name>id</field-name></cmp-field>
            <cmp-field><field-name>name</field-name></cmp-field>
            <cmp-field><field-name>price</field-name></cmp-field>
            <primkey-field>id</primkey-field>
        </entity>
```

With our product bean defined, we can move on to defining the session beans that again start in the same way:

```
        <session>
         <ejb-name>Cart</ejb-name>
         <home>com.wrox.store.ejb.cart.CartHome</home>
         <remote>com.wrox.store.ejb.cart.Cart</remote>
         <ejb-class>com.wrox.store.ejb.cart.CartBean</ejb-class>
```

The next property that we need to define for a session bean is the type of session that we require – stateful or stateless. Our cart is a stateful session bean because it is going to store those products that the customer has selected for purchase.

Finally, we need to declare whether we are using container managed or bean managed transactions, not to be confused with bean or container managed persistence. Instead, this defines whether the container should initiate and manage transactions, or whether the bean should so this. Once again, this is another important topic that is out of the scope of this chapter, details of which can be found in the references listed at the end of the chapter. For the sake of our simple example, we'll assume that we're using container managed transactions:

```
            <session-type>Stateful</session-type>
            <transaction-type>Container</transaction-type>
        </session>
```

The definition of our customer bean is very similar to that of our cart bean:

```
        <session>
          <ejb-name>Customer</ejb-name>
          <home>com.wrox.store.ejb.customer.CustomerHome</home>
          <remote>com.wrox.store.ejb.customer.Customer</remote>
          <ejb-class>com.wrox.store.ejb.customer.CustomerBean</ejb-class>

          <session-type>Stateful</session-type>
          <transaction-type>Container</transaction-type>
        </session>

      </enterprise-beans>

    </ejb-jar>
```

941

Binding in JNDI

Now that we've defined the core details of our EJBs, the next step is to tell jBOSS the JNDI names with which we wish to bind each of the home interfaces. These are the names that our clients (the JSPs, JavaBeans and custom tags) will use to lookup the appropriate home for each of our EJBs. This file is called `jboss.xml` and although it is specific to jBOSS, it simply ties a bean to a unique, well known name. As there could be more than one set of EJBs deployed in the server, it's important to choose unique names not only for our application but for the server as a whole. For this reason, we are using a hierarchical naming structure:

```xml
<?xml version="1.0"?>

<jboss>

  <enterprise-beans>

    <entity>
      <ejb-name>Product</ejb-name>
      <jndi-name>store/ProductHome</jndi-name>
    </entity>

    <session>
      <ejb-name>Cart</ejb-name>
      <jndi-name>store/CartHome</jndi-name>
    </session>

    <session>
      <ejb-name>Customer</ejb-name>
      <jndi-name>store/CustomerHome</jndi-name>
    </session>

  </enterprise-beans>

</jboss>
```

Deploying in jBoss

Now that we've written these two files, deploying the beans in jBOSS is easy. Compile the classes with the following JAR files in your `CLASSPATH`:

- ❏   `%CATALINA_HOME%\common\lib\servlet.jar`

- ❏   `%JBOSS_HOME%\client\ejb.jar`

- ❏   `%JBOSS_HOME%\client\jboss-client.jar`

- ❏   `%JBOSS_HOME%\lib\ext\activation.jar`

All we need to do is build a JAR file with the contents and structure as follows:

```
com
  wrox
    store
      exception
        AuthorizationException.class
      ejb
        AbstractEntityBean.class
```

```
            AbstractSessionBean.class
            cart
               Cart.class
               CartBean.class
               CartHome.class
            product
               Product.class
               ProductBean.class
               ProductHome.class
            customer
               Customer.class
               CustomerBean.class
               CustomerHome.class
      META-INF
         ejb-jar.xml
         jboss.xml
```

Assuming that you're running jBOSS as described above, the final step is to copy the JAR file into the `%JBOSS_HOME%\deploy` directory. If everything is set up correctly, you will see jBoss deploying your EJBs.

Now that you have deployed your EJBs, it is time to test them.

The Upload Class

In order to test your EJBs we must store some book information using JNDI:

```java
import java.rmi.RemoteException;
import java.util.*;

import javax.ejb.*;
import javax.naming.*;
import javax.rmi.PortableRemoteObject;

import com.wrox.store.ejb.product.*;

public class Upload {

   public static void main(String[] args) {

      // setup the JNDI properties
      System.setProperty("java.naming.factory.initial",
                         "org.jnp.interfaces.NamingContextFactory");
      System.setProperty("java.naming.provider.url", "localhost:1099");


      try {
```

First we have to lookup the product home:

```java
         InitialContext ctx = new InitialContext();
         ProductHome home = (ProductHome)
                PortableRemoteObject.narrow(ctx.lookup("store/ProductHome"),
                                            ProductHome.class);
         Product product;
```

If there are any existing products, remove them all:

```
        Collection coll = home.findAll();
        Iterator it = coll.iterator();
        while (it.hasNext()) {
          product = (Product)it.next();
          product.remove();
        }

        System.out.println("Removed all existing products.");
```

In order to test our EJBs we must create some sample products:

```
        product = home.create("1");
        product.setName("Professional JSP");
        product.setPrice(59.99);

        product = home.create("2");
        product.setName("Professional Java Server Programming J2EE Edition ");
        product.setPrice(64.99);

        product = home.create("3");
        product.setName("Professional Java Programming");
        product.setPrice(59.99);

        System.out.println("Added products.");
```

Finally, we need to display the products to make sure they got inserted:

```
        coll = home.findAll();
        it = coll.iterator();
        while (it.hasNext()) {
          product = (Product)it.next();
          System.out.println(product.getName() + " - " + product.getPrice());
        }
      } catch (NamingException ne) {
        System.out.println(ne.getMessage());
      } catch (FinderException fe) {
        System.out.println(fe.getMessage());
      } catch (RemoveException rve) {
        System.out.println(rve.getMessage());
      } catch (CreateException ce) {
        System.out.println(ce.getMessage());
      } catch (RemoteException re) {
        System.out.println(re.getMessage());
      }
    }
  }
```

The Test Class

Once we have some book data stored in JNDI we can test our EJBs:

```
import java.rmi.RemoteException;
import java.util.*;

import javax.ejb.*;
import javax.naming.*;
import javax.rmi.PortableRemoteObject;

import com.wrox.store.ejb.product.*;

public class Test {

  public static void main(String[] args) {

    // setup the JNDI properties
    System.setProperty("java.naming.factory.initial",
                       "org.jnp.interfaces.NamingContextFactory");
    System.setProperty("java.naming.provider.url", "localhost:1099");

    try {
      // look up the product home
      InitialContext ctx = new InitialContext();
      ProductHome home = (ProductHome)PortableRemoteObject.narrow
                         (ctx.lookup("store/ProductHome"),
                          ProductHome.class);
```

Once the home has been looked up, all the products that are known to the system are displayed:

```
      Product product;
      Collection coll = home.findAll();
      Iterator it = coll.iterator();
      while (it.hasNext()) {
        product = (Product)it.next();
        System.out.println(product.getName() + " - " + product.getPrice());
      }
    } catch (NamingException ne) {
      System.out.println(ne.getMessage());
    } catch (FinderException fe) {
      System.out.println(fe.getMessage());
    } catch (RemoteException re) {
      System.out.println(re.getMessage());
    }
  }
}
```

Running the Test

Ensure that %JBOSS_HOME%\client\ejb.jar, %JBOSS_HOME%\client\jboss-client.jar, and ch24.jar are in your CLASSPATH, and run the Upload class to create the entity beans, followed by the Test class to check that everything has deployed correctly.

Accessing EJB from JSP

Now that we've looked at how the various EJBs in our example system were built and deployed, we'll now move on to show how they can be used in the application, and from within the JavaServer Pages themselves.

JSP and Stateful Session Beans

The usual way to bind an object to the HTTP session would be to use the `<jsp:useBean>` tag. This allows you to bind a named, scoped instance of an object to the session and subsequently use it throughout the pages in your application. If an instance with the name you specified doesn't exist, the default no arguments constructor is called and the resulting instance is bound to the session.

This is all well and good except that remote objects cannot be instantiated by calling the no arguments constructor. Instead, the object must be created on the server and the just remote reference passed back to the client. For this reason, another approach is needed.

To create a new instance of an EJB, you must call the appropriate 'create' method on the home interface. Creating a new instance of the cart for a new customer would mean a call to the `create()` method on the `CartHome` interface.

As when using RMI, the reference returned should be cast back to the interface and not the implementation. This is because the remote reference (or stub) is really a proxy for the remote object on the server. This auto-generated stub implements the remote interface, but in fact passes on those calls to the remote object running on the server. To create a new instance in a JSP, typically you would have to write a scriptlet or custom tag to check whether an instance of your EJB already existed and conditionally create and bind it to the HTTP session:

```
<%
    // try to find existing cart instance tied to session
    Cart cart = (Cart)session.getAttribute("cart");

    if (cart == null) {
        // create a new context and perform the JNDI lookup
        InitialContext ctx = new InitialContext();
            (CartHome) PortableRemoteObject.narrow(ctx.lookup("store/CartHome"),
                                            CartHome.class);

        // create a new cart and bind to session
        cart = cartHome.create();
        session.setAttribute("cart", cart);
    }
%>
```

While this is not bad in any way, it does clutter up the page with code that will only be executed once during the lifetime of a session. The other question is that how would we know when the session had been invalidated or expired so that the remote reference can be released?

As discussed in Chapter 16, version 2.3 of the Java Servlet specification introduces the ability to register listeners for specific events that occur during the life of a web application. The one we are particularly interested in here is the `javax.servlet.http.HttpSessionListener`, having two methods that get called when a session is created and destroyed:

```
public interface HttpSessionListener {

  public void sessionCreated(HttpSessionEvent e);
  public void sessionDestroyed(HttpSessionEvent e);


}
```

This is useful because when a new session is created, we can create a new cart and tie it into the session. When the session is subsequently destroyed for any reason, we can grab the cart that we previously created and ensure that it gets cleaned up and destroyed.

The SessionListener Class

In essence, our scriptlet or custom tag that checks for the existence of a cart can now be written as follows. It may be more code, but we now have a reusable, maintainable object with much more flexibility over what happens when the session is created and destroyed:

```
package com.wrox.store.servlet;

import java.rmi.RemoteException;

import javax.ejb.*;
import javax.naming.*;
import javax.rmi.PortableRemoteObject;
import javax.servlet.*;
import javax.servlet.http.*;

import com.wrox.store.ejb.cart.*;

public class SessionListener implements HttpSessionListener {

  public void sessionCreated(HttpSessionEvent e) {
    Cart cart;

    try {

        // create a context and peform the JNDI lookup
        InitialContext ctx = new InitialContext();
        CartHome cartHome =
          (CartHome) PortableRemoteObject.narrow(ctx.lookup("store/CartHome"),
                                                 CartHome.class);

        // create a cart and bind it to the session
        cart = cartHome.create();
        e.getSession().setAttribute("cart", cart);
    } catch (CreateException ce) {
        System.out.println(ce.getMessage());
    } catch (NamingException ne) {
        System.out.println(ne.getMessage());
    } catch (RemoteException re) {
        System.out.println(re.getMessage());
    }
  }

  public void sessionDestroyed(HttpSessionEvent e) {
```

```
    try {

        // get the existing cart out of the session
        Cart cart = (Cart) e.getSession().getAttribute("cart");

        if (cart != null) {

            // and remove it from the EJB container
            cart.remove();
        }
    } catch (RemoveException rve) {
        System.out.println(rve.getMessage());
    } catch (RemoteException re) {
        System.out.println(re.getMessage());
    }
}

}
```

JSP and Entity Beans

There are several different ways that entity beans can be accessed from JSPs, each with their own benefits and drawbacks. Although the examples show how to access EJBs from JSPs, the principles are applicable to accessing the other APIs within the J2EE. The examples that follow show the various ways in which the catalog page of our online shopping store could be written.

From a high level, our JSP will lookup the product home interface, use it to find all of the products and display these in a table on the page.

Scriptlets

Our first (and simplest) example embeds all of the necessary Java code into a scriptlet in the JSP. Using scriptlets in your JSPs is usually discouraged in favor of encapsulating the functionality in JavaBeans or custom tags to make it much more reusable. However, for proof of concept developments and prototypes, it is a quick an easy way of achieving a visible end result.

The Scriptlet JSP

Accessing an EJB from a scriptlet is no different from the Java code we used earlier to lookup the cart home; scriptlet.jsp contains the following:

```
<%@ page import="java.util.*" %>

<%@ page import="javax.naming.*" %>
<%@ page import="javax.rmi.PortableRemoteObject" %>

<%@ page import="com.wrox.store.ejb.product.*" %>

<%
    // create a new context and perform the lookup
    InitialContext ctx = new InitialContext();
    ProductHome home = (ProductHome)PortableRemoteObject.narrow(
        ctx.lookup("store/ProductHome"), ProductHome.class);
```

```
   // find all the products and iterate, displaying each in the table
   Product product;
   Collection coll = home.findAll();
   Iterator it = coll.iterator();
   while (it.hasNext()) {
     product = (Product)it.next();
%>
   <tr>
   <td><%= product.getName() %></td>
   <td align="right">$<%= product.getPrice() %></td>
   <td align="right"><input type="text" size="2" maxlength="2"
     name="quantity_<%= product.getId()%>" value=""></td>
   </tr>
<%
   }
%>
```

First of all (and because we're writing a scriptlet), we are required to import the various classes that we'll be using. As with the cart examples, we then create an `InitialContext` object and use it to look up a reference to our `ProductHome` using the well-known name that was defined during deployment. Once we have this reference, we can use the `findAll()` method to get a collection of all of the products in our system. In fact it's a collection of remote references to `ProductBean` instances on the EJB server and this means that the calls to the `getName()`, `getPrice()` and `getId()` methods are actually all remote method calls.

So once we have a collection, we can then iterate over the collection and generate the HTML in the usual way – with a mixture of HTML and Java expressions surrounded by `<%= %>` tags.

As you can see, there is a fair amount of Java code inside the JSP that will be executed every time the page is requested. While the quantity of Java code isn't really a problem in this example, the number of remote method calls could be. There are a few ways of reducing the number of remote method calls when dealing with EJBs, such as returning coarse-grained value objects – JavaBeans containing a read-only version of the internal state.

Taking our `ProductBean` class as an example, instead of calling the `getName()` and `getPrice()` methods on the remote object across the network, we could have a single remote method called `getDetails()` that returns a simple Java object. This object could have two properties (one each for the name and price), with the appropriate getter methods, therefore reducing the number of remote method calls to just one.

However, we are still left with the remote lookup of the product home and although we could cache this reference in an instance variable on the page, the lookup code is still in the page. From a maintainability perspective, this is undesirable because every page that needs to use a remote object will require the same code. Let's take a look at another approach.

JavaBeans as Wrappers

Our next example uses a regular JavaBean to encapsulate the lookup to the home interface, and thereafter essentially acts as a proxy by forwarding calls onto the remote object.

The ProductManager Class

Our default, no argument constructor is used to create the initial context and lookup the bean through JNDI as shown in our previous examples. What's different this time is that we're actually saving the reference for use later on. Just as our real product home has finder methods, our JavaBean has the same finder methods with one line of code that passes the requests through to the remote object. Our methods throw the same exceptions as our real home interface so that if something does go wrong, the standard JSP error handling mechanism can be used:

```java
package com.wrox.store.ejb.product;

import java.rmi.RemoteException;
import java.util.Collection;

import javax.ejb.*;
import javax.naming.*;
import javax.rmi.PortableRemoteObject;

public class ProductManager {

  private ProductHome productHome;

  public ProductManager() throws NamingException, RemoteException {
    InitialContext ctx = new InitialContext();

    // look up home and keep hold of the reference
    productHome =
      (ProductHome) PortableRemoteObject
        .narrow(ctx.lookup("store/ProductHome"), ProductHome.class);
  }

  public Collection findAll() throws FinderException, RemoteException {
    return productHome.findAll();
  }

  public Product findByPrimaryKey(String id)
        throws FinderException, RemoteException {
    return productHome.findByPrimaryKey(id);
  }

}
```

The Bean JSP

As our wrapper is a regular JavaBean with a no argument constructor, we now use it within our JSPs in conjunction with the standard `<jsp:useBean>` tag as `bean.jsp` demonstrates:

```jsp
<%@ page import="java.util.*" %>

<%@ page import="com.wrox.store.ejb.product.*" %>

<jsp:useBean id="productManager"
  class="com.wrox.store.ejb.product.ProductManager" scope="page"/>
<%
  Collection coll = productManager.findAll();
```

```
    Product product;
    Iterator it = coll.iterator();
    while (it.hasNext()) {
      product = (Product)it.next();
%>
      <tr>
      <td><%= product.getName() %></td>
      <td align="right">$<%= product.getPrice() %></td>
      <td align="right"><input type="text" size="2" maxlength="2"
        name="quantity_<%= product.getId()%>" value=""></td>
      </tr>
<%
    }
%>
```

Again, because we are using some Java code in the page, we need to import the appropriate classes. However, because we've encapsulated the JNDI lookup in our bean, the number of classes that we are required to import has been greatly reduced.

To recap, the <jsp:useBean> tag allows you to bind named, scoped instances of a JavaBean to a particular name and make use of it elsewhere in the page. In our example, we're binding it to a page-scoped instance called "productManager" which we can use to get a collection of remote references in the same way as in our scriptlet example.

However, having the wrapper as page scoped means that an instance will be created every time the page is requested, again meaning that the lookup will be performed on every request. By changing the scope in the <jsp:useBean> tag to session or application, we instantly reduce the number of times the JNDI lookup is performed to once per session, or once per application respectively. The following snippet shows the bean used as session scoped:

```
<jsp:useBean id="productManager"
    class="com.wrox.store.ejb.product.ProductManager" scope="session"/>
```

By moving the lookup code out of the page, we've increased the maintainability of our system and provided an easy way to reduce the number of JNDI lookups that are performed. However, we still have a fair amount of Java code in the page to build up the table of products so let's take at look at our final example that makes use of tags.

Custom tags

Our last example shows how we can remove all (well most!) of the Java code from our JSP. We can do this by replacing the Java code that performs the iteration with a custom tag that does this for us. As we've already seen in Chapters 9 and 10, version 1.2 of the JSP specification brings another interface with which to build custom tags – javax.servlet.jsp.tagext.IterationTag. It extends the regular Tag interface and adds a method called doAfterBody() that is called after the body of the tag has been processed, making it easy to tell the container whether another iteration is required.

Our iterator tag will have three required attributes:

❑ id
As with the <jsp:useBean> tag, the name of the variable into which each of the elements we are iterating over will be placed

❑ className
    The fully qualified class name of the objects

❑ iterator
    A reference to a `java.util.Iterator`

The first two attributes are static values, defined in the page, while the third is a runtime expression.

The TLD Entry

The XML describing the tag (in the taglib descriptor file `taglib.tld`) therefore looks like this:

```
<tag>
  <name>iterator</name>
  <tagclass>com.wrox.store.tag.IteratorTag</tagclass>
  <teiclass>com.wrox.store.tag.IteratorTagExtraInfo</teiclass>
  <info>Performs iteration on a JSP</info>

  <attribute>
    <name>id</name>
    <required>true</required>
    <rtexprvalue>false</rtexprvalue>
  </attribute>

  <attribute>
    <name>className</name>
    <required>true</required>
    <rtexprvalue>false</rtexprvalue>
  </attribute>

  <attribute>
    <name>iterator</name>
    <required>true</required>
    <rtexprvalue>true</rtexprvalue>
  </attribute>
</tag>
```

The IteratorTag Class

Let's now look at how the tag can be implemented:

```
package com.wrox.store.tag;

import java.util.Iterator;

import javax.servlet.jsp.*;
import javax.servlet.jsp.tagext.*;

public class IteratorTag extends TagSupport implements IterationTag {

  private String id;
  private String className;
  private Iterator iterator;

  public int doStartTag() throws JspException {
    if (iterator.hasNext()) {
```

```
        // if there are elements, put the first one into the
        // page under the name provided by the "id" attribute
        pageContext.setAttribute(id, iterator.next());

        // and include the body
        return EVAL_BODY_INCLUDE;
      } else {

        // there are no elements so skip the body
        return SKIP_BODY;
      }
    }

    public int doAfterBody() throws JspException {
      if (iterator.hasNext()) {

        // if there are more elements, put the next one into the
        // page under the name provided by the "id" attribute
        pageContext.setAttribute(id, iterator.next());

        // and instruct the JSP engine to re-evaluate the body
        // of this tag
        return EVAL_BODY_AGAIN;
      } else {

        // there are no more elements so skip the body
        return SKIP_BODY;
      }
    }

    public void setId(String s) {
      this.id = s;
    }

    public void setClassName(String s) {
      this.className = s;
    }

    public void setIterator(Iterator it) {
      this.iterator = it;
    }
  }
```

As when building other tags, we have some JavaBean style setters for the attributes – id, className, and iterator. We then have the doStartTag() and doAfterBody() methods that check whether there are more elements to iterate over and if so, the next one is placed as an attribute into the page under the name provided through the id attribute.

The IteratorTagExtraInfo Class

What you've probably noticed is that the className parameter is not used in our tag. This is because it is actually used by the 'extra info' class defined for our tag. This class is required for our tag because we need to tell the container that we are putting an object back into the page for subsequent use later on. The container needs to know the name of this object, it's type, and where it will be in scope. Chapters 9 & 10 give a full explanation of how this all works, but for completeness, the code for our 'extra info' class is shown below:

```
package com.wrox.store.tag;

import javax.servlet.jsp.tagext.*;

public class IteratorTagExtraInfo extends TagExtraInfo {

  public VariableInfo[] getVariableInfo(TagData data) {
    return new VariableInfo[] {
      new VariableInfo(data.getId(), data.getAttributeString("className"),
                      true, VariableInfo.AT_END)
    };
  }


}
```

The Tag JSP

Once the tag has been built and deployed, we can use it on our catalog page tag.jsp to iterate over the collection of remote Product references as follows:

```
<%-- import the tag library --%>
<%@ taglib uri="http://www.wrox.com/taglib" prefix=" chap24" %>

<jsp:useBean id="productManager"
  class="com.wrox.store.ejb.product.ProductManager" scope="page"/>

<chap24:iterator id="product" className="com.wrox.store.ejb.product.Product"
  iterator="<%= productManager.findAll().iterator() %>">
  <tr>
  <td><jsp:getProperty name="product" property="name"/></td>
  <td align="right">$<jsp:getProperty name="product"
    property="price"/></td>
  <td align="right"><input type="text" size="2" maxlength="2"
    name="quantity_<jsp:getProperty name="product" property="id"/>"
    value=""></td>
  </tr>
</chap24:iterator>
```

In the JSP fragment above, we can pass an iterator over the collection of all products returned from the ProductManager bean into our tag. Each product will be placed into the page, referenced by the variable name "product" and with a type of Product – the interface. What this means is that we can now use the standard <jsp:getProperty> tag to extract the name, price, and id of each product within the body of the <wrox:iterator> tag. After all, the methods on our EJB use the JavaBean naming conventions.

The resulting JSP is much shorter, cleaner, less confusing and more maintainable from both the developer's perspective, and that of the web author whose job it would be to turn this page into a creative masterpiece. Another benefit is that we now have a reusable tag that can be used on other pages and other web applications.

Accessing JNDI from JSP

Using a JavaBean is a good way of wrapping up the services provided by a remote object. However, a drawback to this solution is that our `ProductManager` bean is very much tied into the `ProductHome` interface meaning additional wrappers would have to be written for additional remote objects that we need to look up. One way to address this would be to parameterize the required information so that any remote object could be looked up through the naming service. While this would work, a more appropriate solution would be to use a custom tag.

Taking the `<jsp:useBean>` as our model, let's define the attributes that would be required for a tag that allows us to use remote beans in our JSP:

- ❑   `id` – again, the name of the variable on the page

- ❑   `jndiName` – the name to which the remote object is bound

- ❑   `className` – the fully qualified class name of the resulting instance

The TLD Entry

For this example, the attributes are all static and the definition of the tag in the `taglib.tld` file would look like this:

```
<tag>
  <name>useRemoteBean</name>
  <tagclass>com.wrox.store.tag.UseRemoteBeanTag</tagclass>
  <teiclass>com.wrox.store.tag.UseRemoteBeanTagExtraInfo</teiclass>
  <info>Inserts a remote reference into the page </info>

  <attribute>
    <name>id</name>
    <required>true</required>
    <rtexprvalue>false</rtexprvalue>
  </attribute>

  <attribute>
    <name>jndiName</name>
    <required>true</required>
    <rtexprvalue>false</rtexprvalue>
  </attribute>

  <attribute>
    <name>className</name>
    <required>true</required>
    <rtexprvalue>false</rtexprvalue>
  </attribute>
</tag>
```

The UseRemoteBeanTag Class

As we've previously seen, all that's required to look up an object using JNDI is to create an `InitialContext`, lookup the remote object by its well-known name, and finally cast it to the appropriate interface. The code for our new tag is as follows:

```
package com.wrox.store.tag;

import java.rmi.RemoteException;

import javax.naming.*;
import javax.rmi.PortableRemoteObject;
import javax.servlet.jsp.*;
import javax.servlet.jsp.tagext.*;

public class UseRemoteBeanTag extends TagSupport {

  private String id;
  private String jndiName;
  private String className;

  public int doStartTag() throws JspException {
    try {
      InitialContext ctx = new InitialContext();
      Object remoteBean = null;

      Class remoteClass = Class.forName(className);

      // look up home and keep hold of the reference
      remoteBean = PortableRemoteObject.narrow(ctx.lookup(jndiName),
                                               remoteClass);

      pageContext.setAttribute(id, remoteBean);
    } catch (ClassNotFoundException cnfe) {
      throw new JspException(cnfe.getMessage());
    } catch (NamingException ne) {
      throw new JspException(ne.getMessage());
    }

    return EVAL_BODY_INCLUDE;
  }

  public void setId(String s) {
    this.id = s;
  }

  public void setJndiName(String s) {
    this.jndiName = s;
  }

  public void setClassName(String s) {
    this.className = s;
  }

}
```

Once again, our tag has some standard JavaBean-style setters, but this time only implements the
doStartTag() method. This is called when the starting tag is encountered and it's this that looks up the
remote object, checks it's of the appropriate class and sets an attribute on the JSP page. Instead of looking up
a remote object with a specific name and class, we've created an abstraction with which to lookup any remote
object using JNDI. The name to which the object is bound is passed in to our tag as an attribute, and by using
a little Java reflection we can dynamically load the appropriate class and ensure that our remote object is of
the correct type.

The UseRemoteBeanTagExtraInfo Class

Because we're setting an attribute on back into the JSP, an 'extra info' class is again required:

```java
package com.wrox.store.tag;

import javax.servlet.jsp.tagext.*;

public class UseRemoteBeanTagExtraInfo extends TagExtraInfo {

  public VariableInfo[] getVariableInfo(TagData data) {
    return new VariableInfo[] {
      new VariableInfo(data.getId(), data.getAttributeString("className"),
                  true, VariableInfo.AT_END)
    };
  }

}
```

The JNDI JSP

Now we have the ability to lookup any remote object, we can write yet another variation of the catalog page, jndi.jsp, in our online shopping store example:

```jsp
<%-- import the tag library --%>
<%@ taglib uri="http://www.wrox.com/taglib" prefix=" chap24" %>

<chap24:useRemoteBean id="productHome"
 className="com.wrox.store.ejb.product.ProductHome"
 jndiName="store/ProductHome"/>

<chap24:iterator id="product" className="com.wrox.store.ejb.product.Product"
 iterator="<%= productHome.findAll().iterator() %>">
  <tr>
  <td><jsp:getProperty name="product" property="name"/></td>
  <td align="right">$<jsp:getProperty name="product"
    property="price"/></td>
  <td align="right"><input type="text" size="2" maxlength="2"
    name="quantity_<jsp:getProperty name="product"
  property="id"/>"value=""></td>
  </tr>
</chap24:iterator>
```

This time, we replace the `<jsp:useBean>` with our custom `<useRemoteBean>` tag. By using the same `id` attribute, we don't even have to change any of the JSP that builds the table of products. What we must ensure though is that the `className` attribute of the tag represents the interface and not the implementation, as once again we will be dealing with the reference, or stub, that points to the remote object.

The Complete Online Store

Now that we have all the pieces of functionality in place, we can finish implementing our online bookstore.

The Welcome Page

When first accessing the online store, we would like to have a choice as to which of the above methods we use to access the store. Therefore we need a default index page where we can make our choice:

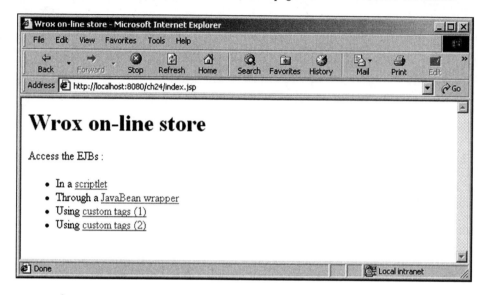

The contents of index.jsp are as follows:

```
<%@ include file="header.jsp" %>

<p>
Access the EJBs :
<ul>
  <li>In a <a href="catalog.jsp?catalogPage=scriptlet.jsp">scriptlet</a>
      </li>
  <li>Through a <a href="catalog.jsp?catalogPage=bean.jsp">JavaBean
      wrapper</a></li>
  <li>Using <a href="catalog.jsp?catalogPage=tag.jsp">custom tags
      (1)</a></li>
  <li>Using <a href="catalog.jsp?catalogPage=jndi.jsp">custom tags
      (2)</a></li>
</ul>
</p>

<%@ include file="footer.jsp" %>
```

As you can see, this page simply gives us a choice of the four EJB access methods we have implemented so far. In addition, we need simple header and footer pages to give the site a more uniform look.

`header.jsp` contains the page header:

```
<%-- find the user's cart that is bound to the HTTP session --%>
<jsp:useBean id="cart" class="com.wrox.store.ejb.cart.Cart"
 scope="session"/>

<html>
<head>
<title>Wrox online store</title>
</head>

<body>

<p>
<h1>Wrox online store</h1>
</p>
```

Finally, `footer.jsp` contains the page footer:

```
</body>
</html>
```

The Catalog Page

Once a choice has been made about which EJB access method we will use, the current catalog page is shown to the user to allow them to make purchases:

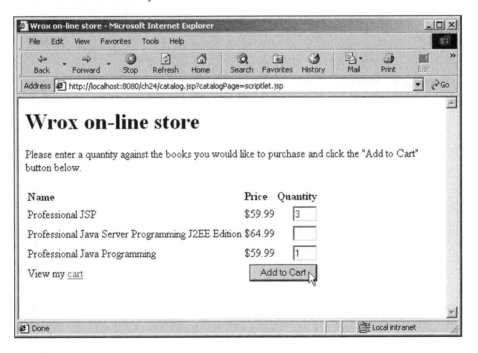

The Catalog JSP

First of all, the `catalog.jsp` checks which JSP should be used to generate the table of products. The default is `scriptlet.jsp`. Once this has been decided, the table of products is created and the user makes a selection:

```jsp
<%@ include file="header.jsp" %>

<%
    String catalogPage = request.getParameter("catalogPage");
    if (catalogPage == null || catalogPage.length() == 0) {
      catalogPage = "scriptlet.jsp";
    }

    System.out.println("Using " + catalogPage + " to render the catalog");
%>

<p>
Please enter a quantity against the books you would like to purchase and click the
"Add to Cart" button below.

<form action="cart.jsp" method="post">
<table>
  <tr>
    <td><b>Name</b></td>
    <td><b>Price</b></td>
    <td><b>Quantity</b></td>
  </tr>

  <jsp:include page="<%= catalogPage %>"/>

  <tr>
    <td>View my <a href="cart.jsp">cart</a></td>
    <td colspan="2" align="right">
      <input type="submit" value="Add to Cart"></td>
  </tr>

</table>
</form>
</p>

<%@ include file="footer.jsp" %>
```

Submitting the Order

When the user submits the order, the shopping cart page is displayed. This is where the user gives delivery and credit card details, before confirming the order:

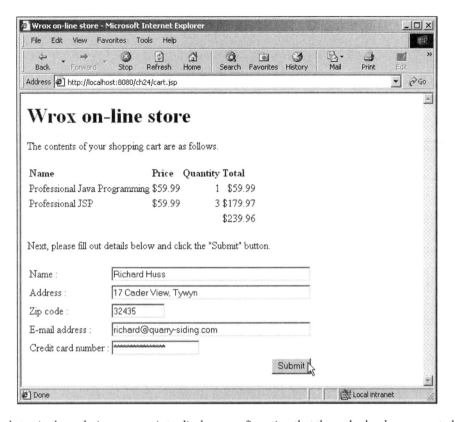

The final step in the ordering process is to display a confirmation that the order has been accepted:

The Cart JSP

When the user is happy with the order, he is taken to the shopping cart page, `cart.jsp`:

```
<%-- imports --%>
<%@ page import="java.util.*" %>

<%@ page import="javax.ejb.*" %>
<%@ page import="javax.naming.*" %>
<%@ page import="javax.rmi.PortableRemoteObject" %>
```

```jsp
<%@ page import="com.wrox.store.ejb.cart.*" %>
<%@ page import="com.wrox.store.ejb.product.*" %>

<%@ include file="header.jsp" %>

<p>
The contents of your shopping cart are as follows.

<form action="submit.jsp" method="post">
<%
    InitialContext ctx = new InitialContext();
    ProductHome home = (ProductHome)PortableRemoteObject.narrow
                            (ctx.lookup("store/ProductHome"),
                                ProductHome.class);
    Product product;
    int quantity;
```

First of all, the JSP finds out how many products there were on the catalog page:

```jsp
int numberOfProducts = 0;
if (request.getParameter("numberOfProducts") != null) {
  numberOfProducts = Integer.parseInt
                            (request.getParameter("numberOfProducts"));
}
```

The quantity parameters are then looped over, and those products where the quantity is greater than zero are added to the cart:

```jsp
String param;
for (int i = 1; i <= numberOfProducts; i++) {
  try {
    param = request.getParameter("quantity_" + i);

    if (param == null || param.length() == 0) {
      param = "0";
    }

    quantity = Integer.parseInt(param);
  } catch (NumberFormatException nfe) {
    quantity = 0;
  }

  if (quantity > 0) {
    product = home.findByPrimaryKey("" + i);
    cart.add(product, quantity);
  }
}
%>
```

The user's purchases are listed along with the total price of the order. If they wish to finish their transaction, they must fill in their details, and click the 'Submit' button:

```
<table>
  <tr>
    <td><b>Name</b></td>
    <td><b>Price</b></td>
    <td><b>Quantity</b></td>
    <td><b>Total</b></td>
  </tr>

<%
    String id;
    Iterator it = cart.getProducts().iterator();
    while (it.hasNext()) {
      product = (Product)it.next();
      quantity = cart.getQuantity(product);
%>
  <tr>
    <td><%= product.getName() %></td>
    <td align="right">$<%= product.getPrice() %></td>
    <td align="right"><%= quantity %></td>
    <td align="right">$<%= quantity * product.getPrice() %></td>
  </tr>
<%
    }
%>

    <tr>
      <td colspan="4" align="right">$<%= cart.getTotal() %></td>
    </tr>

</table>
</p>

<p>
Next, please fill out details below and click the "Submit" button.
</p>

<p>
<table>

  <tr>
    <td>Name : </td>
    <td><input type="text" name="name" value="" size="48"></td></tr>
  <tr>
    <td>Address : </td>
    <td><input type="text" name="address" value="" size="48"></td>
  </tr>
  <tr>
    <td>Zip code : </td>
    <td><input type="text" name="zipCode" value="" size="10"></td>
  </tr>
  <tr>
    <td>E-mail address : </td>
    <td><input type="text" name="emailAddress" value="" size="48"></td>
  </tr>
  <tr>
    <td>Credit card number : </td>
```

```
      <td><input type="password" name="creditCardNumber" value=""
               size="19"></td>
   </tr>

   <tr>
     <td colspan="2" align="right"><input type="submit" value="Submit"></td>
   </tr>

  </table>

  </form>
  </p>

  <%@ include file="footer.jsp" %>
```

The Submit JSP

submit.jsp confirms the order and places the order details in the customer EJB:

```
  <%@ include file="header.jsp" %>

  <p>
  <%
      // create a new customer object amd set the properties
      InitialContext ctx = new InitialContext();
      CustomerHome customerHome = (CustomerHome)PortableRemoteObject.narrow
                                  (ctx.lookup("store/CustomerHome"),
                                   CustomerHome.class);

      Customer customer = customerHome.create();

      customer.setName(request.getParameter("name"));
      customer.setAddress(request.getParameter("address"));
      customer.setZipCode(request.getParameter("zipCode"));
      customer.setEmailAddress(request.getParameter("emailAddress"));
      customer.setCreditCardNumber(request.getParameter("creditCardNumber"));

      try {
        // now submit order ... this method call wraps up the order
        // submission process such as e-mailing the customer with
        // a confirmation
        cart.submitOrder(customer);
  %>

  Thank you for your order, please click here to return to the <A
  href="index.jsp">catalog</a>.

  <%
      } catch (AuthorizationException ae) {
  %>
  Sorry ... you're credit card could not be authorized.
  <%
      }
  %>
  </p>

  <%@ include file="footer.jsp" %>
```

Note that we have yet to implement the confirmation e-mail function of the online store. This will be the subject of our next section.

Deploying the Web Application

Set up your web application as normal in the `%CATALINA_HOME%\webapps\ch24` directory and follow these steps to deploy the online store web application:

- ❑ Copy `ejb.jar`, `jboss-client.jar`, `jnp-client.jar` and `jta-spec1_0_1.jar` from `%JBOSS_HOME%\client` and the EJB deployment JAR file into `%CATALINA_HOME%\webapps\ch24\WEB-INF\lib`

- ❑ Edit `%CATALINA_HOME%\conf\sever.xml` and add this line:

```
<Context path="/ch24" docBase="ch24" debug"0"/>
```

- ❑ Start Tomcat with jBoss still running

- ❑ Point your web browser to `http://localhost:8080/ch24/index.jsp`

Accessing JavaMail and JMS

To round off our look at how to access some of the J2EE APIs from JSP, we're going to take a quick look at JavaMail. Thankfully, the techniques shown earlier are applicable to this API too. For example, you could build a façade for the JavaMail API that provides a simple interface with which to send confirmation e-mails to customers. Not only this, but the JavaBean could also ensure that all messages are sent out from a particular address.

Although the same principles apply, we should ask the question of what this means for our architecture. Using a JavaBean to wrap up the access to these APIs is a great way of creating a developer friendly, reusable component. However, the APIs are still being accessed from the web tier, which raises a few questions about the security and accessibility of those services.

For example, are the web server and mail server on the same side of the firewall and if not, is the mail server accessible from the web server? If the firewall is only configured to allow IIOP traffic through (calls to our remote objects), then trying to access the mail server with SMTP isn't going to work. One solution to this problem is to wrap up access to these APIs using a stateless session bean.

Stateless session beans provide the highest performance of all the EJBs. Because they don't need to maintain any state, the EJB container can create as many instances as it sees fit in order to handle a high number of concurrent requests. Moving this kind of processing to the middle tier therefore makes sense not only from an architectural viewpoint (it can be reused by many types of clients), but also in terms of performance and scalability, and from sound OOP guidelines.

In the architecture diagram that we saw earlier, we mentioned that stateless session beans could be used to wrap up the functionality required to send confirmation e-mails to customers, and messages containing the details of a customer's order to the third party fulfillment center. The code example that follows shows how such a bean can be implemented, deployed and used in our online store.

The Mail Bean

Building a stateless session bean for mail is pretty much the same as building a stateful session bean like the cart that we saw earlier. In order to compile these classes, add `%JBOSS_HOME%\lib\ext\mail.jar` and `%JBOSS_HOME%\lib\activation.jar` to your CLASSPATH. Also remember to add the three new files to your deployment JAR file.

The Mail Interface

To start with, let's define the business (or remote) interface for our mail bean. It will have just one public method providing the ability for us to send e-mails to a specific customer:

```
package com.wrox.store.ejb.mail;

import java.rmi.RemoteException;

import com.wrox.store.ejb.customer.Customer;

public interface Mail extends javax.ejb.EJBObject {

  public void sendConfirmation(Customer customer)
    throws RemoteException;

}
```

The MailBean Class

Next, we have the implementation of our session bean:

```
package com.wrox.store.ejb.mail;

import java.io.UnsupportedEncodingException;
import java.util.*;
import java.rmi.RemoteException;

import javax.mail.*;
import javax.mail.internet.*;
import javax.activation.*;

import com.wrox.store.ejb.customer.Customer;

public class MailBean extends com.wrox.store.ejb.AbstractSessionBean {
```

Note that you must customize the following line to match your set up:

```
public static final String SMTP_HOST = "smtp.yourdomain.com";

public static final String SENDER_NAME = "Order confirmations";
public static final String SENDER_EMAIL_ADDRESS =
  "confirmations@yourdomain.com";

public void sendConfirmation(Customer customer) throws RemoteException {
  StringBuffer message = new StringBuffer();
```

```
        message.append("Hello ");
        message.append(customer.getName());
        message.append(" and thank you for your order. ");
        message.append("It will be dispatched in the next 24 hours.");

        sendMessage(customer.getEmailAddress(),
          "Confirmation of your order", message.toString());
      }

    private void sendMessage(String recipient, String subject,
      String message) {

      // setup the e-mail session for this bean
      Properties props = new Properties();
      props.put("mail.smtp.host", SMTP_HOST);
        Session session = Session.getDefaultInstance(props, null);

      try {
        // create a message and try to send it
        Message msg = new MimeMessage(session);
        msg.setFrom(new InternetAddress(SENDER_EMAIL_ADDRESS, SENDER_NAME));

        msg.setRecipient(Message.RecipientType.TO,
          new InternetAddress(recipient));

        msg.setSubject(subject);
        msg.setSentDate(new Date());
        msg.setText(message);

        Transport.send(msg);
      } catch (UnsupportedEncodingException uee) {
        System.out.println(uee);
      } catch (MessagingException me) {
        System.out.println(me);
      }
    }
  }

}
```

As we can see, the bean makes use of a private method to actually create the e-mail message and send it to the customer's e-mail address. This means that our remote interface could be easily extended at a later date to include methods to send other e-mails. Creating an e-mail message using JavaMail simply involves creating a new e-mail session, creating a new message object, setting the appropriate properties (such as the sender's name and address, recipient, subject and message) and then sending the message using a transport agent.

The MailHome Interface

The final step in building our mail bean is the home interface. As shown below, our home interface only allows new beans to be created:

```
package com.wrox.store.ejb.mail;

import java.rmi.RemoteException;

import javax.ejb.CreateException;
```

```
public interface MailHome extends javax.ejb.EJBHome {

  public Mail create() throws CreateException, RemoteException;

}
```

Deploying the Mail Bean

When it comes to deploying our bean, we simply need to insert the new definition of the bean into the `ejb-jar.xml` file that we saw earlier. The `<session-type>` tag represents that our bean is stateless this time:

```
<session>
  <ejb-name>Mail</ejb-name>
  <home>com.wrox.store.ejb.mail.MailHome</home>
  <remote>com.wrox.store.ejb.mail.Mail</remote>
  <ejb-class>com.wrox.store.ejb.mail.MailBean</ejb-class>

  <session-type>Stateless</session-type>
  <transaction-type>Container</transaction-type>
</session>
```

Now that we've wrapped up the ability to send e-mails, all we need to do now is call it. We could call if from our JSP, but for the reasons outlined previously, we are going to call it from another EJB – the cart bean. When the customer submits their order, the `submitOrder()` method of the cart bean gets called to perform all of the business logic to authorize the credit card, etc. Once this has all been done successfully and the order placed, we can use the new mail bean to e-mail the customer. With this in mind, the new `submitOrder()` is shown below:

```
public void submitOrder(Customer customer)
        throws AuthorizationException, RemoteException {

  // send the user an e-mail with the contents of their order
  try {
    // look up the product home
    InitialContext ctx = new InitialContext();
    MailHome home = (MailHome)PortableRemoteObject.narrow
      (ctx.lookup("store/MailHome"), MailHome.class);

    // create a mail bean and send the e-mail
    Mail mail = home.create();
    mail.sendConfirmation(customer);
  } catch (NamingException ne) {
    System.out.println(ne.getMessage());
  } catch (CreateException ce) {
    System.out.println(ce.getMessage());
  } catch (RemoteException re) {
    System.out.println(re.getMessage());
  }

  // and empty the cart
  products.clear();
}
```

The confirmation e-mail should therefore look something like this:

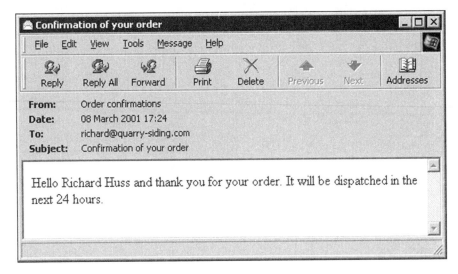

We're not accessing the mail bean (and therefore JavaMail) from the JSP, instead it's being accessed from the session bean containing the business logic for submitting an order. Putting this code here is not only a solution for the security and accessibility problems described above, but it means that we can now modify and extend the workflow in our cart bean, and more importantly, ensure that the order is submitted and that the process or submitting an order is done in one transaction on the middle-tier.

Although we've not shown use of the Java Message Service (JMS), the same principles as those just shown are applicable. For example, a message bean could be written that asynchronously sends an XML message to the order fulfillment house. Again, this could be written as a stateless session bean, a call to which could be inserted into the `submitOrder()` method of the cart bean. A good point of reference to further details and code examples on JMS is an upcoming book in the Wrox Professional Series, *Professional JMS*, ISBN 1861004931.

Summary

In this chapter, we've introduced the Java 2 Enterprise Edition (J2EE) and discussed the role of the primary APIs in terms of what they provide, and why they are important in the context of a web-based application.

We then moved on to a simple online store that could be designed using direct data access and then by illustrated how EJBs could be introduced into the architecture. In doing so, we mentioned some of the benefits and drawbacks of each architecture, including security, maintainability and performance. Following this, we took a closer look at our example application, showing how the EJBs were built and deployed into jBOSS 2.0 before exploring how they could be used from JSPs with the following techniques:

❑   Scriptlets

❑   JavaBeans as wrappers

❑   Custom tags

We then extended our custom tags example to build a generic way of accessing JNDI from a JSP, before wrapping up with a section on accessing JavaMail. Although it can be accessed from a JSP, this section introduced the concept of stateless session beans for reasons of security, accessibility and reuse. While this chapter has concentrated on the interaction between JSP and the other J2EE technologies, there is much, much more to the J2EE. Some good references for further information include:

❑ The J2EE home page on the Sun Microsystems website (http://java.sun.com/products/j2ee/)

❑ Another book in this series, *Professional Java Server Programming J2EE Edition* (ISBN 1-861004-65-6)

That just about wraps up our coverage of the J2EE web tier – we've covered a lot of ground, from writing most basic Servlets and JSPs, through custom tags, filters, event listeners, and the other web components, to architectural considerations and the wider J2EE environment. We hope this book has inspired you to get stuck into developing with the latest Java-based web technologies – enjoy!

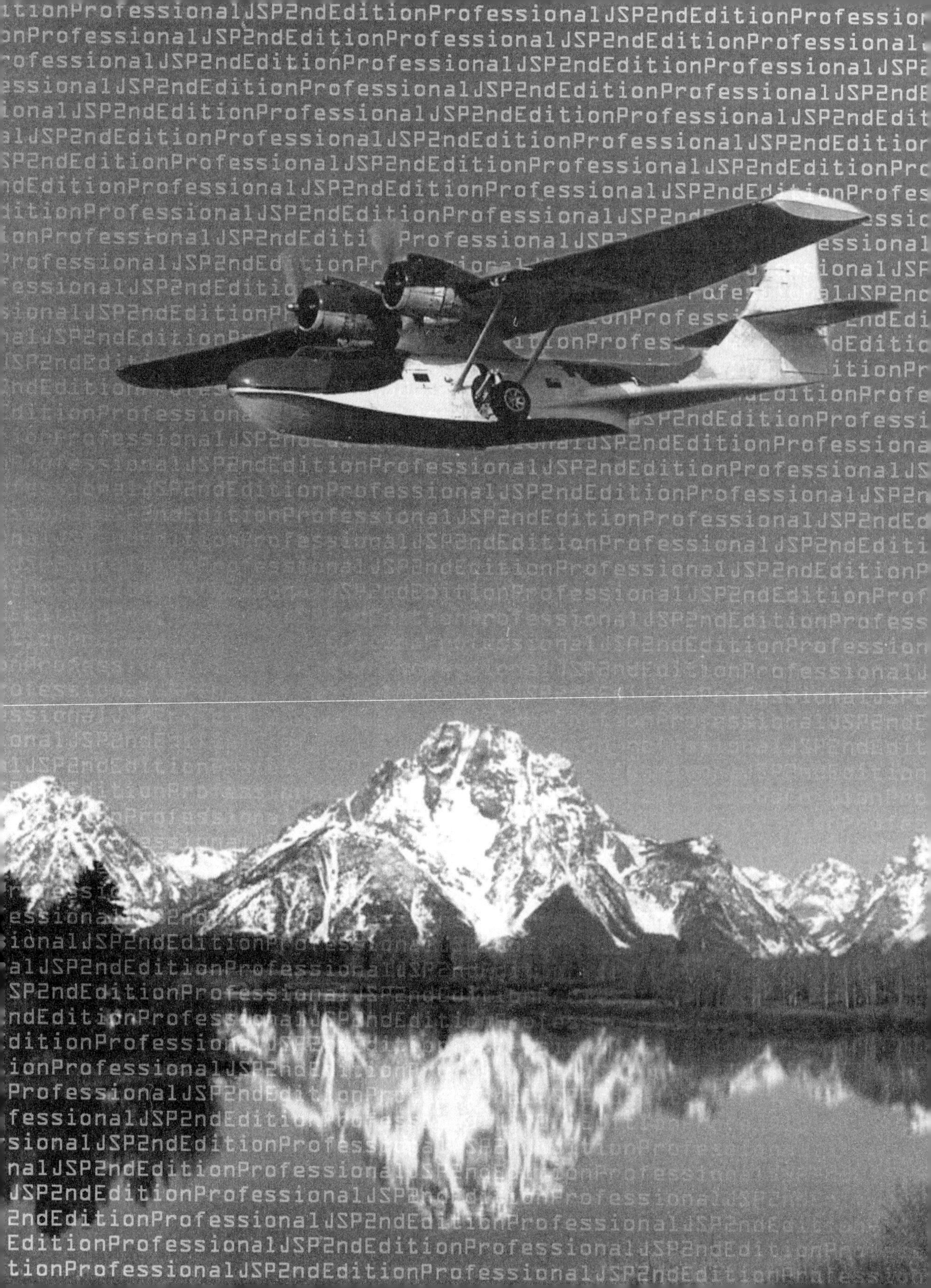

Installing a Servlet/JSP Environment

In this appendix we'll discuss the basics of how to install and configure a Java web container (a Servlet/JSP engine). We will consider three products:

❑　Tomcat 4.0, the latest version of the open-source JSP and Servlet Reference Implementation. Tomcat 4.0 is the main web container that is used in this book.

❑　Tomcat 3.2.1, which supports the older JSP 1.1 and Servlet 2.2 specifications.

❑　JRun 3.0, a commercial product. (A free, non-expiring version is available for development but not deployment.)

Installing Tomcat 4.0

While there are many Servlet and JSP engines available (as of this writing, Sun's 'Industry Momentum' page at http://java.sun.com/products/jsp/industry.html lists nearly 40), we have chosen to focus our attention on Tomcat 4.0. Tomcat is produced by the Apache Software Foundation's Jakarta project, and is freely available at http://jakarta.apache.org/tomcat/.

Since Tomcat is primarily used by programmers, its open-source development model is of particular benefit as it brings the developers and users close together. If you find a bug, you can fix it and submit a patch; if you need a new feature, you can write it yourself, or suggest it to the development team. Tomcat is also the reference implementation of the JSP and Servlet specifications, version 4.0 supporting the latest Servlet 2.3 and JSP 1.2 versions. (Version 3.2.1 is the current version of the Servlet 2.2/JSP 1.1 reference implementation.) Many of the principal developers are employed by Sun Microsystems, who are investing considerable manpower into ensuring that Tomcat 4.0 provides a high-quality, robust web container with excellent performance.

A Word on Naming

The naming of Tomcat 4.0 components can be a little confusing, with the names **Tomcat**, **Catalina**, and **Jasper** all flying around. So, to avoid any problems with terminology:

❑ **Catalina** is a Servlet container – that is, an environment within which Java Servlets can be hosted.

❑ **Jasper** is the JSP component of Tomcat – in fact, it's just a Servlet that understands how to process requests for JSP pages.

❑ **Tomcat** comprises Catalina, plus Jasper, plus various extra bits and pieces including batch files for starting and stopping the server, some example web applications, and mod_webapp.

❑ **mod_webapp** is the component that will allow you to connect Tomcat to the Apache web server. Catalina includes a web server of its own, but you may also wish to connect it to an external web server to take advantage of Apache's extra speed when serving static content, or to allow you to run JSP or Servlet-based applications alongside applications using other server-side technologies such as PHP. As of this writing mod_webapp is in alpha-testing, but expect it to become stable soon. In time, connectors for other major web servers should also appear.

Basic Tomcat Installation

These steps describe installing Tomcat 4.0 on a Windows 2000 system, but the steps are pretty generic; the main differences between platforms will be the way in which environment variables are set.

As this book goes to press, Tomcat 3.0 Beta has just been released. Tomcat 4.0 cannot be finally released until the Servlet 2.3 and JSP 1.2 specifications have been finalized by the Java Community Process. Until this happens you should use the most recent 'milestone' or Beta version.

❑ You will need to install the Java 2 Standard Edition software development kit, if you have not already done so; JDK 1.3 can be downloaded from http://java.sun.com/j2se/1.3/.

❑ Download a suitable Tomcat 4.0 binary release from http://jakarta.apache.org/tomcat/ – the file will be called something like jakarta-tomcat-4.0-xx.zip. (Other archive formats are available which may be more suitable if you are on a Unix-type platform.) For Beta 3 the xx will be b3.

❑ Unzip the file you downloaded into a suitable directory. On a Windows machine, unzipping into C:\ will create a directory named C:\jakarta-tomcat-4.0-xx containing the Tomcat 4.0 files.

❑ Create CATALINA_HOME and JAVA_HOME environment variables pointing to the directories where you installed the Tomcat and Java 2 SDK files – typical values are C:\jakarta-tomcat-4.0-xx for CATALINA_HOME and C:\jdk1.3 for JAVA_HOME.

Under Windows 2000, environment variables are set using the **System** control panel. On the **Advanced** tab, click on the **Environment Variables...** button. In the resulting dialog box, add CATALINA_HOME and JAVA_HOME as system variables:

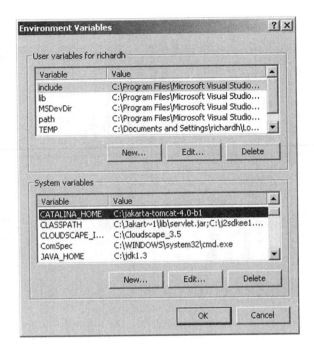

These environment variables allow Tomcat to locate both its own files (using CATALINA_HOME), and the Java 2 SDK components it needs, notably the Java compiler, (using JAVA_HOME).

If you are using Windows 98, environment variables are set by editing the C:\autoexec.bat file. Add the following lines:

```
set CATALINA_HOME=C:\jakarta-tomcat-4.0-xx
set JAVA_HOME=C:\jdk1.3
```

Under Windows 98 you will also need to increase the environment space available, by right-clicking on your DOS prompt window, selecting **Properties**, going to the **Memory** tab, and setting the initial environment to 4096 bytes.

❏   Start Tomcat by running the startup.bat batch file (startup.sh on Unix-type systems), which can be found in the %CATALINA_HOME%\bin directory (in other words, the bin directory inside the directory where Tomcat is installed).

Tomcat will start up and print some status messages:

❑ We now have Tomcat 4.0 up and running, using its internal web server (on port 8080). Point your web browser at http://localhost:8080/; you should see the default Tomcat home page:

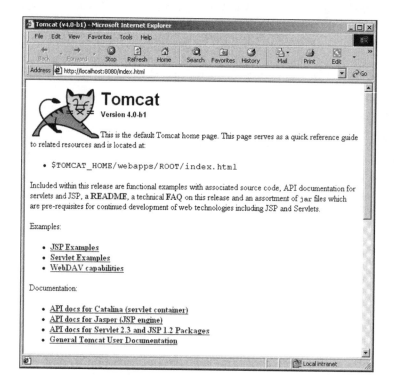

Spend some time exploring the examples and documentation provided with Tomcat.

❏ To shut down Tomcat, run the `shutdown.bat` batch file (`shutdown.sh` on Unix-type systems), again from the `%CATALINA_HOME%\bin` directory.

The Tomcat 4.0 Directory Structure

Looking inside our Tomcat installation directory we find a few text files, and various directories:

❏ `bin` contains Windows batch files and Unix shell scripts for starting and stopping Tomcat, and for other purposes, together with the `bootstrap.jar` JAR file needed for the first stage of starting Tomcat.

❏ `classes` is not created by default, but if it exists any `.class` files it contains will be visible to all web applications.

❏ `common` contains Java code needed by all parts of Tomcat: `.jar` files (Java library files) in the `common\lib` directory, and `.class` files in `common\classes`. Notable among the `.jar` files is `servlet.jar`, which contains the classes defined by the Servlet 2.3 and JSP 1.2 specifications. You will need to have `servlet.jar` listed in your `CLASSPATH` environment variable when compiling classes (for example, Servlets) that use these APIs.

❏ `conf` contains Tomcat's configuration files, notably `server.xml` (used to configure the server – which hostname and port number to use, which web applications to deploy, etc.) and the server-wide `web.xml`.

> Note that settings in the server-wide **web.xml** file (located in **%CATALINA_HOME%\conf**) apply to the whole server, but that this behavior is not mandated by the Servlet specification. Applications making use of it will not be portable to other servlet containers.

❏ `jasper` contains `.jar` files containing parts of the JSP engine.

❏ `lib` is populated with various `.jar` files (library files) required by web applications, including parts of the JSP engine. You can add your own `.jar` files here and they will be visible to all web applications.

❏ `logs` is where Tomcat places its log files. Logging is configured in `server.xml`.

❏ `server` contains the files comprising Catalina, and other required libraries: `.jar` files in `server\lib`, and `.class` files in `server\classes`.

❏ `src` contains the source code for Tomcat, along with the documentation (interspersed with the source code).

❏ `webapps` is the location where Tomcat looks for web applications to deploy. Any `.war` file placed here, or any expanded web application directory structure stored within the directory, will automatically be deployed when Tomcat starts up.

The URL path under which the application is deployed will correspond to the name of the `.war` file or directory; for example, if you place a `myapplication.war` file or a `myapplication` directory within `webapps`, Tomcat will automatically deploy it as http://localhost:8080/myapplication/.

The automatic deployment settings may not suit your application, in which case you may prefer to store the application outside the webapps directory and configure it as desired using server.xml.

❑ work is used by Tomcat to store temporary files, notably the .java source files and compiled .class files created when processing JSPs.

Note that this directory structure has changed slightly since the Tomcat 4.0 Beta 1 release.

Tomcat 4.0 Configuration

The Tomcat documentation has improved considerably compared to early versions and should be your first stop if you need to configure Tomcat in any way. However, there are a few steps that are sufficiently common that we cover them here.

Deploying a Web Application

There are two ways to tell Tomcat to deploy a web application:

❑ As mentioned above, you can deploy an application simply by placing a .war file or an expanded web application directory structure in the %CATALINA_HOME%\webapps directory.

❑ However, the default settings may not be suitable for your application, in which case it will be necessary to edit %CATALINA_HOME%\conf\server.xml and add a <Context> element for your application.

The default server.xml file is well commented, and you should read these to familiarize yourself with the contents of this file. Various additional elements, not shown or described here but included in the default server.xml, provide for logging and other similar functionality, and define authentication realms. The default server.xml also includes commented-out sections illustrating how to set up a secure (HTTPS) connector, and to set up database-driven authentication realms. It also includes elements that work together with the mod_webapp Apache module.

The outline structure of server.xml is as follows:

```
<Server>
  <Service>
    <Connector/>
    <Engine>
      <Host>
        <Context/>
      </Host>
    </Engine>
  </Service>
</Server>
```

At the top level is a <Server> element, representing the entire Java Virtual Machine. It may contain one or more <Service> elements:

```
<Server port="8005" shutdown="SHUTDOWN" debug="0">
```

A `<Service>` element represents a collection of one or more `<Connector>` elements that share a single 'container' (and therefore the web applications visible within that container). Normally, that container is an `<Engine>` element:

```
<Service name="Tomcat-Standalone">
```

A `<Connector>` represents an endpoint by which requests are received and responses are returned, passing them on to the associated `<Container>` (normally an `<Engine>`) for processing. This `<Connector>` element creates a non-secure HTTP/1.1 connector, listening on port 8080:

```
<Connector className="org.apache.catalina.connector.http.HttpConnector"
           port="8080" minProcessors="5" maxProcessors="75"
           acceptCount="10" debug="0"/>
```

An `<Engine>` element represents the Catalina object that processes every request, passing them on to the appropriate `<Host>`:

```
<Engine name="Standalone" defaultHost="localhost" debug="0">
```

The `<Host>` element is used to define the default virtual host:

```
<Host name="localhost" debug="0" appBase="webapps">
```

A `<Context>` element is used to define an individual web application:

```
<Context path="/examples" docBase="examples" debug="0"
         reloadable="true">
</Context>
```

The attributes of the `<Context>` element are:

❑ path determines the URL prefix where the application will be deployed. In the example above, the application will be found at http://localhost:8080/examples/.

❑ docBase specifies the whereabouts of the .war file or expanded web application directory structure for the application. Since a relative file path is specified here, Tomcat will look in its webapps directory (this was configured in the `<Host>` element, above) but an absolute file path can also be used.

❑ debug specifies the level of debugging information that will be produced for this application.

❑ reloadable intimates whether the container should check for changes to files that would require it to reload the application. When deploying your application in a production environment, setting its value to "false" will improve performance, as Tomcat will not have to perform these checks.

```
    </Host>

  </Engine>

</Service>

<!-- Snip details of service for the mod_webapp connector -->

</Server>
```

The Manager Application

Tomcat 4.0's default configuration includes a web application that allows web applications to be deployed, undeployed, and reloaded while Tomcat is running. This application is installed by default in the /manager web application, and contains four commands:

- ❑ http://localhost:8080/manager/list lists all web applications currently deployed in this virtual host.

- ❑ http://localhost:8080/manager/install?path=/myapp&war=mywar deploys the web application specified by the war request parameter, at the context path given by the path parameter.

- ❑ http://localhost:8080/manager/reload?path=/myapp reloads all the Java classes in the specified web application. This works even if automatic class reloading is disabled.

- ❑ http://localhost:8080/manager/remove?path=/myapp shuts down and undeploys the specified web application.

When specifying a web application to the 'deploy' command, the value of the war request path must have one of these forms:

- ❑ file:/absolute/directory/path – the absolute path to the directory containing the unpacked web application.

- ❑ jar:file:/absolute/path/to/mywar.war!/ – a URL specifying the absolute path to the .war file.

- ❑ jar:http://host:port/path/to/mywar.war!/ – a URL specifying the location of the HTTP-accessible .war file.

- ❑ http://localhost:8080/manager/sessions?path=/myapp lists sessions for the specified web application.

- ❑ http://localhost:8080/manager/start?path=/myapp starts the specified web application.

- ❑ http://localhost:8080/manager/stop?path=/myapp stops the specified web application.

Before you can use the manager application you need to set up a user in tomcat-users.xml with the role manager:

```
<tomcat-users>
  <user name="tomcat" password="tomcat" roles="tomcat" />
  <user name="role1"  password="tomcat" roles="role1"  />
  <user name="both"   password="tomcat" roles="tomcat,role1" />
  <user name="admin"  password="adminpassword" roles="manager" />
</tomcat-users>
```

With this addition, the manager application works just fine:

Getting Help

If you need help with Tomcat 4.0, and this appendix and the documentation just haven't helped, your first port of call should be the Tomcat web site, http://jakarta.apache.org/tomcat/. There are two mailing lists dedicated to Tomcat issues:

❑ tomcat-user, for Tomcat's users – this is where you can ask questions on configuring and using Tomcat. The Tomcat developers should be on hand to help out as necessary.

❑ tomcat-dev, which is where the developers themselves lurk. If you decide to get stuck in with contributing to improving Tomcat itself, this is where the action is.

Installing Tomcat 3.2.x

If you do not require the new features of the JSP 1.2 and Servlet 2.3 specifications, you may prefer to use the older Tomcat 3.2.x family. (As this book goes to press, version 3.2.1 is the latest released version in this family, and 3.2.2 is in beta testing.) Basic installation of Tomcat 3.2.1 is rather similar to that for Tomcat 4.0, described above – the main differences are:

❑ Obviously, you need to download the Tomcat 3.2.1 binary release from http://jakarta.apache.org/tomcat/ – the file will be called something like jakarta-tomcat-3.2.1.zip.

❑ The environment variables you need to create are TOMCAT_HOME (rather than CATALINA_HOME) and JAVA_HOME. Typical values are C:\jakarta-tomcat-3.2.1 for TOMCAT_HOME and C:\jdk1.3 for JAVA_HOME.

❑ The batch files to start and stop Tomcat are found in the %TOMCAT_HOME%\bin directory – startup.bat to start the server, and shutdown.bat to stop it. (For Unix-type systems, the relevant scripts are startup.sh and shutdown.sh.)

❑ Tomcat 3.2.1 comes with two Apache modules, the elderly mod_jserv and the more recent mod_jk. Configuration of these is rather more complex than for mod_webapp, but is covered extensively in the documentation that comes with the release.

981

Installing JRun 3.0

JRun was the first servlet and JSP engine, and remains today the most widely adopted. The most recent release, JRun 3.0, includes an EJB server implementation with integrated transaction and messaging server; the J2EE specifications supported include EJB 1.1, JTA 1.0, JMS 1.0, Servlet 2.2 and JSP 1.1. JRun was written by Live Software, which was purchased by the Allaire Corporation in 1999.

Obtaining JRun

JRun ships in the three product variations:

❏   **Developer**: Free, non-expiring copy for development. Includes full Servlet/JSP and EJB/JTA/JMS functionality, unlimited number of JVMs but restricted to three concurrent connections. Not licensed for deployment.

❏   **Professional:** Includes full Servlet/JSP functionality, unlimited number of JVMs and concurrent connections. Licensed for commercial deployment.

❏   **Enterprise:** Includes full Servlet/JSP and EJB/JTA/JMS functionality, unlimited number of JVMs and concurrent connections, HTTP clustering. Licensed for commercial deployment.

You may download a copy from http://commerce.allaire.com/download. Choose the file that corresponds to your operating system; the main difference between them is that they have different installers.

Installation

JRun is written entirely in Java and has installers for Windows 95/98/NT/2000 (SP3 or greater), Solaris 2.6, 7, Red Hat Linux 6.x, HP-UX 11.0, IBM AIX 4.2, 4.3, SGI IRIX 6.5, Compaq UNIX Tru64 4.0. JRun is known to work on other platforms. This appendix will walk through the Windows installation: however, the install process is essentially the same for any operating system because all prompt for the same questions.

In Windows, invoke either the `setup.exe` or `jr30.Exe` file which will kick-off the Windows install-shield. JRun will install by default to `C:\Program Files\Allaire\JRun`; choose the full-install option, which includes Servlet/JSP and EJB/JTA/JMS servers, documentation and sample applications.

In Windows, JRun can be installed as either a service or application. It is recommended that you install JRun as an application on your development servers, and register it as a service on production servers. This is because there is no easy way to kill a service, which you may want to do during development. During the install, you will also be asked to select your Java runtime environment. On Windows platforms, Sun's JDK or JRE 1.3 is supported, as well as versions 1.2 and 1.1: however, note that the EJB/JTA/JMS functionality requires 1.2 or later. This is the case for most other vendors' Java Virtual Machines as well. You will not be able to complete the install without a Java runtime.

You will be asked to specify the port number for the JRun Administration Server, so use port 8000, the default port number. (The default web site will run on port 8100) Next, create a password for the administrator account. Finally, you will be asked if you want to connect to an external web-server.

JRun can work as either a stand-alone engine using its built-in HTTP server, or as an add-on to an existing HTTP server using a connector. The most common external web-servers are supported, including Microsoft IIS & PWS, Apache, Netscape Enterprise, Netscape FastTrack, Netscape iPlanet, Website Pro, and Zeus Web Server. We will explain this later. Select I'll configure my web server later and click Finish. This should launch a new browser window which will prompt you to log into the JRun Management Console using the user name admin and whatever password you supplied during installation. To do this manually, open the browser window (use Internet Explorer or Netscape 4.0 or later) then open the page http://localhost:8000/index.jsp.

The figure below shows the JRun Administration Console, a web-based interface where you can manage your entire application. This includes WAR file deployment, configuring JDBC data sources, creating web apps, re-starting the server, and much more. On the left side bar there is a tree-view controller that shows the different JRun server instances currently running, and for each server instance there are various configuration panels associated with the server, such as JDBC Data Sources, Java Settings, Web Applications, etc.

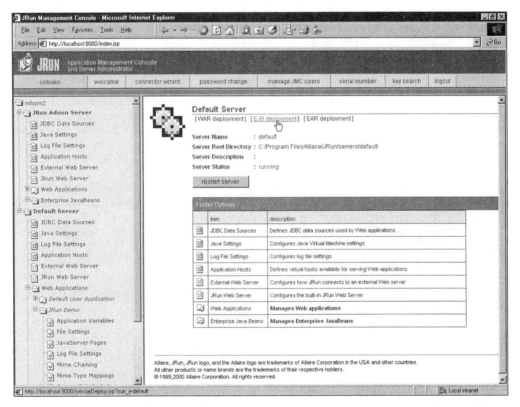

To understand the layout of the Administration Console, it's easiest to look at the JRun architecture diagram shown below. JRun has multiple independent servers. Each JRun server instance runs within its own JVM. Within the JVM, there is an instance of an HTTP server, Servlet, and JSP engine, as well as an EJB server with integrated transactions and messaging, all running in process:

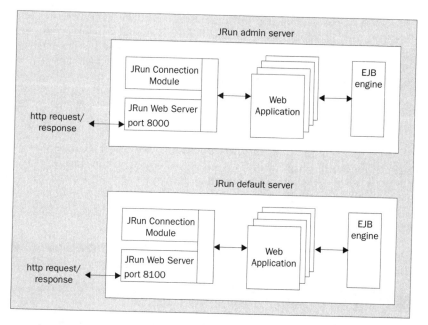

There are several reasons for this approach, including improved security and stability of the system. When you install JRun for the first time, two JRun servers are started up automatically, the Admin Server and the Default Server; you may create additional server instances at any time. The entire JRun Management Console is actually a web application that is deployed on the Admin server; by default it listens for HTTP requests on port 8000.

The default server has several sample applications, and listens for HTTP requests on port 8100. You can quickly verify that the default server's servlet engine is running by invoking one of the sample servlets located at http://localhost:8100/demo/index.html. You should deploy your applications to the default server, or create new server instances and deploy on those servers. You should not deploy other applications on the Administration port, as you might want to consider restricting access to the Administration Console. This can be done by clicking on **JRun Web Server | Client IP Filter** on the Admin Server and listing out the IP addresses that should be granted access. Note that all HTTP listening port numbers can be changed in the Management Console by clicking on **JRun Web Server | Web Server Port** for the desired server instance.

Connecting to an External Web Server

As mentioned earlier, JRun includes connectors for the most common web servers. While some of these web servers may include support for Servlets, one advantage of using JRun is that the Servlet engine itself is portable. If you connect to an external web server, then you are registering JRun as a filter to the external web server; the external server is configured to figure out which requests JRun should service, and JRun and the external server communicate on some specified port. In this case we will connect to Microsoft IIS: however, it is a similar process for all web servers. A connector wizard that walks you through the basic steps facilitates the process of connecting to an external web server; this is shown on the following page. Be sure to install the connector to the server that hosts your application, usually the default server. In general, you should not connect an external web server to the Admin Server because it is not supposed to be hosting your web applications.

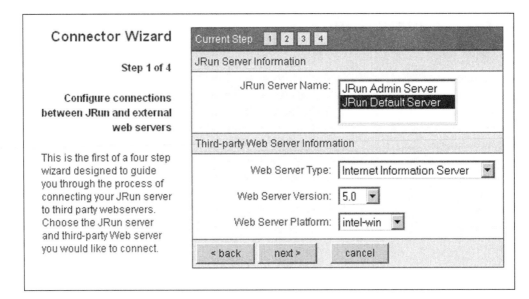

To start the connector wizard, from the left hand menu of the Management Console, expand a server tree and click on **External Web Server**. Follow the instructions on the screen – some tips are listed here:

❏   Shut down the external web server. In Windows, stop the WWW Publishing Service from the services panel; simply clicking the stop button from the Microsoft Management Console is not sufficient, as it does not unlock the dll files, resulting in a failed connection.

❏   Start the JRun Management Console (JMC).

❏   Run the JRun Connector Wizard to create a JRun Connection Module that manages the connection between the web server and the default JRun server. When asked to specify the server connector port, pick any unused port like 53001. This is the port that JRun and the external-web server will then use to communicate. If the JRun server and external web server are not on the same machine, make sure that the port isn't blocked by a firewall.

❏   You will need to choose a directory where the connection module is to be installed. The Wizard requests the scripts directory for IIS, which is normally `c:\Inetpub\Scripts` by default.

❏   Start the external web server and (restart) the default JRun server.

❏   Verify the connection between JRun and the web server by launching one of the sample Servlets through the connector at http://localhost/demo/index.html.

While this is just a basic configuration, there are many other possibilities. The relationship between a JRun server and an external server can be 1:1, many:1, 1:many or many:many. See the advanced configuration guide for more details, available at http://www.allaire.com/Documents/ under JRun Docs.

JRun 3.0 Directory Structure

The JRun 3.0 directory structure reflects the Servlet 2.2 specification, and is shown in the adjacent screenshot:

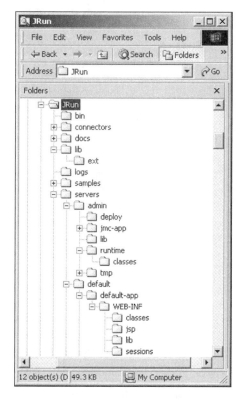

The /servers directory has a subdirectory for each server instance; in this case there are subdirectories for the Admin and Default servers inside which are subdirectories for each web application. Web applications follow the arrangement laid down in the Servlet 2.2 specification, namely that each application has a special directory called WEB-INF, which is not visible to external clients. Place all your class files (Servlets, JavaBeans, etc.) associated with the current application in the WEB-INF/classes directory, or if they are package declared, re-create the directory structure using the WEB-INF/classes directory as the root.

Any class libraries packaged in jar files can be placed in the WEB-INF/lib directory. To invoke a servlet, use the /servlet invoker mapping. (For example, http://localhost:8100/demo/servlet/SnoopServlet invokes the SnoopServlet class of the demo-app, located in JRun\servers\default\demo-app\WEB-INF\classes directory, belonging to the demo application). Alternatively you may create servlet mappings or aliases in either the Management Console by clicking Default Server | Web Applications | JRun Demo | Servlet URL Mappings, or by manually editing the web.xml file associated with the application, located in the WEB-INF directory for that application.

Creating an Application

The easiest way to create a new web application is to use the Create New Application wizard. Just specify which server you are creating the application for, the application name, URL, and root directory as illustrated in the opposite figure:

Note that JRun will automatically create a WEB-INF directory in the application root directory where you can place your .class files and .jar files.

Under the Hood

For those who prefer using property files rather than user interfaces to manage an application, we always have the option of modifying properties manually. It is always a good idea to back up your files first. JRun has a very simple property file hierarchy.

In the /lib directory, there is a global.properties file which contains all of the default settings for all JRun server instances. These properties can be over-ridden at either a server-level in the local.properties file in the /servers/<server_name> directory, and again at the application level in the webapp.properties file located in the WEB-INF directory of the web-application. The following is an excerpt from the global.properties file. This is where you would configure JRun session management: for example, you can specify if you would like to persist session data to a file or relational database, specify the database drivers, the frequency of updates, etc. Any line that begins with a # mark is ignored:

```
######################################################################
## session services
######################################################################

# Session management service.
# to enable these deprecated methods:
#    Enumeration SessionContext.getIds()
#    HttpSession getSession(String id)
# use allaire.jrun.session.JRunSessionService instead.
session.class=allaire.jrun.session.WebappSessionService
# Invalidation time is the default session inactivity timeout.
# If the session is not accessed, it will be expired. This value
# can be set on each session by calling HttpSession.setMaxInactiveTime()
# specified in minutes.
session.invalidationtime=30
```

```
# true if sessions should be persisted when the server is terminated.
session.persistence=true

# What to do with session data when class files change. Values are
# reload, drop, or ignore. Only valid if session.persistence=true
session.persistence.classchange=reload

# true if sessions should be swapped out of memory to a storage service
session.swapping=false

# How often the session pool should be checked for sessions that should
# be swapped to a storage service, specified in seconds
session.swapinterval=10

# The approximate number of sessions that will be allowed in memory
# before swapping to a storage service. Due to delays in the swapinterval
# and sessions that may not be serializable, the actual maximum may
# differ. If 0, all session data will be written out immediately upon
# the completion of the request. session.swapping must be 'true' in order
# for this property to take effect.
session.maxresident=9999999

# The name of the storage service to use for session persistence
# and/or swapping
session.persistence.service=file
session.persistence.file.class=allaire.jrun.session.FileSessionStorage
session.persistence.file.path={webapp.rootdir}/WEB-INF/sessions

# JDBCSessionStorage provider
session.persistence.jdbc.class=allaire.jrun.session.JDBCSessionStorage
session.persistence.jdbc.JDBCDriver=sun.jdbc.odbc.JdbcOdbcDriver
session.persistence.jdbc.JDBCConnectionURL=jdbc:odbc:JRunSessions
# The table name to use
session.persistence.jdbc.JDBCSessionTable=sessions
# A key prefix to keep all server keys unique
session.persistence.jdbc.JDBCSessionIDPrefix={jrun.server.name}-
# The column names to use. The JDBCSessionIDColumn must be a VARCHAR
# type while the JDBCSessionDataColumn must be able to handle
# binary long data
session.persistence.jdbc.JDBCSessionIDColumn=id
session.persistence.jdbc.JDBCSessionDataColumn=data

# settings for cookie-based sesssion tracking
session.cookie.maxage=-1
session.cookie.secure=false
session.cookie.active=true
session.cookie.domain=
session.cookie.comment="JRun Session Tracking Cookie"
session.cookie.path=/
session.cookie.name=jsessionid
```

As you can see, the property files are self-explanatory and you are encouraged to look around at some of the highly configurable features such as a performance monitor that can be used to identify bottlenecks, a customizable logger, and much more.

Getting Help

❑ JRun Support Forum:
http://forums.allaire.com/JRunconf/index.cfm

❑ JRun Developer Center:
http://www.allaire.com/developer/jrunreferencedesk/

❑ Knowledge Base:
http://www.allaire.com/Support/KnowledgeBase/SearchForm.cfm

❑ Online Documentation:
http://www.allaire.com/Documents/

❑ JRun-Interest list:
http://www.egroups.com/group/jrun-interest/

While this section highlights some of the key points in order to get started, complete product documentation is in the docs directory, and includes a setup guide, samples guide, and a comprehensive *Developing Applications in JRun* book in PDF format. An advanced configuration covering ISP and OEM installation and other advanced topics has been posted to the online documentation. The Knowledge Base articles are highly recommended as they are mostly written by JRun engineers.

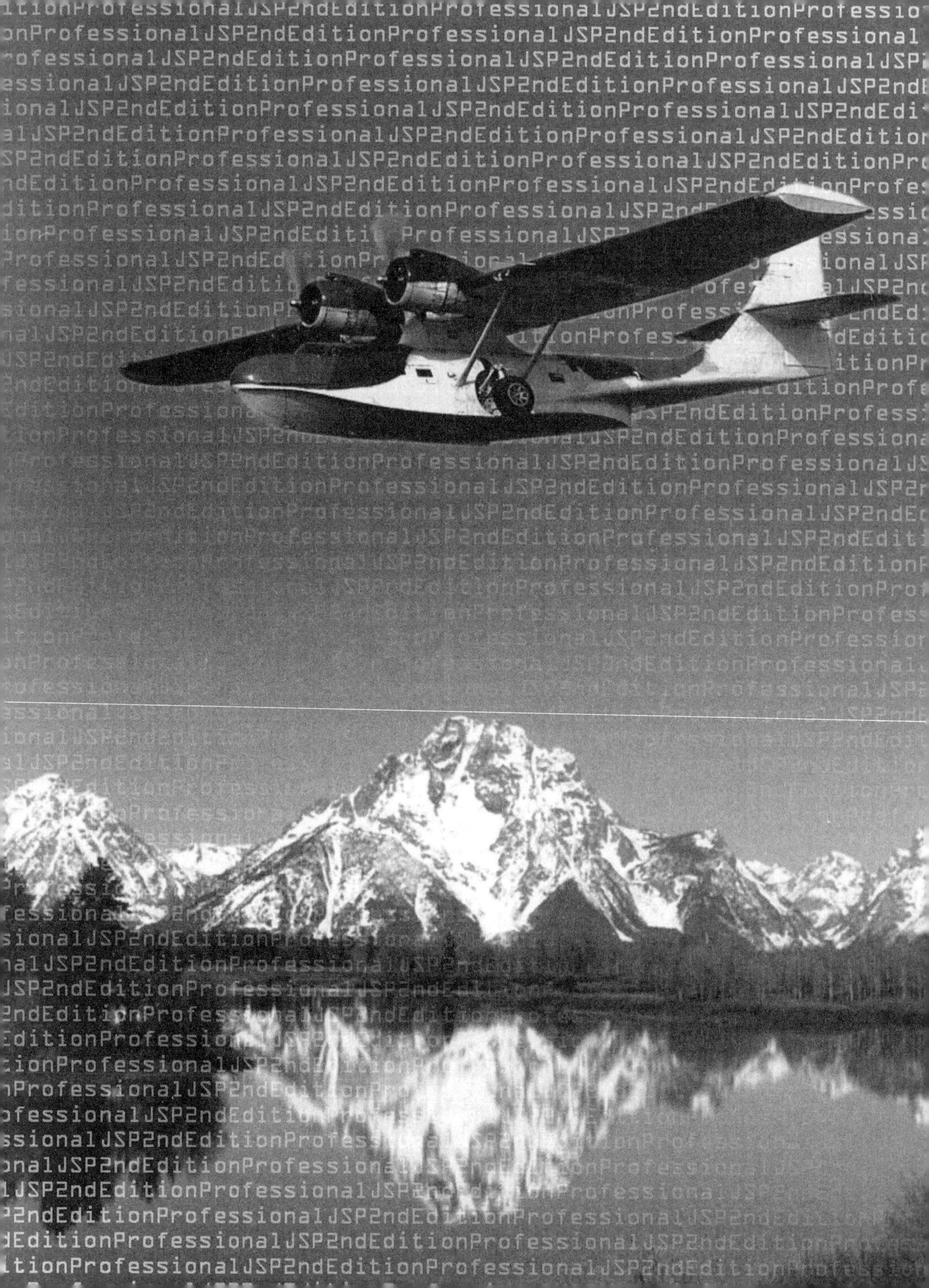
ProfessionalJSP2ndEdition

B

JSP Reference

This appendix reviews the syntax for JavaServer Pages 1.2, as described in the Proposed Final Draft specification. The intention is to provide a reference that is complete and useful, but more compact than the specification. (The JSP 1.2 Proposed Final Draft specification weighs in at 243 pages!)

> **JSP specifications from version 1.0 upwards are available from**
> **http://java.sun.com/products/jsp/.**

A word on the syntax of the syntax:

❏ *Italics* show what you'll have to specify.

❏ **Bold** shows the default value of an attribute. Attributes with default values are optional, if you're using the default. Sometimes, where the default value is a little complicated, we use **default** to indicate that the default is described in the following text.

❏ When an attribute has a set of possible values, those are shown delimited by |.

Preliminaries

Before we get stuck into the details, a few miscellaneous observations.

URL Specifications

URLs specified within JSP tags can be of two sorts:

❑ **Context-relative** paths start with a "/"; the base URL is provided by the web application to which the JSP belongs. For example, in a web application hosted at http://localhost:8080/appB/, the URL "/urlspec.jsp" refers to http://localhost:8080/appB/urlspec.jsp.

❑ **Page-relative** paths are interpreted relative to the JSP page in which they occur.

Comments

Two sorts of comments are allowed in JSPs, in addition to comments in Java code – JSP and HTML:

```
<!-- HTML comments remain in the final client page.
     They can include JSP expressions.
-->

<%-- JSP comments are hidden from the final client page --%>
```

Directives

Directives are instructions to the JSP container regarding page properties, importing tag libraries, and including content within a JSP.

The page Directive

The page directive specifies attributes for the page – all the attributes are optional, as the essential ones have default values, shown in bold.

```
<%@ page language="java"
         extends="package.class"
         import="package.class, package.*, ..."
         session="true|false"
         buffer="none|default|sizekb"
         autoFlush="true|false"
         isThreadSafe="true|false"
         info="Sample JSP to show tags"
         isErrorPage="true|false"
         errorPage="ErrorPage.jsp"
         contentType="TYPE|
                     TYPE; charset=CHARSET|
                     text/html; charset=ISO-8859-1"
         pageEncoding="default"
%>
```

❑ The default buffer size is defined to be *at least* 8kb.

❑ The errorPage attribute contains the relative URL for the error page to which this page should go if there's an un-handled error on this page.

❑ The specified error page file must declare isErrorPage="true" to have access to the Exception object.

❑ The contentType attribute sets the MIME type and the character set for the response.

❑ The `pageEncoding` attribute defines the character encoding for the JSP page. The default is
that specified in the `contentType` attribute, or `"ISO-8859-1"` if none was specified there.

```
<%@ page language="java"
         isErrorPage="true" %>

<html>
<body>
<!-- The fully-qualified class that is the exception -->
<%= exception.toString() %>
<br>
<!-- The exception's message to the world -->
<%= exception.getMessage() %>
</body>
</html>
```

The taglib Directive

The `taglib` directive defines a tag library namespace for the page, mapping the URI of the tag library
descriptor to a prefix that can be used to reference tags from the library on this page.

```
<%@ taglib uri="/META-INF/taglib.tld" prefix="tagPrefix" %>

...

<tagPrefix:tagName attributeName="attributeValue" >
  JSP content
</tagPrefix:tagName>

<tagPrefix:tagName attributeName="attributeValue" />
```

The include Directive

There are two include tags – the `include` directive and the `jsp:include` action.

The `include` directive includes a static file at translation time, adding any JSP in that file to this page
for runtime processing:

```
<%@ include file="header.html" %>
```

See also the `jsp:include` action.

Scripting Elements

Scripting elements are used to include snippets of Java code within a JSP: to declare variables and
methods, execute arbitrary Java code, and display the result of Java expressions.

Declarations

The following syntax allows you to declare variables and methods for the page. These are placed in the generated Servlet *outside* the _jspService() method, in other words variables declared here will be instance variables of the Servlet:

```
<%!
    int i = 0;
    char ch = 'a';
    boolean isTrue(boolean b) {
      // Is this true?
    }
%>
```

Scriptlets

Scriptlets enclose Java code (on however many lines) that is evaluated within the generated Servlet's _jspService() method to generate dynamic content:

```
<%
    // Java code
%>
```

Take care when using adjacent scriptlet blocks – this code:

```
<% if(user.isLoggedIn) { %>
    <p>Hi!</p>
<% } %>
<% else { %>
    <p>Please log in first...</p>
<% } %>
```

is not legal since the line break between the <% } %> and <% else { %> scriptlet blocks is treated as template text to be returned to the client.

Expressions

Expressions return a value from the scripting code as a String to the page:

```
<p>Hello there,
<%= userName %>
Good to see you.</p>
```

Standard Actions

The standard actions provide various facilities for manipulating JavaBeans components, including and forwarding control to other resources at request-time, and generating HTML to use the Java Plug-in.

<jsp:useBean>

The <jsp:useBean> tag checks for an instance of a bean of the given class and scope. If a bean of the specified class exists it references it with the id, otherwise it instantiates it. The bean is available within its scope with its id attribute.

You can include code between the <jsp:useBean> tags, as shown in the second example – this code will only be run if the <jsp:useBean> tag successfully instantiated the bean:

```
<jsp:useBean id="aBeanName"
             scope="page|request|session|application"
             typeSpecification
/>
```

or:

```
<jsp:useBean id="anotherBeanName"
             scope="page|request|session|application"
             typeSpecification
   <jsp.setProperty name="anotherBeanName"
                    property="*|propertyName" />
</jsp:useBean>
```

There is a lot of flexibility in specifying the type of the bean (indicated by typeSpecification above). You can use:

❑ class="package.class"

❑ type="typeName"

❑ class="package.class" type="typeName" (and with terms reversed)

❑ beanName="beanName" type="typeName" (and with terms reversed)

where:

❑ typeName is the class of the scripting variable defined by the id attribute; that is, the class that the Bean instance is cast to (whether the class, a parent class or an interface the class implements).

❑ beanName is the name of the Bean, as used in the instantiate() method of the java.beans.Beans class.

<jsp:setProperty>

The <jsp:setProperty> tag we used above sets the property of the bean referenced by name using the value:

```
<jsp.setProperty name="anotherBeanName"
                 propertyExpression
/>
```

The *propertyExpression* can be any of the following:

- ❏ property=`"*"`
- ❏ property=`"propertyName"`
- ❏ property=`"propertyName"` param=`"parameterName"`
- ❏ property=`"propertyName"` value=`"propertyValue"`

Where:

- ❏ The * setting tells the tag to iterate through the `request` parameters for the page, setting any values for properties in the Bean whose names match parameter names.
- ❏ The `param` attribute specifies the parameter name to use in setting this property.
- ❏ The `value` attribute can be any runtime expression as long as it evaluates to a `String`.
- ❏ Omitting `value` and `param` attributes for a property assumes that the Bean property and `request` parameter name match.
- ❏ The `value` attribute `String` can be automatically cast to `boolean`, `byte`, `char`, `double`, `int`, `float`, `long`, and their class equivalents. Other casts will have to be handled explicitly in the Bean's set`PropertyName`() method.

<jsp:getProperty>

The final bean-handling action is <`jsp:getProperty`>, which gets the named property and outputs its value for inclusion in the page as a `String`:

```
<jsp:getProperty name="anotherBeanName" property="propertyName" />
```

<jsp:param>

The <`jsp:param`> action is used within the body of <`jsp:forward`>, <`jsp:include`>, and <`jsp:plugin`> to supply extra name-value parameter pairs. It has the following syntax:

```
<jsp:param name="parameterName" value="parameterValue" />
```

<jsp:forward>

To forward the client request to another URL, whether it be an HTML file, JSP or Servlet, use the following syntax:

```
<jsp:forward page="relativeURL" />
```

or:

```
<jsp:forward page="relativeURL" >
  <jsp:param name="parameterName" value="parameterValue" />
</jsp:forward>
```

Where:

- ❏ The `page` attribute for `<jsp:forward>` can be a runtime expression

- ❏ The `value` attribute for `<jsp:param>` can be a runtime expression

`<jsp:include>`

The `<jsp:include>` action includes a static or dynamically-referenced file at runtime:

```
<jsp:include page="relativeURL" flush="true|false" />
```

or:

```
<jsp:include page="relativeURL"
            flush="true" >
  <jsp:param name="parameterName" value="parameterValue"/>
</jsp:include>
```

Where:

- ❏ The `page` attribute can be the result of some run-time expression.

- ❏ The optional `flush` attribute determines whether the output buffer will be flushed before including the specified resource. The default value is `"false"`. (Note that in JSP 1.1 this attribute was mandatory and the only permissible value was `"true"`.)

- ❏ The `jsp:param` tag allows parameters to be appended to the original request, and if the parameter `name` already exists, the new parameter `value` takes precedence, in a comma-delimited list.

`<jsp:plugin>`

The `<jsp:plugin>` action enables the JSP to include a bean or an applet in the client page. It has the following syntax:

```
<jsp:plugin type="bean|applet"
            code="class"
            codebase="classDirectory"
            name="instanceName"
            archive="archiveURI"
            align="bottom|top|middle|left|right"
            height="inPixels"
            width="inPixels"
            hspace="leftRightPixels"
            vspace="topBottomPixels"
            jreversion="1.2|number"
            nspluginurl="pluginURL"
            iepluginurl="pluginURL" >
  <jsp:params>
    <jsp:param name="parameterName" value="parameterValue">
  </jsp:params>
  <jsp:fallback>Problem with plugin</jsp:fallback>
</jsp:plugin>
```

Most of these attributes are direct from the HTML spec – the exceptions are `type`, `jreversion`, `nspluginurl` and `iepluginurl`.

❑ The name, `archive`, `align`, `height`, `width`, `hspace`, `vspace`, `jreversion`, `nspluginurl`, and `iepluginurl` attributes are optional

❑ The `<jsp:param>` tag's value attribute can take a runtime expression

❑ The `jreversion` is the Java Runtime Environment specification version that the component requires

❑ `nspluginurl` and `iepluginurl` are the URL where the Java plugin can be downloaded for Netscape Navigator and Internet Explorer

Implicit Objects

See Appendix C for details of the Servlet and JSP classes, and their methods.

Implicit object	Type	Scope
application	javax.servlet.ServletContext	Application
session	javax.servlet.HttpSession	Session
request	javax.servlet.ServletRequest	Request
pageContext	javax.servlet.jsp.PageContext	Page
out	javax.servlet.jsp.JspWriter	Page
config	javax.servlet.ServletConfig	Page
exception	java.lang.Throwable	Page
page	java.lang.Object	Page
response	javax.servlet.ServletResponse	Page

Predefined Attributes

The Servlet and JSP specifications define a number of special request and context (application) attributes.

Security-related Attributes

These attributes are only available when a request has been made over SSL.

javax.servlet.request.cipher_suite

`javax.servlet.request.cipher_suite` is a request attribute of type `String` containing the cipher suite used for an SSL request.

javax.servlet.request.key_size

`javax.servlet.request.key_size` is a request attribute of type `Integer` containing the bit size that was used for an SSL request.

javax.servlet.request.X509Certificate

`javax.servlet.request.X509Certificate` is a request attribute of type `java.security.cert.X509Certificate` containing any certificate associated with an SSL request.

Inclusion-related Attributes

These attributes are available when a Servlet or JSP is accessed via a `RequestDispatcher.include()` or a `<jsp:include>`.

javax.servlet.include.request_uri

`javax.servlet.include.request_uri` is a request attribute of type `String` containing the URI under which this included Servlet or JSP is being accessed.

javax.servlet.include.context_path

`javax.servlet.include.context_path` is a request attribute of type `String` containing the context path of the URI under which this included Servlet or JSP is being accessed.

javax.servlet.include.servlet_path

`javax.servlet.include.servlet_path` is a request attribute of type `String` containing the servlet path of the URI under which this included Servlet or JSP is being accessed.

javax.servlet.include.path_info

`javax.servlet.include.path_info` is a request attribute of type `String` containing the path info of the URI under which this included Servlet or JSP is being accessed.

javax.servlet.include.query_string

`javax.servlet.include.query_string` is a request attribute of type `String` containing the query string of the URI under which this included Servlet or JSP is being accessed.

javax.servlet.error.Servlet_name

`javax.servlet.error.Servlet_name` is a request attribute of type `String` containing the name of the Serrvlet that threw an exception.

Servlet Error Page Attributes

These attributes are only available within an error page declared in `web.xml`.

javax.servlet.error.status_code

`javax.servlet.error.status_code` is a request attribute of type `Integer` containing the status code of the Servlet or JSP that caused the error.

javax.servlet.error.exception_type

`javax.servlet.error.exception_type` is a request attribute of type `Class` that contains the type of the exception thrown by the Servlet or JSP. It is now redundant with the introduction of the `javax.servlet.error.exception` attribute.

javax.servlet.error.message

`javax.servlet.error.message` is a request attribute of type `String` containing the message contained within the exception thrown by the Servlet or JSP. It is now redundant with the introduction of the `javax.servlet.error.exception` attribute.

javax.servlet.error.exception

`javax.servlet.error.exception` is a request attribute of type `Throwable` containing the exception thrown by the Servlet or JSP.

javax.servlet.error.request_uri

`javax.servlet.error.request_uri` is a request attribute of type `String` containing the URI of the request that caused the Servlet or JSP to throw an exception.

JSP Error Page Attributes

This attribute is available within error pages declared in a JSP's `<%@ page %>` directive.

javax.servlet.jsp.jspException

`javax.servlet.jsp.jspException` is a request attribute of type `Throwable` containing the exception thrown by the JSP.

Temporary File Directory Attribute

This attribute allows a web application to make use of a temporary working directory.

javax.servlet.context.tempdir

`javax.servlet.context.tempdir` is a context attribute of type `java.io.File` referencing a temporary working directory that can be used by the web application.

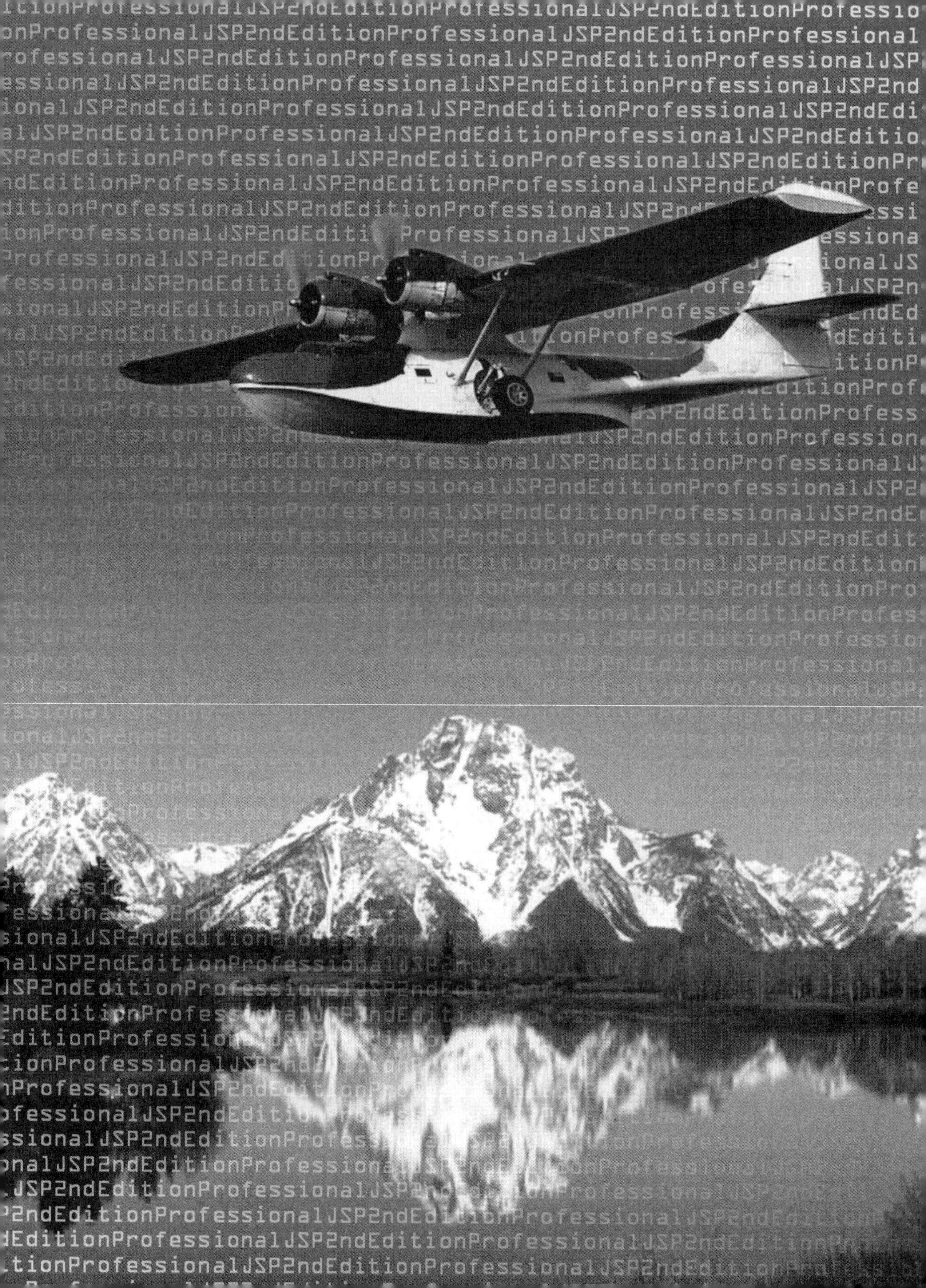
ProfessionalJSP2ndEdition

C

API Reference

This appendix describes the Java classes and interfaces defined in the JSP 1.2 and Servlet 2.3 specifications. These are contained in four packages:

- ❏ `javax.servlet` contains classes and interfaces related to Servlet programming.
- ❏ `javax.servlet.http` contains classes and interfaces related specifically to Servlets using the HTTP protocol.
- ❏ `javax.servlet.jsp` contains classes and interfaces related to JSP.
- ❏ `javax.servlet.jsp.tagext` contains classes and interfaces for programming JSP tag extensions.

In many cases, the actual objects passed will be instances of container-specific implementations of interfaces specified here, or concrete subclasses of abstract classes specified here.

javax.servlet

The `javax.servlet` package provides interfaces and classes that support Servlet programming in the broadest, non-protocol-specific, sense. It includes the `Servlet` interface, which all Servlets must ultimately implement.

javax.servlet Interfaces

Filter

```
public interface Filter
```

A `Filter` component can intercept a request to a resource to perform filtering tasks. The `Filter` interface has three methods.

```
public void init(FilterConfig filterConfig)
        throws ServletException
```

`init()` is called when the filter is instantiated, and is passed a `FilterConfig` object containing configuration information about the filter's environment.

```
public void destroy()
```

`destroy()` is called when the filter is taken out of service.

```
public void doFilter(ServletRequest request,
                     ServletResponse response,
                     FilterChain chain)
        throws java.io.IOException, ServletException
```

`doFilter()` is called each time a request is received for a resource for which this filter is registered. An implementation would typically examine the request object, then either invoke the next object in the `FilterChain` by calling `chain.doFilter()` (optionally wrapping the request and response objects) or generate the response itself.

FilterChain

```
public interface FilterChain
```

A `FilterChain` represents the series of filters to be invoked during a request to a resource. The `FilterChain` interface has one method.

```
public void doFilter(ServletRequest request,
                     ServletResponse response)
        throws java.io.IOException, ServletException
```

`doFilter()` either invokes the next filter in the chain, or (if this is the last filter in the chain) invokes the filtered resource itself.

FilterConfig

```
public interface FilterConfig
```

A `FilterConfig` object is used by the Servlet container to pass configuration information to a filter while it is being initialized. The `FilterConfig` interface has four methods.

```
public String getFilterName()
```

`getFilterName()` returns the name of the filter, as declared in `web.xml`.

```
public ServletContext getServletContext()
```

`getServletContext()` returns the `ServletContext` in which this filter is running.

```
    public String getInitParameter(String name)
```

getInitParameter() returns a String containing the named initialization parameter, or null if there is no such parameter.

```
    public java.util.Enumeration getInitParameterNames()
```

getInitParameterNames() returns an Enumeration containing the names of the initialization parameters.

RequestDispatcher

```
    public interface RequestDispatcher
```

A RequestDispatcher is an object that sends requests to the appropriate resource (Servlet, HTML file, etc.) within the server. The Servlet creates the RequestDispatcher object, which is used as a wrapper around a particular resource. A RequestDispatcher object was intended to wrap Servlets, but can be used to wrap any type of resource on a server. The RequestDispatcher interface has two methods.

```
    public void forward(ServletRequest request,
                        ServletResponse response)
            throws ServletException, java.io.IOException
```

foward() forwards a client request to another resource (Servlet, HTML file, etc.). This method allows a Servlet to serve as a 'request processor', performing some preliminary work before sending the request to the resource that will ultimately respond to it. The forward() method can be used if the Servlet has not already opened a PrintWriter or ServletOutputStream back to the client machine. If an output stream has been created, use the include() method instead. The request and response must be either the same objects that were passed to this Servlet's service() method, or ServletRequestWrapper or ServletResponseWrapper subclass instances that wrap them.

```
    public void include(ServletRequest request,
                        ServletResponse response)
            throws ServletException, java.io.IOException
```

include() allows a resource to be included in the response to a client request. This method is used to include some content to the response after the response has been initiated by opening a PrintWriter or ServletOutputStream back to the client machine. The request and response must be either the same objects that were passed to this Servlet's service() method, or ServletRequestWrapper or ServletResponseWrapper subclass instances that wrap them.

Servlet

```
    public interface Servlet
```

Every Servlet must implement the Servlet interface. It declares the methods that govern the life cycle of the Servlet as well as methods to access initialization parameters and information about the Servlet. The Servlet interface has five methods.

```
    public void init(ServletConfig config)
            throws ServletException
```

`init()` is called when the Servlet is put into service. The `ServletConfig` object is used to provide the Servlet with initialization parameters.

```
public ServletConfig getServletConfig()
```

`getServletConfig()` returns the `ServletConfig` object associated with the Servlet. A `ServletConfig` object contains parameters that are used to initialize the Servlet.

```
public void service(ServletRequest req,
                    ServletResponse res)
        throws ServletException, java.io.IOException
```

`service()` is called to respond to a request from a client machine. The code representing what the Servlet is supposed to do is placed in this method, which is only called after the `init()` method has completed successfully.

```
public String getServletInfo()
```

`getServletInfo()` returns a `String` containing useful information about the Servlet. By default, this method returns an empty `String`, but it can be overridden to provide more useful information.

```
public void destroy()
```

`destroy()` is called when the Servlet is being taken out of service, allowing the Servlet to release any resources associated with it.

ServletConfig

```
public interface ServletConfig
```

A `ServletConfig` object is used to pass initialization parameters (name-value pairs) to a Servlet during its initialization. The `ServletConfig` interface declares four methods, which can access the parameters, as well as returning the name of the Servlet and its associated `ServletContext` object. A `ServletContext` object contains information about the server on which the Servlet resides.

```
public String getServletName()
```

`getServletName()` returns the name of the Servlet. If the Servlet is unnamed, the method will return the Servlet's class name.

```
public ServletContext getServletContext()
```

`getServletContext()` returns the `ServletContext` object associated with the invoking Servlet. A `ServletContext` object contains information about the environment in which the Servlet is running.

```
public String getInitParameter(String name)
```

`getInitParameter()` returns the value of the specified initialization parameter, or `null` if the parameter does not exist.

```
    public java.util.Enumeration getInitParameterNames()
```

getInitParameterNames() returns an Enumeration of String objects containing the names of all of the Servlet's initialization parameters.

ServletContext

```
    public interface ServletContext
```

The ServletContext interface declares 23 methods that a Servlet uses to communicate with its host server, of which four are deprecated. The methods declared in this interface allow a Servlet to obtain information about the server on which it is running.

```
    public ServletContext getContext(String uripath)
```

getContext() returns the ServletContext object for the resource at the specified path on the server. The path argument is an absolute URL beginning with "/".

```
    public int getMajorVersion()
```

getMajorVersion() returns the major version of the Java Servlet API that the server supports. For servers supporting version 2.3 of the Servlet specification, this method will return 2.

```
    public int getMinorVersion()
```

getMinorVersion() returns the minor version of the Java Servlet API that the server supports. For servers supporting version 2.3 of the Servlet specification, this method will return 3.

```
    public String getMimeType(String file)
```

getMimeType() returns the MIME type of the specified file or null if the MIME type cannot be ascertained. Typical return values will be "text/plain", "text/html", or "image/jpg".

```
    public java.util.Set getResourcePaths(String path)
```

getResourcePaths() returns all the paths to resources in the specified subdirectory of the web application as Strings beginning with a "/". The path must start with "/".

```
    public java.net.URL getResource(String path)
            throws java.net.MalformedURLException
```

getResource() returns a URL object that is mapped to the specified path, or null if there is no resource mapped to the path. The path must begin with "/" and is interpreted relative to the current context root.

```
    public java.io.InputStream getResourceAsStream(String path)
```

getResourceAsStream() returns the resource at the specified path as an InputStream object.

```
    public RequestDispatcher getRequestDispatcher(String path)
```

getRequestDispatcher() returns a RequestDispatcher object that acts as a wrapper around the resource located at the specified path. The path must begin with "/", and is interpreted relative to the current context root.

```
public RequestDispatcher getNamedDispatcher(String name)
```

getNamedDispatcher() returns a RequestDispatcher object that will be wrapped around the named Servlet.

```
public void log(String msg)
public void log(String message,
                Throwable throwable)
```

log() is used to write a message to the Servlet engine's log file. The second version writes both an explanatory message and a stack trace for the specified Throwable exception to the log file.

```
public String getRealPath(String path)
```

getRealPath() returns a String object containing the real path, in a form appropriate to the platform on which the Servlet is running, corresponding to the given virtual path. An example of a virtual path might be "/blah.html".

```
public String getServerInfo()
```

getServerInfo() returns a String object containing information on the server on which the Servlet is running. At a minimum, the String will contain the Servlet container name and version number.

```
public String getInitParameter(String name)
```

getInitParameter() returns a String object containing the value of the specified initialization parameter, or null if the parameter does not exist.

```
public java.util.Enumeration getInitParameterNames()
```

getInitParameterNames() returns a Enumeration containing the initialization parameters associated with the invoking ServletContext object.

```
public Object getAttribute(String name)
```

getAttribute() returns the value of the specified attribute name. The return value is an Object or sub-class if the attribute is available to the invoking ServletContext object, or null if the attribute is not available.

```
public java.util.Enumeration getAttributeNames()
```

getAttributeNames() returns an Enumeration containing the attribute names available to the invoking ServletContext object.

```
public void setAttribute(String name,
                         Object object)
```

setAttribute() binds a value to a specified attribute name.

```
public void removeAttribute(String name)
```

removeAttribute() makes the specified attribute unavailable to the invoking ServletContext object. Subsequent calls to the getAttribute() method for this attribute will return null.

```
public String getServletContextName()
```

getServletContextName() returns the name of the web application, as specified in the <display-name> element in web.xml.

```
public Servlet getServlet(String name)
       throws ServletException
public java.util.Enumeration getServlets()
public java.util.Enumeration getServletNames()
public void log(Exception exception,
                String msg)
```

These methods are deprecated.

ServletContextAttributeListener

```
public interface ServletContextAttributeListener
  extends java.util.EventListener
```

An object implementing ServletContextAttributeListener can be registered to receive notification when attributes are added to, removed from, or replaced in the ServletContext. This interface declares three methods.

```
public void attributeAdded(ServletContextAttributeEvent scab)
```

attributeAdded() is called when an attribute is added to the ServletContext. It is passed a ServletContextAttributeEvent containing information about the event.

```
public void attributeRemoved(ServletContextAttributeEvent scab)
```

attributeRemoved() is called when an attribute is removed from the ServletContext. It is passed a ServletContextAttributeEvent containing information about the event.

```
public void attributeReplaced(ServletContextAttributeEvent scab)
```

attributeReplaced() is called when a ServletContext attribute is replaced. It is passed a ServletContextAttributeEvent containing information about the event.

ServletContextListener

```
public interface ServletContextListener
    extends java.util.EventListener
```

An object implementing `ServletContextListener` can be registered to receive notification when the `ServletContext` is initialized or destroyed. This interface declares two methods.

```
public void contextInitialized(ServletContextEvent sce)
```

`contextInitialized()` is called when the `ServletContext` is initialized. It is passed a `ServletContextEvent` containing information about the event.

```
public void contextDestroyed(ServletContextEvent sce)
```

`contextDestroyed()` is called when the `ServletContext` is destroyed. It is passed a `ServletContextEvent` containing information about the event.

ServletRequest

```
public interface ServletRequest
```

The `ServletRequest` interface contains 25 methods that are used to provide client request information to a Servlet; of which one is deprecated. This information can include parameter name-value pairs, attributes, and an input stream. A `ServletRequest` object is passed to the `service()` method defined in the `Servlet` interface, as well as the `forward()` and `include()` methods from the `RequestDispatcher` interface.

```
public Object getAttribute(String name)
```

`getAttribute()` returns the value of the specified request attribute name. The return value is an `Object` or subclass if the attribute is available to the invoking `ServletRequest` object, or `null` if the attribute is not available.

```
public java.util.Enumeration getAttributeNames()
```

`getAttributeNames()` returns an `Enumeration` containing the attribute names available to the invoking `ServletRequest` object.

```
public String getCharacterEncoding()
```

`getCharacterEncoding()` returns a `String` object containing the character encoding used in the body of the request, or `null` if there is no encoding.

```
public void setCharacterEncoding(String env)
        throws java.io.UnsupportedEncodingException
```

`setCharacterEncoding()` overrides the character encoding used in the body of this request.

```
    public int getContentLength()
```

getContentLength() returns the length of the body of the request in bytes, or −1 if the length is not known.

```
    public String getContentType()
```

getContentType() returns a String object containing the MIME type ("text/plain", "text/html", "image/gif", etc.) of the body of the request, or null if the type is not known.

```
    public ServletInputStream getInputStream()
            throws java.io.IOException
```

getInputStream() returns a ServletInputStream object that can be used to read the body of the request as binary data.

```
    public String getParameter(String name)
```

getParameter() returns a String object containing the value of the specified parameter, or null if the parameter does not exist.

```
    public java.util.Enumeration getParameterNames()
```

getParameterNames() returns a Enumeration containing the parameters contained within the invoking ServletRequest object.

```
    public String[] getParameterValues(String name)
```

getParamterValues() is used when a parameter may have more than one value associated with it. The method returns a String array containing the values of the specified parameter, or null if the parameter does not exist.

```
    public java.util.Map getParameterMap()
```

getParameterMap() returns a Map containing the request parameters.

```
    public String getProtocol()
```

getProtocol() returns the name and version of the protocol used by the request. A typical return String would be "HTTP/1.1".

```
    public String getScheme()
```

getScheme() returns the scheme ("http", "https", "ftp", etc.) used to make the request.

```
    public String getServerName()
```

getServerName() returns a String object containing the name of the server that received the request.

```
public int getServerPort()
```

getServerPort() returns the port number that received the request.

```
public java.io.BufferedReader getReader()
        throws java.io.IOException
```

getReader() returns a BufferedReader object that can be used to read the body of the request as character data.

```
public String getRemoteAddr()
```

getRemoteAddr() returns a String object containing the IP address of the client machine that made the request.

```
public String getRemoteHost()
```

getRemoteHost() returns a String object containing the name of the client machine or the IP address if the name cannot be determined.

```
public void setAttribute(String name,
                         Object o)
```

setAttribute() binds a value to a specified attribute name. Note that attributes will be re-set after the request is handled.

```
public void removeAttribute(String name)
```

removeAttribute() makes the specified attribute unavailable to the invoking ServletRequest object. Subsequent calls to the getAttribute() method for this attribute will return null.

```
public java.util.Locale getLocale()
```

getLocale() returns the preferred locale of the client that made the request.

```
public java.util.Enumeration getLocales()
```

getLocales() returns an Enumeration containing, in descending order of preference, the locales that are acceptable to the client machine.

```
public boolean isSecure()
```

isSecure() returns true if the request was made using a secure channel, for example HTTPS.

```
public RequestDispatcher getRequestDispatcher(String path)
```

getRequestDispatcher() returns a RequestDispatcher object that acts as a wrapper around the resource located at the specified path. The path must begin with "/" and can be a relative path.

```
public String getRealPath(String path)
```

This method is deprecated – use ServletContext.getRealPath() instead.

ServletResponse

```
public interface ServletResponse
```

The ServletResponse interface declares 13 methods that are used to assist the Servlet in sending a response to the client machine.

```
public String getCharacterEncoding()
```

getCharacterEncoding() returns a String object containing the character encoding used in the body of the response. The default is "ISO-8859-1", which corresponds to Latin-1.

```
public ServletOutputStream getOutputStream()
        throws java.io.IOException
```

getOutputStream() returns a ServletOutputStream object that can be used to write the response as binary data.

```
public java.io.PrintWriter getWriter()
        throws java.io.IOException
```

getWriter() returns a PrintWriter object that can be used to write the response as character data.

```
public void setContentLength(int len)
```

setContentLength() sets the length of response body.

```
public void setContentType(String type)
```

setContentType() sets the content type of the response sent to the server. The String argument specifies a MIME type and may also include the type of character encoding, for example "text/plain; charset=ISO-8859-1".

```
public void setBufferSize(int size)
```

setBufferSize() requests a buffer size to be used for the response. The actual buffer size will be at least this large.

```
public int getBufferSize()
```

getBufferSize() returns the buffer size used for the response, or 0 if no buffering is used.

```
public void flushBuffer()
        throws java.io.IOException
```

`flushBuffer()` causes any content stored in the buffer to be written to the client. Calling this method will also commit the response, meaning that the status code and headers will be written.

```
public void resetBuffer()
```

`resetBuffer()` clears the content of the response buffer without clearing the headers or status code. It will throw an `IllegalStateException` if the response has been committed.

```
public boolean isCommitted()
```

`isCommitted()` returns `true` if the response has been committed, meaning that the status code and headers have been written.

```
public void reset()
```

`reset()` clears the status code and headers, and any data that exists in the buffer. If the response has already been committed, calling this method will cause an exception to be thrown.

```
public void setLocale(java.util.Locale loc)
```

`setLocale()` specifies the locale that will be used for the response.

```
public java.util.Locale getLocale()
```

`getLocale()` returns the locale that has been assigned to the response. By default, this will be the default locale for the server.

SingleThreadModel

```
public interface SingleThreadModel
```

The `SingleThreadModel` interface declares no methods. A Servlet that implements this interface will allow only one request at a time to access its `service()` method. The server will achieve this by either synchronizing access to a single instance of the Servlet, or by assigning a separate instance of the Servlet for each request.

javax.servlet Classes

GenericServlet

```
public abstract class GenericServlet
  extends Object
    implements Servlet, ServletConfig, java.io.Serializable
```

The GenericServlet class defines a generic, protocol-independent Servlet. It provides implementations of the methods declared in the Servlet and ServletConfig interfaces. Because GenericServlet is an abstract class, a GenericServlet object is never created. To create a generic Servlet, a class must be written that extends the GenericServlet class and overrides the service() method.

> public **GenericServlet**()

This constructor does nothing. The init() methods are used for Servlet initialization.

> public void **destroy**()

destroy() unloads the Servlet from the server's memory and releases any resources associated with it.

> public String **getInitParameter**(String *name*)

getInitParameter() returns the value of the specified initialization parameter from the ServletConfig object associated with the invoking GenericServlet object.

> public java.util.Enumeration **getInitParameterNames**()

getInitParameterNames() returns an Enumeration of String objects containing the names of all of the Servlet's initialization parameters.

> public ServletConfig **getServletConfig**()

getServletConfig() returns the ServletConfig object associated with the invoking GenericServlet sub-class object. A ServletConfig object contains parameters that are used to initialize the Servlet.

> public ServletContext **getServletContext**()

getServletContext() returns the ServletContext object associated with the invoking GenericServlet subclass object. A ServletContext object contains information about the environment in which the Servlet is running.

> public String **getServletInfo**()

getServletInfo() returns a String containing useful information about the Servlet. By default, this method returns an empty String. It can be overridden to provide more useful information.

> ```
> public void init(ServletConfig config)
>         throws ServletException
> public void init()
>         throws ServletException
> ```

init() is called when the Servlet is loaded into the address space of the server. If a ServletConfig object is specified, it can be used to provide the Servlet with initialization parameters. The no-argument version is provided as a convenience, for subclasses to override.

```
public void log(String msg)
public void log(String message,
                Throwable t)
```

log() is used to write a message to the Servlet's log file. The second version writes an explanatory message and a stack trace for the specified Throwable exception to the log file.

```
public abstract void service(ServletRequest req,
                             ServletResponse res)
        throws ServletException, java.io.IOException
```

service() is called to respond to a request from a client machine. The code representing what the Servlet is supposed to do is placed in this method. Because this method is declared abstract, a concrete implementation must be provided by a concrete (non-abstract) subclass of GenericServlet.

```
public String getServletName()
```

getServletName() returns the name of the invoking GenericServlet object.

ServletContextAttributeEvent

```
public class ServletContextAttributeEvent
    extends ServletContextEvent
```

A ServletContextAttributeEvent is the event object used when an attribute is added to, removed from, or replaced in the ServletContext.

```
public ServletContextAttributeEvent(ServletContext source,
                                    String name,
                                    Object value)
```

The constructor simply requires references to the ServletContext in which the event took place, and the name and value of the attribute.

```
public String getName()
```

getName() returns the name of the new/removed/replaced attribute.

```
public Object getValue()
```

getValue() returns the value of the new/removed/replaced attribute.

ServletContextEvent

```
public class ServletContextEvent
    extends java.util.EventObject
```

A ServletContextEvent is the event object used when a ServletContext is created or destroyed.

```
public ServletContextEvent(ServletContext source)
```

The constructor takes a reference to the `ServletContext` in question.

```
public ServletContext getServletContext()
```

`getServletContext()` returns `ServletContext` in which the event took place.

ServletInputStream

```
public abstract class ServletInputStream
    extends java.io.InputStream
```

The `ServletInputStream` class is used to read binary data from a client request when the HTTP POST and PUT methods are used. It provides a single method in addition to those in `InputStream`, which reads the data one line at a time.

```
protected ServletInputStream()
```

This constructor does nothing. Because `ServletInputStream` is an abstract class, a `ServletInputStream` object is never created directly.

```
public int readLine(byte[] b,
                    int off,
                    int len)
        throws java.io.IOException
```

`readLine()` reads data one line at a time and stores it in a `byte` array (b). The read operation starts at the specified offset (off) and continues until the specified number of bytes is read (len), or a new line character is reached. The new line character is stored in the byte array as well. The method returns −1 if the end-of-file is reached before the specified number of bytes is read.

ServletOutputStream

```
public abstract class ServletOutputStream
    extends java.io.OutputStream
```

The `ServletOutputStream` class is used to write binary data to a client machine. It provides overloaded versions of the `print()` and `println()` methods that can handle primitive and `String` datatypes.

```
protected ServletOutputStream()
```

This constructor does nothing. Because `ServletOutputStream` is an abstract class, a `ServletOutputStream` object is never created directly.

```
public void print(String s)
        throws java.io.IOException
public void print(boolean b)
        throws java.io.IOException
public void print(char c)
        throws java.io.IOException
public void print(int i)
```

```
        throws java.io.IOException
public void print(long l)
        throws java.io.IOException
public void print(float f)
        throws java.io.IOException
public void print(double d)
        throws java.io.IOException
```

print() prints the specified primitive datatype or String to the client, without a carriage return/line feed at the end.

```
public void println(String s)
        throws java.io.IOException
public void println(boolean b)
        throws java.io.IOException
public void println(char c)
        throws java.io.IOException
public void println(int i)
        throws java.io.IOException
public void println(long l)
        throws java.io.IOException
public void println(float f)
        throws java.io.IOException
public void println(double d)
        throws java.io.IOException
```

print() prints the specified primitive datatype or String to the client, followed by a carriage return/line feed.

```
public void println()
        throws java.io.IOException
```

The no-argument version of println() simply writes a carriage return/line feed to the client.

ServletRequestWrapper

```
public class ServletRequestWrapper
   extends Object
     implements ServletRequest
```

ServletRequestWrapper provides an implementation of ServletRequest that can be subclassed when it is desired to adapt in some way the request to a Servlet. By default, its methods call the same methods on the wrapped request object.

```
public ServletRequestWrapper(ServletRequest request)
```

The constructor creates a ServletRequestWrapper around the specified ServletRequest object.

```
public ServletRequest getRequest()
```

getRequest() returns the wrapped ServletRequest.

```
    public void setRequest(ServletRequest request)
```

setRequest() sets the ServletRequest to be wrapped.

```
    public Object getAttribute(String name)
    public java.util.Enumeration getAttributeNames()
    public String getCharacterEncoding()
    public void setCharacterEncoding(String enc)
            throws java.io.UnsupportedEncodingException
    public int getContentLength()
    public String getContentType()
    public ServletInputStream getInputStream()
            throws java.io.IOException
    public String getParameter(String name)
    public java.util.Map getParameterMap()
    public java.util.Enumeration getParameterNames()
    public String[] getParameterValues(String name)
    public String getProtocol()
    public String getScheme()
    public String getServerName()
    public int getServerPort()
    public java.io.BufferedReader getReader()
            throws java.io.IOException
    public String getRemoteAddr()
    public String getRemoteHost()
    public void setAttribute(String name,
                             Object o)
    public void removeAttribute(String name)
    public java.util.Locale getLocale()
    public java.util.Enumeration getLocales()
    public boolean isSecure()
    public RequestDispatcher getRequestDispatcher(String path)
    public String getRealPath(String path)
```

These methods, unless overridden in a subclass, call the equivalent method on the wrapped ServletRequest.

ServletResponseWrapper

```
    public class ServletResponseWrapper
      extends Object
        implements ServletResponse
```

ServletResponseWrapper provides an implementation of ServletResponse that can be subclassed when it is desired to adapt in some way the response from a Servlet. By default, its methods call the same methods on the wrapped response object.

```
    public ServletResponseWrapper(ServletResponse response)
```

The constructor creates a ServletResponseWrapper around the specified ServletResponse object.

```
    public ServletResponse getResponse()
```

getResponse() returns the wrapped `ServletResponse`.

```
public void setResponse(ServletResponse response)
```

setResponse() sets the `ServletResponse` to be wrapped.

```
public String getCharacterEncoding()
public ServletOutputStream getOutputStream()
        throws java.io.IOException
public java.io.PrintWriter getWriter()
        throws java.io.IOException
public void setContentLength(int len)
public void setContentType(String type)
public void setBufferSize(int size)
public int getBufferSize()
public void flushBuffer()
        throws java.io.IOException
public boolean isCommitted()
public void reset()
public void resetBuffer()
public void setLocale(java.util.Locale loc)
public java.util.Locale getLocale()
```

These methods, unless overridden in a subclass, call the equivalent method on the wrapped `ServletRequest`.

javax.servlet Exceptions

ServletException

```
public class ServletException
  extends Exception
```

ServletException is a general exception thrown by Servlets in difficulty.

```
public ServletException()
public ServletException(String message)
public ServletException(String message,
                          Throwable rootCause)
public ServletException(Throwable rootCause)
```

The constructors allow a `String` message and/or a `Throwable` representing the root cause of the problem to be encapsulated.

```
public Throwable getRootCause()
```

getRootCause() returns the `Throwable` that was the root cause of this exception.

UnavailableException

```
public class UnavailableException
extends ServletException
```

`UnavailableException` is thrown by a Servlet to indicate that it is unavailable, either permanently or temporarily.

```
public UnavailableException(String msg)
```

This constructor indicates that the Servlet is permanently unavailable. The `String` parameter is a message describing the problem.

```
public UnavailableException(String msg,
                            int seconds)
```

This constructor indicates that the Servlet is temporarily unavailable. It must be passed a `String` describing the problem, and an estimate in seconds of how long the Servlet will be unavailable. (Zero or a negative number indicate that it is impossible to estimate.)

```
public boolean isPermanent()
```

`isPermanent()` returns `true` if the Servlet is permanently unavailable.

```
public int getUnavailableSeconds()
```

`getUnavailableSeconds()` returns the estimated number of seconds that the Servlet will be unavailable.

```
public UnavailableException(Servlet Servlet,
                            String msg)
public UnavailableException(int seconds,
                            Servlet Servlet,
                            String msg)
public Servlet getServlet()
```

These constructors and methods are deprecated.

javax.servlet.http

The `javax.servlet.http` package provides classes and interfaces that are used to create HTTP protocol-specific Servlets. The abstract class `HttpServlet` is a base class for user-defined HTTP Servlets and provides methods to process HTTP DELETE, GET, OPTIONS, POST, PUT, and TRACE requests. The `Cookie` class allows objects containing state information to be placed on a client machine and accessed by a Servlet. The package also enables session tracking through the `HttpSession` interface.

javax.servlet.http Interfaces

HttpServletRequest

```
public interface HttpServletRequest
  extends ServletRequest
```

The HttpServletRequest interface extends ServletRequest to provide methods that can be used to obtain information about a request to an HttpServlet.

```
public static final String BASIC_AUTH
public static final String FORM_AUTH
public static final String CLIENT_CERT_AUTH
public static final String DIGEST_AUTH
```

These String constants are used to identify the different types of authentication that may have been used to protect the Servlet. They have the values "BASIC", "FORM", "CLIENT_CERT", and "DIGEST" respectively.

```
public String getAuthType()
```

getAuthType() returns the name of the authentication scheme used in the request, or null if no authentication scheme was used.

```
public Cookie[] getCookies()
```

getCookies() returns an array containing any Cookie objects sent with the request, or null if no cookies were sent.

```
public long getDateHeader(String name)
```

getDateHeader() returns a long value that converts the date specified in the named header to the number of milliseconds since January 1, 1970 GMT. This method is used with a header that contains a date, and returns −1 if the request does not contain the specified header.

```
public String getHeader(String name)
```

getHeader() returns the value of the specified header expressed as a String object, or null if the request does not contain the specified header.

```
public java.util.Enumeration getHeaders(String name)
```

getHeaders() returns an Enumeration containing all of the values associated with the specified header name. The method returns an empty enumeration if the request does not contain the specified header.

```
public java.util.Enumeration getHeaderNames()
```

getHeaderNames() returns an Enumeration containing all of the header names used by the request.

```
public int getIntHeader(String name)
```

getIntHeader() returns the value of the specified header as an int. It returns -1 if the request does not contain the specified header, and throws a NumberFormatException if the header value cannot be converted to an int.

```
public String getMethod()
```

getMethod() returns the name of the HTTP method used to make the request. Typical return values are "GET", "POST", or "PUT".

```
public String getPathInfo()
```

getPathInfo() returns any additional path information contained in the request URL. This extra information will be after the Servlet path and before the query string. It returns null if there is no additional path information.

```
public String getPathTranslated()
```

getPathTranslated() returns the same information as the getPathInfo() method, but translated into a real path.

```
public String getContextPath()
```

getContextPath() returns the part of the request URI that indicates the context path of the request. The context path is the first part of the URI and always begins with the "/" character. For Servlets running in the root context, this method returns an empty String.

```
public String getQueryString()
```

getQueryString() returns the query string that was contained in the request URL, or null if there was no query string.

```
public String getRemoteUser()
```

getRemoteUser() returns the login of the user making the request, or null if the user has not been authenticated.

```
public boolean isUserInRole(String role)
```

isUserInRole() returns a true if the authenticated user has the specified logical role, or false if the user is not authenticated.

```
public java.security.Principal getUserPrincipal()
```

getUserPrincipal() returns Principal object representing the authenticated user, or null if the user is not authenticated.

```
public String getRequestedSessionId()
```

getRequestedSessionId() returns the session ID that was specified by the client, or null if the request did not specify an ID.

```
public String getRequestURI()
```

getRequestURI() returns a subsection of the request URL, from the protocol name to the query string.

```
public StringBuffer getRequestURL()
```

getRequestURL() reconstructs the URL used to make the request including the protocol, server name, port number, and path, but excluding the query string.

```
public String getServletPath()
```

getServletPath() returns the part of the request URL that was used to call the Servlet, without any additional information or the query string.

```
public HttpSession getSession(boolean create)
public HttpSession getSession()
```

getSession() returns the HttpSession object associated with the request. By default, if the request does not currently have a session, calling this method will create one. Setting the boolean parameter create to false overrides this.

```
public boolean isRequestedSessionIdValid()
```

isRequestedSessionIdValid() returns true if the session ID requested by the client is still valid.

```
public boolean isRequestedSessionIdFromCookie()
```

isRequestedSessionIdFromCookie() returns true if the session ID came in from a cookie.

```
public boolean isRequestedSessionIdFromURL()
```

isRequestedSessionIdFromURL() returns true if the session ID came in as part of the request URL.

```
public boolean isRequestedSessionIdFromUrl()
```

This method is deprecated.

HttpServletResponse

```
public interface HttpServletResponse
  extends ServletResponse
```

The `HttpServletResponse` interface extends the functionality of the `ServletResponse` interface by providing methods to access HTTP-specific features such as HTTP headers and cookies.

```
public static final int SC_CONTINUE
public static final int SC_SWITCHING_PROTOCOLS
public static final int SC_OK
public static final int SC_CREATED
public static final int SC_ACCEPTED
public static final int SC_NON_AUTHORITATIVE_INFORMATION
public static final int SC_NO_CONTENT
public static final int SC_RESET_CONTENT
public static final int SC_PARTIAL_CONTENT
public static final int SC_MULTIPLE_CHOICES
public static final int SC_MOVED_PERMANENTLY
public static final int SC_MOVED_TEMPORARILY
public static final int SC_SEE_OTHER
public static final int SC_NOT_MODIFIED
public static final int SC_USE_PROXY
public static final int SC_BAD_REQUEST
public static final int SC_UNAUTHORIZED
public static final int SC_PAYMENT_REQUIRED
public static final int SC_FORBIDDEN
public static final int SC_NOT_FOUND
public static final int SC_METHOD_NOT_ALLOWED
public static final int SC_NOT_ACCEPTABLE
public static final int SC_PROXY_AUTHENTICATION_REQUIRED
public static final int SC_REQUEST_TIMEOUT
public static final int SC_CONFLICT
public static final int SC_GONE
public static final int SC_LENGTH_REQUIRED
public static final int SC_PRECONDITION_FAILED
public static final int SC_REQUEST_ENTITY_TOO_LARGE
public static final int SC_REQUEST_URI_TOO_LONG
public static final int SC_UNSUPPORTED_MEDIA_TYPE
public static final int SC_REQUESTED_RANGE_NOT_SATISFIABLE
public static final int SC_EXPECTATION_FAILED
public static final int SC_INTERNAL_SERVER_ERROR
public static final int SC_NOT_IMPLEMENTED
public static final int SC_BAD_GATEWAY
public static final int SC_SERVICE_UNAVAILABLE
public static final int SC_GATEWAY_TIMEOUT
public static final int SC_HTTP_VERSION_NOT_SUPPORTED
```

These constants represent the status codes defined in the HTTP specification (see Appendix F for further details).

```
public void addCookie(Cookie cookie)
```

`addCookie()` adds the specified cookie to the response (more than one cookie can be added).

```
public boolean containsHeader(String name)
```

`containsHeader()` returns `true` if the response header includes the specified header name. This method can be used before calling one of the `set()` methods to determine if the value has already been set.

```
public String encodeURL(String url)
```

encodeURL() encodes the specified URL by including the session ID or returns it unchanged if encoding is not needed. All URLs generated by a Servlet should be processed through this method to ensure compatibility with browsers that do not support cookies.

```
public String encodeRedirectURL(String url)
```

encodeRedirectURL() encodes the specified URL or returns it unchanged if encoding is not required. This method is used to process a URL before sending it to the sendRedirect() method.

```
public void sendError(int sc,
                      String msg)
       throws java.io.IOException
public void sendError(int sc)
       throws java.io.IOException
```

sendError() sends an error response back to the client machine using the specified error status code. A descriptive message can also be provided. This method must be called before the response is committed (in other words, before the status code and headers have been written).

```
public void sendRedirect(String location)
       throws java.io.IOException
```

sendRedirect() redirects the client machine to the specified URL. This method must be called before the response is committed (in other words, before the status code and headers have been written).

```
public void setDateHeader(String name,
                          long date)
```

setDateHeader() sets the time value of a response header for the specified header name. The time is the number of milliseconds since January 1, 1970 GMT. If the time value for the specified header has been previously set, the value passed to this method will override it.

```
public void addDateHeader(String name,
                          long date)
```

addDateHeader() adds a response header containing the specified header name and the number of milliseconds since January 1, 1970 GMT. This method can be used to assign multiple values to a given header name.

```
public void setHeader(String name,
                      String value)
```

setHeader() sets a response header with the specified name and value. If the value for the specified header has been previously set, the value passed to this method will override it.

```
public void addHeader(String name,
                      String value)
```

`addHeader()` adds a response header with the specified `name` and `value`. This method can be used to assign multiple values to a given header name.

```
public void setIntHeader(String name,
                             int value)
```

`setIntHeader()` sets a response header with the specified name and `int` value. If the `int` value for the specified header has been previously set, the value passed to this method will override it.

```
public void addIntHeader(String name,
                             int value)
```

`addIntHeader()` adds a response header with the specified name and `int` value. This method can be used to assign multiple values to a given header name.

```
public void setStatus(int sc)
```

`setStatus()` sets the return status code for the response. The status code should be one of SC_ACCEPTED, SC_OK, SC_CONTINUE, SC_PARTIAL_CONTENT, SC_CREATED, SC_SWITCHING_PROTOCOLS, or SC_NO_CONTENT.

```
public String encodeUrl(String url)
public String encodeRedirectUrl(String url)
public void setStatus(int sc,
                         String sm)
```

These methods are deprecated.

HttpSession

```
public interface HttpSession
```

The `HttpSession` interface provides methods that define a session between a client and server, despite the stateless nature of the HTTP protocol. The session lasts for a specified time period and can encompass more than one connection or page request from the user. The methods declared by this interface allow the access of information about the session and enable the binding of objects to sessions. The bound object can contain the state information that each request should be able to access.

```
public long getCreationTime()
```

`getCreationTime()` returns the time when the session was created in milliseconds since midnight Jan 1, 1970 GMT.

```
public String getId()
```

`getId()` returns a `String` object containing a unique identifier for this session.

```
public long getLastAccessedTime()
```

getLastAccessedTime() returns the last time a client request associated with the session was sent. The return value is the number of milliseconds since midnight Jan 1, 1970 GMT.

```
public void setMaxInactiveInterval(int interval)
```

setMaxInactiveInterval() specifies the number of seconds the server will wait between client requests before the session is invalidated. If a negative value is passed to this method, the session will never time out.

```
public int getMaxInactiveInterval()
```

getMaxInactiveInterval() returns the number of seconds the server will wait between client requests before the session is invalidated. A negative return value indicates the session will never time out.

```
public Object getAttribute(String name)
```

getAttribute() returns the Object bound to the specified name in this session, or null if it doesn't exist.

```
public java.util.Enumeration getAttributeNames()
```

getAttributeNames() returns an Enumeration of String objects containing the names of all the objects bound to this session.

```
public void setAttribute(String name,
                         Object value)
```

setAttribute() binds an Object to the specified attribute name, in this session. If the attribute name already exists, the Object passed to this method will replace the previous Object.

```
public void removeAttribute(String name)
```

removeAttribute() removes the Object bound to the specified name from this session.

```
public void invalidate()
```

invalidate() invalidates the session and unbinds any objects bound to it.

```
public boolean isNew()
```

isNew() returns true if the server has created a session that has not yet been accessed by a client.

```
public HttpSessionContext getSessionContext()
public Object getValue(String name)
public String[] getValueNames()
public void putValue(String name,
                     Object value)
public void removeValue(String name)
```

These methods have been deprecated.

HttpSessionActivationListener

```
public interface HttpSessionActivationListener
```

Objects implementing the HttpSessionActivationListener interface will be informed when the session they are bound to is going to be passivated and activated, for example when a session is going to be persisted or migrated to another Virtual Machine.

```
public void sessionWillPassivate(HttpSessionEvent se)
```

sessionWillPassivate() is called when the session is about to be passivated.

```
public void sessionDidActivate(HttpSessionEvent se)
```

sessionDidActivate() is called when the session has just been activated.

HttpSessionAttributeListener

```
public interface HttpSessionAttributeListener
  extends java.util.EventListener
```

An object implementing HttpSessionAttributeListener can be registered to receive notification when attributes are added to, removed from, or replaced in the HttpSession.

```
public void attributeAdded(HttpSessionBindingEvent se)
```

attributeAdded() is called when an attribute is added to the HttpSession. It is passed an HttpSessionBindingEvent containing information about the event.

```
public void attributeRemoved(HttpSessionBindingEvent se)
```

attributeRemoved() is called when an attribute is removed from the HttpSession. It is passed an HttpSessionBindingEvent containing information about the event.

```
public void attributeReplaced(HttpSessionBindingEvent se)
```

attributeReplaced() is called when an HttpSession attribute is replaced. It is passed an HttpSessionBindingEvent containing information about the event.

HttpSessionBindingListener

```
public interface HttpSessionBindingListener
  extends java.util.EventListener
```

The methods declared in the HttpSessionBindingListener interface are called when an object is bound to or unbound from a session.

```
public void valueBound(HttpSessionBindingEvent event)
```

valueBound() is called when an object is being bound to a session.

```
public void valueUnbound(HttpSessionBindingEvent event)
```

valueUnbound() is called when an object is being unbound from a session.

HttpSessionContext

```
public interface HttpSessionContext
```

This interface is deprecated.

```
public HttpSession getSession(String sessionId)
public java.util.Enumeration getIds()
```

These methods are deprecated.

HttpSessionListener

```
public interface HttpSessionListener
```

An object implementing HttpSessionListener can be registered to receive notification when an HttpSession is created or destroyed.

```
public void sessionCreated(HttpSessionEvent se)
```

sessionCreated() is called when a session is created. It is passed an HttpSessionEvent containing information about the event.

```
public void sessionDestroyed(HttpSessionEvent se)
```

sessionDestroyed() is called when a session is destroyed. It is passed an HttpSessionEvent containing information about the event.

javax.servlet.http Classes

Cookie

```
public class Cookie
  extends Object
    implements Cloneable
```

A Cookie is an object that resides on a client machine and contains state information; each cookie has a name, a single value, and some other optional information. Cookies can be used to identify a particular user and provide information such as name, address, account number, etc. They are sent by a server to a Web browser, saved on the client machine, and can later be sent back to the server.

The optional information that can be attached to a cookie includes an expiration date, path and domain qualifiers, a version number, and a comment. The expiration date specifies when the cookie will be deleted from the client machine. If no date is given, the cookie is deleted when the session ends.

A Servlet sends cookies to a browser using the `addCookie()` method defined in the `HttpServletResponse` interface, which adds fields to the HTTP response header. The browser returns cookies to the Servlet by adding fields to the HTTP request header, and the cookies can be retrieved from a request by invoking the `getCookies()` method defined in the `HttpServletRequest` interface.

```
public Cookie(String name,
              String value)
```

This creates a `Cookie` object with a specified `name` and `value`. The name must consist only of alphanumeric characters. Once the name is set by the constructor, it cannot be changed.

```
public void setComment(String purpose)
```

`setComment()` changes or sets the comment associated with the `Cookie` object. A `Cookie` can contain a comment that is normally used to describe the purpose of the `Cookie`.

```
public String getComment()
```

`getComment()` returns the comment associated with the `Cookie` object, or `null` if there is no comment.

```
public void setDomain(String pattern)
```

`setDomain()` sets the domain name within which the `Cookie` will be visible.

```
public String getDomain()
```

`getDomain()` returns the domain name set for the `Cookie` object.

```
public void setMaxAge(int expiry)
```

`setMaxAge()` sets the length of time in seconds that the `Cookie` will persist on the user's machine. A negative value means the `Cookie` will not be stored on the user's machine and will be deleted when the browser terminates. A value of zero means the `Cookie` will be deleted immediately.

```
public int getMaxAge()
```

`getMaxAge()` returns the length of time in seconds that the `Cookie` will persist on the user's machine. A return value of –1 indicates that the cookie will persist until the browser shuts down.

```
public void setPath(String uri)
```

`setPath()` specifies the path on the server where the browser will return the `Cookie` object. The `Cookie` will also be visible to all subdirectories of the specified path.

```
    public String getPath()
```

getPath() returns the path on the server where the browser will return the Cookie object.

```
    public void setSecure(boolean flag)
```

setSecure() specifies whether the browser should send the Cookie object using a secure protocol. The default is false, meaning the Cookie will be sent using any protocol.

```
    public boolean getSecure()
```

getSecure() returns true if the browser will send the Cookie object using a secure protocol.

```
    public String getName()
```

getName() returns the name of the Cookie object.

```
    public void setValue(String newValue)
```

setValue() changes the value of the Cookie object.

```
    public String getValue()
```

getValue() returns a String containing the value of the Cookie object.

```
    public void setVersion(int v)
```

setVersion() sets the version number of the protocol with which the Cookie complies: 0 for the original Netscape specification, or 1 for cookies compliant with RFC 2109.

```
    public int getVersion()
```

getVersion() returns 0 if the invoking Cookie object complies with the original Netscape specification, or 1 if it complies with RFC 2109.

```
    public Object clone()
```

clone() overrides the clone() method from the Object class to return a copy of the Cookie object.

HttpServlet

```
    public abstract class HttpServlet
      extends GenericServlet
        implements java.io.Serializable
```

The HttpServlet class extends GenericServlet to provide functionality tailored to the HTTP protocol. It provides methods for handling HTTP DELETE, GET, OPTIONS, POST, PUT, and TRACE requests. Like the GenericServlet class, the HttpServlet class provides a service() method, but unlike the GenericServlet class the service() method is rarely overridden since the default implementation of service() dispatches the request to the appropriate handler method.

A concrete subclass of HttpServlet must override at least one of the methods defined in the HttpServlet or GenericServlet classes. The doDelete(), doGet(), doPost(), and doPut() methods are the ones most commonly overridden.

```
public HttpServlet()
```

This constructor does nothing. Because HttpServlet is an abstract class, an HttpServlet object is never created directly.

```
protected void doGet(HttpServletRequest req,
                     HttpServletResponse resp)
        throws ServletException, java.io.IOException
```

doGet() is called by the server via the service() method to handle an HTTP GET request. A GET request allows a client to send form data to a server. With the GET request, the form data is attached to the end of the URL sent by the browser to the server as a query string. The amount of form data that can be sent is limited to the maximum length of the URL.

```
protected void doHead(HttpServletRequest req,
                      HttpServletResponse resp)
        throws ServletException, java.io.IOException
```

doHead() is called by the server via the service() method to handle an HTTP HEAD request. A HEAD request allows a client to retrieve only the response headers, rather than the body.

```
protected void doPost(HttpServletRequest req,
                      HttpServletResponse resp)
        throws ServletException, java.io.IOException
```

doPost() is called by the server via the service() method to handle an HTTP POST request. A POST request allows a client to send form data to a server. With the POST request, the form data is sent to the server separately instead of being appended to the URL. This allows a large amount of form data to be sent.

```
protected void doPut(HttpServletRequest req,
                     HttpServletResponse resp)
        throws ServletException, java.io.IOException
```

doPut() is called by the server via the service() method to handle an HTTP PUT request. A PUT request allows a client to place a file on the server and is conceptually similar to sending the file to the server via FTP.

```
protected void doDelete(HttpServletRequest req,
                        HttpServletResponse resp)
        throws ServletException, java.io.IOException
```

doDelete() is called by the server via the service() method to handle an HTTP DELETE request. A DELETE request allows a client to remove a document or Web page from a server.

```
protected void doOptions(HttpServletRequest req,
                         HttpServletResponse resp)
        throws ServletException, java.io.IOException
```

doOptions() is called by the server via the service() method to handle an HTTP OPTIONS request. An OPTIONS request determines which HTTP methods the server supports and sends the information back to the client by way of a header.

```
protected void doTrace(HttpServletRequest req,
                       HttpServletResponse resp)
        throws ServletException, java.io.IOException
```

doTrace() is called by the server via the service() method to handle an HTTP TRACE request. A TRACE request returns the headers sent with the TRACE request back to the client. This can be useful for debugging purposes. This method is rarely overridden.

```
protected long getLastModified(HttpServletRequest req)
```

getLastModified() returns the time the requested resource was last modified. The return value is the time in milliseconds since midnight Jan 1, 1970.

```
protected void service(HttpServletRequest req,
                       HttpServletResponse resp)
        throws ServletException, java.io.IOException
public void service(ServletRequest req,
                    ServletResponse res)
        throws ServletException, java.io.IOException
```

The service() methods receive HTTP requests and send them to the appropriate do() method. They are generally not overridden.

HttpServletRequestWrapper

```
public class HttpServletRequestWrapper
    extends ServletRequestWrapper
      implements HttpServletRequest
```

HttpServletRequestWrapper provides an implementation of HttpServletRequest that can be subclassed when it is desired to adapt in some way the request to a Servlet. By default, its methods call the same methods on the wrapped request object.

```
public HttpServletRequestWrapper(HttpServletRequest request)
```

The constructor creates an HttpServletRequestWrapper around the specified HttpServletRequest object.

```
public String getAuthType()
public Cookie[] getCookies()
public long getDateHeader(String name)
public String getHeader(String name)
public java.util.Enumeration getHeaders(String name)
public java.util.Enumeration getHeaderNames()
public int getIntHeader(String name)
public String getMethod()
public String getPathInfo()
public String getPathTranslated()
```

```
public String getContextPath()
public String getQueryString()
public String getRemoteUser()
public boolean isUserInRole(String role)
public java.security.Principal getUserPrincipal()
public String getRequestedSessionId()
public String getRequestURI()
public StringBuffer getRequestURL()
public String getServletPath()
public HttpSession getSession(boolean create)
public HttpSession getSession()
public boolean isRequestedSessionIdValid()
public boolean isRequestedSessionIdFromCookie()
public boolean isRequestedSessionIdFromURL()
public boolean isRequestedSessionIdFromUrl()
```

These methods, unless overridden in a subclass, call the equivalent method on the wrapped
HttpServletRequest.

HttpServletResponseWrapper

```
public class HttpServletResponseWrapper
    extends ServletResponseWrapper
      implements HttpServletResponse
```

HttpServletResponseWrapper provides an implementation of HttpServletResponse that can be
subclassed when it is desired to adapt in some way the request to a Servlet. By default, its methods call the
same methods on the wrapped request object.

```
public HttpServletResponseWrapper(HttpServletResponse response)
```

The constructor creates an HttpServletResponseWrapper around the specified
HttpServletResponse object.

```
public void addCookie(Cookie cookie)
public boolean containsHeader(String name)
public String encodeURL(String url)
public String encodeRedirectURL(String url)
public String encodeUrl(String url)
public String encodeRedirectUrl(String url)
public void sendError(int sc,
                        String msg)
        throws java.io.IOException
public void sendError(int sc)
        throws java.io.IOException
public void sendRedirect(String location)
        throws java.io.IOException
public void setDateHeader(String name,
                            long date)
public void addDateHeader(String name,
                            long date)
public void setHeader(String name,
                        String value)
```

```
public void addHeader(String name,
                          String value)
public void setIntHeader(String name,
                             int value)
public void addIntHeader(String name,
                             int value)
public void setStatus(int sc)
public void setStatus(int sc,
                          String sm)
```

These methods, unless overridden in a subclass, call the equivalent method on the wrapped HttpServletResponse.

HttpSessionBindingEvent

```
public class HttpSessionBindingEvent
    extends HttpSessionEvent
```

An HttpSessionBindingEvent represents an object being added to, removed from, or replaced in an HttpSession.

```
public HttpSessionBindingEvent(HttpSession session,
                                 String name)
public HttpSessionBindingEvent(HttpSession session,
                                 String name,
                                 Object value)
```

Creates an HttpSessionBindingEvent object. The session and name are the parameters to which the HttpSessionBindingEvent object is bound or unbound.

```
public HttpSession getSession()
```

getSession() returns the session associated with the object that is bound or unbound.

```
public String getName()
```

getName() returns the name associated with the object that is bound or unbound.

```
public Object getValue()
```

getValue() returns the value of the attribute being added, removed or replaced. (If the attribute was replaced, getValue() returns the attribute's old value.)

HttpSessionEvent

```
public class HttpSessionEvent
    extends java.util.EventObject
```

HttpSessionEvent represents an event for changes to a session.

```
        public HttpSessionEvent(HttpSession source)
```

The constructor must be passed a reference to the HttpSession to which the event relates.

```
        public HttpSession getSession()
```

getSession() returns the session attached to this event.

HttpUtils

```
        public class HttpUtils
          extends Object
```

This class has been deprecated.

```
        public HttpUtils()
        public static java.util.Hashtable parseQueryString(String s)
        public static java.util.Hashtable parsePostData(int len,
                                                ServletInputStream in)
        public static StringBuffer getRequestURL(HttpServletRequest req)
```

The constructor and methods have been deprecated.

javax.servlet.jsp

The javax.servlet.jsp package contains interfaces and classes defined in the JavaServer Pages specification. Many of these classes are intended to be used by the JSP engine, rather than within a JSP.

javax.servlet.jsp Interfaces

JspPage

```
        public interface JspPage
          extends Servlet
```

The JspPage interface provides two methods that are used to initialize and destroy a JSP.

```
        public void jspInit()
```

jspInit() is called when the JspPage object is created. It can be used to initialize the JspPage.

```
        public void jspDestroy()
```

HttpJspPage

```
        public interface HttpJspPage
          extends JspPage
```

The Servlet class representing all HTTP JSP pages implements the `HttpJspPage` interface. It defines the `_jspService()` method, which is called by the JSP container to generate the page content.

```
public void _jspService(HttpServletRequest request,
                        HttpServletResponse response)
       throws ServletException, java.io.IOException
```

`_jspService()` provides an HTTP protocol-specific implementation of the `service()` method. The JSP engine generates this method automatically, based on the contents of the JSP source file.

javax.servlet.jsp Classes

JspEngineInfo

```
public abstract class JspEngineInfo
   extends Object
```

The `JspEngineInfo` class is used to obtain information on the current JSP engine.

```
public JspEngineInfo()
```

Since the `JspEngineInfo` class is abstract, a `JspEngineInfo` object is not created directly. Subclasses of `JspEngineInfo` can call this constructor.

```
public abstract String getSpecificationVersion()
```

`getSpecificationVersion()` returns a `String` containing the version number, for example `"1.2"`, of the JSP specification supported by the engine. The return value is `null` if the specification version is unknown.

JspFactory

```
public abstract class JspFactory
   extends Object
```

The `JspFactory` class provides methods for creating or specifying objects that are used to support JSP development, including `JspEngineInfo` and `PageContext` objects.

```
public JspFactory()
```

Since the `JspFactory` class is abstract, a `JspFactory` object is not created directly. Subclasses of `JspFactory` can call this constructor.

```
public static void setDefaultFactory(JspFactory deflt)
```

`setDefaultFactory()` is used to change the default `JspFactory` object. This method can only be called by the JSP engine at runtime.

```
        public static JspFactory getDefaultFactory()
```

getDefaultFactory() returns a reference to the current default JspFactory object.

```
        public abstract PageContext getPageContext(Servlet Servlet,
                                                   ServletRequest request,
                                                   ServletResponse response,
                                                   String errorPageURL,
                                                   boolean needsSession,
                                                   int buffer,
                                                   boolean autoflush)
```

getPageContext() returns a PageContext object for the requesting Servlet to process the specified request and response. The errorPageURL is the URL of the error page of the JSP, or null if there is no error page. needsSession is true if the JSP is participating in a session, and if autoFlush is true the buffer will automatically flush to the output stream on buffer overflow.

```
        public abstract void releasePageContext(PageContext pc)
```

releasePageContext() releases the specified PageContext object, resulting in the PageContext.release() method being called. It should be invoked prior to returning from the _jspService() method of a JSP class.

```
        public abstract JspEngineInfo getEngineInfo()
```

getEngineInfo() returns a JspEngineInfo object that can access information about the current JSP engine.

JspWriter

```
        public abstract class JspWriter
          extends java.io.Writer
```

The JspWriter class provides a character output stream that can be used by a JSP object. It provides overloaded versions of the print() and println() methods that can handle primitive and String datatypes.

```
        public static final int NO_BUFFER
        public static final int DEFAULT_BUFFER
        public static final int UNBOUNDED_BUFFER
```

These constants define various special buffer sizes to pass to the JspWriter constructor.

```
        protected int bufferSize
        protected boolean autoFlush
```

These fields are used internally by the JspWriter class.

```
        protected JspWriter(int bufferSize,
                            boolean autoFlush)
```

The JspWriter class is abstract, so a JspWriter object is not created directly. This constructor can be used by subclasses of JspWriter.

```
public abstract void newLine()
        throws java.io.IOException
```

newLine() writes a system-dependent newline character to the output stream.

```
public abstract void print(boolean b)
        throws java.io.IOException
public abstract void print(char c)
        throws java.io.IOException
public abstract void print(int i)
        throws java.io.IOException
public abstract void print(long l)
        throws java.io.IOException
public abstract void print(float f)
        throws java.io.IOException
public abstract void print(double d)
        throws java.io.IOException
public abstract void print(char[] s)
        throws java.io.IOException
public abstract void print(String s)
        throws java.io.IOException
public abstract void print(Object obj)
        throws java.io.IOException
```

print() prints the specified primitive datatype, Object or String to the client without a carriage return/line feed character at the end. If an Object argument is passed, it is converted to a String using the String.valueOf() method.

```
public abstract void println()
        throws java.io.IOException
public abstract void println(boolean x)
        throws java.io.IOException
public abstract void println(char x)
        throws java.io.IOException
public abstract void println(int x)
        throws java.io.IOException
public abstract void println(long x)
        throws java.io.IOException
public abstract void println(float x)
        throws java.io.IOException
public abstract void println(double x)
        throws java.io.IOException
public abstract void println(char[] x)
        throws java.io.IOException
public abstract void println(String x)
        throws java.io.IOException
public abstract void println(Object x)
        throws java.io.IOException
```

println() prints the specified primitive datatype, Object or String to the client followed by a carriage return/line feed character at the end. The no-argument version simply writes a carriage return/line feed. If an Object argument is passed, it is converted to a String using the String.valueOf() method.

```
public abstract void clear()
        throws java.io.IOException
```

`clear()` clears the contents of the buffer; it throws an exception if some data has already been written to the output stream.

```
public abstract void clearBuffer()
        throws java.io.IOException
```

`clearBuffer()` clears the contents of the buffer, but does not throw an exception if some data has already been written to the output stream.

```
public abstract void flush()
        throws java.io.IOException
```

`flush()` flushes the output buffer and sends any bytes contained in the buffer to their intended destination. `flush()` will flush all the buffers in a chain of `Writers` and `OutputStreams`.

```
public abstract void close()
        throws java.io.IOException
```

`close()` flushes and then closes the output stream.

```
public int getBufferSize()
```

`getBufferSize()` returns the size in bytes of the output buffer.

```
public abstract int getRemaining()
```

`getRemaining()` returns the number of bytes still contained in the buffer.

```
public boolean isAutoFlush()
```

`isAutoFlush()` returns `true` if the buffer flushes automatically when an overflow condition occurs.

PageContext

```
public abstract class PageContext
    extends Object
```

The `PageContext` class provides access to the various scopes associated with a JSP, and various utility methods for JSPs.

```
public static final int PAGE_SCOPE
public static final int REQUEST_SCOPE
public static final int SESSION_SCOPE
public static final int APPLICATION_SCOPE
```

These constants represent the various scopes accessible from a JSP.

```
public static final String PAGE
public static final String PAGECONTEXT
public static final String REQUEST
public static final String RESPONSE
public static final String CONFIG
public static final String SESSION
public static final String OUT
public static final String APPLICATION
public static final String EXCEPTION
```

These `String` constants are used internally by `PageContext`.

```
public PageContext()
```

The `PageContext` class is abstract, so a `PageContext` object is not created directly. This constructor can be used by subclasses of `PageContext`.

```
public abstract void initialize(Servlet Servlet,
                                ServletRequest request,
                                ServletResponse response,
                                String errorPageURL,
                                boolean needsSession,
                                int bufferSize,
                                boolean autoFlush)
        throws java.io.IOException, IllegalStateException,
               IllegalArgumentException
```

`initialize()` is called to initialize a `PageContext` object. The `errorPageURL` is the URL of the error page of the JSP; this can be set to `null` if there is no error page. `needsSession` is `true` if the JSP is participating in a session, and if `autoFlush` is `true` the buffer will automatically flush to the output stream on buffer overflow.

```
public abstract void release()
```

`release()` resets the internal state of the `PageContext` object by releasing all internal references. This method is usually called by the `releasePageContext()` method of the `JspFactory` class.

```
public abstract void setAttribute(String name,
                                  Object attribute)
public abstract void setAttribute(String name,
                                  Object o,
                                  int scope)
```

`setAttribute()` stores the attribute name and associated `Object` at the specified scope. If no scope is provided, page scope is used. The parameter `scope` should be one of the scope constants defined above.

```
public abstract Object getAttribute(String name)
public abstract Object getAttribute(String name,
                                    int scope)
```

getAttribute() searches for the named attribute at the specified scope and returns its value as an Object, or null if the attribute name is not found. If no scope is specified, page scope is searched. The parameter scope should be one of the scope constants defined above.

```
public abstract Object findAttribute(String name)
```

findAttribute() searches the page, request, session, and application scopes for the named attribute and returns its value as an Object, or null if the attribute name is not found.

```
public abstract void removeAttribute(String name)
public abstract void removeAttribute(String name,
                                     int scope)
```

removeAttribute() removes the Object associated with the specified attribute name from the specified scope; if no scope is specified, all scopes are searched. The parameter scope should be one of the scope constants defined above.

```
public abstract int getAttributesScope(String name)
```

getAttributesScope() returns the scope of the specified attribute as one of the scope constants defined above. If the attribute is not found, 0 is returned.

```
public abstract java.util.Enumeration getAttributeNamesInScope(int scope)
```

getAttributeNamesInScope() returns an Enumeration containing all of the attribute names in the specified scope. The parameter scope should be one of the scope constants defined above.

```
public abstract JspWriter getOut()
```

getOut() returns the JspWriter object used to generate the client response (the out implicit object in the JSP).

```
public abstract HttpSession getSession()
```

getSession() returns the current HttpSession object (the session implicit object in the JSP).

```
public abstract Object getPage()
```

getPage() returns the Servlet implementing this JSP (the page implicit object in the JSP).

```
public abstract ServletRequest getRequest()
```

getRequest() returns the current ServletRequest object (the request implicit object in the JSP).

```
public abstract ServletResponse getResponse()
```

getResponse() returns the current ServletResponse object (the response implicit object in the JSP).

```
public abstract Exception getException()
```

getException() returns any Exception for which this JSP is acting as an error page (the exception implicit object in the JSP).

```
public abstract ServletConfig getServletConfig()
```

getServletConfig() returns the current ServletConfig object (the config implicit object in the JSP).

```
public abstract ServletContext getServletContext()
```

getServletContext() returns the current ServletContext object (the application implicit object in the JSP).

```
public abstract void forward(String relativeUrlPath)
        throws ServletException, java.io.IOException
```

forward() forwards the current request to the target resource at the specified relative URL path.

```
public abstract void include(String relativeUrlPath)
        throws ServletException, java.io.IOException
```

include() causes the resource at the specified relative URL path to be included as part of the current response.

```
public abstract void handlePageException(Exception e)
        throws ServletException, java.io.IOException
public abstract void handlePageException(Throwable t)
        throws ServletException, java.io.IOException
```

handlePageException() processes a page-level exception. The exception can be re-directed to the specified error page for the JSP or handled inside the method itself.

```
public BodyContent pushBody()
```

pushBody() returns a new BodyContent object, saves the current JspWriter object, and updates the "out" page attribute.

```
public JspWriter popBody()
```

popBody() returns the JspWriter object saved by a previous call to pushBody() and updates the "out" page attribute.

javax.servlet.jsp Exceptions

JspException

```
public class JspException
    extends Exception
```

JspException is an exception type used by the JSP engine; an uncaught JspException will cause control to pass to an error page.

```
public JspException()
public JspException(String msg)
public JspException(String message,
                    Throwable rootCause)
public JspException(Throwable rootCause)
```

The constructors allow a String message and/or a Throwable representing the root cause of the problem to be encapsulated.

```
public Throwable getRootCause()
```

getRootCause() returns the Throwable that was the root cause of this exception.

JspTagException

```
public class JspTagException
    extends JspException
```

JspTagException is thrown by tag handlers when an unrecoverable error occurs; this will cause control to pass to the error page.

```
public JspTagException(String msg)
public JspTagException()
```

The constructors allow an optional String message to be encapsulated.

javax.servlet.jsp.tagext

The javax.servlet.jsp.tagext package provides interfaces and classes that support the creation of JSP custom tags.

javax.servlet.jsp.tagext Interfaces

Tag

```
public interface Tag
```

Tag is the basic interface that must be implemented by a tag handler class, providing lifecycle methods and methods that are invoked at the start and end tags.

```
public static final int SKIP_BODY
public static final int EVAL_BODY_INCLUDE
public static final int SKIP_PAGE
public static final int EVAL_PAGE
```

SKIP_BODY indicates that evaluation of the tag body should be skipped.

EVAL_BODY_INCLUDE indicates that the tag body should be evaluated into the existing output stream.

SKIP_PAGE indicates that the rest of the page should be skipped.

EVAL_PAGE indicates that page evaluation should continue.

```
public void setPageContext (PageContext pc)
```

setPageContext() specifies the current PageContext object, and is called prior to calling the doStartTag() method.

```
public void setParent (Tag t)
```

setParent() specifies the parent (nesting) Tag of this Tag.

```
public Tag getParent ()
```

getParent() returns the parent (nesting) Tag of this Tag.

```
public int doStartTag ()
        throws JspException
```

doStartTag() is called to process a custom tag's start tag. It should return EVAL_BODY_INCLUDE or BodyTag.EVAL_BODY_BUFFERED if the tag's body should be evaluated, or SKIP_BODY otherwise. EVAL_BODY_INCLUDE indicates that body (if any) should be evaluated into the current "out" JspWriter; BodyTag.EVAL_BODY_BUFFERED is only valid if the tag handler implements BodyTag.

```
public int doEndTag ()
        throws JspException
```

doEndTag() is called to process a custom tag's end tag. It should return either EVAL_PAGE, in which case processing continues, or SKIP_PAGE if the rest of the page should be skipped.

```
public void release ()
```

release() is called to release a tag handler after it has been used.

IterationTag

```
public interface IterationTag
    extends Tag
```

IterationTag is the interface that must be implemented by the tag handler class for an iteration tag.

```
public static final int EVAL_BODY_AGAIN
```

EVAL_BODY_AGAIN indicates that the tag body should be evaluated again.

```
public int doAfterBody()
        throws JspException
```

doAfterBody() is called after the tag's body content has been processed. It should return either EVAL_BODY_AGAIN to request a further iteration over the body, or SKIP_BODY to request that no further body processing take place.

BodyTag

```
public interface BodyTag
    extends IterationTag
```

IterationTag must be implemented by the tag handler class for a body tag.

```
public static final int EVAL_BODY_TAG
```

This constant is deprecated: use EVAL_BODY_BUFFERED or IterationTag.EVAL_BODY_AGAIN instead.

```
public static final int EVAL_BODY_BUFFERED
```

EVAL_BODY_BUFFERED indicates that a new BodyContent object should be created into which to evaluate the tag body.

```
public void setBodyContent(BodyContent b)
```

setBodyContent() sets the BodyContent object that will be used in conjunction with the evaluation of the tag's body.

```
public void doInitBody()
        throws JspException
```

doInitBody() is called before the tag's body is evaluated.

TryCatchFinally

```
public interface TryCatchFinally
```

TryCatchFinally is implemented by a tag handler that needs additional exception handling within the generated Servlet for the JSP. All accesses to the tag handler will be enclosed within a try-catch-finally block and the relevant TryCatchFinally methods called within the catch and finally blocks.

```
public void doCatch(Throwable t)
        throws Throwable
```

doCatch() is called if Throwable occurs within a tag body or in the Tag.doStartTag(), Tag.doEndTag(), IterationTag.doAfterBody(), or BodyTag.doInitBody() methods.

```
public void doFinally()
```

doFinally() is always invoked after doEndTag() for any tag handler class implementing Tag, IterationTag or BodyTag.

javax.servlet.jsp.tagext Classes

BodyContent

```
public abstract class BodyContent
    extends JspWriter
```

The BodyContent class extends the capability of the JspWriter class to allow the processing and retrieval of body evaluations.

```
protected BodyContent(JspWriter e)
```

The constructor will be called by the generated Servlet.

```
public void flush()
        throws java.io.IOException
```

flush() overrides the method defined in the JspWriter class. A BodyContent object is not allowed to flush.

```
public void clearBody()
```

clearBody() clears the body associated with the invoking BodyContent object.

```
public abstract java.io.Reader getReader()
```

getReader() returns the result of the body content as a Reader.

```
public abstract String getString()
```

getString() returns the result of the body content as a String.

```
public abstract void writeOut(java.io.Writer out)
        throws java.io.IOException
```

writeOut() writes the result of the body content into the specified output stream.

```
    public JspWriter getEnclosingWriter()
```

getEnclosingWriter() returns the JspWriter object enclosing this BodyContent object.

BodyTagSupport

```
    public class BodyTagSupport
        extends TagSupport
            implements BodyTag
```

The BodyTag class extends the functionality of TagSupport to provide a base class for body tag handlers.

```
    protected BodyContent bodyContent
```

bodyContent holds a reference to the BodyContent object for this tag.

```
    public BodyTagSupport()
```

Creates a BodyTagSupport object. Subclasses of BodyTagSupport are required to provide a no-argument constructor that calls this constructor.

```
    public int doStartTag()
            throws JspException
```

doStartTag() returns EVAL_BODY_BUFFERED; it should be overridden if necessary in subclasses to provide appropriate behavior.

```
    public int doEndTag()
            throws JspException
```

doEndTag() returns EVAL_PAGE; it should be overridden if necessary in subclasses to provide appropriate behavior.

```
    public void setBodyContent(BodyContent b)
```

setBodyContent() stores the BodyContent object that will be used in conjunction with the evaluation of a tag's body.

```
    public void doInitBody()
            throws JspException
```

doInitBody() does nothing; it should be overridden if necessary in subclasses to provide appropriate behavior.

```
    public int doAfterBody()
            throws JspException
```

doAfterBody() returns SKIP_BODY; it should be overridden if necessary in subclasses to provide appropriate behavior.

```
    public void release()
```

release() resets the state of the tag handler.

```
    public BodyContent getBodyContent()
```

getBodyContent() returns the BodyContent object for this tag handler.

```
    public JspWriter getPreviousOut()
```

getPreviousOut() returns the enclosing JspWriter object.

PageData

```
    public abstract class PageData
      extends Object
```

A PageData object contains translation-time information about a JSP's XML document form, for example for passing to a TagLibraryValidator.

```
    public PageData()
```

The constructor takes no arguments.

```
    public abstract java.io.InputStream getInputStream()
```

getInputStream() returns an InputStream from which can be obtained the XML document form of the JSP.

TagAttributeInfo

```
    public class TagAttributeInfo
      extends Object
```

The TagAttributeInfo class represents a tag attribute at translation time.

```
    public static final String ID
```

ID represents the ID.

```
    public TagAttributeInfo(String name,
                            boolean required,
                            String type,
                            boolean reqTime)
```

Creates a TagAttributeInfo object. The name is the name of the attribute, required is true if the attribute is required, type is the name of the type of attribute, and reqTime is true if the attribute can be a request-time attribute.

```
public String getName()
```

getName() returns the attribute name.

```
public String getTypeName()
```

getTypeName() returns the name of the attribute type.

```
public boolean canBeRequestTime()
```

canBeRequestTime() returns true if the attribute can hold a request-time value.

```
public boolean isRequired()
```

isRequired() returns true if the attribute is required.

```
public static TagAttributeInfo getIdAttribute(TagAttributeInfo[] a)
```

getIdAttribute() is a convenience method that examines an array of TagAttributeInfo objects looking for "id".

```
public String toString()
```

toString() returns a String representation of the TagAttributeInfo object.

TagData

```
public class TagData
    extends Object
        implements Cloneable
```

A TagData object contains the name-value pairs of the attributes associated with a tag at translation time.

```
public static final Object REQUEST_TIME_VALUE
```

REQUEST_TIME_VALUE represents an attribute value that is not known at translation time since it is a runtime expression.

```
public TagData(Object[][] atts)
public TagData(java.util.Hashtable attrs)
```

Creates a TagData object. The attribute name-value pairs for the TagData object can be provided using either a 2D Object array or a Hashtable.

```
public String getId()
```

getId() returns the value of the id attribute, or null if it does not exist.

```
public Object getAttribute(String attName)
```

getAttribute() returns the value of the specified attribute.

```
public void setAttribute(String attName,
                         Object value)
```

setAttribute() sets the value of the specified attribute.

```
public String getAttributeString(String attName)
```

getAttributeString() returns the value of the specified attribute as a String.

```
public java.util.Enumeration getAttributes()
```

getAttributes() returns an Enumeration containing all the attributes of this tag.

TagExtraInfo

```
public abstract class TagExtraInfo
    extends Object
```

A TagExtraInfo object contains additional information associated with a custom tag.

```
public TagExtraInfo()
```

Since the TagExtraInfo class is abstract, a TagExtraInfo object is not created directly. Subclasses of TagExtraInfo can call this constructor.

```
public VariableInfo[] getVariableInfo(TagData data)
```

getVariableInfo() returns an array of VariableInfo objects containing information on scripting variables defined by the tag.

```
public boolean isValid(TagData data)
```

isValid() returns true if the attributes associated with the specified TagData object are valid at translation time. Request-time attributes are indicated as such.

```
public final void setTagInfo(TagInfo tagInfo)
```

setTagInfo() sets the TagInfo object that is associated with the invoking TagExtraInfo object.

```
public final TagInfo getTagInfo()
```

getTagInfo() returns the TagInfo object associated with the TagExtraInfo object.

TagInfo

```
public class TagInfo
  extends Object
```

A TagInfo object contains any information associated with a custom tag.

```
public static final String BODY_CONTENT_JSP
public static final String BODY_CONTENT_TAG_DEPENDENT
public static final String BODY_CONTENT_EMPTY
```

These constants denote JSP, tag-dependent, or empty tag body content.

```
public TagInfo(String tagName,
               String tagClassName,
               String bodycontent,
               String infoString,
               TagLibraryInfo taglib,
               TagExtraInfo tagExtraInfo,
               TagAttributeInfo[] attributeInfo)
```

Creates a TagInfo object from the information contained in a JSP 1.1-format TLD. The tagName is the name given to the tag, the tagClass is the name of the tag handler class, the bodyContent provides information about the body content of these tags (one of the constants defined above), and the infoString is an optional String containing information about this tag.

```
public TagInfo(String tagName,
               String tagClassName,
               String bodycontent,
               String infoString,
               TagLibraryInfo taglib,
               TagExtraInfo tagExtraInfo,
               TagAttributeInfo[] attributeInfo,
               String displayName,
               String smallIcon,
               String largeIcon,
               TagVariableInfo[] tvi)
```

Creates a TagInfo object from the information contained in a JSP 1.2-format TLD. The tagName is the name given to the tag, the tagClass is the name of the tag handler class, the bodyContent provides information about the body content of these tags (one of the constants defined above), and the infoString is an optional String containing information about this tag.

```
public String getTagName()
```

getTagName() returns the name of the tag.

```
public TagAttributeInfo[] getAttributes()
```

getAttributes() returns an array of TagAttributeInfo objects containing information on the tag attributes.

```
public VariableInfo[] getVariableInfo(TagData data)
```

getVariableInfo() returns an array of VariableInfo objects containing information on the scripting objects created by the tag at runtime.

```
public boolean isValid(TagData data)
```

isValid() returns true if the attributes associated with the specified TagData object are valid at translation time. Request-time attributes are indicated as such.

```
public void setTagExtraInfo(TagExtraInfo tei)
```

setTagExtraInfo() sets the TagExtraInfo object for the tag.

```
public TagExtraInfo getTagExtraInfo()
```

getTagExtraInfo() returns the TagExtraInfo object, if any, associated with the tag.

```
public String getTagClassName()
```

getTagClassName() returns the name of the tag handler class.

```
public String getBodyContent()
```

getBodyContent() returns a String containing information about the body content of the tag.

```
public String getInfoString()
```

getInfoString() returns the information string, if any, associated with the tag.

```
public void setTagLibrary(TagLibraryInfo tl)
```

setTagLibrary() sets the TagLibraryInfo object associated with the tag.

```
public TagLibraryInfo getTagLibrary()
```

getTagLibrary() returns the TagLibraryInfo object associated with the tag.

```
public String getDisplayName()
```

getDisplayName() returns the display name of the tag.

```
public String getSmallIcon()
```

getSmallIcon() returns the path to the tag's small icon.

```
public String getLargeIcon()
```

getLargeIcon() returns the path to the tag's large icon.

```
public TagVariableInfo[] getTagVariableInfos()
```

getTagVariableInfos() returns the array of TagVariableInfo objects associated with the tag.

```
public String toString()
```

toString() returns a String representation of the invoking TagInfo object.

TagLibraryInfo

```
public abstract class TagLibraryInfo
   extends Object
```

A TagLibraryInfo object contains information on the tag library associated with a tag.

```
protected String prefix
protected String uri
protected TagInfo[] tags
protected String tlibversion
protected String jspversion
protected String shortname
protected String urn
protected String info
```

These instance variables contain information about the tag library.

```
protected TagLibraryInfo(String prefix,
                         String uri)
```

Creates a TagLibraryInfo object.

```
public String getURI()
```

getURI() returns a String containing the URI from the taglib directive for this library.

```
public String getPrefixString()
```

getPrefixString() returns the prefix that is assigned to this tag library.

```
public String getShortName()
```

getShortName() returns the preferred short name for this tag library.

```
public String getReliableURN()
```

getReliableURN() returns a String containing a reliable URN for this tag library.

```
public String getInfoString()
```

getInfoString() returns the information string, if any, associated with the tag library.

```
public String getRequiredVersion()
```

getRequiredVersion() returns the required version of the JSP container.

```
public TagInfo[] getTags()
```

getTags() returns an array of TagInfo objects containing information about all of the tags contained in this tag library.

```
public TagInfo getTag(String shortname)
```

getTag() returns a TagInfo object for the specified tag.

TagLibraryValidator

```
public abstract class TagLibraryValidator
    extends Object
```

A TagLibraryValidator is a translation-time validator for a tag library, which uses the XML document form of a JSP.

```
public TagLibraryValidator()
```

Since TagLibraryValidator is an abstract class, this constructor will not normally be directly called.

```
public void setInitParameters(java.util.Map map)
```

setInitParameters() sets the initialization parameters for the TagLibraryValidator.

```
public java.util.Map getInitParameters()
```

getInitParameters() returns the initialization parameters for the TagLibraryValidator.

```
public String validate(String prefix,
                       String uri,
                       PageData page)
```

validate() validates a JSP page, and is passed the prefix and URI of the tag library within the page, and a PageData object representing the page itself. It returns an error message, or null if there are no errors.

```
public void release()
```

release() releases any data held by the TagLibraryValidator.

TagSupport

```
public class TagSupport
  extends Object
    implements IterationTag, java.io.Serializable
```

The TagSupport class provides a convenient implementation of the IterationTag interface.

```
protected String id
protected PageContext pageContext
```

TagSupport uses these instance variables to store the id and PageContext associated with this tag.

```
public TagSupport()
```

Creates a TagSupport object. Subclasses of TagSupport are required to provide a no-argument constructor that calls this constructor.

```
public static final Tag findAncestorWithClass(Tag from,
                                              Class klass)
```

findAncestorWithClass() uses the getParent() method in Tag to find the instance of a given tag class that is closest to this tag.

```
public int doStartTag()
        throws JspException
```

doStartTag() returns SKIP_BODY; it should be overridden if necessary in subclasses to provide appropriate behavior.

```
public int doEndTag()
        throws JspException
```

doEndTag() returns EVAL_PAGE; it should be overridden if necessary in subclasses to provide appropriate behavior.

```
public int doAfterBody()
        throws JspException
```

doAfterBody() does nothing; it should be overridden if necessary in subclasses to provide appropriate behavior.

```
public void release()
```

release() resets the state of the tag.

```
public void setParent(Tag t)
```

setParent() sets the sets the parent, or nesting, tag.

```
        public Tag getParent()
```

getParent() returns the parent, or nesting, tag for the current tag.

```
        public void setId(String id)
```

setId() sets the value of the "id" attribute.

```
        public String getId()
```

getId() returns the value of the "id" attribute.

```
        public void setPageContext(PageContext pageContext)
```

setPageContext() specifies the PageContext object associated with the tag.

```
        public void setValue(String k,
                             Object o)
```

setValue() sets the value of the specified attribute.

```
        public Object getValue(String k)
```

getValue() returns the value of the specified attribute.

```
        public void removeValue(String k)
```

removeValue() removes the specified attribute from the tag.

```
        public java.util.Enumeration getValues()
```

getValues() returns an Enumeration containing all of the tag attributes.

TagVariableInfo

```
        public class TagVariableInfo
          extends Object
```

A TagVariableInfo object contains translation-time variable information obtained from the TLD file

```
        public TagVariableInfo(String nameGiven,
                               String nameFromAttribute,
                               String className,
                               boolean declare,
                               int scope)
```

This creates a TagVariableInfo object using the information from the TLD file.

```
public String getNameGiven()
```

getNameGiven() returns the body of the <name-given> TLD element.

```
public String getNameFromAttribute()
```

getNameFromAttribute() returns the body of the <name-from-attribute> TLD element.

```
public String getClassName()
```

getClassName() returns the body of the <variable-class> TLD element.

```
public boolean getDeclare()
```

getDeclare() returns the body of the <declare> TLD element.

```
public int getScope()
```

getScope() returns the body of the <scope> TLD element.

VariableInfo

```
public class VariableInfo
   extends Object
```

A VariableInfo object contains information on the scripting variables that are created or modified by a tag at runtime.

```
public static final int NESTED
public static final int AT_BEGIN
public static final int AT_END
```

These constants denote the scopes available for scripting variables. If a variable is given the NESTED scope, it is visible within the start and end tags. If a variable is given the AT_BEGIN scope, it is visible after the start tag. If a variable is given the AT_END scope, it is visible after the end tag.

```
public VariableInfo(String varName,
                    String className,
                    boolean declare,
                    int scope)
```

Creates a VariableInfo object. The declare parameter is true if the variable is new and may require a declaration. The scope must be one of the scope constants defined above.

```
public String getVarName()
```

getVarName() returns the name of the scripting variable.

```
public String getClassName()
```

`getClassName()` returns the name of the class of the scripting variable.

```
public boolean getDeclare()
```

`getDeclare()` returns `true` if the variable is new and may require a declaration.

```
public int getScope()
```

`getScope()` returns the scope of the scripting variable.

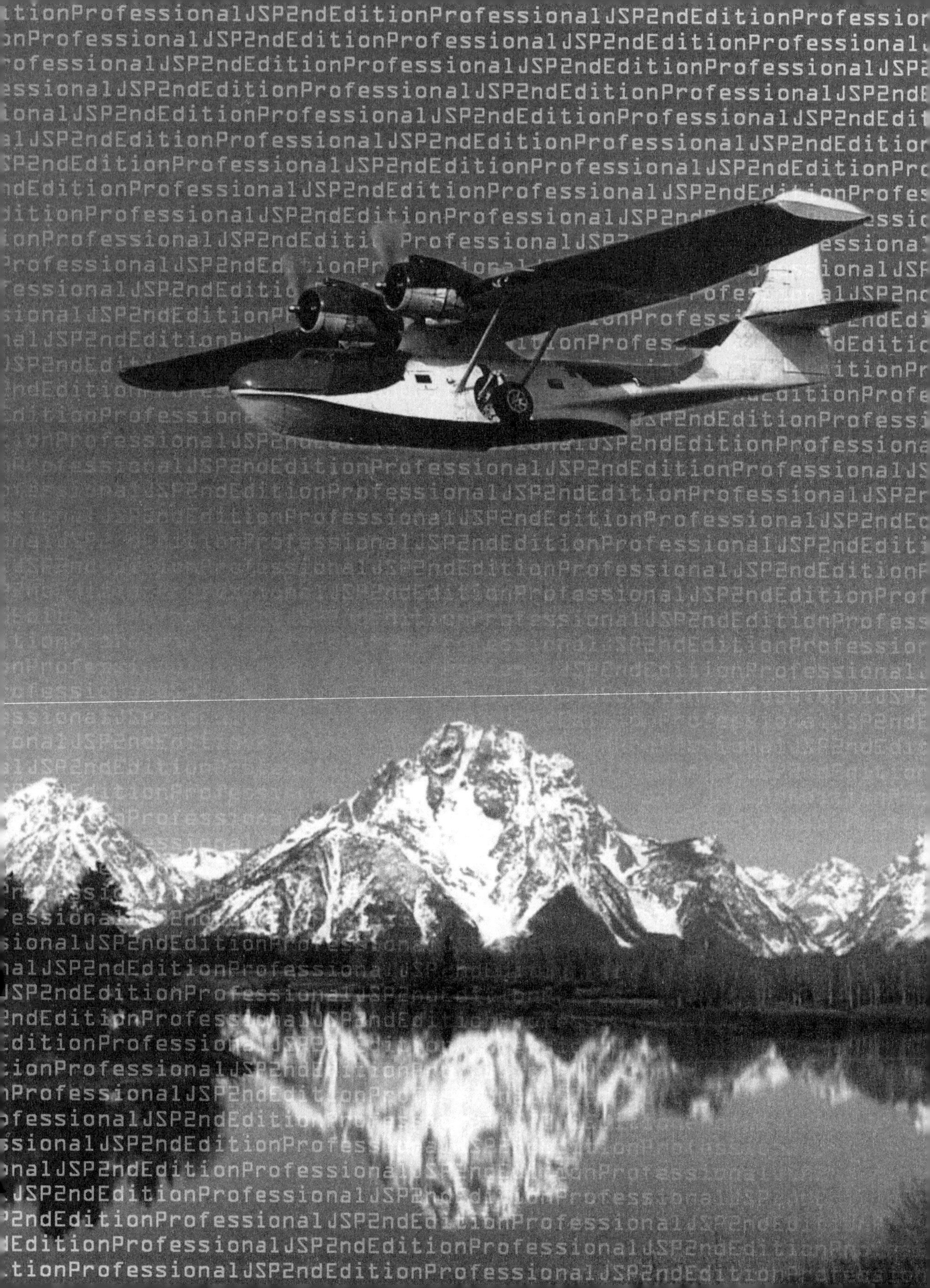

D

Document Type Definitions

This appendix documents the two main document type definitions in the Servlet 2.3 and JSP 1.2 specifications: the web application deployment descriptor (web.xml) and tag library descriptor (.tld) files.

For full details, and for the XML format for JSP files, consult the Servlet and JSP specifications at http://java.sun.com/products/servlet/ and http://java.sun.com/products/jsp/.

Web Application Deployment Descriptor

The DOCTYPE declaration at the head of a Servlet 2.3 web application deployment descriptor (web.xml) file should be:

```
<!DOCTYPE web-app
  PUBLIC "-//Sun Microsystems, Inc.//DTD Web Application 2.3//EN"
  "http://java.sun.com/j2ee/dtds/web-app_2_3.dtd">
```

Note that within the web.xml file the ordering of elements is significant; failure to have the elements in the correct order is a common problem, especially when moving an application from an old web container that used a non-validating XML parser to a more recent one that does validate the XML. (In Servlet 2.3, validation of the web.xml file is recommended.)

Servlet 2.3-compatible web containers are also required to accept a web.xml file using the Servlet 2.2 format; this is included as an appendix to the Servlet 2.3 specification.

Common Elements

The `<description>`, `<display-name>`, and `<icon>` elements can occur in several places within web.xml and we will describe them only once, here.

<description>

The `<description>` element is used in a number of places within the web.xml file to provide a description of its parent element.

<display-name>

The `<display-name>` element contains a short name for its parent element, for GUI tools to display.

<icon>

The `<icon>` element references icons (GIF and JPEG formats must be accepted by tools) that will be used by a GUI tool to represent its parent element. It contains:

❑ An optional `<small-icon>` element containing the location within the application of a 16x16 pixel icon

❑ An optional `<large-icon>` element containing the location within the application of a 32x32 pixel icon

The <web-app> Root Element

The `<web-app>` element is the root element of the web.xml file. It contains:

❑ An optional (in other words 0 or 1) `<icon>` element

❑ An optional `<display-name>` element

❑ An optional `<description>` element

❑ An optional `<distributable>` element

❑ 0 or more `<context-param>` elements

❑ 0 or more `<filter>` elements

❑ 0 or more `<filter-mapping>` elements

❑ 0 or more `<listener>` elements

❑ 0 or more `<servlet>` elements

❑ 0 or more `<servlet-mapping>` elements

❑ An optional `<session-config>` element

❑ 0 or more `<mime-mapping>` elements

❑ An optional `<welcome-file-list>` element

❑ 0 or more `<error-page>` elements

❑ 0 or more `<taglib>` elements

- ❏ 0 or more `<resource-env-ref>` elements
- ❏ 0 or more `<resource-ref>` elements
- ❏ 0 or more `<security-constraint>` elements
- ❏ An optional `<login-config>` element
- ❏ 0 or more `<security-role>` elements
- ❏ 0 or more `<env-entry>` elements
- ❏ 0 or more `<ejb-ref>` elements
- ❏ 0 or more `<ejb-local-ref>` elements

Sub-elements of \<web-app\>

The permissible sub-elements of `<web-app>` (other than those already described) are as follows:

\<distributable\>

The `<distributable>` element, if present, declares that this web application can be deployed in a distributed servlet container.

\<context-param\>

The `<context-param>` element declares a context initialization parameter. It contains:

- ❏ A `<param-name>` element containing the parameter's name
- ❏ A `<param-value>` element containing the parameter's value
- ❏ An optional `<description>` element (see earlier description)

\<filter\>

The `<filter>` element declares a filter. It contains:

- ❏ An optional `<icon>` element
- ❏ A `<filter-name>` element containing the filter's name
- ❏ An optional `<display-name>` element
- ❏ An optional `<description>` element
- ❏ A `<filter-class>` element containing the filter's class name
- ❏ 0 or more `<init-param>` elements containing initialization parameters for the filter

Each `<init-param>` element contains:

- ❏ A `<param-name>` element containing the parameter name
- ❏ A `<param-value>` element containing the parameter value
- ❏ An optional `<description>` element

\<filter-mapping>

The \<filter-mapping> element is used to map a filter to a servlet or a set of URLs. It contains:

❑ A \<filter-name> element containing the name of a filter declared by a \<filter> element

❑ Either a \<url-pattern> element containing a URL pattern to match, or a \<servlet-name> element containing the name of a servlet declared by a \<servlet> element

\<listener>

The \<listener> element is used to declare an application listener. It contains:

❑ A \<listener-class> element containing the listener's class name.

\<servlet>

The \<servlet> element declares a servlet. It contains:

❑ An optional \<icon> element.

❑ A \<servlet-name> element containing the servlet's name.

❑ An optional \<display-name> element.

❑ An optional \<description> element.

❑ Either a \<servlet-class> element containing the listener's class name, or a \<jsp-file> element containing the location within the web application of a JSP file.

❑ 0 or more \<init-param> elements.

❑ An optional \<load-on-startup> element indicating that the servlet should be loaded when the web application starts up, and containing an optional positive integer value indicating the order in which servlets should be started. If a \<jsp-file> was specified, then the JSP should be precompiled and loaded.

❑ An optional \<run-as> element.

❑ 0 or more \<security-role-ref> elements.

Each \<init-param> element contains:

❑ A \<param-name> element containing the parameter name.

❑ A \<param-value> element containing the parameter value.

❑ An optional \<description> element.

The optional \<run-as> element contains:

❑ An optional \<description> element.

❑ A \<role-name> element specifying the security role that should be propagated to EJBs.

A \<security-role-ref> element maps a role name called from within the servlet, and the name of a security role defined for the web application. It contains:

❑ An optional \<description> element.

❑ A \<role-name> element containing the role name used within the servlet.

❑ A \<role-link> element containing the name of a role defined in a \<security-role> element.

<servlet-mapping>

The <servlet-mapping> element maps a servlet to a URL pattern. It contains:

❑ A <servlet-name> element containing the name of a servlet declared by a <servlet> element

❑ A <url-pattern> element containing a URL pattern to match

<session-config>

The <session-config> element configures the session tracking for the web application. It contains:

❑ An optional <session-timeout> element containing the default session timeout for this web application, which must be a whole number of minutes

<mime-mapping>

The <mime-mapping> element maps a filename extension to a MIME type. It contains:

❑ An <extension> element containing a filename extension

❑ A <mime-type> element containing a defined MIME type

<welcome-file-list>

The <welcome-file-list> element defines an ordered list of welcome files. It contains:

❑ 1 or more <welcome-file> elements containing a filename to use as a welcome file

<error-page>

The <error-page> element maps an error code or exception type to a resource ('error page') to use if that error condition arises. It contains:

❑ Either an <error-code> element containing an HTTP error code, or an <exception-type> element containing the class name of a Java exception type

❑ A <location> element containing the location of the error page resource within the web application

<taglib>

The <taglib> element declares a JSP tag library. It contains:

❑ A <taglib-uri> element containing a URI to identify the tag library

❑ A <taglib-location> element containing the location within the web application of the tag library descriptor file (.tld file)

<resource-env-ref>

The <resource-env-ref> element declares that the web application references an administered object. It contains:

❑ An optional <description> element

❑ A `<resource-env-name>` element containing the name of the resource environment

❑ A `<resource-env-ref-type>` element containing the type of the resource environment reference – J2EE web containers are required to support `javax.jms.Topic` and `javax.jms.Queue`

`<resource-ref>`

The `<resource-ref>` element declares that the web application references an external resource. It contains:

❑ An optional `<description>` element.

❑ A `<res-ref-name>` element containing the name of the resource factory reference.

❑ A `<res-type>` element specifying the type of the data source.

❑ A `<res-auth>` element indicating whether the application code signs on to the resource programmatically, or whether the container should sign on based on information supplied by the application deployer. Contents must be either `Application` or `Container`.

❑ An optional `<res-sharing-scope>` element specifying whether connections can be shared. Contents must be either `Shareable` (the default) or `Unshareable`.

`<security-constraint>`

The `<security-constraint>` element applies security constraints to one or more collections of web resources. It contains:

❑ An optional `<display-name>` element

❑ One or more `<web-resource-collection>` elements

❑ An optional `<auth-constraint>` element

❑ An optional `<user-data-constraint>` element

A `<web-resource-collection>` element identifies a set of resources within the application; it can be qualified by specifying particular HTTP method(s). (By default, the security constraint applies to all HTTP methods.) It contains:

❑ A `<web-resource-name>` element containing the name of the web resource collection

❑ An optional `<description>` element

❑ 0 or more `<url-pattern>` elements, each containing a URL pattern to match

❑ 0 or more `<http-method>` elements, each containing the name of an HTTP method

An `<auth-constraint>` element indicates that certain user roles should be permitted to access these web resources. It contains:

❑ An optional `<description>` element

❑ 0 or more `<role-name>` elements each containing a role referenced in a `<security-role-ref>` element, or the special name * that indicates all roles in this application

A `<user-data-constraint>` element indicates how data transmitted between the client and the application should be protected. It contains:

❑ An optional `<description>` element.

❑ A `<transport-guarantee>` element containing the text NONE, INTEGRAL, or CONFIDENTIAL. NONE means that no transport guarantee is required, INTEGRAL means that the data must not be able to be changed in transit, and CONFIDENTIAL means that others should not be able to view the data.

`<login-config>`

The `<login-config>` element configures the authentication mechanism for this application. It contains:

❑ An optional `<auth-method>` element specifying the authentication mechanism. Must contain the text BASIC, DIGEST, FORM, or CLIENT-CERT.

❑ An optional `<realm-name>` element specifying the realm name for HTTP basic authorization.

❑ An optional `<form-login-config>` element to configure form-based authentication. Contains a `<form-login-page>` element specifying the login page, and a `<form-error-page>` element specifying the error page used if login is unsuccessful.

`<security-role>`

The `<security-role>` element declares a security role used in the web application's security-constraints. It contains:

❑ An optional `<description>` element

❑ A `<role-name>` element containing the name of the role

`<env-entry>`

The `<env-entry>` element declares an application's environment entry. It contains:

❑ An optional `<description>` element.

❑ An `<env-entry-name>` element containing the environment entry's name.

❑ An optional `<env-entry-value>` element containing the environment entry's value.

❑ An `<env-entry-type>` element containing the environment entry value's Java type. Legal values are java.lang.Boolean, java.lang.String, java.lang.Integer, java.lang.Double, and java.lang.Float.

`<ejb-ref>` and `<ejb-local-ref>`

The `<ejb-ref>` element declares a reference to an Enterprise JavaBean, while `<ejb-local-ref>` declares a local EJB reference. It contains:

❑ An optional `<description>` element

❑ An `<ejb-ref-name>` element containing the JNDI name of the EJB

❑ An `<ejb-ref-type>` element containing the expected type of the EJB, either Entity or Session

- ❏ A `<home>` element containing the type of the EJB's home interface, or a `<local-home>` element for a local reference
- ❏ A `<remote>` element containing the type of the EJB's remote interface, or a `<local>` element for a local reference
- ❏ An optional `<ejb-link>` element specifying that this EJB reference is linked to the named EJB in the encompassing J2EE application

Document Type Definition

Here's the DTD for the Web Application Deployment Descriptor:

```
<!ELEMENT web-app (icon?, display-name?, description?, distributable?,
                   context-param*, filter*, filter-mapping*, listener*,
                   servlet*, servlet-mapping*, session-config?,
                   mime-mapping*, welcome-file-list?, error-page*, taglib*,
                   resource-env-ref*, resource-ref*, security-constraint*,
                   login-config?, security-role*, env-entry*, ejb-ref*,
                   ejb-local-ref*)>
<!ELEMENT filter (icon?, filter-name, display-name?, description?,
                  filter-class, init-param*)>
<!ELEMENT filter-name (#PCDATA)>
<!ELEMENT filter-class (#PCDATA)>
<!ELEMENT filter-mapping (filter-name, (url-pattern | servlet-name))>
<!ELEMENT icon (small-icon?, large-icon?)>
<!ELEMENT small-icon (#PCDATA)>
<!ELEMENT large-icon (#PCDATA)>
<!ELEMENT display-name (#PCDATA)>
<!ELEMENT description (#PCDATA)>
<!ELEMENT distributable EMPTY>
<!ELEMENT context-param (param-name, param-value, description?)>
<!ELEMENT param-name (#PCDATA)>
<!ELEMENT param-value (#PCDATA)>
<!ELEMENT listener (listener-class)>
<!ELEMENT listener-class (#PCDATA)>
<!ELEMENT servlet (icon?, servlet-name, display-name?, description?,
                   (servlet-class|jsp-file), init-param*, load-on-startup?,
                   run-as?, security-role-ref*)>
<!ELEMENT servlet-name (#PCDATA)>
<!ELEMENT servlet-class (#PCDATA)>
<!ELEMENT jsp-file (#PCDATA)>
<!ELEMENT init-param (param-name, param-value, description?)>
<!ELEMENT load-on-startup (#PCDATA)>
<!ELEMENT servlet-mapping (servlet-name, url-pattern)>
<!ELEMENT url-pattern (#PCDATA)>
<!ELEMENT session-config (session-timeout?)>
<!ELEMENT session-timeout (#PCDATA)>
<!ELEMENT mime-mapping (extension, mime-type)>
<!ELEMENT extension (#PCDATA)>
<!ELEMENT mime-type (#PCDATA)>
<!ELEMENT welcome-file-list (welcome-file+)>
<!ELEMENT welcome-file (#PCDATA)>
<!ELEMENT taglib (taglib-uri, taglib-location)>
<!ELEMENT taglib-uri (#PCDATA)>
<!ELEMENT taglib-location (#PCDATA)>
```

```
<!ELEMENT error-page ((error-code | exception-type), location)>
<!ELEMENT error-code (#PCDATA)>
<!ELEMENT exception-type (#PCDATA)>
<!ELEMENT location (#PCDATA)>
<!ELEMENT resource-env-ref (description?, resource-env-ref-name,
                            resource-env-ref-type)>
<!ELEMENT resource-env-ref-name (#PCDATA)>
<!ELEMENT resource-env-ref-type (#PCDATA)>
<!ELEMENT resource-ref (description?, res-ref-name, res-type, res-auth,
                        res-sharing-scope?)>
<!ELEMENT res-ref-name (#PCDATA)>
<!ELEMENT res-type (#PCDATA)>
<!ELEMENT res-auth (#PCDATA)>
<!ELEMENT res-sharing-scope (#PCDATA)>
<!ELEMENT security-constraint (display-name?, web-resource-collection+,
                               auth-constraint?, user-data-constraint?)>
<!ELEMENT web-resource-collection (web-resource-name, description?,
                                   url-pattern*, http-method*)>
<!ELEMENT web-resource-name (#PCDATA)>
<!ELEMENT http-method (#PCDATA)>
<!ELEMENT user-data-constraint (description?, transport-guarantee)>
<!ELEMENT transport-guarantee (#PCDATA)>
<!ELEMENT auth-constraint (description?, role-name*)>
<!ELEMENT role-name (#PCDATA)>
<!ELEMENT login-config (auth-method?, realm-name?, form-login-config?)>
<!ELEMENT realm-name (#PCDATA)>
<!ELEMENT form-login-config (form-login-page, form-error-page)>
<!ELEMENT form-login-page (#PCDATA)>
<!ELEMENT form-error-page (#PCDATA)>
<!ELEMENT auth-method (#PCDATA)>
<!ELEMENT security-role (description?, role-name)>
<!ELEMENT security-role-ref (description?, role-name, role-link)>
<!ELEMENT role-link (#PCDATA)>
<!ELEMENT env-entry (description?, env-entry-name, env-entry-value?,
                     env-entry-type)>
<!ELEMENT env-entry-name (#PCDATA)>
<!ELEMENT env-entry-value (#PCDATA)>
<!ELEMENT env-entry-type (#PCDATA)>
<!ELEMENT ejb-ref (description?, ejb-ref-name, ejb-ref-type, home, remote,
                   ejb-link?)>
<!ELEMENT ejb-ref-name (#PCDATA)>
<!ELEMENT ejb-ref-type (#PCDATA)>
<!ELEMENT home (#PCDATA)>
<!ELEMENT remote (#PCDATA)>
<!ELEMENT ejb-link (#PCDATA)>
<!ELEMENT ejb-local-ref (description?, ejb-ref-name, ejb-ref-type,
                         local-home, local, ejb-link?)>
<!ELEMENT local (#PCDATA)>
<!ELEMENT local-home (#PCDATA)>
<!ELEMENT run-as (description?, role-name)>
```

In addition, all elements have an implied id attribute, for example:

```
<!ATTLIST web-app id ID #IMPLIED>
```

Tag Library Descriptor

The DOCTYPE declaration at the head of a JSP 1.2 tag library descriptor (.tld) file should be:

```
<!DOCTYPE taglib
PUBLIC "-//Sun Microsystems, Inc.//DTD JSP Tag Library 1.2//EN"
"http://java.sun.com/j2ee/dtds/web-jsptaglibrary_1_2.dtd">
```

Note that the ordering of elements within a tag library descriptor file is significant, and failure to have the elements in the correct order is a common problem.

JSP 1.2-compatible web containers are also required to accept a .tld file using the JSP 1.1 format; this is included as an appendix to the JSP 1.2 specification.

Common Elements

The <description>, <display-name>, <large-icon>, and <small-icon> elements can occur in several places within web.xml and so we will describe them only once – here.

<description>

The <description> element contains a description of the enclosing element.

<display-name>

The <display-name> element contains a short name for its parent element, for GUI tools to display.

<large-icon>

The <large-icon> element contains the location within the tag library of a 16x16 pixel JPEG or GIF image denoting the enclosing element.

<small-icon>

The <small-icon> element contains the location within the tag library of a 32x32 pixel JPEG or GIF image denoting the enclosing element.

The <taglib> Root Element

The <taglib> element is the root element of a .tld file. It contains:

- ❑ A <tlib-version> element
- ❑ A <jsp-version> element
- ❑ A <short-name> element
- ❑ An optional <uri> element
- ❑ An optional <display-name> element
- ❑ An optional <small-icon> element

- ❑ An optional `<large-icon>` element
- ❑ An optional `<description>` element
- ❑ An optional `<validator>` element
- ❑ 0 or more `<listener>` elements
- ❑ 1 or more `<tag>` elements

Sub-elements of `<taglib>`

The permissible sub-elements of `<taglib>` (other than those already described) are as follows:

`<tlib-version>`

The `<tlib-version>` element contains the version number of the tag library.

`<jsp-version>`

The `<jsp-version>` element contains the JSP version that the tag library requires (`1.2` by default).

`<short-name>`

The `<short-name>` element contains a short name for the tag library.

`<uri>`

The `<uri>` element contains a URI uniquely identifying the tag library.

`<validator>`

The `<validator>` element defines a validator to check that a JSP page uses the tag library correctly. It contains:

- ❑ A `<validator-class>` element containing the name of the `TagLibraryValidator` class
- ❑ 0 or more `<init-param>` elements
- ❑ An optional `<description>` element

An `<init-param>` element defines initialization parameters for the validator, and contains:

- ❑ A `<param-name>` element containing the parameter name
- ❑ A `<param-value>` element containing the parameter value
- ❑ An optional `<description>` element

`<listener>`

The `<listener>` element defines an event listener for the web application using the tag library. It contains:

- ❑ A `<listener-class>` element containing the name of the listener class

\<tag\>

The \<tag\> element defines a tag. It contains:

- ❏ A \<name\> element containing the tag's name

- ❏ A \<tag-class\> element containing the name of the tag handler class

- ❏ An optional \<tei-class\> element containing the name of the TagExtraInfo class for the tag

- ❏ An optional \<body-content\> element describing the body content of the tag: either tagdependent, JSP, or empty

- ❏ An optional \<display-name\> element

- ❏ An optional \<small-icon\> element

- ❏ An optional \<large-icon\> element

- ❏ An optional \<description\> element

- ❏ 0 or more \<variable\> elements

- ❏ 0 or more \<variable\> elements

- ❏ An optional \<example\> element giving an example of the tag's use

A \<variable\> tag declares that this tag defines a scripting variable. It contains:

- ❏ Either a \<name-given\> element containing the name of the scripting variable, or a \<name-from-attribute\> element containing the name of the tag attribute that will give the scripting variable's name at runtime.

- ❏ An optional \<variable-class\> element containing the class of the scripting variable. The default is java.lang.String.

- ❏ An optional \<declare\> element whose contents indicate whether the scripting variable is to be defined; the default is true.

- ❏ An optional \<scope\> element whose contents indicate the scope of the scripting variable. Possible values are NESTED (the default), AT_BEGIN, or AT_END.

- ❏ An optional \<description\> element.

An \<attribute\> element defines an attribute of the tag. It contains:

- ❏ A \<name\> element containing the name of the attribute.

- ❏ An optional \<required\> element whose contents indicate whether the attribute is required or optional. Legal values are true, false (the default), yes, and no.

- ❏ An optional \<rtexprvalue\> element whose contents indicate whether the attribute value can be a run-time expression scriptlet rather than a static value. Legal values are true, false (the default), yes, and no.

- ❏ An optional \<type\> element containing the type of the attribute's value. (For static values, this is always java.lang.String.)

- ❏ An optional \<description\> element.

Document Type Definition

Here's the DTD for a Tag Library Descriptor file:

```
<!NOTATION WEB-JSPTAGLIB.1_2 PUBLIC
         "-//Sun Microsystems, Inc.//DTD JSP Tag Library 1.2//EN">
<!ELEMENT taglib (tlib-version, jsp-version, short-name, uri?,
                display-name?, small-icon?, large-icon?, description?,
                validator?, listener*, tag+) >

<!ATTLIST taglib
      id ID #IMPLIED
      xmlns CDATA #FIXED "http://java.sun.com/JSP/TagLibraryDescriptor"
>

<!ELEMENT tlib-version (#PCDATA) >
<!ELEMENT jsp-version (#PCDATA) >
<!ELEMENT short-name (#PCDATA) >
<!ELEMENT uri (#PCDATA) >
<!ELEMENT description (#PCDATA) >
<!ELEMENT validator (validator-class, init-param*, description?) >
<!ELEMENT validator-class (#PCDATA) >
<!ELEMENT init-param (param-name, param-value, description?)>
<!ELEMENT param-name (#PCDATA)>
<!ELEMENT param-value (#PCDATA)>
<!ELEMENT listener (listener-class) >
<!ELEMENT listener-class (#PCDATA) >
<!ELEMENT tag (name, tag-class, tei-class?, body-content?, display-name?,
              small-icon?, large-icon?, description?, variable*,
              attribute*, example?) >
<!ELEMENT tag-class (#PCDATA) >
<!ELEMENT tei-class (#PCDATA) >
<!ELEMENT body-content (#PCDATA) >
<!ELEMENT display-name (#PCDATA) >
<!ELEMENT large-icon (#PCDATA) >
<!ELEMENT small-icon (#PCDATA) >
<!ELEMENT example (#PCDATA) >
<!ELEMENT variable ( (name-given | name-from-attribute), variable-class?,
                    declare?, scope?, description?) >
<!ELEMENT name-given (#PCDATA) >
<!ELEMENT name-from-attribute (#PCDATA) >
<!ELEMENT variable-class (#PCDATA) >
<!ELEMENT declare (#PCDATA) >
<!ELEMENT scope (#PCDATA) >
<!ELEMENT attribute (name, required? , rtexprvalue?, type?, description?) >
<!ELEMENT name (#PCDATA) >
<!ELEMENT required (#PCDATA) >
<!ELEMENT rtexprvalue (#PCDATA) >
<!ELEMENT type (#PCDATA) >
```

In addition, all elements have an implied id attribute, for example:

```
<!ATTLIST tlib-version id ID #IMPLIED>
```

E

JSP and Servlet Version History

This book has been based largely on the JSP 1.2 and Servlet 2.3 Proposed Final Draft specifications. However, many servers still only support older versions of the specifications, often JSP 1.1 and Servlet 2.2. To help complete the picture, this appendix describes the main changes that have occurred to the JSP specification since version 1.0, and to the Servlet specification since version 2.0. For full details you should consult the specifications themselves, available at http://java.sun.com/products/jsp/ for JSP and http://java.sun.com/products/servlet/ for the Servlet API.

Changes in JSP 1.2

The major changes in the JSP 1.2 specification, relative to JSP 1.1, are:

- ❑ `<jsp:include>` can now specify `flush="false"`
- ❑ The XML view of a JSP is now available for input and validation
- ❑ Validation of tag libraries was enhanced
- ❑ The `IteratorTag` interface was added to allow custom tags to iterate over their body without needing to use a `BodyContent` object
- ❑ A tag library can now declare event listeners
- ❑ `TagExtraInfo` classes are now no longer needed in the most common cases
- ❑ The `TryCatchFinally` interface to allow tag handlers to provide better exception handling
- ❑ An implicit URI-to-TLD mapping was introduced for tag libraries packaged as a JAR file; a JAR file can now contain multiple tag libraries
- ❑ The `pageEncoding` attribute was added to the page directive

Changes in JSP 1.1

The major changes in the JSP 1.1 specification, relative to JSP 1.0, are:

- ❑ The custom tag mechanism was added
- ❑ Flush was made a mandatory attribute of `<jsp:include>`, with "true" as the only valid value
- ❑ Parameters were added to `<jsp:include>` and `<jsp:forward>`
- ❑ JSP pages can now be compiled into Servlet classes that are portable between JSP containers
- ❑ `JspException` and `JspTagException` were added
- ❑ JSP 1.1 is based on Servlet 2.2, where JSP 1.0 was based on Servlet 2.1
- ❑ The XML view of a JSP was introduced

Changes in Servlet 2.3

The major changes in the Servlet 2.3 specification, relative to Servlet 2.2, are:

- ❑ Application events (Chapter 16) were added to the specification
- ❑ Servlet filtering (Chapters 14 and 15) were added to the specification
- ❑ The request and response can now be wrapped by a filter, or for a `RequestDispatcher` invocation
- ❑ It is now a requirement that Servlet 2.3 containers provide a Java 2 runtime environment (in other words, JDK 1.2.x or later)
- ❑ Web applications can now declare their dependency on installed Java extensions
- ❑ Various fixes were made to the internationalization facilities

In addition, various API changes were made.

Changes in Servlet 2.2

The major changes in the Servlet 2.2 specification, relative to Servlet 2.1, are:

- ❑ The web application concept, the `web.xml` file, and the standardized directory structure, were introduced, along with web application archive (`.war`) files
- ❑ Response buffering was introduced
- ❑ The concept of distributable servlets was introduced
- ❑ `ServletContext` initialization parameters were introduced
- ❑ The `RequestDispatcher` API was expanded to allow a `RequestDispatcher` to be obtained by name or using a relative path

❏ Improvements were made to the internationalization facilities with the introduction of `getLocale()` and `getLocales()` methods to the `ServletRequest` and `ServletResponse` interfaces

❏ The naming conventions within `HttpSession` were improved by deprecating `getValue()`, `getValueNames()`, `setValue()`, and `removeValue()` and introducing `getAttribute()`, `getAttributeNames()`, `setAttribute()`, and `removeAttribute()`

Changes in Servlet 2.1

The major changes in the Servlet 2.1 specification, relative to Servlet 2.0, are:

❏ `ServletContext` attributes were introduced, allowing global objects to be shared between servlets

❏ The `RequestDispatcher` interface was introduced allowing servlets to forward and nest requests

❏ In connection with this, request attributes were introduced to allow information to be associated with a particular request

❏ Additional header-processing methods were added to `HttpServletRequest` and `HttpServletResponse`

❏ Additional security methods were added to the request objects

❏ `ServletResponse` buffering was enhanced

❏ The `ServletContext` methods `getResource()` and `getResourceAsStream()` were introduced

❏ The `ServletContext` methods `getServlet()`, `getServletNames()`, and `getServlets()` were deprecated for security reasons

❏ The `HttpSessionContext` class was deprecated, along with the `HttpSession` method `getSessionContext()`

Various minor API changes were made, including changes to logging and the ability to process multi-valued request parameters.

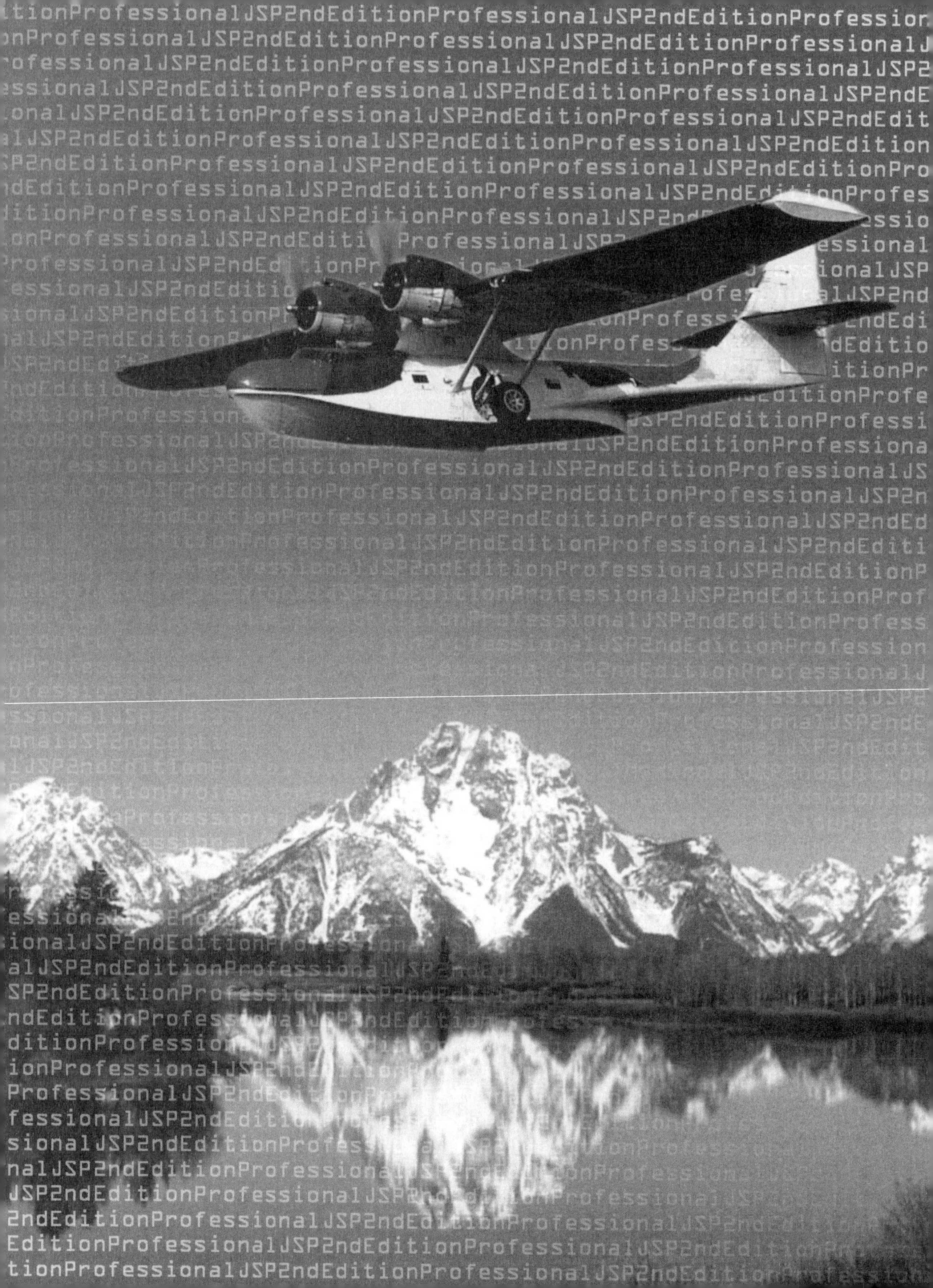
ProfessionalJSP2ndEdition

HTTP Reference

The Hypertext Transfer Protocol (HTTP) is an application-level protocol for distributed hypermedia information systems. It is a generic, stateless protocol, which can be used for many tasks beyond its use for hypertext. A feature of HTTP is the typing and negotiation of data representation, allowing systems to be built independently of the data being transferred.

The first version of HTTP, referred to as HTTP/0.9, was a simple protocol for raw data transfer across the Internet. HTTP/1.0, as defined by RFC 1945 improved the protocol by allowing messages to be in a MIME-like format, containing meta-information about the data transferred and modifiers on the request/response semantics. The current version HTTP/1.1, first defined in RFC 2068 and more recently in RFC 2616, made performance improvements by making all connections persistent and supporting absolute URLs in requests.

URL Request Protocols

A URL is a pointer to a particular resource on the Internet at a particular location and has a standard format as follows:

```
Protocol Servername Filepath
```

In order, the three elements are the protocol used to access the server, the name of the server, and the location of the resource on the server. For example:

```
http://www.mydomain.com/
https://www.mydomain.com:8080/
ftp://ftp.mydomain.com/example.txt
mailto:me@world.com
file:///c:/Windows/win.exe
```

The `servername` and `filepath` pieces of the URL are totally dependent on where files are stored on your server and what you have called it, but there are a standard collection of protocols, most of which you should be familiar with:

- ❑ **http:** Normal HTTP requests for documents.
- ❑ **https:** Secure HTTP requests. The specific behavior of these depends on the security certificates and encryption keys you have set up.
- ❑ **javascript:** Executes JavaScript code within the current document.
- ❑ **ftp:** Retrieves documents from an FTP (File Transfer Protocol) server.
- ❑ **file:** Loads a file stored on the local (Client) machine. It can refer to remote servers but specifies no particular access protocol to remote file systems.
- ❑ **news:** Used to access Usenet newsgroups for articles.
- ❑ **nntp:** More sophisticated access to news servers.
- ❑ **mailto:** Allows mail to be sent from the browser. It may call in assistance from a helper application.
- ❑ **telnet:** Opens an interactive session with the server.
- ❑ **gopher:** A precursor to the World Wide Web.

This book exclusively makes use of the first two of these.

HTTP Basics

Each HTTP client (web browser) request and server response has three parts: the request or response line, a header section, and the entity body.

Client Request

The client initiates a web page transaction – client page request and server page response – as follows:

The client connects to an HTTP-based server at a designated port (by default, 80) and sends a request by specifying an HTTP command called a **method**, followed by a document address, and an HTTP version number. The format of the request line is:

```
Method          Request-URI     Protocol
```

For example:

```
GET    /index.html    HTTP/1.0
```

uses the GET method to request the document /index.html using version 1.0 of the protocol. We'll come to a full list of HTTP Request Methods later.

Next, the client sends optional header information to the server about its configuration and the document formats it will accept. All header information is sent line by line, each with a header name and value in the form:

```
Keyword: Value
```

For example:

```
User-Agent:    Lynx/2.4 libwww/5.1k
Accept:        image/gif, image/x-xbitmap, image/jpeg, */*
```

The request line and the subsequent header lines are all terminated by a carriage return/linefeed (`\r\n`) sequence. The client sends a blank line to end the headers.

Finally, after sending the request and headers the client may send additional data. This data is mostly used with the `POST` method. This additional information is called a **request entity**. Finally a blank line (`\r\n\r\n`) terminates the request. A complete request might look like the following:

```
GET /index.html HTTP/1.0
Accept: */*
Connection: Keep-Alive
Host: www.w3.org
User-Agent: Generic
```

HTTP Request Methods

HTTP request methods should not be confused with URL protocols. The former are used to instruct a web server how to handle the incoming request, while the latter define how client and server talk to each other. In version 1.1 of the HTTP protocol there are seven basic HTTP request methods:

Method	Description
OPTIONS	Used to query a server about the capabilities it provides. Queries can be general or specific to a particular resource.
GET	Asks that the server return the body of the document identified in the Request-URI.
HEAD	Responds similarly to a GET, except that no content body is ever returned. It is a way of checking whether a document has been updated since the last request.
POST	This is used to transfer a block of data to the server in the content body of the request.
PUT	This is the complement of a GET request and stores the content body at the location specified by the Request-URI. It is similar to uploading a file with FTP.
DELETE	Provides a way to delete a document from the server. The document to be deleted is indicated in the Request-URI.
TRACE	This is used to track the path of a request through firewalls and multiple proxy servers. It is useful for debugging complex network problems and is similar to the traceroute tool.

Server Response

The HTTP response also contains three parts.

Firstly, the server replies with the status line containing three fields: the HTTP version, status code, and description of status code in the following format:

```
Protocol    Status-code    Description
```

For example, the status line:

```
HTTP/1.0    200    OK
```

indicates that the server uses version 1.0 of the HTTP in its response. A status code of 200 means that the client request was successful.

After the response line, the server sends header information to the client about itself and the requested document. All header information is sent line by line, each with a header name and value in the form:

```
Keyword: Value
```

For example:

```
HTTP/1.1 200 OK
Date: Wed, 19 May 1999 18:20:56 GMT
Server: Apache/1.3.6 (Unix) PHP/3.0.7
Last-Modified: Mon, 17 May 1999 15:46:21 GMT
ETag: "2da0dc-2870-374039cd"
Accept-Ranges: bytes
Content-Length: 10352
Connection: close
Content-Type: text/html; charset=iso-8859-1
```

The response line and the subsequent header lines are all terminated by a carriage return/linefeed ($\r\n$) sequence. The server sends a blank line to end the headers. Again, we'll return to the exact meaning of these HTTP headers.

If the client's request is successful, the requested data is sent. This data may be a copy of a file, or the response from a CGI program. This result is called a **response entity**. If the client's request could not be fulfilled, additional data sent might be a human-readable explanation of why the server could not fulfil the request. The properties (type and length) of this data are sent in the headers. Finally, a blank line ($\r\n\r\n$) terminates the response. A complete response might look like the following:

```
HTTP/1.1 200 OK
Date: Wed, 19 May 1999 18:20:56 GMT
Server: Apache/1.3.6 (Unix) PHP/3.0.7
Last-Modified: Mon, 17 May 1999 15:46:21 GMT
ETag: "2da0dc-2870-374039cd"
Accept-Ranges: bytes
Content-Length: 10352
Connection: close
```

```
Content-Type: text/html; charset=iso-8859-1

<!DOCTYPE HTML PUBLIC "-//W3C//DTD HTML 4.0 Transitional//EN"
"http://www.w3.org/TR/REC-html40/loose.dtd">
<html>

   ...

</html>
```

In HTTP/1.0, after the server has finished sending the response, it disconnects from the client and the transaction is over unless the client sends a `Connection: KeepAlive` header. In HTTP/1.1 however, the connection is maintained so that the client can make additional requests, unless the client sends an explicit `Connection: Close` header. Since many HTML documents embed other documents as inline images, applets, and frames, for example, this persistent connection feature of HTTP/1.1 protocol will save the overhead of the client having to repeatedly connect to the same server just to retrieve a single page.

Status Codes

The HTTP server reply status line contains three fields: HTTP version, status code, and description in the following format. Status is given with a three-digit server response code. Status codes are grouped as follows:

Code Range	Meaning
100-199	Informational
200-299	Client request successful
300-399	Client request redirected, further action necessary
400-499	Client request incomplete
500-599	Server errors

Informational (1XX)

This class of status code consists only of the status line and optional headers, terminated by an empty line. HTTP/1.0 did not define any 1XX status codes.

100 Continue

The client should continue with its request. This is an interim response that is used to inform the client that the initial part of the request has been received and has not yet been rejected by the server. The client should send the rest of the request or ignore this response if the request has already completed. The server sends a final response when the request is fully completed.

101 Switching Protocols

The server understands the client's request for a change in the application protocol being used on this connection, and is willing to comply with it.

Client Request Successful (2XX)

These status codes indicate that the client's request was successfully received, understood, and accepted.

200 OK

The request has succeeded. The server's response contains the requested data.

201 Created

The request has been carried out and a new resource has been created. The URI(s) returned in the entity of the response can be used to reference the newly created resource.

202 Accepted

The request has been accepted but not yet fully processed. The request may or may not eventually be acted upon, since it might be disallowed when the processing actually takes place.

203 Non-Authoritative Information

The returned information in the entity-header is not the definitive set coming from the origin server, but instead comes from a local or a third-party copy.

204 No Content

The server has carried out the request but does not need to return an entity-body. Browsers should not update their document view upon receiving this response. This is useful code for an image-map handler to return when the user clicks on the useless or blank areas of the image.

205 Reset Content

The browser should clear the form that caused the request to be sent. This response is intended to allow the user to input actions via a form, followed by the form being cleared so the user can input further actions.

206 Partial Content

The server has carried out a partial GET request for the resource. This is used in response to a request specifying a Range header. The server must specify the range included in the response with the Content-Range header.

Redirection (3XX)

These codes indicate that the user agent needs to take further actions for the request to be successfully carried out.

300 Multiple Choices

The requested URI corresponds to any one of a set of representations; for example, the URI could refer to a document that has been translated into many languages. Agent-driven negotiation information is provided to the user agent so that the preferred representation can be selected and the user agent's request redirected to that location.

301 Moved Permanently

The requested resource has been assigned a new permanent URI, and any future references to this resource should use one of the returned URIs in the Location header.

302 Found

The requested resource resides temporarily under a different URI. The Location header points to the new location. The client should use the new URI to resolve the request but the old URI should be used for future requests, since the redirection may not be permanent.

303 See Other

The response to the request can be found at a different URI that is specified in the Location header, and should be retrieved using a GET method on that resource.

304 Not Modified

The client has performed a conditional GET request using If-Modified-Since header, but the document has not been modified. The entity body is not sent and the client should use its local copy.

305 Use Proxy

The requested resource must be accessed through a proxy whose URI is given in the Location field.

Client Request Incomplete (4xx)

The 4xx class of status code is intended for cases where the client seems to have made an error.

400 Bad Request

The request could not be understood by the server due to badly formed syntax.

401 Unauthorized

The result code is given along with the WWW-Authenticate header to indicate that the request lacked proper authorization, and the client should supply proper authentication when the requesting the same URI again.

402 Payment Required

This code is reserved for future use.

403 Forbidden

The server understood the request, but is refusing to fulfill it. The request should not be repeated.

404 Not Found

The server has not found anything matching the Request-URI. If the server knows that this condition is permanent then code 410 (Gone) should be used instead.

405 Method Not Allowed

The method specified in the Request-Line is not allowed for the resource identified by the Request-URI.

406 Not Acceptable

The resource identified by the request can only generate response entities which have content characteristics incompatible with the accept headers sent in the request.

407 Proxy Authentication Required

This code indicates that the client must first authenticate itself with the proxy, using the Proxy-Authenticate header.

408 Request Timeout

The client did not produce a request within the time that the server was prepared to wait.

409 Conflict

The request could not be completed because of a conflict with the current state of the resource.

410 Gone

The requested resource is no longer available at the server and no forwarding address is known.

411 Length Required

The server is refusing to accept the request without a defined Content-Length from the client.

412 Precondition Failed

The precondition given in one or more of the IF request-header fields evaluated to false when it was tested on the server.

413 Request Entity Too Large

The request entity is larger than the server is willing or able to process.

414 Request-URI Too Long

The Request-URI is longer than the server is willing to interpret.

415 Unsupported Media Type

The entity body of the request is in a format not supported.

Server Error (5xx)

These response status codes indicate cases in which the server is aware that it has made an error or cannot perform the request.

500 Internal Server Error

The server encountered an unexpected condition, which prevented it from fulfilling the request.

501 Not Implemented

The server does not support the functionality required to fulfill the request.

502 Bad Gateway

The server, while acting as a gateway or a proxy, received an invalid response from the upstream server it accessed while trying to carry out the request.

503 Service Unavailable

The server is unable to handle the request at the present time due to a temporary overloading or maintenance of the server.

504 Gateway Timeout

The server, while acting as a gateway or proxy, did not receive a response from the upstream server within the time it was prepared to wait.

505 HTTP Version Not Supported

The server does not (or refuses to) support the HTTP protocol version that was used in the request message.

HTTP Headers

HTTP headers are used to transfer information between the client and server. There are four categories of header:

Header Type	Meaning
General	Information that is not related to the client, server or HTTP protocol
Request	Preferred document formats and server parameters
Response	Information about the server
Entity	Information on the data that is being sent between the client and server

General and Entity headers are same for both client and servers. All headers follow the `Name: value` format. Header names are case insensitive. In HTTP/1.1, the value of headers can extend over multiple lines by preceding each extra line with at least one space or tab. All headers are terminated by a carriage-return newline sequence (`\r\n`).

General Headers

These header fields have general applicability for both request and response messages, but do not apply to the entity being transferred. These header fields apply only to the message being transmitted.

Cache-Control: Directives

Caching directives are specified in a comma-separated list. They fall into 2 categories, **request-based** and **response-based**. The following tables list the allowed directives.

Request directives

Directive	Meaning
no-cache	Do not cache the information.
no-store	Remove the information from volatile storage as soon as possible after forwarding it.
Max-age = seconds	The client is willing to accept a response whose age is no greater than the specified time in seconds.
Max-stale [= seconds]	If Max-stale is assigned a value, then the client is willing to accept a response that has exceeded its expiration time by no more than the specified number of seconds. The client will accept a stale response of any age if no value is assigned.
Min-fresh = seconds	Indicates that the client is willing to accept a response that will still be fresh for the specified time in seconds.
only-if-cached	This directive is used if a client wants a cache to return only those responses that it currently has stored, and not to reload or revalidate with the origin server.

Response directives

Directive	Meaning
No-transform	Caches that convert data to different formats to save space or reduce traffic should not do so if they see this directive.
cache-extension	Cache extension tokens are interpreted by individual applications and ignored by the applications that don't understand them.
Public	Indicates that the response may be cached by any cache.
Private	Indicates that all or part of the response message is intended for a single user and must not be cached by a shared cache.
must-revalidate	A cache must not use an entry after it becomes stale to respond to a subsequent request, without first revalidating it with the origin server.
proxy-revalidate	The proxy-revalidate directive has the same meaning as the must-revalidate directive, except for private client caches.
Max-age = seconds	This directive may be used by an origin server to specify the expiry time of an entity.

Connection: options

The header allows the sender to specify options that are to be used for a particular connection and must not be communicated by proxies over further connections. HTTP/1.1 defines the close connection option to allow the sender to signal that the connection will be closed after the response has been completed.

Date: date-in-rfc1123-format

Represents the date and time at which the message was originated. The field value is sent in RFC 1123-date format. An example is:

```
Date: Sat, 16 Oct 1999 19:24:31 GMT
```

Pragma: no-cache

When a request message contains the Pragma: no-cache directive, an application should forward the request to the origin server even if it has a cached copy of what is being requested.

Trailer: header-fields

This header indicates that the given set of header fields is present in the trailer of a message encoded with chunked transfer-coding.

Transfer-Encoding: encoding-type

Transfer-coding values are used to indicate an encoding transformation that has been, can be, or may need to be applied to an entity-body in order to ensure 'safe transport' through the network.

Upgrade: protocol/version

This header allows the client to specify to the server what additional communication protocols it supports and would like to use. If the server finds it appropriate to switch protocols, it will use this header within a 101 (Switching Protocols) response.

Via: protocol receiver-by-host [comment]

This header must be used by gateways and proxies to indicate the intermediate protocols and recipients between both the user agent and the server on requests, and the origin server and the client on responses.

Warning: warn-code warn-agent warn-text

This header carries extra information about the status or transformation of a message that might not be present in the message.

Request Headers

These header fields allow the client to pass additional information about the request, and about the client itself, to the server.

Accept: type/subtype [; q=value]

This header specifies which media types are acceptable for the response. Accept headers can be used to indicate that the request is limited to a small set of specific types, as in the case of a request for an in-line image. The q=value parameter ranges from 0 to 1 (with 1 being the default) and is used to indicate a relative preference for that type. For example:

```
Accept: text/plain; q=0.5, text/html; q=0.8
```

Accept-Charset: charset [; q=value]

This header is used to indicate which character sets are acceptable for the response. The q=value parameter represents the user's preference for that particular character set.

Accept-Encoding: encoding-types [; q=value]

This header restricts the content-codings that are acceptable in the response. The q=value parameter allows the user to express a preference for a particular type of encoding.

Accept-Language: language [; q=value]

This header restricts the set of natural languages that are preferred as a response to the request. Each language may be given an associated preference with the q=value parameter.

Authorization: credentials

This provides the client's authorization to access the URI. When a requested URI requires authorization, the server responds with a WWW-Authenticate header describing the type of authorization required. The client then repeats the request with proper authorization information.

Expect: 100-continue | expectation

This header indicates that particular server behaviors are required by the client. A server that cannot understand or comply with any of the expectation values in the Expect field of a request will respond with an appropriate error status.

From: email

This header contains an Internet e-mail address for the human controlling the requesting user agent.

Host: host [:port]

This header specifies the Internet host and port number of the resource being requested.

If-Match:

A client that has previously obtained one or more entities from the resource can include a list of their associated entity tags in this header field to verify that one of those entities is current.

If-Modified-Since: date-in-rfc1123-format

This header specifies that the URI data should be sent only if it has been modified since the date given.

If-None-Match: entity-tags

This header is similar to the If-Match header, but is used to verify that none of those entities previously obtained by the client is current.

If-Range: entity-tag | date

If a client has a partial copy of an entity in its cache, it can use this header to retrieve the rest of the entity if it is unmodified, or the whole entity if it has changed.

If-Unmodified-Since: date-in-rfc1123-format

This specifies that the URI data should only be sent if it has not been modified since the given date.

Max-Forwards: number

This header limits the number of proxies and gateways that can forward the request.

Proxy-Authorization: credentials

The Proxy-Authorization request-header field allows the client to identify itself (or its user) to a proxy that requires authentication.

Range: bytes=n-m

Using this header with a conditional or unconditional GET allows the retrieval of one or more sub-ranges of an entity, rather than the entire entity.

Referer: url

The `Referer` request-header field allows the client to specify the URI of the resource from which the Request-URI was obtained.

TE: transfer-encoding [; q = val]

The `TE` request-header field indicates which extension transfer-codings the client is willing to accept in the response. If the keyword 'trailers' is present then the client is willing to accept trailer fields in a chunked transfer-coding.

User-Agent: product | comment

This header contains information about the user agent originating the request. This allows the server to automatically recognize user agents and tailor its responses to avoid particular user agent limitations.

Response Headers

The response-header fields allow the server to pass additional information about the response that cannot be placed in the status line. These header fields give information about the server and about further access to the resource identified by the Request-URI.

Accept-Ranges: range-unit | none

This header allows the server to indicate its acceptance of range requests for a resource.

Age: seconds

This header contains the sender's estimate of the amount of time since the response was generated at the origin server.

Etag: entity-tag

This header provides the current value of the requested entity tag.

Location: URI

This is used to redirect the recipient to a location other than the Request-URI to complete the request.

Proxy-Authenticate: scheme realm

This header indicates the authentication scheme and parameters applicable to the proxy for this Request-URI.

Retry-After: date | seconds

This is used by the server to indicate how long the service is expected to be unavailable to the requesting client.

Server string

The `Server` header contains information about the software that the origin server used to handle the request.

Vary: * | headers

This header specifies that the entity has multiple sources and may therefore vary according to specified list of request headers. Multiple headers can be listed separated by commas. An asterisk means another factor other than the request headers may affect the response that is returned.

WWW-Authenticate: scheme realm

This header is used with the 401 response code to indicate to the client that the requested URI needs authentication. The value specifies the authorization scheme and the realm of authority required from the client.

Entity Headers

Entity-header fields define meta-information about the entity-body or, if no body is present, about the resource identified by the request.

Allow: methods

This header is used to inform the recipient of valid methods associated with the resource.

Content-Encoding: encoding

This header indicates what additional content coding has been applied to the entity-body, and hence what decoding must be carried out in order to obtain the media-type referenced by the Content-Type header field.

Content-Language: languages

The `Content-Language` header describes the natural language(s) of the intended audience for the enclosed entity.

Content-Length: n

This header indicates the size of the entity-body. Due to the dynamic nature of some requests, the content-length is sometimes unknown and this header is omitted.

Content-Location: uri

The `Content-Location` header supplies the resource location for the entity enclosed in the message when that entity may be accessed from a different location to the requested resource's URI.

Content-MD5: digest

This header contains an MD5 digest of the entity-body that is used to provide an end-to-end message integrity check (MIC) of the entity-body. See RFC 1864 for more details.

Content-Range: bytes n-m/length

The `Content-Range` header is sent with a partial entity-body to specify where in the full entity-body the partial body should come from.

Content-Type: type/subtype

This header describes the media type of the entity-body sent to the recipient. In the case of the HEAD method, it describes the media type that would have been sent had the request been a GET.

Expires: RFC-1123-date

The `Expires` header gives the date and time after which the response is considered stale.

Last-Modified: RFC-1123-date

This header indicates the date and time at which the origin server believes the variant was last modified.

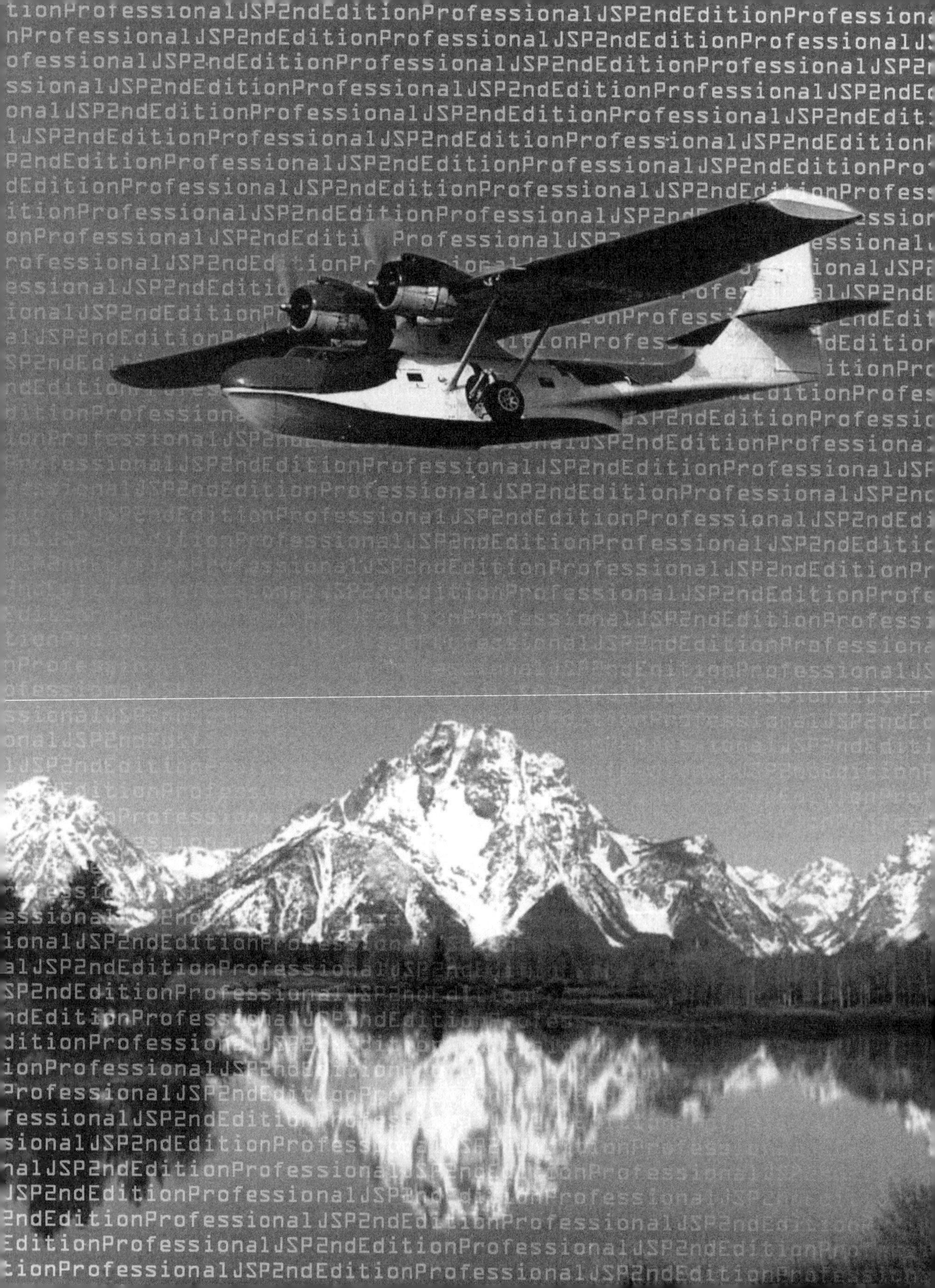
ProfessionalJSP2ndEdition

JSP for ASP Developers

If you're an Active Server Page (ASP) developer and you're unfamiliar with JSP and the Java language then you have may have looked at some of the chapters in this book and thought the examples that you have been faced with were pretty complex. You would have been right; Java is a complex language with vast potential for error but it can be extremely beneficial if you're prepared to look at a new language with open eyes. For an ASP developer, JSP is an excellent way to get into the Java language as it's very familiar territory.

This appendix is aimed at demonstrating some of the real similarities and very confusing differences between the ASP (Microsoft VBScript based) language and the JSP (Java based) language. We will concentrate on MS VBScript here, but if you're already very familiar with JScript then the transition to JSP should be relatively straightforward for you, with some hurdles obviously, but none so high as to hit your chin on.

This appendix will not turn you into the ultimate ASP/JSP developer and it's not designed to; it is important to realize that the rest of the book is key in understanding the concepts behind JSP and Java. What this chapter will do is show some of the pitfalls, differences, and advantages in trying out JSP when your experience is firmly bound to ASP.

For an ASP developer unfamiliar with C syntax or JScript, the leap into Java and JSP from VBScript and ASP can be a daunting prospect. This causes some problems as the difference between VBScript and Java is quite substantial, when you add in scriptlets and beans on top of that it can become rather frustrating.

In this appendix, in order to help reduce the confusion, we'll be looking at the following things:

- ❏ Similarities and differences between ASP and JSP
- ❏ Using JavaBeans
- ❏ Tag libraries

❏ Different approaches to datatypes

❏ Databases

❏ Error handling

❏ Java COM Interoperability

❏ Java in .NET

Similarities and Differences

If we ignore the differences in the underlying language itself for a moment, it becomes clear that both ASP and JSP deliver a very similar type of functionality. They both reside on the server and are called via typical HTTP or even TCP/IP requests, they can both use a complex set of component objects and third party utilities, they both use tags to allow code to be manipulated to output HTML or XML (or indeed XHTML), they both have session tracking, and database interaction, and they both allow for the separation of presentation layers from business and data layers.

Although on first sight ASP and JSP carry many similarities, there are conversely some interesting misconceptions about ASP that are often driven by a complete misunderstanding of the ASP language by people adverse to it, and likewise by hardened ASP fans. ASP is based on ISAPI and uses COM components and DLLs that can be developed in any COM compliant language. The favorites are probably VB, C++, and Delphi, but they can also be developed in Java using the JDK if you know what to do with .java files to use them as COM objects.

In contrast, JSP uses JavaBeans at the component layer, based on Java as the component architecture. Both of them come with a plethora of development tools: Visual Café, Visual Studio, and a personal favorite of mine TextPad32. The biggest difference I see between the two is JSP's native handling of the Java API that makes it very extensible as a language in comparison to ASP, without having to become a COM developer.

JSP through Java and ASP via one of its native scripting languages (VBScript or JSCript) have come with many strengths and weaknesses but if you're an ASP developer, the language comes with a really strong reason not to change. Primarily it is a lot easier to learn and remain skilled in because it's a loosely defined language based on VBA and COM technology you're probably already familiar with.

Microsoft ASP (as opposed to Chilli ASP, http://www.chillisoft.com, which runs on many web servers) is also very tightly linked to the IIS server and most ASP developers need a really in depth understanding of IIS to make the best use of the technology. If you tie that to a high skill level in a COM language and the multitude of pre-supplied ASP native components (such as AdRotator) that JSP does not have then it becomes a very mature and very powerful integrated tool set. The Microsoft .NET platform takes this even further although its server side pre-defined component set is obviously very new.

There are still many reasons to look at the Java language and JSP in particular from an ASP coder's perspective; my favorite reason is the 'learn one language – implement anywhere approach'. The other is that Java is low level enough to handle threads very easily that can be very difficult from ASP alone. The key reason is that as a developer you should always consider the other side of the fence and looking at JSP when all you know is ASP is without a doubt the best way to approach learning Java.

A note to remember before you embark on any JSP programming, and one that often causes a lot of frustration: JSP, unlike VBScript, is case sensitive.

Common Ground

There are some common elements between the two languages that we need to go over to stop any confusion before we begin. Most of the things mentioned here would be familiar to an experienced ASP developer but they need to be covered for you to understand some of the subtle differences between JSP and ASP in these everyday elements and these include:

- ❏   Scripting elements
- ❏   Adding comments
- ❏   Includes
- ❏   The `response` object
- ❏   The `request` object
- ❏   The `session` object
- ❏   The `application` object

Before we can really do any of this, we need to consider getting an operational environment set up so that we can work our way through the samples provided in this appendix.

Setting up our JSP Engine

For the purpose of this appendix we will make use of the open source Tomcat server, which at the time of writing can be found at http://jakarta.apache.org/tomcat/index.html. I will assume that you have already set up your version of the JDK and it functions correctly, hence your CLASSPATH and JAVA_HOME environment variables are already pointing to the correct areas.

We'll be using Tomcat 3.2.1 for this appendix. There are specific reasons for choosing this version of Tomcat; the primary one of course is that it is free to use. While I would probably not recommend it for a commercial organization where traffic is massive, for determining whether you can make use of this technology from an ASP developer's perspective it's really excellent. The second main reason is that it can integrate quite seamlessly with Internet Information Server (4 and 5) to enable you to integrate a JSP solution alongside your existing ASP based environment via a single ISAPI DLL plug-in.

To install Tomcat into IIS you need a couple of component parts available from the Jakarta web site:

- ❏   Tomcat (3.2.1)
- ❏   `isapi_redirect.dll`

We are not going to use the latest Tomcat 4 version for this section although it is referenced in other sections of this book. There is a specific reason for this: at the time of writing, Tomcat 4 does not yet come with an ISAPI plug-in for IIS, which we will cover soon and is the main driver for this installation section.

You can download the latest (non beta/alpha) build from the following address, http://jakarta.apache.org/builds/jakarta-tomcat/release/v3.2.1/bin/jakarta-tomcat-3.2.1.zip.

Once you have the ZIP, simply unzip it to the root of your C drive. You can choose an alternative drive and path if you wish but you will have to change some of the settings referenced in the following sections. I would recommend that you rename the installation directory from `c:\jakarta-tomcat-3.2.1` to `c:\jakarta-tomcat` so you have less tweaking to do with some of the Tomcat files.

Following the installation there are some environment variables that you need to set:

- ❑ TOMCAT_HOME = C:\jakarta-tomcat

- ❑ CLASSPATH should include a reference to your TOMCAT_HOME\lib\servlet.jar file as shown below:

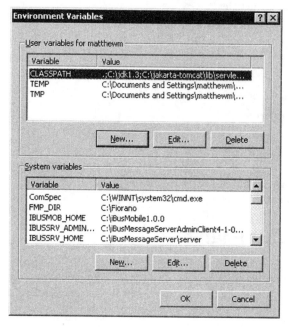

On NT 4 these can be added in Control Panel | System; on Windows 2000 these can be added in Control Panel | Advanced | Environment Variables.

Run Tomcat by using the C:\jakarta-tomcat\bin\startup.bat and shut it down using C:\jakarta-tomcat\bin\shutdown.bat. Tomcat by default will listen to Port 8080 for connection requests so you can test your installation by pointing a browser at http://localhost:8080, the result should resemble that shown in the following screenshot:

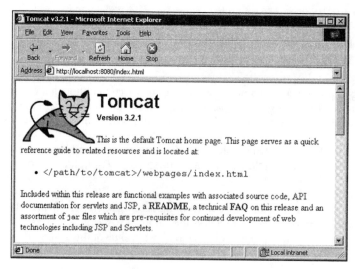

Now that you have an installed and working version of Tomcat you can happily run Servlets and JSPs on your Windows 2000 or NT4 Server. Incidentally, this installation also functions very well on workstations and other flavors of Windows.

Installing the ISAPI Redirector

Perhaps you noticed that you had to provide a specific port number to connect to Tomcat. This is where the ISAPI plug in fits into the build to enable you to request pages via the default port (80) used by Internet Information Server.

The ISAPI DLL is a Visual C++ version 6.0 DLL that hooks into IIS to perform redirection from the ASP engine to the JSP engine when a file handled by the JSP engine is requested. This means that you don't have to specify port numbers on the URL line to reach a separate port that your JSP/Servlet engine is listening to. In simple terms it works based on the file extensions of the page being requested and IIS simply passes the JSP request to Tomcat on your behalf, which is what the ISAPI filter does for ASP pages.

At the time of writing, the redirector can be downloaded from the following URL, http://jakarta.apache.org/builds/jakarta-tomcat/release/v3.2.1/bin/win32/i386/isapi_redirect.dll.

The DLL can be placed in any directory, but it is suggested that you use the `C:\inetpub\Scripts` directory.

Open the Microsoft Management Console for the IIS server and add a new virtual directory called `jakarta` that points to the directory where you stored the `isapi_redirect.dll`. This new directory must be assigned the Scripts and Executables permission under Execute Permissions. Most of this should be apparent when you look at the IIS setting in MMC and the IIS help files can explain these settings further.

Installing the redirector is easy. It does, however, involve manually adding some registry entries. The easiest way to add to the registry is via a registry file outlined below:

```
REGEDIT4

[HKEY_LOCAL_MACHINE\SOFTWARE\Apache Software Foundation\Jakarta Isapi
Redirector\1.0]
"extension_uri"="/jakarta/isapi_redirect.dll"
"log_file"="C:\\jakarta-tomcat\\logs\\iis_redirect.log"
"log_level"="debug"
"worker_file"="C:\\jakarta-tomcat\\conf\\workers.properties"
"worker_mount_file"="C:\\jakarta-tomcat\\conf\\uriworkermap.properties"
```

This file comes with Tomcat and can be found in the `\conf` directory. It is worth noting that it does not exist until you actually start Tomcat, so you need to start and stop Tomcat to create the file. It is called `iis_redirect.reg-auto` and you should rename it to `iis_redirect.reg`. Double click on it to add it to the registry and say yes to any prompts.

The registry file shown is making certain assumptions:

❑ Tomcat was installed into a directory called `jakarta-tomcat`. If you are using the `.reg` file generated by Tomcat you should not need to change this.

❑ A virtual directory in IIS was created called `jakarta`.

❑ The `uriworkermap.properties` file described in the `.reg` file has the correct version of the JDK that you are using listed, if not then change it using a text editor. You may need to change the `workermap.properties` file also.

You need to add a filter to your web server to allow IIS to pass any requests for JSPs via the default port to the correct Jakarta ISAPI plug in. You can add this to the master web server; the filter is then available for all virtual servers in the same machine:

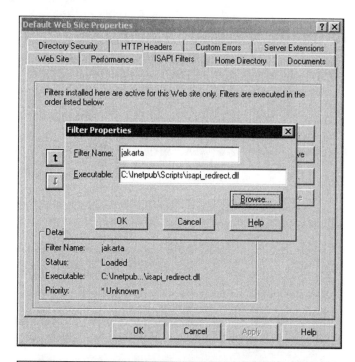

Once you have the registry set up and the filter in place in IIS, your machine requires the IIS Services to be restarted. Once your server has been restarted, your filter list should look something like the following screenshot, with the filter showing a green up arrow rather than red. If the filter does not show a green arrow, it is probably due to a spelling mistake in the registry entries. The best debugging approach is to re-evaluate the instructions above, paying particular attention for any spelling mistakes:

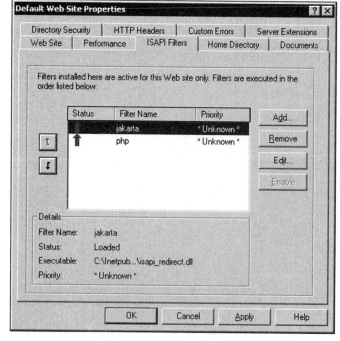

Start Tomcat as described above, open a browser and try the following URL,
http://localhost/examples/jsp/num/numguess.jsp.

The result should be something similar to the following:

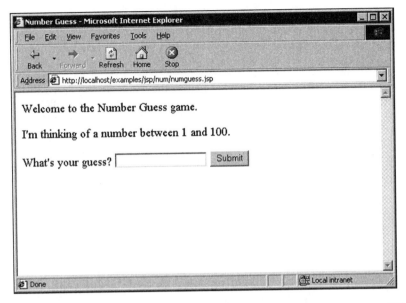

Now we have Tomcat configured and running with IIS, you have the choice to run your JSPs, your ASPs, and your HTML pages etc. through IIS. You need to bear in mind that you require Tomcat to be running for the redirector to work. Of course as the examples are designed to work with or without the IIS Redirector you can choose to follow them without going through IIS.

You can install Tomcat as a service if you choose to, and instructions for this at the time of writing can be found on the Tomcat site at the following URL,
http://jakarta.apache.org/cvsweb/index.cgi/~checkout~/jakarta-tomcat/src/doc/NT-Service-howto.html.

JSP Scripting Elements

You will probably want to add some dynamic content to your JSP files rather than simply serving up static HTML or JavaScript driven HTML pages and like ASP this is done through the use of Scripting Tags or scriptlets (defined below).

Like ASP tags, JSP tags are very flexible and provide the developer with the opportunity to encapsulate tasks that would be difficult or time-consuming to program. They are designed to save you time but you will probably still want to use scripting language fragments to supplement the JSP tags. All JSP scripting elements let you insert Java code into the Servlet that is generated from the current JSP the first time it is requested, or at each subsequent source code change.

The scripting languages that are available to you depend on the JSP engine you are using. With Sun's JSP reference implementation you must use the Java programming language for scripting. Although other vendors' JSP engines may include support for other scripting languages, such as JRun having support for JPython scripting, this is becoming increasingly rare as development teams adhere more stringently to a common syntax.

There are three basic types of scripting element that can be used to enable access to either the JSP underlying object model or to the Java language:

- ❑ Expression Scriptlets
- ❑ Code Scriptlets
- ❑ Declaration Scriptlets

Expression Scriptlets

A JSP expression is the same as a `response.write` using the VBScript `<% =Expression %>` shortcut syntax. This is evaluated at run-time and the result inserted into any output, be it HTML, WML, XML etc. It is used like the VBScript equivalent to insert Java values directly into the output and has the same form: `<%= Java Expression %>`.

The Java expression is evaluated, converted to a string, and inserted in the page. This evaluation is performed at run-time when the page is requested. For example, the following shows the date/time that the page was requested:

```
Current Date: <%= new java.util.Date() %>
```

Or in VBScript:

```
Current time: <%= Date() %>
```

To simplify the level of coding required there are a number of predefined script objects. These objects are discussed in more detail later, but for the purpose of expressions and understanding where they fit in relation to VBScript, the most important ones which you should recognize and need to be aware of are:

Object	Description
request	The HttpServletRequest
response	The HttpServletResponse
session	The HttpSession associated with the request (if any)
out	The PrintWriter used to send output to the client (the response.write command of the JSP world – covered later)

Here's an example of one of the objects that would typically be found in the `Request.ServerVariables("")` collection of VBScript:

```
Remote hostname: <%= request.getRemoteHost() %>
```

In JSP, it's just a property of the `request` object, which implies that you need to do some homework in identifying where the properties and methods normally available in specific ASP objects you're used to, can be found in JSP.

As new as it is, JSP goes a little further than ASP in looking to the future when dealing with scripts. With the rapid acceptance of XML, JSP has got a bit of a jump-start over VBScript in that XML authors can use an alternative syntax for their JSP expressions:

```
<jsp:expression>
Java Expression
</jsp:expression>
```

Remember that XML elements, unlike HTML ones, are case sensitive. I always prefer to use lowercase, you can choose to use either as long as you are consistent.

Code Scriptlets

As in VBScript, these are code sections that may exist between script tags:

```
<% some JSP or ASP code %>.
```

These are inserted into the HTML code and can be used as methods (or functions) or even to process the whole page. A good example in VBScript of when to use this type of scriptlet would be when we embed scripts or functions within an ASP page between HTML to provide some database data for a drop down list box. The same capability is available in JSP. In JSP, like ASP, scriptlets have the following form:

```
<html>
  <body>
    <% Java Code %>
  </body>
</html>
```

Scriptlets by default have access to the same automatically defined variables as expressions. If you wanted output to appear in the page above, you would use the out variable.

```
<html>
  <body>
    <%
      String strStringThing = "Hello ASP from JSP" ;
      out.println("A Message to ASP: " + strStringThing);
    %>
  </body>
</html>
```

Like ASP, the code inside a scriptlet gets inserted into the JSP page; raw HTML outside the scriplet start or end tag will be compiled to out.print commands when it compiles to a Servlet. ASP does not do this; the parser ignores information found outside the tags and simply returns the processed data as part of the response.stream.

As in the expressions tag, the XML equivalent is:

```
<jsp:scriptlet>
  String strStringThing = "Hello ASP from JSP" ;
  out.println("A Message to ASP: " + strStringThing);
</jsp:scriptlet>
```

Declaration Scriptlets

A declaration is the VBScript equivalent of `DIM` and has the following form `<%!  %>`:

```
<html>
  body>
    <%! int myVar = 0; %>
  </body>
</html>
```

Declarations do not generate any output and are normally used for scoping variables within JSP expressions or scriptlets, unlike VBScript declarations which are required for variables. It's also used to declare methods and could be described as being similar to using an include file in VBScript to get access to a set of common functions.

The XML equivalent is:

```
<jsp:declaration>
  int myVar = 0;
</jsp:declaration>
```

What's the Difference?

It's confusing that declarations, expressions, and scriptlets have a very similar syntax and can be used in a very similar fashion. If you are familiar with VBScript already, however, the relationship between these tags is less confusing.

Here are some examples of the differences and similarities.

Declarations

These contain one or more variable or method declarations that end or are separated by semicolons:

```
<%! String s = "A String"; %>
<%! int a, b; long c; %>
```

You must declare a variable or method in a JSP before you use it in the page. There are no on-the-fly declarations like in VBScript without `Option Explicit` set.

The scope of any declaration is usually the JSP file it is called in. If the JSP file includes other JSP files using the `<%@ include %>` directive (covered later) then the included files come within the scope of that declaration.

Expressions

These can contain any language expression that is valid in the scripting language of the Servlet engine you're using. Note the lack of a semicolon when using the `<%=` expression syntax which is a bit of an exception to Java as it normally demands a semicolon on the end of each line. If you use a semicolon here you will generate an internal Servlet compile error:

```
<%= a + b + c %>
<%= new java.util.Date()%>
```

Like ASP, expressions are evaluated from left-to-right and you can write any amount of code lines between an expression's start and end tags. Multi-line expressions require the semicolon and not adding it will generate an Internal Servlet compile error:

```
<%
String sString = "Fred";
out.print(sString);
%>
```

Comments

In Both ASP and JSP comments are processed before content is sent to the browser. Unlike ASP, JSP does not use the apostrophe-style comments supported by VBScript; you have to switch to the JScript equivalent of //.

Hence the ASP page:

```
<%
'This line is a comment.
'This line is also a comment.
Response.write "This line is not a comment"
'This line is also a comment.
%>
```

Would convert to this JSP page:

```
<%
//This line is a comment.
//This line is also a comment.
out.print("This line is not a comment");
//This line is also a comment.
%>
```

You can still use HTML comments to add remarks to an HTML page using the traditional HTML syntax:

```
<!--comment -->
```

As in ASP, comments outside the tags are returned to the browser and are visible if the user views the source HTML. Like ASP you still have to get the <% and %> tags located correctly to use HTML commenting:

```
<%
//This line is a comment.
//This line is also a comment.
%>
<!—html comment -->
```

```
<%
out.print("This line is not a comment");
//This line is also a comment.
%>
```

Java comes with a pretty good utility for converting comments in Java files to HTML help documents called Javadoc. Sadly, Javadoc doesn't work for JSP. That's not much of a loss really if you're thinking of switching languages: what you don't have already can't be that much of a loss. It's worth remembering Javadoc, though, for when you need to document the multitude of class files you're likely to write in the future.

The Include Directive

In ASP, the include directive is slightly different to the JSP equivalent. To include a file you would use the #include directive. For example, to insert a file named header.asp into an HTML page when it is requested, you would use the following directive in the ASP:

```
<!-- #include file="header.asp" -->
<%
' some other ASP code
%>
```

In this example, the file header.asp must be in the same directory as the including file. The HTML file that contains the #include directive must be a published file in your Web site.

Of course, contrary to popular belief,it's almost possible in ASP to perform dynamic includes using if statements:

```
<% if request.querystring("includechoice")="1" then %>
<!--#include file="1.asp"-->
<% else %>
<!--#include file="2.asp"-->
<% end if %>
```

Just like ASP, JSP has the include directive but there are two distinct versions:

One is with the <%@ include %> directive (same as the ASP #include), primarily for fixed includes like HTML footers and the like:

```
<html>
  <body>
    <%@include file="1.htm"%>
  </body>
</html>
```

The other is with the <jsp:include/> file directive, but this directive comes with some extra options and performs a *dynamic* JSP include, sending the request and response to the specified page and including its *output* in the response. The included page is specified with the page attribute. The flush attribute specifies whether or not to flush the output buffer, although since the JSP 1.1 specification you can't have a value of false, nor can you leave it out, which is a bit odd really as leaving it out causes a compile error. In JSP 1.2, a false value is allowed, and is in fact the default.

The following example demonstrates how to perform an include using the `<jsp:include/>` element rather than the `<%@ include %>` directive. It generates a random integer every time the page is accessed. If the number is odd, it loads `time.jsp` that ironically provides the system time; if the number is even, it loads `string.jsp`, which by no feat of real magic gives a string back.

The Include JSP

```
<%! java.util.Random random =
    new java.util.Random(System.currentTimeMillis()); %>
<% if (random.nextInt() % 2 != 0) { %>
<jsp:include page="Time.jsp" flush="true"/>
<% } else { %>
<jsp:include page="String.jsp" flush="true"/>
<% } %>
```

The Time JSP

```
<%@ page import="java.util.Date" %>
<%
  Date now= new Date();
  out.print(now.getHours() + ":" + now.getMinutes());
%>
```

The String JSP

```
<%= "Hmm...." %>
```

The Response Object

Any ASP developer with a bit of experience in the language will be familiar with the `response` object, and you would normally use it to control the information you send to a user. This includes sending information directly to the browser, redirecting the browser to another URL, or setting cookie values. It is very similar when you are looking at JSP. The language comes with everything you would normally use although obviously syntactically different and sometimes located either in a different place or called in a different way.

Let us assume for a moment that we are looking to do nothing more than set the content type of the page details returned to the browser following a page request.

When the web server typically returns a file to a browser, it tells the browser what type of content is contained in the response stream. This enables the browser to determine whether it can display the contents itself or invoke another application. For example, if the Web server returns a PDF, HTML, or a Word file, the browser must be able to start a copy of Adobe or Word to display the page or choose to display it only as HTML or text.

In ASP, you would use the `ContentType` property of the `response` object to set the HTTP content type string for the content you send to the browser:

```
<% Response.ContentType="text/html" %>
```

In JSP, however, we find the `ContentType` object in the `page` directive property:

```
<%@ page ContentType="text/html" %>
```

This really tells us nothing more than not to assume that we will find everything in JSP where it exists in ASP. Fortunately, Sun provide a small .pdf file called the Syntax card that is very useful in determining where some of these methods and properties can be found. At the time of writing the latest version can be found at: http://java.sun.com/products/jsp/pdf/card11a.pdf.

response.write

Probably the most noticeable difference occurs with the VBScript `response.write` method, which is probably the most utilized method in VBScript. The relationship to the `write` object in JSP is a bit obscure as it is a property of the `javax.servlet.servletResponse` object. This object is normally used for sending output from within a Servlet. This means that it is typically not used by JSP developers (remember that JSP compiles to a Servlet, and you could just write your server code directly into a Servlet).

Consequently what you really need to refer to in place of `response.write` is the `out.print()` method which belongs to the `out` object. It has a number of useful methods available: `clearBuffer()`, `flush()`, `getBufferSize()`, and `getRemaining()`, which all enhance its value.

For the ASP developer, the most useful of course is `print()`. Although very useful, `out.print()` isn't really equivalent to `response.write`, but is essential nonetheless. Consider this ASP code:

```
<%

Dim Str
Str = "Testing Out";

Response.write(Str & 1 & "<br>")
Response.write(Str & 2 & "<br>")
Response.write(Str + cstr(3) + "<br>")
Response.write(Str & cstr(4) + "<br>")

%>
```

Taking account of this, the above VBScript example would become the following JSP example. Also notice the difference between the way output is concatenated with VBScript allowing the mixed concatenation operator (assuming compatible types of course) and JSP retaining the C++ style + syntax:

```
<%

String str = "Testing Out";

out.print(str + 1 + "<br>");
out.print(str + 2 + "<br>");
out.print(str + 3 + "<br>");
out.print(str + 4 + "<br>");

%>
```

In relation to outputting text, it's also worth noting that the ASP 3.0 VBScript "With" block has no equivalent in JSP.

The Request Object

Form processing in JSP is pretty similar to handling the same type of data in ASP, and like ASP is very easy. In JSP there are four collections available in the request object:

- ❏ Cookies
- ❏ Form
- ❏ QueryString
- ❏ ServerVariables

The ClientCertificate collection is not available in JSP, as it is in ASP. I would suggest that you read up on the Java Authentication and Authorization Service (JAAS) for an understanding of Java security at http://java.sun.com/products/jaas.

To cover the request object, we will concentrate on the Form and QueryString collections. Let's work our way through a simple form processing example consisting of two pages; FormsProcessing.jsp that produces a HTML page with an input field and FaveWordResults.jsp that produces some output following a GET action.

The FormsProcessing JSP

```html
<html>
<head><title>JSP Interaction Explanation for ASP Coders</title></head>
  <body>
    <table border="0" width="500">
      <tr>
        <td width="120">   </td>
        <td width="500">
          <h1>Hello ASP coder. What's your favorite word?</h1>
        </td>
      </tr>
      <tr>
        <td width="120"   </td>
        <td width="500">
          <form method="get" action="FaveWordResults.jsp">
          <input type="text" name="faveWord" size="25">
          <br>
          <input type="submit" value="Submit">
          <input type="reset" value="Reset">
        </td>
      </tr>
          </form>
    </table>
  </body>
</html>
```

The FaveWordResults JSP

```html
<html>
<head>
<title>Feedback Results</title>
</head>
  <body>
```

```
    <h2>Hey, my favourite word is
    <%
    // Get form fields passed in from the form submission
    String word = request.getParameter("faveWord");
    out.println(word);
    %>
    too...how strange </h2>

  </body>
</html>
```

Saving and calling `Formsprocessing.jsp` provides a screen similar to that shown below:

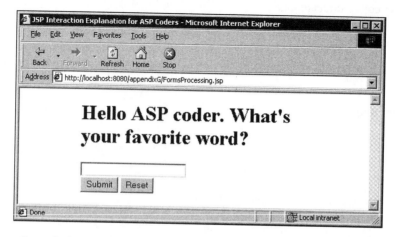

Less than complicated, the screen only requests a single input and, as the HTML code shows, sends the data to `FaveWordResults.jsp`. The results should be pretty similar to that shown in the following screenshot:

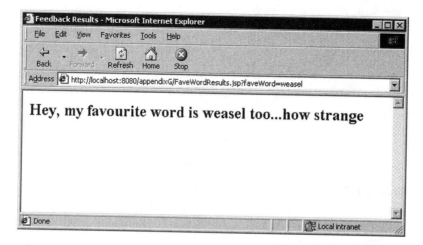

The excellent thing about handling data through the `request` object in JSP is that it doesn't matter whether the data is passed via GET or POST, the processing method is the same using the `getParameter()` method. Unlike ASP which utilizes two objects (`queryString` and `Form`), this allows the code to be written using a common syntax that can handle either POST or GET without worrying about whether your dealing with the `Forms` or `QueryString` collections.

There are some disadvantages to this, in that with only one collection to query from (as opposed to two in ASP) you cannot deal with both `queryString` data and form data submitted via a single post submission.

The JSP `request` object comes with a set of methods that coincide somewhat to the `request.servervariables` collection in ASP. A comprehensive list of ASP `servervariables` can be found at http://msdn.microsoft.com/library/psdk/iisref/vbob5vsj.htm at the time of writing. The JSP collection we will show here:

Collection Item	Method
Request Method	`request.getMethod()`
Request URI	`request.getRequestURI()`
Request Protocol	`request.getProtocol()`
Servlet path	`request.getServletPath()`
Path info	`request.getPathInfo()`
Path translated	`request.getPathTranslated()`
Query string	`request.getQueryString()`
Content length	`request.getContentLength()`
Content type	`request.getContentType()`
Server name	`request.getServerName()`
Server port	`request.getServerPort()`
Remote user	`request.getRemoteUser()`
Remote address	`request.getRemoteAddr()`
Remote host	`request.getRemoteHost()`
Authorization scheme	`request.getAuthType()`
The browser you are using is	`request.getHeader("User-Agent")`
	(Can return any header not just user agent)

Calling them is as simple as the following example:

```
<html>
  <body>
    The remote host is <%=request.getRemoteHost() %>
  </body>
</html>
```

Session and Application Object

The `session` object in ASP is one of the most useful and utilized objects available in creating state in an ASP application. It's safe to say it's pretty invaluable to ASP's capability for RAD. Traditional methods like hidden text fields in HTML forms have been superseded by the ability of ASP to maintain state in this simple but superb object. If you bear in mind what was discussed earlier about the use of loosely defined variables, the ability to simply stuff objects into the `session` object and maintain state is a very strong feature of ASP.

JSP has its own `session` object and it's relatively easy to use, even for someone not used to JSP. Like ASP, JSP has a number of implicit objects that don't need to be declared and `session` is one of them. Like ASP, the `session` object is useful for applications where several pages have to pass values between each other in order to make the application work. A shopping cart is an ideal example of a system where state is usually required.

I don't want to spend much more time on the `session` object, as it's pretty self-explanatory if you are already familiar with it in ASP. If you're not familiar with the ASP `session` object, at the time of writing an explanation can be found at, http://msdn.microsoft.com/library/psdk/iisref/vbob12d0.htm.

For the sake of clarity we'll go through a small example consisting of three pages. The first page (`Session1.jsp`) is a simple JSP consisting only of HTML that displays a form asking for a word. It will submit to `Session2.jsp` and set a session variable containing the word (a note of caution – don't forget to enable cookies in the browser).

The Session1 JSP

```
<html>
<title>
Session1.jsp
</title>
<body>
<form method=post action="Session2.jsp">
Give me a word?
<input type=text name="theWord">
<P>
<input type=submit value="SUBMIT">
</form>
</body>
</html>
```

This will result in something similar to this:

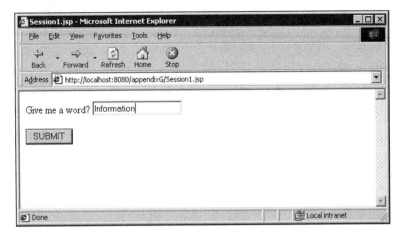

The second page (`Session2.jsp`) uses the `request` object we have already covered to set the session variable to the value of the `theWord` HTML input text field and place the value in the `session` object.

The Session2 JSP

```
<html>
<head>
<title>
Session2.jsp
</title>
</head>
<body>
<%! String word=""; %>
<%
word = request.getParameter("theWord");
session.putValue("theSessionWord", word);
%>

Storing Word <i> <%= word %> </i> to the session object
<p>

</body>
</html>
```

This gives the result:

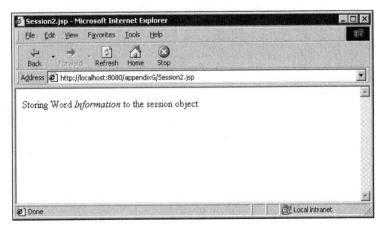

The third page is a JSP page that simply displays the session value. We won't even link to this, you can just call it.

The Session3 JSP

```
<html>
<head>
<title>
Session3.jsp
</title>
</head>
<body>
<%
String word = (String) session.getValue("theSessionWord");
%>
The Magic Word was <br><%= word %>
</body>
</html>
```

Now you will get:

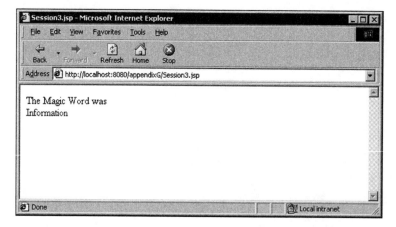

Items that are stored and retrieved from the `session` object are not allowed to be primitive data types (like `int` or `double`); rather they must be cast to their true object form (`Integer`, `Double`). If you have only ever used VBScript you might not know about primitive data types. A very good explanation of them at the time of writing can be found at
http://java.sun.com/docs/books/tutorial/java/nutsandbolts/datatypes.html.

So we have a `session` object, do we also have an `application` object? Well the answer is no, you need to step down another level to make use of the Servlet class.

Application Object

Like ASP, JSP files may need to maintain site-wide application values while each client uses and manipulates the same copy of these values. ASP uses the `application` object, which is similar to the `session` object but contains values available to all user sessions, and JSP uses something called the `ServletContext` object that can also contain values available to all sessions.

In order to get a better idea of how the `ServletContext` object is used, let's look at an example.

The Application1 JSP

```
<%! String Item= new String("MyString"); %>
<%! String appStr = new String(); %>


<%

//set the application value
getServletContext().setAttribute("appstrexample", Item);

// retrieve the application value
appStr = (String) getServletContext().getAttribute("appstrexample");
%>

The value of appStr = <%=appStr%>
```

Running the example should result in something similar to that shown in the following screenshot:

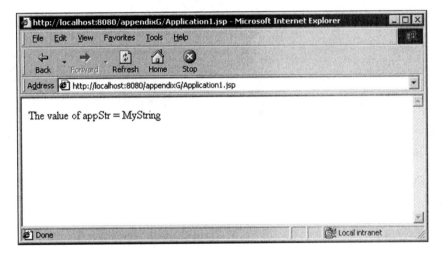

Applications variables are handled in a similar manner to sessions (that is, they use no primitive types). Add on the need to deal with the Servlet container and using the application layer can become quite difficult for inexperienced developers as you have to become very familiar with type casting, object handling and exception handling.

For a VBScript developer this can be very difficult given how easy it is to cast type between variant objects. My recommendation is to stick to strings until you're comfortable with casting objects to other types. We cover this to some degree a little later but until you have experimented a bit with the language the example below will show one way to work with `String` objects at the application layer in dealing with, retrieving and manipulating strings to represent other object types.

The Application2 JSP

```
<%! Integer IntItem= new Integer(33); %>
<%! String AppValueReturned; %>
<%! Integer AppToInteger; %>


<%
//set the application value
```

```
getServletContext().setAttribute("appIntexample", ""+ IntItem);

// retrieve the application value
AppValueReturned = (String) getServletContext().getAttribute("appIntexample");

// convert back to an Int
try {
AppToInteger = Integer.valueOf(AppValueReturned);
}
catch(NumberFormatException e){};

%>

The value of AppToInteger = <%= ""+ AppToInteger%><p>

Consequently, the value of application1.jsp's app variable is
<%= (String) getServletContext().getAttribute("appstrexample")%>
```

The output should be similar to that shown in the following screenshot:

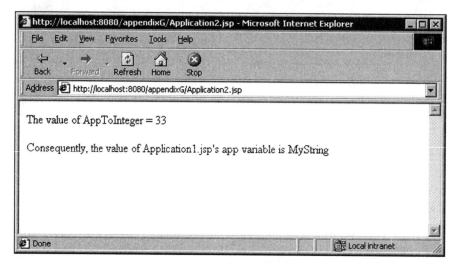

In this example, the following line of code from `Application1.jsp` makes the variable `Item` available as `appstrexample`:

```
getServletContext().setAttribute("appstrexample", Item);
```

This variable is retrieved through this line in `Application2.jsp`:

```
<%= (String) getServletContext().getAttribute("appstrexample")%>
```

This is where the similarity on common objects really ends, the common ground elements may be enough to get you started with JSP producing dynamic pages, but there is more to it than that.

One key thing that you really need to get to grips with subsequently, that is really likely to confuse you, is the use of JavaBeans.

Making Use of JavaBeans

If you're already familiar with developing components, in VB or C++ for instance, then you should have a reasonable understanding of ActiveX and COM. I tend to think of beans as a mix between a VB Class file and a VB ActiveX DLL. If you have used VBScript for a while you are likely to be familiar with COM components. You may have used a set of pre-provided components or even written your own.

For those unfamiliar with the concept of components, they are used to extend the power of your scripts by providing compact, reusable, and secure means of gaining access to things the ASP scripting language does not provide. Without realizing it, you're probably already using components in ASP. For example, the ADO Database Access component in ASP enables scripts access to databases. COM components are very powerful as you can call components from any script or programming language that supports Automation (COM components are Automation servers).

Java makes use of components in the form of beans and this includes both visible and invisible beans – the equivalent of ActiveX controls (typically visible) and ActiveX DLL's (typically invisible). It's a good choice for developing or assembling network-aware solutions for mixed hardware and operating system environments, although I feel it takes a lot of management; not all cross platform JSP/Servlet engines use the same versions of the JSP engine (1.1 or 1.2 etc.) so you need to keep on top of version control. In ASP you normally don't have to worry about this unless you update your scripting language with a new release from Microsoft.

In the ASP environment, it's not that common for developers to integrate Java and ASP unless you are a pretty advanced developer looking to do something a little out of the ordinary. If you are that troubled fellow then it is worth remembering that JavaBeans can actually integrate with ActiveX. Beans can talk to COM via a bridge into other component models such as ActiveX. Software components that use JavaBeans are therefore portable to COM compliant applications including Internet Explorer, Visual Basic, Microsoft Word, Lotus Notes, and others.

At the time of writing, a very good explanation of bridging to VB can be found at http://java.sun.com/products/plugin/1.2/docs/script.html but we are not going to concentrate on that here. We will cover the basics of a bean and help you get up to speed with adding a bean to your JSP examples.

JavaBean Example

As a simple example we will create a `CarCost` bean. It has two simple properties:

❑ Car

❑ Cost

Like a VB class, the properties of the bean are set and retrieved by property SET and property GET methods. The bean will allow you to set the cost for your dream car (if only) and could be used as the database extraction layer. In reality this is where you would add your business logic to feed back to your JSP page that would contain your presentation logic.

The CarCost Class

```
package com.wrox.projsp.appG.carbeans;

// this line (above) is really important, it defines the
```

```
  // directory that the bean exists in

public class CarCost {

  // our car cost bean
  String car;
  double cost;

  // set the car type
  public void setCar(String carName) {
    this.car = carName;
  }

  // get back the car type
  public String getCar() {
    return (this.car);
  }

  // set the car cost
  public void setCost(double carCost) {
    this.cost = carCost;
  }

  // get back the car cost
  public double getCost() {
    return (this.cost);
  }
}
```

To use our bean in a JSP we will use the `<jsp:useBean>` XML tag. When you request a bean in a JSP, the runtime engine searches for any existing beans already instantiated in scope. If none exists it instantiates a new bean based on the class name of the bean requested.

To deploy your bean, you need to put it somewhere that the JSP engine will look for beans. An ActiveX DLL relies on the registry to identify the DLL's location. Beans on the other hand reside where your particular Servlet settings dictate.

Since the bean is in the `com.wrox.projsp.appG.carbeans` package and is part of the `AppendixG` web application, we will put it in the `%TOMCAT_HOME%\webapps\AppendixG\WEB-INF\classes\com\wrox\projsp\appG\carbeans` directory.

Typically, the JSP that calls a bean doesn't live with the bean, as the engine expects them to be elsewhere. Normally this is configurable based on the JSP engine you use. I have created a directory called `\cartest` under the `C:\jakarta-tomcat\webapps\appendixG\jsp` directory to hold the JSPs that will demonstrate the bean working. Also, to confuse the issue slightly, unlike JSP, beans have to be compiled. I will assume that you have an appropriate JDK or JSDK and know how to compile a Java class file, so compile your bean source and place the class in the `carbeans` directory.

The CarTest JSP

```
<html>
<head>
<title>
Bean Test
```

```
    </title>
    </head>

    <body>

    <jsp:useBean id="carBean" scope="session"
                class="com.wrox.projsp.appG.carbeans.CarCost" />

    Setting the Car cost and the Car Type:<p>

    <% carBean.setCar("Ford");
       carBean.setCost(2000);
    %>
    Bean values have been set <p>

    Getting the Car cost and the Car Type:<p>
    State is: <%= carBean.getCar() %> <br>
    Rate is: <%= carBean.getCost() %>

    </body>
    </html>
```

Calling the JSP page will provide a result similar to that shown below:

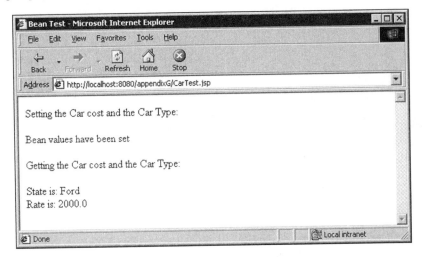

So how does it work?

Within the `<jsp:useBean>` tag there are several attributes. This is very much in line with VBScript where you instantiate most DLLs with a fixed `Server.CreateObject` method, as shown here:

```
    <%
    Set ID = Server.CreateObject("myTestObject.MyTestClass").
    %>
```

The bean options are pretty much the same as the ASP options for `createObject` in so far as the bean has an ID. For our `CarCost` bean the `id` attribute is set to `carBean` intuitively within the `<jsp:useBean>` tag:

```
<jsp:useBean id="carBean"
```

This part of the XML tag is used to identify the bean throughout the JSP page.

The `scope` attribute indicates how the bean remains in scope:

```
<jsp:useBean id="carBean" scope="session"
```

For ASP and JSP you could have assigned the object to the `session` object, the `application` object, or the `page` object. You don't need to explicitly add this to a session variable as you would with ASP; the Servlet engine knows to make this available to the session when it reads the `scope` tag.

VBScript example:

```
<%
Set Session("ID") = Server.CreateObject("myTestObject.MyTestClass")
%>
```

The `class` attribute indicates the class file representing the bean added onto the end of the package file. If you are not familiar with Java packages, it is nothing more than the directory name where the bean's class file lives:

```
<jsp:useBean id="carBean" scope="session"
             class="com.wrox.projsp.appG.carbeans.carCost" />
```

Notice that for the `<jsp:useBean>` tag we used the XML short notation of `/>` to close the tag instead of the usual `</jsp:useBean>`. You can of course change this if you wish. In ASP the class settings are covered by the registry entry in Windows with the `myTestObject.MyTestClass` covering the 'package' and the 'class' file which makes the object available via COM.

I would strongly recommend you take a look at the FAQ provided by Sun about beans as it covers a lot of information relevant to ActiveX developers looking at using beans. At the time of writing the URL is http://java.sun.com/products/javabeans/FAQ.html.

Tag Libraries

If you're comfortable with the concept of JavaBeans in relation to ActiveX and ASP, then you may be very interested to read about tag libraries, which one could argue were brought in to solve a historical problem. While JSPs are a great mechanism for delivering dynamic Web-based content, like ASP, they can suffer from the potential for excessive scripting. Too much functionality is bespoke, and often gets written as complex scripts with HTML, WML, or some other required type of output embedded deep within the script tags. This creates an unnecessary dependency on the page or layout designers to understand the code required for producing a specific output.

To try to alleviate the problem and allow developers to develop code and page designers to design pages, JSP has been extended with tag libraries. Like HTML, JSP has the concept of tags as its building block. Tags are already available to you as a JSP developer; an example would be the tags that actually imply a script block. While it is a sensible argument to say that this set of predefined tags are all that is required to build websites with dynamic content, you are likely to find yourself duplicating some functionality into your JSPs.

Tag libraries are a feature of JSP 1.1; a tag library is a collection of custom tags that permit a set of custom actions to occur. These custom actions enable you as a developer to build (or acquire) libraries of reusable JSP tags that can encapsulate common behavior.

Chapters 8 to 11 cover more details on tag libraries and creating your own custom tags.

Historically in ASP the common solution to this was either to produce a DLL of common functions, or to make use of an ever expanding include file containing a library of functions, or even worse a library of libraries. For some reason the concept of utility embedded script classes in ASP never really took off and it's quite understandable as they were a bit odd to work with. Microsoft re-approached the problem and tag libraries surface quite radically in the .NET framework in the guise of 'server-side custom controls'. If you are already familiar with the .NET controls, you will see that they look and act very much like tag libraries.

Tag Libraries vs. JavaBeans

Here is where some confusion with tag libraries begins to occur. The ability to remove the common functionality from one JSP and reuse it in other pages can sound very much like the concept of JavaBeans. However, defining a JavaBeans tag in your JSP code only provides the ability to bind to an instance of a bean and then get/set those instances' properties. JavaBeans do not remove the need for the page developer to embed the appropriate Java code inside a scriptlet to call methods on JavaBeans.

If we compare the two, server-side JavaBeans are non-visual components and relate very closely to ActiveX DLLs. They are ideal for holding data or manipulating data. Tags on the other hand can represent actions on a page and can generate dynamic output or control the page in some way. To understand this better, the current equivalent of a tag library in the COM world would be an ActiveX DLL bound to the ASP object model. This could interact directly with the `request` and `response` objects to produce output directly to the screen or output stream.

Like .NET controls and COM DLLs, a key difference between JavaBeans and tag libraries is that tags are much more aware of the environment in which they are running. That includes the page context (containing the request, response, etc.) and the Servlet context of the web application in which the tag is running. JSP custom tags can use those contexts to access the HTTP session information, and also to make use of JavaBeans that contain session and/or business state.

All custom tags implement the `javax.servlet.jsp.tagext.Tag` interface, and have the following basic properties:

- ❑ Can be passed attributes from the calling page.

- ❑ Have access to all the objects available to JSPs.

- ❑ Can modify the response generated by the calling page.

- ❑ Can communicate with each other. You can create and initialize a JavaBean component, create a variable that refers to that bean in one tag, and then use the bean in another tag.

- ❑ Can be nested within one another, allowing for complex interactions within a JSP.

So, how do I write a custom tag, I hear you ask? Well there is more to creating a custom tag than creating a JavaBean, and more to creating a simple custom tag than a simple DLL, and more to custom tags than .NET controls, but it's a refined technique that seems to work well once you get your head around it. There are lots of examples available to show you how to make a custom tag and consequently a tag library, and Chapters 8-11 cover them to some degree of depth.

As ASP (Pre .NET) has no real comparison to tag libraries, we will concentrate on getting you started on tag libraries from the perspective of the ASP.NET developer, re-working a .NET C# custom control into an equivalent Java custom tag for JSP.

We will begin with the actual dynamic page used to call the control, which is in fact an ASPX extension page, `SimpleControl.aspx`. The first two lines demonstrate the actual binding to the control via the appropriate namespace, and assigns a name to it for use within the page via a `TagPrefix.`:

```
<%@ Register TagPrefix="SimpleControlSamples"
             Namespace="SimpleControlSamples" %>
<html>
    <body>
        <form method="POST" action="SimpleControl.aspx" runat=server>
            <SimpleControlSamples:Simple id="MyControl" runat=server/>
        </form>
    </body>
</html>
```

We require a .NET custom control and we will use a very simple example called `SimpleControlSamples`, which most aspiring Java developers should easily understand. Here is the custom control that outputs a fixed string of HTML:

```
using System;
using System.Web;
using System.Web.UI;

namespace SimpleControlSamples {

    public class Simple : Control {

        protected override void Render(HtmlTextWriter output) {
            output.Write("<H2>Hello from a Simple TagLib!</H2>");
        }
    }
}
```

In the .NET world, to make this example functional the control requires a simple compilation, ensuring a reference exists during compilation to the `System.Web.dll` library file:

```
csc /t:library /out:SimpleControlSamples.dll /r:System.Web.dll
```

All you require to make this control active and available is for it to reside in the `\bin` directory of the web root in which the control will be available. The JSP custom tag equivalent requires a little more work to make it functional.

The ExampleTag Class

We will begin with the basic tag library code; we need to create a `%TOMCAT_HOME%\webapps\AppendixG\WEB-INF\classes\com\wrox\projsp\appG\tagpackage\tags` directory for the code:

Then create the following `ExampleTag.java` file in the `\tags` directory, and compile the file:

```
package com.wrox.projsp.appG.tagpackage.tags;

import javax.servlet.jsp.*;
import javax.servlet.jsp.tagext.*;
import java.io.*;

public class ExampleTag extends TagSupport {
  public int doStartTag() {
    try {
      JspWriter out = pageContext.getOut();
      out.print("Hello from a Simple TagLib!");
    } catch (IOException ioErr) {
      System.out.println("Error in ExampleTag: " + ioErr);
    }

    return (SKIP_BODY);
  }
}
```

As you can see, there is no more code required than for the .NET control but there are additional steps needed. Where the .NET control required compilation, the custom tag also requires describing to Tomcat, providing information that tells Tomcat how to reference the tag library. In Java this information is called a **Tag Library Descriptor** file (TLD), and is like providing the NT registry with information for a COM DLL in ASP.

The taglib TLD

The following descriptor file `taglib.tld` should be in the `appendixG\WEB-INF` directory:

```
<?xml version="1.0" encoding="ISO-8859-1" ?>
<!DOCTYPE taglib PUBLIC
        "-//Sun Microsystems, Inc.//DTD JSP Tag Library 1.1//EN"
        "http://java.sun.com/j2ee/dtds/web-jsptaglibrary_1_1.dtd">
<taglib>
  <tlibversion>1.0</tlibversion>
  <jspversion>1.1</jspversion>
  <shortname>SimpleControlSamples</shortname>
  <info>
    A Basic tag library
  </info>

  <tag>
    <name>simple</name>
    <tagclass> com.wrox.projsp.appG.tagpackage.tags.ExampleTag</tagclass>
    <info>Simple Tag example</info>
  </tag>
<!-- Other tags defined later... -->
</taglib>
```

The HelloWorld JSP

We also require a JSP to demonstrate the use of our custom tag, which we'll call `HelloWorld.jsp`, as shown below:

```
<!DOCTYPE HTML PUBLIC "-//W3C//DTD HTML 4.0 Transitional//EN">
<HTML>
<HEAD>
<%@ taglib uri="taglib.tld" prefix="SimpleControlSamples" %>
```

```
</HEAD>
<BODY>
Before the tag
<h1>
<SimpleControlSamples:simple />
</h1>
After the tag

</BODY>
</HTML>
```

Pointing your browser at the page should result in something very much like the following screenshot:

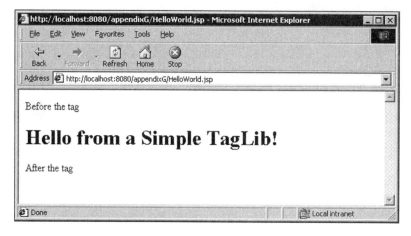

We do not go any deeper into tag libraries as they are covered in some detail earlier in the book, in Chapters 8 to 11. This section should at least demonstrate how similar they are to technologies you may already be familiar with like .NET controls.

The Different Approach to Datatypes

One of the things I love about VBScript is that it is a very lazy language when it comes to declaring data types. By lazy I mean it doesn't force or even expect specific declarations of variable types, in fact if you use VBScript, all variables in ASP are of type `Variant` and you don't even have to name them by default before assigning them. For those of you reading this appendix from a Java perspective, a `Variant` is a special kind of data type that can contain any type of data, depending on how it's used. Because `Variant` is the only data type in VBScript, it's also the data type returned by all functions in VBScript.

At its simplest, a `Variant` in VBScript can contain either numeric or string information. A `Variant` behaves as a number when you use it in a numeric context, and as a string when you use it in a string context (One, Two, Three, etc.). That is, if you're working with data that looks like numbers (1,2,3,etc.), VBScript assumes that it is numbers and does the thing that is most appropriate for numbers. Similarly, if you're working with data that can only be string data, VBScript treats it as string data. Of course, you can always make numbers behave as strings by enclosing them in quotation marks (`"use the string"`). This is naturally a very attractive but very unusual approach to handling data types and still allows the developer to cast a variant to its real type.

A `Variant` can also disseminate information about the specific nature of numeric information. For example, you can have numeric information that represents a date or a time. When used with other date or time data, the result is always expressed as a date or a time. Of course, you can also have a rich variety of numeric information ranging in size from boolean values to huge floating-point numbers.

These different categories of information that can be contained in a `Variant` are called **subtypes**. Most of the time, you can just put the kind of data you want in a `Variant`, and the `Variant` behaves in a way that is most appropriate for the data it contains and that includes arrays and objects which makes it extremely powerful but not as efficient as native datatypes. This is because the interpreter needs to check types before using them, for example to add two variants together the interpreter needs to convert them to integers.

The following table shows the subtypes of data that an ASP `Variant` can contain:

Subtype	Description
Empty	`Variant` is un-initialized. Value is 0 for numeric variables or a zero-length string (`" "`) for string variables.
Null	`Variant` intentionally contains no valid data.
Boolean	Contains either `True` or `False`, `1` or `0`.
Byte	Contains integer in the range 0 to 255.
Integer	Contains integer in the range -32,768 to 32,767.
Currency	-922,337,203,685,477.5808 to 922,337,203,685,477.5807.
Long	Contains integer in the range -2,147,483,648 to 2,147,483,647.
Single	Contains a single-precision, floating-point number in the range -3.402823E38 to -1.401298E-45 for negative values, 1.401298E-45 to 3.402823E38 for positive values.
Double	Contains a double-precision, floating-point number in the range 1.79769313486232E308 to −4.94065645841247E−324 for negative values; 4.94065645841247E−324 to 1.79769313486232E308 for positive values.
Date (Time)	Contains a number that represents a date between January 1, 100 to December 31, 9999.
String	Contains a variable-length string that can be up to approximately 2 billion characters in length.
Object	Contains an object.
Error	Contains an error number.

JSP on the other hand retains purity in its declaration and handling of datatypes. While very advantageous, purity sadly is not cheap and the cost comes in the form of a substantial development consideration for migrating VBScript developers in taking you back to a more traditional approach to data types.

The following table shows the Primitive datatypes that a JSP variable can contain. Notice that these are not subtypes as in the ASP table, nor are they a reference to an object like a string is in Java:

Keyword	Description	Size/Format
Byte	Byte-length integer	8-bit two's complement
Short	Short integer	16-bit two's complement
Int	Integer	32-bit two's complement
Long	Long integer	64-bit two's complement
Float	Single-precision floating point	32-bit IEEE 754
Double	Double-precision floating point	64-bit IEEE 754
Char	A single character	16-bit Unicode character
Boolean	A boolean value (true or false)	True or false

Hence the cost becomes apparent. All variables in the Java language must have a datatype declared for them before you (or the server) compile the code or an error will occur. This is similar to setting `Option Explicit` in VBScript to force declaration of the variables. The primary difference is the lack of subtypes in the Java language and of course the slight difference in how you declare the actual variable itself. There is a key advantage to being forced down this route: it is a very easy to debug and maintain code as it is easier to identify data types and track them through the code. It also increases performance.

The DataTypes JSP

Let's look at an example of what we can get from datatypes in JSP. The following code for `DataTypes.jsp` declares a number of different datatypes, populates them, and displays their values:

```
<html>
<body>

<%
  // the common variables
  byte largestByte = Byte.MAX_VALUE;
  short largestShort = Short.MAX_VALUE;
  int largestInteger = Integer.MAX_VALUE;
  long largestLong = Long.MAX_VALUE;

  // real numbers for handling interesting things like money
  float largestFloat = Float.MAX_VALUE;
  double largestDouble = Double.MAX_VALUE;

  // other primitive types
  char aChar = 'S';
  boolean aBoolean = true;


  // write some output - the equivalent of response.write("output")

  out.print("The largest byte value is " + largestByte+ "<br>");
  out.print("The largest short value is " + largestShort+ "<br>");
  out.print("The largest integer value is " + largestInteger+ "<br>");
  out.print("The largest long value is " + largestLong+ "<br>");
```

```
    out.print("The largest float value is " + largestFloat+ "<br>");
    out.print("The largest double value is " + largestDouble+ "<br>");

    if (Character.isUpperCase(aChar)) {
      out.print("The character " + aChar + " is upper case."+ "<br>");
    } else {
      out.print("The character " + aChar + " is lower case." + "<br>");
    }

    out.print("The value of aBoolean is " + aBoolean + "<br>");

%>


</body>
</html>
```

A variable's data type determines the values that the variable can contain and the operations that can be performed on it. In the above example, the following declares that `largestInteger` is an integer (`int`):

```
int largestInteger
```

In ASP, the equivalent declaration for an integer variable could contain anything from a `string` to an `int` or an `object`, and the compiler doesn't really care. It's actually very clever at working it out – but it does not encourage good development practice by not giving you the choice to use anything other than variant:

```
<%
Dim largestInteger
%>
```

Pointing your browser at `DataTypes.jsp` should produce something very similar to the following screenshot:

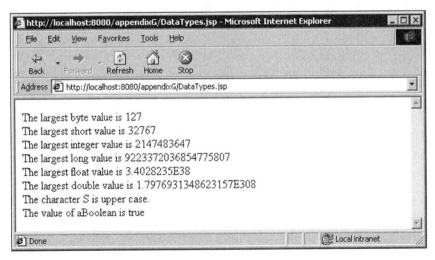

The largest byte value is 127
The largest short value is 32767
The largest integer value is 2147483647
The largest long value is 9223372036854775807
The largest float value is 3.4028235E38
The largest double value is 1.7976931348623157E308
The character S is upper case.
The value of aBoolean is true

Integers in JSP can contain only integral values that may be positive or negative. Just like ASP you can perform arithmetic operations, such as addition, on integer variables but only against other integers, hence strings in JSP can only be concatenated to other strings so you need to consider how to convert types from one to the other. In VBScript it is very easy as I'm sure you're familiar with the many functions provided for subtype conversion:

```
<%

Dim myStringValue
Dim myIntValue

MyStringValue = "25"
MyIntValue = 25

response.write CInt(MyStringValue) + myIntValue

%>
```

In JSP however, it is an entirely different thing but some methods are provided to help you out. I'll provide a few simple examples here to help you better understand the differences between how Java and VB Script handle conversions.

The TypeConvert JSP

The following example, `TypeConvert.jsp`, converts a `String` to an `int`, and back again:

```
<html>
<body>
<%

    // first we'll assign a value to a previously declared int
    int i = 50;
    // and then to a previously declared but Empty String
    String str = "";

    // then we can convert between the different types

    out.print("integer to String:<br>");
    str = Integer.toString(i);
    out.print(str + "<br>");

    out.print("String to integer:<br>");
    i = Integer.valueOf(str).intValue();
    out.print(i + "<br>");

    out.print("Another Approach for String to integer:<br>");
    i = Integer.parseInt(str);
    out.print(i + "<br>");

%>
</body>
</html>
```

The `String` class itself does not provide methods for conversion between a String to a floating point, integer, or other numerical type. However, the classes `Integer`, `Float`, `Double` and `Long` provide a class method named `ValueOf()` that converts a String to an object of that type. You can also use the method `Integer.parseInt()` from the `Integer` class as shown above.

The result if you were to run the example should look something like this:

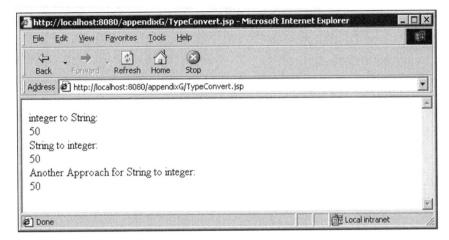

As a last point with regards to datatypes, the Java programming language, unlike ASP, has two major categories of data types: **primitive** and **reference**.

A variable of primitive type contains a single value of the correct size and format for its declared type: a number, character, or Boolean value. The value of an `int` is 32 bits of data, the value of a `char` is 16 bits of data formatted as a Unicode character, and so on.

In ASP, classes, arrays, and objects all exist as `Variants`, while an array, class, or interface in JSP is a reference type. The value of a reference type variable, in contrast to that of a primitive type, is a reference to the value or set of values represented by the variable. A reference is traditionally called a **pointer** and it relates to the to VB API "`addressOf`" operator to reference the value in memory, in C++ it would be a pointer but in JSP (unlike C++) we don't need to go that low level to get to its address. A reference type value is not the array or the object itself, but rather a way to reach it.

Databases

If you have been developing in ASP for a while, you have probably used the Microsoft Data Access Components (MDAC) in one form or another. For any ASP developer, ADO or OLEDB components provide a very easy-to-use, programmatic level of access to all types of data located anywhere. The latest version of MDAC in Windows 2000 is very advanced and, given how easy it is to use, could be considered one of the strongest features of ASP. MDAC has moved on to new heights with Windows 2000 and encompasses a new set of providers for accessing across multiple platforms and includes the ability to perform LDAP queries.

Future releases of MDAC will encourage the migration to a new cross platform access medium known as SOAP (the Simple Object Access Protocol). In case you're interested you can find in-depth information about SOAP at http://www.develop.com/soap.

SOAP combines HTTP and XML into a single solution to provide a whole new level of interoperability. For example, clients written in Microsoft Visual Basic can easily invoke CORBA services running on Linux boxes, web clients can invoke code running on archaic mainframes, and Macs can start invoking Perl objects running on Unix.

While some interoperability is achieved today through cross-platform bridges for specific technologies, if SOAP becomes a ratified standard, bridges will no longer be necessary. JSP (at the time of writing) does not use SOAP; it doesn't even use true ODBC which is grim if you're an ASP developer. If you are looking to utilize databases then you are typically going to do one of two things:

❑ Use a JDBC/ODBC bridge

❑ Or use a pure JDBC driver

We will concentrate on the JDBC/ODBC bridge here as Chapter 13 covers JDBC to an in-depth level and I don't think we need to cover this in any great detail. The other reason is that as an ASP developer you will probably already be familiar with ODBC.

We will start by looking at two simple examples, one for ASP and one for JSP. Both of them do nothing more than extract and display data from a very simple MS Access database called `countrydb.mdb` (available in the code download for this appendix). The database has one table called `countries` that has two fields in it, `ID` and `Name`. `ID` is an `AutoNumber` field, `name` is a `Text` field of length 50, and there are four records in the database containing four country names.

Here is the `Database.asp` file, which will display the names of the countries from the `name` field:

```
<%

set dbConnection = Server.CreateObject("ADODB.Connection")
cnStr = "Provider=Microsoft.Jet.OLEDB.3.51; Data Source=" &
server.mappath("countrydb.mdb")
dbConnection.Open cnStr

Set rs = dbConnection.Execute("Select * from countries")

    Do while not rs.eof
    response.write  rs.fields("name") & "<BR>"
    rs.movenext
     loop

rs.close
dbConnection.close

set rs = nothing
set dbConnection = nothing

%>
```

If you intend to try and run the ASP examples, you will naturally require an ASP configuration on your server that is capable of executing the code. As this appendix is aimed at existing ASP developers I am making a bit of an assumption that you may already have that. However, if you're a drop in Java developer looking to try the ASP examples alongside the JSP examples you may need a good reference; *Beginning Active Server Pages 3.0* ISBN 1861003382, and *Professional Active Server Pages 3.0*, ISBN 1861002610, both from Wrox Press are good places to look.

The Database JSP

Now, let's see the equivalent code for JSP (`Database.jsp`):

```
<%@ page import="java.util.*" %>
<%@ page import="java.awt.*" %>
<%@ page import="java.sql.*" %>

<%

String url = "jdbc:odbc:countrydb";
String user = "";
String password = "";

try {

  Class.forName("sun.jdbc.odbc.JdbcOdbcDriver");
  Connection con = DriverManager.getConnection(url, user, password);
  Statement stmt = con.createStatement();
  ResultSet rs = stmt.executeQuery("Select * from countries");

  while (rs.next()) {
    String result = rs.getString("name");
  %>
  <%= result %><BR>
  <%

  }
  rs.close();


} // end the try

catch (Exception e) {
  System.out.println(e);
} // end the catch


%>
```

Running either example produces very similar results:

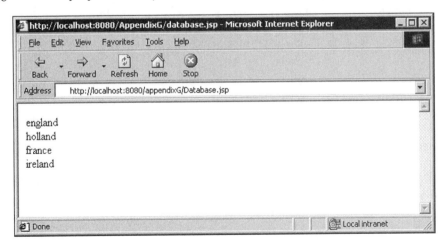

If we look at the two examples, apart from a modicum of different syntax they are pretty much the same thing. However, the biggest difference between them is that the ASP example uses a File DSN defined in the code lines:

```
cnStr = "Provider=Microsoft.Jet.OLEDB.3.51; Data Source=" &
server.mappath("countrydb.mdb")
```

In JSP you cannot use a file DSN to call an ODBC bridge because file DSNs are native to ADO under Windows; you have to configure a system DSN for the JDBC driver to successfully invoke the bridge to Access. For this example, the DSN is called countrydb and it needs to point to the Access database.

This can be identified by the different setting for the DSN in the JSP:

```
String url = "jdbc:odbc:countrydb";
```

The other major difference is the try and catch error trapping that is required for database access in JSP demonstrated below. This is a new feature to VBScript in ASP 3.0, but it is a bit of a fundamental element of Java and you should take note of it as you'll see it appear a lot in all Java code:

```
try {

// do the code

catch (Exception e) {
  System.out.println(e);
} // end the catch
```

Error handling is covered in more detail later in this appendix.

Extending the Example

The example with the country databases is hardly taxing; it is intended to demonstrate how easy it is to utilize the JDBC to ODBC bridging capabilities.

What we will do with the example is include it in a bean example that simply demonstrates adding a piece of JDBC/ODBC bridging code into a bean to separate the presentation from the data extraction. This is the same as moving your business logic into an ActiveX DLL to separate the presentation and business in ASP. As an extra step, we'll make use of some of the other things we have previously been through:

❑ request object

❑ out object

❑ type conversion

The DBCallingForm JSP

We will look at the example in the order we would use it. The first file we use is called DBCallingForm.jsp, although it is pure HTML. HTML would probably be faster (no initial compile) but it means you typically only need to work in one editor:

```
<html>
<head><title>
JSP Bean Business Logic Encapsulation Explanation for ASP Coders
</title></head>
<body>
  <table border="0" width="500">
    <tr>
      <td width="120">   </td>
      <td width="500">
        <h1>Which Country are you looking for?</h1>
      </td>
    </tr>
    <tr>
      <td width="120"   </td>
      <td width="500">
        <form method="get" action="DBBeanCall.jsp">
        <input type="text" name="dbIDNumber" size="25">
        <br><br>
        <input type="submit" value="Submit">
        <input type="reset" value="Reset">
      </td>
    </tr>
        </form>
  </table>
</body>
</html>
```

Running DBCallingForm.jsp gives us something akin to the following screenshot:

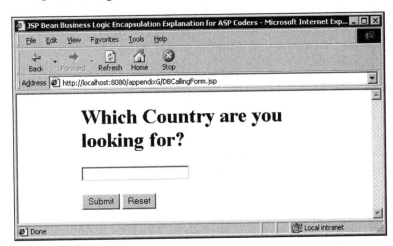

The DBBeanCall JSP

Next we have the form-processing page DBBeanCall.jsp that takes the input data, instantiates and interacts with the bean:

```
<html>
<head>
<title>
Integrated Database Bean Test
```

```
    </title>
    </head>

    <body>

    <jsp:useBean id="dbBeanID" scope="request"
                 class="com.wrox.projsp.appG.dbbeans.dbBeanClass" />

    <%
      String myID = request.getParameter("dbIDNumber");
    %>

    <h3>
    Getting the Country for Country ID Number <%=myID%>:<p>

    <%
      out.print(dbBeanID.getCountry(Integer.parseInt(myID)));
    %>
    </h3>

    </body>
    </html>
```

As you can see, we have included the dbIDNumber from the input page:

```
    <%
      String myID = request.getParameter("dbIDNumber");
    %>
```

We make specific use here of out.print and revisit the need for type conversion to call the getCountry() method of the bean while passing a value to of the bean using:

```
    <%
      out.print(dbBeanID.getCountry(Integer.parseInt(myID)));
    %>
```

The dbBeanClass Class

Finally, we need the bean that queries the database and gets us the information. Like the last bean example, we'll need to put this in a directory that mimics the package structure, and then compile it:

```
    package com.wrox.projsp.appG.dbbeans;

    // this line is really important, it defines the
    // directory that the bean exists in

    import java.util.*;
    import java.awt.*;
    import java.sql.*;

    public class dbBeanClass {

      // a var for holding values
      String country = "";
```

```
    // get back the country back
    public String getCountry(int countryNumber) {

        String url = "jdbc:odbc:countrydb";
        String user = "";
        String password = "";

        try {

            Class.forName("sun.jdbc.odbc.JdbcOdbcDriver");
            Connection con = DriverManager.getConnection(url, user, password);
            Statement stmt = con.createStatement();
            ResultSet rs =
                stmt.executeQuery("SELECT name FROM countries WHERE ID ="
                                  + countryNumber);

            while (rs.next()) {
                String result = rs.getString("name");
                country = result;
            }
            rs.close();

            if (country == "") {
                country = "No record Found for " + countryNumber;
            }


        }    // end the try

        catch (Exception e) {
            country = "There was an error " + e;
        }    // end the catch

        return (this.country);


    }

}
```

If we look at the code, the bean wrappers "`package com.wrox.projsp.appG.dbbeans`" and "`public class dbBeanClass`" are added to the JSP scriptlet `Database.jsp`. The code is also syntactically different as we are working in a Java class rather than JSP scriptlet. Notice the import statements:

```
import java.util.*;
import java.awt.*;
import java.sql.*;
```

These have changed from the earlier JSP scriptlet statements:

```
<%@ page import="java.util.*" %>
<%@ page import="java.awt.*" %>
<%@ page import="java.sql.*" %>
```

We are also making a different use of get and set methods; in fact we aren't even using set, and get has changed to take an input parameter of type integer, defined with:

```
public String getCountry(int countryNumber)
```

The code does still use the same DSN defined earlier, thus a call to getCountry() with an appropriate integer identifying the ID of a specific country will return a string containing the country name.

We have also changed the SQL statement to contain the countryNumber being passed from DBBeanCall.jsp:

```
ResultSet rs =
   stmt.executeQuery("SELECT name FROM countries WHERE ID ="
                      + countryNumber);
```

This is the same as you would do it in VBScript; you may however have chosen to use the & operator which is preferred in ASP.

We have also added a simple empty record check to inform the user if they ask for an ID that does not exist:

```
if (country == "") {
   country = "No record Found for " + countryNumber;
}
```

In addition to that error trap we also modified the try – catch block to be user friendly to some degree by changing the returned error message in case there is an error in the database query:

```
country = "There was an error " + e;
```

As you can see, there is not a lot of difference between the bean and the JSP scriptlet; the main difference is that you have separated the business logic from the presentation of the results. You could now change the bean as necessary without affecting how the results get presented to the end user.

The initialization parameters for the bean are self-explanatory and are covered in the earlier beans section. We have changed the scope of the bean for this example, as we don't want it to be so persistent. There is no specific reason for this except that we are passing it a value for a database call and showing a different scope choice in action. This would be a good opportunity for you to experiment with scope and see what differences you can create and see how it relates to the creation of database object scope in ASP.

Calling the JSP page, with a value for getCountry() of 2 for returns holland as the country that matches that ID (at least it does in my database as holland has the country number 2):

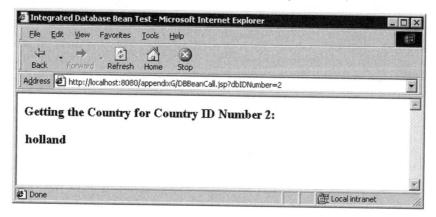

The last thing we included in this example and have not discussed at any length is exception or error handling.

Handling Errors in ASP and JSP

ASP VBScript and JSP don't look at errors in the same way. If a JSP or Java application is well written and something unexpected occurrs, the code will probably throw an exception and display a suitable error. When IIS encounters an error when it's running VBScript it will generate a 500;100 error.

After a 500;100 custom error is generated, IIS will create an instance of the ASPError or Err object which describes the error condition. Typically coders had to manipulate the error object with On Error Resume Next and it was a bit limiting. ASP 3.0 however comes with a try – catch type of exception handling similar to that in Java, but to use it you have to use JScript. The JScript try – catch statement provides a way to handle some or all of the possible errors that may occur in a given block of code, while still running code as shown below:

```
function NumberTryCatch(num) {
  try {
    if (num == 20) // Evalute argument.
      throw "number equals 20";
    else throw "number not 20";
  } catch(e) {
      return e;
  }
}

document.write(NumberTryCatch(17));
```

If errors occur that are not handled by the developer, JScript simply provides its normal ASPError object message to a user, as if there was no error handling. This is a very useful capability but it does mean that you have to switch between language handling in ASP.

Just like a JScript application in ASP, exceptions that occur while a JSP application is running are called **runtime exceptions**. Runtime exceptions are relatively easy to handle in a JSP application. You can use the exception object in a special type of JSP called an **error page**, where you display the exception's name and class, its stack trace, and a useful message. You use what is called the **directive tag** to add the isErrorPage="true" directive at the top of the JSP to declare it as the error handling page:

```
<%@ page isErrorPage="true" %>
```

By using the Java exception.getMessage() in the error page it's possible to display the appropriate message that was caught by the exception handler.

The Exception JSP

We will modify our database JSP scriptlet to trigger an un-handled runtime exception error in the database call by modifying the url String to create a badly named ODBC DSN name by removing the letter "b" from the end of countrydb and stripping out the try – catch elements of the scriptlet. We'll call this Exception.jsp, as presented below:

```
<%@ page errorPage="ErrorPage.jsp" %>
<%@ page import="java.util.*" %>
<%@ page import="java.awt.*" %>
<%@ page import="java.sql.*" %>


<%
```

```
String url = "jdbc:odbc:countryd";
String user = "";
String password = "";

  Class.forName("sun.jdbc.odbc.JdbcOdbcDriver");
  Connection con = DriverManager.getConnection(url, user, password);
  Statement stmt = con.createStatement();
  ResultSet rs =  stmt.executeQuery("Select * from countries");

  while (rs.next()) {
    String result = rs.getString("name");
    %>
    <%= result %><BR>
    <%

  }
  rs.close();

%>
```

The ErrorPage JSP

The `ErrorPage.jsp` file contains the following code:

```
<html>

<body>
  <%@ page isErrorPage="true" %>
  <h3> The exception <%= exception.getMessage() %>
  shows there was an error that was handled by ErrorPage.jsp</h3>
</body>
</html>
```

The result of calling `Exception.jsp` should be similar to that shown in the following screenshot:

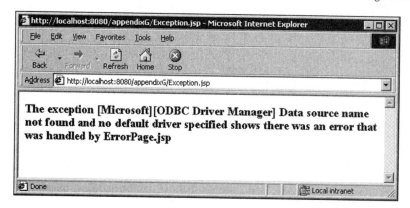

One thing to remember is that some methods demand a `try – catch` and cannot function or compile without one, you need to watch for these. Even when they are not demanded, try to catch your exceptions, it promotes good practice and gets you into the habit of good code management.

Java COM Interoperability

There are a number of tools available that facilitate Java and COM interoperability, but most are very difficult to actually get working, or are seen as quite expensive.

If your background is in COM, you may well have a number of existing objects you would like to utilize in a JSP based solution, and that is not typically an easy task. The Jacob project is an open source Java-COM Bridge that allows you to hook into COM from Java quite easily without having to write anything very convoluted, and therefore makes the task of talking to COM from Java easier.

Jacob can be obtained freely from http://users.rcn.com/danadler/jacob/, and it has quite a following in the open source community.

To demonstrate its usefulness to VBScript developers looking at utilizing JSPs or Servlets, we will modify and implement an example Servlet that is provided with Jacob. The example will show how a Servlet from Tomcat can issue an actual VBScript command to the Microsoft ScriptControl COM object and have the VBScript evaluated, passed to the COM object, executed and the results returned to the browser window.

You must be running on Windows for this to work. You must also have the ScriptControl pre-installed before running the Servlet. You can obtain the ScriptControl at the time of writing free from http://msdn.microsoft.com/scripting/default.htm?/scripting/scriptcontrol/scdown.htm although you will have to register to do so.

To get Jacob working with Tomcat we require only two files from the binary distribution of Jacob:

❑ `Jacob.dll`
This should be placed in your path; I would suggest your `winnt` directory.

❑ `Jacob.jar`
This needs to be added to your classpath; I would suggest you place this in the `C:\jakarta-tomcat\lib` directory and modify the classpath accordingly as shown earlier.

Depending on your installation of Tomcat, you may also need to modify the `tomcat.policy` (`catalina.policy` in Tomcat 4.0) file, found in the `jakarta-tomcat\conf` directory, adding the highlighted line to the example webapp policy as shown below:

```
// Example webapp policy
// By default we grant read access on webapp dir and
// write in workdir
grant codeBase "file:${tomcat.home}/webapps/appendixG" {
    permission java.net.SocketPermission "localhost:1024-", "listen";
    permission java.util.PropertyPermission "*", "read";
    permission java.security.AllPermission;
};
```

Restart Tomcat – it should now be capable of handling calls to COM objects from within a Servlet as we will demonstrate.

The JacobScript Class

Create a new file called `JacobScript.java` containing the following in the `C:\jakarta-tomcat\webapps\appendixG\WEB-INF\classes` directory, and compile it:

```java
import javax.servlet.*;
import javax.servlet.http.*;
import java.io.*;

import com.jacob.com.*;
import com.jacob.activeX.*;

public class JacobScript extends javax.servlet.http.HttpServlet {
  public void doGet(HttpServletRequest req,
                    HttpServletResponse res) throws ServletException {
    PrintWriter out = null;
    try {
      res.setContentType("text/html");
      out = res.getWriter();

      // display a form
      out.println("<h2>This example invokes the COM Object " +
                  "MSScriptControl.ScriptControl</h2>");
      out.println("<h2>The Servlet allows you to enter a VBScript " +
                  "Expression<br /> " +
                  "and get back the results of the call to COM</h1>");
      out.println("As a suggestion, try passing a simple calculation " +
                  "such as 35+17");
      out.println("<form method=\"POST\" " +
                  "action=\"/appendixG/servlet/JacobScript\">");
      out.println("<input name=\"expr\" type=\"text\" width=64>");
      out.println("<input type=\"submit\">");
      out.println("</form>");
    } catch (Exception e) {
      e.printStackTrace();
      out.println("<H2>Error:" + e + "</H2>");
    }
  }
}

  public void doPost(HttpServletRequest req, HttpServletResponse res)
                                        throws ServletException {
    PrintWriter out = null;

    try {
      res.setContentType("text/html");
      out = res.getWriter();

      // get what they typed in
      String expr = (String) req.getParameter("expr");

      // make sure we have a session
      HttpSession session = req.getSession(true);
      Object sControl = null;
      if (session.isNew()) {

        // initialize the control and store it on the session
        String lang = "VBScript";
        ActiveXComponent sC =
          new ActiveXComponent("MSScriptControl.ScriptControl");
        sControl = sC.getObject();
        Dispatch.put(sControl, "Language", lang);
```

```
        session.putValue("control", sControl);
    } else {
        sControl = session.getValue("control");
    }
    Variant result = Dispatch.call(sControl, "Eval", expr);

    // display a form
    out.println("<h1>Enter a VBScript Expression</h1>");
    out.println("<form method=\"POST\" " +
                "action=\"/appendixG/servlet/JacobScript\">");
    out.println("<input name=\"expr\" type=\"text\" value=\"" + expr
                + "\" width=64>");
    out.println("<input type=\"submit\">");
    out.println("</form>");
    out.println("<H1>Jacob Response:</H1>");
    out.println("<H2>" + result + "</H2>");
    } catch (Exception e) {
    e.printStackTrace();
    out.println("<H2>Error:" + e + "</H2>");
    }
  }
}
```

You should now have an operational Servlet capable of talking to the COM object using the Servlet code outlined below:

```
ActiveXComponent sC = new ActiveXComponent("MSScriptControl.ScriptControl");
```

Requesting the Servlet will produce something similar to the following screenshot:

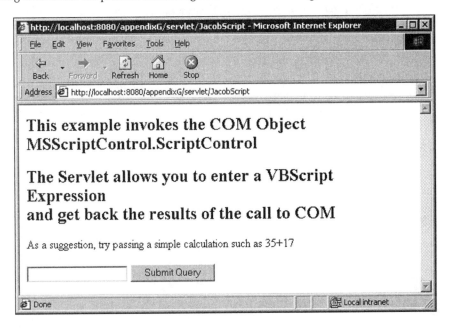

If we do indeed satisfy the request of the Servlet and submit to it the value 35+17, results akin to the following should be provided to us:

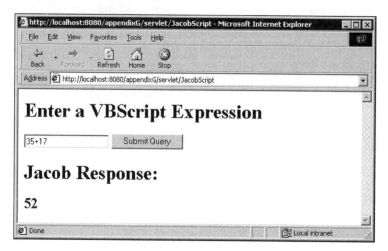

The Jacob ZIP file contains a number of very useful examples to help you work out how to invoke various COM objects and get a feel for its usefulness in making use of COM in your mixed environment.

Java in .NET

As you can probably imagine, this question is too much to be covered at this stage in a book focused on JSP. If you're faced with a conflict of direction as an ASP developer, and you're unsure as to whether you can make use of Java then be assured – Java works in .NET based ASP, and JSP, like ASP, works alongside .NET.

If you plan carefully, anything you develop as a Java class can potentially be re-used in an ASP.NET based solution with little or no re-work. Employing a technique familiar to most COM developers called Late Binding allows .NET to use Java COM.

ASPX code like ASP code allows you to make use of a registered Java class as you would any legacy COM object. We will demonstrate this with a simple but effective example. Naturally, to test this you will require a suitable .NET environment (the Beta will suffice) configured.

The javaNET ASPX

Create an ASPX page called `javaNet.aspx` with the following contents:

```
<%@ Page Language="VB" ClientTarget="downlevel" %>
<%@ Import Namespace="System.Web.Util" %>
<%
  Dim XYZ as Object

  XYZ = Server.CreateObject("javaNET")

  Response.Write(XYZ.sayHello())

%>
```

The javaNET Class

Create the Java class file for use by the ASPX page, javaNET.java, and compile it:

```java
import java.io.*;

public class javaNET {

  public String sayHello() {
    String ret = "Hello from Java in .NET";
    return ret;

  }

}
```

Once compiled, the Java class file needs to be moved (if it's not already there) to the winnt/Java/trustlib directory of your web server. You now need to register the class file using a Microsoft tool called JavaReg available at the time of writing from http://www.microsoft.com/java in the Microsoft JDK or from the Wrox Press download area. For instructions on redistribution of JavaReg please refer to http://www.microsoft.com/java/sdk/40/default.htm.

To actually perform the registration you simply need to type the following in a command window and press return:

```
javareg /register /class:javaNET /progid:javaNET
```

This will hopefully return a success message; if you are not successful there are two likely causes:

❑   Your .NET installation is corrupted and needs a reinstall

❑   Your registration details are incorrect

Calling the ASPX page will return the results from the call to the sayHello() java method as shown in the following screenshot:

As you can see, you can indeed utilize Java in a .NET based solution, so your time spent looking at JSP and Java won't be wasted.

Summary

Reading through the examples demonstrated in this appendix, ASP and JSP can seem very similar and on first sight they are. That makes it a bit easier for you as an ASP developer to look at how you could make use of the language. There are however many differences between the two technologies.

JSP is still missing lots of component functionality native to ASP, and especially to ASP.NET but the adoption of tag libraries will continue to ease this problem. Some Servlet engines (IBM Websphere for instance) come with a comprehensive set of add in beans and reusable tag libraries to add additional functionality not offered by JSP alone to address problems like this, clearly showing that the Java language is flexible enough to allow you to bridge most gaps. You should not become overconfident in the simplicity of some of the examples shown here, especially given the familiarity with the common ASP objects:

- ❑ Scripting
- ❑ Comments
- ❑ Includes
- ❑ Response object
- ❑ Request object
- ❑ Session object

For an aspiring VBScript or .NET developer, significantly adding to the learning curve of JSP is Java's underlying object-oriented (OO) nature that may well be completely alien to you given the loosely defined nature of VBScript as a language. This is a problem you will also likely face with .NET if you are unfamiliar with OO development and aren't well versed in COM. This object-orientation is somewhat responsible for the power and flexibility of the language, but it does carry a steep learning curve. JSP also has some fancy features we have not touched on in this appendix. In reality the topic of JSP for ASP developers is far too much for a single appendix but hopefully it's managed to get you started.

If you are looking for some additional reading Sun have written a short white paper 'Comparing JavaServer Pages and Microsoft Active Server Pages Technology'. It compares some of the elements of both technologies; I, however, think the document is a bit misleading as it deliberately compares the two technologies inaccurately in favor of JSP, but it's a useful supplement to the chapter. You can find it at http://java.sun.com/products/jsp/jsp-asp.html.

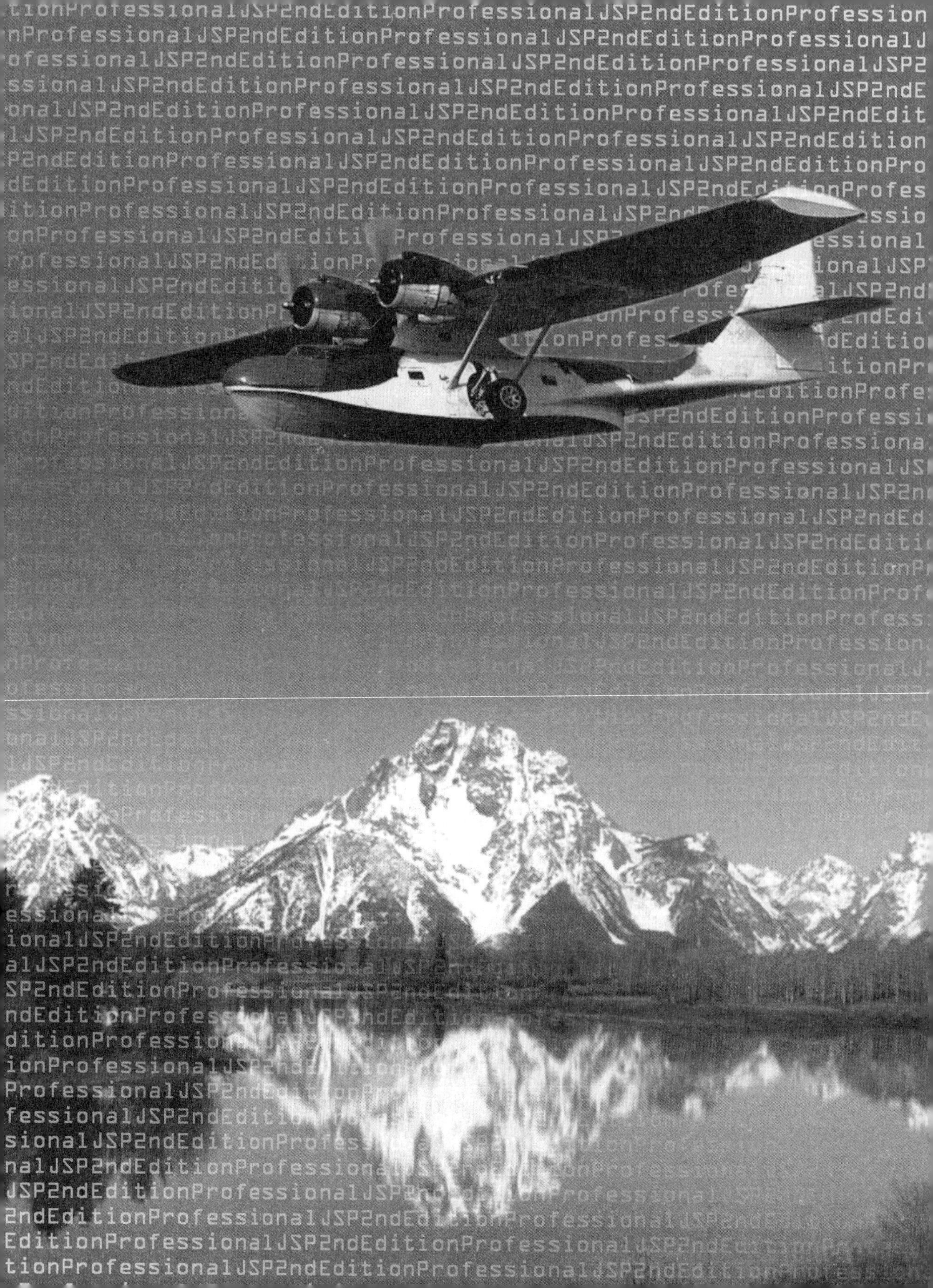
ProfessionalJSP2ndEdition

Software Licenses

This appendix contains the texts of the software licenses used by code quoted in this book:

❏ The Apache Software License (which covers Tomcat, Struts, and all other Jakarta projects), also available at http://www.apache.org/LICENSE.txt

❏ The Gnu Lesser General Public License Version 2.1 (which covers the code used in Chapters 8 and 12), also available at http://www.gnu.org/copyleft/lesser.html

The Apache Software License

```
/* ========================================================================
 *
 *             The Apache Software License,   Version 1.1
 *
 *        Copyright (c) 1999, 2000  The Apache Software Foundation.
 *                    All rights reserved.
 *
 * ========================================================================
 *
 * Redistribution and use in source and binary forms,  with or without modi-
 * fication, are permitted provided that the following conditions are met:
 *
 * 1. Redistributions of source code  must retain the above copyright notice
 *    notice, this list of conditions and the following disclaimer.
 *
 * 2. Redistributions  in binary  form  must  reproduce the  above copyright
 *    notice,  this list of conditions  and the following  disclaimer in the
 *    documentation and/or other materials provided with the distribution.
```

```
*
* 3. The end-user documentation  included with the redistribution,  if any,
*     must include the following acknowlegement:
*
*       "This product includes  software developed  by the Apache  Software
*        Foundation <http://www.apache.org/>."
*
*     Alternately, this acknowlegement may appear in the software itself, if
*     and wherever such third-party acknowlegements normally appear.
*
* 4. The names  "The  Jakarta  Project",  "Tomcat",  and  "Apache  Software
*     Foundation"  must not be used  to endorse or promote  products derived
*     from this  software without  prior  written  permission.  For  written
*     permission, please contact <apache@apache.org>.
*
* 5. Products derived from this software may not be called "Apache" nor may
*     "Apache" appear in their names without prior written permission of the
*     Apache Software Foundation.
*
* THIS SOFTWARE IS PROVIDED "AS IS" AND ANY EXPRESSED OR IMPLIED WARRANTIES
* INCLUDING, BUT NOT LIMITED TO,  THE IMPLIED WARRANTIES OF MERCHANTABILITY
* AND FITNESS FOR  A PARTICULAR PURPOSE  ARE DISCLAIMED.  IN NO EVENT SHALL
* THE APACHE  SOFTWARE  FOUNDATION OR  ITS CONTRIBUTORS  BE LIABLE  FOR ANY
* DIRECT,  INDIRECT,  INCIDENTAL,  SPECIAL,  EXEMPLARY,  OR  CONSEQUENTIAL
* DAMAGES (INCLUDING,  BUT NOT LIMITED TO,  PROCUREMENT OF SUBSTITUTE GOODS
* OR SERVICES;  LOSS OF USE,  DATA,  OR PROFITS;  OR BUSINESS INTERRUPTION)
* HOWEVER CAUSED AND  ON ANY  THEORY  OF  LIABILITY,  WHETHER IN  CONTRACT,
* STRICT LIABILITY, OR TORT  (INCLUDING NEGLIGENCE OR OTHERWISE) ARISING IN
* ANY  WAY  OUT OF  THE  USE OF  THIS  SOFTWARE,  EVEN  IF  ADVISED  OF THE
* POSSIBILITY OF SUCH DAMAGE.
*
* ==========================================================================
*
* This software  consists of voluntary  contributions made  by many indivi-
* duals on behalf of the  Apache Software Foundation.  For more information
* on the Apache Software Foundation, please see <http://www.apache.org/>.
*
* ==========================================================================
*/
```

The Gnu Lesser General Public License, Version 2.1

GNU LESSER GENERAL PUBLIC LICENSE
Version 2.1, February 1999

Copyright (C) 1991, 1999 Free Software Foundation, Inc.
    59 Temple Place, Suite 330, Boston, MA 02111-1307 USA
Everyone is permitted to copy and distribute verbatim copies
of this license document, but changing it is not allowed.

[This is the first released version of the Lesser GPL. It also counts
as the successor of the GNU Library Public License, version 2, hence
the version number 2.1.]

Preamble

The licenses for most software are designed to take away your
freedom to share and change it. By contrast, the GNU General Public
Licenses are intended to guarantee your freedom to share and change
free software--to make sure the software is free for all its users.

This license, the Lesser General Public License, applies to some
specially designated software packages--typically libraries--of the
Free Software Foundation and other authors who decide to use it. You
can use it too, but we suggest you first think carefully about whether
this license or the ordinary General Public License is the better
strategy to use in any particular case, based on the explanations below.

When we speak of free software, we are referring to freedom of use,
not price. Our General Public Licenses are designed to make sure that
you have the freedom to distribute copies of free software (and charge
for this service if you wish); that you receive source code or can get
it if you want it; that you can change the software and use pieces of
it in new free programs; and that you are informed that you can do
these things.

To protect your rights, we need to make restrictions that forbid
distributors to deny you these rights or to ask you to surrender these
rights. These restrictions translate to certain responsibilities for
you if you distribute copies of the library or if you modify it.

For example, if you distribute copies of the library, whether gratis
or for a fee, you must give the recipients all the rights that we gave
you. You must make sure that they, too, receive or can get the source
code. If you link other code with the library, you must provide
complete object files to the recipients, so that they can relink them
with the library after making changes to the library and recompiling
it. And you must show them these terms so they know their rights.

We protect your rights with a two-step method: (1) we copyright the
library, and (2) we offer you this license, which gives you legal
permission to copy, distribute and/or modify the library.

To protect each distributor, we want to make it very clear that
there is no warranty for the free library. Also, if the library is
modified by someone else and passed on, the recipients should know
that what they have is not the original version, so that the original
author's reputation will not be affected by problems that might be
introduced by others.

Finally, software patents pose a constant threat to the existence of
any free program. We wish to make sure that a company cannot
effectively restrict the users of a free program by obtaining a
restrictive license from a patent holder. Therefore, we insist that
any patent license obtained for a version of the library must be
consistent with the full freedom of use specified in this license.

Most GNU software, including some libraries, is covered by the ordinary GNU General Public License. This license, the GNU Lesser General Public License, applies to certain designated libraries, and is quite different from the ordinary General Public License. We use this license for certain libraries in order to permit linking those libraries into non-free programs.

When a program is linked with a library, whether statically or using a shared library, the combination of the two is legally speaking a combined work, a derivative of the original library. The ordinary General Public License therefore permits such linking only if the entire combination fits its criteria of freedom. The Lesser General Public License permits more lax criteria for linking other code with the library.

We call this license the "Lesser" General Public License because it does Less to protect the user's freedom than the ordinary General Public License. It also provides other free software developers Less of an advantage over competing non-free programs. These disadvantages are the reason we use the ordinary General Public License for many libraries. However, the Lesser license provides advantages in certain special circumstances.

For example, on rare occasions, there may be a special need to encourage the widest possible use of a certain library, so that it becomes a de-facto standard. To achieve this, non-free programs must be allowed to use the library. A more frequent case is that a free library does the same job as widely used non-free libraries. In this case, there is little to gain by limiting the free library to free software only, so we use the Lesser General Public License.

In other cases, permission to use a particular library in non-free programs enables a greater number of people to use a large body of free software. For example, permission to use the GNU C Library in non-free programs enables many more people to use the whole GNU operating system, as well as its variant, the GNU/Linux operating system.

Although the Lesser General Public License is Less protective of the users' freedom, it does ensure that the user of a program that is linked with the Library has the freedom and the wherewithal to run that program using a modified version of the Library.

The precise terms and conditions for copying, distribution and modification follow. Pay close attention to the difference between a "work based on the library" and a "work that uses the library". The former contains code derived from the library, whereas the latter must be combined with the library in order to run.

GNU LESSER GENERAL PUBLIC LICENSE
TERMS AND CONDITIONS FOR COPYING, DISTRIBUTION AND MODIFICATION

0. This License Agreement applies to any software library or other program which contains a notice placed by the copyright holder or other authorized party saying it may be distributed under the terms of this Lesser General Public License (also called "this License"). Each licensee is addressed as "you".

A "library" means a collection of software functions and/or data prepared so as to be conveniently linked with application programs (which use some of those functions and data) to form executables.

The "Library", below, refers to any such software library or work which has been distributed under these terms. A "work based on the Library" means either the Library or any derivative work under copyright law: that is to say, a work containing the Library or a portion of it, either verbatim or with modifications and/or translated straightforwardly into another language. (Hereinafter, translation is included without limitation in the term "modification".)

"Source code" for a work means the preferred form of the work for making modifications to it. For a library, complete source code means all the source code for all modules it contains, plus any associated interface definition files, plus the scripts used to control compilation and installation of the library.

Activities other than copying, distribution and modification are not covered by this License; they are outside its scope. The act of running a program using the Library is not restricted, and output from such a program is covered only if its contents constitute a work based on the Library (independent of the use of the Library in a tool for writing it). Whether that is true depends on what the Library does and what the program that uses the Library does.

1. You may copy and distribute verbatim copies of the Library's complete source code as you receive it, in any medium, provided that you conspicuously and appropriately publish on each copy an appropriate copyright notice and disclaimer of warranty; keep intact all the notices that refer to this License and to the absence of any warranty; and distribute a copy of this License along with the Library.

You may charge a fee for the physical act of transferring a copy, and you may at your option offer warranty protection in exchange for a fee.

2. You may modify your copy or copies of the Library or any portion of it, thus forming a work based on the Library, and copy and distribute such modifications or work under the terms of Section 1 above, provided that you also meet all of these conditions:

a) The modified work must itself be a software library.

b) You must cause the files modified to carry prominent notices stating that you changed the files and the date of any change.

c) You must cause the whole of the work to be licensed at no charge to all third parties under the terms of this License.

d) If a facility in the modified Library refers to a function or a table of data to be supplied by an application program that uses the facility, other than as an argument passed when the facility is invoked, then you must make a good faith effort to ensure that, in the event an application does not supply such function or table, the facility still operates, and performs whatever part of its purpose remains meaningful.

1153

(For example, a function in a library to compute square roots has a purpose that is entirely well-defined independent of the application. Therefore, Subsection 2d requires that any application-supplied function or table used by this function must be optional: if the application does not supply it, the square root function must still compute square roots.)

These requirements apply to the modified work as a whole. If identifiable sections of that work are not derived from the Library, and can be reasonably considered independent and separate works in themselves, then this License, and its terms, do not apply to those sections when you distribute them as separate works. But when you distribute the same sections as part of a whole which is a work based on the Library, the distribution of the whole must be on the terms of this License, whose permissions for other licensees extend to the entire whole, and thus to each and every part regardless of who wrote it.

Thus, it is not the intent of this section to claim rights or contest your rights to work written entirely by you; rather, the intent is to exercise the right to control the distribution of derivative or collective works based on the Library.

In addition, mere aggregation of another work not based on the Library with the Library (or with a work based on the Library) on a volume of a storage or distribution medium does not bring the other work under the scope of this License.

3. You may opt to apply the terms of the ordinary GNU General Public License instead of this License to a given copy of the Library. To do this, you must alter all the notices that refer to this License, so that they refer to the ordinary GNU General Public License, version 2, instead of to this License. (If a newer version than version 2 of the ordinary GNU General Public License has appeared, then you can specify that version instead if you wish.) Do not make any other change in these notices.

Once this change is made in a given copy, it is irreversible for that copy, so the ordinary GNU General Public License applies to all subsequent copies and derivative works made from that copy.

This option is useful when you wish to copy part of the code of the Library into a program that is not a library.

4. You may copy and distribute the Library (or a portion or derivative of it, under Section 2) in object code or executable form under the terms of Sections 1 and 2 above provided that you accompany it with the complete corresponding machine-readable source code, which must be distributed under the terms of Sections 1 and 2 above on a medium customarily used for software interchange.

If distribution of object code is made by offering access to copy from a designated place, then offering equivalent access to copy the source code from the same place satisfies the requirement to distribute the source code, even though third parties are not compelled to copy the source along with the object code.

5. A program that contains no derivative of any portion of the Library, but is designed to work with the Library by being compiled or linked with it, is called a "work that uses the Library". Such a work, in isolation, is not a derivative work of the Library, and therefore falls outside the scope of this License.

However, linking a "work that uses the Library" with the Library creates an executable that is a derivative of the Library (because it contains portions of the Library), rather than a "work that uses the library". The executable is therefore covered by this License. Section 6 states terms for distribution of such executables.

When a "work that uses the Library" uses material from a header file that is part of the Library, the object code for the work may be a derivative work of the Library even though the source code is not. Whether this is true is especially significant if the work can be linked without the Library, or if the work is itself a library. The threshold for this to be true is not precisely defined by law.

If such an object file uses only numerical parameters, data structure layouts and accessors, and small macros and small inline functions (ten lines or less in length), then the use of the object file is unrestricted, regardless of whether it is legally a derivative work. (Executables containing this object code plus portions of the Library will still fall under Section 6.)

Otherwise, if the work is a derivative of the Library, you may distribute the object code for the work under the terms of Section 6. Any executables containing that work also fall under Section 6, whether or not they are linked directly with the Library itself.

6. As an exception to the Sections above, you may also combine or link a "work that uses the Library" with the Library to produce a work containing portions of the Library, and distribute that work under terms of your choice, provided that the terms permit modification of the work for the customer's own use and reverse engineering for debugging such modifications.

You must give prominent notice with each copy of the work that the Library is used in it and that the Library and its use are covered by this License. You must supply a copy of this License. If the work during execution displays copyright notices, you must include the copyright notice for the Library among them, as well as a reference directing the user to the copy of this License. Also, you must do one of these things:

a) Accompany the work with the complete corresponding machine-readable source code for the Library including whatever changes were used in the work (which must be distributed under Sections 1 and 2 above); and, if the work is an executable linked with the Library, with the complete machine-readable "work that uses the Library", as object code and/or source code, so that the user can modify the Library and then relink to produce a modified executable containing the modified Library. (It is understood that the user who changes the contents of definitions files in the Library will not necessarily be able to recompile the application to use the modified definitions.)

b) Use a suitable shared library mechanism for linking with the Library. A suitable mechanism is one that (1) uses at run time a copy of the library already present on the user's computer system, rather than copying library functions into the executable, and (2) will operate properly with a modified version of the library, if the user installs one, as long as the modified version is interface-compatible with the version that the work was made with.

c) Accompany the work with a written offer, valid for at least three years, to give the same user the materials specified in Subsection 6a, above, for a charge no more than the cost of performing this distribution.

d) If distribution of the work is made by offering access to copy from a designated place, offer equivalent access to copy the above specified materials from the same place.

e) Verify that the user has already received a copy of these materials or that you have already sent this user a copy.

For an executable, the required form of the "work that uses the Library" must include any data and utility programs needed for reproducing the executable from it. However, as a special exception, the materials to be distributed need not include anything that is normally distributed (in either source or binary form) with the major components (compiler, kernel, and so on) of the operating system on which the executable runs, unless that component itself accompanies the executable.

It may happen that this requirement contradicts the license restrictions of other proprietary libraries that do not normally accompany the operating system. Such a contradiction means you cannot use both them and the Library together in an executable that you distribute.

7. You may place library facilities that are a work based on the Library side-by-side in a single library together with other library facilities not covered by this License, and distribute such a combined library, provided that the separate distribution of the work based on the Library and of the other library facilities is otherwise permitted, and provided that you do these two things:

a) Accompany the combined library with a copy of the same work based on the Library, uncombined with any other library facilities. This must be distributed under the terms of the Sections above.

b) Give prominent notice with the combined library of the fact that part of it is a work based on the Library, and explaining where to find the accompanying uncombined form of the same work.

8. You may not copy, modify, sublicense, link with, or distribute the Library except as expressly provided under this License. Any attempt otherwise to copy, modify, sublicense, link with, or distribute the Library is void, and will automatically terminate your rights under this License. However, parties who have received copies, or rights, from you under this License will not have their licenses terminated so long as such parties remain in full compliance.

9. You are not required to accept this License, since you have not signed it. However, nothing else grants you permission to modify or distribute the Library or its derivative works. These actions are prohibited by law if you do not accept this License. Therefore, by modifying or distributing the Library (or any work based on the Library), you indicate your acceptance of this License to do so, and all its terms and conditions for copying, distributing or modifying the Library or works based on it.

10. Each time you redistribute the Library (or any work based on the Library), the recipient automatically receives a license from the original licensor to copy, distribute, link with or modify the Library subject to these terms and conditions. You may not impose any further restrictions on the recipients' exercise of the rights granted herein. You are not responsible for enforcing compliance by third parties with this License.

11. If, as a consequence of a court judgment or allegation of patent infringement or for any other reason (not limited to patent issues), conditions are imposed on you (whether by court order, agreement or otherwise) that contradict the conditions of this License, they do not excuse you from the conditions of this License. If you cannot distribute so as to satisfy simultaneously your obligations under this License and any other pertinent obligations, then as a consequence you may not distribute the Library at all. For example, if a patent license would not permit royalty-free redistribution of the Library by all those who receive copies directly or indirectly through you, then the only way you could satisfy both it and this License would be to refrain entirely from distribution of the Library.

If any portion of this section is held invalid or unenforceable under any particular circumstance, the balance of the section is intended to apply, and the section as a whole is intended to apply in other circumstances.

It is not the purpose of this section to induce you to infringe any patents or other property right claims or to contest validity of any such claims; this section has the sole purpose of protecting the integrity of the free software distribution system which is implemented by public license practices. Many people have made generous contributions to the wide range of software distributed through that system in reliance on consistent application of that system; it is up to the author/donor to decide if he or she is willing to distribute software through any other system and a licensee cannot impose that choice.

This section is intended to make thoroughly clear what is believed to be a consequence of the rest of this License.

12. If the distribution and/or use of the Library is restricted in certain countries either by patents or by copyrighted interfaces, the original copyright holder who places the Library under this License may add an explicit geographical distribution limitation excluding those countries, so that distribution is permitted only in or among countries not thus excluded. In such case, this License incorporates the limitation as if written in the body of this License.

13. The Free Software Foundation may publish revised and/or new versions of the Lesser General Public License from time to time. Such new versions will be similar in spirit to the present version, but may differ in detail to address new problems or concerns.

Each version is given a distinguishing version number. If the Library specifies a version number of this License which applies to it and "any later version", you have the option of following the terms and conditions either of that version or of any later version published by the Free Software Foundation. If the Library does not specify a license version number, you may choose any version ever published by the Free Software Foundation.

14. If you wish to incorporate parts of the Library into other free programs whose distribution conditions are incompatible with these, write to the author to ask for permission. For software which is copyrighted by the Free Software Foundation, write to the Free Software Foundation; we sometimes make exceptions for this. Our decision will be guided by the two goals of preserving the free status of all derivatives of our free software and of promoting the sharing and reuse of software generally.

NO WARRANTY

15. BECAUSE THE LIBRARY IS LICENSED FREE OF CHARGE, THERE IS NO WARRANTY FOR THE LIBRARY, TO THE EXTENT PERMITTED BY APPLICABLE LAW. EXCEPT WHEN OTHERWISE STATED IN WRITING THE COPYRIGHT HOLDERS AND/OR OTHER PARTIES PROVIDE THE LIBRARY "AS IS" WITHOUT WARRANTY OF ANY KIND, EITHER EXPRESSED OR IMPLIED, INCLUDING, BUT NOT LIMITED TO, THE IMPLIED WARRANTIES OF MERCHANTABILITY AND FITNESS FOR A PARTICULAR PURPOSE. THE ENTIRE RISK AS TO THE QUALITY AND PERFORMANCE OF THE LIBRARY IS WITH YOU. SHOULD THE LIBRARY PROVE DEFECTIVE, YOU ASSUME THE COST OF ALL NECESSARY SERVICING, REPAIR OR CORRECTION.

16. IN NO EVENT UNLESS REQUIRED BY APPLICABLE LAW OR AGREED TO IN WRITING WILL ANY COPYRIGHT HOLDER, OR ANY OTHER PARTY WHO MAY MODIFY AND/OR REDISTRIBUTE THE LIBRARY AS PERMITTED ABOVE, BE LIABLE TO YOU FOR DAMAGES, INCLUDING ANY GENERAL, SPECIAL, INCIDENTAL OR CONSEQUENTIAL DAMAGES ARISING OUT OF THE USE OR INABILITY TO USE THE LIBRARY (INCLUDING BUT NOT LIMITED TO LOSS OF DATA OR DATA BEING RENDERED INACCURATE OR LOSSES SUSTAINED BY YOU OR THIRD PARTIES OR A FAILURE OF THE LIBRARY TO OPERATE WITH ANY OTHER SOFTWARE), EVEN IF SUCH HOLDER OR OTHER PARTY HAS BEEN ADVISED OF THE POSSIBILITY OF SUCH DAMAGES.

END OF TERMS AND CONDITIONS

How to Apply These Terms to Your New Libraries

If you develop a new library, and you want it to be of the greatest possible use to the public, we recommend making it free software that everyone can redistribute and change. You can do so by permitting redistribution under these terms (or, alternatively, under the terms of the ordinary General Public License).

To apply these terms, attach the following notices to the library. It is safest to attach them to the start of each source file to most effectively convey the exclusion of warranty; and each file should have at least the "copyright" line and a pointer to where the full notice is found.

    <one line to give the library's name and a brief idea of what it does.>
    Copyright (C) <year> <name of author>

    This library is free software; you can redistribute it and/or
    modify it under the terms of the GNU Lesser General Public
    License as published by the Free Software Foundation; either
    version 2 of the License, or (at your option) any later version.

    This library is distributed in the hope that it will be useful,
    but WITHOUT ANY WARRANTY; without even the implied warranty of
    MERCHANTABILITY or FITNESS FOR A PARTICULAR PURPOSE. See the GNU
    Lesser General Public License for more details.

    You should have received a copy of the GNU Lesser General Public
    License along with this library; if not, write to the Free Software
    Foundation, Inc., 59 Temple Place, Suite 330, Boston, MA 02111-1307 USA

Also add information on how to contact you by electronic and paper mail.

You should also get your employer (if you work as a programmer) or your school, if any, to sign a "copyright disclaimer" for the library, if necessary. Here is a sample; alter the names:

  Yoyodyne, Inc., hereby disclaims all copyright interest in the
  library `Frob' (a library for tweaking knobs) written by James Random Hacker.

  <signature of Ty Coon>, 1 April 1990
  Ty Coon, President of Vice

That's all there is to it!

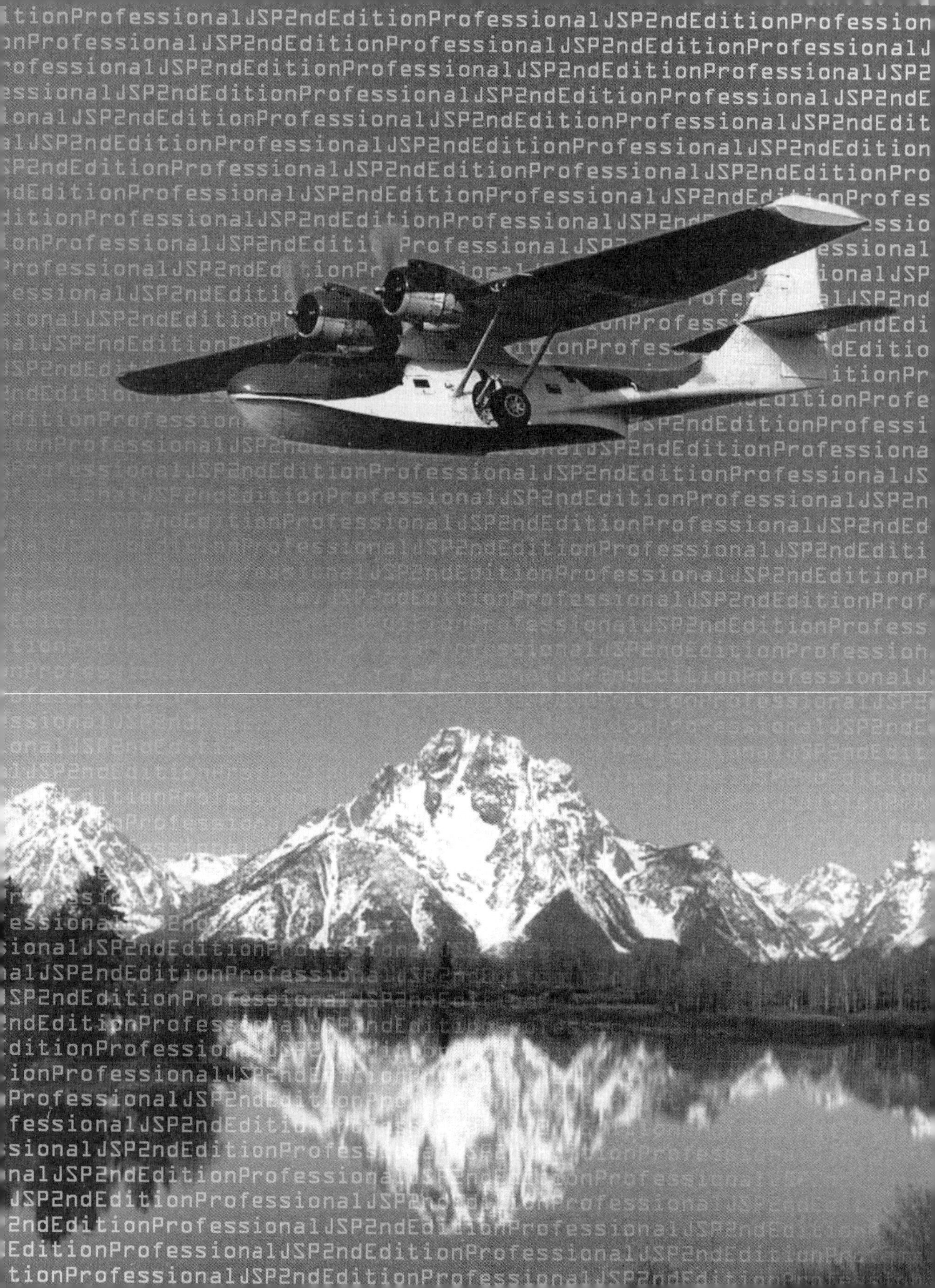

Index

A Guide to the Index

The index is arranged hierarchically, in alphabetical order, with symbols preceding the letter A. Most second-level entries and many third-level entries also occur as first-level entries. This is to ensure that users will find the information they require however they choose to search for it.

F

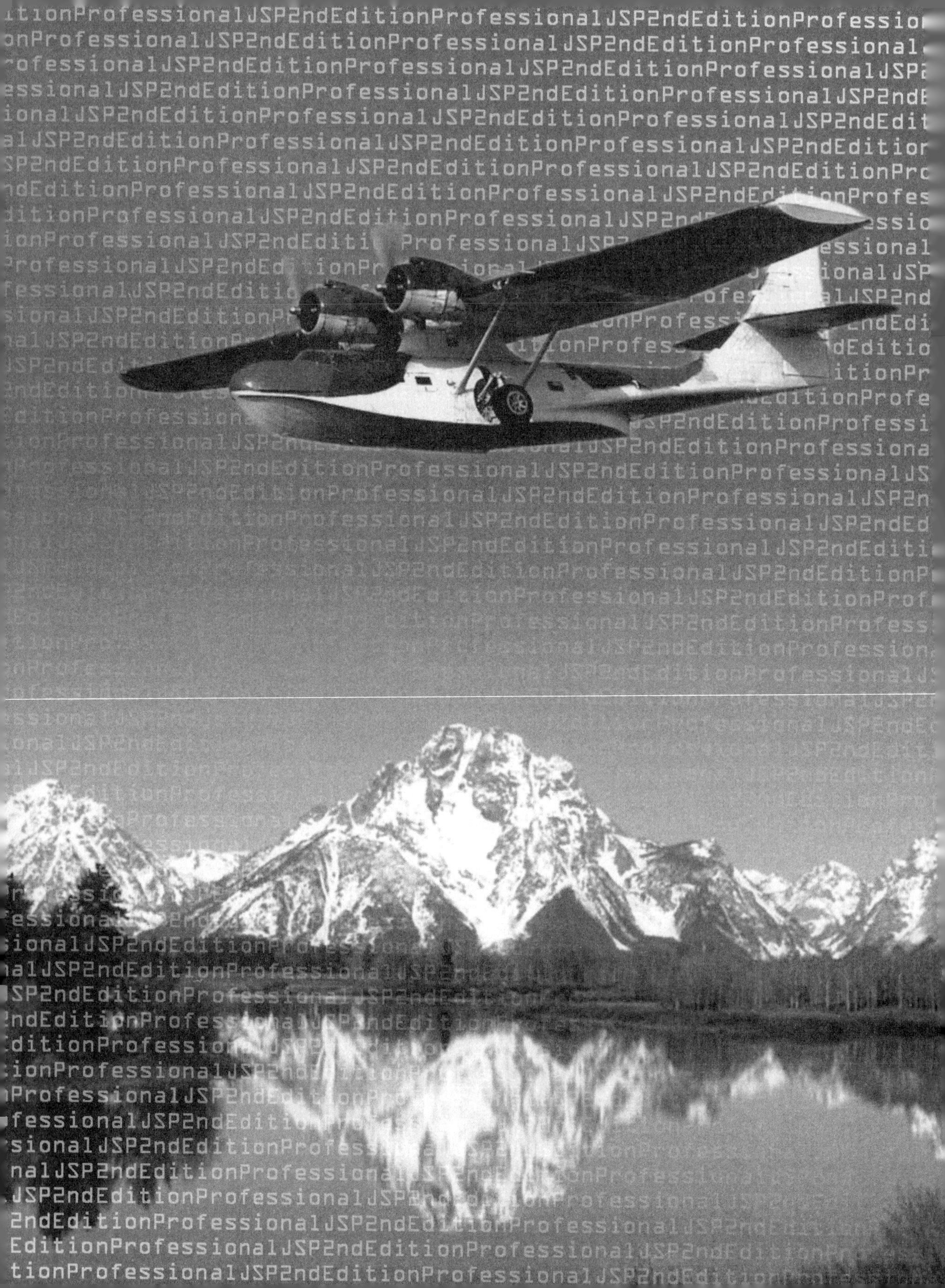
ProfessionalJSP2ndEdition